October 16–19, 2016
Austin, Texas, USA

**Association for
Computing Machinery**

Advancing Computing as a Science & Profession

CHI PLAY 2016

Proceedings of the 2016 Annual Symposium on
Computer-Human Interaction in Play

Sponsored by:
ACM SIGCHI

**Association for
Computing Machinery**

Advancing Computing as a Science & Profession

The Association for Computing Machinery
2 Penn Plaza, Suite 701
New York, New York 10121-0701

Copyright © 2016 by the Association for Computing Machinery, Inc. (ACM). Permission to make digital or hard copies of portions of this work for personal or classroom use is granted without fee provided that copies are not made or distributed for profit or commercial advantage and that copies bear this notice and the full citation on the first page. Copyright for components of this work owned by others than ACM must be honored. Abstracting with credit is permitted. To copy otherwise, to republish, to post on servers or to redistribute to lists, requires prior specific permission and/or a fee. Request permission to republish from: permissions@acm.org or Fax +1 (212) 869-0481.

For other copying of articles that carry a code at the bottom of the first or last page, copying is permitted provided that the per-copy fee indicated in the code is paid through www.copyright.com.

Notice to Past Authors of ACM-Published Articles
ACM intends to create a complete electronic archive of all articles and/or other material previously published by ACM. If you have written a work that has been previously published by ACM in any journal or conference proceedings prior to 1978, or any SIG Newsletter at any time, and you do NOT want this work to appear in the ACM Digital Library, please inform permissions@acm.org, stating the title of the work, the author(s), and where and when published.

ISBN: 978-1-4503-4456-2 (Digital)

ISBN: 978-1-4503-4686-3 (Print)

Additional copies may be ordered prepaid from:

ACM Order Department
PO Box 30777
New York, NY 10087-0777, USA

Phone: 1-800-342-6626 (USA and Canada)
+1-212-626-0500 (Global)
Fax: +1-212-944-1318
E-mail: acmhelp@acm.org
Hours of Operation: 8:30 am – 4:30 pm ET

Printed in the USA

CHI PLAY 2016 Chairs' Welcome

It is our great pleasure to welcome you to the third *ACM SIGCHI Annual Symposium on Computer-Human Interaction in Play - CHI PLAY '16. See more at:* http://chiplay.org.

CHI PLAY is an international and interdisciplinary conference series for researchers and professionals across all areas of play, games, and human-computer interaction (HCI), we call it: "player-computer interaction." CHI PLAY highlights and fosters discussion of current high-quality research in games and HCI. It forms the foundations for the future of digital play. This year is the third year of the symposium, which is already proving to be a premier forum for presentation of research results and experience reports on leading-edge issues of novel game interaction, player experience evaluations, neurogaming, gamification, exertion games, games user research, player psychology, social game systems, serious games, game developer applications, interaction design, and theory. The mission of the symposium is to share insights into game interaction design and analysis that fulfill the needs of developers, researchers, and designers and identify new directions for future research and development in HCI and games. CHI PLAY gives researchers and practitioners a unique opportunity to share their perspectives with others interested in the various aspects of HCI in games. The symposium provides a meeting place for practitioners and academics where participants present and discuss peer-reviewed academic papers and the latest breaking results and approaches from industry.

The call for papers attracted submissions from Asia, Australia, Europe, North America, and South America. We selected a program committee of experts in human-computer interaction and game research to lead the scientific review process. All full papers were blind reviewed by peer reviewers as well as a committee member. Accepted papers are published in the ACM Digital Library. The program committee reviewed and accepted the following:

Venue or Track	Reviewed	Accepted	
Full Technical Papers	124	36	29%
Works-In-Progress	50	35	70%

Putting together CHI PLAY '16 was a team effort. We are extremely thankful to the contributors of this conference: our staff of this event, our partners, our volunteers, the authors who submitted their high quality work to our conference and provided the content of the program, the program committee, who managed the reviews on a short timeline, our reviewers who ensured a high-quality conference, and our local organizing committee.

We hope that you will find this program interesting and thought-provoking and that the event will provide you with a valuable opportunity to share ideas with other researchers and practitioners from institutions around the world.

Anna Cox
CHI PLAY '16 General Co-Chair
University College London, UK

Zach Toups
CHI PLAY '16 General Co-Chair
New Mexico State University, USA

Regan Mandryk
CHI PLAY '16 Technical Program Co-Chair
University of Saskatchewan, Canada

Paul Cairns
CHI PLAY '16 Technical Program Co-Chair
University of York, York UK

CHI PLAY 2016 Papers Chairs' Welcome

We are delighted to present the papers track for the third edition of the vibrant CHI PLAY conference. As the games industry has grown over the last few decades, so has research in games and play within HCI. In keeping with the previous CHI PLAY conferences, we received a large number of high-quality and diverse submissions, reflecting the strength and creativity of researchers in the field of player-computer interaction.

To realize the best possible program, we put together an international Program Committee of 28 experts from Canada, the United States, Europe, the United Kingdom, Asia, and Australia. Each paper submitted to CHI PLAY was assigned to two members of the program committee; one as the primary associate chair and one as the secondary associate chair. These program committee members together solicited external reviewers for each paper, with each paper receiving three or more full reviews. In addition, the secondary associate chair was available to provide an additional review in cases where the reviewers were divided on their opinion or where the paper was rated as borderline for acceptance. The primary associate chair synthesized the reviewers' opinions and wrote a meta-review to provide feedback to authors. The papers chairs made the final decisions in consultation with the Program Committee. Because of the volume of high-quality submissions, the bar was high; accepted papers comprise excellent research and innovative ideas, on par with the quality and creativity expected of a venue sponsored by SIGCHI. The overall acceptance rate for the conference was 29% with a total of 36 papers and notes accepted.

We thank all authors who submitted their work for consideration. We also particularly thank our external reviewers whose efforts are fundamental to the peer review process and who make the CHI PLAY community thrive. Finally, we reserve our greatest appreciation for the members of the Program Committee — without their dedication this conference would not be possible.

Vero vanden Abeele
CHI PLAY '16 Papers Co-Chair
KU Leuven, Belgium

Daniel Johnson
CHI PLAY '16 Papers Co-Chair
Queensland University of Technology, Australia

Table of Contents

Session 3: Purposeful Games

Session Chair: Florian 'Floyd' Mueller *(RMIT University)*

Session 4: New interactions

Session Chair: Nikki Crenshaw *(University of California, Irvine)*

Session 5: Tools for Design

Session Chair: Guenter Wallner *(University of Applied Arts Vienna)*

Session 6: Rewarding Play

Session Chair: Lennart Nacke *(University of Waterloo)*

Session 7: Playing Together

Session Chair: Jo Iacovides *(The Open University)*

Session 8: Play

Session Chair: Peta Wyeth *(Queensland University of Technology)*

CHI PLAY 2016 Conference Organization

General Chairs: Anna Cox *(University College London, UK)*
Zachary O. Toups *(New Mexico State University, USA)*

Technical Program and
Proceedings Chairs: Regan L. Mandryk *(University of Saskatchewan, Canada)*
Paul Cairns *(University of York, UK)*

Papers and Notes: Daniel Johnson *(Queensland University of Technology, Australia)*
Vero vanden Abeele *(KU Leuven, Belgium)*

Works-in Progress: Conor Linehan *(University College Cork, Ireland)*
Luc Geurts *(KU Leuven, Belgium)*

Student Game Competition: Charlene Jennett *(University College London, UK)*
Joshua Tannenbaum, *(University of California Irvine, USA)*

Workshops and Courses: Guenter Wallner *(University of Applied Arts Vienna, Austria)*
Kathrin Gerling *(Lincoln University, UK)*

Doctoral Consortium: Peta Wyeth *(Queensland University of Technology, Australia)*
Florian 'Floyd' Mueller *(Royal Melbourne Institute of Technology, AU)*

Publicity and Social Media: Nicole Crenshaw *(University of California Irvine, USA)*
Roger Altizer *(University of Utah, USA)*

Student Volunteers: Josh Andres *(IBM Research, Australia)*
Erik Harpstead *(Carnegie Mellon University, USA)*

Local Arrangements: Jo Iacovides *(University College London, UK)*
Sarah Spofford *(Electronic Arts, Austin, USA)*
Bill Hamilton *(Texas A&M University, USA)*

PLAY/Demos: Jose Zagal *(University of Utah, USA)*
Frank Lee *(Drexel University, USA)*

Industry Speakers and
Sponsorship: Lennart Nacke *(University of Waterloo, Canada)*
Andre Thomas *(Texas A&M University, USA)*

Things I Wish Game Researchers Would Do (Or Do More): A View from an Occasional Scientist and Hardcore Gamer

Jaime Madigan
http://www.psychologyofgames.com
jamie@psychologyofgames.com

ABSTRACT

Academic research on video games is flourishing, but to some of us watching from the outside (or at most from just inside the doorway) in it seems that researchers still haven't gotten to some notable issues and questions that are critically important to those of us who play games and those who make them. Specifically, research in major journals seems to overrepresent issues around violence, education, addiction, gamification, physical health, and a handful of other topics.

These are important and worthwhile subjects for study, so we're lucky to have it. But left out are other topics that game developers can put directly to use and which players can use to approach their hobby on their own terms. For example, how games can foster enjoyable competition, how they can get players to spend money (or not) on in-app purchases, how to craft feedback systems that get players to adopt and persist in goals, how to reduce cheating, and how players share. These "little picture" issues are a gold mine for academic research and would be well received by the end users of research. In addition, other areas of psychology already have models and theories about human behavior that can be extended to the context of gaming and HCI.

This presentation will focus on on the speaker's experience thinking about these kinds of questions over the years and provide some examples of how they are being approached in some circumstances with generous help from other areas of psychology, communications, economics, and neighboring fields. It will also argue why they are worthy of being studied scientifically and rigorously.

ACM Classification Keywords

H.5.1. Information Interfaces and Presentation (e.g. HCI): Multimedia Information Systems: Artificial, augmented, and virtual realities

Author Keywords

Games research; psychology.

CHI PLAY '16, October 16 - 19, 2016, Austin, TX, USA

© 2016 Copyright held by the owner/author(s).

ACM ISBN 978-1-4503-4456-2/16/10.

DOI: http://dx.doi.org/10.1145/2967934.2967936

BIOGRAPHY

Jamie Madigan Ph.D. has become an expert on the psychology of video games and seeks to popularize understanding of how various aspects of psychology can be used to understand why games are made how they are and why their players behave as they do. Madigan has written extensively on the subject for various magazines, websites, blogs, his own site at http://www.psychologyofgames.com, and in his 2015 book *Getting Gamers: The Psychology of Video Games and Their Impact on the People Who Play Them.* He has also consulted with game development companies and talked at conferences about how game developers can incorporate psychology principles into game design and how players can understand how it affects their play. Finally, he has appeared as an expert on the psychology of video games in dozens of print, radio, and web outlets such as *The Wall Street Journal, USA Today, The Washington Post, The Chicago Tribune, Time Magazine, Wired Magazine, The Atlantic,* and others.

The Gamer Motivation Profile:
What We Learned From 250,000 Gamers

Nick Yee
Quantic Foundry
nick@quanticfoundry.com

Abstract

Gamers are not a monolithic group; gaming preferences and motivations vary among gamers in important ways. An empirical model of gaming motivations allows developers and researchers to create more effective and engaging experiences for entertainment and serious games.

We developed an online app and used an iterative process to create the Gamer Motivation Profile. Using survey data from over 250,000 gamers worldwide, we used factor analysis to develop an empirical framework of gaming motivations and a validated tool to measure those motivations.

We identified 6 clusters of gaming motivations: Action (Excitement & Destruction), Social (Collaboration & Competition), Mastery (Strategy & Challenge), Achievement (Power & Completion), Creativity (Design & Discovery), and Immersion (Story & Fantasy).

In this talk, we'll first describe the motivations we identified, present findings on the higher-order relationships among these motivations, how they vary by gender and age, and how they are related to the Big 5 personality traits.

Respondents to the Gamer Motivation Profile also listed specific games they've enjoyed playing. In the second part of the talk, we'll present case studies of how we have applied this game audience data within the game industry to provide actionable insights for game marketing and production.

Author Keywords: Gaming motivations; factor analysis; quantitative methods.

Short Bio

Nick Yee is the co-founder and analytics lead of Quantic Foundry. For over a decade, he has conducted research on the psychology of gaming and virtual worlds using a wide variety of methods. At Stanford University, he used immersive virtual reality to explore how avatars can change the way people think and behave. At the Palo Alto Research Center (PARC), he applied social network analysis and predictive analytics to examine large-scale World of Warcraft data.

He was a senior research scientist in Ubisoft's Gamer Behavior Research group where he combined data science and social science methods to generate actionable player insights for different game development teams. At Quantic Foundry, he leads the research and development of new tools for quantifying the motivations of game audiences. He is the author of "The Proteus Paradox: How Online Games and Virtual Worlds Change Us—And How They Don't".

CHI PLAY 2016, October 16–19, 2016, Austin, Texas, USA.
ACM ISBN 978-1-4503-4456-2/16/10.
DOI: http://dx.doi.org/10.1145/2967934.2967937

Play, Participation and Empowerment: Design strategies and dilemmas

Annika Waern
Dept. of Informatics and Media
Uppsala University
Uppsala, Sweden
annika.waern@im.uu.se

ABSTRACT

The activity of play has transformative power. When a design invites play, it encourages co-creation and empowers participants to take control over their own experience. Yet, just as game design strives to create challenges that are fun to overcome, play design also strives to create specific, unique experiences - and those experiences will only be available if players to a certain extent succumb to the intentions of designers. Finding the balance between player and designer initiative is thus not straightforward. In this presentation I will discuss example designs that have managed - and some that haven't - eliciting some of the design strategies that can be brought to aid. I will also pose the critical question: does this transformative power reach out of play? Are the powers of play revolutionary - or not?

Author Keywords

Play; Participation; Empowerment; Transgressive play; Creative play; Conformant play; Explorative play

ACM Classification Keywords

H.5.m. Information interfaces and presentation (e.g., HCI): Miscellaneous.

AUTHOR BIOGRAPHY

Annika Waern is professor and chair of Human - Computer Interaction at Uppsala University. She has a long-standing background in design research on games and play within HCI as well as the international game research community, most notably through her groundbreaking work on pervasive games. Recently, prof. Waern has turned her focus to designing for play for children as well as for adults, looking into among as diverse areas as the playful design of science center experiments, outdoor play environments and live role-playing games.

CHI PLAY '16 CD-ROM, October 16-19, 2016, Austin, TX, USA
ACM 978-1-4503-4456-2/16/10.
http://dx.doi.org/10.1145/2967934.2967935

Ranking Practices and Distinction in League of Legends

Yubo Kou
Purdue University
West Lafayette, Indiana, USA
kou2@purdue.edu

Xinning Gui
University of California, Irvine
Irvine, USA
guix@uci.edu

Yong Ming Kow
City University of Hong Kong
Hong Kong SAR, China
yongmkow@cityu.edu.hk

ABSTRACT

Player ranking is a common feature of competitive online games, but little research work has closely examined the ways it mediates player practices within this game genre. In this paper, we present a qualitative study of player practices around ranking in League of Legends (LoL), published by Riot Games and currently one of the most popular eSports games. We found that ranking is a cornerstone of LoL's competitive gaming practices, shaping the ways players distinguished and narrated their game experiences, thus engendering a culture of collaboration and competition through distinction.

Author Keywords

League of Legends; ranking; player experience; Multiplayer online battle arena; MOBA.

ACM Classification Keywords

H.5.m. Information interfaces and presentation (e.g., HCI): Miscellaneous.

INTRODUCTION

Player ranking is an essential feature of competitive online games. A ranking score, calculated based on wins and losses of competitive play, is often considered an indicator of player skill, and serves the dual purpose of motivating players, as well as matchmaking players with similar skills [15]. Apart from research examining general players commitment and engagement [19,20,38], little work has examined why player ranking is so central to competitive gaming. Specifically, we study the extent player ranking mediates social practices and social structure.

We examined player experience with the ranking system in League of Legends (LoL), a team-based competitive game published by Riot Games [28]. Our study consists of semi-structured interviews and an analysis of player forum discussions. We adopted a grounded theory approach to explore the role of ranking in player experience. By adopting Bourdieu's concept of *distinction* [5], we went

CHI PLAY '16, October 16-19, 2016, Austin, TX, USA
© 2016 ACM. ISBN 978-1-4503-4456-2/16/10.. $15.00
DOI: http://dx.doi.org/10.1145/2967934.2968078

beyond earlier findings of ranking as a motivator for player engagement and retention by reporting that player ranking contributed to the formation of social stratification and stereotypes within the LoL community, was incorporated into player narratives of their performance and progress, and impacted the practices of learning and collaboration. Ranking shapes player experience in important ways, which should be considered carefully in game design.

RELATED WORK

Ranking has long been analyzed as an important type of achievement contributing to players' engagement [20,35,38], retention [6,8], and in-game progression [1,14,36]. Much gamification research has adopted ranking as a design feature to motivate players [10,16,17,32].

Previous studies have revealed social practices related to ranking up. For example, people chose to team up with skilled friends for a better chance of winning [13,25,26]. Players with deeper game knowledge might even collude to cheat ranking systems [7,37].

LEAGUE OF LEGENDS

With 67 million monthly active players [34], League of Legends is one of the most popular online games. As a Multiplayer online battle arena (MOBA) game, LoL is match-based rather than presenting a persistent world. Each match occurs between two teams and lasts between 30 – 50 minutes. A typical team contains five players who are selected randomly from a large pool of available players. During a match, players controls their characters (or champions) to destroy their opponents' base, or force them to surrender. During battles, each player gains experience points and gold by killing non-player characters (NPCs) or opponents. Learning to collaborate with strangers in a relatively short time is challenging for video game players [2,11,12,21]. Toxic behaviors are common within such online transient teams [4,18,22,23,33].

LoL ranks players into several tiers: Bronze (about 40.77% of players), Silver (37.54%), Gold (14.38%), Platinum (5.99%), Diamond (1.22%), Master (0.05%), and Challenger (0.02%)[1]. Each of the former six tiers is further divided into five divisions. A division contains 100 league points (LP) that players can gain or lose after a match. On the other hand, players of the latter two tiers participate in a different tournament format designed for the "the most elite players and teams" [29].

---

[1] Data obtained on April 18, 2016 from: http://na.op.gg/statistics/tier/

METHODS

This study belongs to a larger project investigating LoL players' social experience. The study contains 16 semi-structured interviews with North American LoL players between 2013 and 2015. Participants had at least two years' experience playing ranked games during the time of interview. One player's rank was Diamond, three were Platinum, five were Gold, four were Silver, and three were Bronze. We recruited the participants by directly contacting them in game, recruiting on forums, and snowball sampling. Interviews generally lasted between 30 minutes to one hour. We asked them why they played ranked games, what were their strategies to improve their rank, and what a ranking meant to them. We searched forum posts that discussed ranking in Reddit's LoL sub-forum[2] and LoL's official forum[3], using keywords such as "ranking," "bronze," "silver," "gold," "platinum," "diamond," "master," and "challenger." In total we collected 37 posts from the former and 32 posts from the latter.

We took a grounded theory approach to analyze the data [31]. We first read the data and used our initial perceptions to generate a starting list of codes, which included ideas about players' perception of ranking and their strategies of ranking up. From there, we returned to the data to conduct a systematic analysis of the themes that arose. After several iterations of coding, we identified a central phenomenon in the data – how ranking is associated with elements of social experience. With this frame in mind, we returned to the data to systematically analyze these elements which we will discuss in the next section.

FINDINGS

In this section, we discuss how ranking influenced player experience in LoL in three different aspects: social stratification and stereotypes, player narratives, and learning and collaboration.

Formation of Social Stratification and Stereotypes

During our interviews, specific ranks were frequently mentioned when our study participants referred to a particular player such as an in-game friend or an offline connection. For example, a participant started answering our questions by saying, "I have a Diamond friend… Another friend who has been in Silver one for a long time thought…" Another participant said, "a Gold I met in normal recommended Zed mid, so I…" In these instances, participants used a specific rank such as "Diamond," "Silver one," or "Gold" to refer to an individual player. A rank became an important descriptor of players.

For players, a specific rank often suggested much more information than a skill level. Stereotypes were formed around different ranks. For example, when asked to explain what "Diamond" meant, a participant said, "they are pretty hardcore, knowing the pros and cons of many champions,

[2] https://www.reddit.com/r/leagueoflegends

[3] http://boards.na.leagueoflegends.com/en/

and sometimes arrogant!" "Bronze" according to many participants, did not just indicate a low skill at LoL. They used "Bronze" to refer to players who played mindlessly, often raged in game, refused to learn, and showed little interest in cooperating with teammates. From participants' perspective, the stereotypes of ranks differed along several dimensions such as in-game collaboration and learning, such as skill, knowledge, temper, personality, willingness to cooperate, and awareness of teammates.

Players' accounts oftentimes sustained such stereotypes. For example, here is an excerpt from a Reddit post:

> *Before, I was the stereotypical feeding bronze who would autolock a champion either mid or ADC. Back then, League of Legends was a game I played carelessly. I would always find myself in hopeless duels with champions that far outmatched me. After getting sick of blaming everything on Gods creation for my failures I decided to try and get out of my low elo [computed ranking].*

"Autolock" refers to the somewhat "abrupt" behavior of determining a champion and a role without communicating with teammates. This player identified with the Bronze stereotype, admitted his shortcomings, and sought to improve his future rank as determined by the ranking system. In such cases, social positioning represented by player ranks suggested players what kind of players they are, and with whom they are playing with.

Foundation of Player Narratives

Higher ranks supplied players sense of achievement and gratification. As a participant said, "I'm proud about reach[ing] Gold in the first season I played." Another participant mentioned, "I once mentioned to a friend that I was Platinum in League. He immediately said, 'oh, that's very cool man! Very cool! Very few can reach that high.' I was very glad to hear that." This echoed the study of Birk et al. that player self-esteem is positively associated with player perception of competence [3].

Such achievements were so central to players' experience, that when they described themselves to others, they often construct narratives which emphasized not only their present rank, but also the trajectory of ranks changing through their gaming history. Here is an excerpt from a Reddit post:

> *I played Annie every chance I got and placed somewhere around mid-silver (1300 ish elo). Before the pre-season ended, I was at 1576, which was low gold… I played … for about 800-900 ~ Annie games. When season 3 kicked off I was put into Gold V. From there, after playing 536 Annie Games, I reached platinum V… After 930 Annie Games, I reached Diamond V… After 1,438 Annie Games, I reached Diamond 1… So now after 1,960 Annie Games I've reached Challenger.*

"Annie" is a champion in LoL. For this player, the "Challenger" rank indicated his present skill level. But his story also emphasized a history of diligent effort and persistent play that afforded his present rank, which he cared much about. Similarly, a participant noted:

> *I got my Diamond border this season. Every time I see it in the loading screen, it reminds me of the great moments when I made a big play and changed the game... The bad moments when a single teammate ruined the whole game... the amazing people I have played with. Some have become my friends and even now we still play together.*

Like this player, many participants have played hundreds or thousands of matches in order to reach a desired rank. They kept track of rank gains and losses after each match. The long-term endeavor enriched and complicated their feelings for their ranks. A rank was associated with many precious memories, such as memorable gaming moments and friendship. As such, the rank became part of the narratives of LoL players.

Players did not always attempt to improve their ranks, especially after they reached their perceived limits. A participant who was at Diamond explained:

> *After reaching Diamond V, I didn't play ranked as frequently as before. I didn't want to be demoted to Plat[inum] again. I know I can't get to Master or Challenger anyway, and Diamond V and Diamond I have exactly the same rewards... So I and some people I knew just sat at 0 lp till the end of the season.*

The player was aware that by playing more games, there was a risk that he may slide down the rank, and lost his Diamond status. Thus, he became pragmatic and conservative after reaching a desired rank. Such mentality was also reported by our participants who were at Platinum and Gold, who deemed a higher goal unrealistic. While LoL currently does not include the design of dynamic difficulty [9] for balancing player goal and commitment, participants themselves negotiated the situation through means such as controlling playtime.

Players' conservatism goes against the agenda of Riot Games which profits from frequent player participation. The company thus introduced a decay mechanism, in which a Platinum or Diamond player, after 28 days of inactivity, will be removed from the official league table, and will lose part of his LP score every seven days of further inactivity [29]. But our participants reportedly worked around this decay mechanism by playing only one ranked match every four weeks, which they claimed to be effective dealing with the mechanism.

Structuring of Learning and Collaboration
Ranking influenced LoL players' practices of learning and collaboration in concrete ways.

Learning
Our participants reported generally trusting the advice from players with a higher rank. Many participants admitted that they mostly watched the streams or videos of professional players or at least Diamond players, and preferred to read guides written by people that were Diamond or above. A participant explained:

> *I would probably think twice before believing anything said from a Silver. I mean, why he is stuck in Silver if he does everything right... It would be much convincing if the advice is from a pro.*

Another participant even went into further details to explicate the differences among Diamond players. He said:

> *Diamond I is definitely much better than Diamond V. Diamond V's skill is just around high Plat or something. Diamond I players are essentially playing with professionals or semi-professionals. This is why I like to get answers from Diamond Is.*

Ranking thus contributed to the formation of a social hierarchy along which knowledge about LoL was formed and passed. This echoed with Kow and Young's observation of the StarCraft eSport community where knowledge diffusion happened from expert players to ordinary ones [24].

However, participants also stressed the specialty of each individual rank. While participants thought highly of the opinions of high-ranked players, they also stressed critical thinking when applying some "pro advice" to their own play. For example, a participant said:

> *The Diamond/Platinum mentality doesn't always work at low tiers like Bronze... If you want to climb up in Bronze, you have to play aggressively and try to make big plays. Winning your lane and then moving to the team fight phase is simply not enough in Bronze and Silver. By the time you reach 200 cs in 20 minutes, you probably find all the rest of your team get stomped.*

"Cs" means the number of opponent NPCs killed by a player. Here, LoL players were also aware that each ranked league might also favor distinct strategies, thus influencing what constituted knowledge and learning in each league.

Collaboration
Ranking influenced player collaboration. Players judged their teammates based on the latter's ranking information. LoL provides application program interfaces (APIs) that allow public access to players' profile, setting, and history [30], leading to the emergence of a number of third-party websites, or player dossiers [27]. These websites allow people to check any player's ranking information such as win rate, current rank, match history, and performance.

LoL players used these websites to learn about teammates' capability and strengths. They then utilized these insights to influence their teammates. A player noted:

Manipulate your teammates to play one of their top two roles... Go to lolking.net and open up a tab for every one of your 4 teammates. Click on "Ranked Stats," then sort by "Wins." Your new goal in life is to get your teammates to play one of their top 2 roles, you can judge by their wins with champs (if they also have a positive win rate). Force your teammates into their best role if at all possible... Juggle roles to maximize win rate and therefore win chance.

The player discussed steps he used to influence teammates' decisions to optimize team performance. If teammates were uncooperative and picked unfamiliar champions or roles, players would anticipate a larger chance of loss. A common countermeasure is to quit as soon as possible, which may abort a match. A player wrote:

I prefer op.gg [a third party website], and I'm not afraid to dodge when it's clear to me that 2+ lanes are in a position to get rocked. Save yourself the time, the LP, and the potential tilt and just walk around for a few minutes instead. I feel like I jumped from Silver IV to Silver I simply by dodging the games that were "lost" in the champ select. That, and the release of cinderhulk Amumu [a skin for the champion Amumu].

"Tilt" in LoL refers to the downgraded mentality and rationality after a series of losses. In this case, ranking became a deciding factor in player choice of whether or not to play, and how in collaboration.

DISCUSSION AND CONCLUSION

We have discussed how the inclusion of a player ranking system mediated LoL players' perception of social strata in the game, and their interactions with other players. Clues of this social structure can be found in player conversations, learning, and collaborative play. Many participants reported trusting opinions and advice from people with a higher rank. A participant was pressured to improve his rank because "all my friends are either Diamond or high Plat."

Importantly, player ranking is such an important representation in competitive games—especially its position to organize competitive gaming communities—that within it we may conjecture to contain degree of unfairness especially when social biases do not reflect reality of players' true abilities and potentials, as Bourdieu noted:

Commonplaces and classificatory systems are thus the stake of struggles between the groups they characterize and counterpose, who fight over them while striving to turn them to their own advantage. [5]

Players may be unhappy over the ranking system for various reasons. Participants who were demoted to or decayed to a lower rank expressed their frustration and fear of being unable to return to the old rank. Players with limited time may take a pragmatic attitude towards ranking, and further constrain their playtime and investment in the game. Ranking thus can have negative influence over player participation, posing critical questions into the design of "fair" ranking systems. Apart from the demotion and decay mechanisms, game designers need to explore ways of accommodating players' diversity and background.

Unlike in the real world, in which there are "dominant" social classes influencing knowledge creation [5], online forums surrounding games appear to be self-organized, but nonetheless still contains features of a knowledge hierarchy. This hierarchy is socially constructed, based on perception of stereotypes regarding skill, knowledge, mentality, and personality of player ranks. Players with higher ranks possess more authority in defining knowledge, such as how a champion should be played and what items to buy. However, players also perceived the limitations of this top-down knowledge diffusion—not attending to specific playstyle and team dynamics required at lower ranks. Participants who had successfully climbed up one or two tiers stressed the difference in play strategies at different tiers, for example, a participant said, "In Bronze and Silver I just spammed Master Yi. In Gold I paid more attention to my team composition when picking my champions."

With players' deep engagement, a rank is no longer just a skill indicator and a motivator. It reminds participants of the high and low points of their ranking history, such as the first time they reached Gold or the two times they were demoted from Platinum. Five participants explicitly mentioned being proud of the win rate of a particular champion, or a winning streak of 10 games. While each game passes quickly, these memories remain with players for a long time. Players dossiers such as those third-party websites are helpful in presenting more information about past gameplay besides a current rank. However, the precious moments of one player might differ greatly from another, making them difficulty to instantiate in a universal interface. The design of ranking systems might consider more power and freedom on the player side, allowing players to generate content within ranking systems.

While Medler's analysis of player dossier shows its instrumental value in enabling players to analyze past gameplay and increase social capital [27], we point to the value of such systems and the like in preserving an experience in which a player not only find distinction from others, but also derives pleasure from reminiscing and appreciating his own history of play. We suggest that such experience might be a critical component of player experience in competitive games. More research is needed to explore what constitutes proper ways of interacting with one's own data and what role design can play in this interaction.

ACKNOWLEDGMENTS
The work described in this paper was partially supported by grants from City University of Hong Kong (Project No. 7004583).

REFERENCES

1. Jeffrey Bardzell, Jeffrey Nichols, Tyler Pace, and Shaowen Bardzell. 2012. Come meet me at Ulduar: progression raiding in world of warcraft. *Proceedings of the ACM 2012 conference on Computer Supported Cooperative Work - CSCW '12*, ACM Press, 603–612. http://doi.org/10.1145/2145204.2145296

2. Shaowen Bardzell, Jeffrey Bardzell, Tyler Pace, and Kayce Reed. 2008. Blissfully productive: grouping and cooperation in world of warcraft instance runs. *Proceedings of the ACM 2008 conference on Computer supported cooperative work - CSCW '08*, ACM Press, 357–360. http://doi.org/10.1145/1460563.1460621

3. Max V. Birk, Regan L. Mandryk, Matthew K. Miller, and Kathrin M. Gerling. 2015. How Self-Esteem Shapes our Interactions with Play Technologies. *Proceedings of the 2015 Annual Symposium on Computer-Human Interaction in Play - CHI PLAY '15*, ACM Press, 35–45. http://doi.org/10.1145/2793107.2793111

4. Jeremy Blackburn and Haewoon Kwak. 2014. STFU NOOB!: predicting crowdsourced decisions on toxic behavior in online games. *Proceedings of the 23rd international conference on World wide web - WWW '14*, ACM Press, 877–888. http://doi.org/10.1145/2566486.2567987

5. Pierre Bourdieu. 1984. *Distinction: A Social Critique of the Judgement of Taste*. Routledge & Kegan Paul.

6. Dongseong Choi and Jinwoo Kim. 2004. Why People Continue to Play Online Games: In Search of Critical Design Factors to Increase Customer Loyalty to Online Contents. *CyberPsychology & Behavior* 7, 1: 11–24.

7. Mia Consalvo. 2007. Cheating: gaining advantage in videogames. 246.

8. Thomas Debeauvais, Bonnie Nardi, Diane J. Schiano, Nicolas Ducheneaut, and Nicholas Yee. 2011. If you build it they might stay: retention mechanisms in World of Warcraft. *Proceedings of the 6th International Conference on Foundations of Digital Games - FDG '11*, ACM Press, 180–187. http://doi.org/10.1145/2159365.2159390

9. Alena Denisova and Paul Cairns. 2015. Adaptation in Digital Games: The Effect of Challenge Adjustment on Player Performance and Experience. *Proceedings of the 2015 Annual Symposium on Computer-Human Interaction in Play - CHI PLAY '15*, ACM Press, 97–101. http://doi.org/10.1145/2793107.2793141

10. Sebastian Deterding, Miguel Sicart, Lennart Nacke, Kenton O'Hara, and Dan Dixon. 2011. Gamification: using game-design elements in non-gaming contexts. *Proceedings of the 2011 annual conference extended abstracts on Human factors in computing systems - CHI EA '11*, ACM Press, 2425–2428. http://doi.org/10.1145/1979742.1979575

11. Scott Donaldson. 2015. Mechanics and Metagame: Exploring Binary Expertise in League of Legends. *Games and Culture*: 1–19. http://doi.org/10.1177/1555412015590063

12. Lina Eklund and Magnus Johansson. 2010. Social Play? A study of social interaction in temporary group formation (PUG) in World of Warcraft. *DiGRA Nordic*.

13. Maria Frostling-Henningsson. 2009. First-Person Shooter Games as a Way of Connecting to People: "Brothers in Blood." *CyberPsychology & Behavior* 12, 5: 557–562.

14. Alex Golub. 2010. Being in the World (of Warcraft): Raiding, Realism, and Knowledge Production in a Massively Multiplayer Online Game. *Anthropological Quarterly* 83, 1: 17–45. http://doi.org/10.1353/anq.0.0110

15. Thore Graepel and Ralf Herbrich. 2006. Ranking and Matchmaking: How to rate players' skills for fun and competitive gaming. *Game Developer Magazine*.

16. Juho Hamari, Jonna Koivisto, and Harri Sarsa. 2014. Does Gamification Work? -- A Literature Review of Empirical Studies on Gamification. *47th Hawaii International Conference on System Sciences*, 3025–3034.

17. Gwo-Jen Hwang, Po-Han Wu, and Chi-Chang Chen. 2012. An online game approach for improving students' learning performance in web-based problem-solving activities. *Computers & Education* 59, 4: 1246–1256. http://doi.org/10.1016/j.compedu.2012.05.009

18. Magnus Johansson, Harko Verhagen, and Yubo Kou. 2015. I Am Being Watched By The Tribunal-Trust and Control in Multiplayer Online Battle Arena Games. *Proceedings of the 10th International Conference on the Foundations of Digital Games*.

19. Kirsi Pauliina Kallio, Frans Mäyrä, and Kirsikka Kaipainen. 2011. At Least Nine Ways to Play: Approaching Gamer Mentalities. *Games and Culture* 6, 4: 327 –353. http://doi.org/10.1177/1555412010391089

20. Daniel King, Paul Delfabbro, and Mark Griffiths. 2009. Video Game Structural Characteristics: A New Psychological Taxonomy. *International Journal of Mental Health and Addiction* 8, 1: 90–106. http://doi.org/10.1007/s11469-009-9206-4

21. Yubo Kou and Xinning Gui. 2014. Playing with strangers: understanding temporary teams in League of Legends. *Proceedings of the first ACM SIGCHI annual symposium on Computer-human interaction in play - CHI PLAY '14*, ACM Press, 161–169. http://doi.org/10.1145/2658537.2658538

22. Yubo Kou and Bonnie Nardi. 2013. Regulating Anti-Social Behavior on the Internet: The Example of League of Legends. *iConference 2013 Proceedings*: 616–622. http://doi.org/10.9776/13289

23. Yubo Kou and Bonnie Nardi. 2014. Governance in League of Legends: A Hybrid System. *Foundations of Digital Games*.

24. Yong Ming Kow and Timothy Young. 2013. Media technologies and learning in the starcraft esport community. *Proceedings of the 2013 conference on Computer supported cooperative work - CSCW '13*: 387–398. http://doi.org/10.1145/2441776.2441821

25. Elizabeth Losh. 2008. In polite company: rules of play in five Facebook games. *Proceedings of the 2008 International Conference in Advances on Computer Entertainment Technology - ACE '08*, ACM Press, 345–351. http://doi.org/10.1145/1501750.1501832

26. Li Lu, Cuihua Shen, and Dmitri Williams. 2014. Friending your way up the ladder: Connecting massive multiplayer online game behaviors with offline leadership. *Computers in Human Behavior* 35: 54–60. http://doi.org/10.1016/j.chb.2014.02.013

27. Ben Medler. 2011. Player Dossiers: Analyzing Gameplay Data as a Reward. *the international journal of computer game research* 11, 1.

28. Riot Games. 2008. *League of Legends*. Retrieved from http://na.leagueoflegends.com/

29. Riot Games. 2016. RANKED PLAY FAQ. Retrieved from https://support.riotgames.com/hc/en-us/articles/204010760-Ranked-Play-FAQ#h8

30. Riot Games. 2016. Riot Games API. Retrieved from https://developer.riotgames.com/

31. John C. Scott and Barney G. Glaser. 1971. The Discovery of Grounded Theory: Strategies for Qualitative Research. *American Sociological Review* 36, 335. http://doi.org/10.2307/2094063

32. Sepandar Sepehr and Milena Head. 2013. Competition as an element of gamification for learning: an exploratory longitudinal investigation. *Proceedings of the First International Conference on Gameful Design, Research, and Applications - Gamification '13*, ACM Press, 2–9. http://doi.org/10.1145/2583008.2583009

33. Kenneth B. Shores, Yilin He, Kristina L. Swanenburg, Robert Kraut, and John Riedl. 2014. The identification of deviance and its impact on retention in a multiplayer game. *Proceedings of the 17th ACM conference on Computer supported cooperative work & social computing - CSCW '14*, ACM Press, 1356–1365. http://doi.org/10.1145/2531602.2531724

34. Paul Tassi. 2014. Riot's "League of Legends" Reveals Astonishing 27 Million Daily Players, 67 Million Monthly. *Forbes*. Retrieved from http://www.forbes.com/sites/insertcoin/2014/01/27/riots-league-of-legends-reveals-astonishing-27-million-daily-players-67-million-monthly/#e24f30d35111

35. T.L. Taylor. 2003. Power gamers just want to have fun. *Instrumental play in a MMOG*.

36. D. Williams, Nicolas Ducheneaut, Li Xiong, Yuanyuan Zhang, Nick Yee, and Eric Nickell. 2006. From Tree House to Barracks: The Social Life of Guilds in World of Warcraft. *Games and Culture* 1, 4: 338–361. http://doi.org/10.1177/1555412006292616

37. Jeff Yan and Brian Randell. 2005. A systematic classification of cheating in online games. *Proceedings of 4th ACM SIGCOMM workshop on Network and system support for games - NetGames '05*, ACM Press, 1–9. http://doi.org/10.1145/1103599.1103606

38. Nick Yee. 2006. Motivations for Play in Online Games. *CyberPsychology & Behavior* 9: 772–775. http://doi.org/10.1089/cpb.2006.9.772

The Influence of Virtual Agents on Player Experience and Performance

Katharina Emmerich
Entertainment Computing Group
University of Duisburg-Essen, Germany
katharina.emmerich@uni-due.de

Maic Masuch
Entertainment Computing Group
University of Duisburg-Essen, Germany
maic.masuch@uni-due.de

ABSTRACT

This paper contributes a systematic research approach as well as findings of an empirical study conducted to investigate the effect of virtual agents on task performance and player experience in digital games. As virtual agents are supposed to evoke social effects similar to real humans under certain conditions, the basic social phenomenon social facilitation is examined in a testbed game that was specifically developed to enable systematical variation of single impact factors of social facilitation. Independent variables were the presence of a virtual agent (present vs. not present) and the output device (ordinary monitor vs. head-mounted display). Results indicate social inhibition effects, but only for players using a head-mounted display. Additional potential impact factors and future research directions are discussed.

ACM Classification Keywords

K.8.0. Personal Computing: General – Games

Author Keywords

player experience; social facilitation; virtual agent; performance; social impact

INTRODUCTION

Playing games has been a social experience ever since. People use games to socialize, to compete with each other or to learn and train. That applies to *digital* games as well: Playing together with others and social aspects of games in general are among the main motivators to play digital games [29, 22]. While early models of player experience in digital games focused the individual experience of one player, social aspects like the influence of other players, audiences and their behavior during a gaming session are more recently considered as an important part of the overall player experience in game user research [6, 25, 20]. However, players of digital games do not necessarily interact with other real players but also with artificial intelligence and virtual characters. In this context, De Kort et al. [6] explicitly include mediated co-presence as well as the presence of agents and virtual co-players as *sociality*

characteristics of a gaming setting in their framework of social player experience. While the term *agent* is not uniformly defined in computer science (cf. [28]), in the context of this paper a *virtual agent* is considered as a computer-controlled social entity that can feature different representations (mostly visual) and different levels of agency (ranging from being completely passive to autonomously acting based on a complex artificial intelligence system). Agents thus have to be distinguished from *avatars*, which are also social entities but controlled by humans [19]. Research regarding virtual agents in virtual environments supports the conclusion that virtual agents are supposed to trigger basic social reactions as well, provided that they are identified as social entities [24, 3]. Human-like social cues, a human-like outward appearance and a corresponding behavior automatically and unconsciously result in sublime attributions, which in turn effect our behavior [18]. That seems to be true even if the conscious appreciation of the degree of anthropomorphism does not result in identifying the agent as a human, that is to say even if the agent is consciously considered as not being a human [18].

In line with these assumptions, the work presented in this paper suggests that social effects of playing digital games are not limited to the presence of other real players but also apply to the presence of virtual social entities like virtual agents. Accordingly, basic social phenomena like the established social facilitation effect [9] are supposed to be observable in digital games as well. Knowledge about those effects may reveal the social impact of virtual agents and will inform future game design processes, for instance of games for learning that may include virtual agents. In the following, the theoretical foundation regarding social facilitation and virtual agents is introduced and a methodological approach to systematically test social facilitation in digital games is presented. Finally, results of a first study carried out to gain insights into the social impact of agents in games are discussed.

THE SOCIAL FACILITATION EFFECT

In the field of social psychology there are diverse examples of social impact factors and effects that influence people while they are not even aware of it. The social facilitation theory is one of the oldest and impressively demonstrates how the mere presence of another person has an effect on behavior: An individual shows an altered level of performance in a task if another conspecific is present in contrast to attending to the task alone. First observations of racing cyclists and children who should turn a fishing reel as fast as possible showed significantly increased speed if the task was performed next to each other compared to being alone [26]. Later, faster performances in co-working scenarios and free association and writing tasks were found, but while the quantity was enhanced, there was a decrease of the quality of answers [2]. Manifold following studies in diverse application areas show similar results and indicate that the presence of others may not only improve performance but can also have the opposite effect, depending on various aspects like the kind of task and performance measure (see e.g. [9], [4] and [1] for comprehensive overviews). Hence, while in the narrow sense (and as implied by the wording) the social facilitation effect describes an enhancement of performance in the presence of others, it is today rather used as a broader term for any kind of change in performance, also inhibition, due to the fact of not being alone [1].

Despite intense research, the questions why people react to the presence of others like they do and under which conditions co-presence acts facilitating or inhibiting are still not definitely answered. Early research was highly influenced by Zajonc, who postulated the first comprehensive theory particularly accounting for the opposite effects of social facilitation [30]. According to his drive theory, the presence of others influences behavior by raising the level of arousal, which, in turn, leads to an enhancement of dominant responses. Dominant responses are those which are well-learned or automatically executed. In case of easy or learned tasks, this strategy is supposed to result in appropriate and performant behavior, while it will presumably fail in difficult or unfamiliar situations. Hence, Zajonc puts emphasis on the quality of the task as an indicator for facilitation or inhibition, respectively. Other theories followed trying to give different explanations to the effect (see [9] for an overview). While discussing all relevant theories and possible explanations in detail is beyond the scope of the paper at hand, it can be concluded from literature review that the precise processes underlying social facilitation are not yet completely clarified, but that nevertheless processes of *arousal*, *attention* and *social valuation* in some combination are very likely to determine social facilitation effects [9].

Social Facilitation, Digital Media and Virtual Agents
Social phenomena like social facilitation are not limited to "real" social contexts but are supposed to also be induced by digital representations of social entities, including virtual agents. Accordingly, social facilitation was investigated in media scenarios and virtual worlds as well. Hall and Henningsen [10] conducted a study to examine whether a computer icon is capable of triggering social facilitation in typing tasks. They used the default paperclip computer icon of Microsoft Word and found an overall social inhibition effect on the difficult version of the task, but no significant facilitation in case of the easy task. Furthermore, they observed a gender effect: Women perceived more evaluation potential and displayed inhibition effects due to the presence of the icon, while men showed opposite tendencies. Results of a study by Rickenberg et al. [21] also display social inhibition effects due to virtual animated characters on websites.

Hoyt et al. [13] carried out a study to replicate social facilitation effects in an immersive virtual environment. They varied the perceived agency of the virtual observers by differentiating between avatars (virtual characters controlled by a human being) and agents (controlled by the computer system). Participants had to solve a novel or learned task of pattern recognition or categorization in a virtual laboratory environment using a head-mounted display (HMD). Social inhibition was found for avatars and unlearned tasks, but not for the presence of agents. The authors argue that the evaluative character of avatars may foster social effects on performance, while virtual agents with low perceived agency do not trigger evaluation apprehension and thus no social facilitation [13]. Zanbaka et al. [31] compared the influence of a real person, a projected digital agent and a digital agent on task performance in math tasks in an immersive virtual environment using a HMD. In contrast to the study of Hoyt et al. [13], social inhibition effects were revealed in all three conditions, although no evaluation apprehension was provoked, implying that there is no difference between the influence of virtual and real persons. Hayes et al. [12] varied the type of view between 1st and 3rd person view as well as the gender of the present agent. Although there was no significant main effect of audience type on task performance, trends were found that indicate an inhibition effect in the case of complex tasks and a facilitation effect on simple task in the presence of a female agent. Thus, the gender of the audience might also be an influential factor.

Taken together, these exemplary studies provide evidence that virtual agents may evoke social facilitation effects under certain circumstances. However, findings are inconsistent. At least some of these contradictory findings may be due to the variation in the design of the agents. According to Krämer [18] the acceptance of virtual agents is dependent on their characteristics, particularly voice and natural nonverbal behavior. In a similar way Blascovich et al. [3] define two factors of social influence in immersive virtual environments, namely behavioral realism and social presence. It can be suggested that the appearance and behavior of the virtual agent significantly influences the social effect it has on a person.

In the context of digital games Kappen et al. [16] investigated the effect of different types of audiences on the player experiences of co-located players and found that both negative and positive audiences increased game engagement of the players. Furthermore, Bowman et al. [5] found a facilitation effect for players of an easy version of a first-person shooter game in the presence of a real audience. While these studies point out the applicability of social facilitation on digital gaming tasks, they deal with the impact of real-world audiences observing the players and do not account for the presence of virtual social entities. In sum, though experiences so far indicate that social facilitation is likely to also occur in gaming scenarios, it is not yet studied regarding virtual agents in digital games. In order to be able to systematically investigate that, it is first necessary to identify the range of possible impact factors that may influence the effect in order to include them as variables in further research.

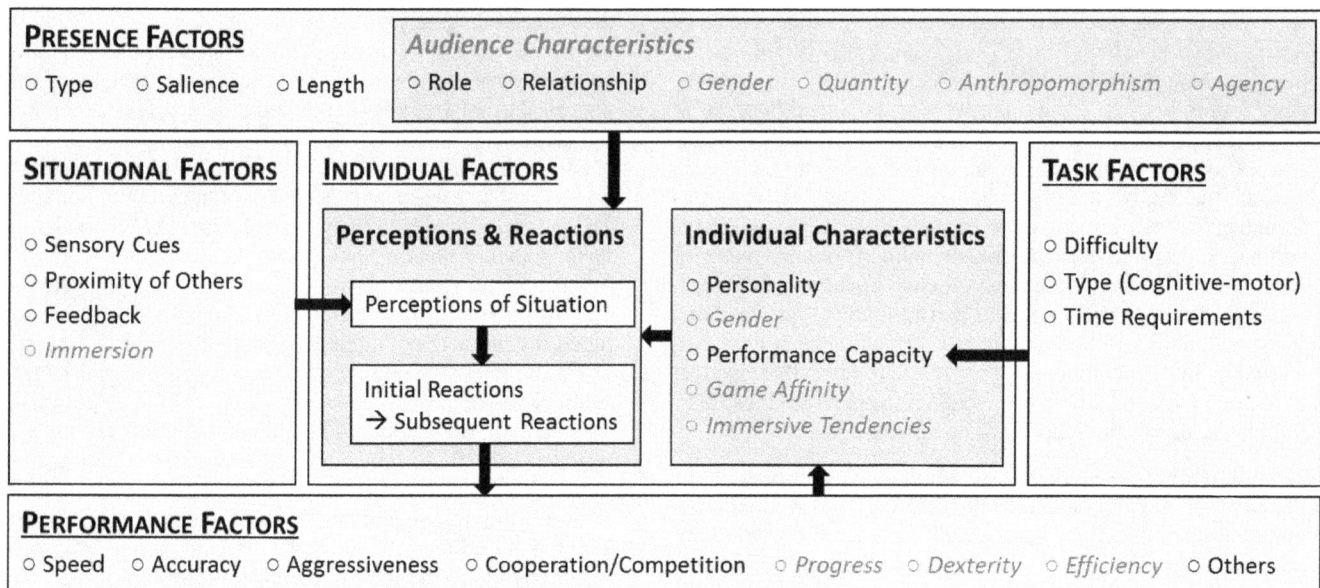

Figure 1. Integrative Model of Social Facilitation by Aiello et al. (2001), adapted to virtual agents in games; changes to the original model are indicated by italic green font.

Possible Impact Factors: An Integrative Model of Social Facilitation

A very suitable groundwork for summarizing possible impact factors of social facilitation is provided by Aiello et al. [1]. They take up the theoretical classifications of Guerin [9], critically reflect the most popular theories regarding social facilitation and finally result in a comprehensive framework for examining social facilitation effects. Instead of favoring a single theory, they put emphasis on the importance of investigating the influence of different variables of the setting and distinguish five categories of potentially influencing factors:

- **Presence factors** include the type, salience and length of presence as well as the role of the other person(s) and their relationship with the individual.
- **Situational factors** like sensory cues, the proximity and the feedback of the others as well as the organizational climate are supposed to also mediate social facilitation.
- **Task factors** include difficulty, characteristics or the type of task (like cognitive or motor tasks) and time requirements. These factors especially account for the inconsistent findings regarding social facilitation in different contexts and different tasks.
- **Individual factors** are further differentiated into more stable characteristics like personality and performance capacity (defining to which degree the person is usually able to perform the task at hand) on the one hand and concrete perceptions and reactions in the current situation on the other hand. Perceptions include social processes like social comparison and evaluation, self-awareness and distraction, and thus account for many explanation theories of social facilitation. Reactions are subdivided into initial and subsequent reactions, where initial reactions also include physiological arousal and cognitive processes.

- **Performance factors** describe the kind of performance that is observed. While speed or accuracy have been investigated in diverse studies, other aspects like cooperation or helpfulness may be influenced differently.

Figure 1 gives an overview of the main impact factors regarding social facilitation and their influence on each other based on the integrative model by Aiello and Douthitt [1]. While the original model accounted for general aspects regarding social facilitation effects, it can be extended and slightly adapted with focus on digital games and virtual agents based on prior findings (marked green and italic in Figure 1). The main change is proposed concerning presence factors: A differentiation is suggested between attributes of the presence itself and particular characteristics of the audience. As the audience can also be represented by a virtual agent, the aspects *perceived agency* and *anthropomorphism* are added, as those factors are supposed to highly influence how the agent is perceived and evaluated [3, 13]. Anthropomorphism is not necessarily related to a human-like outer appearance, but can also be achieved by realism of behavior or voice implementation. Furthermore, the aspects *gender of the audience* (which might be male, female or indistinguishable) and *quantity* (how many social entities comprises the audience) might influence social effects.

Gender of the task-performing individual should also be accounted for, particularly in combination with the sex of the agent (cf. [12, 10]). Furthermore, *game affinity* and *immersive tendencies* are considered as potential individual impact factors accounting for the special context of digital games and virtual environments. Immersive tendencies are supposed to effect the degree to which a person is immersed by an environment [27], while game affinity may mediate performance

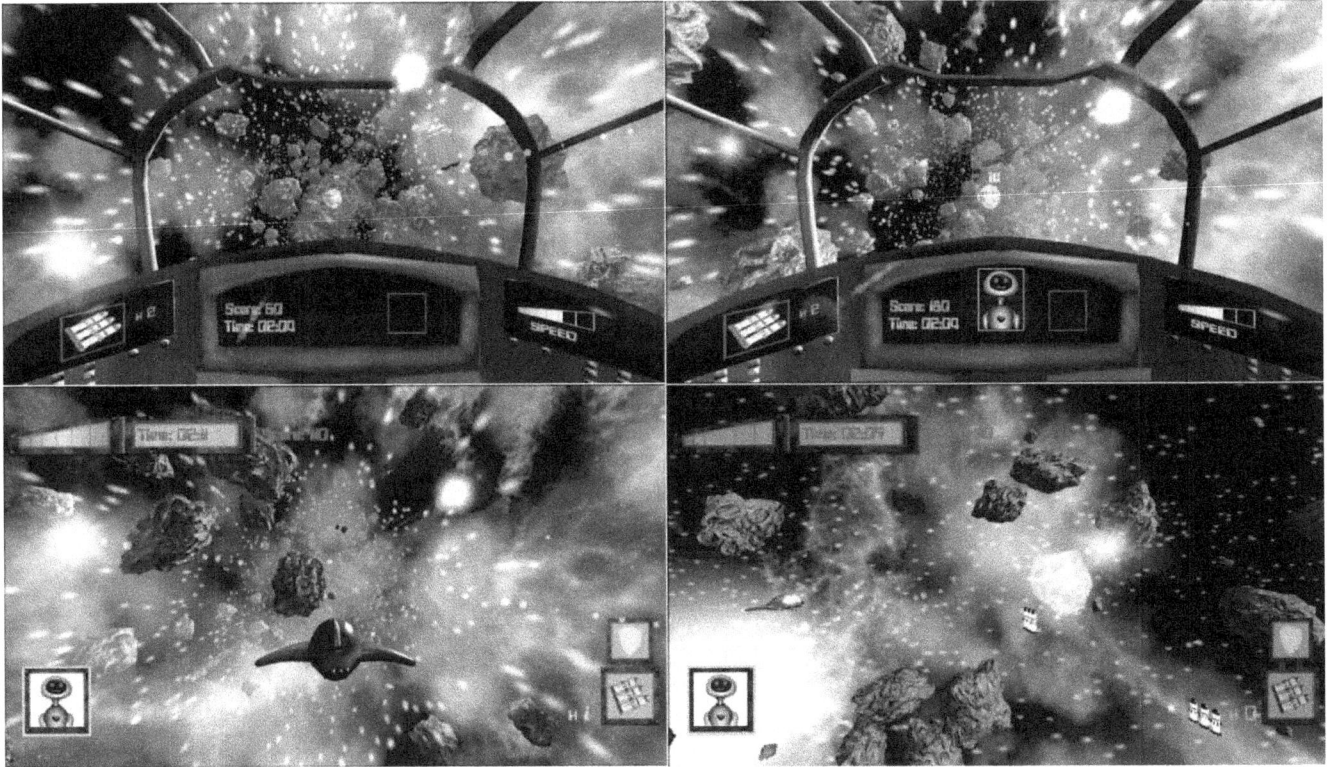

Figure 2. Screenshots of different game versions. Top: 1st-person perspective without agent (left) and with agent (right). Bottom: 3rd-person 3D perspective (left) and 2D graphical perspective (right), both with agent.

capacity. Moreover, there are some more performance measures often found in games, namely *progress*, *dexterity* and *efficiency*. Finally, an additional situational factor related to virtual worlds is *immersion*, as the degree of immersion is supposed to influence feelings of presence, that is to say the feeling of actually being in the virtual world [31].

At this point, some of the concepts and terms mentioned here, namely those related to *immersion* and *presence*, have to be defined more precisely in order to avoid misunderstandings. Those concepts are often considered in game user research and in the context of virtual reality (VR) environments, but not uniformly defined and sometimes even used synonymously [8]. Following the disambiguation of Slater [23] we see immersion as the objective quality of an interactive system to deliver sensory cues to the human sensory system. Hence, the more the system occupies a person's perception, the more immersive it is. Presence, on the other hand, is often described as the feeling of actually being in the virtual world and perceiving it as real, and can be seen as a result of immersion [23]. A VR system with a head mounted display (HMD) for instance is more immersive than a common computer monitor, and thus supposed to convey a higher feeling of presence. A higher feeling of presence, in turn, might increase the social influence of an audience. Therefore, immersion is considered as a situational factor in the adapted model of social facilitation, as it is supposed to be an influential quality of the system that is used to play a game, while the feeling of presence is part of the

resulting individual perception. This notion of presence is not to be confused with the meaning of the term *presence factors* in the integrative model, because in the model *presence* does not refer to the subjective feeling of the user but objectively describes by whatever means the audience is present.

TESTBED GAME FOR THE INVESTIGATION OF SOCIAL FACILITATION

In order to investigate the impact of the presence of virtual agents on performance and player experience in digital games, a comprehensive game environment was designed and implemented using the *Unity3D* engine. The advantage of using a specifically developed game environment for research purposes is threefold: First of all, it makes it possible to purposefully manipulate an independent variable of interest, while keeping all other aspects constant to ensure comparable results of dependent variables among game versions. Second, it allows researchers to systematically investigate various aspects of the game and the setting that may mediate the effect of social facilitation and related effects in a comparable environment. Hence, results of all studies using the same testbed can be checked against each other. Finally, the environment enables automatic logging of relevant data: The game automatically logs the configuration that was applied in a gaming session and furthermore records all relevant game events and states (e.g. the player's score, collected items and whether the goal was reached within time). The core of the testbed

13

Game Aspect	Related Variable	Range/Variation
Difficulty (*Task factors*)	number of obstacles	any number possible (0 - ∞)
	number of resources	any number possible (0 - ∞)
	speed	any level of speed possible (0 - ∞)
	length of each play round	any length possible (0 - ∞ sec.)
Agent (Presence factors)	presence	visible vs. not visible
	animation	animated agent vs. static agent
	valency of feedback	neutral vs. positive vs. negative
	feedback type	visual vs. auditory vs. no feedback
	gender	indistinguishable vs. female vs. male
Appearance (*Situational factors*)	graphical perspective	2D sidescroller vs. 3D
	player perspective	first person vs. third person
Interface (*Situational factors*)	output device	Oculus Rift (HMD) vs. monitor display
	controls	controller vs. keyboard

Table 1. Overview of adaptable aspects of the testbed game *Spacetastic*.

environment introduced here is a simple space shooter game, called *Spacetastic*, which can be adapted in various ways by manipulating a number of variables.

Basic Game Design

The single-player game *Spacetastic* resembles classic space shooter games (cf. screenshots in Figure 2): The player has to navigate a small, damaged spaceship through a determinate space corridor filled with asteroids. The main objective is to reach the Earth at the end of the corridor in a given time before the ship gets completely broken. The spaceship moves at a predefined speed, but every time the player collides with an asteroid speed is decreased for a while, hence the main task of players is to dodge the obstacles and find a safe way through. Collectible items like speed rings, protective shields and oxygen bottles support the player, furthermore rockets can be picked up and used to shoot and destroy single asteroids.

One core aspect of the investigation of social facilitation is the assessment of performance. In the context of games, there are several kinds of possible performance measures, like speed, progress, efficiency and dexterity. Mostly, the applied type of performance depends on the genre and the main mechanics of the game. For this testbed game, it was decided to operationalize performance by means of score and speed due to the consideration that a setting with a predefined timespan allows for comparable playing sessions between individual players. The problem with other measures like progress would be that playing time and challenge could differ significantly between players in a study and that might in turn effect the overall experience and confound results regarding social effects. Accordingly, a player score is calculated and displayed during the game. If the player reaches the goal before time runs out, the time that is left is converted into points. Besides, collected items and destroyed asteroids increase the score.

Adaptability and Variations

Based on preliminary findings in social facilitation research, special focus was laid on the design and implementation of a

highly adjustable game that can serve as a testbed for related studies. Hence, the simple game setting was enriched by a number of adaptable features as shown in Table 1. Those aspects for the most part correspond with the potential impact factors defined in the adapted integrative model of social facilitation (cf. Figure 1): It is possible to vary task factors by changing the level of difficulty (depending on the number of game objects and speed) and time requirements. Presence factors are addressed by the customizability of the virtual agent and its behavior. In this context, feedback type and animation do account for the factor of anthropomorphism, while the valency of feedback defines the role of the agent and may control evaluation apprehension. If the agent is present, a visual representation is displayed in the bottom middle cockpit of players (cf. Figure 2), which differs regarding gender aspects. Besides, situational factors are variable in terms of the game's appearance and the interfaces that are used. For instance, the game is playable both in a 3D and a 2D mode, and the player's perspective can be varied between first-person and third-person view (cf. Figure 2). Furthermore it is possible to adapt the level of immersion of the game by using a HMD, the Oculus Rift, as a highly immersive output device.

EVALUATION OF SOCIAL FACILITATION IN DIGITAL GAMES

The testbed game *Spacetastic* described above was used in a first study aiming at investigating the influence of a virtual agent on players with special focus on social facilitation effects. In the following, the underlying hypotheses, applied methods and results are described and discussed.

Hypotheses

As the adapted integrative model of social facilitation (cf. Figure 1) illustrates, there is a whole range of factors that might have an impact on social facilitation effects and thus should be considered and systematically investigated in experiments in order to assess their impact value. In order to make a first steps towards such an undertaking, a study was conducted focusing

Figure 3. Robotic, gender-neutral agent representation used in the study.

on two potential factors: the presence of a virtual agent per se, and the degree of immersion offered by the game setting. Research has demonstrated that a person's performance is influenced by the presence or absence of others in many different contexts. The review of literature has shown that this effect seems to also apply to robots and virtual agents under certain circumstances, but prior results are inconsistent. Hence, the first intention of the study at hand is to generally test whether performance in the game is influenced by the presence of the agent, hypothesizing the following:

- H1: The mere presence of a virtual agent significantly influences players' performance in the game in the sense of social facilitation or inhibition effects.

Furthermore, the influence of immersion is taken into account, since a higher degree of immersion is assumed to foster the social impact of virtual agents (cf. [31]). Accordingly, a highly immersive HMD interface is supposed to increase the feelings of presence and thereby to intensify effects of social facilitation or inhibition. It is thus hypothesized the following:

- H2.1: The use of a HMD leads to a higher perception of presence.
- H2.2: The performance of players using a HMD is more strongly influenced by the presence of a virtual agent in the sense of social facilitation or inhibition effects than the performance of players using no HMD.

Study Design and Methodology
Based on the formulated hypotheses, a 2x2 between-subject design was used to investigate the influence of the two variables *presence of agent* (no agent vs. visible agent) and *output device* (monitor display vs. HMD), resulting in four experimental groups. The game was adapted regarding those aspects, while all other variables were kept constant. In terms of difficulty, a medium number of obstacles and resources as well as a medium speed level were chosen. Three levels, each lasting three minutes, were generated. The structure of all levels (placement of obstacles and resources) was identical for all players. Due to the planned use of the Oculus Rift as a HMD, the 3D first-person perspective was selected for all four conditions. The game was controlled by a common Xbox360-controller. In the two experimental conditions which included a virtual agent, a visual and animated presentation of a robotic, gender-neutral agent (see Figure 3) was displayed

as a hologram at the bottom of the cockpit and delivered neutral auditory feedback regarding the course of the game (e.g. "What happened?" in case of collision with an asteroid). To test whether mere presence of an agent is enough to induce social facilitation effects, the agent did not directly interact with the player and had no influence on the course of the game.

Procedure and applied measures
Figure 4 gives an overview of the course of the study session and the sequence of the applied questionnaires. Each participant was welcomed and randomly differentiated into one of the four experimental conditions after signing a consent to participate. A first questionnaire assessed demographic data, gaming habits, prior experiences with the Oculus Rift (if provided) as well as relevant aspects of health to ensure unimpaired eyesight, appropriate concentration and the absence of any disease (e.g. epilepsy) that might endanger participants during the playing session, especially if the Oculus Rift was to be used. Then, the game was introduced by a short text supplemented with screenshots and figures. It covered the short story of the game, the game's goal, a description of the game world and all objects as well as a short manual of the controls. After reading the instructions, participants were asked to play three levels of the game. In the two conditions with the Oculus Rift, the interface was adapted to the individual player and its functionality was also shortly explained. During the whole playing session the player was left alone, while the examiner waited outside the room in order to avoid any social facilitation effect due to his/her presence. The logging feature of the game was active all the time, hence score, collected items and time were recorded automatically for each level. Score was assessed as the main indicator of performance. Players were allowed to make small pauses between game rounds and had to let the examiner know when the third level was finished.

Subsequently, another couple of questionnaires was presented about how players experienced the game. The first was the Igroup Presence Questionnaire (IPQ) [14] to assess the degree of presence, meaning the feeling of being present inside the virtual game world. The IPQ consists of the four dimensions *general presence*, *spatial presence*, *involvement* and *experienced realism*. If the Oculus Rift was used, some questions about the experience related to it were put, e.g. whether the Oculus Rift was comfortable to wear or rather unpleasing, to which degree it added to a positive experience and how impressive the sensory impression was. Following this, all participants were asked to complete the core module of the Game Experience Questionnaire (GEQ) [15] to assess different aspects of the overall experience, including the eight dimensions *competence*, *sensory and imaginative immersion*, *flow*, *tension*, *challenge*, *negative affect* and *positive affect*. In the two conditions that included the virtual agent, three more corresponding questionnaires followed: First, the *social presence module* (SPGQ) from the GEQ [7] was used in order to assess how the presence and influence of the agent was experienced. Additionally, four scales from the Networked Minds Questionnaire (NMQ) [11] were applied. Those included all questions regarding the dimensions *co-presence*, *attentional allocation* and *perceived behavioral interdependence* as well as three items related to the dimension *perceived*

OR & Agent	OR & no Agent	No OR & Agent	No OR & no Agent
Randomized assignment to one experimental condition			
Questionnaires regarding social demographics, physical and mental health and gaming experience and habits			
Questionnaire regarding prior experience with OR			
Playing Session (3 levels, each lasting 3 minutes)			
Igroup Presence Questionnaire (IPQ)			
Questionnaire regarding OR experience			
Game Experience Questionnaire (GEQ)			
Social Presence in Games Questionnaire (SPGQ) Networked Minds Questionnaire (NMQ) Agent Attribution		Social Presence in Games Questionnaire (SPGQ) Networked Minds Questionnaire (NMQ) Agent Attribution	
Immersive Tendencies Questionnaire (ITQ) Simulator Sickness Questionnaire (SSQ) Questionnaire regarding game usability			

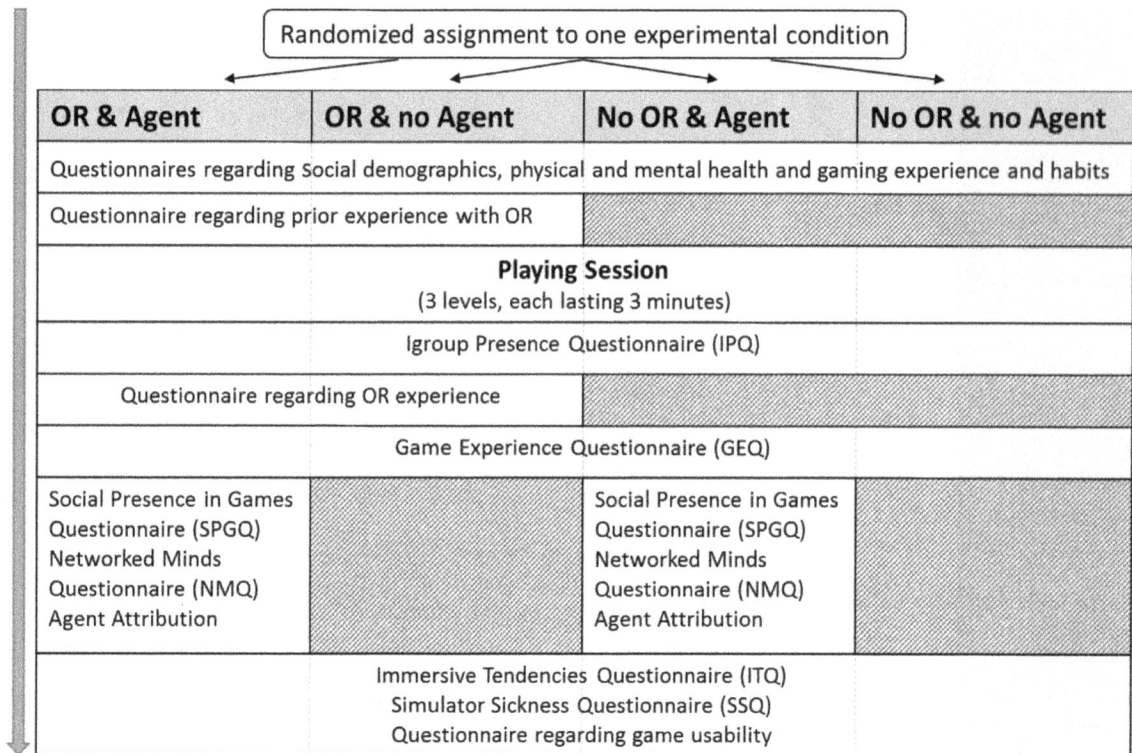

Figure 4. Overview of study procedure and applied measures (OR= Oculus Rift).

message understanding. Altogether those agent-related questions are supposed to give insight into how players perceived the presence and relevance of the agent and their interaction with it. Furthermore, participants were asked to evaluate the agent's character by scoring a range of 30 single adjectives like *pleasant*, *supportive* and *threatening*. Besides, participants of all conditions completed the Immersive Tendencies Questionnaire (ITQ) [27] and the Simulator Sickness Questionnaire (SSQ) [17]. Those questions were applied in order to control for individual differences regarding immersive tendencies and susceptibility, which may influence the overall results. Finally, some questions referred to the quality and usability of the game to ensure that the gaming experience was not interfered by design flaws or inappropriate controls. Participants were then debriefed and released.

Results

A number of 81 persons (41 females) aged between 19 and 48 years (M=26.06, SD=5.53) took part in the study. All four experimental groups were comparable regarding gender and age distribution. Participants were recruited in the context of the university, hence most participants were students (n=52) or employees (n=22). Additionally, three apprentices, two school pupils and two unemployed persons participated.

Manipulation check

In order to check the manipulations and basic assumptions regarding the four different study conditions, it has to be ensured that for one thing participants noticed the presence of the agent in the two audience conditions and that for another thing

perceived feelings of presence were significantly higher in the two Oculus Rift groups. Social presence of the agent was assessed using the SPGQ and the NMQ. As related data was not normally distributed (indicated by Kolmogorov-Smirnoff-tests), non-parametric tests were used to test for significant differences. Mann-Whitney-U-tests comparing the two agent groups regarding all items of the SPGQ and the NMQ show no significant differences (all p's >.240), indicating that the Oculus Rift did not significantly influence the perceived presence of the agent. Accordingly, participants in both groups were aware of the presence of the agent and moreover experienced the agent's presence in a similar way. Due to that, mean values of both agent groups regarding SPGQ and NMQ are summarized for further analysis. In order to check whether the agent was noticed by the players, it is informative to have a look at single items of the Networked Minds Questionnaire which were rated on a 7-point Likert scale (ranging from "*not at all*" to "*absolutely*"): The item "*I noticed the robot*" received a mean value of M=4.37 (SD=2.07) and the item "*The presence of the robot was obvious to me*" was rated with a mean value M=5.02 (SD=1.84). The mean values are slightly above average and thus imply that the agent was apparently noticed, but seemed to be not in the attentional focus of the players. Calculated results of the sub-scales of the NMQ support this impression, as they are all rather low or neutral (rated on a 7-point Likert scale): co-presence M=4.18 (SD=1.23), attentional allocation M=3.78 (SD=.97), perceived behavioral interdependence M=2.75 (SD=1.31) and perceived message understanding M=3.41 (SD=1.00). Similarly, values of the

	Mean Group 1 (OR Agent) (N = 22)	Mean Group 2 (OR no Agent) (N = 21)	Mean Group 3 (No OR Agent) (N = 19)	Mean Group 4 (No OR no Agent) (N = 19)	ANOVA F	p	Eta squared
Score Level 1	567,27	727,62	668,42	703,68	1.260	.294	.047
Score Level 2	759,09	956,19	944,21	913,68	1.416	.245	.052
Score Level 3	793,64	985,24	1005,26	970,53	1.389	.253	.051
Total Score	2120,00	2669,05	2617,89	2587,89	1.592	.198	.058

Table 2. Mean values of scores of all four conditions and results of the ANOVA (OR = Oculus Rift).

three dimensions of the SPGQ, which were assessed on a 5-point Likert scale, also tend to be low: empathy $M=1.46$ ($SD=.48$), negative feelings $M=1.31$ ($SD=.36$) and behavioral involvement $M=1.70$ ($SD=.57$). Overall, it is concluded that although the agent was noticed, players did not seem to feel a strong connection to the agent or any kind of influence or distraction by the agent's presence. Aside from that, results of the evaluation of the agent's character by scoring a range of 30 single adjectives indicate that the agent was perceived as rather neutral and passive altogether, as intended by design.

Perceived presence was measured using the IPQ. Results of a Mann-Whitney-U-test comparing the groups with and without Oculus Rift display that all dimensions of presence were rated significantly higher by Oculus Rift players: general presence ($U=479.00$, $z=-3.26$, $p=.001$), perceived spatial presence ($U=367.50$, $z=-4.26$, $p<.001$), involvement ($U=405.50$, $z=-3.93$, $p<.001$) and experienced realism ($U=528.50$, $z=-2.74$, $p=.006$). As those values are highly significant, it can be concluded that the Oculus Rift led to higher feelings of presence, thus the first part and precondition of hypothesis 2 (H2.1) is supported. Besides, presence values tend to be slightly higher than average (except for experienced realism) in all conditions, indicating that the game in general was satisfactorily immersive. In sum, manipulations of both independent variables worked as intended.

Control variables
As it has to be precluded that potential differences in the four experimental conditions regarding the main hypotheses are caused by unintended interfering variables, a number of control variables has been assessed. As the Kolmogorov-Smirnoff-test indicates that data is not normally distributed regarding the following control variables, Kruskal-Wallis one-way analyses of variance were calculated for comparing all groups in terms of prior gaming experience, immersive tendencies and simulator sickness. There were no significant differences found between groups for any of those variables: Gaming experience ($H(3)=1.56$, $p=.668$), all four ITQ sub-scales (focus: $H(3)=2.40$, $p=.494$; involvement: $H(3)=1.10$, $p=.777$; emotions: $H(3)=1.05$, $p=.788$; games: $H(3)=1.81$, $p=.613$) as well as both SSQ sub-scales (nausea: $H(3)=3.02$, $p=.388$; oculomotor: $H(3)=1.19$, $p=.756$) were thus comparable for all groups and may not account for any differences found in performance or immersion of players. In addition, simulator sickness values were rather low in general (the means for each item were lower than the mean value of the scale, i.e. <2), thus

it can be concluded that player experience was not impaired by unpleasant feelings of simulator sickness.

Besides, participants' ratings of the game's quality and usability indicate that there were no crucial problems with the controls (e.g. the mean score of the item "*the controls were easy to handle*" was $M=3.05$ ($SD=.77$) on a 4-point Likert scale) and that the game was rated rather positive overall, e.g. indicated by the items "*I liked the game world*" ($M=2.81$, $SD=.73$), "*I think the game is exciting*" ($M=2.62$, $SD=.86$) and "*I would like to play the game again*" ($M=2.84$, $SD=.94$). Kruskal-Wallis analyses of all single items show no significant differences between the experimental groups (all p's >.165). Hence all participants rate the game similarly and rather positive. Finally, it was tested whether the Oculus Rift device compromises players' well-being and comfort during play. All related items, which had to be rated on a 4-point Likert scale, indicate positive sensations, e.g. "*I felt comfortable wearing the Oculus Rift*" ($M=2.86$, $SD=.86$) and "*I think the Oculus Rift increased the fun of the game*" ($M=3.35$, $SD=.92$). Thus, the device was accepted and not perceived as annoying. Moreover, there was no significant difference between the two Oculus Rift groups as shown by Mann-Whitney-U-tests for all items (all p's >.286).

Test of hypotheses
After having checked the successful manipulation of experimental conditions and having precluded interference of results by confounding variables, the main hypotheses can be tested. Since an overall difference in performance among the groups is expected (H1), mean scores of participants are compared. As the Kolmogorov-Smirnov-test indicates normally distributed data, first a one-way ANOVA is calculated comparing scores of all three playing rounds as well as the total score among all four conditions (see Table 2). Contradictory to hypothesis one, results show no significant overall difference between groups regarding the mean scores in round one ($F(3,77)=1.26$, $p=.294$), round two ($F(3,77)=1.42$, $p=.245$), round three ($F(3,77)=1.39$, $p=.253$) or the total score ($F(3,77)=1.59$, $p=.198$).

To examine the influence of the Oculus Rift on performance, summarized mean scores of the two groups playing with the HMD are compared to the summarized mean scores of the two groups playing without Oculus Rift by performing an Independent Samples t Test (see Table 3). Though there is a tendency that all mean scores are higher in the conditions without HMD, those differences are not significant, either,

	Mean Oculus Rift Groups (Groups 1+2, N = 43)	**Mean No Oculus Rift Groups** (Groups 3+4, N = 38)	t	p	Cohen's d
Score Level 1	645,58	686,05	.605	.547	.135
Score Level 2	855,35	928,95	.923	.359	.206
Score Level 3	887,21	987,89	1.149	.255	.256
Total Score	2388,14	2602,89	1.020	.311	.227

Table 3. Results of the Independent Samples t Test comparing summarized mean scores of the two Oculus Rift groups (groups 1 and 2) and the summarized scores of the groups without Oculus Rift (groups 3 and 4).

for scores in round one ($t(65.214)=.61$, $p=.547$), round two ($t(79)=.92$, $p=.359$), round three ($t(64.164)=1.15$, $p=.255$) and total scores ($t(79)=1.02$, $p=.311$).

Finally, with respect to hypothesis 2 (H2.2), scores in the Oculus Rift conditions and in the conditions without Oculus Rift are analyzed separately in order to focus the influence of the agent without comparing different devices. An Independent Samples t Test comparing scores of both Oculus Rift conditions (see Table 4) displays significant differences regarding the scores in round one ($t(41)=2.29$, $p=.027$), round two ($t(41)=2.13$, $p=.040$), round three ($t(41)= 2.11$, $p=.041$) as well as regarding the total score ($t(41)=2.39$, $p=.022$). The calculated effect sizes indicate medium effects (all > .60). The same is calculated for comparing the scores of the two groups that played without Oculus Rift (see Table 5), but in contrast no significant differences are found for round one ($t(36)=.31$, $p=.757$), round two ($t(36)=.23$, $p=.818$), round three ($t(36)=.23$, $p=.817$) or the total score ($t(36)=.08$, $p=.934$).

	t	p	Cohen's d
Score Level 1	-2,287	.027	.698
Score Level 2	-2.125	.040	.648
Score Level 3	-2.105	.041	.642
Total Score	-2.387	.022	.728

Table 4. Results of the Independent Samples t Test comparing score values of the two groups that used the HMD: group 1 (Oculus Rift and Agent) and group 2 (Oculus Rift and no Agent).

	t	p	Cohen's d
Score Level 1	-.312	.757	.101
Score Level 2	.232	.818	.075
Score Level 3	.233	.817	.076
Total Score	.084	.934	.027

Table 5. Results of the Independent Samples t Test comparing score values of the two groups that did not use the HMD: group 3 (no Oculus Rift and Agent) and group 4 (no Oculus Rift and no Agent).

Further results

Data assessed by the GEQ is supposed to provide additional insights into the experience of participants during playing the game. Kruskal-Wallis-tests are applied to investigate whether there are any differences regarding the sub-scales of the GEQ between groups. Significant differences appear for the sub-scales flow ($H(3)=12.88$, $p=.005$) and negative affect

($H(3)=10.99$, $p=.012$). To further examine those differences, Mann-Whitney-U-tests with Bonferroni correction (significance level $p=.0083$) are calculated. Results show that participants who played with Oculus Rift and agent scored higher on the flow scale ($M=3.70$) than those who played without oculus but with agent ($M=2.40$) ($U=86.00$, $z=-3.22$, $p=.001$). This is in line with the higher immersion found in the Oculus Rift conditions. In terms of negative affect, participants who played with Oculus Rift and agent showed significantly lower values than participants playing without HMD but with agent ($U=108.00$, $z=-2.79$, $p=.005$) and the group who played with Oculus Rift but without agent ($U=99.50$, $z=-3.00$, $p=.003$).

After grouping and summarizing the values of the two conditions playing with the Oculus Rift and the two conditions playing on a usual screen, respectively, Mann-Whitney-U-tests reveal that players in the Oculus Rift conditions felt significantly less competent compared to the other group ($U=607.00$, $z=-1.99$, $p=.047$). The same was found for negative affect ($M=1.50$, $U=540.00$, $z=-2.72$, $p=.007$). In contrast, flow was higher ($U=84.00$, $z=-2.83$, $p=.004$) for Oculus players, as already indicated above.

Discussion of Results

Results show that there is no overall effect of the presence of the agent on player performance: Neither social facilitation nor inhibition effects could be detected based on the comparison of all four study conditions. Accordingly, hypothesis H1 is not supported by these findings. However, further analyses reveal that the presence of the agent seems to have affected players' performance if they were wearing the HMD: Performance was significantly worse if the agent was present, indicating an inhibition effect. This can be interpreted in line with the hypothesis that the performance of players using a HMD is more strongly influenced by the presence of the virtual agent (H2.2): It can be argued that the lack of differences regarding performance between the two conditions without HMD indicates just a weak (or no) social influence of the agent, which is increased by the application of the Oculus Rift, leading to a stronger (detectable) effect in the two HMD conditions. Hence, H2.2 is not disproved but requires further investigation in future studies to test whether this assumption is true.

The question arises why there was a measurable social influence of the agent in the Oculus Rift conditions, while it could not be detected regarding players at a common monitor. Interference of control variables was precluded, hence results can not be ascribed to a lack in conspicuousness of the agent, simulator sickness, problems with the game controls or dissimilar distribution of participants' relevant individual characteristics (e.g. immersive tendencies). There were two noticable differences found: Based on the analyses of the IPQ data and the flow values, immersion was significantly higher in the Oculus Rift conditions, as expected (H2.1). Hence, a higher immersion might have led to higher feelings of presence and an intensified perception of the agent, which, in turn, might have increased the agent's inhibitory effect. However, another difference was found regarding feelings of competence. Oculus Rift players felt less competent during play than the other participants. This might also account for the results, as less perceived competence might be an indicator for experienced difficulty: If the difficulty of the task was higher due to the HMD, social inhibition is more likely to occur. The GEQ sub-scale for challenge, in contrast, displayed similar values for all groups, which does not support the latter assumption, but does not completely preclude it either. Whether the differences in performance are caused by varying perceived levels of difficulty or by differences in immersion (or both) in combination with the presence of the agent should be examined in a follow-up study.

There are also some limitations of the study that have to be considered when interpreting the results and that especially have to be taken into account for the planning of future studies. First, the virtual agent that was designed for the game has not been evaluated in a preliminary study. It was assumed that the agent appears as a neutral, non-evaluative social entity due to an indistinguishable sex and indifferent visual and auditory feedback. Though it seems that it worked out as intended in this case, future variations of the agent's appearance optimally should be verified before the actual experiment is conducted. Similarly, the level of difficulty should be assessed in pre-tests by measuring both perceived difficulty (self-reports) and actual performance in different variations of the game in order to be able to identify easy and difficult configurations. Since that was not done beforehand in this case, making a clear statement about the difficulty of the applied levels is not possible. Finally, a larger sample size might benefit the detection and clarification of effects.

CONCLUSION AND FUTURE WORK
The study presented here contributes relevant research results regarding social facilitation in digital games in particular and the complex field of social player experience in general. Findings indicate a potential impact of virtual agents as social entities on player performance and player experience under certain conditions, as social inhibition was detected in the immersive version of the space-shooter game. At the same time, this article illustrates the demand for further systematical investigation of social effects in digital games.

The introduced testbed game is a promising approach for this purpose and offers various possibilities to examine social facilitation effects evoked by virtual agents. It will be applied in future studies, making use of the other adaptable aspects like the player's perspective or the appearance of the agent. While the agent in the present study was designed as neutral as possible (no distinguishable gender, neutral feedback and comments regarding game events), other configurations

may have different effects. For instance, a more human-like appearance and the degree of perceived anthropomorphism may result in higher attributed social features and thus in an increased social effect. Furthermore, future research should include different levels of difficulty, which was not accounted for in the experiment reported here. However, the testbed game also entails some limitations: The genre chosen is just one of many existing game genres that feature very different characteristics. Hence, results are not generalizable to other games and genres. In this context, it might be particularly interesting to investigate whether other kinds of game mechanics and tasks show other results for social facilitation. While the testbed game presented here is focused on motor abilities and dexterity, a player's performance in cognitive or social tasks might be influenced differently by the presence of others.

Interesting subsequent questions will be whether or not the mere presence of an agent is really enough to cause significant social facilitation effects as once proposed by Zajonc (1965) and if social effects are stable or rather short-termed. Potential wear-out effects should be investigated. All those research suggested here is supposed to be highly relevant as it may lead to new implications regarding the use of virtual agents in digital games as well as in virtual environments that might be applied for learning or training purposes and in working contexts. In general, the work presented in this article underlines the potential impact of virtual social entities and shows that virtual agents may indeed influence us like real persons do.

ACKNOWLEDGMENTS
We especially thank a group of students of the University of Duisburg-Essen who supported the design and evaluation process, namely Maxim Babinski, Karol Barton, Kathrin Bischof, Robert-Duc Le, Ersen Tuerkyilmaz, Andre Waschk and Julia Winkler, as well as all participants of our study.

REFERENCES
1. John R. Aiello and Elizabeth A. Douthitt. 2001. Social facilitation from Triplett to electronic performance monitoring. *Group Dynamics: Theory, Research, and Practice* 5, 3 (2001), 163–180. DOI: http://dx.doi.org/10.1037/1089-2699.5.3.163

2. Floyd H. Allport. 1920. The influence of the group upon association and thought. *Journal of Experimental Psychology* 3, 3 (1920), 159–182. DOI: http://dx.doi.org/10.1037/h0067891

3. Jim Blascovich, Jack Loomis, Andrew C. Beall, Kimberly R. Swinth, Crystal L. Hoyt, and Jeremy N. Bailenson. 2002. TARGET ARTICLE: Immersive Virtual Environment Technology as a Methodological Tool for Social Psychology. *Psychological Inquiry* 13, 2 (2002), 103–124. DOI: http://dx.doi.org/10.1207/S15327965PLI1302{_}01

4. Charles F. Bond and Linda J. Titus. 1983. Social facilitation: A meta-analysis of 241 studies. *Psychological Bulletin* 94, 2 (1983), 265–292. DOI: http://dx.doi.org/10.1037/0033-2909.94.2.265

5. Nicholas David Bowman, Rene Weber, Ron Tamborini, and John Sherry. 2013. Facilitating Game Play: How

Others Affect Performance at and Enjoyment of Video Games. *Media Psychology* 16, 1 (2013), 39–64. DOI: http://dx.doi.org/10.1080/15213269.2012.742360

6. Yvonne A. W. De Kort and Wijnand A. Ijsselsteijn. 2008. People, places, and play. *Computers in Entertainment* 6, 2 (2008), 1. DOI: http://dx.doi.org/10.1145/1371216.1371221

7. Yvonne A. W. De Kort, Wijnand A. Ijsselsteijn, and Karolien Poels. 2007. Digital games as social presence technology : development of the social presence in gaming questionnaire (SPGQ). In *Proceedings of the 10th Annual International Workshop on Presence*. 195–203.

8. Laura Ermi and Frans Mäyrä. 2005. Fundamental Components of the Gameplay Experience: Analysing Immersion. In *DiGRA '05 - Proceedings of the 2005 DiGRA International Conference: Changing Views: Worlds in Play.* http://www.digra.org/wp-content/uploads/digital-library/06276.41516.pdf

9. Bernard Guerin. 1993. *Social facilitation.* Cambridge University Press and Editions de la Maison des Sciences de l'homme, Cambridge [England] and New York, N.Y. and Paris.

10. Byron Hall and David Dryden Henningsen. 2008. Social facilitation and human–computer interaction. *Computers in Human Behavior* 24, 6 (2008), 2965–2971. DOI: http://dx.doi.org/10.1016/j.chb.2008.05.003

11. C. Harms and F. Biocca. 2004. Internal consistency and reliability of the networked minds social presence measure. *Seventh Annual International Workshop: Presence 2004* (2004).

12. Austen L. Hayes, Amy C. Ulinski, and Larry F. Hodges. 2010. That Avatar Is Looking at Me! Social Inhibition in Virtual Worlds. In *Intelligent virtual agents*, Jan Allbeck, Norman Badler, Timothy Bickmore, Catherine Pelachaud, and Alla Safonova (Eds.). Lecture notes in computer science Lecture notes in artificial intelligence, Vol. 6356. Springer, Berlin, 454–467. DOI: http://dx.doi.org/10.1007/978-3-642-15892-6{_}49

13. Crystal L. Hoyt, Jim Blascovich, and Kimberly R. Swinth. 2003. Social inhibition in immersive virtual environments. *Presence: Teleoperators and Virtual Environments* 12, 2 (2003), 183–195. DOI: http://dx.doi.org/10.1162/105474603321640932

14. Igroup Project Consortium. 2016. Igroup Presence Questionnaire (IPQ). (2016).

15. Wijnand A. Ijsselsteijn, Yvonne A. W. De Kort, and Karolien Poels. manuscript in preparation. The Game Experience Questionnaire: Development of a self-report measure to assess the psychological impact of digital games. (manuscript in preparation).

16. Dennis L. Kappen, Pejman Mirza-Babaei, Jens Johannsmeier, Daniel Buckstein, James Robb, and Lennart E. Nacke. 2014. Engaged by boos and cheers. In *Proceedings of the first ACM SIGCHI annual symposium on Computer-human interaction in play*, Lennart E.

Nacke and T. Nicholas C. Graham (Eds.). ACM, NY, USA, 151–160. DOI: http://dx.doi.org/10.1145/2658537.2658687

17. Robert S. Kennedy, Norman E. Lane, Kevin S. Berbaum, and Michael G. Lilienthal. 1993. Simulator Sickness Questionnaire: An Enhanced Method for Quantifying Simulator Sickness. *The International Journal of Aviation Psychology* 3, 3 (1993), 203–220. DOI: http://dx.doi.org/10.1207/s15327108ijap0303{_}3

18. Nicole C. Krämer. 2008. *Soziale Wirkungen virtueller Helfer: Gestaltung und Evaluation von Mensch-Computer-Interaktion* (1. aufl. ed.). Kohlhammer, Stuttgart.

19. Kristine L. Nowak and Frank Biocca. 2003. The Effect of the Agency and Anthropomorphism on Users' Sense of Telepresence, Copresence, and Social Presence in Virtual Environments. *Presence: Teleoperators and Virtual Environments* 12, 5 (2003), 481–494. DOI: http://dx.doi.org/10.1162/105474603322761289

20. Thorsten Quandt. 2014. *Multiplayer: The social aspects of digital gaming.* Routledge studies in European communication research and education, Vol. 3. Routledge, London and New York.

21. Raoul Rickenberg and Byron Reeves. 2000. The effects of animated characters on anxiety, task performance, and evaluations of user interfaces. In *Proceedings of the SIGCHI conference on Human Factors in Computing Systems*, Thea Turner and Gerd Szwillus (Eds.). ACM, NY, USA, 49–56. DOI: http://dx.doi.org/10.1145/332040.332406

22. Richard M. Ryan, C. Scott Rigby, and Andrew Przybylski. 2006. The Motivational Pull of Video Games: A Self-Determination Theory Approach. *Motivation and Emotion* 30, 4 (2006), 344–360. DOI: http://dx.doi.org/10.1007/s11031-006-9051-8

23. Mel Slater. 2003. A note on presence terminology. *Presence Connect* 3, 3 (2003).

24. Lee Sproull, Mani Subramani, Sara Kiesler, Janet Walker, and Keith Waters. 1996. When the Interface Is a Face. *Human-Computer Interaction* 11, 2 (1996), 97–124. DOI: http://dx.doi.org/10.1207/s15327051hci1102{_}1

25. Jari Takatalo, Jukka Häkkinen, Jyrki Kaistinen, and Göte Nyman. 2010. Presence, Involvement, and Flow in Digital Games. In *Evaluating user experience in games*, Regina Bernhaupt (Ed.). Springer, London and New York, 23–46. DOI: http://dx.doi.org/10.1007/978-1-84882-963-3{_}3

26. Norman Triplett. 1898. The Dynamogenic Factors in Pacemaking and Competition. *The American Journal of Psychology* 9 (1898), 507–533.

27. UQO Cyberpsychology Lab. 2004. Immersive Tendencies Questionnaire (ITQ). (2004).

28. Michael Wooldridge and Nicholas R. Jennings. 1995. Intelligent Agents: Theory and Practice. *Knowledge Engineering Review* 10 (1995), 115–152.

29. Nick Yee. 2006. Motivations for play in online games. *Cyberpsychology & behavior : the impact of the Internet, multimedia and virtual reality on behavior and society* 9, 6 (2006), 772–775. DOI: http://dx.doi.org/10.1089/cpb.2006.9.772

30. Robert B. Zajonc. 1965. Social Facilitation. *Science, New Series* 1965, Volume 149, No. 3681 (1965), 269–274.

31. Catherine Amine Zanbaka, Amy Catherine Ulinski, Paula Goolkasian, and Larry F. Hodges. 2007. Social responses to virtual humans. In *Proceedings of the SIGCHI Conference on Human Factors in Computing Systems*, Mary Beth Rosson and David Gilmore (Eds.). ACM, NY, USA, 1561. DOI: http://dx.doi.org/10.1145/1240624.1240861

Visualizations for Retrospective Analysis of Battles in Team-based Combat Games – A User Study

Günter Wallner
University of Applied Arts Vienna
Institute of Art & Technology
guenter.wallner@uni-ak.ac.at

Simone Kriglstein
Vienna University of Technology
Institute for Design & Assessment of Technology
simone.kriglstein@tuwien.ac.at

ABSTRACT

Team-based combat games rank among the most popular genres of online games. Their competitive and skill-based gameplay requires players to develop new and constantly refine existing skills in order to succeed and stay ahead of the game. Players of such games are thus showing increased interest in training visualizations which allow them to review their own gameplay, to learn from others, and assist them in building their skills. This research contributes to the emerging area of player-centric visualization by evaluating three different types of visualizations geared toward retrospective analysis of team battles. For that purpose an online survey was developed and disseminated to the player community. Our results, based on 41 responses, provide insights into how the assessed training visualizations score in terms of informational content and design, player preference, how correctly the visualizations can be interpreted, and how suitable they are for different analysis purposes.

ACM Classification Keywords

K.8.0 General: Games; H.5.m Information Interfaces and Presentation (e.g. HCI): Miscellaneous

Author Keywords

Player-centric visualization; information visualization; gameplay analysis; user study; team-based games.

INTRODUCTION

Nearly all games use some sort of visual representation to convey important information about the current in-game state to the player. Players, on the other hand, rely on these visualizations to assess their current performance, to make informed decisions, and ultimately to advance through the game (cf. [29]). Data visualization in games takes on a variety of forms, ranging from simple representations such as health bars or glyph-based approaches to depict the number of remaining lives or ammunition to more complex visualizations, for instance, graph-based approaches to represent skill and technology trees. While such status representations may

be the most obvious use of visualizations in games, visualizations can serve other purposes as well. The rise of online gaming and e-sports has led to increased competition among players and growing interest in visualizations to monitor, analyze, and subsequently to improve their gameplay, hereafter referred to – following the terminology of Bowman et al. [1] – as visualizations for training. This particularly holds true for games where gameplay is largely skill-based such as shooters or real-time strategy games (cf. [15]). Game developers have recognized this growing interest in in-game data and have started to expose in-depth data and statistics either in-game, on websites, or through dedicated application programming interfaces. This, in turn, has prompted the player community to develop customized analysis and visualization tools. Yet, despite the ubiquitous presence and importance of data visualization in games, research in this area is still surprisingly scarce (see also [1, 29]), particularly with respect to visualizations for training. There is currently a lack of empirical studies on how well available visualizations for training convey the information and how useful they are for gauging and reflecting upon gameplay.

In this work we contribute to this line of research by evaluating three different types of visualizations intended for retrospective analysis of battles in team-based combat games, that is, games where two teams of players compete for certain objectives. Team-based combat games are among the most popular genres of online games, encompassing games such as the *Battlefield* series [6], *League of Legends* [9], or *World of Tanks* [26]. In the present study we are focusing on the latter game which has been chosen for several reasons. First, *World of Tanks (WoT)* captures all the data necessary to re-simulate a battle and stores this data in so-called replay files which, secondly, resulted in an active player community building tools for extracting, analyzing, and visualizing the data contained in these replays. The goal of this paper is to provide insights into (i) how well the three evaluated visualizations are perceived with respect to cartographic and data visualization design principles such as clarity, accurateness, and aesthetics, (ii) how these visualizations rank in terms of personal preference, readability, and battle representation, (iii) how correctly they can be interpreted, and (iv) how suitable they are for different types of tasks. In order to reach these objectives an online survey was devised and promoted on *WoT* related message boards. However, we would like to stress that since the core gameplay mechanics are similar across objective-based team games and because the investigated visualizations are

CHI PLAY '16 CD-ROM, October 16–19, 2016, Austin, TX, USA
Copyright is held by the owner/author(s). Publication rights licensed to ACM.
ACM 978-1-4503-4456-2/16/10. . . $15.00
DOI: http://dx.doi.org/10.1145/2967934.2968093

not specific to *WoT* we believe that our results also apply to other, similar, games as well. Our findings are a step toward a better understanding of how helpful these visualizations are and can thus inform and provide guidance for the design of useful player-centric visualizations of gameplay data.

RELATED WORK

Information visualization techniques for visualizing in-game data have been reviewed by several authors [1, 15, 29]. Medler and Magerko [15] discuss how visualizations can support and promote play. Bowman et al. [1], drawing upon the work of Medler and Magerko [15], proposed a framework for classifying visualizations in games along five dimensions, including target audience (e.g., players, developers) and primary purpose. The latter distinguishes between visualizations for debugging and balancing, communication, for displaying information regarding status or progression, and training. Zammitto [29], focusing on in-game interfaces for status display, analyzed games of different genres to identify which visualization techniques are used to display information and how well the information is presented. While all these surveys highlight the importance of information visualization for games there is also a shared sentiment that research in this area is still in a relatively early stage. Visualizations for conveying status information in games, for example, in the form of head-up displays (HUDs) have received perhaps the most attention so far. However, work in this space mostly centers around aspects of immersion and less on how effective the data is visualized. For example, Llanos and Jørgensen [23] conducted a qualitative study, involving semi-structured interviews and observation, to assess the influence of the superimposed HUD in *Assassin's Creed* on the players' sense of involvement. Iacovides et al. [12] examined how immersion in a first-person shooter game is affected by interacting with a diegetic and non-diegetic interface. In terms of effectiveness, however, we are only aware of the recent work by Peacocke et al. [19] who assessed the effectiveness of diegetic interfaces for displaying ammunition compared to HUDs with respect to player performance in first person shooter games.

The focus of this paper is on visualizations for the purpose of training. In this regard, especially the visual analytics system proposed by Hoobler et al. [11] is worth mentioning as it is also concerned with helping players to understand the game dynamics unfolding in team-based shooters. The proposed system offers various types of overlays, allowing observers to analyze, among others, player paths, lines of fire, and the location of forces. As such it shares certain similarities with the visualizations used in the present study. However, no user study has been performed to evaluate the effectiveness of the system. Perhaps the work most related to ours is the recent user study by Kriglstein et al. [14] who assessed the suitability of heatmaps and cluster maps for interpreting gameplay and how these representations perform with respect to time efficiency, correctness, suitability, and player preference. However, the investigated visualizations focused on two specific gameplay aspects of shooter games – namely death locations and weapon usage – whereas the visualizations used in our study are broader in scope in that they aim to give a more comprehensive overview of the complete course of a battle.

EVALUATION

The overall goal of our study was to assess the utility of different types of visualizations for analyzing and understanding the course of a battle. Specifically we address the following research questions (RQ):

RQ1: How well do the investigated visualization types represent the gameplay data with respect to cartographic and data visualization design principles? How do players perceive the quality of these visualizations? Is the assessment influenced by age, experience with the game, or familiarity with maps?

RQ2: How do the investigated visualizations rank in terms of personal preference, readability, and their depiction of the flow of battle? Is the ranking influenced by age, experience with the game, or familiarity with maps?

RQ3: How correctly are the different visualization types interpreted by the players?

RQ4: For which analysis tasks are the visualizations suited?

World of Tanks (*WoT*)

WoT [26] is a war-themed massively multiplayer online game in which two teams compete against each other for military objectives, usually capturing the enemies team's base or destroying all enemy units. Each player controls a single tank or another armored vehicle. Once a tank is destroyed the player is out of the game and cannot rejoin the battle, i.e., there is no respawn mechanic.

Datasets

WoT offers players the possibility to record replays of battles. A replay contains all necessary information to re-simulate a battle, including unit movements and data about which players caused damage to enemy tanks. However, a single replay file only contains complete information about the units of the recording players' team. Details on enemy units are only included as long as they are within the field of view of one of the team members. As such two replay files – one from each team – are necessary to generate a complete record of a battle. To obtain such pairs of replays we searched the repository of the *Wargaming.net League Europe Bronze Series* [7] for matches were both teams uploaded a replay file. In the end, we selected three matches (to keep the length of the survey reasonable while at the same time allowing for counterbalancing), two played on the map *Cliff* and one played on the map *Steppes*. We will refer to these datasets as CLIFF-1, CLIFF-2, and STEPPES in the following. *Cliff* features a mountainous landscape with valleys and peeks while *Steppes* is largely covered by open fields and small hills. Movements on the former map are thus more confined whereas unit trajectories contained in the STEPPES dataset are more dispersed. All three matches were played in *Assault* game mode, where one team has to defend two bases against the other for a duration of seven minutes. On the other hand, the attacking team wins if it captures either of the two bases. Alternatively, each team can also be victorious by destroying all enemy tanks. A team is comprised of seven players (i.e., units). Lastly, the obtained replay files were converted into JSON files for further processing using the *WoT Replay Parser* [24].

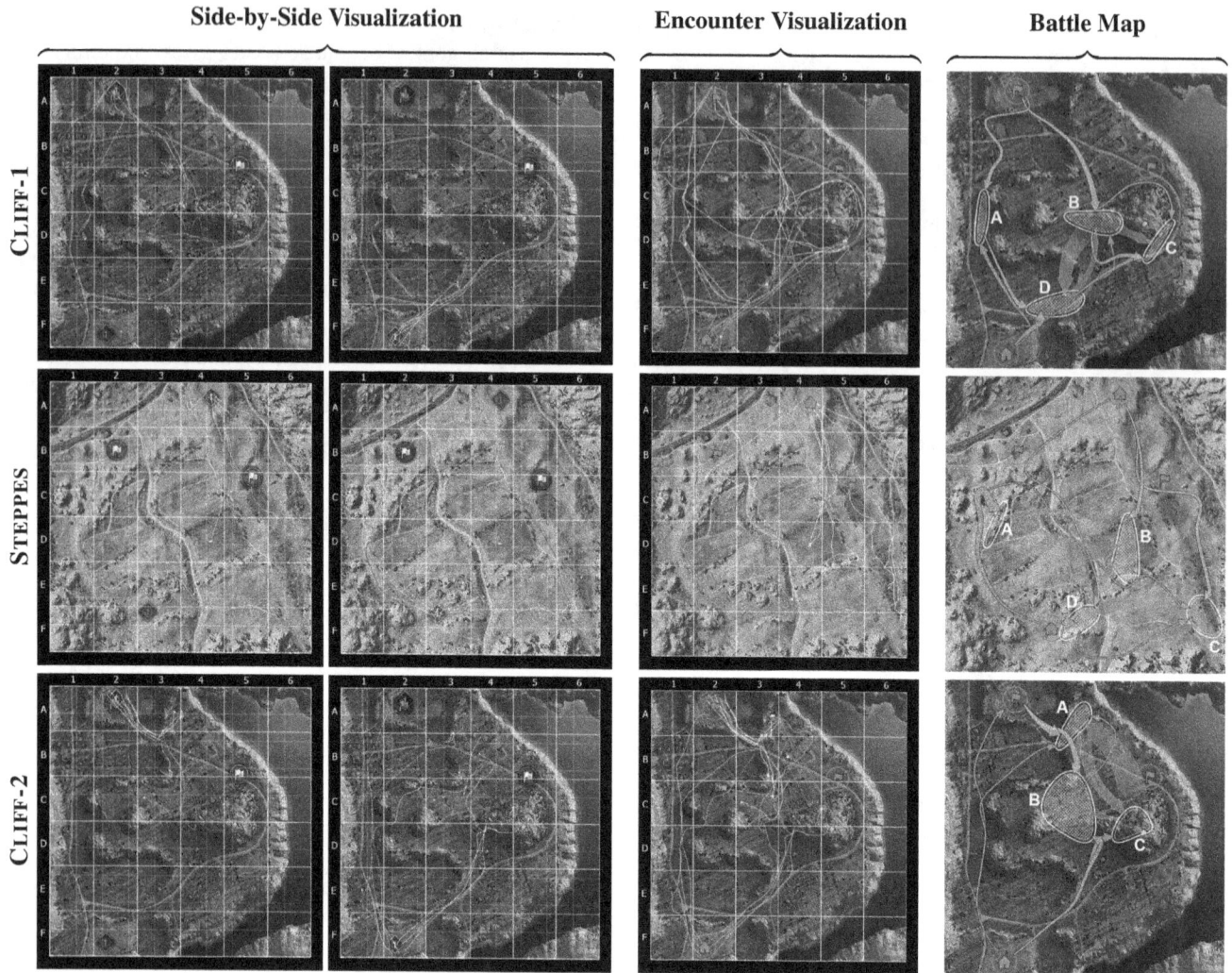

Figure 1. Overview of the different visualizations used in the evaluation. Grids and labels have been added to avoid ambiguities when referring to positions or areas in the task descriptions.

Visualization Types

For each dataset we generated three visualizations which are explained in detail in the following.

Side-by-Side Visualization (SSV)

The *WoT Replay Parser* [24] offers the possibility to convert replay files into different types of visualizations, including a visualization that shows the trajectories of individual units and their death locations (see Figure 1, left column). Trajectories are rendered using individual points and are color-coded: green trajectories correspond to units of the recording player's team and red trajectories show movements of the enemy team when within the field of view of one of the recording player's teammates. The blue trajectory reflects the path of the recording player itself. Death locations are marked with small yellow dots. Spawn points and bases are depicted using icons. This is the only one of the three investigated visualizations which allows player to assess where units of the enemy team have been spotted. It can be considered to be the prevalent visualization for *WoT* replays (apart from heatmaps) and is used by the popular statistics website *vBAddict* [3].

However, as it is based on a single replay it only conveys what was known to the recording player's team. Thus, *vBAddict* offers a so-called *versus view* for matches were replays of both teams have been uploaded. This view juxtaposes to the two visualizations horizontally. We used the same side-by-side arrangement for our evaluation (cf. Figure 1, left column).

Encounter Visualization (EV)

Juxtaposition designs as used by the above visualization are known to rely on the viewers memory to draw connections between objects (cf. [10]) which may make it difficult to get a complete view of a battle. For this reason, we included a visualization which combines the data of both replay files into a single map instead of using separate views for each team (see Figure 1, middle column). To facilitate this process, we created a small tool which extracts the complete movement data of each unit from two JSON files. No simplification was performed on the movement data, that is, the paths have the same accuracy as in the *Side-by-Side Visualization (SSV)*. Trajectories are rendered using straight line segments and are colored in light blue or light red depending on the team the unit belongs to. Spawn points and bases are represented by icons similar to those used by the *SSV*.

This is also the only visualization which explicitly shows the lines of fire which we suppose are helpful for understanding the nature of encounters. In the following we will thus refer to it as *Encounter Visualization (EV)*. Lines of fire are not directly stored in the replay file rather the file contains time-stamped damage events. This time-stamp is used to reconstruct the position of the two involved units at that time from the movement data. The respective shooting and target position are then connected with an arrow pointing toward the target. Based on the team membership of the attacker the arrow is colored in dark blue or dark red. Similar to the *SSV*, death locations are indicated by yellow rectangles. Generally speaking, this visualization offers the largest amount of information in a single map. Contrary to the *SSV* it is, however, not possible to see where enemy units have been spotted.

Battle Map (BM)

So-called *battle maps (BMs)* have long been used by military planners to develop and review strategies for military operations. Likewise, battle maps have also commonly been employed by historians to visually convey the course of a battle. For example, Davis et al. [5] provide an extensive compilation of maps of battles of the *American Civil War*. Moreover, *BM*-like representations are already used by tools (e.g., [18, 20]) to help players of team-based combat games to visually plan and convey team tactics and strategies. We thus believe that such a representation may also be valuable for post-hoc battle analysis. The design and level of detail of a battle map is not strictly defined, it is left to the discretion of the mapmaker what information and how much detail to include in the map (e.g., troop movements, lines of defense, fortifications, etc.). However, battle maps usually focus on the manoeuvres of organizational units such as corps, divisions, or squads rather than of individual units.

We devised an algorithm that automatically creates a battle map from a pair of replay files (cf. Figure 1, right column). These maps show troop movements, major sites of combat (areas with a high density of shooting and target locations), as well as long distance attacks between these combat sites. We will not elaborate upon the technical details here but the basic idea behind the algorithm can be summarized as follows: First combat sites are extracted from the shooting and target locations using DBSCAN clustering [8]. Next, troop movements are derived by first transforming the input trajectories into simplified semantic trajectories (i.e. sequences of landmarks, see, e.g., [28]) and then aggregating these semantic trajectories based on their similarity. Lastly, attacks between combat sites are determined by examining the shooting and target locations of damage events. Visually, troop movements are depicted using colored arrows whose width is proportional to the number of involved units. Arrow heads indicate the direction of movement. Combat sites are enclosed by a closed white curve with the enclosed area being cross-hatched if close combat (i.e., units within the same site attacking each other) occurred. Long-range attacks between combat sites are also visualized using directed arrows. The

width of these arrows indicates the amount of shots fired to give an impression of the strength of the attack. Again, these arrows are color-coded to show which army was responsible for the attack. Again, icons are used to depict team bases and spawn points.

Among the three evaluated visualizations this one has the highest level of abstraction, offering a more concise and high-level view of a battle. However, this also comes at the cost of reduced accuracy. For example, due to the grouping of trajectories subtleties in the movement of individual units are not discernible any more. Neither can the precise firing lines or exact death locations be inferred from this visualization.

Tasks

For each visualization and dataset we devised 10 tasks in the form of true/false statements. To this end, labels for regions of interest were added to each *BM* and grid squares, denoted A1 to F6, were superimposed on the *SSV* and *EV* to make it easier to refer to specific locations on the maps (cf. Figure 1) and, in turn, prevent ambiguities in the statements. The statements itself were influenced by *WoT's* basic battle mechanics that players need to know to succeed in the game (gathered through an informal review of game-related websites), by what data can be extracted from the replay files, and by what data is visualized in existing *WoT* battle visualizations. In particular the statements covered questions about troop movements and their strength (e.g., *Team 1 moved units to area A then moved on to area C*; *Starting from their spawn point Team 2 moved more units to D1 than to E3*), direction and strength of attacks (e.g., *Team 1 attacked units of Team 2 located in area C from area A*; *Attack rate of Team 2 from area A to B was larger than from D to B*), succession of movements and attacks (e.g., *Team 2 moved units to area C then attacked units located in area B and A*), and death locations (e.g., *Units of Team 1 got killed in sector E6*; *Both teams lost units in sector E3*). It should also be emphasized, that, as a matter of course, these statements varied slightly from visualization to visualization since 1) these were based on three different battles and 2) because not all types of statements were applicable to each type of visualization (e.g., the *SSV* does not show information about the direction of attacks).

Procedure

For data collection we administered an online questionnaire which was publicized through various *WoT* related message boards[1] and kept active for approximately one month. Responses to the survey were anonymous and participants received no compensation for participation in the study. The survey itself consisted of three parts. The first part posed general questions about demographics (age and gender), their familiarity with maps in general, and their experience with *WoT* (namely, number of battles fought, earned experience points, self-perceived expertise, and clan membership).

The second part covered the visualizations itself. It started with a description of the game mode the visualizations are based on (in case some of the participants are not familiar

---

[1] http://forum.worldoftanks.eu, http://forum.wotlabs.net, https://www.reddit.com/r/WorldofTanks

with it) and then presented the three types of visualizations (*BM*, *EV*, and *SSV*) in counterbalanced order. To counteract learning effects further no two visualizations were based on the same dataset. For example, a participant which received the CLIFF-1 dataset for the *BM* would receive the CLIFF-2 dataset for the *EV* and the STEPPES dataset for the *SSV* or vice versa. For each visualization participants had to first complete the respective 10 tasks (true or false, RQ3) and then rate the visualization on a five-point scale anchored by *poor* (1) and *excellent* (5) with respect to seven quality measures (RQ1), in particular, *clarity* (i.e. is the information displayed easily interpretable), *readability* (i.e. are the different visual elements easily discernible), *informativeness*, *aesthetic appeal*, *accurateness* (i.e. how accurate is the data such as movement data displayed), *usefulness* (for gameplay analysis), and *ease of extraction* (i.e. how easily can information be extracted from the visualization). These measures were chosen based on cartographic and data visualization principles (e.g., [4, 16, 25]) and the problem domain of gameplay analysis. The tasks had to be completed before participants could rate the visualization to ensure that they have spent some time with the representation before assessing it. In addition, a legend – explaining the displayed visual elements and the utilized color-coding – was provided for each visualization.

The last part of the survey asked participants to rank the visualization types in terms of personal preference, perceived readability, and according to how well they depict the course of battle (RQ2). Participants were also requested to explain their ranking in each case. Lastly, participants were able to share their views and opinions on the types of questions for which the different visualizations are most useful (RQ4). All open-ended questions were optional. Before launching the survey a pre-test with two participants was conducted to estimate the duration of the questionnaire and to identify potential problems. Based on this feedback we revised the phrasing of some statements to avoid ambiguities and added the ability to enlarge the visualizations in a pop-up window. The entire survey took about 30 minutes to complete.

Sample
In total, 41 players between 15 and 51 years of age ($M = 27.1$, $STD = 9.8$) completed the survey with 37 being male and four respondents being female. One participant indicated to have red-green color blindness. Asked about their familiarity with maps on a 5-point scale anchored by 1 (not at all familiar) and 5 (extremely familiar), 17.1% rated themselves with a score of 3, 53.6% with a score of 4, and 29.3% with 5. With regard to *WoT* experience, participants reported to have fought between 1854 and 35,847 battles ($M = 12,067$, $STD = 8641$) and to have between 255 and 25,710,640 ($M = 6,744,663$, $STD = 6,493,609$) experience points. As such the survey attracted mainly intermediate and experienced players. This is also reflected by the players self-assessment of their *WoT* expertise. On a five-point scale anchored by 1 (novice) and 5 (expert), only three respondents self-rated their expertise with a 2. The majority (44%) gave themselves a score of 4 and about equal proportions (27% and 22%) a score of 3 and 5. 31 participants stated to be a member of a clan.

RESULTS
In the following analysis all responses to rating scales are treated as ordinal values and thus analyzed using non-parametric statistics (using a significance level of .05). Responses to open-ended questions were examined using qualitative content analysis [22] by two researchers in an iterative process. On the one hand participants' responses were analyzed to identify common reasons why the participants ranked the visualization the way they did and on the other hand to explore their views and opinions about the types of questions for which the different visualizations are most useful.

Rating (RQ1)
First, we assessed if the dataset influenced participants' ratings of the three visualization types. In case of the *BM* visualization a Kruskal-Wallis H test showed no statistically significant differences in the ratings of the seven criteria between the three different datasets ($p > .05$ in each case). Similarly, no significant differences in the ratings for the *EV* were found. However, in case of the *SSV* ratings of clarity ($\chi^2(2) = 7.065$, $p = .029$) and readability ($\chi^2(2) = 6.138$, $p = .046$) were significantly different. Post-hoc comparisons using Mann-Whitney U tests with Bonferroni adjustment ($\alpha = .0167$) only showed a significant difference between the ratings of the STEPPES ($Mdn = 2$) and CLIFF-2 ($Mdn = 3$) dataset with regard to clarity ($U = 50.0$, $p = .011$) with a medium effect size of $r = .47$. This could perhaps be attributed to the fact that the more dispersed trajectories on the *Steppes* map made comparisons between the two maps more difficult. In general, however, the ratings were not influenced by the particular dataset. As such we will not distinguish between the different datasets in the following analysis.

Figure 2 shows a boxplot of the descriptive statistics of the quality measures across all three datasets for each visualization type. For each criterion we tested if the ratings differed significantly across the three types of visualizations using a Friedman test. If the Friedman test was significant at the .05 level, follow-up pairwise comparisons were performed using Wilcoxon signed-rank tests with Bonferroni correction ($\alpha = .0167$) for multiple comparisons. Effect sizes were estimated for significant findings with $r = Z / \sqrt{N}$, where N is the total number of observations. In addition, a Spearman rank correlation was performed to assess the effect of age (due to the predominance of males in our sample we refrain from analyzing the influence of gender), *WoT* experience (specifically, number of experience points as we think these better reflect a player's skill than the number of battles fought), and familiarity with maps on the ratings. For brevity, we will only report statistically significant results in the following.

Clarity
The Friedman test revealed a statistically significant difference in perceived clarity depending on the visualization type, $\chi^2(2) = 11.46$, $p = .003$. Post-hoc analysis showed that the *BM* was rated higher than the *EV* ($Z = -2.707$, $p = .007$) and the *SSV* ($Z = -2.619$, $p = .009$). In both cases the effect size can be considered moderate (in terms of Cohen's criteria [2]) with values of $r = .30$ and $r = .29$, respectively. It can be reasonable assumed that the more abstracted, and less detailed,

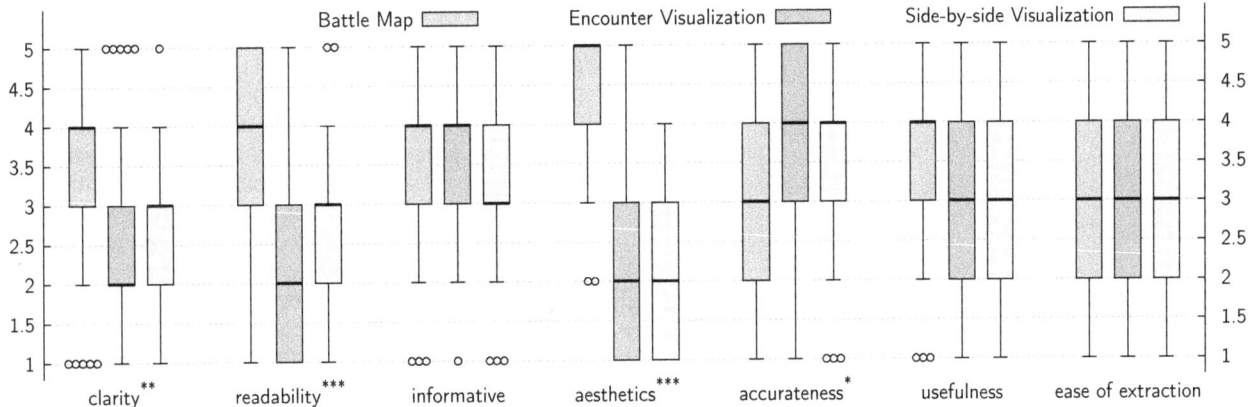

Figure 2. Boxplot showing the median, interquartile range, and maximum and minimum (whiskers) of the players' ratings of the different visualization types with respect to seven different criteria (*, **, * significant differences in ratings at $p < .05$, $p < .01$, $p < .001$).**

representation of the *BM* contributed to the greater perceived clarity. No significant correlations were observed.

Readability

Ratings of readability differed significantly across the three visualizations with $\chi^2(2) = 30.5$, $p < .001$. Again, the *BM* was rated more favorable than the *EV* ($Z = -4.128$, $p < .001$) and the *SSV* ($Z = -4.215$, $p < .001$), with moderate effect sizes of $r = .46$ and $r = .47$. This is most likely because the *BM* is – due to aggregating the data – less cluttered in comparison with the other visualizations which both plot all unit trajectories individually. Interestingly, there was a moderate negative correlation between the number of experience points and the perceived readability of the *SSV* ($r_s = -.474$, $p = .002$), that is, players with more experience assessed the readability of the *SSV* lower than those with less experience.

Informativeness

All three visualizations were considered to be equally informative. Nonetheless, participants with more experience points tended to give lower ratings in case of the *EV* ($r_s = -.325$, $p = .038$) and the *SSV* ($r_s = -.436$, $p = .004$).

Aesthetic appeal

Statistical analysis revealed significant differences in the aesthetic ratings of the three visualizations types ($\chi^2(2) = 58.53$, $p < .001$). The *BM* scored considerable higher in terms of aesthetics than the other two types with $Z = -5.281$, $p < .001$ (*EV*) and $Z = -5.348$, $p < .001$ (*SSV*). Effect sizes were medium to large in both cases with $r = .58$ and $r = .59$. No significant correlations were found.

Accurateness

In terms of accuracy, results also indicate significant differences in the ratings among the three conditions ($\chi^2(2) = 7.702$, $p = .021$). Not surprisingly, the accurateness of the *BM* was rated lower than that of the *EV* ($Z = -2.748$, $p = .006$) with a moderate effect size of $r = .30$. This can be attributed to the fact that this representation abstracts from the original input data to provide a more aggregated view of the battle. Less obvious, given that both the *EV* and the *SSV* visualize the unaltered data as stored in the replays, is the higher

rating of the *EV* ($Z = -2.148$, $p = .032$). This may probably be due the fact that the juxtaposition of the two maps hinders accurate comparisons of trajectories from different teams (e.g., how close to each other have enemy units been). Also, the *EV* shows the lines of fire and as such it provides more accurate information on which player caused damage to (or destroyed) another unit. However, effect size was rather low with $r = .24$. Correlation analysis also showed that players with more experience points tended to rate the accurateness of the *SSV* lower ($r_s = -.483$, $p = .001$). Experienced players are likely to put greater importance on accurate information and the side-by-side view, as pointed out above, makes accurate comparisons between trajectories or death locations more difficult.

Usefulness

Participants considered all three visualizations equally useful for gameplay analysis, with no significant differences between them. However, the rating of the *SSV* was influenced by the *WoT* experience of the respondents, with more experienced players considering it less useful ($r_s = -.466$, $p = .002$). In addition, older participants tended to rate the usefulness of the *BM* representation higher than younger respondents ($r_s = .360$, $p = .021$).

Ease of extraction

Ratings did not significantly differ between the visualizations. However, participants with more experience points tended to find it a bit easier to extract information from the *EV* than players with less experience ($r_s = .357$, $p = .022$). This visualization is perhaps the most complex of the three as it shows the most information in a single drawing and more experience with the game is likely to prove helpful for extracting information from it. Surprisingly, familiarity with maps was weakly negatively correlated with the rating scores for the *SSV* ($r_s = -.384$, $p = .013$), that is, participants who had more experience with maps found it more difficult to get information out of this representation. Although this may seem counter-intuitive at first we suspect that people who use maps more regularly expect to find all necessary information in a single map and thus felt that comparing two views complicates matters. However, this is mainly speculative and needs

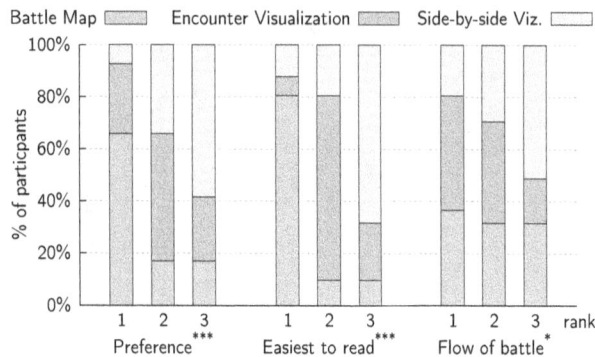

Figure 3. Ranking of the three investigated visualizations with respect to personal preference, readability, and how well they depict the flow of battle (*, * significant differences in the rankings at $p < .05$, $p < .001$).**

to be confirmed in further studies. No correlations were found for the *BM* representation, suggesting that its interpretation is equally easy for less experienced players or players with less practice in reading maps.

Ranking (RQ2)

Figure 3 shows the ranking of the three visualizations with respect to personal preference, perceived readability, and how well participants thought the visualizations represent the course of a battle. In all three instances the ranking did not correlate significantly with age, familiarity with maps, nor with *WoT* experience (i.e., number of experience points). In some ways this is surprising as we would have expected that more experienced players would prefer visualizations with a higher level of detail.

Personal Preference

A Friedman test showed a statistically significant difference in the ranking of the visualization types with respect to personal preference ($\chi^2(2) = 20.54$, $p < .001$). The *BM* was preferred to most ($Mdn = 1$) followed by the *EV* ($Mdn = 2$) and lastly the *SSV* ($Mdn = 3$). However, agreement among raters, measured using Kendall's W (0 – no agreement to 1 – complete agreement), was weak (based on Schmidt's [21] guidelines) with $W = .25$. Post-hoc analysis with Wilcoxon signed-rank tests and Bonferroni correction ($\alpha = .0167$) revealed significant differences between the *BM* and the *SSV* ($Z = -3.903$, $p < .001$, $r = .43$) as well as between the *EV* and the *SSV* ($Z = -2.834$, $p = .005$, $r = .31$).

Respondents reported that they preferred the *BM* representation because of its good readability (stated 11 times) and because of its more abstract and general overview of the battle which allowed them to quickly access information (12x). The visual design of the *BM* also played an important role for the participants (6x), highlighting that it is the *shiniest* and *has the nicer graphics*. However, the lack of detail was the main reason for many participants to rank it lower (13x). Respondents, for example, complained that *precise movements cannot be determined*, that there is *no info on which tanks died where*, or that *battles zones/troop concentrations are vague*. With respect to the *EV*, participants valued the higher level of detail the most (10x), especially emphasizing the accurate

representation of movements (5x) and the depiction of firing lines (5x). The non-significant differences between the *BM* and *EV* can thus most likely be attributed to the fact that some participants prefer more details while others are more interested in a general overview. This would also explain the low inter-rater agreement. On the downside, the resulting decrement in readability (6x) and problems with cluttering (5x) had a negative effect on participants' preference toward the *EV*. The *SSV* was clearly the least preferred with participants mainly reporting drawbacks, primarily the lack of readability due to being confusing or unclear (4x) and its reliance on two juxtaposed maps (3x). Three participants also disliked the graphical representation itself. In summary, readability, level of detail, as well as the graphical design itself seem to have been to most important factors for the participants.

Readability

Results of the Friedman test also indicated significant differences in the ranking of the visualizations in terms of readability ($\chi^2(2) = 34.39$, $p < .001$) with moderate agreement among players (Kendall's $W = .42$). Again, the *BM* was ranked first ($Mdn = 1$), followed by the *EV* ($Mdn = 2$) and the *SSV* ($Mdn = 3$). Pair-wise Wilcoxon signed-rank tests showed significant differences between the *BM* and the *EV* ($Z = -4.274$, $p < .001$, $r = .47$) and between the *BM* and the *SSV* ($Z = -4.486$, $p < .001$, $r = .49$).

This is in line with the results of the readability rating, where the *BM* was also rated significantly better than the other two visualizations. Statements of the participants also reflect their preference toward the *BM* in terms of readability, stating that it is easy to read and interpret (11x) and that it offers a quick overview of the battle (6x). Participants especially appreciated the clean design of the *BM* (8x), stressing, among others, that *the large, bold markers of the Battle Map, while less precise, clearly and concisely convey the information* and that it is *clear even when both teams meet*. Others liked the visual design and graphics (3x) and the clear depiction of engagement zones (3x). The other two representations were less well received in terms of readability. Participants found the *EV* to be quite cluttered (5x) and noted that it takes more effort to read (4x). Likewise, the ranking of the *SSV* was influenced by similar reasons, participants again mentioning visual clutter (3x) and that the additional displayed information (in contrast to the *BM*) makes it harder to read (3x). Interestingly, and contrary to our expectations, the separate maps for each team were not mentioned explicitly by the participants as reason for ranking it lower. While each map in itself is not as crowded as the *EV* we would have expected that the effort for comparing the maps would impede their perceived readability.

Flow of Battle

Contrary to above, players were much more indecisive (cf. Figure 3) about which visualization type most effectively conveys the progression of a battle. This impression is backed by the statistical analysis which – although showing significant differences ($\chi^2(2) = 7.17$, $p = .028$) – yielded a very weak agreement among raters ($W = .087$) which precludes us from drawing any confident conclusions about the ranking.

As the qualitative content analysis revealed this ambivalence in player preference most likely stems from different conceptions of how much details should be included in a visualization in order to effectively convey the battle progress. While some participants were in favor of the *BM* due to its more abstract representation (7x), others complained about the lack of detail (4x), noting, for example, that its representation is *too broad and vague to give anything other than general ideas*. In contrast, some respondents were positive about the detailed data provided by the *SSV* (8x). Others, in turn, were more apprehensive, expressing concerns that it contains too much information, making the representation harder to read (5x). For instance, one respondent highlighted that it *takes considerably more effort*. Likewise, players were fond of the level of detail provided by the *EV* (7x). One participant, for example, stated that it gives the *best picture of how the battle took place from location to distance of engagement*. On the other hand, two respondents were worried about the visualization being too cluttered or confusing. In comparison with the *SSV* two participants found that the *EV*'s approach of combining the information of both teams in a single map is beneficial for understanding the flow of battle. However, three respondents felt the exact opposite, noting that the separate views of the *SSV* allow to infer *what was known to each team* and to see *who was spotted and where*.

Correctness (RQ3)

In this section we will look at how well the posed tasks could be answered by the participants with each of the three visualization types. For that purpose, we calculated for each task the percentage of participants who gave the correct response. In the following, we will primarily focus our discussion on tasks that appeared to be particularly hard to solve, i.e., tasks where the percentage of correct answers was one standard deviation below the mean correctness.

Side-by-Side Visualization

On average, the number of correct answers for a task was provided by 78.1% ($STD = 20.6\%$) of the participants with four out of the 30 tasks falling below the mean minus one standard deviation threshold of 57.5%. More specifically, these statements were only answered correctly by 33.3% to 46.7% of the respondents. In contrast to the other two visualization types these statements were not of a common type but instead were quite varied asking about death locations, unit positions, and unit movements. We could not identify any particular causes for the poor result in these four instances as other similar questions were answered more correctly. However, we suspect that the color-coding gave rise to confusions and thus increased the chance of errors. Each map renders the battle from the perspective of one team using the same colors to depict units of the own and enemy team. This means, for example, that in one map green refers to members of the first team and in the other map to the units of the second team. Moreover, it is known that relationships between elements of separate views are not always easy to see (cf. [10, 13]). Together, these two drawbacks may have complicated matters and may also explain the large variation in overall correctness rates by statement. Generally, statements purely about unit movements (10 statements) were, on average, answered

correctly by 81.8% of the participants while questions concerned with death locations (11 statements) were answered less correctly (74.5%) – probably because not every death location is marked in each map.

Encounter Visualization

Tasks were, on average, answered correctly by 80.9% ($STD = 15.4\%$) of the respondents. Especially four statements caused difficulties for the participants with the percentage of correct answers ranging from 40.0% to 64.3%. Three of these four statements asked about the direction of attacks (mean correctness of 52.5%). Generally, this type of question caused less problems as seven similar statements where answered correctly by a much higher proportion of, on average, 74.5%. However, in these three particular instances the areas under consideration were rather congested and thus visually cluttered. This likely impeded participants' ability to clearly recognize the sometimes partly occluded arrow heads. Moreover, dense regions make it more difficult to locate the unit trajectory from which an attack arrow is actually originating from since the start position of a firing line is not explicitly marked. The fourth statement – correctly answered by 58.3% of the respondents – asked about the direction of movement. Generally, we would have expected that such tasks pose more difficulties as the visualization provides no explicit indication of the movement direction. However, two very similar questions also inquiring specifically about the direction of a single unit were answered correctly by all and almost all (83.3%) participants. It should be emphasized, however, that the movements in the professional replays we used were generally straightforward and goal-directed. On the other hand, replays from beginners, may include more complicated and *tangled* trajectories with lots of detours and are thus likely to complicate this task. With this in view, the clarity of the visualization could possible be enhanced further by, for example, using indicators such as equidistant arrows or comets – which have been shown to work well for visualizing complex trajectories (see [17]) – to encode the direction of units.

Battle Map

On average, tasks were solved correctly by 84.3% ($STD = 16.2\%$) of the participants. However, five tasks – all of them concerned with troop movements – were seemingly difficult to solve with only 40.0% to 64.3% of the respondents providing the correct answer. In four cases the difficulties most likely arose due to the overlapping of movement arrows of the same color (e.g., the red arrows in the CLIFF-1 map, cf. Figure 1) as similar statements about movement not affected by overlapping were mainly answered correctly. However, in two instances the difficulties may have also occurred because of participants being uncertain if troops engaged in a battle (arrow heads pointing toward the battle region) or just passed through the area at a time while the battle did not last (movement arrows crossing through beneath the battle region). In case of the fifth statement with a correctness of 64.3% we first hypothesized that participants were mistaking the attack arrow for showing a troop movement but since all other questions involving both arrows types did not cause major problems we suspect that some participants did not carefully read this statement. Statements dealing with the direction (6 statements) and strength of attack (2 statements) were answered correctly by almost all participants (92.5% and 95.8% on average, respectively). In summary, the visualization seems to be easy to read with mainly overlappings being responsible for the misinterpretations.

Suitability (RQ4)

Participants were asked for which types of questions they think the different visualization types are most useful. Using qualitative content analysis the following seven major categories of analysis tasks emerged:

Battle Summary: Questions concerned with getting a quick overview of the course of a battle were assigned to this category. This includes, for example, questions such as *How did the particular battle happen?* as well as questions about the *general flow of a battle* and *overall match progress.*

Map Strategy: Questions regarding map-specific strategies and tactics fell into this category. Respondents, for example, deemed some visualizations helpful for *learning how to play a map* or to identify *safe routes.*

Areas of Interest: This category contains questions related to specific locations such as areas of conflict, choke points, or areas of troop concentrations. Examples include: *Where did major fights take place? Where were dangerous zones? Where were the majority of allied/enemy tanks located?*

Team movement: Questions relating to this category focus on team-specific strategies and tactics. This comprises questions like: *What was the general positioning of the teams? How did the teams split up?* or *How did each team deploy and engage each other during the battle?*

Unit Movement and Positioning: Questions about individual movements of units and their positions such as about *what movements were made by each tank* fell into this category.

Combat: This category includes all questions which deal with the particulars of combat such as: *Which positions were used to shoot? Where were the firing lines?* or *Who shot at who and from where?*

Reconnaissance: Questions concerned with obtaining information about enemy activities or enemy presence such as about *effective spotting locations* or about *where enemy tanks were spotted* were grouped under this category.

Table 1 lists the number of statements falling within each category grouped by visualization type. As Table 1 shows, the BM was judged to be very suited for getting a quick summary of a battle and to learn about map-specific strategies whereas the other two visualizations were not deemed very useful for these purposes. This is in line with the preference findings where participants especially valued the abstract representation of the BM for its readability and its ability to quickly convey information. While participants found all three visualizations appropriate for answering questions about areas of interest these types of questions were mostly mentioned with regard to the BM. The clear delineation of areas with densely

Category	Side-by-Side Visualization	Encounter Visualization	Battle Map
Battle Summary	1	4	8
Map Strategy	2	4	12
Areas of Interest	8	8	18
Team Movement	10	3	11
Unit Mov. and Pos.	5	11	0
Combat	0	11	5
Reconnaissance	13	0	0

Table 1. Task categories derived through qualitative content analysis ($N = 41$) and number of statements by visualization type.

distributed shooting and hit locations in the BM representation helps to quickly recognize zones of activity and thus facilitates such tasks. Questions concerning the analysis of team movements were most often named in connection with the BM and the SSV. In case of the former the movement arrows of the BM offer a concise overview of team movements and troop strengths of both teams while the separate views of the latter seem to draw the attention to the behavior of individual teams, for example, one participant remarked that it is more useful *for seeing what an individual team did, rather than the interaction of both teams.* Team-related questions were far less mentioned with regard to the EV. One likely reason for this is that the increased clutter impairs the ability to understand the interplay between team members. However, the EV was considered to be particularly well suited if the positioning and movement of individual units is from interest. None of the participants found the BM adequate for this type of questions which is, however, not surprising as movements of individual units are not discernible. Combat-related questions were mainly associated with the EV and – to a lesser degree – also with the BM representation, albeit for different reasons. The BM was appreciated for investigating general attack patterns and the fierceness of attacks (macro analysis) while the EV was found suitable for reviewing the details of combat such as information about the exact shooting positions, firing lines, and cross fire (micro analysis). The clear advantage of the SSV is that it is the only visualization type which supports reconnaissance questions. Scouting and exposing enemy tanks is an important gameplay mechanic in WoT (cf. [27]) and information related to this aspect cannot be deduced from the other two visualization types.

DISCUSSION

In the following we briefly summarize and discuss our findings with regard to our four research questions.

RQ1: With respect to aesthetics, readability, and clarity the BM was rated most favorable by the participants. In contrast, the EV was considered to be the most accurate visualization. All three visualization types were considered equally useful for gameplay analysis – although for different analysis tasks (see RQ4 below) – and equally informative, that is, all three types convey relevant, but partly different, information useful for understanding team matches. Likewise, ease of information retrieval was considered to be similar for the three visualization types which is also confirmed by the average task correctness rates (see RQ3 below).

RQ2: Asked about their personal preference, participants strongly preferred the *BM* and the *EV* over the *SSV*, primarily because of the good readability and general overview offered by the former and the high level of detail provided by the *EV*. It is worthwhile to note at this point that the visual design was also a major reason for the participants to rank the *BM* higher. Hence, training visualizations for players should not only strive to be as informative as possible but also to be visually appealing. Rankings according to readability reinforce the findings from RQ1, that is, the *BM* was considered best while visual clutter emerged as a decisive factor for ranking the other two visualizations lower. Training visualizations, like visualizations in general, should display information in a clean and accessible manner and should be conceived in a way that minimizes visual clutter. Queried about which visualization type they think best conveys the course of battle, participants expressed no clear preference for either type. Our results suggest that this indecisiveness is most likely caused by different opinions about how much detail is required to understand a battle. We had expected that more experienced players put higher importance on accuracy and detail than less experienced players. However, our results do not support this hypothesis. It seems likely that demand for accuracy rather depends on personal interest and preference, but this should be investigated further.

RQ3: Task correctness was high for all investigated visualization types and all three types were interpreted equally well. Nevertheless, all of them have potential for further improvements. In case of the *BM* readability could, for example, be enhanced by replacing movement arrows that partly run along the same path by arrows that can bifurcate and reconnect in order to avoid overlappings. The *EV* would benefit from reducing the visual clutter caused by the lines of fire and by explicitly marking their start and end positions while the *SSV* may be improved by using a better color scheme (e.g., using the same color for the same team in both views) and by providing means (e.g., explicit linking) to help players recognize the relations between the two maps.

RQ4: In terms of suitability it can be said that the *BM* visualization is most well suited for gaining a general understanding of a battle, including high-level information about areas of conflict or other regions of interest, team movements, and overall map strategy. Contrary, the *EV* and the *SSV* are both suited for questions that focus on detail (e.g., exact death locations, lines of fire). Whereas the former is more suited for combat related questions and for analyzing the movements and positioning of individual units the team-centric approach of the latter makes it more appropriate for analyzing the behavior of one particular team and aspects of reconnaissance.

Concerning the limitations of this study it should be highlighted that while our participants varied considerably in terms of experience with *WoT*, none of the participants can be considered to be a complete novice. Therefore, our results are more representative for players at an intermediate and advanced level. Secondly, this study relied on a single game – namely *WoT* – and results may vary slightly across team-based combat games. However, since we have deliberately not included *WoT* specific data (e.g., tank classes) in the visualizations and instead focused on general battle mechanics (unit movements, encounters, troop strengths, . . .) which are shared by many team-based shooters, MOBAs, and – to a certain extend – RTS games, we strongly believe that our results are of interest and applicable to other related games as well. However, it can also be safely assumed that different types of games or genres impose different requirements on training visualizations. Consequently, it would thus be useful to investigate how the requirements and informational needs of players differ across genres. Third, as pointed out earlier, statements for each map were adapted to reflect the course of events and the information depicted in the maps. This fact makes it difficult to draw comparisons between the three investigated types of visualizations in terms of ease of interpretation. Nonetheless, our results provide insights into how well the different visualization convey the information and support different kind of tasks. It should also be kept in mind that due to the use of true/false statements – which were mainly chosen to keep the duration of the online survey within reasonable limits – we could only assess specific facts about a battle. Further work may thus examine sense-making with these visualizations in more depth, e.g., by prompting participants to articulate the observations they can derive from the maps and by comparing these explanations with the actual battle. Likewise, the present evaluation is limited in the sense that it does not offer insights into how effective the visualization types are in terms of skill-building. More research is needed to a) evaluate the effectiveness of training visualizations and b) to identify appropriate means and indicators which can be used for that purpose. Lastly, it is worth noting that we focused on static visualizations in this study as many of the visualizations currently targeted toward players offer only limited or no possibilities for interaction such as the *SSV* used by the *WoT* community. However, it can be reasonably assumed that interactive visualizations are likely to be even more effective for exploring multidimensional datasets like the ones used in this study. While this can be seen as a limitation of our study, we think that the results presented here can provide valuable guidance for the design of interactive combat visualizations. Future work may explore possibilities which allow players to customize training visualizations to their needs and to investigate approaches to automatically adapt the representation of the visualization such that it best suits a given analytical task.

CONCLUSIONS

The user study reported in this paper contributes to a better understanding of player-centric visualizations, particularly visualizations for retrospective analysis of battles in team-based combat games. Our results shed light on the strengths and weaknesses of the investigated visualizations, their usefulness for answering various gameplay-related questions, and their ease of interpretation. However, while our study provides evidence that all three evaluated visualizations are useful for gameplay analysis it also highlights that none of them could satisfy all participants. When viewed from this perspective, our results show that players constitute a heterogeneous group of individuals that have diverse and sometimes contradictory demands, expectations, and preferences with regard to training visualizations.

REFERENCES

1. Brian Bowman, Niklas Elmqvist, and T.J. Jankun-Kelly. 2012. Toward Visualization for Games: Theory, Design Space, and Patterns. *IEEE Transactions on Visualization and Computer Graphics* 18, 11 (2012), 1956–1968.

2. Jacob Cohen. 1988. *Statistical Power Analysis for the Behavioral Sciences* (2 ed.). L. Erlbaum Associates.

3. Marius Czyz. 2016. vBAddict. http://www.vbaddict.net/. (2016). Accessed: April, 2016.

4. Clodoveu A. Davis, Jr. and Alberto H. F. Laender. 1999. Multiple Representations in GIS: Materialization Through Map Generalization, Geometric, and Spatial Analysis Operations. In *Proc. of the 7th ACM International Symposium on Advances in Geographic Information Systems*. ACM, 60–65.

5. George B. Davis, Leslie J. Perry, Joseph W. Kirkley, and Calvin D. Cowles. 2003. *The Official Military Atlas of the Civil War*. Barnes & Noble.

6. EA DICE. 2002. Battlefield (series). Game [PC]. (10 September 2002). Electronic Arts, Redwood City, USA.

7. Electronic Sports League. 2016. Wargaming.net League Europe Bronze Series. http://play.eslgaming.com/worldoftanks/europe/wot/open/bronze-series/. (2016). Accessed: April, 2016.

8. Martin Ester, Hans P. Kriegel, Jorg Sander, and Xiaowei Xu. 1996. A Density-Based Algorithm for Discovering Clusters in Large Spatial Databases with Noise. In *2nd International Conference on Knowledge Discovery and Data Mining*, Evangelos Simoudis, Jiawei Han, and Usama Fayyad (Eds.). AAAI Press, 226–231.

9. Riot Games. 2009. League of Legends. Game [PC]. (27 October 2009). Riot Games, Los Angeles, USA.

10. Michael Gleicher, Danielle Albers, Rick Walker, Ilir Jusufi, Charles D. Hansen, and Jonathan C. Roberts. 2011. Visual Comparison for Information Visualization. *Information Visualization* 10, 4 (2011), 289–309.

11. Nate Hoobler, Greg Humphreys, and Maneesh Agrawala. 2004. Visualizing Competitive Behaviors in Multi-User Virtual Environments. In *Proc. of the Conference on Visualization*. IEEE, 163–170.

12. Ioanna Iacovides, Anna Cox, Richard Kennedy, Paul Cairns, and Charlene Jennett. 2015. Removing the HUD: The Impact of Non-Diegetic Game Elements and Expertise on Player Involvement. In *Proc. of the 2015 Annual Symposium on Computer-Human Interaction in Play*. ACM, 13–22.

13. Waqas Javed and Niklas Elmqvist. 2012. Exploring the Design Space of Composite Visualization. In *Proc. of the IEEE Pacific Visualization Symposium*. IEEE, 1–8.

14. Simone Kriglstein, Günter Wallner, and Margit Pohl. 2014. A User Study of Different Gameplay Visualizations. In *Proc. of the SIGCHI Conference on Human Factors in Computing Systems*. ACM, 361–370.

15. Ben Medler and Brian Magerko. 2011. Analytics of Play: Using Information Visualization and Gameplay Practices for Visualizing Video Game Data. *Parsons Journal for Information Mapping* 3 (2011), 1–12. Issue 1.

16. Rameshwar Prasad Misra and Attur Ramesh. 1989. *Fundamentals of Cartography*. Concept Publishing Company.

17. Rudolf Netzel, Michel Burch, and Daniel Weiskopf. 2014. Comparative Eye Tracking Study on Node-Link Visualizations of Trajectories. *IEEE Transactions on Visualization and Computer Graphics* 20, 12 (2014), 2221–2230.

18. newnetwork.cc. 2014. Map Tactic. http://maptactic.com/. (2014). Accessed: July, 2016.

19. Margaree Peacocke, Robert J. Teather, Jacques Carette, and I. Scott MacKenzie. 2015. Evaluating the Effectiveness of HUDs and Diegetic Ammo Displays in First-person Shooter Games. In *Proc. of IEEE Games Entertainment Media Conference (GEM)*. IEEE, 1–8.

20. Pyratron Studios. 2016. StratSketch. https://stratsketch.com/. (2016). Accessed: July, 2016.

21. Roy C. Schmidt. 1997. Managing Delphi Surveys Using Nonparametric Statistical Techniques. *Decision Sciences* 28, 3 (1997), 763–774.

22. Margrit Schreier. 2012. *Qualitative Content Analysis in Practice*. SAGE Publications, London, UK.

23. Ciro Llanos Stein and Jørgensen Kristine. 2011. Do Players Prefer Integrated User Interfaces? A Qualitative Study of Game UI Design Issues. In *Proc. of the 2011 DiGRA International Conference: Think Design Play*. DiGRA/Utrecht School of the Arts.

24. Jan Temmerman. 2016. World of Tanks Replay Parser. https://github.com/evido/wotreplay-parser. (2016). Accessed: April, 2016.

25. Edward R. Tufte. 2001. *The Visual Display of Quantitative Information* (2 ed.). Graphics Press.

26. Wargaming. 2011. World of Tanks. Game [PC]. (12 April 2011). Wargaming, Nicosia, Cyprus.

27. Wargaming.net. 2016. World of Tanks Battle Mechanics. http://wiki.wargaming.net/en/Battle_Mechanics. (2016). Accessed: April, 2016.

28. Josh Jia-Ching Ying, Wang-Chien Lee, Tz-Chiao Weng, and Vincent S. Tseng. 2011. Semantic Trajectory Mining for Location Prediction. In *Proc. of the 19th ACM SIGSPATIAL International Conference on Advances in Geographic Information Systems*. ACM, 34–43.

29. Veronica Zammitto. 2008. Visualization Techniques in Video Games. In *Proc. of Electronic Information, the Visual Arts, and Beyond*. 267–276.

The Convergence of Player Experience Questionnaires

Alena Denisova
Department of Computer
Science, University of York
York, United Kingdom
ad595@york.ac.uk

A. Imran Nordin
Institute of Visual Informatics,
The National University of
Malaysia, UKM Bangi
Selangor, Malaysia
imran.nordin@gmail.com

Paul Cairns
Department of Computer
Science, University of York
York, United Kingdom
paul.cairns@york.ac.uk

ABSTRACT

Player experience is an important field of digital games research to understand how games influence players. A common way to directly measure players' reported experiences is through questionnaires. However, the large number of questionnaires currently in use introduces several challenges both in terms of selecting suitable measures and comparing results across studies. In this paper, we review some of the most widely known and used questionnaires and focus on the immersive experience questionnaire (IEQ), the game engagement questionnaire (GEQ), and the player experience of need satisfaction (PENS), with the aim to position each of them in relation to each other. This was done through an online survey, in which we gathered 270 responses from players about their most recent experience of a digital game. Our findings show considerable convergence between these three questionnaires and that there is room to refine them into a more widely applicable measure of general game engagement.

ACM Classification Keywords

K.8.0 [Personal Computing]: General - Games.

Author Keywords

Player experience; immersion; engagement; player experience of need satisfaction; questionnaires; PENS; IEQ; GEQ.

INTRODUCTION

Flow, presence, engagement, immersion, and fun are amongst most commonly used terms to describe the experience people have when playing digital games [2]. Many methods to evaluate these experiences exist. These include objective measures, such as heart rate measurements, electromyography (EMG) and electrodermal activity (EDA), but these are hard to map to the subjective experience of players. More appropriate subjective measures are also used, such as interviews, focus groups, and surveys, but these can lack standardisation and comparability. Questionnaires are useful standardised research instruments that allow quantification of the subjective

experience under consideration, while being relatively easy to deploy [1]. Like the more objective measures, the use of questionnaires ensures consistency and uniformity of collected data, because the same specific aspects are considered by all participants in all studies.

There are, however, a few drawbacks of using questionnaires to measure player experience. Nordin et al. [12] named the challenges researchers face when looking for the most appropriate questionnaire. Amongst these, they note, is the ability to persuade participants to treat the questionnaires seriously, and the scale upon which participants answer them. Moreover, it is important to consider the wording of questions, so it does not reduce the face validity of the questionnaires [1].

Player experience is a multi-faceted experience. Theories, and their corresponding questionnaires, aim to address each unique concept in great detail. While some questionnaires measure broader experiences, such as engagement and immersion in games [3, 11], which take into account most aspects of gaming, others focus more on a specific facet of experience, e.g. narrative immersion or social presence [7, 13].

On the one hand, the variety of questionnaires allows researchers to focus on a specific aspect of games. At the same time, the various questionnaires show considerable conceptual, and in some cases actual, overlap, while supposedly measuring apparently different experiences. This leads to a confusion as to whether they in fact do the same job. The plurality of questionnaires also reduces the ability to compare the outcomes of player experience studies. The aim of this work is to see empirically how three of the most widely used questionnaires conceptually converge or diverge. The goal is not to say that there should be only one questionnaire, but instead to evaluate whether questionnaires with similar aims to measure engagement in digital games produce consistent and correlated results. This empirical work also helps to determine which aspects of these questionnaires work well and which do not. As a result, we also suggest improvements to the extant tools for quantifying a general game engagement.

MEASURING PLAYER EXPERIENCE

Many existing player experience theories use their own questionnaires to quantify the experience one is having when playing digital games. While the theories aim to focus on a specific aspect of player experience unique to each concept, the overlap between the theories is evident. Similarly, the measuring tools each theory uses have much in common in their questions and

CHI PLAY '16, October 16 - 19, 2016, Austin, TX, USA
Copyright is held by the owner/author(s). Publication rights licensed to ACM. ACM
978-1-4503-4456-2/16/10 $15.00
DOI: http://dx.doi.org/10.1145/2967934.2968095

Questionnaire	Components
Immersive Experience Questionnaire (IEQ)[11]	Cognitive Involvement, Emotional Involvement, Real World Dissociation, Challenge, Control
Game Engagement Questionnaire (GEQ/GEngQ)[3]	Absorption, Flow, Presence, Immersion
Player Experience of Need Satisfaction (PENS)[14]	Competence, Autonomy, Relatedness, Controls, Presence/Immersion

Table 1. Questionnaires measuring player experience after playing a digital game.

components, as seen in Table 1, which contains a summary of the three widely known and used questionnaires and their components. These three questionnaires aim to measure immersion either as a component of player experience, like in the case of the GEQ and the PENS, or as a whole experience, as the IEQ does.

In addition to these three questionnaires, some examples of other important questionnaires used to measure player experience include the Game Experience Questionnaire (GExpQ) [10], GameFlow [16], the questionnaire used to measure immersion by Ermi and Mäyrä [9], as well as more broad concepts like Flow [6], and Presence [17] questionnaires. Such a large number of existing questionnaires poses a challenge for new researchers, who may not necessarily be familiar with every specific detail of each theory. Choosing one is therefore often based on their availability: questionnaires like the GExpQ or the immersion questionnaire by Ermi and Mäyrä are not readily available to the researchers. So eventually only the easily accessible questionnaires tend to be used for measuring player experience. There is also a question of reliability. To obtain reliable results it is imperative that the data is gathered using a reliable questionnaire. However, some of the available questionnaires are not statistically validated, and as a result cannot be presumed trustworthy.

We, therefore, decided to focus on the three tools outlined above based on their dominant use in gaming research, their availability, and the conceptual overlap. The GEQ (GEngQ) [3] and the IEQ [11] are both available publicly and are set up in a similar fashion to evaluate player experience. The GEQ was developed to assess the deep engagement of violent video game players, and it consists of 19 positively worded questions answered on a 7-point Likert scale. The questionnaire is formulated in such a way that the engagement is a unidimensional experience, which ranges up from immersion to flow.

The IEQ is used to measure the levels of immersion experienced by players. It has been used extensively across a diverse array of different use cases and game genres, for example [5,

8]. The IEQ uses 5-point Likert scale questions to measure player experience, but is specifically focused on the notion of immersion when playing games. It uses a combination of positively and negatively worded statements, adding an additional layer of accuracy. The overall score is composed of a summary of the results from the positive questions, and the inverted results of the negative. The development of the IEQ also suggested that there are five factors underlying immersion, but in practice, immersion is treated as a unidimensional concept with the factors framing the interpretation of the results.

Another questionnaire frequently used to quantify the experience of playing digital games is the player experience of need satisfaction (PENS). The questionnaire contains 19 items, where it reviews the experience in terms of 5 components, such as competence, autonomy, relatedness, immersion/presence, and intuitive controls. All but one are measured using 3-item scales (apart from immersion, which is a 9-item scale), ranked on a 7-point Likert scale. It has been statistically validated [15], however the questionnaire is copyrighted and therefore is not readily available to researchers.

An item-by-item analysis shows some similarities between all three of these questionnaires. It is reasonable to expect some correlation between the results obtained using them. However, all three are also described as measuring differing concepts, with the PENS in particular addressing five ostensibly unrelated aspects of player experience. The question is to what extent these questionnaires do in fact measure different concepts.

EXPERIMENTAL METHOD

The aim of the present study was to compare three of the most widely used questionnaires measuring player experience: the IEQ, the GEQ, and the PENS. For this, their questions were combined into an online survey, which was distributed in a number of online gaming forums in order to gather responses from a variety of digital game players.

Participants

Overall, the study gained 287 respondents, where 17 entities had to be omitted due to the age restrictions imposed by the ethical clearance of the study, leaving 270 valid responses from 30 women, 232 men, 1 person who identified themselves as other gender, and 3 people who did not report their gender. Their average age was 26.42 years ($SD = 6.66$, min/max: 18/63). Participants were mostly native English speakers, and were from a total of 32 countries. They had a varied level of previous experience of playing digital games, averaging 17.5 years of gaming ($SD = 6.63$).

Participants were invited to complete the survey, in which they had to reflect on their most recent experience of playing a digital game, which they entered before taking the survey. Overall, over 100 titles were entered, with some of the most popular games being "The Witcher 3" (13), "Dark Souls" series (8), "League of Legends" (4), "FIFA" series (8), "DOTA 2" (19), "Fallout 4" (9), "Counter-Strike" series (7) and "Enter the Gungeon" (9). Other titles listed were from a variety of genres, including role-playing games (RPGs), action games, and action-adventure games of various kinds, simulations, strategy,

		IEQ	GEQ	PENS (Total)	PENS				
					Competence	Autonomy	Relatedness	Immersion	Controls
		$M = 141.56$ $SD = 22.71$	$M = 67.90$ $SD = 16.61$	$M = 94.84$ $SD = 20.46$	$M = 15.40$ $SD = 3.46$	$M = 15.60$ $SD = 3.83$	$M = 11.61$ $SD = 4.30$	$M = 36.61$ $SD = 11.86$	$M = 15.62$ $SD = 3.85$
	IEQ	–							
	GEQ	0.804**	–						
	PENS (Total)	0.813**	0.692**	–					
	Competence	0.573**	0.405**	0.592**	–				
	Autonomy	0.595**	0.428**	0.697**	0.443**	–			
PENS	Relatedness	0.461**	0.421**	0.683**	0.237**	0.333**	–		
	Immersion	0.705**	0.666**	0.902**	0.323**	0.500**	0.586**	–	
	Controls	0.524**	0.369**	0.546**	0.547**	0.399**	0.163**	0.270**	–

Table 2. Pearson r correlations of questionnaire scores ($N = 270$, ** $p < 0.01$).

and racing games. To incentivise the participants we offered them to be entered into a prize draw raffle to win Steam or Amazon vouchers worth £20, depending on their preference.

Materials

The questions from the IEQ, GEQ, and PENS questionnaires were merged to produce a single unified questionnaire that was delivered through Google Forms. Because each questionnaire had different question formats that might confuse participants, the items from all three were presented as standard Likert-type statements in the present tense (as in the GEQ). For example, a question in the original version of the IEQ reading as: "To what extent did you find the game easy?" was rephrased to: "I find the game easy" to match the conventions of the other two questionnaires. All items had a 7-point Likert scale anchored at the ends with Strongly Disagree and Strongly Agree. The order of the questions was randomised in Google forms for each participant in order to avoid order-effects.

At the end of the questionnaire, there was an open-ended field for comments. This was not extensively used but, where appropriate, these responses are reported on.

Design and Procedure

The link to the survey was distributed on various online forums, such as the Steam Users' Forum, Twitter, and relevant Facebook groups, with the aim to gather responses from a diverse audience of digital game players. Each participant was briefed on the usage of the data in accordance with the ethical clearance provided on the study. After this they were asked to reflect back on their most recent experience of playing a digital game and to choose answers that best reflected their experience.

RESULTS AND DISCUSSION

Scale reliability was performed to ensure internal consistency for each questionnaire using Cronbach's α. Additionally, item-total correlations were considered to identify items with weaker coherence to the overall scales they belonged to. These are not reported here for brevity. Correlations between scales and their components were all calculated using Pearson's product correlations.

Scale Reliability and Principle Component Analysis

The collected data was used to perform reliability analyses on the questionnaires: the IEQ, the GEQ, PENS Competence, Autonomy, Relatedness, Immersion, and Controls scales. Internal consistency measures of reliability (Cronbach's α) for the IEQ and the GEQ yielded high levels of internal consistencies of 0.91 and 0.85, respectively.

Each of the PENS factors also had high levels of reliability: 0.74 for competence, 0.78 for autonomy, 0.88 for immersion, 0.80 for intuitive controls. However, relatedness had a lower internal consistency of 0.62, which can be considerably improved to 0.81 if one of the items is removed. Additionally, internal consistency of the PENS as a single scale was evaluated, yielding alpha of 0.90.

The PENS was not designed to be a uni-dimensional scale, and we recognise that high alpha is not a valid indicator of unidimensionality. We, therefore, conducted the Principal Component Analysis (PCA) on the 21 items with oblique rotation (direct oblimin). Analysis of the Measure of Sampling Adequacy suggested that the weak Relatedness item seen previously was not suitable for PCA and it was removed from further analysis. The scree plot strongly suggested two factors accounting for more than 50% variance and the structure matrix also suggested two clear factors, the first composed of Immersion and Relatedness ($\alpha = 0.90$) and the second of Autonomy, Competence, and Control ($\alpha = 0.84$). Details of the analysis are on our website[1].

This suggests that across the wide range of games considered by our participants, PENS does not automatically divide into five clear factors, but in this context has only two factors. It would be worth more substantially exploring the PENS to better understand why the conceptual differences underlying the scales are not seen in the PENS scores here.

Scale Correlations

Overall, there were high positive correlations between the pairs of the IEQ, the GEQ, and the PENS Immersion scales, as shown in the Table 2. The results obtained using the IEQ and the GEQ scales were highly correlated: 0.804. Similarly, the IEQ and the GEQ were also positively significantly correlated with the results from the PENS Immersion/Presence: 0.705

---

[1]sites.google.com/a/york.ac.uk/questionnaires/

and 0.666, respectively. The high correlation between the IEQ and the GEQ suggests that engagement and immersion are in fact addressing the same underlying aspect of player experience. Similarly, data gathered using the immersion scale of the PENS questionnaire also greatly correlated with results obtained using the other two. These findings are not surprising considering that engagement is often perceived as a part of immersive experience [4], and all three scales had questions of a similar nature.

Similarly, there was a positive significant correlation between players' perception of competence and to what extent they found the controls intuitive, according to the results collected using the PENS. As competence questions concerned players' perceived level of skill and challenge in the game, and controls questions were more relevant to the challenge players face when using the controls, it is fair to assume that there is a correlation between the two factors as they broadly address challenge, regardless of its nature. Having appropriate levels of challenge is important for the players to have a positive gaming experience, as reflected in the correlation between the competence and controls data and the IEQ results.

Autonomy, as it is measured in the PENS questionnaire, is described in terms of the amount of freedom and the interesting options the game offers their players. These questions were similar to the emotional involvement, as it is measured in the IEQ. Having interesting choices in the game also contributes to the overall experience, as it is also seen in the high correlation between autonomy and the IEQ and GEQ results. Similarly, there was a positive correlation between autonomy and relatedness. The two come hand in hand in games that offer opportunities for emotional involvement, and a storyline, in which the player can develop relationships with other players.

Given the high statistical reliability of the overall PENS scale, this was also treated as a single scale and compared to the other questionnaires and showed correlations of 0.813 and 0.692 with the IEQ and the GEQ, respectively. Interestingly, even the total scores of the items of the PENS scale that are not part of the Immersion component also correlated with the IEQ and GEQ, $r = 0.750$ and $r = 0.569$, respectively. This suggests it too is measuring engagement. From consideration of the questionnaire items, this is not so surprising. There is a large overlap between the themes of questions used in all three questionnaires, which address such aspects as physical and mental challenge, intuitive controls, emotional involvement (including relationships with other players, the storyline and aesthetics), sense of time, and a sense of being in the game world.

Problematic Items
Although the questionnaires produced coherent results, there were a few drawbacks. Some unreliable items became evident during the analysis of the collected data, such as questions asking players about their relationships with other players (PENS). As many single-player games do not provide opportunities for this experience, this question was viewed as confusing, and players left comments such as (P13): "Some of the questions, for example the ones asking about my relationship to other player, didn't apply to a lot of the game (single player) games I prefer playing" and (P99): "The questions that you were asking seemed to target more of a triple A game audience with world building or even more aptly a MMO or MMORPG I find those games to focus far more on relationship building, immersion and blurring the lines between reality and fantasy." As a whole however, relatedness to the "others was not always inapplicable, as many RPG games offer players opportunities to build relationships with other characters that can be valuable to the player. This perhaps suggests why one of the PENS relatedness questions did not function as well in the Relatedness scale where the other two did.

Another issue mentioned in the comments was about the fact that not all games have a clear ending, as one of the IEQ items concerns players' desire to "win" the game. Similarly, not all digital games are aimed at eliciting emotional responses, and therefore some items in the IEQ and the PENS were deemed inappropriate. A League of Legends player described his experience as something more akin to a sports player during a football match (P241): "The appeal of it isn't like Skyrim or The Witcher in the sense I want to be immersed in another world but more of the sense you get when you play a sport. I will be with a group of friends and out go "out" to play to forget about our worries and responsibilities bonding at the same time."

Moreover, some of the questions seemed out of place to some respondents, such as "I feel scared" item in the GEQ, which does not necessarily apply to many games. Vaguely phrased questions, such as "I feel different" (GEQ) also provided too many opportunities for interpretation, as well as the following item: "Things seem to happen automatically" (GEQ). These items also did not have strong correlations with the others.

CONCLUSION
Overall, the analysis of the collected data suggests that although there is much correlation between the three widely used questionnaires, there is potential for improvement. As different game genres elicit different aspects of gaming experience, the questionnaires in their present form are not fully applicable to all kinds of digital games. As things currently stand, all three seem to function as reasonable measures of player engagement in a game. However, we suggest that there is the opportunity to develop a more refined questionnaire based on these three, which is both a good measure of engagement and not dependent on the game or game type being played. This would not only allow more robust findings, but increase the comparability of studies in different contexts. There is some room to consider nuanced differences between aspects of engagement, for example, through relatedness or challenge but the IEQ and GEQ are not currently construed as addressing those nuances. In conclusion, in their present form, the questionnaires can be used equally reliably to measure player engagement generally. However, we argue that there should be a unified method, which allows us to evaluate players' experience in a variety of digital games without discriminating against games that do not have all such aspects. To do so, more research is needed to unveil the individual differences in games based on the theme, content, and styles of play.

REFERENCES

1. A. Adams and A. Cox. 2008. Questionnaires, in-depth interviews and focus groups. In *Research methods for human-computer interaction*, P. Cairns and A. Cox (Eds.). Cambridge University Press, Cambridge, UK, 17–34.

2. R. Bernhaupt, M. Eckschlager, and M. Tscheligi. 2007. Methods for evaluating games: how to measure usability and user experience in games?. In *Proceedings of the international conference on Advances in computer entertainment technology*. ACM, 309–310.

3. J. Brockmyer, C. Fox, K. Curtiss, E. McBroom, K. Burkhart, and J. Pidruzny. 2009. The development of the Game Engagement Questionnaire: A measure of engagement in video game-playing. *Journal of Experimental Social Psychology* 45, 4 (2009), 624–634.

4. E. Brown and P. Cairns. 2004. A grounded investigation of game immersion. In *CHI '04 extended abstracts on Human factors in computing systems*. 1297–1300.

5. A. Cox, P. Cairns, P. Shah, and M. Carroll. 2012. Not doing but thinking: the role of challenge in the gaming experience. In *Proceedings of the 2012 ACM annual conference on Human Factors in Computing Systems*. ACM, 79–88.

6. M. Csikszentmihalyi. 1998. *The flow experience and its significance for human psychology*. Cambridge University Press, Cambridge, UK, Chapter In: Optimal experience: psychological studies of flow in consciousness, 15–35.

7. Y. De Kort, W. A IJsselsteijn, and K. Poels. 2007. Digital games as social presence technology: Development of the Social Presence in Gaming Questionnaire (SPGQ). *Proceedings of PRESENCE* 195203 (2007).

8. A. Denisova and P. Cairns. 2015. First Person vs. Third Person Perspective in Digital Games: Do Player Preferences Affect Immersion?. In *Proceedings of the 33rd Annual ACM Conference on Human Factors in Computing Systems*. ACM, 145–148.

9. L. Ermi and F. Mäyrä. 2005. Fundamental components of the gameplay experience: Analysing immersion. *Worlds in play: International perspectives on digital games research* 37 (2005), 2.

10. W. IJsselsteijn, K. Poels, and Y. de Kort. 2008. The Game Experience Questionnaire: Development of a self-report measure to assess player experiences of digital games. *TU Eindhoven, Eindhoven, The Netherlands* (2008).

11. C. Jennett, A. Cox, P. Cairns, S. Dhoparee, A. Epps, T. Tijs, and A. Walton. 2008. Measuring and defining the experience of immersion in games. *International journal of human-computer studies* 66, 9 (2008), 641–661.

12. I. Nordin, A. Denisova, and P. Cairns. 2014. Too Many Questionnaires: Measuring Player Experience Whilst Playing Digital Games. *Seventh York Doctoral Symposium on Computer Science & Electronics* 69 (2014).

13. H. Qin, P.L.P. Rau, and G. Salvendy. 2009. Measuring player immersion in the computer game narrative. *Intl. Journal of Human–Computer Interaction* 25, 2 (2009), 107–133.

14. S. Rigby and R. Ryan. 2007. The player experience of need satisfaction (PENS) model. *Immersyve Inc* (2007).

15. R. Ryan, S. Rigby, and A. Przybylski. 2006. The motivational pull of video games: A self-determination theory approach. *Motivation and Emotion* 30, 4 (2006), 344–360.

16. P. Sweetser and P. Wyeth. 2005. GameFlow: a model for evaluating player enjoyment in games. *Computers in Entertainment (CIE)* 3, 3 (2005), 3–3.

17. B. Witmer and M. Singer. 1998. Measuring presence in virtual environments: A presence questionnaire. *Presence: Teleoperators and virtual environments* 7, 3 (1998), 225–240.

Do Field Dependence–Independence Differences of Game Players Affect Performance and Behaviour in Cultural Heritage Games?

George E. Raptis
HCI Group
Department of Electrical and
Computer Engineering
University of Patras, Greece
raptisg@upnet.gr

Christos A. Fidas
Department of Cultural
Heritage Management and
New Technologies
University of Patras, Greece
fidas@upatras.gr

Nikolaos M. Avouris
HCI Group
Department of Electrical and
Computer Engineering
University of Patras, Greece
avouris@upatras.gr

ABSTRACT

Stimulated by a large number of different theories on human cognitive processing, suggesting that individuals have different habitual approaches in retrieving, recalling, processing and storing information, this paper investigates the effect of field dependence/independence with regards to game players' performance in the context of a cultural heritage game. Thirty two participants took part in an in-lab study and were classified as field dependent or independent based on a cognitive style elicitation instrument. Quantitative analysis methods were used to examine gaming performance in terms of game completion time, information seeking and items collection. The results revealed statistically significant differences in task completion time and in crucial information retrieval situations. Findings are expected to provide useful insights for practitioners and researchers with the aim to design more user–centric cultural heritage games.

ACM Classification Keywords

H.1.2. User/Machine Systems : Human factors; Human information processing

Author Keywords

Cognitive Styles; Field Dependence/Independence; Cultural Heritage; Games; Player Analytics; Game Design

INTRODUCTION

Immersive technologies and video games are widely used in order to enrich visitors' experience in cultural heritage environments. Therefore, this domain has been the focus of various research endeavours throughout the recent years [9, 14, 18, 33], as technological advances have contributed towards intelligent and sophisticated digital solutions. Numerous cultural heritage games have been developed [4, 28] aiming to engage players in immersive and playful experiences, often combined with learning goals. In the aforementioned context, game designers are usually trying to scaffold informal learning activities embracing information processing tasks, such as information seeking, comprehension, recall and knowledge acquisition, in the game mechanics. Given that the aforementioned information processing tasks are basically human cognitive tasks, it is interesting to investigate the effect of human cognitive differences in information processing on gaming performance during a cultural heritage game.

Motivation and Theoretical Background

The high–level motivation underlying our work is investigating whether certain game designers' decisions, such as gameplay rules, interaction mechanisms and information structure and presentation, favour specific user groups, who share common information processing attributes, in game contexts embracing human information processing tasks.

The theoretical background of this work is mainly based on theories of individual differences in cognitive styles and abilities [12, 23, 41], suggesting that individuals have preferred ways of seeking, representing, processing and retrieving information, which are related to their individual cognitive skills and abilities, e.g. information process speed and memory load. Several researchers have focused on high–level cognitive processes in order to explain empirically the observed differences in information quest, representation, process and retrieval [24, 35]. Such high–level processes are the cognitive styles and a number of them have been developed and studied over the years [1, 23, 34, 41].

One of the most well established and validated [5, 7] cognitive styles is the Field Dependence/Independence style [41]. It is a single dimension model with the field dependence lying on the one side, and the field independence on the other. The individuals described as field dependent (FD) tend to prefer personal orientation, be holistic, have difficulties in distinguishing details from other information around them and perform better on inductive tasks [41]. On the other hand, the individuals described as field independent (FI) tend to prefer impersonal orientation, be analytical, pay attention to details and tend to easily separate simple elements and structures from the surrounding context [41].

CHI PLAY 2016, October 16–19, 2016, Austin, Texas, USA.
Copyright © 2016 ACM ISBN 978-1-4503-4456-2/16/10 ... $15.00.
DOI: http://dx.doi.org/10.1145/2967934.2968107

RELATED WORK

Video games are closely related to cognitive skills and styles in terms of visual or spatial attention, memory load, verbal representation, etc. [6, 16]. In video gaming contexts the players usually need to solve problems, overcome challenges and interact with the game environment in multiple ways in order to progress and succeed, and thus several cognitive skills are utilised [37, 38]. McDaniel and Kenny in their recent study [27] investigated the impact of FD/FI cognitive style on students' preconceived impressions and enjoyment of video games during a learning activity, and found that there is a difference on the perceived difficulty of playing between FD and FI individuals, with FDs demonstrating a general reluctance towards using games for learning activities. Similar results derived from Naudet et al. [29], who studied the effect of players' cognitive style on a social network game playing in a cultural heritage environment. However, both studies focused on overall gaming experience of the participants, and not on the gaming performance, e.g. game completion time.

METHOD

Time Explorer

In order to further elaborate our research motivation, we selected *Time Explorer*[1], a well–known and multiple award winning web based game provided by British Museum, which integrates multiple game mechanisms and genres, such as adventure, action and problem solving tasks, requiring players to perform several information processing tasks through gameplay such as information seeking, comprehension, recall and knowledge acquisition.

The objective of the game is to travel back in time to explore ancient civilisations and recover precious treasured objects. During the game, the players navigate in a room, performing information seeking and retrieval tasks such as quests for helpful items and facts. In order to solve problems to proceed in the game, and answer the final riddle to save the precious treasured object the players are required to reflect on acquired knowledge incorporating information comprehension, recall and acquisition tasks. The aforementioned tasks are reflected on specific gaming performance metrics, which form the overall score. In particular, the score is measured based on the game completion time, the number of items discovered and whether or not the in–game puzzle solved throughout the gameplay, which are the dependent variables of our study.

Null hypotheses

To provide valuable insights related to our motivation, we formed the following null hypotheses, for which we were suspecting that the main effects would reveal which design aspects of Time Explorer favour specific user types (FD/FI).

- $H0_1$: there is no significant difference regarding the time needed to complete the game between FD and FI players;

- $H0_2$: there is no significant difference regarding the items discovered throughout the game between FD and FI players;

- $H0_3$: there is no significant difference in puzzle discovery throughout the game between FD and FI players.

_____
[1] http://www.britishmuseum.org/games/GreatCourt.swf

Procedure

The first stage of the study procedure involved the recruitment of the participants, who had to meet a set of minimum requirements. In particular, they should a) be engaged with online gaming activities more than twelve hours per week; b) have no previous experience in playing Time Explorer; and c) have never taken the Group Embedded Figures Test (GEFT) before. After the recruitment, five study sessions were scheduled at times convenient for the participants. The individuals of each session were firstly asked to complete a short questionnaire about demographic information, and then they proceeded to the GEFT sessions, which were facilitated by the researchers and had a total duration of fifteen minutes.

Next, the game session took place in a usability lab. Each participant played an introductory level of the game, Ancient Rome, in order to familiarise with the controls and the overall game environment. The main phase of the game followed, where the players had to rescue a porcelain vase in Imperial China. The time allocated for the game was twenty five minutes in total. At the end, a semi structured interview followed in order to ask questions about participants' behaviour and understand their incentives during the game. Ten minutes were allocated to this phase. Prior to the main study, a pilot study was carried out in order to test the environmental components, the study instruments and the flow and the participants' behaviour, aiming to adjust the study parameters.

Participants

Participants were recruited from the institution during the spring semester of 2016. In total, thirty two students were recruited, eight female (25%) and twenty four male (75%), aged between eighteen and thirty years old (mean age = 22 years old, SD = 4 years). All participants played single player web based games more than twelve hours per week. Furthermore, the participants were explicitly asked to specify whether they had played Time Explorer before, and no previous experience on the selected game was reported.

Instruments

Group Embedded Figures Test

To determine the participants' cognitive styles, the Group Embedded Figures Test (GEFT) [30] was used. The test consisted of three sections, and during each of them, the participants had to identify simple forms within complex patterns in a given time. The first section included seven items and the time limit was two minutes. Its purpose was to familiarise the participants with the test process, and hence it was not considered in the total score. The next two sections consisted of nine items each and five minutes were allocated to each. The score is calculated by adding the number of simple forms correctly identified in the second and third section, thus the score range is between 0 and 18. During the administration and scoring of the GEFT, the directions about the materials, the test procedure, scoring and time limits, described in the scoring template [42], were firmly followed.

Participants' average performance on the GEFT was 12.59 (SD = 3.39), distributed normally according to Shapiro–Wilk test (p = 0.36). The classification of participants into FD or FI

Group Statistics				
Group	N	Mean	Std. deviation	Std. error mean
FD	15	206.20	57.486	14.843
FI	17	277.29	64.634	15.676

Independent Samples Test				
t	df	Sig. (2-tailed)	Mean Difference	Std. Error Dif
-3.268	30	.003	-71.094	21.751

Table 1. Independent samples test results.

is based on a cut–off score, which however is not identified in the original work [30]. A number of classification procedures have been developed [10, 25] and for the scope of this study the mean score was adopted as the cut-off score.

Therefore, the cut–off score was determined to be 12, meaning that the participants who scored 12 or lower were classified as FD, and those who scored from 13 to 18 as FI. Based on the aforementioned classification scheme, fifteen participants were classified as FD and seventeen as FI. It is important to stress that the frequencies of users' scores on the GEFT test in our sample is comparably similar to general public GEFT test scores as shown in several studies which embraced individuals with different demographics [3, 5, 11, 19, 22, 36].

ANALYSIS OF RESULTS

The effect of FD/FI on completion time

To examine whether the hypothesis $H0_1$ is rejected or not, the independent–samples t–test was used. More specifically, this test was used to determine whether there is a difference between the FD and FI individuals regarding the completion time, and whether it is statistically significant. There is only one dependent variable, i.e. completion time, which is measured at the continuous level. There is also only one independent variable which consists of two categorical and independent groups, i.e. FD and FI cognitive styles.

There were no significant outliers in the FD and FI groups as it was visually inspected on the produced box–plots. Next, the Shapiro–Wilk test was used in order to validate that completion times for FD and FI groups were normally distributed (p > 0.05). Finally, and since there was homogeneity of variances, as assessed by Levene's test for equality of variances (p = 0.747), the t–test with equal variances was run and its results are displayed in Table 1. The completion time of the FD participants was less (206.20 ± 57.49) than the time needed by the FI participants (277.29 ± 64.63) in order to complete the game, a statistically significant difference of 71.094 (95%), t(30) = 3.268 and p = 0.003.

The effect of FD/FI on the number of items discovered

To examine whether there is a statistically significant difference regarding the items discovered by the participants during the game, based on their group, the Mann–Whitney U test was selected. In order to meet the assumption related to the study data it should be determined whether the two distributions have the same shape. A visual inspection of the shapes of the

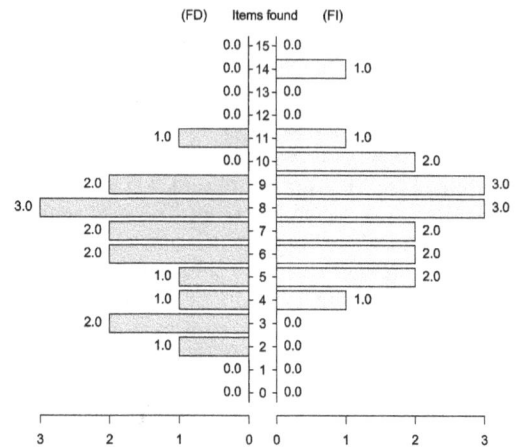

Figure 1. Number of items discovered by the participants

distribution illustrated on the histogram of Figure 1, reveals that the shapes are not the same. The Mann-Whitney U test which was run to determine if there were differences in the number of items discovered by the FD participants (mean rank = 6.40, sd = 2.586) and FI participants (mean rank = 8.00, sd = 2.500), revealed that there was no statistically significant difference between the two groups (U = 86.5, z = -1.560, p = 0.123) using an exact sampling distribution for U.

The effect of FD/FI on whether the puzzle discovered

To examine whether there is a statistically significant difference regarding the discovery of the puzzle which would provide the participants with crucial hints in order to answer the final question and complete the game, Fisher's Exact test was selected. The results of the study revealed that only four (26.7%) FD individuals discovered and solved the puzzle. On the other hand, twelve (70.7%) FI individuals found and solved the puzzle. There was a statistically significant association between cognitive style and the discovery of the in–game puzzle by Fisher's exact test (p = 0.032).

Behavioural patterns of FD/FI players

A few behavioural patterns were identified among the participants of each group. In particular, the two groups followed different approaches in order to complete their tasks. FD individuals tended to seek information in a timely manner and with less moves, whereas FI individuals spent more time when seeking and processing information, as they followed a more analytical approach. Moreover, FD individuals tried more often to correlate acquired knowledge, such as revealed objects, with riddles required to proceed to next game stages, whereas FD individuals followed a more intrinsic approach, being primarily reliant on guesses. Furthermore, FI individuals tended to use the inventory more often, as they wanted to have a clear picture of the gathered items. Also, the fact that most of the FD participants did not access the puzzle stage and found a few hidden items, could be due to their difficulty to perceive objects as separate from the field [24, 41]. The afore mentioned findings are in line with the results derived from our qualitative analysis [32].

DISCUSSION AND INTERPRETATIONS

Quantitative analysis uncovered observable differences between the game–playing approaches of FD and FI individuals. The study revealed a statistically significant difference in completion time between FD and FI participants, which is on a par with the findings of studies in other application domains, such as learning and web search [5, 31]. This difference could be attributed to the different approach of problem solving the two groups followed. FI individuals generally require external help to solve a problem [41], which in this case is to finish the game, therefore they were in the lookout for help while playing, such as using the inventory more often or discovering more items. This finding is confirmed in our previous work [32], with FI individuals accessing more often the inventory to find clues on how to proceed, while FD individuals followed a more inherent approach, verifying their intrinsic nature [41]. In addition, FD individuals are generally less inclined to find objects or cues, as they have difficulty in detecting details, which could explain that they found less items than FI participants.

On the other hand, FI individuals tend to develop self–defined goals, while FD individuals require external ones. An example of such behaviour is that the FI participants found more objects than the FD participants while playing. Moreover, most of the FI participants discovered and solved the in–game puzzle, whereas most of the FD players did not. Given that finding hidden objects and solving the puzzle was not a prerequisite for finishing the game, FI participants spent more time trying to find all the objects and solved the puzzle, while they collected less points. This finding is mainly explained by their analytical nature [41]. Despite FI participants discovered more items than the FD, the difference is not statistically significant which can be attributed to the participants' unawareness of whether the items were required in order to progress in the game, but also to the fact that most items were hidden in obvious spots, and thus they were easily distinguishable. In general, FD individuals focused on the external goal, i.e. find the vase, spending less time in exploring the level and concentrated on the cues that allowed them to proceed more quickly.

The analytical nature of the FI individuals enabled them to solve the puzzle that provided critical hints for answering the final question and rescuing the object. Solving the puzzle required information acquired when collecting specific objects of the game, which the FD participants did not detect, as they tended not to pay attention to detail. In addition, the FI participants' engagement in the puzzle solving, could explain the more time they needed to complete the game, in comparison to FD players. Finally, the complexity of the game did not allow for validating other characteristics of the two cognitive style groups such as complex problem solving performance.

Design Implications and Generalizability

The contribution of the paper entails two important aspects; theory and application. Regarding theory, the study provides evidence that socio-cognitive theories, like FD/FI, can be considered as applicable analysis frameworks in understanding deeper player interactions. Regarding application, the analysis and discussion of results underpinned the value for considering cognitive styles as a human design factor, in both design and run time, in order not to design games that unintentionally favour a specific group, e.g. the Time Explorer designers' decision of non–mandatory discovery of objects and puzzles in order to complete the game favoured FI players in terms of acquired information and FD players in terms of completion time. Given that future studies will further shed light on such effects,they can drive the design of games that adapt to individual cognitive styles by using sophisticated techniques, such as classification tools based on eye tracking mechanisms in AR/VR environments.

Regarding the generalisability of our work, we expect that similar effects will be replicated in the contexts of different game genres, contributing to the study's external validity, as long as the game activity involves in large extend information seeking, retrieval, comprehension, recall and knowledge acquisition tasks. Specifically within the cultural heritage domain, given that user population is culturally diverse, e.g. Time Explorer players span among different cultures, and that users from different nations/cultures have different cognitive processing style abilities [2, 8, 15, 21], we argue that adapting and personalizing design to this aspect may contribute to improvements of cultural heritage gaming experiences for diverse audiences.

CONCLUSION

The purpose of this study was to investigate the effects of field dependence/independence cognitive styles on gamers' performance and behaviour when playing cultural heritage games. The findings of the study revealed a main effect of cognitive differences on task completion time and the discovery of crucial items. No effect on the exploration of the game environment and the discovery of helpful items was identified.

Validity of the study and limitations

An important limitation is related to the rather limited number and non–varying user profiles of the sample since undergraduate and postgraduate students were recruited for conducting the study. However, as mentioned previously the sample distribution towards their FD/FI styles reflects the general public distribution. Given that high level cognitive styles of individuals rarely change throughout adult lifespan [13, 40], the observed main effects of this study would possibly apply for other age groups (e.g., 30–40). There is also a gender imbalance in our sample, but despite the fact that there are mixed outcomes in the literature about the gender effect on FD/FI classification [17, 20, 26, 39], our study has not shown a gender effect towards FD/FI distribution within our sample, as the distribution of GEFT scores was normal. Nevertheless, similar research attempts are required in order to acquire a deeper understanding about the effects of human cognitive factors on performance and user behaviour in cultural heritage games, and thus, increase the external validity of this research.

ACKNOWLEDGEMENTS

We would like to thank SIGCHI offering us the SIGCHI Student Travel Grant (SSTG) program and providing us financial assistance to present our work at CHI PLAY '16.

REFERENCES

1. Christopher W. Allinson and John Hayes. 1996. The cognitive style index: A measure of intuition-analysis for organizational research. *Journal of Management studies* 33, 1 (1996), 119–135. DOI: http://dx.doi.org/10.1111/j.1467-6486.1996.tb00801.x

2. Christopher W. Allinson and John Hayes. 2000. Cross–national differences in cognitive style: implications for management. *International Journal of Human Resource Management* 11, 1 (2000), 161–170. DOI:http://dx.doi.org/10.1080/095851900340042

3. Arif Altun and Mehtap Cakan. 2006. Undergraduate students' academic achievement, field dependent/independent cognitive styles and attitude toward computers. *Journal of Educational Technology and Society* 9, 1 (2006), 289.

4. Eike Falk Anderson, Leigh McLoughlin, Fotis Liarokapis, Christopher Peters, Panagiotis Petridis, and Sara de Freitas. 2010. Developing serious games for cultural heritage: a state–of–the–art review. *Virtual reality* 14, 4 (2010), 255–275. DOI: http://dx.doi.org/10.1007/s10055-010-0177-3

5. Charoula Angeli, Nicos Valanides, and Paul Kirschner. 2009. Field dependence–independence and instructional–design effects on learners' performance with a computer–modeling tool. *Computers in Human Behavior* 25, 6 (2009), 1355–1366. DOI: http://dx.doi.org/10.1016/j.chb.2009.05.010

6. Andy Boyan and John L. Sherry. 2011. The Challenge in Creating Games for Education: Aligning Mental Models With Game Models. *Child Development Perspectives* 5, 2 (2011), 82–87. DOI: http://dx.doi.org/10.1111/j.1750-8606.2011.00160.x

7. Dane M. Chapman and Judith G. Calhoun. 2006. Validation of learning style measures: implications for medical education practice. *Medical education* 40, 6 (2006), 576–583. DOI: http://dx.doi.org/10.1111/j.1365-2929.2006.02476.x

8. Lian-Hwang Chiu. 1972. A cross–cultural comparison of cognitive styles in Chinese and American children. *International Journal of Psychology* 7, 4 (1972), 235–242. DOI:http://dx.doi.org/10.1080/00207597208246604

9. Tanguy Coenen, Lien Mostmans, and Kris Naessens. 2013. MuseUs: Case Study of a Pervasive Cultural Heritage Serious Game. *J. Comput. Cult. Herit.* 6, 2, Article 8 (May 2013), 19 pages. DOI: http://dx.doi.org/10.1145/2460376.2460379

10. Edward E Cureton. 1957. The upper and lower twenty–seven per cent rule. *Psychometrika* 22, 3 (1957), 293–296. DOI:http://dx.doi.org/10.1007/BF02289130

11. Gregory A. Davis. 2006. Learning style and personality type preferences of community development extension educators. *Journal of Agricultural Education* 47, 1 (2006), 90. DOI: http://dx.doi.org/10.5032/jae.2006.01090

12. Andreas Demetriou, George Spanoudis, Michael Shayer, Antigoni Mouyi, Smaragda Kazi, and Maria Platsidou. 2013. Cycles in speed-working memory–G relations: Towards a developmental–differential theory of the mind. *Intelligence* 41, 1 (2013), 34–50. DOI: http://dx.doi.org/10.1016/j.intell.2012.10.010

13. Jack Demick and Seymour Wapner. 1991. Field Dependence-Independence in Adult Development and Aging. In *Field Dependence-independence Bio–psycho–social Factors Across the Life Span*, Seymour Wapner and Jack Demick (Eds.). Lawrence Erlbaum Associates, Mahwah NJ, USA, Chapter 12, 245–268.

14. Josef Froschauer, Dieter Merkl, Max Arends, and Doron Goldfarb. 2013. Art History Concepts at Play with ThIATRO. *J. Comput. Cult. Herit.* 6, 2, Article 7 (May 2013), 15 pages. DOI: http://dx.doi.org/10.1145/2460376.2460378

15. Martin Graff, Jo Davies, and Maggy McNorton. 2004. Cognitive style and cross cultural differences in internet use and computer attitudes. *European Journal of Open, Distance and E-Learning* 7, 2 (2004).

16. C. Shawn Green and Daphne Bavelier. 2012. Learning, Attentional Control, and Action Video Games. *Current Biology* 22, 6 (2012), R197 – R206. DOI: http://dx.doi.org/10.1016/j.cub.2012.02.012

17. Colin J. Hamilton. 1995. Beyond sex differences in visuo-spatial processing: The impact of gender trait possession. *British Journal of Psychology* 86, 1 (1995), 1–20. DOI: http://dx.doi.org/10.1111/j.2044-8295.1995.tb02542.x

18. Mauricio Hincapie, Christian Diaz, Maria Zapata, and Camilo Mesias. 2016. Methodological Framework for the Design and Development of Applications for Reactivation of Cultural Heritage: Case Study Cisneros Marketplace at Medellin, Colombia. *J. Comput. Cult. Herit.* 9, 2, Article 8 (Jan. 2016), 24 pages. DOI: http://dx.doi.org/10.1145/2827856

19. Jon-Chao Hong, Ming-Yueh Hwang, Ker-Ping Tam, Yi-Hsuan Lai, and Li-Chun Liu. 2012. Effects of cognitive style on digital jigsaw puzzle performance: A GridWare analysis. *Computers in Human Behavior* 28, 3 (2012), 920–928. DOI: http://dx.doi.org/10.1016/j.chb.2011.12.012

20. Rob N. Hughes. 1981. Sex differences in Group Embedded Figures Test performance in relation to sex-role, state and trait anxiety. *Current Psychological Research* 1, 3-4 (1981), 227–234. DOI: http://dx.doi.org/10.1007/BF03186733

21. Simy Joy and David A. Kolb. 2009. Are there cultural differences in learning style? *International Journal of intercultural relations* 33, 1 (2009), 69–85. DOI: http://dx.doi.org/10.1016/j.ijintrel.2008.11.002

22. Mohammad Khatib and Rasoul Mohammad Hosseinpur. 2011. On the validity of the Group Embedded Figure Test (GEFT). *Journal of Language Teaching and Research* 2, 3 (2011), 640–648. DOI: http://dx.doi.org/10.4304/jltr.2.3.640-648

23. Michael Kirton. 1976. Adaptors and innovators: A description and measure. *Journal of applied psychology* 61, 5 (1976), 622. DOI: http://dx.doi.org/10.1037/0021-9010.61.5.622

24. Maria Kozhevnikov. 2007. Cognitive styles in the context of modern psychology: toward an integrated framework of cognitive style. *Psychological bulletin* 133, 3 (2007), 464. DOI: http://dx.doi.org/10.1037/0033-2909.133.3.464

25. Mojtaba Maghsudi. 2007. The interaction between field dependent/independent learning styles and learners' linguality in third language acquisition. *Interactive Multimedia Electronic Journal of Computer-Enhanced Learning* 7, 5 (2007), 1–23.

26. Laura J. Massa, Richard E. Mayer, and Lisa M. Bohon. 2005. Individual differences in gender role beliefs influence spatial ability test performance. *Learning and Individual Differences* 15, 2 (2005), 99–111. DOI: http://dx.doi.org/10.1016/j.lindif.2004.11.002

27. Rudy McDaniel and Robert Kenny. 2013. Evaluating the relationship between cognitive style and pre-service teachers' preconceived notions about adopting console video games for use in future classrooms. *International Journal of Game-Based Learning (IJGBL)* 3, 2 (2013), 55–76. DOI: http://dx.doi.org/10.4018/ijgbl.2013040104

28. Michela Mortara, Chiara Eva Catalano, Francesco Bellotti, Giusy Fiucci, Minica Houry-Panchetti, and Panagiotis Petridis. 2014. Learning cultural heritage by serious games. *Journal of Cultural Heritage* 15, 3 (2014), 318–325. DOI: http://dx.doi.org/10.1016/j.culher.2013.04.004

29. Yannick Naudet, Angeliki Antoniou, Ioanna Lykourentzou, Eric Tobias, Jenny Rompa, and George Lepouras. 2015. Museum Personalization Based on Gaming and Cognitive Styles: The BLUE Experiment. *International Journal of Virtual Communities and Social Networking (IJVCSN)* 7, 2 (2015), 1–30. DOI: http://dx.doi.org/10.4018/IJVCSN.2015040101

30. Philip K. Oltman, Evelyn Raskin, and Herman A. Witkin. 1971. *Group Embedded Figures Test.* Consulting Psychologists Press, Palo Alto CA, USA.

31. Ruth A. Palmquist and Kyung-Sun Kim. 2000. Cognitive style and on-line database search experience as predictors of Web search performance. *Journal of the American Society for Information Science* 51, 6 (2000), 558–566. DOI: http://dx.doi.org/10.1002/(SICI)1097-4571(2000)51:6<558::AID-ASI7>3.0.CO;2-9

32. George E. Raptis, Christos A. Fidas, and Nikolaos M. Avouris. 2016. A qualitative analysis of the effect of wholistic-analytic cognitive style dimension on the cultural heritage game playing. In *Proc. 7th International Conference on Information, Intelligence, Systems and Applications (IISA)*. IEEE, Chalkidiki, Greece.

33. Stefan Rennick-Egglestone, Patrick Brundell, Boriana Koleva, Steve Benford, Maria Roussou, and Christophe Chaffardon. 2016. Families and Mobile Devices in Museums: Designing for Integrated Experiences. *J. Comput. Cult. Herit.* 9, 2, Article 11 (May 2016), 13 pages. DOI: http://dx.doi.org/10.1145/2891416

34. Richard J. Riding and Indra Cheema. 1991. Cognitive styles–an overview and integration. *Educational psychology* 11, 3-4 (1991), 193–215. DOI: http://dx.doi.org/10.1080/0144341910110301

35. Richard J. Riding and Eugene Sadler-Smith. 1997. Cognitive style and learning strategies: Some implications for training design. *International Journal of Training and Development* 1, 3 (1997), 199–208. DOI: http://dx.doi.org/10.1111/1468-2419.00020

36. Kent A. Rittschof and Wendy L. Chambers. 2005. Instructional Favoritism? Field Dependence-Independence Does Not Consistently Predict Self–Perceptions or Teaching Preferences. *Online Submission* (2005).

37. Hannah Schmitt, Jutta Kray, Michael Schmitz, and Mert Akbal. 2015. Training While Playing?: Enhancing Cognitive Control Through Digital Games. In *Proceedings of the 2015 Annual Symposium on Computer-Human Interaction in Play (CHI PLAY '15)*. ACM, New York, NY, USA, 685–690. DOI: http://dx.doi.org/10.1145/2793107.2810322

38. Kamran Sedig and Robert Haworth. 2014. Interaction Design and Cognitive Gameplay: Role of Activation Time. In *Proceedings of the First ACM SIGCHI Annual Symposium on Computer-human Interaction in Play (CHI PLAY '14)*. ACM, New York, NY, USA, 247–256. DOI: http://dx.doi.org/10.1145/2658537.2658691

39. Robert M. Torres and Jamie Cano. 1994. Learning styles of students in a college of agriculture. *Journal of Agricultural Education* 35, 4 (1994), 61–66.

40. Herman A. Witkin, Donald R. Goodenough, and Stephen A. Karp. 1967. Stability of cognitive style from childhood to young adulthood. *Journal of personality and social psychology* 7, 3p1 (1967), 291. DOI: http://dx.doi.org/10.1037/h0025070

41. Herman A Witkin, Carol Ann Moore, Donald R Goodenough, and Patricia W Cox. 1975. Field–dependent and field–independent cognitive styles and their educational implications. *ETS Research Bulletin Series* 1975, 2 (1975), 1–64. DOI: http://dx.doi.org/10.1002/j.2333-8504.1975.tb01065.x

42. Herman A. Witkin, Philip K. Oltman, Evelyn Raskin, and Stephen A. Karp. 1971. *Group Embedded Figures Test – Scoring Template/Key.* Consulting Psychologists Press, Palo Alto CA, USA.

Blood and Violence: Exploring the Impact of Gore in Violent Video Games

Louise Ashbarry; Benjamin Geelan; Kristy de Salas; Ian Lewis
School of Engineering and ICT
University of Tasmania, Hobart, Australia
Louisea0@utas.edu.au, Benjamin.Geelan@utas.edu.au, Kristy.deSalas@utas.edu.au,
Ian.Lewis@utas.edu.au

ABSTRACT

Violence is a key element in video games and despite the extensive research in video game violence, there is still a debate on its psychophysiological effect. There is a lack of understanding on the elements of video game violence that influence aggression. The present pilot study examines the effect of blood and gore in a first-person shooter with participants playing in one of the two conditions, with or without blood and gore. To assess the effect of blood and gore, and thus violence, a number of elements were measured including physical arousal, individual differences, personality, and game experience. The results suggested that blood and gore had no effect on aggression-related associations and cognitive processes. The findings did suggest that previous game experience had a significant effect on increased physiological arousal when engaging in violent content featuring blood and gore. Furthermore, a personality trend emerged showing an effect on arousal and cognitive processes. As the study was preliminary, definitive conclusions cannot be drawn, however the findings warrant further investigation.

Author Keywords

Violence, Video Games, Aggression, Arousal, Psychophysiology, Blood, Gore, Player Experience.

INTRODUCTION

With the ubiquity of technology, it is becoming essential to find viable social implications of video game violence, with over 70% of Australians playing video games [1]. It is speculated that individuals will experience aggressive thoughts or express aggressive behaviours after engaging with video game violence [2-5], which may have a relationship with other antisocial behaviours such as engaging in violent crime, street fights and domestic

CHI PLAY '16 CD-ROM, October 16 - 19, 2016, Austin, TX, USA
Copyright is held by the owner/author(s). Publication rights licensed to ACM.
ACM 978-1-4503-4456-2/16/10...$15.00
DOI: http://dx.doi.org/10.1145/2967934.2968111

violence [6]. Despite the number of studies being conducted in this area, there is not yet sufficient evidence to suggest convincingly the nature of the relationship between violent video games and real world aggressive behaviours. This contention is particularly evident in the debate surrounding whether the relationship, if any, is causal (i.e. violent video games cause aggressive behaviours), or correlative (i.e. people with predispositions to aggression enjoy violent video games) [2,3,7,8,9].

One of the core criticisms of violent video games that is proposed to contribute towards increased aggression is the representation of violence and gore. While there is currently no evidence to suggest that depictions of gore or blood in violent video games increase aggression, depictions of blood and gore in other forms of media has been found to increase physiological arousal, such as an individual's heart rate, perspiration and discomfort level [10]. Furthermore, the amount of blood present in violent media content has been found to increase physical aggression [11,12]. Therefore, this study aims to investigate the influence that depictions of blood and gore in a violent video game have upon the levels of physiological arousal and levels of aggression, and explores possible relationships with real world aggressive behaviours.

Video Game Violence and Aggression

In the context of behaviour, aggression is widely defined as physical or verbal behaviour that is intended to harm other people and may result in an individual conducting violent behaviour [5,13]. Violence differs from aggression, with violence being a subtype of physical aggression and incorporating a physical behaviour which is likely to cause severe bodily harm or even death [5,13]. Aggressive behaviour is learnt passively meaning that exposure to violent media affects an individual whether they intended to learn the behaviour or not [14]. It is suggested that individuals learn how to respond to the violent stimuli through media, and that an abnormal or anti-social response can be reinforced with repeated exposure. In previous research, it has been found that high levels of aggressive behaviour were demonstrated in rejected social groups, and those that exhibited less academic interest and motivation [6]. A commonly used model to explain the learning of aggressive behaviour is the General Aggression Model.

General Aggression Model (GAM)

The General Aggression Model (GAM) is a widely used model which can describe the influence of violence on aggression [15]. The model is based on a social-cognitive approach to aggression and attempts to explain the social learning of behavioural sequences [15, 18]. According to GAM, the process of learning and reinforcement of violent stimuli influences the acquisition of aggressive perceptions, cognitions and emotions [5, 15]. An accumulation of research has used the GAM to support the claim that exposure to video game violence is positively associated with the expression of aggression and increased physiological arousal in individuals [2,7,8,15]. Previous research found that after playing video games participants became less physiologically aroused to violence; thus desensitized [8]. The desensitization theory explains that the initial negative perceptual, cognitive and physiological responses to blood and gore becomes habituated with repeated exposure to violence [4]; which may reduce individuals expressing empathy for the suffering of others [8].

Confounding Evidence of GAM

Recently, research showed that the GAM did not hold true as participants that were exposed to violent stimuli did not express a significant bias towards aggressive words [17].

A supporting study found that the expression of aggression positively related to exposure of video game violence; conversely there was no socialization effect contradicting GAM [19]. Additionally, it was found that video game violence did not have any effect on a range of factors such as physiological arousal, aggressive cognitions or behaviour, and post-game affect [18]. Contradicting research has used the Catalyst Model to explain alternative explanations of perceived aggressive responses while engaging in video game violence.

Catalyst Model

An opposing model to GAM is the Catalyst model which is less used within research. The Catalyst Model focuses on innate motivation, biological dispositions and environmental factors which may foster aggression [9]. An aggressive personality is claimed to be mostly developed by biological and genetic dispositions [9]. Previous research has found that the stronger the aggressive responses are in the biological and environmental context, the higher chance an individual will express aggression [18]. In addition, the Catalyst Model highlights that the role of media violence is a correlated relationship with expressed aggression, as individuals who are prone to violence may act aggressively when confronted with similar violence in media. Thus, individuals that have an aggressive personality may be more attracted to violent media.

When comparing the GAM and Catalyst Model, the distinct strength of the GAM is its in-depth social-cognitive theory approach, and its popularity in media research. The concerns of GAM are highlighted through the Catalyst Model. The biological influences on aggression are not considered in depth within GAM, which may undermine its prediction of violent content effects. The vast majority of video game research selected the GAM as it is more suitable than the Catalyst Model. The relationship between aggressive behaviour and video game violence is greatly focused on exposure to gaming elements and as an avenue for individuals to experience violence. Thus, as the GAM is based on social learning the majority of research uses the GAM, and is considered to be the most appropriate model for this project.

Effects of Blood and Gore on Arousal

Previous research found that a key element to a positive gaming experience is the game's virtual blood and gore [8]. It was reported that the "bloody" version of Mortal Kombat sold seven times more than the version which had less blood and gore [20]. As a concern, the level of blood and gore present in a video game may further increase the physiological arousal and aggressive behaviour demonstrated by an individual [16]. To support this concern, the study investigated the presence of blood in video games and found that blood is a factor that may increase aggression [16]. Research has additionally found that participants who play a violent video game without blood have lower levels of physical aggression than participants who play with blood [11-12].

Assumptions and Research Questions

Previous research has focused on the relationship between violent content and aggressive behaviour. As there have been contradictory findings, the current pilot study examines identified assumptions and aims to provide further evidence to clarify the debate, as well as acting as a foundation to future investigations. Based on the past literature, the following hypotheses and research question were derived:

- H0. There is no difference in physiological arousal between playing a violent video game with and without gore.

- H1. Individuals will experience a greater level of physiological arousal to a violent video game featuring gore than a violent video game without gore.

- H2. Players with video game experience will have lower levels of physiological arousal to violent stimuli in video games than players with no or little video game experience.

- RQ. What patterns of physiological arousal are associated with different levels of blood and gore in video games, as measured by self-reporting and machine?

METHODOLOGY

Participants

Participants ($N = 30$; 22 male and 8 female) were recruited from the general population of Tasmania via recruitment advert, and distributed via email, poster and social media.

The population size of the study was based on research which identified that testing 30 representative participants for a pilot study is recommended for the purpose of scale development (i.e conducting further research), thus 30 participants was selected for this study [21]. A total of 60% percent were undergraduate students from the University of Tasmania. The participants were equally divided between the experimental condition (n=15), which featured blood and gore in a violent video game, and the control group, which did not feature blood and gore in a violent video game. Gender was equally distributed over the two conditions, X^2 (3, $N = 30$) = 7.5, p < 0.01. The mean age of participants was 31.53 years ($SD = 11.17$), aligning with the average age of Australian Games being 33 years [1].

Stimulus Material

As the objectives of this study are to examine the effects, if any, that representations of blood and gore have upon arousal and aggressive cognitions during video game play, it was considered most appropriate that the stimulus video game selected be inherently violent within both the experimental and the control conditions. Minimising potential experimental confounds is highly desirable [22], therefore it was considered appropriate to use a single game across experimental conditions and simply manipulate the level of blood and gore within that game. Likewise, games of a more casual nature may not display or represent blood and gore regularly enough or in such a way that would necessarily produce measurable influences on physiological arousal experienced by players.

While most, if not all, video games would logically increase physiological arousal to some extent, inherently violent video games can be demonstrated to do so to a significantly larger extent, with factors such as time pressures and enemy activities increasing stress and excitement [23], and potentially other factors such as blood and gore playing a role. However, this level of arousal is, relative to the capacity of the human body, reasonably low [24], and there is logically considerable scope for more nuanced factors such as the level of gore to have additional effects on arousal. Finally, the controversies and debates surrounding video game violence and influences on aggression are predominantly centred around games with high levels of violence [23]. It was therefore considered most appropriate to use an innately violent video game within this study.

Selection of the video game within this study considered several factors, including: having easily noticeable levels of blood and gore displayed within typical game play, having the option reduce or remove blood and gore; being a relatively modern game graphically; having the ability for all participants to play through identical game segments; having the ability for participants to select from multiple weapon choices; and the game being available on the Windows PC platform. Though several alternative video games were considered, Serious Sam 3: Before First Encounter [25] was considered appropriate for this study as it fulfilled all requirements to a greater degree than other games considered. *Serious Sam 3: Before First Encounter* [25] follows the protagonist Sam as he fights against numerous enemies in wide-open environments. The primary objective of the violent video game is to travel to an end location on each level, killing enemies to survive along the way.

The participants were required to play a tutorial and walk through the game terrain, a desert town in Egypt, while fighting opponents along the way. Participants witnessed the same story elements and barriers so that they had to continue on the same path. Difficulty level remained consistent throughout the procedure being 'Normal' to allow both novice and expert players the opportunity to perform well. If the participant struggled on 'Normal' difficulty (died more than twice), the difficulty was reduced to 'Easy' to avoid the participant experiencing unnecessary frustration.

The blood and gore directly emitted from the bodies was red, however the blood and gore was not displayed in the control condition. Without blood and gore, there were no cadavers as bodies simply faded away, the rag-doll effect did not occur, there was no blood splatter when the enemy was taking damage and there was no blood present on the weapon as the result of violent acts. The game environment featured some blood splatter on the walls which could not be modified, and therefore stayed consistent between the experimental groups. Sounds of pain were heard when an enemy was killed, in both experimental conditions. Figure 1 illustrates the difference between killing an enemy between the experimental and control condition.

Figure 1: A scene from the video game used, Serious Sam 3: Before First Encounter (left: control setting with no blood splatter and absent cadaver, right: blood and gore present).

Physiological Arousal

To measure physiological arousal a Polar H7 Bluetooth Heart Rate Strap was used along with a mobile phone to record heart rate. The Polar H7 Bluetooth Heart Rate Strap is a non-invasive device used to measure a participant's heart rate. The participant was required to wear the device around the chest. Note that when an individual is aroused there is an increase in the rate at which the heart is beating due to stimulation of the sympathetic nervous system.

Cognitive Associations

The GAM, being based on social-cognitive approaches to understanding aggressive behaviours [15,18], posits the finite cognitive resources of the individual are focused towards aggressive patterns of thought during or following exposure to violent forms of media, resulting in the individual recognising or attending to aggressive or violent prompts more readily than non-aggressive prompts [15]. As this cognitive association effect has been demonstrated repeatedly within violent video games, the measurement of variations in cognitive association attendance is considered a valid and reliable instrument for assessing state aggression in video games [18,23,28].

The Lexical Decision Task (LDT) is a statistically validated instrument for assessing variations in cognitive associations [18], and involves displaying series of aggressive words, neutral words, and non-words in random orders and asking participants to identify the words as either being words or non-words, with the latency and accuracy of identification providing metrics for the level of cognitive attendance [18]. Therefore, this study used a LDT after exposure to the violent video game to measure variations in accessibility of aggressive associations after exposure to either violent or non-violent video game content.

The aggressive and neutral words used within the LDT were adapted from previous research [14] and the non-words were generated using the database from another study [26]. Participants were shown 52 words of various lengths, referred to as letter strings, and were required to indicate if the string was an English word or if it was a non-word. In total there were 13 aggressive words (e.g. "gunfire"), 13 neutral words (e.g. "gossip") and 26 non-words (e.g. "grurmp"). The response time and accuracy was used as indicators of aggressive-related associations. A higher accessibility of aggression-related associations was indicated by a faster response time and accuracy in response to the letter strings.

Demographic Influence

A demographic questionnaire designed for the study was used to assess factors that may influence a participant's response. Participants were required to select the most appropriate answer that reflected their social background. The questions were categorised into age, employment status, education, ethnicity, gender and previous video game experience (e.g. hours spent per week playing video games).

Game Experience Questionnaire (GEQ)

An evaluation participant engagement in the violent video game was measured by the Game Experience Questionnaire (GEQ), [27]. The 32-item GEQ is a questionnaire requiring participants to rate each item on a 5-point Likert scale, where 1 = "strongly disagree" and 5 = "strongly agree".

The items are positively worded questions; for example, "I thought it was fun". Overall engagement scores were calculated by summing all of the items to determine an engagement score. Note that higher scores indicate higher engagement [29].

Big Five Inventory of Personality

A 44 short-phase item Big Five Inventory (BFI) was used to assess personality [30]. Participants rated each item on a 5-point scale, where 1 = "disagree strongly" and 5 = "agree strongly". Each short-phase related to a personality factor which is tested on five personality scales being: extraversion, individuals who enjoy human interactions and are generally talkative; agreeableness, an individual who is warm, friendly and tactful; conscientiousness, people who are thorough, careful and organised; neuroticism, a person who demonstrates anxiety, fear and moodiness; and openness, an individual with an appreciation of art, emotion and imagination [31]. Overall personality was calculated by summing all of the categorised items to determine personality score (note that the highest scored category determined personality type).

Procedure

Upon completion of the consent form, participants undertook the demographic questionnaire which consisted of 11 questions. Participants were then randomly allocated into either the experimental condition, being blood and gore, or the control group, being absent blood and gore. Participants were required to wear a Polar H7 Bluetooth Heart Rate Strap positioned on the chest area. Play time lasted for approximately 15 minutes (no longer than 20 minutes) which included a tutorial. Once participants finished playing the mission, the Pulse H7 Bluetooth Heart Rate Strap was removed and the participants undertook a Lexical Decision Task (LDT). 52 proper English words (13 aggressive, 13 neutral) and 26 of non-word letter string practice trials were conducted. For the LDT, participants interacted with a keyboard using their left index finger and right ring finger to press the key "E" to identify it was a proper English word and "I" to identify it was a non-word.

Finally, the participants undertook the last two surveys, Game Experience Questionnaire and Big Five Inventory. At the end of the study the participants were debriefed.

RESULTS

Physiological Arousal

A two-way between subjects' analysis of variance (ANOVA) was conducted on heart rate to compare the effect of gore in the control and experimental conditions. There was no significant effect on average, minimum and maximum heart rate for the two conditions, $F(1,2) = 18.8$, $p = .05$. There was a significance between average, minimum and maximum heart rate within each condition, $F(1,2) = 80.02$, $p<.05$, see Table 1. Regression analyses did not reveal any significant predictor or model for the heart rate measurements.

	Heart Rate		
Condition	Minimum	Average	Maximum
Experimental	84.60	78.73	93.73
Control	79.73	76.67	89.07

Table 1: Mean heart rates in beats per minute, recorded during game play for both conditions.

Cognitive Associations

Latency and correctness in identifying aggressive, neutral and non-words were tested by a two-way between subjects' ANOVA, to compare the effect of gore on aggression-related cognitions in the control and experimental conditions. In the experimental condition there was a significant effect of word latency between the three word types, $F(1,2) = 5212.93$, $p < 0.01$. Additionally, in the control group there a similar significant effect of word latency between the three word types, $F(1,2) = 472.98$, $p <.01$. To investigate the trend further, a paired-samples t-test was conducted to compare response latencies in both the control and experimental conditions.

Although the experimental group correctly identified neutral words with lower latency on average than the control group ($M= .94$, $SD =.08$ and $M = .85$, $SD=.25$ respectively), this difference was not significant ($t(17)=1.35$, $p=.097$). The experimental group also identified aggressive words with lower latency on average than the control group ($M=561.19$, $SD=.09$ and $M=538.52$, $SD=177.41$ respectively), however this difference was also not significant ($t(26)=.40$, $p=.347$). Similarly, paired-sample t-tests were conducted to compare latency for aggressive words, and latency and correctness for neutral words, showing no significant effect.

Previous Video Game Experience

The participants were categorized as being 'experienced players' (n=16), who indicated spending more than six hours playing video games a week, and 'inexperienced players' (n=14), spending less than six hours playing video games a week. A paired-samples t-test was conducted to compare average heart rate, response latency and response

Measure	Experimental		Control	
	Aggres.	Neutral	Aggres.	Neutral
Latency	561.19 (131.20)	562.30 (173.67)	538.52 (177.4)	525.10 (190.81)
Correctness	95 (.09)	94 (.08)	89 (.21)	85 (.25)

Table 2: Mean and Standard Deviations (in brackets) of latency in milliseconds, and accuracy in %, when responding to aggressive or neutral words during the Lexical Decision Task for both conditions.

correctness in both the control and experimental conditions. There was a significant effect in average heart rate between experienced ($M=90.00$, $SD=13.04$) and inexperienced ($M=78.57$, $SD=9.83$) players in the gore condition; $t(13)=1.93$, $p < .05$. Additionally, there was also a significant effect within the control condition ($t(6)=1.64$, $p=.047$), showing that experienced players correctly identified words more frequently than inexperienced players ($M=.98$, $SD=.04$ and $M=.74$, $SD=.22$ respectively), and with lower response latency.

During Gameplay Experience

There was an observed trend that on average, participants experienced a high level of immersion in both the control ($M =2.37$, $SD = .91$) and experimental conditions ($M=2.48$, $SD=.91$). A higher level of tension was reported in the control condition ($M=1.88$, $SD=.83$) than the experimental condition ($M=1.42$, $SD=.79$) on average, which did not have a significant effect; $t(28)=1.54$, $p=.07$. The reported average ratings for each condition is provided in Table 4.

Emotion	Condition Rating	
	Control	Experimental
Competence	1.33 (.62)	1.20 (.62)
Immersion	2.37 (.91)	2.48 (.91)
Flow	1.84 (.63)	1.84 (.65)
Tension	1.88 (.83)	1.42 (.79)
Challenge	1.59 (.76)	1.23 (.92)
Negative	1.50 (.80)	1.37 (.83)
Positive	2.04 (.81)	1.66 (.64)

Table 3: Emotions experienced during gameplay highlighting the different average ratings between conditions, where higher rates reflect a high level of emotion experienced.

Personality

There were three core personalities identified in the population being agreeableness (n=6), conscientiousness (n=8) and openness (n=16). A paired-sample t-test showed a significant effect that participants with an openness personality (*M*=459.82, *SD*=112.62) had a faster latency (response time) to aggressive words than participants with an agreeableness personality (*M*=659.18, *SD*=82.70) in the experimental condition; t(9)=2.76, p<.05. Furthermore, a significant effect showed that participants with an openness personality (*M*=459.82, *SD*=112.62) had a faster latency to aggressive words than participants with a conscientious personality (*M*=605.42, *SD*=5.97) in the experimental condition; t(10) = 2.21, p < .05. The average latency time for each personality is given in Figure 2.

Within the control condition, participants with an agreeableness personality (*M*=0.97, *SD*=0.05) responded more accurately (correctness) to aggressive words than participants with a conscientious personality (*M*=0.90, *SD*=0.04); t(4)=2.20, p< .05. For all participants, these trends were supported with agreeableness personalities (*M*=.99, *SD*=.03) having higher accuracy than openness personalities (*M*=.88, *SD*=.21); t(17) = 1.89, p < .05. Additionally, agreeableness personalities (*M*=.99, *SD*=.03) having higher accuracy than conscientious personalities (*M*=.93, *SD*=.07) for all participants; t(12) = 1.90, p < .05.

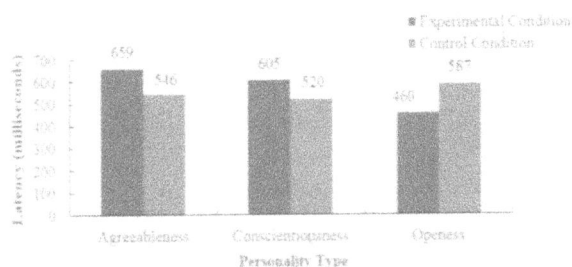

Figure 2: The mean latency recorded for aggressive words, showing personality differences between both conditions.

DISCUSSION

The results of the pilot study supported the null hypotheses for both the experimental condition, with gore, and control condition, without gore. Participants in the gore condition did not experience a significantly higher arousal level, with both groups demonstrating similar arousal responses. There was little difference in the mean heart rates between the gore and no gore conditions, resulting in the rejection of the first alternative hypothesis, supporting some existing studies [17-18] and contradicting other studies [10-12]. Experienced gore players demonstrated a higher level of physiological arousal than inexperienced players, rejecting the second alternative hypothesis and contradicting the theory of desensitization [4,8]. It is plausible that experienced players expressed higher levels of physical arousal in response to blood and gore as a result from previous learnt aggressive responses, which may be explained by using the General Aggression Model (GAM).

The GAM explains that learning and reinforcement of video game violence, influences the acquisition of aggressive perceptions, cognitions and emotions [5,15]. However, a second plausible explanation is simply that players

experienced with violent video games prefer video games that depict violence and gore, which would possibly support a correlative relationship between video game violence and increased levels of arousal. For example, there was approaching trends to show that experienced players were more accurate and faster to identify aggressive words than inexperienced players. Furthermore, as the experienced individuals experienced a higher level of physiological arousal, it may be suggested that these individuals enjoy violent video games, which is supported with the frequent engagement of similar games. Again however, these subtle differences may be caused by external factors, such as increased reaction times in experienced video game players.

Ultimately the research acted as a preliminary study that sought to find patterns of physiological response to blood and gore in video games to warrant further investigation. The results suggest that violent stimuli, that featured blood and gore, did not have a significant effect on individuals' physiological arousal and aggressive cognitions. There was a significant effect in response latency to different types of words (aggressive, neutral and non-word); however, no further significant effects were found while comparing the experimental and control conditions. This trend supports the findings of previous research [17-18], which also found that bloody violence did not promote higher levels of aggressive behaviour. However, the absence of a measured impact does not necessarily imply that the inclusion of blood and gore do not have any effect on arousal or aggression. Further examination including a wider range of measures and a larger participant sample would need to be conducted, generating sufficient evidence to formulate a strong conclusion.

The results of the study may provide some support for the suggestion that the GAM is appropriate in explaining learnt and reinforced aggressive behaviour as experienced players demonstrated a higher level of arousal in response to blood and gore, however further studies should be conducted in these areas before this assumption can be made. In contrast, a personality trend emerged supporting the Catalyst Model. Participants with a high openness personality (individuals who are artistic, emotional and imaginative), expressed a faster latency in processing aggressive words than both participants with a conscientious personality (a thorough, careful and organised person), and agreeableness personality (a warm, friendly and tactful individual), [31]. Within the control condition, a significant effect showed that agreeableness personalities were able to respond more correctly to aggressive words than participants with a conscientious personality.

The results suggest that personality may be a key factor in the expression of aggression in response to video game violence. This significant effect was also apparent when comparing all participants. Additionally, it was reported that participants reported a higher tension (emotional strain) in the no gore condition. A higher level of tension may have occurred as without blood and gore the participant may have focused more on level completion and other competitive factors.

A strength of this study was that participants had the average age of 32 years, being roughly representative of the average age of Australian Games which is 33 years [1]. Thus the current research used a reasonably normal sample of the expected gamer population in Australia unlike previous studies [7,11,16] that only measure young undergraduate age males. Additionally, unlike previous research [6,7,11,16], both male and female participants were tested.

Limitations and Future Research

While the research was successful in achieving its aims, there were some limitations that need to be considered. Firstly, despite having a similar number of participants to existing studies in this area [17], this study was necessarily limited to a relatively small sample size and would have benefited from a larger sample. As the intention of the study was to provide a reasonable foundation for further investigations, a larger secondary study should build upon the results by including a larger participant population. Secondly, the research was limited to testing participants that were over the age of eighteen being a mature audience, where adolescents may exhibit a different psychophysiological reaction to violent video games due to possible biological and social structure to a mature audience. Lastly, the data collected is potentially limited by the equipment used, and future research should be conducted using a wider range of psychophysiological equipment and including a number of additional measures, such as body temperature, respiration rate, electroencephalography (EEG) and electrodermal activity (EDA). Additional measures would add further accuracy in determining the relationships and respective influences of gore in video games.

Although no definitive conclusion can be drawn, the results of the present study imply that representations of blood and gore within violent video games may not have a significant effect on aggressive behaviour. It would appear that the violent stimuli, regardless of the blood and gore, results in heightened levels of physiological arousal and is not determined by factors such as gender and age. Such knowledge may assist social sciences in understanding the trend that frequent interaction with video games, increases psychophysiological response to gore. Knowing that the probability of such an interference may possibly result in the demonstration of higher aggressive behaviour, and may influence further game research to investigate if there is a risk with frequent engagement with video games in adults.

Furthermore, future game research could determine if the response is learned and as a personality trend emerged, future game research could investigate the effects of personality on expressing aggression.

CONCLUSION

The present study examined the effect of violent content on in-game arousal levels, aggression-related associations, individual differences and game experience. The results indicated that, at least within the context of this study, representation of blood and gore within violent content had no effect on physiological arousal, nor did it appear to have any significant influence on aggression-related associations and cognitive processes, although definitive conclusions cannot be drawn without further investigation. Previous game experience also appeared to have a significant effect on increased psychophysical arousal when engaging in violent content featuring gore. Furthermore, a personality trend emerged showing that an openness personality demonstrated faster cognitive processing of aggressive words than conscientious and agreeableness personalities. It was reported that participants in the control condition (no blood and gore) experienced higher levels of tension which may be a result of changed player goals and focus. Thus, previous game experience, personality and player goals should be considered as important influential factors in future game research with the current results acting as a foundation for these future studies and contributing to the debate surrounding video game violence.

REFERENCES

1. J.E. Brand, P.Lorentz, and Mathew, T. 2014. *Digital Australia 2014*, Queensland, Australia. Retrieved April 17, 2016, http://www.igea.net/wp-content/uploads/2013/11/Digital-Australia-2014-DA14.pdf.

2. C. A. Anderson, and B. J. Bushman. 2001. Effects of violent video games on aggressive behavior, aggressive cognition, aggressive affect, physiological arousal, and prosocial behavior: A meta-analytic review of the scientific literature. *Psychological science* 12, 5: 353-359. doi: 10.1111/1467-9280.00366.

3. C.A. Anderson, N.L. Carnagey, M. Flanagan, A.J. Benjamin Jr., J. Eubanks, and J.C. Valentine. 2004. Violent video games: Specific effects of violent content on aggressive thoughts and behavior. *Advances in Experimental Social Psychology* 36, 1: 200-251. doi: 0065-2601/04.

4. J.B. Funk, H.B. Baldacci, T. Pasold, and J. Baumgardner. 2004. Violence exposure in real-life, video games, television, movies, and the internet: is there desensitization? *Journal of Adolescence* 27, 1: 23-39. doi:10.1016/j.adolescence.2003.10.005.

5. D.A. Gentile, and B.J. Bushman. 2012. Reassessing media violence effects using a risk and resilience approach to understanding aggression. *Psychology of Popular Media Culture* 1, 3:138-152. http://dx.doi.org/10.1037/a0028481.

6. G.A. Waas. 1987. Aggressive rejected children: Implications for school psychologist. *Journal of Psychology* 25, 4: 383-388. doi:10.1016/0022-4405(87)90039-2.

7. B.D. Bartholow, B.J. Bushman, and M.A. Sestir. 2006. Chronic violent video game exposure and desensitization to violence: Behavioral and event-related brain potential data. *Journal of Experimental Social Psychology* 42, 4: 532-539. doi:10.1016/j.jesp.2005.08.006.

8. N.L. Carnagey, C.A. Anderson, and B.J. Bushman. 2007. The effect of video game violence on physiological desensitization to real-life violence. *Journal of Experimental Social Psychology* 43, 3: 489-496.   doi:10.1016/j.jesp.2006.05.003.

9. C.J. Ferguson, S.M. Rueda, A.M. Cruz, D.E. Ferguson, S. Fritz, and S.M. Smith. 2008. Violent video games and aggression: causal relationship or byproduct of family violence and intrinsic violence motivation? *Criminal Justice and Behavior* 35, 3: 311-332. doi: 10.1177/0093854807311719.

10. L.R. Huesmann. 2007. The Impact of Electronic Media Violence: Scientific Theory and Research. *The Journal of Adolescent Health: Official Publication of the Society for Adolescent Medicine* 41, 6: 6-13. doi:10.1016/j.jadohealth.2007.09.005.

11. C.P. Barlett, J.H. Harris, and Bruey, C. 2008. The effect of the amount of blood in a violent video game on aggression, hostility, and arousal. *Journal of Experimental Social Psychology* 44, 3: 539-546. doi: 10.1016/j.jesp.2007.10.003.

12. K.M. Farrar, M. Krcmar, and K.L. Novak. 2006. Contextual features of violent video games, mental models, and aggression. *Journal of Communication* 56, 2: 387-405. doi: 10.1111/j.1460-2466.2006.00025.x.

13. B.J. Bushman, M.Gollwitzer, and C. Cruz. 2014. There is broad consensus: Media researchers agree that violent media increase aggression in children, and pediatricians and parents concur. *Psychology of Popular Media Culture* 4, 3: 200-214. http://dx.doi.org/10.1037/ppm0000046.

14. J.A. Maier, and D.A. Gentile. 2012. Learning Aggression through the Media: Comparing Psychological and Communication Approaches. In *The Psychology of Entertainment Media: Blurring the lines between Entertainment and Persuasion*, Taylor and Francis, 291-305.

15. C. A. Anderson, and B. J. Bushman. 2002. The effects of media violence on society. *Science* 295, 5564: 2377-2379. doi: 10.1126/science.1070765.

16. M.E. Ballard, and J.R.Wiest. 1996. Mortal Kombat: The effects of violent video game play on males' hostility and cardiovascular responding. *Journal of Applied Social Psychology* 26, 8: 717-730. doi: 10.1111/j.1559-1816.1996.tb02740.x.

17. W. Bösche. 2015. Violent video games prime both aggressive and positive cognitions. *Journal of Media Psychology* 22, 4: 139-146. http://dx.doi.org/10.1027/1864-1105/a000019.

18. J. Kneer, M. Elson, and F. Knapp. 2016. Fight fire with rainbows: The effects of displayed violence, difficulty, and performance in digital games on affect, aggression, and physiological arousal. *Computers in Human Behavior* 54, 1: 142-148. doi:10.1016/j.chb.2015.07.034.

19. J. Breuer, J. Vogelgesang, T. Quandt, and R. Festl. 2015. Violent Video Games and Physical Aggression: Evidence for a Selection Effect among Adolescents. *Psychology of Popular Media Culture* 4, 4: 1-24. http://dx.doi.org/10.1027/1864-1105/a000019.

20. Jeffrey H. Goldstein. 1998. *Why we watch: The attractions of violent entertainment.* Oxford University Press.

21. G. A. Johanson, and G. P. Brooks. 2009. Initial scale development: sample size for pilot studies. Educational and Psychological Measurement 70, 3: 394-400. doi: 10.1177/0013164409355692.

22. M. B. Brewer, and W. D. Crano. 2014. "Research Design and Issues of Validity", in *Handbook of Research Methods in Social and Personality Research*, 2nd ed., H Reis and C Judd, Eds. 2014.

23. M. Elson, and C. Ferguson. 2014. Twenty-Five Years of Research on Violence in Digital Games and Aggression. European Psychologist 19, 1: 33-46.

24. J. Cacioppo, L. Tassinary, and G. Berntson. *Handbook of Psychophysiology*. Cambridge University Press. New York, USA. 2007.

25. Croteam. 2011. *Serious Sam 3: Before First Encounter*. (22 November 2011). Devolver Digital, Untied States of America. Played 25 January 2016.

26. K. Rastle, J. Harrington, and M. Coltheart. 2002. 358,534 nonwords: The ARC nonword Database. *Quarterly Journal of Experimental Psychology* 55, 4: 1339-1362. doi: 10.1080/02724980244000099.

27. J.H. Brockmyer, C.M. Fox, K.A. Curtiss, E. McBroom, K.M. Burkhart, and J.N. Pidruzny. 2009. The development of the Game Engagement Questionnaire: A measure of engagement in video game-playing. *Journal of Experimental Social Psychology* 45, 4: 624-634. doi:10.1016/j.jesp.2009.02.016.

28. A.K. Przybylski, E. L. Deci, C. S. Rigby, and R. M. Ryan. Competence-impeding electronic games and

players' aggressive feelings, thoughts, and behaviors. Journal of Personality and Social Psychology 106, 3: 441-457.

29. A.I. Nordin, A. Denisova, and P. Cairns. 2014. Too Many Questionnaires: Measuring Player Experience Whilst Playing Digital Games. *Seventh York Doctoral Symposium on Computer Science and Electronics* 69, 1: 69-75.

30. O.P. John, E.M. Donahue, and R.L. Kentle. 1991. *The Big Five Inventory-Versions 4a and 54*. University of California, Berkeley, Institute of Personality and Social Research.

31. O.P. John, and S. Srivastava. 1999. The Big-Five trait taxonomy: History, measurement, and theoretical perspectives. In *Handbook of personality: Theory and research*, Guilford Press, 102-13.

2084 – Safe New World: Designing Ubiquitous Interactions

Julian Frommel*, Katja Rogers*, Thomas Dreja, Julian Winterfeldt,
Christian Hunger, Maximilian Bär, Michael Weber
Ulm University
Ulm, Germany
{firstname.lastname}@uni-ulm.de

ABSTRACT

This paper investigates a concept for highly ubiquitous game interactions in pervasive games. Pervasive gaming is increasingly popular, but steadily improving mobile and ubiquitous technologies (e.g. smartwatches) have yet to be utilised to their full potential in this area. For this purpose, we implemented *2084 – Safe New World*; a pervasive game that allows particularly ubiquitous gameplay through micro interactions of varying duration. In a lab study, different interaction techniques based on gestures and touch input were compared on two mobile devices regarding usability and game input observability. A second study evaluated the player experience under more realistic circumstances; in particular, it examined how well the game can be integrated into everyday life, and tested boundaries of social acceptance of ubiquitous interactions in a pervasive spy game.

ACM Classification Keywords

K.8.0. General: Games; H.5.2. User Interfaces: Interaction styles (e.g., commands, menus, forms, direct manipulation)

Author Keywords

pervasive games; game interaction; ubiquitous interaction; social acceptance; player experience; usability; observability; smartwatch

INTRODUCTION

In recent years, pervasive games have seen a rise in popularity; e.g. *Ingress* [26] is very popular and has been attracting large numbers of players for years. *Pokemon Go* [27] is another pervasive game that enjoyed a very successful start upon its recent release [32]. While there are a variety of different definitions for the genre of pervasive games [4, 14, 24, 29], they usually have in common that the game's virtual world is in some way interwoven with the real world. However, the degree of this integration varies quite a lot from game to game. Pervasive games often cannot be very well integrated into the daily life of the players. In a lot of pervasive games, players must actively decide to play a game session, e.g. through

* These authors contributed equally to this contribution.

Figure 1. A player of the pervasive game *2084 – Safe New World* interacting with the game without interrupting his everyday life.

deliberate exploration of a portal in *Ingress*. In this paper, we present the concept of particularly ubiquitous pervasive games, i.e. pervasive games that are interwoven more unobtrusively into everyday life.

In order to achieve a high degree of integration into everyday life, it is important that a particularly ubiquitous pervasive game does not enforce game sessions that are entirely separate from the everyday activities of the players. For that purpose, players should be able to interact with the game via interactions with brief durations, before returning to their current activities, ideally with only a bare minimum of interruption to these. Thus, interaction with the game ideally consists of short and spread-out interactions rather than long clearly-defined periods of game play. In order to provide a well-rounded gaming experience, however, it is necessary that the interactions are embedded into a larger game metaphor. Thus, we argue for a game that is *always-on*, which can be realized by an extension of the game's temporal and spatial dimensions, e.g. through the mixed-reality hybrid game space that is inherent to the pervasive game genre. Consequently, interaction with the game takes place within this larger game metaphor and is often triggered by external factors such as for example temporal, spatial or even social circumstances. This design allows for the desired integration of the pervasive game into players' everyday lives, as the temporal, spatial and social features are not fixed factors but remain flexibly triggered.

We implemented the concept in *2084 – Safe New World*, a multiplayer pervasive spy game. Players are always part of the game's alternate reality, i.e. they become spies in a futuristic world in which data is used as currency. The players can interact with the game, i.e. with the other players, through two game modes: the *battle* and the *shadowing* mode. The *battle* mode employs a player-vs.-player paradigm using symmetrical micro interactions, i.e. both players can perform the same game input. This mode requires that players are potentially able to see each other and is thus triggered by physical proximity to another player. In the *shadowing* mode, a player has to stay in close proximity to another player (following them if necessary) for as long as possible, while attempting to not be noticed. This mode is also indirectly triggered by physical proximity of other players, but due to its slightly longer interaction time requires the player to actively indicate readiness to participate. The player that is followed, however, participates passively in this interaction and interacts with the system only when they suspect they are being followed. Thus, both game modes contribute to the game's integration into the players' everyday life in slightly different ways, in that game interactions can take place anywhere and anytime. Further, the game mechanics encourage brief interactions for which players often do not have to interrupt their non-gaming tasks during daily life at all, or can return to them very quickly.

The contribution of this paper consists of the following:

- the design of interactions for technology-based pervasive games including such that involve wearables which are particularly challenging because of their limited interaction space

- an empirical contribution in form of a user study exploring the effects of interaction methods in technology-based pervasive games on observability, usability, and social acceptance

- a second empirical contribution with a user study evaluating the social acceptability of playing a smartwatch-based pervasive game in a natural setting

RELATED WORK

The genre of pervasive games is an ambiguous domain, encompassing several overlapping or contradictory categories depending on the researcher's favoured definition [14, 7]. Most of them, however, involve the merging of a virtual and physical space into a hybrid game world, through spatial, temporal, or social expansion [24] of the so-called magic circle [39]. In 2007, Nieuwdorp published a detailed analysis of the terms used in this genre, in particular, the confusion over two different perspectives on "pervasiveness": technological (i.e. the focus lies on the technologies used, showing close ties with the genre's origins in pervasive computing) vs. cultural (with a focus on game world properties) [29]. Following her recommendation, we do not attempt to find the best suited label for the type of pervasive games we are investigating, but rather will describe the ways in which our concept is pervasive.

The focus of this paper lies on games that are *always-on*, i.e. the player can at any point in their daily lives be engaged in active gameplay (i.e. temporal and spatial pervasiveness). Active gameplay is triggered by player proximity, with a focus on player-vs.-player interaction, although players' identities are not generally known (social pervasiveness). While there are many pervasive games that affect social acceptability, e.g. *Killer – Game of Assassination* [16], in the following we focus on technology-enabled pervasive games.

Temporal and Spatial Dimensions

For the purpose of integrating our concept into a broader classification, we discuss dimensions of temporal and physical pervasiveness with the help of several examples. Some games are pervasive only in the physical sense, but not the temporal; the player can partake in the game at any location, but only at certain times. Any casual mobile game that enforces or restricts the times of gameplay can be considered part of this category. For example, *Clash of Clans* [40] features many periods during which the players can do nothing but wait, e.g. until the construction of a game object is complete. Other games are similarly temporally restricted, but additionally enforce a physical setting. For instance, the mobile multi-player game *Pirates!* [6] focuses on player-to-player proximity to trigger battles in a seafaring narrative. The game is temporally restricted (i.e. event-based [23]), but also physically restricted to a delimited area. Games such as *Mogi* [17] feature temporal pervasiveness, but physical restriction to a city, i.e. Tokyo. In this location-aware mobile game, players collect virtual objects located in the physical city space.

The addition of physical pervasiveness to this kind of game is exemplified by *Botfighters* [2] and *Alien Revolt* [37]. The latter was investigated in an early case study by De Souza E Silva. In this game, players are notified of each other's presence at a 3km range, while player-vs.-player fights are triggered when within 200m. The success of these fights is based on distance, luck, and equipment; the objective is to gain as many points as possible through winning fights. As such, their game principle is quite similar to part of our own, in that they feature player-vs.-player battles triggered by proximity. Similarly, *Ingress* (see [20] for an overview) gained popularity quite rapidly several years ago, and consists of geographic battles between opposing teams. Another game in this temporally and physically pervasive category is called *Feeding Yoshi*: this game is set up to be long-term and wide-area. Players collect points by growing and collecting fruit in the environment in order to feed Yoshi creatures. Player proximity triggers the opportunity to swap fruits.

Social Acceptance

The issue of social acceptance is especially problematic for pervasive games, as by definition they expand on traditional boundaries of play. The spatial expansion in particular means that players will likely encounter non-players during the game. Further, the social expansion mentioned previously blurs the line between the identity of players and non-players: players cannot be certain who is part of the game; sometimes, non-players are even actively involved through the game mechanics. The issue is further complicated by the fact that socially acceptable gameplay differs significantly between individuals [30]. Much like the definition of pervasive games, the issue of social acceptance can also viewed from two perspectives: technological and cultural, i.e. the acceptance of specific interactions in public, and the acceptance of playful behaviour in general. Playful behaviour is generally seen as positive, but nevertheless is subject to many social conventions. Certain interaction methods and devices may similarly be frowned upon or draw attention in certain situations, although there is little research comparing social acceptance for specific interaction and device combinations. The case study on *Feeding Yoshi*, for instance, discussed players feeling odd walking around with a PDA device. One player described being asked by a stranger if they were lost, and many reported strange looks: "the distinctive [...] movements required by the game would draw attention" [3]. Similar feelings can be expected for interaction with smartwatches as they are a new technology as PDAs were then. The involvement of bystanders has significant implications on privacy, as discussed by Niemi et al. [28] with a focus on design factors, e.g. ways of ensuring informed consent to participation, to whichever degree. They also found opinions on such privacy issues are highly subjective, and differ particularly between adults and adolescents, potentially hinting at a generational attitude shift. On a similar note, a study by Friedman et al. [13] indicates that people generally expect a modicum of privacy even in public. In-game social conventions also occur; players of *Mogi* developed the expectation of acknowledgement of other players' proximity (apologizing for delays in such). Face-to-face meetings were often suggested, but generally declined.

Our game concept includes a *shadowing* mode in which players are required to follow each other. This is a particularly difficult subject for social acceptance. For instance, *Mogi* game designers discussed safeguards against stalking (a case study of a suspicious proximity event in *Mogi* is discussed by Licoppe and Inada in a different paper [18]). However, other researchers have encouraged the use of playful interactions proxemic to bystanders and/or in public spaces. Mueller et al. [25] report that the breaking of social or cultural norms may be permitted or even thrilling, and cite examples such as *Twister* [21], their own *Musical Embrace* [25], and *WarDriving* [5] as such examples. In summary, the issue of social acceptance for pervasive games is difficult, but important, and requires a case-by-case analysis.

Ubiquitous Gesture Interaction
The nature of our game concept requires the design and implementation of ubiquitous interactions for the game mechanisms. We consider interactions ubiquitous when they fall in line with Weiser's vision of ubiquitous computing: unobtrusive and simple, so as to become part of everyday life [41]. Yet the game also requires that the interactions potentially be distinguishable by players in viewing distance. This necessitates a fine balancing in the interaction design. Further, for user acceptance, feedback appears to be particularly important for hands-free and eyes-free interaction methods [34, 9, 19], requiring a two-part consideration of interaction design: both the interaction itself and the type of feedback used should be considered socially acceptable. Nowadays, almost everyone carries a smartphone or a watch (smart or otherwise), or even a combination thereof. The interaction with these systems should thus not be obtrusive in and of itself, as the general public is accustomed to it. However, the least obtrusive method for this interaction is not immediately clear. The list of potential methods for human-computer interaction is long and varied, and even the reduction to two devices – the smartphone, and the smartwatch – leaves a lot of possibilities. The options include speech, gestures, haptics, and additional pointing devices, as well as various combinations thereof.

Social acceptability is considered an important factor in human-computer interaction, and researchers of this topic have discovered a multitude of variables that influence it, among them user type and culture [22]. Rico and Brewster [33] investigated various interaction methods in regards to their social acceptability through an in-the-wild study, and discovered that subtle movements are generally more socially acceptable, as are gestures which pass for everyday movements. The importance of small motions for greater social acceptability in gestures is echoed by Linjama et al. [19] and Ronkainen et al. [34]. Nevertheless, depending on the use case, the degree of noticeability and social acceptance for a specific interaction method may vary significantly. For instance, wrist rotations were found to be generally quite acceptable by Rico and Brewster, whereas participants in a study by Wiliamson et al. [42] reported feeling uncomfortable using this in public. Wiliamson et al. distinguish between different types of public settings: those with transient spectators (passersby) and those with sustained onlookers (e.g. being stuck in the same public transport carriage). Further dimensions to device input could be achieved, for example through adding degrees of freedom to the smartwatch's face, allowing more focused interactions [44]. However, this addition would require both hands, and may cross the line to becoming *too* easily distinguishable.

Pervasive Wearable Games
There is an increasing amount of games for use on wearable devices, however, many are simply the adaptation of already existing games for use on a new device, such as the puzzle game *2048 Wear* [10]. Yet the use of a wearable device offers many possibilities for pervasive games. Some games are of course more suited to this kind of adaptation than others; for example, the previously mentioned *Ingress*, one of the most popular pervasive games, has been extended to allow gameplay with Android Wear smartwatches [38]. Another game that features a pervasive element is *Sonic Dash 2* - this game is for mobile devices, but can be extended with an Apple Watch app that bestows helpful skills in-game for reaching a daily step goal [12].

So far, it seems that few games are designed explicitly with the properties of a wearable medium in mind. Nevertheless, we will discuss two games that exhibit such properties. Real-time interactive fiction games have found newfound popularity on the smartwatch with games such as *Lifeline* and *Spy Watch*. In *Lifeline* [1] (100,000-500,000 installs as of April 2016), the player has to help a crashlanded astronaut survive on a distant planet, by answering messages delivered through notifications on the player's watch. The principle of *Spy Watch* [8] is similar: the player acts as the handler of a fictional spy agent by sending instructions, and replying to questions sent through the watch's notifications system. This kind of game works well as a ubiquitous game that is played via micro interactions throughout everyday life. However, smartwatches are still not particularly prevalent among the general population, as shown by a recent survey by Shirazi and Henze [36]. This survey also showed how users rate the importance of notifications on various devices when considered for certain categories, among them games; 67.7% of 440 participants did not choose any device for the games category. Together, this may indicate that users require more experience with smartwatch games before they associate gaming with such devices.

THE GAME: 2084 - SAFE NEW WORLD

The main objective of this game consists of a high degree of integration into daily life, i.e. a particularly ubiquitous pervasive game. The concept is thus based on micro interactions with mobile and wearable devices, in order to provide a game that is *always on* – through two game modes with a total of three kinds of interactions. The first game mode provides a player-vs.-player mechanism, triggered by the system based on player proximity. The game input is contributed via micro interactions and is symmetrical, i.e. game interaction is the same for both players in this mode. The second game mode is asymmetrical, in that it consists of two different variants – passive and active – each with its own game interaction. The passive version occurs when a player comes to suspect that the second game mode is active; they can then attempt to verify this via a micro interaction. The active version consists of attempting to practise the second game mode unnoticed by another nearby player for as long as possible. This variant thus necessitates a longer game interaction, and is player-initiated.

Game Narrative

As suggested by the title *2084 – Safe New World*, the game takes place in a dystopian future in the year 2084, in which all traditional currencies have collapsed, and work is performed by machines. People pay with data, which has become the de facto currency. Therefore, the game's main goal is to collect as much data from other players as possible. It can be either be gained by theft i.e. "hacking" other players (*battle* mode), or generated by spying on them (*shadowing* mode).

Game Modes

The *battle* mode is triggered by player proximity, and was designed with symmetrical micro interactions for easier integration in everyday life. A battle occurs when two players are approximately in viewing distance of each other, i.e. up to a distance of about 100 meters between players. Both players are notified of the battle simultaneously through a vibration pattern on their device. The underlying concept of the battle is based on the well known game *Rock-Paper-Scissors*. Players must choose between three different game inputs: *SISSR-Virus*, *RocKit!* and *Paper worm*. The game allows a specific time frame for the game input; thus, the players do not have to perform their gestures simultaneously and have the opportunity to potentially identify and observe their opponents. A later input increases the chance to observe the opponent player and react accordingly. However, exceeding the time frame results in forfeiture of the battle. Strategies like hiding or feigning a gesture can increase the chance to win.

Compared to the battles, the active *shadowing* mode requires more effort. The user has to follow another player and stay as close as possible without being noticed and unmasked. This interaction is therefore inherently less integrated into the player's everyday life. The passive variant of *shadowing*, however, consists of a player noticing their follower, and unmasking them via a micro interaction, thus potentially achieving a similar degree of integration as the *battle* mode interaction. While the *shadowing* mode is activated, the *battle* mode is disabled and a map appears on the player's interface, to show where nearby players are located. The spatial approximation of these positions is re-calculated periodically via Bluetooth, to ensure that the user has to be within a range of about 10 meters to the other player to collect data. A countdown of five seconds appears once data collection begins, and has to be restarted by the player to avoid unmasking. The shadowing player is unmasked if the countdown runs out or the player being shadowed pushes the discover button. Thus, the *shadowing* mode provides an engaging social game experience for both player roles of this game mode.

System Architecture

As the game was designed to be played on several devices simultaneously, a client-server approach was chosen to connect all players and their devices. Each player runs the game as a background process on an *Android* smartphone; notifications only appear when in-game actions occur. If the player uses a smartwatch as their primary device, it will connect to the smartphone and act as an additional display for notifications and an input device for interactions. Each smartphone instance connects to the central server running *NodeJS* and *MongoDB*, providing a *HTTP REST API*. Push notifications are sent via the Google Cloud Messaging services. A custom transport layer was created for the communication between smartphone and smartwatch to provide a Bluetooth serialisation mechanism. For example, the map display is implemented via the *OSMDroid*[1] package on both devices. The smartphone downloads the map tiles directly as image files, whereas the smartwatch, lacking the internet connection, uses a custom wrapper to use the smartphone as the map file source.

Location Awareness

One of the most important aspects of the implementation consisted of location tracking. Using just GPS and the central server to evaluate positions did not yield reliable results in terms of visibility and distance. The server was unaware of visibility issues due to buildings or vegetation, yet the game design required players to be notified when they were within viewing distance. Thus the GPS locations were combined with peer-to-peer based wireless communication to create a more reliable tracking system. From the game's perspective, players move inside 200 by 200 meters cells within a larger grid, and only communicate with the server when they move between cells, or the server requests faster updates for the *shadowing* mode. To accommodate edge cases, such as a player moving along the border of two cells, the server always includes neighbouring cells in its location checks.

To determine whether two players are approaching each other, the game relies on Wi-Fi Direct technology: as soon as there are players in adjacent cells, their devices start periodically broadcasting and discovering Wi-Fi Direct services. As soon as a discovery is successful, each device knows that another player is nearby, and a battle is triggered. Early tests showed that the signal can reach up to 100 meters under ideal circumstances, but with obstacles such as buildings, detection may

---

[1]OSMDroid project, version: 5.1 (Release: 24.01.2016), `https://github.com/osmdroid/osmdroid`

occur at much shorter distances. With these signal propagation properties, the game can more reliably detect physical visibility between players.

While a suitable choice for the *battle* mode, Wi-Fi Direct was not sufficient for the *shadowing* mode. For this mode, Bluetooth technology was deployed instead. As soon as a player enters the *shadowing* mode, all players' devices in the surrounding cells are instructed to activate a Bluetooth server. The shadowing player then acts as a client and tries to connect to the others periodically. With each connection, a cache of in-game data is generated and awarded to the player. Compared to Wi-Fi Direct, Bluetooth can work with a much faster refresh interval and requires much shorter distances for connections due to its different propagation properties, making it ideal for the interactions of the shadowing mode.

Using this three-component approach to location awareness, the game is able to provide a reliable system for tracking multiple players, and at the same time account for physical visibility due to player surroundings.

Interaction Methods
Related work indicates that providing ubiquitous interactions in the context of pervasive gaming requires interaction methods to be simple and unobtrusive in order to become part of everyday life. In total, four different interaction methods were implemented for the *battle* mode. Two of these methods were based on gestures; a wrist rotation interaction for the smartwatch, and a knock-based interaction method for the smartphone. Both devices were also equipped with a touch-based user interface for comparison of the two gesture interactions with touch interactions. The touch-based user interface design offers three simple buttons for the game input during the *battle* mode. An overview of these interaction methods is illustrated in Figure 2. Active gameplay in the *shadowing* mode is based mainly on a map view to locate nearby players. Since the player's attention in this game mode is already focused on the device's display to identify opposing players, this game mode provides only the touch-based interaction method.

The design of the gesture-based interaction for the *battle* mode takes social acceptability into consideration by choosing gestures of modest spatial scale, yet also tries to provide a degree of observability to enhance gameplay. Both gesture-based interaction methods are based on a fixed user-independent gesture language, to contribute to fair gameplay by preventing users from defining their own advantageous gestures.

Smartwatch Gestures
As wrist-worn devices, smartwatches offer a more direct and less interruption-prone access than smartphones, which are commonly carried in a pocket. The *battle* mode requires the distinction of three different game inputs. These game inputs are communicated as the same single gesture and can be distinguished by the number of its repetitions, to supply a set of three gestures. To perform these gestures, players have to rotate their wrist (wearing the smart watch) one to three times. Wrist rotation can be regarded as a subtle and mostly *secretive* [31] in-air gesture, fitting our need for an unobtrusive, non-disruptive and socially acceptable gesture

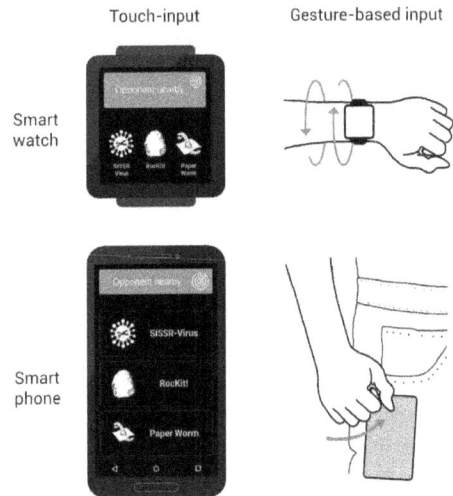

Figure 2. The four different interactions methods of the *battle mode*: touch-based input on a smartwatch *(smartwatch UI)* and on a smartphone *(smartphone UI)*, as well as gesture-based input on smartwatch *(smartwatch gestures)* and smartphone *(smartphone gestures)*.

set [33]. This gesture set is characterized by the rotational movement of the smartwatch around the x-axis of the device's coordinate system. This allows the utilisation of the internal gyroscope and a reduction of the relevant sensor data from three to one dimension. We applied and adapted a kinematic feature-based gesture recognition approach by Xian et al. [43], which includes the classification of gestures by the number of extreme values in the sensor signal (thus no training data is needed). With this approach, the characteristics of each gesture are analyzed beforehand and gesture recognition can be performed based on rules. Our implementation uses an activation threshold to ignore random hand movement and a cool-down period triggered by a deactivation threshold to stop the sample analysis. Extreme values in the sensor data are detected by using minimum distance thresholds and a rotation energy threshold. During pre-processing, the data is smoothed with a low-pass filter to ignore irrelevant small peaks or sensor noise. To further support the player with an unobtrusive type of interaction feedback, the smartwatch and the connected smartphone confirm the performed game input with a gesture-specific vibration pattern upon successful recognition.

Smartphone Gestures
For the gesture-based interaction with the smartphone, game balancing required an approach that equals the wrist rotation for smartwatch users in terms of required effort, social acceptance and observability. In particular, players should be able to interact with the game without having to take their smartphone out of their pocket or purse for every battle. We hypothesized that these requirements may be well met by knock gestures: instead of rotating their wrist, players knock on their smartphones up to three times. Knocks seemed to be well recognizable, they are relatively unobtrusive and non-disruptive in daily life. There is little research on this topic, yet, previous work indicates that the area of the interaction [15, 11] and the interaction method itself, i.e. slapping the phone in the pocket, can be considered socially acceptable [22].

The implementation is based on *KnockKnock*[2], which offers knock detection for *Android* smartphones by combining accelerometer and microphone sensor data to detect simultaneous peaks in volume and device movement. While the detection rate of *KnockKnock* was acceptable, too much force had to be applied in knocking on the phone. However, lower thresholds resulted in a drastic increase of false positives while walking. To address this issue, we implemented a simple form of activity recognition that blocks detection while the noise level caused by device movement exceeds a certain threshold. Nevertheless, preliminary evaluations showed that it was nearly impossible to detect single knock events when false positives are not acceptable, even given higher thresholds. Therefore, the smartphone gesture language was designed with double-knocks. A double-knock corresponds to one wrist rotation. Vibration feedback is given after each double-knock and at the end of the game input.

STUDY 1

A user study was conducted in a controlled lab setting in order to examine the interaction methods for the *battle* mode and the general player experience thereof. The study aimed to investigate how the interaction methods that were deemed suitable for the concept performed with regard to observability, usability, and social acceptance, as these variables were considered important for an overall positive playing experience. Further, the study examined the social acceptance and player experience of the *battle* mode in general.

Participants

The sample of this study consisted of 16 university students (12 male, 4 female) with an average age of 25.94 years ($SD = 2.82$). They were mostly from a background related to computer science. The participants were recruited in pairs in order to guarantee that they at least knew each other, which they confirmed in a demographic questionnaire. 13 participants reported that they had not heard of pervasive games. After reading a generic definition, 12 participants reported that they had never played pervasive games. Regarding mobile gaming habits, only three participants reported that they never play games on their mobile phones.

Procedure

The study took place in a lab setting in a conference room. Initially, the two participants were introduced to the background story of *2084 – Safe New World* and the general concept behind the *battle* mode. Players stated their consent and completed a short demographic questionnaire. They were then positioned face to face at marked positions at a distance of five meters which was deemed a compromise between a realistic playing scenario and optimal conditions to observe the other player.

The participants played the *battle* mode for each of the interaction methods consecutively. To avoid carry-over effects, the order of interaction methods was counterbalanced per pair of participants using a Latin square. For each of the interaction methods, the participants first watched a short introduction

[2]KnockKnock by Turtum & Lien, 05.04.2016, https://github.com/KybDP/KnockKnock

video demonstrating how to use the method. They then played three test runs against each other to ensure that they were well acquainted with the use of the interaction method. Subsequently they played five battles. For the first four battles of each interaction method, the participants were asked to stay face to face at the marked position without employing any gaming strategies such as turning away or hiding their input, to guarantee optimal conditions for observability. In the final battle for every interaction method, players were encouraged to employ gaming strategies as they wanted. After every battle the players recorded the game input they had wanted to perform and the input they suspected their opponent had executed on a questionnaire next to the playing area. They could select from a list with the three possible game inputs and *"not sure"*. Further, participants completed a short questionnaire after they finished all five battles for an interaction method in order to assess the suitability for everyday life and social acceptance. Two participants that wore trousers without pockets were provided aprons with pockets in order to simulate realistic conditions for the *smartphone gesture* condition. A third participant used the pockets of their jacket for this interaction. Finally, participants completed a concluding questionnaire in which they stated their subjective experience of the game and the *battle* mode in specific.

Results

Interaction Observability

After each battle, participants stated the input they had wanted to perform and the input they suspected their opponent had executed. The *mean observability* of each interaction method per participant was calculated by comparing these values and calculating the mean. The observability of the first four battles of each interaction method was calculated separately from the observability of the fifth battle, as gaming strategies influenced the overall observability greatly (see Table 1). A Friedman's ANOVA showed that the interaction method had a significant effect on the observability of the first four rounds, $\chi^2(3) = 23.894, p < .001$. Post hoc tests revealed that *smartphone gestures* were significantly more easily observable than *smartwatch UI*. Further, *smartwatch gestures* were significantly more observable than *smartphone UI* and *smartwatch UI*. There was no significant effect of the interaction method on observability in the fifth round where participants were encouraged to employ gaming strategies, $\chi^2(3) = 4.1351, p > .05$.

Interaction Usability

The interaction methods were examined with regard to their usability of selecting the desired input for the game. For this purpose, the input that players wanted to perform was compared to the input registered by the system, i.e. constituting the input recognition rate. A Friedman's ANOVA revealed a significant effect of the interaction method on the recognition rate, $\chi^2(3) = 26.2, p < .001$. Post hoc tests showed that the recognition rate of *smartphone gestures* was significantly lower than the rate of *smartphone UI* and *smartwatch UI*. While another Friedman's ANOVA showed significant effects of the interaction method on the recognition rate for the fifth battle including gaming strategies, $\chi^2(3) = 9.6923, p < .05$, the pair-wise comparisons showed no significant effects.

	Smartphone UI	Smartwatch UI	Smartphone Gesture	Smartwatch Gesture
optimal conditions	20% (23%)	17% (18%)	44% (25%)	61% (27%)
with gaming behavior	25% (45%)	25% (45%)	12% (34%)	44% (51%)

Table 1. The mean observability (and standard deviations) (1) under optimal conditions and (2) with gaming behavior for every interaction method in the *battle* mode (values range from 0 to 100%).

Further, participants indicated the subjective usability of each method via agreement on a 7-point Likert scale (1 – *strongly disagree* to 7 – *strongly agree*) to the statement *I had no problems performing a game action*. A Friedman's ANOVA showed that the interaction method had a significant effect on players' ratings, $\chi^2(3) = 25.538, p < .001$. Post hoc tests revealed that only *smartphone gestures* were rated significantly worse than *smartphone UI* and *smartwatch UI*.

Social Acceptance of Interaction

Regarding the social acceptability of the interaction schemes, participants were asked to indicate their agreement to different statements on a 7-point Likert scale (1 – *strongly disagree* to 7 – *strongly agree*). In particular, the participants rated how comfortable they would feel using each interaction method in public (*Using this interaction in public would make me feel uncomfortable.*), how they would feel when noticing other players using it (*Players using this interaction would draw negative attention.*), and the suitability of the interaction in daily life (*This interaction is unsuitable for certain situations.*).

Friedman's ANOVAs were conducted on the participants' subjective ratings. The interaction method significantly influenced the perceived comfortableness, $\chi^2(3) = 24.713, p < .001$. Post hoc tests showed that participants would feel significantly less comfortable using *smartphone gestures* in public compared to *smartphone UI* and *smartwatch UI*. A significant effect was found for the players' rating regarding drawing negative attention, $\chi^2(3) = 23.167, p < .001$. Participants rated *smartphone gestures* significantly higher for drawing negative attention in comparison with *smartphone UI* and *smartwatch UI*. Regarding the suitability of the interaction in everyday situations, there was a significant effect of the interaction method as well, $\chi^2(3) = 14.186, p < .01$. Pair-wise comparisons revealed that only *smartwatch UI* was rated significantly more suitable than *smartphone gestures*.

General Evaluation of the Battle Mode

Participants were asked if they thought that generally they could integrate the *battle* mode well in their daily life on a 7-point Likert scale (1 – *strongly disagree* to 7 – *strongly agree*). The results show that participants thought they could integrate the *battle* mode well in their life ($M = 5.06, SD = 1.18$). Participants were undecided if they would have to disable the *battle* mode in many situations ($M = 3.75, SD = 1.48$), but they mostly agreed that there are several situations in which they would disable it ($M = 5.62, SD = .96$). Finally, participants had to indicate their agreement with several statements regarding their playing experience of the game in general. Specifically, they were asked how much fun they had (*Enjoyment*), how difficult they found the game (*Difficulty*), if they would like to continue playing (*Intention I*), if they would like to play the game again (*Intention II*), if they would recommend the game

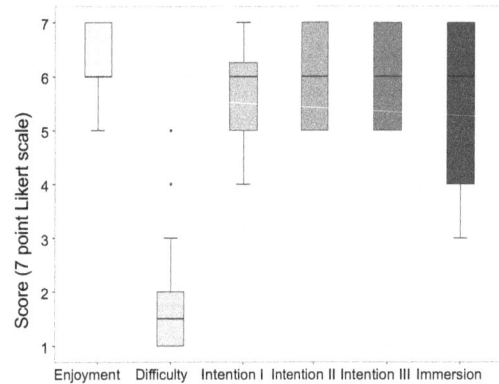

Figure 3. Results showing the gaming-experience of the *battle* mode measured by self-reported enjoyment, difficulty, intention to play and immersion.

to their friends (*Intention III*) and if they had felt immersed in the game (*Immersion*). The results (see Figure 3) show that the game generally did offer an enjoyable playing experience for the players.

Discussion

The results of this study showed that the interaction methods employing *gesture* paradigms were more observable under optimal conditions than the interaction methods that used *UIs*. When considering the setting of the study, i.e. a setting in which players stood face to face this is not too surprising. This might have differed in a setting that allowed for more observability of the *UI* interaction methods, e.g. scenarios that allow shoulder surfing. But for the presented game concept, a setting as the one in the study is more realistic and thus suitable for examination.

Concerning usability, the interaction with *smartphone gestures* performed worst objectively and subjectively. This may be due to several reasons, such as the very unfamiliar interaction scheme, the fact that three participants did not wear trousers with pockets, or just technical difficulties, as the recognition of input was often rather difficult. On the other hand, the *UI* interaction methods obviously provided the objectively best results for gameplay as there were no difficulties regarding the recognition of input. These interaction methods were also subjectively rated best as they performed with the least amount of errors and the interaction was familiar to all participants. The *smartwatch gestures* interaction, however, also performed quite well and not significantly different than the *UI* interaction methods, objectively and subjectively.

Regarding social acceptability of the interaction methods, *smartphone gestures* performed worst, while the *UI* interaction methods performed best. This might stem from the familiarity of the interaction as well, as touchscreen interaction is common in public while the *smartphone gestures* was new for the participants. Further, they might fear that the interaction would not work as reliably as other interactions. Again, *smartwatch gestures* performed a little worse than the *UI* interaction methods, but not significantly so. As this interaction actually might be less obvious than interacting with a touchscreen, the worse performance compared to the *UI* interactions might stem from the unfamiliarity and the fact that the interaction was pretty obvious in the setting of the study.

We therefore concluded that the interaction that provides the best trade-off between observability, usability and social acceptance is the most suitable for the presented game concept. *Smartwatch gesture* performed best with regard to observability together with *smartphone gesture* compared to the *UI* interaction methods, and also performed on par with the *UI* methods with regard to usability and social acceptance. We further suspected that the interaction would perform better with increasing familiarity and appear less obvious in a non-lab setting. Due to this and well balanced trade-off between the factors mentioned above, we decided that the *smartwatch gesture* interaction method was the most suitable to further evaluate the presented concept in a more realistic setting.

STUDY 2

In order to evaluate the game concept in a less controlled setting, we conducted a second study to investigate player reactions in scenarios simulating in-the-wild usage. The study had two objectives: investigating a) how well players are able to identify each other in both the *battle* and *shadowing* mode, and b) the social acceptability of playing the two modes in public. Based on the results of the first study, the second study was conducted only with the *smartwatch gestures* interaction method, as it provided the best trade-off between observability, usability and social acceptance. The *unmasking* option was deactivated for this study. As discussed in the section on related work, it is important that the gesture interaction remains as unobtrusive as possible for greater acceptability. The *shadowing* mode is particularly problematic, as the following of another person can look suspicious. A very high rate of successful player identification in the wild is also crucial, so as to not involve bystanders.

Methodology

The second study began with an introductory briefing wherein each participant was informed of the game concept. A video tutorial demonstrated the *smartwatch gesture* interaction method. The participants were then asked to participate in three mock battles with the instructor, as well as a trial run of shadowing the instructor. Before the study continued, they were asked to fill in a demographic survey. Subsequently, participants were asked to play the game while following a predefined route consisting of three stages:

- Stage 1: Walking from the exit of building A to the terrace of building B, where another (known) instructor was waiting.

Unknown to the participant, a previously unseen actor engaged in *shadowing* of the participant during this stage (starting with a distance of approx. 15m, consistently reducing this until

overtaking the participant shortly before the first checkpoint). Additionally, the instructor waiting at the checkpoint (i.e. a known potential opponent) initiated a battle with the participant while the actor passed them.

- Stage 2: Walking through the cafeteria inside building B and performing a dummy task, i.e. looking up the price of an item.

During this stage, participants had to respond to an unknown opponent in *battle* mode once they reached a certain point in the cafeteria. The cafeteria was always filled with a minimum of five other bystanders when the study was conducted.

- Stage 3: Following an unknown player in *shadowing* mode; the task was to correctly identify the player, and follow them as long as possible.

The part of the final unknown player was performed by an actress who was instructed to walk at the same pace for each study iteration. She always stopped at the half-way point between the two buildings to search inside her purse, in order to evoke a scenario that was as realistic as possible to what can be expected in real-life gameplay. An actress was chosen for this part, as opposed to a male actor, as we expect the reactions to social acceptability to differ based on gender.

For each stage, the participants did not know in advance what was going to happen; however they were informed that the game would be running in its entirety, i.e. any game events could potentially occur. They were also instructed to attempt to identify their opponent (in case of either game mode) and their game input (in case of a battle). At each checkpoint, the participants were asked whether they had battled anyone or been shadowed, and then told whether the latter had been the case. After the final stage, the participants were escorted back to the starting point for a concluding questionnaire.

Participants

A total of eight participants (2 female, 6 male) were recruited for the second study, with an average age of 23.1 ($SD = 2.26$), none of whom had participated in the first study. The players were asked about their gaming habits; three participants reported having played a pervasive game before; three others denied playing any games on mobile devices. Regarding smartwatch experience, four participants reportedly had never used a smartwatch before, three participants had used one at least once, and one indicated frequent use.

Measures

At all checkpoints, the participants were asked to fill in a brief questionnaire with the questions *Do you think that somebody shadowed you while walking to this checkpoint?* and *Did a battle occur while walking to this checkpoint?* If the answer to either question was yes, they were asked to indicate the identity of their assumed opponents. After being informed whether they had actually been followed, they were asked to indicate how they had felt about the experience on a 7-point Likert scale (1 – *strongly disagree* to 7 – *strongly agree*), i.e. *I felt uncomfortable, I was embarrassed, I was scared, I felt as if I had no control, It was entertaining* and *It was funny*. After the final stage, the participants were asked to rate (on the same scale) how well they thought the game modes could be integrated into their daily life, as well as general questions regarding their enjoyment of the game, and two questions regarding passive and active shadowing (*I do not want to be shadowed by others* and *I would not want to shadow others*).

Results

Overall, the participants rated the game highly for overall enjoyment ($M = 6.25$, $SD = 0.71$), feeling immersed ($M = 5.25$, $SD = 1.91$), and wanting to play again ($M = 6.25$, $SD = 1.03$).

Player Identification

In the first stage, the battle was initiated by a known potential opponent. Seven of eight participants noticed that the battle occurred, and five correctly identified their opposing player. They attributed this to the instructor's wrist rotation, the look to the wrist, and eye contact. During the second stage, two battles did not occur in time due to roaming issues between access points. Two of the six remaining participants successfully identified the unknown opponent. Regarding player identification in the *shadowing* mode, three of eight participants noticed the shadowing player. In the second stage, however, two participants declared that they had been followed despite this not being the case; one of them indicated a bystander with a laptop had appeared suspicious. Similarly, three participants felt that they had been shadowed in the final stage (one reported the feeling of being followed, another suspected a bystander who by coincidence had also been at the second stage). For the active shadowing task, two participants followed the wrong person, once because one participant unfortunately recognised one of the observers as someone they associated with the project.

Reaction to Shadowing

After the first stage (when the participants actually had been followed), the majority of participants tended to disagree with the negative reactions to being followed (*uncomfortable*: $M = 3.38$, $SD = 1.60$; *embarrassing*: $M = 2.38$, $SD = 1.06$; *scared*: $M = 2.00$, $SD = 1.19$; *lack of control*: $M = 2.50$, $SD = 1.19$), while the positive emotional reactions received noticeably higher ratings (*entertaining*: $M = 6.00$, $SD = 0.53$; *funny*: $M = 5.75$, $SD = 0.71$). The active following of another player in the third and final stage received similar results (*uncomfortable*: $M = 3.38$, $SD = 2.06$; *embarrassing*: $M = 2.62$, $SD = 1.50$; *scared*: $M = 2.00$, $SD = 1.07$; as opposed to *entertaining*: $M = 5.88$, $SD = 0.99$, *funny*: $M = 6.00$, $SD = 0.75$). These affective results are summarised in Figure 4.

Integration into Daily Life

The battle mode received significantly higher scores ($M = 5.88$, $SD = 0.83$) for fitting well into the participants' daily life compared to shadowing ($M = 4.50$, $SD = 1.69$), $t(7) = 2.43$, $p < 0.05$, $r = 0.68$. Overall, both modes averaged a positive score for this item. The scores for feeling uncomfortable with either interaction were generally low, with a slightly higher mean for shadowing ($M = 3.38$, $SD = 1.69$) than the battle mode ($M = 2.25$, $SD = 1.49$). This difference was not significant. Regarding the participants' estimation of non-usage (*I would have to disable the battle/shadowing mode in many situations*), the battle mode received lower scores ($M = 3.50$,

$SD = 1.41$) than the shadowing mode ($M = 4.38$, $SD = 1.51$), albeit not significantly so. Participants generally would not oppose participating in either active or passive shadowing. They were more inclined towards participating in active shadowing ($M = 2.63$, $SD = 1.06$) than passive shadowing ($M = 3.13$, $SD = 1.73$).

Discussion

The *battle* mode appears to allow for reasonably high rates of player identification when the player knows who is potentially an opponent. This rate is reduced with entirely unknown opponents. Less than half of participants noticed the shadowing in the first stage, but the ones that did notice were all able to identify their follower. Interestingly, this mode may foster a degree of paranoia, as indicated by some participants' continued belief that they had been followed even during the stages when this did not in fact occur. Regarding active *shadowing*, the player identification rates were also high. However, as two participants followed the wrong person, and as this game mode can be considered socially more problematic, player identification may have to be supported more strongly for active *shadowing*. Future research will likely require qualitative evaluation of the social acceptability for this mode (including for non-players). The overall reaction to both the active and passive *shadowing* mode was nevertheless quite positive.

Both modes were well received regarding integration into the participants' daily life, and how they would feel using either mode in public. The *battle* mode's significantly higher scores for integration support the hypothesis that this mode exemplifies a socially acceptable micro interaction, whereas the asymmetric *shadowing* mode partly requires a longer interaction. This is also indicated by the estimation of non-usage; the *battle* mode would have to be disabled less often (although this was not a significant difference). Interestingly, for the distinction between active and passive shadowing, the participants disagreed more strongly with not wanting to actively shadow people than not wanting to be shadowed, i.e. they preferred the active to the passive *shadowing* mode, and tended to disagree with not wanting to use either.

LIMITATIONS & SUMMARY

The concept of the presented paper aims for a high integration of pervasive games into everyday life. However, players frequently use games as a means of diversion or to break away from their life [35]. Thus it may seem contradictory to aim for such an integration. However, such games are not meant to replace the recreational aspects of "regular" entertainment games, but can rather be used as gaming experiences that augment the enjoyment of players' daily lives.

Regarding the comparison of interaction methods in the first study, the choice for the interaction with the best trade-off may not actually be the best for real-life pervasive game deployment. There are also many other potential interaction paradigms, as well as devices, that could be investigated. In the conducted studies, participants reported that they could integrate the game modes of *2084 – Safe New World* (to varying degrees) well into their lives. However, this is a subjective estimation based on relatively short gameplay experiences. To

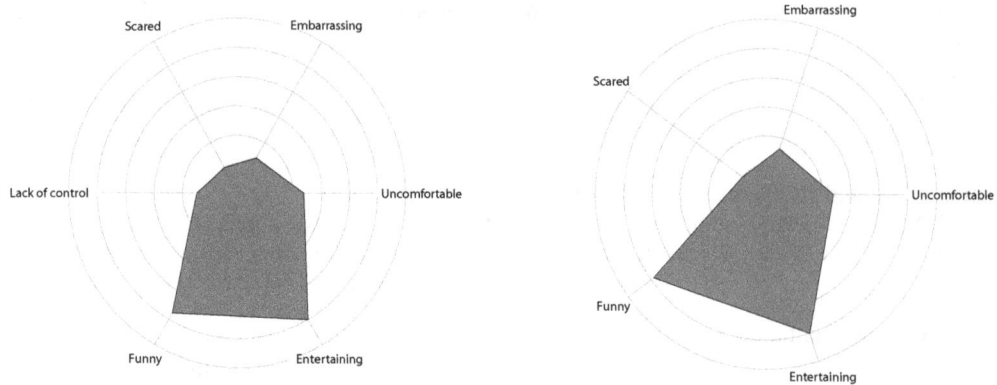

Figure 4. Spider plot of mean values for participants' emotional reactions to being followed by other players (left) and following other players (right) in the *shadowing* mode. The *Lack of control* item was only used for the passive *shadowing* mode.

evaluate if the concept holds up for real-life pervasive gaming, it is of course necessary to conduct a long-term field study.

Part of the concept is based on the assumption that integration of a pervasive game into players' everyday lives relies on social acceptability of game interaction. Thus, this aspect was examined via the participants' subjective rating regarding this construct. However, social acceptability is a concept that is hard to conceptualize and subsequently difficult to assess. Potentially, the subjective estimates of social acceptability do not really indicate if players will in fact be comfortable using such a game in public. The concept of games that are *always-on* can lead to several challenges only remotely addressed in this paper. These include technical issues such as the effect on battery life of mobile devices, issues regarding the privacy of players, as well as how the implementation of a not-available feature in an *always-on* concept would influence the multiplayer aspects of the game. Further, the player-vs.-player paradigm requires a user-base of a certain size, which is a limitation inherent to multiplayer games in which interaction is triggered by proximity and thus requires nearby players. This is in fact one major limitation of the concept and cannot be mitigated through AI-controlled "fake players" alone, as the game concept requires that players actually encounter opposing players in the real world.

The studies' results showed that a pervasive game that is integrated in the players' daily lives has to adhere to certain guidelines as providing the possibility to turn off the *always-on* aspect for specific social circumstances as well as supplying support for player identification. Finally, while the studies revealed that players had positive gaming experiences, this is not indicative of the game's ability to provide sustained long-term enjoyment, yet this is crucial for a temporally pervasive game. Thus, in future work we plan to extend the overall game to include systems that provide a more complete experience, for example through the addition of a more in-depth progression system or location-based items.

CONCLUSION

In this paper we presented a concept for pervasive games that can integrate thoroughly into players' everyday life. This is realised by the combination of a strong degree of ubiquity (the game is *always-on*) and of the interactions which are brief enough to not overly interrupt the players everyday activities. The concept was implemented in the prototypical pervasive multiplayer game *2084 – Safe New World*, which comprises two game modes: (1) a player-vs.-player *battle* mode that utilizes micro interactions and (2) a *shadowing* mode that aimed to test boundaries of social acceptability. A lab study confirmed that the *battle* mode was well received by participants. It further revealed that gesture interaction on a smartwatch provided the best trade-off between usability, subjective social acceptance and observability of the compared interaction methods for this game mode. A second user-study simulating in-the-wild usage suggests that both game modes of *2084 – Safe New World* can be integrated into players' everyday lives, and further showed that, within the game construct, shadowing other players can be socially acceptable. The effect on non-players requires further investigation. In conclusion, while more research on long-term in-the-wild usage is necessary, the studies suggest that the micro interactions can provide enjoyable gaming experiences for players of pervasive games. Further, this concept need not suffer unduly from issues of negative social acceptance, as long as the game mechanics adhere to criteria such as support of player identification and ubiquitous interactions.

Acknowledgements

This work was conducted as part of the project "Serious Games - Skill Advancement Through Adaptive Systems" which is funded by the Carl Zeiss Foundation.

REFERENCES

1. 3 Minute Games LLC. 2016. *Lifeline*. Game [Android Wear]. (21 December 2016). Seattle, USA.

2. It's Alive. 2001. *Botfighters*. Game [Mobile Phone]. (2001). It's Alive, Stockholm, Sweden.

3. Marek Bell, Matthew Chalmers, Louise Barkhuus, Malcolm Hall, Scott Sherwood, Paul Tennent, Barry Brown, Duncan Rowland, Steve Benford, Mauricio Capra, and Alastair Hampshire. 2006. Interweaving Mobile Games With Everyday Life. In *Proceedings of the SIGCHI conference on Human Factors in computing systems*. ACM, 417–426.

4. Steve Benford, Carsten Magerkurth, and Peter Ljungstrand. 2005. Bridging the physical and digital in pervasive gaming. *Commun. ACM* 48, 3 (2005), 54–57.

5. Hal Berghel. 2004. Wireless infidelity I: War driving. *Commun. ACM* 47, 9 (2004), 21–26.

6. Staffan Björk, Jennica Falk, Rebecca Hansson, and Peter Ljungstrand. 2001. Pirates! Using the physical world as a game board. In *Proceedings of Interact*. 423–430.

7. Staffan Björk and Johan Peitz. 2007. Understanding pervasive games through gameplay design patterns. In *Situated Play, Proceedings of DiGRA 2007 Conference*. 440–448.

8. Bossa Studios. 2015. *Spy Watch*. Game [Apple Watch]. (9 June 2015). London, UK.

9. Stephen Brewster, Joanna Lumsden, Marek Bell, Malcolm Hall, and Stuart Tasker. 2003. Multimodal 'Eyes-free' Interaction Techniques for Wearable Devices. In *Proceedings of the SIGCHI conference on Human factors in computing systems*. ACM, 473–480.

10. Stephane Coutant. 2015. *2048 - Android Wear*. Game [Android]. (14 November 2015). Scoutant.org, Meylan, France.

11. David Dobbelstein, Philipp Hock, and Enrico Rukzio. 2015. Belt: An Unobtrusive Touch Input Device for Head-worn Displays. In *Proceedings of the 33rd Annual ACM Conference on Human Factors in Computing Systems*. ACM, 2135–2138.

12. Allegra Frank. 2015. Sonic helps you work on your fitness with Sonic Dash 2 Apple Watch companion. `http://www.polygon.com/2015/10/8/9477313/sonic-dash-2-sonic-boom-apple-watch`. (2015). Online; accessed: 06 April 2016.

13. Batya Friedman, Peter H Kahn Jr, Jennifer Hagman, Rachel L Severson, and Brian Gill. 2006. The Watcher and the Watched: Social Judgments About Privacy in a Public Place. *Human-Computer Interaction* 21, 2 (2006), 235–272.

14. Steve Hinske, Matthias Lampe, Carsten Magerkurth, and Carsten Röcker. 2007. Classifying Pervasive Games: On Pervasive Computing and Mixed Reality. *Concepts and Technologies for Pervasive Games–A Reader for Pervasive Gaming Research* 1 (2007), 20.

15. Paul Holleis, Albrecht Schmidt, Susanna Paasovaara, Arto Puikkonen, and Jonna Häkkilä. 2008. Evaluating Capacitive Touch Input on Clothes. In *Proceedings of the 10th International Conference on Human Computer Interaction with Mobile Devices and Services*

(MobileHCI '08). ACM, New York, NY, USA, 81–90. DOI:`http://dx.doi.org/10.1145/1409240.1409250`

16. Steve Jackson. 1998. *Killer, The Game of Assassination*. Steve Jackson Games.

17. Christian Licoppe and Yoriko Inada. 2006. Emergent uses of a multiplayer location-aware mobile game: The interactional consequences of mediated encounters. *Mobilities* 1, 1 (2006), 39–61.

18. Christian Licoppe and Yoriko Inada. 2009. Mediated proximity and its dangers in a location aware community: a case of 'stalking'. *Digital cityscapes: Merging digital and urban playspaces* (2009), 100–128.

19. Jukka Linjama, Jonna Hakkila, and Sami Ronkainen. 2005. Gesture Interfaces for Mobile Devices – Minimalist Approach for Haptic Interaction. In *CHI Workshop: Hands on Haptics: Exploring Non-Visual Visualisation Using the Sense of Touch*.

20. Marta Majorek and Marta du Vall. 2015. Ingress: An Example of a New Dimension in Entertainment. *Games and Culture* (2015), 1–23.

21. Milton Bradley Company and Winning Moves. 1966. *Twister*. Game [Board game]. (1966). Milton Bradley Company, Springfield, Massachusetts, USA.

22. Calkin S Montero, Jason Alexander, Mark T Marshall, and Sriram Subramanian. 2010. Would You Do That? – Understanding Social Acceptance of Gestural Interfaces. In *Proceedings of the 12th international conference on Human computer interaction with mobile devices and services*. ACM, 275–278.

23. Markus Montola. 2011. A ludological view on the pervasive mixed-reality game research paradigm. *Personal and Ubiquitous Computing* 15, 1 (2011), 3–12.

24. Markus Montola, Jaakko Stenros, and Annika Waern. 2009. *Pervasive games: theory and design*. Morgan Kaufmann Publishers Inc., CA, USA.

25. Florian Mueller, Sophie Stellmach, Saul Greenberg, Andreas Dippon, Susanne Boll, Jayden Garner, Rohit Khot, Amani Naseem, and David Altimira. 2014. Proxemics Play: Understanding Proxemics for Designing Digital Play Experiences. In *Proceedings of the 2014 conference on Designing interactive systems*. ACM, 533–542.

26. Niantic, Inc. 2013. *Ingress*. Game [Android]. (14 December 2013). San Francisco, U.S.

27. Niantic, Inc. 2016. *Pokémon Go*. Game [Android, iOS]. (6 July 2016). The Pokémon Company, San Francisco, U.S. Played July 2016.

28. Jenny Niemi, Susanna Sawano, and Annika Waern. 2005. Involving Non-Players in Pervasive Games. In *Proceedings of the 4th decennial conference on Critical computing: between sense and sensibility*. ACM, 137–140.

29. Eva Nieuwdorp. 2007. The Pervasive Discourse: An Analysis. *Computers in Entertainment (CIE)* 5, 2 (2007), 13.

30. Johan Peitz, Hannamari Saarenpää, and Staffan Björk. 2007. Insectopia: Exploring Pervasive Games Through Technology already Pervasively Available. In *Proceedings of the international conference on Advances in computer entertainment technology*. ACM, 107–114.

31. Stuart Reeves, Steve Benford, Claire O'Malley, and Mike Fraser. 2005. Designing the Spectator Experience. In *Proceedings of the SIGCHI Conference on Human Factors in Computing Systems (CHI '05)*. ACM, New York, NY, USA, 741–750. DOI: http://dx.doi.org/10.1145/1054972.1055074

32. Reuters. 2016. Pokemon Go Has Added $7.5 Billion to Nintendo's Market Value. (2016). http://fortune.com/2016/07/11/pokemon-go-nintendo-market-value/.

33. Julie Rico and Stephen Brewster. 2010. Usable Gestures for Mobile Interfaces: Evaluating Social Acceptability. In *Proceedings of the SIGCHI Conference on Human Factors in Computing Systems*. ACM, 887–896.

34. Sami Ronkainen, Jonna Häkkilä, Saana Kaleva, Ashley Colley, and Jukka Linjama. 2007. Tap Input as an Embedded Interaction Method for Mobile Devices. In *Proceedings of the 1st international conference on Tangible and Embedded Interaction*. ACM, 263–270.

35. John L Sherry, Kristen Lucas, Bradley S Greenberg, and Ken Lachlan. 2006. Video Game Uses and Gratifications as Predictors of Use and Game Preference. *Playing video games: Motives, responses, and consequences* 24 (2006), 213–224.

36. Alireza Sahami Shirazi and Niels Henze. 2015. Assessment of Notifications on Smartwatches. In *Proceedings of the 17th International Conference on Human-Computer Interaction with Mobile Devices and Services Adjunct*. ACM, 1111–1116.

37. Adriana De Souza E Silva. 2008. Alien Revolt (2005-2007): A Case Study of the First Location-Based Mobile Game in Brazil. *Technology and Society Magazine, IEEE* 27, 1 (2008), 18–28.

38. Nick Statt. 2015. Augmented-reality game Ingress arriving on Android Wear watches. http://www.cnet.com/uk/news/augmented-reality-game-ingress-arrives-on-android-wear-watches/. (2015). Online; accessed: 06 April 2016.

39. Jaakko Stenros. 2012. In Defence of a Magic Circle: The Social and Mental Boundaries of Play. In *Proceedings of DiGRA Nordic 2012 Conference*.

40. Supercell. 2012. *Clash of Clans*. Game [Android]. (2 August 2012). Supercell, Helsinki, Finland.

41. Mark Weiser. 1991. The Computer for the 21st Century. *Scientific American* 265, 3 (1991), 94–104.

42. Julie R Wiliamson, Andrew Crossan, and Stephen Brewster. 2011. Multimodal Mobile Interactions: Usability Studies in Real World Settings. In *Proceedings of the 13th international conference on multimodal interfaces*. ACM, 361–368.

43. Wan Xian, Paula Tarrío Alonso, Ana M. Bernardos Barbolla, Eduardo Metola Moreno, and Jose Ramon Casar Corredera. 2012. User-independent accelerometer-based gesture recognition for mobile devices. *Advances in Distributed Computing and Artificial Intelligence Journal* 1, 3 (December 2012), 11–25. http://oa.upm.es/16199/

44. Robert Xiao, Gierad Laput, and Chris Harrison. 2014. Expanding the Input Expressivity of Smartwatches with Mechanical Pan, Twist, Tilt and Click. In *Proceedings of the SIGCHI Conference on Human Factors in Computing Systems*. ACM, 193–196.

Evaluating Display Modalities Using a Mixed Reality Game

Hitesh Nidhi Sharma[1], Zachary O. Toups[1], Igor Dolgov[2], Andruid Kerne[3], Ajit Jain[3]
[1]Play & Interactive Experiences for Learning Lab, Dept. Computer Science, New Mexico State University
[2]Perception, Action, & Cognition in Mediated Artificial & Natural Environments Lab, Dept. Psychology,
New Mexico State University
[3]Interface Ecology Lab, Dept. Computer Science & Engineering, Texas A&M University
hitesharmaa@gmail.com, z@cs.nmsu.edu, id@nmsu.edu, andruid@ecologylab.net, ajit@ecologylab.net

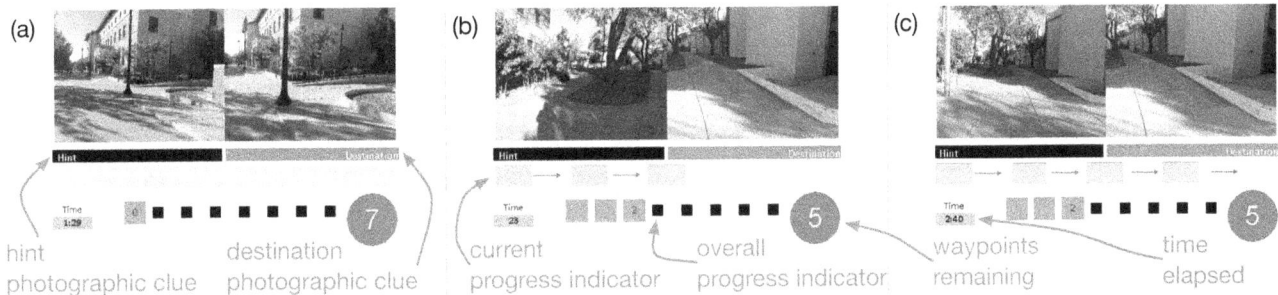

Figure 1. The *PhotoNav* game user interface, showing player progress along a course, guided by a hint photographic clue to a destination photographic clue. UI components populate the bottom. The current progress indicator shows the advancement of a player toward the current waypoint. The overall progress indicator shows progression along all the waypoints. In: (a) the player starts at the first waypoint (7 waypoints remain), (b) the player moves from 2nd to the 3rd waypoint (5 waypoints remain), (c) the player continuing progression nearing the current destination (5 waypoints remain).

ABSTRACT

We design and study a mixed reality game, *PhotoNav*, to investigate wearable computing display modalities. We study game play, varying display modality: head-mounted, handheld, and wrist-worn. *PhotoNav* requires the player to split attention between the physical world and display by using geotagged photographs as clues for navigation. Our results showed that participants using the head-mounted display exhibited poor performance in one of the courses and that players preferred handheld and wrist-worn displays, likely due to their familiarity with them. We derive design implications from the study and discuss problems faced in designing mixed reality games and interfaces that require users to split their attention.

ACM Classification Keywords

H.5.1. Information Interfaces and Presentation (e.g. HCI): Multimedia Information Systems: Artificial, augmented, and virtual realities

Author Keywords

Display modalities; mixed reality; wearable; handheld display; head-mounted display; wrist-worn display.

CHI PLAY '16, October 16 - 19, 2016, Austin, TX, USA

© 2016 Copyright held by the owner/author(s). Publication rights licensed to ACM.
ISBN 978-1-4503-4456-2/16/10. . . $15.00

DOI: http://dx.doi.org/10.1145/2967934.2968090

INTRODUCTION

Handheld displays, in the form of smartphones and gaming devices, are common in many parts of the world; wrist-worn and head-mounted displays (HMDs) have begun to proliferate. Open questions remain about the ability of wearable computers to enhance performance, improve situation awareness, and reduce mental workload. Already, cases where users split their attention between the physical world and digital data arise in urban contexts, where individuals attend to devices and the environment simultaneously (e.g., reading email and walking). New use cases for wearable computers emerge beyond mundane scenarios, such as disaster responders with wearables for local sensor telemetry and incoming warnings displayed on facemasks or soldiers with information displays built into helmets.

To address these use cases and study the best designs for wearables moving forward, the present research tests wearable computer designs using mixed reality games to better understand how they impact human performance in the physical world. We develop *PhotoNav*, a game that engages players both in an information device and in the physical world. We use this game to investigate *display modality*: the relationship between the display and the user's body. We test HMD, handheld, and wrist-worn display modalities which act as proxies for devices available on the market (e.g., HMD mobile devices, smartwatches, and smartphones, respectively). We expect HMD to perform better due to shorter shift in attention.

In our mixed reality game, a player chooses a path through physical environments, seeking out waypoints using *photo-*

graphic clues. The game UI shows two photographs: one of the destination and one hint taken nearby, the vantage point of which will advance the user toward the destination waypoint. The game is designed such that the player must use the photographs, and not other UI components, to traverse the environment. The UI components have been designed to provide useful status information while making them useless for direct navigation, forcing reliance on the photographic clues.

A key component of the game's UI design, in order to simulate wearable computing use cases, is to split the player's attention between device and the physical world. The photographic clues provide a tension: they are necessary to determine where to go, but draw attention away from scanning the physical world in search of the next clue. The current research builds on our prior pilot study [38].

We proceed to connect together background. We then describe our custom wearable computer, used for the present game, as well as game mechanics and design of *PhotoNav*. We describe a user study, discuss implications for design, and present conclusions.

BACKGROUND

The background for this project combines research into wearable computing, game design, mixed reality, splitting attention, and navigation.

Mobile and Wearable Computing

Little scholarly attention has been paid to non-handheld mobile display modalities, likely due to the lack of practical wearable designs [8, 11, 20], until recently. While smartphones and tablets have become commonplace in many countries, everyday wearable technologies are just beginning to proliferate through wrist-worn displays (e.g. Pebble, Apple Watch, Android Wear) and HMDs (Google Glass, Microsoft HoloLens, Meta Pro, Sony SmartEyeglass).

Wearable computers distribute computing technology across the body [26, 41]. While we have seen a recent increase in the commercial availability of wearable technologies, the present research uses a modular, backpack wearable, that serves as a development platform for multiple mixed reality scenarios with a minimal set of hardware. Wearables incorporating general purpose computing, location and direction sensors, head tracking, and/or HMDs, were pioneered by Mann, Starner, Feiner, MacIntyre, and others for the applications of personal, day-to-day augmentation [40], data collection [27], location-based information gathering [15], and/or gaming [30, 45].

Although HMDs have been compared to desktop and large-scale displays [37,39,42], there is a knowledge gap in wearable contexts. HMDs enable the user to access information directly in the visual field, but users must merge the visual field and computer display [49, 50]. Moreover, social pressures may impact appropriateness of device use [34].

Two prior empirical studies compared display modalities [47, 52]. Yeh et al.'s simulated mission study [52] showed that participants detected targets better using a handheld navigation aid over a helmet-mounted one; display clutter diminished performance. Vadas et al. [47] undertook a mobile in-the-laboratory [1] study in which participants used either an HMD, a handheld e-ink display, or a backlit handheld display to read while walking. The HMD fared worst for walking performance, but not reading comprehension, due to participants' split attention.

Numerous other studies have compared pilots' performance using head-up and head-down displays [14]. Unlike HMDs, head-up displays (HUDs) are fixed inside the cockpit/cabin while HMDs effectively track users' head movements. A head-down display is analogous to a handheld or wrist-worn one, except that the handheld or wrist-worn display may be moved, where the head-down display is fixed.

Game Design

Game play fundamentally involves making decisions. A *game mechanic* is a designed set of rules through which a player makes a choice, advancing toward an outcome [36]. Rules constrain play, rendering it meaningful. The *core mechanics* are the set of game mechanics engaged repeatedly.

Mixed Reality

Systems that connect physical and virtual reality in some meaningful way through sensors and databases, are *mixed realities* [6, 7, 9, 29]. These range from augmented reality, in which 3D imagery is integrated with a perspective on the physical world, as with most HUDs, to augmented virtuality, in which physical-world artifacts and spaces are integrated into a virtual world. Mixed reality systems offer the opportunity to create *embodied* interfaces [12], in which participants create meaning through hybrid digital / physical experiences.

The present research involves *mobile* mixed reality, which provides the user a location-specific experience [3, 15, 16]. Users are tracked with GPS-based location sensors [10,16,53], which drive the player's experience of the virtual world. The user's physical-world location is mapped to a virtual-world location isomorphically.

Splitting Attention

Many tasks require users to split attention when they need to focus on the physical world and a display interface simultaneously (e.g., reading email while walking, navigating using a map). As wrist-worn displays and HMDs also help to accomplish similar tasks, we investigate which display modality works best when users need to split their attention. Trevisan et al. showed that when real and virtual worlds interact, designers must focus a user's attention on one or the other [46], pointing out that the ability to focus is affected by UI design. We investigate intentional splitting of attention as a part of gameplay, making decisions about where to focus a game mechanic.

Navigation

In a prior study [31], a pedestrian navigation assistant was developed to compare view-based wayfinding using pictures to incidental learning using map-based wayfinding; the study showed that users developed good knowledge of routes while using both map-based and view-based navigation assistance. Beeharee et al. [5] found that geo-annotated photographs aid pedestrians in following routes. They augmented photographs

Figure 2. Top-down view of photographic clue selection algorithm as a player progresses through a space rich with clues. Potential clues are shown with their reverse orientation arc (so standing within a clue's arc suggests one could see the physical world the photograph represents). Clues that are closest and whose reverse orientation arc align with the orientation of the player, as determined by the head-mounted compass, are selected. In (a), the simplest case, where the nearest clue is in view; in (b) a nearby clue outside of view is selected because no clues are in view; in (c) an image that should be visible is selected over other, nearer clues.

with direction cues to minimize navigational ambiguities [4]. May et al. [28] studied requirements of pedestrians within an urban context and identified that providing information at key decision points and confirming correct decision are useful mobile navigation features. In the present study, we provide navigational clues through photographs.

PHOTONAV DESIGN

We designed *PhotoNav* to evaluate the utility of display modalities in demanding situations by purposefully splitting the player's attention between physical world and device. The physical world forms a component of the digital game. We constructed the game to provide minimal information to the player for decision making, using photographic *clues* to guide players through a course. The game was designed to be playable with any display modality.

Wearable Computer

We developed a modular wearable computer that combines computing, tracking, feedback, and minimal direct user interaction; Figures 3 and 4 show the wearable. We use this wearable, rather than existing commercial solutions, due to its flexibility and ease-of-development. We use GPS to obtain player location, while a forehead-mounted compass provides head tracking. The wearable incorporates an HMD and a small wired display, which can either be handheld or strapped onto an arm to act as a wrist-worn display. While modern smartwatch interfaces are smaller in size, given the nature of the study, the same wired display was used as a wrist-worn display as it would be difficult to compare two different user interfaces. Feedback is provided to the user using the active display modality. Details are provided in the apparatus section.

Core Mechanics

PhotoNav is a location-aware game in which a player moves through a physical environment with the goal of finding hidden waypoints using photographic clues. The *core mechanics*, about which players make decisions, are freely moving through the environment, paying activating the display, exploring, and seeking out the clues provided.

Each round of *PhotoNav* is played on a *course* (several of which are run for a study). Courses consist of a sequence of *waypoints* and a collection of *photographic clues*: geotagged and oriented photographs. *Hint photographic clues* are algorithmically selected at runtime such that, if the player advances

toward the photographed location, s/he will be closer to the destination. Each waypoint has a single *destination photographic clue*. As the player moves, system provides new hints. Players accrue score based on finding each waypoint quickly.

Game Interface and Photographic Clues

The game interface is designed to provide only sufficient information for the player to make informed decisions about where to move. The *PhotoNav* UI is minimal (Figure 1), the majority of it consists of photographic clues. As the player moves, the hint photographic clue updates. After finding the destination, the waypoint is updated and a new destination photographic clue is shown.

The game program selects clues based on the player's likelihood of seeing them, using a photographic clue selection algorithm (Figure 2). The algorithm uses two arcs: the forward viewing arc of the player, calculated from GPS location and compass orientation, and the viewable arc of each photograph, calculated from the photograph's geotag and *inverse* orientation. The selection criteria assume that a person in the viewable arc of the photograph, looking in the direction the photo was taken, will be able to see the photographed scene. To make selection more robust, *PhotoNav* will pick the nearest image if the player is not within any photograph's viewable arc. The maximum distance between the player and an image is fixed at 30 meters, and the view arcs are all 60 degrees. Photographic clue images are taken in advance of the game, during the same season as play, to minimize the differences between photographs and the physical world.

Feedback

The game UI provides supporting contextual information, including two progress indicators; Figure 1 shows the interface in a variety of progression points. The current progress indicator shows the progress of a player towards the current waypoint at a low resolution (only five states). The coarse-grained nature of the current progress indicator prevents its use as the sole means of navigation.

The display also includes an overall progress indicator at the bottom of the screen that shows total progress of the player. The progress indicator provides a series of blocks, as well as a single numerical value showing the remaining waypoints.

These UI cues are minimal and obfuscated: as player progresses, *hint* photographic clues change. The feedback does **not** tell the player which direction to move; the player needs to make a decision based on the surrounding and clues.

Player Input

The player's direction and location are constantly monitored by the *PhotoNav* software to maintain and progress the game state. The player does not need to provide direct input to the game to play, but a handheld chording keyboard (Figure 3 right) is used to activate the display and allow the player to indicate that s/he is already familiar with the destination.

The player can activate the display by holding down a button on the chording keyboard; otherwise, the display is blank. This requires players to explicitly indicate when they need to see the display; we use this as a proxy for the player's attention. By determining the total time players activate the display, we aim to find out how often players use the display or how it affects player performance.

For data-collection purposes, a familiarity button allows players to mark the current section of the course as familiar if they can reach the destination without hints. When the button is pressed, a countdown timer is used to confirm familiarity. If the button is held for 10 seconds, the systems registers player's familiarity with the immediate waypoint.

Supporting Systems and Implementation

The *PhotoNav* system is comprised of three components: the *PhotoNav* game itself, the NavCurator support application, and the *PhotoNav* Capture support application. While the *PhotoNav* game is our focus, the NavCurator and *PhotoNav* Capture applications were used to develop game courses and collect images for *PhotoNav*.

PhotoNav Game Implementation Details

PhotoNav is built in Java and runs on the wearable computer using a single active display modality (any other displays are blank). The hardware implementation drives the game resolution, which uses the maximum resolution of the HMD: 640×480 pixels. As the player starts the game, an interface is shown that provides a clue and a destination, both of which are images that are shown on the screen as shown in Figure 1.

The waypoints that make up each course are stored in an XML file, which references a collection of geotagged photographs. The XML file is generated by the experimenter using NavCurator. The S.IM.PL Libraries [17, 18] were used for de-/serialization to create, manage, and read the XML configuration files. The file only contains information about the waypoints, the clue and destination photographic hints are determined by the *PhotoNav* application at runtime.

PhotoNav can be run in two different modes: game mode and simulation mode. In the game mode, a player puts on a wearable computer and moves through real physical locations to explore the game. In simulation mode, *PhotoNav* uses Google Earth[1] as a GPS emulator. The location data is then sent to *PhotoNav* application, which updates the images based on the acquired location data. This provides for an efficient way to test *PhotoNav* without having to be at real locations.

NavCurator Support Application

NavCurator is a Java application developed to create courses for *PhotoNav*. Users import geotagged images, markers of which are overlaid on top of aerial photographs. NavCurator is built on the NASA World Wind Platform[2], which displays aerial photographs and satellite imagery of the globe. The imported images are plotted with their image direction. Users draw courses and the *PhotoNav* clue-selection algorithm identifies which images apply to the course. The created course can then be packaged up and exported to *PhotoNav*.

PhotoNav Capture Support Application

PhotoNav Capture is an Android application developed to accurately capture geotagged images and supply the player with enough context data to support creating courses in the NavCurator. Capture utilizes the in-built compass and GPS sensor of a tablet to tag images with location and direction information. It shows the player a map with photograph markers, so that the player can determine if enough photographs have been taken to cover an area. The images are saved in the tablet's internal memory and are transferred to a computer for NavCurator to plot and export *PhotoNav*-usable courses.

METHODS

The *PhotoNav* experiment was conducted with two conditions: display modality and course. Courses were specially designed sequences of waypoints that players needed to visit in order. Display modality was varied quasi-randomly among participants, but courses were always run in the same order owing to their geographic locations (Course A ended near Course B, which ended near Course C; see Figure 5 (optimal paths) to see the course layouts and how they connect). If courses were run out-of-order, participants would have had to walk through potentially future courses on the way to a course.

Apparatus

The wearable computer (Figures 3, 4) provides computation via a back-mounted notebook computer, tracking through a suite of sensors, and feedback through an HMD or handheld display (the latter of which may be used as a wrist-worn display). The wearable is built into a lightweight frame custom developed by Mystery Ranch[3]. Attached to the lower-back of the pack was a Dell Inspiron Mini 9 910 notebook, (Windows XP Operating System, 1 GHz Intel Atom processor, 1 GB RAM, 5 GB hard drive).

While the wearable has other sensors built-in, *PhotoNav* used a GPS and compass, both of which were head-mounted on the HMD mount. The GPS receiver was a Qstarz BT-Q818XT 10Hz Bluetooth GPS receiver, connected to the computer via Bluetooth. An OceanServer OS5000-S digital compass was used for head tracking, connected to the notebook via a USB cable bound to the HMD cables. A Twiddler 3 chording keyboard / mouse is used as an input device for the game. The Twiddler is connected to the notebook computer via Bluetooth.

---

[1] https://www.google.com/earth/

[2] http://worldwind.arc.nasa.gov/java/

[3] http://www.mysteryranch.com

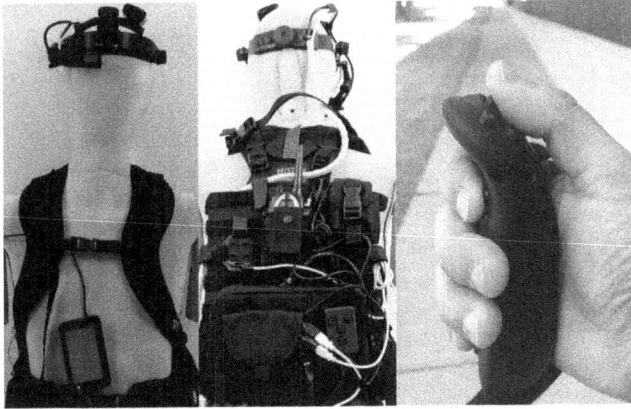

Figure 3. Front (left) and back (middle) views of the wearable computer. The wearable consists of: front: a monocular, see-through HMD with compass and GPS attached and a tethered handheld display; back: interconnects and a notebook computer. View of the chording keyboard, Twiddler (right): players used the thumb to record familiarity and the forefinger to bring up the interface.

Display Modalities

The wearable includes two displays to cover the three display modalities: an HMD and an external monitor that can be handheld or wrist-worn. The handheld device was a 4.3-inch Century LCD-4300U LCD display connected as an external monitor via a USB port to the notebook computer. The same LCD display was strapped to the hand of the participant to function it as a wrist-worn display as shown in Figure 4.

When we began developing the wearable computer in 2009, we considered a number of displays for the HMD modality. Tested systems included the Icuiti 920M, Vuzix Tac Eye, i-Port EX, and Liteye LE-750A; more recently, we tested a Google Glass Explorer Edition and Sony Smart Eyeglasses. The Liteye was chosen due to its ability to be used with corrective lenses, its extensive range of focus, and its ability to have the display placed in flexible locations. The display is monocular and see-through with a polarizing filter to reduce glare from the sun and adjustable brightness levels.

Display Modality Conditions

Three display modalities represented the three conditions in the study. In all conditions, the configuration of the wearable was held the same, with the appropriate display activated. In this way, we are not measuring the ergonomic impact of components of the wearable.

Course Design

Before taking the photographs, it was necessary to design the courses. There are many factors to be taken in consideration while choosing an outdoor space for any mixed reality system, especially player safety and the affordances [32] of the environment. We ensured a high density of photographic hints to keep players engaged and provide adequate feedback. We designed three courses which we expected to be unfamiliar to players.

All courses were developed with the following characteristics:

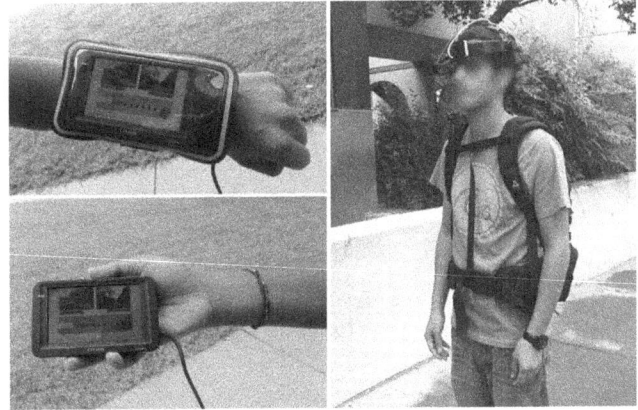

Figure 4. A player putting on a wrist-worn display (top left), player using a handheld display (bottom left). A participant putting on the HMD and wearable computer (right).

- were in pedestrian-safe areas;

- primarily featured open overhead space to avoid urban-canyon effects and/or other GPS interference [10, 53];

- were selected from the New Mexico State University (NMSU) campus;

- feature seven waypoints (including the starting point); and

- contain at least three turns of approximately $90°$.

The individual characteristics of the courses were as follows:

- **Course A:** 334 meters, 304 photographs, 3 turns. Passed near the following landmarks: Foster Hall, Young Hall, Hardman & Jacobs Undergraduate Learning Center and Domenici Hall.

- **Course B:** 345 meters, 290 photographs, 4 turns. Passed near the following landmarks: Business Complex, Aggie Memorial Tower, Dove Hall, Hardman & Jacobs Undergraduate Learning Center, and parking lot 11.

- **Course C:** 259 meters, 200 photographs, 4 turns. Passed near the following landmarks: Clara Belle Williams Hall, CHSS Annex, Speech Center.

Figure 5 (optimal paths) shows the layout of the courses, including the turns and how they connect in sequence.

As players rely on photographic clues to reach the waypoints, *PhotoNav* Capture was used to take pictures. The photos were captured such that there were about one photo per two meters, providing sufficient density to have hint photographic clues on and around the course.

Subject Recruitment and Study Protocol

The research protocol was approved by the NMSU IRB (protocol #12948). Participants from NMSU were invited via flyers and emails to participate. Participants were not compensated.

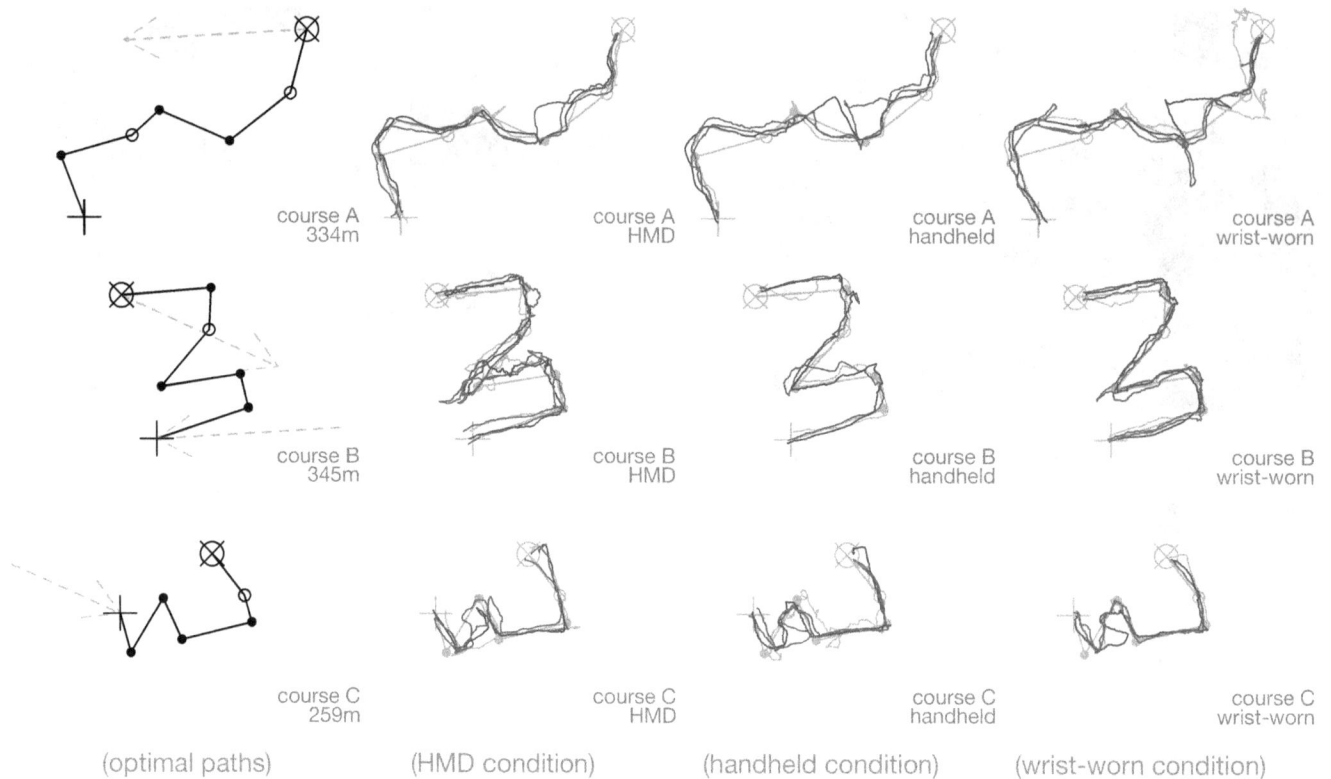

Figure 5. A visualization of the optimal paths and actual paths taken in the user study. Courses are arrayed vertically (A–C); optimal paths are in the leftmost column with display modalities in the right three. Starting points are marked with a plus (+), end points marked with a circle-X (⊗). Waypoints are indicated as filled circles for turns of approximately 90°; open circles for others. For the optimal paths, gray arrows indicate how courses connect together in a sequence. Colors are not mapped to data, only for distinguishing traversed paths.

As *PhotoNav* is played outdoors, players were first invited to a computer lab where participants provided informed consent. A video was then shown to introduce them to the game and its rules. The video explained the game interface, game mechanics, and instructions to operate the chording keyboard and how to focus on the HMD. We chose to use a video introduction, rather than tutorial, to avoid biasing participants toward a particular modality. The use of a video ensured that participants did not gain actual experience using the system prior to playing the game. The participants were then asked to complete a demographics and a navigation questionnaire. The demographics questionnaire consisted of age, gender, education. The navigation questionnaire addressed experience navigating, familiarity with GPS devices, and mixed reality games. It captured participants' navigation preferences and self-rating of prior navigation experiences using GPS and maps: the usage context (e.g. car, pedestrian).

Data Collection

During the user study, an XML-based log file recorded participants' game data, capturing game state, sensor state, and interaction state during each play. For game state, the log file recorded participant's time to reach each waypoint and current game progress. Sensor state consisted of GPS and compass data, which were taken at 1Hz: GPS coordinates, GPS health data (e.g., dilution of precision, number of satellites tracked), and compass orientation. We recorded the duration of time

the UI was active (i.e., the player held the UI activate button on the Twiddler) and participants' indication of familiarity with the destination waypoints (i.e., when the player held the familiarity button for 10 seconds, the destination was marked familiar).

We asked the participants to fill out multiple ordinal questions after each session with each display modality. The Likert-scale questions we analyze for the present phase of research are the following:

1. How easy / difficult was it to view photographic clue on the display?
   ["very easy", "easy", "neutral", "difficult", "very difficult"];

2. Rate the display in matching images to the outside world:
   ["very easy", "easy", "neutral", "difficult", "very difficult"];

3. Rate the display in ease of viewing the interface:
   ["very easy", "easy", "neutral", "difficult", "very difficult"];

4. How safe did you feel while using the device and walking along the way points?
   ["very safe", "safe", "neutral", "unsafe", "very unsafe"];

5. Before the study, how familiar were you with the course?
   ["very unfamiliar", "unfamiliar", "neutral", "familiar", "very familiar"];

6. Where did you focus the most in the interface?
   [Multiple allowed: "destination", "hint", "time", "overall progress", "current progress"].

We also asked participants how enjoyable they found the game.

EXPERIMENT EXECUTION

In fall and winter of 2015, a study was conducted on *PhotoNav* with 12 volunteers (5 female) from the student population of NMSU. Participants' ages ranged from 24–35 years old ($M = 27$, $SD = 3.4$). All participants were graduate students. All participants had used smartphones; none reported prior use of HMD or smartwatch. The study used a within-subjects design with display condition (HMD, handheld display, wrist-worn display) counterbalanced.

The wearable itself is unchanged for the conditions, only the active display is switched so that ergonomics of the wearable impact all conditions evenly. The participants were asked to follow the courses based on the game UI for the condition's display modality.

DATA ANALYSES

The XML data logs, generated from the *PhotoNav* game, were processed to determine each participant's time to reach each waypoint. From this, we calculated the average course traversal speed of each player (defined as the course distance divided by course completion time). Additionally, each player's location data were compared to the optimal path of the course (i.e., an optimal path was generated by using shortest distance between each waypoint, shown in Figure 5. Root-mean-square distance (RMSD) error was computed to investigate how much participants deviated from the optimal path. We calculated the percentage of time the UI was active during course traversal by each participant. Questionnaire data were compiled for statistical analyses.

Statistical Analyses

The independent variable was display modality and was manipulated within-subjects. The dependent variable was average course traversal speed, rather than completion time, since the latter was confounded by course length and difficulty. RMSD and the percentage of time participants actively used the *PhotoNav* interface were included in the analyses as covariates. Rather than a traditional analysis of variance (ANOVA), a linear mixed-model analysis was employed due to the presence of time-varying covariates in the design and partial data loss from one participant. While linear-mixed model techniques are relatively new, they are equally effective and more robust than traditional ANOVAs [21]. The complete linear-mixed model contained a single fixed factor, display modality, and the two aforementioned covariates. In addition, we used nonparametric Chi-square tests (Friedman and Wilcoxon signed-rank) to examine responses to the questionnaire.

All participants completed the courses successfully using each interface. Movement data were successfully recorded from 11 of the 12 participants, with partial data loss for the final participant (values for RMSD and interface usage were unavailable in the handheld condition only; other values were captured). The data loss was minor and discovered late. Our choice of

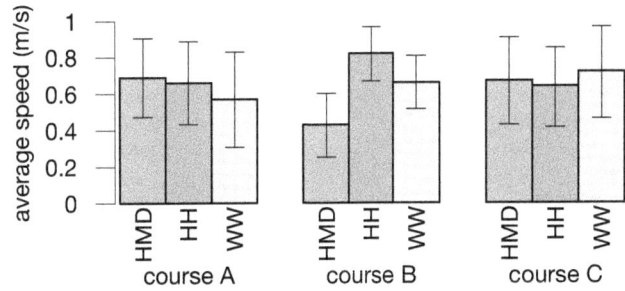

Figure 6. Estimated marginal means of player speed on each course with each display modality, accounting for covariates; error bars denote 95% confidence interval. (Note that HH is handheld and WW is wrist-worn.)

linear mixed models analysis is robust to missing data and allowed us to retain this participant in our analyses.

RESULTS

Movement Data

A visualization of the actual paths taken by players compared to the optimal paths appears in Figure 5. For Course B, the analysis revealed a significant effect of display modality, $[F(2, 5.58) = 6.44, p = .035]^4$. Sidak-adjusted pairwise comparisons showed that participants traversed the course significantly faster using the handheld display ($M = .82$) when compared with the HMD ($M = .43$); performance for the wrist-worn display ($M = .66$) did not differ from the others. However, there was no effect of display modality in Course A $[F(2, 4.1) = .30, p = .76]$ nor in Course C $[F(2, 5.28) = .17, p = .85]$ (Figure 6). RMSD and the percentage of time that participants actively utilized the UI did not covary significantly with average course traversal speed (A RMSD: $[F(1, 4.53) = 3.74, p = .12]$, A UI use: $[F(1, 5.38) = 2.24, p = .19]$; B RMSD: $[F(1, 5.47) = 1.34, p = .30]$, B UI use: $[F(1, 3.69) = 1.86, p = .25]$; C RMSD: $[F(1, 5.78) = 1.20, p = .32]$, C UI use: $[F(1, 6.94) = 2.08, p = .19]$).

Questionnaire Results

We conducted Friedman and Wilcoxon signed-ranked (Chi-square) tests on participants questionnaire responses (questions described previously): ease of viewing clues, sense of safety, ease of viewing, and ease of matching. The sole independent variable was display modality. Figure 7 shows participant's rankings of different display modalities.

The Friedman test revealed significant differences in participants' rankings of the ease of viewing clues with the three interface modalities $[\chi^2(2) = 6.62, p = .037]$. Wilcoxon signed-rank tests on each pair of modalities revealed significant differences between rankings of the HMD ($M = 2.75$) and wrist-worn ($M = 3.92$) modalities $[z = -2.14, p = .032]$, and marginal differences in rankings between HMD ($M = 2.75$) and handheld ($M = 3.92$) modalities $[z = -1.85, p = .064]$. No difference in participants' rankings was observed between the handheld and wrist-worn modalities $[z = 0]$.

Similarly, there was a significant effect of display modality $[\chi^2(2) = 7.00, p = .030]$ for participants' perceived safety

---

[4]Note that fractional degrees of freedom are standard in linear mixed-model analyses [43].

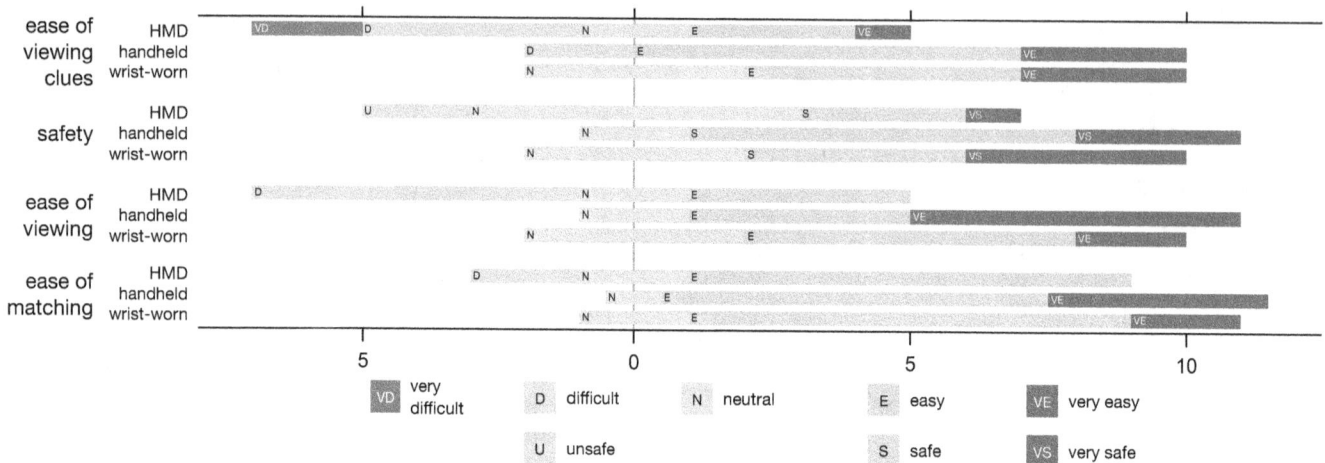

Figure 7. Participants' rankings of display modalities for ease of viewing hints, safety, ease of viewing in general, and ease of matching with the environment. X-axis is the counts of each response by participants. Results indicate that the HMD is *not* favored by participants.

while navigating the courses using *PhotoNav*. Wilcoxon signed-rank tests on each pair of modalities revealed significant differences between rankings of the HMD ($M = 3.50$) and handheld ($M = 4.10$) modalities [$z = -2.33$, $p = .020$], and marginal differences in rankings between HMD ($M = 3.50$) and wrist-worn ($M = 4.00$) modalities [$z = -1.73$, $p = .084$]. No difference in participants' rankings was observed between the hand-held and wrist-worn modalities [$z = .38$, $p = .705$].

For ease of viewing, the effect of display modality was significant [$\chi^2(2) = 6.54$, $p = .038$]. Wilcoxon signed-rank tests on each pair of modalities revealed significant differences between rankings of the HMD ($M = 2.83$) and handheld ($M = 4.33$) modalities [$z = -2.44$, $p = .015$], and significant differences in rankings between HMD ($M = 2.83$) and wrist-worn ($M = 3.83$) modalities [$z = -2.18$, $p = .029$]. There was a marginal difference in participants' rankings between the hand-held ($M = 4.33$) and wrist-worn ($M = 3.83$) modalities [$z = -1.90$, $p = .058$].

Likewise, for ease of matching *PhotoNav* images with the outside world, the effect of display modality was significant [$\chi^2(2) = 6.74$, $p = .034$]. Wilcoxon signed-rank tests on each pair of modalities revealed significant differences between rankings of the HMD ($M = 3.50$) and handheld ($M = 4.25$) modalities [$z = -2.07$, $p = .038$], and marginal differences in rankings between handheld ($M = 4.25$) and wrist-worn ($M = 4.00$) modalities [$z = -1.73$, $p = .083$]. No difference in participants' rankings was observed between the HMD and wrist-worn modalities [$z = -1.511$, $p = .131$].

Additionally, we asked each participant what display modality they would prefer for outdoor navigation, 7 preferred handheld, 3 preferred wrist-worn, and 2 preferred head-mounted display. In response to which UI elements the participants focused on, to which participants could respond with multiple answers, we found that the hint photographic clue was mentioned 10 times; the current progress indicator 4 times; the overall progress indicator 4 times; and the destination photographic hint 1 time. None mentioned the time indicator.

For game enjoyment, across 36 ratings (12 participants × 3 courses) no participants indicated that the game was "unenjoyable", 3 indicated "somewhat unenjoyable", and 2 were "neutral"; of the remaining 31: 14 considered the game "enjoyable" and 17 "very enjoyable".

Course Familiarity

Across all participants and courses, the familiarity button was only used twice. After completing each course, participants were asked about their familiarity with the course. Across 36 ratings (12 participants × 3 courses) participants never indicated that they were "very familiar" or "familiar", 14 were "neutral", 10 were "unfamiliar" and 12 were "very unfamiliar".

DISCUSSION

In our study, we found that participants preferred using handheld or wrist-worn displays, but we also know that this is what participants are familiar with using in their everyday lives. It might be possible that features of our particular courses might have impacted the results. The study provided insights into the design of interfaces for wearables and mixed reality systems.

Analyzing Game Design

Overall, the data suggest the design of *PhotoNav* is successful. Participants' lack of familiarity with the courses suggests that course designs were effective, though an alternative explanation is that the workload of indicating familiarity was too high. Lack of familiarity indicates that participants would be reliant on the game, rather than their prior experience, to traverse the environment. Further, most participants paid attention to the hint view, which is the part of the UI we expect them to use to play. Participants reported that *PhotoNav* was fun.

Issues with Head-Mounted Displays

Our data suggest that there remain challenges for using HMDs in the physical world. In the present research, we observed issues with ambient light (e.g., sunlight) and challenges in merging the visual field. The HMD conditions performed the poorest, and were least preferred by participants.

The prior research in this space aligns with our findings. The study conducted by Vadas et al. [47] found that the HMD's walking performance was worst. Similarly, Yeh et al. [52] observed that handheld displays performed better than HMDs. Our prior pilot study [38] of *PhotoNav* also showed that handheld performed better than HMD.

Ambient Light
Due to the use of a see-through HMD, one of the difficulties of outdoor experiments was found to be ambient light and glare caused by the sun. We observed that participants used their hands to block the ambient light while using the HMD so they could view the interface clearly. This aligns with a prior finding on the *ARQuake* game [44] that points out that bright sunlight makes it difficult to differentiate some colors from natural surroundings. Kerr et al. [19] also point out difficulty in viewing display because of bright sunlight. Since our game involves comparing images, some parts of the photographic clues might not have been clearly visible to participants in bright sunlight. Even though the HMD had a polarizing light filter to cut down on glare, and our prototyping experiments found it to be the best available with regards to sunlight, participants found it difficult to match images or see the UI.

Four out of 12 participants indicated that bright lights made it difficult to view images while using HMDs. P4 mentioned:

> ...HMD screen is transparent, which makes it difficult to see the hints under bright lights. I would suggest the screen to be made less transparent.

Challenges in Merging the Visual Field
When using the HMD, some participants mentioned that they found it difficult to match images because it was challenging to merge their visual field with the display. P11 mentioned:

> For HMD, it was hard for me to concentrate on the system image while the view of the physical surrounding were presented on the background.

In the case of handheld or wrist-worn displays, the display is opaque and users can view information without distraction. Some studies have tried to provide recommendations on interface design to maximize visual recognition of interface elements. A study conducted by Gabbard et al. [24], studied six background textures commonly found in outdoor environments and six drawing styles and provide recommendations on colour choices and drawing style. Renkewitz et al. [35] conclude that colour and size of fonts used in HMDs should vary according to background, and they provide recommendations on optimal font size. Peterson et al. [35] found that selection time during visual search task is reduced by distributing overlapping labels in depth.

Context of Use
The *PhotoNav* UI was held constant across display modalities to avoid introducing bias, yet, Vogl et al. [48] concluded that interface design should be based on device and use context. Yeh et al. [52] found that clutter on HMDs rendered it less effective than handhelds with similar information. When we

take this with the data on the weakness of the HMD in *PhotoNav*, it suggests that handheld or wrist-worn devices can be designed to provide more complex information (e.g., the norm for smartphones), while HMD use cases should minimize information and use *micro-interactions* (see next section).

In the conducted experiment, there were significant differences among the display modalities solely when participants traversed Course B. Courses A and C had many open areas, so players' freedom within the game rules resulted in larger number of decisions about where to go. Course B primarily ran in open spaces between buildings (not close enough to interfere with GPS), thus, players needed to make fewer decisions in the movement core mechanic. In addition, since participants were not provided a tutorial session, we expect that they acclimated to *PhotoNav* during Course A, where participants were getting used to the game interface and the nature of the mixed reality game. The pre-questionnaire showed that none of the participants had played mixed reality games before.

Device Familiarity
Our data suggest that participants' prior device experience biases their experience of display modality. We recorded display familiarity in pre-questionnaire and participants were not familiar with HMDs or wrist-worn displays; but were familiar with handheld displays. At the same time, handheld displays performed the best and were preferred by participants. Three participants said that they preferred the handheld device due to habitual use of a smartphone; P7 mentioned:

> I was comfortable using the handheld display during the game because it was familiar to a smartphone and it was easy to handle it using my hand without putting pressure on any other body part like my wrist or head.

Despite the HMD offering the ability to see a player's surroundings, the familiarity of the handheld devices enables adept use by participants that they consider safe.

Social Acceptance
An informal observation was that participants were concerned about social acceptance of the wearable computer. Some participants preferred not to play the game during weekdays because of pedestrian crowd. They did not feel comfortable wearing the HMD in a crowded area. Profita et al. [34] surveyed 1,200 participants to analyze social acceptability of HMDs in a public setting. They examined how participant's judgment on the use of HMDs changed when information about HMD user's disability was made known. Their findings reveal that if the device was being used to support a person with a disability, HMD use was more socially acceptable.

DESIGN IMPLICATIONS
We derive design implications for wearable computers supporting mixed reality games based on our data with *PhotoNav*.

Display Opacity
See-through HMDs enable users to observe the physical environment; this is assumed to support situation awareness. Beyond issues with ambient light, problems with merging the visual field, especially with monocular displays, might pose

a distraction while viewing information on the HMD. In fact, our participants found that the HMD inhibited their sense of safety, suggesting that the HMD did not support environment situation awareness.

One design choice might be to develop a modal display that can be almost opaque when information is displayed and see-through when it is not. This would enable users to focus on the display for information, and maintain situation awareness when focus is elsewhere. A study by Laramee and Ware [22] also suggested that monocular transparent HMDs are not very useful in dynamically changing environments. We thus argue for the value of opaque displays, at least for monocular HMDs when there is a need to display complex information on the HMD screen. Future iterations of the *PhotoNav* experiment will test see-through and opaque displays.

Detail Depends on Modality
Our data, taken with prior work, suggest that information detail should depend heavily on display modality. We expect that HMD use cases should focus on *micro-interactions*, events that take place briefly (i.e., four seconds or less) [2], rather than interfaces with prolonged interaction. Micro-interactions should be based on screen elements that are easy to spot on the HMD, with minimal detail. A study conducted by Vogl et al. [48] on everyday use of head-worn computers also suggested that HMDs should be used for micro-interactions. Further bolstering this point is an earlier study by Oulasvirta et al. [33], which showed users' attention span for a mobile device is about 4–8 seconds.

Since many outdoor use cases of display modalities require users to split their attention, we suggest that in case of viewing tasks, UIs should be designed for micro-interactions. We suggest that handheld displays can still have complex interactions compared to HMDs since handhelds provide less distractions as UI is not merged with the environment. Further experiments are needed to determine how details in interfaces should be adapted based on display modalities.

Static Interfaces
The *PhotoNav* interface is an information-display interface: players did not need to navigate the UI for further information. Our questionnaire results suggest that players focused mostly on the hint photographic clue and the current progress indicator. The results suggest that immediate contextual information is crucial for tasks requiring split attention.

Affordances and Constraints of Physical-World Spaces
Norman considers how artifacts enable action through affordances and prevent action through constraints [32]; these properties apply to physical-world environments as well. We advise designers of mixed reality games to consider the physical world context of play not just as *found objects* [23] that afford physical gameplay or facilitate safety, but as an essential object, to which the player *always* attends, leverages, and engages with, as a component of play. For example, many photographic clues did not contain images that showed names of buildings, this was done to introduce more challenge to the players by utilizing nature of the environment.

MacIntyre identifies *aura* of places as the intangible significance of a physical location [25], which has implications for the narratives one might develop in a space. In prior systems (e.g., [13, 51]) location becomes vital part of mixed reality experience that connects participants to a narrative.

We observe that weather plays a big part in scheduling a mixed reality game, as many times the game session had to be canceled prior to the start because of cold weather. The game had to be run during the daytime so this limited gameplay schedule. Standard digital games that can be played in PCs, consoles or mobile phone do not come with constraints of weather, sunlight or daylight, the nature of outdoor mixed reality games make it challenging to reach a mass audience.

CONCLUSION
In this paper, we described a mixed reality game, *PhotoNav*, in which participants navigate the physical world, guided by photographic clues. The game design is aimed at investigating the architecture of wearable computers, specifically selecting the best display modality for navigation. Furthermore, we presented the results of a user study, in which participants played *PhotoNav* while traversing different courses using three distinctive display modalities.

Our results showed that handheld displays performed better in one of the courses and users preferred handheld as well. While we expected the HMD to outperform other modalities, we discovered the opposite. Factors that might have resulted in players poor performance included ambient sunlight and participants' inability to discern information displayed on the interface. Lack of familiarity with the display modality also likely contributed to the HMD's failure.

Our data, synthesized with the literature, suggest a number of design implications for mixed reality systems. The see-through nature of some HMDs inhibits readability, which suggests that such displays should be opaque when data is displayed. The level of detail that should be used in a UI depends on the display modality: HMDs are best suited to low-detail information that changes infrequently. Finally, spaces afford and constrain action, and physical space should be deeply incorporated into the design of mixed reality games.

Open questions remain about how UIs can best adapt, in terms of design and detail, to match context of use and type of device. As new and improved HMDs become more mainstream, investigation of HMDs that adapt their transparency according to ambient light and root their design on micro-interactions might be useful. In light of the UIs' context dependency and display modalities, accurate comparison of such modalities while optimizing their design remains a big challenge.

ACKNOWLEDGMENTS
We thank all of our research subjects. Author Sharma wishes to thank Sultan A. Alharthi for helping with video development. Author Toups wishes to thank NMSU for its financial support of his team. This material is based upon work supported by the National Science Foundation under Grant Nos. IIS-0803854, IIS-0742947.

REFERENCES

1. Daniel Ashbrook, Kent Lyons, James Clawson, and Thad Starner. 2009. *Smart Clothing: Technology and Applications*. CRC Press, Chapter Methods of Evaluation for Wearable Computing, 229–248.

2. Daniel Lee Ashbrook. 2010. *Enabling Mobile Microinteractions*. Ph.D. Dissertation. Massachusetts Institute of Technology.

3. Ronald T. Azuma. 1999. The Challenge of Making Augmented Reality Work Outdoors. In *Mixed Reality: Merging Real and Virtual*. Springer-Verlag, 379–390.

4. Ashweeni Beeharee and Anthony Steed. 2007. Minimising pedestrian navigational ambiguities through geoannotation and temporal tagging. In *Human-Computer Interaction. Interaction Platforms and Techniques*. Springer, 748–757.

5. Ashweeni Kumar Beeharee and Anthony Steed. 2006. A Natural Wayfinding Exploiting Photos in Pedestrian Navigation Systems. In *Proceedings of the 8th Conference on Human-computer Interaction with Mobile Devices and Services (MobileHCI '06)*. ACM, New York, NY, USA, 81–88. DOI: http://dx.doi.org/10.1145/1152215.1152233

6. Steve Benford, Andy Crabtree, Martin Flintham, Adam Drozd, Rob Anastasi, Mark Paxton, Nick Tandavanitj, Matt Adams, and Ju Row-Farr. 2006. Can you see me now? *ACM Transactions on Computer-Human Interaction* 13, 1 (2006), 100–133. DOI: http://dx.doi.org/10.1145/1143518.1143522

7. Steve Benford and Gabriella Giannachi. 2011. *Performing Mixed Reality*. MIT Press.

8. Olav W. Bertelsen and Christina Nielsen. 2000. Augmented Reality As a Design Tool for Mobile Interfaces. In *Proceedings of the 3rd Conference on Designing Interactive Systems: Processes, Practices, Methods, and Techniques (DIS '00)*. ACM, New York, NY, USA, 185–192. DOI: http://dx.doi.org/10.1145/347642.347714

9. Elizabeth M. Bonsignore, Derek L. Hansen, Zachary O. Toups, Lennart E. Nacke, Anastasia Salter, and Wayne Lutters. 2012. Mixed reality games. In *Proceedings of the ACM 2012 conference on Computer Supported Cooperative Work Companion (CSCW '12)*. ACM, New York, NY, USA, 7–8. DOI: http://dx.doi.org/10.1145/2141512.2141517

10. Gaetano Borriello, Matthew Chalmers, Anthony LaMarca, and Paddy Nixon. 2005. Delivering Real-world Ubiquitous Location Systems. *Commun. ACM* 48, 3 (March 2005), 36–41. DOI: http://dx.doi.org/10.1145/1047671.1047701

11. Bo Dahlbom and E. Ljungberg. 1998. Mobile informatics. *Scandinavian Journal of Information Systems* 10 (1998), 227–234.

12. Paul Dourish. 2001. *Where the Action Is: The Foundations of Embodied Interaction* (1st ed.). MIT Press, Cambridge, MA, USA.

13. Steven Dow, Jaemin Lee, Christopher Oezbek, Blair MacIntyre, Jay David Bolter, and Maribeth Gandy. 2005. Exploring Spatial Narratives and Mixed Reality Experiences in Oakland Cemetery. In *Proceedings of the 2005 ACM SIGCHI International Conference on Advances in Computer Entertainment Technology (ACE '05)*. ACM, New York, NY, USA, 51–60. DOI: http://dx.doi.org/10.1145/1178477.1178484

14. Steven Fadden, Patricia May Ververs, and Christopher D. Wickens. 1998. Costs and benefits of head-up display use: A meta-analytic approach. In *Proceedings of the Human Factors and Ergonomics Society Annual Meeting 1998*, Vol. 42. 16–20.

15. Steven Feiner, Blair MacIntyre, Tobias Hollerer, and Anthony Webster. 1997. A Touring Machine: Prototyping 3D Mobile Augmented Reality Systems for Exploring the Urban Environment. In *ISWC '97: Proceedings of the 1st IEEE International Symposium on Wearable Computers*. IEEE Computer Society, 208–217.

16. Jeffrey Hightower and Gaetano Borriello. 2001. Location Systems for Ubiquitous Computing. *Computer* 34, 8 (2001), 57–66. DOI: http://dx.doi.org/10.1109/2.940014

17. Andruid Kerne, Yin Qu, Andrew M. Webb, Sashikanth Damaraju, Nic Lupfer, and Abhinav Mathur. 2010. Meta-metadata: A Metadata Semantics Language for Collection Representation Applications. In *Proceedings of the 19th ACM International Conference on Information and Knowledge Management (CIKM '10)*. ACM, New York, NY, USA, 1129–1138. DOI: http://dx.doi.org/10.1145/1871437.1871580

18. Andruid Kerne, Zachary O. Toups, Blake Dworaczyk, and Madhur Khandelwal. 2008. A Concise XML Binding Framework Facilitates Practical Object-oriented Document Engineering. In *Proceedings of the Eighth ACM Symposium on Document Engineering (DocEng '08)*. ACM, New York, NY, USA, 62–65. DOI: http://dx.doi.org/10.1145/1410140.1410152

19. Steven J. Kerr, Mark D. Rice, Yinquan Teo, Marcus Wan, Yian Ling Cheong, Jamie Ng, Lillian Ng-Thamrin, Thant Thura-Myo, and Dominic Wren. 2011. Wearable Mobile Augmented Reality: Evaluating Outdoor User Experience. In *Proceedings of the 10th International Conference on Virtual Reality Continuum and Its Applications in Industry (VRCAI '11)*. ACM, New York, NY, USA, 209–216. DOI: http://dx.doi.org/10.1145/2087756.2087786

20. Steinar Kristoffersen and Fredrik Ljungberg. 1998. Representing modalities in mobile computing. *Proceedings of Interactive applications of mobile computing* (1998).

21. Charlene Krueger and Lili Tian. 2004. A Comparison of the General Linear Mixed Model and Repeated Measures ANOVA Using a Dataset with Multiple Missing Data Points. *Biological Research For Nursing* 6, 2 (2004), 151–157. DOI: http://dx.doi.org/10.1177/1099800404267682

22. Robert S. Laramee and Colin Ware. 2002. Rivalry and Interference with a Head-mounted Display. *ACM Trans. Comput.-Hum. Interact.* 9, 3 (Sept. 2002), 238–251. DOI: http://dx.doi.org/10.1145/568513.568516

23. Lucy R. Lippard. 1971. Marcel Duchamp. In *Dadas on Art: Tzara, Arp, Duchamp, and Others*, Lucy R. Lippard (Ed.). Dover Publications, Inc., 139–154.

24. Mark A. Livingston, Joseph L. Gabbard, J. Edward Swan II, Ciara M. Sibley, and Jane H. Barrow. 2013. Basic perception in head-worn augmented reality displays. In *Human factors in augmented reality environments*. Springer, 35–65.

25. Blair MacIntyre, Jay David Bolter, and Maribeth Gandy. 2004. Presence and aura of meaningful places. In *7th Annual International Workshop on Presence (PRESENCE 2004)*. 36–43.

26. Steve Mann. 1997. Wearable computing: A first step toward personal imaging. *Computer* 30, 2 (1997), 25–32.

27. Steve Mann, Jason Nolan, and Barry Wellman. 2003. Sousveillance: Inventing and using wearable computing devices for data collection in surveillance environments. *Surveillance & Society* 1, 3 (2003), 331–355.

28. Andrew J. May, Tracy Ross, Steven H Bayer, and Mikko J. Tarkiainen. 2003. Pedestrian navigation aids: Information requirements and design implications. *Personal and Ubiquitous Computing* 7, 6 (2003), 331–338.

29. Paul Milgram and Fumio Kishino. 1994. A taxonomy of mixed reality visual displays. *IEICE Transactions on Information and Systems* E77-D, 12 (1994), 1321–1329.

30. Keith Mitchell, Duncan McCaffery, George Metaxas, Joe Finney, Stefan Schmid, and Andrew Scott. 2003. Six in the city: Introducing Real Tournament - a mobile IPv6 based context-aware multiplayer game. In *NETGAMES '03: Proceedings of the 2nd Workshop on Network and System Support for Games*. ACM Press, 91–100. DOI: http://dx.doi.org/10.1145/963900.963909

31. Stefan Münzer, Hubert D. Zimmer, Maximilian Schwalm, Jörg Baus, and Ilhan Aslan. 2006. Computer-assisted navigation and the acquisition of route and survey knowledge. *Journal of Environmental Psychology* 26, 4 (2006), 300–308. DOI: http://dx.doi.org/10.1016/j.jenvp.2006.08.001

32. Don Norman. 2013. *The Design of Everyday Things: Revised and Expanded Edition* (revised 2013 ed.). Basic Books.

33. Antti Oulasvirta, Sakari Tamminen, Virpi Roto, and Jaana Kuorelahti. 2005. Interaction in 4-second Bursts: The Fragmented Nature of Attentional Resources in Mobile HCI. In *Proceedings of the SIGCHI Conference on Human Factors in Computing Systems (CHI '05)*. ACM, New York, NY, USA, 919–928. DOI: http://dx.doi.org/10.1145/1054972.1055101

34. Halley Profita, Reem Albaghli, Leah Findlater, Paul Jaeger, and Shaun K. Kane. 2016. The AT Effect: How Disability Affects the Perceived Social Acceptability of Head-Mounted Display Use. In *Proceedings of the 2016 CHI Conference on Human Factors in Computing Systems (CHI '16)*. ACM, New York, NY, USA, 4884–4895. DOI: http://dx.doi.org/10.1145/2858036.2858130

35. Helge Renkewitz, Verena Kinder, Mario Brandt, and Thomas Alexander. 2008. Optimal font size for head-mounted-displays in outdoor applications. In *Information Visualisation, 2008. IV'08. 12th International Conference*. IEEE, 503–508.

36. Katie Salen and Eric Zimmerman. 2004. *Rules of Play: Game Design Fundamentals*. MIT Press, Cambridge, MA, USA.

37. Beatriz Sousa Santos, Paulo Dias, Angela Pimentel, Jan-Willem Baggerman, Carlos Ferreira, Samuel Silva, and Joaquim Madeira. 2009. Head-mounted display versus desktop for 3D navigation in virtual reality: A user study. *Multimedia Tools and Applications* 41, 1 (2009), 161–181. http://dx.doi.org/10.1007/s11042-008-0223-2

38. Hitesh Nidhi Sharma, Zachary O. Toups, Ajit Jain, and Andruid Kerne. 2015. Designing to Split Attention in a Mixed Reality Game. In *Proceedings of the 2015 Annual Symposium on Computer-Human Interaction in Play (CHI PLAY '15)*. ACM, New York, NY, USA, 691–696. DOI:http://dx.doi.org/10.1145/2793107.2810289

39. Sarah Sharples, Sue Cobb, Amanda Moody, and John R. Wilson. 2008. Virtual reality induced symptoms and effects (VRISE): Comparison of head mounted display (HMD), desktop and projection display systems. *Displays* 29, 2 (2008), 58–69.

40. Thad Starner, Steve Mann, Bradley Rhodes, Jeffery Levine, Jennifer Healey, Dana Kirsch, Roz Picard, and Alex Pentland. 1997. Augmented Reality Through Wearable Computing. *Presence* 6, 4 (Winter 1997), 386–398.

41. Thad Eugene Starner. 1999. *Wearable computing and contextual awareness*. Ph.D. Dissertation. Massachusetts Institute of Technology. http://dx.doi.org/10.1162/pres.1997.6.4.386

42. Colin Swindells, Barry A. Po, Ima Hajshirmohammadi, Brian Corrie, John C. Dill, Brian D. Fisher, and Kellogg S. Booth. 2004. Comparing CAVE, wall, and desktop displays for navigation and wayfinding in complex 3D models. In *Proceedings of the Computer Graphics International*. IEEE Computer Society, 420–427. DOI: http://dx.doi.org/10.1109/CGI.2004.1309243

43. Kunio Takezawa. 2014. *Learning Regression Analysis by Simulation*. Springer Japan, Tokyo, Chapter Linear Mixed Model, 269–294. DOI: http://dx.doi.org/10.1007/978-4-431-54321-3_6

44. Bruce Thomas, Ben Close, John Donoghue, John Squires, Phillip De Bondi, Michael Morris, and Wayne Piekarski. 2000. ARQuake: An outdoor/indoor augmented reality first person application. In *Wearable Computers, The Fourth International Symposium on*. 139–146. DOI: http://dx.doi.org/10.1109/ISWC.2000.888480

45. Bruce Thomas, Ben Close, John Donoghue, John Squires, Phillip De Bondi, and Wayne Piekarski. 2002. First Person Indoor/Outdoor Augmented Reality Application: ARQuake. *Personal Ubiquitous Computing* 6, 1 (Jan. 2002), 75–86. DOI: http://dx.doi.org/10.1007/s007790200007

46. Daniela G. Trevisan, Monica Gemo, Jean Vanderdonckt, and Benoît Macq. 2004. Focus-based Design of Mixed Reality Systems. In *Proceedings of the 3rd Annual Conference on Task Models and Diagrams (TAMODIA '04)*. ACM, New York, NY, USA, 59–66. DOI: http://dx.doi.org/10.1145/1045446.1045458

47. Kristin Vadas, Kent Lyons, Daniel Ashbrook, Ji Soo Yi, Thad Starner, and Julie Jacko. 2006. *Reading on the Go: An Evaluation of Three Mobile Display Technologies*. Technical Report GIT-GVU-06-09. Georgia Institute of Technology.

48. Anita Vogl, Nicolas Louveton, Rod McCall, Mark Billinghurst, and Michael Haller. 2015. Understanding the everyday use of head-worn computers. In *Human System Interactions (HSI), 2015 8th International Conference on*. IEEE, 213–219.

49. Christopher D. Wickens. 1997. Attentional issues in head-up displays. *Engineering psychology and cognitive ergonomics:* 1 (1997), 3–21.

50. Christopher D. Wickens and Jeffry Long. 1995. Object versus space-based models of visual attention: Implications for the design of head-up displays. *Journal of Experimental Psychology: Applied* 1, 3 (1995), 179.

51. Jason Wither, Rebecca Allen, Vids Samanta, Juha Hemanus, Yun-Ta Tsai, Ronald Azuma, Will Carter, Rachel Hinman, and Thommen Korah. 2010. The westwood experience: connecting story to locations via mixed reality. In *2010 IEEE International Symposium On Mixed and Augmented Reality-Arts, Media, and Humanities (ISMAR-AMH)*. IEEE, 39–46.

52. Michelle Yeh, James L. Merlo, Christopher D. Wickens, and David L. Brandenburg. 2003. Head up versus head down: The costs of imprecision, unreliability, and visual clutter on cue effectiveness for display signaling. *Human Factors: The Journal of the Human Factors and Ergonomics Society* 45, 3 (2003), 390–407.

53. Jean-Marie Zogg. 2007. *Essentials of Satellite Navigation - Compendium*. Technical Report GPS-X-02007-C. u-blox AG.

Roles People Play: Key Roles Designed to Promote Participation and Learning in Alternate Reality Games

Elizabeth Bonsignore[1], Derek Hansen[2], Kari Kraus[1], Amanda Visconti[3], and Ann Fraistat[1]

[1]Human-Computer Interaction Lab
University of Maryland,
College Park, MD 20742 USA
{ebonsign,kkraus}@umd.edu

[2] School of Technology
Brigham Young University
Provo, UT, USA
dlhansen@byu.edu

[3]Purdue Libraries
Purdue University
West Lafayette, IN, USA
aviscont@purdue.edu

ABSTRACT

In this paper, we outline specific roles that are used by designers of Alternate Reality Games (ARGs) to help promote and sustain player participation and provide educational scaffolding. These roles were derived through analysis of a representative sample of ARGs and two case studies of small scale, education-based ARGs. In particular, we found that the approach that designers take to incorporate in-game protagonists ("protagonist-by-proxies" and "protagonist-mentors") can influence the ways in which 1) players gain access to the disparate narrative and ludic elements within an ARG and 2) designers can integrate collaborative learning opportunities authentically into the narrative and gameplay.

Author Keywords

Alternate Reality Games; serious games; design; collaboration; participation; social roles.

ACM Classification Keywords

K.4.0 [Computers and Society]: General; K.3.0 [Computers and Education]: General.

INTRODUCTION

Identifying key roles that individuals play in games is an important research strand in human-computer interaction (HCI) and related fields in the social sciences [32]. Studies that inform our understanding of social roles have been applied to improve the design of social technologies [40,52,70] as well as enhance cooperative, multiplayer game play [7,57,61,76]. This paper extends research on the design and influence of social roles in multiplayer games with a focus on a popular collaborative play experience known as the Alternate Reality Game (ARG).

An ARG is a form of transmedia storytelling [33] whose narrative context is not bound within any single communications platform or media type. An ARG is also a type of pervasive game, with interactive elements that are "woven into the fabric of the real world" [8:1], such as messages and clues that are scattered and hidden in billboards, in websites, phone calls, text messages, or books [39,45]. If *Alice in Wonderland* were adapted as an ARG, for example, a player might receive a text message from the Rabbit that contains GPS coordinates to an encrypted clue, which the player could upload to a discussion forum for other players to help decode, then email the results to the Mad Hatter to advance the story.

Player collaboration is a primary design goal for ARG designers, who strive "to create puzzles and challenges that no single person could solve on their own" [46:203]. Indeed, players in ARGs often successfully navigate the same problems that workers in knowledge organizations[1] face, such as making sense of disparate data distributed across multiple media, or defining and coordinating problem-solving tasks [15,25,39,46]. Players in the ARG, *I Love Bees* (*ILB*) organized themselves into different sub-groups, each representing competing theories about story data they had collected, in order to determine the best interpretation and collective plan of action [46,57]. Because of the success with which players collectively operate in many ARGs, they also offer insight into potential designs for collaborative methods and tools that support knowledge organizations and learning communities [8,25,39,58]. By "learning communities," we refer to diverse social groups that emphasize social interaction, active and situated learning [19,71]), and can be formal (e.g., in a school, classroom, or professional organization), or informal (e.g., an after-school club, social media network) [42].

Although successful collaborations are a key characteristic of ARGs, many ARGs fail to 1) attract sufficient participation and/or 2) promote and scaffold learning (especially for younger or more inexperienced players). For example, two ARG design teams targeting youth and young adults in informal learning contexts struggled to recruit players [69,73]. Despite a strong marketing plan and a

---

[1] We define knowledge organizations as those whose primary interactions depend on the transfer of information, typically via communications technologies [6,25,66].

CHI PLAY '16, October 16-19, 2016, Austin, TX, USA

© 2016 ACM. ISBN 978-1-4503-4456-2/16/10...$15.00

DOI: http://dx.doi.org/10.1145/2967934.2968108

robust mixed reality design, Sylvan et al. [69] were not able to develop and sustain an adequate player base for their environmental science game for older teens (15-17 years old), *Canaries in a Coalmine*. Although the registration page for Canaries logged 2000 – 3000 visits during its initial launch (August 2011), only 75 players actually registered; approximately 20 players posted content; and only 10 players engaged in the chat sessions required to advance the game's storyline [69]. Even after the designers revised and re-released the game based on lessons learned from the first release, "a sustainable community did not form" [69:5]. Similarly, *ARGOSI*, an ARG that targeted undergraduate students (18-21 years old), failed to recruit and sustain a substantial player base [N. Whitton, personal interview, January 2011]. *ARGOSI* was designed to support undergraduate students as they transition into university life and learn to use library/research resources at a university in the U.K. While several hundred students were targeted, only about 10-20 students completed the ARG [73].

Relatedly, participation patterns in some ARGs reveal how designers can miss the mark for promoting productive collective action and learning, and instead, create an echo chamber of player opinions and attitudes that may appear effective in the ARG's fictional context, but would be ineffectual or even erroneous when applied to "real-world" problem-solving situations [31]. For example, players in *World Without Oil* (*WWO*) [18] shared personal narratives about their efforts to survive a global oil crisis that added a human interest touch to community efforts; however, they often failed to develop effective sustainability solutions that were grounded in factual, evidence-based research [30].

Consequently, investigating the social roles that ARG creators integrate into their designs to promote and sustain participation can inform the design and implementation of future ARGs and similar transmedia experiences, especially in learning contexts [8,25,46,57]. Categorizing these social roles can also enhance our understanding of the ways in which problem-solving communities self-organize and offer options for designers to explicitly engineer mechanisms for more productive roles into future designs [25,47,57]. While previous, focused studies of specific ARGs have laid the groundwork for such categorizations [15,25,31,45,57], the research presented in this paper aims to extend these individual accounts by developing a broader framework of social roles that support participation in ARGs overall.

This paper makes the following contributions to games-based research and social computing design. First, we identify specific social roles that are considered critical by ARG designers for engaging and sustaining player interest, participation, and collaborative sense-making (i.e., how social groups work toward a shared understanding of a situation or problem, and develop strategies to address it [4,17,59]). To do so, we studied a select sample of past ARGs and interviewed several ARG designers, focusing our analysis on the question, *"What key social roles have ARG designers used to promote and sustain participation, and model positive learning behaviors within learning communities?"* Second, we present two case studies to examine how specific roles from our framework were designed into the storylines for two ARGs that target youth (13 – 17 years old). Of note, the two case studies were implemented in two different learning contexts: 1) a middle school social studies class and 2) a public library summer reading program. Our case studies detail the ways in which ARG designers tried to integrate characters that modeled positive and productive learning behaviors.

RELATED WORK
We situate our study within the context of previous studies on social roles in ARGs and similar mixed reality experiences. We also draw from research in videogames to lay the groundwork for our study's approach.

Related Research on Roles in ARGs and Mixed Reality Experiences
Current research on ARGs largely attends to actual game play and player participation [15,45,46], and their implications for design [57,76]. Several studies have conducted detailed qualitative analyses, offering thick descriptions of the ways in which ARG player communities self-organize to solve problems [24,58] or develop community resources to support collaboration and sense-making [15].

For example, Peyton et al. [57,58] analyzed the military language and culture that *ILB* players adopted to collect and make sense of scattered clues as they propelled their play toward a successful endgame. These roles were determined by leadership behaviors that were mapped to military tropes: players organized themselves into "platoons", "squads", and "armies" or advocated for promotion of peer players to higher ranks like "general" or "lieutenant" [58]. Similarly, based on her analysis of multiple ARGs, Dena [15] developed a typology of game resources that players create to support their sense-making, along with a framework regarding the types of players who create these resources. Player-created "tiers of interaction" [15] include story fragment aggregators or recaps (e.g., "trails" or game guides), puzzle-solving tools (e.g., code charts, alphanumeric converters, and decryption toolsets such as those found at ARG community sites like "Unfiction," http://www.unfiction.com/resource/otools/). From an educational perspective, player-produced game resources are exemplary forms of participatory culture and community knowledge production [8,15,34], because they reformulate and remix ARG designer content (i.e., "primary producer") into formats that enable novice and non-players to access and enjoy distributed, often complex narratives. Indeed, some studies have found that spectators, or more passive consumers of ARGs and related mixed reality games represent a social position that is just as important to designers to consider as other more active roles [5,53].

The military roles that *ILB* players assumed as they tackled its puzzles and challenges offered a productive self-organizing strategy that has attracted the interest of knowledge management organizations [24,25] and education communities [36,51,73]. In contrast, Jafarinaimi et al.'s [30,31] analysis of the roles players assumed in *WWO* underscores the educational limitations of an ARG design that failed to attract players with opinions and data that expanded beyond the narrow set of sustainability practices continually proposed by the design team.

Instead, the player roles that Jafarinaimi et al. [30] identified reflect the *WWO* designers' inability to sustain meaningful participation. For example, *Toe-dippers*, *Late-comers*, and *Drop-outs* [30] were able to quickly and easily contribute to the *WWO's* community dialogue on sustainability due to an easy-to-use online site design and the low barrier to entry that its designers gave ("Tell us YOUR story"). However, these players did not consistently contribute and typically stopped playing after a short time (e.g., one week). Furthermore, most of the *Regulars* and members of the design team did not offer feedback that challenged players to move beyond micro-sustainable actions (e.g., ride a bike to work) or extended their knowledge about sustainability in general (e.g., find and share factual resources rather than offer subjective, often misleading personal stories). The player roles that Jafarinaimi et al. [30] identified from *WWO* participation profiles suggests strategies for designing ARGs that result in more innovative problem-solving solutions; however, [30] stopped short of examining how designers might design and implement ARG character-based roles to promote more meaningful participation. In addition, the inconsistent cycles of participation that *WWO* players exhibited [31] underscores a challenge that designers of ARGs [69], related community-based games [50] and online communities alike [41,44] must address: what social roles, toolsets, or other components can be integrated into these experiences to promote and sustain participation?

In their investigation of the design of a mixed reality game related to ARGs, Gonzales et al. [21] found that even "a wacky, volunteer scavenger hunt" like the "Greatest International Scavenger Hunt the World Has Ever Seen" (*GISHWHES*) revealed the same sorts of "user roles" that have been found in professional IT organizations [21:955]. The main difference between scavenger-hunt-based games like GISHWHES and ARGs is the primacy of story, and the player community's role in enacting the story as they interact with its transmedia elements. From a learning perspective, designers of the mixed reality game, *Operation: Citadel*, defined various roles for the docents who helped guide players through a history-based experience in a national historic site [76].

Overall, these studies have analyzed player participation patterns to derive their role sets from the roles and behaviors that *players* and player communities assume to collaborate and support their own engagement. In contrast, our study shifts its analytic focus to the ways in which *designers* endeavor to create and employ characters within the ARG narrative to promote participation and collaboration. We also examine the ways in which ARG designers can craft special player roles during gameplay to monitor and enhance player engagement. Furthermore, these studies focus their analysis on specific ARGs. Our study's goal is to build upon their analysis by examining a broader sample of ARG to derive a more generalized framework that may be used by designers of ARGs and similar collaborative game-based experiences, such as *GISHWHES* [21] and Operation Citadel [76].

Related Research on Roles in Videogames

From a traditional videogame design perspective, many game-based learning studies over the past decade have investigated the ways in which role-playing activities (e.g., "playing an environmental scientist") enable players to adopt epistemic frames, or ways of knowing and working within specific in-game contexts that can transfer to "real world" contexts [62,63]. This learning sciences' work has emphasized the knowledge-building [64] and scientific inquiry practices [67] of youth players as they develop their own identities while assuming different social roles in multiplayer videogames [65]. Similarly, our case-study analysis explores the ways in which various social roles that designers create can help advance design-based research on technology-mediated social participation [60] and learning in learning communities such as ARGs.

More broadly, Isbister [29] established videogame design considerations for crafting in-game characters (i.e., non-player characters or NPCs) that can promote higher engagement and participation by players. To develop her "common social roles" taxonomy, Isbister [29] examined videogame NPCs along several design dimensions that lead to role formation, such as:

- *Power dynamics and hierarchies* (e.g., "minions" are designed to engage in unthinking service and loyalty to a player or group of players);

- *Interdependence* due to complementary abilities and overlapping or competing objectives (e.g., "allies" and "enemies" may possess similar levels of skill, but an enemy's goals run counter to player objectives);

- *Defining interaction moments* (e.g., "minions" mirror player excitement over successes or cheer when the player faces obstacles; "mentors" act as player guides by providing training or new information that players need).

Our case-study analysis of the roles that ARG designers create is grounded in Isbister's framework [29]. The social roles we identified are closely related to the psychology-based naming conventions that [29] established (e.g., "allies," "enemies"), but we use terms that hew more closely to the narrative roots of ARGs (e.g., protagonist, antagonist). In addition, we use the case studies to highlight ways in which ARG characters can be designed to enact their roles across Isbister et al.'s dimensions (e.g., specific interaction moments and power hierarchies).

The remainder of our paper will proceed as follows. First, we provide a brief summary of designer-created roles from a sample of existing ARGs. Next, we review two case studies on the roles and behaviors assumed by ARG characters and players to promote player participation and collaborative learning. Finally, we touch on limitations of our current analysis and plans for future work.

METHODS

The analysis presented in this paper is part of a larger design-based research project to explore ARGs as collaborative sense-making systems and authentic, participatory learning environments [7,8,10,11,26]. For this paper's more focused study, the following research question guided our analysis: *"What key social roles have ARG designers used to promote and sustain participation, and model positive learning behaviors within learning communities?"*

We designed our study in two phases, using a qualitative, case-study approach [74]:

1. Our goal for the initial part of this study was to identify and categorize community roles that exist in ARGs, whether they are: 1) created by designers prior to game launch or 2) crafted to emerge during gameplay. To that end, we analyzed a sample of existing ARGs and transmedia experiences and solicited interviews from designers of these ARGs and transmedia experiences.

2. In the second part of our study, we reviewed the design processes followed by two different ARG teams who were developing their experiences for teenagers learning contexts (a classroom in a public middle school and a public library's summer reading program).

Data Collection

We followed a purposeful sampling strategy [13] to select a set of existing ARGs and transmedia experiences for our analysis, using the following criteria:

- *Identified as "seminal" or model ARGs by designers and scholars.* For example, *The Beast* is commonly referred to as the "first" large-scale ARG [39,45], and *ILB* was both an early ARG and a wildly successful marketing campaign (over 100,000 active players and 3 million more casual players and observers) [39,45,46].

- *Distinguished by mission or purpose.* For example, early ARGs served as marketing tools in the entertainment industry. Others were designed to raise awareness of and mobilize action in response to major social issues, such as an impending global oil shortage (*WWO*) [31,47] or disaster preparedness and solving the world's clean water crisis (*Urgent Evoke*) [20,27,47]. A small number were designed with educational goals in mind, such as information literacy practices and environmental science (*ARGOSI; Black Cloud*) [51,73].

- *Distinguished by primary narrative delivery platform.* A growing number of print books extend their stories into other media, such as character blogs, websites for fictional businesses, working phone numbers and email addresses (*Cathy's Book; Personal Effects: Dark Art* [8,28,68]. While these book-based ARGs feature active online community sites where readers/players can share information, personal interpretations, and questions, they can be experienced with little to no online interactions.

We selected at least two ARGs in each category to review in detail, focusing on the social roles and behaviors that designers developed for in-game characters and game runners. We also conducted a literature review for available research studies and design documents such as archived player community websites (e.g., urgentevoke.com) and player walkthroughs (e.g., *Lostpedia*) related to our sample.

In addition to the sample of existing ARGs that we reviewed, we also analyzed interview recordings and transcripts for a diverse set of 17 game designers and researchers who have experience producing ARGs or studying ARGs and similar immersive learning experiences. Eight of the interviewees are established professionals in the entertainment industry (transmedia designers and producers). The rest of the participants included game studies scholars, librarians, and museum professionals. Two of the ARG experts have produced ARGs specifically for undergraduate-level educational environments [36,73]; three have produced ARGs targeted for teenagers and tweens [16,51,56,72]; and one designed ARGs to support informal learning in museums [22,23]. Our diversity of ARG designers helped us gain insights about professional practice, as well as non-professional contexts such as secondary school environments.

To evaluate how designers *applied* elements of our community roles' framework in practice, we used a case study framework [74] to investigate two small-scale ARGs. They were both targeted at younger players (13-17 years old) in learning contexts. The first ARG case study (C1) was designed for a formal education environment: a middle school social studies classroom. The second ARG case study (C2) included two ARGs that were played across two summers as part of public library summer reading program. The design team for C1 included the authors (university researchers and a creative writer), while the design team for C2 was comprised of two youth service librarians at a public library and three teenagers (12-16 years old).

Data Analysis

Because our study included qualitative sources of data such as interviews, recordings of design meetings (for our two design cases, C1 and C2), field notes from design sessions (C1, C2) and gameplay with study participants (C1), we used a qualitative coding approach. Our iterative coding approach was inspired by grounded theory [12,13], in that we did not have preconceived categories. Rather, we let the data drive the categories that emerged. We coded data collaboratively to help reduce the biases of any single researcher. We focused our analyses on the social roles and behaviors that designers developed for in-game characters and game runners.

KEYSTONE ROLES USED BY ARG DESIGNERS

Based on our analysis of existing ARGs and interviews with experienced ARG designers, we identified five types of *keystone* roles that designers have developed. *Keystone species* are those whose presence is essential to the survival of an ecosystem [49]. In ARGs, keystone species (i.e., roles) can help players become and remain engaged as they progress from launch to endgame. We divided our keystone roles into two categories:

- *Narrative-Centric, defined pre-game.* These roles include characters who are integrated into the narrative pre-game and whose social roles remain distinct from players throughout gameplay. Three social roles fall within this category: 1) the "*Protagonist-by-Proxy*", a character who is part of the overall narrative but works as a close ally and informant to the player community [3]; and 2) the "*Protagonist-Mentor*" who acts as the ARG's help system and authority figure, often directing the players to complete specific missions and offering training or advice that enables them to do so; and 3) the "*Antagonist*" (whether an individual "villain" or organization), that can serve as a primary source of conflict to engage potential players to participate and existing players to become more invested in helping the protagonists [37,77].

- *Gameplay-Centric, designed for and emerging post-launch.* These ARG social roles may be established and assigned pre-game, but very little narrative content or player interaction is developed pre-game. These roles are activated for engagement after the game is launched. Members of the ARG design team who assume these gameplay-centric roles have been dubbed *Gamerunners*, since they essentially drive gameplay once the ARG is launched. Two social roles fall within the *Gamerunner* category: 1) *Community Conduits*, who are responsible for dynamically reporting player activity to designers; and 2) *Planted, or Proxy Players* who may be introduced as characters within the narrative, but who interact with the player community as insiders and often, player role-models and guides.

Because our case studies focus on the design of the narrative-centric keystone roles of protagonist-by-proxy and protagonist-mentor, we address the gameplay-centric social roles first. We highlight the ways in which these roles were implemented by drawing upon our sample of existing ARGs and interview transcripts. Since these designer-created roles are closely related to the ARG player community from a functional perspective, we also touch on the ways in which ARG players have assumed similar gameplay roles to promote participation and support sense-making.

GamePlay-Centric (Gamerunner) Roles

Because of the ways in which ARGs distribute content, a key problem is keeping track of what is being found, who is finding it, what they are doing with it, and how it fits into the overall story. For designers, the question is: how do we connect our players to the distributed narrative content, and with each other? For players, the question is: how do we collectively keep track of what we have, and how does it fit into the mystery we are unraveling? The solution on both sides has been a social one: make sure someone is watching, responding to, and preserving community interactions. This role is best described as a *conduit* that ensures any and all interaction data about gameplay is being shared effectively and efficiently among ARG designers and players, and among players themselves. In ARG design circles, the role of the community conduit is known variously as the Community Lead (*ILB*), Participation Architect (*WWO*), Community Liaison (*WWO*), or Moderator (*The Beast*).

During *The Beast*, the core design team shared the responsibility of monitoring and responding to any and all player reactions [S. Stewart, personal interview, Dec 17, 2010]. For their next ARG venture, *ILB*, the same design team felt the community-monitoring task was so important that they recruited a "Community Lead." The *ILB* Community Lead was responsible for checking "every known source of information written about the game, including discussion groups, …mainstream media and blogs" [39:39]. The community lead would also file a daily report that the design team would use to make "instant story updates and adjustments as needed" [39:40]. Since then, a Community Lead or Community Liaison has been a standard member of the ARG design team. *WWO* listed three Community Liaisons and one "Participation Architect" in its project team credits [18]. Jane McGonigal, *WWO*'s Participation Architect, called it "a fancy way of saying my job was to help make sure every single player found a way to contribute meaningfully to the collaborative effort" [47:305]. Community Leads can be a primary means for ARG design teams to engage and sustain player participation.

Player communities have devised their own equivalent forms of community support. These players are typically more active players who establish themselves as forum or chat room moderators. They help organize content and categories on community wikis or other game-based repositories, and tend to "bring new players and lurkers into the community through fun and welcoming discussion" [45:46]. Community leads and/or moderators can be instrumental to players in terms of keeping track of information [15] or recruiting new participants with skills the existing community might be lacking (e.g., asking who knows how to read esoteric lute tablatures in *The Beast*) [S. Stewart, personal interview, Dec 17, 2010]. Community liaisons in player communities have also become key figures in the preservation and evolution of ARGs as a genre. Several early player community leads moved on to become ARG designers themselves, while others established and maintain prominent ARG gaming/critique communities (e.g., Unfiction, ARGnet, and ARGology).

The role of *proxy-player* emerged through our analysis of ARGs with more open-ended narrative structures [11] whose design goals are often to raise awareness around a social issue (e.g., *WWO, Urgent Evoke*). For example, members from the WWO design team seeded the community site and other social media with the initial news of an impending oil crisis. During the game, these proxy players created blog posts alongside players, encouraged existing players to contribute their coping stories and strategies, and invited potential players to join. The proxy-player role includes a subset called *Mentors*, who are essentially "super-players" or volunteers who are charged with welcoming and orienting new players, encouraging players individually to sustain participation, and providing feedback to ARG Community Conduits throughout the game. For example, in addition to designating community leads and proxy players within its own design team, *Urgent Evoke* also recruited *Mentors*, special players who publicly championed one or more fellow players [2].

It is important to note that the support functions that community conduits, proxy-players and mentors provide are not unique to ARGs – other studies have identified individuals who serve similar roles, such as founders/leaders [40], mediators [44,54] and elders, or mentors [38].

Narrative-Centric: Protagonist-by-Proxy
The "*protagonist-by-proxy*" is a core keystone species – and staple interactive dynamic – used by ARG designers as they develop an ARG storyline. Novelist/screenwriter and transmedia author, J.C. Hutchins, coined the phrase to evoke the ways in which ARG players function as "both passenger and driver of the narrative" [3]. The protagonist-by-proxy is an ARG character who seems to discover the story in tandem with the players. During game-play, the player is presented with the same artifacts and information – such as URLs, copies of documents, photographs, email addresses, or phone numbers – as the in-game protagonist. Players have the chance to unearth secrets that this character may not have, but needs, and s/he has the means to communicate new information to the players. The protagonist-by-proxy often asks players for help in solving some problem that is initially perplexing, but increasingly threatening.

For example, in *ILB*, the web-master of the site asked players for help in getting rid of what looked like a hacking program that was breaking her site. In *ARGOSI*, a college student named Viola asks for help in uncovering the mystery of a letter that she found in her grandmother's attic. From an information literacy perspective, the protagonist-by-proxy often models productive information-seeking and problem-solving behaviors that the players can emulate. In

Personal Effects: Dark Art (*PE:DA*), for example, the in-game protagonist Zach enlists the information search and retrieval skills of Rachael, his girlfriend, who is also a "fact-checker" for the New York Journal-Ledger. Similarly, in the *Cathy's Book* transmedia series for young adult readers, the lead protagonist, Cathy, has a best friend, Emma, who models expert information search and retrieval skills, similar to *PE:DA*'s Rachael for players to emulate.

Players often see the in-game protagonists as people "just like them," and are motivated to regard them as both mentors and investigative partners. At times, the in-game protagonist not only seems like a partner in the player community, s/he actually breaks into the "real-world" of the players. The actress who portrayed Rachel Blake, the in-game protagonist in the *Lost Experience*, participated as an audience member in Comic-Con 2006. During a panel with the producers of the Lost TV show, she took an active part in the question and answer period, causing a scene that drew cheers from other audience members when she accused the producers of hiding information about the Hanso Foundation, a fictional organization within the *Lost Experience* narrative [43].

Narrative-Centric: Protagonist-Mentor
Just as videogame narratives benefit from including characters who act as the gameplay "help system" [29] or game guide, ARGs designers implement protagonist-mentors. These narrative-centric social roles support player sense-making from a more authoritative vantage point than the protagonist-by-proxy. As a player ally who is uncovering information alongside the player, the protagonist-by-proxy is typically unable to provide higher level, omniscient information about the game narrative, or training guidance and advice on game challenges. A protagonist-mentor offers a character-driven device that authentically fulfills this role. This role has been most evident in ARGs created with learning goals in mind. For example, in *ARGOSI*, the protagonist-by-proxy, Viola, needed help to navigate the university library databases that would help her solve the map-based puzzles that she encountered throughout the game [N. Whitton, personal interview, Jan 2011]. Because the ARG was also promoting information literacy activities for new university freshmen, the *ARGOSI* design team wanted to establish that there was an authoritative, credible educational resource to support gameplay [N. Whitton, personal interview, Jan 2011]. The protagonist-mentor, Percy Root, who was a fictional librarian at the local university, was created to fulfill this role. His blog posts were publicized at the beginning of the ARG, and provided links to Viola's main website as well as pointers to university databases and helpful tips about using them. Similarly, the character Alchemy, the leader of the social action movement in Urgent Evoke, was featured in the ARG's trailer and introduced the first mission and gameplay guidelines. In *Black Cloud*, an ARG designed to introduce youth in an urban public high school to urban air pollution issues, the protagonist-mentor was not a person,

but an anthropomorphized "cloud" that provided players the means to monitor and improve air quality in their neighborhood [51]. Our case study analysis provides more detail regarding the protagonist-mentor role.

Narrative-Centric: Antagonist

In literary studies, the antagonist represents ideals that directly oppose the protagonist [14]. Antagonists can be a single character/person, a group of people, an organization or institution, or even an idea that serves as a major source of conflict for the in-game protagonist, and by extension, the player in an ARG. Like the protagonist-by-proxy, well-designed antagonists can motivate potential players to participate and become more invested in helping a protagonist.

The fictional Hanso Foundation from the *Lost Experience* was the same shadowy group depicted in the *LOST* television series and represents a classic antagonist organization. *The Lost Experience* players not only supported their protagonist-in-proxy Rachel Blake in face-to-face settings, as noted earlier, they also contributed to her online efforts to uncover the Hanso Foundation's secret and shady practices (by cataloguing information found across the Internet in game-resources such as *LOSTpedia*) [48]. Similarly in *ILB*, players gradually uncovered and shared details about the antagonist Artificial Intelligence (AI) character, the Flea, which turned out to be the source of the protagonist's memory loss and an espionage AI built by the *Covenant*. In the HALO videogame whose story was the backdrop for ILB, the *Covenant* was a fictional military alliance of alien races and portrayed the ARG's major antagonist [46].

C1: ARCANE GALLERY OF GADGETRY (AGOG)

Our first case study details the ways in which we designed a protagonist-by-proxy into an ARG developed for a formal education setting and targeted for teenagers (13-15 years old). The participants in the case study included the design team (five adult researchers and one creative writer) and 60 eighth grade students who played the game (13-15 years old) along with their teacher and school librarian. The game itself took place over a 2-week period in a public school in the U.S [7,10]. The students played primarily during American History class sessions (daily classes, Monday-Friday, 50 minutes each). Slightly fewer boys participated than girls: 44% boys (n=26), 56% girls (n=34).

Data collected and analyzed for C1 included field notes recorded by the authors/*AGOG* designers during gameplay, meeting notes from design sessions (before and during gameplay), player interaction logs stored on the *AGOG* community site, and a player survey given to players during a post-game debrief/focus group. The post-game player survey collected demographic data on the players (gender, ethnicity) and posed short answer, open-ended questions about the ways in which players used specific design features/tools available on the *AGOG* player community website, and game-based activities and features they liked, disliked, and found challenging (or not).

AGOG was launched when university researchers recruited middle school students to help inspect a set of historical documents and artifacts for the Smithsonian museum. To join the game, students accepted the researchers' invitation to become part of a modern version of a special society that was allegedly established by Benjamin Franklin, a prominent, "founding father" figure in U.S. history. The players then learned that their primary responsibility as key members of Franklin's *Junto of Enlightened Naturalists and Inventors for a United Society* (JENIUS) was to curate a special subset of inventions from the U.S. Patent Office known as the Arcane Gallery of Gadgetry (*AGOG*). As they progressed through the game, players discovered that several *AGOG* documents carried clues to a secret message whose pieces they had to collaboratively find, decode, reassemble, and share with an in-game protagonist, "April," to help prevent a devastating reversal in historical events (a change in the outcome of the U.S. Civil War). April was designed as a mechanism for presenting story bits to players, pointing out clues, and sharing in their efforts to decode Morse-encoded and encrypted messages that would help them "save history" (as described by several players during the post-game focus group and survey). April's primary function as a protagonist-by-proxy emerged gradually throughout the design evolution of *AGOG*.

Midway through the design process, as the narrative and player challenges were being developed, we explored multiple design options to fragment and then distribute the narrative in ways that were accessible to teen players (e.g., with partial information on the community wiki, with clues embedded in facsimiles of historical documents) [10]. Most of these solutions, however, required that players take the initiative to find and read the wiki data to uncover the clues. As the *AGOG* creative writer, Ann Fraistat, noted in her post-game interview, these passive, text-based narrative elements required little "interaction" from players beyond reading about them. They covered a rich, complex mythology and backstory, but players could not directly interact with them as they could with a "live" character:

"My first task was to create the 'narrative bible'... it was like, oh, yes, I'll go write sort of like a history novel, y'know? When we started talking about how to actually design this game and incorporate players (laughs). ...It made me think about-- for our teen players-- how it would be great to have some kind of grounding force. ...A lot of the narrative components were more the mythology side of things, and we had trouble reconciling all that mythology with the fact the players need to **play** *this game, and the mythology wasn't really* **playable***. April was a playable narrative element that we could put in there that would ground it for middle schoolers. It was important to me to try to make her cool, even in the setting of this, y'know, like it's hard when you're trying to relate to some kids who might be kind of like, "eh, school, whatever." I was hoping to help pull them in by having someone who they could relate to a little bit* (A. Fraistat, personal interview, June, 2011).

Thus, April Gravure ("April G." to players) was created as *AGOG's* protagonist-by-proxy, whose main function was to share expository elements via videos and personal blog posts. Based on databased traces of player activity on the community site and a post-game survey, April's video blog posts proved to be one of the most engaging design elements for players. They would often replay April's daily video blog posts multiple times to ensure that they uncovered all the clues they thought she might reveal to them. Figure 1 shows players watching (and re-watching) April's latest post.

Figure 1: Teen players listen carefully (and repeatedly) to April's daily video blog about *AGOG's* mysteries.

In addition to meting out story events via almost daily videos and personal blog posts, April modeled information search behaviors that the players' librarian and teacher were trying to promote (e.g., [1]. and helped respond to players' requests for help via, interactive chats with players [7,9]. Almost 20% of the chat messages on the *AGOG* player community site involved players asking April for specific help on game missions and badges, or voicing their support. For example:

1) Henry >> April: *"Hii April, my name is henry and these missions are hard especially cryptographer first mission"*

April >> Henry: *"Hey Henry. Yeah, the one with all the morse code... People from the last class said you guys had some JENIUS people there today, right?"*

2) Ben05 >> April (asking for her help to make out the morse code sketched out in her notebook (a picture of which she included in a blog post): *"As a chryptotographer, it is difficult to read your morse code. please give me a hint"*

April >> Ben05: *"Blake, here's the morse code broken down: -- . ...- --. . ... / . - -.-. .-. --- ... ... / - .. -- ."*

3) Kailee >> April: *"hey how r u doin... i know im with u"*

April >> Kailee: *"I'm doing okay--safe for now! How's training going?"*

Kailee >> April: *"its goin ok for now! i saw ur video its great and ill do anything 2 help ... i just need allitle help on my missions"*

Kailee >> April (at end of a class session): *"yeee april nice talkin 2 ya!!!!!!!!!! talk 2 u 2marrow!!!!!!!!"*

April also provided an engaging and accessible means for following and piecing together the fragmented narrative and related factual historical elements [7,9]. As evidenced by chat messages during the game, during the post-game focus group in which players engaged in a final live video chat with April, and the post-game survey, most players exhibited a strong connection to their protagonist-by-proxy. Several players noted that April was a major reason why they participated: *"I helped April G"*; *"I tapped the code for April"*; and *"April was in trouble and we had to help her."*

To support the players' perspective of April "as one of them," April was portrayed as a student. However, to support the middle school teens' aspirations to interact with older, more experienced youth, April was a 21-year old college sophomore. Her college-age status piqued the interest of several players: during the end-of-game focus group the research team held for *AGOG*, a handful of the male players inquired whether April had a boyfriend.

A fictional Ambassador to JENIUS provided players with guidance as the *protagonist-mentor*. The JENIUS Ambassador was depicted as an all-knowing leader in the society, and provided information to players at pre-scripted stages in the narrative. For example, he introduced the players to the tenets of JENIUS (e.g., importance of respect for others and careful evaluation of information). He also delivered the game's Final Mission orders and presented endgame congratulations. Because the Ambassador was characterized as a stereotypical authority figure, his interaction with the players was one-way only. He did not engage in dialogue with them, but presented direction via pre-recorded podcasts. Players were initially interested in the JENIUS Ambassador when April wondered aloud how he had earned so many badges, or JENIUS training certifications: several players investigated his profile page to find out more about the badges that they might earn. Many showed and shared their pride when he mentioned specific individuals by name, based on training missions they had completed.

A secret society known as the Scientific Confederate Alliance for Revolution (SCAR) presented players (and April) with an *antagonist* organization who, like *AGOG's* protagonist-mentor, the Ambassador, never interacted directly with players, but were referred to indirectly in clues on the community site, or overheard in a conversation recorded by a hidden April on her phone. SCAR offered excitement and motivation for many players, as demonstrated in this excerpt from a player blog post:

Ben: *"As you know, last week we observed April G's notes on her phone recording. The morse code translated out to be Message Across Time. This is obviously linked to the*

Kairograph, which can send messages in the past, present, and future. SCAR is obviously on the hunt for this. We need April to write that message on the 15th!!!!! We need to work together for clues & find out why SCAR wants April. You can talk to me about my blog at Ben05."

C2: SUMMER READING PROGRAM MYSTERIES

Our second case study followed the design process used by two public librarians and three teens as they developed two ARGs (over the course of two summers) to promote their summer reading programs. This case study offers a design-based view into the evolution of approaches that the public library team employed to make the traditional ARG format more accessible to youth (13-17 years old) and to encourage greater participation by their local community in library events.

For the first ARG, known as *"Find Chesia,"* the librarians and teen designers attempted to follow design principles applied to adult-based ARGs, but found that, rather than engaging their target population of tweens and teens in a collaborative sense-making adventure, they were confused by the lack of direction and concerned with Internet privacy issues [H. Owings, personal interviews, November 2010 and September 2012]. For example, the lead adult designer, a youth services librarian, received feedback from her library's "Teen Advisory Board" that most individuals who attempted to play were unsure that they would be allowed to follow the Twitter feed that was established for one of the in-game protagonists, because they were not allowed by their parents to create accounts on social media networks such as Twitter. The teen designers themselves also noted that they were uncomfortable playing some of the online characters that they had developed for the game narrative, because they were adult characters, not teenagers like themselves. They reported that much of their apprehension stemmed from discussions at school and at home about the dangers of misrepresenting yourself online [H. Owings, personal interviews, November 2010 and September 2012]. As a result, initial participation in the ARG itself was quite low (less than 10), with less than 5 players actually completing the ARG.

The following year, the library design team developed an ARG whose multimedia content was delivered primarily through one community website ("The Mystery Guest", [16]). Furthermore, the protagonist-by-proxy model that they employed presented the teen designers as players themselves, who found clues and shared their thoughts and questions for the rest of the player community in more "natural voices" than the first ARG [H. Owings, personal interview, September 2012]. Not only did the teen designers feel more comfortable, the target teen players also felt more connected to these in-game characters, given their closeness in age and vernacular [H. Owings, personal interview, September 2012].

The lead librarian also decided to include an additional authoritative in-game character, to help provide the direction and guidance that the previous ARG lacked. As she concluded, *"In an adult-run game, if there's not clear*

directions, adults might take the initiative to create [their own] directions... but teens really, they're just, well, they're in a culture of education and they are looking for directions on how to do [ARGs]...Once they know the structure they are more than happy to respond. We found that with a librarian character, they had someone to look to that would give them direction...whereas our teen characters kind of filled in the storyline" [H. Owings, personal interview, September 2012]. The C2 design team also dubbed the Librarian character as *"the voice of reason"* for players, who could *"give hints on how you would answer the problem, or how you might find the solution...things that we didn't do in the beginning, because we thought [teens] could figure it out on their own"* [H. Owings, personal interview, September 2012]. Community participation jumped by a factor of four—to about 23 players total—with eight core players throughout the 12 week summer ARG [16]. Feedback from the library's Teen Advisory Board was also more complimentary: teens reported higher levels of engagement and enjoyment.

DISCUSSION AND DESIGN IMPLICATIONS

Considering the protagonist-by-proxy and protagonist-mentor from Isbister's design dimensions, which organized NPC roles by *power dynamics* (least to most dominant) and *defining interaction moments*, both case studies offer ARG designers with strategies for using these roles to engage players and promote their sustained participation.

In particular, both case studies highlight narrative-based character design techniques for crafting a protagonist-by-proxy who possesses characteristics that are *relatable* to an ARG's target demographic. Like Isbister's *sidekick* and *ally* roles, protagonists-by-proxy are peers, "unequivocally on the player's side" [29:234] and can "make the player really feel he or she has a back-up and help give the player the feeling of being on a supportive team" [29:237]. For example, April was a student, like *AGOG's* middle school players. She fretted about her skill and effectiveness in tackling JENIUS training missions in the same ways that the teen players did. Similarly, the teen designers in C2 who acted as proxy players (rather than adult characters) in their second ARG were more comfortable and more accessible to their peer player audience. In contrast, the Ambassador (C1) and Librarian (C2), as protagonist-mentors, conveyed "far more power in the game world" and took a "leadership role in guiding the player" [29:238], and is analogous to Isbister's own *Mentor* role.

Beyond the character-specific, narrative features that define the protagonist-by-proxy and protagonist-mentor roles, designers can use different media platforms/channels to underscore their *power dynamics* and enable specific types of *defining interaction moments*. A protagonist-mentor like the JENIUS Ambassador remained dominant, not just in title and temperament, but also in the media he used to communicate with players. He always prescribed player actions and tasks; his communication was one-way and omniscient. Players never "chatted" with the Ambassador; likewise, they never "saw" him in a video as they could with April. April used the same media channels as *AGOG's* players, and her video blogs were created with a homegrown, hanging-out-in-my-bedroom quality that is familiar to most teenagers. Many of the key moments between April and players occurred due to the dynamic, "live" interaction afforded by the *AGOG* community site's Chat feature, coupled with the fact that the April was active during the times that the middle school players were most active (during their *AGOG* class sessions).

As noted in several communications genre analysis and new media studies [35,55,75], different media support "different communicative practices" [35:519], and can represent "the purpose, content, participants, location, timing and form of communicative action" [75]. Different media platforms/channels afford different directionality, volume, and timing (e.g., one-to-one, one-to-many; synchronous, asynchronous) [35]. Future ARG designers could establish more ways for the more authoritarian protagonist-mentor to exploit one-to-many, asynchronous media, while a protagonist-by-proxy and proxy player – on the same communicative level as players – would gravitate toward peer-to-peer or many-to-many, synchronous platforms.

While April was viewed very much as a peer and ally to *AGOG's* players, she was also slightly older and wiser (college sophomore), someone who the players might aspire to in high school and beyond. Thus, April could also serve as a model for the learning behaviors that *AGOG* was trying to promote. She would explicitly guide player actions, giving them new story information and ideas for what to do with it, as well as summarize the "story so far." In short, April provided the positive feedback that Jafarinaimi et al. [30,31] found missing in their analysis of the design weaknesses of *WWO* that limited productive player participation practices.

Like player-produced game resources that enable non-players to access and enjoy distributed, often complex ARG narratives [15], the protagonist-by-proxy and protagonist-mentor roles offer interactive means for players to access and learn from ARG content. These key roles can help designers create experiences that fulfill the participatory learning promise that many ARG proponents have touted.

LIMITATIONS
The roles we have described do not reflect a comprehensive typology of the social roles and associated interaction behaviors that can be engineered within ARGs and similar community-based transmedia experiences. Just as multiple types of social roles (or characters) exist in video games [29] and related collaborative gaming communities [46,76], ARG designers can and do integrate a number of character-based roles that were not covered in detail here. For example, in more traditional video games and role-playing games, antagonist or enemy roles are often covered in great detail [29]. Indeed, the enemy role can be "one of the most popular and enduring NPC types in [video] games" [29:241] that can engage existing players or incite new players to participate. In this paper, we focused our analysis on ARG community roles that influence player participation through largely

positive interaction, such as "protagonist-by-proxy" and "protagonist-metnor," both of which act as allies to the player. The *antagonist* role, while identified and touched on, was given only cursory review for its potential effect on player engagement and learning.

CONCLUSION AND FUTURE WORK
We have identified several "keystone species," or specific roles and associated behaviors that designers can implement to positively impact player participation in ARGs and similar interactive transmedia storytelling experiences. Specifically, we have highlighted approaches used for incorporating these roles in ARGs designed for learning contexts. In contrast to previous studies of ARGs that focus on social roles and behaviors assumed and enacted by players/player communities, our analysis reveals social roles explicitly created by designers. Designer-crafted social roles can be integrated into the ARG narrative (e.g., protagonist-by-proxy) and enacted during game play (community conduits, proxy-players). Our study builds upon early work such as Yule et al. [76], who describe the role of docents in a mixed reality game designed to promote visitor engagement with a historic site.

The keystone roles we have outlined hold implications for use in the design and play of ARGs for learning. Educators (whether in informal or formal education contexts) or older students could assume roles as community leads and encourage more hesitant players. The protagonist-by-proxy could be used to model target literacy practices as well as motivate players on a peer-to-peer level. Due to the protagonist-by-proxy's narrative-centric role, much of the character's interactive content can be created in advance of game launch and thus offer opportunities for reuse. We are currently developing and experimenting with a more comprehensive design typology of ARG social roles and associated modes of interaction within a larger, NSF-funded project to design ARGs that support Science, Technology, Engineering, Arts, and Math (STEAM) learning.

ACKNOWLEDGEMENTS
We thank the designers we interviewed; C2's librarian and teen designers; and the C2 teachers, librarian, and students who supported *AGOG*. In addition, we gratefully acknowledge the NSF for funding EAGER IIS-0952567.

REFERENCES
1. American Association of School Librarians (AASL). 2008. *Standards for the 21st-Century Learner in Action*. American Association of School Librarians, Chicago, IL.

2. Alchemy. 2010. Welcome EVOKE Mentors! *EVOKE Blog*. Retrieved October 11, 2011 from http://blog.urgentevoke.net/2010/02/28/welcome-evoke-mentors/

3. Michael Anderson. 2008. An Interview with JC Hutchins: Personal Effects. *ARGNet: Alternate Reality Gaming Network*. Retrieved November 1, 2011 from

http://www.argn.com/2008/11/an_interview_with_jc_hu
tchins_personal_effects/

4. Chris Baber, Dan Andrews, Tom Duffy, and Richard
McMaster. 2011. Sensemaking as narrative:
Visualization for collaboration. *VAW2011, University
London College.*

5. Steve Benford, Andy Crabtree, Martin Flintham, et al.
2011. Creating the spectacle: Designing interactional
trajectories through spectator interfaces. *ACM Trans.
Comput.-Hum. Interact.* 18, 3: 1–28.

6. Frank Blackler. 1995. Knowledge, knowledge work and
organizations: An overview and interpretation.
Organization studies 16, 6: 1021–1046.

7. Elizabeth Bonsignore, Derek Hansen, Kari Kraus, et al.
2012. Alternate Reality Games: Platforms for
Collaborative Learning. *The Future of Learning:
Proceedings of the 10th International Conference of the
Learning Sciences (ICLS 2012) – Volume 1, Full
papers,* International Society of the Learning Sciences,
251–258.

8. Elizabeth Bonsignore, Derek Hansen, Kari Kraus, and
Marc Ruppel. 2012. Alternate Reality Games as
Platforms for Practicing 21st-Century Literacies.
International Journal of Learning and Media 4, 1: 25–
54. http://doi.org/10.1162/IJLM_a_00086

9. Elizabeth Bonsignore, Derek Hansen, Kari Kraus,
Amanda Visconti, June Ahn, and Allison Druin. 2013.
Playing for real: designing alternate reality games for
teenagers in learning contexts. *Proceedings of the 12th
International Conference on Interaction Design and
Children,* ACM, 237–246.

10. Elizabeth Bonsignore, Kari Kraus, Amanda Visconti,
Derek Hansen, Ann Fraistat, and Allison Druin. 2012.
Game design for promoting counterfactual thinking.
*Proceedings of the SIGCHI Conference on Human
Factors in Computing Systems, Austin, TX,* ACM,
2079–2082.

11. Elizabeth Bonsignore, Vicki Moulder, Carman
Neustaedter, Derek Hansen, Kari Kraus, and Allison
Druin. 2014. Design tactics for authentic interactive
fiction: insights from alternate reality game designers.
*Proceedings of the 32nd annual ACM conference on
Human factors in computing systems,* ACM, 947–950.

12. Kathy Charmaz. 2005. Grounded Theory in the 21st
Century: Applications for Advancing Social Justice
Studies. In *The Sage Handbook of Qualitative Research*
(3rd ed.). Sage Publications, Thousand Oaks, CA, 507–
535.

13. John W. Creswell. 2007. *Qualitative inquiry & research
design: choosing among five approaches.* Sage
Publications, Thousand Oaks.

14. J. A. Cuddon, Rafey Habib, and Matthew Birchwood.
2013. *A dictionary of literary terms and literary theory.*
John Wiley & Sons, Hoboken, N.J.

15. Christy Dena. 2008. Emerging Participatory Culture
Practices: Player-Created Tiers in Alternate Reality
Games. *Convergence* 14, 1: 41–57.
http://doi.org/10.1177/1354856507084418

16. Jane Doh. 2010. Interview with Mystery Guest 2010
Creator Heather Owings | ARGNet: Alternate Reality
Gaming Network. *ARGNet: Alternate Reality Gaming
Network.* Retrieved May 31, 2013 from
http://www.argn.com/2010/09/interview_with_mystery_
guest_2010_creator_heather_owings/

17. Tom Duffy, Chris Baber, and Neville Stanton. 2013.
Measuring collaborative sensemaking. *Proceedings of
the 10th International Conference on Information
Systems for Crisis Response and Management.*

18. Ken Eklund. 2007. WWO: Credits and Contact. *World
Without Oil (WWO).* Retrieved March 10, 2011 from
http://www.worldwithoutoil.org/metacontact.htm

19. Scott Freeman, Sarah L. Eddy, Miles McDonough, et al.
2014. Active learning increases student performance in
science, engineering, and mathematics. *Proceedings of
the National Academy of Sciences* 111, 23: 8410–8415.

20. Edmond Gaible and Amitabh Dabla. 2010. *Project
Evaluation: EVOKE.* The Natoma Group, Oakland, CA.
Retrieved from
http://siteresources.worldbank.org/EDUCATION/Resou
rces/ProjectEVOKE-evaluation-final-16oct11.pdf

21. Joseph A. Gonzales, Casey Fiesler, and Amy Bruckman.
2015. Towards an Appropriable CSCW Tool Ecology:
Lessons from the Greatest International Scavenger Hunt
the World Has Ever Seen. *Proceedings of the 18th ACM
Conference on Computer Supported Cooperative Work
& Social Computing,* ACM, 946–957.

22. Georgina Bath Goodlander. 2009. Fictional Press
Releases and Fake Artifacts: How the Smithsonian
American Art Museum is Letting Game Players
Redefine the Rules. *Museums and the Web 2009:
Proceedings,* Archives & Museum Informatics.
Retrieved from
http://www.archimuse.com/mw2009/papers/goodlander/
goodlander.html

23. Goodlander, Georgina. 2008. *Ghosts of a Chance
Alternate Reality Game (ARG).* Smithsonian American
Art Museum, Washington, D.C.

24. David Gurzick, Brian Landry, and Kevin F. White.
2010. Alternate reality games and groupwork.
*Proceedings of the 16th ACM international conference
on Supporting group work,* ACM, 303–304.

25. David Gurzick, Kevin F. White, Wayne G. Lutters,
Brian M. Landry, Caroline Dombrowski, and Jeffery Y.
Kim. 2011. Designing the future of collaborative
workplace systems: lessons learned from a comparison
with alternate reality games. *Proceedings of the 2011
iConference,* ACM, 174–180.

26. Derek Hansen, Elizabeth Bonsignore, Marc Ruppel,
Amanda Visconti, and Kari Kraus. 2013. Designing

reusable alternate reality games. *Proceedings of the SIGCHI Conference on Human Factors in Computing Systems*, ACM, 1529–1538.

27. Robert Hawkins. 2010. EVOKE -- a crash course in changing the world. *World Bank on ICT use in Education*. Retrieved from http://blogs.worldbank.org/edutech/evoke-a-crash-course-in-changing-the-world

28. J. C. Hutchins and Jordan Weisman. 2009. *Personal effects: dark art*. St. Martin's Griffin, New York.

29. Katherine Isbister. 2006. *Better game characters by design: a psychological approach*. Elsevier/Morgan Kaufmann, Amsterdam ; Boston.

30. Nassim Jafarinaimi and Eric M. Meyers. 2015. Collective Intelligence or Group Think?: Engaging Participation Patterns in *World without Oil*. *Proceedings of the 18th ACM Conference on Computer Supported Cooperative Work & Social Computing*, ACM, 1872–1881.

31. Nassim Jafarinaimi, Eric M. Meyers, and Allison Trumble. 2014. Designing Meaningful Participation: Analyzing Contribution Patterns in an Alternate Reality Game. *Proceedings of the 18th International Conference on Supporting Group Work*, ACM, 306–309.

32. Isa Jahnke. 2010. Dynamics of social roles in a knowledge management community. *Computers in Human Behavior* 26, 4: 533–546. http://doi.org/10.1016/j.chb.2009.08.010

33. Henry Jenkins. 2006. *Convergence culture: where old and new media collide*. New York Univ. Press, New York NY.

34. Henry Jenkins, Katie Clinton, Ravi Purushotma, Alice J Robinson, and Margaret Weigel. 2006. *Confronting the Challenges of Participatory Culture: Media Education for the 21st Century*. MacArthur Foundation, Chicago, IL.

35. K. B. Jensen and R. Helles. 2011. The internet as a cultural forum: Implications for research. *New Media & Society* 13, 4: 517–533. http://doi.org/10.1177/1461444810373531

36. Margeaux Johnson, Amy G. Buhler, and Chris Hillman. 2010. The Library is Undead: Information Seeking During the Zombie Apocalypse. *Journal of Library Innovation* 1, 2: 29–43.

37. Suzanne Keen. 2003. *Narrative form*. Palgrave Macmillan, New York.

38. Amy Jo Kim. 2006. *Community building on the web: Secret strategies for successful online communities*. Peachpit Press.

39. Jeffrey Y. Kim, Jonathan P. Allen, and Elan Lee. 2008. Alternate reality gaming. *Communications of the ACM* 51, 2: 36–42.

40. Robert E. Kraut and Andrew T. Fiore. 2014. The role of founders in building online groups. *Proceedings of the 17th ACM conference on Computer supported cooperative work & social computing*, ACM, 722–732.

41. Robert E. Kraut and Paul Resnick. 2011. *Building successful online communities: evidence-based social design*. MIT Press, Cambridge, Mass.

42. Oscar T. Lenning and Larry H. Ebbers. 1999. *The powerful potential of learning communities: improving education for the future*. Graduate School of Education and Human Development, George Washington University, Washington, DC.

43. Lostpedia. Rachel Blake. *Lostpedia - The Lost Encyclopedia*. Retrieved January 5, 2012 from http://lostpedia.wikia.com/wiki/Rachel_Blake

44. Kurt Luther, Casey Fiesler, and Amy Bruckman. 2013. Redistributing leadership in online creative collaboration. *Proceedings of the 2013 conference on Computer supported cooperative work*, ACM, 1007–1022.

45. Adam Martin, Brooke Thompson, and Tom Chatfield. 2006. *Alternate Reality Games White Paper – IGDA ARG SIG*. Retrieved January 23, 2015 from http://www.christydena.com/wp-content/uploads/2007/11/igda-alternaterealitygames-whitepaper-2006.pdf

46. Jane McGonigal. 2008. Why I Love Bees: A Case Study in Collective Intelligence Gaming. In *The Ecology of Games: Connecting Youth, Games, and Learning*, Katie Salen (ed.). MIT Press, Cambridge, MA, 199–227.

47. Jane McGonigal. 2011. *Reality is broken: why games make us better and how they can change the world*. Penguin Press, New York.

48. Jason Mittell. 2009. Sites of Participation: Wiki fandom and the case of Lostpedia. *Transformative Works and Cultures*. http://doi.org/10.3983/twc.2009.0118

49. Bonnie A. Nardi, and Vicki L. O'Day. 2000. *Information Ecologies: Using Technology with Heart*. MIT Press, Cambridge, MA.

50. Carman Neustaedter and Tejinder K. Judge. 2012. See it: a scalable location-based game for promoting physical activity. *Proceedings of the ACM 2012 conference on Computer Supported Cooperative Work Companion*, ACM, 235–238.

51. Greg Niemeyer, Antero Garcia, and Reza Naima. 2009. Black cloud: patterns towards da future. *Proceedings of the 17th ACM international conference on Multimedia*, ACM, 1073–1082.

52. R.D. Nolker and L. Zhou. 2005. Social Computing and Weighting to Identify Member Roles in Online Communities. *2005 IEEE/WIC/ACM International Conference on Web Intelligence*, IEEE, 87–93. http://doi.org/10.1109/WI.2005.134

53. Kenton O'Hara, Hazel Grian, and John Williams. 2008. Participation, collaboration and spectatorship in an alternate reality game. *Proceedings of the 20th Australasian Conference on Computer-Human Interaction Designing for Habitus and Habitat - OZCHI '08*, 130. http://doi.org/10.1145/1517744.1517787

54. Kazuo Okamura, Wanda J. Orlikowski, Masayo Fujimoto, and JoAnne Yates. 1994. Helping CSCW applications succeed: the role of mediators in the context of use. *Proceedings of the 1994 ACM conference on Computer supported cooperative work*, ACM, 55–65.

55. Wanda J. Orlikowski and JoAnne Yates. 1994. Genre Repertoire: The Structuring of Communicative Practices in Organizations. *Administrative Science Quarterly* 39, 4: 541–574.

56. Heather Owings. 2009. Building an ARG | The Gaming Life. *School Library Journal [online]*. Retrieved from http://www.slj.com/2009/12/opinion/the-gaming-life/building-an-arg-the-gaming-life/#_

57. Tamara Peyton, Alyson L. Young, and Wayne Lutters. 2013. Playing with leadership and expertise: military tropes and teamwork in an arg. *Proceedings of the SIGCHI Conference on Human Factors in Computing Systems*, ACM, 715–724.

58. Tamara Peyton, Alyson Leigh Young, and Wayne Lutters. 2013. The militarization of teamwork in alternate reality gaming. *Proceedings of the 2013 conference on Computer supported cooperative work companion*, ACM, 255–258.

59. Peter Pirolli and Daniel M. Russell. 2011. Introduction to this special issue on sensemaking. *Human–Computer Interaction* 26, 1–2: 1–8.

60. Jennifer Preece and Ben Shneiderman. 2009. The reader-to-leader framework: Motivating technology-mediated social participation. *AIS Transactions on Human-Computer Interaction* 1, 1: 13–32.

61. Antti Salovaara, Mikael Johnson, Kalle Toiskallio, Sauli Tiitta, and Marko Turpeinen. 2005. Playmakers in multiplayer game communities: their importance and motivations for participation. *Proceedings of the 2005 ACM SIGCHI International Conference on Advances in computer entertainment technology*, ACM, 334–337.

62. David W. Shaffer. 2006. Epistemic frames for epistemic games. *Computers & Education* 46, 3: 223–234. http://doi.org/10.1016/j.compedu.2005.11.003

63. David Williamson Shaffer. 2004. Epistemic frames and islands of expertise: learning from infusion experiences. *Proceedings of the 6th international conference on Learning sciences*, International Society of the Learning Sciences, 473–480.

64. Kurt Squire. 2006. From Content to Context: Videogames as Designed Experience. *Educational Researcher* 35, 8: 19–29.

65. Kurt Squire. 2008. Open-Ended Video Games: A Model for Developing Learning for the Interactive Age. In *The Ecology of Games: Connecting Youth, Games, and Learning*, Katie Salen (ed.). MIT Press, Cambridge, MA, 167–199.

66. William H. Starbuck. 1992. Learning by knowledge-intensive firms. *Journal of management Studies* 29, 6: 713–740.

67. Constance Steinkuehler and Sean Duncan. 2008. Scientific Habits of Mind in Virtual Worlds. *Journal of Science Education and Technology* 17, 6: 530–543. http://doi.org/10.1007/s10956-008-9120-8

68. Sean Stewart, Jordan Weisman, and Cathy Brigg. 2006. *Cathy's book: if found call (650 266-8233)*. Running Press, Philadelphia, Pa.

69. Elisabeth Sylvan, James Larsen, Jodi Asbell-Clarke, and Teon Edwards. 2012. The Canary's Not Dead, It's Just Resting: The Productive Failure of a Science-Based Augmented-Reality Game. *Proceedings of Games + Learning + Society (GLS 8.0)*, ETC Press, 31–37.

70. Jennifer Thom-Santelli, Michael J. Muller, and David R. Millen. 2008. Social tagging roles: publishers, evangelists, leaders. *Proceedings of the SIGCHI Conference on Human Factors in Computing Systems*, ACM, 1041–1044.

71. Etienne Wenger. 1998. *Communities of practice: learning, meaning, and identity*. Cambridge University Press, Cambridge, U.K.; New York.

72. Andrew Whitacre. 2011. "VANISHED": Smithsonian and MIT to Launch Sci-Fi Infused Interactive Mystery Event. *MIT Comparative Media Studies Archives*. Retrieved from http://cms.mit.edu/news/2011/02/vanished_smithsonian_and_mit_l.php

73. Nicola Whitton. 2008. Alternate reality games for developing student autonomy and peer learning. *Proceedings of Learners in the Co-creation of Knowledge (LICK)2008*, Edinburgh Napier University, 32–40. Retrieved October 14, 2010 from http://lick2008.wikispaces.com/file/view/Strand+1+-+Nicola+Whitton+-+V1+Paper.pdf

74. Robert K. Yin. 2009. *Case study research: design and methods*. Sage, Los Angeles Calif.

75. Takeshi Yoshioka, George Herman, JoAnne Yates, and Wanda Orlikowski. 2001. Genre taxonomy: A knowledge repository of communicative actions. *ACM Trans. Inf. Syst.* 19, 4: 431–456.

76. Daniel Yule, Bonnie MacKay, and Derek Reilly. 2015. Operation Citadel: Exploring the Role of Docents in Mixed Reality. *Proceedings of the 2015 Annual Symposium on Computer-Human Interaction in Play*, ACM, 285–294.

77. Dolf Zillmann. 1995. Mechanisms of emotional involvement with drama. *Poetics* 23, 1–2: 33–51. http://doi.org/10.1016/0304-422X(94)00020-7

A Breathtaking Journey. On the Design of an Empathy-Arousing Mixed-Reality Game

Martijn J.L. Kors[1,2], Gabriele Ferri[1], Erik D. van der Spek[2], Cas Ketel[2], Ben A.M. Schouten[1,2]

[1]Amsterdam University of Applied Sciences
Play and Civic Media Research Group
Amsterdam, The Netherlands
{m.j.l.kors, g.ferri, b.a.m.schouten}@hva.nl

[2]Eindhoven University of Technology
Department of Industrial Design
Eindhoven, The Netherlands
{m.j.l.kors, e.d.v.d.spek, bschouten}@tue.nl,
c.ketel@student.tue.nl

ABSTRACT

Persuasive games exist for a wide variety of objectives, from marketing, to healthcare and activism. Some of the more socially-aware ones cast players as members of disenfranchised minorities, such as migrants, prompting them to 'see what they see'. In parallel, a growing number of designers has recently started to leverage immersive technologies to enable the public to temporarily inhabit another person, to 'sense what they sense'. From these two converging perspectives, we hypothesize a still-uncharted space of opportunities at the crossroads of games, empathy, persuasion, and immersion. Following a Research through Design approach, we explored this space by designing A Breathtaking Journey, an embodied and multisensory mixed-reality game providing a first-person perspective of a refugee's journey. A qualitative study was conducted with a grounded theory/open coding methodology to tease out empathy-arousing characteristics, and to chart this novel game design space. As we elaborate on our analysis, we provide insights on empathic mixed-reality experiences, and conclude with offering three design opportunities: visceral engagement, reflective moments and affective appeals, to spur future research and design.

Author Keywords

Mixed Reality; Augmented Virtuality; Virtual Reality; Persuasive Games; Games; Empathy; Persuasion; Multisensory; Immersion; Visceral Engagement

ACM Classification Keywords

H.5.1 [Multimedia Information Systems] Artificial, Augmented and Virtual Realities. K.8.0 [Personal Computing] Games. H.1.2 [User/Machine Systems] Human Factors.

CHI PLAY '16, October 16-19, 2016, Austin, TX, USA.
© 2016 ACM. ISBN 978-1-4503-4456-2/16/10...$15.00
DOI: http://dx.doi.org/10.1145/2967934.2968110

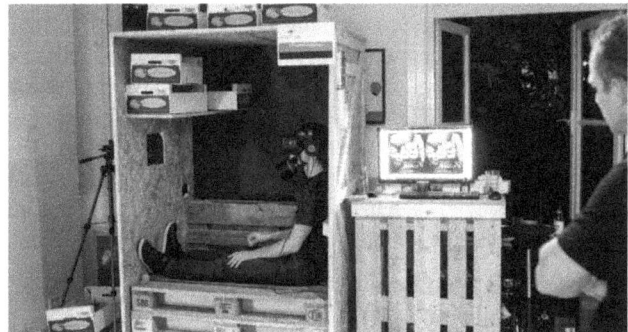

Figure 1. ABTJ at the Dutch VR Days 2015 (Amsterdam, NL)

INTRODUCTION

According to a recent meta-analysis, American college students exhibit a relatively sharp decline in empathy since the early 2000s, especially in relation to the abilities of empathic concern and perspective taking [42]. While the possible causes for this decline are manifold, a part of it might be related to the media and technology we increasingly expose ourselves to (e.g. social networks, reality TV, or digital games [42]). Furthermore, there is a concern that, though contested (e.g. [67]), repeated engagement with the content of violent video games may lead to lower empathy [3]. At the same time however, evidence has emerged that games can influence real world attitudes, also towards more desirable outcomes (or at least desirable to the designers of such games) [86]. These games, more commonly known as persuasive games, could therefore potentially also be used to improve the empathic abilities of the players. The underlying mechanisms, especially in terms of how to design for empathy-arousing experiences in games, are still poorly understood however. With a Research through Design [88] approach and a Grounded Theory [2] methodology this paper aims to shed light on how multisensory immersive experiences, and the subsequent identification with the game's protagonist, could be used to arouse empathy. Finally, we propose a set of design opportunities to guide future design and research endeavors.

PERSUASIVE INTERACTIONS

The use of games for persuasion has gained widespread acceptance. A subset of these leverages persuasion not for expressly commercial or promotional purposes, but to temporarily put players in the role of specific characters – for example the disadvantaged, marginalized or dispossessed – to communicate "how does it feel" to be in certain conditions. In parallel, many HCI solutions have been developed over the years exploring empathy as a desired outcome, for instance game-based training aids for people within the autistic spectrum. Here we aim to connect these two sets, namely: 1) games that foster empathic connections to promote attitude change, and 2) HCI artifacts designed to elicit empathy as a main objective, often through playful interactions. In the following paragraphs, we further unpack these two points of view on empathy and digital artifacts. The first one is slightly more functionalistic and foregrounds empathy as a desirable means to leverage in persuasion. The second brings aesthetic experiences to the forefront, and explores artifacts aiming at altering users' perceptions, thus producing empathic effects. The two perspectives are not mutually exclusive, as they situate the same phenomena (empathy-induction) in different contexts (applied games and aesthetic artifacts). We now outline these two views, before presenting a device situated in the middle ground.

Empathy-Oriented Persuasive Games
The use of empathy-arousal as persuasive appeal in legacy media is not uncommon, presenting struggles or happiness (e.g. people fleeing from a war torn-country or someone overcoming an illness), and has been effectively used to change or reinforce related attitudes and behaviors [26,40,73,74]. Although games might not have received the same amount of attention as other forms of media when it comes to empathy, they do present a unique array of opportunities to foster empathy [9,14,28,36]. Through their interactivity [81], goal driven nature [45] and various opportunities for role-taking [63], games already present a compelling toolkit for stimulating empathy. As Boltz et al. [15] argue, "well-designed empathy games can also encourage [players] to evaluate choices and consequences, and to question the system a game represents". Games that use empathy-arousing appeals to change or reinforce attitudes belong to the field of Persuasive Games. Bogost coined the term "persuasive games", to describe digital games "that mount procedural rhetoric effectively" [13]. However, this definition was quickly contested for being too narrow, ignoring other possible persuasive dimensions games can encompass [35]. Based on earlier work, unfolding the persuasive gameplay experience [44], we settle for a more general description and refer to persuasive game as 'interactive entertainment designed to shape how the player thinks and feels about reality'.

Current research in game design and education [15,32,77] is exploring how game systems may stimulate the cognitive and affective aspects of empathy. This may empower players to explore alternate points of view and foster a sense of shared similarity and empathic concern for individuals and groups with whom they may not have direct contact (e.g. experiences of trauma, illness, migration, war…). Belman and Flanagan [9] point at PeaceMaker [37] as an exemplar artifact that is at the same time a game: "Cognitive empathy is involved in gameplay [...] To make progress [...] players have to consider the perspectives of a variety of stakeholders, rather than only that of their own side. [...] The game requires one to think carefully about the perspectives of a wide range of stakeholder groups [...] Policy decisions that agitate a stakeholder group too much can potentially derail the peace process." Games such as PeaceMaker [37], Darfur is Dying [68], Hush [4] and more recent games such as This War of Mine [1] and Spec Ops: The Line [87] do not only ask players to empathize with certain game characters, they also present the player with arguments that might cause one to think and feel differently about the people, events or situations represented in these games [44].

Several possible qualities have been named to increase the impact of such persuasive gameplay on a macro level [44], namely Engagement (and Immersion), Credibility and Relevance. For our current research on persuasive games it is in particular the design of engaging and immersive gameplay (i.e. degrees of involvement with a game [17,76]) that present an interesting quality [44], even more so as such experiences have already shown to be conducive for changing or reinforcing attitudes in other fields such as narrative persuasion [21,76], with indication for empathy as facilitating component [84] and as factor to help increase the likelihood such experiences lead to real world prosocial behavior [39]. While engagement and immersion can be strengthened through captivating narratives [48], we might also employ immersive technologies to stimulate similar experiences [21,33]. Through immersive technologies (e.g. head-mounted displays) we can experience a sense of 'presence' in an alternate reality, tricking our brain into thinking that we are somewhere other (a virtual world) than the physical world our bodies actually reside in [20,33,82]. With this feeling of being "somewhere" else, the feeling to stand in "someone" else's shoes becomes possible, which in turn presents ample opportunity to also think and feel like this other person (i.e. empathy). Although little is known about the effects of a mediated 'presence' on persuasion, the concept is captivating [21] and increasingly relevant for the field of persuasive games, in particular due to the recent rise and popularity of virtual reality (VR).

Empathy-Oriented Playful HCI
Similarly, to game design/game studies, empathy is not a new concept for researchers in some domains of HCI. In this part, we focus on artifacts that – while not being full-fledged games – still leverage a degree of playfulness in engaging their users [12,71]. Specifically, the interplay between immersive technology and phenomenology is opening new design spaces: the rapid and widespread diffusion of VR and wearables has made it feasible and relatively affordable to create a variety of artifacts making one experience someone else's phenomenological

perceptions. Design research has drawn upon pragmatist phenomenology to argue that interacting with technology in society "requires us to understand the experiences of [a] person in relation to ourselves and it is [there] that we identify empathy" [27]. To illustrate this, we propose here two approaches to empathy-oriented playful HCI: first immersive journalism, and then wearable devices that modify the perception of one's own body. As we present our selected examples, we categorize them as "playful" inasmuch they are not games, but they are not functionalistic tools either: as Lucero et al. argue, *"playfulness is a mindset whereby people approach everyday, even mundane, activities with an attitude similar to that of paidia" [49]*.

De la Peña et al. [62] discuss the possibilities of "immersive journalism", a form of mediated first-person experience of a journalistic reportage, *"[allowing] the participant [...] to actually enter a virtually recreated scenario representing the news story [that] affords the participant unprecedented access to the sights and sounds, and possibly feelings and emotions" [62]*. In this vein, Arora and Pousman developed Clouds Over Sidra [6], a 360° film in partnership with the United Nations, following Sidra, a twelve year old girl, living in the Za'atari camp in Jordan. On the production company's website, co-director Arora describes: *"by leveraging breakthrough technologies, such as virtual reality, we can create solidarity with those who are normally excluded and overlooked, amplifying their voices and explaining their situations" [6]*. And, indeed, filmmaker and digital artist Chris Milk has recently argued for VR constituting an "empathy machine" [56]. When playing Clouds Over Sidra, *"[you're sitting there in [Sidra's] room, watching her, you're not watching it through a television screen, you're not watching it through a window, you're sitting there with her [...] when you look down, you're sitting on the same ground that she's sitting on [...] and because of that, you feel her humanity in a deeper way: you empathize with her in a deeper way" [56]*.

In addition to using technology to alter the viewpoint of the viewer, technological devices can also be used to stimulate the other senses and thereby alter one's own bodily perception, with the objective of literally feeling what someone else might perceive. Marshall et al. [51] and Benford and colleagues [11] have experimented with devices built around military-style gas masks, fitted with wireless breath sensors and cameras. They report [51] on a horror-themed maze visited by volunteers wearing sensors-equipped gas masks, who were remotely observed by other participants through their video feeds and breathing sounds. Semi-structured interviews showed the remote participants experiencing heightened fear, arguably because of their empathic bond with the volunteers inside the horror labyrinth. In a later study [11], they present Breathless, a physical installation for three participants wearing breath sensors. Breathless prompts one participant to sit on a swing, another to control its rhythm and the last one to

observe them from afar - and they all had to synchronize (in different ways according to their role) their breathing and their movements. Qualitative analyses of the collected data points at an empathic relationship created between the participants by means of their shared perceptions.

An Opportunity Space: Presence, Empathy, Persuasion
The examples and literature discussed so far suggest that 'presence' may be an effective vehicle to support persuasion, to change or reinforce attitudes, and to think or feel differently about objects or issues [60,64]. As such, it is surprising that immersive technologies, particularly in combination with empathy-arousal as persuasive appeal, are still largely absent from the repertoire of games designed to persuade [89]. On one hand, we see a variety of applied games following the footsteps of PeaceMaker [37], fostering empathy by presenting carefully simulated sequences of strategic actions and reactions. At the same time, Marshall et al. [51], Benford et al. [11] and De la Peña et al. [62] exemplify an approach to empathy that is more grounded in playful immersion and in the sense of presence it produces. There are both the technical opportunity and the urgent need for merging these approaches and examine the design of immersive applied games for empathy. For these reasons, an exploratory Research through Design (RtD) [88] process was launched to examine the problem space, produce relevant concepts and test them on an experimental artifact, on which we report in the following section.

A BREATHTAKING JOURNEY
A Breathtaking Journey (ABTJ) is a mixed-reality game, meant to arouse empathy for refugees. ABTJ was born out of a project with Amnesty International the Netherlands [90] in 2014 and 2015, in which we set the objective to explore how interactive media could help motivate people to change or reinforce attitudes towards human rights related issues [43]. The design of ABTJ draws inspiration from empathy-supporting games for change such as Hush [4] or Madrid [29] from art-games such as The Graveyard [83], as well as from unusual immersive experiences such as Taphobos [18]. ABTJ places the player in the shoes of a refugee who is fleeing from a war-torn country, hiding in the back of a truck, to reach a safe haven (fig. 1 and 2). The virtual experience of ABTJ, delivered through a head-mounted display and over-the-ear headphones, is augmented with a range of physical elements including a mask (housing a breathing sensor and a scent diffuser), a tangible contraption mimicking the inside of a truck, an unbalance motor to simulate movement and a controlled shutter to drop objects on the player during the game. The combination of both virtual and real elements effectively positions ABTJ as a Mixed-Reality [10] game. It is particularly close to the concept of Augmented-Virtuality, which is situated towards the Virtual-Reality end of Milgram and Kishino's Reality-Virtuality continuum [55]. Augmented-Virtuality refers to the integration of real world objects into a predominantly virtual world, as opposite to Augmented-Reality where virtual elements are integrated

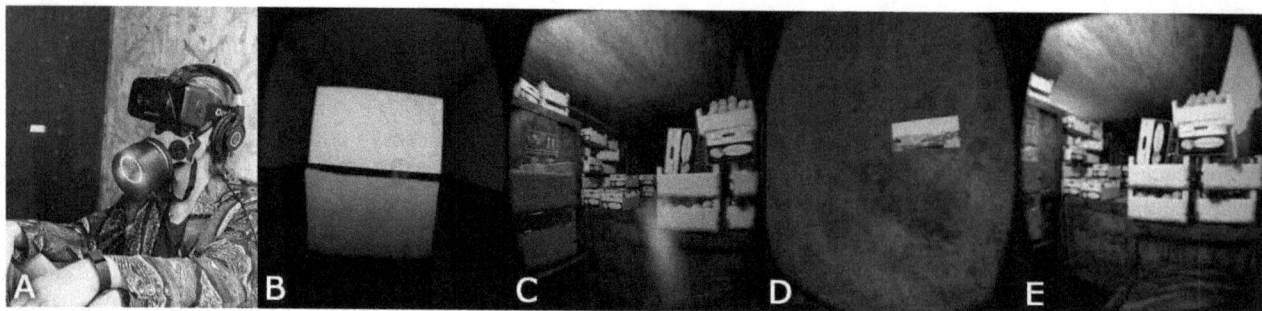

Figure 2A-2E. A: Participant wearing a head-mounted display, a mask to diffuse scent and measure breathing, and over-the-ear headphones. B: Dream scene. C: Driving scene. D: Window on the side of the truck. E: Door of the truck is being opened.

into a predominantly real world. Although the term Augmented-Virtuality is seldom used (and, when it appears, it often refers to the integration of live visuals from reality into a virtual world) we could also consider the inclusion of live physical elements, such as the use of real world gravity, acceleration, wind, mass, materials, scent and temperature, as possible augmentations of the virtual world. This particular format affords the creation of an alternate (virtual) world, completely authored by the designer (through computer generated visuals and audio), all the while supplemented with real, physical, elements (that are still difficult to fabricate digitally) to address additional senses, enhance the experience, and most importantly increase the player's sense of 'presence' [23].

As a RtD [88] project, ABTJ addresses the aforementioned gap between applied games and "empathy machines" by designing a game that (a) generates a sense of presence through embodied and multisensory elements, (b) suggests complex emotions and visceral reactions, and (c) stimulates users to interpret the embedded told-narrative.

Technology

In what follows, we describe how ABTJ provides players with outputs that are 1) audio-visual, 2) tactile, vestibular, and proprioceptive, 3) olfactory. For that last point, we also address the use of an anemometer as a novel input device.

For audio-visual stimuli, we used an Oculus Rift Development Kit 2 head-mounted display [59], providing the player with low latency head/positional tracking and a stereoscopic visual of the virtual environment. It was combined with isolating over-the-ear Audio Technica ATH-M40x [7] headphones, providing simulated spatial audio. Tactile, vestibular, and proprioceptive elements required a more complex setup. By placing users in a wooden crate (roughly 120x100x140cm), we were able to map the virtual world represented in ABTJ with a player's physical surroundings (fig. 1). By precisely superimposing the virtual environment onto the physical contours of the contraption, players are able to actually touch and feel what their avatars might perceive in the virtual world. To create a sense of movement we positioned the the contraption on a suspension system, which simulates a realistic sense of driving via a heavy unbalanced motor situated in a protected compartment underneath the player. Furthermore,

to add an extra physical component to the installation, a pair of mandarins is automatically dropped on the player's leg, triggered by a specific in-game event. For olfactory stimuli, and to use the player's breathing as an input, we created a wireless device that closely resembling a gasmask (fig. 2A). The device houses two independently controllable ultrasonic scent diffusers. These diffusers use electronic frequencies to create fast vibrations that vaporize essential oils (mandarin in this case) into the user's airstream. The device also houses an anemometer (wind sensor based on a hot-wire technique) to measure the player's breathing. All sensors and actuators are interfaced to the computer over a (wireless) serial connection using an Arduino microprocessor [5]. We used the Unreal (Game) Engine 4 [25] to drive the narrative, process interactions, facilitate in the communication between sensors, actuators and the game code, and real-time render the virtual environment.

Gameplay

We created an embedded narrative to frame the experience, but, at the same time, we decided to keep it at a minimum to better foreground and explore the multisensory and immersive aspects of ABTJ. The game is divided in two scenes, spanning five minutes overall. We refer to them as the "dream scene" (an auto-diegetic narrative introducing part of the protagonist's background) and the "driving scene" (representing the protagonist hidden in a truck). During the entire game, the player is free to move and look around within the physical boundaries of the contraption, while subtle visual elements are rendered in sync with the input of the anemometer (fig. 2C). Although the game has a single script for the embedded narrative, the player's gender determines the gender of the protagonist and corresponding narration (the auto-diegetic voice).

In the "dream scene" (fig. 2B) the player has no virtual body and floats mid-air in a dark room. A movie (with an outline filter applied) is projected on a white virtual wall, and an auto-diegetic voice tells about a raid kidnapping the protagonist's brother. Then, the movie shows a boat drifting off at sea, with the protagonist's voice telling how he/she escaped the country, how the boat he/she was on sank not far from shore, leaving the protagonist as one of the few survivors. The player sees water rising from below to above his or her head (fig. 2B), as if being submerged and drowning, after which the environment turns black, and the protagonist explains that continuing the journey through an overland route is the only option left.

The "driving scene" (fig. 2C) begins with the player waking up, hidden in a truck that is transporting mandarins. The diffusers in the mask are activated and disperse the soothing scent of mandarins. A small window on the right side of the crate exists both in the physical and in the virtual worlds, and players can touch it and peek outside over a Middle Eastern/Balkan scenario [see Figure 2D]. After several minutes the truck is stopped, players hear a patrol questioning the driver, and an off-voice tells to be quiet and not to breathe. The door on the side of the truck swings open (fig. 2E), the cargo is being inspected, but nothing suspicious is found. When the door closes again several mandarins fall down, alarming the patrol, who consequently inspects the truck a second time. This time however, depending on whether the player is quiet and breathing, the system determines whether the protagonist is able to avoid detection, or not. For this study, both endings are virtually identical, fading the environment to gray, presenting the result of whether the player was caught or not, and ending with the auto-diegetic voice wishing a better future for those in a similar situation.

STUDY

ABTJ was deployed at three tech-oriented public events in Western Europe for a total of six days, between October and December of 2015. Of these events, one was free and two required only a small entrance fee. Furthermore, all three events had a focus on popularizing new technology, thus attracting a diverse population. This is an exploratory deployment study, with which we aimed at putting our RtD device "in the wild" and capture spontaneous reactions, with a grounded theory / open coding approach [2]. The objective was to probe reactions vis-à-vis empathy, embodiment and persuasive emotional appeals, to inform the future design of empathic and persuasive experiences through immersion.

We used an open-ended face-to-face interview protocol [22], formulated for attitude measurement [50,64], in combination with a photo elicitation interview protocol [34]. Interviews were conducted either in English or in Dutch. The interview script aimed at a better understanding a participant's attitudes and empathy (or lack thereof) towards non-European migrants. Photo elicitation was added specifically to frame the responses of participants from the perspective of a refugee, as the concept that empathy includes the communicating of one's own understanding within a particular perspective [85]. Six photo portraits depicting middle-Eastern people were selected from Flickr [91] by two researchers independently based on their diversity and their low degree of emotional face expressions.

Recruitment, Grouping and Interview Scripts

Inclusion in this study required participants to be over 18 years old, and agree to be recorded during the interview. All participants included in the study were from Western-European countries, in specific the Netherlands, Belgium, Germany and England. We randomly created two groups: prospective participants were approached either when waiting in line before experiencing ABTJ (Group 1), or immediately afterwards (Group 2). Given the limitations of field studies [66], we were particularly cautious not to prime participants before playing ABTJ, and therefore decided to only interview participants either before (Group 1) or after (Group 2) playing ABTJ. Priming participants from group 1, giving them opportunity to reflect on the plight of refugees or to spark a discussion with other participants waiting in line, before actually playing ABTJ, could dilute our qualitative understanding of ABTJ's effects on how participants elaborate on their experience afterwards. Group 1 is essentially our baseline group to assess the attitude of people, who did not try ABTJ, towards refugees at the given time and place, whereas responses from group 2, after playing ABTJ, contribute to the qualitatively evaluation of ABTJ's effects.

A total 70 people participated in the study, Group 1 had a total of 32 participants (13 females, 19 males,) with an average interview duration of 59 seconds per participant, Group 2 had 38 participants (13 females, 25 males) with an average interview duration of 93 seconds per participant. The two sets are of different size as not all the people approached ultimately gave consent to be interviewed.

After participants from Group 1 selected one of the six fictional characters ("whose journey do you want to experience?"), they were prompted to elaborate on the character's story, feelings, thoughts, hopes, and beliefs. The interview for Group 2 was identical, with modifications only to tenses (e.g. "whose journey did you just experienced?"). We specifically inquired how the character would think and feel as a method to understand participants' self-expressed attitude from the perspective of a refugee [50]. In our case, an attitude's cognitive components refer to the beliefs, thoughts and attributes held by participants vis-à-vis the refugee's narrative presented by our game. The affective components refer to the feelings and emotions assigned to these cognitive component [64].

We do acknowledge that a field setting (vs. a controlled lab study) might include greater distraction for participants, but it does also offer a more natural setting with greater realism and a more representative population sample [66]. Since participants were completely isolated from the environment during the experience, we found the advantages of a field setting to outweigh the disadvantages. Additionally, with a field setup we aimed for more accurate insights on future real-world application of empathy-arousing experiences as persuasive appeal (e.g. for NGOs and charities that promote their work at public events).

Analytical Procedures, Coding Schemes and Concepts

We used a qualitative form of analysis through grounded theory / open coding [2], informed by humanistic HCI [8], and informed by narratological [69,70] and pragmatist [54] analytical methodologies. The data resulting from the interviews is a combination of both English and Dutch voice recorded responses. The transcriptions were first coded according to participant's number, gender, choice of character, and whether a response belonged to either Group 1 or Group 2. After this coding, the responses were translated to English, and then we performed a thematic analysis on the textual data following a grounded theory / deductive approach [16]. Two researchers performed our preliminary coding independently, and we converged on four significant coding schemes to account for the recurring themes in our dataset (Socially-Shared Narrative Schemas, Post-hoc Narrative Interpolations, Emotional Markers, and Embodied Feelings). In the following, we present a brief outline of the theoretical grounding for each code.

Our study probes how participants recounted their experience as a refugee in ABTJ (Group 2), or how they envisioned being a refugee would be (Group 1). Doing so, we align with Ryan's [69,70] definition of "narrative quality" or "storiness", which is "a sort of cognitive template at work in many different media, [...] evoking specific cognitive effects in its interpreters' minds" [41]. In the wake of founding metaphors such as Janet Murray's holodeck [57] or Brenda Laurel's computers as theatrical performances [46], the practice of computer game design has significantly evolved in the past decades and produced outstanding interactive artifacts that merge playful competition with nuanced storytelling structures. Indeed, there are several ways in which interactive experiences and games allow players to expand beyond the embedded told-narrative [38]. In specific, we leverage our interview questionnaires and photo-elicitations to tease out the different interpretations of the experience with ABTJ by different participants and, by coding and analyzing participants' responses, we look for correlations between narrative effects and interaction.

We also examined markers signaling emotions in our participants' responses, with a specific interest in the cognitive and affective components [50] used to describe a perspective on migrants either before or after the experience. We coded emotional statements with Power and Dalgleish's [65] 'factor model for correlated basic emotions', as it elaborates on the strong connection between emotions and goals, which in turn fits well within the often goal-oriented nature of games [45]. Although we followed the categorization (both primary and secondary emotions) as presented by Power and Dalgleish's [65] as overarching structure, we also used the more complete list of secondary and tertiary emotions as introduced by Shaver et al. [72] and Parrott [61] for this coding. After coding the explicitly pronounced emotions we additionally decided to code several sentences that essentially describe certain (complex) emotions inexplicitly (i.e. as a result from sentence structure). We finally coded expressions of embodied feelings in our dataset. The notion of embodiment draws from a long tradition in philosophy and phenomenology: "our experience of ourselves and our world is always embodied and involves [...] feelings that are typically unnoticed though [...] indispensable for our proficient functioning" [75]. Generally, embodiment in HCI indicates the feedback from a body interacting with an environment. Dourish [24] understand embodiment as "grounded in and emerging out of everyday, mundane experience" which is "directed towards [...] practical tasks" and providing "a source of meaning". In practice, we coded expressions in our data describing interactions between players and their environment, including quotes from participants telling about not only their own physical body acting upon parts of the device (e.g. the breathing sensor, the wooden crate...), but also about their avatar's simulated body interacting with the virtual environment.

ANALYSIS
We now produce a qualitative analysis of the data collected throughout our study. As this is an exploratory deployment, we went in as much as possible "as a blank slate", with the objective of capturing data for a study based in grounded theory. After transcribing and translating the data, a preliminary open coding was performed (by two researchers independently). Here we report on four significant coding schemes that emerged from our reading (Socially-Shared Narrative Schemas, Post-hoc Narrative Interpolations, Emotional Markers, Embodied Feelings), that we use as lenses to access our participants' experience through the narratives they produced.

Socially-Shared Narrative Schemas
The themes of migration from Africa and the Middle East, and of refugees escaping war-torn countries have been significantly present in Western media in the past decades, often becoming a polarizing topic in social and cultural discourses. Expressly leaving aside the political implications of these subjects, as a first step in our study we probed for spontaneous narratives about migrants from a group of our participants that had not yet interacted with ABTJ. With this first coding scheme, we teased out quotes from participants who produced coherent narratives about the experience of being a migrant without having interacted with ABTJ. Participants in Group 1 (interviewed before interacting with the artifact) were shown a diverse set of photo portraits, and asked to choose one. In a short open-ended interview, they were asked to envision and tell a short narrative from the point of view of the selected character, including events, contexts, thoughts and feelings. The participants themselves acknowledge the influence of mass media – as Peter (pseudonym, #33, Male, Group 1, Portrait 4) notes: *"This is of course [...] borrowed from the news, so I don't really have an idea about her on a personal level..."*

We observe some recurring narrative structures across these data – stories that, despite containing negative elements, are also about determination, willpower and the fight for a better future. Emma (pseudonym, #37, Female, Group 1,

Portrait 2) proposes: *"It looks like she is holding something. I think she is like a person who has demonstrated or up and against something in her country, and eh, and therefore she is kind of strong, will power and because of that, as a consequence, she has to flee her country. She might have some children, and a husband. Maybe her husband is dead, and eh, her children might already be somewhere and she is protesting and wants to change something in the country she comes from."* In addition, Kevin (pseudonym, #79, Male, Group 1, Portrait 2) elaborates: *"I think he is about the same age as I am, so I think he is a student and I think he is looking for the best future, just as we look at our future here in the Netherlands. He will seek this better future possibly in Europe or somewhere else where it's safe because I think you have the best change to be secure, be safe, and have a better future in countries or states like the European Union or the United States or comparable countries."*

Whereas some participants also produced very short and generic descriptions, the examples proposed here show some articulated (albeit stereotypical) ones. There seems to be a recurring narrative schema at work here, arguably ingrained in some mainstream media representation of migrants and refugees. Thematic nuclei in these archetypical structures include the escape from a war-torn country to avoid violence or persecution; embarking on a long, difficult and stressful journey trying to reach a safe haven; worries about what the future might bring; and having to leave family behind in the process. Let us now return to the embedded narrative programmed into ABTJ: for the purpose of our study, that storyline was designed to be as generic as possible, without deviations from a canon of refugee stories. It mentions the protagonist's brother's abduction, the decision to flee the country, a dangerous journey by sea and a ride in the back of truck, hiding in a small space between crates – all elements that fit into the socially-shared narrative schema outline above, of which Emma's and Kevin's quotes demonstrate an implicit knowledge.

After having compared ABTJ's narrative design with a general basic socially-shared response to a narrative photo elicitation technique, we will now proceed to examine how it was later reconceptualized by participants after having interacted with ABTJ.

Narrative Interpolation
The concept of narrative interpretation, or the creation of a story-like account of first-person experiences, is not new in digital media and game studies [38,69,70], and also constitutes the basis for a number of research methods leveraged in HCI practice, from experience sampling to diary studies. In this section, we report on not only how participants narrated their experience interacting with ABTJ, but also how they spontaneously interpolated it by adding extra details not explicitly present in the system.

In our data, we highlighted portions that clearly refer to the diegetic world represented in ABTJ, but at the same time do not exist in the embedded narrative. Following the same protocol of Group 1, participants in Group 2 (interviewed after interacting with the artifact) were shown photo portraits, asked to choose one, and told that the person depicted was also the one they "enacted" during the experience. Then, they were asked to tell a short narrative from the point of view of the selected character. Mark (pseudonym, #47, Male, Group 2, Portrait 3) produces these interpretations, not literally and immediately connected to the embedded narrative: *"[It was] you make yourself very, very small, very insignificant, you sit in a corner behind boxes, your window is very small."* Daniel (pseudonym, #31, Male, Group 2, Portrait 3) further expands: *"Well, I guess that I felt how anxious it is to endure the journey, and constantly on the lookout to avoid being discovered, be sent back, or murdered [...] Especially when it [the truck] was stopped. Because in the beginning I thought, it is going quite well, look a bit out of the window, and let everything just pass by. And when the door really opened it started to feel quite tense. It was the moment I was also pointed out to hold my breath when I thought, oh yeah, then I was suddenly totally pulled into the experience, oh yes, this is how it is, quite exciting what's happening here. [...] I really thought, oh this is the moment that I should really remain quiet because otherwise I might soon be discovered."*

These quotes demonstrate how our participants interpolated the narrative they experience by adding details not originally present in the embedded script. Neither the narrating voice of ABTJ, nor the on-screen action depicts the protagonist making himself/herself *"very, very small"* (Mark), or *"being constantly on the lookout"* or *"[starting] to feel quite tense"* (Daniel). And, yet, these interpolations do make sense within the overall narrative, and the two participants were arguably using them as a means to interpret and convey their own personal experience with ABTJ. However, if we simply lump these phenomena together, we risk keeping them opaque: to address them more effectively, we need to isolate them and apply additional coding schemes specifically on that subset of data, thus teasing out other salient characteristics.

Emotional Markers
We discovered participants leveraging a broad variety of linguistic markers to indicate emotions within the narrative accounts/interpolations they produced of their ABTJ experience. To examine them more in detail, we made a first broad pass coding emotional statements utilizing Power and Dalgleish's [65] 'factor model for correlated basic emotions'. This categorization includes Happiness, Fear, Sadness, Anger and Disgust as primary emotions, and was later expanded following Shaver et al. [72] and Parrott [61] to account for more complex ones (e.g. loneliness, despair, relief, distress, pride).

The following quotes present some examples of emotional markers we teased out from within parts that are clearly narrative interpolations. On the one hand, we observe a broad palette of markers, ranging from simple to ones that are more complex. For example, Emily (pseudonym, #12, Female, Group 2, Portrait 4) reports: *"[it was] very exciting, tense, especially, yes, you especially are very vigilant, and pay attention. I did not quite know where [the character] came from, but with the water you feel some kind of shortness of breath."* (note: she is referring to the part in ABTJ representing water rising around the protagonist). Frank (pseudonym, #4, Male, Group 2, Portrait 3) mentions an ambiguous condition: *"Ehm. She was sad, but also happy. She was the only survivor of a ship which sunk. And then she was really just very anxious, and especially when she was almost discovered."* Other participants similarly use *"anxious"*, *"tense"* (Benjamin, pseudonym), or *"scared"* (Brian, Anna and Sarah, pseudonyms), *"afraid"* and *"nervous"* (Arthur).

In addition to this, we also observe other more nuanced expressions that convey an emotional connotation coupled with other components that are rooted in physical and/or narrative contexts, such as *"But the [interesting] experience is especially the part when you are locked up in that truck and that you are in her skin. Smell helps, and I felt that I was there, found that it works well"* (Linda) or *"you feel trapped"* (Paul). Whereas the previous examples (e.g. feeling fear) may emerge from a simple open coding, we need to consider multiple dimensions to account for these more complex ones.

Embodied Feelings

If we temporarily collect all the strands of this analysis so far, we notice – throughout many of the narrative interpolations produced by our participants – an abundance of expressions pointing to one's own body, to body parts and to bodily characteristics. This prompted us to apply another specific code to tease out how our participants leveraged embodied terms and expressions to convey better specific feelings, emotions and perceptions.

A first recurring theme involving embodiment is the sense of being physically constricted, almost to the point of claustrophobia. Susan (pseudonym, #4, Female, Group 2, Portrait 4) mentions *"If you are sitting there [note: hidden in a truck] for a whole day it should be awful, I never really realized, I never, it feels quite small, claustrophobic. [...] I didn't really feel fear, it was more desperation."* Others talk about being *"locked up [...] and [...] in her skin"* (Linda), *"your contact with the outside world is minimal. Uh, yeah, and you feel trapped"* (Paul) and *"you realize how lonely one must feel [...]this confined perspective"* (Lily).

Different participants elaborated on being prompted by the installation to control their breathing, such as *"It was the moment I was also pointed out to hold my breath when I thought, oh yeah, I was suddenly totally pulled into the experience, oh yes, this is how it is, quite exciting what's happening here"* (Daniel). But breathing was also pointed out to be something on which the device and the embedded

story have an indirect effect: for example, Emily refers to the scene in which the protagonist is getting submerged in water and reports that *"[in] the water you feel some kind of short[ness] of breath"* – it should be mentioned that the device worn by users was not actively restricting their airflow in any way. The emphasis that participants placed on bodily feelings and on physical sensations in their recounting of the experience is significant. It suggests how a first-person mixed-reality experience may provide players with a repertoire of embodied feelings – even those not explicitly mentioned in the embedded narrative – over which they may elaborate.

The four coding schemes, and related observations, that emerged from our exploratory study are partially surprising. We found evidence of participants clearly situating their experience in the contemporary mass-media discourse (Code 1: Socially-Shared Narrative Schemas), and yet being well-disposed to interpreting freely and add to the embedded narrative (Code 2: Narrative Interpolation). This suggests not only a promising level of engagement, but also the use of the immersive experience as an "activator", some kind of a catalyst that users leverage to tell original stories about migrants. The third and fourth coding schemes (Emotional Markers and Embodied Feelings) are interesting for their distribution, as they often co-occur in our dataset. This suggests that emotions and physical stimuli, real or simulated, may mutually influence and reinforce each other. We observe many of the foundational components of empathic relationships emerging from the data we collected, further motivating the exploratory agenda of designing for empathic appeals with immersive technology. We point at these elements as an ideal middle ground between the two fields we outlined in the beginning – persuasive games for humanitarian empathy, and provocative aesthetic experiences – and we see further potential and a yet-understudied problem space at the overlapping of the two. We will now extrapolate three design opportunities and related concepts, supported from our RtD process, deployment and analyses, which we offer to the design community as an input for future works.

DESIGN OPPORTUNITIES

Following our observations and analysis, we can discern three different game design opportunities to stimulate empathy arousal in virtual reality. These are visceral engagement, moments of reflection, and affective appeals.

Visceral Engagement

The concept of viscerality has already been explored in HCI design, as exemplified by Norman [58] describing the "visceral level" of an artifact as its look, feel, sound and, more in general, its material components as they support and orient its intended functions. He argues that humans "are exquisitely attuned to receive powerful emotional signals from the environment that get interpreted automatically at the visceral level" [58]. This seems to derive from a metaphorical understanding of the term "visceral" as in the colloquial "gut feeling", and it is not the only possible connotation we may assign to this concept. Stark reminds us of the etymology of visceral: "affecting inward feelings, and [stemming] from the Latin words *visceralis* or internal, and *viscera*, plural of *viscus* [which means] internal organ, inner parts of the body" [80]. For example, Benford et al. [11], Levisohn et al. [47] and Byrne et al. [19] have already begun exploring aesthetic experiences produced by stimuli acting on users' bodily core, such as breathing, sweating [11] and vertigo [19]. Indeed, the data we collected demonstrate how our participants often conceptualized their experiences in peculiar ways, resonating with this second meaning of viscerality. This is clearly still a much underexplored design space, whose study has been made timely by the rapid diffusion of immersive, tangible, and wearable technologies. Our study and related literature point at clear opportunities for new designs; a design space characterized by viscerally engaging experiences that are insuppressible and intense, difficult to name, feelings that are excited from outside of our bodies, but are felt deep inside. The vertigo caused by the fear of heights, the uneasiness of gazing in a stranger's eyes, the sense of weightlessness and breathlessness in a rollercoaster may be good examples of this opportunity space. We support this proposal by pointing at two moments in ABTJ that have consistently been described through expressions denoting visceral engagement - the part where the user is submerged in water and the part where the player sits between crates, looking outside, while the truck is driving. Both parts provide multisensory experiences that go beyond the audio-visual (the proprioceptive feelings of breathing and of being constricted between crates), that have an inward directionality (inhalation, pressure), and are uncomfortable, if not threatening, to the user's avatar. For example, a participant said she experienced a shortness of breath when visually submersed in water, even though the mask did not restrict airflow. The other moment, when sitting in the truck, participants presented experiences that relate to the feeling of being trapped, cramped and claustrophobic, some explaining that this made them feel very small and insignificant. Being able to create these intense moments provides a compelling case for using immersive technologies, and in particular multisensory/embodied mixed-reality experiences, to explore complex feelings that are otherwise difficult to convey. This could indeed allow a deeper, more empathic relationship with the characters represented.

Although visceral engagement remains an underexplored area, we propose that one can stimulate visceral reactions by taking away players' agency of bodily freedom, creating a sense of confinement through physical space and objects, or acting of biofeedback during gameplay, for example analyzing the players' breathing to determine game progression. Discomfort and suspense are another aspect to consider. For example, we observed some of our participants waiting in line before ABTJ being (unnecessarily) worried about the game possibly restricting

their airflow – an element that relates to the uncomfortableness of the "Rising Action", first described by Benford et al. [11].

A Moment of Reflection

Mixed-Reality experiences do not only offer the possibility to sense and feel being "somewhere" else, but also to sense and feel being "someone" else, in first-person experiences that are much more immersive than other screen-based media. Temporarily "inhabiting" other people's perspectives, sensing what they sense and potentially feeling what they feel would seem to address most characteristics required for an empathic experience. However, a fundamental question emerges: when we adopt someone else's point of view through an immersive device, with whom are we empathizing? With the person we "temporarily inhabit"? With other people entering our field of view? Clouds Over Sidra, whose gameplay has been described as "you're sitting there in her room, [...] when you look down, you're sitting on the same ground that she's sitting on" [56], clearly favors this second opportunity. We wonder whether there might be more potential in immersive technologies than what we are using now: can players empathize with their avatars? ABTJ, an essentially solitary experience, has explored this specific opportunity.

And yet, an issue surfaces: if empathizing is the process with which one understands unjudgmentally the experiences, the feelings, and the difficulties of another person, then this is made more complicated by a first-person perspective which does not immediately provide the participants with "someone to empathize with" other than with oneself. As Bob (pseudonym, #27, Male, Group 2, Portrait 2) mentions *"I think I played as myself"*. This process would require reflection and introspection, to allow users to separate themselves from the character. However, reflecting in games is non-trivial, as creating a rich experience leads to a "flow paradox", where being more involved with gameplay can lead to less critical reflection [79]. Does this mean that immersive and interactive first-person experiences that promote empathy are unlikely? On the contrary, as a future design opportunity, we point at empathic relationship with one's own avatar as a still understudied possibility to examine. As a prerequisite, we emphasize the usefulness of leaving a moment of reflection to participants. We argue that this would give them the chance of using the material they experienced to empathize. In our study, this chance was actively evoked through the post-questionnaire (to collect further data, a debriefing session would have been necessary [31] but in a natural setting these follow-up sessions are not easily organizable). But *in lieu* of a formal debriefing, we found that some participants spontaneously used the two-minutes of ABTJ when the protagonist just sits in the moving truck without any told-narrative or challenges as an opportunity to reflect. Some participants report that this moment offered a chance to drift away in thoughts, almost like a mindful experience. This might have actually also presented a moment of reflection and deeper processing: a moment in which participants had the time to relate their virtual experiences to someone else's experiences in reality, realizing how lonely and claustrophobic such a journey would feel for a refugee. Very recently, a similar argument has been put forward by Marsh, in the context of learning about the great barrier reef [52].

We underline how the majority of narrative expansions and reported visceral reactions took place in that specific moment. We call for designers to create pockets of downtime, where people cannot (or, more preferably, do not wish to) do anything else than experience. The inclusion of mundane activities that create moments of apparently meaningless action could be a yet-underconsidered resource for these kinds of retrospection and introspection.

Affective Appeals

About a decade ago, Bogost argued that games have unique persuasive powers mainly due to their capacity to make arguments through their rules and procedures – a characteristic he named Procedural Rhetoric. Procedural Rhetoric is "The art of persuasion through rule-based representations and interactions rather than the spoken word, writing, images or moving pictures", focusing instead on "using processes persuasively" [13]. Although it is argued that games can use other dimensions for persuasion as well [30,35,44], none is as exclusive to games as procedural rhetoric. However, now with the rapid diffusion of immersive technology we might have an additional, more emotionally engaging, aspect that is unique to games, which is the experience of a mediated presence.

Our analysis suggests multiple ways designers can use mixed-reality to strengthen the affective appeal of their game, in particular through embodied multisensory experiences. Tying back to Bogost's use of rhetoric [13], we wonder whether multisensory and affective persuasive appeals may function in the same way as visual enthymemes [78]. For future designs, we point at the use of scents as a means of pulling players into the experience, or to create discomfort by including less pleasant scents. Affective appeals might also leverage fear/terror as ways to set up a type of persuasive argument (enthymeme). However, with highly immersive (multisensory) experiences, saddening or frightening experiences can be quite overwhelming, and designers should therefore be cautious to avoid events that could possibly cause great distress [53]. To illustrate, for an early prototype of ABTJ we experimented with scents like smoke and mold, which we discontinued for the final prototype as it proved too unbearable to endure.

CONCLUSIONS

With the recent rise of virtual and mixed reality, many questions surfaced on the potential of immersive technologies to influence how we think and feel about reality, with in particular the captivating potential to foster empathy by having players inhabit another person's perspective. But despite the strong interest from industry, already labeling virtual reality as "the empathy machine" [56], little research has actually focused on the arousal of empathy through immersive experiences, and subsequent persuasive processes. Following a Research through Design approach we created A Breathtaking Journey, a multisensory mixed-reality game that provides the player with a first-person perspective of a refugee's journey. A qualitative study was conducted on three tech-oriented public events, followed with with a grounded theory/open coding methodology to tease out empathy-arousing characteristics, and to chart this novel game design space. We observed reactions coherent with the characteristics of empathic responses, and formulated three design opportunities for further applications and research in this field. We offer these, stimulating visceral reactions, introducing moments of reflection, and leveraging affective appeals, as a contribution for future work.

The first design opportunity relates to the stimulation of viscerally-engaging experiences. Our study and related literature point to a design space characterized by visceral feelings, insuppressible and intense, difficult to name, sensations that are excited from outside of our bodies, but are felt deep inside. These feelings are difficult to mediate through legacy media and seem to require a sense of presence. The second opportunity space relates to a moment of reflection. Immersive technology can support the temporarily first-person "inhabiting" of another person's perspective, sensing what they sense and feel what they feel. This seems to address most characteristics of empathic experiences, guiding players to empathize with their avatars. Our study points at a way to overcome this issue by introducing a moment of reflection, the inclusion of down-time to temporarily slow down the pace of the experience, and offer players a mindful moment to acknowledge the other person they are inhabiting. The third opportunity space relates to the affective appeals of immersive technology. In our study we found that participants primarily expand through emotions, rather than logic. This is partly due to the setup of the design, but also a clear indication that immersive technology is able to convey complex emotional experiences such as loneliness and insignificance quite effectively.

There is clearly much more research and design work to do in this application domain, whose opportunities are far from being exhausted. We exposed a still untapped potential for (persuasive) game design research and applied game design, presenting both an exemplar prototype and three opportunities to guide further design and research. In this vein, we urgently call for game designers, interaction designers, immersive journalists, and hardware makers to seriously consider the emerging opportunities of a more empathic way of designing immersive experiences.

ACKNOWLEDGEMENT

This research is part of the project "Persuasive gaming. From theory-based design to validation and back", funded by the Netherlands Organization for Scientific Research.

REFERENCES

1. 11 Bit Studios. 2014. *This War of Mine*. Retrieved from http://www.11bitstudios.com/games/16/this-war-of-mine

2. Anne Adams, Peter Lunt, and Paul Cairns. 2008. A qualititative approach to HCI research. In *Research Methods for Human-Computer Interaction*, Paul Cairns and Anna Cox (eds.). Cambridge University Press, Cambridge, UK, 138–157.

3. Craig A. Anderson, Akiko Shibuya, Nobuko Ihori, et al. 2010. Violent video game effects on aggression, empathy, and prosocial behavior in eastern and western countries: a meta-analytic review. *Psychological bulletin* 136, 2: 151–173.

4. Jamie Antonisse and Devon Johnson. 2013. *Hush*.

5. Arduino. 2015. Arduino Microprocessor. Retrieved from https://www.arduino.cc

6. Gabo Arora, Barry Pousman, and Chris Milk. 2015. *Clouds over Sidra*. Vrse. Retrieved from http://with.in/watch/clouds-over-sidra

7. Audio-Technica. 2014. ATH-M40x. Retrieved from http://www.audio-technica.com/cms/headphones/75b2f282c93a7651

8. Jeffrey Bardzell and Shaowen Bardzell. 2015. Humanistic HCI. *Synthesis Lectures on Human-Centered Informatics* 8, 4: 1–185.

9. Jonathan Belman and Mary Flanagan. 2010. Designing games to foster empathy. *International Journal of Cognitive Technology* 15, 1: 11.

10. Steve Benford and Gabriella Giannachi. 2011. *Performing Mixed Reality*. The MIT Press.

11. Steve Benford, Chris Greenhalgh, Gabriella Giannachi, Brendan Walker, Joe Marshall, and Tom Rodden. 2012. Uncomfortable Interactions. *Proceedings of the SIGCHI Conference on Human Factors in Computing Systems*, ACM, 2005–2014.

12. Mark A. Blythe, Kees Overbeeke, Andrew F. Monk, and Peter C. Wright (eds.). 2005. *Funology: From Usability to Enjoyment*. Springer Netherlands.

13. Ian Bogost. 2007. *Persuasive games: The expressive power of videogames*. Mit Press.

14. Ian Bogost. 2011. *How to do things with videogames*. U of Minnesota Press.

15. Liz Owens Boltz, Danah Henriksen, and Punya Mishra. 2015. Rethinking Technology & Creativity in the 21st Century: Empathy through Gaming--Perspective Taking in a Complex World. *TechTrends* 59, 6: 3.

16. Virginia Braun and Victoria Clarke. 2006. Using thematic analysis in psychology. *Qualitative research in psychology* 3, 2: 77–101.

17. Emily Brown and Paul Cairns. 2004. A Grounded Investigation of Game Immersion. *CHI '04 Extended Abstracts on Human Factors in Computing Systems*, ACM, 1297–1300.

18. James Brown, Kathrin Gerling, Patrick Dickinson, and Ben Kirman. 2015. Dead Fun: Uncomfortable Interactions in a Virtual Reality Game for Coffins. *Proceedings of the 2015 Annual Symposium on Computer-Human Interaction in Play*, ACM, 475–480.

19. Richard Byrne, Joe Marshall, and Florian Floyd Mueller. 2016. Designing the Vertigo Experience: Vertigo As a Design Resource for Digital Bodily Play. *Proceedings of the TEI '16: Tenth International Conference on Tangible, Embedded, and Embodied Interaction*, ACM, 296–303.

20. Karl-Erik Bystrom, Woodrow Barfield, and Claudia Hendrix. 1999. A Conceptual Model of the Sense of Presence in Virtual Environments. *Presence: Teleoperators and Virtual Environments* 8, 2: 241–244.

21. Jordan M. Carpenter and Melanie C. Green. 2012. Flying with Icarus: narrative transportation and the persuasiveness of entertainment. *Psychology of entertainment media, 2nd edn. Routledge, Florence*: 169–194.

22. John W. Creswell. 2014. *Research design: Qualitative, quantitative, and mixed methods approaches*. Sage publications.

23. H. Q. Dinh, N. Walker, L. F. Hodges, Chang Song, and A. Kobayashi. 1999. Evaluating the importance of multi-sensory input on memory and the sense of presence in virtual environments. *Virtual Reality, 1999. Proceedings., IEEE*, 222–228.

24. Paul Dourish. 2001. *Where the Action is: The Foundations of Embodied Interaction*. MIT Press, Cambridge, Massachusetts.

25. Epic Games. 2015. *Unreal Engine 4*. Retrieved from www.unrealengine.com

26. J. E. Escalas and B. B. Stern. 2003. Sympathy and empathy: Emotional responses to advertising dramas. *The Journal of consumer research*.

27. Salvatore Fiore, Peter Wright, and Alistair Edwards. 2005. A Pragmatist Aesthetics Approach to the Design of a Technological Artefact. *Proceedings of the 4th Decennial Conference on Critical Computing: Between Sense and Sensibility*, ACM, 129–132.

28. Mary Flanagan. 2009. *Critical Play: Radical Game Design*. MIT Press.

29. Gonzalo Frasca. 2004. *Madrid*. Retrieved from http://www.newsgaming.com/games/madrid

30. Gonzalo Frasca. 2007. Play the message: Play, game and videogame rhetoric. *Unpublished PhD dissertation. IT University of Copenhagen, Denmark*.

31. Rosemary Garris, Robert Ahlers, and James E. Driskell. 2002. Games, Motivation, and Learning: A

Research and Practice Model. *Simulation & gaming 33*, 4: 441–467.

32. Marientina Gotsis, Judith Piggot, Diana Hughes, and Wendy Stone. 2010. SMART-games: A Video Game Intervention for Children with Autism Spectrum Disorders. *Proceedings of the 9th International Conference on Interaction Design and Children*, ACM, 194–197.

33. D. Grigorovici. 2003. Persuasive Effects of Presence in Immersive Virtual Environments. *In G. Riva, F. Davide, & W. IJsselsteijn (Eds.), Being there: Concepts, effects and measurement of presence in synthetic environments.*

34. Douglas Harper. 2002. Talking about pictures: A case for photo elicitation. *Visual Studies 17*, 1: 13–26.

35. Teresa de la Hera Conde-Pumpido. 2013. A Conceptual Model for the Study of Persuasive Games. *Proceedings of DiGRA 2013.*

36. Ioanna Iacovides and Anna L. Cox. 2015. Moving Beyond Fun: Evaluating Serious Experience in Digital Games. *Proceedings of the 33rd Annual ACM Conference on Human Factors in Computing Systems*, ACM, 2245–2254.

37. ImpactGames. 2007. *PeaceMaker*. Retrieved from http://www.peacemakergame.com

38. Henry Jenkins. 2004. Game design as narrative architecture. *Computer 44*, 3: 118–130.

39. Dan R. Johnson. 2012. Transportation into a story increases empathy, prosocial behavior, and perceptual bias toward fearful expressions. *Personality and individual differences 52*, 2: 150–155.

40. Dena M. Jones. 1997. Advertising Animal Protection. *Anthrozoös 10*, 4: 151–159.

41. Hartmut Koenitz, Gabriele Ferri, Mads Haahr, Diğdem Sezen, and Tonguç İbrahim Sezen. 2015. *Interactive Digital Narrative: History, Theory and Practice.* Routledge.

42. Sara H. Konrath, Edward H. O'Brien, and Courtney Hsing. 2011. Changes in dispositional empathy in American college students over time: a meta-analysis. *Personality and social psychology review: an official journal of the Society for Personality and Social Psychology, Inc 15*, 2: 180–198.

43. Martijn Kors. 2015. Towards Design Strategies for the Persuasive Gameplay Experience. *Proceedings of the 2015 Annual Symposium on Computer-Human Interaction in Play*, ACM, 407–410.

44. Martijn Kors, Erik van der Spek, and Ben Schouten. 2015. A Foundation for the Persuasive Gameplay Experience. *Proceedings of the 10th Foundations of Digital Games Conference (FDG '15).*

45. Petri Lankoski. 2007. Goals, affects, and empathy in games. *Philosophy of computer games.*

46. Brenda Laurel. 1991. *Computers as Theatre*. Addison-Wesley.

47. Aaron Levisohn, Jayme Cochrane, Diane Gromala, and Jinsil Seo. 2007. The Meatbook: Tangible and Visceral Interaction. *Proceedings of the 1st International Conference on Tangible and Embedded Interaction*, ACM, 91–92.

48. Amy Shirong Lu, Tom Baranowski, Debbe Thompson, and Richard Buday. 2012. Story Immersion of Videogames for Youth Health Promotion: A Review of Literature. *Games for health journal 1*, 3: 199–204.

49. Andrés Lucero, Evangelos Karapanos, Juha Arrasvuori, and Hannu Korhonen. 2014. Playful or Gameful?: creating delightful user experiences. *Interactions 21*, 3: 34–39.

50. Gregory Maio and Geoffrey Haddock. 2009. *The psychology of attitudes and attitude change*. Sage.

51. Joe Marshall, Brendan Walker, Steve Benford, et al. 2011. The Gas Mask: A Probe for Exploring Fearsome Interactions. *CHI '11 Extended Abstracts on Human Factors in Computing Systems*, ACM, 127–136.

52. Tim Marsh. 2016. Slow serious games, interactions and play: Designing for positive and serious experience and reflection. *Entertainment computing 14*: 45–53.

53. Tim Marsh and Brigid Costello. 2013. Lingering Serious Experience as Trigger to Raise Awareness, Encourage Reflection and Change Behavior. *Persuasive Technology*, Springer Berlin Heidelberg, 116–124.

54. John McCarthy and Peter Wright. 2004. Technology As Experience. *Interactions 11*, 5: 42–43.

55. Paul Milgram and Fumio Kishino. 1994. A taxonomy of mixed reality visual displays. *IEICE transactions on information and systems 77*, 12: 1321–1329.

56. Chris Milk. 2015. *How virtual reality can create the ultimate empathy machine*. TED. Retrieved April 18, 2016 from https://www.ted.com/talks/chris_milk_how_virtual_reality_can_create_the_ultimate_empathy_machine?language=en

57. Janet Horowitz Murray. 1997. *Hamlet on the holodeck: The future of narrative in cyberspace*. Simon and Schuster.

58. Donald A. Norman. 2005. *Emotional design: Why we love (or hate) everyday things*. Basic books.

59. Oculus. 2014. Oculus Development Kit 2. Retrieved from https://www.oculus.com/en-us/dk2

60. Daniel J. O'keefe. 2002. *Persuasion: Theory and research*. Sage Publications.

61. W. Gerrod Parrott. 2001. *Emotions in social psychology: Essential readings*. Psychology Press.

62. Nonny de la Peña, Peggy Weil, Joan Llobera, et al. 2010. Immersive Journalism: Immersive Virtual Reality for the First-Person Experience of News. *Presence: Teleoperators and Virtual Environments* 19, 4: 291–301.

63. Wei Peng, Mira Lee, and Carrie Heeter. 2010. The Effects of a Serious Game on Role-Taking and Willingness to Help. *The Journal of communication* 60, 4: 723–742.

64. Richard M. Perloff. 2008. *The dynamics of persuasion: communication and attitudes in the twenty-first century*. Lawrence Erlbaum Associates, New York.

65. Mick Power and Tim Dalgleish. 2008. *Cognition and emotion: From order to disorder (2nd ed.)*. Psychology Press.

66. Stanley Presser, Jennifer M. Rothgeb, Mick P. Couper, et al. 2004. *Methods for Testing and Evaluating Survey Questionnaires*. John Wiley & Sons.

67. Andrew K. Przybylski, Edward L. Deci, Edward Deci, C. Scott Rigby, and Richard M. Ryan. 2014. Competence-impeding electronic games and players' aggressive feelings, thoughts, and behaviors. *Journal of personality and social psychology* 106, 3: 441–457.

68. Susana Ruiz, Ashley York, Mike Stein, Noah Keating, and Kellee Santiago. 2006. *Darfur is dying*. Retrieved from http://www.darfurisdying.com

69. Marie-Laure Ryan. 2001. *Narrative As Virtual Reality: Immersion and Interactivity in Literature and Electronic Media*. Johns Hopkins University Press, Baltimore, MD, USA.

70. Marie-Laure Ryan. 2015. *Narrative as Virtual Reality 2: Revisiting Immersion and Interactivity in Literature and Electronic Media*. JHU Press.

71. B. A. M. Schouten, Menno Deen, and M. M. Bekker. 2010. Playful Identity in game design and open ended play. *Proceedings of the Homo Ludens conference*.

72. P. Shaver, J. Schwartz, D. Kirson, and C. O'Connor. 1987. Emotion knowledge: further exploration of a prototype approach. *Journal of personality and social psychology* 52, 6: 1061–1086.

73. Mary Lou Shelton and Ronald W. Rogers. 1981. Fear-Arousing and Empathy-Arousing Appeals to Help: The Pathos of Persuasion. *Journal of applied social psychology* 11, 4: 366–378.

74. L. Shen. 2011. The effectiveness of empathy-versus fear-arousing antismoking PSAs. *Health communication*.

75. Richard Shusterman. 2014. Somaesthetics. In *The Encyclopedia of Human-Computer Interaction, 2nd Ed.*

76. Michael D. Slater and Donna Rouner. 2002. Entertainment—Education and Elaboration Likelihood: Understanding the Processing of Narrative Persuasion. *Communication theory: CT: a journal of the International Communication Association* 12, 2: 173–191.

77. Toby Smethurst and Stef Craps. 2014. Playing with Trauma: Interreactivity, Empathy, and Complicity in The Walking Dead Video Game. *Games and Culture*. http://doi.org/10.1177/1555412014559306

78. Omar Sosa-Tzec, Erik Stolterman, and Martin A. Siegel. 2015. Gaza Everywhere: Exploring the Applicability of a Rhetorical Lens in HCI. *Proceedings of The Fifth Decennial Aarhus Conference on Critical Alternatives*, Aarhus University Press, 69–72.

79. Kurt D. Squire. 2005. Educating the fighter: buttonmashing, seeing, being. *On The Horizon - The Strategic Planning Resource for Education Professionals* 13, 2: 75–88.

80. Luke Stark. 2015. Making Values Visceral. *Aarhus Conference 2015 Workshop: "Charting the Next Decade for Value Sensitive Design.*

81. Sharon T. Steinemann, Elisa D. Mekler, and Klaus Opwis. 2015. Increasing Donating Behavior Through a Game for Change: The Role of Interactivity and Appreciation. *Proceedings of the 2015 Annual Symposium on Computer-Human Interaction in Play*, ACM, 319–329.

82. Jonathan Steuer. 1992. Defining Virtual Reality: Dimensions Determining Telepresence. *The Journal of communication* 42, 4: 73–93.

83. Tale of Tales. 2008. *The Graveyard*. Retrieved from http://tale-of-tales.com/TheGraveyard/index.html

84. Tom Van Laer, Ko De Ruyter, Luca M. Visconti, and Martin Wetzels. 2014. The extended transportation-imagery model: A meta-analysis of the antecedents and consequences of consumers' narrative transportation. *The Journal of consumer research* 40, 5: 797–817.

85. T. Wiseman. 1996. A concept analysis of empathy. *Journal of advanced nursing* 23, 6: 1162–1167.

86. Pieter Wouters, Erik D. Van der Spek, and Herre Van Oostendorp. 2009. Current practices in serious game research: A review from a learning outcomes perspective. *Games-based learning advancements for multi-sensory human computer interfaces: techniques and effective practices*: 232–250.

87. Yager Development. 2012. *Spec Ops: The Line*. Retrieved from http://www.specopstheline.com

88. John Zimmerman, Jodi Forlizzi, and Shelley Evenson. 2007. Research Through Design As a Method for Interaction Design Research in HCI. *Proceedings of the SIGCHI Conference on Human Factors in Computing Systems*, ACM, 493–502.

89. Games for Change. *Games for Change*. Retrieved April 18, 2016 from http://www.gamesforchange.org

90. Amnesty International | Voor de mensenrechten. *Amnesty International Nederland*. Retrieved September 10, 2014 from https://www.amnesty.nl

91. Flickr, a Yahoo company. *Flickr*. Retrieved October 4, 2015 from https://www.flickr.com

Say Cheese! Games for Successful Academic and Student Networking

Emily I M Collins
School of Psychology
University of Birmingham,
Birmingham, B15 2TT, UK
e.collins.2@bham.ac.uk

Anna L Cox
UCL Interaction Centre,
Gower Street, London,
WC1E 6EA, UK
anna.cox@ucl.ac.uk

Frank Lee
Drexel University 3141
Chestnut Street Philadelphia
PA, USA
fjl@drexel.edu

ABSTRACT

Networking is a vital but stressful aspect of academic life, one which digital games may be able to make more playful. Existing examples of networking games require players to interact as part of the game-play, and therefore do not bypass the stressful part of networking. In contrast, many other games successfully encourage interaction between players whilst avoiding causing stress to the players. Flashbulb is a networking game that only requires a photograph of another player to be taken in order to progress. Players can choose whether to start a conversation depending on the target and situation. Thematic analysis of interviews with Flashbulb players found that despite not including an icebreaking *requirement,* it encouraged networking and widened the scope of those spoken to. The act of photographing players promoted conversations without forcing players to engage in uncomfortable discussions. We make recommendations for the design of future iterations of networking games.

Author Keywords

Digital games; networking; icebreaker games

ACM Classification Keywords

H.5.m. Information interfaces and presentation (e.g., HCI): Miscellaneous; K.8.0 General: Games; H.5.2 User Interfaces: User Centred Design; H.5.3 Group and Organization Interfaces: Synchronous interaction

INTRODUCTION

Getting to know new people within a community is a vital aspect of a successful career in research [33] and is one of the main objectives for attending academic conferences [38]. Similarly, new students stand to benefit from getting to know their classmates to share ideas, form professional relationships and work together effectively in group

CHI PLAY '16, October 16-19, 2016, Austin, TX, USA
ACM 978-1-4503-4456-2/16/10.
http://dx.doi.org/10.1145/2967934.2968096

assignments. It can also serve less formal purposes such as feeling part of an academic community. However, many people find networking stressful and sometimes avoid it all-together [34]. Situations that involve meeting new people can be fraught with concerns about how to initiate and maintain conversations with other attendees whom you know little about. As a result, ice-breaking activities have become popular in course inductions and conference sessions which aim to overcome this problem by structuring the social interaction. Whilst such activities make it socially acceptable to initiate a conversation with a stranger, they do little to alleviate the discomfort felt by the participants. Moreover, these interventions are often met with a negative response. Previous studies show that students do not like ice-breaker activities on the first day of a course, despite wanting to get to know other students [17]. There is therefore a need to better explore ways in which networking can be supported as an integral part of events such as student orientations and conferences.

One possibility is to develop and utilize games which encourage and incorporate social interaction in a way that does not form a compulsory part of game-play, but is instead supportive of it. The recent success of games such as Pokémon Go highlight how this may be a successful approach; anecdotal reports suggest that while the structure of the game does not necessitate interactions between players, this is occurring regardless [13,15]. Players are put in a real-life situation as part of the in-game activity and when encountering other players, they have the option of capitalizing on the shared experience of playing and can easily strike up conversation. Alternatively, if they do not wish to do this, they can continue playing without talking to anyone without any detriment to the gameplay. This could result in a rather anti-social game, but to the contrary, numerous media reports suggest that players are often interacting, and relationships are forming from incidental meetings of likeminded players [13,15].

If these kinds of enjoyable, non-compulsory, interactions could be incorporated into games that are specifically designed to promote networking, this may be particularly effective. In this paper we describe the design and evaluation of a game, Flashbulb [11], that facilitates social interaction without forcing players into uncomfortable situations. This work makes several contributions. First, it examines whether Flashbulb itself is successful in supporting networking and identifies the areas in which it could be improved for future events. A second, wider contribution is to the field's understanding of whether games without an in-built conversation requirement can still be successful in providing opportunities for conversations to occur. We argue that a focus on breaking the ice is not necessary within the game itself, as simply playing a game may be helpful in getting people to interact and get to know each other. Knowing that others have consented to play makes it easier and less stressful for individuals to engage in related social interaction, especially when it is apparent that most people's motivations for playing will involve wanting to meet or talk to other people.

The paper subsequently outlines several design implications derived from the findings of these interviews, which stand to benefit those designing games with a similar aim of promoting social interaction. For example, the awkwardness of taking photographs of one another was for many a catalyst for self-driven conversation, and this has interesting implications for the kinds of tasks these games should involve. We suggest initial low barriers of entry should be incorporated together with additional incentives for deeper conversation (beyond those relating to the immediate task) and that future game design should aim to bridge the gap between game and non-game interactions by making it easier for players to communicate once the game has finished.

RELATED WORK

Networking

There are many contexts in which networking and meeting new people are both useful and expected. For instance, attending conferences and discussing research with peers is integral to a successful career in research [33], and evidence suggests that feeling a sense of cohesion and community can significantly impact on course retention rates [35,37]. This has been found to be particularly important for those who find themselves in the minority amongst their classmates, whether in relation to race or gender [8,37], but this can also be countered by programs that promote social interaction between students [8]. A substantial amount of learning (both as a student and in a professional context) occurs through the development and utilization of social networks, which also stands to benefit the wider organization to which connected individuals belong [23]. Therefore, encouraging networking and informal discussions is something that needs to be supported at events such as conferences and orientation days. However, it is not guaranteed that this will happen in the most effective manner possible.

A primary issue is that at events such as orientations and conferences, impromptu discussions and networking opportunities do not occur at the same rate for all attendees. For example, those who are more extravert or are native speakers of the language spoken at the event are at an advantage, as are conference delegates of a higher social or professional status who already have an established

reputation in the field [25]. Consequently, more junior attendees, who arguably stand to benefit the most from extending their professional network, may find it more difficult to strike up conversation. Studies into networking activities at these events also suggest that those who have presented talks are approached substantially more than attendees who did not present [32]. First of all, this suggests that delegates who are not giving papers may be at a disadvantage when it comes to meeting new people, but it also indicates that once a delegate has seen someone presenting their work, it becomes easier to strike up conversation with them; those in the audience will know the person's name, their affiliation and will have a good idea of their research interests. With such details, delegates may feel more comfortable approaching these people and will have a number of suitable topics or questions with which conversation can be initiated.

This initiation of conversation has been argued to be the most difficult aspect of networking [34]. In part, this is due to the need to overcome the sense of awkwardness associated with approaching new people, but also due to having to identify the best way to start conversation without any prior knowledge. Guidelines on how to successfully network at conferences suggest a range of openers depending on who you are approaching (e.g. [34]), such as asking for opinions on conference keynotes or bringing up an interesting topic of debate relating to one of the talks. Nevertheless, even with such conversations in mind, it remains difficult to find a reason to approach a particular person, as well as mitigate the risk that they will not be receptive to such an out-of-the-blue introduction.

Technology for networking

These issues, as well as other practical restrictions of academic events (such as the inability to discuss the current presentation with other people watching it), have led both individuals and organizers to utilise technology in these contexts. The ubiquitous nature of smartphones and WiFi connectivity mean that smartphones have been the main focus of technologies that enhance the conference experience. Technology has been developed to supplement other aspects of the conference experience, for example by providing information on the conference sessions and presenters, and contact information of other delegates [1]. Furthermore, the use of Twitter is well documented. Research suggests that attendees use it as a "back channel" [7,24,31], although Chen [7] reports that this is primarily used to notify attendees of information and not to promote discussions between them. While using Twitter in this manner may increase an individual's visibility (or highlight others they should try to meet) at an event [22,31], it does not necessarily support or encourage real life interactions. Existing social networking applications may therefore not be best suited to creating new connections, and as a vital and difficult aspect of conference attendance, specialist applications have been designed to fill this gap.

The majority of applications and technologies that have been developed for conferences have focused on sharing information of the event itself (such as Conferator which also shows the location of attendees [1]), exchanging contact or profile information based on proximity (e.g. MobiClique [26]), or indeed both (e.g. Find & Connect [38]). These are undoubtedly useful in maximising time spent at the event through ensuring that interesting talks can be attended and that connections that have been made can be followed up on later. However, considering that it is the initiation of these conversations that can be the most challenging part of the process [34], technologies are also needed to support this aspect too.

Games for networking
One possible approach that has demonstrated promise is the use of digital games. There is a growing body of evidence to suggest that in-game socializing can have a number of benefits, including a more immersive gaming experience [6] and more effective stress relief [9] than non-social games. Social games have also been argued to ease some of the anxieties associated with talking to people in offline contexts, particularly for people who find socializing especially stressful (e.g.[10,18,20,21]).

This may be particularly useful for networking, and introducing playful components in these contexts has shown to be effective [5,30] and there is a rising trend of utilising digital games in these contexts [27,36]. Games like Snag 'em [27] and CHI PLAYGUE [36] have been developed with this application in mind, and have shown success in encouraging and supporting interactions [14,27]. However, these games tend to require the player to initiate some form of social interaction in order to play the game. Snag 'em requires players to create a profile and select tags that apply to them which could refer to hobbies, interests or something else that is relevant to the situation in which it is being played, such as workplace or research team. Then, they are presented with "missions" that ask players to find others with a particular tag. For example, players might have to identify someone who plays guitar. While this promises to assist with the task of locating particular attendees of interest, this might still be difficult for those who find the initiation of the interaction daunting. Similarly, CHI PLAYGUE, which was originally developed for the CHI PLAY'15 conference, requires players to scan barcodes on the badges of other attendees in order to "infect" or "cure" players, depending on whether they are aiding the Earthling or Alien teams. Once again, while this provides motivation to approach people and an excuse for starting a conversation, there is still the requirement that players actually start a conversation in order to play the game. This cannot be avoided, irrespective of the personality of the player, the people they are playing with or the situations in which they are playing.

Conversely, games that tend to encourage socializing rarely have inter-player communication at the centre of gameplay; the focus tends to be on a central task that is enhanced or facilitated by interaction, but not dependent on it. For example, the recent release of Pokémon Go has seen numerous media reports discussing the social nature of the game and how relationships are being forged as a result of playing [13,15]. This is despite no in-game requirement for socialising.

Games such as these further demonstrate the success that integrating gaming features into real world behaviours can have in a number of areas (e.g. in encouraging reductions in sedentary behaviours [16]). Moreover, they establish the ability of such games to incentivize and normalize behaviours that may otherwise feel unappealing, awkward or stressful [2,27], which could include networking.

THE GAME: FLASHBULB
Flashbulb (the focus of the present paper), takes a different approach to existing networking games. It is a social game designed for large groups of people in order to maximise the opportunities to meet and to break the ice. It is played on mobile devices, and players take on the role of a "paparazzo". The game provides assignments to photograph other players (chosen at random), the successful submission of which results in points.

Figure 1. Account creation screen for Flashbulb.

Figure 2. The "target" screen on which players are shown who they need to photograph next.

The first stage of the gameplay is an account creation screen (see Figure 1). Here, the players enter their name, contribute a photo of themselves and enter in other profile information such as their affiliation and research interests. Once this is completed, the user can start playing, and will be shown their first target (see Figure 2), a randomly chosen user from the same event. The player will be able to see their target's photograph, their name and the information they entered when creating their account. The task for the player is to locate this person and to take and submit a photograph of them in order to receive their points. A manual assessment process consequently judges whether the photograph submitted is indeed the person it is supposed to be, and if not, the player is informed that they should submit a different photograph.

The player also has the option to skip their target if they cannot find the person, although if they choose to do this, that target will never appear again and so this reduces the potential for scoring. Players have access to information on the time remaining at the event, leaderboards (see Figure 3), and their current rank within the game. They can also update their profile information at any point during the game.

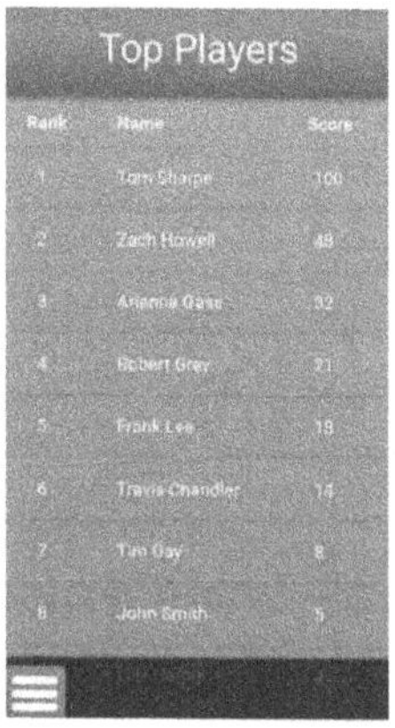

Figure 3. The scoreboard for Flashbulb showing the names of the top players and their scores.

In contrast to other games with the same aim, players only need to take a photo of another person in order to participate in the game. This could feasibly occur in the absence of the awkwardness of starting conversation with a stranger, but would also leave subsequent social interaction open as a possibility. This approach provides a low barrier to entry and one that might feel less stressful (and thus more appealing) to participate in, particularly for individuals who feel less comfortable in social situations. For these people, knowing that there is a way of playing that does not require constant initiation of communication may make it more attractive to play, and may increase the opportunities for networking when they do choose to start a conversation. That said, it is not just the more introverted people that may find this approach beneficial. For many people, willingness to participate socially is not something that remains fully consistent in all situations. Although an individual's behavior will remain somewhat consistent with their overall personality traits, the exact manner and extent to which these traits are expressed will differ depending on the wider context [29], and on the personality of the conversation partner [12]. Additionally, even an extravert who feels very at ease in social situations may encounter some people that they will find intimidating and may be reluctant to speak to. For instance, a postgraduate student being asked to interact with a high ranking conference organizer or head of department could be a very difficult situation for the student to navigate, and they may wish to avoid having to do this. Therefore, in Flashbulb, players have the option to alter the way they play the game on a target-by-target basis, and could therefore choose to strike up conversations with certain players but can also avoid being penalized if one target is someone they simply feel unable to converse with.

The ability to adjust the level of difficulty within the game is an approach that is well-documented in a range of existing games. If a game is too difficult or stressful to play, the game risks losing its ability to be entertaining, and the player may simply quit. As a result many games allow for variations in the level of difficulty, provide cheats that permit players to bypass certain obstacles or, in the case of many role-playing games, let them avoid tasks they do not wish to pursue in favor of those they enjoy. For instance, Mass Effect [3], a third person shooter game, allows players to spend resources in lieu of completing mini games in order to pick locks, should they wish to move on quicker or if they find the mini-games too difficult. Similarly, in Metal Gear Solid V [19], if a player's character dies too many times, the game provides the option of making the character invisible to enemies (through the use of a chicken hat) in order to make the mission easier to complete.

Flashbulb has the capability of following a similar route: whilst it aims to motivate and assist people in engaging in conversations, it also allows users to avoid this should they wish to. The game has a low barrier to entry; points are accrued by taking photographs of other players, which can be achieved by initiating conversation if the player is willing and comfortable, or alternatively, they can just take the photograph and move on.

There are several possible outcomes of incorporating a voluntary social component. One possibility is that it will players to adapt their strategy, thus relieving some of the stress of networking; individuals can approach those they feel comfortable with but will also not be at a disadvantage if they do not wish to strike up conversation with a particular target, perhaps because they are too senior or because they are in the middle of a group conversation. Players can continue to accrue points and the game could still support networking in a less forced and stressful manner.

However, the lack of encouragement to actually converse with other players may also make it an ineffective icebreaker; simply photographing other players and not developing any of these interactions into a conversation would not be useful to individuals hoping to find out more about the other people at the event.

We therefore investigated whether such a game might be able to encourage and support networking. The first stage was to determine whether people engaged with the game. In order to investigate this, we deployed it at a conference and at a postgraduate student program orientation day, two situations in which networking are main goals of the attendees.

DEPLOYMENT EVENTS

The game was deployed at two events. In September 2015 a group of students and academic staff were asked to play as part of a student orientation day. They were encouraged to download the game at the start of the day and a specific time in the schedule (a networking lunch) was identified for playing the game.

In October 2015 the game was also deployed at the CHI PLAY 2015 conference. The game was made available for download during the first day of the conference. The game was played throughout the second day of the conference.

	Student orientation	Academic conference
Profiles created	47	16
Active players	45	16
Profile updates	6	11
Photos submitted	397	106
Photos accepted	338	86
Targets skipped	19	1

Table 1. Descriptive statistics for players at the student orientation and academic conference.

Although there were very different numbers of people playing at the two events, Table 1 demonstrates that, of those who expressed an interest in playing by downloading the game and creating a profile, almost all became active players.

The 47 people who downloaded the game at the student orientation day represented approximately 98% of the people in attendance. In contrast, the 16 people who downloaded the game at the conference represented just ~9% of the people in attendance. This difference is not so surprising. Those at the student orientation day were primarily new students who did not know anyone else: their motivation to get to know each other was likely to be high. However, the conference delegates consist of an existing community of academics, many of whom already know each other from other events.

There is a large difference between the two groups in terms of the number of profile updates that were made during the gameplay. Only ~13% of players at the orientation day updated their profile, whilst ~69% of the players at the conference did so. This further suggests different motivations for playing in the two groups. Perhaps students were motivated in order to get to know who everyone was whilst conference delegates are more concerned with projecting a particular image, communicating particular information about themselves or connecting with people with similar research interests.

The mean number of photos submitted by players at each of the events is very similar (student orientation = 8.8, conference = 7), suggesting comparable levels of engagement with the game. Similarly low percentages of targets were skipped at the two events. We therefore concluded that it would be reasonable to interview players from both events and look for common themes across the transcripts.

The descriptive statistics presented in table 1 suggest that the players at both events were engaged in and perceived value and enjoyment in the game. However, these data do not enable us to determine whether players felt that the game achieved its aim in terms of facilitating networking, or whether they had chosen to adapt their game strategy depending on the targets they had been assigned. In order to investigate these aspects we decided to interview players about their experiences.

EXPERIENCE EVALUATION

Participants

A total of nine participants were recruited (five of whom were female) to be interviewed about their experiences of playing the game. Five were recruited from the student cohort who had played Flashbulb at their course orientation day, and four were conference delegates who had played the game at the CHI Play'15 conference. All were given a £10/$15 Amazon voucher in exchange for their participation in the study.

Procedure

Semi-structured interviews were conducted, mostly over Skype due to the geographical location of the interviewees. However, two of the student sub-group were instead interviewed in person at their university as per their request. Interviews took between 20 and 45 minutes and were recorded and transcribed for analysis.

The interview questions covered motivations for playing, experiences and strategies in relation to different aspects of the game, and whether the game resulted in conversations, as well as probes for more details of how and when they occurred.

Analysis

The transcripts were analyzed using Thematic Analysis in line with the procedure outlined by Braun and Clarke [4].

Results

Several themes emerged from the interview data. These were:

- *Starting conversations* - Flashbulb was most appealing for and apparently successful at allowing individuals to start conversations;
- *Consenting to awkwardness* - Players felt that the task was potentially awkward but that it became fun as everyone taking part had consented to it;
- *Continuing conversations* - Conversations tended to remain superficial and did not always continue beyond the task;

- *A need for greater support* - Players wanted the game to assist more in taking conversation beyond the immediate requirements of the task;
- *Fit with the event* - Players noted that the game's success in encouraging networking relied on it fitting well with the event's geography, nature, cohort and schedule.

We outline each of these below.

Starting conversations

Participants reported that the application was especially useful for providing an excuse to strike up conversations in situations that would normally require a specific reason to start talking to someone. This appeared to be the case for people who found socializing enjoyable:

"While I don't mind talking to most people it was really nice to have an additional reason to just start a random conversation so I really liked excuses to just go around to everyone and be like "hi how are you?" – P1, student

But also for those who were less comfortable with social situations:

"And for somebody who is on the shyer side it makes it easier to approach people. You know who you are approaching, you know their name and also when you see them in the program then you've made a facial, you recognize that person." – P6, conference attendee

"I don't interact with people very well so it was a good excuse for me to chat to people and have a reason to go up to people and start talking to them. Sometimes, especially in things like that you…it can be difficult to go up to people and know what to say, and initiate a conversation with them." – P2, student

This is in line with previous research which has argued that people find it easier to introduce themselves to others when it is as part of a game-based task rather than simply for the sake of networking [27].

Conversing with a wider range of people

Because of this lower barrier to starting conversations, participants also reported that the application encouraged them to talk to people they may have otherwise not interacted with. This could be due to a perceived lack of shared interests:

"…You would eventually get to know the people that interest you at the end, like if you had similar backgrounds or interests, I don't know, but the other ones that you would never have to contact them. Maybe this was a chance to talk to other people as well" – P8, student

Or the person being well-known or in a position of authority:

"I had my supervisor as one of my targets so it was good talking to her more. I guess with people who are more

higher up it's a bit intimidating but I still think it's a good way to start talking to them." – P5, student

This suggests that games which go above and beyond simply matching players based on interests may be especially beneficial. Although players express a preference for meeting like-minded or similarly employed people, it appears that this diversity in networking opportunities is one of the particular benefits of a game-based approach. Opportunities for discussions and socializing between people of different levels (for instance, students and educators) has been argued to be invaluable for the professional development of both parties [23], and this therefore appears to be a particular benefit of this kind of system.

Opting out of intimidating conversations

However the apprehension associated with talking to other, more well-known players did sometimes restrict the extent to which this opportunity was utilized:

"At first there were some people that were like I guess bigger names that I was shy to approach and there wasn't lots of conversation there but mostly because I was shy!" – P7, conference attendee

"Amongst students it was OK but then I had [a staff member] once…I'm sure some people would embrace the opportunity to go up to him, but for me I was a little shy and so…I dunno…it made me feel kind of weird." – P5, student

This indicates that players are utilizing the option to just play the game and not continue conversation beyond this if the situation does not feel right. One conclusion to be drawn from this might be that the game should attempt to not only open up a line of communication between people of varying statuses, but also mitigate the anxiety associated with acting on this. However, in practice this would be a very difficult task considering how well ingrained academic hierarchies are. Consequently, ensuring that opportunities are present to interact with better-known players and providing an opportunity to opt out of conversations if necessary may be sufficient. One possibility might be to attempt to integrate suggestions for openings or appropriate conversation topics for players of different rankings according to job titles, for example. Advice on how to network at conferences tend to differentiate the kinds of conversation starters that would be appropriate for delegates of different levels (for example, fellow PhD students and professors) [34]. Therefore applications such as this may wish to similarly provide more tailored support, appreciating that an individual's networking strategy is likely to depend a lot on the person they are approaching.

Consenting to awkwardness

Although participants did find the actual act of taking photographs or having theirs taken strange (*"I personally don't like being…having a photo taken of me, so I just kind of felt awkward"* P5, student), many participants felt that this was not as stressful as it otherwise would have been due to the fact that it was incorporated in the game:

"It's always a bit embarrassing having your photo taken but it was so quick and everyone was doing it so you didn't feel like you were in the spotlight or anything." – P1, student

Moreover, they knew others would have needed to have been aware of the requirements of the game when signing up. They were consequently able to perceive participation as consent in relation to being approached and having photographs taken:

"Felt a little bit awkward but y'know, we're all playing it, right, so it's kind of fine." – P9, Conference attendee

One possible conclusion to be drawn from this is that the actual task does not need to be something people naturally feel comfortable with in more conventional contexts for it to be effective. In fact, as we will discuss in the following section, it may be beneficial for the task to feel somewhat awkward.

Continuing conversations

Whether or not these initiated conversations resulted in longer discussions seemed to differ very much between participants. Most participants did report to continue conversations beyond simply asking for a photograph

"You wouldn't just snap a photo and not say anything at all, you'd at least say Hi how are you, can I take your picture." – P1, student

"With some people I talked about some paper sessions or some other unrelated things so sometimes I just went to people that I knew, that I know from before, and I had to take a selfie of them, and I used the chance to talk about them when are we going for lunch today or where are we going for dinner tonight, or when are you flying back." - P4, conference attendee.

Consequently, despite no game-based incentive for initiating conversation, players still chose to do so. This was sometimes because it made the interaction less awkward.

"I tried not to [just take a photograph and leave] because I felt awkward when people did that to me so like, "oh, I hope that was a good picture...ha ha" y'know? Just sort of awkward about it so I tried to always make some sort of conversation about something" P7, conference attendee

This suggests that conversation was initiated as a way of countering the awkwardness, whereas in more conventional networking situations, this in itself is the most difficult [34]. Subsequently, it is possible that incorporating an additional, slightly unusual task (in this case, taking a photo of a stranger) distracts from the stress caused by needing to start a conversation. Moreover, the fact that the game itself did not directly incentivize continuing communication between

players may have had the effect of making it feel like a personal choice; removing any sense of coercion or direct expectation could have reduced some of the stress usually experienced in these situations. This once again provides support for the use of games in these situations, as providing a distraction and allowing for what feel like incidental interactions are not usual features of conventional networking.

Conversations taking over from the game

Some participants reported that at one point, conversations actually took over from the game and this was therefore what they shifted their attention to.

"Initially I wanted to do that, like I need to be one of the top three people, but as I interact with people around and the students around who are playing the same game, I begin to seek out more interaction and just get to know them better, so the gamification was less prioritized and I just wanted to socialize." – P3, student

"I kind of played it at the start and then I kind of forgot about it because I was getting into conversations" – P1, student

"My one single reason for playing was to beat [the conference organizer] at the game. But I think in the end the score wasn't as important to me as, like, I just want to play and meet people" – P7, conference attendee

This also has the implication that while scoring is a necessary part of the gaming experience in this context, it is not the only incentive. Support for this also comes from several participants that reported a dip in interest once it became evident that they would not be ranking highly in terms of score. Therefore highlighting the importance of and positive outcomes of the social aspect may be especially beneficial in encouraging players to continue to use the came for socializing.

Depth of conversations

However, the majority reported that the resultant conversations tended to remain superficial.

"Just small talk - hey did you enjoy the conference, will you go to the next session...Not really deep philosophical topics, but small talk is OK I think". – P4, conference attendee

"Yeah but not long conversations, like oh yeah where are you from, or I don't know, what is your background, or how are you, or is it your first time in London, something like that and then OK, bye. This kind of thing." P8, conference attendee

"Since everybody knew what was going on, we were just kind of like "hey! My name is [participant 5]" and like a short introduction, but nothing beyond just names." – P5, student

Increasing familiarity

And therefore, the outcomes tended to be more to do with familiarity than growing friendships.

"It was fun trying to track up the points and introduce yourself to the other person but it didn't lead to the deeper connection I would have hoped for, in the way that other parts of the conference did, the non-playful parts maybe." - P6, conference attendee.

"I think it depended on the classmate, some there would be talking afterward but I think for the most part, not too much. I think it did help though to break the ice. At least you're familiar with people's faces and names kind of, so in that sense I think it definitely helps." – P5, student

"The interactions with the game was like a precursor to later, longer interactions but the longer interactions I don't think were directly part of the game experience at the time, like instant." – P9, conference attendee

This is not necessarily a bad thing, as evidence suggests that familiarity with an individual can eventually lead to more favorable opinions [28], and sometimes simply being aware of who someone is may be beneficial. However, there was also a widespread awareness of there being participants who simply were not interested in any interaction beyond those directly relating to the game itself.

"I wanted to get to know these people better but sometimes someone would be really focused on the game, and so it would get glanced over and they'd run away." - P3, student

"Well, most people just like called my name and then took a picture, or said 'smile' or something like that. There was a couple of people that were like "Oh, hi, have you met... blah blah, nice to meet you!" which was really pleasant but sometimes I'd be like "why are you taking my picture? Oh yeah, the game"." – P7, conference attendee.

A need for greater support

Many of the participants felt that there needed to be more support from the application, particularly in relation to prompting players to continue conversations beyond taking the photographs.

"I think I kind of forgot about the feature where it says 'ask me about...', maybe that could have popped up after you took the photo or something just to give people an extra sort of conversation starter, or a conversation continuer or something like that." – P1, student

"If you had to ask a person a question, or I don't know, tell them something other than "can I take your picture" or something like that. So you had a purpose for asking them something about themselves or something like that." – P8, conference attendee

"I could see a potential in it. I feel like if there was some more facilitation around it, or some more information in it,

it could be a great networking game." – P6, conference attendee

Fit with the event

There was also an appreciation for the notion of fit.

The group

Some participants mentioned this in relation to the group, in particular that a minimum number of people playing to maintain interest...

"After one day you found all the people. I think the game would work best with a minimum of 40 or 50 people." – P4, conference attendee

...as well as the specific interests and commonalities of the group:

"It was easier to talk to people with Flashbulb and maybe it was just the fact that we all have the common...we're all on the same course." – P3, MSc student

"I think the real benefit of that was not networking but because it was a game and CHI Play was a conference about games, so it was an opportunity to try a game research prototype of another institution." – P4, conference attendee

Timings

Timings seemed to also be important to the interviewees, who argued that dedicated time to concentrate on playing and suitable opportunities to get engaged may have maximized the utility of the application.

"It also was during lunch time as well so people were hungry. If that time was truly dedicated to just playing the game I'm pretty sure people would have been more engaged but it kind of overlapped like break time and lunch time and so people were sitting down to eat." – P5, student

"Being at a conference, there are times when you can't do that stuff. You just can't! And so maybe unleashing that in a different time, like just before lunch when there is an immediate opportunity to be able to do that stuff" – P6, conference attendee

Geography of the venue

The nature of the rooms themselves were also highlighted as important:

"It was pretty nice as we were all in this one room and then we can identify people quickly just because we're not separated or in different parts of the building." – P3, student

"It seemed to kind of be people in the vicinity so like the next couple of people that popped up were standing quite close to me anyway, so we didn't really have to...like if you were in a bit of a group chat for a minute, you didn't really have to break that which was quite good" – P1, student

"Well, I mean, right at the start, there were only so many people playing, you just sort of got everybody because we're all there at the coffee break together. The fact there were two coffee breaks sort of did break that up a little bit because it's like "oh they're not in this room, let me go look in the other room"." – P9, conference attendee

Therefore, implementation of these games also needs to consider the wider context beyond the game itself.

DISCUSSION

Flashbulb was successful in supporting players in *starting conversations* by providing an excuse to approach someone in order to take their photograph. This is despite the fact that photos that were taken from a distance were appropriate and there was no requirement from the game that players actually initiated conversations with other players. Players seemed to utilize this, adjusting the level of conversation to the situation (e.g. if the people they were talking to were in a group), and to the target (e.g. keeping stressful conversations with well-known academics brief), as well as interacting with people who were playing despite not wanting to engage in conversation. This suggests that the low barrier to play was successful in allowing for a wide variety of possible strategies that were able to be adapted to suit the individual situation of the player at that particular time. The game was also successful in supporting players in *continuing conversations* beyond the verbal exchange. However, conversations tended to remain superficial and did not always continue beyond the task and therefore participants identified *a need for greater support* in taking conversation beyond the immediate requirements of the task. Players also noted the importance of the game *fitting with the event* in that the game's success in encouraging networking relied on there being appropriate opportunities in the schedule of the event to take part in the game and to engage in conversation with other players.

Therefore, Flashbulb appears to be a successful tool in promoting networking at both student orientation days and academic conferences, with a few possible areas for improvement in terms of providing greater support and ensuring a good fit with the event. More generally, these findings also corroborate the notion that social interaction does not need to be at the core of the gameplay for this to be something the game can support. Giving players options to adapt strategies and to opt out of stressful situations while still providing an excuse or opportunity to strike up conversation if they so wish, may widen the appeal and improve the success of these games.

Implications for design

Based on these findings, there are two main suggestions for the future development of Flashbulb and other ice-breaking games.

Support further conversation (not just initial contact)
The initial act of starting conversation has been argued to be one of the more challenging aspects of networking [34]. However, participants in this study reported that despite Flashbulb making this aspect easier, there were still barriers that prevented these interactions becoming something more meaningful; the game provided a reason to ask someone for a photograph but it relied on the individual to take the conversation beyond this, something that still felt awkward or misplaced for some of the players. Therefore, we suggest that networking games include some provision for conversation continuing beyond the main task of the game (in this case, taking a photograph of another player). Participants interviewed in this study recommended including additional tasks that necessitated a discussion about hobbies or research interests, for example a mini-game that requires players to guess or find out specific details about their target before being awarded their point. Providing this extra level of in-game support above and beyond initiating contact may allow players to feel better able to extend conversation to a greater degree than observed in the present study.

Bridge the gap between game and non-game interactions
Participants reported that the conversations they had as a result of the game tended to remain superficial and did not lead to any stronger relationships. We argue that this is not a failing of the game per se, as friendships are unlikely to blossom from one initial conversation regardless of the context. However, ice-breaking games should aim to facilitate further discussions and opportunities for contact; one participant in particular reported that although they met another player through the game itself, it was the subsequent chance meetings with that individual that led to the discovery of shared interests and the development of a professional relationship. Therefore, we argue that games such as this should supplement gameplay with opportunities to utilize this newfound familiarity. One way this could be included is through the application making it easy to share contact details or links to social networking profiles. Academic relationships (for both researchers and postgraduate students) are often maintained through social networks such as Twitter and Facebook, and applications with the sole purpose of sharing these details have reported success in assisting with networking [1,38].

Limitations

The present study has several limitations. The most notable is the small, self-selected sample who were interviewed. Alongside issues of generalizability, it is also possible that only those who especially enjoyed the game came forward to participate, skewing the present conclusions in a positive direction. As not all of the responses we analyzed were complimentary and suggestions for improvement were outlined, we believe that this did not substantially conflate our conclusions. However, future research may wish to make more specific attempts to recruit players who were indifferent to or disliked the game in question.

As the interviews relied heavily on participants' memory of the event at which they played Flashbulb, attempts were made to interview them as soon after the event as possible. In practice, this was usually around a month after with the maximum amount of time being two months. Participants did not seem to have many issues recalling the game or their reactions to it, but it remains possible that certain details were forgotten. Therefore more immediate data collection would benefit future work in this area.

CONCLUSIONS

In this paper we describe the application of the networking game Flashbulb at a student orientation day and at an academic conference. Interviews with players after these events indicate that it is a promising tool in supporting networking particularly in terms of its ability to provide an excuse to approach a wide range of individuals. Arguably, it is precisely the low barrier to entry that is its success here, and the fact that social interaction is not the central aim of the gameplay. This means that players are able to apply different strategies for acquiring the photo of each of their targets, something that is rarely an option in games that have interaction at their center. If they are allocated a target who they feel particularly concerned about approaching they can choose either to skip that target all together, or else to photograph the target from afar. In contrast, when they are allocated a target who they do not feel intimidated by, they are able to use the game as an excuse to approach the target and start a conversation. Interestingly, the awkwardness of the task at hand (namely, taking a photograph) also appeared to enhance the game's ability to encourage networking, as players felt it was simply to strange a thing to do without also striking up conversation.

However, creating in-game incentives for players to continue discussions beyond the immediate task at hand and ensuring that it is deployed in suitable surroundings are important in its success as a networking tool. Moreover, future games with this aim should also consider addressing ways in which the game could provide an opportunity for players to continue to develop professional relationships beyond the game, such as allowing the exchange of contact details or social media profiles.

ACKNOWLEDGMENTS

We would like to thank Jo Iacovides for her helpful comments, as well as everyone who participated in the interviews.

REFERENCES

1. Atzmueller, M., Kibanov, M., and Scholz, C. Conferator – A Ubiquitous System for Enhancing Social Networking at Conferences. *Proceedings of the International UIS Workshop*, (2015), 1–4.

2. Baranowski, T., Buday, R., Thompson, D.I., and Baranowski, J. Playing for real: Video games and stories for health-related behavior change. *American Journal of Preventative Medicine 34*, 1 (2008), 74–82.

3. BioWare. *Mass Effect*. Microsoft Game Studios, Washington, U.S., 2007.

4. Braun, V. and Clarke, V. Braun, V ., Clarke, V . Using thematic analysis in psychology. *Qualitative Research in Psychology 3*, (2006), 77–101.

5. Butterfield, J. and Pendegraft, N. Gaming techniques to improve the team- formation process. *Team Performance Management 2*, 4 (1996), 11–20.

6. Cairns, P., Cox, A.L., Day, M., Martin, H., and Perryman, T. Who but not where: The effect of social play on immersion in digital games. *International Journal of Human-Computer Studies 71*, 11, (2013), 1069-1077.

7. Chen, B. Is the Backchannel Enabled ? Using Twitter at Academic Conferences. *2011 Annual Meeting of the American Educational Research Association (AERA)*, (2011), 1–13.

8. Cohoon, J.M. Toward improving female retention in the computer science major. *Communications of the ACM 44*, 5 (2001), 108–114.

9. Collins, E. and Cox, A.L. Switch on to games: Can digital games aid post-work recovery? *International Journal of Human-Computer Studies 72*, 8-9 (2014), 654–662.

10. Desjarlais, M. and Willoughby, T. A longitudinal study of the relation between adolescent boys and girls' computer use with friends and friendship quality: Support for the social compensation or the rich-get-richer hypothesis? *Computers in Human Behavior 26*, 5 (2010), 896–905.

11. Drexel University Entrepreneurial Game Studio. *Flashbulb*. 2014. http://egs.excite.drexel.edu/projects/flashbulb/

12. Eaton, L.G. and Funder, D.C. The creation and consequences of the social world: an interactional analysis of extraversion. *European Journal of Personality 17*, 5 (2003), 375–395.

13. Feldman, B. Pokémon Go Is an Okay Game, But a Great Social Network. *New York Magazine*, 2016. http://nymag.com/selectall/2016/07/pokemon-go-is-an-okay-game-but-a-great-social-network.html.

14. Finkelstein, S.L., Hicks, A., Barnes, T., and Charlotte, U.N.C. SNAG : Using social networking games to increase student retention in computer science. *Proceedings of the fifteenth annual conference on Innovation and technology in computer science education*, (2010), 142-146.

15. Francisco, E. Complete Strangers are Meeting By the Dozens Because of 'Pokémon GO.' *Inverse*, 2016. https://www.inverse.com/article/18049-pokemon-go-is-creating-real-life-friendships.

16. Gao, Y., Gerling, K.M., Mandryk, R.L., and Stanley, K.G. Decreasing sedentary behaviours in pre-adolescents using casual exergames at school. *Proceedings of the first ACM SIGCHI annual symposium on Computer-human interaction in play - CHI PLAY '14*, (2014), 97–106.

17. Henslee, A.M., Burgess, D.R., and Buskist, W. Student preferences for first day of class activities. *Teaching of Psychology 33*, 3 (2006), 189–207.

18. Hussain, Z. and Griffiths, M.D. Gender swapping and socializing in cyberspace: An exploratory study. *CyberPsychology & Behavior 11*, 1 (2008), 47–53.

19. Kojima-Productions. *Metal Gear Solid V: Ground Zeroes*. Konami Digital Entertainment, Japan, 2014.

20. Kowert, R.. and Oldmeadow, J.A. Social reputation: Exploring the relationship between online video game involvement and social competence. *Computers in Human Behavior 29*, 4 (2013), 1872–1878.

21. Kowert, R.. and Oldmeadow, J.A. Playing for social comfort: Online video game play as a social accommodator for the insecurely attached. *Computers in Human Behavior 53*, (2015), 556–566.

22. Kwok, R. A conference in your pocket. *Nature 498*, (2013), 395–397.

23. de Laat, M. *Enabling professional development networks: How connected are you?* Open Universiteit, 2012.

24. Letierce, J., Passant, A., Breslin, J.G., and Decker, S. Using twitter during an academic conference: The #iswc2009 use-case. *Proceedings of the Fourth International AAAI Conference on Weblogs and Social Media*, (2010), 279–282.

25. Mccarthy, J.F., Nguyen, D.H., Mccarthy, J.F., et al. Augmenting the social space of an academic conference. *Proceedings of the 2004 ACM conference on Computer supported cooperative work - CSCW '04* (2004), 39-48.

26. Pietiläinen, A.-K., Oliver, E., LeBrun, J., Varghese, G., and Diot, C. MobiClique: Middleware for mobile social networking. *Proceedings of the 2nd ACM workshop on Online social networks - WOSN '09*, (2009), 49–54.

27. Powell, E., Stukes, F., Barnes, T., and Lipford, H.R. Snag'em: Creating community connections through games. *Proceedings of the 2011 IEEE International Conference on Privacy, Security, Risk and Trust and IEEE International Conference on Social Computing (PASSAT/SocialCom)*, (2011), 591–594.

28. Reis, H.T., Maniaci, M.R., Caprariello, P.A., Eastwick, P.W., and Finkel, E.J. Familiarity does indeed promote attraction in live interaction. *Journal of Personality and Social Psychology 101*, 3 (2011), 557–570.

29. Roberts, B.W. and Donahue, E.M. One personality, multiple selves: Integrating personality and social roles. *Journal of Personality 62*, 2 (1994), 199–218.

30. Rogers, Y. and Brignull, H. Subtle ice-breaking: Encouraging socializing and interaction around a large public display. *Workshop on Public, Community. and Situated Displays*, Citeseer (2002).

31. Ross, C., Terras, C., Warwick, M., and Welsh, A. Enabled backchannel: Conference Twitter use by Digital Humanists. *Journal of Documentation 67*, (2011), 214–237.

32. Scholz, C., Atzmueller, M., Stumme, G., Barrat, A., and Cattuto, C. New insights and methods for predicting face-to-face contacts. *WSM 2013*, (2013), 563–572.

33. Stobbe, M., Mishra, T., and Macintyre, G. Breaking the ice and forging links: The importance of socializing in research. *PLoS Comput Biol 9*, 11 (2013), 1–3.

34. Streeter, J. Networking in academia: Generating and enhancing relationships with your acquaintances and colleagues will create a diverse network of sponsors eager to help you succeed. *EMBO reports 15*, 11 (2014), 1109–1112.

35. Tinto, V. Taking retention seriously: Rethinking the first year of college. *NACADA Journal 19*, 2 (1999), 5–9.

36. Tondello, G.F., Wehbe, R.R., Stahlke, S.N., Leo, A., Koroluk, R., and Nacke, L.E. CHI PLAYGUE : A Networking Game of Emergent Sociality. *The ACM SIGCHI Annual Symposium on Computer-Human Interaction in Play (CHI PLAY)*, (2015), 791–794.

37. Treisman, U. Studying students studying calculus: A look at the lives of minority mathematics students in college. *College Mathematics Journal 23*, (1992), 362–372.

38. Zuo, X., Chin, A., Fan, X., et al. Connecting people at a conference: A study of influence between offline and online using a mobile social application. *2012 IEEE International Conference on Green Computing and Communications*, (2012), 277–284.

Trust Me: Social Games are Better than Social Icebreakers at Building Trust

Ansgar E. Depping, Regan L. Mandryk, Colby Johanson, Jason T. Bowey, Shelby C. Thomson

Department of Computer Science, University of Saskatchewan

Saskatoon, SK, S7N 5C9, Canada

{firstname.lastname}@usask.ca

ABSTRACT

Interpersonal trust is one of the key components of efficient teamwork. Research suggests two main approaches for trust formation: personal information exchange (e.g., social icebreakers), and creating a context of risk and interdependence (e.g., trust falls). However, because these strategies are difficult to implement in an online setting, trust is more difficult to achieve and preserve in distributed teams. In this paper, we argue that games are an optimal environment for trust formation because they can simulate both risk and interdependence. Results of our online experiment show that a social game can be more effective than a social task at fostering interpersonal trust. Furthermore, trust formation through the game is reliable, but trust depends on several contingencies in the social task. Our work suggests that gameplay interactions do not merely promote impoverished versions of the rich ties formed through conversation; but rather engender genuine social bonds.

Author Keywords

Trust; distributed teams; online game; social play

ACM Classification Keywords

K.8.0 [Personal Computing]: General - Games.

INTRODUCTION

The performance of project teams depends on many factors; one of the key factors is the interpersonal trust – the "willingness to be vulnerable based on positive expectations about the actions of others" [39] – that exists between team members [15,56]. Low interpersonal trust in project teams can lead to collaboration problems, including poor decision making, hampered information exchange, increased risk of misunderstandings, and higher personal conflict [23,15]. Higher trust on the other hand, leads to organizations that work more efficiently, and adapt more quickly to changing circumstances [15,68]. For project teams that work in a face-to-face context, there are multiple established methods of facilitating trust development; team-building activities such as social

CHI PLAY '16, October 16-19, 2016, Austin, TX, USA
© 2016 ACM. ISBN 978-1-4503-4456-2/16/10…$15.00
DOI: http://dx.doi.org/10.1145/2967934.2968097

icebreaker games, ropes courses, and even trust falls – part of the quintessential team-building movie montage – have been shown to be effective at facilitating trust development within collocated project teams [34].

Literature suggests two underlying strategies for facilitating trust development. First, developing the feeling that another team member is trustworthy assists with trust development [69,56], and can be scaffolded through personal information exchange [70] and feelings of similarity [19]. Second, the situational context can assist with trust development – situations that involve interdependence and mutual risk promote trust building [27,56]. In collocated teams, both strategies can be employed to facilitate trust formation among team members. For example, social icebreakers enable information exchange and a feeling of similarity, while the trust fall represents the epitome of risk and interdependence.

However, geographically-distributed project teams are becoming increasingly common, as many knowledge workers are able to telecommute and do not have to live in the city in which they work [47]. The rise of distributed project teams raises the question of how trust development is affected by the online virtual interactions that replace face-to-face communication. Research shows that trust is more difficult to achieve in distributed teams, especially in the initial phases of a project [2,28,29]. Trust develops more slowly in distributed teams [27], and once developed, it is also more fragile and easily damaged [70]. These findings call for effective strategies to facilitate trust development in distributed teams. However, traditional strategies that engender trust formation are difficult to transfer to distributed digital communication. From a purely practical perspective, access to team-building activities is limited when team members are distributed in that the activity itself has to be feasible in an online context. As such, current online trust-building approaches use the strategy of promoting trustworthiness, facilitated through personal information exchange [56]. However, current systems fail to employ the second strategy of promoting risk and interdependence – the online equivalent of ropes courses or trust falls are not available to facilitate trust development in distributed teams.

Considering the various social activities that people already participate in online, we argue that there is potential in multiplayer online games to allow players to experience risk and interdependence in a safe and playful environment, addressing the situational context of trust. While the stakes in a game might not have real-world consequences, the vulnerability that is developed, and the need for cooperation with other team members are real. Given their popularity, capacity to help players feel connected [59,66], and ability to simulate risk and interdependence, there is reason to believe that online multiplayer games can be used to facilitate trust building in distributed project teams. Previous literature has already indicated that groups will accept online multiplayer games as a team-building activity [16,36,44], and also provides design guidelines for collaborative games whose purpose is team building [16,44]. However, previous literature has not evaluated the ability of games to enable trust formation.

Previous literature and theoretical frameworks on trust formation suggest that online games can be a viable alternative to current interventions based on personal information exchange. Our goal was to determine whether or not a game could compete with a social task at building trust. First we developed an online puzzle-based multiplayer game that employs interdependence and creates risk, and we then determined whether it could build trust between distributed strangers. We also created a social task that promotes personal information exchange and similarity development to represent the standard in online team-building. We compared the game to the social icebreaker task in an online experiment with 34 pairs of strangers conducted through the web browser using voice chat. Our results showed that:

- Overall, our game is more effective than a social task at building trust between distributed strangers.

- Our game is as effective as a social task at facilitating interpersonal interaction, including the development of relational depth, affect, and interpersonal involvement.

- Trust formation in the game is reliable, whereas the efficacy of the social task is contingent on several factors:

  - Personality–the game works equally well for everyone, whereas the social task works less well for individuals low in propensity to trust or agreeableness.

  - Enjoyment of the experience–the game works equally well for everyone regardless of whether or not they enjoyed it; however, the social task does not work well for people who did not enjoy it.

- The efficacy of our game for building trust is also not affected by age, gender, or gaming experience, suggesting that it is an option with broad demographic appeal.

Our work shows that our game not only worked better for trust development than a social task in general, but that trust development in the game was robust to individual personality characteristics, task enjoyment, and interpersonal experience, whereas trust development in the social task was sensitive to these factors. As such, online social games should be considered as an approach to foster trust-building in distributed project teams. The relationships built through gameplay are sometimes considered as impoverished versions of the rich bonds that are created through conversation. We contribute to a growing body of work suggesting that games can facilitate deep and meaningful social bonds.

RELATED LITERATURE

We propose that games can be used to facilitate trust development in distributed teams. The increasing technological support for telecommuting along with the dearth of skilled workers in certain fields means that more workplace teams are integrating geographically-remote workers or allowing team members to work from home [47]. Ensuring that distributed members of a team are well integrated is essential for the productivity and well-being of the entire team [15,56]. In this section, we present the arguments about the importance of trust development for distributed teamwork, describe how trust is developed, present technologies (including games) that facilitate trust development, and describe how games are used to foster relationship building.

Why Trust is Important

Interpersonal trust is believed to be one of the key factors influencing the performance and efficiency of both face-to-face and distributed teams [1,5,7,12,20,28,29,52,63,64]. Trust is most commonly defined as a "willingness to be vulnerable based on positive expectations about the actions of others" [39]. When trust is low within a work group, collaboration problems may occur. Low trust is associated with poor decision-making [22,23,56], a lack of sharing relevant information with team members [10,56], a tendency to avoid coordination with team members [24,61], increased misunderstandings, and escalating conflicts [22,23, 56]. High trust among team members has been shown to have positive effects on team communication [3,11,14], team identification [40,48,54], negotiations among dyads [58,33], conflict resolution [11,49,68], individual performance [54,53], and team performance [14,15,68].

How Trust is Developed

Russman et al. [56] proposed a model of trust development that can be applied to face-to-face and distributed teams. Following Zolin et al. [69], they distinguish between *trust* and *trustworthiness*. Interpersonal *trust* is conceptualized as a state that determines whether the trustor engages in trusting behavior towards the trustee, whereas trustworthiness is conceptualized as the trustor's perception of how trustworthy the trustee is. Interpersonal trust as a state is determined by the perceived trustworthiness of the trustee [60,69], but also by the characteristics of the trustor (e.g., the inherent propensity to be trusting, mood) [55,39,67,56], and the situational context (e.g., perceived risk) [56,69,37,27].

The trust state determines whether the trustor engages in trusting behavior for each interaction. If the consequences of an interaction were positive, perceived trustworthiness of the trustee increases, which impacts the trust state in future interactions [56]. Trust is therefore built through repeated feedback loops of trust state, trusting behavior, and positive consequences. Because of these self-enhancing properties, researchers stress the importance of initial trust building right at the formation of work groups [56,69,71,28,29].

Trust Development in Distributed Teams

A large body of research has shown that distributed teams face difficulties in building and sustaining trust

[28,29,65,2,70]. These challenges and their effects on inter-personal trust can be summarized in three groups:

First, trust formation works differently when teams are not collocated. Distributed teams tend to have less information about trustworthiness available and fewer chances for personal communication, which leads to assessments of trustworthiness based on stereotypes and generalizations [27,32]. These initial assessments of trustworthiness are harder to change ('sticky'), and heavily impact interpersonal trust, further stressing the importance of initial trust formation in distributed teams [69,70,56]. Second, interpersonal trust that does get built tends to be more fragile and easily damaged in distributed teams than the more robust trust that is based on an extensive history of shared experiences [2,27,65,70,56]. Third, the overall levels of interpersonal trust and trustworthiness appear to be lower in distributed teams, and team members appear to need higher initial trust to engage in collaborative behaviour [56,69].

Current Methods of Building Trust in Distributed Teams

Trustworthiness. In order to engender trust formation in distributed teams, interventions often aim to compensate for the lack of personal and background knowledge in distributed teams [19,56,70,46]. The goal of these interventions is to enhance the initial assessment of trustworthiness. Team members are sometimes encouraged to *exchange personal information* or supply information on trust warranting properties. The sharing of personal information has been shown to increase the perceived trustworthiness of other group members. This in turn facilitates trust formation and allows for a more robust and stable trust in distributed teams [56]. Zolin et al. [70] found a positive impact of personal information exchange on perceived trustworthiness, and Feng et al. [19] argue that helping group members to find similarities amongst each other promotes interpersonal trust.

Characteristics of the trustor. Other factors that will influence interpersonal trust are characteristics of the trustor, such as personality traits. Research has shown that there is an *inherent propensity to trust* that determines how easily someone trusts people in general [55,39,67]. While personality plays a role in trust formation, it is not something that can be changed easily. Therefore, trust-building interventions don't generally address this aspect of trust formation; however, the role of individual characteristics has to be acknowledged in trust-building interventions.

Context. The other factor that strongly affects interpersonal trust formation is situational context. Research on context properties shows that two concepts are important to facilitate trust formation: *risk* and *interdependence* [27,56]. Risk can be described as an uncertainty about the outcome of an interaction [56]. Interpersonal trust is required when the trustor has a potential gain or loss through the interaction with the trustee. The higher the stakes, the more trust is needed to compensate the uncertainty. An ideal context will therefore provide an appropriate risk/trust ratio that encourages the trustor to risk cooperatively engaging with the trustee. Be-cause new teams often have low initial trust [56] toward each other, starting with low risks might be recommendable. Interdependence is the extent to which a trustor is dependent on the actions of the trustee [27]. If the actions of another person are irrelevant for the personal outcome of the trustor, then trust is neither necessary nor will it form through the interaction [27,56]. If a context involves risk and high interdependence, the trustor is vulnerable to the actions of the trustee. According to current models of trust formation, this vulnerability, in combination with positive experiences, should lead to an increase in perceived trustworthiness and in turn interpersonal trust [69,56].

To our knowledge, current approaches for trust building in virtual teams ignore contextual factors. Current approaches of information exchange (e.g., personal profiles, group chats) don't encourage team members to be vulnerable towards their team members. We believe collaborative games can be an ideal setting for team members to experience risk and interdependence in a safe and playful environment. While the stakes in games might not have real world consequences, the feeling of vulnerability and the need for cooperation with other team members are real.

Digital Games as Team Building Exercises

Research has started to investigate whether or not games are a viable form of team building for distributed teams. Research has shown that in-game performance and effort influence how team members feel about their partner [9]. The access to online 3D virtual worlds has inspired studies investigating their potential to support collaborative work. Ellis et al. [16] propose the use of playful group activities in the virtual world *Second Life* to increase cohesion in groups. The study doesn't evaluate the effectiveness of these games to enhance group cohesion or trust, but focuses on the design challenges and frameworks that are relevant when designing games for team building. Lewis, Ellis and Kellogg [36] used a game to investigate leadership behavior. Chat interviews with the groups suggested that games should be considered as a viable team-building intervention. Similar results were shown by Bozanta et al. [4], suggesting that playing a game in a 3D virtual world can have positive effects on group identification and team building.

Nasir et al. [44,45] compared the group interaction of three face-to-face groups that played an icebreaking game before a group exercise to three face-to-face groups that did not interact before the group exercise. Their research indicates that playing an icebreaking game has, for the most part, positive effects on group communication in terms of talking activity, and group member participation. Because of the very low sample size, it is difficult to generalize these results to distributed team building. While these results point to the potential benefits of games as icebreakers in subsequent face-to-face collaborations, it is unclear if their results can be transferred to distributed teams. Furthermore, only the first pilot study [44] compared a game condition with a non-game icebreaker condition. The promising initial results were not verified in the actual study [45].

Together all of these results seem to indicate that games are potentially suitable team-building activities for distributed teams. The current literature also suggests that groups accept games as a viable team building exercise, even in a business context [4]. Previous work has provided solid design guidelines for collaborative games [44,45,16]. These guidelines have partially been derived from literature on educational games and partially derived from qualitative analysis of collaborative game play. Literature is in agreement that the game should be cooperative in the sense that players should be working towards the same goal, they should be required to come up with communication strategies in order to play successfully, and they should fulfill different roles within the game [16,44]. Keeping theories on trust formation in mind, it becomes evident that these are all game mechanics that enhance the interdependence of the game. Literature also suggests to keep the difficulty low and employ easy to use interfaces. [16,44].

Following these guidelines, a game should be an interdependent task that rewards or even requires coordination and cooperation. Players should also have the chance to take risks with other players within the safe space of a playful interaction. The risk of winning or losing in a game has no real life consequences. We therefore think it is optimal to encourage players to take risks despite low initial trust. The artificial vulnerability that cooperative games create could be ideal for players to *rehearse trust* in a playful environment that encourages trusting behavior. We therefore think that games can be used specifically to foster trust in distributed teams. This approach does not involve information exchange to increase perceived trustworthiness and is therefore quite different from current trust-building interventions. In the next section, we describe a study that tested our assumptions and investigated whether a game can compete with the trust-building properties of a task designed for personal information exchange.

EXPERIMENT

We conducted an online experiment to explore whether games can facilitate trust development in distributed teams. In our experiment, half of the participants played a game to facilitate trust development. To compare our game to a control condition, the remaining participants completed a social icebreaker task used for developing trust.

Labyrinth Game

We created *Labyrinth* (see Figure 1), a networked, cooperative 2-player, asymmetric role puzzle game implemented using the Unity3D game Engine. Labyrinth is played on a tiled board where each tile comprises a piece of a maze (a road through a lake of lava).

Players start on fixed positions within the maze as either the *Pusher* or *Collector*. Moving along the road, the pair's goal is to enable the Collector to collect all of the gems, which appear at fixed locations around the maze. The Pusher can reconfigure the maze by sliding tiles horizontally or vertically, by holding the Shift key and walking towards a wall to

"push" the row or column. To foster coordination and communication (over voice chat) between the players, they can only see the other player character's location on the board if they are close to each other; otherwise the other player is invisible. Four rocks are also scattered across the map for players to use as landmarks when communicating locations [62]. The maze's initial configuration was designed such that players would have to work together to effectively move the rows and columns to collect all of the gems. Players completed 4 rounds of 2 minutes, alternating playing as the Pusher or Collector. After each round the participants were given their score with a grade (bronze, silver, gold, or platinum) to give performance feedback.

The mechanics of the game were specifically designed to satisfy the guidelines for developing trust proposed by literature. Players were working together toward the same goal of collecting all of the gems. They were given different but complementary roles. Communication between the players was necessary to coordinate which path to take, to communicate player location, and to strategize. We made the input straightforward, using only arrow keys and shift. The level design was simple enough that most gems could be accessed with a single wall push.

Social Icebreaker Task

For our non-game control condition, we implemented an online version of a social icebreaker task in Construct 2, using WebRTC for the networking. We designed a set of questions that were presented to both participants and that they were encouraged to ask each other over voice chat. In total, the social task included 30 questions. Participants had to talk for at least 15 seconds after the presentation of a question before they could advance to the next question; this feature was included to ensure that participants did not run out of system-presented content during the duration of the social icebreaker task. They could also dwell on questions for as long as they liked and there were no constraints placed on the content of their conversations.

This social task was designed to stimulate conversation and information exchange. As described in the related literature section, social interaction and exchange of personal information about team members is a current method of developing trust in distributed teams [56]. We created the questions with specific criteria in mind. We did not want participants to feel uncomfortable providing personal information, so we avoided questions that included age, address, or place of work. We also avoided questions about controversial or divisive topics, such as religion or politics. To support conversational flow, the questions were phrased openly so that participants were encouraged to give longer and more elaborate answers than a simply yes or no answer (e.g., "Where did you grow up?", "If you had a year off with pay, what would you do?", "When you are stressed out, what do you do to relax?"). We tested our icebreaker questions in a pilot study and found that the social task worked well to facilitate communication between distributed strangers online. We also observed reoccurring questions the pilot participants asked and included them in final version. (e.g., "How long have you been working on Mechanical Turk?", "What kind of hits do you usually do?").

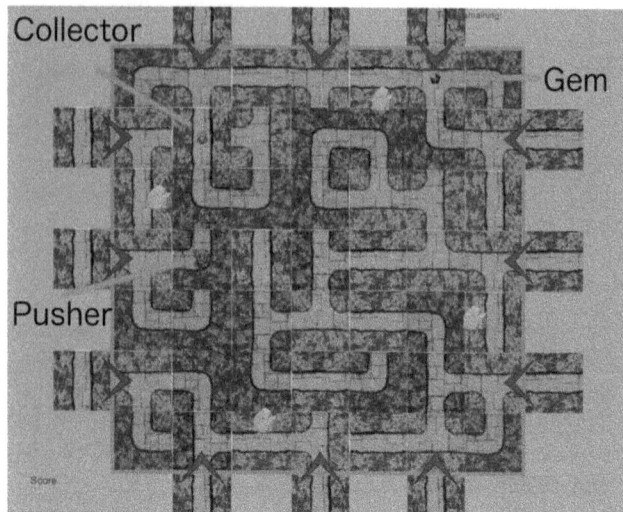

Figure 1: Annotated image of game board

Measures

First, we measured interpersonal trust between the participant and their partner as our main outcome measure. Based on literature on interpersonal trust formation, we expected characteristics of the participants to affect trust formation. Therefore we measured individual propensity to trust and the big five personality dimensions. We were also interested in how the participants perceived the social interaction. We drew from early communication research and distinguished the content of the social interaction from the relational aspects of communication [31,13]: Any given interaction can be analyzed in terms of what it reveals about the relationship between the two participants [13]. Because these are abstract dimensions independent of content, they allow us to compare the two very different tasks in terms of how they impact relational communication. Finally, to understand how trust formation interacts with the experience of the trust development task, we measured how participants experienced the task (game or social task) by including established experience measures from games user research. Unless otherwise mentioned all item responses were measured on a 7-point-Likert scale:

Interpersonal Trust: Most scales for interpersonal trust are designed for close romantic relationships [50,35,30]. We selected 5 items from the Rempel trust scale [50] (e.g., *"I could count on my partner to be concerned about my welfare."*), 4 items from the Dyadic Trust scale [35] (e.g., *"I feel that my partner can be counted on to help me."*) and 2 items from the Specific Interpersonal Trust Scale [30] (e.g., *"I could expect my partner to tell the truth."*) to have enough items appropriate for our setting of loose platonic relationships. Our interpersonal trust scale was an internally consistent measurement of trust (Cronbach's α=.922, M=5.46, SD=.93).

Propensity to Trust: We measure general propensity to trust as proposed by Yamagichi [67]. The 6-item questionnaire (M=4.94, SD=.93) asks participants to rate statements such as *"Most people are basically honest."*.

Ten-Item Personality Inventory (TIPI): We assessed personality using the TIPI [18]. The questionnaire measures the personality dimensions commonly known as the Big Five [26]: extraversion (M=3.87, SD=1.60), agreeableness (M=5.50, SD=1.20), openness to new experiences (M=5.66, SD=1.19), conscientiousness (M=5.79, SD=1.07) and neuroticism (M=2.52, SD=1.31) .

Intrinsic Motivation Inventory (IMI): IMI used a 5-point-Likert scale to measures the interest/enjoyment (M=4.14, SD=.67), effort/importance (M=4.44, SD=.48), pressure/tension (M=2.43, SD= .93), and perceived competence (M=3.42, SD=1.09) felt during a task [41].

Relatedness: We used the relatedness subscale from the Player Experience of Needs Satisfaction (PENS) scale to assess perceived satisfaction of relatedness (M=3.71, SD=.68) on a 5-point-Likert scale [57].

Relational Communication Scale (RCS): We measure relational communication with a selected set of subscales from the RCS [13]. We measure involvement (M=5.13, SD=1.26), affect (M=48, SD=1.08), similarity/depth (M=4.62, SD=1.13), receptivity/trust (M=5.70, SD=.87), and formality (M=3.17, SD=1.12).

Participants and Deployment Platform

The study was deployed on Amazon's Mechanical Turk (MTurk) crowdsourcing platform. MTurk connects paid workers to *Human Intelligence Tasks* (HITs) and has been shown to be a reliable research tool [38]. We had 52 pairs of participants in our study; however, one participant left after the task, resulting in 103 participants completing the full study. Participants completed informed consent and were compensated with $2.50 for the 15-20 minute study.

During the deployment of the study, we encountered client-side networking errors that caused technical difficulties for many of our participants (due likely to low-bandwidth connections). We excluded participants from the study if their voice chat did not work or the experimental platform froze. Some of the remaining participants also experienced minor networking issues – particularly in the game condition because it required real-time networking. The debrief comments and the voice chat recordings indicate that these issues clearly impacted the play experience. We will address these shortcomings in the discussion.

Procedure

Participants began with instructions about the expectation that they have a working microphone, they will be recorded, they should be free to interact with a partner for 10 uninterrupted minutes, and that the Unity Web Player plugin was required. Participants completed the trait questionnaires and then proceeded to a matchmaking page that matched people based on the order they arrived. Once participants were matched, the pair was randomly assigned to complete either the icebreaker or labyrinth game task.

The icebreaker started as soon as audio communication was established and both participants pressed a button to indicate they were ready. It lasted 8 minutes. A countdown timer showed for the last 10 seconds of the task before participants were automatically redirected to the remaining questionnaires so that they could say goodbye.

The labyrinth game had a 90-second tutorial video that played before participants were connected to each other. After the video, the audio chat was established and written instructions were also provided. The game began only once it had finished loading for both participants and lasted for 8 minutes. Following the experiment, participants completed the remaining questionnaires and completed a debrief page.

Data Analyses
We excluded participants for being noncompliant in filling out the questionnaires. We identified non-compliance if participants had zero variance in their answers or spent less than one-second per item on average on our main outcome scale (interpersonal trust). In total, we excluded 37 participants due to the previously-mentioned technical issues and non-compliance, leaving 67 participants: 31 male (age: m = 35.18, SD = 9.65, min = 23, max 64).

To test our hypotheses, we used SPSS to perform multivariate analysis of variance (MANOVA) for comparison of means and multivariate regression analysis to investigate moderating effects. We analyzed our data on the individual level and not dependent on pair membership. For all subsequent analyses, we ran a post-hoc power analysis using G-Power. Given our sample size of 67, an α set to 0.05, and estimated small effect sizes (f = 0.10), our statistical power was above 0.90 thereby allowing us to assume the null hypothesis when no significant differences were found [17].

RESULTS
Of 67 remaining participants, 35 experienced the social task and 32 the game. The difficulties experienced while playing the game led to some teams performing rather poorly during the game. Over all four rounds, teams collected on average 15.65 gems (SD = 6.97; min = 7, max = 30). Because poor performance could potentially influence trust formation, we median split teams into high and low performing teams and compared their interpersonal trust scores using ANOVA: there was no effect of performance on trust formation (F=.965, p<.334, η^2=.03).

Q1. Does the game work better than the social task at building interpersonal trust?
To determine the effects of task on trust development, we conducted a MANOVA with task (social, game) as a between-subjects factor on trust development, on establishing relational communication, and on generating satisfaction of relatedness. The MANOVA revealed an overall significant effect of task ($F_{1,29}$=6.76, p<.001, η^2=.45); we investigate each individual measure in the following sections.

Building Trust
The MANOVA revealed a significant effect of task on trust development ($F_{1,65}$=13.5, p<.001, η^2=.17), showing that the game was significantly better at supporting trust development than the social task (see Figure 2).

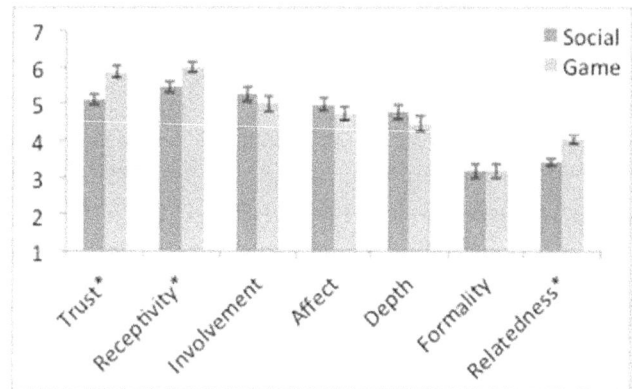

Figure 2. Main effects of condition on interpersonal trust, relational communication, and task experience.

Relational Communication
The MANOVA revealed a significant effect of task on the receptivity and trust subscale of the relational communication scale ($F_{1,65}$=7.51, p=.008, η^2=.10), showing that the game produced greater receptivity than the social task (see Figure 2). The receptivity subscale measures an individual's perception of the sincerity, honesty, openness, and willingness to listen of their partner.

There was no difference between the game and social task on involvement ($F_{1,65}$=0.65, p=.424) – which measures an individual's perception of the enthusiasm and interest of their partner, affect ($F_{1,65}$=.81, p=.371) – the warmth and closeness of their partner, depth ($F_{1,65}$=1.4, p=.244) – the friendliness, similarity, depth of conversation, and desire for further communication of their partner, or formality ($F_{1,65}$=.003, p=.954) – how casual/formal they perceived their partner to be (see Figure 2).

Although the social task was comprised of sharing personal information – whereas the game was comprised of enacting cooperative and interdependent game mechanics – there was no advantage of the social task in any aspects of relational communication.

Relatedness and Experience
The MANOVA revealed a significant effect of task on perceived relatedness ($F_{1,65}$=15.6, p<.001, η^2=.19), showing that the game was significantly better at satisfying the psychological need for relatedness than the social task (see Figure 2). There were also significant differences for perceived competence ($F_{1,65}$=53.30, p<.000, η^2=.45), and tension ($F_{1,65}$=6.57, p<.01, η^2=.09). Perceived competence was higher in the social task and perceived tension was higher in the game. We partially attribute these results to the technical difficulties during gameplay, but also to the fact that a conversation in our context is a familiar task with low pressure. The other task experience measures showed no differ-

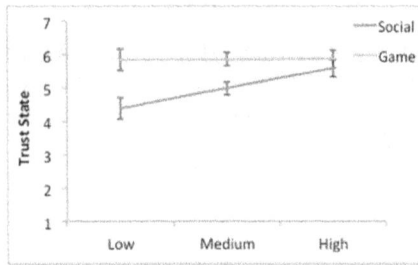

Figure 3: Interaction of propensity to trust (low, medium, high) with condition on interpersonal trust.

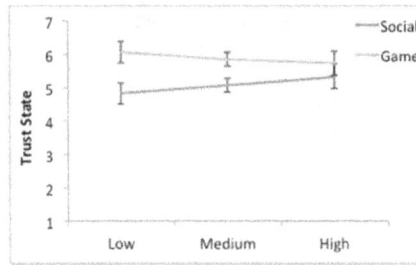

Figure 4: Interaction of agreeableness (low, medium, high) with condition on interpersonal trust.

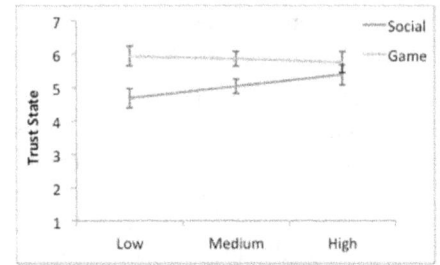

Figure 5: Interaction of condition and enjoyment (low, medium, high) on interpersonal trust.

ences: interest/enjoyment ($F_{1,65}$=2.56, p<.114, η^2=.04), and effort ($F_{1,65}$=2.56, p<.114, η^2=.00).

Q2. Do the trust-building advantages of the game depend on individual characteristics?

We showed that the game works better than the social task overall at building trust amongst distributed strangers (Q1) We further investigated whether the efficacy of games was dependent on demographic variables (e.g., gamers, women) or particular traits (e.g., extroverts, people who are inherently trusting) as is suggested by literature of trust formation [56]. To investigate the role of the continuous demographic factors, we conducted moderated regressions in which we investigated whether the prediction of trust by task (game, social task) was moderated by the demographic or personality factor of interest (see Data Analyses section).

In each of the regressions, task (game or social) significantly predicts trust; however, the role of the moderating factor varies. To investigate the role of the categorical demographic factors (i.e., gender and gaming experience), we conducted univariate analysis of variance.

Age

The moderated regression shows that task (game or social) predicts trust (β=.75, p<.001). However, age does not predict trust (β=.01, p=.284), nor does it moderate the effect of task on trust (p=.265).

Gender

To investigate the effect of gender on trust, we conducted a univariate analysis of variance (ANOVA) with gender (male, female) and task (game, social) as two between-subjects factors; because gender was collected as a categorical and not continuous variable, we could not conduct a moderated regression (note that although we provided other options, participants all answered either male or female). The ANOVA shows a significant main effect of task (game or social) on trust ($F_{1,63}$=11.8, p=.001, η^2=.16). Although we also see a significant main effect of gender on trust ($F_{1,63}$=4.84, p=.031, η^2=.07), it does not interact with task ($F_{1,63}$=0.44, p=.511). The main effect of gender shows that women (N=36, mean =5.70, SD=0.74) develop more trust than men (N=31, mean=5.18, SD = 1.06) in our sample.

Gaming Experience

Gaming experience was collected using an ordinal scale (from not at all through to every day). We divided partici-

pants into two groups – those who played multiple times per week or more (N=45) and those who played once per week or less (N=22). We conducted a univariate ANOVA with gaming experience and task as two between-subjects factors. As expected, the ANOVA shows a significant main effect of task (game or social) on trust ($F_{1,63}$=15.8, p<.001, η^2=.20). There was no main effect of gaming experience on trust ($F_{1,63}$=0.99, p=.324); however, there was a marginally significant interaction with task ($F_{1,63}$=3.74, p=.057, η^2=.06). The interaction showed that the game was significantly better than the social task at generating trust for people with less gaming experience (p=.001), but only marginally better for people with more experience (p=.078).

Propensity to Trust

We conducted a moderated regression with task (game, social) as the predictor of trust state, moderated by an individual's propensity to trust (trait). As expected, task significantly predicted trust development (β=.878, p<.001). General propensity to trust also significantly predicted trust development (β=.348, p=.004). In addition, propensity to trust moderated the effect of task on trust development (p=.009). As Figure 3 shows, for people with low (p<.001) or medium (p<.001) propensity to trust, the social task performed significantly worse than the game; however, for people high in propensity to trust, the social task did not perform worse than the game (p=.294). In other words, the game works equally well for people regardless of their general propensity to trust; however, the efficacy of the social task declines with an individual's propensity to trust.

Personality

We conducted five moderated regressions – one for each of the big five personality factors. As expected, in each case, task predicted trust. However, personality was not a significant predictor of trust: Extraversion (β<.001, p=.999), Agreeableness (β=.022, p=.846), Conscientiousness (β=.076, p=.481), Neuroticism (β=-.040, p=.653), and Openness (β=-.076, p=.526). In addition, Extraversion (p=.254), Conscientiousness (p=.433), Neuroticism (p=.653), and Openness (p=.805) did not moderate the prediction of trust. Agreeableness marginally moderated the effect of task on trust development (p=.079). Similar to the effect of propensity to trust, for people with low (p<.001) or medium (p<.001) agreeableness, the social task performed significantly worse than the game; however, for people high in agreeableness, the social task did not perform significantly worse than the game (p=.426) (see Figure 4).

Q3. Do the trust-building advantages of the game depend on the experience during the task?

In addition to investigating whether the effect of task on trust development was affected by demographic factors, we wondered whether or not trust depended on the participants' experience of the task. To investigate the role of task experience, we conducted moderated regressions in which we investigated whether the prediction of trust by task (game, social task) was moderated by experience as measured by the intrinsic motivation inventory, which measures experienced enjoyment, invested effort, perceived competence, and experienced pressure. In each of the regressions, task (game or social) significantly predicts trust; however, the role of the moderating factor varies.

Enjoyment: We conducted a moderated regression with task (game, social) as the predictor of trust state, moderated by an individual's experienced enjoyment of the task. As expected, task significantly predicted trust development (β=.812, p<.001). Experienced enjoyment did not directly predict trust development (β=.201, p=.207); however, enjoyment did moderate the effect of task on trust development (p=.040). As Figure 5 shows, for people who experienced low (p<.001) or medium (p<.001) enjoyment, the social task performed significantly worse than the game; however, for people with high enjoyment, the social task did not perform significantly worse than the game (p=.233). In other words, the game works equally well for people regardless of their experienced enjoyment of it; however, the efficacy of the social task declines with a decline in experienced enjoyment.

Invested Effort: The moderated regression shows that task predicts trust (β=.76, p<.001), as expected. However, invested effort does not predict trust (β=.243, p=.279), nor does it moderate the effect of task on trust (p=.799). **Perceived competence** does not predict trust (β=.253, p=.076), nor does it moderate the effect of task on trust (p=.187). **Experienced tension** does predict trust (β=-.342, p=.002), showing that increases in experienced tension decrease the development of trust. However, tension does not moderate the effect of task on trust (p=.349).

Q4. Do the trust-building advantages of the game depend on the interpersonal experience?

The efficacy of the social task was sensitive to task experience, whereas the game was not. We were also interested in whether the efficacy of the tasks might be sensitive to the relationship developed. As such, we conducted moderated regressions of task on trust development with experienced relational communication (i.e., receptivity, involvement, affect, depth, and formality) as moderators.

As expected, task predicted trust development in all cases. In addition, all aspects of relational communication except formality (β=.059, p=.628) also predicted trust development (Receptivity: β=.286, p=.003; Involvement: β=.513,

p<.001; Affect: β=.276, p=.012; Depth: β=.335, p<.001). This suggests that relational communication is an important factor for interpersonal trust formation. However, none of the interpersonal relationship factors moderated the effect of the task on trust development (Receptivity: p=.739; Involvement: p=548; Affect: p=.958; Depth: p=.286; Formality: p=.778). The effect of task on trust is therefore independent of relational communication.

As mentioned above, relational communication did not change based on our conditions (except for receptivity, which increased as a result of playing the game).

DISCUSSION

We summarize our results, explain why the game works so well at facilitating trust, and discuss the implications of our findings in the broader context of games and interaction.

Summary of Results

The goal of this study was to investigate whether or not games are a legitimate option for fostering interpersonal trust in distributed teams. We compared a multiplayer co-operative game to a social task that was designed to facilitate casual conversation and personal information exchange – a strategy proposed by current literature on trust formation. Although both solutions helped to facilitate trust formation, our game appeared to be more effective than our social task. This was not only true for interpersonal trust but also for how much the task satisfied relational needs and how receptive/trusting the partner was perceived to be.

A closer look at our results gives us an understanding of why a game is overall more effective than a social task. Under ideal conditions, our social task was as effective as our game for facilitating interpersonal trust. However, the effectiveness of our social task was sensitive to characteristics of the trustor as well as to the experience of the task, suggesting that when a team member is inherently less inclined to be trusting or doesn't enjoy social tasks, their ability to foster trust may break down. A similar trend was seen in the personality trait of agreeableness, which measures how socially harmonious people are. The notion that interpersonal trust formation is affected by characteristics of the trustor is coherent with literature on interpersonal trust [67,56,27]. Our results let us conclude that personal information exchange *can* be very effective at fostering trust; however, its effectiveness is fragile and dependent on circumstance. In contrast to this fragility, the game's ability to foster trust was robust to these factors.

The effectiveness of our game was unchanged by any of the measurements we collected in this study. The inherent propensity to trust, enjoyment of the game, or agreeableness did not affect its power to make people feel safe with one another. The effectiveness of the game was also not compromised by age or gender. Although there was a marginally-significant interaction with game play frequency, the results showed that the game was better than the social task for both frequent gamers and less-frequent gamers, but the magnitude of the difference was weaker for game enthusiasts, suggesting that games are a viable option for all demographics and levels of experience in games. These results suggest that games such as ours are the more reliable form of fostering trust among team members.

Equally interesting are the constructs that weren't changed by the task. We compared pairs that were talking about each other's preferences and personalities with pairs that talked about where to go on a game board or which tile to push. However we did not observe any differences in involvement, affect, depth, and formality. This is consistent with literature on relational communication, which suggests that the content of a conversation is distinct from its emotional and relational components [31,13]. The results suggest that a game is as effective at fostering a relational connection between two people as a social conversation.

Why Does the Game Work?

The results clearly indicate that a game has the power to facilitate interpersonal trust between players. Considering that the conversations in these games were without any meaning or consequence to the players' lives, these results may seem surprising. One might argue that the interaction that occurs between players in online games might be considered as an impoverished form of communication, and as a result, online games should not be effective at facilitating trust development. Unless games are intentionally designed to promote personal information exchange or similarity development through their mechanics, the limited amount of conversation that does occur will generally be about events in the game. We now explore the idea that a game is in fact a legitimate social interaction that can be optimal for trust formation. In particular, we focus on two components of play: the game's ability to simulate risk and interdependence, and the idea of game moves as conversational turns.

Simulating Risk and Interdependence

As described above, the formation of trust requires an appropriate amount of risk (i.e., consistent with the current level of trust between the individuals) and interdependence between two partners. A game is an artificial environment that can be designed specifically to create interdependence. Following existing frameworks on collaborative game design [16,44], we implemented mechanics like asymmetrical roles and the need for information exchange (e.g., position on the board) to induce interdependence between the players. In terms of risk, poor performance in the game had no real life consequences for the players. Because the stakes were artificial, the risk was relatively low, thereby ideal for initial trust formation between strangers who have no existing interpersonal trust. The conditions we created in our game therefore allow players to *rehearse* or *perform* cooperation and trusting behavior. These activity-based interactions build a relational connection through experiences, rather than through shared knowledge or similarities.

Game Moves as Conversational Turns

Although not explicitly about trust formation, similar patterns of relationship building to ours have been observed in Internet play rooms [42], MUDs [43], and virtual reality games [6]. In these examples, players didn't communicate explicitly about non-game content; however, they still created social bonds. McEwan et al [42] argue that moves within the game *"are legitimate forms of human contact which create a shared experience through an (albeit stylized) form of human interaction"*. The notion that players can communicate nonverbally through the game is reflected in our recordings of the game sessions. Players would sometimes suddenly say "Good Idea!" or "Ah, now I get it" without the other player having proposed anything, clearly responding to a nonverbal game move. The game adds richness to computer-mediated communication by allowing for extra channels of communication (i.e., game moves as conversational turns). Our results suggest that these interactions create relational bonds between players that are as strong as those created through explicit verbal conversation.

Fragility of Conversation vs. Robustness of Games

We showed that the effect of social conversation on interpersonal trust is fragile because it is vulnerable to personality and enjoyment of the conversation. Games appear to be robust against these contingencies. We believe the reason for this robustness is due to the activity-based nature of social interaction within games. Based on literature on trust formation, personal information exchange facilitates trust because this information is *trust warranting* and highlights similarities between partners. These effects are however dependent on the content of the interaction. If the information exchanged is not trust warranting or only highlights differences between the partners, the interaction is not likely to facilitate trust formation. Some partners might not want to exchange information because they are generally more private or don't enjoy these kinds of interactions. In contrast, the social interactions in games are independent of content or explicit communication. Relational bonds are formed through action and game-related communication. These activity-based interactions appear to foster relational bonds between partners as well as personal communication, while being free of the contingencies that content-based interactions depend on.

What should be said about the properties of the game

Our game was strongly affected by networking issues, which made the game more frustrating and difficult than we expected. This is reflected in the results. Performance in terms of gems collected was lower than we expected, and participants in the game condition scored low on competence and high on tension. Comments from the debrief as well as the recordings of the game session confirm that many participants experienced a frustrating, 'buggy' game, rather than the playful experience we intended. The results of this study have to be interpreted with this in mind. Nevertheless, our results showed strong effects that support arguments for the effectiveness of our game. Submitted comments and the recorded conversations indicated that dealing with a 'buggy' game made the players bond over how frustrating and challenging the game was. Literature suggests that frustration in games can have positive consequences on player experience [21]. Our results show that performance, perceived competence, and enjoyment don't impact trust formation directly, supporting at least the assumption that the game doesn't have to be 'fun' or satisfy competence to facilitate trust. Social identity theory suggests that creating an 'out-group', which can be considered the common enemy, strengthens the cohesion of the 'in-group' [60] – in our case, the players can be considered as the in-group and the game system as the out-group. Alternatively, the frustration might have hampered an otherwise even more effective trust building intervention. Based on previous frameworks for team building games [16,44], frustration and poor usability should be avoided. The results support the assumption that increased tension inhibits trust formation. The role of frustration on trust formation in team building games is an interesting area of future research.

Design Implications

Our results suggest that online multiplayer games should be considered as a potential team-building activity to facilitate trust formation in distributed project teams; however, there are implications to other collaborative relationships and to aspects of interpersonal relationships beyond trust.

Games have long been used as a means of supporting social interaction. Family board game nights, tabletop gaming in board game stores, or weekly bridge meet-ups among friends can help us satisfy our psychological need for relatedness [57] and create shared experiences that draw us closer [8,25]. Online multiplayer games have the additional advantage of allowing distributed friends and families to maintain a connection—for example, people enhancing their friendship through play of social network games [66] or seniors playing online poker together to stay connected [59]. Trust is not just important in distributed project teams, but is valuable in many types of relationships. Consider, for example, an online dating site. Users who are matched chat via text to get to know one another before deciding whether or not to meet for a date. Our results suggest that playing an online game together might help potential couples to develop a trusting bond or to develop positive relational communication patterns. Or consider families who are geographically separated from one another. Playing a networked game may help develop that trusting bond between, for example, a grandparent and their grandchild who lives in a different part of the world. Future work is needed to determine whether our results can be applied into contexts beyond distributed project teams.

Limitations and Future Work

Although our results strongly suggest the potential of games as trust-building activities, there are limitations in our study that should be addressed in future work. First we have to acknowledge the already discussed technical problems and the effects on our manipulations. The potential influence of in-game frustration on our results and the question of how well a non-frustrating game could facilitate interpersonal trust should be investigated. Second, we treated participants as individuals, when they were part of a dyad, and therefore not entirely independent. This also prevented us from inves-

tigating the effects of matchmaking. An interesting direction for future research would be to investigate the effect of team constellations (e.g., same sex vs. mixed dyads). Third, our method for measuring trust was a modified scale. Even though its metric properties made it a viable measure for trust, future research should try a more multi-methodological approach to measuring trust. Other studies investigating trust have, for example, implemented social dilemmas based on game theory to measure trust behaviorally [2,51]. Using these methods, it is possible to make assumptions about the fragility of trust, which is suggested to be a problem in distributed teams [2,50]. Future research could investigate the effect of games on the 'thickness or fragility' of trust compared to social tasks. Fourth, our results must be generalized with caution. Effects we found in this study might be specific to the mechanics implemented in our labyrinth game. Further research should investigate the effects of other games containing different game mechanics and narrative elements. Fifth, we attribute the results of this study to the game in general. Our findings raise the follow-up question of which mechanics or properties of the game specifically caused our results. Future research should further investigate what properties of the game (e.g., cooperation, interdependence, risk, frustration, playfulness) were the cause of our results. Lastly, we investigated dyads. While using dyads to investigate small group dynamics is a viable research method, future research should aim to investigate the effects of a game in bigger teams.

CONCLUSIONS

Based on current literature on trust development, we proposed that context factors like risk and interdependence could facilitate trust formation in distributed teams. We argued that games are an optimal medium to induce an appropriate amount of risk and a need for interdependent interaction between team members. In this paper, we showed that a game designed with these properties in mind could compete with a social task that was designed to facilitate trust through personal information exchange. In fact, it was better at facilitating trust than the social task. Our game was also as good as the social task in promoting relational communication between the partners in terms how involved or affectionate they perceived one another. These results support the notion that interactions in games, while being focused on the game itself, are as efficient at facilitating social bonds as social conversations. Our findings also suggest an explanation as to why games were better at fostering trust than the social task. Under optimal conditions, the conversations in the social task could effectively bring participants closer together. However, the efficacy of the conversation was vulnerable to a set of contingencies, whereas our game facilitated trust regardless of age, gender, personality, or experience. We conclude that games are simply more robust against factors that threaten the efficacy of social icebreakers.

The relationships built through gameplay are sometimes considered as impoverished versions of the rich bonds that are created through conversation. We contribute to a growing body of work recognizing the ability of games to shape and foster online social relationships, facilitating the development of deep and meaningful social bonds.

ACKNOWLEDGMENTS

Thanks to NSERC for funding, our participants, and the Interaction Lab for feedback. Thanks also to Sigrid, Horst, Miriam and Anna.

REFERENCES

1. M. Beer, F. Slack, and G. Armitt. 2003. Community building and virtual teamwork in an online learning environment. In *36th Annual Hawaii International Conference on System Sciences, 2003. Proceedings of the*. Institute of Electrical & Electronics Engineers (IEEE). http://dx.doi.org/10.1109/hicss.2003.1173639

2. Nathan Bos, Judy Olson, Darren Gergle, Gary Olson, and Zach Wright. 2002. Effects of four computer-mediated communications channels on trust development. In *Proceedings of the SIGCHI conference on Human factors in computing systems Changing our world, changing ourselves - CHI 02*. Association for Computing Machinery (ACM). http://dx.doi.org/10.1145/503376.503401

3. W. Boss. 1978. Trust and Managerial Problem Solving Revisited. *Group & Organization Management* 3, 3 (sep 1978), 331--342. http://dx.doi.org/10.1177/105960117800300306

4. Aysun Bozanta, Birgul Kutlu, Nuket Nowlan, and Shervin Shirmohammadi. 2012. Multi User Virtual Environments and Serious Games for Team Building. *Procedia Computer Science* 15 (2012), 301--302. http://dx.doi.org/10.1016/j.procs.2012.10.086

5. P. Brown. Technology and trust in teams. In Proceedings Academia/Industry Working Conference on Research Challenges 00. Next Generation Enterprises: Virtual Organizations and Mobile/Pervasive Technologies. AIWORC00. (Cat. No.PR00628). Institute of Electrical & Electronics Engineers (IEEE). http://dx.doi.org/10.1109/aiworc.2000.843266

6. Barry Brown and Marek Bell. Play and Sociability in There: Some Lessons from Online Games for Collaborative Virtual Environments. In *Computer Supported Cooperative Work*. Springer Science Business Media, 227--245. http://dx.doi.org/10.1007/1-4020-3898-4_11

7. G. Corbitt, L.R. Gardiner, and L.K. Wright. 2004. A comparison of team developmental stages, trust and performance for virtual versus face-to-face teams. In *37th Annual Hawaii International Conference on System Sciences, 2004. Proceedings of the*. Institute of Electrical & Electronics Engineers (IEEE). http://dx.doi.org/10.1109/hicss.2004.1265157

8. Kathrin, Gerling, and Regan L. Mandryk. "Designing video games for older adults and caregivers." (2014). In *Meaningful Play 2014*, East Lansing, MI, USA. 24 pages

9. Laura A. Dabbish. 2008. Jumpstarting relationships with online games. In *Proceedings of the ACM 2008 conference on Computer supported cooperative work - CSCW 08*. Association for Computing Machinery (ACM). http://dx.doi.org/10.1145/1460563.1460620

10. T. K. Das and Bing-Sheng Teng. 1998. Between Trust and Control: Developing Confidence in Partner Cooperation in Alliances. *The Academy of Management Review* 23, 3 (jul 1998), 491. http://dx.doi.org/10.2307/259291

11. Carsten K. W. De Dreu, Ellen Giebels, and Evert Van de Vliet. 1998. Social motives and trust in integrative negotiation: The disruptive effects of punitive capability. *Journal of Applied Psychology* 83, 3 (1998), 408--422. http://dx.doi.org/10.1037/0021-9010.83.3.408

12. Virginia Dignum, and Rogier M. Van Eijk. 2005. Towards a model to understand the influence of trust in knowledge sharing decisions. In *Workshop on Trust AAMAS*, vol. 5.

13. James Price Dillard, Denise Haunani Solomon, and Mark Palmer. 1999. Structuring the concept of relational communication. *RCMM* 66, 1 (mar 1999), 49--65. http://dx.doi.org/10.1080/03637759909376462

14. Kurt T. Dirks. 1999. The effects of interpersonal trust on work group performance. *Journal of Applied Psychology* 84, 3 (1999), 445--455. http://dx.doi.org/10.1037/0021-9010.84.3.445

15. Kurt T. Dirks and Donald L. Ferrin. 2001. The Role of Trust in Organizational Settings. *Organization Science* 12, 4 (aug 2001), 450--467. http://dx.doi.org/10.1287/orsc.12.4.450.10640

16. Jason B. Ellis, Kurt Luther, Katherine Bessiere, and Wendy A. Kellogg. 2008. Games for virtual team building. In *Proceedings of the 7th ACM conference on Designing interactive systems - DIS 08*. Association for Computing Machinery (ACM). http://dx.doi.org/10.1145/1394445.1394477

17. Franz Faul, Edgar Erdfelder, Axel Buchner, and Albert-Georg Lang. 2009. Statistical power analyses using GPower 3.1: Tests for correlation and regression analyses. *Behavior Research Methods* 41, 4 (nov 2009), 1149--1160. http://dx.doi.org/10.3758/brm.41.4.1149

18. Mark G. Ehrhart, Karen Holcombe Ehrhart, Scott C. Roesch, Beth G. Chung-Herrera, Kristy Nadler, and Kelsey Bradshaw. 2009. Testing the latent factor structure and construct validity of the Ten-Item Personality Inventory. *Personality and Individual Differences* 47, 8 (dec 2009), 900--905. http://dx.doi.org/10.1016/j.paid.2009.07.012

19. Jinjuan Feng, Jonathan Lazar, and Jenny Preece. 2004. Empathy and online interpersonal trust: A fragile relationship. *Behaviour & Information Technology* 23, 2

(mar 2004), 97--106. http://dx.doi.org/10.1080/01449290310001659240

20. K. Furumo and J.M. Pearson. 2006. An Empirical Investigation of How Trust, Cohesion, and Performance Vary in Virtual and Face-to-Face Teams. In *Proceedings of the 39th Annual Hawaii International Conference on System Sciences (HICSS06)*. Institute of Electrical & Electronics Engineers (IEEE). http://dx.doi.org/10.1109/hicss.2006.51

21. Kiel M Gilleade and Alan Dix. 2004. Using frustration in the design of adaptive videogames. In *Proceedings of the 2004 ACM SIGCHI International Conference on Advances in computer entertainment technology - ACE 04*. Association for Computing Machinery (ACM). http://dx.doi.org/10.1145/1067343.1067372

22. Päivi Häkkinen. 2004. What Makes Learning and Understanding in Virtual Teams So Difficult? *CyberPsychology & Behavior* 7, 2 (apr 2004), 201--206. http://dx.doi.org/10.1089/109493104323024465

23. Francis Hartman. 2000. The role of trust in project management. In Proceedings of PMI Research Conference 2000: PM Research at the turn of the millennium, pp. 23-28.

24. James D. Herbsleb, Audris Mockus, Thomas A. Finholt, and Rebecca E. Grinter. 2000. Distance, dependencies, and delay in a global collaboration. In *Proceedings of the 2000 ACM conference on Computer supported cooperative work - CSCW 00*. Association for Computing Machinery (ACM). http://dx.doi.org/10.1145/358916.359003

25. Hamilton A. Hernandez, T.C. Nicholas Graham, Mallory Ketcheson, Adrian Schneider, Zi Ye, Darcy Fehlings, Lauren Switzer, Virginia Wright, Shelly K. Bursick, and Chad Richards. 2014. Design and evaluation of a networked game to supportsocial connection of youth with cerebral palsy. In *Proceedings of the 16th international ACM SIGACCESS conference on Computers & accessibility - ASSETS 14*. Association for Computing Machinery (ACM). http://dx.doi.org/10.1145/2661334.2661370

26. E. Tory Higgins. 1987. Self-discrepancy: A theory relating self and affect. *Psychological Review* 94, 3 (1987), 319--340. http://dx.doi.org/10.1037/0033-295x.94.3.319

27. Y.-T.C. Hung, A.R. Dennis, and L. Robert. 2004. Trust in virtual teams: towards an integrative model of trust formation. In *37th Annual Hawaii International Conference on System Sciences, 2004. Proceedings of the*. Institute of Electrical & Electronics Engineers (IEEE). http://dx.doi.org/10.1109/hicss.2004.1265156

28. Sirkka L. Jarvenpaa, Kathleen Knoll, and Dorothy E. Leidner. 1998. Is Anybody out There? Antecedents of Trust in Global Virtual Teams. *Journal of Management Information Systems* 14, 4 (mar 1998), 29--64. http://dx.doi.org/10.1080/07421222.1998.11518185

29. Sirkka L. Jarvenpaa, and Dorothy E. Leidner. 1998. Communication and trust in global virtual teams. *Journal of Computer-Mediated Communication* 3, no. 4: 0-0.

30. Cynthia Johnson-George and Walter C. Swap. 1982. Measurement of specific interpersonal trust: Construction and validation of a scale to assess trust in a specific other. *Journal of Personality and Social Psychology* 43, 6 (1982), 1306--1317. http://dx.doi.org/10.1037/0022-3514.43.6.1306

31. D. Jones, Paul Watzlawick, Janet Helmwick Bevin, and Don D. Jackson. 1969. Pragmatics of Human Communication: A Study of Interactional Patterns, Pathologies, and Paradoxes. *Man* 4, 3 (sep 1969), 471. http://dx.doi.org/10.2307/2798146

32. Prasert Kanawattanachai and Youngjin Yoo. 2002. Dynamic nature of trust in virtual teams. *The Journal of Strategic Information Systems* 11, 3-4 (dec 2002), 187--213. http://dx.doi.org/10.1016/s0963-8687(02)00019-7

33. Melvin J Kimmel and et al. 1980. Effects of trust, aspiration, and gender on negotiation tactics. *Journal of Personality and Social Psychology* 38, 1 (1980), 9--22. http://dx.doi.org/10.1037/0022-3514.38.1.9

34. Cameron Klein, Deborah DiazGranados, Eduardo Salas, Huy Le, C. Shawn Burke, Rebecca Lyons, and Gerald F. Goodwin. "Does team building work?." *Small Group Research* (2009).

35. Robert E. Larzelere and Ted L. Huston. 1980. The Dyadic Trust Scale: Toward Understanding Interpersonal Trust in Close Relationships. *Journal of Marriage and the Family* 42, 3 (aug 1980), 595. http://dx.doi.org/10.2307/351903

36. Sheena Lewis, Jason B. Ellis, and Wendy A. Kellogg. 2010. Using virtual interactions to explore leadership and collaboration in globally distributed teams. In *Proceedings of the 3rd international conference on Intercultural collaboration - ICIC 10*. Association for Computing Machinery (ACM). http://dx.doi.org/10.1145/1841853.1841856

37. Niklas Luhmann, 2000. Familiarity, confidence, trust: Problems and alternatives. *Trust: Making and breaking cooperative relations*, 6, 94-107.

38. Winter Mason, and Siddharth Suri. "Conducting behavioral research on Amazon's Mechanical Turk." *Behavior research methods* 44, no. 1 (2012): 1-23.

39. R. C. Mayer, J. H. Davis, and F. D. Schoorman. 1995. An Integrative Model of Organizational Trust. *Academy of Management Review* 20, 3 (jul 1995), 709--734. http://dx.doi.org/10.5465/amr.1995.9508080335

40. D. J. McAllister. 1995. Affect-and cognition-based trust as foundations for interpersonal cooperation in organizations. *Academy of Management Journal* 38, 1 (feb 1995), 24--59. http://dx.doi.org/10.2307/256727

41. Edward McAuley, Terry Duncan, and Vance V. Tammen. 1989. Psychometric properties of the Intrinsic Motivation Inventory in a competitive sport setting: A confirmatory factor analysis. *Research quarterly for exercise and sport* 60, no. 1: 48-58.

42. Gregor McEwan, Carl Gutwin, Regan L. Mandryk, and Lennart Nacke. 2012. "I'm just here to play games": social dynamics and sociality in an online game site. In *Proceedings of the ACM 2012 confer- ence on Computer Supported Cooperative Work* (CSCW '12). ACM, 549-558. http://dx.doi.org/10.1145/2145204.2145289

43. Jack Muramatsu and Mark S. Ackerman. 1998. Computing, Social Activity, and Entertainment: A Field Study of a Game MUD. *Computer Supported Cooperative Work (CSCW)* 7, 1-2 (mar 1998), 87--122. http://dx.doi.org/10.1023/a:1008636204963

44. Maaz Nasir, Kelly Lyons, Rock Leung, and Ali Moradian. 2013. Cooperative Games and Their Effect on Group Collaboration. In *Design Science at the Intersection of Physical and Virtual Design*. Springer Science Business Media, 502--510. http://dx.doi.org/10.1007/978-3-642-38827-9_43

45. Maaz Nasir, Kelly Lyons, Rock Leung, Anthea Bailie, and Fred Whitmarsh. 2015. The effect of a collaborative game on group work. In *Proceedings of the 25th Annual International Conference on Computer Science and Software Engineering*, pp. 130-139. IBM Corp.

46. Judith S. Olson and Gary M. Olson. 2000. i2i trust in e-commerce. *Commun. ACM* 43, 12 (dec 2000), 41--44. http://dx.doi.org/10.1145/355112.355121

47. B. Perry. "Virtual Teams Now a Reality. Two out of Three Companies Say They Will Rely More on Virtual Teams in the Future. Retrieved 5 October 2009." (2008).

48. R. Pillai. 1999. Fairness Perceptions and Trust as Mediators for Transformational and Transactional Leadership: A Two-Sample Study. *Journal of Management* 25, 6 (dec 1999), 897--933. http://dx.doi.org/10.1177/014920639902500606

49. Thomas W. Porter and Bryan S. Lilly. 1996. The effects of conflict, trust, and task commitment on project team performance. *Int Jnl of Conflict Management* 7, 4 (apr 1996), 361--376. http://dx.doi.org/10.1108/eb022787

50. John K. Rempel, John G. Holmes, and Mark P. Zanna. 1985. Trust in close relationships. *Journal of Personality and Social Psychology* 49, 1 (1985), 95--112. http://dx.doi.org/10.1037/0022-3514.49.1.95

51. Irene Rae, Leila Takayama, and Bilge Mutlu. 2013. In-body experiences. In *Proceedings of the SIGCHI Conference on Human Factors in Computing Systems - CHI 13*. Association for Computing Machinery (ACM). http://dx.doi.org/10.1145/2470654.2466253

52. A. M. L. Raes, Marielle G. Heijltjes, Ursula Glunk, and A. R. Roe. 2006. *Conflict, trust, and effectiveness in teams performing complex tasks: A study of temporal patterns*. METEOR, Maastricht research school of Economics of Technology and Organizations.

53. G. A. Rich. 1997. The Sales Manager as a Role Model: Effects on Trust, Job Satisfaction, and Performance of Salespeople. *Journal of the Academy of Marketing Science* 25, 4 (sep 1997), 319--328. http://dx.doi.org/10.1177/0092070397254004

54. Sandra L. Robinson. 1996. Trust and Breach of the Psychological Contract. *Administrative Science Quarterly* 41, 4 (dec 1996), 574. http://dx.doi.org/10.2307/2393868

55. Julian B. Rotter. 1967. A new scale for the measurement of interpersonal trust1. *J Personality* 35, 4 (dec 1967), 651--665. http://dx.doi.org/10.1111/j.1467-6494.1967.tb01454.x

56. Ellen Rusman, Jan van Bruggen, Peter Sloep, and Rob Koper. 2010. Fostering trust in virtual project teams: Towards a design framework grounded in a TrustWorthiness ANtecedents (TWAN) schema. *International Journal of Human-Computer Studies* 68, 11 (nov 2010), 834--850. http://dx.doi.org/10.1016/j.ijhcs.2010.07.003

57. Richard M. Ryan, C. Scott Rigby, and Andrew Przybylski. 2006. The motivational pull of video games: A self-determination theory approach. *Motiva- tion and emotion* 30, no. 4: 344-360.

58. Paul H. Schurr and Julie L. Ozanne. 1985. Influences on Exchange Processes: Buyers Preconceptions of a Sellers Trustworthiness and Bargaining Toughness. *J CONSUM RES* 11, 4 (mar 1985), 939. http://dx.doi.org/10.1086/209028

59. Nicholas Shim, Ronald Baecker, Jeremy Birnholtz, and Karyn Moffatt. "TableTalk Poker: an online social gaming environment for seniors." In *Proceedings of the International Academic Conference on the Future of Game Design and Technology*, pp. 98-104. ACM, 2010.

60. Martin Tanis and Tom Postmes. 2005. A social identity approach to trust: interpersonal perception, group membership and trusting behaviour. *European Journal of Social Psychology* 35, 3 (2005), 413--424. http://dx.doi.org/10.1002/ejsp.256

61. Stephanie Teasley, Lisa Covi, M. S. Krishnan, and Judith S. Olson. 2000. How does radical collocation help a team succeed?. In *Proceedings of the 2000 ACM conference on Computer supported cooperative work - CSCW 00*. Association for Computing Machinery (ACM). http://dx.doi.org/10.1145/358916.359005

62. Uddin, Md Sami, Carl Gutwin, and Benjamin Lafreniere. "HandMark Menus: Rapid Command Selection and Large Command Sets on Multi-Touch Displays."

63. Joseph B. Walther. 1995. Relational Aspects of Computer-Mediated Communication: Experimental Observations over Time. *Organization Science* 6, 2 (apr 1995), 186--203. http://dx.doi.org/10.1287/orsc.6.2.186

64. Joseph B. Walther, U. Bunz, and N.N. Bazarova. 2005. The Rules of Virtual Groups. In *Proceedings of the 38th Annual Hawaii International Conference on System Sciences*. Institute of Electrical & Electronics Engineers (IEEE). http://dx.doi.org/10.1109/hicss.2005.617

65. Jeanne M. Wilson, Susan G. Straus, and Bill McEvily. 2006. All in due time: The development of trust in computer-mediated and face-to-face teams. *Organizational Behavior and Human Decision Processes* 99, 1 (jan 2006), 16--33. http://dx.doi.org/10.1016/j.obhdp.2005.08.001

66. Donghee Yvette Wohn, Cliff Lampe, Rick Wash, Nicole Ellison, and Jessica Vitak. "The" S" in social network games: Initiating, maintaining, and enhancing relationships." In *System Sciences (HICSS), 2011 44th Hawaii International Conference on*, pp. 1-10. IEEE, 2011.

67. Toshio Yamagishi and Midori Yamagishi. 1994. Trust and commitment in the United States and Japan. *Motivation and Emotion* 18, 2 (jun 1994), 129--166. http://dx.doi.org/10.1007/bf02249397

68. Akbar Zaheer, Bill McEvily, and Vincenzo Perrone. 1998. Does Trust Matter? Exploring the Effects of Inter-organizational and Interpersonal Trust on Performance. *Organization Science* 9, 2 (apr 1998), 141--159. http://dx.doi.org/10.1287/orsc.9.2.141

69. Roxanne Zolin, Pamela J. Hinds, Renate Fruchter, and Raymond E. Levitt. 2002. Trust in Cross-functional, global teams. *Center for Integrated Facility Engineering, Stanford University, Working Paper* 67.

70. Roxanne Zolin, Renate Fruchter, and Pamela J. Hinds. 2003. Communication, trust and performance: The influence of trust on performance in A/E/C cross-functional, geographically distributed work.

71. Roxanne Zolin, Pamela J Hinds, Renate Fruchter, and Raymond E Levitt. 2004. Interpersonal trust in cross-functional, geographically distributed work: A longitudinal study. *Information and Organization* 14, 1 (jan 2004), 1--26. http://dx.doi.org/10.1016/j.infoandorg.2003.09.002

Collaborative Solving in a Human Computing Game Using a Market, Skills and Challenges

Olivier Tremblay-Savard
University of Manitoba
Winnipeg, Canada
tremblao@cs.umanitoba.ca

Alexander Butyaev
McGill University
Montreal, Canada
butyaevaa@gmail.com

Jérôme Waldispühl
McGill University
Montreal, Canada
jeromew@cs.mcgill.ca

ABSTRACT

Crowdsourcing with human-computing games is now a well-established approach to help solving difficult computational problems (e.g. Foldit, Phylo). The current strategies used to distribute problems among participants are currently limited to (i) delivering the full problem to every single user and ask them to explore the complete search space (e.g. Foldit), or (ii) decomposing the initial problem into smaller sub-problems and aggregate the solutions returned by gamers (e.g. Phylo). The second approach could be used to explore larger search spaces while harnessing collective intelligence, but popular crowdsourcing systems making use of the Amazon Mechanical Turk deliberately forbid communication between participants to avoid group-think phenomena. In this paper, we design a novel multi-player game-with-a-purpose, and analyze the impact of multiple game mechanisms on the performance of the system. We present a highly collaborative human-computing game that uses a market, skills and a challenge system to help the players collectively solve a graph problem. The results obtained during 12 game sessions of 10 players show that the market helps players to build larger solutions. We also show that a skill system and, to a lesser extent, a challenge system can be used to influence and guide the players towards producing better solutions. Our collaborative game-with-a-purpose is open-source, and aims to serve as a universal platform for further independent studies.

ACM Classification Keywords

H.5.3 Group and Organization Interfaces

Author Keywords

Game-with-a-purpose; Human computing; Collaboration; Crowdsourcing; Graph problem; Market; Trading game; Skills; Challenges.

INTRODUCTION

Human-computation and crowdsourcing are now perceived as valuable techniques to help solving difficult computational problems. In order to make the best use of human skills in

these systems, it is important to be able to characterize the expertise and performance of humans as individuals and even more importantly as groups. Currently, crowd-computing approaches make use of popular platforms such as Amazon Mechanical Turk (AMT) [1, 24] or Crowdcrafting [21]. The initial problem is decomposed into smaller sub-tasks that are distributed to individual workers and then aggregated to build a solution. This is also the case in popular scientific human-computing games such as Phylo [12, 18]. Importantly, these systems prevent any interaction between workers in order to prevent groupthink phenomena and bias in the solution [22]. However, such constraints are necessarily limiting the capacity of the system to harness the cognitive power of crowds and make full benefit of collective intelligence. For instance, iterative combinations of crowdsourced contributions can help enhancing creativity [30]. Similarly, the presence of a broad spectrum of expertise in a crowdsourcing community has been shown to increase innovation and the advance of knowledge in the group [2]. The usefulness of parallelizing workflows has also been suggested for tasks accepting broad varieties of answers [20].

The benefits of developing recommendation systems or co-ordination methods in collaborative environments has been demonstrated [15, 3, 31]. Therefore, in order to gain expressivity and improve their performance, the next generation of human-computation systems will certainly need to implement mechanisms to promote and control the collaboration between workers. Nonetheless, before transitioning to this model, it is important to first estimate the potential gains in productivity, and quantify the usefulness of the mechanisms and incentives to promote collaborative solving and prevent groupthink. A first step in this direction was made recently: mathematical models have been used to simulate the interactions between the participants of crowdsourcing projects in order to estimate the optimal group size depending on the difficulty of the problem [5], and analyze the effect of repeated encounters on the reactive strategies of competing groups that can attack and sabotage each other [23].

Computer games are now a widely used and effective media to complete crowdsourcing tasks [16]. Multiple studies already investigated the impact of design on human-computing tasks [17, 10, 11]. Incidentally, they are also an excellent and potentially powerful framework to study collaborative work.

Historically, computation on graphs has proven to be a good model to study the performance of humans in solving complex combinatorial problems [14]. Experiments have been conducted to evaluate the dynamics of crowds collaborating at solving graph problems [13] but still, little is known about the efficiency of the various modes of interaction.

In this paper, we propose a formal framework to study human collaborative solving. We embed a combinatorial graph problem into a novel multiplayer game-with-a-purpose [27, 7], which will be used to engage participants and analyze collective performances. More precisely, we design a market game in which players can sell and buy solutions or bits of information, and couple this platform with (i) a skills system to enhance the efficiency of specific gaming strategies and (ii) a challenge system to guide the work of the crowd.

Most existing simultaneous collaborative games rely on two or three players trying to agree on an annotation of an image [27, 8, 28], a song [29, 19], a video [6] or a text [4]. In other crowdsourcing projects, collaboration between workers is iterative [26, 25, 9]. To the best of our knowledge, it is the first time that a market system is proposed to allow simultaneous collaborative solving by a large group of people.

We developed this market game to investigate the validity of the following hypotheses.

Hypotheses

The development of the game with its three main features, *i.e.* the market, the skills and the challenge system, was based on those four hypotheses:

1. A market system will help the players build longer solutions.
2. A skill system is useful to orient the players into doing specific actions that are beneficial to the game and other players.
3. A challenge system is effective in encouraging the players to do a specific action in the game.
4. The collected solutions are larger when all the three features are present in a game session, independently of the players' personal skills.

To test those hypotheses, we conducted a study on 120 participants using different variants of our market game. Our results confirm the benefits of using a trading platform to produce better solutions. Interestingly, we also found that a skills system helps to promote actions that are favorable to the collective solving process, but that the efficiency of a skill is reduced if it is designed to help solve one of the primary objectives of the game. Finally, we observed that a precise parametrization of challenges (i.e. finding an appropriate difficulty, nor too easy, nor too difficult) is required to result in an improvement of the quality of the collective work.

Our game is freely available at http://csb.cs.mcgill.ca/market-computing, and can be used as a platform for further independent studies.

PROBLEM

The game was implemented to solve a graph problem, which is the problem of finding maximal cliques in a multigraph. In simpler terms, the goal is to find subsets of vertices in the graph such that any two distinct vertices in the subsets are connected. In the case of this problem, we are dealing with a multigraph, which is simply a graph that can have multiple parallel edges. Let $G(V, E)$ be a multi-colored graph, where each vertex $v \in V$ has a set of colors $c(v)$. There is a colored edge $e = (v, u) \in E$ between the vertices v and u for every color in $c(v) \cap c(u)$ (*i.e.*, one for every color that they have in common). In other words, there is no colored edge between two vertices v and u for which $c(v) \cap c(u) \neq \emptyset$. Let $|C|$ be the total number of colors in the graph. The problem is then the one of finding maximal cliques for each possible n number of colors (where $1 \leq n \leq |C|$), *i.e.* cliques in which all the edges (and vertices) have the same n colors. A simple exact algorithm can solve the problem in $O(|V|2^{|C|})$. We make the conjecture that it is also the worst time complexity of the problem.

This problem was chosen for two reasons. First, it can be solved quickly by a computer when the number of colors is small, thus making it possible to compute the exact solution and measure the percentage of the solution that is found by the players in a game session. Second, this problem can easily be translated into a color matching game, which takes advantage of the ability of human perception. Indeed, since the colored edges between the vertices are given implicitly by the colors of the vertices, it is possible to show the players only the colored vertices. To solve the problem, the players have to find the largests sets of circles with colors in common, for all possible subsets of colors.

Note that it is not our goal to compare the performance of players with the performance of computers in solving this problem. With a limited number of colors (like six in our tests), the exact algorithm can solve the problem in seconds. For this study, we required a problem that was structured enough so that we could easily calculate the optimal solution and evaluate the performance of the players depending on what features were on or off and also the effect of the different features on the quality of solutions.

PRESENTATION OF THE GAME

Goal of the game

The main objective of the game is to build *sequences* (*i.e.* sets) of circles (circles represent vertices of the graph) that (i) are as long as possible and (ii) contain as many colors in common as possible. Circles used by the players to build the sequences either come random packages bought from the system or they come from another player through the market. The sequences can then be sold to the system for a certain amount of game money, which is determined by a scoring function that takes into account the length and the number of colors in common of the sequence.

The players continuously have to fill up their "hand" by buying circles, create the best sequences of circles from their hand and sell them to the system for in-game money. Figure 1 shows the gameplay loop and how the inclusion of the market system and challenges affect it.

Scoring function

The score of a sequence sold to the system is equal to $baseScore_n * seqLength^2$, where $baseScore_n$ is a base score

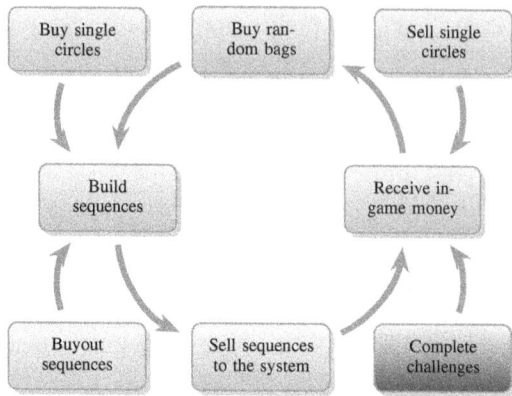

Figure 1. Gameplay loop diagram. The green boxes represent the actions that the players can make when there are no challenges and no market. The orange (resp. blue) boxes represent the actions that are allowed when the market (resp. challenge system) is present and how they interact with the gameplay.

depending on the number of colors in common (see Table 1) and *seqLength* is the length of the sequence. The base scores were calculated based on the exact solution for the graph that was generated for the tests (see section Generating the graph for a description of the graph that was used) in such a way to give a reward that is proportional to the difficulty of building the sequence. More precisely, we calculated the average length L_n of all solutions for each n number of colors. The base score is simply the reciprocal of this average ($1/L_n$) multiplied by a balancing factor (505 in our case). The balancing factor was chosen in order to get a score of 500 for a sequence of length 10 with only one color in common, which is exactly the price of two random packages of circles. Also notice that the value of a sequence is exponential in relation to its length, which is to encourage players to build the longest possible sequences.

Number of colors	0	1	2	3	4	5	6
Base score	0	5	14	26	40	55	72

Table 1. Value of the base score depending on the number of colors in common

The idea behind the scoring function is simple. Building simple short sequences with few colors in common can be done very quickly without much effort, so the score of those sequences is low. On the other hand, building long sequences with a lot of colors in common takes longer, so a high score is given to those sequences. Hence there is a tradeoff for the players between creating and selling many simple sequences, or creating and selling fewer more complex sequences.

Game interface

The game client and the server were built in Java 1.7. As shown in Figure 2, the game interface can be divided into 3 parts: the player information panel, the game panel and the market panel.

A: Player information panel

This panel simply contains information on the player's wallet, the current level of the player and has three buttons, allowing the player to open dialogs showing information on the current challenge, the skills (see section Skills for a description of the

available skills) and the leaderboard. One experience point is given to the player for each game dollar that he/she wins. The player can lose game money, but cannot lose experience points (experience points can only go up). Every time a player levels-up, he/she gets a skill point that can be used to improve any of the skills.

B: Game panel

The first component of the game panel is the 'My sequence' panel, which shows the current sequence that is being built by the player. The maximum size of a sequence is 10. Colors in common in the sequence are indicated by a thick black border surrounding the colors in the circles. Players can use the arrows to switch between the different sequence slots (2 sequence slots are available at the start of the game). The current value of the sequence is shown at the right, and the price for adding one more circle with the same colors in common is shown right below in gray. Finally, the sell button allows the player to sell the current sequence to the system: the sequence then disappears and the money is given to the player. Selling a sequence is equivalent to submitting a solution to the system.

The second component is the 'My hand' panel, which can contain up to 20 circles. Players can add a circle to the sequence by clicking on it. Circles are represented by their colors and by a price label (in a black box). The price corresponds to the current value of the circle on the market. Clicking on the price label sells the circle to the highest bidder on the market. Circles that are bought from a random package or from other players are sent to the hand.

The 'Awaiting to get sold' is where the circles are sent just before being sold to the highest bidder. If the bid disappears before the transaction is completed, the 'sold' circle will stay there. The player can then click on it to cancel the selling and put it back in the hand.

Finally, the bottom panel is a news feed, showing information on the game state, like the remaining time to complete the challenge and the last transactions completed by the player.

C: Market panel

At the top of the market panel, buttons allow the player to create bids for circles or to buy random packages (or bags) of circles. The 'Random bag' costs $250 and contains 5 circles with fewer colors. The 'Premium bag' costs $500 and contains 5 circles with a higher chance of getting circles with many colors.

Right below the buttons is the 'Automatic bids' panel, which allows the player to get automatic bids for circles corresponding to the sequences that he or she is building. A percentage of profit for the price of the automatic bids can be set with the slider. The profit is defined as the money the player would make by adding one more circle with the same colors in the current sequence (difference between the gray and black prices above the Sell button).

The 'My bids' panel shows all the bids that the player currently has on the market. The bid price is shown below the circle (in the black box). On the right side of the circle is the number of sequences with the same colors that the player can buy from other players (in the blue box). Clicking on the blue box opens a window showing the list of sequences that can be bought. Buying a sequence from another player is called a 'buyout' (see the following subsection for a more detailed description of buyouts).

Finally, the last panel at the bottom shows the last circle or sequence that was bought by the player.

Market

The market has three functions: (i) allow the players to exchange circles through a bidding system, (ii) allow players to buy sequences built and sold by other players so that they can be improved, and (iii) merge together sequences of length 10 to create super circles that are then put back in the game.

For every subset of colors, the server has a list of all the bids that are currently on the market. The value of the highest bid on the market is shown below every circle under the possession of the players. When a circle is sold by a player, it is sent through the server to the highest bidder.

Buyouts work differently. Players cannot bid on sequences, but the server holds for two minutes all the sequence that have been sold by the players. During those two minutes, other players can buy the sequences for a price that is equal to 150% of the initial score of the sequence. When a buyout is made, the bonus game money is sent to the player who initially sold the sequence to the system.

Finally, the game system creates a super circle every time a sequence of length 10 is sold by a player. A super circle of level 2 (representing 10 circles) counts as two circles when put in a sequence. Super circles can be of any level (a sequence of 10 super circles of level 2 form a super circle of level 3, and so on). The idea behind the creation of the super circles was to remove the limitation of the maximum sequence size imposed by the game interface.

Skills

Four different skills were implemented in the game. One skill point is awarded to a player when he or she levels up, which can then be put in any of the four skills. The maximum level of each skill is six (there are six levels of bonuses). Each skill was put in the game as a way to guide the player in doing actions that are beneficial to the system or to the other players:

- *Buyout King*: lowers the price of buying a sequence from another player (goal: encourage buyouts);
- *Color Expert*: gives a bonus to selling sequences that have more than one color in common (goal: push players to build more multicolored sequences);
- *Sequence Collector*: gives an additional sequence slot (goal: give more space to encourage the creation of longer sequences with more colors in common);
- *Master Trader*: gives a bonus to selling circles to other players (goal: promote the selling of individual circles).

Challenge system

We implemented a challenge system that analyzes the recent actions of the players and creates a new challenge every five minutes. The five challenge types are:

- *Sell/buy circles*: requires the players to sell or buy circles;
- *Buyout sequences*: requires the players to buy sequences from other players;
- *Minimum number of colors*: requires the players to sell sequences with at least a certain number of colors in common;
- *Minimum sequence length*: requires the players to sell sequences with a minimum sequence length;
- *Specific colors in common*: requires the players to sell sequences with a specific subset of colors in common.

Basically, the system continuously monitors the activities of the players and decreases or increases the probabilities of each challenge type. The next challenge is then selected using a multinomial sampling on these probabilities. The number of times T that the challenge-related action must be completed is selected randomly between 2 and 4. The prize that is awarded for completing the challenge is equal to $1500 * T$.

EXPERIMENTS

Independent and dependent variables

In the context of this study, there were three independent variables: the market (present; not present), the skills (present; not present) and the challenges (present; not present). Instead of trying all 8 possible combinations of independent variables, we decided to focus on four game conditions:

1. All features present (or A)
2. Everything except the market, hereafter referred to as "No Market" (or NM)
3. Everything except the skills, hereafter referred to as "No Skills" (or NS)
4. Everything except the challenges, hereafter referred to as "No challenges" (or NC)

Focusing on those four playing conditions allowed us to repeat each experiment more times with different groups of players. Moreover, the goal was to evaluate the importance of every game feature by removing them one at a time and evaluating the effect on the results obtained by the players.

As for the dependent variables, we were interested in measuring the following:

1. Percentage of the problem solved
2. Total experience points earned by the players
3. Average sequence length of the sequences created by the players ($\sum_{i=1}^{TS} sL_i / TS$)
4. Average number of colors in common of the sequences created by the players ($\sum_{i=1}^{TS} nbC_i / TS$)
5. Proportion of sequences of more than one color in common created by the players ($(TS - T1C)/TS$)
6. Number of circles sold individually to another player
7. Number of sequences bought from other players (buyouts)

where TS is the total number of sequences sold by all players during a session, sL_i is the sequence length of sequence i, nbC_i is the number of colors in common of sequence i and $T1C$ is the total number of sequences of one color sold by all players during a session.

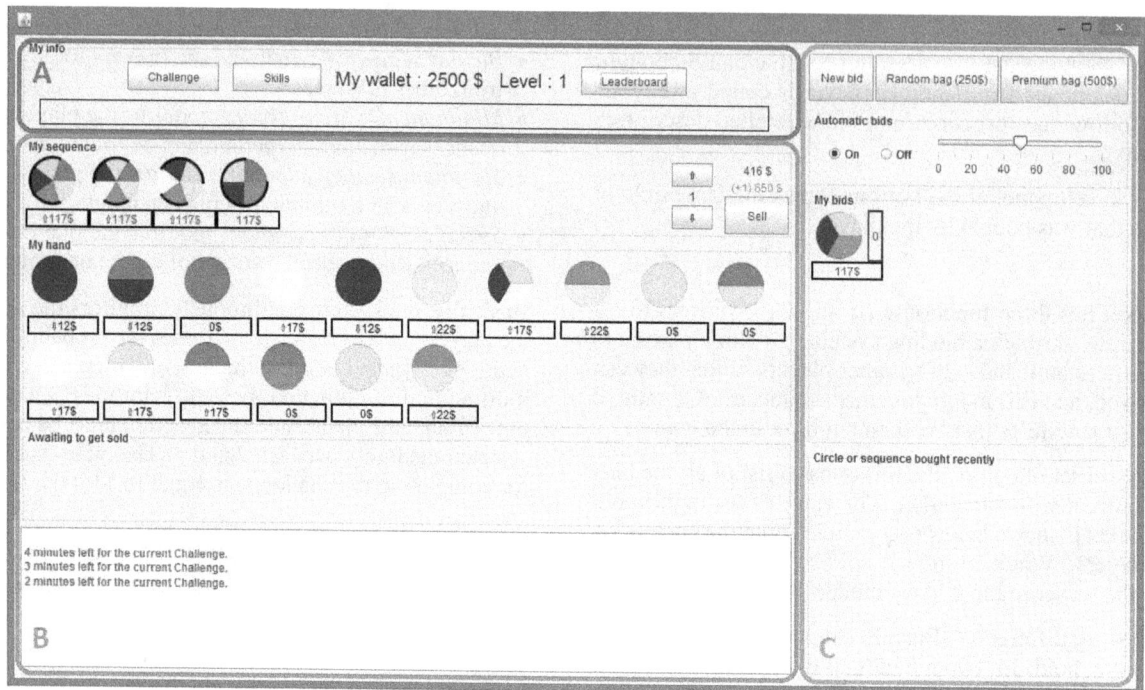

Figure 2. The game interface, separated in three panels. Panel A (inside the red box) is the player information panel. Panel B (inside the green box) is the game panel. Panel C (inside the orange box) is the market panel.

Game sessions

We recruited 120 people in total to test our game. Out of those 120 participants, 35% were female and 65% were male. Their average age was 25.7 and average video gaming time per week was 4.7 hours. Roughly 75% of the participants were undergrad students from McGill University and University of Montreal. The other 25% were grad students and volunteers recruited through social media. Out of all the participants, about half of them were currently studying or working in computer science.

We divided the participants into groups of 10 and repeated three times each of the four game conditions presented in the previous subsection. Each participant was playing the game for the first time, except for some people that were invited as replacements to deal with last minute cancellations. Before starting each game session, the players were shown a document explaining the rules of the game and the interface. The participants were told that they were playing a human computing game that aims to solve a graph problem, but the mathematical problem in question was not described to the players. They were also asked to fill in a questionnaire so that we could get information on the participants, such as their age, their abilities at puzzle solving and their experience with video games for example. For all the experiments, the game session lasted 45 minutes.

Generating the graph

We generated one random colored multigraph that we used for all the 12 tests. Since the edges in the graph depend entirely on the colors of the vertices, it is sufficient to generate only the colored vertices. For the tests, a graph containing 300 vertices and 6 different colors was generated. To randomly select the

number of colors for each vertex, a geometric distribution of parameter $p = 0.5$ was used, so that the vertices with a lot of colors are rarer. Once the number of colors was selected for the vertex, the set of colors was selected uniformly.

RESULTS AND DISCUSSION

Testing hypothesis 1: the efficiency of the market

The market system we implemented in the game allows the players to exchange circles and partial solutions (in the form of buyouts). The main goal of the market is to help the players in building longer sequences.

As shown in Figure 3, the three game sessions in which we had the lowest average of sequence lengths (for all the sequences sold by all the players) are the ones that were played without the market, with averages of 4.40 for NM, 4.19 for NM-2 and 4.63 for NM-3. Even if we consider the super circles (the special circles that are actually 10 circles combined into one), the average sequence lengths for those three sessions are still the lowest ones, with values of 4.90 for both NM and NM-2, and 5.40 for NM-3.

Since the distribution of the lengths for all the sequences sold to the system during a game session do not follow a normal distribution, we used a non-parametric test (Kruskal-Wallis) to verify if the sequence lengths of the different game sessions seem to come from the same distributions. The Kruskal-Wallis test revealed a significant effect of the game conditions on the sequence lengths without considering super circles ($\chi^2(11) = 1391.7$, $p < 2.2E - 16$) and also when considering super circles ($\chi^2(11) = 1388.4$, $p < 2.2E - 16$).

134

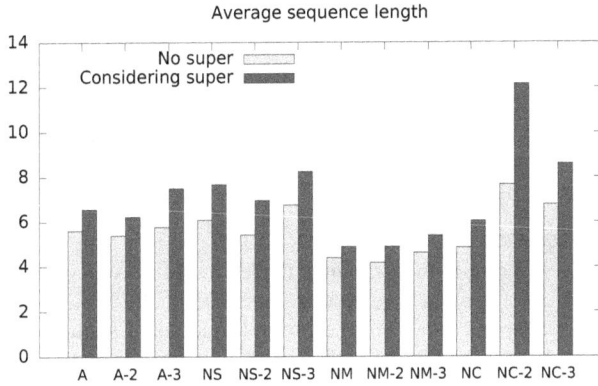

Figure 3. Average sequence length for every game session, not considering the super circles and considering the super circles (e.g. a super circle of level 2 in a sequence represents 10 circles in the solution). 'A', 'A-2' and 'A-3' represent the tests with all the features on; 'NS', 'NS-2' and 'NS-3' represent the tests without the skills; 'NM', 'NM-2' and 'NM-3' represent the tests without the market; 'NC', 'NC-2' and 'NC-3' represent the tests without the challenges.

We then made a post hoc test (Dunn's test) to do pairwise comparisons between all the groups. With or without considering super circles, all the game conditions were shown to be significantly different ($p < 0.01$), except a few shown in table 2. Note that the strongest similarities are found between the three 'All' groups and the three 'No market' groups. Some of the 'No skills' experiments are found to be similar to the 'All' groups, which could indicate that the presence of the skills have a very limited effect on the sequence length. The NC experiment is found to be similar to two 'No market' groups, but that can be explained by the fact the players for the NC experiment were very weak (as can be seen by the total experience gained during that session in Figure 10).

Note that even in the two sessions (A and NC) for which we had the smallest total experience (which is a way to evaluate the strength of the players; see Figure 10), the averages of sequence lengths were higher than the ones of the 3 game sessions without the market, even though we had some very strong groups for NM-2 and NM-3 (as shown by the total XP in Figure 10). Those observations confirm that the market is helping the players in the creation of longer sequences.

	A-2	A-3	NS	NS-2	NS-3	NM	NM-2	NM-3
A	n/s	n		n/s				
A-2		n		n/s				
A-3			n/s					
NC						n		n/s
NC-3					n/s			
NM							n/s	n

Table 2. Similar groups of sequence length distributions, as reported by Dunn's test. An 'n' in the table represents a similar pair when not considering super circles, and an 's' in the table represents a similar pair when considering super circles.

Testing hypothesis 2: the benefits of a skill system

We implemented the skill system for two reasons: (i) to give the players more incentive to accumulate experience points as fast as possible, because the reward for leveling-up is an additional skill point, and (ii) to influence indirectly the players into doing actions that are either improving the solutions collected by the system or helpful to the other players (which in the end will also improve the solutions). In our game, two skills were related to the market (*Buyout King* and *Master Trader*) and two skills were related to building sequences (*Color Expert* and *Sequence Collector*). In the following paragraphs, we will analyze how those four skills affected the strategies and actions of the players. Note that when some players lost all their money in the game, they had to start a new game. In our results, we count both new games as if they were played by different players, since the players who restart might choose a different set of skills the second time. That explains why the total number of players is larger than 120. Players of the 'No skills' game condition were considered and put automatically in the without skill group.

Buyout King

The *Buyout King* skill allows the players to reduce the price of buying a sequence from another player (which we call a buyout). The idea behind this skill was to encourage the players to buy small sequences built by other players so that they could improve them before selling them back to the system. In other words, a buyout is the action of buying a partial solution made by another player in order to improve it.

Figure 4-left shows statitics for the players who have put at least one skill point in the *Buyout King* skill and the players who did not use the skill at all. We were interested in the number of buyouts that the players with the skill were making compared to the rest of the players. Note that since this skill is related to the market, we did not consider the 'No market' sessions for these results.

The median value for players who spent a skill point in the *Buyout King* skill is 15, while the median value for the players without the skill is 1.5, indicating that half of the players without the skill did not use the buyout at all or used it only once. Since the distribution of the number of buyouts is not following a normal distribution (the Shapiro-Wilk test rejected the null hypothesis with $p = 2.6E - 10$), we used a Mann-Whitney's U test to compare the medians of the two groups. We found a significant effect of the presence of this skill on the medians ($U = 1629.5$, $p = 0.004$, effect size $r = 0.28$).

Master Trader

The *Master Trader* skill allows the players to get bonus money in addition to the regular market price for each circle they sell individually. This skill was put in the game in order to increase the activity on the market by encouraging more players to send the circles that they don't need to players who need it the most.

Figure 4-right shows statistics for the players who have put at least one skill point in the *Master Trader* skill and all the other players. We were interested in comparing the number of individual circles that were sold to another player for the two different categories. Once again, since this skill depends on the presence of the market, we did not consider the 'No market' experiments in the results shown.

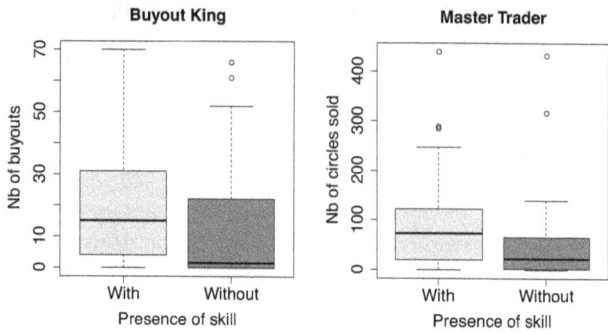

Figure 4. Left: Boxplot of the number of buyouts made by players with (37 players) and without (66 players) the *Buyout King* skill. Right: Boxplot of the number of circles sold individually by players with (33 players) and without (70 players) the *Master Trader* skill.

The median value for the players who had selected the *Master Trader* skill (73) is more than three times larger than the one for the rest of the players (21.5). Since the distribution of the number of circles sold individually is not following a normal distribution (the Shapiro-Wilk test rejected the null hypothesis with $p = 5.3E - 13$), we used a Mann-Whitney's U test to compare the medians of the two groups. We found a significant effect of the presence of the *Master Trader* skill on the medians ($U = 1633.5$, $p = 7.2E - 4$, effect size $r = 0.33$).

Color Expert

The *Color Expert* skill gives a bonus multiplier to the scoring function for sequences with more than one color in common. This skill was implemented in order to give extra motivation to build sequences with many colors in common, since they are harder to build. Indeed, more focus is needed from the player to match many circles with more than one color in common.

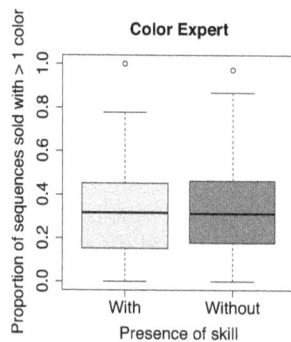

Figure 5. Boxplot of the proportion of sequences with more than one color in common sold by players with (94 players) and without (49 players) the *Color Expert* skill.

In Figure 5, we show the comparison of the proportion of multicolored sequences sold by players with the *Color Expert* skill and players without it. Interestingly, the median values for both groups are almost identical: 0.317 (or 31.7%) for the players with the skill and 0.313 (or 31.3%) for the players without the skill. The distribution of the proportion of multicolored sequences was not normal (the Shapiro-Wilk test rejected the null hypothesis with $p = 0.3E - 4$), so we did a Mann-Whithney's U test to compare the medians. As

expected, the test failed to reject the null hypothesis that the values were sampled from the same distribution ($p = 0.89$).

We conclude that the *Color Expert* skill does not affect the behavior of the players. This can be explained by the fact that one of the main goals of the game is to create sequences with as many colors in common as possible, whether the player selects this skill or not.

Sequence Collector

Every point in the *Sequence Collector* skill gives an additional slot to build a sequence. Because of the limited size of the player's hand and the limited number of sequence slots, it's hard to build long sequences with many colors in common. It is for both the sequence length and the number of colors in common that we added the *Sequence Collector* skill in the game.

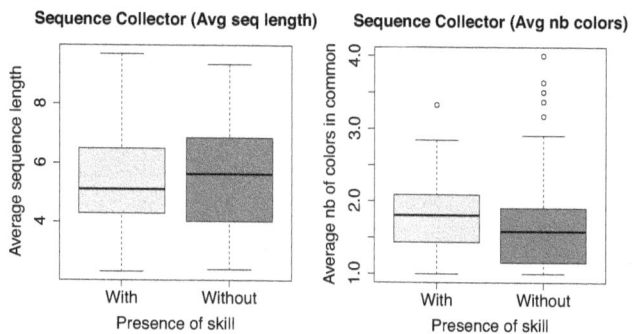

Figure 6. Boxplots of the average sequence length (left) and the average number of colors in common (right) of sequences built by players with (60 players) and without (83 players) the *Sequence Collector* skill.

We first compared the average sequence length of sequences built by players with the *Sequence Collector* skill and the ones built by the rest of players (see Figure 6-left). While the median value for the players without the skill (5.63) is a little bit larger than the one for the players with the skill (5.12), the averages of both groups are actually similar (5.61 and 5.56 in the same order). Since the distribution of the average sequence lengths were not normal (the Shapiro-Wilk test rejected the null hypothesis with $p = 0.0057$), we did a Mann Whitney's U test to compare the medians of both groups. The test failed to reject the null hypothesis that the values were sampled from the same distribution ($p = 0.69$). Thus, there is no evidence that the *Sequence Collector* skill helps players build longer sequences. This tends to confirm what we mentioned earlier (in Section Testing hypothesis 1): the presence of the skills in general does not seem to affect the length of the sequences built by players. Once again, this can be explained by the fact that selling long sequences is one of the two main goals of the game, and is one of the main components of the scoring function.

We then compared the average number of colors in common of the sequences built by players with and without the *Sequence collector* skill (see Figure 6-right). The median value for the players without the skill (1.58) is 12% lower than the one for the players with the skill (1.80). Since the distribution of the average number of colors in common is not following a normal distribution (the Shapiro-Wilk test rejected the null hypothesis with $p = 1.2E - 7$), we used a Mann-Whitney's U test to compare the medians of the two groups and we found a significant effect of the presence of this skill on the medians ($U = 3113$, $p = 0.01$, effect size $r = 0.21$). The *Sequence collector* skill is thus helping players to build sequences with more colors, by allowing them to store unfinished sequences of multiple colors in the additional slots until they are able to complete them.

Testing hypothesis 3: the usefulness of the challenge system

The challenge system was implemented to analyze the current state of the game and guide the players towards doing actions that are currently needed. As mentionned previously, five different challenge types were implemented in the game (see Section Challenge system for the complete list). In order to analyze the effect of the challenges on the way the participants were playing, for each challenge type, we compared the relevant statistics of the game during the challenge with the rest of the game session (when a different challenge was available).

Note that we are considering here only the nine sessions in which the challenges were present and that the Sell/buy and Buyout challenges were disabled during the session without the market.

Minimum number of colors challenge

To measure the effect of the *Minimum number of colors challenge* on the game, we compared the average number of colors of the sequences built by the players when the challenge was active and when it was not. The different averages for each game session are presented in Figure 7. In all the game sessions except A-3 and NM, the average number of colors in common is higher when the challenge is active.

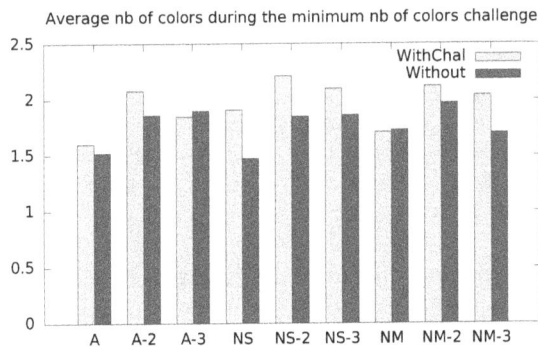

Figure 7. **Average number of colors in the sequences with and without the *Minimum number of colors challenge* active. 'A', 'A-2' and 'A-3' represent the tests with all the features present, 'NS', 'NS-2' and 'NS-3' represent the tests without the skills, and 'NM', 'NM-2' and 'NM-3' represents the tests without the market.**

The distribution of the averages of the number of colors in common for all the game sessions considered here is normal (Shapiro-Wilk $p = 0.79$), allowing us to use a Welch's t-test to compare the means for both groups, *i.e.* 1.96 colors in common during the challenge and 1.76 during the rest of the time. The test confirmed a significant effect of the presence

of the challenge on the average number of colors in common ($t(16) = 2.19$, $p = 0.04$, Cohen's $d = 1.03$).

Minimum sequence length challenge

In order to analyze the effect that the *Minimum sequence length challenge* had on the game, we compared the average sequence length during the challenge and when a different challenge was active for all the game sessions. As shown in Figure 8, the presence of this challenge increased the average sequence length in all the game sessions except the three sessions with all the features.

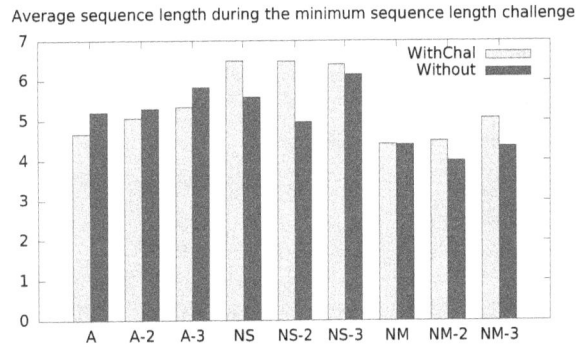

Figure 8. **Average sequence length with and without the *Minimum sequence length challenge* active. 'A', 'A-2' and 'A-3' represent the tests with all the features present, 'NS', 'NS-2' and 'NS-3' represent the tests without the skills, and 'NM', 'NM-2' and 'NM-3' represents the tests without the market.**

The means of all the average sequence lengths during the challenge and for the rest of the time are 5.38 and 5.08 respectively. Since the distribution of the averages of sequence lengths is normal (Shapiro-Wilk $p = 0.27$), we used a Welch's t-test to compare those means, but the test wasn't able to prove that those means are significantly different ($t(16) = 0.79$, $p = 0.44$).

Although there is not a statistically significant difference between the two groups, we can generally see a small effect for six of the nine groups with challenges. The fact that we observe the opposite effect in the three game sessions with all the features is very surprising, but hard to explain. One possible explanation could be that when all the features are present, the players have more to think about and check the challenges a little bit less.

Sell/buy challenge

For the *Sell/buy challenge*, we were interested in comparing the number of individual circles sold on the market per minute when the challenge was active and when it was not. The results, presented in Figure 9, don't show a clear trend. Indeed, in half of the game sessions, the number of circles sold per minute is higher during the challenge, while it's the opposite for the other half of the game sessions.

Once again, the numbers of circles sold per minute in the six different game sessions follow a normal distribution (Shapiro-Wilk $p = 0.26$), so we used a Welch's t-test to compare the means of both groups, which are 13.18 during the challenge and 12.73 during the rest of the time. The t-test failed to reject

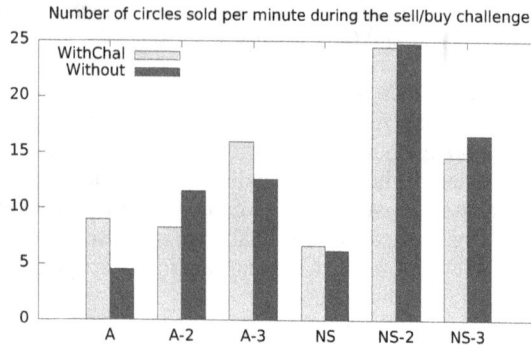

Figure 9. Number of individual circles sold on the market per minute with and without the _Sell/buy challenge_ active. 'A', 'A-2' and 'A-3' represent the tests with all the features present, and 'NS', 'NS-2' and 'NS-3' represent the tests without the skills.

the null hypothesis that both means are the same ($t(10) = 0.11$, $p = 0.91$).

We believe that the main reason why there doesn't seem to be any difference between the two groups is that most people were able to complete this type of challenge without really changing anything to their normal behavior. This challenge was simply too easy, because most of the players are always selling or buying (through the bids) at least 2 or 4 circles every five minutes (the length of a challenge).

Buyout challenge

The _Buyout challenge_ appeared only once in total in all the three gaming session with challenges and with the market. Thus, we don't have a significant amount of data to analyze the effect of this challenge. The reason why this challenge almost never appeared is because players were always using the buyout, which greatly reduced the probability of showing this challenge.

Specific colors in common challenge

The _Specific colors in common challenge_ is also difficult to analyze because it was completed only 8 times in total during the nine sessions with challenges, despite appearing 11 times throughout those nine experiments. This can be explained by the fact that it was the hardest challenge. All the other challenges are more general and can be completed by doing actions that are not specific to a certain subset of colors. Even if the market should be helpful in finding circles with the required subset of colors, it seems highly probable that the players felt that this type of challenge was too hard and almost never tried to complete it.

Testing hypothesis 4: percentage of the problem solved as a measure of the importance of different game features

One of the research goals was to measure the impact of each feature by analyzing how much of the problem can be solved by the players in each of the game sessions. Our initial hypothesis was that players who have access to all the game features should be able to solve more of the problem.

Interestingly, we observed a larger than expected variance in the participants' personal skills which made it sometimes

difficult to compare one game session with another in terms of the percentage of the problem that was solved. Indeed, some players quickly understood all the rules of the game and how to maximize their score, while others struggled to make points during the whole session, even with our help.

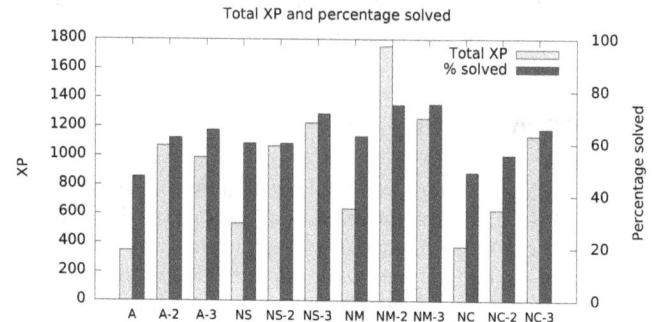

Figure 10. Total game experience and percentage of the problem solved for each of the 12 game sessions. 'XP' represents experience points. 'A', 'A-2' and 'A-3' represent the tests with all the features on; 'NS', 'NS-2' and 'NS-3' represent the tests without the skills; 'NM', 'NM-2' and 'NM-3' represent the tests without the market; 'NC', 'NC-2' and 'NC-3' represent the tests without the challenges.

As shown in Figure 10, the percentage of the problem that was solved varies from 48% to 75% in all the different experiments. In particular, the differences observed for experiments with the exact same game conditions (sometimes up to a 18% difference) demonstrates that we cannot simply use the percentage of the exact solution found as a way to measure the impact of a feature. Moreover, the top five sessions in terms of percentage solved (all sessions with more than 65%) come from the four different game conditions.

We used linear regression to test if the percentage of the problem solved is, to some extent, directly proportional to the total experience points accumulated by all the players during a session, which is a good way to measure the skills of the players during each session. The linear function obtained (graph not shown) had a coefficient of correlation $r = 0.89$, which shows a strong level of correlation. Thus, it suggests that the participants' skill level has a greater effect on the size of the collected solutions than the game features alone.

Understanding what makes a good player

Based on the questionnaire filled by the players before playing the game, and the global leaderboard of all the players from all the sessions put together, we tried to find similarities between the top players. Table 3 shows the most interesting differences between the top 12 players and the rest of the players. In the questionnaires, players had to indicate their age category (between 21 and 25 for example), their own evaluation of their puzzle solving abilities and a range of hours spent playing video games every week.

The average age of the two groups of players was calculated by taking the middle point of the age categories. The average age of the top 12 players was about 2.5 years younger than the one of the other players. For the puzzle solving self evaluation, the players could choose a level between 1 and 5 (5 being the strongest). The average level of the top 12 players was 3.67, compared to 2.90 for the others. As we did with the age categories, we computed averages of time spent playing video games every week using the middle point of the categories. The top 12 players were playing roughly 2.5 times more every week than the rest of the players.

	Top 12 players	Others
Age	23.42	25.99
Self evaluation (0-5)	3.67	2.90
Game time (hrs)	10.00	4.11

Table 3. Average statistics on the top 12 players vs the others.

We also looked at the mean age, mean video game time per week, and mean puzzle solving self evaluation for each of the 12 groups. We used linear regression to measure the correlation between those mean values and the total experience points gained by all the players of the groups. Mean age and mean video game time per week have a moderate level of correlation with total experience ($r = -0.67$ and $r = 0.58$ respectively), while mean self evaluation only exhibits a weak level of correlation with total experience ($r = 0.39$).

CONCLUSION

We implemented a human computing game that uses a market, skills and challenges in order to solve a problem collaboratively. The problem that is solved by the players in our game is a graph problem that can be easily translated into a color matching game. The total number of colors used in the tests was small enough so that we were able to compute an exact solution and evaluate the performance of the players. We organized 12 game sessions of 10 players with four different game conditions (three times each).

Our tests showed that the market is a useful tool to help players build longer solutions (sequences, in our case). We also observed that weaker players can benefit from the market: it allows them to make larger contributions on average than stronger players without the market. In other words, the market allows participants of any skill level to be more productive. In addition, it also makes the game more dynamic and players mentioned that they really enjoyed this aspect of the game.

Our results also showed that skills in general are helpful to influence and guide the players into doing specific actions that are beneficial to the system and other players. We have found that skills are more efficient in their role of guiding the players if they are not directly related to the main goal of the game: the *Color Expert* skill for example did not affect the proportion of multicolored sequences built by the players.

The results on the challenges indicate that they can be useful to promote an action in the game (*Minimum number of colors in common* for example), but in order to be effective, the difficulty needs to be well-balanced. Challenges that are too easy (*Sell/buy challenge* for example) or too hard (*Specific colors in common challenge* for example) do not affect the game significantly.

Although the great variability in the participants' personal skills made it very difficult to make direct comparisons between the different game conditions in regards to the percentage of the solutions found, we showed that the percentage solved is proportional to the total experience gained by all players during a game session. Therefore, the percentage of the problem solved is clearly not only dependent on the features present in the game, but also on the participants' ability to be good at the game.

The analysis of the best players tends to show that younger players who play video games on a regular basis and have a strong self evaluation of their puzzle solving skills are able to understand the rules of the game and find winning strategies faster than the average participant.

In the context of a human computing game, where participants are contributing for free, players' perception and statisfaction with the gameplay is very important. We asked the players in the questionnaire to rate their experience with the game and the average score was 71.6%, which is significantly above average. We also gathered some feedback when we were talking to the participants after the sessions. Since the game has no end in itself (we decided to limit the sessions to 45 minutes), some players mentioned that it is very addictive. Competing against other players to be at the top of the leaderboard was also a powerful motivation for the players. Obviously, we also had some negative comments: some players found the game hard to understand, while some very good players found it too easy. Overall, it is quite interesting to see that players enjoyed the game in its current state without any extensive effort put into visual aesthetics.

Another important point for a collaborative game like ours is scalability. In the tests that we have done during the development of the game, we have noticed that having more players is actually beneficial to the system. There are more sellers and buyers on the market, which results in a market that is a lot more dynamic (bidders get their circles faster, prices change more often, etc.). A more dynamic market allows different strategies to be equally profitable (e.g. some players can decide to focus on the Master Trader skill that boosts prices for selling circles, and then focus entirely on selling individual circles to other players). We are planning as future work to build an online version of the game that would be available 24/7. This will allow us to analyze the differences in gameplay and quality of solutions between peak hours (with possibly thousands of players at the same time) and normal hours.

ACKNOWLEDGMENTS

First and foremost, the authors wish to thank all the players who made this study possible. The authors would also like to thank Jean-François Bourbeau, Mathieu Blanchette, Derek Ruths and Edward Newell for their help with the initial design of the game, and Alexandre Leblanc for his helpful advice on the statistical tests. The authors wish to thank Silvia Juliana Leon Mantilla and Shu Hayakawa for their help with the organization of the game sessions and the recruitment of participants. This work was made possible by grants from CIHR (BOP-130836), Genome Canada, NSERC (386596-10), and FRQNT.

REFERENCES

1. Michael Buhrmester, Tracy Kwang, and Samuel D. Gosling. 2011. Amazon's Mechanical Turk: A New Source of Inexpensive, Yet High-Quality, Data? *Perspectives on Psychological Science* 6, 1 (2011), 3–5. DOI:http://dx.doi.org/10.1177/1745691610393980

2. Marija Mitrović Dankulov, Roderick Melnik, and Bosiljka Tadić. 2015. The dynamics of meaningful social interactions and the emergence of collective knowledge. *Scientific Reports* 5, 12197, Article 12197 (2015). DOI: http://dx.doi.org/10.1038/srep12197

3. Steven Dow, Anand Pramod Kulkarni, Scott R. Klemmer, and Björn Hartmann. 2012. Shepherding the crowd yields better work. In *CSCW '12 Computer Supported Cooperative Work, Seattle, WA, USA, February 11-15, 2012.* 1013–1022. DOI: http://dx.doi.org/10.1145/2145204.2145355

4. Nathan Green, Paul Breimyer, Vinay Kumar, and Nagiza F. Samatova. 2010. PackPlay: Mining Semantic Data in Collaborative Games. In *Proceedings of the Fourth Linguistic Annotation Workshop (LAW IV '10).* Association for Computational Linguistics, Stroudsburg, PA, USA, 227–234. http://dl.acm.org/citation.cfm?id=1868720.1868757

5. Andrea Guazzini, Daniele Vilone, Camillo Donati, Annalisa Nardi, and Zoran Levnajić. 2015. Modeling crowdsourcing as collective problem solving. *Scientific Reports* 5, 16557, Article 16557 (2015). DOI: http://dx.doi.org/10.1038/srep16557

6. Michiel Hildebrand, Maarten Brinkerink, Riste Gligorov, Martijn van Steenbergen, Johan Huijkman, and Johan Oomen. 2013. Waisda?: Video Labeling Game. In *Proceedings of the 21st ACM International Conference on Multimedia (MM '13).* ACM, New York, NY, USA, 823–826. DOI: http://dx.doi.org/10.1145/2502081.2502221

7. Chien-Ju Ho, Tsung-Hsiang Chang, and Jane Yung-jen Hsu. 2007. PhotoSlap: A Multi-player Online Game for Semantic Annotation. In *Proceedings of the Twenty-Second AAAI Conference on Artificial Intelligence, July 22-26, 2007, Vancouver, British Columbia, Canada.* 1359–1364. http://www.aaai.org/Library/AAAI/2007/aaai07-215.php

8. Chien-Ju Ho, Tao-Hsuan Chang, Jong-Chuan Lee, Jane Yung-jen Hsu, and Kuan-Ta Chen. 2010. KissKissBan: A Competitive Human Computation Game for Image Annotation. *SIGKDD Explor. Newsl.* 12, 1 (Nov. 2010), 21–24. DOI:http://dx.doi.org/10.1145/1882471.1882475

9. Chang Hu, Benjamin B. Bederson, and Philip Resnik. 2010. Translation by Iterative Collaboration Between Monolingual Users. In *Proceedings of the ACM SIGKDD Workshop on Human Computation (HCOMP '10).* ACM, New York, NY, USA, 54–55. DOI: http://dx.doi.org/10.1145/1837885.1837902

10. Panagiotis G Ipeirotis and Evgeniy Gabrilovich. 2014. Quizz: targeted crowdsourcing with a billion (potential) users. In *Proceedings of the 23rd international conference on World wide web.* ACM, 143–154.

11. Geoff Kaufman, Mary Flanagan, and Sukdith Punjasthitkul. 2016. Investigating the Impact of 'Emphasis Frames' and Social Loafing on Player Motivation and Performance in a Crowdsourcing Game. In *Proceedings of the 2016 CHI Conference on Human Factors in Computing Systems.* ACM, 4122–4128.

12. Alexander Kawrykow, Gary Roumanis, Alfred Kam, Daniel Kwak, Clarence Leung, Chu Wu, Eleyine Zarour, Phylo players, Luis Sarmenta, Mathieu Blanchette, and Jérôme Waldispühl. 2012. Phylo: a citizen science approach for improving multiple sequence alignment. *PLoS One* 7, 3 (2012), e31362. DOI: http://dx.doi.org/10.1371/journal.pone.0031362

13. Michael Kearns. 2012. Experiments in social computation. *Commun. ACM* 55, 10 (2012), 56–67. DOI: http://dx.doi.org/10.1145/2347736.2347753

14. Michael Kearns, Siddharth Suri, and Nick Montfort. 2006. An experimental study of the coloring problem on human subject networks. *Science* 313, 5788 (Aug 2006), 824–7. DOI:http://dx.doi.org/10.1126/science.1127207

15. Aniket Kittur and Robert E. Kraut. 2008. Harnessing the wisdom of crowds in wikipedia: quality through coordination. In *Proceedings of the 2008 ACM Conference on Computer Supported Cooperative Work, CSCW 2008, San Diego, CA, USA, November 8-12, 2008.* 37–46. DOI:http://dx.doi.org/10.1145/1460563.1460572

16. Markus Krause and René Kizilcec. 2015. To Play or Not to Play: Interactions between Response Quality and Task Complexity in Games and Paid Crowdsourcing. In *Third AAAI Conference on Human Computation and Crowdsourcing.*

17. Markus Krause, Aneta Takhtamysheva, Marion Wittstock, and Rainer Malaka. 2010. Frontiers of a Paradigm: Exploring Human Computation with Digital Games. In *Proceedings of the ACM SIGKDD Workshop on Human Computation (HCOMP '10).* ACM, New York, NY, USA, 22–25. DOI:http://dx.doi.org/10.1145/1837885.1837893

18. Daniel Kwak, Alfred Kam, David Becerra, Qikuan Zhou, Adam Hops, Eleyine Zarour, Arthur Kam, Luis Sarmenta, Mathieu Blanchette, and Jérôme Waldispühl. 2013. Open-Phylo: a customizable crowd-computing platform for multiple sequence alignment. *Genome Biol* 14, 10 (2013), R116. DOI: http://dx.doi.org/10.1186/gb-2013-14-10-r116

19. Edith Law and Luis von Ahn. 2009. Input-agreement: A New Mechanism for Collecting Data Using Human Computation Games. In *Proceedings of the SIGCHI Conference on Human Factors in Computing Systems (CHI '09).* ACM, New York, NY, USA, 1197–1206. DOI: http://dx.doi.org/10.1145/1518701.1518881

20. Greg Little. 2010. Exploring iterative and parallel human computation processes. In *Proceedings of the 28th International Conference on Human Factors in Computing Systems, CHI 2010, Extended Abstracts Volume, Atlanta, Georgia, USA, April 10-15, 2010.* 4309–4314. DOI: http://dx.doi.org/10.1145/1753846.1754145

21. Daniel Lombrana, Marvin Reimer, Alejandro Dominguez, James Doherty, Jorge Correa, Clara Sanchez-Puga, and Alvaro Suarez Perez. 2015. http://crowdcrafting.org/. (2015). http://crowdcrafting.org/

22. Jan Lorenz, Heiko Rauhut, Frank Schweitzer, and Dirk Helbing. 2011. How social influence can undermine the wisdom of crowd effect. *Proc Natl Acad Sci U S A* 108, 22 (May 2011), 9020–5. DOI: http://dx.doi.org/10.1073/pnas.1008636108

23. Koji Oishi, Manuel Cebrian, Andres Abeliuk, and Naoki Masuda. 2014. Iterated crowdsourcing dilemma game. *Scientific Reports* 4, 4100, Article 4100 (2014). DOI: http://dx.doi.org/10.1038/srep04100

24. Gabriele Paolacci, Jesse Chandler, and Panagiotis G. Ipeirotis. 2010. Running Experiments on Amazon Mechanical Turk. *Judgment and Decision Making* 5, 5 (2010), 411–419.

25. Massimo Poesio, Jon Chamberlain, Udo Kruschwitz, Livio Robaldo, and Luca Ducceschi. 2013. Phrase Detectives: Utilizing Collective Intelligence for Internet-scale Language Resource Creation. *ACM Trans. Interact. Intell. Syst.* 3, 1, Article 3 (April 2013), 44 pages. DOI: http://dx.doi.org/10.1145/2448116.2448119

26. Jimmy Secretan, Nicholas Beato, David B. D Ambrosio, Adelein Rodriguez, Adam Campbell, and Kenneth O. Stanley. 2008. Picbreeder: Evolving Pictures Collaboratively Online. In *Proceedings of the SIGCHI Conference on Human Factors in Computing Systems (CHI '08)*. ACM, New York, NY, USA, 1759–1768. DOI: http://dx.doi.org/10.1145/1357054.1357328

27. Luis von Ahn and Laura Dabbish. 2004. Labeling images with a computer game. In *Proceedings of the 2004 Conference on Human Factors in Computing Systems, CHI 2004, Vienna, Austria, April 24 - 29, 2004.* 319–326. DOI: http://dx.doi.org/10.1145/985692.985733

28. Luis von Ahn, Ruoran Liu, and Manuel Blum. 2006. Peekaboom: A Game for Locating Objects in Images. In *Proceedings of the SIGCHI Conference on Human Factors in Computing Systems (CHI '06)*. ACM, New York, NY, USA, 55–64. DOI: http://dx.doi.org/10.1145/1124772.1124782

29. Borui Wang and Jingshu Chen. 2013. Visimu: A Game for Music Color Label Collection. In *Proceedings of the Adjunct Publication of the 26th Annual ACM Symposium on User Interface Software and Technology (UIST '13 Adjunct)*. ACM, New York, NY, USA, 93–94. DOI: http://dx.doi.org/10.1145/2508468.2514726

30. Lixiu Yu and Jeffrey V. Nickerson. 2011. Cooks or cobblers?: crowd creativity through combination. In *Proceedings of the International Conference on Human Factors in Computing Systems, CHI 2011, Vancouver, BC, Canada, May 7-12, 2011.* 1393–1402. DOI: http://dx.doi.org/10.1145/1978942.1979147

31. Haoqi Zhang, Edith Law, Rob Miller, Krzysztof Gajos, David C. Parkes, and Eric Horvitz. 2012. Human computation tasks with global constraints. In *CHI Conference on Human Factors in Computing Systems, CHI '12, Austin, TX, USA - May 05 - 10, 2012.* 217–226. DOI: http://dx.doi.org/10.1145/2207676.2207708

Opening the Black Box of Play: Strategy Analysis of an Educational Game

Britton Horn
Northeastern University
Boston, Massachusetts
bhorn@ccs.neu.edu

Amy K. Hoover
Northeastern University
Boston, Massachusetts
amy.hoover@gmail.com

Jackie Barnes
Northeastern University
Boston, Massachusetts
jacqbarn@gmail.com

Yetunde Folajimi
Northeastern University
Boston, Massachusetts
yetundeofolajimi@gmail.com

Gillian Smith
Northeastern University
Boston, Massachusetts
gi.smith@northeastern.edu

Casper Harteveld
Northeastern University
Boston, Massachusetts
c.harteveld@northeastern.edu

ABSTRACT

A significant issue in research on educational games lies in evaluating their educational impact. Although game analytics is often leveraged in the game industry, it can also provide insight into player actions, strategy development, and the learning process in educational games separate from external evaluation measures. This paper explores the potential of game analytics for learning by analyzing player strategies of an educational game that is designed to support algorithmic thinking. We analyze player strategies from nine cases in our data, combining quantitative and qualitative game analysis techniques: hierarchical player clustering, game progression visualizations, playtraces, and think-aloud data. Results suggest that this combination of data analysis techniques provides insights into level progression and learning strategies that may have been otherwise overlooked.

ACM Classification Keywords

H.5.1 Information Interfaces and Presentation (e.g., HCI): Multimedia Information Systems—*Evaluation/methodology*; K.3.2 Computers and Education: Computer and Information Science Education—*Computer science education*; K.8.0 Personal Computing: General—*Games*

Author Keywords

educational games; computational thinking; playtrace analysis; evaluation.

INTRODUCTION

Through the emerging field of *game analytics* [8] (analogous to *learning analytics* [37]), methods for both evaluating gameplay and analyzing player behavior have been dramatically expanding [27]. Rather than evaluating learning outcomes through external evaluations alone (e.g. , questionnaires and tests), recent approaches investigate player actions logged during gameplay to provide insights into the learning processes of players [25, 12, 13]. A significant challenge in game analytics and educational game design lies in successfully combining traditional methods of assessing knowledge with tracking and analyzing behavioral telemetry for the purposes of both assessing learning and improving the design of educational games.

This paper contributes to analyzing educational games with game analytics by exploring player strategies in *GrACE*, an educational puzzle-based game for middle school aged students (11-13 years old) that is designed to support algorithmic thinking [20]. While many educational games such as *CodeCombat* [4], *Robocode* [29], and *Robozzle* [24] also focus on supporting algorithmic thinking, they often emphasize the structure and syntax of computer programming rather than addressing the core planning and strategy development processes. *GrACE* on the other hand, supports algorithmic thinking by presenting players with a puzzle analogous to solving a typical computer science problem (i.e., finding the minimum spanning tree). Through navigating and solving multiple puzzles, the goal is for players to learn both the data structure and the step-wise algorithm for solving it.

One obstacle in game analytics is that it is often difficult to correctly interpret the meaning of player data [18]. To interpret the meaning of player actions in *GrACE*, we take the approach of triangulating findings by combining quantitative hierarchical cluster analysis of player actions with a qualitative analysis of playtraces supported by concurrent think-aloud data and progression visualizations. We found that our mixed-methods approach helped discover emergent player strategies and how the game mechanics may have supported such strategies, findings that may not have been visible through traditional assessments or game analytics alone. Our work unveils prevalent player strategies by "opening the black box of play" using this triangulation approach, building a deeper understanding of how players learn and progress in the game, and aiding

CHI PLAY '16, October 16-19, 2016, Austin, TX, USA

© 2016 ACM. ISBN 978-1-4503-4456-2/16/10. . . $15.00

DOI: http://dx.doi.org/10.1145/2967934.2968109

decisions in the (re)design process of building an effective educational game.

BACKGROUND
This section elaborates on why game analytics should be considered when developing and evaluating educational games. It also discusses existing playtrace analysis techniques used in commercial and educational games.

Game Analytics for Educational Games
Although there is a long and rich history of developing games for education, such games often lack rigorous evaluation [14]. While used in game development, evaluating learning using game analytics is relatively new. Given time constraints of educators or researchers to distribute and evaluate traditional assessments, or code interview data, game analytics is a promising alternative to efficiently and automatically evaluate performance and learning. In fact, some scholars argue that game data itself is an assessment of learning (provided that appropriate metrics have been defined) [36]. Shaffer and Gee [35] even state that "We have been designing games for learning when we should have been designing games for testing" (p. 3). As evidence of how game data can act as an assessment of learning, one recent study showed a strong correlation between game performance and external test measures [17].

Further, analyzing game data should not only determine whether a design works, but also *how* it works. For example, in a study that analyzed both efficacy measures as well as game data [15], it was found that the game was an effective training intervention, but looking closely at the playtraces indicated that players consistently made the same errors, suggesting the design itself could be improved. Asking only efficacy questions can discount other aspects of player experience and potentially result in incorrect conclusions. Given this, game analytics can facilitate data-driven game development, which can expose design problems at an early stage. Although such data-driven design is becoming increasingly common in the industry [8], it is not yet a common practice for educational games. Data-driven game development has the potential to assist in the formative evaluation of achieving learning objectives [14].

Tools and Methods for Playtrace Analysis
Many methods have been used for playtrace analysis [10], including traditional observational studies [19] as well as videotaping play and interview sessions [1], all of which are qualitative in nature and are difficult to use in analyzing large-scale playtest data [3]. In contrast, statistical and machine learning techniques have been used to track and categorize players in, among others, *Bioware* [6], *Forza Motorsport* [33], and *World of Warcraft* [7] by leveraging raw game data. For these quantitative approaches, scholars developed and validated aggregate metrics from the raw data to measure game states or player behavior [8], such as the number of attempts or level difficulty.

Using such metrics to describe player behavior has also been applied to educational games. For example, Serrano-Lugano et al. [34] introduce a scalable two-step approach where they first define simple generic metrics that could be applied to any educational game and then build game-specific assessment rules based on combinations of these metrics. They found that their approach is valid for identifying where players get confused, but it does not give insight into *how* to address player confusion, likely due to a lack of understanding of why players behave in a certain way [18].

In addition, to better understand player decisions during gameplay and how player choices differed from what designers expected, a playtrace of an educational game has been done using conceptual feature extraction methods drawn from log data [12]. Researchers created various models that break gameplay down into individual cognitive tasks (or knowledge components) and assess which of these models is the best descriptor of player learning throughout the game. Though this work aims to gain insights into the dynamics of learning in an educational game, it relies solely upon logged game data and performing statistical regressions to better understand predictor variables.

To decode *how* players play games, tools have been developed to visualize player trajectories. In fact, two existing efforts, *Playtracer* [3, 26] and *Glyph* [28], have both supported the qualitative and quantitative analysis of an educational puzzle game through state graphs to identify common play patterns. *Playtracer* calculates the distance of states to the goal, whereas *Glyph* uses defined player actions as the edges connecting the game states. Even with these tools, it is a challenge to decide how to define game states, their relationships to one another, and to interpret the data being visualized.

Historically, playtrace analyses have developed from small-scale qualitative studies to large-scale quantitative studies. The latter was enabled with the arrival of game analytics and the need to study larger data sets; however, this came at the cost of meaning, which has been the strength of traditional playtrace studies. In our work, we pursued a mixed-methods approach to address the issue of interpretation in analyzing player strategies in *GrACE*.

DESIGN
GrACE is a puzzle game with a vegetable-collecting narrative designed to encourage algorithmic thinking. Algorithmic thinking involves thinking about problems abstractly, identifying common traits so that they can be treated as a class of problems instead of a single instance, and building sequences of instructions as solutions. It is a logical method of problem solving that can also be applied in areas outside computing [40]. Because *GrACE* is being developed in part to interest girls in computer science, the puzzle genre is chosen based on research suggesting it is appealing to girls [11, 31]. Furthermore, the puzzle genre is one of the top two genres played by teens [22] and like much of the computer science discipline, is about logically solving complex problems [16].

Specifically, *GrACE* aims to illustrate the potential of teaching algorithmic thinking through puzzles analogous to finding the minimum spanning tree (MST) of a graph, a core problem in computer science. These MST-based puzzles were chosen over other possibilities for their ease of visual representation, the existence of many algorithms to solve the problem, and

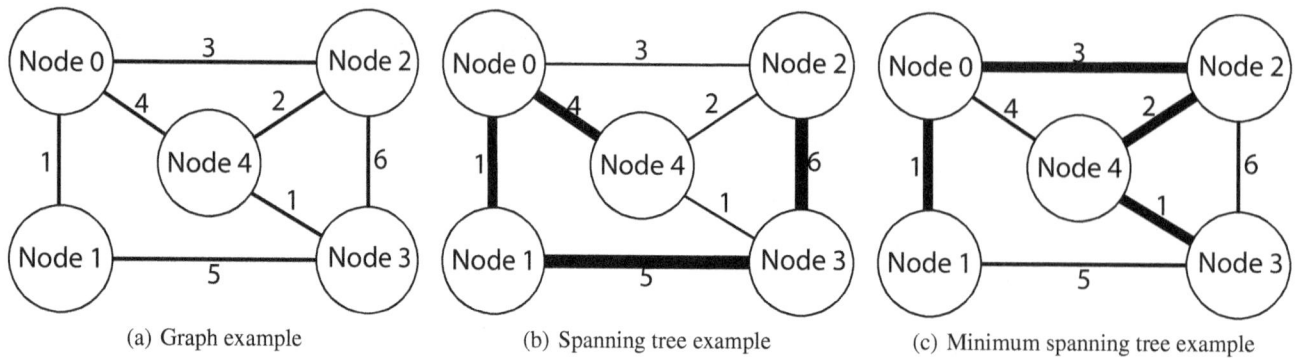

(a) Graph example   (b) Spanning tree example   (c) Minimum spanning tree example

Figure 1. Each connected graph such as the example in (a) has a variety of spanning trees, including the ones in (b) and (c). Because the cost of the path illustrated in (b) is 16 and that shown in (c) costs 7, (c) represents a less costly path and in this case represents the minimum spanning tree.

that even finding an incorrect solution (i.e., a spanning tree that is not minimal) involves algorithmic thinking.

Abstractly, the MST-based puzzles in *GrACE* are represented as graphs, which are a collection of nodes connected by edges. Each edge has an associated cost as shown in Figure 1(a), which shows an abstract MST puzzle. Players travel from one node to another along the edges that connect them. The cost of including an edge in the solution is represented by the number above the traveled edge. For example, in Figure 1(a), the cost of the edge between Node 0 and Node 2 is three.

In these graphs, players can travel along any edge connected to the node they are currently visiting. To indicate a particular edge should be considered in the solution of the puzzle, players can flag the edge when visiting the nodes connected to it. The darkened edges in Figure 1(b) like the edge connecting Node 0 and Node 4 represent such flagged edges.

A "spanning tree" is formed when a player visits all of the nodes and flags edges such that each node is only connected to the others once (as shown in Figure 1(b)). While a graph can have many different spanning trees, those with minimal cost are a MST (shown in Figure 1(c)). The abstract goal in *GrACE* is for players to find a MST by traveling along and flagging the least costly path where each node is connected to the others exactly once.

To avoid computer science jargon and create an interesting and relevant context, solving the MST-based puzzles centers around a narrative with two characters, Scout the mouse and Hopper the rabbit, whose combined goal is to collect all possible vegetables while expending the least amount of energy. In this narrative, burrows represent the graph nodes where each burrow contains a vegetable. The graph edges are tunnels that Hopper can dig to collect the vegetables. The cost of each tunnel is represented by the number of rocks through which Hopper must dig.

In the game, players control the character Scout, who traverses the graph while simultaneously placing flags on the edges to indicate which tunnels the character Hopper should dig. Scout the mouse is too small to dig but is able to traverse the graph unlike Hopper the rabbit. Scout shows Hopper where tunnels

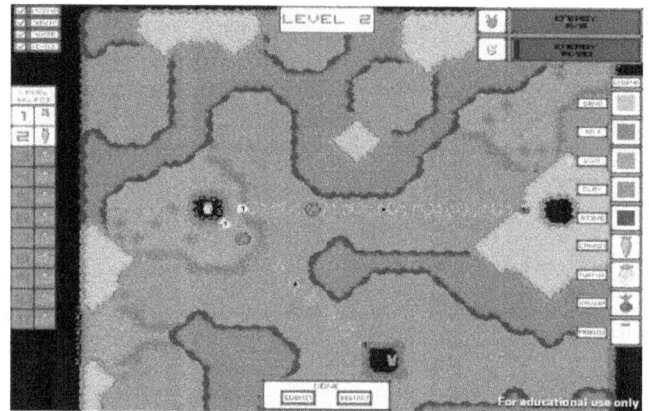

Figure 2. Screenshot of *GrACE* ©Northeastern University. This puzzle currently shows three nodes (as other nodes may be revealed later) with two edges, both with a cost of one, indicated by the arrow and number of rocks. Flagging involves literally placing a flag in the middle of an edge. On the top right are Hopper's and Scout's energy levels, to the left are the level select options, and at the bottom the submit button.

should be dug by flagging paths. At any point during the game, players may place or remove a flag on an edge.

Once players think they have explored the graph sufficiently and found the best possible solution, Hopper will dig tunnels along the flagged path, and collect the vegetables. The total cost of the flagged paths represents the amount of work for Hopper to dig tunnels, and if this is more than Hopper's available energy (represented as an energy bar) then players have not found an MST, which is necessary to successfully complete the puzzle and proceed to the next level.

Scout also has an energy bar which decreases with every action the player takes (moving, flagging, unflagging). For completing the level, Scout's amount of energy is not relevant except if she runs out, because in that case players will have to try again. Scout's energy has been included to encourage players to explore puzzles efficiently, and thereby algorithmically.

To simulate the way computers "think" through the problem node by node while keeping track of discovered edges and their weights, players initially can only see the starting node and the nodes which are directly connected to it. Players choose an edge to traverse at which point the new node and its connections are revealed. By slowly revealing the entirety of the graph, players are encouraged to develop an algorithmic approach which helps them solve more complex problems that would be challenging with only visual inspection.

Once all nodes have been explored and desired edges flagged, the player may submit their answer by clicking the "Submit" button. A correct answer sends the player to the next level which will contain more nodes and edges than the previous, while an incorrect answer leaves several options: the player may edit their submitted answer (which will continue to reduce Scout's available energy), restart the level, or replay any previously successfully submitted puzzles.

METHOD

To both explore how well *GrACE* encourages algorithmic thinking and to evaluate the ability of players to solve MSTs, this paper analyzes game data collected from a pilot study with *GrACE* [20]. Results from traditional external evaluation measures indicated a moderate improvement in scores after playing. Gameplay metrics were also considered (e.g., time for completion of each level, the number of correct and incorrect submitted solutions, and the number of levels completed), and indicated that participants tended to stumble at particular levels, with some never completing a level past the fifth (out of 11). Because some participants completed all eleven puzzles and some did not, a difference in strategies (and learning) may explain the variety in progress. To analyze players' strategies, we selected a small sample of participants and performed an in-depth analysis using qualitative and quantitative techniques.

Our approach combines a quantitative hierarchical clustering of player actions over the course of the game with a qualitative analysis of playdata that we call *retrospective player sense-making* collected through concurrent think-aloud data. Retrospective player sense-making involves reconstructing what a player did in the game by examining their playtrace step-by-step, noting observations along the way. Cluster analysis in particular is susceptible to issues of interpretation and trial-and-error [38, 39], so the advantage of this combined approach is that findings can be triangulated. Also, the think-aloud data may provide insights into players' in-the-moment perceptions and goals. Playtraces alone only help infer *what* players did rather than *why* they did it. Overall, our goal was to understand the divergence of player trajectories beyond quantitative game data. That is, we wanted to get an idea of why some players got stuck on certain levels and others were able to progress easily.

Study Context

The pilot study [20] was implemented as a programmed three-hour activity in a two-week summer program at Northeastern University that focuses on STEM education and retention for underserved and underrepresented minorities. Talented middle school students (ages 11 through 13) are selected to participate in this free of charge program. The original study was a 2x2 experimental design, where students received a prequestionnaire and pretest at the start. Following an explanation of how to play the game (without mentioning MSTs or the game's relationship to computer science), participants were randomly assigned to one of the conditions and played the game for about an hour. If students finished playing all levels, they were encouraged to repeat past levels and attempt to minimize the energy used by Scout the mouse. The activity ended with a postquestionnaire and posttest, followed by a group discussion.

Selection of Case Studies

Out of the 43 students who participated with the consent of their parents in the pilot study, we selected nine. These nine students participated in the same condition and played the same puzzles making it possible for us to perform an in-depth comparative analysis on how they played. For these selected students, ages ranged from 11 to 13 ($M = 12.2$, $SD = 1.06$). Four students identified themselves as female and five as male. Additionally, one student identified as Hispanic or Latino, three as Asian, one as Black or African American, two as White, and one as "other" (with one participant preferring not to answer). Each student indicated interest and experience playing games (e.g. video games, board games, sports), with some indicating that they played games several times a day while others only played every few weeks. Therefore, the selected nine students were diverse in terms of their socio-demographics and frequency of play (see also Table 1).

Data Collection

Of relevance to this paper is that players were asked to complete a postquestionnaire on their game experience with *GrACE* as well as a pretest and posttest to assess their algorithmic thinking. The postquestionnaire measured play experience with four 7-point Likert items focused on enjoyment and four on difficulty. The resulting composite scores range from 4 to 28, and are both reliable and valid [20].

The tests were developed to measure conceptual understanding of the MST and involved a multiple choice assessment of nine test questions with four choice options. All test questions were phrased in the context of a specific MST puzzle such as deciding what edge to add, what edge to remove, and what needs to be corrected. Test scores were calculated by providing one point per correctly answered question. Thus, with nine questions students could get a maximum score of nine points. The pre- and posttest differed in the exact questions asked, but were the same type.

The game data logged for each player was collected and each player also received a USB voice recorder to record their talk while playing. We encouraged students to think-aloud while playing so we could infer from their talk why they are playing in a certain way.

Analysis

The analysis considers players' strategies and progression through cluster analysis and retrospective player sense-making. For the cluster analysis, each playtrace was first converted to a string representing the sequence of actions performed. For instance, if a player successfully completed a level by starting at Node 0, moving to Node 1, flagging that edge, and then submitting their answer, these actions would be represented as "Start Node0, Move Node0 Node1 Edge1, Flag Edge1, Submit Correct." These strings are then compared by calculating the

Levenshtein string edit distance between them [23, 30], which counts the number of additions, substitutions, and deletions necessary to convert one string to the other. This number indicates the similarity between strings of playtraces.

For the retrospective player sense-making, we considered player strategies for each level and how these strategies evolved as players attempted each new level. We also used level progression visualizations to observe where players got stuck and puzzle features that may explain why. Once patterns emerged, we worked to better understand these patterns by supplementing initial findings with in-the-moment audio recordings of players during the game experience.

Strategy Analysis

For the strategy analysis, playtraces are compared to a standard algorithm for finding the MST of a graph called Prim's [32], which maintains and grows a tree by incrementally selecting the lowest cost edge encountered. Only edges that connect previously unconnected nodes are added to the MST solution and the process is repeated until all of the nodes are connected. If players solve the puzzles according to Prim's, it shows that *GrACE* helps to solve computational problems algorithmically. Other algorithmic approaches are possible, but Prim's was chosen as the golden standard algorithm because it directly aligns with our game mechanics.

We first performed a hierarchical cluster analysis to tease out different play styles used by *GrACE* players. Because the number of emergent strategies was not known *a priori* and hierarchical clustering operates without a predetermined number of clusters, each player run is hierarchically clustered based on the edit distances from one another and from the solution found by Prim's algorithm. Since sorting through qualitative data is time consuming, the idea is that clustering helps target the runs and level structures that need additional analysis with retrospective player sense-making.

For the retrospective player sense-making individual strategies were analyzed by retracing player steps by hand. This analysis involved redrawing on paper how players played each puzzle. Although this exercise seems tedious compared to watching a video of a player, the actual act of replaying the player steps on paper encourages us as researchers to imagine how players were making sense of the puzzle while playing, and therefore what strategies they were employing. In analyzing, the player steps were compared to a single run of Prim's algorithm on the same level.

Progression Analysis

Levels in *GrACE* are designed to increase in difficulty through the progression of the game, where difficulty is based on increasing numbers of nodes and edges. Levels with many failed player submissions indicate the challenge it posed to players. Progression visualizations can help evaluate whether the puzzles are progressively more difficult and where players first display some misunderstanding. We used a similar progression visualization method as Linehan et al. [25] who used it to detail how novel skills are introduced in a progressive manner.

An example of our player progression visualization method is shown in Figure 3. Each progression visualization represents

Participant	Pre	Post	Fun	Diff	Freq	Strategy
Red	NA	7	H	M	L	D
Orange	5	6	H	L	L	IT
Yellow	8	9	M	M	H	D
Green	8	8	L	H	M	IT
Blue	5	8	L	M	H	E
Indigo	7	5	H	L	M	D
Violet	3	4	H	H	M	D
Brown	8	9	M	L	L	D
Maroon	5	7	H	L	L	D

Table 1. The nine participants and their questionnaire results from the pilot study and predominant strategy from analyzing their gameplay. Questionnaire scores include pretest (Pre) and posttest (Post) scores (each ranges from 0 to 9), enjoyment (Fun) of *GrACE* (composite score ranging from 4 to 28), how difficult (Diff) they perceived *GrACE* (also from 4 to 28), how often they played games (Freq), and their predominant strategy (Strategy) during their initial playthrough of the game. Enjoyment and difficulty are listed in terms of Low < 14 (L), Medium = 14-20 (M), or High > 20 (H). Freq of game play ranges from 1 to 6 ("Never or Almost Never" to "Several Times a Day"). Freq is listed by Low = 1 or 2 (L), Medium = 3 (M) or High = 4 or 5 (H). There are three strategies: deliberate (D), exploratory (E), or iterative testing (IT).

a single playthrough of the game, but may not necessarily include completion of each level. For instance, Progression 1 in Figure 3 is an incomplete playthrough where the player never reached Level 6. Each dot represents a particular puzzle. The dot on the far left indicates Level 1 and on the far right Level 11. Lines connecting puzzles that arc upwards show forward progression in the game (e.g., moving from Level 1 to Level 2). Lines that arc downward are backward progressions (e.g., moving from Level 5 to Level 2) and indicate a replay of a previously completed puzzle. Loops starting and ending at the same dot are replays of the current level. The arc size (height and line width) and the boldness of the line are proportional to the number of times an answer for a particular level is submitted. For example, Progression 1 in Figure 3 has a large, wide loop on Level 5 illustrating that the level was attempted many times. Progression 2 in Figure 3 illustrates a player who progresses through the levels from Level 1 to Level 11 without replaying a current or previous level.

Qualitative Analysis of Think Aloud Data

To better understand the player experience and address the emergent questions that arose from the aforementioned analyses, we analyzed the approximately hour-long recordings for each of the nine participants. Any audible utterances were transcribed and time-stamped, to later compare with game actions taken during the same time. The transcripts were investigated in two ways: 1) the talk was searched for evidence of strategy articulation during the trajectory of the players' experience and 2) the transcripts were used to align utterances to player action patterns at specific points of gameplay.

RESULTS

Results in this section explore the emergent strategies players exhibited and how well they can solve and learn MSTs through *GrACE*. Each player is represented by one of the following colors: Red, Orange, Yellow, Green, Blue, Indigo, Violet, Brown, Maroon. Each player's pretest, posttest, enjoyment

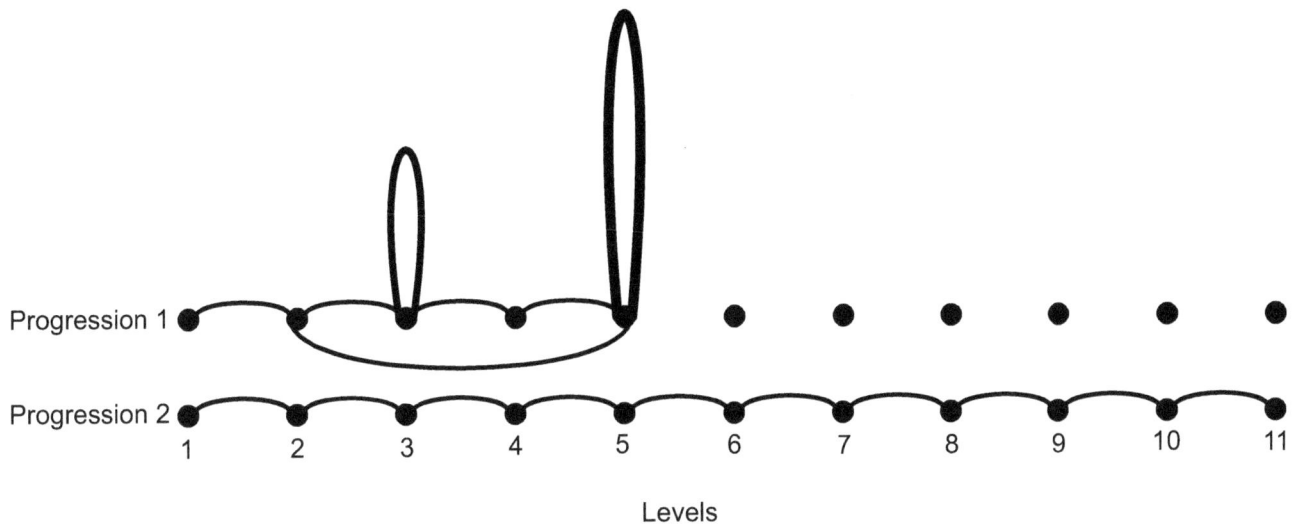

Figure 3. Example Player Progressions. Progression 1 shows a player progressing from level 1 to 2 to 3, repeating level 3 a few times, then progressing from 3 to 4 to 5, repeating level 5 many times, and finally going back to retry level 2. The player then quits playing at this point. Progression 2 shows a player progressing from level 1 all the way to level 11 without repeating any levels. Arcs above the dots indicate forward progression and arcs below the dots indicate a player going back to a previous puzzle.

of the game, assessment of its difficulty, frequency of game playing in general, and strategy is reported in Table 1. All but two individuals showed improvement from pretest to posttest (Green and Indigo). The table further shows diversity in how players experienced the game with no clear relationships between any of the measures, which indicates that these external measures may not provide the necessary insight to explain for these results, and that their actual play needs to be explored. The only interesting observation that can be inferred from the table is that it seems that players who play few games (Red, Orange, Brown, and Maroon) in their free time seem to find the game more fun and less difficult.

A broad overview of how players progressed through the game can be inferred from the progression visualizations in Figure 4. For instance, it is apparent that Green experienced difficulty grasping the game concepts as he completed only up to Level 5, and made multiple attempts from higher levels to go back and repeat lower levels. That idea is supported by the player's audio data expressing frustration and his expressed low enjoyment and high difficulty in playing the game. Similarly, though Blue never attempted to solve levels before her current level, her highest completed level is Level 9 and has a low enjoyment too. Blue, however, did seem to make the most visible improvement on the tests.

Evaluating successful players is less straightforward. For instance, because Red, Orange, Yellow, Indigo, Brown, and Maroon completed the game multiple times, they appear to have implemented an efficient strategy; however, further analysis of each player on each level leads to three emergent strategies called the 1) deliberate strategy, 2) exploratory strategy, and 3) iterative testing strategy. These strategies are indeed similar to previous research that grouped player strategies in response to challenge in the process of learning in single player games (trial and error, experiment, repetition, stop and think, and take the hint) [21]. A deliberate strategy typically indicates

the player has a clear understanding of how to solve the puzzle by flagging as they move, and an iterative testing strategy typically indicates player experimentation or that the player is having difficulty solving the puzzles. An exploratory strategy is often an intermediate strategy where players explore large portions of the map before flagging any edges. The following analysis is broken up into analyzing these player behaviors at each level.

Play Analysis in Level 1

To help players understand basic gameplay in *GrACE*, Level 1 is based on the simple graph illustrated in Figure 6(a). It has two nodes, called Node 0 and Node 1 and one connection with a weight of one. Depending on their current position, players can either move left or right, and flag or unflag the path until their energy runs out. Solving this puzzle indicates a basic understanding of game mechanics.

All players eventually solve Level 1 with the least amount of moves, most on their first try. In fact, in the clustered representation of successful Level 1 attempts shown in Figure 5, each player has at least one run of Level 1 clustered with the computer's solution obtained through Prim's Algorithm. In this level, however, many also experiment with the mechanics. For instance, Yellow whose first run is solved near perfectly, begins experimenting with Level 1 on the second run. While in the first run, Yellow solves the puzzle by moving from Node 1 to Node 0, flagging the path and then submitting on the first try. In subsequent attempts, the player tests the game functionality figuring out whether it is necessary to move to each node and if a path can be flagged before moving to it.

Several users did have difficulty understanding these basic game mechanics, only reaching a solution after several attempts. Only three actions are necessary to solve this puzzle, yet Orange performed ten actions in the first two runs of the level, both unsuccessful. On the third try of Level 1, the cor-

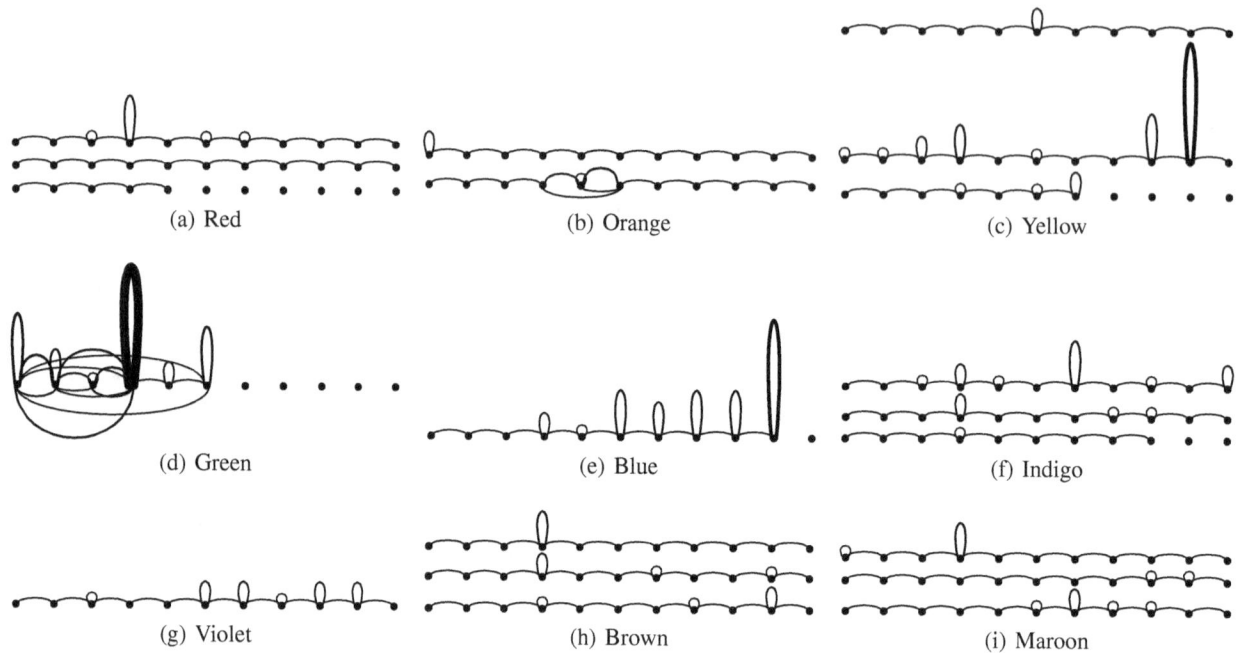

Figure 4. Progression visualizations over the 11 levels by player, where Level 1 is represented on the leftmost dot, and Level 11 the rightmost. Arcs above the dots indicate that players are advancing to the next level, while arcs starting and ending at same the dot represent that players are repeating that level. Then, arcs below the dots show players going back to solve levels that they have already solved. The arc size (height and line width) and the boldness of the line indicates the number of times a particular progression is repeated. In a set, the topmost progression is a player's first playthrough. The bottom progression is the final playthrough.

rect solution is found in nine tries, seemingly through trial and error. Eventually on the fourth run the puzzle is solved in three actions: move, flag, and submit.

Play Analysis in Level 3

Level 2 mostly reinforces the concepts that nodes must be visited, edges flagged and new information about a node's connections is discovered by visiting it. Level 3, on the other hand, challenges players to selectively choose edges to flag, important for identifying MSTs. Shown in Figure 6(b), a correct solution is moving between all the nodes, flagging connections between Nodes 0 and 1 and Nodes 1 and 2.

Though Red and Green start with a deliberate strategy, seemingly understanding flagging edges with minimum weights, once both encounter an "Out of Energy" error they retry the puzzle. During the second try in the same run, Red explores crossing the highest weight edge several times before running out of energy again, but eventually submits the correct answer. Similarly, Green submits the correct solution the second time Level 3 is played, but does not experiment with crossing the higher weight. Audio data suggests that Green grasps the goal of efficiency when exploring the graph. While playing Level 3, he utters "I'm not even sure how you do it...But, I don't need to go over there. Then, I run out of energy." Though he is likely still learning navigational affordances in the game, he appears to be attending to the energy constraints encountered by moving. Similarly, despite his actions Red acknowledges energy constraints, saying "...Too much time exploring."

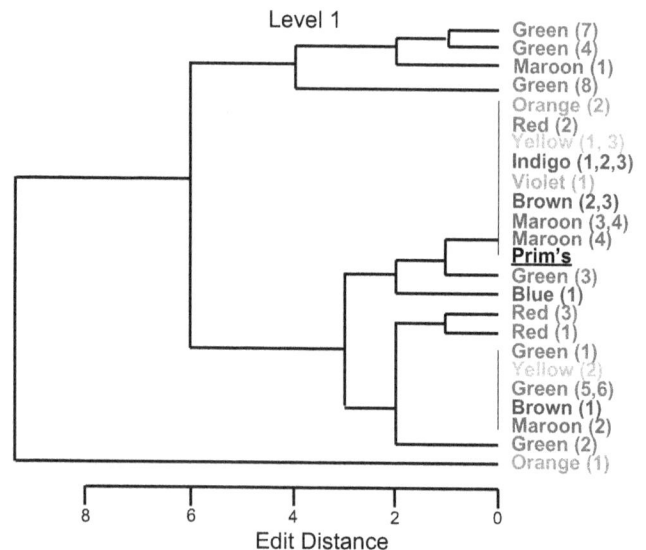

Figure 5. Clustering of *successful* playtraces for Level 1. Colored labels on the right indicate the player ID and run number. Some players completed one run (Blue and Violet) while others completed many (Green).

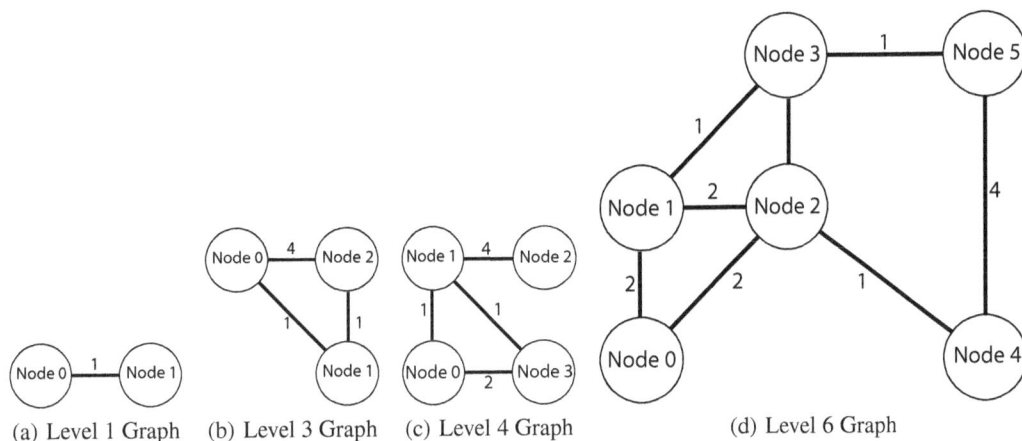

(a) Level 1 Graph   (b) Level 3 Graph   (c) Level 4 Graph   (d) Level 6 Graph

Figure 6. Graph depictions of levels in *GrACE*. Levels in *GrACE* can be abstracted into graphs, where each node represents a burrow for the character to investigate for vegetables and each edge the path to a particular burrow. The goal is for players to plot a path so that each burrow is visited with the least amount of cost, or that is, the goal is to find a MST of the graph. The significant Levels 1, 3, 4, and 6 are depicted.

Yellow, Brown, Orange, and Indigo also all execute deliberate strategies while Violet and Maroon who had previously executed deliberate strategies start each run in Level 3 by exploring all of the nodes and then flagging them in an exploratory style. Blue previously implemented an iterate and test strategy, but for this level switched to exploratory.

This is the first level where players rerun levels to achieve the most efficient solution (i.e., one completed in the least amount of steps). Only Yellow and Green find the solution on their first attempts. Most players eventually converge on the Prim's solution, yet Orange and Blue never find a solution comparable to Prim's.

Play Analysis in Level 4
With a total of four nodes and four edges compared to Level 3's three nodes and three edges, Level 4 shown in Figure 6(c) produces even greater challenges to the players. Furthermore, in this level it is possible to select two edges not connected to the same node. It is evident from the progression visualizations that Level 4 presents the first big hurdle for players with most having an increased number of attempts on their first playthrough of the game. The correct solution involves flagging a path of weight 4 between Nodes 1 and 2, and choosing not to connect Nodes 0 and 3 with weight 2. The other two paths with weight 1 should be flagged instead.

Initially, players struggle to only connect the lowest weight edges. For example, Blue and Violet begin by flagging all of the edges, while Maroon connects all of the nodes and excludes an edge, but does so without regard for which has the lowest weight. Interestingly, on a second playthrough of the game, Maroon solves the puzzle in a number of steps similar to that calculated by Prim's.

Perhaps because all lowest cost weights in previous levels were 1, it is possible that some players faced difficulty flagging the only connection to Node 2, which has a weight of 4. Everyone eventually solves Level 4, however, only Yellow, Brown, and Maroon present solutions comparable to Prim's. Of these players, only Yellow solves it like Prim's on the first

try. These players perform the best throughout the remaining levels, with Yellow and Brown scoring perfectly on the posttest, and Maroon improving more than others (except for Blue). Interestingly, Maroon found it more enjoyable than Yellow and Brown, possibly because she learned more.

Play Analysis in Level 6
Pictured in Figure 6(d), Level 6 is a graph with six nodes and eight edges, and is the first to present a node connected to four other nodes, testing the player's ability to choose which edge for the node should be flagged. Level 5, the last that all players were able to solve, presented at most three edge selections at any given node and had two fewer nodes overall.

Even Yellow who had previously solved each level easily and optimally took three tries to solve the puzzle. Starting at Node 2, on her first try, Yellow moved along a shortest path to Node 4, flagged it, and then moved to Node 5 across a path of weight 4. She flagged the higher weight path after visiting Node 5, meaning this weight was chosen after seeing the cheaper connection to Node 5 from Node 3. From Node 5, she went to Node 3, flagged the path and then moved to Node 1. After moving from Node 1 to Node 0, Yellow ran out of energy and restarted the level.

Since Yellow previously seemed to understand the necessity of choosing the lowest cost path, it is notable that she chose the weight path of value 4 connecting Nodes 4 and 5. Though she eventually finds the correct answer, the confusion is reflected across other players. For instance, although Violet starts deliberately moving and flagging, after the first submission fails, he explores and iterates and tests until six submissions later he finds the right answer.

When comparing to the answer found by Prim's algorithm, for this level the edit distance from any given solution is greater than zero, with Brown's second try and Maroon's second and third tries being the closest. However, Orange, Yellow, Indigo, and Brown were all eventually able to complete Level 6 with only one more action than Prim's algorithm.

Play Analysis Levels 7 through 11

Levels 7 through 11 continue to reinforce the concepts introduced by previous levels, challenging the players' existing strategies on more difficult puzzles. Players who have already discovered the deliberate strategy described in Table 1 have little trouble completing these levels, while those with exploratory and iterative testing strategies struggle with the additional nodes and edges.

Level 9 is the last level Blue completes, perhaps because Level 10 jumps to eight nodes, 13 edges, and a maximum connectivity of six, versus the six nodes, ten edges, and maximum connectivity of five seen in Level 9. The average connectivity of a node decreases slightly (3.30 to 3.25), but the highest connectivity of a node increases from 5 to 6.

Inspecting the clusters indicates that Red, Orange, and Violet begin to diverge from Prim's algorithm at Level 7, and Red and Orange continue this pattern until the end. Interestingly, Red and Orange sat next to each other while playing the game and were frequently talking to each other during game play, although they were instructed to solve the problems on their own—a fact highlighted only through audio data. Importantly, their similarity in play was detectable in their game actions. Their conversation included critique of the game—first Red then Orange posited that they found "a bug." Red explained that the game "says I'm wrong when it in actuality I was right." Later, he repeated "the last few levels I had the right answer and it said try again." Occasionally Orange asks Red for help and Red is continuously vocal in discussing his critiques with researchers. Through clustering of their playtraces and retrospective player sense-making, the difficulty they faced solving levels in *GrACE* is evident.

Indigo, Maroon, Brown, and Yellow continued to solve the puzzles in a manner similar to Prim's algorithm. Interestingly, Violet seemed to be implementing a deliberate strategy followed by an amount of guessing and checking, and by Level 11 the strategy was clearly cemented. Violet's progression in Level 10, began to hint that the main ideas were being learned.

In fact, our analysis suggests that over the course of the game, most students learn to visit all of the nodes in the MST, prefer traveling on shorter paths to avoid running out of energy, the concept of a spanning tree, and how to find the MST.

DISCUSSION

Our results highlight that including game data in analysis can shed light onto findings from traditional measures in addition to giving a better understanding of what players actually do. However, in some cases it raises more questions such as in the interesting case of Blue. In this section, we focus on discussing our findings for what made levels more or less difficult and the emergent player strategies and their implications for educational game design.

Although this work represented analysis of data for a particular game, future work will focus on its scalability to larger data sets and different games. For instance, with data from more players, an archetype clustering [5] can be performed helping sort the data into small enough subsets to perform meaningful hierarchical clustering.

Level Complexity and Progression

To avoid boredom and frustration, and to support learning effectively, it is important that the difficulty of levels increases steadily over time. However, through the progression analysis in this paper it is apparent that Level 6 was the first to present such a significant challenge to players that some could not successfully complete it. By tracing through individual player actions and examining the level structure (i.e., its underlying graph), part of the challenge appeared to be the increase in the number of nodes and edges from that in Level 5 (i.e., from four nodes to six nodes and five edges to seven).

Interestingly, while Level 11 also increased the number of nodes and edges from that in Level 10, this increase posed less of a challenge to players. While an explanation for this difference could in part be that those who were struggling most never reached Levels 10 and 11, further analysis across all levels in the progression reveals that in fact the biggest predictor of challenge lies in the number of choices available to players at a given node (i.e., the number of edges connected to a node). The number of edges connected to the node with the greatest amount of choices represents the maximum connectivity of the underlying graph. Although increasing the number of nodes and edges can lead to increased maximum connectivity, alone it is only a secondary indicator of difficulty. In fact, Levels 4, 6, 8, and 10 all saw increased maximum connectivity and were the levels players struggled with the most. Before our analysis, it was thought level difficulty could be sufficiently represented by the number of nodes and edges; however, a detailed trace analysis revealed the primary indicator of level difficulty as the graph's maximum connectivity.

Although the issue of maximum connectivity of a graph is specific to graph-based games, the process of discovering this phenomenon is not. We suggest that designers of educational games add into their development cycle a phase exploring where players get stuck, identifying the factors that contribute to challenges for those players, and then modifying and retesting the level progression. Through application of this procedure, designers can adjust the progression in an effort to reduce player frustration and increase learning.

That said, it is an open question to designers if reducing frustration needs to be aimed for. Blue is an interesting case. She did not enjoy the game and did not progress as far in the game as others, yet made the most visible improvement. Although Blue is a single case, in our other analyses with *GrACE* [9] we found a similar paradox: that players who did not enjoy it seemed to be the ones most benefiting from it. Regardless of how to deal with frustration, it will be beneficial to designers to understand what makes their game really difficult.

Player Strategy

Player strategies were determined through the mixed-methods approach described in this paper. We discuss how we determined such strategies and what they mean in the context of other findings. In addition, we discuss the implications for educational game design, and focus on the importance of game mechanics in encouraging (or hindering) learning and determining the appropriate measures of success.

Determining Strategies

Whether a player solved a level is important information in analyzing an educational game, but to explore learning it is crucial to understand *how* players solved the problem. Although player strategies are often discerned through laborious qualitative studies [21], the mixed-methods approach presented in this paper reduced time spent analyzing the qualitative data by allowing us to focus on critical game events and problematic levels. Clustering players' game actions combined with playtrace and audio analysis led us to determine that six of the nine players employed a deliberate strategy while two used an iterative testing method and one used an exploratory strategy.

When characterizing player strategies, it is difficult to conclusively state why particular actions were taken, but some evidence exists as to why player experiences diverged. For example, there appear to be trends related to player engagement as shown in Table 1. Player strategy appears independent to either their enjoyment or perception of difficulty. Looking at Orange and Green, who both took iterative approaches, Orange had a low rating of difficulty with a high rating of enjoyment. Green had a high rating of difficulty and a low rating of enjoyment. At least for the iterative approach, strategy development does not appear related to enjoyment or difficulty; however, both players had a gain of either 0 or 1, and so it may be the case that iterative strategies did not support learning. These are potential trends that need to be explored further.

Although surprising, improvement in score does not appear to be driven by enjoyment of the game. Counter-intuitively, those who played games more often rated the game at a medium or high difficulty, and medium and low enjoyment. One might expect that frequent gamers might enjoy a new game, and would find it less difficult than other players. These patterns require further investigation, but one hypothesis is that the players may have perceived the game as an educational task, rather than a true game, and the very logical nature of the task compared to the games they usually play, may have affected their engagement, learning (e.g., despite low engagement, Blue was one of two participants with high frequency of gaming, but was also the participant who gained most from pre to post), and potentially strategy development.

Interleaving Game Mechanics, Strategy, and Learning

Another important finding is the impact of game mechanics on learning. For example, Violet initially began with an efficient strategy, but was often confused by the game mechanic that required visiting all burrows before submitting a correct answer. Even though he sometimes began with a deliberate and correct strategy, when he failed to visit all burrows, his answer was judged as incorrect leading him to doubt his original strategy. Educational games that allow multiple strategies to lead to success should carefully consider their game mechanics' interactions with player strategies and how those impact learning. It is important to support all valid strategies and give proper feedback at failure points, which may vary based on strategy.

Metrics for Success

Another issue is developing appropriate metrics for success. As seen in previous playtrace research [2], trace length (number of actions) was insufficient to determine difficulty (or player success) of levels. In *GrACE*, some players successfully completed levels in as few actions as possible whereas others adopted a more exploratory strategy and would successfully complete levels using more actions than required. Neither of these strategies coincided with a more successful approach as they both successfully completed the levels.

Additionally, players could be equally efficient but have playtraces clustered separately. This was seen on Level 6 between Orange, Yellow, Indigo, and Brown. Only two were grouped with Prim's algorithm even though they all had identical efficiency and trace length. Although our original intent was to allow players to find their own algorithm since many exist for solving the MST problem, it became evident upon playtrace analysis that an additional measure of success (e.g., number of actions taken) is required during gameplay to encourage a more algorithmic approach than guess-and-check. In our game, the measure of success for efficiency—Scout's energy—was not reinforced enough since we didn't want to limit players to only one algorithm. Because of this, players would hardly ever run out of energy even with an iterative testing strategy. We encourage other algorithmic thinking game designers to implement similar measures of success to ensure a player must be algorithmic to be successful. In fact, this approach can be extended to any game where designers want players to exhibit a particular behavior.

CONCLUSION

In this research we have detailed the analysis from nine individuals playing *GrACE*, an educational puzzle game emphasizing algorithmic thinking. Our research outlines insights gained through the use of a mixed-methods strategy for gameplay analysis that triangulates data from four perspectives: think-aloud voice recordings, qualitative playtrace analysis we call *retrospective player sense-making*, level progression visualizations and quantitative clustering on player actions. We have shown how a mixed-methods approach can be applied to an educational game and how it helped us gain insights that may have been overlooked or incorrectly inferred without game analytics or using a single method to analyze playtraces. Finally, data-driven design and evaluation of an educational game has allowed us to detect problem areas early in the design phase where steps can still be taken to correct shortcomings. We hope that future game designers—educational and otherwise—take into consideration the benefits of mixed-methods approaches to game analytics and develop appropriate metrics for success that will ensure the game designer's goals are met.

ACKNOWLEDGMENTS

We want to thank the Northeastern STEM Center for Education for integrating our pilot study in their summer program and Christopher Clark and Oskar Strom who helped create the game. This material is based upon work supported by the National Science Foundation under Grant No. 1422750.

REFERENCES

1. Mike Ambinder. 2009. Valve's approach to playtesting: The application of empiricism.

2. Erik Andersen, Sumit Gulwani, and Zoran Popović. 2013. A Trace-Based Framework for Analyzing and

Synthesizing Educational Progressions. In *Proceedings of the SIGCHI Conference on Human Factors in Computing Systems*. ACM, 773–782.

3. Erik Andersen, Yun-En Liu, Ethan Apter, Francois Boucher-Genesse, and Zoran Popović. 2010. Gameplay Analysis Through State Projection. ACM, 1–8.

4. CodeCombat. 2016. CodeCombat: Learn to Code by Playing a Game. (2016).

5. Adele Cutler and Leo Breiman. 1994. Archetypal analysis. *Technometrics* 36, 4 (1994).

6. Phillip DeRosa. 2007. Tracking player feedback to improve game design. *Gamasutra* (2007).

7. Nicholas Duchenaut, Nick Yee, Eric Nickel, and Robert J. Moore. 2006. Building an MMO with mass appeal: A look at gameplay in World of Warcraft. *Game Developer Magazine* 1 (2006), 281–317.

8. Magy Seif El-Nasr, Anders Drachen, and Alessandro Canossa. 2013. *Game analytics: Maximizing the value of player data*. Springer Science & Business Media.

9. Yetunde Folajimi, Britton Horn, Jacqueline Barnes, Amy Hoover, Gillian Smith, and Casper Harteveld. 2016. A Cross-Cultural Evaluation of a Computer Science Teaching Game. In *Proceedings of Games+Learning+Society*. ETC Press, Pittsburgh, PA.

10. Tracy Fullerton. 2008. *Game Design Workshop: A playcentric Approach to Creating Innovative Games* (2nd ed.). Morgan Kaufmann.

11. Bradley S Greenberg, John Sherry, Kenneth Lachlan, Kristen Lucas, and Amanda Holmstrom. 2010. Orientations to video games among gender and age groups. *Simulation & Gaming* 41 (2010), 238–259.

12. Erik Harpstead and Vincent Aleven. Using Empirical Learning Curve Analysis to Inform Design in an Educational Game. In *Proceedings of the 2015 Annual Symposium on Computer-Human Interaction in Play (CHI PLAY 2015)*. ACM Press, 197–207.

13. Erik Harpstead, Christopher J MacLellan, Vincent Aleven, and Brad A Myers. 2015. Replay Analysis in Open-Ended Educational Games. In *Serious Games Analytics*, Christian Sebastian Loh, Yanyan Sheng, and Dirk Ifenthaler (Eds.). Springer International Publishing, 381âĂŞ399.

14. Casper Harteveld. 2011. *Triadic game design: Balancing reality, meaning and play*. Springer Science & Business Media.

15. Casper Harteveld. 2012. *Making Sense of Virtual Risks*. IOS Press.

16. Casper Harteveld, Gillian Smith, Gail Carmichael, Elisabeth Gee, and Carolee Stewart-Gardiner. 2014. A Design-Focused Analysis of Games Teaching Computer Science. In *Proceedings of Games+Learning+Society 10*. Madison, WI.

17. Casper Harteveld and Steven Sutherland. 2015. The goal of scoring: Exploring the role of game performance.. In *Proceedings of the 2015 ACM Conference on Computer-Human Interaction*.

18. Eric Hazan. 2013. Contextualizing Data. In *Game Analytics*. Springer, 477–496.

19. David Hilbert and David Redmiles. 2000. Extracting usability information from user interface events. *Comput. Surveys* 32, 4 (2000), 384–421.

20. Britton Horn, Christopher Clark, Oskar Strom, Hilery Chao, Amy J. Stahl, Casper Harteveld, and Gillian Smith. 2016. Design insights into the creation and evaluation of a computer science educational game. In *Proceedings of the 47th ACM Technical Symposium on Computer Science Education (SIGCSE)*. ACM Press, Memphis, TN.

21. Ioanna Iacovides, Anna L Cox, Ara Avakian, and Thomas Knoll. Player Strategies: Achieving Breakthroughs and Progressing in Single-player and Cooperative Games. In *Proceedings of the First ACM SIGCHI Annual Symposium on Computer-Human Interaction in Play (CHI PLAY 2014)*. ACM Press, 131–140.

22. Amanda Lenhart and Pew Internet & American Life Project. 2008. *Teens, Video Gaming and Civics*. Technical Report.

23. Vladimir I Levenshtein. 1966. Binary Codes Capable of Correcting Deletions, Insertions and Reversals. *Soviet Physics - Doklady* 10, 8 (1966), 707–710.

24. Frederick WB Li and Christopher Watson. 2011. Game-based concept visualization for learning programming. In *Proceedings of the third international ACM workshop on Multimedia technologies for distance learning*. ACM, 37–42.

25. Conor Linehan, George Bellord, Ben Kirman, Zachary H Morford, , and Bryan Roche. Learning Curves: Analysing Pace and Challenge in Four Successful Puzzle Games. In *Proceedings of the First ACM SIGCHI Annual Symposium on Computer-Human Interaction in Play (CHI PLAY 2014)*. ACM Press, 181–190.

26. Yun-En Liu, Erik Andersen, Richard Snider, Seth Cooper, and Zoran Popović. 2011. Feature-based Projections for Effective Playtrace Analysis. In *Proceedings of the 6th International Conference on Foundations of Digital Games (FDG '11)*. ACM, New York, NY, USA, 69–76.

27. Christian Sebastian Loh, Yanyan Sheng, and Dirk Ifenthaler. 2015. *Serious Games Analytics: Methodologies for Performance Measurement, Assessment, and Improvement*. Springer.

28. Truong-Huy Dinh Nguyen, Magy Seif El-Nasr, and Alessandro Canossa. 2015. Glyph: Visualization Tool for Understanding Problem Solving Strategies in Puzzle Games. *Foundations of Digital Games (FDG)* (2015).

29. Jackie O'Kelly and J Paul Gibson. 2006. RoboCode & problem-based learning: a non-prescriptive approach to teaching programming. *ACM SIGCSE Bulletin* 38, 3 (2006), 217–221.

30. Joseph C Osborn, Ben Samuel, Joshua Allen McCoy, and Michael Mateas. 2014. Evaluating play trace (dis)similarity metrics. In *10th AAAI Conference on Artificial Intelligence and Interactive Digital Entertainment*.

31. Mikki H Phan, Jo R Jardina, Sloane Hoyle, and Barbara S Chaparro. 2012. Examining the Role of Gender in Video Game Usage, Preference, and Behavior. In *Proceedings of the Human Factors and Ergonomics Society Annual Meeting*. SAGE Publications, 1496–1500.

32. Robert C. Prim. 1957. Shortest Connection Networks And Some Generalizations. *Bell System Technical Journal* 36 (Nov. 1957), 1389–1401.

33. Ramon Romero. 2008. Successful instrumentation: Tracking attitudes and behviors to improve games. In *Game DeveloperâĂŹs Conference*.

34. Angel Serrano-Laguna, Javier Torrente, Pablo Moreno-Ger, and Baltasar FernÃąndez-Man. 2014. Application of Learning Analytics in Educational Videogames. *Entertainment Computing* 5 (2014), 313–322.

35. David Williamson Shaffer and James Paul Gee. 2012. The Right Kind of GATE: Computer games and the future of assessment. *Technology-based assessments for 21st century skills: Theoretical and practical implications from modern research. Charlotte, NC: Information Age Publishing* (2012).

36. Valerie Shute and Matthew Ventura. 2013. *Stealth assessment: Measuring and supporting learning in video games*. MIT Press, Cambridge, MA.

37. George Siemens and Ryan S J d Baker. 2012. Learning Analytics and Educational Data Mining: Towards Communication and Collaboration. In *Proceedings of the 2nd International Conference on Learning Analytics and Knowledge*. ACM, 252–254.

38. Catherine A Sugar and Gareth M James. 2003. Finding the Number of Clusters in a Dataset: An Information-Theoretic Approach. *J. Amer. Statist. Assoc.* (2003), 750–763.

39. Robert L Thorndike. 1953. Who belongs in the family? *Psychometrika* 18 (Dec. 1953), 267–276.

40. Allen Tucker, Fadi Deek, Jill Jones, Dennis McCowan, Chris Stephenson, and Anita Verno. 2006. *ACM K-12 CS Model Curriculum*. Computer Science Teachers Association.

PAWdio: Hand Input for Mobile VR using Acoustic Sensing

Majed Al Zayer
malzayer@cse.unr.edu

Sam Tregillus
tregillus@cse.unr.edu

Eelke Folmer
efolmer@cse.unr.edu

Human+ Lab - Computer Science - University of Nevada

ABSTRACT

Hand input offers a natural, efficient and immersive form of input for virtual reality (VR), but it has been difficult to implement on mobile VR platforms. Accurate hand-tracking requires a depth sensor and performing computer vision on a smartphone is computationally intensive, which may degrade the frame rate of a VR simulation and drain battery life. PAWdio is a novel 1 degree of freedom (DOF) hand input technique that uses acoustic sensing to track the relative position of an earbud from a headset that the user holds in their hand. PAWdio requires no instrumentation and its low computational overhead assures a high frame rate. A user study with 18 subjects evaluates PAWdio with button input that is commonly available on VR adapters. Results with a 3D target selection task found a similar accuracy and usability, a significantly slower performance, but higher immersion for PAWdio. We discuss limitations and game applications of PAWdio.

ACM Classification Keywords

I.3.7 Graphics: 3D Graphics and Realism–Virtual Reality;

Author Keywords

Acoustic sensing, virtual reality; games; immersion; hand tracking; head-mounted display; switch input; natural input

INTRODUCTION

Smartphone VR adapters, such as Google Cardboard, have a potential to bring VR to the masses as they can turn the now-ubiquitous smartphone into a head-mounted VR display at a low cost. A criticism of current mobile VR apps is that they only deliver simple "look-and-see" or "rollercoaster" -like experiences [6] as the input options of mobile VR adapters are limited [14, 26]. Google Cardboard requires users to hold the adapter with both hands to limit the head rotation speed to the torso, which helps mitigate simulation sickness, [5], but limits the use of a controller. Google Cardboard features a single button that is either activated using magnetic sensing [22] or through an internal mechanism that generates a touchscreen input. Due to these constraints, mobile VR apps largely rely on gaze input -facilitated using the smartphone's inertial sensors. This leads to using GUI elements, such as gaze or stare buttons, whose usage has been found to be detrimental to immersion [9] when compared to conventional input.

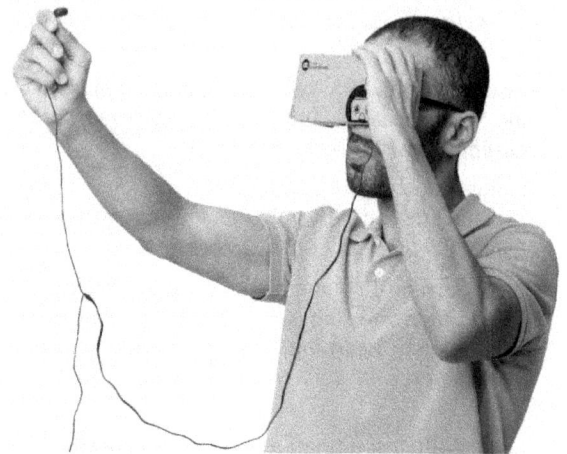

Figure 1. PAWdio appropriates a pair of ordinary in-ear headphones to track the position of the hand. The user holds a single earbud in their hand that produces an inaudible tone. Doppler shifts are used to determine the velocity of the earbud from or towards the phone, which is then used to manipulate the Z-position of a virtual hand that is attached to the user's gaze pointer.

The hand is the most natural input device for direct manipulation in VR [7], and is considered more immersive than using a controller. Hand input, however, has been difficult to implement on mobile VR platforms. Marker-less hand tracking is feasible on a smartphone [2] but its accuracy is subject to background and illumination changes, something that occurs frequently as VR users often turn their head to look around. Smartphone cameras have a small field of view; limiting hand-tracking to a small area, which may be detrimental to immersion. Robust hand-tracking usually requires an external depth sensor (i.e., Leap Motion) and because this sensor is powered by the smartphone it reduces battery life significantly. Mobile computer vision apps are generally computationally intensive [8], which may create lag or degrade the frame rate of the VR simulation that runs on the same smartphone. This is undesirable, as a high frame rate is required to maintain immersion and minimize simulation sickness [17].

This paper addresses a need for low-cost, immersive forms of input on mobile VR by presenting PAWdio; a one DOF hand tracking technique that uses acoustic sensing. PAWdio is low cost as it can be implemented using an ordinary pair of in-ear headphones. It doesn't require any training or calibration while having a low computational overhead that assures a high frame rate. PAWdio was found to be just as efficient and accurate as the standard single button input for selecting targets but was found considerably more immersive. PAWdio enables immersive implementations of various game related actions, such as; grabbing, punching, pushing or thrusting and throwing.

BACKGROUND

Acoustic sensing uses properties of sound such as the Doppler effect to provide user input [21]. Compared with vision based sensing it can be implemented with little computational overhead [11]. Speakers and microphones on current smartphones are capable of producing and recording audio up to 24kHz [16]. The human hearing range lies between 20Hz to 20kHz, which degrades as the result of aging; and the highest frequency a typical adult can hear is 15kHz [24]. Acoustic sensing methods using the [15-21kHz] spectrum can be implemented on any mobile device and are non-obtrusive to adults. Acoustic sensing methods can be distinguished into passive (only recording) and active (emitting and recording). We survey approaches pertaining to gesture detection and localization.

Acoustic gesture sensing uses Doppler shifts, i.e., changes in frequency of soundwaves that occur due to a positional change between an emitter and a receiver. One-handed gestures in 3D space can be recognized using three low-cost stationary ultrasonic receivers and a hand held transmitter [12]. This approach isn't mobile and relies on custom hardware. SoundWave [10] uses ordinary laptop speakers and microphone to detect various in air hand gestures using observed Doppler shifts and its properties, such as velocity and direction. Dolphin [19] implements this approach on a smartphone. AAMouse [28] localizes a smartphone between two TV speakers that emit different inaudible tones. Doppler shifts and triangulation allows AAMouse to achieve a localization accuracy of 1.4cm using an initial calibration. Phone-to-phone localization with reasonable accuracy ($\approx$10cm) can be implemented using time-difference of-arrival (TDoA) [18] or time of flight (ToF) [20], but these approaches require two mobile devices. Sweepsense [15] detects whether an earbud of a headset has fallen out through the detection of a non-audible tone that is played through each earbud. Acoustic Ruler [1] is an iPhone app that lets users measure the distance from their smartphone to an earbud of their headset. It uses ToF with an audible tone and with an initial calibration claims a resolution of 1mm.

PAWDIO DESIGN

An ideal implementation of hand input for Mobile VR offers 3D input, requires no specialized hardware or prior calibration and offers a low computational overhead to assure a high frame rate with no lag in tracking to maintain a high immersion [17]. PAWdio was designed within these constraints but a compromise had to be made regarding the available degrees of freedom (DOF) of the hand input.

Three dimensional acoustic localization approaches either require a stationary setup [12] or using two devices [20], which is not practical or cost-effective in mobile VR contexts. Instead PAWdio uses more practical and low-cost hardware setup -as introduced by Acoustic Ruler [1]- by appropriating an ordinary set of in-ear headphones to sense the distance of an earbud that the user holds in their hand (see Figure 1 for the hardware setup). This setup has two limitations: (1) because we only acquire a distance to the earbud, this only allows 1 DOF hand input, e.g., a virtual hand can only be moved forwards and backward; and (2) with the headset used for hand tracking, users cannot listen to sounds/music which may be detrimental to the VR experience.

Another constraint is that the microphone and speaker need to be directed at each other for best performance. This is challenging for mobile VR as the smartphone is inside the VR adapter and corrugated cardboard has excellent sound absorption properties. Typically, smartphones feature a pair of microphones for noise cancellation, with a primary microphone located near the mouth and secondary near the ear. When the smartphone is in the adapter, the primary microphone is occluded and pointed towards the user. The location of the second microphone seems to vary (e.g., side, top), but recent smartphones, like the Nexus smartphones, have the second microphone on the back close to the location of the camera. Because most smartphone VR adapters feature a cutout for the camera for AR applications, this conveniently leaves the second microphone unobstructed and aimed towards the hand.

Acoustic localization can be achieved using: TDoA [18], ToF[20] or Doppler shifts [28]. ToF measures the exact time it takes for a sound wave to travel from the emitter to the receiver and then-using the known speed of sound in the air-calculates the absolute distance between them. The use of ToF in a non-real-time operating system, such as Android or iOS, results in large estimation errors [18] as their non-determinism makes it difficult to exactly measure the time when a sound is actually sent or received. Peng et al [18] identified for a smartphone a lower-bound delay of 2.5 ms, which yields an estimation error of $\approx$ 85 cm. Because PAWdio requires estimation distances up to an arm length ($\approx$ 65 cm) using ToF is not feasible. Acoustic Ruler [1] also uses ToF but circumvents timing limitations using a multi-step calibration process, which we deem too cumbersome for PAWdio, as users may want to quickly engage in VR. TDoA does not require absolute timing, but it requires at least two non-coplanar microphones to achieve one-dimensional ranging, which would require a second device. Doppler shifts are the most feasible method for PAWdio as it doesn't rely on precise timing or calibration.

PAWdio emits a pure sine wave with a base frequency (f_0) in the inaudible spectrum [15-21kHz] over the earbud used for hand tracking. Besides being non-obtrusive to adults, this frequency doesn't seem to be susceptible to environmental interference given the ubiquitous application of ultrasonic sensors, such as automatic door openers [15]. The generated wave is recorded with the smartphone's secondary microphone and for analysis in real-time it is divided into chunks of size B. The size of B determines the resolution of the frequency estimation and it dictates the latency of the hand tracking. A larger value for B allows for tracking finer motions of the hand but also increases latency. After an audio chunk is captured, a fast-Fourier transform (FFT) is used convert it from the time domain to the frequency domain. We then extract a frequency spectrum subdomain around the base frequency (f_0) of size W. Within W, we find the frequency component f_{peak} with the highest amplitude. Comparison of f_{peak} and f_0 provides an estimate of the amount of Doppler shift, which allows for estimating the velocity of the hand (v) as follows:

$$v = \frac{c(f_0 - f_{peak})}{f_{peak}} \qquad (1)$$

where c is the speed of sound in air at room temperature. By calculating the time difference between two consecutive sound chunks, t_s, along with the calculated velocity (v), we can estimate the relative displacement (D_p) of the earbud from or towards the phone using: $D_p = v t_s$ Because the physical and virtual worlds are at different scales, we translate the physical displacement D_p to a virtual displacement D_v using a scaling factor α. The virtual hand's X and Y locations are coupled to the user's gaze pointer and its Z location is bounded by a maximum/minimum distance. Sampled changes in v can be associated with scaled displacement values D_v that determine the virtual hand's Z location at each frame.

EVALUATION

Comparing PAWdio to vision based methods is difficult as they offer 3D input; they require additional sensors; and they don't offer acceptable frame rates on mobile devices. We therefore compare PAWdio to single button input that is available on mobile VR platforms, as this is most similar in terms of available hardware. In our study, subjects perform a 3D target selection task by combining PAWdio with gaze input. Fitts' law analysis [23] has been performed for related 3D selection studies [13, 25]. Because PAWdio uses gaze & hand selection, a detailed Fitts' analysis does not generate significant results.

Instrumentation

We used a Cardboard V2 adapter (I AM Cardboard), whose button generates touch input that is considered more reliable than magnetic input [22]. We used a Motorola X Pure Edition smartphone with a Qualcomm Snapdragon 808 CPU with an Adreno 418 GPU which can render 3D simulations at a high frame rate. We used Apple's EarPods for our in-ear headphones. Our game was implemented using Unity 5 and the Google Cardboard for Unity SDK. PAWdio was implemented as a Unity plugin using the TarsosDSP [4] digital sound processing library. Specific to PAWdio's implementation, $18KHz$ was selected for f_0 and 340m/s for c. We experimentally found 8,192 to work best for B to accurately track the moderate motions required to grab an apple with no lag. We found that it is difficult for PAWdio to pick up very fast or very slow motions of the hand as this is difficult to detect using Doppler shifts. For the game, we determined a scaling factor of $\alpha = 5.8$, which moved the hand most realistically. In Unity we did not observe a difference in frame rate between both input options, which demonstrates PAWdio's low computational overhead.

Participants

We recruited 18 participants (9 females, average age 25.2, SD=4.4, 1 left handed) to participate in our user study. None of the subjects self-reported any non-correctable impairments in visual/audio perception or limitations in mobility. Individuals who self-reported to have previously experienced simulator sickness were excluded from participation, as they were at a higher risk of not completing the study. The user study was approved by an IRB. 13 participants had prior experience with VR and 14 had experience with 3D games.

Procedure

To evaluate the performance, accuracy and usability of PAWdio with button input, we conducted a within-subject study using a 3D target acquisition task that was implemented as a game. The use of a game is motivated by that this is a major application area for VR and a game context often allows for eliciting optimal performance. The game consists of a virtual hand whose X, Y position is tied to the gaze pointer and its Z position is controlled by the button or PAWdio. A button click moves the hand forward and another click retracts it and we selected a velocity for the hand that felt most realistic. Using PAWdio, the user's hand motions are directly mapped to forward/backward motions of the virtual hand. Targets, i.e., apples with a fixed size, are generated at a random location on an imaginary sphere around the participant where the virtual hand's movement is bounded by the sphere's boundaries. A gaze pointer is rendered to aid with the X, Y target selection task. The hand grabs the apple when they collide and when the hand is fully retracted, the apple disappears and a new apple is generated at least 60 degrees away from the previous apple. Participants played two sessions of the game each using one of the input methods with a 2-minute break between them. The order in which input method was used first was counterbalanced among participants. To mitigate the effect of the visual search task on overall task performance, we used the same sequence of apples for both sessions. For each session, participants had to collect 10 apples in the training session and 25 in the experiments.

Each participant received a brief tutorial on how the game works with each input method. When using PAWdio, participants were asked to reach out for the apple using their dominant hand like they would in the real world. To avoid picking up unintended motions, we asked users to retract their hand when looking for apples. We also asked users not to extend their arm extremely fast, as such motions were difficult to detect by PAWdio. We measured total task time from the first to the last apple and errors. For the error count, we define an error as any forward movement of the virtual hand that exceeds a given threshold and does not result in grabbing an apple. Both game sessions were video-recorded for analysis. After the trials, basic demographic and qualitative feedback was collected using a questionnaire. The entire session, including training and questionnaire, took about 30 minutes.

Results

A Grubb's test found no outliers and table 1 lists the average results for all users. A paired T-test found that the PAWdio input technique took significantly longer to perform ($t_{19} = -2.64$, $p < .05$) but no statistically significant difference was found for error rate ($t_{19} = 1.88$, $p = .076$).

Input method	Time (s)	SD	Errors	SD
Button	130.82	41.6	1.83	2.4
PAWdio	147.71	55.4	0.83	1.2

Table 1. Average time and errors for all users.

Input	Efficiency	Errors	Learnability	Likeability
Button	4.50 (1.0)	3.61 (1.5)	4.28 (1.1)	4.11 (1.1)
PAWdio	4.28 (.6)	3.17 (1.3)	4.28 (.6)	4.0 (.8)

Table 2. Likert scores for each usability attribute per technique (SD).

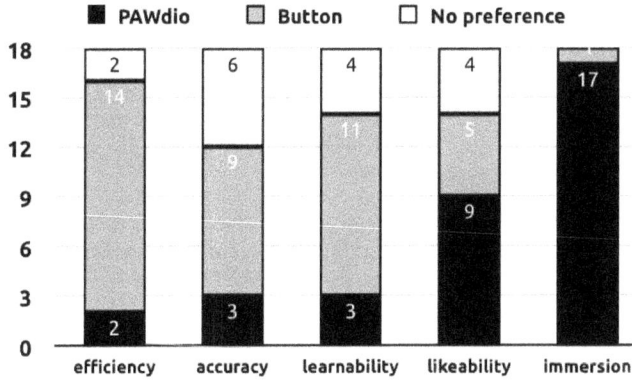

Figure 2. Ranking of input methods based on usability criteria.

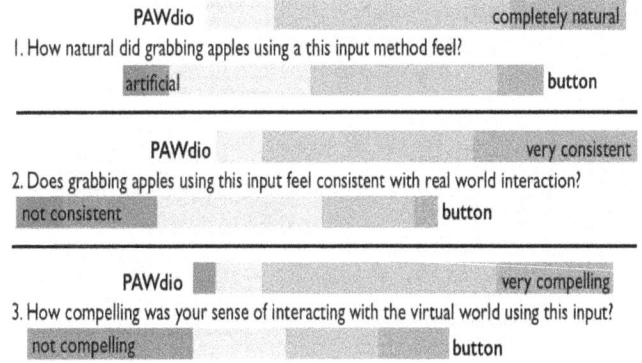

Figure 3. Evaluation of immersion for both input techniques

Qualitative results. After the trial, questionnaires were used to collect qualitative feedback. First, using a 5-point Likert scale, users evaluated each input method on 4 usability criteria: efficiency, accuracy, learnability and likability. Table 2 lists the results and a paired T-test found no statistical significant difference between input methods for any attribute. To assess VR immersion, we selected 3 questions from the Witmer and Singer presence questionnaire [27] who were most closely related to input and which are evaluated on a scale of 1 to 5. Figure 3 lists the questions and results. PAWdio received significantly higher scores ($t_{19} = -2.17(Q1), -5.68(Q2), -2.95(Q3), p < .05(Q1, Q2, Q3)$) . We then let subjects rank each input type on the four usability criteria and VR immersion, where subjects could select "No preference" as a 3rd option. Figure 2 lists the results, and a χ^2 test found the rankings for efficiency ($p = .027$), and overall immersion ($p = .001$) to be statistically significantly different. Finally, participants (# who said this) provided feedback about each input technique. For button input, participants liked its simplicity (6) and that it was easy to learn (3). Button input felt efficient (5) and was easy on the arms (2). Several participants complained that the button input was too sensitive (4) with users unintentionally activating it when they merely rested their finger on the button. PAWdio felt natural and realistic (11) and it allowed for making corrections half-way (2) something that is not possible with button input. Some users expressed that PAWdio was somewhat strenuous to perform (7) and that it was susceptible to some inaccuracy (5), e.g., the hand moving unintentionally.

DISCUSSION

Button input is faster as the virtual hand moves with a fixed speed when the button is pressed, where PAWdio follows the actual position of the user's hand, which takes more time.Surprisingly, users felt the button input was more accurate, but results showed the error rate for button input to be twice that of PAWdio (not significant for $\alpha = .05$ but significant for 0.1). This error was caused by the sensitivity of the button input of the Cardboard adapter we used. Occasionally PAWdio would pick up false positives when the user would turn quickly without moving their arm; which would cause a Doppler shift. Hand input was considered more strenuous than button input, but this is an inherent characteristic of hand input. Though the usability of both input techniques was similar, PAWdio was found to be significantly more immersive, which is important for VR.

LIMITATIONS AND FUTURE WORK

Playing audio is limited when using PAWdio, which is considered essential to immersion. Some earphones may allow for one earbud to be in the ear while the other one can be used for hand tracking; but audio will then be limited to mono. Android allows for playing different audio streams over the earphones or speakers at the same time [3], and this allows for PAWdio to work while playing audio over the speakers. PAWdio uses a frequency that is hearable by children and pets, and f_0 should be set to the highest frequency, e.g., $22Khz$. Because we did not evaluate PAWdio robustness to noise, our results are preliminary. It may be difficult for PAWdio users to activate the button on a VR adapter as they hold an earbud in their hand. We were able to create an alternative input by having users cap the earbud with their thumb. This blocks the ultrasonic tone and its absence/presence can be detected and used for input, i.e., similar to Sweepsense [15]. PAWdio's one DOF hand input is constrained when compared to 3D hand input; PAWdio only tracks a single hand, and very fast or slow motions of the hand are difficult to detect using Doppler shift. However, using different values of B, either faster or slower motions may be detected at the cost of performance. False positives may occur when the user turns quickly, but this is less likely to occur with most VR apps as they typically don't contain a large visual search task, like the game we used for the evaluation. The X, Y position of the virtual hand is tied to the gaze, which may be considered less immersive than 3D hand input. However, Cardboard already requires users to hold the adapter with both hands [5], so requiring the user's hand to remain in the field of view, is not a major constraint.

Despite these limitations, we demonstrated that PAWdio can offer basic hand input without relying on expensive sensors. PAWdio offers a slightly lower performance, but higher immersion than current VR input options. A number of VR demos were developed that demonstrate how PAWdio can be used to enable various "linear" game actions, e.g., punching, throwing object, thrusting a spear or pool cue, opening a door, and pushing or pulling objects.

For future work, we will research how to enhance PAWdio to enable 3D hand input, which is more immersive than 1D hand input. Many in-ear headsets often feature a microphone. When attaching this microphone to an earbud, three distinct speaker-microphone pairs could be defined and it might be possible to triangulate the location of the hand using ToF [20].

REFERENCES

1. Acoustic Ruler, iPhone App https://itunes.apple.com/us/app/acoustic-ruler-pro/id475081963?mt=8.

2. Android hand tracking in OpenCV, https://www.youtube.com/watch?v=1pZbY8naj9Q.

3. Stack overflow: Playing sound over speakers while playing music through headphones http://stackoverflow.com/questions/12017297/playing-sound-over-speakers-while-playing-music-through-headphones.

4. Tarsos: Real-time audio processing framework in java, https://github.com/JorenSix/TarsosDSP.

5. Works with google cardboard guidelines and best practices, http://static.googleusercontent.com/media/www.google.com/en//get/cardboard/downloads/wwgc_best_practices.pdf.

6. Barbagallo, R. How to support gear and google cardboard in one unity3d project, http://ralphbarbagallo.com/2015/05/26/how-to-support-gear-vr-and-google-cardboard-in-one-unity3d-project/.

7. Bowman, D. A., Kruijff, E., LaViola Jr, J. J., and Poupyrev, I. *3D user interfaces: theory and practice.* Addison-Wesley, 2004.

8. Clemons, J., Zhu, H., Savarese, S., and Austin, T. Mevbench: A mobile computer vision benchmarking suite. In *Workload Characterization (IISWC), 2011 IEEE International Symposium on*, IEEE (2011), 91–102.

9. Gowases, T., Bednarik, R., and Tukiainen, M. Gaze vs. mouse in games: The effects on user experience. *Proceedings of the 16th International Conference on Computers in Education (ICCE 2008)* (2008), 773–777.

10. Gupta, S., Morris, D., Patel, S., and Tan, D. Soundwave: using the doppler effect to sense gestures. In *Proceedings of the SIGCHI Conference on Human Factors in Computing Systems*, ACM (2012), 1911–1914.

11. Harrison, C., Tan, D., and Morris, D. Skinput: appropriating the body as an input surface. In *Proc. of the 28th international conference on Human factors in computing systems (CHI '10)*, ACM (2010), 453–462.

12. Kalgaonkar, K., and Raj, B. One-handed gesture recognition using ultrasonic doppler sonar. In *Acoustics, Speech and Signal Processing, 2009. ICASSP 2009. IEEE International Conference on*, IEEE (2009), 1889–1892.

13. Kopper, R., Bowman, D. A., Silva, M. G., and McMahan, R. P. A human motor behavior model for distal pointing tasks. *International journal of human-computer studies 68*, 10 (2010), 603–615.

14. Laput, G., Brockmeyer, E., Hudson, S. E., and Harrison, C. Acoustruments: Passive, acoustically-driven, interactive controls for handheld devices. In *Proceedings of the 33rd Annual ACM Conference on Human Factors in Computing Systems (CHI'15)*, ACM (2015), 2161–2170.

15. Laput, G., Chen, X. A., and Harrison, C. Sweepsense: Ad hoc configuration sensing using reflected swept-frequency ultrasonics. In *Proc. of the 21st International Conference on Intelligent User Interfaces (IUI'16)*, ACM (2016), 332–335.

16. Lazik, P., and Rowe, A. Indoor pseudo-ranging of mobile devices using ultrasonic chirps. In *Proc. of the 10th ACM Conference on Embedded Network Sensor Systems*, ACM (2012), 99–112.

17. Meehan, M., Razzaque, S., Whitton, M. C., and Brooks Jr, F. P. Effect of latency on presence in stressful virtual environments. In *Proc. IEEE Virtual Reality*, IEEE (2003), 141–148.

18. Peng, C., Shen, G., Zhang, Y., Li, Y., and Tan, K. Beepbeep: a high accuracy acoustic ranging system using cots mobile devices. In *Proc. of the 5th international conference on Embedded networked sensor systems*, ACM (2007), 1–14.

19. Qifan, Y., Hao, T., Xuebing, Z., Yin, L., and Sanfeng, Z. Dolphin: Ultrasonic-based gesture recognition on smartphone platform. In *IEEE International Conference on Computational Science and Engineering (CSE)*, IEEE (2014), 1461–1468.

20. Qiu, J., Chu, D., Meng, X., and Moscibroda, T. On the feasibility of real-time phone-to-phone 3d localization. In *Proc. of the 9th ACM Conference on Embedded Networked Sensor Systems*, ACM (2011), 190–203.

21. Raj, B., Kalgaonkar, K., Harrison, C., and Dietz, P. Ultrasonic doppler sensing in hci. *IEEE Pervasive Computing, 2* (2012), 24–29.

22. Smus, B., and Riederer, C. Magnetic input for mobile virtual reality. In *Proc. of the International Symposium on Wearable Computers*, ACM (2015), 43–44.

23. Soukoreff, R. W., and MacKenzie, I. S. Towards a standard for pointing device evaluation, perspectives on 27 years of Fitts' law research in HCI. *International journal of human-computer studies 61*, 6 (2004), 751–789.

24. Stelmachowicz, P. G., Beauchaine, K. A., Kalberer, A., and Jesteadt, W. Normative thresholds in the 8-to 20-khz range as a function of age. *The Journal of the Acoustical Society of America 86*, 4 (1989), 1384–1391.

25. Teather, R. J., and Stuerzlinger, W. Pointing at 3d targets in a stereo head-tracked virtual environment. In *IEEE Symposium on 3D User Interfaces*, (2011), 87–94.

26. Tregillus, S., and Folmer, E. VR-step: Walking-in-place using inertial sensing for hands free navigation in mobile VR environments. In *Proc. of the Conference on Human Factors in Computing Systems (CHI'15)*, (ACM 2016), 1250–1255.

27. Witmer, B. G., and Singer, M. J. Measuring presence in virtual environments: A presence questionnaire. *Presence: Teleoperators and virtual environments 7*, 3 (1998), 225–240.

28. Yun, S., Chen, Y.-C., and Qiu, L. Turning a mobile device into a mouse in the air. In *Proc. of the 13th Annual International Conference on Mobile Systems, Applications, and Services*, ACM (2015), 15–29.

Balance Ninja: Towards the Design of Digital Vertigo Games via Galvanic Vestibular Stimulation

Richard Byrne
Exertion Games Lab
RMIT University
Melbourne, Australia
rich@exertiongameslab.org

Joe Marshall
School of Computer Science
University of Nottingham
Nottingham, UK
joe.marshall@nottingham.ac.uk

Florian 'Floyd' Mueller
Exertion Games Lab
RMIT University
Melbourne, Australia
floyd@exertiongameslab.org

ABSTRACT

Vertigo – the momentary disruption of the stability of perception – is an intriguing game element that underlies many unique play experiences, such as spinning in circles as children to rock climbing as adults, yet vertigo is relatively unexplored when it comes to digital play. In this paper we explore the potential of Galvanic Vestibular Stimulation (GVS) as a game design tool for digital vertigo games. We detail the design and evaluation of a novel two player GVS game, Balance Ninja. From study observations and analysis of Balance Ninja (N=20), we present three design themes and six design strategies that can be used to aid game designers of future digital vertigo games. With this work we aim to highlight that vertigo can be a valuable digital game element that helps to expand the range of games we play.

Author Keywords

Vertigo; play; ilinx; movement-based games; exertion games; vestibular stimulation.

ACM Classification Keywords

H.5.m. Information interfaces and presentation (e.g., HCI): Miscellaneous

INTRODUCTION

Caillois [6] highlights that vertigo is one of the four key categories of games and play, explaining that activities such as spinning around, rock-climbing, skiing and dancing are positive play experiences that arise through the encouragement of disorientating and confusing the players' senses. Digital games have mostly considered vertigo as a negative side effect of bodily play experiences, and should therefore be avoided.

However, some game designers *have* considered vertigo in their designs. In these explorations, visual stimulation is often used in the form of Virtual Reality (VR) to create

Figure 1. *Balance Ninja.*

virtual vertigo experiences, such as rock climbing games [9,13] or to create the illusion that the player is walking over precipices [21]. Non-visual stimulation has also been used such as using physical force feedback to move the players' body through the use of special ride machinery [31], or through combining both visual and physical stimulation to create, for example, an immersive VR skydiving experience [14]. In each of these above examples, vertigo is created as a second-order response to an external stimulation (altered vision, or the physical and forceful movement of the body) to create novel and fun experiences, yet in digital games, designers appear to consider vertigo as a negative effect, and something that has the potential to make players feel nauseous, for example in the case of VR 'simulator sickness'.

In contrast, we believe vertigo could have a role to play in digital games, and in particular, believe that digital technology offers novel opportunities to facilitate unique and engaging play experiences not previously possible. Unfortunately, little has been written concerning the design of digital games that use vertigo as a core design element. Yet, whilst designing for digital vertigo games has not generally been considered in a structured way, recent advances in areas such as VR have led to a resurgence in the development of game designs involving vertigo elements, such as VR flying experiences [8,22]. As such, we believe that now is a good time to explore vertigo within digital games in greater detail.

In order to facilitate this, in this paper, we describe a novel vertigo game system called *Balance Ninja,* which directly stimulates the body's balance organs in order to confuse and disorientate players' senses. We achieve this through the use of Galvanic Vestibular Stimulation (GVS). In *Balance Ninja*, players must battle to keep their balance whilst under GVS stimulation triggered by an opposing player. GVS is a simple and safe way of affecting one's balance by applying a small current (+/-2.5mA) to one's vestibular system [16]. Electrodes placed behind each ear deliver the current and the user feels a *pull* towards the anode, and also feels a loss of balance in that direction. We see GVS as having the potential to take a pivotal role in digital vertigo games and therefore begin our investigation here.

In the following sections we first explore background work on vertigo games and GVS before describing our GVS prototype. The design and implementation of *Balance Ninja* and a description of our user study follows. We employed a thematic analysis of interview and video data captured during the study in order to provide insight into the gameplay experience of *Balance Ninja*. Studying participants' experience of the game allowed us to address our research question: *"how should we design digital vertigo games?"*

With this work we aim to encourage game designers to consider vertigo in their games through making the following contributions:

- A proof of concept design of a vertigo game system.
- Three themes derived from analysis of the player experience of *Balance Ninja*.
- Six design strategies for designers of digital vertigo games, useful for practitioners who want to utilize vertigo in their game design practice.

BACKGROUND

To design digital vertigo games, we must first understand how vertigo has been considered in game design and what it is about vertigo games that people find compelling.

Vertigo can be medically defined as "a sensation of motion <…> in which the individual or the individual's surroundings seem to whirl dizzily" [33]. Intuitively, it would seem that such sensations should be avoided in digital game design. However, we note that these sensations can be the basis for a range of popular non-digital play activities such as skiing, racing fast cars and ballroom dancing [6]. Similarly, sports psychologists highlight that "the pursuit of vertigo" [1] is the main attraction behind certain gameful experiences such as rock climbing [1,25]. We therefore believe that vertigo might also be valuable in digital game design, especially bearing in mind that the role of the body is increasingly considered in digital play experiences. Caillois calls activities that draw on such sensations ilinx or vertigo games [6] and describes them as consisting of "an attempt to momentarily destroy the stability of perception and inflict a kind of voluptuous panic on an otherwise lucid mind" [6](p23). In this work, we lean on Caillois' definition of vertigo games and extend it to include digital games, defining digital vertigo games as:

digital games that digitally alter the stability of player perception, creating a pleasurable panic for the player.

Unfortunately, prior work has suggested that Caillois' thinking is not easy to incorporate into digital games. For example, Salen and Zimmerman highlight that Caillois' vertigo definition "falls outside the boundaries of games" and that the vertigo classification goes "beyond a description of <digital> games" [43]. Conversely, Bateman [2] has discussed the "joy of ilinx", describing how vertigo can actually be a potent force in digital games, suggesting that high speed racing and snowboard simulation games, for example, can heighten the player's enjoyment of the game through artificially inducing a state of vertigo in the players. He notes that the vertigo of digital games is not the nausea-inducing kind, but echoes Caillois' sentiment that it is a "vertiginous" experience. Bateman reflects that "very little has been written about the ilinx of videogames", which further suggests that Caillois' vertigo understanding may have previously proved difficult to translate into digital game design.

We propose that this shortage of literature about drawing on vertigo in digital games is perhaps why designers of body-based physical games have not considered designing games with vertigo as a central design element. For example, designers of exertion games [39] have looked to traditional videogame design whilst moving focus more and more toward the human body, yet do not consider vertigo explicitly. Similarly, Hämäläinen et al. [19] collate several body-based games that consider the use of gravity as a design resource, involving apparatus such as trampolines and gymnastics rings that could indirectly create a feeling of vertigo in players, yet knowledge about vertigo is still limited when it comes to designing body-based games that explicitly draw upon vertigo.

Prior work suggests that current play experiences that facilitate the emergence of vertigo do so as a second-order effect to the body being moved, in other words, an external force moves the player's body to create instability in players' perception that then can result in feelings of vertigo. For example, Cheng et al.'s *Haptic Turk* requires a group of players to physically move another player whilst they 'fly' through a VR world [8]. More commonly, however, players are moved through the use of specialised machines in order to facilitate feelings of vertigo, for example through rollercoasters and other amusement park rides [14,31].

In VR, early experiments identified that people could experience vertigo within a virtual world [34] and more recently there has been interest in creating entertainment and commercial experiences of vertigo through the use of VR. For example the design studio *Inition* presented a virtual vertigo experience [21] requiring participants wearing a 3D headset to walk across a real-world plank that appeared in the VR world to be suspended between two tall buildings. A series of fans were also used to simulate high altitude winds, further enhancing the experience. Similarly, based on the idea of exploring heights in VR, Dufour et al. [13] created a mountain climbing game where players can see a generated mountain terrain via a 3D headset and climb the mountain through controller input. Likewise, *The Climb* [9] also allows players to traverse mountain trails within a VR world. These works exploit acrophobia - a fear of heights - to create a vertigo experience. Exploiting a fear of heights could be one potential way of designing vertigo games, however, Caillois describes vertigo games as causing a *voluptuous* (pleasurable) panic for the player, which suggests to us that there are other opportunities to facilitate vertigo in digital games beyond drawing on uncomfortable interactions [4].

Despite these initial explorations around vertigo experiences, designing for vertigo as a direct part of digital games has not been readily explored. With our work we see an opportunity to address this gap in design knowledge by providing game designers with an understanding of how to design digital vertigo games. As such, we address the research question: *"how should we design digital vertigo games?"*

Galvanic Vestibular Stimulation

Our review of related work highlighted that most existing related games use indirect methods of creating vertigo, i.e. they move the player's body through external forces, provide visual stimulation or draw upon a fear of heights. In this section, we describe an additional technique: Galvanic Vestibular Stimulation (GVS). GVS is a technology that directly affects the player's vestibular system by inducing sensations of vertigo within the inner ear. GVS has the advantage that it is a simple and mobile system that can easily be digitally controlled, and therefore lends itself to being connected with other sensing and game elements.

Traditionally used in physiology [17] and psychology [44], GVS is a digital system that is described by Fitzpatrick and Day as a simple and *safe* way to elicit vestibular reflexes [16]. GVS affects a person's vestibular system and hence their balance through the electrical stimulation of the vestibular system via electrodes placed on the mastoid bones behind each ear. The resulting effect is that wearers feel a *pull* or *sway* towards the positive electrode and thus the system affects one's sense of balance in that direction. Repeated use of GVS results in no deterioration to global function [47], and only minor itching from electrode placement [45].

Designers have considered the possible applications of GVS, for example Nagaya et al. [38] investigated altering a person's visual perception and balance based on the playback of music tuned to the GVS stimulation, whilst Maeda et al. [29] adapted a GVS system to allow one person to affect another's balance via remote control. Maeda et al. [30] have also investigated GVS in VR environments, finding that in a VR setting, GVS can increase one's sense of self-motion. GVS has also been explored as a practical training tool, for example, Moore et al. [35] used GVS as a training tool for astronauts to simulate post-flight effects. Such applications highlight the versatility of GVS and also the control one may

have over the stimulation applied in order to achieve specific effects. Using such a technology in game design could allow designers of body-based games to have control over how the player's body internally reacts to gameplay.

GVS, we propose, could be adapted and used to realise the design of vertigo games. Caillois even suggests that as we get older we seek more exotic and extreme measures to experience the feeling of vertigo he defines - from simply spinning playfully in circles as a child, to needing what he calls "powerful machines" (e.g. spinning fair ground rides), to experience the same feeling as adults [6](p25). Interestingly, Caillois suggests that if a system existed such that it could affect the balance organs of the inner ear (which is what GVS does), such powerful machines may not be necessary anymore [6](p26). With GVS, we have a technology that can facilitate feelings of vertigo and can be digitally controlled. Furthermore, GVS can be mobile and cheap to build (as we demonstrate in the next section), and therefore lends itself to be used in digital games.

GVS PROTOTYPE

Although we initially investigated the possibility of obtaining an off-the-shelf GVS system we were unable to readily locate one, so we chose to look to related work as guidance to inform the creation of our own GVS system. Our prototype was built through an iterative design process and the final version used in the study can be seen in figure 2a.

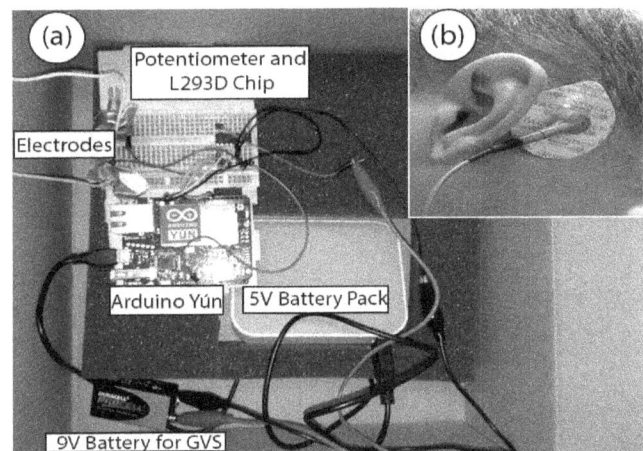

Figure 2. (a) The GVS system used in the study, (b) GVS electrode placement.

For our study we made two identical systems. The circuit of each system consists of one L293D full bridge motor driver chip, which acts as an H-Bridge, allowing us to change which electrode (left or right) is positive. An isolated 9V battery powers the actual GVS circuit, whilst a 5V USB battery pack powers an Arduino Yún microcontroller. For calibration we also included a 10k potentiometer, which allows for fine-tuning the effect felt by participants as explained below. Two 2.5 meter low resistance insulated wires complete the circuit and are attached to the electrodes (see figure 2b).

Safety Considerations

The system was designed for safety reasons such that the maximum current of the GVS system could not go above 2.5 mA. We chose this number since related work indicates good performance from 1 mA - 2.5 mA [17,37], and it is far less than the recommended maximum of 5 mA [10].

Although the GVS circuit is relatively simple (essentially a small current of no more than 2.5 mA alternating via an H-bridge), we made sure that the system would be as safe as possible to use in our study. Also, due to the effect of GVS causing an individual to lose their balance, we took the following precautions when using the system:

- We designed our system to be modular, and thus come apart under physical stress. If a participant were to stumble excessively (which did not happen during our study) we made sure that the cables easily detached from the breadboard. We also used snap-style electrode connectors, which could "pop" off under stress.
- We made sure that no physical obstacles that could cause harm during play were near participants. This included the deliberate choice not to use soft mattresses or crash mats next to the game. As the balance boards are only a few inches from the ground, players recover very quickly by stepping onto solid ground. A soft surface may have caused players to actually stumble and trip when recovering.
- The system was controlled remotely from the researchers laptop (players could not activate it, but could deactivate by detaching themselves), and we ensured a stop button was available to the researcher that would immediately end the game and any stimulation, should a participant feel uncomfortable or in the case of any excessive stumble.
- Two researchers were present during the studies to assist participants if needed.

The above were assumed precautions, and during the study the stop button did not need to be pressed, nor did anyone lose his or her balance in a dangerous way.

BALANCE NINJA

Balance Ninja is a balance game for two players. Both players stand on their own wooden board (which we call a balance board) resting on a shared wooden beam (see figure 1) and both players are attached to their own GVS system. Players also wear a pouch containing a tight-fitting Android mobile phone, and the accelerometer readings taken from the phone affect the other player's GVS system. For example, if player 1 leans to the left, the GVS of player 2 creates a pull to the right for player 2 (and vice versa). The more player 1 leans, the greater the level of stimulation applied to player 2. The maximum stimulation is applied when players are leaning around seven degrees from the vertical, which, although a noticeable lean, is not enough that a player would lose their balance without the extra stimulation being applied.

The object of the game is to cause the opposing player to lose their balance and either step off their board, or touch their

Figure 3. Player 1 (left) smiles as he wins the round when player 2 touches his balance board to the floor.

board to the floor (see figure 3). The game is not turn-based and thus players are free to "attack" at any time. A point is awarded to the winner of the round and the first player to reach five points wins the game. Each round has music playing in the background, the end of which signals that the round is over and a voiceover indicates that, for example, player 1 lost the round and player 2 was awarded the point. Points are displayed on a scoreboard from a laptop visible to both players and spectators.

STUDY PROCEDURE

Before playing *Balance Ninja*, players had to prepare by first attaching the phone pouches around their chests. The electrodes were then attached to the mastoid bones of each participant by either the lead researcher or participants themselves, in which case the lead researcher checked the connection and placement. Next, the GVS systems were calibrated.

As individuals can have a different level of skin impedance it is necessary to calibrate the GVS system. In other words, one player could be affected at a much lower current than another player. To calibrate the system, participants were asked to stand on their balance board one at a time and their GVS system was turned on and the current slowly increased by the researcher until the player lost their balance (by touching their board to the floor). We stopped increasing the current and the maximum setting for that player was derived. Calibrating the system was also a necessary safety precaution since it ensured that players would not experience stimulation higher than their comfort level. This process was then repeated for the second player.

Players were given a one minute practice round to familiarise themselves with balancing on the boards and the GVS sensation. After this practice round the game started properly. Each game session was started and stopped from the researcher's laptop, with music signalling the start of each round and that the GVS systems were activated.

When a point was awarded (i.e. a player won a round) gameplay paused and the systems were deactivated between rounds. Following the game, participants were detached from the GVS system before they were asked to remove the phone pouches and electrodes. They were then invited to take part in a post-game interview with the lead researcher.

Participants

We recruited 20 participants to play *Balance Ninja*, (17 Male, 3 Female), aged between 23 and 51 (M=29, SD=7.4). Participants, on average, played videogames at least 4 hours per week. Only one participant said that they did not play videogames at all. Participants were recruited via the university mailing list, word of mouth, and interest generated from watching the game being played.

Ethical Approval

Ethical approval was obtained prior to the study and precautions were taken to ensure safety to the participants. Each participant was thoroughly briefed and asked to provide informed consent prior to playing the game and taking part in the study. Play sessions occurred in the open atrium of the computer science department of the university, during the working day when first aid personnel were also available.

Data Collection

Data was collected through the use of video and audio recordings of all gameplay sessions, pre and post game setup, and participant interviews. We used both video and audio due to the open nature of the study venue and wanted to ensure responses could later be transcribed correctly. Audio and video was taken with participants' consent and in total around two hours of video and audio were recorded.

After each play session, which lasted typically no more than five minutes, participants were interviewed in pairs using a semi-structured interview schedule, which lasted an average of six minutes. Following the interview, participants were also invited to fill in a short 5-point Likert scale (1 = strongly disagree, 5 = strongly agree) questionnaire about the game to elicit a quantitative understanding of their experience.

Data Analysis

We employed an inductive thematic analysis approach to the data, as described by Braun and Clarke [5]. Participant interviews were transcribed from the audio and video recordings of the interview sessions and the completed transcripts were exported for qualitative analysis. Two researchers independently consulted their own copy of these transcripts. We consider each turn of speech in the transcripts to be 'Units', and thus, excluding interviewer questions, there were a total of 206 Units to consult, each of varying length (short answers and longer responses). In order to garner meaning from these Units, both researchers designated their own codes and description of the codes to the Units as they deemed fit. Following this process, a meeting was held where the researchers consulted and refined their codes until a final agreement resulted in a total of 10 codes. These codes were then further examined and referenced with the transcripts to search for overarching themes, which were again reviewed by both researchers in another meeting. This approach resulted in three overarching themes in total.

RESULTS

In this section we detail the responses to the participant questionnaire and also describe the three overarching themes that we derived from our analysis of the data: Game and GVS Feelings, Balance Ninja Gameplay, and finally, Balance Ninja Technology.

Questionnaire Responses

Likert responses are illustrated in figure 4. Participants generally found the game fun, citing positive responses with a Median (M) of 4 and Median Absolute Deviation (*MAD*) of 0.5, with participants also agreeing that they would play the game again (M = 4, *MAD*=0). Participants had mostly neutral responses to the GVS sensation being uncomfortable (M=2.5, *MAD*=0.5), however, participants mostly agreed that the GVS sensation was subtle (M=4, *MAD*=1). We received mostly neutral responses to participants being in control of their body and also feeling disorientated (M=3, *MAD*=1), and finally, participants mostly found the game difficult to play (M=4, *MAD*=0.5).

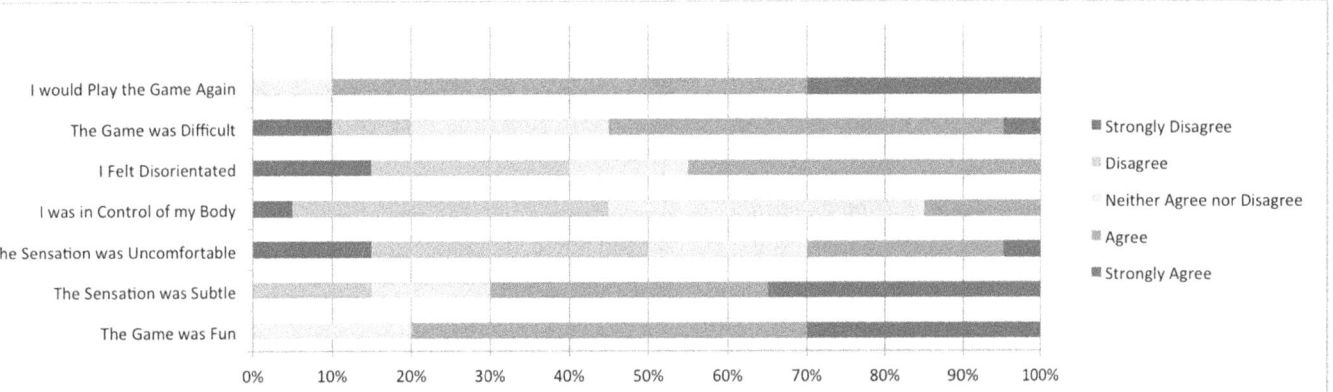

Figure 4. Participant (N=20) responses to *Balance Ninja's* Likert questionnaire.

Theme 1: Game and GVS Feelings

This theme describes 112 of the 206 Units and is divided into four categories: Feeling of GVS (82), After-Effects (9), Vertigo (6) and finally Game Enjoyment (15). We had expected to receive a high number of Units describing GVS as we asked participants how it felt playing the game. However, we did find that participants were eager to discuss the feeling, and often required little prompting to describe their experience of the game and of using GVS.

Feeling of GVS

Participants explained how the GVS sensation was new: *"the feeling itself was really, like new to me, except for when I was drunk!"* *"The best bits were just how weird it was, it was just, like, different"*, *"I've never known <anything> like that before!"* Participants did not appear to find the GVS sensation uncomfortable or unpleasant: *"I wouldn't say uncomfortable in a bad sense. If there was any discomfort it was in the playful sense, so all good"*, *"it didn't hurt, it was very comfortable"*, *"I think it wasn't any feeling of un-comfortableness"*. In fact, participants were often not aware that there was any stimulation being applied: *"I didn't feel anything <laugh> actually. I felt the sensation of not being balanced"*, finding any sense of the stimulation to be subtle in nature: *"mine felt subtle, I didn't know I was falling over until I fell over!"* This is important for us, since we did not want to make an uncomfortable gameplay experience, although some research has shown that uncomfortable interactions can be an attractive design element in games [4,20]. However, it is important to stress that there is obviously a difference between *uncomfortable* and *painful*, and no participants reported the game or the GVS as being painful. The main discomfort reported by the participants was interestingly not the GVS sensation or the gameplay but the process of removing the electrodes.

Feelings of vertigo

When asked if they had experienced vertigo whilst playing, participants generally agreed that they had experienced vertigo: *"after a bit I could definitely feel it as a dizzy-ness, like a vertigo feeling that really made me sway"*, *"I think it's a pretty good approximation <of vertigo>."* *"Vertigo? Yeah it did feel relatively similar actually, the stronger sensations there definitely equate to that kind of feeling"*. Some participants were unsure if they experienced vertigo at first, asking if we actually meant acrophobia: *"vertigo is the fear of heights right?"* However, in such instances we reiterated our definition, which often led participants to agree that they did actually experience vertigo: *"um, I think under your definition for me I did achieve a degree of 'vertigo', yes. That's true, there was disorientation and a definite unusual state about it"*.

After-effects

Although participants did not report any pain or discomfort, some reported on interesting after-effects they experienced, saying that they felt: *"just a bit weird after, yeah"*, *"I kind of, like, almost had to sit down just for a little bit to almost relax for a little bit, but I don't know if that's because we were trying to balance for ages and just standing on firm ground was not a balance thing"*, *"I just felt slightly less control, I felt a little bit wobbly"*. Participants likened the effects to those felt post-exertion, such as: *"<it felt> like coming off a trampoline"*, *"yeah, when you're not on the trampoline <anymore> you feel really weird"*, which could have been due to the nature of using one's legs to keep the board balanced, resulting in muscle fatigue from doing so. To note is that although participants indicated that they experienced some post-game feelings, the feelings did not last very long *"uh afterward you feel a bit of a hangover just for like 10 seconds maybe, 5 or 10 seconds"*. *"When I first stepped off I felt quite awkward, <and> not sure whether to move or stay still for a second, but that cleared quite quickly"*. By the end of the interviews none of the participants showed any sign that they were still experiencing adverse post-game effects, explaining that in the case that they had felt anything after the game, it had subsided quickly as they regained their sense of balance. We also note that a vertigo game such as spinning around in circles leaves the player feeling dizzy for a while afterwards, which is actually the desired result. For our players, playing *Balance Ninja* seems to have resulted in a similar experience.

Game enjoyment

The feelings of vertigo also led to participants expressing how they had enjoyed playing the game *"the best thing was the two occasions I got where it was really clear that the game was actually affecting my sense of balance"*, *"the best bit was when I did feel it, the kind of visceral feeling almost when you actually go: 'actually this thing has made me unbalanced'"*. Participants described the game as cool and fun, *"it was good I enjoyed it"*, *"I think it is really cool"*, *"yeah, it's a cool kind of game, definitely"*, *"that was really good and fun"*. This was really important as we purposefully designed the game to be difficult and physically challenging to play through affecting players' sense of balance, but more importantly we wanted the game to be fun to play.

As well as participants enjoying the sense of their own balance being affected through GVS, participants also expressed that their sense of fun came from their ability to control other players, *"it was fun, as a game perspective trying to make the other person feel what I was feeling"*, *"it was really funny. It kind of made me laugh, looking at <player> trying to balance and trying to throw me over at the same time, and me trying to do the same, it was kind of comical really"*. The post-game questionnaire responses support these findings, showing that participants positively agreed that the game was fun to play.

Figure 5. Player 2 (right) loses the first round, and concentrates on their breathing technique to remain balanced in the next round.

A concern of ours when we decided to use GVS to affect player balance in a digital vertigo game was that players could have found the effect uncomfortable, and, due to the disorientating nature of the game, unpleasant. However, in our game this did not appear to be the case and participants enjoyed playing. Participants offered suggestions for future games, such as a GVS controlled vertigo horror game: *"in a horror game, if you got that feeling at a crucial moment, that would make it a lot more fun, and, like, seem more real"*, suggesting that they would be eager to not only play *Balance Ninja* again, but future digital vertigo games. We also observed a sense of playful engagement emerging between players with participants regularly laughing when they lost and joking with each other at the attempts of another player to cause them to lose their balance. None of the participants wished to stop playing during the study and, as the questionnaire responses suggest, 90% of the participants would play the game again, with the remaining 10% neutral about replaying.

The game also appeared to invoke other gameful states, such as competition, with participants commenting when asked about the best bit: *"winning was the best bit-"* *"-and losing was the worst!"* *"The best bit was that I won! I don't win anything so I'm going to take this one and enjoy it."* *"<The best bit was> winning! <Laughs>"*. These comments about wining and an eagerness to play *Balance Ninja* again suggest to us that participants did view *Balance Ninja* as a game, which further suggests that digital vertigo games could be adopted and appreciated by players and not seen just as novelty experiences. In *Balance Ninja*, participants played in pairs so generally played against their friends or colleagues, which may have also facilitated the sense of competition amongst the participants. However, for vertigo games of more than one player we predict that the co-located nature of these multiplayer vertigo games would likely result in friends playing primarily together, so believe that the sense of competition arose from the gameplay as well as playing with friends. Participants even suggested games that they would like to play with their opposing player in the future, for example that they: *"like<d> the idea there's cerebral gladiators out there <who> don't need sticks to knock people*

over", which refers to a game where players traditionally knock each other off podiums with padded sticks.

Theme 2: Balance Ninja Gameplay
This theme was present in 78 of the 206 Units and we have divided it into four categories: Game Strategies (21), Game Feedback and Difficulty (42) and Game Fairness (15).

Game Strategies
Participants displayed varying tactics to win the game, such as trying to stand still, *"there were definitely times where I felt the best strategy for me was to try and stand as still as possible"* and using their own breathing techniques to remain balanced, *"yeah I did Pilates, <laughs>"*. This particular tactic can be seen in figure 5, where player 2 loses a round, but employs breathing techniques to avoid losing in the next round. Alternatively, for some, the best strategy was not to remain still, but to move in order to put the other player off balance, *"little quick twitches were good"*, *"Yeah that's how he got me!"*

Participants also found that if they distracted themselves and readjusted their focus they could remain balanced, *"well <I> was looking at the ground, because that then made me regain my balance every time I looked at a new spot, so if I <did> it quickly enough I could maintain a balance"*. Participants also expressed how finding the right amount of movement was part of the fun of the experience *"you're trying to knock over the opponent but at the same time you have to be a bit cautious - so it is <a> fun experience"*, also explaining that the learning curve and finding the optimal strategy was important to the gameplay: *"figuring it <the game> out <...>, once you've got a strategy off you go. It definitely was a game, at the end"*, *"if I do this <quick side to side movements>, too much body movement would be costing me to lose"*.

Game Feedback and Difficulty
Despite finding winning tactics, participants did express difficulty in playing the game due to being required to balance, *"so I found balancing on the board quite hard anyway, but it's probably not my naturally good skill set"*, *"if I just stood still I could see the other person swaying and go back and forth, as soon as I tried to do it as well then I*

just couldn't!" Some of the perceived difficulty could be due to the game not providing much feedback to players, *"what's difficult is the fact that I did something in it that affected <the other player>, but I couldn't obviously see that"*, *"yeah sometimes I find it, I'm not sure I'm controlling the other player, am I really controlling him, or <is> he just losing <balance> by himself?"* We did explain to participants that it was leaning the upper body that would affect the opposing player's GVS system, but it apparently seemed more intuitive and a more natural body movement to move the balance board instead: *"also, I wasn't sure if it was tilting the board that got the effect. I knew, because you told me in the beginning, that the phone was the actual tilt sensor, but the natural feeling for me was that I should try tilting the board"*.

This confusion over what player actions controlled the GVS stimulation led to participants suggesting to include visual or audio feedback to confirm the system was working: *"I would have liked some feedback, so I could see what part of my movement was having an effect. Apart from the effect on the other person I wasn't sure if it was actually working"*. With *Balance Ninja* we assumed that seeing the opposing player moving would be feedback enough, but perhaps in some digital vertigo games additional visual feedback may be required, particularly if designers are aiming to alter perception in a non-intuitive way.

Game fairness
Finally participants suggested further improvements. such as ensuring both players started the rounds fairly: *"often when the rounds started, you <player one> were already leaning!"* The GVS systems were activated at the start of each round, so if one player was already leaning then the opposing player would receive a higher level of stimulation than the leaning player from the very start of the game until that player stopped leaning. Interestingly participants also offered ways of making the game harder to play, such as including sensors in the balance board itself: *"so you'd make it harder as you'd have to rock the board without touching the ground"*. This suggested to us that game fairness is subjective, i.e. there were participants who enjoyed the challenge and wanted more, whereas there were other participants who found it too difficult playing against players who had better control over their balance, indicating that for vertigo games, like other body-based games, matching player abilities is something that could be considered.

Theme 3: Balance Ninja Technology
This theme relates to participant discussions concerning the digital and physical technology we used to implement the game. 24 of the 206 Units were described by this theme, which we derived from one category code: Game Technology (24).

Balance Board Setup
In *Balance Ninja* the balance boards were not attached to the beam but placed on top, which led to difficulty for some players in maintaining their balance: *"the balance board itself I thought, perhaps, was not very well designed"*, *"I*

didn't like the wooden thing, it was too easy to fall off and it was too difficult to kind of, reset", and suggested that the boards should have allowed players the ability to lean further: *"I should have been able to lean more before I fell off"*. We observed that at first participants seemed to prefer moving the board whilst keeping their body vertical, but quickly learned that they needed to lean their upper body and try not to move the boards to experience the game and the GVS effect properly. We designed *Balance Ninja* purposefully to encourage this upper body movement and lean, but did not anticipate that participants would find it difficult to grasp at first. Although, participants did offer that they quite liked the way the balance boards facilitated the balance aspect of the gameplay: *"I didn't mind it I thought it was good actually, I thought it was a good balance board for this"*. However, for multiplayer digital vertigo games perhaps consideration needs to be given towards supporting players of different balance abilities, and how the game environment can facilitate this support.

For example, our GVS vertigo game required players to be off-balance to exaggerate the GVS sensation. Simply applying the stimulation is not enough to easily achieve this off-balance sensation. In our experience the affect is exaggerated when in motion (i.e. either off balance or walking). Therefore, in supporting players of different abilities designers would need to consider the best way to make the gameplay environment adaptable to facilitate the off-balance sensation.

Electrodes
Finally, participants described the 'worst' part of the game to be the removal of the electrodes, usually because of their hair getting stuck to the electrode adhesive: *"yeah the worst was trying to get rid of the <electrodes>, <because of> my hair"*, *"it was a bit sore, to be honest but that was partly because I got some hair caught"*. What we found interesting with our study was that participants described only the electrodes as being uncomfortable to remove or the worst part of the game, suggesting that both *Balance Ninja* and the actual GVS sensations were not unpleasant to experience. Unfortunately GVS requires electrodes or some other conductive material to use, in much the same way as similar technology like Electric Muscle Stimulation (EMS) does so. However, we see an opportunity for incorporating this necessary step into the gameplay by encompassing the main game within a compelling narrative that enforces an intro (calibration and setup) phase, and an outro (removal of electrodes) phase to the gameplay.

DISCUSSION: STRATEGIES FOR DESIGNING DIGITAL VERTIGO GAMES
Here we articulate six design strategies that we derived from our data analysis, informed by the recurring themes and participant feedback that we have previously described. These strategies are for designers of future digital vertigo games to guide the development and design of these games, based on our experience and study of *Balance Ninja*.

Design Physical Game Setting to Support Vertigo Stimulation

Some of our participants were able to win repeated rounds of the game by employing tactics that helped them limit the GVS effects. They uncovered these tactics during the course of playing the game, with one player, for example, focusing their vision so that they could concentrate on not losing their balance. With GVS, the effect is weakened when people focus hard on visual balance cues [11], so designers could dampen this tactic by considering visual elements which distract the player, for example by using head mounted displays or blindfolds to remove any visual cues.

Another popular technique was to try and remain as still as possible and focus on not moving. The balance boards were designed specifically to make it so players had to constantly balance. We could make this more pronounced by actuating the surface on which the person is standing, so it occasionally shakes or wobbles, to require the players to respond. Marshall et al.'s breath controlled bucking bronco ride [31] employs a similar tactic, by deliberately jolting riders in an attempt to cause them to fall off once they reach the final difficulty level. In response to our findings we suggest designers of vertigo games would need to consider how to design the game settings to enforce the vertigo effects.

Create an Appropriate Narrative for Digital Vertigo Game Acts

In our game, there were essentially three acts: setup, gameplay and post-game. Setup involved calibration before use, and post-game involved removing the electrodes and the after-effects of GVS stimulation. Considering this, designers could lean on the work of trajectories [3] and videogame narrative [23] to creatively explain why their players must wear a system and engage in a calibration process. For example, a mind control game could involve players trying to gain control over another, requiring them to wear a futuristic helmet with the GVS inside which, in turn, would affect another player. Or, in a supernatural horror game, players could wear mobile GVS systems that activate when an imposing presence is near by, causing them to momentarily lose balance when trying to run away. Designers could also employ the use of trained actors to perform the setup stage, in a role appropriate for the particular digital vertigo game. For example, Yule et al. [48] investigated the role of using docents in mixed-reality games, finding that the role of the docents improved the player experience. These docents were trained in the use of the system and acted as guides who also helped to explain *why* players were performing their particular tasks, all whilst remaining in character. As such, we recommend to designers to consider an appropriate narrative for digital vertigo game acts, and how to support the different acts.

Consider the Type of Feedback Provided to Players due to the Subtlety of Vertigo Sensations

As confirmed in our interviews, GVS is a subtle and nuanced sensation that also suffers from an inherent latency of approximately 200mS [17]. This resulted in a delay in players feeling an effect, which at times could have led to some of our players questioning whether the system was working. Providing simple visual or audio feedback of when the GVS system was working, and what intensity of stimulation was being applied, could have helped to alleviate concerns that the system was not working. However, in other game genres, such as horror games, the subtlety of the sensation and the ambiguity of how the system is affecting players could in fact become the core strength of the game design. Designers of vertigo games who want to create this type of experience could consider ambiguity as a design resource [18] to decide the level of feedback that is most appropriate for their vertigo game. As such, we recommend designers consider if highlighting the subtlety of vertigo through additional feedback in their games is the appropriate choice for the type of digital vertigo game experience that they are trying to create.

Design Digital Vertigo Games for Players of Different Abilities

Some participants discussed that they found balancing on the balance board to be difficult, whereas others found balancing quite easy. Those who found balancing straight forward often said during the interviews that they usually had quite a good understanding of their balance due to sports or meditation activities they frequently pursued, such as Pilates. In multiplayer videogame design balancing players of varying abilities is often achieved by limiting the abilities of experienced players, whilst providing a greater advantage to weaker players [7]. Similarly, exertion games have adapted the effort required from individual players based on the players' level of fitness [36].

However, for multiplayer-digital vertigo games, designers need to consider how the player is affected by two factors: 1) the environment, 2) the stimulation. For example, in *Balance Ninja* simply helping the weaker player to balance by making the board stationary (the environment) would not help if they were also affected strongly by the GVS stimulation. Conversely if a player is good at balancing, giving them a higher level of stimulation than the weaker player may also be unfair as they may be particularly sensitive to the stimulation applied.

For single player digital vertigo games, designers do not need to consider how to match players of different abilities, however, they could perhaps use the game as a training tool such as, for example, helping players learn to ride a unicycle. In exertion games Kajastila et al. [24] found that combining trampoline training with a platform video game improved players trampoline abilities, and perhaps the same could be true for digital vertigo games aimed at improving player balance. Designers would therefore need to consider what type of multiplayer game they want to create and in particular if they want to cater to players of different abilities, similar abilities, or design the game so that it has flexibility to support both ability types.

Design for the Invasive Nature of Digital Vertigo Technology that Affects the Body

Sensing people can often be achieved in a non-invasive manner. For example, the Kinect can be used to detect people's state of balance from a distance [26]. However, technologies such as GVS, EMS [27] or haptics often require some form of direct attachment to the body, such as the gel-electrodes used in *Balance Ninja*. We can see two potential ways designers can respond when using these technologies: the most obvious is to attempt to minimise the invasiveness of the technology, for example by using headbands with embedded conductive foam for GVS; alternatively, we could take the approach of Marshall et al.'s [32] breathing sensor gas masks, where they embrace the discomfort of the sensing method, and make it part of the experience. We suggest designers consider how to design for the invasive nature of balance altering technology for digital vertigo games, and how such technology affects the body.

Use Vertigo Interfaces Sparingly to Avoid Players Becoming Desensitised

Vertigo can be subject to desensitisation effects. These effects are different to simply learning or gaining competence in playing the game, but are more related to players becoming used to and expecting the stimulation. For example, repeated long term exposure to GVS can cause familiarity and an ability to overcome the effects [12]. This means that if vertigo-inducing stimulation is overused, digital vertigo games may no longer be exciting to play. To reduce chances of players becoming overly familiar with the sensation, designers should be mindful of using the vertigo interfaces too excessively. For example, in *Balance Ninja* the intensity of the effect felt by a player was determined by the lean of another player (up to their maximum setting). This added unpredictability to the effect, which prevented players from becoming familiarised with a set pattern, since the effect was related to the movement of the opposing player. Using these interfaces sparingly helps to overcome this effect and reduce chances of desensitisation. For example, stimulation could be used to exaggerate or punctuate specific game moments, and not be continually applied or repeated. As such, we recommend designers use the vertigo interfaces sparingly and at key moments, to avoid players becoming desensitised and familiar with repeated play sessions.

LIMITATIONS

In this paper we have shown that digital vertigo games using GVS can be an exciting and positive gameplay experience. As far as we know, GVS is not currently available as off-the-shelf hardware that can be plugged directly into digital games, however, some researchers have considered patenting the technology for entertainment purposes [15]. It is possible that GVS has perhaps not been made commercially available for entertainment purposes yet as it may be seen as an unpleasant gameplay accessory. However, similar experimental interaction technologies from recent HCI work, such as EMS interaction [28,40] make use of off-the-shelf EMS systems. These systems often come with a warning that medical advice should be sought before using, yet have been adapted into game design and used for entertainment purposes. There also

exists commercially available entertainment games centred on the use of electricity to stimulate players, such as *Lightning Reaction* [49], an electric shock party game for 2 – 4 players where the last player to press a button when a light flashes receives a small electric shock.

Additionally, there is also recent interest in developing vertigo experiences through the use of head mounted displays. For example, researchers have investigated novel ways of using VR in waterparks [41,42] and theme park designers in the UK have built the first virtual reality rollercoaster, called *Galactica* [46,50]. These developments suggest to us that it is now an exciting time to consider the development of digital vertigo games, whether that is through the use of GVS or other stimulation technologies.

With this work we have explored the artificial stimulation of the senses through only one method of stimulation: GVS. Alternative ways of facilitating vertigo in players, such as through visual or physical means, are also of interest to us, and we are currently exploring games that use these methods of stimulation towards the design of a digital vertigo game design space.

CONCLUSION

In this paper we reported on the development of a vertigo game, *Balance Ninja*, which used GVS as its main gameplay interface. Through a thematic analysis of a study with 20 participants we identified three overarching design themes, and articulated these along with six accompanying design strategies for designers of digital vertigo games. We challenge designers to use our findings and strategies to develop their own digital vertigo games, and encourage them to think of how they can use other technologies to explore this newly articulated design space.

We also highlight a gap in research concerning games of vertigo. Whereas vertigo has appeared in games, it has often been a second-order effect and not the intended core game play mechanic. We hypothesised that this was due to a lack of consideration regarding the design of vertigo games. Similarly we highlighted that both vertigo and interfaces such as GVS have not generally been considered from a game design perspective.

With this work, we therefore encourage challenging negative preconceptions, such as vertigo being an unwanted game sensation, and using digital technology to transform the negative effects into positive user experiences. Designers are encouraged to explore the body's limitations and transform them into novel user experience opportunities.

ACKNOWLEDGMENTS

We would like to thank our participants for their involvement in this study, and our reviewers for their thoughtful and useful feedback. Joe Marshall is funded by the Leverhulme Trust (ECF/2012-677).

REFERENCES

1. R B Alderman. 1974. *Psychological Behavior in Sport*. Saunders.

2. Chris Bateman. 2006. The Joy of Ilinx. *Only a Game*. Retrieved December 30, 2015 from http://onlyagame.typepad.com/only_a_game/2006/05/the_joy_of_ilin.html

3. Steve Benford and Gabriella Giannachi. 2008. Temporal trajectories in shared interactive narratives. *Proceedings of the SIGCHI Conference on Human Factors in Computing Systems*, 73–82.

4. Steve Benford, Chris Greenhalgh, Gabriella Giannachi, Brendan Walker, Joe Marshall, and Tom Rodden. 2012. Uncomfortable interactions. *Proceedings of the SIGCHI Conference on Human Factors in Computing Systems*, 2005–2014.

5. Virginia Braun and Victoria Clarke. 2006. Using thematic analysis in psychology. *Qualitative research in psychology 3*, 77–101.

6. Roger Caillois. 1961. *Man, play, and games*. University of Illinois Press.

7. Jared E Cechanowicz, Carl Gutwin, Scott Bateman, Regan Mandryk, and Ian Stavness. 2014. Improving Player Balancing in Racing Games. *Proceedings of the First ACM SIGCHI Annual Symposium on Computer-human Interaction in Play*, ACM, 47–56. http://doi.org/10.1145/2658537.2658701

8. Lung-Pan Cheng, Patrick Lühne, Pedro Lopes, Christoph Sterz, and Patrick Baudisch. 2014. Haptic Turk: A Motion Platform Based on People. *Proceedings of the SIGCHI Conference on Human Factors in Computing Systems*, ACM, 3463–3472.

9. Crytek. 2016. The Climb. Retrieved from http://www.theclimbgame.com/

10. Ian S Curthoys and Hamish Gavin MacDougall. 2012. What galvanic vestibular stimulation actually activates. *Frontiers in neurology 3*.

11. B L Day, A Severac Cauquil, L Bartolomei, M A Pastor, and I N Lyon. 1997. Human body-segment tilts induced by galvanic stimulation: a vestibularly driven balance protection mechanism. *The Journal of Physiology 500*, 661–672.

12. Valentina Dilda, Tiffany R. Morris, Don A. Yungher, Hamish G. MacDougall, and Steven T. Moore. 2014. Central adaptation to repeated galvanic vestibular stimulation: Implications for pre-flight astronaut training. *PLoS ONE 9*, 11.

13. Tristan Dufour, Vincent Pellarrey, Philippe Chagnon, et al. 2014. ASCENT: A First Person Mountain Climbing Game on the Oculus Rift. *Proceedings of the First ACM SIGCHI Annual Symposium on Computer-human Interaction in Play*, 335–338.

14. Horst Eidenberger and Annette Mossel. 2015. Indoor Skydiving in Immersive Virtual Reality with Embedded Storytelling. *Proceedings of the 21st ACM Symposium on Virtual Reality Software and Technology*, 9–12.

15. Jason Evangelho. 2016. Mayo Clinic May Have Just Solved One Of Virtual Reality's Biggest Problems. *Forbes*.

16. Richard C Fitzpatrick and Brian L Day. 2004. Probing the human vestibular system with galvanic stimulation. *Journal of Applied Physiology 96*, 2301–2316.

17. Richard C Fitzpatrick, Daniel L Wardman, and Janet L Taylor. 1999. Effects of galvanic vestibular stimulation during human walking. *The Journal of Physiology 517*, 931–939.

18. William W Gaver, Jacob Beaver, and Steve Benford. 2003. Ambiguity As a Resource for Design. *Proceedings of the SIGCHI Conference on Human Factors in Computing Systems*, 233–240.

19. Perttu Hämäläinen, Joe Marshall, Raine Kajastila, Richard Byrne, and Florian Mueller. 2015. Utilizing Gravity in Movement-Based Games and Play. *Proceedings of the 2015 Annual Symposium on Computer-Human Interaction in Play*, ACM, 67–77.

20. Amy Huggard, Anushka De Mel, Jayden Garner, Cagdas "Chad" Toprak, Alan Chatham, and Florian Mueller. 2013. Musical Embrace: Exploring Social Awkwardness in Digital Games. *Proceedings of the 2013 ACM International Joint Conference on Pervasive and Ubiquitous Computing*, 725–728.

21. Inition. 2014. Future of 3D #5: Oculus Rift Vertigo Experience. Retrieved April 1, 2016 from http://www.inition.co.uk/case_study/future-3d-5-oculus-rift-virtual-reality-experience/

22. Inition. 2014. Built-to-Thrill Wingsuit VR Experience for Nissan. Retrieved April 1, 2016 from http://www.inition.co.uk/case_study/nissan-built-thrill-wingsuit-experience/

23. Henry Jenkins. 2004. Game design as narrative architecture. *Computer 44*.

24. Raine Kajastila, Leo Holsti, and Perttu Hämäläinen. 2014. Empowering the Exercise: a Body-Controlled Trampoline Training Game. *International Journal of Computer Science in Sport*.

25. Gerald S Kenyon. 1968. A conceptual model for characterizing physical activity. *Research Quarterly. American Association for Health, Physical Education and Recreation 39*, 96–105.

26. Belinda Lange, Chien-Yen Chang, Evan Suma, Bradley Newman, Albert Skip Rizzo, and Mark Bolas. 2011. Development and evaluation of low cost game-based balance rehabilitation tool using the Microsoft Kinect sensor. *Engineering in Medicine and Biology Society, EMBC, 2011 Annual International Conference of the IEEE*, 1831–1834.

27. Pedro Lopes, Lars Butzmann, and Patrick Baudisch. 2013. Muscle-propelled Force Feedback: Bringing Force Feedback to Mobile Devices Using Electrical

Stimulation. *Proceedings of the 4th Augmented Human International Conference*, ACM, 231–232. http://doi.org/10.1145/2459236.2459276

28. Pedro Lopes. 2015. Proprioceptive Interaction. *Proceedings of the 8th Ph. D. retreat of the HPI research school on service-oriented systems engineering*, 123.

29. T Maeda, H Ando, T Amemiya, N Nagaya, M Sugimoto, and M Inami. 2005. Shaking the World: Galvanic Vestibular Stimulation As a Novel Sensation Interface. *ACM SIGGRAPH 2005 Emerging Technologies.*

30. T Maeda, H Ando, and M Sugimoto. 2005. Virtual acceleration with galvanic vestibular stimulation in a virtual reality environment. *Virtual Reality, 2005. Proceedings. VR 2005. IEEE*, 289–290.

31. Joe Marshall, Duncan Rowland, Stefan Rennick Egglestone, Steve Benford, Brendan Walker, and Derek McAuley. 2011. Breath control of amusement rides. *Proceedings of the SIGCHI conference on Human Factors in computing systems*, 73–82.

32. Joe Marshall, Brendan Walker, Steve Benford, et al. 2011. The Gas Mask: A Probe for Exploring Fearsome Interactions. *CHI '11 Extended Abstracts on Human Factors in Computing Systems*, ACM, 127–136. http://doi.org/10.1145/1979742.1979609

33. Medical Dictionary. 2016. Medical Definition of Vertigo Retrieved January 6, 2016 from http://c.merriam-webster.com/medical/vertigo.

34. Michael Meehan, Brent Insko, Mary Whitton, and Frederick P Brooks Jr. 2002. Physiological measures of presence in stressful virtual environments. *ACM Transactions on Graphics (TOG) 21*, 645–652.

35. Steven T Moore, Valentina Dilda, and Hamish G MacDougall. 2011. Galvanic vestibular stimulation as an analogue of spatial disorientation after spaceflight. *Aviation, space, and environmental medicine 82*, 535–542.

36. Florian Mueller, Frank Vetere, Martin Gibbs, et al. 2012. Balancing exertion experiences. *Proceedings of the SIGCHI Conference on Human Factors in Computing Systems*, 1853–1862.

37. Naohisa Nagaya, Maki Sugimoto, Hideaki Nii, Michiteru Kitazaki, and Masahiko Inami. 2005. Visual Perception Modulated by Galvanic Vestibular Stimulation. *Proceedings of the 2005 International Conference on Augmented Tele-existence*, 78–84. Retrieved from http://10.1145/1152399.1152415

38. Naohisa Nagaya, Masashi Yoshidzumi, Maki Sugimoto, et al. 2006. Gravity jockey: a novel music experience with galvanic vestibular stimulation. *Proceedings of the 2006 ACM SIGCHI international conference on Advances in computer entertainment technology*, 41.

39. Jasmir Nijhar, Nadia Bianchi-Berthouze, and Gemma Boguslawski. 2012. Does Movement Recognition

Precision Affect the Player Experience in Exertion Games? *Intelligent Technologies for Interactive Entertainment 78*, 73–82.

40. Max Pfeiffer, Tim Dünte, Stefan Schneegass, Florian Alt, and Michael Rohs. 2015. Cruise Control for Pedestrians: Controlling Walking Direction Using Electrical Muscle Stimulation. *Proceedings of the 33rd Annual ACM Conference on Human Factors in Computing Systems*, ACM, 2505–2514.

41. W L Raffe, M Tamassia, F Zambetta, Xiaodong Li, and F Mueller. 2015. Enhancing theme park experiences through adaptive cyber-physical play. *Computational Intelligence and Games (CIG), 2015 IEEE Conference on*, 503–510. Retrieved from http://10.1109/CIG.2015.7317893

42. William L Raffe, Marco Tamassia, Fabio Zambetta, Xiaodong Li, Sarah Jane Pell, and Florian Mueller. 2015. Player-Computer Interaction Features for Designing Digital Play Experiences across Six Degrees of Water Contact. *Proceedings of the 2015 Annual Symposium on Computer-Human Interaction in Play*, 295–305.

43. Katie Salen and Eric Zimmerman. 2004. *Rules of play: Game design fundamentals*. MIT press.

44. Kathrin S Utz, Violeta Dimova, Karin Oppenländer, and Georg Kerkhoff. 2010. Electrified minds: Transcranial direct current stimulation (tDCS) and Galvanic Vestibular Stimulation (GVS) as methods of non-invasive brain stimulation in neuropsychology--A review of current data and future implications. *Neuropsychologia 48*, 2789–2810.

45. Kathrin S Utz, Kathia Korluss, Lena Schmidt, et al. 2011. Minor adverse effects of galvanic vestibular stimulation in persons with stroke and healthy individuals. *Brain Injury 25*, 11: 1058–1069.

46. Jeremy White. 2016. We took a ride on the world's first VR rollercoaster. *Wired*. Retrieved April 18, 2016 from http://www.wired.co.uk/news/archive/2016-03/18/galactica-alton-towers-virtual-reality-rollercoaster-samsung-gear-vr

47. David Wilkinson, Olga Zubko, and Mohamed Sakel. 2009. Safety of repeated sessions of galvanic vestibular stimulation following stroke: A single-case study. *Brain injury 23*, 10: 841–845.

48. Daniel Yule, Bonnie MacKay, and Derek Reilly. 2015. Operation Citadel: Exploring the Role of Docents in Mixed Reality. *Proceedings of the 2015 Annual Symposium on Computer-Human Interaction in Play*, ACM, 285–294. http://doi.org/10.1145/2793107.2793135

49. *Lightning Reactions*. (n.d.) Squirrel Products.

50. Galactica. *Alton Towers*. Retrieved April 17, 2016 from https://www.altontowers.com/theme-park/galactica/

The Emergence of EyePlay:
A Survey of Eye Interaction in Games

Eduardo Velloso
Microsoft Research Centre for Social NUI
The University of Melbourne
eduardo.velloso@unimelb.edu.au

Marcus Carter
Microsoft Research Centre for Social NUI
The University of Melbourne
marcus.carter@unimelb.edu.au

ABSTRACT

As eye trackers become cheaper, smaller, more robust, and more available, they finally leave research labs and enter the home environment. In this context, gaming arises as a promising application domain for eye interaction. The goal of this survey is to categorise the different ways in which the eyes can be incorporated into games and play in general as a resource for future design. We reviewed the literature on the topic, as well as other game prototypes that employ the eyes. We compiled a list of eye-enabled game mechanics and derived a taxonomy that classifies them according to the eye movements they involve, the input type they provide, and the game mechanics that they implement. Based on our findings we articulate the value of gaming for future HCI gaze research and outline a research program around eye interaction in gaming.

Author Keywords
Survey; Eye tracking; Games

ACM Classification Keywords
H.5.m. Information Interfaces and Presentation (e.g. HCI): Miscellaneous

INTRODUCTION

Marty McFly: (showing two boys how to play an arcade game in an idealised 80's vision of 2015) I'll show you, kid. I'm a crack shot at this.
Boy #1: You mean you have to use your hands?
Boy #2: That's like a baby's toy!

Back to the Future Part II (1989)

Gaming is an application domain traditionally receptive to novel input devices, driving their commercial adoption and proliferation. Until recently, eye-enabled games were restricted to research prototypes and student projects, as prices in the order of tens of thousands of dollars made purchasing eye-trackers prohibitive for the consumer market. However, more recent affordable trackers specifically designed for gaming are bringing this technology to the home environment. 2015 represents an

important landmark in this timeline, with the release of *Assassin's Creed Rogue* [68], the first natively gaze-enabled AAA game; and the *SteelSeries Sentry*, the first gaming-specific eye tracker. Emerging VR and AR devices are also increasingly incorporating eye-tracking, as exemplified by the upcoming *FOVE* VR headset.

Eye interaction research has been prolific in HCI and associated fields since the late 1970's, but has typically focused on applications relating to health, user-experience evaluation, marketing, or accessibility. Thus, as we highlight in this paper, current literature has little contribution to its likely commercial success in gaming. Further, as is typical in HCI [10], the gaze-enabled game research that does exist often only utilizes the game element to demonstrate novel interaction techniques or to collect data, frequently without consideration of the game-specific demands or opportunities, and typically without deeper evaluations of the *play* experience.

In this paper we present a survey of 70 works that have interrogated gaze-enabled interaction in the context of games or play, categorizing them based on the 112 individual game mechanics we identify within them, their motivations, and relevance to game design and the games industry. This work contributes (1) a clear vocabulary for discussing and designing eye-based games and play, (2) a comprehensive and practical list of existing gaze-enabled game mechanics, and (3) a critique of gaze-in-games' overemphasis on specific eye-movements and mechanics, and minimal engagement with opportunities for gaze to provide new game experiences.

Based on this comprehensive literature review, we propose the existence of an 'EyePlay' research program as a distinct and emerging field within HCI. Rather than utilizing games as an instrument for peripheral research, EyePlay research is concerned with game experiences that are only possible through eye-based interaction. In the discussion we articulate the boundaries and importance of this emerging research program and distinguish it from marketing, broader HCI and accessibility gaze research involving games.

RELATED WORK

Gaze is a term with many meanings in the literature. In the field of inter-personal communication, it often refers to mutual eye contact [2]. In feminist theory, media studies, and game studies, it relates to the concept of the *male gaze* [57]. Many post-modernist thinkers, such as Sartre, Foucault, and Lacan, presented theories based on the concept of gaze [46]. Consequently, clarity in defining such a fundamental concept/term to eye-tracking in games is necessary. In our discussion, we consider the gaze point to refer to the point in space where the user is looking at. Because our discussion goes beyond just gaze (e.g. eye gestures, winks, blinks, etc.), we opted for the more general term *eye interaction* when referring to the input modality and Turner et al.'s term *EyePlay* to refer to *playful experiences that take input from the eyes* [79] . We use this definition to frame the discussion in the remainder of the paper, excluding from our scope works that use eye tracking for evaluating interface design [7], drawing conclusions about human visual attention [75], and discovering new aspects of human cognition [45], even if these are in games.

Isokoski et al. were the first to overview the use of the eyes for game control, with a focus on assistive interfaces [37]. The authors begin by describing eye movements and their relation to gaming. They classify different works according to how they incorporate eye tracking: emulating mice and keyboards; using additional middleware; modifying the source code of existing games; and building a new game. However, as game engines, level editors, and other prototyping technologies enable the easy creation of new games from scratch, this taxonomy becomes less relevant. In fact, modern eye trackers even offer tools specifically directed at game development (e.g. the *Tobii EyeX* offers an SDK for the *Unity* game engine).

They also discuss possibilities for future implementations based on the requirements for different game genres. The authors propose that positive indicators for the use of eye tracking are 'one-player mode' and 'turn-based gameplay'. Negative indicators are 'online multiplayer', 'online real-time multiplayer', 'continuous position control', 'dissociation of focus of attention and control', and 'large number of commands'. They conclude with an analysis of four case studies. We however disagree with their analysis of indicators based on genre. Though a lot of the challenges identified by Isokoski et al. remain true for trying to retro-fit an existing game for eye tracking use, all the challenges posed by eye tracking can be cleverly solved and incorporated into new games with careful interaction design, regardless of the genre.

Sundstedt surveyed the literature on the topic in the form of notes for a SIGGRAPH course [73], which led to a book about the topic [74]. She describes different works on the topic and discusses three cases studies from her own research that investigate the combination of gaze with voice interaction. Almeida et al. also overviewed the literature, dividing the works into eye tracking as input for video games and visual attention studies in video games [1].

These works provide an excellent starting point for reviewing the related literature. However, they limit the scope of their analysis to the level of the papers surveyed. We take a substantially different approach, by delving into the eye movements, interaction techniques, and individual mechanics implemented in different games. While working at these deeper abstraction levels, we were able to extract a taxonomy of game mechanics that offer game designers a practical toolbox from which to draw when designing eye-enabled games.

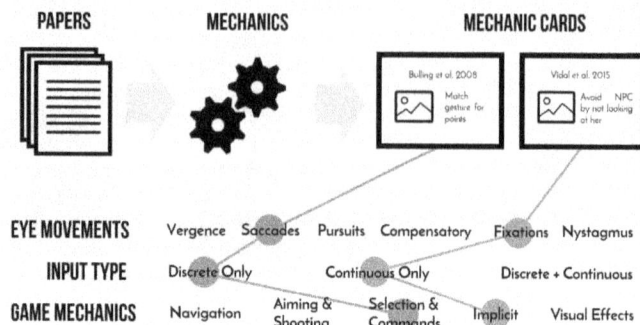

Figure 1. Research methodology: From different works, we extracted individual game mechanics and for each of them, we created a card. We then conducted three analyses, clustering the cards by eye movements involved in the mechanic, the type of input and the type of game mechanic.

METHODOLOGY

EyePlay research is disparate, irregular and often in little conversation with its peers, consequently utilizing a wide variety of terms. Unlike other similar reviews [10, 44], the conference and disciplinary boundaries of this work are unclear, and a strict Boolean-type review would be inappropriate. We started with the initial set of works surveyed in previous reviews [1, 37, 73, 74]. We found more recent papers through Google Scholar and the ACM Digital Library by searching not only for works that are cited by these surveys but also the works that have cited them since. We repeated this process until it converged into the set that we examined. We also searched for videos on YouTube and magazine articles that demonstrated unpublished prototypes of eye-enabled games, and reviewed the official forums and documentation provided by eye-tracker manufacturers.

We compiled a total of 106 papers, videos, and articles. We discarded works that did not present a concrete implementation of a game mechanic controlled by the eyes (e.g. eye tracking for evaluation), coming down to a total of 70 items. For each of them, we annotated individual game mechanics, and created a Game Mechanic card, containing the reference, a summary of the game mechanic and an image that demonstrates it, for a total of 112 cards (see Figure 1). To categorise these mechanics we conducted a series of workshops, in which the authors started with an abstraction level (eye movements, input type, game mechanic) and used a affinity mapping to cluster them. First, we spread all cards on a large whiteboard placed horizontally on a tabletop. We then organised the cards by placing similar mechanics (according to the abstraction level) close to each other. As patterns started to emerge, we connected related mechanics with a marker, until we achieved a map of themes. In accordance with our methodology, these themes were articulated as memos that formed the basis of theory development. As our lines of inquiry developed through the research, we returned to the papers and similarly summarized the papers to identify the motivations, methodologies and contributions of the paper to *EyePlay* research.

As a principal aim of this comprehensive literature review is to contribute a practical foundation for future design and research, we present a bottom-approach for understanding eyes in games. At the lowest level, we look at the **eye movements** that form the building blocks of eye behaviour. These help us understand what are the capabilities and limitations of players eyes when using them for input. One level of abstraction above, we look at how these movements are interpreted in the software side, considering the different **input types**. Finally, we overview how these are incorporated into the game design as concrete **game mechanics**.

EYE MOVEMENTS

Our eyes are limited to specific types of movements. Explanations of how each movement works at a physiological level, and how to identify and track them can be found elsewhere [19, 34]. As these movements are rigid categories, we used them as a basic framework for understanding the different ways the eyes have been enabled in HCI games research.

Fixations: These are movements that stabilise the retina over a stationary object of interest so that its image falls on the fovea of the eyes [19]. As it is analogous to pointing, mechanics that use dwell time for selection leverage this kind of behaviour—by setting a threshold that outlasts the normal fixation length, it is possible to estimate intention. Measuring the length of fixations can also hint at players' attention pattern and other cognitive processes, which can be leveraged for implicit interaction mechanics.

Saccades: These are the rapid movements used in repositioning the fovea as the eyes jump from one fixation to the next [19]. Mechanics that focus on saccades usually involve eye gestures [18], which can be used for gesture matching [8] or mode selection [39]. An advantage of working with saccades is that they can still be detected even with no registration information with the environment, making it well suited for ubiquitous games or trackers that only observe relative movement, such as electrooculography (EOG) ones [8].

Smooth Pursuits: These are the smooth movements that occur when tracking a moving object and keeping the gaze fixated on the target [19]. Whereas saccades are sudden and quick, pursuits are smooth and match the relative velocity of the target. Smooth pursuits cannot be faked—to exhibit this movement, the eyes must be following a moving target. This makes them particularly useful for identifying whether the user is actually following a moving target on the screen by comparing the relative trajectory of the target and of the gaze point. Vidal et al. found that a simple Pearson's correlation coefficient thresholding algorithm can be used for such detection [91]. EyePlay applications include using these movements to calibrate the eye tracker unobtrusively [26, 66] and to select moving targets [24, 91].

Compensatory Eye Movements: These are involuntary smooth movements that occur when moving the head whilst keeping the eyes fixated at the same point in the visual field [19]. Until recently, the use of these movements for HCI was difficult, because eye trackers needed users' heads to remain stationary (some even requiring a chin support) in order to track gaze accurately. However, modern trackers are now robust enough to compensate for head movements, and are able to detect that the user is looking at the same spot, even as they translate and rotate their head. Whereas we did not

find examples of mechanics that leverage this behaviour, the combination of an eye tracker with the 3D head tracking capabilities of depth cameras can enable its incorporation into games. An simple example could be a virtual environment in which the player can direct nods and other head gestures at different NPCs, depending on which avatar she looks at.

Vergence: These movements focus the eyes at a distant target [19]. The further the target, the more parallel the two eyes will be. In HCI, they are particularly useful for transparent displays, as the system can detect whether the user is looking at the foreground (i.e. at the screen) or the background (i.e. through the screen) [92]. Even though, we did not find applications for vergence in games, this could be incorporated into games like *Keyewai* [3] and *Relationship Tunnel Vision* [14], which use a see-through, gaze-enabled display where which players sit across from each other. By observing vergence, the games would be able to detect whether the focus of attention is at the screen or at the other player.

Optokinetic Nystagmus: this is a conjugate eye movement comprised of smooth pursuits interspersed with saccades that enable us to perceive continuously an object that moves across the field of view [19]. These are the movements that happen when we observe a train passing by or we look through the window from inside a moving car. We did not find any direct use of these movements in games, but they nevertheless happen when playing games.

In summary, as eye-tracking technology has improved, more types of eye-movement are increasingly trackable. However, as our review demonstrates, re-articulating the different eye-movements available to game designers is necessary, as *Eye-Play* research has overwhelmingly focused on fixations. By highlighting other types of movements, we hope to uncover new opportunities for novel eye-based game mechanics.

INPUT TYPE

Modern eye trackers can capture a lot of information beyond the gaze point. From an application perspective, the input captured from a sequence of eye movements and gestures can be classified as discrete, continuous, or as a combination of them. From this perspective, we take an abstract approach to examine individual interaction techniques, illustrating them with example mechanics.

Discrete-Only

These are actions that do not incorporate the point-of-regard as input, but use other eye actions as a trigger. They are broadly categorised as Eye Gestures and Eyelid Gestures. *Eye gestures* are comprised of a sequence of saccades that correspond to different commands. In games, eye gestures can be used as an end in itself (e.g. in *EyeMote*, users must repeat the gestures indicated by the game to gain points [8]) or as a replacement for other command triggers. Examples of the latter include selecting different modes of operation [40] and triggering healing and attack spells [4]. Common problems with eye gestures include accidental activation due to the potential overlap with natural search patterns; limited screen real estate for gesture anchors; and saccadic fatigue, as intentional control of saccades is unnatural and tiresome [55].

Eyelid gestures include winks and blinks. Winks are voluntary closures of one of the eyes. Winks have been long proposed as an eyes-only trigger to replace mouse clicks [54], and they have been used in games as a trigger while users aim with a pistol [35]. However, not every user is able to wink voluntarily, with some people only being able to wink with one eye, and some not being able to wink at all [65]. Winking also transmits substantial nonverbal content, signaling collusion, shared secrecy, momentary intimacy , flirtation and trust [52, 56]. As a social gesture, Da Silva et al. implemented a game in which a little girl steals the player's homework, which he can recover by winking at her [15]. Blinking is part of the natural maintenance of the eyes and occur semi-automatically. Therefore, when used for interactive purposes, blinks must be held for longer to distinguish them from natural blinks.

Continuous-Only

These are mechanics that take as input the X and Y coordinates of the point-of-regard on the screen. We identified three ways to implement it: target pursuit, target avoidance, and always-on tracking. *Target pursuit* mechanics are those in which the player actively scans the virtual environments and triggers actions, events or commands by looking at specific objects or regions of the screen. These include triggering social and interactions and attacks with NPCs [3, 13, 78, 90, 95], triggering gaze-contingent objects [27, 70], looking at active regions to control avatar navigation [40, 63, 64, 71, 85, 87] and panning the camera by looking at the edges of the screen [12, 27, 37, 61]

Target Avoidance mechanics are those that require the player to look away from objects of interest or even the entirety of the screen. This can be implemented by requiring players to close their eyes (e.g. in *Invisible Eni* the player can close both eyes to make the avatar disappear and hide from enemies [23]) or by triggering negative actions when the user looks at certain areas of the screen (e.g. in *The Royal Corgi* this is implemented in multiple ways, including looking down to show respect, looking away to distract an annoying NPC, and looking away from an NPC to avoid engaging a conversation [90]). Because we are naturally drawn to moving and salient objects, this can offer players a challenging experience.

In *Always-On* tracking, the X and/or Y coordinates of the gaze point are interpreted continuously. This can be used explicitly to continuously control parameters, in one dimension (e.g. the horizontal position of a *Breakout* or *EyeGuitar* paddle [17, 88]) or more (e.g. absolute position of a character or control [14, 62], or speed and camera rotation [76]). Alternatively, it can be used implicitly by making inferences about players based on their visual attention patterns.

Continuous + Discrete

These are mechanics that use gaze for pointing and an additional modality for confirmation. The additional modality can be eye-based or not. If so, it is appropriate as an accessible input alternative for disabled users. Eye-based confirmation modalities include winks [35], blinks [16, 49, 69, 95] and gestures [37, 39, 69], as discussed before, as well as dwell time [4, 5, 6, 12, 16, 28, 29, 37, 40, 69, 77], smooth pursuits [91, 93], and voluntary changes in pupil size [23]. Other modalities for confirmation include voice [95], hand movement [97], and mechanical triggers, including buttons [67], mouse clicks [5, 6, 16, 28, 29, 36, 43, 48, 67], key presses [12] and gamepad controllers [35, 36].

Each confirmation modality has its advantages and disadvantages. We have already discussed winks, blinks and eye gestures above. Dwell time activation is known to suffer from the *Midas Touch* problem, i.e. unintentional target activation while users scan the environment [42]. Whereas increasing the dwell time thresholds can minimise this problem, it also slows down the interaction and leads to unnatural fixation behaviour. Smooth pursuits are somewhat more natural than selection by dwell time, as the eyes are naturally drawn to moving objects, reducing strain. However, they are also susceptible to unintentional activation and slow selection times. Selection by voluntary changes in pupil size are possible, but difficult. Such changes can be induced by physical activity, self-induced pain, positive emotions, negative emotions, cognitive tasks, focusing gaze and concentration [22]. Voice interaction has the advantage of offering multiple possible actions and make the player feel more immersed, but it can be slow and susceptible to mistakes in the recognition. For an in-depth treatment of voice interaction, see Harris [31]. Mechanical triggers require additional hardware, but offer an inexpensive, fast and intuitive way of triggering actions.

GAME MECHANICS

In this section, we categorise mechanics according to how they are employed as elements of game play. While some are similar and overlapping, our categorisations are meant to assist game designers and thus map to existing mechanics implemented with other modalities. We identified 5 categories which we explore in the following subsections, namely: Navigation, Aiming & Shooting, Selection & Commands, Implicit Interaction, and Visual Effects. Our classification should be seen as a snapshot of current implementations rather than a comprehensive overview of what can be accomplished with the eyes. In concretely categorising what has previously been implemented, we hope to inspire and uncover novel categories of mechanics that can be explored in future work, and assist researchers in avoiding common duplications.

Navigation

Navigation mechanics are those that involve moving the player's avatar through the virtual environment. We identified five subcategories of navigation mechanics: 1:1 mapping, look to go there, virtual buttons, Cartesian spaces, and gradients.

1:1 Mapping: In this mechanic, the player's avatar is positioned exactly where the gaze point is. Because of the jittery and sudden saccadic movements of the eyes, avatars controlled in this fashion tend to "teleport" around the screen. If using this pattern, designers must make sure that this behaviour is supported by corresponding game metaphors. This is usually implemented for non-humanoid avatars, such as in Dorr et al.'s *Breakout*, and in Vickers et al.'s *EyeGuitar* [17, 88]. In both cases, the player is substantiated in the game by a paddle

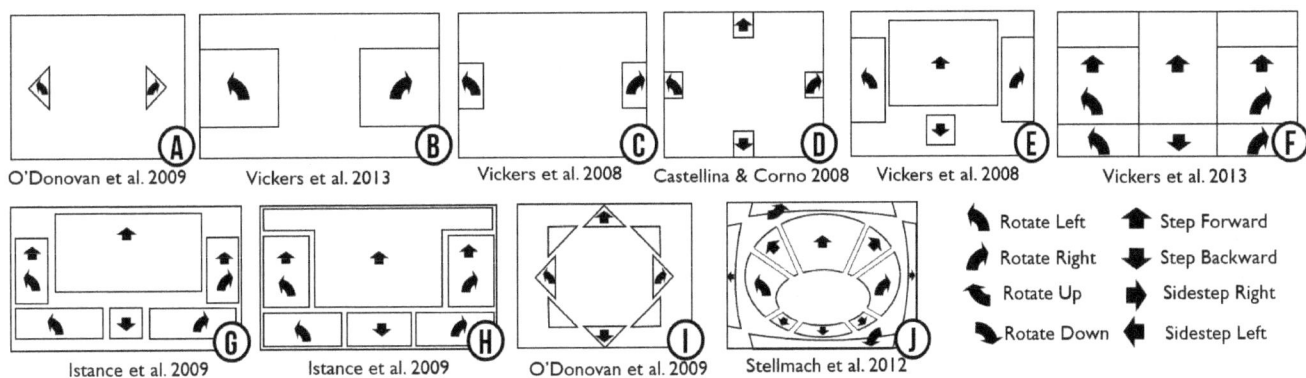

Figure 2. Different designs for navigation interfaces that use virtual buttons, in order of complexity.

whose position is controlled by the horizontal coordinate of the gaze point.

Look to go there: In this mechanic, the player looks to indicate the end position of the avatar (confirmed by dwell time [23] or other modality [67]) and using pathfinding techniques, the game guides the avatar to the desired position. In *Invisible Eni*, players fixate at a point to make the character go there [23]. Smith and Graham implemented this mechanic in the game *Neverwinter Nights*, a third-person RPG with a top-down view [67]. In first-person games this can be implemented by constraining the movement along a pre-defined path and navigating through it by dwelling at anchor points [12].

Virtual Buttons: In this mechanic, gazing at specific regions on the screen triggers a continuous action. This is often implemented by toggling a constant stream of keys, such as WASD. Previous works have explored a wide variety of designs, but there are few empirical comparisons between them, making it difficult to confidently assess what works and what does not. The first decision in the design of virtual buttons regards the **number** of buttons. Examples in the literature range from two [64, 86, 87] to twelve [71]. Designs with two buttons only enable the lateral rotation of the camera. This means that to move their avatars, players have to use a separate modality (e.g. voice commands as in *Rabbit Run* [64]) or use another mode of interaction that enables movement [38]. Additional buttons increase functionality of this mechanic, such as sidestepping, diagonal movement and vertical camera rotation [71].

The second decision regards the **visual feedback**, which can be achieved through opaque buttons, transparent buttons, or through no feedback. Opaque buttons, may communicate their functionality more clearly, but they occlude the content behind them. An example of such implementation can be found in Vickers et al.'s evaluation of the use of a gaze-controlled cursor as input for *Second Life* [84]. Their results show that because of the discrepancy between the locus of control (i.e. the widget) and the locus of attention (i.e. the environment), users would often get distracted and steer the avatar in the wrong direction. Further, because such controls occlude the game, they tend to be small, which can be a challenge for inaccurate trackers. Semi-transparent buttons allow users to see through the widget while still communicating their func-

tionality explicitly [12, 39, 71]. The final alternative is to not display any controls on the screen. A recent trend in game interface design is to move away from persistent on-screen elements of head-up displays (HUDs) towards more immersive and realistic diegetic representations [96], strengthening the case for Virtual Buttons with no on-screen representation. The different designs that implement this pattern aim at leveraging the natural eye behaviours that players present when performing these actions with other controllers. Examples in the literature include controls for *Second Life* and *World of Warcraft* [40, 41, 86, 87].

The third decision relates to the **shape** of the buttons. We found in the literature three major kinds of shapes: triangular [64, 39], rectangular [12, 40, 41, 86, **?**], and elliptical sections [71], with little report of the different usability or justifications of the shapes.

Cartesian space: In this mechanic, the whole screen acts as a Cartesian space where the XY coordinates of the gaze point control the movement. Nielsen et al. implemented this pattern to control a virtual aeroplane [63] (see Figure 3A). However, to fully control an aircraft in 3D space, a third degree-of-freedom is necessary. Hansen et al. assigned this extra degree-of-freedom to the keyboard, and compared different mappings of parameters to the different coordinates of the Cartesian space [30](see Figure 3B). Another possibility of adding additional degrees of freedom is to combine the Cartesian space with virtual buttons at the bottom of the screen, as Tall et al. did for steering a remote control toy car [76] (see Figure 3C).

Gradients: Similarly to *Virtual Buttons*, looking at different areas on the screen triggers movement and camera rotations (see Figure 3). The difference is that in *gradient* patterns, the specific point within the region being gazed at modulates the rate of change of the parameter under control (similarly to *Cartesian spaces*). Because users usually keep their gaze at the centre of the screen, the mapping usually flows from the centre towards the edges, with points further from the centre representing higher values (e.g. of rotation velocity). Stellmach et al. explored different designs for such navigation interfaces [71] (see Figure 3D,E).

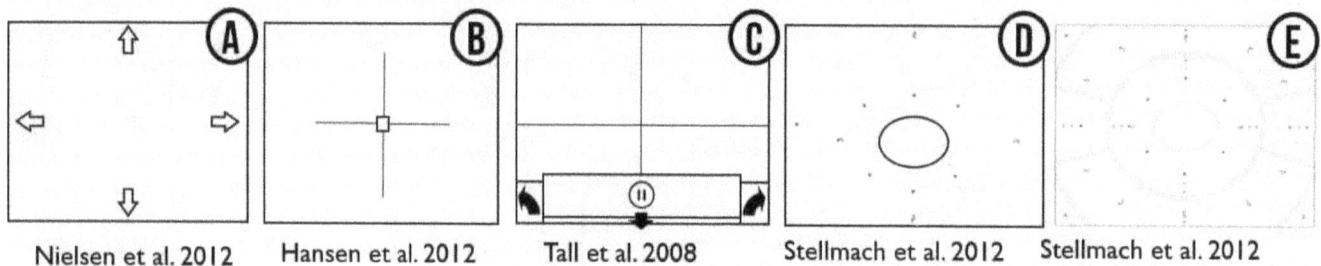

Figure 3. Different designs for navigation interfaces that use gradients and Cartesian spaces, in order of complexity.

Aiming & Shooting

Despite the despair of many concerned parents, shooting is still a widely popular game mechanic. As our eyes are naturally and quickly drawn to points of interest, many games have explored the possibility of augmenting performance by assigning the control of the weapon to players' gaze. In most shooting games, the four parameters of interest are the character's movement, the viewport control, the weapon's aim (the crosshair), and the weapon's trigger. In the previous section, we covered movement mappings to the eyes. In this section, we cover the viewport, crosshair, and trigger mappings. Table 1 shows how different shooting games mapped the eyes to the four shooting-related mechanics.

Viewport: In conventional first- and third-person shooting games the movement, viewport, and crosshair are inherently coupled—the viewport determines both the direction of movement and the aim of the weapons, as the crosshair remains static at a fixed position (usually at the centre). In most games, the movement is assigned to one hand, and the viewport/direction of movement/crosshair to the other hand.

The viewport control works well with mice and joysticks, as these are *relative* input devices—they measure changes in position and orientation, respectively. This translates well in users' mental models of viewport control: for the character to turn right, the player moves the mouse to the right. If she wants to turn a bit more, she moves the mouse a bit more. She can repeat this process until she has to clutch the mouse back to the starting position. An eye tracker, however, is an *absolute* input device. This means that it outputs coordinates in the screen frame of reference. Because of the jittery and sudden nature of eye movements, a 1:1 mapping of gaze to the viewport control is infeasible.

We found two types of implementations for controlling the viewport with the eyes. The first is to scroll to the viewport sideways when the user looks close to the edge of the screen. In this pattern, the closer to the edge of the screen the gaze point is, the faster the camera rotates in that direction. An early example of this feature can be found in the work of Gips in an adventure game for disabled children [27]. Castellina and Corno implemented this camera control technique among many others [12]. Isokoski et al. discuss the implementation of this technique for scrolling the camera sideways in the *Chicken Run* shooting game [37].

Game Title	Mov.	Aim	Cam.	Trigger
Feyerball Mage [82]	Feet	Eyes	Hands	Pinch
Quake II [67]	Keys	Eyes	Eyes	Keys
Half-Life 2 [43]	Keys	Eyes	Eyes	Mouse
Son of Nor	Keys	Eyes	Mouse	Keys
Isokoski et al., 2007 [36]	Keys	Eyes	Mouse	Keys
Half-Life 2[43]	Keys	Eyes	Mouse	Mouse
A.C. Rogue	Keys	Mouse	Eyes	Mouse
Battlefield 3 [81]	Keys	Mouse*	Mouse*	Mouse
Chicken Run [37]	Static	Eyes	Eyes	Look up
Killer Penguins [95]	Static	Eyes	Static	Blink
Eye Asteroids [77]	Static	Eyes	Static	Dwell
Sacrifice [43]	Static	Eyes	Static	Mouse
Leyba et al., 2004[48]	Static	Eyes	Static	Mouse
Lunar Command[67]	Static	Eyes	Static	Mouse
Hülsmann et al., 2011 [35]	Static	Eyes	Static	Pistol
Frog Game[91, 93]	Static	Eyes	Static	Pursuit
Killer Penguins[95]	Static	Eyes	Static	Voice
Hülsmann et al., 2011 [35]	Static	Eyes	Static	Wink
Hülsmann et al., 2011[35]	Static	Pistol	Static	Mouse

Table 1. Mappings for shooting mechanics. Games without a title are indicated by their authors. *Aim and camera are controlled by the mouse, but modulated by gaze.

The second type of implementation is to continuously centre the viewport around the gaze point. This can mean that the camera is entirely controlled by gaze or the mouse acts as the primary control while gaze modulates the speed [81]. This mechanic was first proposed by Smith and Graham in their modification of *Quake 2*. In their game, these movement was controlled by WASD keys, and the camera constantly rotated towards the gaze point at a constant speed [67]. Isokoski et al. had a similar implementation for a FPS, but the camera only rotated towards the gaze point when the player pressed a button on the gamepad [36]. Further, the longer the player pressed this button, the faster was the rotation. In Ubisoft's *Assassin's Creed Rogue* gaze enables players to re-orient their cameras around the third-person avatar using gaze [68].

Aiming: The most common mapping of the eyes in shooting games is assigning the gaze point to control the aim of the weapon. This is a natural mapping, as even in conventional games we tend to look first before shooting the target. In terms of aiming, the crosshair can be controlled directly by the gaze position or controlled by a separate input device and modulated by gaze. As shown in Table 1, most surveyed games use the former implementation. The exception is Velloso et al.'s MAGIC techniques for *Battlefield 3*, in which (rather than having the eyes control the aim directly) the eyes modulated the speed of the aim and viewport, which were primarily controlled by the mouse [81].

Trigger: The final possible shooting-related mechanic that can be controlled by the eyes is to trigger the shots. Whereas any discrete technique could be used for this purpose, we found uses of eye gestures [37], blinks [95], winks [35], dwell time[77], and smooth pursuits [91, 93].

Selection & Commands

Selecting objects and issuing commmands are mechanics existing in virtually every game. We found many diegetic (i.e. belonging to the game world) and non-diegetic instances of eye-based selection and commands. The input type for these mechanics can be discrete-only (e.g. making an eye gesture to invoke a menu) or discrete + continuous (e.g. looking to point and dwelling to select), so similarly to the shooting mechanics discussed above, the interaction techniques can be eyes-only or multimodal.

Pick & Drop: Many board, puzzle, and adventure games implemented mechanics that require the player to move objects around the game space. As this is a mechanic that can be fairly easy to implement, there are many examples in which picking and dropping objects with the eyes is used to demonstrate an eye tracker's capabilities. Examples include card games [97], chess [69], and puzzles [5, 6, 29].

Action Activation: These are mechanics in which a given eye behaviour triggers a generic game action. This can range from throwing healing and attack spells with eye gestures [39] to activating some functionality of in game objects [23]. In particular, it is interesting to think about how other modalities can influence the gameplay when combined with gaze for pointing, especially when the interaction technique matches in-game events. For example, in *Feyereball Mage*, players throw a fireball in the gaze direction by pinching in the air, an action that is repeated by the game avatar [82]. Previous work has shown how voice interaction in games can increase immersion and flow as players' and characters' voices overlap [9]. Analogously, activating actions with the eyes has great potential for merging players' and characters' gaze, consequently increasing immersion.

In-Game Widgets: As a supporting modality, the eyes offer an alternative way to interact with in-game widgets, such as keypads [4] and context menus [12, 78]. This offers a way for separating diegetic and non-diegetic interactions by input modality. For example, whereas primary interactions can remain mapped to conventional controllers, the eyes can support the hands in accomplishing secondary tasks.

Implicit Interaction

Because in eye-enabled applications, the eyes serve the dual purpose of not only providing input to the system, but also capturing information from the environment around us, they reveal a lot about our cognitive states and serve an important social role. Therefore, games can use gaze data implicitly, for example to affect social interactions with NPCs, to trigger environmental effects, and to adapt the game AI.

Social Gaze: Social aspects of gaze have been a huge element of gameplay even for non-digital games: a glance that gives away the poker player's bluff; a killing wink in *Wink Murder*; a constant staring at Europe that can predict that player is about to make an attack in *Risk*. Vidal et al. surveyed the Psychology literature and identified eight gaze behaviours that could be implemented as game mechanics: desire for interaction, avoidance of interaction, apparent distraction, cultural disrespect, dominance test, gaze following trigger, signs of intent, and joint attention. In this work, we clustered the individual mechanics by similarity, finding three clusters of behaviours: Engagement/Disengagement, Dominance/Submission, and Shared Attention.

First, gaze can be used to engage and disengage in conversation with other characters. An example suggested by Tobii is that of a player that enters a tavern and looks at the bartender, who greets him when establishing eye contact [78]. Eye contact can also engage multiple NPC's as in *WAYLA*, a game where the player looks at NPC couples to harmonise their relationship. This pattern can also be used to punish the player, by forcing them to engage in unwanted conversations. In *The Royal Corgi*, the player must avoid an annoying NPC by not looking at her [90]. An even earlier example is in the work of Da Silva et al., in which the player roams around a university lab and must avoid an evil student by looking down [15]. Another negative effect of engagement by eye contact is attracting the attention of enemies. For example, in *Keyewai*, players are stranded in an island, and looking at the native cannibals make them chase the player [3]. In the same way that eye contact can initiate interactions, looking away can terminate them. This effect can be as mild as simply finishing the conversation, but can also have repercussions for subsequent interactions with the NPC. For example, in *The Royal Corgi*, one of the NPCs demands all the player's attention and will get offended if the player looks away [90].

A second popular effect of the eyes on NPCs is that of domination and submission. Humans and other animals perceive eye contact as a dominant behaviour. Taken to one extreme, this prolonged eye contact can indicate a lack of respect in certain cultures. Conversely, lack of eye contact can convey a submissive personality. In games, this pattern has been implemented in several ways. Tobii suggests an Agatha Christie-like scenario in which the player-detective looks at different suspects at a crime scene until prolonged eye contact with the killer makes him panic [78]. In *Shynosaurs*, the title creatures become intimidated and run away after the player looks at them for a certain time [89]. This mechanic can also involve multiple players. In *Keyewai*, both players must look at the cannibal to confuse and repel him [3]. Taken to an extreme, this mechanic can completely freeze an enemy—the so-called *Medusa Effect* [60]. Lankes et al. investigated this mechanic in depth in a platformer game, comparing the effects on the player experience depending on the relation between the player's gaze and the avatar's gaze [47].

The Dominance/Submission pattern has also been implemented in staring competitions with NPCs, which function as a dominance test. In *The Revenge of the Killer Penguins*, the player must stare at an NPC's hypnotic eyes [95] and in *The Royal Corgi*, if the player wins the staring competition, the NPC proceeds to exhibit a submissive behaviour [90]. Conversely to dominant behaviour, it might be in the player's best interest to also show submissive behaviour. In *The Royal Corgi*, to receive support from a certain NPC, the player must look down to show respect [90]. The behaviour required to avoid the evil student in Da Silva et al. can also be interpreted as submissive [15].

A third possible use of social gaze is to indicate shared attention, for example, when the player looks at an object or location during an interaction with an NPC. There are many ways in which this can be interpreted by the game. First, it can be seen as a sign of intent. The premise that guides the design of interaction techniques such as MAGIC pointing [98] is that gaze often precedes action. In a social sense, this can be used by NPCs to predict players future actions. For example, Tobii suggests a football game in which the goalkeeper uses the player's gaze point to predict where he is going to shoot the ball [78]. An even more interesting use case happens when players can use their gaze behaviour to deceive NPCs. For example, to evade the annoying character in *The Royal Corgi*, players can look behind her. The character then gets distracted and looks away, giving the player an opportunity to escape the conversation [90].

Such pattern can add richness and complexity to conversations, by incorporating the context of the interaction. This can be used for positive or negative effects on the relationship with the NPC. An example of a positive effect is that of the conversation with the painter in *The Royal Corgi*. During this conversation, if the player dedicates her attention to this NPC's favourite painting, she can gain his support [90]. Conversely, also in *The Royal Corgi*, one of the NPCs will get angry if the player stares at his wife during the conversation [90].

Responsive Environments: Many games offer mechanics that leverage users' behaviours while exploring the game world to create magical effects. For example, *Eagles Eyes*, showed instructions when players looked at certain objects and displayed weather information when the player looked at the window [27]. In Starker and Bolt's prototype, the game played synthesised speech depending on users' visual attention patterns as they scanned the planet where the story of *The Little Prince* took place [70]. Dechant's horror game *Sophia* triggers scary events as the player looks at different objects in a haunted mansion[1].

Adaptive AI: A third way in which gaze can implicitly influence game play is having the game AI learn from users' visual attention patterns and predict future actions and intentions. For example, Wetzel et al. adapted the AI's strategy in *Hex* [94], Hillaire et al. predicted in which direction players were going to turn when exploring an environment [32], Munoz et al. predicted player's actions in *Super Mario Bros.* [58], and Vesterby triggered different narrative branches depending on which character the user looked at the most [83].

Visual Effects
The last category of uses of eye tracking in games involves how the knowledge of the gaze point can enhance the presentation of the game's visuals to the player. Such effects can range

---
[1]Sophia, https://youtu.be/CRJpxu5NQes

from subtle changes in how graphics are rendered to fully fledged game mechanics.

Depth-of-Field: This subtle effect renders the object being looked at sharply, while blurring objects at different distances. Hillaire et al. implemented gaze-contingent depth-of-field blur in *Quake III* [33] and Mantiuk et al. suggest that the use of players' eyes for this effect does increase their preference over a control condition [51]. This effect improves the perception of 3D objects over flat images, but the quantitative depth information conveyed by this channel is limited [53].

Compensating Camera Motion: Another effect that Hillaire et al. implemented for *Quake III* was based on the focal point [33]. This effect simulates eye movements when walking, such as the vestibulo-ocular reflex, by compensating the camera motion normally created by walking FPS characters based on where the player is looking. The authors suggest that using gaze to compensate this motion is superior to other techniques, improving the sense of immersion and fun.

Hiding and Enhancing: Blinding players is an element of many games, ranging from children's games, such as *Blind Man's Bluff* to more recent exertion games, such as *Reindeer & Wolves* [25]. Knowledge of players' gaze point can be used to create blindness by hiding objects and obscuring the field of view. A common pattern found in games is reducing the field of view with a flashlight metaphor. This mechanic effectively eliminates players peripheral vision, which makes it well suited for horror games [78]. It has also been implemented in Bala et al.'s *Keyewai*, and Velloso et al.'s *StarGazing* [3, 82]. Conversely, the gaze point can be used to enhance visuals. For example, when retro-fitting games to incorporate eye tracking input, interaction with small targets that would be trivial with a mouse, suddenly become a challenge. To address this problem, Istance et al. implemented a magnifier glass that zooms what is underneath, that can be dropped with gaze where fine grained positioning is required. Also, in graphically intensive games, visuals can be rendered from the gaze point outward, allowing faster frame rates and levels of details where they are required, crucial for applications such as VR [20, 59].

DISCUSSION
In this paper, we presented a survey of 70 works that have interrogated eye interaction in the context of games and play—a research agenda we refer to as EyePlay. From them, we distilled 112 individual game mechanics that employ the eyes in some fashion. This contributed a vocabulary for discussing and designing eye-enabled games, and a comprehensive and practical list of existing mechanics that serves as a resource for design and future work.

Our initial analysis was based on the (immutable) physiological nature of eye-movements, finding that research has overwhelmingly focused on fixations, and that little to no research has used more complex eye movements such as vergence and optokinectic nystagmus in gaze-game research. A further categorisation based on input type highlighted the relevance of eyelid gestures (winks and blinks) to EyePlay research, as well as the prevalence of work that has combined gaze with other forms of input to overcome the Midas Touch problem.

Subsequently, we identified and categorised individual game mechanics in the games surveyed according to how the eyes are used in the different games: navigation, aiming & shooting, selection & commands, implicit interaction, and visual effects. Of these, navigation and shooting were respectively the most common applications for gaze-enabled game mechanics in games research. In addition to highlighting commonly repeated applications of gaze in games, this summary provides a rich resource for design through highlighting typical pitfalls, drawbacks and successes.

In our discussion, we draw attention to the fact that even though game interaction design can be seen as a subset of HCI, designing interaction techniques for gaming follows a substantial set of rules and goals that distinguish EyePlay research from HCI research on gaze-based computer interaction. We demonstrate this through highlighting the many ways that HCI 'problems' have been implemented as resources for play in game design. Consequently, we conclude by arguing for the formulation of a formal EyePlay research agenda, as a distinct and emerging field within the CHI Play research community.

Game Design Solutions to HCI Problems

Even though game interaction design can be seen as a subset of HCI, designing interaction techniques for gaming follows a different set of rules and goals. Whereas in most domains, an interaction technique can be appropriately evaluated by measuring completion times and error rates, these metrics are not always adequate for evaluating games as they cannot capture social factors, the state of the user and other emotional, sensorial, cognitive, and behavioural factors that affect the game experience [80]. Moreover, specifically related to input design is the notion that mastering the input technology can be part of the play experience, and sometimes even the game's core mechanic. Examples of the latter include the humorously difficult and frustrating *QWOP*, which challenges players to control individual joints of the characters legs, and *There is Only One Level*, which challenges players' to discover and master unintuitive mappings.

Given that gaze-enabled interaction is harnessing a behaviour already in use—a fact that HCI research has explored extensively—challenging users' natural reactions can create novel game mechanics. Conversely, sometimes leveraging them can create uninspiring play experiences. As the eyes are naturally drawn to moving targets, shooting with the eyes can be both a fun mechanic that leverages users' natural intuitions. However, many games can create fun experiences that go against this natural behaviour. For example, they can force the user to use their peripheral vision to play the game, either by offering positive incentives (e.g. in *Shynosaurs*, players save the cuties by dragging them with the mouse while staring at the Shynosaurs to scare them away [89]) or negative incentives (e.g. in *Virus Hunt*, users must touch the viruses to kill them, but if they look at them, the infection spreads [82]).

However, a natural mapping is no guarantee of a positive game experience. For example, in *Breakout*, players must align the paddle with a bouncing ball to advance in the game. By assigning the control of the paddle to the eyes, Dorr et al. found that all that players had to do was to follow the ball

on the screen to beat the game, which effectively removed all challenge [17]. In fact, after playing the game for two minutes, one of their participants asked when the game would actually start. This is not to say that the challenge to master the interface can be an excuse for poor mappings, but that careful balance between challenge and intuitiveness is paramount for a positive play experience. As a consequence, we look at the game genres that Isokoski et al. recommend against, not with discouragement, but as opportunities for ingenious game design solutions to these HCI problems [37].

The capacity of game design solutions to overcome an input device's shortcomings offers fertile grounds for rethinking the challenges presented by many interaction techniques. In this paper, we consider the three common problems for eye-based interaction found in the literature; the *Midas Touch*, inaccuracies of the tracking, and the double role of the eyes for observation and control [72].

The **Midas Touch** is a well-known problem based on the difficulty of distinguishing between an intentional gaze interaction (for example, selecting a target with dwell) from natural eye behaviour. This leads to the unintentional activation of targets, due to the continuous tracking of the gaze point. A huge number of projects in HCI have addressed this problem, but games can take advantage of it in different ways. On one hand, the game might encourage players to scan the whole environment: in Starker and Bolt's work, the more regions on the planet the player looked at, the more of the story she would uncover [70]. On the other hand, the game can penalise players for looking at certain areas, such as having an enemy chase them in case they look at them [3].

Inaccuracies in gaze tracking come in three forms. First, due to the jittery movement of the eyes, the estimated gaze point is less like a pixel and more like a thumb-sized region on the screen. Second, issues in the calibration can lead to an offset between the ground truth and the estimated gaze point. Third, depending on the tracker's capabilities, a significant delay can be incurred in the estimation which can add perceivable lag in the interaction. Typical HCI solutions to these 'problems' include increasing the size of interactive objects, snapping user's gaze to interactive areas, and 'smoothing' gaze feedback [50].

In game design, these inaccuracies can be dealt with in many ways. In games that require pointing, such as in adventure games, inaccuracies can be dealt with similarly to HCI. However, the dynamic nature of games creates an opportunity for correcting the calibration on-the-fly. For example, by correlating the movement of the eyes with the movement of in-game characters, an algorithm such as Pfeuffer et al.'s *Pursuit Calibration*, would be able to update the calibration dynamically [66]. Second, depending on the game this might not be a problem to begin with. For example, many passive eye-based mechanics can deal elegantly with ambiguity: in the social mechanic in which characters start a conversation with eye contact, a false activation due to inaccuracies could be attributed to the outgoing personality of the NPC, who starts conversations even though no eye contact has been established. Finally, inaccuracies can be leveraged within the game to increase the challenge. This is sometimes desirable in shooter games, where perfect accuracy does not reflect the way in which guns shoot in the real world, and where the mastery of the input device is a core component of the game's challenge.

When eye-tracking is introduced, the eyes serve a **double-role** for observation and input, introducing numerous challenges, from the *Midas Touch* to social and privacy concerns. This duality is very well illustrated by the attention dilemma explored in *Shynosaurs*: on one hand, the player must look at the cuties to place them in the pen, but, on the other hand, players must stare at the Shynosaurs to scare them away [89]. Similarly, the social implications of gaze-monitoring are explored in *The Royal Corgi*, where a gaze towards the Treasurer's attractive wife can get the player in trouble [90].

While we note that these examples are hardly exhaustive, our goal is to highlight how gaze-interaction challenges which HCI has long perceived as shortcomings of the input device can be elegantly incorporated into the game to create novel experiences. Alongside the proliferation of gaze trackers and the NUI game interfaces, the different motivations, methods and contributions of gaze-enabled games research calls for the articulation and formulation of a novel research program.

EyePlay as a Research Program

This paper has so far demonstrated that there is a wide variety of research that has engaged with gaze in games, but that this body of research is often repetitive, disparate, irregular and often in little conversation with its peers. Often this work is motivated by, or situated within, broader HCI gaze research where games are used to evaluate an interaction technique, or gaze for accessibility research. As noted above, the transfer of new knowledge between these domains is not always direct. We argue that, as HCI games research is increasingly established as a distinct research discipline within HCI, and as gaze-tracking devices increase in commercial availability (and look to be embedded in the next generation of VR and AR devices), there is the emergence of a distinct research program within HCI games research, that of EyePlay Research.

EyePlay is thus a research program within HCI games research concerned with game experiences that are only possible through gaze-based interaction. Our call to formalizing the boundaries of this research area in this way is specifically intended to allow researchers to more clearly situate the motivations and goals of their work, avoid duplication and more clearly contribute to game design practice. Our emphasis on game experiences reflect the emergence of HCI games research as distinct from broader HCI work (consider CHI Play, established in 2014, the Games and Play subcommittee at CHI, and also see [10]), allowing for work which considers the creative and ludic potential of interfaces in games, while limiting EyePlay to those types of experiences *only possible through gaze* excludes the excellent and valuable work in research with eyes-only interaction as alternative input for disabled users which is often of little relevance or contribution to the gaming industry-at-large. Despite the breadth of work surveyed in this paper that has explored different means for gaze-only virtual world navigation, none have exceeded the capacity of the keyboard and mouse or game controller.

EyePlay is consequently motivated by improving and creating new game experiences, and the presentation of results that are accessible and relevant to game design practice. This is important because the majority of mechanics surveyed in this paper are aimed at desktop computer use, unsurprising considering both laboratory and consumer grade trackers are aimed at this context. As gaze-tracking becomes increasingly available in consumer devices (such as in the affordable Tobii Eyex, or MSI gaming laptop with built-in gaze tracking), EyePlay research has the potential to contribute meaningfully to game development.

Furthermore, this survey and our articulation of the EyePlay research program draws attention to significant gaps in the potential contribution of gaze-games research to industry. The emerging paradigms of computer interaction (natural user interfaces, virtual and/or augmented reality) are likely to vastly increase the ubiquity of gaze-tracking devices in non-desktop content, in which we found few examples of EyePlay research. Although likely remain too expensive for widespread adoption in the short term, head-mounted VR or AR devices presents prime opportunity for low-impact, high-accuracy inclusion of gaze-tracking, and many of the mechanics identified in our review could immediately be transplanted to these contexts. As games are likely to be a core driver of the adoption of these new computer interfaces, EyePlay presents a clear opportunity for HCI games research to have an impact on this area.

Similarly, even though the current eye tracking capabilities of mobile phones and tablets are substantially inferior to those of desktop eye trackers, recent models offer some rudimentary eye and head tracking capabilities for scrolling. However, several research works have investigated gaze interactions with small screens, including phones [21], tablets [79], and even smart watches [24]. Mobile gaming has completely revolutionised the gaming industry despite not providing input as precise as the mouse or gamepads, due to the size of users' fingers. We believe that even rudimentary eye tracking capabilities can create compelling playful experiences if well designed and distinguishing EyePlay research from HCI, interaction design work—overwhelmingly focused on accuracy [11]—creates a context for this future work.

CONCLUSION

In this paper, informed by an extensive literature review we compiled and classified game mechanics that involve the eyes form three different perspectives. By doing so, we contribute a practical toolbox that game designers can draw from to incorporate in their games and to inspire new ones. Noting that gaze-enabled games research has been highly disparate and conducted over many years, this paper has provided a thorough overview of existing work in order to provide a clear resource for design and highlight common opportunities and pitfalls. In doing so, it becomes clear how the ludic nature of gaze in games calls for a distinct research agenda—EyePlay—which we articulate based on its methods, motivations, research context and contributions. In doing so, we note the existing limitations and gaps in gaze-enabled games research, and call for future work as gaze-interaction continues to proliferate commercially as well as into novel devices and domains.

REFERENCES

1. Samuel Almeida, Ana Veloso, Licínio Roque, and O Mealha. 2011. The eyes and games: A survey of visual attention and eye tracking input in video games. In *Proceedings of SBGames 2011: X Brazilian Symposium of Computer Games and Digital Entertainment*. DOI: http://dx.doi.org/10.13140/RG.2.1.2341.3527

2. Michael Argyle. 2013. *Bodily Communication*. Taylor & Francis.

3. Paulo Bala, Lucilia Noóbrega, Guilherme Neves, Lai's Lopes, Joana Morna, João Camacho, and Cristina Freitas. 2015. Keyewai: Looking at Cooperation in a Holographic Projection Screen. In *Proceedings of the 33rd Annual ACM Conference Extended Abstracts on Human Factors in Computing Systems (CHI EA '15)*. ACM, New York, NY, USA, 61–64. DOI: http://dx.doi.org/10.1145/2702613.2728652

4. Richard Bates, Stephen Vickers, and Howell O Istance. 2010. Gaze interaction with virtual on-line communities: levelling the playing field for disabled users. *Universal Access in the Information Society* 9, 3 (2010), 261–272. DOI:http://dx.doi.org/10.1007/s10209-009-0173-0

5. Roman Bednarik, Tersia Gowases, and Markku Tukiainen. 2009. Gaze interaction enhances problem solving: Effects of dwell-time based, gaze-augmented, and mouse interaction on problem-solving strategies and user experience. *Journal of Eye Movement Research* 3, 1 (2009), 1–10. DOI: http://dx.doi.org/10.16910/jemr.3.1.3

6. Roman Bednarik, Tersia Gowases, and Markku Tukiainen. 2013. Gaze-augmented interaction improves problem-solving: new evidence from verbal protocols. *Behaviour & Information Technology* 32, 8 (2013), 836–844. DOI: http://dx.doi.org/10.1080/0144929X.2012.659216

7. Aga Bojko. 2013. *Eye tracking the user experience: A practical guide to research*. Rosenfeld.

8. Andreas Bulling, Daniel Roggen, and Gerhard Tröster. 2008. *EyeMote — Towards Context-Aware Gaming Using Eye Movements Recorded from Wearable Electrooculography*. Springer-Verlag, Berlin, Heidelberg. 33–45 pages. DOI: http://dx.doi.org/10.1007/978-3-540-88322-7_4

9. Marcus Carter, Fraser Allison, John Downs, and Martin Gibbs. 2015. Player Identity Dissonance and Voice Interaction in Games. In *Proceedings of the 2015 Annual Symposium on Computer-Human Interaction in Play (CHI PLAY '15)*. ACM, New York, NY, USA, 265–269. DOI:http://dx.doi.org/10.1145/2793107.2793144

10. Marcus Carter, John Downs, Bjorn Nansen, Mitchell Harrop, and Martin Gibbs. 2014. Paradigms of Games Research in HCI: A Review of 10 Years of Research at CHI. In *Proceedings of the First ACM SIGCHI Annual Symposium on Computer-human Interaction in Play (CHI PLAY '14)*. ACM, New York, NY, USA, 27–36. DOI: http://dx.doi.org/10.1145/2658537.2658708

11. Marcus Carter, Joshua Newn, Eduardo Velloso, and Frank Vetere. 2015. Remote Gaze and Gesture Tracking on the Microsoft Kinect: Investigating the Role of Feedback. In *Proceedings of the Annual Meeting of the Australian Special Interest Group for Computer Human Interaction (OzCHI '15)*. ACM, New York, NY, USA, 167–176. DOI: http://dx.doi.org/10.1145/2838739.2838778

12. Emiliano Castellina and Fulvio Corno. 2008. Multimodal gaze interaction in 3D virtual environments. *Proceedings of the Conference on Communication by Gaze Interaction (COGAIN)* 8 (2008), 33–37. http://www.cogain.org/

13. Wein Chang, Po-An Shen, Kushal Ponnam, Helena Barbosa, Monchu Chen, and Sergi Bermudez. 2013. WAYLA: Novel Gaming Experience Through Unique Gaze Interaction. In *ACM SIGGRAPH 2013 Emerging Technologies (SIGGRAPH '13)*. ACM, New York, NY, USA, Article 16, 1 pages. DOI: http://dx.doi.org/10.1145/2503368.2503384

14. Mon-Chu Chen, Bong-Keum Jeong, and Victor Rivera. 2015. Relationship Tunnel Vision: Altered Social Interaction Using Eye-Tracking. In *Proceedings of the Ninth International Conference on Tangible, Embedded, and Embodied Interaction (TEI '15)*. ACM, New York, NY, USA, 399–400. DOI: http://dx.doi.org/10.1145/2677199.2690868

15. Matthieu Perreira Da Silva, Vincent Courboulay, and Armelle Prigent. 2007. Gameplay experience based on a gaze tracking system. In *Proceedings of the Conference on Communication by Gaze Interaction (COGAIN)*. 25–28. http://www.cogain.org/

16. Soussan Djamasbi and Siavash Mortazavi. 2015. Generation Y, Baby Boomers, and Gaze Interaction Experience in Gaming. In *System Sciences (HICSS), 2015 48th Hawaii International Conference on*. 482–490. DOI: http://dx.doi.org/10.1109/HICSS.2015.64

17. Michael Dorr, Martin Böhme, Thomas Martinetz, and Erhardt Barth. 2007. Gaze beats mouse: a case study. In *Proceedings of the Conference on Communication by Gaze Interaction (COGAIN)*. 16–19. http://www.cogain.org/

18. Heiko Drewes and Albrecht Schmidt. 2007. Interacting with the Computer Using Gaze Gestures. In *Proceedings of the 11th IFIP TC 13 International Conference on Human-computer Interaction - Volume II (INTERACT'07)*. Springer-Verlag, Berlin, Heidelberg, 475–488. DOI: http://dx.doi.org/10.1007/978-3-540-74800-7_43

19. Andrew T. Duchowski. 2007. *Eye Tracking Methodology: Theory and Practice*. Springer-Verlag New York, Inc., Secaucus, NJ, USA. DOI: http://dx.doi.org/10.1007/978-1-84628-609-4

20. Andrew T Duchowski, Nathan Cournia, and Hunter Murphy. 2005. Gaze-contingent displays: A review. *CyberPsychology & Behavior* 7, 6 (2005), 621–634. DOI: http://dx.doi.org/10.1089/cpb.2004.7.621

21. Morten Lund Dybdal, Javier San Agustin, and John Paulin Hansen. 2012. Gaze Input for Mobile Devices by Dwell and Gestures. In *Proceedings of the Symposium on Eye Tracking Research and Applications (ETRA '12)*. ACM, New York, NY, USA, 225–228. DOI: http://dx.doi.org/10.1145/2168556.2168601

22. Inger Ekman, Antti Poikola, Meeri Mäkäräinen, Tapio Takala, and Perttu Hämäläinen. 2008b. Voluntary Pupil Size Change As Control in Eyes Only Interaction. In *Proceedings of the 2008 Symposium on Eye Tracking Research & Applications (ETRA '08)*. ACM, New York, NY, USA, 115–118. DOI: http://dx.doi.org/10.1145/1344471.1344501

23. Inger M. Ekman, Antti W. Poikola, and Meeri K. Mäkäräinen. 2008a. Invisible Eni: Using Gaze and Pupil Size to Control a Game. In *CHI '08 Extended Abstracts on Human Factors in Computing Systems (CHI EA '08)*. ACM, New York, NY, USA, 3135–3140. DOI: http://dx.doi.org/10.1145/1358628.1358820

24. Augusto Esteves, Eduardo Velloso, Andreas Bulling, and Hans Gellersen. 2015. Orbits: Gaze Interaction for Smart Watches Using Smooth Pursuit Eye Movements. In *Proceedings of the 28th Annual ACM Symposium on User Interface Software & Technology (UIST '15)*. ACM, New York, NY, USA, 457–466. DOI: http://dx.doi.org/10.1145/2807442.2807499

25. Daniel J. Finnegan, Eduardo Velloso, Robb Mitchell, Florian Mueller, and Rich Byrne. 2014. Reindeer &; Wolves: Exploring Sensory Deprivation in Multiplayer Digital Bodily Play. In *Proceedings of the First ACM SIGCHI Annual Symposium on Computer-human Interaction in Play (CHI PLAY '14)*. ACM, New York, NY, USA, 411–412. DOI: http://dx.doi.org/10.1145/2658537.2661309

26. David R. Flatla, Carl Gutwin, Lennart E. Nacke, Scott Bateman, and Regan L. Mandryk. 2011. Calibration games: making calibration tasks enjoyable by adding motivating game elements. In *Proceedings of the 24th annual ACM symposium on User interface software and technology (UIST '11)*. ACM, New York, NY, USA, 403–412. DOI: http://dx.doi.org/10.1145/2047196.2047248

27. James Gips and Peter Olivieri. 1996. EagleEyes: An eye control system for persons with disabilities. In *The Eleventh International Conference on Technology and Persons with Disabilities*. 1–15.

28. Tersia Gowases. 2007. *Gaze vs. Mouse: An evaluation of user experience and planning in problem solving games*. Master's thesis. University of Joensuu, Finland.

29. Teresia Gowases, Roman Bednarik, and Markku Tukiainen. 2008. Gaze vs. mouse in games: The effects on user experience. In *Proceedings of the International Conference on Computers in Education (ICCE)*. APSCE, 773–777.

30. John Paulin Hansen, Alexandre Alapetite, I. Scott MacKenzie, and Emilie Møllenbach. 2014. The Use of Gaze to Control Drones. In *Proceedings of the Symposium on Eye Tracking Research and Applications (ETRA '14)*. ACM, New York, NY, USA, 27–34. DOI: http://dx.doi.org/10.1145/2578153.2578156

31. Randy A. Harris. 2004. *Voice Interaction Design: Crafting the New Conversational Speech Systems*. Elsevier Science.

32. Sébastien Hillaire, Anatole Lécuyer, Gaspard Breton, and Tony Regia Corte. 2009. Gaze Behavior and Visual Attention Model when Turning in Virtual Environments. In *Proceedings of the 16th ACM Symposium on Virtual Reality Software and Technology (VRST '09)*. ACM, New York, NY, USA, 43–50. DOI: http://dx.doi.org/10.1145/1643928.1643941

33. S. Hillaire, A. Lecuyer, R. Cozot, and G. Casiez. 2008. Using an Eye-Tracking System to Improve Camera Motions and Depth-of-Field Blur Effects in Virtual Environments. In *Proceedings of the 2008 IEEE Virtual Reality Conference*. 47–50. DOI: http://dx.doi.org/10.1109/VR.2008.4480749

34. K. Holmqvist, M. Nyström, R. Andersson, R. Dewhurst, H. Jarodzka, and J. Van de Weijer. 2011. *Eye tracking: a comprehensive guide to methods and measures*. Oxford University Press.

35. Felix Hülsmann, Timo Dankert, and Thies Pfeiffer. 2011. Comparing gaze-based and manual interaction in a fast-paced gaming task in virtual reality. In *Proceedings of the Workshop Virtuelle & Erweiterte Realität 2011*.

36. Poika Isokoski, Aulikki Hyrskykari, Sanna Kotkaluoto, and Benoit Martin. 2007. Gamepad and eye tracker input in first person shooter games: Data for the first 50 minutes. In *Proceedings of the Conference on Communication by Gaze Interaction (COGAIN)*. 11–15. http://www.cogain.org/

37. Poika Isokoski, Markus Joos, Oleg Spakov, and Benoît Martin. 2009. Gaze controlled games. *Univers. Access Inf. Soc.* 8, 4 (Oct. 2009), 323–337. DOI: http://dx.doi.org/10.1007/s10209-009-0146-3

38. Howell Istance, Richard Bates, Aulikki Hyrskykari, and Stephen Vickers. 2008. Snap Clutch, a Moded Approach to Solving the Midas Touch Problem. In *Proceedings of the 2008 Symposium on Eye Tracking Research & Applications (ETRA '08)*. ACM, New York, NY, USA, 221–228. DOI: http://dx.doi.org/10.1145/1344471.1344523

39. Howell Istance, Aulikki Hyrskykari, Lauri Immonen, Santtu Mansikkamaa, and Stephen Vickers. 2010. Designing Gaze Gestures for Gaming: An Investigation of Performance. In *Proceedings of the 2010 Symposium on Eye-Tracking Research &; Applications (ETRA '10)*. ACM, New York, NY, USA, 323–330. DOI: http://dx.doi.org/10.1145/1743666.1743740

40. Howell Istance, Aulikki Hyrskykari, Stephen Vickers, and Thiago Chaves. 2009a. For your eyes only: Controlling 3d online games by eye-gaze. In *Proceedings of the 12th IFIP TC 13 International Conference on Human-computer Interaction (INTERACT)*. Springer Berlin Heidelberg, 314–327. DOI: http://dx.doi.org/10.1007/978-3-642-03655-2_36

41. Howell Istance, Stephen Vickers, and Aulikki Hyrskykari. 2009b. Gaze-based Interaction with Massively Multiplayer On-line Games. In *CHI '09 Extended Abstracts on Human Factors in Computing Systems (CHI EA '09)*. ACM, New York, NY, USA, 4381–4386. DOI: http://dx.doi.org/10.1145/1520340.1520670

42. Robert J. K. Jacob. 1990. What you look at is what you get: eye movement-based interaction techniques. In *Proceedings of the SIGCHI conference on Human factors in computing systems: Empowering people (CHI '90)*. ACM, New York, NY, USA, 11–18. DOI: http://dx.doi.org/10.1145/97243.97246

43. Erika Jönsson. 2005. If looks could kill–an evaluation of eye tracking in computer games. *Unpublished Master's Thesis, Royal Institute of Technology (KTH), Stockholm, Sweden* (2005).

44. Jesper Kjeldskov and Connor Graham. 2003. A review of mobile HCI research methods. In *Proceedings of the 5th International Symposium on Human-Computer Interaction with Mobile Devices and Services (Mobile HCI)*. Springer Berlin Heidelberg, 317–335. DOI: http://dx.doi.org/978-3-540-45233-1

45. Daniel T Knoepfle, Joseph Tao-yi Wang, and Colin F Camerer. 2010. Studying Learning in Games Using Eye-tracking. *Journal of the European Economic Association* 7, 2-3 (2010), 388–398. DOI: http://dx.doi.org/10.1162/JEEA.2009.7.2-3.388

46. Henry Krips. 2010. The politics of the gaze: Foucault, Lacan and Žižek. *Culture Unbound: Journal of Current Cultural Research* 2, 1 (2010), 91–102.

47. Michael Lankes, Thomas Mirlacher, Stefan Wagner, and Wolfgang Hochleitner. 2014. Whom Are You Looking for?: The Effects of Different Player Representation Relations on the Presence in Gaze-based Games. In *Proceedings of the First ACM SIGCHI Annual Symposium on Computer-human Interaction in Play (CHI PLAY '14)*. ACM, New York, NY, USA, 171–179. DOI: http://dx.doi.org/10.1145/2658537.2658698

48. J Leyba and J Malcolm. 2004. Eye tracking as an aiming device in a computer game. *Course work (CPSC 412/612 Eye Tracking Methodology and Applications by A. Duchowski), Clemson University* (2004), 14.

49. Chern-Sheng Lin, Chia-Chin Huan, Chao-Ning Chan, Mau-Shiun Yeh, and Chuang-Chien Chiu. 2004. Design of a computer game using an eye-tracking device for eye's activity rehabilitation. *Optics and Lasers in Engineering* 42, 1 (2004), 91 – 108. DOI: http://dx.doi.org/10.1016/S0143-8166(03)00075-7

50. Päivi Majaranta. 2011. *Gaze Interaction and Applications of Eye Tracking: Advances in Assistive Technologies: Advances in Assistive Technologies*. IGI Global.

51. Radosław Mantiuk, Bartosz Bazyluk, and Anna Tomaszewska. 2011. Gaze-dependent depth-of-field effect rendering in virtual environments. In *Proceedings of the Second International Conference on Serious Games Development and Applications*. Springer, 1–12. DOI:http://dx.doi.org/10.1007/978-3-642-23834-5_1

52. Paola Manzini, Abdolkarim Sadrieh, and Nicolaas J Vriend. 2009. On Smiles, Winks and Handshakes as Coordination Devices. *The Economic Journal* 119, 537 (2009), 826–854. DOI: http://dx.doi.org/10.1111/j.1468-0297.2009.02253.x

53. Michael Mauderer, Simone Conte, Miguel A. Nacenta, and Dhanraj Vishwanath. 2014. Depth Perception with Gaze-contingent Depth of Field. In *Proceedings of the SIGCHI Conference on Human Factors in Computing Systems (CHI '14)*. ACM, New York, NY, USA, 217–226. DOI:http://dx.doi.org/10.1145/2556288.2557089

54. Eric Missimer and Margrit Betke. 2010. Blink and Wink Detection for Mouse Pointer Control. In *Proceedings of the 3rd International Conference on PErvasive Technologies Related to Assistive Environments (PETRA '10)*. ACM, New York, NY, USA, Article 23, 8 pages. DOI:http://dx.doi.org/10.1145/1839294.1839322

55. Emilie Møllenbach, John Paulin Hansen, and Martin Lillholm. 2013. Eye Movements in Gaze Interaction. *Journal of Eye Movement Research* 6, 2 (2013), 1–1. DOI: http://dx.doi.org/10.16910/jemr.6.2.1

56. D. Morris. 1994. *Bodytalk: A World Guide to Gestures*. Jonathan Cape Ltd.

57. Laura Mulvey. 1975. Visual pleasure and narrative cinema. *Media and cultural studies: Keyworks* (1975), 393–404. DOI:http://dx.doi.org/10.1093/screen/16.3.6

58. Jorge Munoz, Georgios N Yannakakis, Fiona Mulvey, Dan Witzner Hansen, German Gutierrez, and Araceli Sanchis. 2011. Towards gaze-controlled platform games. In *2011 IEEE Conference on Computational Intelligence and Games (CIG'11)*. 47–54. DOI: http://dx.doi.org/10.1109/CIG.2011.6031988

59. Hunter Murphy and Andrew T Duchowski. 2001. Gaze-contingent level of detail rendering. *EuroGraphics 2001* (2001).

60. Lennart Erik Nacke, Michael Kalyn, Calvin Lough, and Regan Lee Mandryk. 2011. Biofeedback Game Design: Using Direct and Indirect Physiological Control to Enhance Game Interaction. In *Proceedings of the SIGCHI Conference on Human Factors in Computing Systems (CHI '11)*. ACM, New York, NY, USA, 103–112. DOI:http://dx.doi.org/10.1145/1978942.1978958

61. Lennart E Nacke, Sophie Stellmach, Dennis Sasse, and Craig A Lindley. 2009. Gameplay Experience in a Gaze Interaction Game. In *Proceedings of the Conference on Communication by Gaze Interaction (COGAIN)*. The COGAIN Association, Lyngby, Denmark, 49–54. http://www.cogain.org/

62. Lennart E. Nacke, Sophie Stellmach, Dennis Sasse, Joerg Niesenhaus, and Raimund Dachselt. 2011. LAIF: A logging and interaction framework for gaze-based interfaces in virtual entertainment environments. *Entertainment Computing* 2, 4 (2011), 265 – 273. DOI: http://dx.doi.org/10.1016/j.entcom.2010.09.004

63. Anders Møller Nielsen, Anders Lerchedahl Petersen, and John Paulin Hansen. 2012. Gaming with Gaze and Losing with a Smile. In *Proceedings of the Symposium on Eye Tracking Research and Applications (ETRA '12)*. ACM, New York, NY, USA, 365–368. DOI: http://dx.doi.org/10.1145/2168556.2168638

64. Jonathan O'Donovan. 2009. Gaze and Voice Based Game Interaction. *University of Dublin, Trinity College. Master of Computer Science in Interactive Entertainment Technology* (2009).

65. Lyelle L Palmer. 1976. Inability to wink an eye and eye dominance. *Perceptual and motor skills* 42, 3 (1976), 825–826. DOI: http://dx.doi.org/10.2466/pms.1976.42.3.825

66. Ken Pfeuffer, Mélodie Vidal, Jayson Turner, Andreas Bulling, and Hans Gellersen. 2013. Pursuit Calibration: Making Gaze Calibration Less Tedious and More Flexible. In *Proceedings of the 26th Annual ACM Symposium on User Interface Software and Technology (UIST '13)*. ACM, New York, NY, USA, 261–270. DOI: http://dx.doi.org/10.1145/2501988.2501998

67. J. David Smith and T. C. Nicholas Graham. 2006. Use of Eye Movements for Video Game Control. In *Proceedings of the 2006 ACM SIGCHI International Conference on Advances in Computer Entertainment Technology (ACE '06)*. ACM, New York, NY, USA, Article 20. DOI: http://dx.doi.org/10.1145/1178823.1178847

68. Ubisoft Sofia. 2015. *Assassin's Creed Rogue*. Game [Windows]. (10 March 2015).

69. Oleg Špakov. 2005. EyeChess: the tutoring game with visual attentive interface. *Alternative Access: Feelings & Games* (2005), 81–86.

70. India Starker and Richard A. Bolt. 1990. A Gaze-responsive Self-disclosing Display. In *Proceedings of the SIGCHI Conference on Human Factors in Computing Systems (CHI '90)*. ACM, New York, NY, USA, 3–10. DOI:http://dx.doi.org/10.1145/97243.97245

71. Sophie Stellmach and Raimund Dachselt. 2012. Designing Gaze-based User Interfaces for Steering in Virtual Environments. In *Proceedings of the Symposium on Eye Tracking Research and Applications (ETRA '12)*.

ACM, New York, NY, USA, 131–138. DOI: http://dx.doi.org/10.1145/2168556.2168577

72. Sophie Stellmach and Raimund Dachselt. 2013. Still Looking: Investigating Seamless Gaze-supported Selection, Positioning, and Manipulation of Distant Targets. In *Proceedings of the SIGCHI Conference on Human Factors in Computing Systems (CHI '13)*. ACM, New York, NY, USA, 285–294. DOI: http://dx.doi.org/10.1145/2470654.2470695

73. Veronica Sundstedt. 2010. Gazing at Games: Using Eye Tracking to Control Virtual Characters. In *ACM SIGGRAPH 2010 Courses (SIGGRAPH '10)*. ACM, New York, NY, USA, Article 5, 160 pages. DOI: http://dx.doi.org/10.1145/1837101.1837106

74. Veronica Sundstedt. 2012. *Gazing at Games: An Introduction to Eye Tracking Control* (1st ed.). Morgan & Claypool Publishers.

75. Veronica Sundstedt, Matthias Bernhard, Efstathios Stavrakis, Erik Reinhard, and Michael Wimmer. 2013. Visual attention and gaze behavior in games: An object-based approach. In *Game analytics: Maximizing the Value of Player Data*. Springer, 543–583. DOI: http://dx.doi.org/10.1007/978-1-4471-4769-5

76. Martin Tall, Alexandre Alapetite, Javier San Agustin, Henrik H.T Skovsgaard, John Paulin Hansen, Dan Witzner Hansen, and Emilie Møllenbach. 2009. Gaze-controlled Driving. In *CHI '09 Extended Abstracts on Human Factors in Computing Systems (CHI EA '09)*. ACM, New York, NY, USA, 4387–4392. DOI: http://dx.doi.org/10.1145/1520340.1520671

77. Tobii. 2011. *Tobii EyeAsteroids: The Worldâ˘AŹs First Eye-Controlled Arcade Game*. Technical Report. Tobii Technologies.

78. Tobii. 2014. *10 Ways to Use Eye Tracking in Games*. Technical Report. Tobii Technologies. https://www.youtube.com/watch?v=UJEA9Z3SaUo

79. Jayson Turner, Eduardo Velloso, Hans Gellersen, and Veronica Sundstedt. 2014. EyePlay: Applications for Gaze in Games. In *Proceedings of the First ACM SIGCHI Annual Symposium on Computer-human Interaction in Play*. ACM, New York, NY, USA, 465–468. DOI: http://dx.doi.org/10.1145/2658537.2659016

80. Anders Tychsen. 2008. Crafting user experience via game metrics analysis. In *Proceedings of the Workshop Research Goals and Strategies for Studying User Experience and Emotion at the 5th Nordic Conference on Human-computer interaction (NordiCHI)*. 20–22.

81. Eduardo Velloso, Amy Fleming, Jason Alexander, and Hans Gellersen. 2015a. Gaze-Supported Gaming: MAGIC Techniques for First Person Shooters. In *Proceedings of the 2015 Annual Symposium on Computer-Human Interaction in Play (CHI PLAY '15)*. ACM, New York, NY, USA, 343–347. DOI: http://dx.doi.org/10.1145/2793107.2793137

82. Eduardo Velloso, Carl Oechsner, Katharina Sachmann, Markus Wirth, and Hans Gellersen. 2015b. Arcade+: A Platform for Public Deployment and Evaluation of Multi-Modal Games. In *Proceedings of the 2015 Annual Symposium on Computer-Human Interaction in Play (CHI PLAY '15)*. ACM, New York, NY, USA, 271–275. DOI:http://dx.doi.org/10.1145/2793107.2793145

83. Tore Vesterby, Jonas C Voss, John Paulin Hansen, Arne John Glenstrup, Dan Witzner Hansen, and Mark Rudolph. 2005. Gaze-guided viewing of interactive movies. *Digital Creativity* 16, 04 (2005), 193–204.

84. Stephen Vickers, Howell Istance, and R Bates. 2008. Gazing into a Second Life: Gaze-driven adventures, control barriers, and the need for disability privacy in an online virtual world.. In *Proceedings of the 7th International Conference on Disability, Virtual Reality and Associated Technologies (ICDVRAT)*. http://hdl.handle.net/2086/5462

85. Stephen Vickers, Howell Istance, and Michael J. Heron. 2013a. Accessible Gaming for People with Physical and Cognitive Disabilities: A Framework for Dynamic Adaptation. In *CHI '13 Extended Abstracts on Human Factors in Computing Systems (CHI EA '13)*. ACM, New York, NY, USA, 19–24. DOI:http://dx.doi.org/10.1145/2468356.2468361

86. Stephen Vickers, Howell Istance, and Aulikki Hyrskykari. 2013b. Performing Locomotion Tasks in Immersive Computer Games with an Adapted Eye-Tracking Interface. *ACM Transactions on Accessible Computing* 5, 1, Article 2 (Sept. 2013), 33 pages. DOI:http://dx.doi.org/10.1145/2514856

87. Stephen Vickers, Howell Istance, A Hyrskykari, N Ali, and R Bates. 2008. Keeping an eye on the game: Eye gaze interaction with massively multiplayer online games and virtual communities for motor impaired users. (2008). http://hdl.handle.net/2086/5464

88. Stephen Vickers, Howell Istance, and Matthew Smalley. 2010. EyeGuitar: Making Rhythm Based Music Video Games Accessible Using Only Eye Movements. In *Proceedings of the 7th International Conference on Advances in Computer Entertainment Technology (ACE '10)*. ACM, New York, NY, USA, 36–39. DOI:http://dx.doi.org/10.1145/1971630.1971641

89. Mélodie Vidal. 2014. Shynosaurs: A Game of Attention Dilemma. In *Proceedings of the First ACM SIGCHI Annual Symposium on Computer-human Interaction in Play (CHI PLAY '14)*. ACM, New York, NY, USA, 391–394. DOI:http://dx.doi.org/10.1145/2658537.2662979

90. Mélodie Vidal, Remi Bismuth, Andreas Bulling, and Hans Gellersen. 2015. The Royal Corgi: Exploring Social Gaze Interaction for Immersive Gameplay. In *Proceedings of the 33rd Annual ACM Conference on Human Factors in Computing Systems (CHI '15)*. ACM, New York, NY, USA, 115–124. DOI:http://dx.doi.org/10.1145/2702123.2702163

91. Mélodie Vidal, Andreas Bulling, and Hans Gellersen. 2013. Pursuits: Spontaneous Interaction with Displays Based on Smooth Pursuit Eye Movement and Moving Targets. In *Proceedings of the 2013 ACM International Joint Conference on Pervasive and Ubiquitous Computing (UbiComp '13)*. ACM, New York, NY, USA, 439–448. DOI:http://dx.doi.org/10.1145/2493432.2493477

92. Mélodie Vidal, David H. Nguyen, and Kent Lyons. 2014. Looking at or Through?: Using Eye Tracking to Infer Attention Location for Wearable Transparent Displays. In *Proceedings of the 2014 ACM International Symposium on Wearable Computers (ISWC '14)*. ACM, New York, NY, USA, 87–90. DOI:http://dx.doi.org/10.1145/2634317.2634344

93. Mélodie Vidal, Ken Pfeuffer, Andreas Bulling, and Hans W. Gellersen. 2013. Pursuits: Eye-based Interaction with Moving Targets. In *CHI '13 Extended Abstracts on Human Factors in Computing Systems (CHI EA '13)*. ACM, New York, NY, USA, 3147–3150. DOI:http://dx.doi.org/10.1145/2468356.2479632

94. Stefanie Wetzel, Katharina Spiel, and Sven Bertel. 2014. Dynamically Adapting an AI Game Engine Based on Players' Eye Movements and Strategies. In *Proceedings of the 2014 ACM SIGCHI Symposium on Engineering Interactive Computing Systems (EICS '14)*. ACM, New York, NY, USA, 3–12. DOI:http://dx.doi.org/10.1145/2607023.2607029

95. Tom Wilcox, Mike Evans, Chris Pearce, Nick Pollard, and Veronica Sundstedt. 2008. Gaze and Voice Based Game Interaction: The Revenge of the Killer Penguins. In *ACM SIGGRAPH 2008 Posters (SIGGRAPH '08)*. ACM, New York, NY, USA, Article 81, 1 pages. DOI:http://dx.doi.org/10.1145/1400885.1400972

96. Greg Wilson. 2006. Off with their huds!: Rethinking the heads-up display in console game design. *Gamasutra* (2006), 1–2. http://www.gamasutra.com/view/feature/2538/off_with_their_huds_rethinking_.php

97. Michiya Yamamoto, Munehiro Komeda, Takashi Nagamatsu, and Tomio Watanabe. 2011. Hyakunin-Eyesshu: A Tabletop Hyakunin-Isshu Game with Computer Opponent by the Action Prediction Based on Gaze Detection. In *Proceedings of the 1st Conference on Novel Gaze-Controlled Applications (NGCA '11)*. ACM, New York, NY, USA, Article 5, 4 pages. DOI:http://dx.doi.org/10.1145/1983302.1983307

98. Shumin Zhai, Carlos Morimoto, and Steven Ihde. 1999. Manual and Gaze Input Cascaded (MAGIC) Pointing. In *Proceedings of the SIGCHI Conference on Human Factors in Computing Systems (CHI '99)*. ACM, New York, NY, USA, 246–253. DOI:http://dx.doi.org/10.1145/302979.303053

Using Positive or Negative Reinforcement in Neurofeedback Games for Training Self-Regulation

Anke V. Reinschluessel
University of Bremen
Bremen, Germany
a.reinschluessel@gmail.com

Regan L. Mandryk
University of Saskatchewan
Saskatoon, SK, Canada
regan@cs.usask.ca

ABSTRACT

Neurofeedback training can reduce symptoms related to epileptic seizures, attention deficits, and Asperger's Syndrome, and often uses games to motivate participation over the long term needed to see improvements. Most neurofeedback games use negative reinforcement to guide players – i.e., a barrier to progressing in the game is removed when players achieve a desirable state – which is considered to be less effective than reinforcing behaviour through positive feedback when players do well. We investigate whether using positive reinforcement is more successful than negative reinforcement through the design and evaluation of the experience and efficacy of a custom neurofeedback training game. We showed that positive reinforcement was more effective in encouraging players to keep their brain activity regulated. Furthermore it generated more positive affect and motivated more investment of effort in players, suggesting that positive reinforcement in neurofeedback games may provide a better and more effective neurofeedback training experience.

Author Keywords
Biofeedback; neurofeedback; games; reinforcement.

ACM Classification Keywords
K.8.0 [Personal Computing]: General - Games.

INTRODUCTION

Biofeedback training systems encourage a specific mental state in a user through a closed biofeedback loop. The user's physiological state (e.g., heart rate, concentration level) is gathered through sensing hardware, integrated into a computer-based application, and presented back to the user so that they can try to adapt their state [12]. Neurofeedback training – biofeedback training that is driven by a user's brain activity – is gaining prevalence; the research published in this field has accelerated in the last decade and clinical use of neurofeedback training is on the rise. Although there are still questions surrounding the efficacy of neurofeedback training for clinical use [33], research has shown it to be effective in helping people reduce the intensity and duration of epileptic seizures [57], treating attention deficits [26], and decreasing behavioural symptoms of Asperger's Syndrome [59].

Effective neurofeedback training generally requires several weeks of commitment, with a total of 25 to 60 sessions that last 30 to 60 minutes each [21]. Because of the repetitive aspect, neurofeedback training systems often incorporate games into the training system. The motivational pull of games [52] makes them enjoyable to play both over the short term and over the longer term, which could encourage the uptake of neurofeedback training and improve training compliance over the repeated long-term engagement that is needed for effective training [38].

In standard neurofeedback games, the players must maintain a particular cognitive state to make progress or succeed [2,7,21,38,40,56]. This is generally accomplished by adjusting the game's mechanics (i.e., the rules and procedures of play [15]). For example, force fields may prevent a car from moving in a racing game if the player lacks focus. Players respond by self-regulating their brain activity in the desired direction, which helps them learn to self-regulate their brain activity outside of the context of neurofeedback training. Neurofeedback games generally remove barriers – such as screen obfuscations or sluggish controls – to progress or success in the game when the players achieve the right cognitive state. This technique is called *negative reinforcement* [55]. Its goal is to increase the desired behaviour (in our example the focus of players) by removing the negative stimuli (in our example the force fields) if the player is showing the desired behaviour [37]. The player wants to get rid of the aversive stimuli and thereby trains the desired behaviour.

In contrast to that, *positive reinforcement* – the notion of adding a reinforcing stimulus following desired behaviour to make it more likely to occur again – has been shown to significantly increase the person's perception of their own performance, which leads to increased intrinsic motivation to do a task [61]. Positive feedback has also been shown to enhance perceived competence [52], which is an important predictor of game enjoyment, and the effort invested into a game [52]. Positive reinforcement has been used in several exergames, increasing player engagement and commitment

CHI PLAY '16, October 16-19, 2016, Austin, TX, USA
© 2016 ACM. ISBN 978-1-4503-4456-2/16/10...$15.00
DOI: http://dx.doi.org/10.1145/2967934.2968085

and therefore exertion [28, 32]. Negative reinforcement leaves it up to players to discover how to succeed [37], and has been shown to be less effective than positive reinforcement at motivating children to try to succeed in an educational context, fostering dislike for the teacher and the task [63].

To create good neurofeedback training games, designers have to ensure that they are maximizing both *therapeutic efficacy* (i.e., the treatment is working to help player's self-regulate brain activity), and *player engagement*, which can be operationalized as the intrinsic motivation of players in terms of their enjoyment experienced and invested effort [52] – two factors that will promote long-term and repeated use. As clinicians gain interest in neurofeedback training games, we need to ensure that we design them in a principled way that promotes both efficacy and engagement. However, to our knowledge, neurofeedback games in literature generally employ negative reinforcement (e.g., [2,7,21,38,40,56]), despite evidence that positive reinforcement might be better for both the efficacy of training and enjoyment of the game. In addition, we did not find any evidence of studies that have investigated the role of reinforcement type (positive or negative[1]) on the efficacy or engagement of neurofeedback training games. As such, in this paper, we systematically investigated the role of positive versus negative reinforcement on training efficacy and player engagement in neurofeedback training games.

We designed, implemented, and evaluated a neurofeedback training game using a game design in which we could maintain the core mechanic, but integrate the neurofeedback training into gameplay using positive reinforcement, negative reinforcement, and no neurofeedback training (a control condition). We measured brain activity using NeuroSky's MindWave Mobile headset, and chose the theta/low beta ratio in the Electroencephalography (EEG) signal to drive the neurofeedback training component. It has been shown that training people to lower their theta/low beta activity has improved self-regulation in several neurofeedback systems [2,35,42,56]. Participants played our game in a laboratory setting for 15 minutes. We measured player experience through needs satisfaction (i.e., perceived competence, autonomy, relatedness, immersion, and intuitive control) [52], which are constructs that have been shown to promote increased intrinsic motivation (i.e., interest/enjoyment and invested effort) [52], and ultimately changes in positive

affect after play [3]; we use a time-based analysis of the in-game EEG signals as a proxy for measuring effective training over the long-term [38].

We asked and answered four main research questions:

1. Does positive reinforcement work better than negative reinforcement at motivating players to lower their theta/low beta ratio?
2. Are these results being driven by players experiencing more competence, autonomy or immersion in the positive reinforcement condition?
3. Are players enjoying the positive reinforcement condition more or investing more effort?
4. Does the positive reinforcement condition yield more positive affect or less negative affect?

The results of our study showed that the positive reinforcement condition was more successful than the negative reinforcement condition in lowering the theta/low beta EEG ratio. Furthermore, the positive reinforcement version was better at motivating the players in terms of investing more effort than the control condition and also produced more positive affect than the negative reinforcement condition.

Although preliminary, our work shows that neurofeedback games could potentially be more successful if they used positive reinforcement in training. Because of their potential to help improve the health and wellness of a broad range of people in society, it is important that we consider the principles of designing neurofeedback training games to maximize both therapeutic efficacy and player engagement. Our work takes an initial step in this direction.

RELATED WORK

After introducing electroencephalography (EEG), this section covers an overview over the literature related to neurofeedback training, neurofeedback games, and the general cognitive benefits of games. Additionally, we present research about the need to develop positive reinforcement approaches.

Electroencephalography

The brain consists of billions of neurons, which communicate by electrical currents [60]. These electrical currents can be measured using an electroencephalograph (EEG), which places several electrodes on the participant's head. The amount of electrical activity corresponds to the amount of brain activity. Brain activity is usually distinguished by the amplitude and frequency of the signal in comparison to a reference location on the head [45]. Standard EEG devices differentiate the captured signal into different frequency bands. The frequency bands are named alpha (8-13 Hz), beta (13-30 Hz) – again divided into low beta (13-20 Hz) and high beta (20-30 Hz), theta (4-8 Hz), delta (1-4 Hz), and gamma (30-50 Hz). Not all frequency bands show the same activity all the time; they are associated with certain states. Beta activity, for example, is related to alertness, attention, vigilance, and excitatory

---

[1] Note that we are investigating negative versus positive reinforcement (i.e., *increasing the desired behaviour* through the removal of a negative stimulus or addition of a positive stimulus respectively) and not the effects of punishment (i.e., *decreasing an undesirable behaviour* by the addition of a negative stimulus or removal of a positive stimulus). For further explanations we refer to Skinner [55].

problem solving activities while delta is mostly seen during sleep. Theta activity is associated with decreased alertness, drowsiness and lower information processing [45,60].

Neurofeedback Training

In 1976, Lubar et al. [34] showed that it is possible to modulate one's brain activity with neurofeedback and thereby decrease seizure intensity and duration. Based on his findings, neurofeedback training started to be explored to treat various conditions (e.g. Attention Deficit Hyperactivity Disorder (ADHD) [2,42], Fetal Alcohol Spectrum Disorder (FASD) [38], and Asperger's Syndrome [59]). Because video games were available in combination with low-cost home computer systems (e.g. Atari, Apple), and they were fascinating to play (especially for children), researchers started to combine neurofeedback and video games [65].

Lubar et al. [34] originally showed that neurofeedback training could significantly reduce seizure intensity and duration for epilepsy patients, when they focused on increasing the 12-14 Hz activity of EEG referred to as sensorimotor rhythm (SMR). Further research showed similar success in reducing symptoms for seizure patients [21,57], and neurofeedback training began to be explored to treat other conditions. Monastra et al. [41] demonstrated that participants with Attention Deficit Hyperactivity Disorder (ADHD) have a distinctive difference in their brain activity compared to people without ADHD. Specifically, they showed that people diagnosed with ADHD have significantly higher levels of slow-wave (i.e., theta, 4-8 Hz) in relation to fast-wave (i.e., beta, 13-21 Hz) EEG activity. Research focused especially on children with ADHD used different training mechanisms, i.e., suppressing or increasing activity in different frequency bands (e.g., SMR, theta, beta) [2,19,21,35,36,44,56]. The results showed that people who were able to change their brain activity showed significant improvements along several metrics: their results in attention tests (like T.O.V.A.) and intelligence tests for children (e.g., WISC-R) increased, behavioural ratings (assessed for example by the Behavior Assessment System for Children) improved, and feedback from parents and teachers was positive [26,35,42]. Neurofeedback training has proven itself effective not just in case studies, but also in large-scale studies in treating attentional dysfunction [26]. The results of neurofeedback training seem to be sustainable, as shown by follow-up studies after years without continued neurofeedback training [42]. One study demonstrated the positive effect of neurofeedback training with school children that were taking medication to treat the symptoms of ADHD. The positive effect of the altered brain activity was sustained even when the medication was discontinued [43].

In addition to helping people with different medical conditions modulate brain activity, neurofeedback training also showed positive results when used for healthy people who were not diagnosed with a medical condition [21,26,

62,46]. The purpose of the studies was to determine whether neurofeedback training could result in improvements in areas such as memory, sports, and artistic performance [62]. Vernon et al. [62] documented that by training healthy subjects to modulate their SMR/beta and SMR/theta ratios they were able to see improvements in semantic working memory. Other researchers showed that by increasing the low frequency activity in the left hemisphere, the targeting ability in pre-elite archers improved significantly [30]. Finally, researchers showed that the performance of a dancer could be improved with neurofeedback training [50]. For a more detailed review of the possibilities of neurofeedback training, see [62].

Cognitive Benefits of Games

Game elements have been used to increase the motivation to perform a variety of non-game activities – a process known as gamification [11] – but games have also been shown to yield cognitive benefits in and of themselves. For example, researchers have discovered differences in a number of basic cognitive and perceptual abilities between non-gamers and expert gamers, including that gamers are better in tracking objects moving at greater speeds, detecting changes to objects seen previously and performing task-switching more quickly [6,20]. Boot et al. [6] showed the training effect of playing games on a mental rotation task, in which expert gamers outperformed non-gamers; however, with extensive video game practice, the non-gamers improved.

Jaeggi et al. [25] showed that a game with the aim of improving working memory also improved the participant's performance in untrained fluid intelligence tasks. This improvement was sustained three months after training stopped. In addition, within the trained group, there were differences between the children who described the game as having the right amount of difficulty and challenge and the ones who perceived it as overwhelming. The effect of training on the first group was significantly higher than on the second group. Therefore the authors conclude that the perceived difficulty might have a significant impact on how much the children improved.

By letting naïve older adults play a game that trained their multitasking abilities, Anguera et al. [1] demonstrated that training this ability in the elderly could compensate for age-related decreases seen in multitasking abilities. Their neural activity patterns after completing the training were comparable to those observed in younger adults and didn't revert back after training stopped.

Neurofeedback Games

Although playing certain types of games have shown cognitive benefits under certain conditions, our work focuses particularly on the use of neurofeedback games for training purposes. During neurofeedback training, most setups give auditory or visual feedback [26,34], i.e., a sound or/and a light signal that the desired brain frequency threshold was achieved or maintained long enough. Visual feedback could also include points or colour wheels advancing around the periphery [35]. Because a lot of the participants in the studies were children, the researchers tried to make the feedback more fun and the training more engaging. One good way to keep children engaged is through computer games, as they have been shown to capture the attention of children [9]. Therefore instead of staring at a lamp or waiting for an auditory signal, the children had to complete tasks such as: changing the colour of a pole to enable a famous mouse from German TV to jump [21], make a diver sink to reach a treasure [7], make an emoticon smile [2], make a monkey climb a tree for food [2], make a ball blink [2] or make a dolphin dive to the ocean ground to collect coins [56]. Although these are not games by standard definitions (e.g., they don't include an uncertain outcome) [53], they are rather playful applications that provide more fun and engagement than standard training approaches [31]. To introduce more engaging games, researchers at NASA decided to try a different approach and modulated the control of off-the-shelf games using the EEG signal [40]. If the player increased his or her beta activity, the game controller or joystick became more responsive and the player had greater control; whereas, if theta waves increased, the controller was more sluggish [40]. Mandryk et al. [38] developed a similar approach where the view of the game was obfuscated by game-relevant graphics if the player's brain activity was not in the desired theta/low beta range. They deployed their system over 12 weeks of training (3 sessions/week) and noted differences in theta/low beta from the first week of training until the final week of training. Note that each of these approaches use negative reinforcement – players must achieve the desired state (focus) to remove the aversive stimuli (sluggish controls or obfuscating graphics).

There are, of course, also games that use brain input (as measured by EEG) to drive interaction for non-therapeutic purposes (e.g., Brainball [22], the NeuroSky games [47], or the Brainmaster [24] games). NeuroSky and Brainmaster both sell equipment and games for neurofeedback training. NeuroSky's focus is more consumer-oriented, whereas the equipment by Brainmaster takes a more clinical approach. The games are similar in that the player has to reach and maintain the desired brain activity to be able to play.

Use of Positive Reinforcement
As described in the previous section, games for neurofeedback training tend to use negative reinforcement – rather than positive reinforcement – to provide feedback to players. To our knowledge, there are no studies that investigate the differential efficacy of these two approaches in the context of games. Although the literature about comparing positive to negative reinforcement in non-game scenarios is sparse, there are a few results concerning the effectiveness of these two approaches. Two case studies showed that positive reinforcement works better to reduce problem behavior like self-injuring or aggression [10,29]. Siniatchkin et al. showed that both reinforcement strategies

work even when they're unknowingly interchanged, but they highlight that it is important to encourage and reward users, especially when working with children [54]. They note that there should be emphasis on the reinforcement strategy in the feedback process. And Boddy et al. [5] showed that the efficacy of the approaches for learning depend on the person's personality; they suggest that extraverts learn better under positive reinforcement while introverts learn better under negative reinforcement. Similar results were presented by Frank et al. [14], who measured the error-related negativity (ERN) in brain signals. Based on the ERN magnitude, they predicted whether their subject learns better from positive or negative consequences of their decisions. This shows that there is a physiological foundation for exploring both types of reinforcement. In addition, studies in the domain of exergames employing mechanics based on positive reinforcement show improved engagement and levels of exertion [28]. Results from these studies and design guidelines for games for health explicitly advise designers to use positive reinforcement, as negative reinforcement has been shown to demotivate [32,8]. In one particular case, the participants reduced interaction with an exergame to avoid the negative reinforcer [32].

STUDY
To investigate whether positive reinforcement is more engaging and efficacious than negative reinforcement for neurofeedback training games, we designed, implemented, and evaluated a neurofeedback training game using the Unity game development engine [58].

The Game
We chose a game design in which we could maintain the core mechanic in all three designs (positive and negative reinforcement plus control), but integrate the EEG signal into gameplay using both a positive reinforcement and a negative reinforcement mechanic. Our neurofeedback game used an endless runner mechanic (e.g., Disney's Temple Run or Kiloo's Subway Surfers), and was developed using the Unity Development Engine [58]. The primary game mechanic involved an avatar running down an endless street at a speed determined by the game (i.e., not directly controlled by the character), collecting coins and avoiding obstacles, such as buses, cars, and road signs. Whenever the avatar hit an obstacle, it died and the coins that had been collected were reduced by a third. To ensure that participants could keep engaging in gameplay for the full play session, the number of lives was unlimited. To make the game remain challenging over the play session, we implemented 15 patterns of obstacle placement, plus two additional patterns that were used for an initial training and calibration phase. The first 30 seconds of training/ calibration had no obstacles and participants could just explore the controls for moving left ("A"), moving right ("D"), jumping ("W"), and ducking ("S"). In the following 30 seconds, obstacles were arranged in a more challenging pattern. This increase in difficulty was intended to encourage the participants to focus on game play so that we

could gather a baseline measure of their EEG activity. During the calibration phase, the speed of the game avatar was the same for all three conditions.

After the calibration phase, the 15 patterns kept repeating in a fixed order. A blue bar in the bottom right corner (see Figure 1) gave the participants feedback on their concentration level – a higher bar indicated better focus, corresponding to a lower theta/low beta ratio.

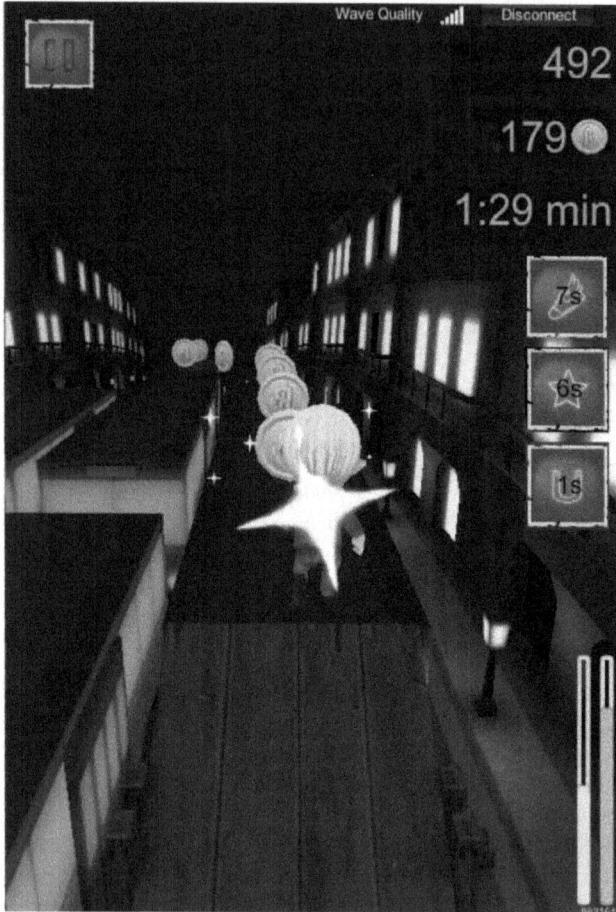

Figure 1. Screenshot of the game, neurofeedback version

Integrating Positive and Negative Reinforcement
Although the core game mechanic was the same regardless of feedback condition, we developed two methods of using the EEG to drive gameplay.

In the positive reinforcement version (*positive condition*), our goal was to reward the player for achieving and maintaining a low theta/low beta ratio without presenting an aversive stimulus to them if they failed to do so. To this end, we integrated power-ups into the game. In addition to the concentration meter, we integrated a power-up meter (the yellow bar in the bottom right corner of Figure 1) that charged up and rewarded players consecutively with one of three temporary power-ups: double jump (immediate ability to jump higher by jumping twice), sprint (immediate ability to run really fast combined with invincibility if obstacles were hit), and magnet (immediate ability to attract all coins

around). Icons were used to represent active power-ups (see Figure 1) to the player. The concentration level set the charging speed of the power-up meter dynamically. As soon as the power-up meter was full, the player gained a power-up for 8 to 12 seconds. If the player died, the power-up meter level was reduced by half and any active power-ups were disabled. In the positive reinforcement condition, the avatar's speed increased until their avatar died, at which point, it was reset to the initial speed of 5 units. The maximum speed was 15 units.

Our goal with the negative reinforcement version (*negative condition*) was to create a game that worked according to the familiar principles in neurofeedback games: if the player didn't maintain a good concentration level, progress in the game was prevented. We chose to manipulate avatar speed as the method of preventing progress. The avatar's speed was set by the player's concentration level: the better the focus, the faster the avatar. If the player's theta/low beta ratio was above a certain threshold, the avatar barely moved at all. In this condition, the yellow bar in the bottom right corner (see Figure 1) showed the avatar's current speed. In the negative condition the three power-ups occurred in a fixed order every five patterns and the player could collect them by running through them.

We also created a version of the game that used no neurofeedback training (*control condition*). As in the positive condition, the game avatar gained speed by making progress in the game without dying. And similar to the negative condition, the player could collect the three power-ups in the game. We included the control condition to determine how the dependent measures were explained simply by the core mechanics of the game without the inclusion of neurofeedback training.

Integrating EEG
NeuroSky's MindWave Mobile headset was used to measure the player's brain activity. It is equipped with a sensor module (ThinkGear AM (TGAM) EEG sensor PCB module) to measure brainwaves on the forehead with dry-electrodes [48]. This device has the advantage that setting it up is quite fast compared to other (off-the-shelf) [13] devices and the electrode on the forehead has direct skin contact regardless of how much hair the participant has on their head. Using NeuroSky's ThinkGear PlugIn for Unity, the raw EEG activity was integrated in the game. The output frequency of the headset's data was once every second. The data output was volatile, which decreased the game experience. Therefore we smoothed the signal using a simple moving average window over three seconds.

To integrate EEG into the game, we used the ratio of theta activity over low beta activity. The baseline *theta/low beta ratio* was used during the game as a reference point to determine how well the participants were focusing and to set the *concentration level* that was used to integrate neurofeedback in both of the game versions. We used the theta/low beta ratio because Monastra et al. [41] showed a difference in this ratio (higher levels of theta EEG relative to low beta EEG activity) for people diagnosed with ADHD compared to those who were not. In addition, this ratio is used for training, because a higher power in the Theta band of EEG is related to decreased attention and low beta activity is related to increases in both hyperactivity and impulsivity [60]. Neurofeedback training has successfully helped in lowering the ratio of theta/low beta activity [2,35,42,56].

During calibration, we measured the theta/low beta ratio and took the minimum as a reference point throughout the game. We mapped the theta/low beta ratio to a 100 % scale, where 0 % means low focus/concentration and 100 % means good concentration. The minimum theta/low beta measured during calibration was set as 90 % concentration to allow for improvement over the game.

To integrate the theta/low beta ratio into the game mechanics we used a sigmoid function to map it to either the avatar speed or the charging speed of the power-up meter. This allowed for a high response when the participants increased their focus from low to medium high. If the player already was highly concentrated, small changes in speed (avatar speed or charging speed of the power-up meter) were visible. Because the theta/low beta ratio data provided by the headset were volatile, we mapped the avatar speed function to discrete categories to provide a better game experience. Based on the sigmoid function, the categories set a maximum speed for different ranges of the theta/low beta ratio. If the player's theta/low beta ratio changed and fell into a different category, the avatar then smoothly accelerated or decelerated until it reached the next threshold. This way of integrating the raw EEG data into the game was shown to create a joyful game experience during pilot testing.

Procedures and Methods

After giving informed consent, participants were randomly assigned to one of the three game conditions. Following this, they completed the Positive and Negative Affect Scale (PANAS), which measures positive affect and negative affect through rating agreement with 20-items (e.g., afraid, excited) on a 5-point scale [64]. PANAS has been successfully used to measure affective states arising from gameplay [4]. Next, the NeuroSky MindWave Mobile was fitted to the participant's head and the game, controls, and specific information related to their particular condition were each explained. The participants were instructed to keep the concentration meter as high as possible during the game by relaxing and focusing. Participants then played the game for 15 minutes.

After finishing the game, the participants completed several post-experiment questionnaires. First, participants completed the PANAS again to measure post-play affect. Following this, they completed the Player Experience of Need Satisfaction (PENS) scale [52], which measures how well the game satisfies needs as described by Self

Determination Theory [51]. Participants rated their agreement with a series of 21 statements on a 5-point scale that described their perceived competence (experience of mastery of game challenges), autonomy (engaging in play under their own volition), relatedness (feeling connected to others), immersion (feeling transported into the game), and intuitive control (feeling that the controls were natural) in the game. We also used the Intrinsic Motivation Inventory (IMI) [39], which measures intrinsic motivation within gameplay through agreement with 18 items using a 5-point scale. The IMI assesses the dimensions of interest-enjoyment, effort-importance, competence (which we left out because we assessed it using the PENS scale), and pressure-tension during play. Finally, we finished with a demographic questionnaire that asked basic questions about the players and their game expertise.

Participants and Apparatus

Fifty-three participants (34 females and 19 males), aged 18 to 49 (mean of 25) were recruited from a local university. One participant was removed due to a calibration error, leaving 19 players in each of the positive and negative conditions and 14 in the control condition, which was included for comparison. Five participants stated they were diagnosed with a condition that affects their ability to concentrate; however, we asked for no further explanation. Inspection of the data from these five participants did not differ significantly from the rest of the sample.

The experiment was conducted in a private room in a laboratory at the University of Saskatchewan. The game was played on an iMac with a 21.5-inch monitor. The resolution was 1920x1080 px and the game had a resolution of 582x835 px.

Data Analyses

All data analyses were performed with IBM SPSS Statistics 23. We performed a Multivariate Analysis of Variance with condition (positive, negative, control) as a between-subjects factor on the PENS scales, IMI scales, and positive and negative affect change from baseline. We controlled for Type 1 error with Bonferroni-corrected (α=.05) pairwise comparisons. We also conducted a repeated-measures ANOVA on the EEG data over time, as described below.

RESULTS

We present our results as organized by our research questions.

Efficacy of Training

Our first research question asked: Does positive reinforcement work better than negative reinforcement at motivating players to lower their theta/low beta ratio?

Figure 2 shows the average theta/low beta ratio for participants in each of the positive and negative conditions (we did not collect brain activity in the control condition) for each minute of play. The figure suggests that participants in the positive condition are better at keeping their theta/low beta ratio low.

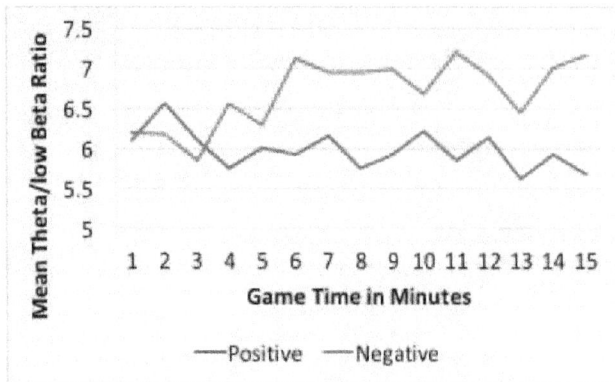

Figure 2. Average theta/low beta ratios over game time

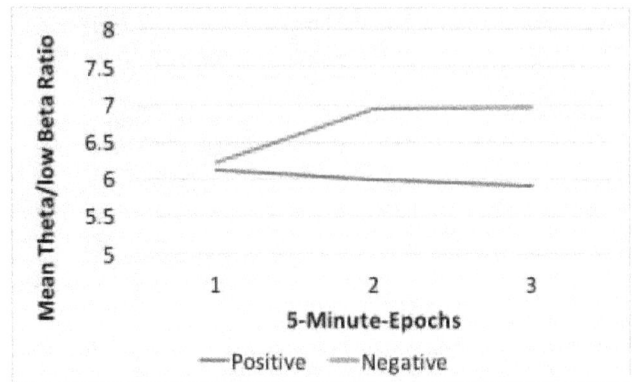

Figure 3. Average theta/low beta ratios for the 5-minute-epochs

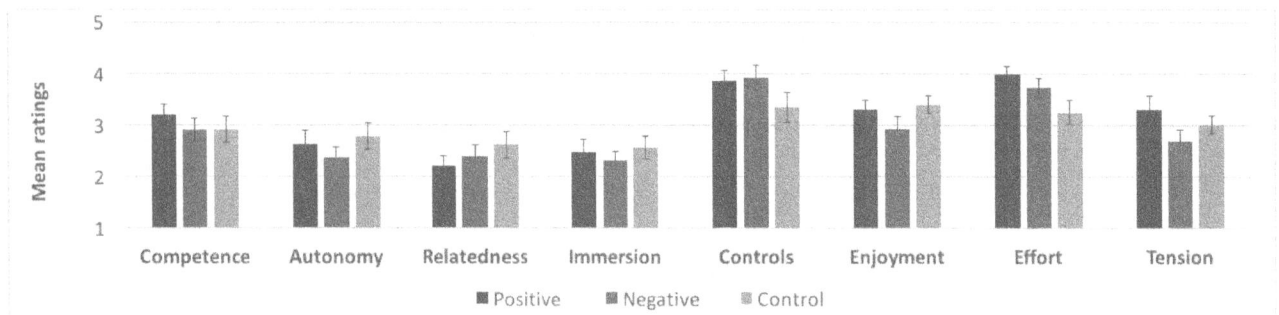

Figure 4. Mean ± SE ratings on the PENS questionnaire and IMI questionnaire (scale 1-5, where 5 indicates more agreement).

To analyze this, we used an epoch analysis with three 5-minutes epochs (beginning is minutes 1-5, middle is minutes 6-10, and end is minutes 11-15). A RM-ANOVA with time as the within-subjects factor and reinforcement (positive, negative) as the between-subjects factor showed no significant main effects of reinforcement ($F_{1,36}=1.42$, p=.242) or time ($F_{2,72}=2.03$, p=.139), but a significant time by reinforcement interaction ($F_{2,72}=4.87$, p=.010, $\eta^2=.119$). Pairwise comparisons (using the Bonferroni correction) revealed that there was no change from epoch one to epoch two (p=.99) or three (p=.99) in the positive condition, but there was significant increase in the theta/low beta ratio in the negative condition for both the first and second epoch (both p=.015); see Figure 3.

Needs Satisfaction during Play

Our second research question asked whether or not the experience of more competence, autonomy or immersion in the positive reinforcement condition was driving these EEG differences; thus we investigated whether in-game needs satisfaction was different depending on reinforcement type.

A multivariate ANOVA with condition (positive, negative, control) as a between-subjects factor on the five measures of in-game needs satisfaction shows no significant effect of game condition on competence ($F_{2,49}=.68$, p=.509), autonomy ($F_{2,49}=.72$, p=.493), relatedness ($F_{2,49}=.78$, p=.465), immersion ($F_{2,49}=.36$, p=.696), or intuitive control ($F_{2,49}=1.48$, p=.239). This suggests that there was no difference in how well the game versions satisfied needs within play. See Figure 4.

Intrinsic Motivation: Enjoyment and Effort

Our third research question asked: are players enjoying the positive reinforcement condition more or investing more effort? As such, we tested whether motivation was different depending on reinforcement type.

A multivariate ANOVA with condition (positive, negative, control) as a between-subjects factor on the measures of intrinsic motivation showed that there was no significant effect of game condition on enjoyment ($F_{2,49}=1.53$, p=.226) or tension ($F_{2,49}=1.85$, p=.168); however, there was a significant effect on effort ($F_{2,49}=3.304$, p=.045, $\eta^2=.12$). Pairwise comparisons (using the Bonferroni correction) showed that the players perceived that they invested more effort in the positive condition than in the control condition (p=.041) and that no other pairwise comparisons were significant; see Figure 4.

Positive and Negative Affect

Our final research question asked whether the positive reinforcement condition yielded more positive affect, thus we investigated whether the resulting affective changes were different depending on reinforcement type.

A multivariate ANOVA with condition (positive, negative, control) as a between-subjects factor on the changes in positive affect and negative affect (i.e., difference from baseline) showed that there was no significant effect of reinforcement type on negative affect ($F_{2,49}=.12$, p=.886); however, there was a significant effect on positive affect ($F_{2,49}=3.614$, p=.034, $\eta^2=.13$). Pairwise comparisons (using the Bonferroni correction) showed positive affect increase was higher in the positive condition than in the negative condition (p=.039); see Figure 5. No other pairwise comparisons were significant.

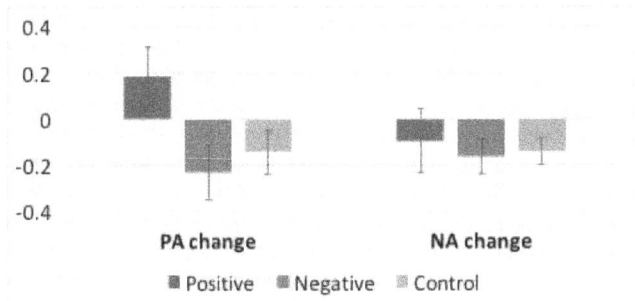

Figure 5. Mean ± SE Positive Affect (PA) and Negative Affect (NA) change from baseline to post-play questionnaire.

Summary of Results

Our results show that using positive reinforcement yielded more effort for players than playing the control game, and that it resulted in greater increases in positive affect than the negative reinforcement condition. In addition, the positive reinforcement condition was better at helping players lower their theta/low beta EEG ratio than the negative condition. As expected, positive reinforcement is better for motivating players and producing positive affect change.

DISCUSSION

Our results suggest that the positive reinforcement condition was more effective at helping players lower their theta/low beta ratio as compared to the negative reinforcement condition. However, we did not find any differences in the needs satisfaction measures, suggesting that all three versions satisfy needs similarly during play. We did find a significant difference in experience regarding the effort invested in the game and positive affect change. In the following section, we will have a closer look at the findings and limitations of this study.

Explanation of Findings on Experience

The results showed that playing the positive condition resulted in significantly higher positive affect change after play as compared to before the game (see Figure 5), whereas the negative condition and the control condition saw reductions in positive affect over the course of play. A higher positive affect has been associated with a state of higher concentration [64], which is corroborated by the lower theta/low beta ratio we measured. It is unclear what the cause of the increase in positive affect was. It is possible that the use of a positive stimulus (i.e., power-ups) generated more positive affect because it is an encouraging game mechanic. It is also possible that effective self-regulation encourages more positive feelings or that the non-significant benefits of positive reinforcement on enjoyment, competence, autonomy, and immersion together translated into significantly more positive affect. More work is needed to derive the sources of the improved affect in the positive reinforcement condition.

A higher positive affect is indicative of pleasurable engagement and we noticed (anecdotally) that only after playing the positive condition did participants mention that it was fun to play. However, we measured enjoyment using the intrinsic motivation scale and found no significant differences between the conditions. Although the mean enjoyment was higher in the positive condition than the negative condition, there was high variance in responses, and the results failed to reach significance. We see a similar trend in the satisfaction of competence and autonomy. The lack of differences regarding need satisfaction might be related to the high variance of response and relatively small sample size; however, they might also be driven by the fact that the game mechanics, dynamics, and aesthetics [23] for the different conditions are almost identical. The player achieves competence and autonomy by mastering the mechanics and dynamics. The aesthetics related to the desirable emotional response in the player likely influence immersion. Player satisfaction of needs in our study was mainly driven by their experience with the game mechanics and controls, and less by the minor variation in gameplay between the positive reinforcement and negative reinforcement conditions. That we saw differences in effort, positive affect change, and efficacy of the training itself in an experiment with such subtle differences between the game conditions is indicative of the potentially powerful differences that can result from positive versus negative reinforcement in neurofeedback training games.

Taking a Closer Look at the EEG Data

A closer look at Figure 2 reveals some interesting observations. During the calibration phase (first game minute) there was no difference between the positive and negative reinforcement conditions – both groups start within a similar theta/low beta ratio range. Positive reinforcement players initially raise their theta/low beta ratio and negative reinforcement players initially lower it. As mentioned previously, the second half of the calibration was intentionally designed to be difficult to play and required a lot of focused attention from the players. After calibration, the game became a little bit easier to play. For the positive condition, there was no instantaneous presentation of a negative reinforcer when they did not stick to the intense concentration, because the avatar kept moving at the same pace. For the negative condition, there was an immediate reduction in speed after calibration if they did not concentrate hard enough (a concentration of at least 70 % was required to maintain speed). But because the avatar did not slow down to its minimum speed immediately and all patterns were still new to them, it might have been easier for them to focus initially. However, in the third minute, the negative reinforcement participants experienced a turning point and an increase of the theta/low beta ratio. It is possible that the demotivation of the avatar slowing down took the participants out of the flow of the game and caused them to lose focus. It could be that it is easier to focus in the game when the avatar moves more quickly. More research is needed to isolate and explain the effects of gameplay on the EEG data.

Figure 2 also demonstrates that the differences between the positive reinforcement condition and the negative reinforcement condition are driven by a rise in theta-low beta in the negative conditions while theta/low beta of the positive group remained flat. This has two implications. First it is unclear whether positive reinforcement is helping players self-regulate attention or whether negative feedback is harming players. Because we did not collect EEG data for the control condition participants, we cannot know how the performance of reinforced players compares to play without any form of neurofeedback training. Second, the goal of neurofeedback training is to help players reduce their theta/low beta ratio. In our most successful approach (the positive reinforcement condition), participants were only able to prevent their ratio from rising. It is possible that the game interferes with the player's ability to focus; however, as neurofeedback training should occur over months with multiple sessions per week, it is more likely that the participants simply needed more time to figure out how to self-regulate.

In the negative reinforcement condition, participants were unable to lower their theta/low beta ratios, or even prevent them from increasing. It is possible that the game mechanic did not translate to effective training. More likely, the inability of participants to exert control over the avatar through self-regulation resulted in demotivation. Participants may have stopped trying because the avatar was progressing so slowly anyways, and they just gave up. One of the biggest criticisms of negative reinforcement is that people don't know how to improve because there is little specificity in being presented with a negative reinforcer for not doing things correctly [63,55]. Our participants may have experienced this lack of specificity and thus were demotivated to continue trying. This hypothesis goes along with the results of Barbero et al., who suspected that demotivation was the reason that participants in their study didn't acquire the skills necessary for controlling a brain-computer interface [3].

Application of the Findings to Neurofeedback Training
Our study examines the EEG data of participants during play, which is likely to predict the positive outcomes related to neurofeedback training over time, i.e., improved self-regulation of attention, improved behaviour, or improved sleep hygiene. It is important in iterative design to have interim measures of evaluation – otherwise, the tight cycles of design, evaluate, iterate would not be possible. EEG collected during play provides a proxy measure as it is the feature being trained; however, full deployments of the training protocol with standard outcome measures and measurement using clinical-grade EEG devices are needed to draw conclusions about the efficacy of training.

Furthermore, although our goal is to build neurofeedback training games for children with attention deficits due to ADHD or FASD, our study was conducted with volunteers in the university environment. Again, it is important to iterate on designs before testing in full deployments, and generating and evaluating ideas with easy-to-access participants is a common practice when designing technologies to help people with special needs. Not only does this help speed progress due to the lack of access to special populations, but it also respects the time and commitment of families looking for solutions for their children with attention deficits. Asking these parents and children for their commitment to a long-term training program that has not been tested in an iterative cycle could provide false hope to people who are trying to improve their lives. This approach of using participants who are not invested in the need for solutions in the early stages of iteratively designing technologies for people with special needs has been shown to be effective for designing games for the elderly (e.g., [16]) and interactive applications for people with mobility disabilities (e.g., [17,18]).

In the end, our goal is to translate our work to people with attention deficits (e.g., ADHD, FASD). Kaiser et al. [26] showed that both healthy people and those diagnosed with ADHD improved doing neurofeedback training based on the T.O.V.A. score, which is an outcome measure of neurofeedback training used for ADHD. Additionally, It was shown [62,49,54] that healthy participants can modulate brain activity using neurofeedback, so it is reasonable to assume that we can translate our approach to people with attention deficits in the future.

Beyond Neurofeedback Training
Although positive reinforcement has not been explored in neurofeedback games, it has been shown to provide value in motivating physical activity during exergame play. Ketcheson et al. [27,28] showed that providing power-ups in a game as a reward for keeping heart rate in the desired range increased the enjoyment of the game, which is in line with our results for neurofeedback games for training. There are many examples of serious games for contexts other than neurofeedback training in which our results apply. Although one of the reasons that current games use negative reinforcement is that positive reinforcement could interfere with existing reward schemata, games designed to motivate behaviour, learning, or dedication might benefit from using positive reinforcement.

Limitations and Future Work
Our results show the positive impact of using positive reinforcement instead of negative reinforcement; however, there are limitations in what we can infer from our study.

First, we do not know whether the positive reinforcement condition is helpful or the negative condition is harmful. Future work will need to differentiate these conditions. Although it may be tempting to collect EEG data in a control condition to make this distinction, EEG data collected in the control condition would not actually be indicative of a typical experimental 'control'. Because players in that condition were not instructed to self-regulate their attention, and had no feedback to actually do so, their EEG data would not reflect a baseline 'control'. It would be difficult to say what the theta/low beta data gathered in a non-feedback condition would represent, as it would not indicate baseline performance. To best understand how our data compares to a control condition, we can only compare to previous work that shows how players lower their theta/low beta ratio through neurofeedback (NF) training. Our participants trained for a short time, and our results suggest future explorations in using positive reinforcement for longer periods of NF training.

Second, the sample size is small. Our goal was to investigate the initial relationship between reinforcement and efficacy of neurofeedback training games. Our results suggest that positive reinforcement is better (using several metrics); however, we plan to conduct a larger study to replicate our findings with sufficient power to determine whether there are small differences in needs satisfaction due to positive or negative reinforcement.

Third, receiving power-ups after a certain amount of time (based on the concentration) was not an instantaneous feedback, in contrast to controlling the avatar speed, which responded quickly to changes in player concentration. Investigating the underlying factors in the design of the two reinforcement types to uncover the source of the differences is important for the long-term generalizability of the work.

Fourth we used an off-the-shelf EEG device, the NeuroSky. Although it provides raw data split into the main frequency bands, it isn't as accurate as a clinical-grade EEG cap with up to 256 electrodes [13]. However, one of its biggest benefits is the fast setup time and placement of the electrode on the forehead [13]; reliable skin contact can be easy established because of the absence of hair at this point. Also the users themselves can adjust it on their head, which is important, as the ultimate goal of neurofeedback games is to make them available for in the home to give broad access to training. Clinics already use lower-grade EEG during training – both in the clinic as well as at home. Finally, we do not use the EEG device to measure cognitive change but to drive interaction with a game during training. To measure pre- and post changes in cognition as a result of an intervention, a clinical-grade EEG would be needed, which we intend to use in our future work.

Finally, training sessions in neurofeedback training usually last 30 to 60 minutes and are repeated several times per week for 20 to 40 sessions. Using one training session of just 15 minutes might be short to indicate potential trends in the efficacy of the training system (although some training sessions only last 20 minutes, including breaks [21]). It has been reported that (healthy) subjects are able to modulate their brain activity within one to five sessions [21,49]. A longer-term deployment is needed to see whether the training is effective and whether or not the initial differences between positive and negative reinforcement hold up over time. It could be that positive reinforcement is

better initially, but that negative reinforcement would work better in the longer term. We will investigate this further. It could also be interesting to combine the positive and negative reinforcement techniques. Previous research showed that using screen obfuscations as a negative reinforcement did not ruin the game experience [38], and therefore combining both approaches could lead to increased variety and challenge – which could help motivate players in the long term.

CONCLUSION
Neurofeedback training has been shown to be effective at reducing symptoms related to epileptic seizures, attention deficits, and Asperger's Syndrome. It often uses games to motivate participation over the long term needed to see improvements. Most neurofeedback games use negative reinforcement to guide players – i.e., they are prevented from progressing or succeeding in the game if they are not in the right state – which is considered to be less effective than reinforcing positive behaviour through feedback when players do well.

We investigated whether using positive reinforcement is more successful than negative reinforcement through the design and evaluation of the experience and efficacy of a custom neurofeedback training game. Using the endless runner mechanic, we implemented two methods of driving gameplay through EEG activity – a positive reinforcement approach that rewarded players with power-ups, and a negative approach that removed a barrier on avatar speed when players showed focus. We demonstrated that positive reinforcement was more effective at encouraging players to keep their brain activity regulated. Furthermore, it generated more positive affect and motivated more investment of effort, suggesting that positive reinforcement in neurofeedback games provides both a better and more effective neurofeedback training experience.

Motivated by the desire design better neurofeedback games for kids with attention deficits, our results also have value for game designers trying to motivate behaviour in other serious contexts, such as persuasive games, learning games, and games designed for behaviour change.

ACKNOWLEDGEMENTS
We thank NSERC for funding, the Interaction Lab at the University of Saskatchewan, and our participants.

REFERENCES
1. Joaquin A Anguera, Jacqueline Boccanfuso, James L Rintoul, Omar Al-Hashimi, Farhoud Faraji, Jacqueline Janowich, Eric Kong, Yudy Larraburo, Christine Rolle, E Johnston, and others. 2013. Video game training enhances cognitive control in older adults. *Nature* 501, 7465 (2013), 97–101.

2. Ali Reza Bakhshayesh, Sylvana Hänsch, Anne Wyschkon, Mohammad Javad Rezai, and Günter Esser. 2011. Neurofeedback in ADHD: a single-blind randomized controlled trial. *European child & adolescent psychiatry* 20, 9 (2011), 481–491.

3. Álvaro Barbero and Moritz Grosse-Wentrup. Biased feedback in brain-computer interfaces. *Journal of neuroengineering and rehabilitation* 7, no. 1 (2010): 1.

4. Max Birk, Regan Mandryk, Matthew Miller, and Kathrin Gerling. 2015. How Self-Esteem Shapes our Interactions with Play Technologies. In *The ACM SIGCHI Annual Symposium on Computer-Human Interaction in Play (CHI PLAY)*. London, UK.

5. John Boddy, Annabel Carver, and Kevin Rowley. Effects of positive and negative verbal reinforcement on performance as a function of extraversion-introversion: Some tests of Gray's theory. *Personality and Individual Differences* 7.1 (1986): 81-88.

6. Walter R Boot, Arthur F Kramer, Daniel J Simons, Monica Fabiani, and Gabriele Gratton. 2008. The effects of video game playing on attention, memory, and executive control. *Acta psychologica* 129, 3 (2008), 387–398.

7. Vratislav Cmiel, Oto Janousek, and Jana Kolarova. 2011. EEG biofeedback. In Proceedings of the 4th International Symposium on Applied Sciences in Biomedical and Communication Technologies. ACM, 54.

8. Sunny Consolvo, David W McDonald, and James A Landay. 2009. Theory-driven design strategies for technologies that support behavior change in everyday life. In *Proceedings of the SIGCHI Conference on Human Factors in Computing Systems*. ACM, 405–414.

9. Thomas H Davenport and John C Beck. 2013. *The attention economy: Understanding the new currency of business*. Harvard Business Press.

10. Iser G. Deleon, Pamela L. Neidert, Bonita M. Anders, and Vanessa Rodriguez-Catter. Choices between positive and negative reinforcement during treatment for escape-maintained behavior."*Journal of Applied Behavior Analysis* 34, no. 4 (2001): 521-525.

11. Sebastian Deterding, Dan Dixon, Rilla Khaled, and Lennart Nacke. 2011. From Game Design Elements to Gamefulness: Defining "Gamification". In *Proceedings of the 15th International Academic MindTrek Conference: Envisioning Future Media Environments (MindTrek '11)*. ACM, New York, NY, USA, 9–15. http://doi.acm.org/10.1145/2181037.2181040

12. W. Alex Edmonds and Gershon Tenenbaum. 2011. *Case Studies in Applied Psychophysiology: Neurofeedback and Biofeedback Treatments for Advances in Human Performance*. Wiley.

13. Joshua I. Ekandem, Timothy A. Davis, Ignacio Alvarez, Melva T. James, and Juan E. Gilbert. "Evaluating the ergonomics of BCI devices for research and experimentation." *Ergonomics* 55, no. 5 (2012): 592-598.

14. Michael J. Frank, Brion S. Woroch, and Tim Curran. "Error-related negativity predicts reinforcement learning and conflict biases." *Neuron* 47.4 (2005): 495-501.

15. Tracy Fullerton. 2014. Game Design Workshop: A Playcentric Approach to Creating Innovative Games, Third Edition. CRC Press.

16. Kathrin Gerling, Kristen Dergousoff, and Regan Mandryk. 2013a. Is Movement Better? Comparing Sedentary and Motion-Based Game Controls for Older Adults. In *Graphics Interface 2013*. Regina, SK, Canada, 133–140.

17. Kathrin M. Gerling, Regan L. Mandryk, and Michael R. Kalyn. 2013. Wheelchair-based game design for older adults. In *Proceedings of the 15th International ACM SIGACCESS Conference on Computers and Accessibility* (ASSETS '13). ACM, New York, NY, USA, , Article 27 , 8 pages. http://doi.acm.org/10.1145/2513383.2513436

18. Kathrin Gerling, Matthew Miller, Regan Mandryk, Max Birk, and Jan Smeddinck. 2014. Effects of Balancing for Physical Abilities on Player Performance, Experience and Self-Esteem in Exergames. In *CHI'14: Proceedings of the 2014 CHI Conference on Human Factors in Computing Systems*. 2201–2210.

19. Holger Gevensleben, Birgit Holl, Björn Albrecht, Dieter Schlamp, Oliver Kratz, Petra Studer, Susanne Wangler, Aribert Rothenberger, Gunther H Moll, and Hartmut Heinrich. 2009. Distinct EEG effects related to neurofeedback training in children with ADHD: a randomized controlled trial. *International Journal of Psychophysiology* 74, 2 (2009), 149–157.

20. C. Shawn Green and Daphne Bavelier. 2003. Action video game modifies visual selective attention. *Nature* 423, no. 6939 (2003): 534-537.

21. Hartmut Heinrich, Holger Gevensleben, and Ute Strehl. 2007. Annotation: Neurofeedback–train your brain to train behaviour. *Journal of Child Psychology and Psychiatry* 48, 1 (2007), 3–16.

22. Sara Ilstedt Hjelm and Carolina Browall. 2000. Brainball-using brain activity for cool competition. In *Proceedings of NordiCHI*, Vol. 7. 9.

23. Robin Hunicke, Marc LeBlanc, and Robert Zubek. 2004. MDA: A formal approach to game design and game research. In *Proceedings of the AAAI Workshop on Challenges in Game AI*, Vol. 4.

24. Brainmaster Technologies Inc. 2015. Neurofeedback Games. (21 September 2015). http://www.brainmaster.com/page/neurofeedback-games/.

25. Susanne M Jaeggi, Martin Buschkuehl, John Jonides, and Priti Shah. 2011. Short-and long-term benefits of

cognitive training. *Proceedings of the National Academy of Sciences* 108, 25 (2011), 10081–10086.

26. David A Kaiser and Siegfried Othmer. 2000. Effect of neurofeedback on variables of attention in a large multi-center trial. *Journal of Neurotherapy* 4, 1 (2000), 5–15.

27. Mallory Ketcheson, Zi Ye, and T.C. Nicholas Graham. 2015. Designing for Exertion: How Heart-Rate Power-ups Increase Physical Activity in Exergames. In *The ACM SIGCHI Annual Symposium on Computer-Human Interaction in Play (CHI PLAY)*. London, UK, 79-89.

28. Mallory Ketcheson, Luke Walker, and T.C. Nicholas Graham. 2016. Thighrim and Calf-Life: a study of the conversion of off-the-shelf video games into exergames. In *Proceedings of the 2016 CHI Conference on Human Factors in Computing Systems*. ACM, 2681–2692.

29. Joseph S. Lalli, Timothy R. Vollmer, Patrick R. Progar, Carrie Wright, John Borrero, Dency Daniel, Christine Hoffner Barthold, Kathy Tocco, and William May. Competition between positive and negative reinforcement in the treatment of escape behavior. *Journal of Applied Behavior Analysis* 32, no. 3 (1999): 285-296.

30. Daniel M Landers, Steven J Petruzzello, Walter Salazar, Debra J Crews, Karla A Kubitz, Timothy L Gannon, and Myungwoo Han. 1991. The influence of electrocortical biofeedback on performance in pre-elite archers. *Medicine & Science in Sports & Exercise* (1991).

31. Mark R Lepper and Thomas W Malone. 1987. Intrinsic motivation and instructional effectiveness in computer-based education. In *Conative and Affective Process Analysis*, Richard E. Snow and Marshall J. Farr (Eds.). Aptitude, learning, and instruction, Vol. 3. L. Erlbaum, 255–286.

32. James J Lin, Lena Mamykina, Silvia Lindtner, Gregory Delajoux, and Henry B Strub. 2006. Fish'n'Steps: Encouraging physical activity with an interactive computer game. In *International Conference on Ubiquitous Computing*. Springer, 261–278.

33. Nicholas Lofthouse, L Eugene Arnold, and Elizabeth Hurt. 2012. Current status of neurofeedback for attention-deficit/hyperactivity disorder. *Current psychiatry reports* 14, 5 (2012), 536–542.

34. Joel F Lubar and WW Bahler. 1976. Behavioral management of epileptic seizures following EEG biofeedback training of the sensorimotor rhythm. *Biofeedback and Self-regulation* 1, 1 (1976), 77–104.

35. Joel F Lubar, Michie Odle Swartwood, Jeffery N Swartwood, and Phyllis H O'Donnell. 1995. Evaluation of the effectiveness of EEG neurofeedback training for ADHD in a clinical setting as measured by changes in TOVA scores, behavioral ratings, and WISC-R performance. *Biofeedback and self-regulation* 20, 1 (1995), 83–99.

36. Judith O Lubar and Joel F Lubar. 1984. Electroencephalographic biofeedback of SMR and beta for treatment of attention deficit disorders in a clinical setting. *Biofeedback and self-regulation* 9, 1 (1984), 1-23.

37. John W Maag. 2001. Rewarded by punishment: Reflections on the disuse of positive reinforcement in schools. *Exceptional children* 67, 2 (2001), 173–186.

38. Regan L Mandryk, Shane Dielschneider, Michael R Kalyn, Christopher P Bertram, Michael Gaetz, Andre Doucette, Brett A Taylor, Alison Pritchard Orr, and Kathy Keiver. 2013. Games as neurofeedback training for children with FASD. In *Proceedings of the 12th International Conference on Interaction Design and Children*. ACM, 165–172.

39. Edward McAuley, Terry Duncan, and Vance V Tammen. 1989. Psychometric properties of the Intrinsic Motivation Inventory in a competitive sport setting: A confirmatory factor analysis. *Research quarterly for exercise and sport* 60, 1 (1989), 48–58.

40. LLC Mindspire. 2001. Helping Video Games "Rewire Our Minds". (2001).

41. Vincent J Monastra, Joel F Lubar, Michael Linden, Peter VanDeusen, George Green, William Wing, Arthur Phillips, and T Nick Fenger. 1999. Assessing attention deficit hyperactivity disorder via quantitative electroencephalography: an initial validation study. *Neuropsychology* 13, 3 (1999), 424.

42. Vincent J Monastra, Steven Lynn, Michael Linden, Joel F Lubar, John Gruzelier, and Theodore J La Vaque. 2006. Electroencephalographic biofeedback in the treatment of attention-deficit/hyperactivity disorder. *Journal of Neurotherapy* 9, 4 (2006), 5–34.

43. Vincent J Monastra, Donna M Monastra, and Susan George. 2002. The effects of stimulant therapy, EEG biofeedback, and parenting style on the primary symptoms of attention-deficit/hyperactivity disorder. *Applied psychophysiology and biofeedback* 27, 4 (2002), 231–249.

44. Tais S Moriyama, Guilherme Polanczyk, Arthur Caye, Tobias Banaschewski, Daniel Brandeis, and Luis A Rohde. 2012. Evidence-based information on the clinical use of neurofeedback for ADHD. *Neurotherapeutics* 9, 3 (2012), 588–598.

45. Lennart E. Nacke. 2013. An Introduction to Physiological Player Metrics for Evaluating Games. In *Game Analytics Game Analytics Maximizing the Value of Player Data*, Magy Seif El-Nasr, Anders Drachen, and Alessandro Canossa (Eds.). Springer, Chapter 26, 585–619

46. Wenya Nan, João Pedro Rodrigues, Jiali Ma, Xiaoting Qu, Feng Wan, Pui-In Mak, Peng Un Mak, Mang I Vai, and Agostinho Rosa. 2012. Individual alpha neurofeedback training effect on short term memory. *International journal of psychophysiology* 86, 1 (2012), 83–87.

47. NeuroSky. 2015a. EEG App - Brain Wave App | NeuroSky Store. (21 September 2015). http://store.neurosky.com/collections/apps.

48. NeuroSky. 2015. EEG Hardware Platforms. (21 September 2015). http://neurosky.com/biosensors/eeg-sensor/biosensors/.

49. Femke Nijboer, Adrian Furdea, Ingo Gunst, Jürgen Mellinger, Dennis J McFarland, Niels Birbaumer, and Andrea Kübler. 2008. An auditory brain–computer interface (BCI). *Journal of neuroscience methods* 167, 1 (2008), 43–50.

50. Joshua Raymond, Imran Sajid, Lesley A Parkinson, and John H Gruzelier. 2005. Biofeedback and dance performance: A preliminary investigation. *Applied Psychophysiology and Biofeedback* 30, 1 (2005), 65–73.

51. Scott Rigby and Richard M Ryan. 2011. *Glued to Games: How Video Games Draw Us In and Hold Us Spellbound*. ABC-CLIO.

52. Richard M Ryan, C Scott Rigby, and Andrew Przybylski. 2006. The motivational pull of video games: A self-determination theory approach. *Motivation and emotion* 30, 4 (2006), 344–360.

53. Katie Salen and Eric Zimmerman. 2004. *Rules of play: Game design fundamentals*. MIT press.

54. Michael Siniatchkin, Peter Kropp, and Wolf-Dieter Gerber. 2000. Neurofeedback – The significance of reinforcement and the search for an appropriate strategy for the success of self-regulation. *Applied psychophysiology and biofeedback* 25, 3 (2000), 167–175.

55. Burrhus Frederic Skinner. 2002. *Beyond Freedom and Dignity*. Penguin Books Limited, Chapter 2, 26–43.

56. Naomi J Steiner, Elizabeth C Frenette, Kirsten M Rene, Robert T Brennan, and Ellen C Perrin. 2014. Neurofeedback and cognitive attention training for children with attention-deficit hyperactivity disorder in schools. *Journal of Developmental & Behavioral Pediatrics* 35, 1 (2014), 18–27.

57. M Barry Sterman. 2000. Basic concepts and clinical findings in the treatment of seizure disorders with EEG operant conditioning. *Clinical EEG and Neuroscience* 31, 1 (2000), 45–55.

58. Unity Technologies. 2015. Unity - Game engine, tools and multiplatform. (21 September 2015). http://unity3d.com/unity.

59. Lynda Thompson, Michael Thompson, and Andrea Reid. 2010. Neurofeedback outcomes in clients with Asperger's syndrome. *Applied psychophysiology and biofeedback* 35, 1 (2010), 63–81.

60. Michael Thompson and Lynda Thompson. 2003. *The neurofeedback book: An introduction to basic concepts in applied psychophysiology*. Association for Applied Psychophysiology and Biofeedback.

61. Richard J Vallerand and Greg Reid. 1984. On the causal effects of perceived competence on intrinsic motivation: A test of cognitive evaluation theory. *Journal of Sport Psychology* 6, 1 (1984), 94–102.

62. David J Vernon. 2005. Can neurofeedback training enhance performance? An evaluation of the evidence with implications for future research. *Applied psychophysiology and biofeedback* 30, 4 (2005), 347–364.

63. Stephen Walker. 1975. *Learning and reinforcement*. Vol. 3. Taylor & Francis.

64. David Watson and Lee Anna Clark. 1999. The PANAS-X: Manual for the positive and negative affect schedule-expanded form. (1999).

65. Nathan Wilkinson, Rebecca P Ang, and Dion H Goh. 2008. Online video game therapy for mental health concerns: a review. *International journal of social psychiatry* 54, 4 (2008), 370–382.

Plant-based Games for Anxiety Reduction

Taiwoo Park
Michigan State University
East Lansing, MI, USA
twp@msu.edu

Tianyu Hu
Age of Learning Inc.
Glendale, CA, USA
ariel9011@gmail.com

Jina Huh
University of California, San Diego
La Jolla, CA, USA
jinahuh@ucsd.edu

ABSTRACT

More and more researchers are finding anxiety and stress as critical health problems influencing quality of life and various illnesses. Studies suggest gardening activities help with anxiety. Our goal is to create engaging ways for people to interact with plants and eventually reduce anxiety and stress. We made three short games employing a person's touch interaction with a plant as the input interface. Each of the three games implements a unique interaction: tapping, patting, and gentle pinching. We then tested the games with ten players, among whom five of them (the plant group) played the games with the plant as the input interface. The other five (the non-plant group) played the games with a pressure sensor board. The plant group showed decreased anxiety with a borderline statistical significance (p=0.054) with Cohen's d of 0.20 (i.e., 'small' effect), while the non-plant group showed a non-significant decrease in anxiety after the gameplay (p=0.65). We further examined which in-game elements contributed to calming the participants as well as the design elements that need to be improved for plant-based games.

Author Keywords

Experimental game, user interface design, anxiety reduction, human-plant interaction.

ACM Classification Keywords

H.5.m. Information interfaces and presentation (e.g., HCI): Miscellaneous.

INTRODUCTION

Handling anxiety and stress has become a significant concern for people dealing with complex tasks and responsibilities in their daily lives. 75% of Americans have experienced symptoms of stress in 2015 [1]. The study also highlighted the importance of emotional support for stress management; 43% of people without emotional support reported that their overall stress has increased in the past year, whereas only 26% of those with emotional support gave similar reports.

One promising medium for such emotional support is plants; calming and peaceful sense caused by caring for plants has been known to help with relaxation. Gardening

CHI PLAY '16, October 16 - 19, 2016, Austin, TX, USA
Copyright is held by the owner/author(s). Publication rights licensed to ACM.
ACM 978-1-4503-4456-2/16/10...$15.00
DOI: http://dx.doi.org/10.1145/2967934.2968094

activities can help reduce depression and stress [11,29]. A recent study showed that people unconsciously experienced calming responses after touching plant foliage [17].

In this paper, we designed and implemented three short games with a hardware prototype enabling touch sensing through plant leaves. We tested the games with student participants to explore potential factors that contribute to reducing anxiety after the interaction with plants as a game controller interface.

Figure 1. Example setting of plant-based game control.

BACKGROUND

Anxiety is an emotional state that includes feelings of apprehension, tension, and worry related to physiological arousal [24]. High anxiety has been known as a risk factor for hypertension [15] and coronary heart disease [12] alongside obesity and unhealthy behaviors such as smoking and binge drinking [28]. Significant causes of high anxiety include psychological stress [24], which can be induced by external stimuli or events [2].

Several types of interventions for anxiety reduction have been proposed and evaluated. Examples include breathing lessons [18], music [16], exercise, and meditation [4,19]. Mobile and sensor technologies facilitated the creation of new approaches, such as mobile acupressure based on on-line social support [20] and body-wide haptic feedback [32].

The potential of living or plant-based interfaces for aesthetic, experimental, and educational uses has been demonstrated by audio-visual embodiment of human touches on a plant [12,20,24,29]. Such exploration has opened an avenue of using plants as interfaces, where we envision a more interactive mode of intervention for health. However, researchers have underexplored using plants as game controller interfaces, especially in the context of anxiety reduction. Our experimental work provides a novel starting point to examining plant-based interfaces and mental health interventions.

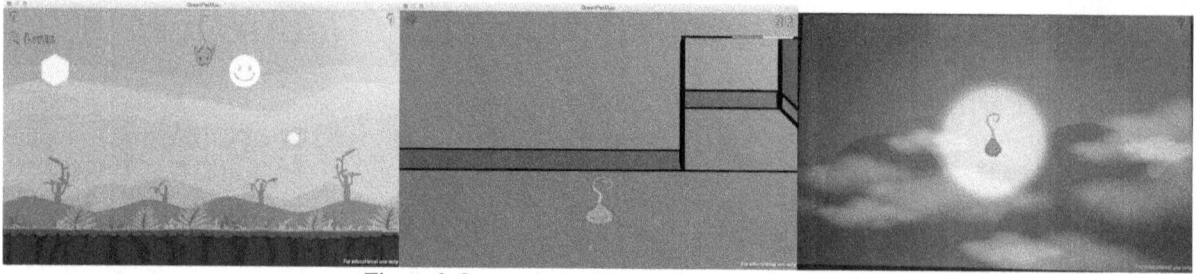

Figure 2. Screenshots of three plant pet games.

PLANT GAMES AND HARDWARE PROTOTYPE

The plant-based games in this paper consist of plant pet games and a touch-sensing controller attached to plants.

Plant Pet Games

We designed three short games on petting plants: The Jump game, the Sleep game, and the Meditation game. These games incorporated the living and responsive nature of plants through a virtual character, called a *"plant pet,"* which requires gentle care. The games employ specific physical input schemes of tapping, patting, and gentle pinching, respectively. We have implemented the three games using the Unity3D game development toolkit.

The Jump game (Figure 2, left). Players tap the plant with fingers to make the pet jump and obtain approaching items. To control the jumping height, the player can change the number of fingers. More fingers can make the plant pet jump higher. The game includes two items; players need to collect blue bubbles, which are nutritious, and players need to avoid red bubbles, which are toxic and will harm the pet.
The Sleep game (Figure 2, middle). The goal of this game is to put the plant pet to sleep by patting the plant slowly and gently. The plant touch sensitivity is set high for this game. Once a player succeeds in maintaining the touch continuously and gently enough, the plant pet will start to sleep. Otherwise, if the player touches with strong force or fails to pat continuously, the pet will get angry and run away. **The Meditation game** (Figure 3, right). In this game, there is a golden halo on the center of the screen, and the player is required to keep the plant pet inside the halo. The plant pet falls down by gravity, and the player gently pinches the plant to lift up the plant pet. The pinching pressure is mapped to the lifting force. Thus, the player needs to carefully adjust their fingers to control the pet. If the pet comes out of the halo within a certain amount of time, the game is over.

Implementation of Plant-based Interface

To develop the plant-based interface, we used touch-sensing controller hardware employing a capacitive-sensing mechanism from an electrode attached to plants. We implemented the touch sensing system with Adafruit Flora, an Arduino-compatible microcontroller. For touch-sensing logic, we used the Arduino Capsense library. We observed that the capacitance value from the electrode changes while a user physically touches a plant's skin. The broader and stronger the touch is, the higher the value will be. We programmed the system to calibrate the range of

capacitance values before each game play, as it may vary depending on player's physical status, such as sweat, the amount of static electricity, the surrounding humidity, and the plant type. Similar implementation may include Makey-Makey [1], however, we discarded it due to its additional requirement of additional 'earth' electrode during interaction.

To evaluate the comparative effectiveness of the plant-based interface, we built another interface to be used as a control condition with a pressure sensor pad. The interactions required for the games were identical to that of the plant interface: tapping, patting, and pinching. The pressure sensor pad was placed slightly beyond the edge of the table to enable pinching.

METHODS

Participants. We recruited graduate students from a US public university in the Midwest through a class email distribution list. Twenty students responded to the recruitment. Our target users were those facing higher anxiety levels. We asked the 20 respondents to complete the State-Trait Anxiety Inventory (STAI) survey [26], which is widely used to test overall anxious response and current anxiety level in a score ranging from 40 to 160. Based on the STAI score, we chose ten candidates who had higher scores than the average of the 20 respondents as the final participants (4 F, 6 M). Five of the participants were randomly selected and assigned to the non-plant group, who played the three short games using the pressure sensor board. The other five were assigned to the plant group, and they played the Plant Pet Game using the plant-based interface.

Study Design and Analysis. The participants played the three games using the controller assigned to their group, either the plant-based interface or the pressure sensor board. Before and after the gameplay, they were asked to complete the STAI survey. A semi-structured interview followed after the end of study. The order of the three games to be played was decided using the Latin Square method. The participants were encouraged to think aloud [31] while playing the three games. The participants were allowed to play the games as long as they wanted. The participants played the games for 10-20 minutes. For the end of study interview, we asked the participants about their overall gaming experiences, including relaxation while gaming as well as perceptions about the gaming interface. We did not

---
[1] www.makeymakey.com

The non-plant group				The plant group			
Player#	STAI score		Δ	Player#	STAI score		Δ
	Pre	Post			Pre	Post	
P1	89	87	−2	P6	94	82	−12
P2	93	96	+3	P7	93	95	+2
P3	110	100	−10	P8	98	81	−17
P4	89	93	+4	P9	107	97	−10
P5	101	100	−1	P10	97	91	−6
Mean	96.4	95.2	−1.2	Mean	97.8	89.2	−8.6
Median	99	96	−1	Median	97	91	−10
SD	9.04	5.45	5.54	SD	5.54	7.36	7.13

Table 1. Pre- and post-test STAI scores for the non-plant group and the plant group.

reveal the purpose of the study to the participants until the end of the study. All think-aloud and interview data were transcribed and analyzed using open coding [27] to examine emerging themes. We then created an affinity diagram [14] for axial coding to understand common themes and patterns across the codes that were generated. We used MemoSort, an online collaborative tool for affinity diagramming.

FINDINGS

We first describe the STAI survey results, followed by the interview results.

STAI Survey

Table 1 shows the STAI survey scores before and after game play. We ran a two-tailed paired t-test for each group to compare the STAI survey scores before and after the gameplay. For the plant group, the difference between the pre-gameplay STAI survey score (M=97.8, SD=5.54) and the post-gameplay STAI survey score (M=89.2, SD=7.36) was at around the borderline to show statistical significance (t(4)=2.70, p=0.054), with a Cohen's *d* of 0.20, which indicates the potential of 'small' effect [7]. In the non-plant group, the differences in the scores for the pre-gameplay STAI survey (M=96.4, SD=9.04) and the post-gameplay STAI survey (M=95.2, SD=5.45) was not significant (t(4)=0.48, p=0.65).

Our findings show that although the sample size is small, playing with the plant interface has a potential to help reduce the anxiety level. With the interview findings below, we discuss potential explanations for our findings.

Perceived effect of the Plant Pet Game

The participants talked about the game as a relaxing activity and how the game should be designed to trade off between boredom and anxiety. The participants also described visual and acoustic aesthetics that could influence their game play.

Repetitive interaction as a relaxing activity

Participants found that the simple and repetitive nature of the game interaction helped them focus and led them to feel relaxed: "*I could concentrate better during jumping game, and felt most calm and peaceful. [...] The simple and repetitive tasks helped me calm*" (P9); "*Focusing on "one thing" helped to concentrate and was also meditative.*" (P2)

This finding agrees with prior studies in that activities involving repetitive muscular movements such as knitting can elicit a "*relaxation response,*" including decreased heart rate, blood pressure, and muscle tension [5].

P10 attempted to intentionally avoid anxiety by modifying the gameplay. P10 avoided looking at the screen to better focus on controlling the plant interface: "*[For the petting game,] staring at the screen made me feel more anxious, since I kept wondering when it would finally fall asleep.*"

Negative responses against anxiety

The goal of the games being to meditate and relax led to a unique limitation in game challenge design. The participants pointed out that anxiety caused by the gameplay might hinder the effect of meditation while playing the game: "*[The meditation game] should not have a losing state if it really wants the players to be meditating.*" (P6) In typical game design, inducing anxiety is frequently employed to motivate players to improve their skills, thereby contributing to player engagement [8].

The participants liked the smiling face of the pet (P1) and the plant pet looking happy (P7) but "*felt sorry when the pet gets pissed*" (P10) and "*didn't like the angry look*" (P8).

Aesthetics

Aesthetics have been recognized as an important element for immersion and pleasure in gameplay [10]. Participants liked the visual aspects of the game for their cute, happy, and harmonious presentation, which contributed to the "*meditative nature*" (P7). They also suggested that an appropriate use of audio feedback could increase the meditation and relaxation effect.

Viewpoints toward interacting with plants

The participants shared opinions about emotionally connecting with the plant-based interface and using plants as interface.

Emotional connection between human and plant

The participants' ownership with the plant could associate with greater anxiety reduction after interacting with the plant interface. P8 brought his own plant to use as the plant interface. P8 had the most significant decrease in STAI score: "*I have a basil in my room. [...] I feel the plant is the only living life in my apartment except me. Since my family is so far away, it feels like my family member is here.*" (P8)

Even with those participants who played with the plant we brought, they started making emotional connections with the plant (P7, P9). For instance, P7 said he "*felt guilty and upset when [he] killed the pet in the Meditation game*" (P7). On the other hand, P6 did not feel any emotional connection with plants in general because she thought "*it is not possible to communicate with plants but possible with animal pets*" (P6). Participants also stated that the low visual similarity between the plant and the pet character of the game could make it difficult to establish a strong emotional connection with the plant (P6, P9).

Plants as interface: some challenges

Initially, the participants found the plant-based interface novel. They had *"never thought that plants can be game controllers"* (P7). P7 also commented on the plant's elastic physical property adding a unique interaction feedback: *"The leaves bouncing back feels like pushing a button."* After the initial feeling of novelty, however, the overall perception of the plant interface was divided. One felt *"weird while touching the plant"* (P8). Another participant felt *"fun and interesting"* (P7), and P6 felt *"not very good [touching the plant] as its texture was not flurry like dogs."*

Some participants had difficulty familiarizing themselves with the plant interface. This difficulty came from not being sure about the strength (P8) and area (P10) of touch and keeping consistent strength of touch (P9). After the Meditation game, P6 felt tired because the game required her to hold her hands in the air. P10 stated that the sweat on her hands increased friction between the hands and the plant, which made her uncomfortable during play.

The participants questioned if the consequences of their interaction caused any harm to the plant's health. For instance, P9 was afraid *"whether touch will harm the plant,"* considering that plants are delicate (P8, P9).

INSIGHTS FOR PLANT-BASED GAMES AND ANXIETY

In this section, we discuss insights in designing and developing plant-based games for anxiety reduction.

Enhancing emotional connections

We learned the participants were anxious about hurting the plants. Especially for those without prior experiences with plants, we suggest plants with relatively bigger leaves, smoother surfaces, and solid structure to ameliorate this problem. Such plants, for example, include succulent plants such as Aloe and Kalanchoe, which are usually considered tough and drought-tolerant [21]. As our participants noted, further emotional connection can be made by appropriating the appearance traits of the plant used as the interface when designing the pet character in the game.

We suggest the use of a personalized storyline between the player and the plant pet character from the beginning of the game, to enhance players' perceived *relatedness* [22]. The game can be customized for common stress inducers, such as money, school, dating, or spousal issues. Games for each stress inducer will be uniquely designed using customized storyline to make the player not feel alone, in accordance with the psychotherapy literature [2]. For example, the pet character can ask the player: *"I just broke up with my boyfriend too. Could you pat me on the back?"* and say *"We will feel better together if you feed me these chocolates!"*

Non-discouraging game design challenges

Our participants noted negative feedback, such as losing or killing the pet, could make them feel more anxious during play. Keeping players engaged in the game while minimizing such negative feedback will be important for anxiety-reducing games. We should rethink using challenges that might discourage the players. An example is a yoga-training program in the Wii Fit game [32], which focuses on meditation. This game provides no explicit negative feedback, and the overall activities in the game progress monotonically. Possible design choices for less negative feedback may include collective and building mechanics such as accumulating achievements over time.

Inspired by the relationship between repetition and relaxation as well as studies on knitting and anxiety [9], we believe that players can master a plant-touching pattern. This task can be an alternative game challenge, especially for anxiety reduction. While knitting, the repetition of knit and purl—when mastered—is known to be highly meditative [9]. Similarly, the fundamental actions of the plant interface, such as tapping and patting, can be employed to create specific action patterns (e.g., tap-tap-pet and so forth) to enhance the meditative effect of the games.

One natural benefit of knitting is its product over a long period of time, such as a sweater for one to wear or a muffler to give to significant others as a gift. Players can choose plant-touching patterns and products that they can create by interacting with plants in a repetitive pattern over a long period of time. Example products include a plant-touching pattern one player can give to another player. This gift-giving, challenge-based feature can help players be motivated to continue engaging with the game.

SUMMARY AND FUTURE WORK

As an earlier attempt, this work allowed us to understand the next steps in plant-based games. First, we need to evaluate how employing plants as interface will influence plants' health. There are a few studies regarding the positive effect of human touch on plant growth [6]. If we find that the interface will not harm the plants, we can envision plant-based games to be a great potential for building mutual care between people and plants. In a broader viewpoint, it may be interesting to explore effect of tangible, living or organic objects as an interface device.

Our study needs to be tested with a larger sample size and groups of users other than students. Future work should also discuss issues of attrition on play engagement and solutions for prolonged involvement with the plant-based games. To clarify actual efficacy of plant-based game play, it will be worthwhile to treat length of play time as a covariate. As well, it may be useful to include other control conditions such as engaging in light exercise or other relaxing activity.

CONCLUSION

We showed the potential of plant-based games on anxiety reduction. We tested the feasibility of plants as interaction devices. As an organic interface, plants provided novel ways to produce emotional connection and mutual care between people and plants. Our work also helped us explore one promising example application in the field of the Internet of Things. The plant interfaces can open a new avenue through which people can find novel ways to relax.

REFERENCES

1. American Psychological Association. Stress in America: Paying With Our Health. Retrieved September 25, 2015 from http://www.apa.org/news/press/releases/stress/2014/stress-report.pdf

2. Jack C. Anchin. 2015. The SAGE Encyclopedia of Theory in Counseling and Psychotherapy. Sage Publication.

3. Aaron Antonovsky. 1979. Health, stress, and coping. Jossey-Bass.

4. Michael S. Bahrke and William P. Morgan. 1978. Anxiety reduction following exercise and meditation. *Cognitive therapy and research*, 2, 4: 323-333.

5. Herbert Benson and Klipper Z. Miriam. 1976. *The relaxation response*. New York: Avon.

6. James F. Cahill, Jeffrey P. Castelli, and Brenda B. Casper. 2002. Separate effects of human visitation and touch on plant growth and herbivory in an old-field community. *American Journal of Botany*, 89, 9: 1401-1409.

7. Jacob Cohen. 1988. Statistical power analysis for the behavioral sciences. Vol. 2. Lawrence Earlbaum Associates.

8. Mihaly Csikszentmihalyi. 1990. Flow: The psychology of optimal experience. Harper and Row.

9. Lisa Dittrich. 2001. Knitting. *Academic Medicine, 76,* 7: 671-671.

10. Laura Ermi and Frans Mäyrä. 2005. Fundamental components of the gameplay experience: Analysing immersion. *Worlds in play: International perspectives on digital games research, 37.*

11. Marianne Thorsen Gonzalez, Terry Hartig, Grete Grindal Pati, Egil W. Martinsen, and Marit Kirkevold. 2010. Therapeutic horticulture in clinical depression: A prospective study of active components. *Journal of Advanced Nursing*, 66, 9: 2002–2013. doi:10.1891/1541-6577.23.4.312

12. Foad Hamidi and Melanie Baljko. 2014. Rafigh: a living media interface for learning games. In*CHI '14 Extended Abstracts on Human Factors in Computing Systems* (CHI EA '14). ACM, New York, NY, USA, 407-410. DOI=http://dx.doi.org/10.1145/2559206.2574772

13. Harry Hemingway and Michael Marmot. 1999. Evidence based cardiology: psychosocial factors in the aetiology and prognosis of coronary heart disease: systematic review of prospective cohort studies. *BMJ: British Medical Journal*, 318, 7196: 1460.

14. Karen Holtzblatt and Sandra Jones. 1993. Contextual inquiry: A participatory technique for system design. *Participatory design: Principles and practices*, 177-210.

15. Bruce S. Jonas, Peter Franks, and Deborah D. Ingram. 1997. Are symptoms of anxiety and depression risk factors for hypertension? Longitudinal evidence from the National Health and Nutrition Examination Survey I Epidemiologic Follow-up Study. *Archives of family medicine*, 6, 1: 43.

16. Wendy EJ Knight and Nikki S. Rickard. 2001. Relaxing music prevents stress-induced increases in subjective anxiety, systolic blood pressure, and heart rate in healthy males and females. *Journal of music therapy*, 38, 4: 254-272.

17. Kazuko Koga and Yutaka Iwasaki. 2013. Psychological and physiological effect in humans of touching plant foliage - using the semantic differential method and cerebral activity as indicators. *Journal of Physiological Anthropology*, 32, 1: 7. doi:10.1186/1880-6805-32-7

18. Diane K. Leggett. 2010. *Effectiveness of a brief stress reduction intervention for nursing students in reducing physiological stress indicators and improving well-being and mental health.* Doctoral dissertation, The University of Utah.

19. Amber Li and C. A. Goldsmith. 2012. The effects of yoga on anxiety and stress. *Altern Med Rev*, 17, 1: 21-35.

20. Pablo Paredes and Matthew Chan. 2011. CalmMeNow: exploratory research and design of stress mitigating mobile interventions. In *CHI '11 Extended Abstracts on Human Factors in Computing Systems* (CHI EA '11). ACM, New York, NY, USA, 1699-1704. http://doi.acm.org/10.1145/1979742.1979831

21. Ivan Poupyrev, Philipp Schoessler, Jonas Loh, and Munehiko Sato. 2012. Botanicus Interacticus: interactive plants technology. In *ACM SIGGRAPH 2012 Emerging Technologies* (SIGGRAPH '12). ACM, New York, NY, USA, , Article 4 , 1 pages. http://doi.acm.org/10.1145/2343456.2343460

22. Richard M. Ryan, C. Scott Rigby, and Andrew Przybylski. 2006. The motivational pull of video games: A self-determination theory approach. *Motivation and emotion* 30, 4: 344-360.

23. Peter Martin Rhind. 2010. Plant Formations in the Eastern Madagascan BioProvince.

24. Jinsil Hwaryoung Seo, Annie Sungkajun, and Jinkyo Suh. 2015. Touchology: Towards Interactive Plant Design for Children with Autism and Older Adults in Senior Housing. In *Proceedings of the 33rd Annual ACM Conference Extended Abstracts on Human Factors in Computing Systems* (CHI EA '15). ACM, New York, NY, USA, 893-898. http://doi.acm.org/10.1145/2702613.2732883

25. Charles D. Spielberger. 1966. Theory and research on anxiety. *Anxiety and behavior, 1.*

26. Charles D. Spielberger. 1983. Manual for the State–Trait Anxiety Inventory (Form Y). Palo Alto, CA: Mind Garden.

27. Anselm Leonard Strauss and Juliet M. Corbin. 1990. *Basics of qualitative research* (Vol. 15). Newbury Park, CA: Sage.

28. Tara W. Strine, Ali H. Mokdad, Shanta R. Dube, Lina S. Balluz, Olinda Gonzalez, Joyce T. Berry, Ron Manderscheid and Kurt Kroenke. 2008. The association of depression and anxiety with obesity and unhealthy behaviors among community-dwelling US adults.*General hospital psychiatry, 30*, 2: 127-137.

29. Tiffany Y. Tang, Relic Yongfu Wang, Yuhui You, Leila Zeqian Huang, and Christine Piao Chen. 2015. Supporting collaborative play via an affordable touching + singing plant for children with autism in China. In *Adjunct Proceedings of the 2015 ACM International Joint Conference on Pervasive and Ubiquitous Computing and Proceedings of the 2015 ACM International Symposium on Wearable Computers* (UbiComp/ISWC'15 Adjunct). ACM, New York, NY, USA, 373-376. DOI: http://dx.doi.org/10.1145/2800835.2800913

30. Roger S. Ulrich, Robert F. Simons, Barbara D. Losito, Evelyn Fiorito, Mark A. Miles, and Michael Zelson. 1991. Stress recovery during exposure to natural and urban environments. *Journal Environmental Psychology. 11*: 201–230.

31. Maarten Van Someren, Yvonne F. Barnard, Jacobijn AC Sandberg. 1994. The think aloud method: A practical guide to modelling cognitive processes (Vol. 2). London: Academic Press.

32. Cati Vaucelle, Leonardo Bonanni, and Hiroshi Ishii. 2009. Design of haptic interfaces for therapy. In *Proceedings of the SIGCHI Conference on Human Factors in Computing Systems* (CHI '09). ACM, New York, NY, USA, 467-470. http://doi.acm.org/10.1145/1518701.1518776

33. Nintendo Co. Ltd. 2007. *Wii Fit* [Wii game]. Kyoto, Japan: Nintendo Co. Ltd.

Point & Teleport Locomotion Technique for Virtual Reality

Evren Bozgeyikli
Tampa, USA
evren@mail.usf.edu

Andrew Raij
Orlando, USA
raij@ucf.edu

Srinivas Katkoori
Tampa, USA
katkoori@mail.usf.edu

Rajiv Dubey
Tampa, USA
dubey@usf.edu

ABSTRACT

With the increasing popularity of virtual reality (VR) and new devices getting available with relatively lower costs, more and more video games have been developed recently. Most of these games use first person interaction techniques since it is more natural for Head Mounted Displays (HMDs). One of the most widely used interaction technique in VR video games is locomotion that is used to move user's viewpoint in virtual environments. Locomotion is an important component of video games since it can have a strong influence on user experience. In this study, a new locomotion technique we called *"Point & Teleport"* is described and compared with two commonly used VR locomotion techniques of walk-in-place and joystick. In this technique, users simply point where they want to be in virtual world and they are teleported to that position. As a major advantage, it is not expected to introduce motion sickness since it does not involve any visible translational motion. In this study, two VR experiments were designed and performed to analyze the *Point & Teleport* technique. In the first experiment, *Point & Teleport* was compared with walk-in-place and joystick locomotion techniques. In the second experiment, a direction component was added to the *Point & Teleport* technique so that the users could specify their desired orientation as well. 16 users took part in both experiments. Results indicated that *Point & Teleport* is a fun and user friendly locomotion method whereas the additional direction component degraded the user experience.

Author Keywords

Virtual reality; locomotion; teleportation.

ACM Classification Keywords

H.5.1. Information interfaces and presentation (e.g., HCI): Multimedia Information Systems: Artificial, augmented, and virtual realities.

INTRODUCTION

Since the development of virtual worlds, researchers have been working on different locomotion techniques.

CHI PLAY '16, October 16-19, 2016, Austin, TX, USA.
© 2016 ACM. ISBN 978-1-4503-4456-2/16/10…$15.00.
DOI: http://dx.doi.org/10.1145/2967934.2968105

Locomotion can be defined as self-propelled movement in virtual worlds [9]. Locomotion is considered as one of the most important interaction components of virtual reality (VR) experiences, since it is a very common and crucial task for moving in 3D virtual environments [2]. Although usually locomotion is not the main goal of VR applications and games, in almost every case some kind of locomotion is required to move the user's viewpoint in the virtual world.

In immersive VR applications, HMDs make it possible for users to control the position and the orientation of the viewpoint by moving their heads. These applications are usually suitable to be explored on foot. But due to the limited physical tracked area, large virtual environments cannot be examined simply by normal walking. In those cases, applications need different locomotion techniques. A poorly designed locomotion technique may distract the user and reduce immersion. It may also introduce motion sickness since locomotion triggers movement which is directly related to motion sickness. In the last few years, with the introduction of new HMDs such as Oculus Rift [20] and HTC Vive [10], and VR goggles that can work with mobile phones like Samsung Gear VR [23] and Google Cardboard [8]; VR games and applications gained a lot of attention and popularity. The developed games and applications use interaction techniques that are specifically designed considering the capabilities of these new devices. Previous generation headsets were capable of tracing the rotation of the head. The games were mainly using video game controllers such as Xbox hand held controllers or keyboards and mice for locomotion [4], [31]. With the recent improvements in HMDs, new generation devices now can track position of the head as well. They also supply hand controllers with real time position and rotation tracking. With these new capabilities, video games started to use real walking as an alternative to the controller based locomotion. But since the tracked area is still limited, games need to use different alternatives for locomotion beyond the physical limitations. One alternative is to limit the virtual space to be similar to the real space. The game focuses on a limited area and game objects and agents come to the user instead of the user moving around [11]. While this is a good approach to keep the user in a restricted area, environmental variety and the user's freedom of locomotion is restrained which would degrade enjoyment until a fully immersive game design is achieved. Another alternative approach is to move the user passively in the virtual world.

In most of the cases, this is done via a vehicle such as a car and a plane. The game may give the control of the vehicle to the user or the vehicle may be controlled automatically. While the vehicle does the transportation, the user focuses on different game objects [27]. Although this is also a clever solution, it limits game design alternatives and is likely to induce motion sickness since the user remains passive while the virtual world moves.

In this study, a new VR locomotion technique we call *"Point & Teleport"* is described and compared with two commonly used VR locomotion techniques: walk-in-place and joystick controller. In *Point & Teleport*, users simply point where they want to be in the virtual world and they are teleported to that position. Locomotion techniques that are similar to *Point & Teleport* are starting to be used in today's new VR games but there are only very few related studies in the literature. Since our technique enables locomotion without real walking, it is suitable for limited tracking areas. Pointing can be done either with hand tracking or with a tracked hand held controller. Main expected advantage of this technique is the reduced motion sickness since there is no visible translation of the virtual world. As a proposed improvement, we designed a variation of the *Point & Teleport* with the additional feature of the direction specification. Both techniques were implemented as simple VR video game like interactive experiments and a user study was performed with 16 participants. This paper presents the design and the implementation of the *Point & Teleport* VR locomotion technique and the user study with the motivation of providing insight to future VR studies and video games.

RELATED WORK

Various locomotion techniques with different characteristics have been evaluated by researchers so far. Some techniques use special devices to sense the locomotion and keep the user in a secure place, while some other techniques use general purpose tracking devices with some possible gestures to control the locomotion along with algorithms to keep the user inside the tracking area. There are also some applications that use general controllers such as joysticks. Each technique has their advantages and disadvantages which may also depend on the aimed application.

U.S. Army's Dismounted Infantry Training Program developed and compared different devices for locomotion in virtual environments [5]. After a group of studies, researchers developed an *"Omni-Directional Treadmill"* to enable walking in any direction freely in virtual worlds. The system is a combination of moving belts that can move together perpendicular to their moving direction. Different studies later developed different Omni-directional treadmills with the same underlying idea [12], [25]. Another approach was to create low friction surfaces so that the users can walk without any actual displacement. This has usually been done by using ball bearings, with the users secured at the center of the locomotion device [15], [29].

With the increasing popularity of HMDs and VR games, similar locomotion devices started to get more attention. Some commercial devices recently announced to be commercially available soon [3], [30]. There are also some unusual locomotion devices that were developed for experimental research studies such as a large sphere that the user gets in and moves in any direction by turning the sphere according to the walking speed and direction [6], [18]; powered shoes [14]; and moving tiles [13]. Although these devices are inventive alternatives for locomotion and proved to offer an immersive and intuitive user experience, they are costly, require learning and good balancing skills, and the users are restrained in an unnatural way.

Another main trend in locomotion is to use general purpose tracking devices to sense user's movements while the user walks freely inside a tracked area. In this method, user's position and direction data is utilized to render the virtual environment from the user's point of view. Since the tracked area is limited, these algorithms must also keep users inside the tracking area, to make continuous interaction possible and to ensure safety of the user. One of the most popular among these techniques is called *redirected walking* [22]. In this technique, user's walking and turning speeds are manipulated to keep the user inside the tracking area. Furthermore, the virtual world is rotated in small amounts so that the user walks in circles although they think that they are walking straight. The unnoticeable limits of these manipulations were studied by Steinicke et al. [26]. Although this algorithm tries to keep the user inside the tracking area, it is possible that the user may occasionally come to the edge of the tracked area. For those cases, different approaches were suggested such as intercepting the application and asking the user to do some movements to go to the center of the tracked area [34] or using distracters to direct the towards the center [21]. Some researchers worked on different algorithms which were designed to change the virtual environment to keep the users inside the tracked area. One example was to change the direction of the doors inside the virtual world while the user was looking elsewhere [28]. Although it seems like a major change at first glance, only 1 out of 77 users could notice this change. Another example was to change the environment layout dynamically [33]. These clever solutions have the limitation of being applicable to only indoor virtual environments.

Furthermore, there are some gesture based locomotion techniques. One of the most popular techniques is called *walk-in-place* [24]. The user marches without actually walking forward and this gesture triggers the locomotion in the virtual world. Usually the virtual walking direction is specified by the user's head direction. Some researchers examined alternative gestures for the walk-in-place technique such as tapping and wiping [19]. Another gesture used for locomotion is leaning [32]. The user leans forward to go forward and leans sides to turn in the virtual word.

Although teleportation is a simple yet powerful possible alternative to the previous locomotion techniques, it has not been quite explored yet. There are a few studies that explored methods related to our proposed *Point & Teleport* locomotion technique. One example developed for CAVE-like environments used teleportation in the virtual world thorough portals [7]. This technique utilized redirected walking and when a user created a portal by using a controller, a conjugate portal gate appeared in the center of the tracked area, so that the user is kept inside the tracked area. Another study used the teleportation approach to help the users walk long distances in the virtual environments [1]. The locomotion was done by real walking, and when the user made a jumping gesture, teleportation was triggered in the head direction. No other studies we are aware of studied teleportation for locomotion in VR.

POINT & TELEPORT TECHNIQUE

To use the *Point & Teleport* technique, users should point to wherever they want to be in the virtual world and the virtual viewpoint will be teleported to that position. In our design, to trigger the teleportation, users should point to the same place or a close vicinity for two seconds. After that, the teleportation is triggered and the virtual avatar is instantaneously moved to that position. An illustration of the *Point & Teleport* technique can be seen in Figure 1 (a).

Implementation

In our implementation, the hand and the shoulder of the user's dominant side are tracked with the optical motion tracking system. The pointing direction is determined as the vector from the virtual shoulder position data to the virtual hand position data. In this approach, the wrist is assumed to be straight. Another alternative approach to determine the pointing direction could be using only the hand position and the orientation data. According to our in-house testing, with the latter approach it is harder to track the user's pointing direction accurately. Small unintentional hand movements or errors in the motion tracking of the hand orientation may cause large displacements at the pointed position. This makes the technique harder to control, which may introduce frustration. When both hand and the shoulder are tracked as in the first approach, the aiming is more accurate and easier to control. Furthermore, the virtual viewpoint is usually close to the vector formed from the shoulder to the hand, which makes aiming easier for the user.

The pointed position in the virtual world is calculated by ray casting. The ray origin is the virtual hand position and the ray direction is the pointing direction calculated by subtracting the virtual position of the shoulder from the virtual position of the hand of the user. The collision detection is performed between the ray and the possible teleportation surfaces. In our case, the only possible surface was the ground of the virtual environment. Once a collision is detected, the position of the collision point is stored. In the next frames, if the distance between the new collision position and the stored position is smaller than a threshold, it is assumed that the user is pointing to the same point constantly, and the timer is

increased by the frame length. If the distance is larger than the threshold, the stored collision position is updated with the new collision position and the timer is reset. If no collision is detected, the stored collision position is cleared until another collision is detected. Balancing the threshold value is important since the larger the threshold is, the larger the tolerance is to the unintentional hand movements. But this comes with the cost of lowered precision when the vicinity of the target is pointed. After in-house testing, we found out that a threshold value similar to the virtual character's bounding capsule diameter worked well, since it will occupy the same virtual space after the teleportation.

In our design, to exclude interfering effects of any additional components, we did not include any controllers to trigger the teleportation. Users needed to point to the same place or a close vicinity for two seconds. Two seconds was decided by in-house testing to be just long enough to eliminate unintentional teleportation instances yet to be short enough not to cause tiredness to the users. Although turned out to be suitable for evaluation, this triggering method may not be suitable for fast paced games. Different designs can use different triggering methods such as hand held controllers.

Activation

Point & Teleport is always active unless the tracked arm is lowered by the user's sides. Since we do not use any handheld controller in our implementation to activate or deactivate the teleportation, we utilized the lowered arm posture to make the teleportation inactive. With this implementation, the users can wait at a constant position in a relaxed posture with their arms lowered. However, this design may not work well for applications in which the user is supposed to do some activities with their hands while waiting. In that case, another gesture or a controller may be utilized to control the activeness of teleportation. Before checking for collision, the angle between the pointing vector and the down vector for the environment is calculated and if the angle is smaller than a threshold, the teleportation is deactivated. This is important for the users to be able to stay in the same position without getting constantly teleported unintentionally. The disadvantage of this approach is that it does not let the users move in very short distances, which was not required in our experiments. If that is required in game design, controller based triggers may work better.

Visual Cues

To make the locomotion more user-friendly, in our implementation, an orange ring overlay is placed on the pointed position in the virtual world if the pointed position is on a possible teleportation surface. This way, the users can easily see where they are pointing at and where they are going to be teleported. The color of this ring is gradually turned into green as long as the user points at the vicinity of the initial position. The color feedback is helpful for users in understanding if they are pointing the same position and how much longer they need to point. Furthermore, a virtual laser beam was displayed that originated from the user's virtual hand and extended towards the ring, parallel to the pointing direction. In our in-house testing, this laser beam helped with the sense of being in control and distance estimation. Without the laser beam, it was difficult to see the ring if the user pointed to a position that was far away from their viewpoint. The color of the laser beam is kept the same with the ring color if the ring is active; otherwise the laser beam's color is kept red, indicating that no possible teleportation surface is pointed currently.

Teleportation

Once the teleportation is triggered by the user, the virtual character and the virtual viewpoint is moved to the pointed position in the virtual world instantaneously. The orientation of the user is kept the same during the teleportation. In our implementation, the user rotates in the virtual world by rotating their bodies in the real world. So the user is able to adjust their orientation after the teleportation. Different approaches were tested in-house before designing the experiment. One approach was to move the virtual character in the virtual world until it reached to the destination point. The speed could be adjusted as an average walking speed or a faster speed. In both these conditions, the approach has introduced motion sickness to the testers. Motion sickness with this approach was not unexpected since the users saw themselves moving in the virtual world while they were standing still in the real world. Another approach was to make the teleportation with a fade-out and fade-in effect in order to help the users cope with the instantly changing virtual world. This approach was found to break immersion and unnecessary since the users did not get overwhelmed by the changing virtual world. In addition, fading introduced wasted time for each teleportation which caused impatience in the testers. The users could expect what to see once they were teleported because they already saw where they were going to be teleported. Hence we suggest that the fading effect may only be resorted to for very crowded virtual worlds in which the teleportation would result in significant change in the environmental visuals.

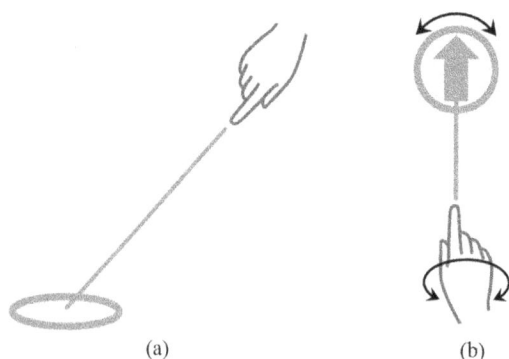

Figure 1: Illustration of the (a) Point & Teleport and (b) Point & Teleport with direction specification techniques.

Teleportation with Direction Specification

In the explained implementation of the *Point & Teleport* so far, the teleportation was performed without any change in the orientation before and after the teleportation. To be able to turn in the virtual world, the users were required to make a real turn after the teleportation. We wondered if we could improve the *Point & Teleport* by adding a direction feature. Hence, a variation of this technique was implemented with a direction specification. With this modified technique, while the users point to a position in the virtual world, they can also specify which direction they want to be facing after the teleportation. For this purpose, in our implementation, a 3D arrow is placed above the ring. The arrow is restricted to x-z plane and the rotation in the y-axis is determined by the rolling axis of the pointing hand (see Figure 1(b)). This way, users can both point to the destination position and specify the direction they will be facing when they are teleported by only using their one arm. After our initial in-house testing, the rolling axis was found to be the easiest for the rotation of the hand to specify the direction among other alternatives in terms of understanding and operating the gesture.

Testing System

An optical tracking system with 12 OptiTrack V100R2 FLEX cameras (640x480 resolution, 100FPS, sub-millimeter accuracy) and passive reflective markers for real time head, hands and feet tracking was used. The tracking area was 2m by 2m. A high resolution HMD (Virtual Realities LLC. VR2200) was used for viewing the virtual world. Our server computer had AMD FX-8150 3.61Ghz Eight-Core CPU, AMD FirePro W600 GPU and 16GB RAM. Implementation was done using the Unity game engine.

EXPERIMENT ONE

In our first experiment, we compared the *Point & Teleport* technique with walk-in-place and joystick controlled locomotion techniques that are commonly used in VR systems. In the walk-in-place technique, locomotion is performed with a marching gesture performed in a constant position. The locomotion direction is controlled by the head orientation. In the joystick control, locomotion is simply controlled by continuously pushing the joystick. For the locomotion direction, the users can either turn their heads or push the joystick sideways.

Objective

The objective of the experiment is to go to the destination points in the virtual environment. The destination points are pointed out using three objects in the virtual world. A circle having 0.6m radius on the ground, a semi-transparent animated textured cylinder of an equal diameter placed on the circle, and an oscillating arrow pointing the destination to emphasize the position (see Figure 2, top). These three objects help the user to see the destination point not only from a large distance but also when they are inside it. The color of these three objects is orange in default. Once the user gets inside the circle, the color of all objects immediately turns into green. This is an important feedback for the users to understand that they are inside the destination point. Once they get into the destination point, a timer for that destination point starts. The user is supposed to stay inside the circle for three seconds. During this interval, the color of all three objects gradually turns into cyan. As the user stays inside the circle for three seconds, the destination point disappears and then appears at another position in the virtual environment. The reason for this forced waiting inside the destination point for three seconds was to incorporate the user's control over starting and stopping the locomotion technique and eliminate unintentional destination point triggering while passing by. The users are required to go to ten destination points with each locomotion technique. After completing the sixth one, some obstacles in the form of pillars are placed in the virtual world. The users are asked not to collide with these static obstacles while going to the destination points. If the users get teleported very close to the obstacles, collision occurred. We did not give any feedback to the users when a collision occurred not to discourage them, but we stored the collision data in the background.

Figure 2: (Top) Experiment one. User points to the destination point. Laser beam and the circle color is close to green, meaning that the user is about to get teleported inside the destination point. (Bottom) Experiment two. User points to the destination point using the direction specification feature. When teleported, the user will be facing the green arrow's

Environment

For the virtual world, a simple 16m by 16m outdoor environment is used. The environment is limited by fence walls of 2.2m height at all sides. After the sixth destination point, 21 cylindrical static obstacles with 0.5m diameter and 2.4m height are placed in the environment. The obstacles

are modelled as roman pillars and the distance between each neighbor pillars is 1.77m (Figure 2, top). The environment is designed as simple as possible yet realistic looking for immersion purposes. No distractors or unexpected objects are used to keep the user's attention only on the locomotion.

Experiment Design

The experiment was designed as within subjects with the independent variable of locomotion technique having three levels (*Point & Teleport*, walk-in-place, joystick). Each user was asked to try all three locomotion techniques with a random order. With each locomotion technique, the users needed to go to ten destination points. The first two destination points for each locomotion technique was considered as training, determined by in-house testing, and not taken into account for the results and data analysis. The next four destination points were tested without obstacles and the last four destination points had static obstacles. The user started the testing at the center of the virtual environment. The first destination point appeared 2m away from the user, since it was the first training destination. The rest of the destination points appeared 4m away from the previous destination point and they required 160 to 210 degrees turns between each destination point. There were predefined destination point sets for each locomotion technique to ensure that no learning effect of the destination points interfered with the collected data. During the testing, data was collected for the time passed for each destination point, collision counts and positions as well as the user's real and virtual positions. After each locomotion technique, the users were asked to fill a survey about usability, presence and motion sickness. At the end of all locomotion techniques, the users were asked to rank their preferences. We built the following four hypotheses for experiment one: **Hypothesis 1:** Point & Teleport will be the best technique in terms of enjoyment. **Hypothesis 2:** Point & Teleport will be less effortful than the walk-in-place technique. **Hypothesis 3:** Point & Teleport will result in the lowest motion sickness results. **Hypothesis 4:** Point & Teleport will result in lower number of collisions with obstacles.

User Study

16 participants (11 male, 5 female) aged between 21 and 35 ($\mu = 26.38$, $\sigma = 3.74$) participated in the experiment. All participants' dominant side was right. All participants had none to minimal previous VR experience. Due to a hardware malfunction in the testing session of one user, their data was discarded and 15 users' data was used in the analysis.

Procedure

The participants entered the testing laboratory, read and signed the consent form and filled out the demographics questionnaire. Then, we explained the users the system and their objective in the experiment. They were told about the destination points, color changing dynamics of the objects and the obstacles after the sixth destination point and trying not to hit them. After that, we helped the participants wear

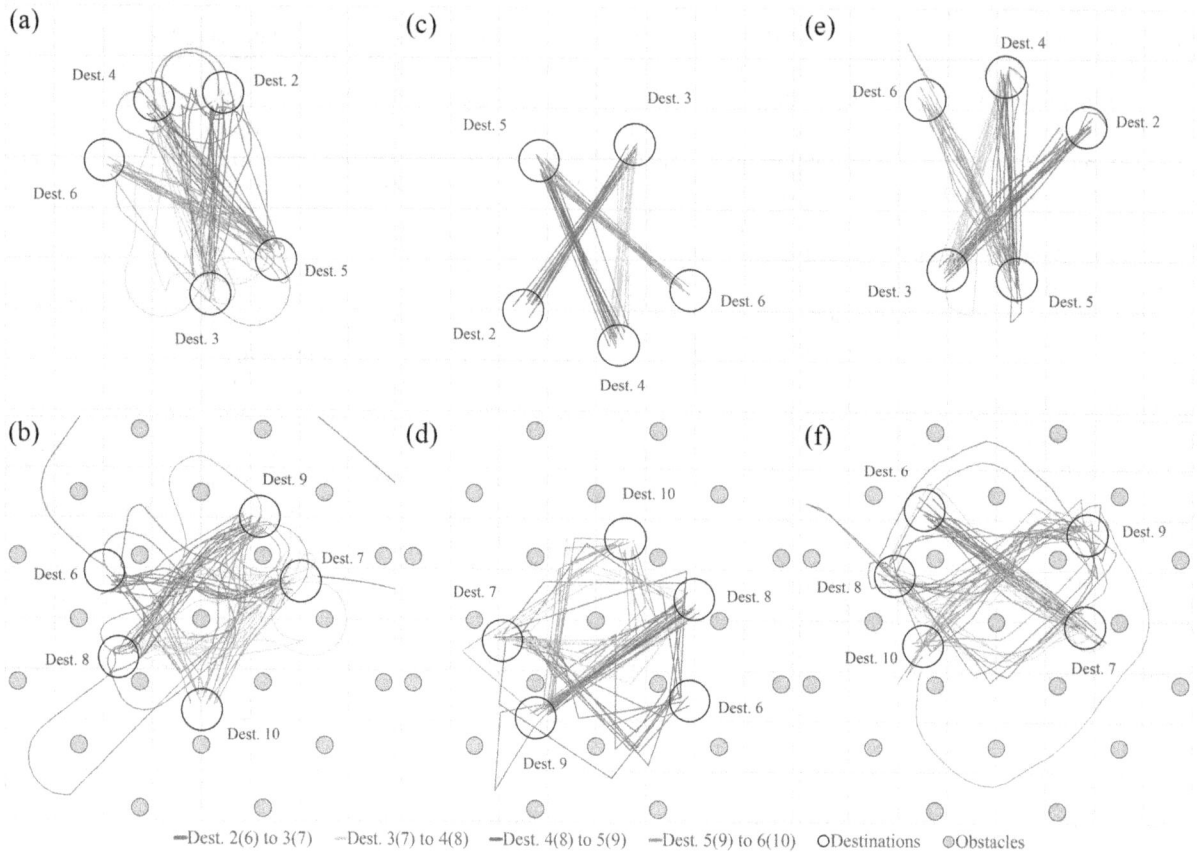

Figure 3: Trajectories of the users' virtual world movements. Joystick (a) without, (b) with obstacles. Point & Teleport (c) without (d) with obstacles. Walk-in-place (e) without (f) with obstacles.

the HMD and the markers for motion tracking and the experiment started. Locomotion methods were assigned to the users randomly but counterbalancing was also done to ensure an even distribution. When the user completed all 10 destination points with a technique, they were given a survey about their experience with that technique. After all techniques were tried, an overall survey was given to the users for the ranking of the methods.

Results

The first two destination points were treated as training and discarded from all data analysis. Trajectories of the virtual world movement of the users are presented in Figure 3. Error bars in all charts are standard error of the mean.

Time to Reach the Destination Points

To analyze the average time it took to reach the destination points with different methods, we divided the data into two groups according to the presence of the obstacles, since the obstacles may have caused longer times (Figure 4). We conducted one way ANOVA analysis and found significant difference between the techniques for both *'without obstacles'* case ($F(2, 12) = 7.707$, $p = 0.001$, F crit. = 3.047) and *'with obstacles'* case ($F(2, 12) = 8.352$, $p = 0.0003$, F crit. = 3.047). When we applied t-tests to pairs of techniques, there was significant difference between *joystick* and *walk-in-place* ($t(14) = -3.455$, $p = 0.001$, Cohen's d = 0.631), and between *Point & Teleport* and *walk-in-place* ($t(14) = -3.256$, $p = 0.001$, Cohen's d = 0.595)

for *'without obstacles'* case. As we examined the techniques for *'with obstacles'* case, t-tests resulted in significant difference between *joystick* and *Point & Teleport* ($t(14) = -4.028$, $p = 0.000$, Cohen's d = 0.735), and between *joystick* and *walk-in-place* ($t(14) = -3.544$, $p = 0.001$, Cohen's d = 0.647).

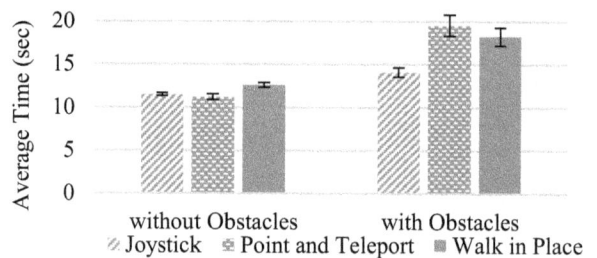

Figure 4: Average time to reach the destination points.

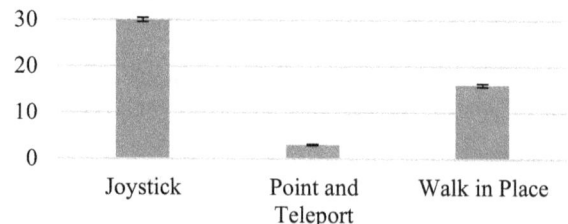

Figure 5: Total number of collisions in the presence obstacles for different locomotion techniques.

Collisions

We looked at how many times the users collided with the obstacle pillars as a measure of their control over the locomotion (Figure 5). One way ANOVA analysis resulted in significant difference between the three techniques ($F_{(2, 12)} = 7.814$, $p = 0.001$, F crit. = 3.22). As we conducted two sample t-tests, there was significant difference between *joystick* and *Point & Teleport* ($t(14) = -4.006$, $p = 0.0004$, Cohen's d = 1.463), and between *Point & Teleport* and *walk-in-place* ($t(14) = 2.402$, $p = 0.023$, Cohen's d = 0.877).

Survey Results on Usability

To analyze the usability of different locomotion techniques, we used a modified version of Loewenthal's core elements of the gaming experience questionnaire [17] with eight different sub categories that are relevant to our evaluation: difficulty of understanding the method, difficulty of operating the method, feeling of being in control while using the method, required effort to use that method, feeling of tiredness the method gave to the user, feeling of enjoyment while using the method, feeling of being overwhelmed while using the method and feeling of frustration the method gave to the user. Each question had answers on a 5 point Likert scale (1: not at all, 5: very much). Results of these eight categories can be seen in Figure 6.

Difficulty of Understanding and Operating the Method

One way ANOVA analysis resulted in significant difference between three techniques ($F_{(2, 12)} = 3.775$, $p = 0.031$, F crit. = 3.22) for difficulty of understanding the locomotion method. Two sample t-tests revealed that the only difference was between *joystick* and *walk-in-place* ($t(14) = -3.024$, $p = 0.005$, Cohen's d = 1.104). No significant difference was found in one way ANOVA analysis between the three techniques ($F_{(2, 12)} = 2.67$, $p = 0.081$, F crit. = 3.22) in terms of difficulty of operating the locomotion technique.

Feeling in Control

As we conducted one way ANOVA analysis, there was no significant difference between the three locomotion techniques ($F_{(2, 12)} = 2.634$, $p = 0.084$, F crit. = 3.22) in terms of the feeling of being in control they provided.

Effort and Tiredness

One way ANOVA analysis resulted in significant difference ($F_{(2, 12)} = 5.630$, $p = 0.007$, F crit. = 3.22) between the three locomotion techniques in terms of the effort it took to use them. Two sample t-tests resulted in significant difference

between *joystick* and *walk-in-place* ($t(14) = -3.286$, $p = 0.003$, Cohen's d = 1.2), and between *Point & Teleport* and *walk-in-place* ($t(14) = -2.055$, $p = 0.049$, Cohen's d = 0.751). As we conducted one way ANOVA analysis to the tiredness data, there was significant difference ($F_{(2, 12)} = 5.851$, $p = 0.006$, F crit. = 3.22). We then conducted two sample t-tests and found significant difference between *joystick* and *walk-in-place* ($t(14) = -3.313$, $p = 0.003$, Cohen's d = 1.21), and between *Point & Teleport* and *walk-in-place* ($t(14) = -2.157$, $p = 0.04$, Cohen's d = 0.788).

Enjoyment, Overwhelmedness and Frustration

One way ANOVA analysis resulted in no significant difference for level of enjoyment ($F_{(2, 12)} = 0.442$, $p = 0.646$, F crit. = 3.22), feeling of being overwhelmed ($F_{(2, 12)} = 0.062$, $p = 0.94$, F crit. = 3.22), and level of frustration ($F_{(2, 12)} = 0.269$, $p = 0.765$, F crit. = 3.22).

Motion Sickness and Presence

To measure motion sickness, a modified version of the Pensacola Diagnostic Criteria survey [16] was used with four levels (0: none, 3: major). The questions measured nauseousness, cold sweating, drowsiness, headache, flushing/warmth and dizziness. One way ANOVA analysis resulted in no significant difference for the motion sickness data ($F_{(2, 12)} = 0.691$, $p = 0.507$, F crit. = 3.22). To measure presence, a modified version of Witmer and Singer's questionnaire [35] was used with four levels (1: not at all, 4: completely). There was no significant difference for level of presence ($F_{(2, 12)} = 0.499$, $p = 0.611$, F crit. = 3.22). Results for motion sickness and presence are presented in Table 1.

	Joystick		Point&Tel.		Walk-in-Place	
	M	**SD**	**M**	**SD**	**M**	**SD**
Motion Sickness	0.067	0.258	0.333	1.047	0.333	0.617
Presence	2.71	0.58	2.87	0.71	2.93	0.58

Table 1. Motion sickness and presence scores.

User Preference

Weighted averages of the user preference ranking scores are presented in Figure 7. *Point & Teleport* got the highest preference score while *walk-in-place* got the lowest. However, as we conducted the Friedman test, no significant difference was found between the ranking scores of the three techniques (χ^2 (2, N = 15) = 2.80, $p = 0.247$).

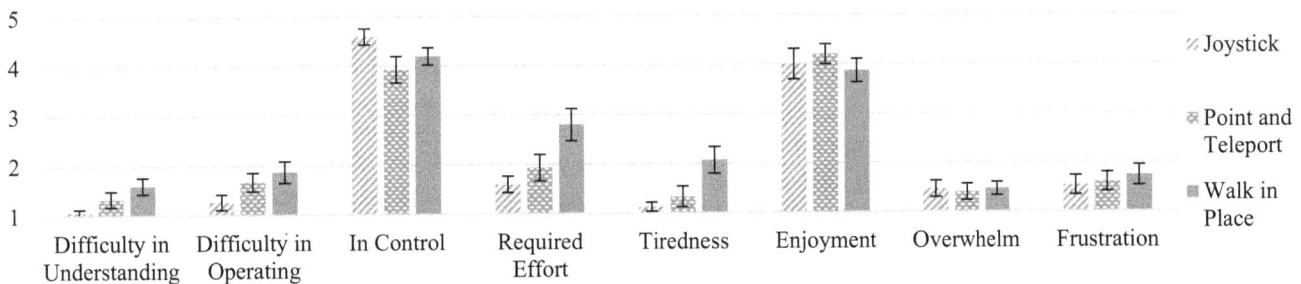

Figure 6: Survey Results for Joystick, Point & Teleport and Walk-in-Place locomotion techniques.

In our experiment, the first two destination points were considered as training and the remaining 8 destination points were used to evaluate the techniques. The training number was determined by in-house testing to give the users enough time for comfortable use of the techniques. Simple design of our experiment and the techniques contributed to the low number of training instances required. As we analyzed the data for any correlation to find out if there was any learning effect in the evaluation, no significant correlation was found between the completion time and the destination order (r(Joystick) = 0.113, r(Point & Teleport) = 0.030, r(Walk-in-Place) = -0.109). This can be considered as an evidence for no learning effect being present in our experiment.

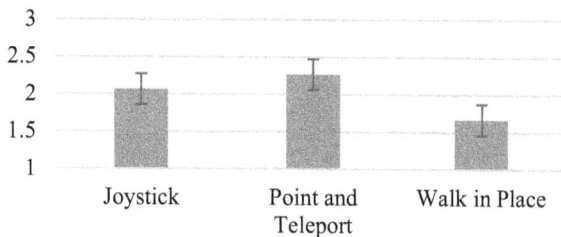

Figure 7: Weighted averages of the user preference ranking.

User Comments

We asked the participants to describe anything they liked, disliked or would like to suggest about each locomotion method. Participants gave many positive comments about the simplicity and usability of *Point & Teleport* "Pointing is very easy and interesting." "Easy to move and avoid obstacles." "This felt more like a video game because I wasn't actually walking to move in VR." "Really cool method. Would be fun for video games." "This method was very easy to use." "I liked the magic wand in my hand." A few users stated that it was a bit challenging using *Point & Teleport* with the obstacle pillars "It was fun and accurate. It got challenging with the columns." "Getting around obstacles was a lot of time. But good for longer, unobstructed distances." For the joystick method, a few users gave positive comments such as "Love this method. No thinking, no effort. Know for sure." There were some negative feedbacks for the joystick as well "It was easier to control the walking but completely conscious that I was controlling from outside." For the walk-in-place method, some users made positive statements "I think it is simple and also have real walk." "Feels more natural when walking and turning at the same time." "While not as easy as joystick, it did feel more immersive." Some users made negative comments about the effort the marching gesture needed in walk-in-place "Needs more effort." "Actually it is intuitive but I cannot walk sideways."

Discussion

When there were no obstacles in the scene, it took similar times to reach the destination points for all three techniques. However, when there were obstacles, it took longer with *Point & Teleport*. We interpret that our triggering method of pointing the same place for two seconds for teleportation may have contributed to this. When the users needed to walk around the obstacles with multiple teleportations, these activation times accumulated. Although we didn't receive any negative comments from the users about the two seconds pointing for teleportation nor observed any impatience in the users while activating the teleportation; we recommend using an instantaneous triggering method such as a controller button in video games that involve many objects to walk around. *Point & Teleport* resulted in significantly lower number of collisions with obstacles than joystick and walk-in-place, which supports Hypothesis 4. This was expected since *Point & Teleport* isn't a process oriented technique. It is rather result oriented. The user only points to where they want to go and does not need to care about the rest. With the other two techniques however, the user needs to control the walking aspect continuously. Walk-in-place was found to be more difficult to understand than the joystick, whereas no difference was found between the *Point & Teleport* and the other two techniques. We interpret this as *Point & Teleport* not exerting significant cognitive load for learning how to use it. All three techniques got high scores for feeling in control and no significant difference was found between them. We interpret this as *Point & Teleport* giving the users a feeling of control as strong as the other two commonly used locomotion techniques. Although joystick got the highest score for the feeling of being in control, we observed that there was a drifting effect in turning with the joystick (see the arcs in Figure 3 (a) and (b)). Although the users could have stopped, turned and then moved forward, they preferred to move forward and turn at the same time, which resulted in unnecessary distances travelled. We did not observe this effect with the other two techniques. Walk-in-place required the users to exert more effort than the other two techniques, which supported Hypothesis 2. Walk-in-place also caused more tiredness in the users than the other two techniques. This can be interpreted as *Point & Teleport* not causing significant effort or tiredness in users, which makes it a favorable candidate for video games in terms of usability. We think that our gesture design may have contributed to this. Lowering the arms while waiting was appreciated by the participants. We think that it is important to keep the users in a relaxed position unless they need to trigger something, to avoid tiredness. *Point & Teleport* enables the users to move very large or small distances with the same minimal effort. It removes the time component from moving inside the virtual world. All techniques got similar scores for enjoyment. While *Point & Teleport* got slightly higher scores, there wasn't evidence to support Hypothesis 1. However, we received very positive comments about the *Point & Teleport* resembling a superpower, being fun and being like a magical experience. The idea of teleportation made the participants excited. Many participants made positive statements about how fun it was like to have a magical power or how cool to emit a laser beam; although what we provided was actually just a simple line. This makes us believe that an embraced theme can contribute greatly to the user experience. Most of the participants made verbal statements such as "Wow" and "Cool" just as we told them the name of the technique. None of the techniques caused feeling of being overwhelmed or frustrated, which makes us think that *Point & Teleport* is a user friendly locomotion technique. All three techniques resulted in low motion sickness results. We couldn't find evidence to support Hypothesis 3. We believe that since the objective of the experiment was designed to be simple to enable the users to concentrate on the locomotion techniques and the environment was also designed to be simple with no moving objects or distractions, not to inject any artificial contributions; the results for the motion sickness turned out to be similar for all techniques. This at least shows that, *Point & Teleport* does not introduce more motion sickness than the two commonly used techniques in static and roomy virtual worlds. We think that *Point & Teleport* may result in lower motion sickness results in more dynamic virtual environments as well since this technique does not present the user locomotion movement of their own, however experiments are needed for scientific and reliable results. We didn't observe any significant effect of the three locomotion techniques on the level of presence. To sum up, experiment results and reactions from the participants make us think that *Point & Teleport* is an intuitive, fun and user friendly way of locomotion with a high potential to be a popular technique in VR video games. We suggest that *Point & Teleport* can be used for low paced adventure or exploration games in which immediate actions such as dodging or moving in small increments aren't necessary. For FPSs, MMORPGs or highly realistic serious games, this technique may not work well.

EXPERIMENT TWO

In our second experiment, *Point & Teleport (P&T)* was compared with a modified version of itself: *Point & Teleport with Direction Specification (P&T w/DS)*. In this modified version, users could specify the direction they would be facing when teleported by rotating their hands in the rolling axis before the teleportation. The same participants who attended experiment one attended the second experiment.

Objective

Experiment two's objective is similar to experiment one. The participants were asked to go to the destination points and wait inside until another destination point appeared somewhere else. Same destination point objects with experiment one were used to designate the target positions. Users completed two trials, each with 6 destination points. One trial was played with *P&T* and the other was played with *P&T w/DS*. Order of the trials was decided randomly with counterbalancing. Destination points of the two trials were different to eliminate any learning effect. The users started the testing at the center of the virtual maze. Each destination point was 8m away from the previous destination point.

Environment

In this experiment, the virtual world was designed as a simple maze (see Figure 2, bottom) to measure effects of the additional direction specification component more effectively. The maze was designed not to be challenging, with 14m length and 14m width. No gaps were placed on the exterior walls so the user could not go outside the virtual maze. The corridors had 2m length for easy navigation. The longest dead-end corridor was 2m long, so the users did not waste too much time if they made wrong path choices. The height of the maze walls was 1.5m, which made it possible for the users to see the destination point from anywhere in the maze. Since the environment was designed as a maze and the maze walls inherently were obstacles, no additional obstacles in the form of pillars were used in this experiment. That's why this experiment had 6 destination points in total.

Experiment Design

Experiment two was also designed as within subjects. Each participant tried both *P&T* and *P&T w/DS* techniques with a random order. Similar to experiment one, first two destination points for each technique were considered as training and discarded, and the remaining four destination points were taken into consideration for evaluation. After each technique, the participants filled out a survey about the technique they tried. After completing both trials, the participants were asked to state their preference between the two techniques on an additional survey question. We built the following hypotheses: **Hypothesis 5:** *P&T w/DS* will give lower average time to reach the destination points. **Hypothesis 6:** *P&T w/DS* will require more effort.

Results

Time to Reach the Destination Points

The average time to reach the destination points are presented in Figure 8. Two sample t-tests resulted in no significant difference ($t(14) = -1.289$, $p = 0.200$, Cohen's d $= 0.235$) in the time it took to reach the destination points.

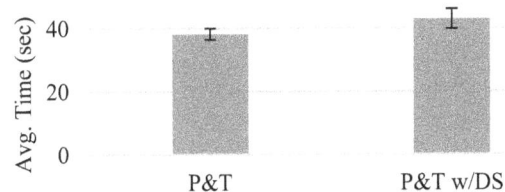

Figure 8: Average time to reach the destination points.

Collisions

In terms of the number of collisions made by the users, two sample t-tests resulted in no significant difference between the two techniques ($t(14) = -1.339$, $p = 0.191$, Cohen's d $= 0.489$). Data can be seen in Figure 9.

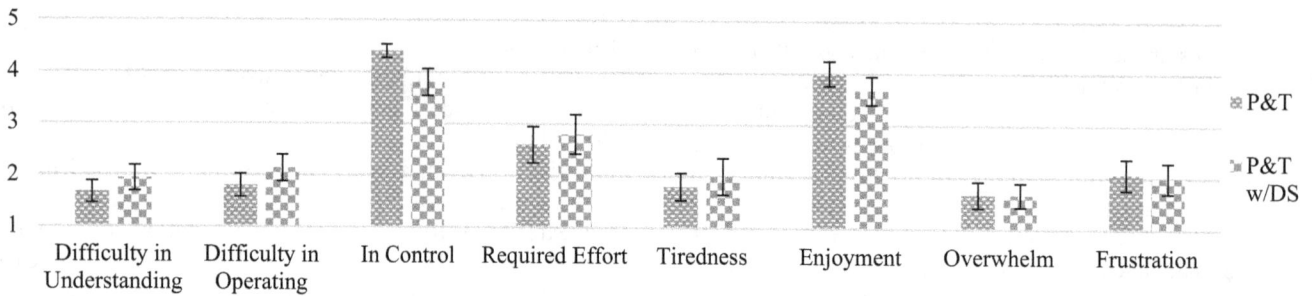
Figure 10: Survey Results for Point & Teleport and Point & Teleport with Direction Specification locomotion techniques.

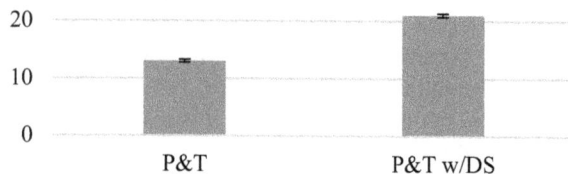
Figure 9: Total number of collisions with maze walls.

Survey Results on Usability

To analyze the usability aspects of the two versions of the *Point & Teleport*, we used the same eight sub categories with experiment one: difficulty in understanding, difficulty in operating, feeling of being in control, required effort to move, feeling of tiredness, enjoyment, being overwhelmed and frustration. Each question had answers on a 5 point Likert scale (1: not at all, 5: very much). Results of these eight categories are presented in Figure 10. As two sample t-tests were conducted, the only significant difference between the two locomotion techniques was in the feeling of being in control (see Table 2). No significant difference was found in terms of motion sickness although P&T w/DS got higher scores (M = 0.47, SD = 1.06) than P&T (M = 0.27, SD = 0.59). Presence results weren't significantly different as well although P&T got slightly higher scores (M = 3.04, SD = 0.52) than P&T w/DS (M = 2.89, SD = 0.50).

User Preference

To analyze the user preference data (Figure 11), we conducted the Friedman test and found no significant difference (χ^2 (1, N = 15) = 0.067, p = 0.796).

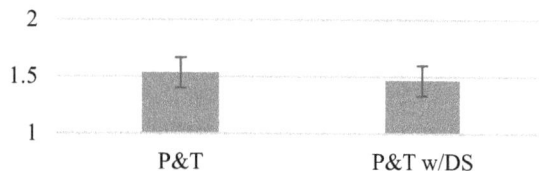
Figure 11: Weighted average user preference ranking.

User Comments

Many users stated preference for P&T over P&T w/DS in their comments "I liked this method [P&T]. It made navigating the maze relatively easy." "I think it is [P&T] better than the first one [P&T w/DS]. I am not very dizzy." "I like pointing and then I look for directions. I think I do it faster this way."

	t	df	p	Cohen's d
Diff. Understand	-0.819	14	0.420	0.299
Diff. Operate	-0.983	14	0.334	0.359
In Control	2.049	14	0.050	0.748
Required Effort	-0.387	14	0.701	0.141
Tiredness	-0.456	14	0.652	0.167
Enjoyment	0.924	14	0.363	0.337
Overwhelm	0.000	14	1.000	0.000
Frustration	0.159	14	0.875	0.058
Motion Sickness	-0.638	14	0.529	0.233
Presence	0.838	14	0.409	0.306

Table 2. T-test results for the survey data of experiment two.

"It was easier overall to reach my destination in this method [P&T]." Only a few users made comments stating preference over *P&T w/DS* such as "I liked the added control of choosing the direction. It made the method feel more efficient." A lot of users complained about feeling dizzy or disoriented with *P&T w/DS* "Might be [P&T w/DS] more confusing than before [P&T]. Difficult to fully realize own orientation after teleporting." "A little bit dizziness for me [with P&T w/DS]." "While I really liked this method [P&T w/DS] over regular teleporting [P&T], the directional controls were a bit touchy. Accordingly, I sometimes felt a little disoriented."

Discussion

Average time to reach the destination points was similar for the two techniques, not supporting Hypothesis 5. In fact, it took more time to reach the destination points with *P&T w/DS* as opposed to what we expected. No difference was observed in the required effort to use the two techniques, not supporting Hypothesis 6, although *P&T w/DS* required slightly more effort. *P&T w/DS* resulted in slightly higher motion sickness results. User preference results were similar between the two techniques. *P&T w/DS* was more difficult to operate and understand. We interpret this as the effect caused from merging two components of moving and rotating into one in this modified version. In the original *P&T*, users controlled the locomotion sequentially; first they moved to the desired location, then they turned to face wherever they wanted. *P&T w/DS* merged these components and induced more cognitive load in users. We received a lot of complaints about the feeling of disoriented and dizziness *P&T w/DS* caused whereas none for the *P&T*. Since *P&T w/DS* changed the environment's orientation instantly, this may have caused disorientation in the users. Hence, we do not recommend using the additional direction specification feature and we recommend keeping *P&T* in its simple form. As possible solutions to disorientation, we recommend using in game mini maps or making the user's previous position marked for a while after they teleport to somewhere else to help them maintain their sense of orientation. To wrap up, although we expected the additional direction specification feature to enhance the *P&T* locomotion technique, experiment results indicated the opposite.

CONCLUSION

In this study, *Point & Teleport* locomotion technique is described and evaluated. Two VR experiments were designed and performed with 16 participants. In experiment one, *Point & Teleport* was compared with walk-in-place and joystick locomotion techniques. In experiment two, a direction component was added to the *P&T* so that the users could specify their post teleportation orientation beforehand. Results indicated that *Point & Teleport* is an intuitive, easy to use and fun locomotion technique. However, the additional direction specification component degraded the user experience. Future work may consist of evaluating the *P&T* in more dynamic, challenging and high paced virtual environments, especially regarding motion sickness and disorientation, exploring the controller triggered version and studying the usability of *P&T* for multiplayer games.

REFERENCES

1. Benjamin Bolte, Gerd Bruder, and Frank Steinicke. 2011. The Jumper Metaphor: An Effective Navigation Technique for Immersive Display Setups. In *Proceedings of the Virtual Reality International Conference* (VRIC) (2011), 1-7.

2. Doug A. Bowman, Ernst Kruijff, Joseph J. Laviola, and Ivan Poupyrev. 2004. *3D User Interfaces: Theory and Practice*. Addison Wesley Longman Publishing Co., Inc.

3. Tuncay Cakmak and Holger Hager. 2014. Cyberith virtualizer: a locomotion device for virtual reality. In *Proceedings of the ACM SIGGRAPH 2014 Emerging Technologies* (Vancouver, Canada2014), ACM, 2614105, 1-1. http://dx.doi.org/10.1145/2614066.2614105.

4. Creative Assembly. 2014. *Alien: Isolation*. Game [Oculus]. (7 October 2014). Sega, Tokyo, Japan.

5. Rudolph P. Darken, William R. Cockayne, and David Carmein. 1997. The omni-directional treadmill: a locomotion device for virtual worlds. In *Proceedings of the Proceedings of the 10th annual ACM symposium on User interface software and technology* (Banff, Alberta, Canada1997), ACM, 263550, 213-221. http://dx.doi.org/10.1145/263407.263550.

6. Kiran J. Fernandes, Vinesh Raja, and Julian Eyre. 2003. Cybersphere: the fully immersive spherical projection system. *Commun.* ACM 46, 9, 141-146. http://dx.doi.org/10.1145/903893.903929.

7. Sebastian Freitag, Dominik Rausch, and Torsten Kuhlen. 2014. Reorientation in virtual environments using interactive portals. In *3D User Interfaces (3DUI), 2014 IEEE Symposium on*, 119-122. http://dx.doi.org/10.1109/3DUI.2014.6798852.

8. Cardboard Google. Retrieved April 15, 2016 from https://www.google.com/get/cardboard/

9. Kelly S Hale and Kay M Stanney, 2014. *Handbook of virtual environments: Design, implementation, and applications*. CRC Press.

10. Htc Vive. Retrieved April 15, 2016 from https://www.htcvive.com/

11. I-Illusions. 2016. *Space Pirate Trainer*. Game [HTC Vive]. (April 5, 2016). I-Illusions, Brussels, Belgium.

12. Hiroo Iwata. 1999. The Torus Treadmill: realizing locomotion in VEs. *Computer Graphics and Applications, IEEE* 19, 6, 30-35. http://dx.doi.org/10.1109/38.799737.

13. Hiroo Iwata, Hiroaki Yano, Hiroyuki Fukushima, and Hirokazu Noma. 2005. CirculaFloor [locomotion interface]. *Computer Graphics and Applications, IEEE* 25, 1, 64-67. http://dx.doi.org/10.1109/MCG.2005.5.

14. Hiroo Iwata, Hiroaki Yano, and Hiroshi Tomioka. 2006. Powered shoes. In *Proceedings of the ACM SIGGRAPH 2006 Emerging technologies* (Boston, Massachusetts2006), ACM, 1179162, 28. http://dx.doi.org/10.1145/1179133.1179162.

15. Huang Jiung-Yao. 2003. An omnidirectional stroll-based virtual reality interface and its application on overhead crane training. *Multimedia, IEEE Transactions on* 5, 1, 39-51. http://dx.doi.org/10.1109/TMM.2003.808822.

16. Ben D Lawson, David A Graeber, Andrew M Mead, and Er Muth. 2002. Signs and symptoms of human syndromes associated with synthetic experiences. In *Handbook of virtual environments: Design, implementation, and applications*, 589-618.

17. Kate Miriam Loewenthal. 2001. *An introduction to psychological tests and scales*. Psychology Press.

18. Eliana Medina, Ruth Fruland, and Suzanne Weghorst. 2008. Virtusphere: Walking in a Human Size VR "Hamster Ball". In *Proceedings of the Human Factors and Ergonomics Society Annual Meeting* 52, 27 (September 1, 2008), 2102-2106. http://dx.doi.org/10.1177/154193120805202704.

19. Niels Nilsson, Stefania Serafin, Morten Laursen, Kasper Pedersen, Erik Sikstrom, and Rolf Nordahl. 2013. Tapping-In-Place: Increasing the naturalness of immersive walking-in-place locomotion through novel gestural input. In *3D User Interfaces (3DUI), 2013*

IEEE Symposium on, 31-38.
http://dx.doi.org/10.1109/3DUI.2013.6550193.

20. Oculus Rift. Retrieved April 15, 2016 from https://www.oculus.com/

21. Tabitha Peck, Henry Fuchs, and Mary Whitton. 2010. Improved Redirection with Distractors: A large-scale-real-walking locomotion interface and its effect on navigation in virtual environments. In *Virtual Reality Conference (VR)*, 2010 IEEE, 35-38. http://dx.doi.org/10.1109/VR.2010.5444816.

22. Sharif Razzaque, Zachariah Kohn, and Mary C Whitton. 2001. *Redirected Walking*. Technical Report. University of North Carolina at Chapel Hill.

23. Samsung - Gear Vr. Retrieved April 15, 2016 from http://www.samsung.com/us/explore/gear-vr/

24. Mel Slater, Anthony Steed, and Martin Usoh. 1995. The virtual treadmill: a naturalistic metaphor for navigation in immersive virtual environments. In *Proceedings of the Selected papers of the Eurographics workshops on Virtual environments '95* (Barcelona, Spain1995), Springer-Verlag, 237143, 135-148.

25. Jan Souman, Paolo Robuffo Giordano, Martin Schwaiger, Ilja Frissen, Thomas Thummel, Heinz Ulbrich, Alessandro De Luca, Heinrich Bulthoff, and Marc Ernst. 2008. CyberWalk: Enabling unconstrained omnidirectional walking through virtual environments. *ACM Trans. Appl. Percept.* 8, 4, 1-22. http://dx.doi.org/10.1145/2043603.2043607.

26. Frank Steinicke, Gerd Bruder, Jason Jerald, Harald Frenz, and Markus Lappe. 2010. Estimation of Detection Thresholds for Redirected Walking Techniques. *IEEE Transactions on Visualization and Computer Graphics* 16, 1, 17-27. http://dx.doi.org/10.1109/tvcg.2009.62.

27. StressLevelZero. 2016. *Hover Junkers*. Game [HTC Vive]. (April 5, 2016). StressLevelZero, Los Angeles, CA, USA.

28. Evan. A. Suma, Seth Clark, David Krum, Samantha Finkelstein, Mark Bolas, and Zachary Warte. 2011. Leveraging change blindness for redirection in virtual environments. In *Virtual Reality Conference (VR),*

2011 IEEE, 159-166. http://dx.doi.org/10.1109/VR.2011.5759455.

29. Minghadi Suryajaya, Tim Lambert, and Chris Fowler. 2009. Camera-based OBDP locomotion system. In *Proceedings of the Proceedings of the 16th ACM Symposium on Virtual Reality Software and Technology* (Kyoto, Japan2009), ACM, 1643938, 31-34. http://dx.doi.org/10.1145/1643928.1643938.

30. David Swapp, Julian Williams, and Anthony Steed. 2010. The implementation of a novel walking interface within an immersive display. In *3D User Interfaces (3DUI), 2010 IEEE Symposium on*, 71-74. http://dx.doi.org/10.1109/3DUI.2010.5444717.

31. Tammeka Games. 2016. *Radial-G : Racing Revolved*. Game [Oculus]. (28 March 2016). Tammeka Games, Brighton, UK.

32. Dimitar Valkov, Frank Steinicke, Gerd Bruder, and Klaus Hinrichs. 2010. A multi-touch enabled human-transporter metaphor for virtual 3D traveling. In *3D User Interfaces (3DUI), 2010 IEEE Symposium on*, 79-82. http://dx.doi.org/10.1109/3DUI.2010.5444715.

33. Khrystyna Vasylevska, Hannes Kaufmann, Mark Bolas, and Evan Suma. 2013. Flexible spaces: Dynamic layout generation for infinite walking in virtual environments. In *3D User Interfaces (3DUI), 2013 IEEE Symposium on*, 39-42. http://dx.doi.org/10.1109/3DUI.2013.6550194.

34. Betsy Williams, Gayathri Narasimham, Bjoern Rump, Timothy P. Mcnamara, Thomas H. Carr, John Rieser, and Bobby Bodenheimer. 2007. Exploring large virtual environments with an HMD when physical space is limited. In *Proceedings of the Proceedings of the 4th symposium on Applied perception in graphics and visualization* (Tubingen, Germany2007), ACM, 1272590, 41-48. http://dx.doi.org/10.1145/1272582.1272590.

35. Bob G. Witmer and Michael J. Singer. 1998. Measuring Presence in Virtual Environments: A Presence Questionnaire. *Presence: Teleoper. Virtual Environ.* 7, 3, 225-240. http://dx.doi.org/10.1162/105474698565686.

"Always a Tall Order": Values and Practices of Professional Game Designers of Serious Games for Health

Jinghui Cheng, Cynthia Putnam, Jin Guo

College of Computing and Digital Media, DePaul University

Chicago, IL, USA

{jcheng13, cputnam, jguo9}@cdm.depaul.edu

ABSTRACT

Serious games for health utilize game media to help players attain health-related goals. Game designers play a crucial role in this growing game genre; they focus on particularly challenging design problems that are not well represented in the literature. In this study, we interviewed 11 professional game designers focused on games for health to explore how they perceived and approached their work. Our findings revealed how our participants considered "success" and the challenges of designing games for health; we also identified various methods and tools used in their practice. Additionally, we found that our participants were very user-centric and tended to focus almost equally on the problem and the solution spaces when approaching game design. The insights presented in this study will be of interest to games for health researchers and designers. This work also contributes to bridging the research-practice gap in the community exploring games as purposeful media.

Author Keywords

Game designer; design practice; game design; games for health; serious game.

ACM Classification Keywords

H.5.m. Information interfaces and presentation (e.g., HCI): Miscellaneous.

INTRODUCTION

In this study, we explored how game designers who focus on serious games for health perceive and approach designing games. Serious games are those designed to "deliver a message, teach a lesson, or provide an experience" [25]; they aim to convey a purposeful goal in addition to entertainment. Serious games for health (or simply games for health, or health games) are a thriving area that targets various types of health related goals. Games in this genre have included games designed to: (1) promote a healthy behavior such as healthy eating or smoking cessation [19,42,43], (2) encourage physical activities (sometimes called exergames) [24,30,38], (3) support rehabilitation activities involved in a therapy [1,8,12], and (4) improve health and wellbeing of elderly populations [16,28]. Accordingly, target audiences for health games are also diverse, including children, elderly adults, people who have health conditions, caregivers, and the general public.

The field of games for health has experienced a rapid growth in the past 30 years [29]; as of this writing, practitioners have created more than 400 published health-related games [11]. This growth has also inspired (and is expedited by) professional and research communities such as the Games for Health Project [31] and the Games for Health Journal [2]. Currently, games for health is an active and flourishing area that attracts diverse professionals including designers, researchers, and medical and healthcare experts.

Game designers play a crucial role in the development of games for health. In their day-to-day practice, they communicate with various stakeholders, research subject matter, interact with target players, and strive to create an engaging experience to convey the purposeful goal. Different from other types of serious games, games for health are often aimed at players with special needs, such as elderly populations and/or people with disabilities. Therefore, games for health designers often face unique and significant challenges to making their end products accessible and engaging to target players while delivering the intended objectives. However, there is little research examining how these designers perceive and overcome these challenges. Game designers have often shared their insights through postmortems (i.e. reflections on a particular game project) and in other venues such as talks in game development conferences [18]. In the field of games for health, however, this type of information sharing is not common, with only a few exceptions (e.g. [7,20,31]). Further, no work has been done to synthesize the knowledge and experiences of this group of game designers.

In this paper, we bridge this gap by accumulating insights from professional game designers who focus on games for health through in-depth interviews. In particular, we were interested in understanding: (1) how the designers judge and perceive success of games for health projects; (2) how they think about and act on the challenges in their work; (3) how they acquired domain knowledge and assessed their games; and (4) what "tools" they used to support their work. For the last point, we adopted Stolterman et al.'s concept of *Designerly Tools* that include concepts, theories, and artifacts that supported design activity [40].

Our work acknowledges a focus in recent Human-Computer Interaction (HCI) research aimed at understanding designers as professional practitioners and exploring the processes and tools that designers use and value in their practice [13,27,41]. A rationale for this approach is that an emphasis on professional designers' experience, including an understanding of their distinctive approach to creative work, will help bridge the research-practice gap in the HCI community and support design education. As such, we argue that understanding the values and practices of game design professionals is a needed first step to explore important Player-Computer Interaction factors such as (a) adaptation of Games User Research methods in serious game design and (b) methods and tools that can better support serious game designers.

Understanding how games for health designers think and act in their work is important for two additional reasons. First, designers of games for health focus on particularly challenging design areas that are not well represented in the literature. As such, we believe that insights obtained from this group of designers can also inform research on serious game design in other areas. Second, cases cited in the literature have identified that game designers' expertise and skills are not always sufficiently stressed in the design of games for health [7,20]. In other words, there has often been a stronger emphasis on meeting the health-related goals than on designing an engaging game experience; this could be a reason why many games for health projects have not been considered successful [6]. As the field matures, emphasizing and understanding game designers' role will become increasingly imperative for the creation of successful games for health.

RELATED WORK
This study is grounded in work related to: (1) games for health research concerned with the balance between player engagement and the game's effectiveness; and (2) research about design practitioners, especially those involving interaction designers and game designers.

Games for Health
Research in games for health has focused on subjects including: (1) healthy behavior [19,42,43], (2) physical activities [24,30,38], (3) rehabilitation [1,8,12], and (4) elderly wellbeing [16,28]. While much of the work in this area is aimed at evaluating the game's effectiveness at addressing the health-related goals, researchers have also investigated player engagement in recent literature. For example, Alankus et al. [1] created nine adjustable games for upper body rehabilitation of patients who have had a stroke; in user studies of these games, they emphasized players' motivation and engagement in addition to the

games' accessibility and efficacy. In another example focused on encouraging physical activity of elementary school children, Penko and Barkley [30] found that a motion-based Wii game generated significantly better physiological outcomes and were preferred by both lean and overweight children when compared to either (1) a traditional "sedentary" Nintendo game with the same theme and (2) physical exercises.

Researchers have also generated design guidelines aimed at increasing game engagement in health games. For example, Flores et al. [12] generated a list of design criteria for stroke rehabilitation games for people who were elderly; the list included criteria focused on entertainment. A stronger focus on engagement has led to the understanding that an effective collaboration between subject matter experts and game designers is important for creating successful games for health [6,12]. For example, Thompson et al. [42] reported a case study of how a close collaboration between game designers and behavioral scientists led to the creation of a promising game that focused on preventing Type 2 diabetes and obesity among youths. Built upon the related literature about the balance between player engagement and the game's effectiveness in games for health, this work is particularly focused on the role of game designers.

Understanding Design Practitioners
Based on studies with practitioners from various areas (e.g. architects and psychotherapists), Schön [37] proposed common characteristics of expert practitioners: (1) expert practitioners consider each practice situation as a unique and undetermined case; and (2) they frequently reframe this situation through "reflection-in-action" (i.e., reflective conversations during practice that is aimed at assessing and adjusting actions in an unfolding situation). Echoing this view, Cross [27] argued that design expertise requires the abilities to solve ill-defined problems and adopt solution-focused strategies. He called for exploring "deep, underlying patterns of how designers think and act." In this study, we aimed to understand how designers of games for health think and act (based on their reflection) to meet the unique and unfamiliar challenges in their work. In the following sections, we review literature aimed at understanding interaction designers and game designers.

Understanding interaction Designers
The HCI community has explored the HCI/UX practitioners' perceptions and practices since the field is inaugurated (e.g. [14,33]). In a seminal paper, Gould and Lewis [14] outlined three principles that defined a "user-centered" approach: (a) early focus on the user, (b) empirical measurement, and (c) iterative design. Aiming to explore how professional practitioners considered these principles, they asked the attendees of a HCI conference to describe the major steps they regard as good practice in their work. Only a small fraction of their participants mentioned the three principles [14].

As the interaction design profession matures, more recent related research has focused on stressing the role of designers and acknowledging their experience and skills [13,32,39–41,46]. A rationale for this approach is that knowledge about designers' values and practices will help bridge the HCI research-practice gap and support design education. For example, Goodman et al. discussed the gap between HCI research and interaction design practice; they proposed a shift in which "HCI researchers turn their attention to producing theories of interaction design practice that resonate with practitioners themselves" [13]. Stolterman et al. also proposed the concept of *Designerly Tools* aimed at exploring "methods, tools, techniques, and approaches that support design activity in a way that is appreciated by practicing designers" [40]. In an exploratory study, the authors found that designers framed tools as having two different purposes: supporting design thinking and supporting creation of an artifact. In addition, designers considered physical or digital tools and conceptual tools (theories and approaches) in the same manner [40]. These insights informed the interview questions in our study.

Understanding Game Designers

How game designers think and work has also been a topic of recent research [4,15,23]. For example, Hagen [15] interviewed six game designers from major game development studios in Sweden to understand how they considered and captured player experience in their work. He found that while all participants considered player experience as an important focus in design, most adopted an "autobiographical design" approach when capturing player experience; i.e., the designers they interviewed mainly relied on their personal and professional experiences when approaching design and rarely leveraged user research methods to understand their target players and assess their games [15]. Related, Manker and Arvola [23] interviewed 27 game designers to understand how they perceived and practiced prototyping to support their design. They found that prototyping helped designers set and clarify the design goals and communicate design ideas to stakeholders.

There are very few studies focused on designers of serious games; many have focused on games for learning (e.g. [17,34]). For example, Isbister et al. [17] interviewed 17 game designers within and beyond the games for learning field to explore how they considered the challenges and best practices in educational game design. Their participants claimed that serious games must be fun first and the serious contents need to be deeply integrated in the game mechanics and goals. Interviewees also expressed concerns about sparse resources (e.g. budget and time) that reduced the designers' abilities to polish their games to a higher level. Delving into the issue of how designers integrate serious contents into gameplay, Ryan and Charsky [34] interviewed 11 serious game practitioners. They identified several factors that influenced the success of this integration; factors included sufficient evaluation, adequate recourses, and client collaboration and understanding. Related to games for health, Mueller and Isbister [18,26] collected game design experts' feedback about design guidelines they had created for movement-based games; the authors asked their participants to evaluate their guidelines' appropriateness, accuracy, and the communicative value. In our literature review, we were unable to find work that directly targeted understanding games for health designers. Our work thus contributes to the literature by focusing on this unique and challenging design terrain.

METHODS

We conducted semi-structured interviews with 11 professional game designers who are currently working in the games for health field. In the following sections, we discuss our recruitment process and participants, our interview protocol, and our data analysis procedure. This study was approved by the Institutional Review Boards at DePaul University to ensure ethical conduct.

Participants

We began the recruitment process by identifying authors or presenters from the Games for Health Journal (22 issues from February 2012 to August 2015) and the Games for Health Conference (2013 and 2014) who were associated with a professional game design studio. We then followed each studio's website and collected names and contact information (if available) of the game designers in the studio. Among the 48 game designers we identified, we were able to obtain an email address contact for 30 designers. We sent recruitment emails to those 30 designers; 11 responded and completed the interview.

Among the 11 participants we interviewed, nine were from the United States (from five states including Illinois, Wisconsin, Pennsylvania, Texas, and California), one was from the Netherlands, and one was from the UK; four out of the 11 designers were female. All participants had a job title that included "designer" or "creative director" and considered game design as their main responsibility. Their professional experience as game designers varied between 3 and 23 years. All participants had actively worked on games for health projects during the past three years; many were designing a game for health at the time of our interview. All but one participant had also worked on game projects beyond games for health, including commercial entertainment games and games for learning. Table 1 summarizes professional experiences of our participants.

While most participants focused on digital games ($N = 8$), two had exclusively worked on tabletop games and the remaining one focused on active games that are played in a real-world space. The health goals participants had considered included promoting a healthy behavior ($N = 5$), addressing a mental health issue (e.g. anxiety) ($N = 4$), increasing awareness or empathy of a health condition (e.g. depression) ($N = 2$), supporting conversations around health related issues (e.g. sex and sexuality among teens) ($N = 2$), and promoting physical exercise ($N = 2$).

Interviews

We conducted the interviews between October and December 2015. All but one interview was conducted via

ID	Job title	Years as game designer	# of games for health designed	% of games for health in all projects
P1	Creative Director	8	7	66%
P2	Head of Game Design	23	3	10%
P3	Senior Game Designer	10	3	20%
P4	Creative Director	15	3	20%
P5	Lead Designer	20	25	80%
P6	Lead Designer	5	2	50%
P7	VP of Design	13	10	50%
P8	Art Director	8	4	25%
P9	Game Designer	9	10	50%
P10	Lead Designer	8	2	30%
P11	Game Designer	3	10	100%

Table 1. Summary of participants' professional experiences (all data were collected at the time of the interview)

phone calls or VoIP; the remaining one was conducted in-person. During the interviews, we asked participants about many aspects as to how they think and act in practice, including: (1) processes they followed to design games for health; (2) their most and least successful games for health projects and their accounts related to successfulness; (3) methods they used to acquire domain knowledge and to explore the needs of their target players; (4) methods they used to evaluate their games; (5) the biggest challenges they considered in games for health design; and (6) the tools they used for designing games for health. Each interview took between 30 and 45 minutes; interviews were audio-recorded and later fully transcribed.

Data Analysis

We adopted a grounded theory approach [9] and followed four steps in analyzing the transcribed interviews.

1. One author conducted structural coding [35] of the interviews to identify the major topics and the corresponding text segments. The topics identified in this step included (1) general approach, (2) success, (3) challenge, (4) domain research and game evaluation, and (5) tools used.

2. Two authors independently analyzed the interviews and inductively coded for salient themes in each structural topic identified in step 1.

3. The two authors discussed their codes and reached an agreement on the themes they identified. They then co-wrote a codebook to describe how to identify those themes; in the codebook, each theme was associated with one or more structural topics.

4. A third author who did not involve in the interviews and the codebook creation process (i.e. a blind coder) used the codebook and deductively coded the interviews. We then calculated inter-rater reliability using Cohen's kappa through binary agreement with the blind coder (i.e. if a theme was identified at least

once within a structural topic in the interview, we coded it "Yes").

FINDINGS

Among all the themes included in our codebook, the average inter-rater reliability based on Cohen's kappa was 0.68 ($SD = 0.27$); a kappa statistic between 0.60 and 0.80 is considered a "substantial" agreement [22]. In the following sections, we only report on themes in which inter-rater reliability was considered substantial or better (Cohen's kappa is 0.60 or greater) *and* at least three participants mentioned the theme. Those themes were categorized into the four overarching topics based on the structural coding: (1) success, (2) challenge, (3) domain research and game evaluation methods, and (4) tools used in design.

Success

We asked participants to describe their most and least successful games for health projects and reflect on why they felt the games were successful or unsuccessful. When discussing this topic, participants mentioned two top-level themes: (1) specifics about *criteria* they considered when determining the success of a game for health and (2) specifics about *factors* that contributed to the successfulness or unsuccessfulness of a game for health. When coding these themes, we consolidated the designers' opinions and reflections on both successful and unsuccessful projects; i.e. similar criteria or factors were discussed in both successful and unsuccessful projects.

Success Criteria

When discussing how they judged the success of a game for health project, participants mentioned standards and criteria that fell into one of the three categories: (a) the game's effectiveness at addressing the targeted health goals, (b) a balance between engagement and efficacy, and (c) adoption and/or publicity of the game.

(a) Eight of our participants considered meeting the game's serious objectives (i.e. the health goals) as a criterion of success. For example, P5 explicitly mentioned that he would generally regard efficacy and effectiveness as the top success measure:

"The measure of success is whether your hypothesis turns out to be true. You know, I could measure success based on unit sales. But you are very limited on that. I would really measure it on efficacy and on effectiveness."

When considering a game designed to support children with an attention deficit hyperactivity disorder (ADHD), P9 discussed its success around clinical tests and meeting the serious goals:

"That is a rare thing – that is it was really tested clinically and validated. ... I think in that case. It was really successful. And I think it really provided the users with all the goals they needed to have with the game."

(b) Five participants also explicitly discussed player experience and considered achieving a balance between player engagement and goal efficacy as a success criterion.

For example, when talking about the same game supporting children with ADHD, P9 also stressed the importance of balancing efficacy with engaging gameplay; he mentioned that this consideration is more associated with his own perspective as a game designer:

"If I look at that project, I think it was one of my biggest successes in terms of how to make a real game that also has these serious elements in it. ... That's always a delicate balance between how serious something gets and how fun it is to play. ... So from my point of view as a designer, it was a really successful game."

P2, a veteran commercial game designer who recently entered the games for health area, discussed the differences between success of a commercial game and a game for health; he emphasized the importance of embedding engagement into the game to support the serious contents:

"We can't typically design a game like you would in entertainment. You would have to look at the learning and health goals, talk with subject matter experts, and come up with very unique ways in order to add that fun factor or engagement in the game. That really is embedded in how those goals come across."

(c) Seven participants mentioned that they considered a wide adoption and/or a considerable publicity as a measure of success. For example, P4 considered a game aimed at helping youths understand medical knowledge as successful because it had *"won some awards."* P8 also mentioned a wide adoption when talking about the success of a unique game that leveraged biofeedback mechanisms for young people to understand and manage anxiety; in addition to the standard mouse and keyboard control, the game reacts to changes in players' physiological state such as pulse and sweat monitored using biofeedback hardware:

"This game has been used in a variety of environments and it's our most requested game. So in that respect, that made it a uniquely successful product for us."

While P9 considered the game for children with ADHD as successful in terms of effectiveness and a balance between player engagement and goal efficacy, he lamented about the low adoption of the game:

"But unfortunately, it wasn't really a success with the rollout. I think not a lot of people actually played the game. ... That's a bit sad."

Success Factors

Participants discussed various factors that contributed to the success of their games. We categorized the factors into four groups: (a) direct interaction with target players, (b) stakeholder communication and cooperation, (c) successful game design elements and design choices, and (d) iteration.

(a) Seven of our participants considered direct interaction with target players as an important factor to achieve success. Many mentioned that including target players in a participatory design process or during playtest sessions had helped them understand the characteristics and needs of their players and/or had provided insightful information for designing the games. For example, when talking about a game to promote healthy behavior for patients who have had a heart failure, P7 mentioned that insights gained from interviews with target players had motivated him to adopt a minimalist game design style that had contributed to the success of the game:

"What we found in our interviews with patients at the beginning of our design process was that even the basic literacy level of many of the patients is super low. ... And people's scientific literacy and medical literacy was even lower. So we really, really simplified it."

(b) Six participants considered the quality of the partnership with other stakeholders (e.g. the client or subject matter experts) and the support they acquired from the stakeholders as a factor contributing to the games' success. For example, P7 mentioned a good partnership with other team members had allowed the designer to embrace his minimalist game design style:

"Luckily we had a team that trusted us and I had a lot of support from the folks we were working with. So we were able to say, 'we are really going to focus on these complete really basic ideas.'"

Some participants also valued the domain and user information provided by the subject matter experts (i.e. medical and healthcare experts) that helped achieve success of the game. For example, P9 emphasized the support he acquired from the client and the subject matter experts:

"We had a team of researchers at our disposal that was really involved in the whole process. ... They knew everything about the subject and we could iterate with them on how we should implement that in the game."

Poor partnership with stakeholders would also negatively affect the game's success. When talking about an unsuccessful game, P9 considered a scenario in which an assertive client can impede a designer's effort to achieve a balance between player engagement and goal efficacy:

"Especially if the client is really pushing its vision on the game through, then you have a game that the client think is great but the users are not that interested about it – players are just not engaged and they don't like to play the game. Then basically it fails to meet the goals that you set for the project."

(c) Seven participants mentioned general game design elements (e.g. narratives, challenge, etc.) or specific design choices when discussing factors contributed to the success of a game. For example, P3 designed an iPad game aimed at supporting youths at risk of sexually transmitted diseases; she mentioned that focusing on narratives and delivering an authentic experience helped to make the game successful:

"We focused on narrative and making important decisions and seeing the outcome of the decisions. ... We

also focused on trying to capture the narrative quality of stories that these players would see in their everyday life, trying to make it feel authentic so that they would be interested – kind of like they were interested in what's happening to themselves and their peers."

P8 also emphasized game narratives in a game for anxiety management; he strived for combining novel technology and narratives to create a unique player experience:

"There is the novel aspect of it: We merged clinical techniques and eastern techniques [of anxiety management] into our own mythic world. So it has a very unique narrative. Also, it's a game that works with the biofeedback device, which a lot of people are not doing."

(d) Three participants explicitly mentioned that design iteration is a key to create successful games. For example, P2 provided an insightful summary of his design philosophy, in which he valued the combination of subject matter expert support, direct interaction with target players, and iteration:

"I got up with that whole idea of, you know, more time with subject matter experts and more time with focus-testing and iterating on design, the better the game would be. I think that's the key in any game for impact."

Challenge

We identified six themes in participants' consideration of the major challenges in games for health design: (a) combining engagement and the serious game goals, (b) consolidating interests of subject matter experts and game designers, (c) evaluating efficacy, (d) working with limited resources, (e) achieving lasting impact and interest, and (f) overcoming stereotypes associated with gaming.

(a) Six participants felt a major challenge in games for health design is to achieve a balance between player engagement and the game's effectiveness at addressing the health goals. On one hand, participants regarded achieving the health goal via an engaging game as challenging. For example, P3 said:

"The biggest challenge is that it's always a tall order. It's not just about designing an engaging game. But you have to really be aware of the research, you have to really investigate the problem, and you have other metrics for success in addition to the game is engaging – you also have to achieve the purpose. So I think there is just a lot more requirements for this kind of game."

On the other hand, many participants also emphasized the difficulty of achieving player engagement in games for health and lamented on the lack of engagement in many current games. For example, P2 mentioned:

"The biggest challenge is making it still feel like a game. It's ultimately its name, you know, a 'game for health', versus a 'task for health'. There are a lot of games out there that are just tasks. So the challenge is trying to

embed that goal in a very playful way ... so it should come across very naturally."

(b) Four participants mentioned that it is often challenging to consolidate the different mindsets, interests, and motivations between the subject matter experts and the designers. For example, P2 talked about the conflicts they often meet and the compromise they often have to make when working with subject matter experts:

"On almost every project we come to this point of compromise, where as game designers, we are trying to add very game-like motivations and trying to embed and hide the serious goals in there, and then the PIs or the subject matter experts are scientists and they are looking at it from science. So they tend to want to just see the serious goals in every interface. So what usually ended up happening is we strip out what we call the fun and engagement part of it and we end up putting in like 'look what you are getting' in your face – because that makes them feel better."

P4 discussed the same issue and felt the severity of the issue *"depends on how well the subject experts understand games."* P5 also emphasized the difficulty to communicate with subject matter experts because of this difference on mindsets and focuses:

"One of the barriers to serious game development is the disconnect between game developers and the serious content providers. They often do not speak the same language or understand each other's areas. ... Especially in healthcare, many of the subject experts are not game players. ... So when talking about games they may understand the words but not be able to relate it to an experience in their own fund of knowledge."

(c) Three participants considered measuring the efficacy of games for health as a major challenge. Participants mentioned various reasons for the difficulty of measuring efficacy. First, it is sometimes difficult to define the proper metrics for efficacy in games for health. Second, a proper measurement requires resources such as time and committed partners that are often limited in games for health projects. Third, a proper evaluation on efficacy is usually done when the game is finished and it has little value to feedback to the design iterations. Mentioning all three reasons, P7 said:

"I think the biggest challenge is measurement – to actually do a pilot and get a scientifically rigorous assessment about whether or not the intervention is successful. The problem we face is also that it takes a long time. It takes a really committed partner. And it's really hard to iterate when you have to wait for six months or a year to get data from a study like that."

(d) Three participants also emphasized that games for health projects usually have to work around limited resources such as time and budget, which poses a considerable challenge. For example, P3 considered limited budget is one reason that constrained the quality of some games for health projects:

"I think one of the biggest challenges is that we have to do more with less. The projects are usually underfunded. ... The typically funded, they are in smaller amounts as compared to traditional entertainment games. ... I think that is one of the reasons why some of these games struggle with quality."

(e) Three participants mentioned that it is often challenging for games for health to achieve sustainable impacts and maintain lasting player interest. P1 also associated this challenge of sustainability with limited budget:

"I think the biggest challenge is promoting lasting change and having a sustainable experience. There is a novelty value to every game – people play it for a while ... and often you come to know that over time this novelty wears off very quickly. ... Since we don't have much money to create a huge game for health, it is a problem using one or two intervention and then people play it for an hour and you are done. So being able to milk that positive benefit of games for a longer amount of time is a huge challenge."

(f) Three participants considered a challenge for games for health is to handle stereotypes associated with gaming. For example, P6 designed a board game aimed at supporting communication around end of life topics; a big challenge he experienced when promoting this game was a stereotype that people think games are not serious:

"Especially at the beginning when we were starting the design of the game and trying to get people interested in it, particularly because this is a very serious topic, people don't think games are appropriate for this kind of thing. ... A few weeks ago, there was a big event where people play the game and afterwards several people came up and said, 'I really enjoyed it. We had a lot of fun. But don't call it a game.' And I think there is a disconnection about what a game is."

Domain Research and Game Evaluation Methods

We asked participants to describe methods they had used to understand the domain and the target players and methods they had used to evaluate their games. We organized these methods into two top-level themes: (1) before-prototype methods and (2) after-prototype methods.

Before-Prototype Methods

Before creating a game prototype, participants mentioned use of various methods to understand the subject matter topic, explore the characteristics and needs of targeted players, and refine the game's objectives. We grouped the before-prototype methods into three major types: (a) get support from subject matter experts, (b) directly interact with target players, and (c) read materials about the domain. These methods eventually supported the designers in brainstorming and prototyping.

(a) All 11 participants acquired some kind of support from subject matter experts before prototyping starts in at least one of their games for health projects. However, the level and the form of subject matter experts' involvement varied.

Some participants gained subject matter experts' help from informal conversations. For example, P1 mentioned that she regularly talked with a medical school professor who focused on the treatment of anxiety disorders to acquire knowledge about this subject.

In contrast, some games for health projects were led by or partnered with a research group focused on the subject matter. For example, P7 mentioned that he usually get subject matter experts' support from this kind of partnership:

"We start with our client and our partner. They often have subject matter experts. So we start there to learn what they believe the context would be. They are not our players – they are not our end audience. But they do inform the criteria for success and what they believe to be the correct objectives."

In some cases, game development studios had hired subject matter experts to support their design. For example, P8 discussed how they hired different types of experts throughout the design process:

"We usually have two levels of experts. We have people who are generalists. They come in early and set the table for the domain. ... We sometimes call them 'storytellers.' They help the whole team get familiar with and start understanding the domain. Then once we drill in, and we start knowing what we are going to focus. We bring in content experts. They really know a lot about specific things. We work with them to make sure what we are doing is accurate."

(b) Seven participants mentioned that they had directly interacted with target players (via e.g. interviews, focus groups, and/or informal conversations) prior to creating a prototype to understand the domain and player needs. For example, P7 stated that he usually conducted interviews with target players before creating a prototype:

"We generally follow a player-centric design process, where we try to do interviews with our target audience up front. ... When we talk to representative players, we were really looking for 'What's their baseline?' You know. 'What are their attitude about the content? What do they know? What don't they know? What do they want to know more about?' We also have general questions about games: 'Do they play games? What kind of games? How do they feel about games?'"

(c) Four participants also mentioned that they read materials such as research papers or books to understand the domain and the target players. For example, when designing a game aimed at supporting youths at risk for sexually transmitted diseases, P3 mentioned that after interacting with subject matter experts they further explored the domain through research materials:

"[After subject experts focus groups,] we then drew from the body of research around behavior change that is long-standing. So we were looking at that research."

After-Prototype Methods

Participants adopted several methods to help evaluate and iterate the prototypes they created. These methods fell into one of the two major categories: (a) playtests that are conducted by the designers themselves and (b) formal research studies that are usually conducted with the support of subject matter experts and focused on game efficacy.

(a) All 11 participants have conducted playtests with target players to help explore the effectiveness, the gameplay, and/or other aspects such as narratives and artwork of their prototypes. The methods participants used in playtests included observations of player behavior ($N = 6$), interviews or focus groups with the players ($N = 5$), surveys during or after playtest sessions ($N = 4$), and remote tests leveraging telemetry data or player diaries ($N = 3$). P9 mentioned all four playtest methods by saying:

"So when you can actually observe it, it gives you the most insight. But we can't always be there. So sometimes we just provide them with the game and they can test it at home. Then they can fill in, for example, surveys online and provide us with feedback. We recently tested a game and let players play it at home. We then had a telephone survey – we call them and ask them how they were doing and how it was the gameplay. So that's a media between seeing it and just letting them fill in the questionnaire."

Participants also expressed concerns with three factors about how to conduct playtest:

1. *Early and often.* Eight of our participants mentioned that they tended to conduct playtests early and often in the development cycle. For example, P7 mentioned: "A*s soon as we had something built, usually our first prototype, we do playtesting with representative players and collect data from it. These then inform our iterative development process. We playtest as much as we can in the course of the development."*

2. *Obscuring the purposeful goal.* Four participants mentioned that they intentionally obscured the purposeful goals of the game from the players during playtests to see if the goal emerges from play. For example, when talking about playtesting a game that aimed at promoting awareness and empathy about people who are living with depression, P1 mentioned: "*In the beginning we didn't tell them because I wanted to see whether the experience came across without their knowing what it was about – did we really captured, with the mechanisms and the game structure alone, that feeling of helplessness of loss and frustration – because that was the point."*

3. *Group/social testing.* Four participants mentioned that they included multiple participants in a same playtest session to encourage feedback. For example, when talking about playtesting a game aimed at helping children understand medical knowledge, P4 said, *"Often we will have kids paired up and you want to get them talk to each other. ... And also, it can be helpful for keeping them honest."*

(b) Three participants mentioned that they collaborated with subject matter experts to conduct formal research studies to evaluate the game's effectiveness at addressing the serious goals. For example, P6 mentioned that a research team they were collaborating with was actively evaluating the game for end of life communication:

"The research team is actually the one that's doing much more in-depth studies of how people play the game. They actually do audio and video recording of every game. And then they have a methodology called the Multiple Goals Framework to assess communication qualities."

Tools Used in Design

We asked participants to discuss tools they had used that supported their design of games for health; we explicitly asked them to consider "physical, digital, and conceptual tools." Participants considered several types of tools that included (a) theoretical frameworks, (b) design philosophy or design process, and (c) early prototyping methods. Very few participants mentioned physical and digital tools.

(a) Seven of our participants mentioned that they have used theoretical frameworks that are either published or internal to the participant's organization to support their design; those frameworks included (1) theories about the domain or the subject matter ($N = 3$), (2) works about game design in general (such as Jesse Schell's game design lenses [36], $N = 3$), and (3) frameworks about serious game design ($N = 2$). For example, P7 mentioned that he had used both published and internal frameworks to support his work:

"We leverage Bloom's taxonomy to think about the learning and behavior change objectives. ... We also developed internally in our studio a model of elements of game for behavior change. And that model certainly informs how we approach the design of a game."

(b) Four participants considered a certain design philosophy or a certain aspect of their design process as a "tool." For example, P7 considered a design process of determining the game's objectives up front as a tool:

"I would say that a tool is really our design process, particularly in the very beginning. ... I mentioned the idea of determining learning objectives and behavior objectives up front. ... That really helps us drive the focus early in the project."

Several participants also mentioned using other existing games as a tool to support inspiration or communication. For example, P2 said:

"When working with the PIs and the researchers, one of the tools is playing other games. ... Because a lot of times the people we were working with aren't gamers. So I think games themselves become tools that helped the communication and design."

(c) Three participants considered early prototyping methods (e.g. using pencil and paper or board game pieces) as tools to support design. For example, P8 considered paper prototyping as a tool to design a digital game:

"A tool is really paper prototyping. Sometimes we even first do it as a board game or a card game."

DISCUSSION

In this study, we explored how game designers who focused on games for health perceived and approached designing games. We argue that the insights presented in this study bridges a current gap between research and practice in the Player-Computer Interaction (PCI) community; that is, our work exposes current values and practices of game design professionals in the context of games for health, which is a needed first step for discussing (1) adaptation of Games User Research (GUR) methods in serious game design and (2) methods and tools that can better support serious game designers. These insights will be of interest not only to games for health researchers and practitioners, but also contribute to understanding about the design of games as purposeful media. In the following sections we discuss the major implications of our study.

Games for Health Designers Are Very User-Centric

In our interviews, we found that most games for health designers valued and practiced Gould and Lewis's three principles of user-centered design, i.e. early focus on the user, empirical measurement, and iterative design [14]. Further, most participants mentioned interviews or focus groups with target players as one of their first steps approaching a game for health project; many also regarded direct user involvement as an important factor that contributed to the success of their games. These findings suggested that games for health designers tend to put a lot of emphasis on early user involvement and user research.

Notably, our finding is inconsistent with Hagen's discoveries about the practice of some commercial entertainment game designers; while limited on sample size, Hagen [15] found that his entertainment-focused game designer participants tended not to leverage early user research in their work. We speculate that the nature of the game projects may have influenced the approaches of the health and entertainment game designers. Target players of games for health often have special health-related attributes that are not familiar to the designers. In addition, many of the user attributes essential to game design (e.g. target users' play preferences) are also unique to the user group (e.g. an elderly population). As a result, it is crucial for the games for health designers to pay special attention to their target players and conduct user research themselves to understand the player attributes.

Our participants also mentioned that they have adapted common GUR methods to fit in the unique context of games for health design. For example, participants told us that they often obscured the health goals in playtesting sessions to see if those goals were embedded in play. Interviewees also discussed how playtesting methods were limited in establishing the efficacy of the game at meeting health goals; as a result, many of our participants resorted to more formal research studies. These insights indicated that adaptation of traditional GUR methods in serious game design is an important area to explore.

Problem-Focused vs. Solution-Focused

Nigel Cross [27] argued that, unlike problem-focused professionals (e.g. scientists), designers usually adopt a solution-focused strategy when approaching a design problem. According to Cross, designers are often faced with ill-defined and ill-structured problems; as a result, they prefer to approach a problem by synthesizing lessons learned from "planning, inventing, making and doing" to create a satisfactory solution. While we found that games for health designers are also generally solution-focused, many participants in our interviews approached game design by exploring both the problem and the solution spaces somewhat equally.

On one hand, all of our participants were committed to iterative prototyping and playtesting when approaching game design. Participants also relied on this iterative process to refine their understanding of the domain and the target users (i.e. the problem space). On the other hand, we also found that many of our participants put a lot of emphasis on before-prototype methods. Many participants devoted considerable effort to explore the subject matter and the needs of the target players even before creating the first prototype. Additionally, we found that some participants put more emphasis on before-prototype methods than others; i.e. there was a spectrum of problem-focused tendency among our participants. In particular, some of our participants mentioned that they strived to clearly define the serious objectives and the efficacy measures of a proposed game before approaching design.

We feel this tendency of approaching design from the problem and the solution spaces somewhat equally is unique to serious game designers; Vasalou et al. [44] also emphasized pre-prototyping efforts when developing an educational game. We speculate that this tendency among games for health designers has two originating sources. First, games for health designers are facing complex problems that are often unfamiliar to them. As such, they often have to acquire a great amount of domain knowledge in order to approach the initial design; this is also associated with their early user focus tendency. Second, games for health designers often work closely with subject matter experts and other stakeholders who are more accustomed to problem-focused approaches. For example, some of the game projects discussed in the interviews were initiated or funded through a research project led by medical professionals. As a result, designers often need to adjust their approaches to maintain effective collaboration and communication with these stakeholders.

Games for Health Design Is a Challenging Area

Entertainment and serious game designers all face significant challenges when considering the design of engaging experiences; however the latter group also have to steer player experience to deliver a purposeful goal. Some of our findings about games for health designers' account for challenges were in agreement with the literature focused on other groups of serious game designers. For example, our findings supported that embedding serious content into an engaging gameplay experience is a crucial but difficult aspect [5,7,34]; in addition, maintaining successful stakeholder collaboration is also important but challenging in serious game projects [6,20].

We have also identified several challenges that are particularly important for games for health designers. For example, when compared to educational games, which are usually focused on delivering specific knowledge or skill, games for health often focus on more subtle (e.g. behavior change) or long-term (e.g. rehabilitation) effects. As such, our participants considered establishing efficacy of the games as a significant challenge. In addition, games for health players are diverse; in some areas (e.g. games for elderly adults), the target users are not typically familiar with the game media. So dealing with stereotypes (and sometimes stigmas) associated with gaming was perceived as a challenging aspect by some of our participants.

When addressing those challenges, our interviewees tended to be more problem-oriented and very user-centric in their practice. However, their user-centered efforts did not always help with some of the prominent challenges such as communicating with subject matter experts and achieving lasting player experiences. These findings indicated that more research is needed to help support games for health designers overcome the challenges interviewees discussed.

Success of Games for Health Is a Complex Issue

While delivering an engaging player experience is usually the success criteria of most entertainment games, our interviewees discussed the success of their games for health projects in more complex ways. When we asked our participants to describe their successful and unsuccessful games, they usually started by qualifying the definition of success and continued in discussing multiple aspects of the project, indicating that they did not consider success as a one-dimensional phenomenon. We speculate that this multi-dimensional and sometimes context-based view of success is associated with the challenges designers meet in their work. For example, designers need to balance the needs of various stakeholders including subject matter experts, clients, players, and/or caregivers when approaching their design vision.

In research that has explored factors contributing to the success of serious games, many have proposed game design elements, such as appropriate challenge and meaningful feedback, as success factors (e.g. [3,21,45]). In our study, however, participants valued process and methodological issues (e.g. interaction with target players, stakeholder communication) over specific game design elements when considering factors leading to success. While we acknowledge game design elements are important components, we call for more research on methodologies and approaches from the games for health and serious game communities.

Tools Are Mostly Theoretical and Conceptual

When discussing tools used to support design, we found that participants took account of major consideration on theoretical frameworks and conceptual approaches. This consideration of theoretical and conceptual tools supports Stolterman et al.'s concept of *Designerly Tools* [40]; i.e. designers value artifacts, methods, and theories similarly as tools. It also resonates with the recent efforts in related literature that explored game designers' accounts of theoretical and conceptual tools [15,18,23]. For example, echoing with Manker and Arvola [23], our participants also considered early prototyping methods as tools to support generating and communicating design ideas. We argue that the designers' emphasis on theoretical and conceptual tools provides insights for both researchers and educators concerned with games for health; i.e. the need to emphasize investigation and teaching about these tools.

Further, very few of our participants mentioned the use of physical or digital tools to support their design. Some participants also expressed dissatisfaction about the lack of design tools. Specifically, our interviewees voiced a need for information tools to help them understand the subject matter and communicate with other stakeholders. We feel that investigating information tools for serious game designers is a valuable future area to explore.

LIMITATIONS AND FUTURE WORK

In this study, we relied on practitioners' reflection on past experiences to explore their values and practices. We recognize that this approach is limited in its ability to understand how designers work "in-action." A longitudinal contextual inquiry would provide supplemental information to this study. In addition, while we aimed to include diverse participants to understand the common themes in their perspectives, exploring how different experience and background can affect designers' perspectives would be compelling future work. In the future, we also plan to examine how theoretical and conceptual tools can support games for health designers. In particular, we are exploring how therapy-centered game design patterns can serve as a tool to support designers focused on games for brain injury rehabilitation [10].

ACKNOWLEDGEMENTS

We thank our participants for their time and Dr. Doris Rusch for her insightful input that guided our protocol. Also, thanks to the DePaul University Research Council for funding this project.

REFERENCES

1. Gazihan Alankus, Amanda Lazar, Matt May, and Caitlin Kelleher. 2010. Towards customizable games for stroke rehabilitation. *Proceedings of the 28th international conference on Human factors in computing systems CHI '10*, ACM Press, 2113–2122. http://doi.org/10.1145/1753326.1753649

2. Tom Baranowski. *Games for Health Journal*. Retrieved from http://www.liebertpub.com/overview/games-for-health-journal/588/

3. Katrin Becker. 2009. Video Game Pedagogy: Good Games = Good Pedagogy. In *Games: Purpose and Potential in Education*. Springer US, Boston, MA, 73–125. http://doi.org/10.1007/978-0-387-09775-6_5

4. Elizabeth Bonsignore, Vicki Moulder, Carman Neustaedter, Derek Hansen, Kari Kraus, and Allison Druin. 2014. Design Tactics for Authentic Interactive Fiction: Insights from Alternate Reality Game Designers. *Proceedings of the 32nd annual ACM conference on Human factors in computing systems - CHI '14*: 947–950. http://doi.org/10.1145/2556288.2557245

5. Amy Bruckman. 1999. Can Educational Be Fun? *Game Developer Conference*, 75–79.

6. Richard Buday, Tom Baranowski, and Debbe Thompson. 2012. Fun and Games and Boredom. *Games for Health Journal* 1, 4: 257–261. http://doi.org/10.1089/g4h.2012.0026

7. Richard Buday. 2015. Games for Health: An Opinion. *Games for Health Journal* 4, 1: 38–42. http://doi.org/10.1089/g4h.2014.0083

8. J. W. Burke, M. D. J. McNeill, D. K. Charles, P. J. Morrow, J. H. Crosbie, and S. M. McDonough. 2009. Optimising engagement for stroke rehabilitation using serious games. *The Visual Computer* 25, 12: 1085–1099. http://doi.org/10.1007/s00371-009-0387-4

9. Kathy Charmaz. 2014. *Constructing Grounded Theory*. SAGE Publications Ltd.

10. Jinghui Cheng, Cynthia Putnam, and Doris C Rusch. 2015. Towards Efficacy-Centered Game Design Patterns For Brain Injury Rehabilitation: A Data-Driven Approach. *Proceedings of the 17th International ACM SIGACCESS Conference on Computers & Accessibility*, ACM Press, 291–299. http://doi.org/10.1145/2700648.2809856

11. Health Games Database. 2016. Health Games Database. Retrieved March 8, 2016 from http://www.cdgr.ucsb.edu/db

12. Eletha Flores, Gabriel Tobon, Ettore Cavallaro, Francesca I. Cavallaro, Joel C. Perry, and Thierry Keller. 2008. Improving patient motivation in game development for motor deficit rehabilitation. *Proceedings of the 2008 International Conference in Advances in Computer Entertainment Technology - ACE '08*, ACM Press, 381–384. http://doi.org/10.1145/1501750.1501839

13. Elizabeth Goodman, Erik Stolterman, and Ron Wakkary. 2011. Understanding interaction design practices. *Proceedings of the 2011 annual conference on Human factors in computing systems - CHI '11*, ACM Press, 1061. http://doi.org/10.1145/1978942.1979100

14. John D Gould and Clayton Lewis. 1985. Designing for Usability : Key Principles and What Designers Think. *Communications of the ACM* 28, 3: 300–311. http://doi.org/10.1145/3166.3170

15. Ulf Hagen. 2011. Designing for player experience : How professional game developers communicate design visions. *Journal of Gaming and Virtual Worlds* 3, 3: 259–275. http://doi.org/10.1.1.194.1417

16. Amanda K. Hall, Enmanuel Chavarria, Vasana Maneeratana, Beth H. Chaney, and Jay M. Bernhardt. 2012. Health Benefits of Digital Videogames for Older Adults: A Systematic Review of the Literature. *Games for Health Journal* 1, 6: 402–410. http://doi.org/10.1089/g4h.2012.0046

17. Katherine Isbister, Mary Flanagan, and Chelsea Hash. 2010. Designing games for learning: insights from conversations with designers. *Proceedings of the 28th international conference on Human factors in computing systems - CHI '10*, ACM Press, 2041–2044. http://doi.org/10.1145/1753326.1753637

18. Katherine Isbister and Florian "Floyd" Mueller. 2015. Guidelines for the Design of Movement-Based Games and Their Relevance to HCI. *Human–Computer Interaction* 30, 3-4: 366–399. http://doi.org/10.1080/07370024.2014.996647

19. Rilla Khaled, Pippin Barr, Ronald Fischer, James Noble, and Robert Biddle. 2006. Factoring culture into the design of a persuasive game. *Proceedings of the 20th conference of the computer-human interaction special interest group (CHISIG) of Australia on Computer-human interaction: design: activities, artefacts and environments - OZCHI '06*, ACM Press, 213. http://doi.org/10.1145/1228175.1228213

20. Rilla Khaled and Gordon Ingram. 2012. Tales from the front lines of a large-scale serious game project. *Proceedings of the 2012 ACM annual conference on Human Factors in Computing Systems - CHI '12*, ACM Press, 69–78. http://doi.org/10.1145/2207676.2207688

21. Fedwa Laamarti, Mohamad Eid, and Abdulmotaleb El Saddik. 2014. An overview of serious games. *International Journal of Computer Games Technology* 2014. http://doi.org/10.1155/2014/358152

22. J Richard Landis and Gary G Koch. 1977. The Measurement of Observer Agreement for Categorical Data. *Biometrics* 33, 1: 159–174. http://doi.org/10.2307/2529310

23. Jon Manker and Mattias Arvola. 2011. Prototyping in

Game Design: Externalization and Internalization of Game Ideas. *BCS-HCI '11 Proceedings of the 25th BCS Conference on Human-Computer Interaction*, British Computer Society, 279–288.

24. Robin Mellecker, Elizabeth J. Lyons, and Tom Baranowski. 2013. Disentangling Fun and Enjoyment in Exergames Using an Expanded Design, Play, Experience Framework: A Narrative Review. *Games for Health Journal* 2, 3: 142–149. http://doi.org/10.1089/g4h.2013.0022

25. David DR Michael and SL Sande Chen. 2005. *Serious games: Games that educate, train, and inform.* Muska & Lipman/Premier-Trade, Mason, OH, USA.

26. Florian Floyd Mueller and Katherine Isbister. 2014. Movement-Based Game Guidelines. *Proceedings of the SIGCHI Conference on Human Factors in Computing Systems - CHI '14*, 2191–2200. http://doi.org/10.1145/2556288.2557163

27. Nigel Cross. 2006. *Designerly Ways of Knowing.* Springer-Verlag, London. http://doi.org/10.1007/1-84628-301-9

28. Rui Nouchi, Yasuyuki Taki, Hikaru Takeuchi, et al. 2012. Brain Training Game Improves Executive Functions and Processing Speed in the Elderly: A Randomized Controlled Trial. *PLoS ONE* 7, 1: e29676. http://doi.org/10.1371/journal.pone.0029676

29. Kyle Orland and Chris Remo. 2008. Games For Health: Noah Falstein On Exergaming History. Retrieved March 8, 2016 from http://www.gamasutra.com/view/news/109512/Games_For_Health_Noah_Falstein_On_Exergaming_History.php

30. Amanda L. Penko and Jacob E. Barkley. 2010. Motivation and physiologic responses of playing a physically interactive video game relative to a sedentary alternative in children. *Annals of behavioral medicine : a publication of the Society of Behavioral Medicine* 39, 2: 162–169. http://doi.org/10.1007/s12160-010-9164-x

31. The Games for Health Project. 2016. The Games for Health Project. Retrieved March 8, 2016 from https://gamesforhealth.org

32. Cynthia Putnam, Aaron Reiner, Emily Ryou, et al. 2016. Human-Centered Design in Practice: Roles, Definitions, and Communication. *Journal of Technical Writing and Communication*. http://doi.org/10.1177/0047281616653491

33. Mary Beth Rosson, Susanne Maass, and Wendy a. Kellogg. 1987. Designing for designers: an analysis of design practice in the real world. *Proceedings of the SIGCHI/GI conference on Human factors in computing systems and graphics interface - CHI '87*, ACM Press, 137–142. http://doi.org/10.1145/29933.30873

34. William Ryan and D Charsky. 2013. Integrating Serious Content into Serious Games. *Foundations of Digital Games*, 330–337.

35. Johnny Saldaña. 2009. *The coding manual for qualitative researchers.* Sage, Thousand Oaks, CA, USA.

36. Jesse Schell. 2008. *The Art of Game Design: A book of lenses.* Morgan Kaufmann, Burlington, MA, USA.

37. Donald A. Schön. 1984. *The Reflective Practitioner: How Professionals Think in Action.* Basic Books.

38. Jeff Sinclair, Philip Hingston, and Martin Masek. 2009. Exergame development using the dual flow model. *Proceedings of the Sixth Australasian Conference on Interactive Entertainment - IE '09*, ACM Press, 1–7. http://doi.org/10.1145/1746050.1746061

39. Hanne Sørum. 2015. Do We Really Emphasize the Users That Much? Explorative Interviews With Interaction Designers. *Norsk konferanse for organisasjoners bruk av IT* 23, 1.

40. Erik Stolterman, Jamie McAtee, David Royer, and Selvan Thandapani. 2008. Designerly Tools. *Undisciplined! Proceedings of the Design Research Society Conference 2008.*

41. Erik Stolterman and James Pierce. 2012. Design Tools in Practice: Studying the Designer-Tool Relationship in Interaction Design. *Proceedings of the Designing Interactive Systems Conference on - DIS '12*, ACM Press, 25. http://doi.org/10.1145/2317956.2317961

42. Debbe Thompson, Tom Baranowski, Richard Buday, et al. 2010. Serious Video Games for Health: How Behavioral Science Guided the Development of a Serious Video Game. *Simulation & gaming* 41, 4: 587–606. http://doi.org/10.1177/1046878108328087

43. Debbe Thompson. 2012. Designing serious video games for health behavior change: current status and future directions. *Journal of Diabetes Science and Technology* 6, 4: 807–811. http://doi.org/10.1177/193229681200600411

44. Asimina Vasalou, Gordon Ingram, and Rilla Khaled. 2012. User-centered research in the early stages of a learning game. *Proceedings of the Designing Interactive Systems Conference on - DIS '12*: 116. http://doi.org/10.1145/2317956.2317976

45. Jeffrey Yim and T. C. Nicholas Graham. 2007. Using games to increase exercise motivation. *Proceedings of the 2007 conference on Future Play - Future Play '07*: 166–173. http://doi.org/10.1145/1328202.1328232

46. Xiao Zhang and Ron Wakkary. 2014. Understanding the role of designers' personal experiences in interaction design practice. *Proceedings of the 2014 conference on Designing interactive systems - DIS '14*, ACM Press, 895–904. http://doi.org/10.1145/2598510.2598556

The Gamification User Types Hexad Scale

Gustavo F. Tondello[1], Rina R. Wehbe[1], Lisa Diamond[2], Marc Busch[2],
Andrzej Marczewski[3], Lennart E. Nacke[1]
[1] HCI Games Group, Games Institute, University of Waterloo, Waterloo, ON, Canada
[2] AIT – Austrian Institute of Technology GmbH, Vienna, Austria
[3] Gamified UK, New Haw, Surrey, England
gustavo@tondello.com, rina.wehbe@uwaterloo.ca, lisa.diamond@ait.ac.at, marc.busch@ait.ac.at,
andrzej@gamified.uk, lennart.nacke@acm.org

ABSTRACT

Several studies have indicated the need for personalizing gamified systems to users' personalities. However, mapping user personality onto design elements is difficult. Hexad is a gamification user types model that attempts this mapping but lacks a standard procedure to assess user preferences. Therefore, we created a 24-items survey response scale to score users' preferences towards the six different motivations in the Hexad framework. We used internal and test-retest reliability analysis, as well as factor analysis, to validate this new scale. Further analysis revealed significant associations of the Hexad user types with the Big Five personality traits. In addition, a correlation analysis confirmed the framework's validity as a measure of user preference towards different game design elements. This scale instrument contributes to games user research because it enables accurate measures of user preference in gamification.

Author Keywords

Gamification; Gameful Design; User Types; Hexad.

ACM Classification Keywords

H.1.2. User/Machine Systems: Human Factors.

INTRODUCTION

Gamification, the use of game design elements in non-game contexts [12], has been operationalised to increase user engagement, activity, and enjoyment. Studies have shown that gamification can lead to positive behavioural changes; however, we currently do not understand the factors influencing user motivation in gamification. For example, Hamari *et al.* identified confounding factors such as the role of the context being gamified and the qualities of the users [17]. To better understand user motivation and to personalize the experience in gameful systems to each user, we propose a scale for preference assessment in gamification.

Personalizing gameful systems to each user is important because personalized interactive systems are more effective than *one-size-fits-all* approaches. Gameful systems are effective when they help users achieve their goals, which often involve educating them about certain topics, supporting them in attitude or behaviour change, or engaging them in specific topics [9]. The efficacy of personalization according to the user's personality traits has been shown in user interface design [33], persuasive technology [24,25], and games [1,34,35]. As a consequence, we believe that personalized gameful systems will be more engaging if they adapt to personality traits or player types [14,15].

Bartle's player typology for Multi-User Dungeons (MUDs) [3] is popularly used in gamification. However, it was created specifically for MUDs and it should not be generalized to other game genres nor to gameful design. To address this problem, Marczewski developed the Gamification User Types Hexad framework [27], based on research on human motivation, player types, and practical design experience. He also suggested different game design elements that may support different user types [28]. However, we still lack a standard assessment protocol for user's preferences based on the Hexad framework. There is also no empirical validation, yet, that associates Hexad user types and game design elements. In this paper, we address these two gaps.

Our work contributes to the field of gameful design[1] in human-computer interaction (HCI) with two related goals. Firstly, we propose and validate a survey measure for scoring user's preferences towards different game design elements according to the Hexad framework. The questions were contributed by experts in scale development, game design, and HCI. We conducted an initial validation with 133 people, which confirmed the survey scale's reliability is within the acceptable limits. Next, we analyzed the correlations between the participants' scores in each of the Hexad user types with their scores on each Big Five personality trait as measured by the BFI-10 [38]. Positive correlations were found for the pairs in which the theoretical background suggested them, which also contributes to validate both the Hexad framework itself and the new survey scale.

---

[1] In this paper, we refer to *gamification* and *gameful design* indistinctively because they frame the same extension of phenomena through different intentional properties [12]. Thus, the Hexad model can be used for both.

Secondly, we evaluate the potential of the Hexad framework as a model to personalize user experience (UX) in gameful systems. We asked participants to score their preferences regarding 32 design elements commonly employed in gameful design and analyzed their correlations with each of the Hexad user types. Overall, positive correlations were found between the Hexad user types and the corresponding game design elements, confirming the usefulness of the Hexad model to personalize gameful systems.

RELATED WORK

Understanding an individual's personality is a multifaceted endeavour. Theories of behaviour and personality are often employed to understand user behaviour and preferences in interactive systems because they provide some insight into motivating factors. Especially, Self-Determination Theory (SDT) [10,40] provides the theoretical background for the Hexad model concerning the expression of both intrinsic and extrinsic motivation. Thus, the Hexad user types are expressions of these distinct motivating factors.

Motivation

Within HCI research, the principles of SDT [10,40–42] are often used as an explanation to provide insights into behaviour motivation. SDT suggests that individual motivation to engage in a task can be located within a range of different grades of internalization. In a simplified model, motivation can be *intrinsic*, i.e., afforded by the individual's perception of a task as enjoyable by itself, or *extrinsic*, i.e., afforded by factors outside of the task, such as expected outcomes that may result from completing the task.

Intrinsic motivation is supported in SDT by three components. *Competence* marks the feeling of having the skills needed to accomplish the task at hand. *Autonomy* means the more in control of a situation a person feels, the more likely they are to succeed. Finally, *relatedness* is the feeling of involvement with others. Additional work in the field by Ryan *et al.* [39] notes the importance of these three pillars and indicates that they can strongly contribute to a person's mental health benefits. Furthermore, the Hexad model is also informed by the evidence that *meaning* (purpose) facilitates internalization, increasing the motivation to carry out uninteresting but important activities [11], and leads to increased happiness and life satisfaction [20,37].

Personality

Previous research has demonstrated that personality has an effect on player types [32] and player preferences of different game genres [23] and gamification elements [21]. Personality also seems to affect how players experience psychological satisfaction in games [22] and presence in virtual reality applications [26]. Thus, we decided to study how different personality traits relate to the Hexad user types.

A common way to analyse people's personalities is via the five-factor model of personality, commonly known as the *Big Five*. The Big Five provides a survey measure of five main categories of personality factors. *Openness* referring to an adventure seeking or an open-to-experience person;

Conscientiousness is related to thought and organization; *Extraversion* or outgoing personality and *Agreeableness* referring to the qualities associated with the person's relation to others; and finally, *Neuroticism* or level of self-security and confidence. We used a short, ten-questions version of the Big Five survey scale (BFI-10, [38]).

Johnson and Gardner [22] have previously studied the relationship between the Big Five personality traits and the fulfillment of psychological needs in video games. They found positive correlations between agreeableness and competence; and openness to experience and autonomy; as well as a negative correlation between emotional stability and presence. Yee *et al.* [45] studied how personality traits affect player behaviour in *World of Warcraft*. They related extraversion with the preference for group activities, agreeableness with more frequent use of emotes and preference for non-combat activities, conscientiousness with the enjoyment of disciplined collections in non-combat settings, neuroticism with a preference for Player vs. Player activities, and openness with curiosity-driven gameplay, such as creating new characters or exploring the game world. Jia *et al.* [21] studied the correlation between the Big Five personality traits and individual gamification affordance elements. They found positive correlations of extraversion with points, levels, and leaderboards; agreeableness with challenges; and conscientiousness with levels and progress; as well as negative correlations of emotional stability (the opposite of neuroticism) with points, badges, progress, and rewards; and openness with avatars.

The Balanced Inventory of Desirable Responding (BIDR) [36] is also often used in scale validation to evaluate people's tendency to bias their self-reported answers in a socially desirable way. The BIDR measures two constructs: self-deceptive enhancement (SDE), or the tendency to give reports that are honest but positively biased, and impression management (IM), or the tendency to deliberately construct a self-presentation to an audience. We used a short, six-questions version of the scale (BIDR-6, [43]).

Personalization in Games and Gameful Design

Personalization can be used in game design to tailor game mechanics to the player or in gameful design to tailor interaction mechanics to the user. Using player or user typologies to understand individual preferences is one of the common approaches for personalization. Thus, several different models exist in the literature. We review some of these most well-known and recent models, which informed the creation of the Hexad model. A more comprehensive review has been done by Hamari and Tuunanen [18].

One of the oldest and most frequently used player type models is Bartle's player type model [3] and its extensions [4]. Bartle identified four player types (Achiever, Explorer, Socialiser, and Killer) for players of Multi-User Dungeons (MUDs) based on what they desired from a MUD.

Yee [46,47] used a factor analysis approach out of questions based on Bartle's player types. His analysis identified three main components of player motivation with ten sub-components: achievement (advancement, mechanics, competition), social (socializing, relationship, teamwork), and immersion (discovery, role-playing, customization, escapism). Like Bartle's model, Yee's components have a strong focus on one specific game genre, Massively Multiplayer Online Role-Playing Games (MMORPGs). It was not created or intended for a broad range of different game genres.

A wider perspective regarding player types is included in the first Demographic Game Design model (DGD1) [6], which is an adoption of the Myers-Briggs Type Indicator (MBTI, [30]) to games. It proposed the player styles Conqueror, Manager, Wanderer, and Participant. The second Demographic Game Design model (DGD2) [5] explored the hard-core to casual dimension, different skill sets, and the preference for single and multiplayer. Although providing valuable insights into player characteristics, both DGD1 and DGD2 are based on a pre-existing psychometric model (MBTI) that is not focused on games. The authors also reported issues related to methodology and data collection.

Emerging from an empirical evaluation of a health game for younger adults, Xu et al. [44] developed five player types: achievers, active buddies, social experience seekers, team players, and freeloaders. These types include both motivational and behavioural factors. However, they have not been investigated regarding their validity to personalize games.

The BrainHex model [31,32] was developed considering previous player typologies and neurobiological research. It introduces seven player archetypes: Achiever, Conqueror, Daredevil, Mastermind, Seeker, Socialiser, and Survivor. It is a promising approach, supplementing existing research with a more diverse array of player types, and it has been initially investigated on its psychometric properties [8] and been used in a number of recent studies in HCI [7,35,48].

While these models are often used in personalizing gameful systems, they were built specifically for game design, thus, their usefulness for gameful design is limited.

Looking at models created specifically for gameful design, Barata et al. [2] studied data regarding student performance and gaming preferences from a gamified university level engineering course and identified four student types related to different gaming preferences: Achievers, Regular Students, Half-hearted Students, and Underachievers.

Barata's model is specific to the domain of gamified learning. Differently, the Hexad model aims at covering a broad range of gameful systems. Therefore, we consider the Hexad model to be potentially suitable for personalization of gameful systems and thus warrant further research.

Gamification User Types Hexad

Marczewski proposed six user types that differ in the degree to which they can be motivated by either intrinsic (e.g., self-realization) or extrinsic (e.g., rewards) motivational factors [27]. Rather than basing the model on observed behaviour, the user types are personifications of people's

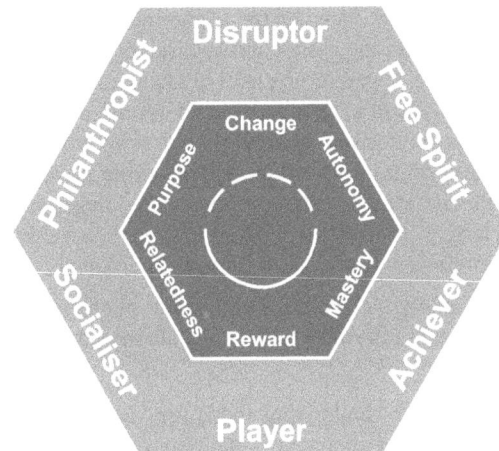

Figure 1. Gamification User Types Hexad [27].

intrinsic and extrinsic motivations, as defined by SDT [41]. Accordingly, the four intrinsically motivated types in the Hexad model are derived from the three types of intrinsic motivation from SDT, namely relatedness, competence, and autonomy, with the addition of purpose [11]. Figure 1 illustrates the six user types from the Hexad model. Below, we list the user types and the game design elements suggested by Marczewski to address the motivations of each type [28], which we investigate in this work.

Philanthropists are motivated by *purpose*. They are altruistic and willing to give without expecting a reward.

Suggested design elements: collection and trading, gifting, knowledge sharing, and administrative roles.

Socialisers are motivated by *relatedness*. They want to interact with others and create social connections.

Suggested design elements: guilds or teams, social networks, social comparison, social competition, and social discovery.

Free Spirits are motivated by *autonomy*, meaning freedom to express themselves and act without external control. They like to create and explore within a system.

Suggested design elements: exploratory tasks, nonlinear gameplay, Easter eggs, unlockable content, creativity tools, and customization.

Achievers are motivated by *competence*. They seek to progress within a system by completing tasks, or prove themselves by tackling difficult challenges.

Suggested design elements: challenges, certificates, learning new skills, quests, levels or progression, and epic challenges (or "boss battles").

Players are motivated by *extrinsic rewards*. They will do whatever to earn a reward within a system, independently of the type of the activity.

Suggested design elements: points, rewards or prizes, leaderboards, badges or achievements, virtual economy, and lotteries or games of chance.

Disruptors are motivated by the triggering of *change*. They tend to disrupt the system either directly or through others to force negative or positive changes. They like to test the system's boundaries and try to push further. This type is derived from SDT, but from empirical observation of this behaviour within online systems. Although disruption can sometimes be negative (e.g., cheaters or griefers), this is not always the case because disruptors can also work to improve the system.

Suggested design elements: innovation platforms, voting mechanisms, development tools, anonymity, anarchic gameplay.

Some motivations underlying these user types are related, but the user types themselves overlap slightly. Achievers and Players are both motivated by achievement, but differ in their focus: Players focus on extrinsic rewards while Achievers focus on competence. Philanthropists and Socialisers are both motivated to interact with other players. However, they differ because a Socialiser's interest is in the interaction itself while a Philanthropist is motivated by interaction to help others. Finally, Free Spirits and Disruptors are both motivated by autonomy and creativity. However, Free Spirits stay within the system limits without a desire to change them and Disruptors seek to expand beyond these boundaries to change the system.

It is also worth noting that, although these motivation clusters are presented as user types, individuals are rarely motivated by one of them exclusively. Although users are likely to display a principal tendency, in most cases they will also be motivated by all the other types to some degree.

There are several ways to use the Hexad model to personalize gameful applications. For example, Jia *et al.* [21] provide design suggestions for gameful applications based on the Big Five traits, but the Hexad model has even more potential for customizing gameful applications since it is modeled after player motivations specific to gameful applications. Designers would be able to screen their target audience using the suggested survey and choose the adequate design elements for each user. In research, the survey can be used to better understand user engagement and enjoyment in studies regarding gameful applications.

METHODOLOGY
We conducted our work in three sequential phases:

1. *survey scale construction*, in which we developed a standard survey response scale for the Gamification User Types Hexad framework;

2. *data collection*, in which we collected responses from an on-line survey with questions related to the Hexad framework, preferences regarding game design elements, and personality tests;

3. *data analysis*, in which we analyzed the responses to accomplish two goals: validate the User Types Hexad scale and evaluate the potential of the Hexad framework to personalize the user experience in gameful systems.

Survey Scale Construction
To design the Gamification User Types Hexad Scale, we followed a systematic approach involving an expert workshop to generate items based on the available framework and a subsequent expert validation process to evaluate and rate items based on their face validity. The new scale is inspired by but is not the same as the previous attempt by Marczewski to create an assessment tool [29], which did not follow a systematic approach and was found to be unreliable. The survey construction phase has already been described in more detail elsewhere [13].

We started the development of the survey with an expert workshop conducted by the Austrian Institute of Technology to generate a pool of items for each of the different Hexad user types. A group of six experts with either an expertise in scale development or game mechanics was introduced to the Gamification User Types Hexad framework [27] through detailed material, explaining each of the different types and the game mechanics they are likely to respond to as suggested by Marczewski [28]. Subsequently, each expert was asked to develop a list of items that would describe each of the user types. Each item aimed to help assess the participant's inclination towards one of the user types. Once this task was completed, the developed items were pooled successively for each type and discussed. As part of these discussions, the defining characteristics were reviewed and the created item pools were extended to cover missing aspects of the respective types as needed.

As the second step of the survey development, we reviewed the list of items created for each type, removing those items that seemed misleading, too broad, too context-dependent, or redundant. A rating form was created for the remaining list of 74 items. We then sent the form out for an expert rating by the group of experts involved in the workshop, as well as to the creator of the Hexad framework, Andrzej Marczewski, and two experts in the fields of HCI and games. The expert jury was asked to judge how well each item represented its gamification user type (along a 6-point scale ranging from "very bad" to "very good") and to comment if any potential issues were observed (e.g., an item insufficiently differentiating between related types). Further, everyone was invited to mention any aspects of the player types they observed as not sufficiently covered. Once all rating forms were returned, we analyzed the ratings (mean, range). Then, we selected the items with the best ratings for a first 30-item version of the survey. The list of survey items is included in the appendix.

Survey Instrument
We conducted an online survey with students of the University of Waterloo, Canada, which was completed in English and contained the following sections:

1. *Demographic information*: age, gender, education level, native country, native language, and self-reported level of English proficiency (to identify possible misunderstandings because of lacking language proficiency).

2. *Hexad User Types survey items*: we asked participants to rate the 30 items related to the six Hexad user types (see appendix) on a 7-point Likert scale and to comment on the items (e.g., to mention any item they found confusing or hard to understand).

3. *Game Elements preferences*: we asked participants to rate how much they are motivated by 32 different game design elements (as used indistinctively in games or gameful applications) on a 7-point Likert scale.

4. *Personality*: the BIDR-6 [43] and the BFI-10 [38] personality surveys using 7-point Likert scales were included to gain insight into potential relationships between user types and personality.

We asked participants for permission to contact them again in a few weeks to answer a follow-up survey aimed at enabling calculation of a test-retest reliability score for the Hexad User Types survey. The follow-up survey contained only the Hexad User Types question section.

Participants
One hundred and thirty-three graduate and undergraduate students from the University of Waterloo, Canada (64 females, 59 males, 10 declined to answer), aged 18–36 ($M = 23.5$ years, $SD = 3.3$ years), volunteered to participate in the online survey. From those 133 respondents, 40 participated in the follow-up survey. They were recruited through the University's mailing lists and bulletin boards and offered a chance to win a CAD$ 50.00 (approximately USD$ 38.00) Amazon gift card in a draw after completing the survey. Informed consent was obtained from all participants. Answers were collected in March 2016. Retest data were collected two weeks after the initial survey.

Regarding English language proficiency, 75 participants reported having English as a native language and 58 reported a variety of different native languages. However, 90 participants reported a native English proficiency level (i.e., some considered themselves as proficient as a native, even not being a native speaker), 36 reported a very good proficiency, and four reported a fair proficiency (three declined to answer). Thus, we operate on the assumption that lack of English proficiency was not a detriment to our study.

Analytical Procedure
We conducted our data analysis in three steps: scale reliability, scale correlation with personality traits, and scale correlation with game design elements. In all cases, we used Kendall's τ to calculate correlations, following Howell's suggestion that it provides the best estimates for nonparametric data [19], as the scores were not normally distributed. However, doing so requires attention to effect size interpretation because the absolute value of τ is usually lower than the values of the more commonly known Pearson's r and Spearman's ρ for the same effect sizes [16]. Therefore, we used the correspondence tables calculated by Gilpin [16] to interpret Kendall's τ effect size according to the approximate Pearson's r equivalent:

- small effect: $\tau = 0.20$ ($\approx r = 0.30$);
- medium effect: $\tau = 0.34$ ($\approx r = 0.50$);
- large effect: $\tau = 0.50$ ($\approx r = 0.70$).

Scale Reliability
We analyzed the scale's internal reliability by separately calculating the Cronbach's α for each one of the six subscales. In addition, we evaluated the individual contribution of each item to its subscale and the participants' comments to decide whether to keep or remove less reliable items. After verifying the scale's reliability, we calculated each participant's score for each of the six Hexad types as the median of the rates reported by the participant for each of the items composing the subscale. These scores were employed for the subsequent tests. To evaluate the test-retest reliability, we separately calculated the bivariate correlation between the original and the retest scores of each subscale using Pearson's r.

Next, we calculated the bivariate correlation coefficients of each user type with all others using Kendall's τ. Considering the Hexad model's theoretical background regarding overlapping user types, we expected the following significant correlations: Achiever with Player, Philanthropist with Socialiser, and Free Spirit with Disruptor.

Finally, we tested the bivariate correlation of each subscale's score with the two scales from the BIDR-6 using Kendall's τ, to verify if participants' responses could have been influenced by a tendency to desirable responding.

Scale Correlation with Personality Traits
First, we analyzed the bivariate correlation between the Big Five personality traits and the BIDR-6 scales to control for acquiescence regarding the BFI-10 scale. We do not present the full results table due to space limitations. We found a significant strong negative correlation between neuroticism and SDE ($\tau = -0.438$, $p < 0.01$); therefore, participants' scores on neuroticism might be underestimated by their tendency to protect their self-esteem. We then analyzed the bivariate correlations between the Hexad scale and the Big Five model of personality traits by separately calculating the correlation coefficient between each pair of Hexad type and personality trait using Kendall's τ. Based on previous literature [21,22,45], we establish the following hypotheses:

H1: The Achiever user type is positively correlated with agreeableness and conscientiousness.

H2: The Free Spirit user type is positively correlated with openness to experience.

H3: The Player user type is positively correlated with extraversion and neuroticism.

In addition, – although this correlation did not appear previously – we can also make the following hypothesis because the Socialiser and Philanthropist types are both based on social interactions:

H4: The Philanthropist and Socialiser user types are positively correlated with extraversion.

Scale Correlation with Game Design Elements

To analyze the correlation of the Hexad types with the set of game design elements, we firstly calculated scores for six sets of game elements, corresponding to the six Hexad types, following the division suggested by Marczewski [28]. We then separately calculated the bivariate correlation between each pair of Hexad type with its corresponding set of game design elements using Kendall's τ.

After initial analysis, we calculated the bivariate correlation of each individual game design element with each of the six Hexad types using Kendall's τ. This was done to evaluate the distribution of the design elements between the Hexad user types and to suggest improvements based on reported preferences. Next, we suggested a new association table between design elements and user types. As a general rule, correlations with a coefficient τ > 0.20 were considered meaningful because this represents the threshold for a small-sized correlation. After creating the new table, we recalculated the scores for each element set and compared them to the original scores to verify improvements.

RESULTS

Our analysis included the following measures, as reported in the Methodology section: scale reliability, distribution of the user types scores, scale correlation with personality traits, and scale correlation with game design elements.

Scale Reliability

Table 1 presents the internal reliability coefficients of each of the subscales, measured by Cronbach's α. After evaluating each subscale's reliability, we analyzed the individual reliability of each item. Two items were found to poorly contribute to their scales: "*I look out for my own interests*" (Player) and "*I like to take changing things into my own hands*" (Disruptor). Moreover, a few participants reported that they could not precisely understand the meaning of the latter Disruptor item. Thus, we removed these two items. We then analyzed the effect of removing the least reliable item of each of the remaining four subscales on their reliabilities. The effects were small (<= 0.008). Thus, we removed the least reliable subscale items, arriving at a final scale with 24 items (four items per subscale). The recalculated internal reliability coefficients for the 24-items scale are presented in Table 1. In addition, the scale correlations for all items are presented later in Table 8.

User Type	5-items subscale	4-items subscale
Philanthropist	0.896	0.893
Socialiser	0.846	0.838
Free Spirit	0.727	0.723
Achiever	0.766	0.759
Disruptor	0.728	0.738
Player	0.689	0.698

Table 1. Internal scale reliability (Cronbach's α) for each of the Hexad User Types in the original 30-items (5 per subscale) and the final 24-items (4 per subscale) surveys.

Table 2 exhibits the test-retest correlation coefficients for each of the subscales, measured by Pearson's r. All subscales presented a high test-retest reliability for the 24-items scale, except for the Player type, which presented a small coefficient. Moreover, results show that removing the least reliable item per subscale represent a small overall improvement in test-retest reliability.

Table 3 presents the bivariate correlation coefficients and significance levels between each Hexad user type and the BIDR subscales. Results show significant weak correlations between Free Spirit, Achiever, and Player with SDE and between Philanthropist and Disruptor with IM (the latter is negative). This seems to suggest that the achievement- and autonomy-oriented subscales might be just slightly overestimated by participants' tendency to protect their self-esteem; and that the philanthropist subscale might be slightly overestimated and the disruptor subscale slightly underestimated by participants' desire to please others.

Table 4 presents the correlation coefficients between each user type and all others. Positive medium-sized correlations were found between the pairs suggested by the theoretical background: Philanthropist with Socialiser, Free Spirit with Disruptor, and Achiever with Player. Furthermore, similar magnitude correlations were also found between Philanthropist and Free Spirit, Achiever and Free Spirit, and Player and Free Spirit. Other significant correlations that appeared were of weaker magnitude.

We also conducted a factor analysis with a maximum-likelihood method and an Oblimin rotation with Kaiser

User Type	5-items subscale	4-items subscale
Philanthropist	0.850 **	0.852 **
Socialiser	0.820 **	0.853 **
Free Spirit	0.483 **	0.631 **
Achiever	0.752 **	0.798 **
Disruptor	0.611 **	0.782 **
Player	0.387 *	0.357 *

$^*p < 0.05.$ $^{**}p < 0.01.$

Table 2. Test-retest reliability (Pearson's r) for Hexad User Types in the original 30-items (5 per subscale) and the final 24-items (4 per subscale) surveys.

User Type	S.D.E.	I.M.
Philanthropist	0.066	**0.135** *
Socialiser	0.042	0.060
Free Spirit	**0.204** **	0.065
Achiever	**0.209** **	0.084
Disruptor	0.021	**-0.173** **
Player	**0.146** *	0.003

$^*p < 0.05.$ $^{**}p < 0.01.$

Table 3. Bivariate correlation coefficients (Kendall's τ) and significance between Hexad user types and desirable responding sub-scales: self-deception enhancement (S.D.E.) and impression management (I.M.).

User Type	Philanthropist	Socialiser	Free Spirit	Achiever	Disruptor
Socialiser	**0.476** **				
Free Spirit	**0.328** **	0.274 **			
Achiever	**0.325** **	0.218 **	**0.465** **		
Disruptor	-0.057	-0.001	**0.249** **	0.045	
Player	0.213 **	**0.307** **	**0.354** **	**0.432** **	0.092

** $p < 0.01$.

Table 4. Bivariate correlation coefficients (Kendall's τ) and significance between each Hexad user type and all others.

normalization. We forced a six factors analysis to evaluate the correspondence of the factors with the Hexad user types. We report the rotated factor loads later in Table 8. We report only factor loads higher than 0.20 to improve readability. Together, the six factors explained 55.1% of the variance in the data. The results show that the six factors correspond to the Hexad types in overall, with some overlapping in the Philanthropist, Free Spirit, and Achiever types, which correspond to the overlaps found between the different user types (see Table 4).

Distribution of the User Types Scores

Table 5 presents the mean and standard deviation of the calculated scores for each of the six user types from the 24-items scale. For better readability, scores are presented as the sum of each item's rates instead of the mean (i.e., the maximum value for each subscale is 28). A visual inspection reveals that the average score for the Disruptor type is considerably lower than the other types. Figure 2 presents the distribution of participants' main Hexad User Type, i.e., the type in which the participant achieved the highest score. These data suggest that the four user types based on intrinsic motivation – Philanthropist, Socialiser, Free Spirit, and Achiever – are similarly common as the main user type, while the Player type is also somewhat common as the main user type, but half as common as the intrinsic types, and the Disruptor type is not at all common as the main user type.

Scale Correlation with Personality Traits

Table 6 presents the bivariate correlations coefficients and significance levels between each Hexad user type and each of the Big Five model personality traits, measured by Kendall's τ. The Philanthropist type is positively correlated with extraversion, supporting hypothesis **H4**, and also with agreeableness, conscientiousness, and openness. The Socialiser type is positively correlated with extraversion, supporting hypothesis **H4**, and also with agreeableness. The Free Spirit type is positively correlated with openness, sup-

porting hypothesis **H2**, and also positively correlated with extraversion and negatively with neuroticism. The Achiever type is positively correlated with conscientiousness; however, it was not found to be correlated with agreeableness. Thus, hypothesis **H1** is only partly supported. This appears to differ from Johnson and Gardner's findings [22]. However, they measured how much players felt competent after gameplay, while our survey scores general user preferences towards different game design elements. Therefore, while both measures are based on the intrinsic need for competence, they are not measuring the same effect. This fact might explain the contradiction. The Disruptor type is negatively correlated with neuroticism. Finally, the Player type is only positively correlated with conscientiousness, thus, hypothesis **H3** was not supported. In summary, our results lead to the following conclusions:

H1: *partly supported*. The Achiever user type was positively correlated with conscientiousness, but not with agreeableness.

H2: *supported*. The Free Spirit user type was positively correlated with openness to experience.

H3: *not supported*. The Player user type was not correlated with either extraversion or neuroticism.

H4: *supported*. The Philanthropist and Socialiser user types were positively correlated with extraversion.

Furthermore, there are three sets of correlations that were not hypothesized but raised from the data: Philanthropist and Socialiser with agreeableness; Philanthropist and Player with Conscientiousness; and Free Spirit and Disruptor with emotional stability (the opposite of neuroticism).

User Type	Mean Score	S.D.
Philanthropist	22.36	4.72
Socialiser	20.33	5.09
Free Spirit	22.09	4.06
Achiever	22.18	3.97
Disruptor	14.94	4.80
Player	20.99	4.08

Table 5. Average scores and SD for each Hexad user type.

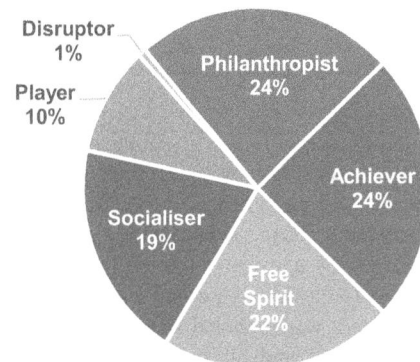

Figure 2. Distribution of participants' Hexad User Type.

User Type	Extraversion	Agreeableness	Conscientiousness	Neuroticism	Openness
Philanthropist	**0.148** *	**0.191** **	**0.159** *	0.013	**0.145** *
Socialiser	**0.290** **	**0.272** **	0.079	-0.073	0.082
Free Spirit	**0.152** *	0.089	0.078	**-0.204** **	**0.215** **
Achiever	-0.005	0.041	**0.255** **	-0.117	0.027
Disruptor	0.038	-0.106	-0.080	**-0.170** **	0.090
Player	0.054	0.121	**0.144** *	-0.054	0.093

* $p < 0.05$. ** $p < 0.01$.

Table 6. Bivariate correlation coefficients (Kendall's τ) and significance of Hexad user types with Big Five personality traits.

Scale Correlation with Game Design Elements

Table 7 presents the game design elements suggested to address the motivations of each user type, together with the correlation coefficients between each user type's mean score and the corresponding design elements' mean score per participant. Overall, the user types were positively correlated with the corresponding game design elements, which confirms the validity of the Hexad model for understanding user preferences towards different elements. The exception was the Philanthropist type, for which no correlation was found with the expected design elements.

We do not present the complete correlation table of the individual game design elements because of space constraints, but it is included in the appendix. The analysis revealed that some design elements presented a higher correlation coefficient with a different user type than that suggested by Marczewski [28] or were correlated with more than one user type. In addition, some design elements only presented insignificant or weak correlations. Thus, we suggest a new association table between user types and game design elements considering, as a general rule, the significant correlations with a coefficient higher than 0.20 (weak or stronger correlations). However, we cannot make a suggestion for the Philanthropist type because we did not encounter design elements significantly correlated with it. Table 7 also exhibits the new association table and the new correlation coefficients after the adjustment. Design elements that were correlated with more than one user type are shown as *Additional Elements*. Moreover, we compare the new correlation coefficients with the previous ones to measure the improvement. Results show that our new suggested association table leads to an overall improvement of 9% over the table suggested by Marczewski.

DISCUSSION
In this section, we discuss the implications of our findings.

Scale Reliability
After evaluating the internal reliability of each subscale, we arrived at a final 24-items survey that represented the optimal format (see Table 8 and the appendix). Results showed a need to improve the Player subscale in future work as both its internal (0.698) and test-retest (0.357) reliabilities were below the desired levels. All other scales achieved the desired reliability, as it was higher than 0.70 for Free Spirit, Achiever, and Disruptor, and higher than 0.80 for Philanthropist and Socialiser.

The correlation analysis between the Hexad user types and the BIDR showed only weak correlations of Free Spirit, Achiever, and Player with self-deceptive enhancement and of Philanthropist and Disruptor with impression management. This is relevant for future work, but this effect was not strong enough to be considered influential to the results.

The correlation analysis of the Hexad user types between themselves showed positive correlations where suggested by the theoretical background (Philanthropist with Socialiser, Free Spirit with Disruptor, and Achiever with Player). Furthermore, we found unexpected correlations between Philanthropist and Free Spirit, Achiever and Free Spirit, as well as Player and Free Spirit, which suggest avenues for further investigation. The factor analysis corroborates these findings and confirms that the scale items correspond to their nominal subscales, with some partial overlaps.

These results collectively confirm that the Hexad user types can be measured empirically and correspond to the expected effects according to their theoretical background. Thus, we reinforce the relevance of the Hexad model for future developments in gameful design and HCI.

Scale Correlation with Personality Traits
Analysis of the correlations between the Hexad user types and personality traits showed significant correlations on most of the pairs where they were suggested by the theoretical background, further contributing to validate the Hexad model. Positive correlations were found of Philanthropist and Socialiser with extraversion, Achiever with conscientiousness, and Free Spirit with openness. Moreover, we found unexpected correlations of Philanthropist and Socialiser with agreeableness, which can be explained by the fact that all are connected with social relations, and of Achiever and Player with conscientiousness, which can help explain their orientation towards goals and rewards. Additionally, Free Spirit and Disruptor were correlated with emotional stability, which seems counter-intuitive. This can be partially explained by a potential deviation on the scores for neuroticism due to self-deceptive enhancement. Thus, these results suggest interesting avenues for further investigation.

Scale Correlation with Game Design Elements
We found positive correlations between all Hexad user types with the expected game design elements, except Philanthropist. These results validate the usefulness of the Hexad framework as a tool to personalize gamified

User Type	Suggested by Marczewski [28]			Improved Associations			Imp.
	Design Elements	τ		Principal Elements	Additional Elements	τ	
Philanthropist	Collection and Trading Gifting Knowledge Sharing Administrative Roles	0.039		-		-	-
Socialiser	Guilds or Teams Social Networks Social Comparison Social Competition Social Discovery	0.257 **		Guilds or Teams Social Networks Social Comparison Social Competition Social Discovery		0.257 **	0%
Free Spirit	Exploratory Tasks Nonlinear Gameplay Easter Eggs Unlockable Content Creativity Tools Customization	0.341 **		Exploratory Tasks Nonlinear Gameplay Easter Eggs Unlockable Content Learning Anonymity Anarchic Gameplay	Customization Challenges Creativity Tools	0.386 **	13%
Achiever	Challenges Certificates Learning Quests Levels or Progression Epic Challenges	0.347 **		Challenges Certificates Quests	Anonymity Learning Badges or Achiev. Levels or Progression	0.362 **	4%
Disruptor	Innovation Platforms Voting Mechanisms Development Tools Anonymity Anarchic Gameplay	0.326 **		Innovation Platforms Voting Mechanisms Development Tools Creativity Tools	Social Competition Anarchic Gameplay Challenges	0.379 **	16%
Player	Points Rewards or Prizes Leaderboards Badges or Achievements Virtual Economy Lotteries or Chance	0.383 **		Points Rewards or Prizes Leaderboards Badges or Achievements Virtual Economy Levels or Progression Collection and Trading	Social Comparison Social Competition Social Discovery Anonymity Challenges Certificates Quests	0.420 **	10%
Overall							9%

** $p < 0.01$.

Table 7. Bivariate correlation coefficients (Kendall's τ) and significance between the Hexad user types and the suggested game design elements for each user type, as well as the percentage of improvement of the new suggestions over the previous ones.

applications because a user's subscale scores predict their preference of different design elements. In addition, we suggested an improved association table between user types and design elements based on the analysis of the correlation coefficients (see Table 7). These results also pointed out to a need for further studies regarding the Philanthropist user type. Its reliability scores were high (> 0.80), which means it is accurately measuring a user personality trait. However, we did not found correspondence to a user's preference of difference game design elements.

LIMITATIONS AND FUTURE WORK

This paper represents the first step toward a standard survey that assesses user preferences for personalization of gamified systems. For this first step, we acquired data from a limited sample to provide a survey validation. Although the sample was large enough for statistical analysis, it was limited to students of one University, which limits generaliza-

tion of the survey to a general population. Thus, our next step will be to repeat this study with a larger sample, including people from different cultural origins and a broader age range to validate the model and survey for the general population. In addition, our reliability analysis revealed a need for improving the Player subscale, which we plan to execute on the next survey iteration. Furthermore, we employed a short scale (BFI-10) to assess participants' personality traits. Since short scales are known to potentially have problems with acquiescence, our results should be validated in future work using a more reliable BFI scale.

Our analysis also suggested some unexpected overlap between the Hexad user types and correlations between user types and personality traits, which we plan to investigate further. Finally, we plan to better understand the impact of the Philanthropist user type in user preference towards gamified systems, which our study did not reveal.

User Type	Item	5-items subscale correlation (*r*)	4-items subscale correlation (*r*)	Rotated Factor Loads					
				1 (A)	2 (P)	3 (S)	4 (D)	5 (R)	6 (F)
Philanthropist (P)	P1	0.786	0.780		**0.418**	0.321			0.468
	P2	0.779	0.775		**0.980**				
	P3	0.733	0.783		**0.437**				0.450
	P4	0.771	0.763		**0.457**	0.338	-0.228		
	P5	0.667	removed						
Socialiser (S)	S1	0.730	0.734			**0.829**			
	S2	0.624	0.617			**0.541**		0.201	
	S3	0.670	0.676			**0.829**			
	S4	0.688	0.662			**0.620**			
	S5	0.569	removed						
Free Spirit (F)	F1	0.529	0.480						**0.514**
	F2	0.491	0.546					0.383	**0.220**
	F3	0.507	0.525	0.319			0.352	0.353	
	F4	0.538	0.496						**0.622**
	F5	0.373	removed						
Achiever (A)	A1	0.603	0.574	**0.359**				0.222	
	A2	0.483	0.485	**0.288**				0.395	
	A3	0.553	0.569	**0.434**				0.211	
	A4	0.612	0.604	**1.042**					
	A5	0.454	removed						
Disruptor (D)	D1	0.579	0.588				**0.671**		
	D2	0.451	0.398				**0.555**		0.249
	D3	0.569	0.569				**0.620**		
	D4	0.523	0.577			-0.213	**0.732**		
	D5	0.323	removed						
Player (R)	R1	0.445	0.459				0.318	**0.521**	
	R2	0.561	0.622				0.255	**0.670**	
	R3	0.359	0.313					**0.304**	
	R4	0.580	0.568					**0.668**	
	R5	0.305	removed						

Table 8. Corrected item-total correlations (*r*) and rotated factor loads (>= 0.20) for each of the Hexad survey items.

SUMMARY AND CONCLUSION

We have presented and validated a standard scale to score users' preferences regarding the six different motivations to use a gameful system according to the Hexad framework: Philanthropist, Socialiser, Free Spirit, Achiever, Disruptor, and Player. The final Hexad scale is composed of 24 items, which together can accurately describe user preferences. Using our survey is more effective than asking users about design elements directly because the survey's goal is to understand more about user psychology in a gamified context than just which game elements they prefer. Furthermore, users are not necessarily gamers and may therefore not be aware of their game preferences and not familiar with game design vocabulary. Therefore, our survey aims to use a common vocabulary. Moreover, correlation analysis of the Hexad user types with different game design elements confirmed the usefulness of the Hexad model as a measure of preferred design elements. This allowed us to suggest a table of game design elements for each user type.

The Hexad User Types framework can be seen as a valid model for personalizing gamified applications after this study. Thus, the survey developed in this paper makes a significant contribution to the areas of HCI and gamification because it will enable researchers and designers to accurately measure user preference for different elements in gameful design.

ACKNOWLEDGMENTS

Gustavo Tondello would like to thank the University of Waterloo and the CNPq, Brazil for funding his research. Rina Wehbe would like to thank the Cheriton School of Computer Science, University of Waterloo, and NSERC for funding her research. This research has received funding from NSERC (RGPIN-418622-2012), SSHRC (895-2011-1014, IMMERSe), and the project GEMPLAY (contract no. 844845), funded by the Austrian Research Promotion Agency. The authors would like to thank Elisa Mekler, Melissa Stocco, and the reviewers for providing feedback.

REFERENCES

1. Sander Bakkes, Chek Tien Tan, and Yusuf Pisan. 2012. Personalised gaming. *Proceedings of The 8th Australasian Conference on Interactive Entertainment Playing the System - IE '12*, ACM, 1–10. http://doi.org/10.1145/2336727.2336731

2. Gabriel Barata, Sandra Gama, Joaquim A.P. Jorge, and Daniel J.V. Gonçalves. 2014. Relating gaming habits with student performance in a gamified learning experience. *Proceedings of the first ACM SIGCHI Annual Symposium on Computer-Human Interaction in Play - CHI PLAY '14*, ACM, 17–25. http://doi.org/10.1145/2658537.2658692

3. Richard Bartle. 1996. Hearts, Clubs, Diamonds, Spades: Players who suit MUDs. *Journal of MUD Research* 1, 1.

4. Richard Bartle. 2005. Virtual Worlds: Why People Play. *Massively Multiplayer Game Development* 2, 1.

5. Chris Bateman, Rebecca Lowenhaupt, and Lennart E Nacke. 2011. Player Typology in Theory and Practice. *Proceedings of DiGRA 2011*.

6. Chris Mark. Bateman and Richard Boon. 2006. *21st Century Game Design (Game Development Series)*. Charles River Media.

7. Max V. Birk, Dereck Toker, Regan L. Mandryk, and Cristina Conati. 2015. Modeling Motivation in a Social Network Game Using Player-Centric Traits and Personality Traits. *Proceedings of User Modeling, Adaptation and Personalization*, Springer, 18–30. http://doi.org/10.1007/978-3-319-20267-9_2

8. Marc Busch, Elke Mattheiss, Rita Orji, Peter Fröhlich, Michael Lankes, and Manfred Tscheligi. 2016. Player Type Models – Towards Empirical Validation. *Proceedings of the 2016 CHI Conference Extended Abstracts on Human Factors in Computing Systems - CHI EA '16*, ACM, 1835–1841. http://doi.org/10.1145/2851581.2892399

9. Marc Busch, Elke Mattheiss, Rita Orji, et al. 2015. Personalization in Serious and Persuasive Games and Gamified Interactions. *Proceedings of the 2015 Annual Symposium on Computer-Human Interaction in Play - CHI PLAY '15*, ACM, 811–816. http://doi.org/10.1145/2793107.2810260

10. Edward L Deci and Richard M Ryan. 1985. *Intrinsic Motivation and Self-Determination in Human Behavior*. Plenum, New York and London.

11. Edward L. Deci, Haleh Eghrari, Brian C. Patrick, and Dean R. Leone. 1994. Facilitating Internalization: The Self-Determination Theory Perspective. *Journal of Personality* 62, 1: 119–142. http://doi.org/10.1111/j.1467-6494.1994.tb00797.x

12. Sebastian Deterding, Dan Dixon, Rilla Khaled, and Lennart E Nacke. 2011. From Game Design Elements to Gamefulness: Defining "Gamification." *Proceedings of the 15th International Academic MindTrek Conference: Envisioning Future Media Environments – MindTrek '11*, ACM, 9–15. http://doi.org/10.1145/2181037.2181040

13. Lisa Diamond, Gustavo F. Tondello, Andrzej Marczewski, Lennart E. Nacke, and Manfred Tscheligi. 2015. The HEXAD Gamification User Types Questionnaire : Background and Development Process. *Workshop on Personalization in Serious and Persuasive Games and Gamified Interactions*.

14. Dan Dixon. 2011. Player Types and Gamification. *CHI 2011 Workshop Gamification Using Game Design Elements in NonGame Contexts*, 12–15.

15. Lauren S. Ferro, Steffen P. Walz, and Stefan Greuter. 2013. Towards personalised, gamified systems: an investigation into game design, personality and player typologies. *Proceedings of the 9th Australasian Conference on Interactive Entertainment: Matters of Life and Death - IE '13*, 1–6. http://doi.org/10.1145/2513002.2513024

16. Andrew R. Gilpin. 1993. Table for Conversion of Kendall's Tau to Spearman's Rho Within the Context of Measures of Magnitude of Effect for Meta-Analysis. *Educational and Psychological Measurement* 53, 1: 87–92. http://doi.org/10.1177/0013164493053001007

17. Juho Hamari, Jonna Koivisto, and Harri Sarsa. 2014. Does gamification work? - A literature review of empirical studies on gamification. *Proceedings of the 47th Annual Hawaii International Conference on System Sciences*, 3025–3034. http://doi.org/10.1109/HICSS.2014.377

18. Juho Hamari and Janne Tuunanen. 2014. Player types: A meta-synthesis. *Transactions of the Digital Games Research* 1, 2. Retrieved April 10, 2016 from http://todigra.org/index.php/todigra/article/view/13

19. David Howell. 2012. *Statistical Methods for Psychology*. Cengage Learning.

20. Veronika Huta and Alan S. Waterman. 2014. Eudaimonia and Its Distinction from Hedonia: Developing a Classification and Terminology for Understanding Conceptual and Operational Definitions. *Journal of Happiness Studies* 15, 6: 1425–1456. http://doi.org/10.1007/s10902-013-9485-0

21. Yuan Jia, Bin Xu, Yamini Karanam, and Stephen Voida. 2016. Personality-targeted Gamification: A Survey Study on Personality Traits and Motivational Affordances. *Proceedings of the 34th Annual ACM Conference on Human Factors in Computing Systems - CHI '16*. http://doi.org/10.1145/2858036.2858515

22. Daniel Johnson and John Gardner. 2010. Personality, Motivation and Video Games. *Proceedings of the 22nd Conference of the Computer-Human Interaction Special Interest Group of Australia on Computer-*

Human Interaction - OZCHI '10, 276. http://doi.org/10.1145/1952222.1952281

23. Daniel Johnson, Peta Wyeth, Penny Sweetser, and John Gardner. 2012. Personality, genre and videogame play experience. *Proceedings of the 4th International Conference on Fun and Games - FnG '12*, ACM, 117–120. http://doi.org/10.1145/2367616.2367633

24. Maurits Kaptein, Panos Markopoulos, Boris De Ruyter, and Emile Aarts. 2015. Personalizing persuasive technologies: Explicit and implicit personalization using persuasion profiles. *International Journal of Human Computer Studies* 77: 38–51. http://doi.org/10.1016/j.ijhcs.2015.01.004

25. Maurits Kaptein, Boris De Ruyter, Panos Markopoulos, and Emile Aarts. 2012. Adaptive Persuasive Systems: A Study of Tailored Persuasive Text Messages to Reduce Snacking. *ACM Transactions on Interactive Intelligent Systems* 2, 2: 1–25. http://doi.org/10.1145/2209310.2209313

26. Silvia Erika Kober and Christa Neuper. 2013. Personality and Presence in Virtual Reality: Does Their Relationship Depend on the Used Presence Measure? *International Journal of Human-Computer Interaction* 29, 1: 13–25. http://doi.org/10.1080/10447318.2012.668131

27. Andrzej Marczewski. 2015. User Types. In *Even Ninja Monkeys Like to Play: Gamification, Game Thinking & Motivational Design*. CreateSpace Independent Publishing Platform, 69–84.

28. Andrzej Marczewski. 2015. Gamification Mechanics and Elements. In *Even Ninja Monkeys Like to Play: Gamification, Game Thinking & Motivational Design*. CreateSpace Independent Publishing Platform, 165–177.

29. Andrzej Marczewski. 2015. Marczewski's User Type Test. *Gamified UK*. Retrieved July 20, 2016 from http://gamified.uk/UserTypeTest2015/user-type-test.php

30. Isabel Briggs Myers. 1962. *The Myers-Briggs Type Indicator*. Consulting Psychologists Press, Palo Alto, CA.

31. Lennart E Nacke, Chris Bateman, and Regan L Mandryk. 2011. BrainHex: Preliminary Results from a Neurobiological Gamer Typology Survey. In *Proceedings of the 10th International Conference on Entertainment Computing - ICEC 2011*. Springer Berlin Heidelberg, 288–293. http://doi.org/10.1007/978-3-642-24500-8_31

32. Lennart E Nacke, Chris Bateman, and Regan L Mandryk. 2014. BrainHex: A Neurobiological Gamer Typology Survey. *Entertainment Computing* 5, 1: 55–62. http://doi.org/10.1016/j.entcom.2013.06.002

33. Oded Nov and Ofer Arazy. 2013. Personality-targeted design: theory, experimental procedure, and preliminary results. *Proceedings of the 2013 Conference on Computer Supported Cooperative Work - CSCW '13*, ACM, 977–984. http://doi.org/10.1145/2441776.2441887

34. Rita Orji, Regan L. Mandryk, Julita Vassileva, and Kathrin M. Gerling. 2013. Tailoring persuasive health games to gamer type. *Proceedings of the SIGCHI Conference on Human Factors in Computing Systems - CHI '13*, 2467–2476. http://doi.org/10.1145/2470654.2481341

35. Rita Orji, Julita Vassileva, and Regan L. Mandryk. 2014. Modeling the efficacy of persuasive strategies for different gamer types in serious games for health. *User Modeling and User-Adapted Interaction* 24, 5: 453–498. http://doi.org/10.1007/s11257-014-9149-8

36. Delroy L. Paulhus. 1984. Two-component models of socially desirable responding. *Journal of Personality and Social Psychology* 46, 3: 598–609. http://doi.org/10.1037/0022-3514.46.3.598

37. Christopher Peterson, Nansook Park, and Martin E. P. Seligman. 2005. Orientations to happiness and life satisfaction: the full life versus the empty life. *Journal of Happiness Studies* 6, 1: 25–41. http://doi.org/10.1007/s10902-004-1278-z

38. Beatrice Rammstedt and Oliver P. John. 2007. Measuring personality in one minute or less: A 10-item short version of the Big Five Inventory in English and German. *Journal of Research in Personality* 41, 1: 203–212. http://doi.org/10.1016/j.jrp.2006.02.001

39. Richard M. Ryan, Edward L. Deci, and Maarten Vansteenkiste. 2016. Autonomy and Autonomy Disturbances in Self-Development and Psychopathology: Research on Motivation, Attachment, and Clinical Process. In *Developmental Psychopathology*, Dante Cicchetti (ed.). Wiley, 1–54. http://doi.org/10.1002/9781119125556.devpsy109

40. Richard M. Ryan and Edward L. Deci. 2000. Self-determination theory and the facilitation of intrinsic motivation, social development, and well-being. *The American Psychologist* 55, 1: 68–78. http://doi.org/10.1037/0003-066X.55.1.68

41. Richard M. Ryan and Edward L. Deci. 2000. Intrinsic and Extrinsic Motivations: Classic Definitions and New Directions. *Contemporary Educational Psychology* 25, 1: 54–67. http://doi.org/10.1006/ceps.1999.1020

42. Richard M. Ryan, C. Scott Rigby, and Andrew Przybylski. 2006. The motivational pull of video games: A self-determination theory approach. *Motivation and Emotion* 30, 4: 347–363. http://doi.org/10.1007/s11031-006-9051-8

43. Niels Winkler, Martin Kroh, and Martin Spiess. 2006. Entwicklung einer deutschen Kurzskala zur zweidimensionalen Messung von sozialer Erwünschtheit. *DIW-Diskussionspapiere* 579. Retrieved April 10, 2016 from http://www.econstor.eu/handle/10419/18472

44. Yan Xu, Erika Shehan Poole, Andrew D. Miller, et al. 2012. This is not a one-horse race: understanding player types in multiplayer pervasive health games for youth. *Proceedings of the ACM 2012 conference on Computer Supported Cooperative Work - CSCW '12*, ACM, 843–852. http://doi.org/10.1145/2145204.2145330

45. Nick Yee, Nicolas Ducheneaut, Les Nelson, and Peter Likarish. 2011. Introverted Elves & Conscientious Gnomes: The Expression of Personality in World of Warcraft. *Proceedings of the Annual Conference on Human Factors in Computing Systems - CHI '11*, ACM, 753–762. http://doi.org/10.1145/1978942.1979052

46. Nick Yee, Nicolas Ducheneaut, and Les Nelson. 2012. Online gaming motivations scale: development and validation. *Proceedings of the 2012 ACM annual conference on Human Factors in Computing Systems - CHI '12*, ACM, 2803–2806. http://doi.org/10.1145/2207676.2208681

47. Nick Yee. 2006. Motivations for Play in Online Games. *CyberPsychology & Behavior* 9, 6: 772–775. http://doi.org/10.1089/cpb.2006.9.772

48. Virgil Zeigler-Hill and Sean Monica. 2015. The HEXACO model of personality and video game preferences. *Entertainment Computing* 11: 21–26. http://doi.org/10.1016/j.entcom.2015.08.001

APPENDIX A. SURVEY ITEMS

User Types		Items	5-items subscale correlation (r)	4-items subscale correlation (r)
Philanthropist	P1	It makes me happy if I am able to help others.	0.786	0.780
	P2	I like helping others to orient themselves in new situations.	0.779	0.775
	P3	I like sharing my knowledge.	0.733	0.783
	P4	The wellbeing of others is important to me.	0.771	0.763
	~~P5~~	~~I feel good taking on the role of a mentor.~~	0.667	removed
Socialiser	S1	Interacting with others is important to me.	0.730	0.734
	S2	I like being part of a team.	0.624	0.617
	S3	It is important to me to feel like I am part of a community.	0.670	0.676
	S4	I enjoy group activities.	0.688	0.662
	~~S5~~	~~It is more fun to be with others than by myself.~~	0.569	removed
Free Spirit	F1	It is important to me to follow my own path.	0.529	0.480
	F2	I often let my curiosity guide me.	0.491	0.546
	F3	I like to try new things.	0.507	0.525
	F4	Being independent is important to me.	0.538	0.496
	~~F5~~	~~I prefer setting my own goals.~~	0.373	removed
Achiever	A1	I like defeating obstacles.	0.603	0.574
	A2	It is important to me to always carry out my tasks completely.	0.483	0.485
	A3	It is difficult for me to let go of a problem before I have found a solution.	0.553	0.569
	A4	I like mastering difficult tasks.	0.612	0.604
	~~A5~~	~~I am very ambitious.~~	0.454	removed
Disruptor	D1	I like to provoke.	0.579	0.588
	D2	I like to question the status quo.	0.451	0.398
	D3	I see myself as a rebel.	0.569	0.569
	D4	I dislike following rules.	0.523	0.577
	~~D5~~	~~I like to take changing things into my own hands.~~	0.323	removed
Player	R1	I like competitions where a prize can be won.	0.445	0.459
	R2	Rewards are a great way to motivate me.	0.561	0.622
	R3	Return of investment is important to me.	0.359	0.313
	R4	If the reward is sufficient I will put in the effort.	0.580	0.568
	~~R5~~	~~I look out for my own interests.~~	0.305	removed

How to use the scale:

1. Ask users to rate how well each item describes them in a 7-point Likert scale.
    a. Use only the 24 items numbered from 1-4 in each subscale.
    b. Items must be presented without identifying the corresponding type and, if possibly, in random order.
2. Separately add the scores of the items corresponding to each subscale.

APPENDIX B. CORRELATIONS OF THE HEXAD USER TYPES WITH GAME DESIGN ELEMENTS

Suggested by Marczewski	Game Element	Improved Associations					
		Socialiser	Free Spirit	Achiever	Disruptor	Player	Philanthropist
Philanthropist	Collection and Trading	.153*	.148*	.172*		**.259****	
	Gifting	.163*				.207**	
	Knowledge sharing	.184**	.138*		.167*	.231**	
	Administrative roles				.199**		
Socialiser	Guilds or Teams	**.179****			.169*	.192*	
	Social networks	**.150****			.197**	.143*	
	Social comparison or pressure	**.152****				.239**	
	Social competition	**.216****	.249**	.161*	**.320****	.239**	
	Social discovery	**.205****			.179**	.217**	
Free Spirit	Exploratory tasks		**.352****			.152**	.139*
	Nonlinear gameplay		**.221****				.179*
	Easter eggs	.137*	**.246****		.153**	.162*	
	Unlockable or rare content		**.225****			.149*	.140*
	Creativity tools		**.230****		.252**		
	Customization		**.198****		.136**	.162**	
Achiever	Challenges		**.412****	**.463****	**.207****	**.317****	.212**
	Certificates	.142*	**.200****	**.229****		**.228****	
	Learning		**.391****	**.215****			
	Quests		.236**	**.266****		**.245****	
	Levels or Progression	.170*	.204**	**.239****		**.302****	
	Boss battles						
Player	Points	.168*	.201**	.172**		**.259****	
	Rewards or Prizes		.139*	.167**		**.301****	
	Leaderboards	.199*			.170**	**.276****	
	Badges or Achievements	.164*		.208**		**.271****	
	Virtual economy					**.273****	
	Lotteries or Games of chance	.148*				**.190****	
Disruptor	Innovation platforms				**.302****	.166*	
	Voting mechanisms				**.236****	.138*	
	Development tools				**.294****	.144*	
	Anonymity		**.318****	**.289****		.211*	
	Anarchic gameplay		**.285****		**.268****		

Notes.
All correlations measured by Kendall's τ. Only significant correlations are shown.
The bold cells in each column mark the new suggestions of game design elements to support each Hexad user type.
* $p < 0.05$.   ** $p < 0.01$.

Towards a Taxonomy for the Clarification of PCG Actors' Roles

Rui Craveirinha
Department of Informatics
Engineering
University of Coimbra,
Portugal
rui.craveirinha@gmail.com

Nuno Barreto
Department of Informatics
Engineering
University of Coimbra,
Portugal
nbarreto@dei.uc.pt

Licinio Roque
Department of Informatics
Engineering
University of Coimbra,
Portugal
lir@dei.uc.pt

ABSTRACT

This work proposes a novel classification system that clarifies the multiple role configurations in the context of video-game design production involving use of Procedural Content Generation (PCG) methods. Specifically, the role that designers can have, either by the direct PCG-game design or via interaction with PCG-tools, and its consequent impact on PCG's output. Towards this effect, a taxonomy is specified that synthesizes existing PCG taxonomies so that it lists all possible roles and impact that each actor - the Human Designer, the Computational Algorithm and the Human Player - can have in PCG's evaluation and generation processes.

ACM Classification Keywords
HCI Theory

Author Keywords
Procedural Content Generation, Computational Creativity, Game Design

INTRODUCTION

Procedural Content Generation (PCG) is a not a new method in game design practices. Though PCG solutions have been around for decades [11], their impact on game design roles and procedures is, we argue, still undeveloped. Recently, there has been a surge of research in this area, yet despite the proposal of several models and taxonomies, there lacks a unified perspective for identifying and cataloguing a PCG system, particularly, in a way that allows clear understanding of how humans can interact with them in a game production context.

Our view is that PCG can be understood in three distinct ways. One, as a computational creativity agent that replaces the human author in the production of a video-game or part of its content, a **"PCG designer"**. Two, as a tool to used by human

CHI PLAY 2016, October 16–19, 2016, Austin, Texas, USA.
Copyright is held by the owner/author(s). Publication rights licensed to ACM.
ACM ISBN 978-1-4503-4456-2/16/10 ...$15.00.
http://dx.doi.org/10.1145/2967934.2968086

creators during video-game production, with procedurally generated content being incorporated into a video-game, a **"PCG design tool"**. And three, as part of a finished video-game artefact that features in-game content generation, a **"PCG game"**, designed by humans with or without aid of **"PCG design tools"**. And yet, existing PCG surveys and taxonomies [33, 39, 11, 28] do not elaborate on this distinction, classifying methods without ever taking into consideration how designers can interact with PCG methods during video-game design and production. Therefore, this work seeks to propose a classification system that allows for a clarification of the multiple role configurations that human designers, PCG algorithms and players can have in the context of PCG-aided video-game design and production. Towards this end, we will synthesize and redesign existing taxonomies in a way that highlights divergent approaches.

In the next section, we briefly overview existing PCG taxonomies, discuss their perspectives, how they complement each other, and analyse how they could be more inclusive and clarifying in our perspective. Then, we proceed to propose a synthesis of these taxonomies, with a focus on identifying the roles both human agents, designers and players, and of computational agents (the PCG methods) interact in video-game creation. We discuss how to classify PCG solutions according to this model, and discuss its strengths and weaknesses.

PROCEDURAL CONTENT GENERATION TAXONOMIES

Togelius et al. [33] proposed a taxonomy of PCG approaches and then surveyed existing examples accordingly, arriving at five dialectical factors that constitute their classification system. 'Online versus Offline' refers to when generation occurs, 'Necessary versus Optional Content' clarifies what type of game content is being generated, and 'Random Seeds versus Parameter Vectors', 'Stochastic versus Deterministic' and 'Constructive versus Generate-and-Test' elaborate on the procedural generation method. They further define 'Search-Based Content Generation', a sub-type of 'Generate-and-Test', evaluation is on a quantitative real-number scale. Finally, they elaborate on different types of 'Evaluation Functions' of PCG approaches, distinguishing 'Direct', 'Simulation-based' and 'Interactive' types.

Further expansion was made in a follow-up work on Experience Driven Procedural Content Generation (EDPCG for short) [39], a *"generic and effective approach for the optimization of user (player) experience"* with player experience being understood as *"the synthesis of affective patterns elicited and cognitive processes generated during gameplay"*. There are four main components to EDPCG: Player Experience Modeling (how player experience is modelled as a function of the interaction between game content and player), Content Quality (how generated content is qualitatively assessed based on modelled experience), Content Representation (how content is represented to the algorithm), and Content Generator (the algorithm that searches through content space so as to optimize player experience). Their taxonomy is established according to this new framework, with different alternative approaches in the four components.

Hendrikx et al. [11] surveyed and provide a taxonomy of existing PCG for games based on a twin perspective, content type versus generation method. In respect to content type, they present a hierarchical categorization (which is further subdivided): Game Bits, Game Space, Game Systems, Game Scenarios, Game Design, and Derived Content. Also, six large families of fundamental generation methods used in both literature and development praxis are established: Pseudo Random Number Generators, Generative Grammars, Image Filtering techniques, Spatial Algorithms, Modelling and Simulation of Complex Systems and Artificial Intelligence, with further sub-categorizations to each of these.

Smith [28], after over-viewing several PCG games and research projects, proposed an analytical framework and corresponding vocabulary for understanding the role of PCG in games, from a design point of view. She starts by listing 5 categories for content generation approaches, based on the procedural aspects of algorithms' generation: Optimization, Constraint Satisfaction, Grammar Approaches, Content Selection and Constructive Generators. Smith's view is that PCG methods can be encompassed as integral part of a game experience, and consequently, aims to study PCG from a design perspective; she therefore uses a design model, MDA (Mechanics, Dynamics and Aesthetics) for the taxonomy. She identified four PCG Mechanics. Building Blocks, the various ways human design knowledge can be represented and incorporated into the procedural content generator. Game Stage, which identifies when PCG occurs, either before game-play or during game-play. Interaction-type refers to how the generator takes (or does not take) into account players' interactions so as to determine what content is created. Player experience refers to how player experience is impacted and conceived in the perspective of the procedural content generator. Smith [28] goes on to elaborate on how player dynamics and aesthetics are impacted by PCG mechanics.

TAXONOMICAL ISSUES
We believe each positioning for a PCG research reflects a different sensibility, and frames methods in their respective taxonomies accordingly. While the value of these taxonomies is indisputable, we have some reservations to their internal logic, nomenclature and consequent coverage. Hendrikx et al. [11] only factored method and content type, and ended up with a very conceptually narrow Taxonomy, useful in listing

existing solutions in the industry, but not particularly powerful in terms of providing a space for classification of innovative PCG methods, or for finding identifying traits that inform us of the nature of each method outside of its generation algorithm and output. Take, for instance, the family of Experience-Driven PCG methods [39]: despite the firm heterogeneity of possible solutions, they would be lumped together and categorized under the AI category, with only their algorithmic basis and content type serving to distinguish between themselves through sub-categorization, when, for example, Yannakakis et al.'s [39] taxonomy identifies several distinctive characters that inform us on their procedural aspects and that go well beyond simple mentioning of their algorithm. Furthermore, Hendrikx et al's [11] nomenclature is at times problematic: the aforementioned AI category illustrates this fact, as all other categories make reference to AI algorithms, only of different families. To conclude, we think that methods and output are valid characteristics to form a PCG taxonomy, but are not enough to capture the wide diversity of qualitatively different solutions.

Yannakakis et al's [39] EDPCG taxonomy fares much better in terms of identifying key characters for categorization of PCG approaches. Its division of EDPCG into four distinct components - Player Experience Modelling, Content Quality, Content Representation and Content Generator - with several different traits in each, allows for a finer, more meaningful system for classification and identifying of different solutions. Furthermore, it has an advantage in that it clarifies how players and player-derived data are factored into existing PCG solutions, something amiss in [11]. Some problems remain however. First and foremost, there is a distinct lack of inclusiveness: admittedly, this is a quality inscribed by design. By only addressing EDPCG solutions, a vast scope of different-minded solutions (say, any classical PCG solution with no player interaction) get left either uncategorised (for lacking any of the characteristics that conform to the four defining components of this model) or simply poorly defined, whenever their distinguishing features sit outside the four characters.

In respects to the latter, we find at least two striking examples: both Sentient Sketchbook, by [38] and Tanagra [29] involve subject interaction which defies both the Player denomination in 'Player Experience Modelling' (as subjects behave like creators and not players, constructing the end-solution in tandem with PCG systems), as well as its taxa, existing none where a role of active design of the solution can be properly framed. This brings a crucial question of how would video-game producers appropriate EDPCG systems. No hint is given in these works as to what sort of control of content generation would be afforded to designers and programmers, whether they would have to code their own variant of these systems, adapt them by providing base-content to fill out gaps, or if there would be significant parametrization of these methods. The way EDPCG is proposed, the human designer seems to have no part to play. It is our position that there is no reason why this should be so. Again, it must be stressed that these are not a problems with the EDPCG taxonomy in of itself, merely a stating that its scope that was never intended to be abusively generalized to the whole spectre of PCG solutions, therefore making it inadequate for the broader categorization that is needed to establish.

Smith's [28] own taxonomy broadens the inclusiveness of previous efforts, and fixing some issues, while providing greater detail on the distinguishing features of each solution (besides other contributions). However, it still has its share of problematic choices. We start with a repeat of the subject role issue; Smith considers the human designer to an extent previously absent from taxonomies, especially when she addresses the Building Blocks mechanic. Nonetheless, when she considers interaction with the PCG system she only addresses Player Interaction, from whence we surmise that in her model Smith conceives of the designer only in the creation of the PCG system in of itself, with no interaction of an outside designer with the PCG-system, making the PCG-game (per her own nomenclature) the end-artefact in of itself (and not a tool for support in design, as is common in several practices [11]). When it comes to the words "human" and "user" it is not always makes it clear whether she is referring to player or designer, hence pointing in the direction that the only human agent interacting with the PCG system is the player.

So there is not accounting for a wider breadth of contexts and roles that PCG can offer; to [28] PCG in games seems limited only to games with incorporated PCG systems (a PCG game), and not games produced with PCG algorithms (PCG as design tool). There are arguments in favour that the two should not be mixed, but the other taxonomies did engulf these two approaches (even if they did not mark any lines between them), and in good reason, as the same PCG algorithms can be appropriated in these two contexts. As a consequence, because of this positioning, designers role when interacting with PCG was not fully taken into account.

It is our opinion that these previous efforts in categorization should be assembled together, expanded upon and improved, with their discrepancies solved. Furthermore, we wish to propose a perspective on PCG that enables a clarification of the roles that both human and computational agent can embody, both in terms of content generation and evaluation.

TAXONOMY PROPOSAL

Expanding upon [28], we aim to establish a vocabulary that facilitates and enriches communication between the different practitioners and researchers of the field. We also wanted, for reasons of our own research, to detail the multiple role configurations of roles of human and computer actors when using procedural content generation, with particular emphasis on the human author, a factor we think that has remained implicit in previous taxonomies. It is our opinion that this clarification is a necessary first step in studying how PCG impacts both creative and procedural aspects of the game design practice, as well as players' experience.

In order to clarify the context of this proposal, we must put forward our own understanding of what constitutes Procedural Content Generation for video-games, seeing as this limits the scope of our problem. To [39], PCG is the *"creation of content automatically, through algorithmic means"*. We wish to expand on this definition so as to highlight how human creators

can interact with these systems, and so we must broaden the automatic clause. Thus, we define Procedural Content Generation as the process by which an algorithmic method can, autonomously or semi-autonomously, be capable of generating video-game content. We define content as any component part of a video-game, or a complete or incomplete video-game artefact or prototype. Because this definition amplifies the notions of content beyond its original meaning, we will use the term solution to refer to the output of a PCG method, be it content or otherwise. With this definition, we can include all the variants and families of PCG: **"PCG designer"**, **"PCG (as a) design tool"** and a **"PCG games"**.

This taxonomical proposal results from a process of synthesis and expansion of preceding taxonomies, maintaining, whenever possible, common grounds to them and incorporating their unique aspects, while adding any we found lacking. Complementing the study of these taxonomies, we list state of the art PCG methods in research, and commercial games that were created with PCG methods or that included PCG in them, forwarding these as examples of each classification branch whenever needed. Terms and branches from previous taxonomies were maintained and fused together, though effort was made to adapt, simplify and improve the end result. We sought to strike a balance between inclusiveness, communicability, understandability, and categorization accuracy.

Generation vs. Evaluation

We separate the content-generation act into two moments: solution generation (proper) and solution evaluation. Because this division is a crucial quality of our taxonomy, and it can be seen as controversial, what follows is a succinct justification of this choice supported by creativity literature and a survey of existing PCG methods.

Csikszentmihalyi [8] studied human creativity, and found that the creative act was composed of a recursive process, laden with repeated loops around a set of five steps: preparation, incubation, insight, evaluation and elaboration. We think the three first steps can be analogically understood as a generation procedure: you take knowledge from an area (preparation) and try out different, improbable combinations (incubation) until a pattern or a fitting solution emerges (insight). Then, a form of evaluation of the solution's quality has to be made in order to decide on its merits; this determines whether or not work is forwarded to further refining of said solution (elaboration). The relevance of evaluation in creative computer systems is, for example, advocated in [18], where it is argued that a *"genuine evolutionary artificial artist (...) requires (...) a system that is able to "perceive" an artwork, and perform an evaluation of the piece"*. In Computational Creativity systems, that seek to emulate or parabolise human creative processes, this distinction is very common. Besides *"generating new material"*, these systems include the responsibility to develop or employ the means to *"assess the value of the artefacts"* they produce [5]. Similarly, co-creativity methods, which pair human and computational, include *"the evaluation of the final (or possibly intermediate) outcomes and the evaluation of the co-creative processfor the generation of outcomes, solutions, or items"*[38]. Procedural content generation methods are in-

Actor \ Role	Evaluation	Generation
Designer	None Implicit { Editorial Control, PCG Design Explicit { Quality Assessment, Quality Definition	None Configuration { Method Selection, Method Parametrization, Content Parametrization Base-Design { Idea, Experiential Chunk, Template, Component Patterns, Subcomponent Co-Design Meta-Design
Computer	None Implicit Explicit { Content-based { Heuristics, Simulation-Based, Experience Inference }, Player Experience-based	Content-type { Derived, Scenarios, Systems, Space, Decorative, Design Strategy { Optimization, Constraint Satisfaction, Grammar Derivation, Content Selection, Constructive Phase { Design-Time, Pre-play, Play-time
Player	None Implicit { Preference Inference, Experience Model-based Explicit { Preference, Experience Self-Evaluation	None Game-play Parametrization Co-Design

Figure 1. Taxonomy used to clarify actors roles in PCG methods.

scribed in these traditions, and thus tend to reveal this pattern of generation and evaluation. This is evident in generate-and-test and search-based content generation [33], all experience driven content generation [39] and constraint-based methods. All these, besides generating content, also have procedures to either assess its quality or at least validate it. Despite this, not all methods have algorithmic evaluation; constructive and grammar generators, for instance. However, we would argue that there are other forms of implicit or explicit validation of solutions' quality: either pre-emptively inscribed in the generator's algorithm as it was being created - so that it would tend to give results that the human designer found valuable (more on this in the next section) - or have their output evaluated by human designers, that then proceed to either include or discard generated content in their design.

The added value in separating these two phases lies in being able to identify, with accuracy how each actor impacts the end-result, as the qualitative aspect of it depends on whether or not they interfere with each phase, and in what role. This also allows us to track in detail, the responsibilities of the different actors in terms of the quality of a play experience mediated thanks to PCG systems. By **Generation** we understand all processes with the goal of creation, recreation or iteration of a game content solution, irrespective of its validity or quality. **Evaluation** refers to any procedures or acts, be they formal or

informal, that end up determining the attributed value of any generated solution, in a way that guides the creative generation process in subsequent iterations.

Description

Figure 1 shows a visual representation of the various categories for this Taxonomy. It is a 3 by 2 table, in which rows correspond to the different actors, and columns to the two PCG roles they can enact, evaluation and generation. In each cell lie all the alternatives for a specific combination of Role and Actor. Possibilities, unless otherwise stated are *not* mutually-exclusive, with several possible combinations being possible. Note however that one specific cell, **Computer Generation**, is an exception, and has a further subdivision into three sub-taxonomies, each pertaining to a particular aspect of that role-actor combination.

Classifying PCG methods according to this model requires only that a specific question be answered for each combination: how does the Actor (Designer, Computer and Player) impact the Role (of Evaluation or Generation) in the context of this PCG method? If one fills out the type of impact each actor has or lacks in these six combinations, then PCG methods interaction with human actors in a game design context is made clear. The following subsections have descriptions of each branch and each categorization possibility.

Designer x Computer x Player

The main addition of this taxonomical model is the direct and explicit enunciation of how Human and Computers interact in PCG powered design contexts. This serves to further distinguish between different PCG alternatives, as methods in which PCG algorithms act as the primary creative force in the process, will have a greater prominence of the computational role face the designers', whereas co-creativity alternatives and PCG as tool alternatives will be more balanced.

By **Designer** we mean all human creators that directly impact the design of the game during production and before it is released to the public; this includes everyone that interacts with the PCG system, from game and level designers to programmers. This branch then seeks to enumerate all content that is created by human beings that interacts with the computational algorithm, which can then alter, expand, blend, and reconstruct it; it also includes the impact humans have in the creation and/or use of the PCG system itself. It is our stance that an excessive focus on Players and Player Experience Modelling has left Designers' role in the use and creation of PCG solutions sorely undeveloped. By attributing a role to their participation in PCG enabled design processes, we clarify and make explicit their impact in PCG solutions, and establish a clear path for communication between researchers and designers.

By **Player**, we mean any human who plays the game after its release. Note that in some cases ("Minecraft" [24], "Dwarf Fortress" [1]", "Little Big Planet"[10]), players can interact with the game in a way that changes its experiential content, be it thanks to level editors or procedural content generators that come with the game, making their role seem akin to that of designers; despite this, for the purposes of this taxonomy, they are players and only players. Player experience data has an especially big role in EDPCG solutions [39], and therefore needs to be taken into account. We use the term **Computer** to refer to all algorithms that are executed either during game production or during game-play, that with complete or partial autonomy, can generate game content. This excludes any computational tool which is directed by a human and has no end-result autonomy, such as modelling and level editors, etc.

Designer x Evaluation

In this section we list all aspects in which a designer can impact the evaluation processes of a PCG enabled video-game. **None** refers to examples where the computational agent does not take into account any Designer feedback into evaluation processes. The aesthetic evaluation of resulting solutions is decided by computational algorithmic processes and/or player input. For the Designer to have no impact in this category, it is also absolutely necessary that he was not the designer of the PCG solution (see below). For such a case, we use the **Implicit** categorization: this means any way that the designer might indirectly affect how solutions are evaluated by the designer-computer-player complex. Finally, **Explicit** refers to all the possible ways in which the designer overtly impacts how solutions are evaluated.

The basic and most common form of implicit Designer Evaluation is **Editorial Control**. When designing aided by any

tool, creators can select which solutions get used, discarding partial or complete work at any time; the same holds true for procedurally generated design solutions. Irrespective of the quality attributed by computational algorithm and/or players, designers thus reveal an implicit act of evaluation on their part. We did not find accounts that reveal this effect in action, but it is highly likely that when using PCG tools in the development phase designers will often repeat procedural processes, so as to obtain the best results.

Another alternative we find is the one in which the designer takes part in the process of designing the PCG system itself, **PCG-Design**. If creators of a game program their own PCG method and code its procedures in a way that it somehow implicitly promotes certain qualities in generated solutions and demotes others, then this is an implicit form of solution evaluation impacted by designers, even though no formal evaluation method may be held. This is potentially the case if designers program Constructive, Grammar algorithms, for instance, which have no computational evaluation method, but tend to seek out specific kind of solutions as if they were (implicitly) evaluating content, and pursuing it.

Explicit Evaluation refers to cases in which designers are the ones attributing quality to generated solutions. The most direct approach is designer **Quality Assessment**, which are those cases in which procedural generation methods present solutions to designers so they can then evaluate it in some way, by either selecting which solutions to pursue or which quality value is attributed. Interactive evaluation is common in evolutionary art (see [31] for a survey on several), though less frequent in respects to games [39]. Examples include a meta-generator of level generators [14], where users evaluate a generator via its generated level sets, and a system for generating game buildings where users define which (high-quality) buildings are evolved [19].

Quality Definition refers to cases in which the designer does not attribute quality to solutions himself, but defines the way in which the PCG system will automatically assess each solution's quality. In evolutionary art, we know of at least two examples in which human users can *"express their intentions through the design of fitness functions"* [17, 16]. In the Author-crentric approach to PCG, designers get to model, via a user-interface, the PCG's evaluation function [7]. Besides this work proposal, we are not aware of any PCG approach that gives designers the power to map-out how evaluation takes place indirectly, though considering how many PCG solutions use Experience Models (see [39]), there is no reason why these should not offer the possibility to establish multiple levels of configuration and manipulation by designers; and in fact, Togelius et al. [33] assume this possibility of evaluation function personalisation in their work. As a simple prototypical example, imagine a PCG solution for a Mario level generator where designers could define a weighted sum fitness function, attributing weights to content's classification as fun, challenging or frustrating by the models in [23]; different designers could thus express their preference in terms of design through distinct combinations of weights.

To conclude the **Quality Definition** branch we put forth only a sub-classification that views to clarify the degree of impact that the designer can have in his definition of the Quality evaluation function. Namely, we propose a qualitative distinction between cases in which designers can parametrize aspects of a pre-existent quality function, **Parametrization** (in [16] an application for the creation of non-photorealistic renderings of images features a User Interface for human-led parametrization of the fitness function), and **Design** for extreme cases in which designers can finely detail their quality function using whatever data-sources the procedural content generator affords as basis (of the latter, we know of only one example, the Author-centric PCG approach [7]). Further sub-categorization of this branch could be made by listing the types of base-data used in the designer' defined evaluation function, but we place the qualitative nature of these in the Computer x Evaluation cell, to avoid repetition.

Designer x Generation

This branch refers to all creative impact that a designer can have in the production process of a PCG powered video-game, that can be related to the use of PCG techniques. The designer can have four major types of generation impact. **None** corresponds to cases in which the computational system would create, with absolute autonomy from the designer, every aspect of the video-game content in question, without using any designer-authored content. Also, the algorithm would have to show independence and unpredictability in respects to human designers, i.e. having been programmed by someone other than them. Though we could find no prototypical case today of this type of PCG as designer, there is no reason why the possibility should not come to pass, and many authors in PCG seem to be headed in that direction.

Configuration refers to when the games' creators interact in some way with a pre-programmed PCG method that offers some degree of customization to its operation. Three sub-types of impact were identified. **Method Selection** is for when a particular PCG tool offers different methodological alternatives to its generation algorithm. One notable example outside of video-games is landscape generator Terragen [30], which allows users to chose which algorithm to employ in land and cloud generation (Subdivide and Displace, Perlin Noise, etc). **Method Parametrization** refers to when procedural aspects can be configured in the generator, for example, include a system for generating game buildings where users can parametrize he genetic operators' strength and likelihood [19], or alternatives such as the Author-centric PCG approach, where full control of the evolutionary algorithm's parameters is given [7].

Content Parametrization goes beyond just selecting or parametrizing the algorithm type, being reserved to PCG approaches where the output is functionally dependent on a set of input parameters, and these offer *"clear and predictable result for the output"* [27]. **Parametrization** is available in Terragen [30], as several features that determine the end-result can be selected a priori (percentage levels of Realism, Smoothing, Glaciation, Canyonism). Another example from evolutionary art comes from [17], where *"control is given to the*

users by allowing them to specify the rendering details of selected pieces". We found other examples for video-games with **Content Parametrization**, but these were for player use and will be listed accordingly, though the logic is quite the same. Grome, a terrain generator [25] is an interesting example of PCG as it allows all types of parametrization.

Base Design is the branch where all human-authored content that computational generation methods need in order to find new solutions is listed. Quality of end-artifact can be positively affected by high-quality of base design elements[5] which is why proper identification of human authored elements is so relevant. All known PCG systems use as a base some sort of human-authored basis on top of which they will operate. These can be of multiple types, but we adapted a selection of classification terms from Smith's [28] 'Building Blocks' mechanics category, while adding **Idea** for cases in which designers forward high-level concepts as a basis for the system to generate solutions.

Examples of PCG systems where computers require designers to forward an **Idea** can be seen in both ANGELINA [6] and Nelson and Mateas' [22] system. These require a thematic input of some sort to come from a human agent. In the former case this is just a word (or multiple words which the system then derives a single word), and in the latter it uses verb and/or noun. These are then conceptually incorporated into the generation system which abides by them as themes.

As per Smith [28], **Experiential Chunks** are large building blocks for content designed by human authors, that can by themselves, be experienced by players; **Templates** are a generalized form of experiential chunk where human designers left 'blank' spaces for the computer to fill in; **Component patterns** are human designed components that are small enough that by themselves do not greatly impact player experience; **Subcomponents** is in reference of generators that operate at the subcomponent level, using the same building blocks as a human designer would. For further detail and examples, please refer to [28].

Co-design is for when PCG methods assign both computational and human actors preponderance in the creative act. Examples such as Sentient Sketchbook [38] and Tanagra [29] are paradigmatic examples approaches where Designers are co-creators, manually authoring new content on top of procedurally generated one and then feeding the generator human-authored solutions, in an iterative creative process. This is qualitatively different from Base-design, which describes cases where only the computational agent operates on top of human authored content, and the interaction stops at that point. Note however that when content generation occurs in game production, it is not strictly needed for a system to actually support co-design, as designers can always take computational output and refine it manually.

Finally, **Meta-design** refers to design production cases where designers create their own custom-made PCG algorithm, so that it then in turn generates game's content. Game creators programming their own PCG system is a standard practice in commercial ventures (e.g. quest generation in "Skyrim"

[35], map generation in "Minecraft" [36]; (see [11] for further examples). Because it is equally common in some content types to see producers use general purpose methods that were not created by them (examples: Speedtree, a foliage generator [13] and Grome, a terrain generator [25], both are outsourced to game studios), this category serves to distinguish between these cases, as the Meta-design class is specific to the former, in which case it should be highlighted, as it underlines greater designer control in the generation process.

Computer x Evaluation

This division refers to all solution evaluation processes that are carried out automatically and autonomously by the computational agent. Note that many of the possible methods in this section assume human input of some kind, so this branch should be read in conjunction to both Designer and Player Evaluation.

None: PCG methods might not have any computational impact on content evaluation. Hypothetically, this would be a case in which all content evaluation would be carried out either by designers in production-time or by players in play-time, or in cases where the generator affords no means of content evaluation. It is possible that the PCG algorithm may bias the generation process by some **Implicit** process, that makes it seem like there is some form of computational content evaluation. Though we could not find any overt example of this effect, we think it is bound to be a PCG feature in some cases and should this classification should be kept open for it. The most explored category is, naturally, **Explicit** forms of Computer Evaluation where the computational agent enacts some formal act of content quality judgement. Two types of explicit evaluation carried out by computers, **Content-based** and **Player Experience-based**.

Content-based refers to any evaluation that takes into consideration intrinsic aspects of the generated content. Say the system is generating a platform game level, if the evaluation module is looking at qualities like the numbers and placement of enemies, pits and other obstacles, and then using these elements as indicators of quality of the solution, then evaluation is explicit and content-based. In terms of Yannakaki et al.'s [39] taxonomy, this is the equivalent to their Direct Content Quality assessment.

Also somewhat akin to Yannakakis et al.'s [39] work, we propose to sub-divide **Content-based** evaluation into three types: **Heuristics Simulation-based** and **Experience Inference**, which are identical Theory-Driven, Simulation-based and Data-driven categories [39], respectively (changes in names are meant to open-up, simplify and make each category's meaning clearer). **Heuristics** is for when evaluation functions map a functional relationship between intrinsic features and content quality. This is typically based on some theoretical basis as per [39] though there is no reason why Designers cannot establish ad-hoc functions of this type. **Simulation-based** refers to cases when evaluation is based on simulated game-play data, extracted from artificial agents walkthroughs.

Finally, **Experience Inference** is for when structural content component qualities are mapped as being predictive of affec-tive states or other experiential qualities, and thus used as basis for content evaluation. **Player Experience-based** also follows [39], and refers to when the PCG system evaluates solutions not based on the intrinsic qualities of the solution, but based on actual player experience data that is then transformed into a measure of solution quality. For further detail on the previous categories, and examples, please refer to [39].

Computer x Generation

It is in this branch where the bulk of PCG occurs: in the automatic algorithmic processes that permit computers to generate new content and new artefacts. As expected, Computer generation hosts the bulk of possibilities. We follow Hendrikx et al. (2013) in the sense that we believe that there must be an identification of both the algorithm family used to generate solutions (what we name **Strategy**, as in the generation strategy used) and the nature of the generated content, the **Content-type**. Also, we add **Phase**, to identify when generation occurs, as per [33].

Content-Type

We followed Hendrikx et al.'s [11] classification of single-layered content types, but adapted it somewhat for easier reading and more accurate categorization. **Derived**, **Scenarios** and **Space** were maintained as is and their meaning remains untouched. The class Bits name was replaced by the more meaningful term **Decorative** (taken from [28]), but the original definition remains, as elementary units of game content that the player, usually, does not directly engage with; these include cosmetic elements such as textures, sound and vegetation, but also simple behaviour (i.e. the way objects interact with each other and the environment).

Hendrikx et al.'s [11] Game Design layer is here replaced with one of its subcategories, **System Design**, as the modelling of real-life phenomena represented in the game, such as ecosystems and entity behaviour. This change was based on two reasons. First, the words game design tend to be used at a broader scope level, as in meaning the entirety of a video-game's design, making it a poor choice of terms. Second, it conflated two heterogeneous types of content, **System Design** (referring to *"patterns underlying the game and game rules"* [11]), and World design, meaning *"the design of a setting, story, and theme"* [11]. We argue that examples of the latter can be separated and included in the **Scenarios** content, seeing as that has a subcategory for Story content. **Scenarios** describes the way and order in which events unfold, typically story-related content, but also level sequences and puzzles. **Space** refers to the environment where game-play takes place in, mostly map and terrain geography. Finally, **Derived Content** is all content that is a side-product of the game world, such as news and broadcasts which communicate game-events and player leader-boards. For examples and further clarification on these categories, refer to [11].

Besides these, PCG methods can go beyond just generating content, and can create (complete or partial) **Design** prototypes, as well as fully fledged video-games. These will typically assemble or operate on several different layers of content, and can operate with different generation methods; notable research examples include ANGELINA [6] and [22]. In these cases, it is the composited whole that is, in fact, generated. We then reserve the term **Design** for these cases, as it makes classification clearer.

Strategy

Strategy answers the question of How the computational agent proceeds to generate content. In this, we followed Smith's categorization, mainly for her better choice of representative and easily communicable classes, namely **Optimization**, **Constraint Satisfaction**, **Grammar Derivation**, **Content Selection** and **Constructive**; for further examples and clarification of these categories see [28]). **Optimization** methods *"treat the design process as a search for the combination of elements that best fit some criteria"* [28]. Examples include [32, 37], and all methods that use search-based algorithms and similar approaches.

Constraint Satisfaction approaches are based on the declarative specification of both the properties and constraints that define the content that is to be generated (see "Facade" [20], Tanagra [27], and "Left 4 Dead" [34] as examples). **Grammar** approaches refer to when content is generated by an expansion of grammar-like rules. **Content Selection**, a humble approach which relies on the simple act of sampling content (from a larger database) and then presenting it to the player. Though assuredly debatable, this category has been proposed by [28], and it was used with notable effect in the commercial game "LSD: Dream Emulator" [26, 15]. **Constructive** generators build content by assembling with a predetermined process previously constructed building blocks.

Phase

Understanding when procedural generation occurs is crucial in our understanding of the role of Designers and players. Togelius et al. [33] defined this with two categories, 'Online versus Offline', that distinguish whether generation occurs during game development, or while players are playing games. Smith [28] however, seems to have a different interpretation of these terms, as she utilizes them and she shifts the off-line term from *"during game development"* [33], to what *"happens before a unit of play experience begins"* [28] which, considering her examples, means after production and release, but before game-play proper occurs, as when players are navigating pre-game menus. To provide some systematization of the phases in which PCG occurs, in a way that bridges the gap between the different taxonomies, we propose a change from an Off-line vs On-line dichotomy, to a three-way branch: **Design-time**, **Pre-play** and **Play-time**.

Design-time refers to Togelius et al.'s [33] off-line, a phase in the development cycle of the video-game where it is still not finished. PCG can be used in this phase as either a tool for development of a non-PCG powered game, or as part of PCG-powered game (or, more likely, a bit of both). In this phase, player data may be collected as part of creating an intrinsic evaluation function, but apart from that specific case, we consider players do not interact with the PCG system.

Pre-play refers to our interpretation of Smith's [28] off-line variation - referring to when procedural generation occurs in a released game, but before players game-play experience in itself starts; examples range from [21] to [1]. **Play-time** refers to on-line generation: when a released game has content that is being generated as game-play occurs, maybe even as a consequence of how it occurs. Commercial examples include "Minecraft" [24], that has on-line generation of landscape data, "Borderlands" weapon generation [2] and "Skyrim's" [12] Radiant quest system. For research examples of both off-line and on-line variations, see [33, 39].

Player x Evaluation

Every player action with the finished video-game artefact that affects how generated content is evaluated falls in this branch. Like before, these three categories refer to whether nor not there is player evaluation, and if there is, if it is an **Explicit** act on their part (usually, but not necessarily, measured by some form of questionnaire), or an **implicit** form of evaluation derived from their behaviour (usually, but not necessarily, analysed through game-play metrics). **Implicit** types include two possibilities **Preference-inference** and **Experience-based**.

Preference-inference refers to when some player action or behaviour betrays their liking a particular quality in generated content, which generators can afterwards map to a value in their evaluation procedures. In [33] an example is forwarded of a PCG shooter by Hastings et al. where a weapon generation system evaluates content based on how often players fire them. In this case, evaluation is not based on any experience model, but on the logic that using a given item betrays preference, and generation should promote solutions identical to those that players like.

Experience Model-based is for when behaviour is mapped to some experiential concept - an emotion, an idea, a type of behaviour, for example - and this can then be used as basis for new content (see, for example experience models in [23]). Commercial examples include "Left4Dead" [3], where a director AI controls game events and seeks to modulate player tension, stress, pacing, conflict and difficulty [34].

Explicit refers to when PCG systems use subject-data - typically in the form of questionnaires - to determine how to appraise generated content and generate new content. When players get to evaluate the content they are playing in terms of their quality (attributing a score to content, or valuing content by comparison of different alternatives), we say that players contribute in to evaluation in terms of **Preference**. We have found no example of this, but it seems an obvious path to explore. **Experience Self-evaluation** is for cases in which players evaluate their own experience, but do not judge it in terms of what they want or prefer, so the generator can adapt its output to players affective state. These distinctions between Preference and Experience is may give rise to contention. We propose them because they offer very different design mindsets and can be used in different design contexts. Whatever data-source used, one serves to maximize player satisfaction, the other to adapt and modulate players experience.

Player x Generation

This branch refers to every player interaction with a video-game that can impact content generation. **None** refers to PCG methods which do not take into account any Player actions in order to generate new solutions. **Game-play** refers to when **Play-time** PCG takes into account in-game interactions so as to select which type of content to subsequently generate. These are not actions used to value game content, nor represent player attempts to determine generated content, but cases where PCG-games react to player actions so as to reply with dynamic consequences (usually **Systems** content generators that view the maintenance of a believable and complex game-world). Examples include "Blade Runner" [4] and "Facade" [20], and "Skyrim's" [12] procedural quest generation system.

Parametrization (per [28]) is analogous to Designer's **Content Parametrization**. Examples include map generation "Civilization IV" [21] where players can determine map's topological features, or in "Dwarf Fortress" [1] where they can determine key game-play map elements (history, size, number of civilizations, sites, beasts, savagery and mineral occurrence). Another example is "Murder" [9], a procedural detective game, where an initial screen allows players to parametrize several aspects of the experience (names of characters, murder date and location, etc.).

Co-design is for cases in which players can create or edit content in conjunction with the computational agent. Though there are no commercial examples we could find of this type, Tanagra [29] and Sentient Sketchbook [38], if incorporated in a finished game and opened up to players, would be of this kind. Given the prominence of in-game level editors, their integration with a PCG system acting as a co-designer seems like a logical next step.

DISCUSSION

PCG systems do not exist in a vacuum; as far we know, there has yet to be a computational creative system capable of generating content without some form of human input. Hence, until the day we create autonomous creative systems, we need to research how humans can interact with these systems. Thus far in this research area, there has been a great deal of focus both on novel methods for content generation and how these can better fulfil player needs, without forming a clear picture of how designers fit with these systems. This taxonomy offers a first blueprint on how to categorize human interaction with these systems, while simultaneously synthesizing previous taxonomies into a more expressive model.

We believe that for PCG methods to yield results, they must be designed, first and foremost, with human factors in mind, as there is great potential for humans and computers to complement each other, minimizing their flaws and potentiating the resulting creative output. Towards that end, more study needs to be directed at understanding how humans can interact with these systems, and this taxonomy aids in that regard, providing a clear way for classifying PCG methods in respects to what modes of interaction they afford human creators.

This taxonomy can also be appropriated as a reference when studying of other applications that use computational creativity systems, or in broader terms, any application used in creative activities that has some degree of autonomy.

To conclude, this role clarification shows that there are many undeveloped areas of research, as we could find very few PCG methods for video-games that fit some of the new classes in this taxonomy. Namely, systems with Explicit Designer-centred Evaluation (both in terms of Quality Assessment and Quality Definition), forms of Designer Generation Configuration (especially Content Configuration), and last but not least, Co-Design approaches that can capitalize on human designers creativity.

ACKNOWLEDGMENTS
This work was financed under PhD Scholarship number SFRH/BD/75196/2010 awarded by the FCT - Fundação de Ciências e Tecnologia.

REFERENCES
1. Tarn Adams. 2006. Dwarf Fortress. Bay 12 Games, Windows. (2006).

2. Matthew Armstrong. 2009. Borderlands. Gearbox Software, Xbox 360. (2009).

3. Mike Booth. 2008. Left 4 Dead. Turtle Rock Studios, Xbox 360. (2008).

4. Louis Castle. 1997. Blade Runner. Westwood Studios, PC CD-ROM. (1997).

5. Simon Colton and Geraint A. Wiggins. 2012. Computational Creativity: The Final Frontier?. In *ECAI (Frontiers in Artificial Intelligence and Applications)*, Luc De Raedt, Christian Bessière, Didier Dubois, Patrick Doherty, Paolo Frasconi, Fredrik Heintz, and Peter J. F. Lucas (Eds.), Vol. 242. IOS Press, 21–26.

6. Michael Cook and Simon Colton. 2014. Ludus Ex Machina: Building A 3D Game Designer That Competes Alongside Humans. In *Proceedings of the Fifth International Conference on Computational Creativity (ICCC2014)*. International Association for Computational Creativity.

7. R. Craveirinha, L.L. Santos, and Licinio Roque. 2013. An Author-Centric Approach to Procedural Content Generation. In *ACE 2013 the 10th International Conference in Advances in Computer Entertainment Technology*.

8. Mihály Csíkszentmihályi. 1997. *Creativity: flow and the psychology of discovery and invention*. HarperPerennial.

9. Grant Harrison and Jason Kingsley. 1990. Murder! U.S. GOLD, Amiga C64. (1990).

10. Mark Healey and David Smith. 2008. Little Big Planet. Media Molecule, Playstation 3. (2008).

11. Mark Hendrikx, Sebastiaan Meijer, Joeri Van Der Velden, and Alexandru Iosup. 2013. Procedural Content Generation for Games: A Survey. *ACM Trans. Multimedia Comput. Commun. Appl.* 9, 1 (2013), 1:1–1:22.

12. Todd Howard. 2011. The Elder Scrolls V: Skyrim. Bethesda Game Studios, Xbox 360. (2011).

13. IDV. 2016. SpeedTree. (2016). http://www.speedtree.com/ Online; accessed February 1st 2016.

14. M. Kerssemakers, J. Tuxen, J. Togelius, and G.N. Yannakakis. 2012. A procedural procedural level generator generator. In *Computational Intelligence and Games (CIG), 2012 IEEE Conference on*.

15. LSDWiki. 2016. LSD: Dream Emulator. (2016). http://dreamemulator.wikia.com/ Online; accessed February 1st 2016.

16. Penousal Machado and Hugo Amaro. 2013. Fitness Functions for Ant Colony Paintings. In *Proceedings of the fourth International Conference on Computational Creativity (ICCC)*.

17. Penousal Machado, Tiago Martins, Hugo Amaro, and Pedro H. Abreu. 2014. *Evolutionary and Biologically Inspired Music, Sound, Art and Design: Third European Conference, EvoMUSART*. Springer Berlin Heidelberg, Chapter An Interface for Fitness Function Design.

18. Penousal Machado, Juan Romero, María Luisa Santos, Amílcar Cardoso, and Bill Manaris. 2004. *Applications of Evolutionary Computing EvoWorkshops Proceedings*. Springer Berlin Heidelberg, Chapter Adaptive Critics for Evolutionary Artists.

19. Andrew Martin, Andrew Lim, Simon Colton, and Cameron Browne. 2010. *Applications of Evolutionary Computation EvoApplicatons, Proceedings, Part I*. Springer Berlin Heidelberg, Chapter Evolving 3D Buildings for the Prototype Video Game Subversion.

20. Michael Mateas and Andrew Stern. 2003. Facade: An Experiment in Building a Fully-Realized Interactive Drama. In *Game Developers Conference*.

21. Sid Meier. 2005. Civilization IV. Firaxis Games, PC. (2005).

22. Mark J. Nelson and Michael Mateas. 2007. Towards Automated Game Design. In *Congress of the Italian Association for Artificial Intelligence*.

23. Chris Pedersen, Julian Togelius, and Georgios N. Yannakakis. 2009. Modeling player experience in super mario bros. In *Proceedings of the 5th international conference on Computational Intelligence and Games (CIG'09)*. IEEE Press, 132–139.

24. Markus Persson. 2011. Minecraft. Mojang, PC Download. (2011).

25. QuadSoftware. 2016. SpeedTree. http://www.quadsoftware.com/. (2016). Online; accessed February 1st 2016.

26. Osamu Sato. 1998. LSD. Asmik Ace Entertainment, Playstation. (1998).

27. Gillian Smith. 2012. *Expressive Design Tools: Procedural Content Generation for Game Designers*. Ph.D. Dissertation. UC Santa Cruz.

28. Gillian Smith. 2014. Expressive Design Tools: Procedural Content Generation for Game Designers. In *Proceedings of the ACM CHI Conference on Human Factors in Computing Systems*.

29. Gillian Smith, Jim Whitehead, and Michael Mateas. 2010. Tanagra: An Intelligent Level Design Assistant for 2D Platformers.. In *AIIDE*. The AAAI Press.

30. Planetside Software. 2016. Terragen 3. (2016). planetside.co.uk/ Online; accessed February 1st 2016.

31. Hideyuki Takagi. 2001. Interactive Evolutionary Computation: Fusion of the Capabilities of EC Optimization and Human Evaluation. *Proc. IEEE* 89, 9 (2001).

32. Julian Togelius, Renzo De Nardi, and Simon M. Lucas. 2006. Making racing fun through player modeling and track evolution. In *in Proceedings of the SAB'06 Workshop on Adaptive Approaches for Optimizing Player Satisfaction in Computer and Physical Games*. 70.

33. Julian Togelius, Georgios N. Yannakakis, Kenneth O. Stanley, and Cameron Browne. 2011. Search-Based Procedural Content Generation: A Taxonomy and Survey. *Computational Intelligence and AI in Games, IEEE Transactions on* 3, 3 (2011).

34. WikiA. last retrieved February 2016. Left4Dead. (last retrieved February 2016). http://left4dead.wikia.com/wiki/The_Director

35. Wikipedia. 2016a. The Elder Scrolls V: Skyrim. (2016). https://en.wikipedia.org/wiki/The_Elder_Scrolls_V:_Skyrim Online; accessed February 1st 2016.

36. Wikipedia. 2016b. Minecraft. (2016). https://en.wikipedia.org/wiki/Minecraft Online; accessed February 1st 2016.

37. Georgios N. Yannakakis and John Hallam. 2007. Towards Optimizing Entertainment in Computer Games. *Appl. Artif. Intell.* 21 (2007), 933–971. Issue 10.

38. Georgios N Yannakakis, Antonios Liapis, and Constantine Alexopoulos. 2014. Mixed-initiative co-creativity. In *Proceedings of the ACM Conference on Foundations of Digital Games*.

39. Georgios N. Yannakakis and Julian Togelius. 2011. Experience-Driven Procedural Content Generation. *IEEE Transactions on Affective Computing* 99 (2011).

Playtesting with a Purpose

Judeth Oden Choi[1], Jodi Forlizzi[1], Michael Christel[2], Rachel Moeller[1], MacKenzie Bates[3], Jessica Hammer[1] [2]

[1]HCI Institute, Carnegie Mellon University, Pittsburgh, USA
[2]ETC, Carnegie Mellon University, Pittsburgh, USA
[3]Sledgehammer Games, Foster City, USA
{jochoi, forlizzi, christel, hammerj}@cs.cmu.edu, rmoelle@andrew.cmu.edu, itbmac@yahoo.com

ABSTRACT

Playtesting, or using play to guide game design, gives designers feedback about whether their game is meeting their goals and the player's expectations. We report a case study of designing, deploying, and iterating on a series of playtesting workshops for novice game designers. We identify common missteps made by novice designers and address these missteps through the concept of purposefulness, understanding why you are playtesting as well as how to playtest. We ground our workshops in the development of rich player experience goals, which inform playtest design, data collection and iteration. We show that by applying methods taught in our workshops, novice game designers leveraged playtest methods and tools, employed playtesting and data collection methods appropriate for their goals, and effectively applied playtest data in iterative design. We conclude with lessons learned and next steps in our research on playtesting.

Author Keywords

Game design; playtesting; game design education; game user research.

ACM Classification Keywords

H.5.m. Information interfaces and presentation (e.g., HCI): Miscellaneous; I.2.1 Applications and Expert Systems (H.4, J); K.3.2 Computer and Information Science Education.

INTRODUCTION

Involving users in the process of game design and development is important, especially with the increasing complexity of digital games. Often this is done in the form of usability testing, which ensures that different disciplines develop a shared vision of the game, and that the features of the game are easily understood by users.

Game User Research, a growing community of user experience researchers, game developers and academic researchers, have developed a number of tools and methods to address the unique challenge of testing games. These methods help game developers better understand the player experience.

However, game user testing methods are not as widely applied or understood in industry as one would hope. A recent paper by Washburn et al. out of Microsoft Research, reviewed 155 postmortems shared on gamasutra.com [17] and discovered that most often when testing was listed under "what went wrong" developers cited a lack of testing. Our own review of the 72 postmortems shared on gamasutra.com since 2010 revealed that 28% of developers expressed some desire to have conducted more testing. Perhaps more telling is one of Washburn et al.'s key takeaways: "For a better development process, game developers should invest time in the beginning of the project planning and designing. Game developers should also build prototypes during development, and if possible continue building off of these prototypes using an iterative process" [17].

We observed first-hand in our work that student teams struggled with integrating playtesting into the iterative design process. Therefore, we set out to identify the biggest playtesting challenges teams faced, to develop a curriculum that helped teams meet these challenges, and to understand the curriculum's impact.

To do so, we assembled an interdisciplinary team of game designers, computer scientists, designers, and educators. We first conducted primary research to discover and assess what existing game design and development curricula and resources exist for game design teams who are not affiliated with a particular company. Informed by these resources, we conducted a literature review and interviews with game designers. We then used our findings to develop a series of playtesting workshops: Explore, Refine, and Prove. We ran these workshops in the context of a graduate program focused on game design and development twice during the 2014-2015 academic year, evaluating the playtesting outcomes, interviewing faculty and student stakeholders, and debriefing within our group. In observing students' progress with playtesting, we identified common missteps, such as trouble with applying data collected from a playtest to advance game design. The common theme of these missteps was a lack of *purposefulness* in playtesting.

CHI PLAY '16, October 16-19, 2016, Austin, TX, USA
© 2016 ACM. ISBN 978-1-4503-4456-2/16/10...$15.00
DOI: http://dx.doi.org/10.1145/2967934.2968103

Therefore, we created a second iteration of the workshops, focusing on "playtesting with a purpose." We emphasized 1) setting player experience goals, 2) making and testing hypotheses about how design decisions support those goals, and 3) using playtesting data in a persuasive way.

In this paper, we report a case study of designing, deploying, and iterating on these playtesting workshops. We show how purposeful playtesting, designing playtests to address a designer's specific set of questions, positively impacts an iterative game design process, and that novice game designers struggle in this area. We provide evidence that with support for purposeful playtesting, novices can leverage playtest methods and tools, selecting and executing testing and data collection methods appropriate for their goals, and effectively applying playtest data in iterative design. We conclude with lessons learned and next steps in our research on playtesting.

RELATED WORK
Games are experiences created by rules [3]. These rules set the parameters within which players make choices and perform actions, referred to as game mechanics [3]. Art, narrative, and system design create the context for the rules and mechanics, allowing the player to make meaning from the gameplay. Taken together, all the elements of a game holistically form a system that shapes the player's experience [14].

Player engagement with the rule system cannot always be predicted from the set of rules itself; there must be freedom for players to make choices, mess around, and, unsurprisingly, play [27]. Even in the most cohesive system, the player sometimes behaves in unexpected ways and finds unintended meaning in the game. These unexpected interactions between the player and the game system are a form of emergent play [4].

Game design employs an ecology of approaches, such as design, storytelling, performance, psychology, behavioral economics, and computer science to create this holistic experience [14, 28, 29]. It is inherently multidisciplinary and often requires the coordination of diverse practices and processes. Balancing the interdependencies within the game system and across the design process is challenging, and an iterative design process is commonly used [14]. In an iterative design process, the prototype is tested, analyzed, refined and then the cycle repeats [31]. Effective user testing is employed to engage both with elements that games share with other types of interactive software systems, such as art or usability, and also with game rules and mechanics [15].

Game User Research
Game User Research (GUR) is a growing community bringing together user experience researchers, game developers, and academic researchers to help improve the player experience [9]. GUR attempts to understand and measure how the play experience meets the designer's goals and the player's expectations [9].

Researchers have developed a number of heuristics to understand the player experience, such as flow [8], presence [22], immersion [16], engagement [5], enjoyment [30] and challenge and enjoyment [1]. Through the study of the player experience, GUR has developed and applied a number of quantitative and qualitative methods, instruments and tools to the study of games. For example, think-aloud protocols applied from cognitive science are used to understand the mental process of players [20]. The RITE (Rapid Iterative Testing and Evaluation) method was developed by Microsoft to fold usability testing into their iterative development process [23]. PLAY is a set of heuristics adapted from usability testing for the play experience [10]. Playtesting, the study of hands-on play [24], has been evaluated through physiological measures [2], and with a number of validated questionnaires based off of sets of heuristics, such as immersion, engagement and challenge [18].

GUR methods have been widely adopted by the gaming industry. Microsoft developed the RITE method during the development of *Halo I*. In RITE when a player identifies a problem, the developers address the problem immediately before testing the game further. Large game companies such as Valve incorporate observation, biometric data, and game metrics to draw conclusions about players [2]. Riot Games is famous for conducting A/B testing in *League of Legends* to understand what factors reduce negative player behavior [6]. Heat maps are used to visualize where and how often player deaths occur in first-person shooters [11] in order to identify excessively or unintentionally challenging areas of the game. These examples demonstrate not only the utility of GUR to the game industry, but also the variety of ways it can be applied.

Playtesting as a Method
Game development includes the process from a designer's first sketch through the marketing and release of a digital game. The game development process can be divided into four phases: concept, pre-production, production, and quality assurance [13].

Playtesting evolved from product research methods at firms such as Disney and LucasArts and, because of this, is a method often used late in the development process, as the game nears release [9]. However, game educators and game textbooks suggest that playtesting should be part of an iterative design process starting from the beginning of the design process. In her game design text, Fullerton says that, "Playtesting is something that the designer performs throughout the entire design process to gain an insight into whether or not the game is achieving your player experience goals" [12]. Schell also advocates for early playtesting, "The whole point of playtesting is to make clear to you that some of the decisions you were completely comfortable with are completely wrong. You need to find these things out as soon as possible, while there is still time to do something about them" [29].

Schell differentiates playtesting from other kinds of testing, such as usability testing or quality assurance testing, as "the kind of testing designers care about most" [29]. Playtesting guides the design of a playful experience by generating detailed feedback to the development team about if and how the game fulfills the player experience goal. In game design textbooks, "playtesting" seems to be the term of art. Although it was developed from the product research context, game design educators understand playtesting more broadly as a tool to gain insight on the player experience.

Teaching Playtesting

In teaching playtesting, we incorporated GUR methods and the insights of game educators about playtesting as an end-to-end process. We therefore researched both GUR curricula and playtesting curricula. We discovered that game design textbooks provide high-level descriptions of playtesting, but they do not detail the process. At best, the entire process is summarized in a chapter [12]. Courses are offered at the college and graduate level on game research methods, but those materials are not publicly available. Individual lectures that are public, such as those by Lewis-Evans or Ambinder [19, 2], provide little pedagogical support. Recently Pulsipher has published a lecture-based course on playtesting at udemy.com [26], but it provides no hands-on activities or feedback.

In response to these findings, we set out to develop a playtesting curriculum for game designers that was detailed, pedagogically appropriate for designers, hands-on, and publicly available. We provided a detailed focus on methods, from designing and running a playtest, to collecting data and applying data to design. We drew materials from game design texts and GUR methods. Within our workshops we provided hands-on opportunities to practice skills and apply methods taught to student game designers.

To develop the workshops, we engaged in an iterative design process of our own. Spanning three iterations over three years, we have developed insights into effective playtesting teaching and the common missteps of novice game designers.

CONTEXT OF THE WORKSHOPS

The Entertainment Technology Center (ETC) is a two-year professional graduate program that focuses on game development, interactive entertainment research, design, and production. In the spring of year one and in each semester of year two, students complete a semester-long interdisciplinary design project focused on designing and developing a digital game or interactive experience. Teams typically are comprised of 5-8 members with diverse backgrounds in art, programming, game design, writing, and producing.

Each project team partners with a real-world client to produce a working digital prototype of an original game or experience. Clients range from local schools and hospitals,

to energy companies and AAA video game design studios. Similarly, the types of experiences teams produce vary from games for entertainment, to interactive museum installations, to serious and educational games.

At the beginning of each semester, teams receive a project brief from the client. Project briefs vary in specificity. It is typical for teams to meet with their clients weekly or every two weeks throughout the semester to ensure that they are meeting the client's expectations. In this context playtesting data is an important tool for communicating with clients, as project teams act much like small design studios.

Two faculty advisors are assigned to meet regularly with project team. Additionally, four checkpoints during the course of the semester involve the entire ETC faculty in evaluating and providing feedback on games in progress.

Curriculum design

To address the lack of publicly available playtesting curricula and to complement game design perspectives on playtesting with GUR methods, we developed a detailed, process-driven and hands-on playtesting curriculum. To determine the specific issues that our curriculum should address, we conducted interviews with game design students and faculty.

We heard from the faculty that students did not seem invested in playtesting. They seemed to be "checking a box," and had difficulty allocating time and resources to playtesting. Students expressed their anxieties about playtesting: they did not know where to start, had not received hands-on practice with playtesting and were afraid of making mistakes.

Faculty agreed that student playtesting needed to start earlier in the design process. However, both students and faculty revealed a tension in the perception of playtesting: some viewed it as intuitive observation of play, while others viewed it as a rigorous research method. There was also a deep concern that student teams did not know how to apply data collected in playtesting to the next iteration of their prototypes.

Informed by the literature, interviews with game designers, and our collective expertise, it became apparent that playtesting did not require a single method, but a set of methods that could be applied differently at different stages in the game design process.

Workshop design process

The workshop series was developed in collaboration with experts from a variety of disciplines, including game designers, HCI researchers, and educators. The workshop was piloted in Fall 2014 with students in a game design studio course. The workshop series was significantly redesigned and ran during the Spring 2015 semester with students completing the ETC's semester-long game design projects. The three playtesting workshops were scheduled to align with project timelines. They were redesigned again and run in the Spring 2016 semester with ETC students completing semester-long projects.

Participants
At the beginning of the Spring 2015 and 2016 semesters, we were provided with a list of 18 ETC student teams and projects. All student teams were invited to attend the voluntary workshop series. After the workshop series, we observed a subset of teams conducting public playtests and followed up with interviews when possible.

	Attended at least 1 workshop	Attended all workshops	Playtest observations	Interviews
2015	16 teams	7 teams	8 teams	6 teams
2016	18 teams	8 teams	8 teams	2 teams

Table 1. Overview of teams who participated in the Spring 2015 and Spring 2016 workshops, including how many teams were observed playtesting and were interviewed.

2015 WORKSHOPS
Based on our research, we developed a series of playtesting workshops that focused on playtesting methods and addressed the faculty's key concerns: 1) playtesting should start earlier in the design process; 2) students needed practice and feedback on playtesting skills; 3) students needed to apply more rigor to playtesting; and 4) students did not always seem invested in playtesting. To address these concerns, we: developed one workshop dedicated to exploratory playtesting, built hands-on activities and opportunities for feedback into every workshop, emphasized rigorous experiment and data collection methods, and demonstrated how playtesting was relevant to each member of a multidisciplinary team.

Skills across three workshops
The game development process can be divided into four phases: concept, pre-production, production, and quality assurance [13]. We identified questions that designers are commonly faced with in each stage and explored how they use play to investigate those questions. For example, we asked: how do game designers use play to conceptualize a game? To iterate on a game? And to evaluate a game?

These questions became the basis for three workshops: Explore, Refine and Prove. The workshops continued to develop around the theme of "The Right Playtest at the Right Time." In each workshop, we practiced three core skills: asking good questions, choosing appropriate methods, and applying data to design. We used these skills to show similarities between the Explore, Refine, and Prove playtest approaches.

Physical Set-up
Tables and chairs were arranged around the room. On each table were a variety of post-it notes, paper and markers. Project teams sat together at a table. At the front of the room we played our slide presentation. Teams displayed their activity posters (e.g. composition box) on the wall near their tables. During the workshop, we alternated between lectures, team discussions and exercises, and adding to or notating the posters on the wall.

Explore
In the Explore workshop, we introduced exploratory playtesting techniques. Exploratory playtesting incorporates a broad set of practices used by game designers to better understand the player population and their motivations, the environment or context where the game will be played, and/or the design space within which a game is situated. Exploratory playtest methods include "playstorming," a process where game rules are generated on the fly during play; creating and testing low fidelity prototypes of a game or of a subset of game features; modifying existing game systems; or creating a scaled down digital prototype of a game. By studying players playing the game prototypes, designers discover and clarify their player experience goals and the game design features they believe will achieve those goals.

We developed a visual organization tool called the "composition box" (based loosely on a method of devising works for the theatre [7]) to help designers visualize their design space and goals. Student designers framed their composition box poster with a description of the game. Within the box the designers list the "ingredients" that might go into designing the game. These ingredients can be divided into three basic categories: 1) needs, 2) inspiration, and 3) experience. After listing the ingredients, designers outlined their player experience goals in terms of type of play (e.g. cooperative or competitive), tone, or emotions. This encouraged collaboration between the designers by sharing their expectations, creating common references, and identifying holes in their collective knowledge for further exploration.

Refine
The Refine workshop introduced playtesting methods to help teams iterate on an existing game during development. At this stage in the design process, teams had homed in on a set of game design and player experience goals and were iterating on ways to achieve those goals through their design choices. In this workshop we covered 1) posing important, accurate and answerable questions, 2) designing playtests to investigate those questions, and 3) practicing data collection techniques.

The Refine workshop began with a continuation of the composition box exercise. This time teams were asked to bring their composition box back to the workshop setting and to identify one player experience goal to frame a new composition box poster. By narrowing down the list of possible ingredients they generated in "Explore," they filled the new box with a recipe of features that they hypothesized would achieve the player experience goal, including game mechanics, narrative elements, art, and important context about the stakeholders and the play environment. Teams then brainstormed questions about the possible interactions and effectiveness of the features in their recipe. We used these questions throughout the workshop to shape each team's research questions and playtest design.

In the second half of the workshop, we introduced data collection methods and skills. We practiced these skills by running playtests on three modified Uno decks. Participants practiced observing behavior and asking follow-up interview questions. We drew connections between observed behavior and the different mechanics of each modified Uno deck. Participants then crafted survey questions which we workshopped to reduce bias. For example, one participant asked, "How fair do you think the game is?" which after some discussion we revised to, "How much do you feel chance plays a role in the game?"

Prove

The Prove workshop focused on conducting playtests with an eye toward communicating with stakeholders. When designers have refined their games to the point where they can make claims about the player experience, it is possible to run playtests to evaluate those claims. Playtest results might be informative to players and clients, but may also serve to resolve conflicts about design within the team. We discussed experiment design methods including A/B testing, pre- and post-tests, and using in-game metrics to reveal patterns of play. We practiced communicating the strengths of your game by situating it within a body of literature and explicating your design process.

Each team began the workshop by listing the claims they could make about their game, then the evidence that it would take to support that claim, and finally the stakeholder to whom they needed to communicate the claim. Next, teams were asked to consider what that stakeholder would find persuasive. After introducing different models of experiment design, the majority of the workshop was spent in consultation with the teams as they designed a playtest that could best test their claims.

Data Collection

Data on teams' development process was collected during

Team name	Game topic
Team S	Game on socially sensitive topic for undergraduates
Team F	Cooperative game for families
Team J	Science game for elementary school classrooms
Team K	Enhanced storybook for middle school readers
Team B	Game to empower children with a health condition
Team D	A live game on global issue

Table 2. Overview of teams and game topics from 2015.

the Spring 2015 semester. We investigated uptake of the workshops using a variety of methods: observations of playtesting processes, interviews with students and faculty advisors, and collection and analysis of a variety of artifacts, including materials created during the playtesting workshops, weekly activity logs, and weekly reports generated for faculty.

Midway through the semester, we approached a cross-section of teams who attended at least one workshop for permission to study their game design process. Eight teams agreed to be observed while conducting playtests, and six of these teams agreed to interviews and to having their workspace documented. Faculty advisors for the six teams interviewed were approached for additional interviews; four teams' advisors agreed. For the purpose of this study, team names are anonymized, but the topic of their game is not.

Observation

We observed eight teams playtesting for two hours at a public playtesting event, which took place mid-semester. During this event, each team conducted 2-6 playtest sessions with unique sets of playtesters. Playtesters were members of the public who were age-appropriate for each game. We took structured notes and photographs of playtesting set ups, procedures and data collection methods. We collected teams' playtesting documents, including scripts, gameplay instructions, surveys and interview protocols.

Late in the semester, design teams invited faculty into their studios to play and critique games. We shadowed two faculty members as they critiqued the teams' games and experiences included in our study. We documented the state of the game, the faculty's critique, and the design teams' discussion of their process.

Interviews

In the final two weeks of the design process, we conducted closing interviews with six teams (Table 1) and the advisors of four of those teams. Topics included the role of playtesting in their design process and how playtesting data was used to iterate on teams' games. Interviews with advisors were used to provide an expert view on the use of playtesting in the game design and development process.

Data analysis

We triangulated our findings from these data sources. Using Atlas TI software, we quantitatively analyzed interview transcripts, design artifacts and observations of playtesting sessions, using a grounded theory approach [25]. We analyzed the data to identify important concepts including how playtesting was applied and how the resulting data was used to drive the design. This resulted in 86 concepts, which were organized into three final themes.

PITFALLS TO PLAYTESTING

Our workshops were designed to teach game designers a suite of playtesting methods to be applied at different points in the design process. In each of the three stages, we guided students through the process of 1) asking good questions; 2) choosing appropriate playtesting methods; and 3) applying playtesting data to their designs. However, through our post-workshop observations of each team's playtests, evaluation of playtesting and game design materials, and interviews with 6 teams and the advisors to 4 of the teams, we discovered that novice design teams faced stumbling blocks during each of these steps.

Setting goals and asking questions

Asking good playtesting questions was difficult for some teams because they did not have a clear concept of what their games should achieve and had not set specific player experience goals. Player experience goals help designers conceptualize "the type of experience" they want the player to have [12]. Player experience goals provide a lens through which to make design decisions and to evaluate a game. Pagulayan discusses the role of the designer in interpreting user data, stating that "the designer holds the vision for their creation as well as the vision for what makes their game fun. [...] it is only the designer who can recognize when the player experience is not being experienced as intended" [23].

We noticed that setting specific player experience goals provided a frame for designing good playtests and interpreting playtest data.

Team B was charged by their client to make a game to empower children with a health condition. The team struggled with the idea of empowerment, which could have been a rich area for inspiration. Instead of asking targeted research questions around feelings of empowerment, their playtests hinged on survey questions drawn from an established engagement questionnaire. Engagement questions such as these are intended to give the designers an overall feel for how well their game is received; however, research has shown that users commonly over-report satisfaction, and this effect is likely exacerbated in children [13]. In the absence of other data, Team B used high engagement scores as a defense of their game design. When asked what the design team learned from the survey, the producer replied, "We mostly got that the game was engaging, for the most part." When pushed to identify data from their playtesting that informed a design decision the producer said, "We based a lot of parts of our game on stuff that we know that work for children." In the absence of usable data and with the reassurance of high engagement scores, the team had no reason to iterate further on their design based on playtesting. Instead they relied on internalized assumptions about what children like to guide them. In the end, they squandered the opportunity to learn about their player population and iterate on their gameplay.

Choosing appropriate methods

Some teams set player experience goals, but did not connect those goals to the design of their playtests; they therefore struggled to choose appropriate playtesting methods. The data that they collected was divorced from their core gameplay experience, so they struggled to use the data to inform the next iteration of their games.

Designing playtests that tested gameplay proved difficult for several novice teams. For example, Team K created a playful storybook experience, in which they wanted the player to feel as though "the page is magic." Despite designing a number of mechanics that activated the page, the development team had difficulty identifying and testing the features of the game that contributed to the "magical" feel. Instead they designed tests that were divorced from the core mechanic. For example, they designed an A/B test to measure reading comprehension of the game versus reading comprehension of a digital text. However, they lacked the resources to create a controlled experiment with a large enough sample size to claim any difference in learning. Not only were their results inconclusive, but they walked away from the test without generating any data that helped them iterate on their game design.

Next they designed a usability test, where they asked children to go on a "scavenger hunt" to find and play with all of the responsive features in the app. The scavenger hunt created an environment one designer described as "competitive reading." By introducing this element of competition and reducing the emphasis on the reading experience, the usability test divorced the game mechanics from the player experience they were designing for. In the usability test, hypertext features were rated as highly usable, and the team used this data to defend their design decision. Their faculty advisors, however, felt strongly that hypertext, by directing the player to a new page, went against their design aesthetic that the page itself is magic and alive: "Your design goal is not usability. Your design goal is a magical experience. And — 'but our demographic testing showed that nobody had trouble with it!' — that's not the question." In the end, the team followed the advice of their advisors, which focused on player experience goals, over their playtesting data, which measured only usability, and removed the hypertext features.

In fact, we found that development teams across the board struggled to playtest their game's core mechanic. It is easier to test art, usability, narrative, character design, or other features of a game. When teams were able to playtest game mechanics, they did so by connecting specific player experience goals to game mechanics they believed would support that experience. In other words, player experience goals seemed to be an important mediating factor in creating successful playtests.

Applying data to an iterative design process

Other teams, especially those with low-fidelity prototypes or attempting to measure the intended impact of their game, also struggled to apply the data they collected to the design of their games.

Playtesting with low fidelity prototypes

Teams embraced the idea of running early playtests — in theory. For example, Team S commented on how running early playtests was the most valuable thing they learned across the playtesting workshops: "I understand the importance of playtesting. And I understand what it can teach you and show you about your product. But it hadn't occurred to me to playtest the idea first. So for me personally, once you talked about it, it was, like, 'duh!'" More broadly, eleven of the fifteen teams expressed intentions of conducting exploratory playtests in their weekly newsletters. However, only four teams actually followed through.

One reason for this discrepancy was that teams did not know what they were trying to learn from their prototypes. Schell asserts that "Every prototype should be designed to answer a question and sometimes more than one" [29]. Because teams did not define the problems the prototype could help them solve, they either decided against designing low-fidelity prototypes, unable to justify investing the time and resources, or they built prototypes but did not know how to interpret data generated from playtesting with the prototype.

Team D created a paper prototype for a location-based mobile game. After running the playtest, the designers were frustrated with the results, reporting that "the paper prototyping just couldn't stand up to the processing that needed to happen in a mobile experience." However, once they built the digital prototype the problems revealed in paper prototyping persisted. After some reflection, they realized that "if we had dug into the reasons why that (the failure of the paper prototype) was happening we probably would have identified a lot earlier that that part was just too complicated in the first place."

Measuring for impact and gameplay

Some games in our sample were transformational games, intended to change the player in some way. While measuring the impact of transformational games is important, focusing too tightly on impact during the semester-long design process often distracted teams from iterating on game mechanics and core interactions. This tension was demonstrated above in case of Team K. However, for some teams, impact and gameplay were closely intertwined, and for these teams interpreting data was particularly complicated. Team S designed a game on a socially sensitive topic for undergraduates. Several questions in their survey and interview protocol attempted to measure learning or a shift in attitude. Often players reported little learning: "some people are very confident… and they know what they would do, so when we asked, 'Did this teach you anything?' They said 'not really.'" These results were disappointing for the team and caused conflict about how to move forward. In order to iterate on their design, they had to ask themselves hard questions about what the mechanics were designed *to do* and what kind of experience they wanted players to have. They came to understand that: "I think being able to gauge the effectiveness is going to be difficult, because it's going to be long term. We're trying to effect long-term change." They realized that instead of trying to cause attitude change, the real goal of the game was to spark conversation. With this knowledge they shifted their playtests to measure the

willingness of the player to discuss the sensitive subject matter of the game and was able to use this data to iterate on important features of the characters and dialogue.

PLAYTESTING WITH A PURPOSE

We designed the first round of playtesting workshops to encourage game design students to playtest early and often as part of an iterative design process. Based on the literature and our problem-finding interviews with faculty and students, we focused on introducing and practicing a range of playtesting methods, selecting the appropriate method to fit one's playtesting question and stage of development and then applying the data to the next iteration of a game prototype.

We initially believed that students needed more information and practice with playtesting tools and methods; however, we found that what students were actually lacking was *purposefulness*, a deep understanding of the purpose of their games, their design choices and how to test them. Game designers, whether designing for entertainment or for transformation, make design choices based on their goals; their playtest design should be just as intentional.

The pitfalls we identified across the game design teams suggested that designers did not necessarily struggle with *how to playtest*, but rather with understanding *why they were playtesting*. Novice game designers demonstrated an understanding, for example, of data collection methods and reducing experimenter bias, but struggled at a more fundamental level with problems of purpose. Without good goals, teams could not articulate the purpose of their games, much less test them. Without purposeful questions, teams playtested using methods they were comfortable with, instead of choosing the best method to fit their purpose. When teams collected data without having a clear plan, they struggled to make sense of the data and apply it to their design.

In response to our findings, we re-designed the workshops for the Spring 2016 semester. We address the major changes below.

Workshop redesign

We redesigned the workshops to fit the theme "playtesting with a purpose". Table 3 summarizes the main design iteration made in the workshops.

These changes were implemented both as uniform changes across all three workshops, and as specific changes to the content of each workshop to address the three pitfalls we observed. For example, to address choosing appropriate methods across all three workshops, we added pro and con lists to each method we presented, and an in depth example of how professional or novice designers have applied it. We also addressed "choosing appropriate methods" head-on in the Refine workshop with a hands-on activity to help students connect goals to specific questions and methods for answering them. Each of the three pitfalls informed the redesign of the workshops' content in the following way:

	Fall 2014 workshop	Revisions in 2014-2015	Revisions in 2015-2016
Overall		• Employ equal case studies from industry and academic projects • Create an overarching structure: 1) introduction, 2) asking good questions, 3) choosing appropriate methods, 4) applying data to design, 5) drafting an action plan	• Emphasize player experience goals • Develop pre-workhsop activities; leveraged to reveal playtesting goals • Develop a rubric to guide in method selection
Explore	• Introduce playtesting as part of an iterative design process • Explore a design space through prompts, bodystorming, & improv • Perform exercises in playful bodystorming and improvisation techniques.	• Focus on problem selection and asking open-ended questions • Remove bodystorming exercises • Add pre-workshop composition box activity • Add Plex Cards ideation exercise around player experience	• Provide more structure in the composition box activity. • Link exploratory methods to "what you know" about your design space • Streamline Plex Card player experience exercise
Refine	• Focus on asking an important, answerable and accurate questions • Introduce designing with stakeholder needs in mind • Exercise on persona development • Introduce affinity diagram as method to interpret playtest data	• Focus on developing player experience goals • Uno game mod used as a playtest observation exercise • Practice crafting and asking interview questions	• Bridge activity to craft a "recipe" of ingredients that serve player experience goals • Integrate methods more fully • Allow time to discuss action plans in the workshop.
Prove/ Persuade	• Focus claims/evidence structure • Introduce designer's judgment as a way to advance game design	• Add lecture on reliability and validity • Add examples of experimenter bias • Add pros and cons for each testing method	• Change workshop name from "Prove" to "Persuade" • Divide methods into two groups: experimental (A/B, pre/post) and expertise (expert panels, designer's judgment).

Table 3. Overview of revisions across three iterations of workshops.

Explore

Realizing both how difficult and how important it is for designers to set meaningful and specific goals for their games, we redesigned the explore workshop to better support setting player experience goals. While keeping the composition box exercise as a pre-workshop activity, we restructured it with a focus on exploring player experience goals, what you want the player to feel, think or do.

In the workshop, we suggested four starting points for the game design process and linked them to pre-production research methods: 1) Observe: if you know your target population, conduct field observations or design a playtest of a typical game for your population, 2) Probe: if you are starting with an idea for art or other assets, begin testing it to learn how potential players respond to it, 3) Test: if you know your core mechanic, create a low fidelity prototype or mod of an existing game and begin playtesting, 4) Co-design: if you are working with stakeholders to create a specific experience or impact, introduce play and the language of games into your relationship early.

Next, we used Plex cards to introduce different types of play experiences, such as competition, control or fellowship

[21]. Students selected a card and created a mind map with this player experience in the center. They distilled their insights and added these notes to the output of their composition box, adding to their understanding of their player experience goals.

We repeated this simple framework of starting with what you know, identifying the gaps in your knowledge through research, and then adding to your understanding of the desired player experience in the pre-workshop and Plex card activities. We also demonstrated how to apply exploratory playtesting methods to this framework and led students in designing an exploratory playtest.

Refine

To help students select appropriate playtesting methods, we first revisited their player experience goals, hypothesized how specific game features affect the player experience and then determine which playtesting method to use.

In the pre-workshop activity, we provided more structure on how to create a composition box recipe for a prototype: 1) Frame the composition box with a player experience goal; 2) Fill the box with the set of features, or "ingredients," you hypothesize will support the player experience goal (consider affect, themes, environment, objects, mechanics, relationships, and events); and 3) Pull from the composition box sketches for a prototype incorporating these features.

Throughout the workshop, students practiced asking questions about how their set of ingredients supported their player experience goals. These questions were developed first through observation of play (e.g. What evidence are you looking for?), then through asking interview questions of players, and finally by writing survey questions.

Prove to Persuade

We reframed the Prove workshop as Persuade because we recognized that novice designers, especially those designing transformational games, felt intense pressure to prove that their games were successful and impactful. This need to validate one's designs can stymie the iteration process and make it difficult to pivot. In Persuade we focused on making a persuasive claim about a game based on evidence in order to elicit the support of stakeholders.

Of the four methods we taught, two were experimental methods, A/B testing and pre/post testing, and two were open-ended methods based on expertise, expert panels and designer's judgment. In practice, even with extensive playtesting, design decisions come down to judgment calls. We recognized the role of expertise in the design process to dissuade novice designers from running unproductive playtests, or simply "checking the box" without purpose. We provided examples of making a persuasive case for your game both based on data and through a clearly developed design rationale.

Data Collection

We investigated uptake of the workshops using a variety of methods: observations of playtesting processes, interviews with students, and collection and analysis of a variety of artifacts, including materials created during the workshops, materials displayed in student's workspace, and materials created in support of playtests after the workshops.

Data collection for this semester is ongoing. To date we have observed 8 teams playtesting and have conducted semi-structured interviews with 2 teams.

Team name	Game topic
Team L	VR public speaking simulation
Team H	Problem-solving game for boys

Table 4. Overview of teams and game topics from 2016.

EVIDENCE OF IMPACT

By observing the activities of design teams (Table 4), we can see that intervening at the level of *purpose* rather than *method* leads to the design of playtests that are more relevant to the designers and inform further iteration on their game prototypes. We have looked at design teams' activities rather than outcomes because we aimed to improve the process by which playtests are designed.

Specificity

We have observed that teams can identify more specific design elements within their prototype. Specificity demonstrates an awareness of their design choices and reflects the purposefulness of those choices. We see evidence of specificity in the materials generated across the workshops.

Providing more structure to the composition box exercise allowed teams to think about their game concept, their player experience goals and how their design choices support those goals more analytically. We observed students express more unique and purposeful player experience goals in their workshop materials. When asked to develop player experience goals the 2015 teams tended toward blanket statements, such as "fun and engaging," "to empower children," or "enhance a storybook." 2016 teams, on the other hand, demonstrated more nuance in their goals, showed greater consideration of the player's emotional experience, and pointed toward actionable design choices. For example, a team developing a VR experience to practice public speaking sought to create a game that dealt with feelings of "tension and anxiety" and gave the player "self confidence for presentations." A game geared toward elementary school boys wanted players to feel "powerful, accomplished and smart."

We observed an increase in analytical thinking, manifested through the specificity of students' playtest design. For example, when asked what evidence they needed to collect to test their claims, a 2015 team designing a storybook experience answered "observation," "surveys," and "test reading comprehension," whereas a 2016 team designing a VR training simulation, said they would measure "volume, pauses, eye gaze tracking, and time management."

Ability to pivot

Pivoting in the design process helps designers get unstuck and innovate. In order to pivot, a designer needs a deep understanding of both their goals and the design space. Pivoting is evidence that a development team is making a purposeful turn based on what they have learned through the iterative process of prototyping and playtesting.

From the teams who attended the workshops, we identified teams who attempted to pivot. We selected teams for case studies on pivoting based on availability for interviews.

Pivoting goals

Team L (2016) demonstrated an ability to pivot, shifting player experience goals and design aesthetic based on player feedback. As with many VR experiences, Team L believed that immersion, the feeling that the player was present in a real world, was the most salient feature of their VR training simulation. In their first set of playtests, they focused on how natural, realistic and believable the interaction was. However, they realized that to operate as a training simulation, the readability, credibility and applicability of the feedback provided to the player was of paramount importance. They then ran playtests that focused on how and when feedback was displayed to the player and noticed that because head-tracking stood in for eye-tracking (a constraint of the mobile VR technology), players had difficulty trusting feedback on their gaze. To alleviate this problem the team added a crosshair to the screen, signaling to the player where they are looking at all times. This reduced the realism of the experience, and arguably detracted from a sense of immersion in a virtual world. The claim/evidence/stakeholder framework introduced in the workshop assisted the reevaluation of their goals. They then dedicated their second round of playtesting to evaluating feedback to the player, and turned their focus to the quality of the experience as a training simulation.

In contrast, because Team K (2015) tested for factors such as reading comprehension and usability divorced from the player experience, they were unable to prioritize the player experience in their design choices. Instead it was their advisor who intervened to preserve the player experience of interacting with a "magic" page. Team K struggled to design playtests that served their purpose, while Team L designed purposeful playtests.

Pivoting gameplay

Team H (2016) designed a problem-solving game for elementary school boys. Their goal was for players to feel empowered, to demonstrate self-determination and feelings of competency, but also to practice computational thinking. They began iterating on a paper prototype based on a Pac-man-like chase mechanic. Team H playtested their prototype once a week at an elementary school. Playtesting with paper prototypes went well, but when they transferred to a digital prototype, players overwhelmingly wanted to attack the enemy and lost sight of the problem-solving objectives. To address this issue they returned to the paper prototype and went through seven more iterations of mechanic and level design, playtesting each one, before finding one that struck the right balance between a fighting game, thus fulfilling the goals of feeling empowered, and a strategy game, fulfilling the goal of practicing computational thinking. Team H went into each of their weekly playtests with a prototype of their "best guess" at this balance, and every week they collected actionable data from their playtests that informed the next iteration.

Compare Team H's methodical and analytical process of finding the right balance between empowerment and challenge in their game to Team B's (2015) reliance on user engagement surveys and their own heuristics. Team H approached each playtest as an opportunity to iterate meaningfully on their design, while Team B, despite their efforts to apply validated methods, was unable to generate data that truly informed their design.

LIMITATIONS

We believe that the workshops represent an approach to playtesting that contribute to our understanding of game development and to game design education. However, our research has some limitations: workshops were conducted at one institution with a relatively small sample of student game designers; and, although faculty did not express any discernable differences in ability or attitude between the class of 2015 and 2016, we cannot rule out the possibility that students in the 2016 workshops started the semester with greater expertise.

CONCLUSION

We conducted research to improve the process of game design and development. We first focused on training students in testing methods, but found that the real need was to understand the overarching player experience, then to create a research plan that supported delivering that experience. We demonstrated how purposeful playtesting, designing playtests to address a designer's specific set of questions, positively impacts an iterative game design process. We provide evidence that by applying methods taught in our workshops, novices leveraged playtest methods and tools, selecting and executing playtesting and data collection methods appropriate for their goals, and effectively applied playtest data in iterative design.

Purposefulness is the hard part of playtesting. Being purposeful requires more than sound experimental methods, survey writing skills or good heuristics to incorporate feedback from the player in an iterative game design process. It requires that the designers have a vision for their game, can translate that vision into design choices, and can design purposeful playtests to test their goals and the player's expectations. Our workshops provided evidence that structuring playtesting methods with the purpose of understanding the overarching game experience is useful, and may even result in more innovative games. Designing these workshops in the context of a graduate program, provided us insight into how much there is still to understand about when, how and why game developers apply testing methods.

Future work in this area can address several research trajectories. First, we can conduct similar work with other populations of game designers who face resource challenges (e.g. indie and transformational game designers) to further validate our findings across populations. Second, we can develop tools and methods to support game designers, such as we have begun to do with the composition box, and recommend best practices for playtest processes. Third, we can develop testable models of the playtest process that will help us generalize our insights. We seek to understand not just *how* to support game designers in playtesting in ways that produce better games, but in understanding *why* certain types of playtesting processes work. Finally, we will continue to iterate and evaluate our playtesting workshops. We offer this work to the community, with the hopes that we can collectively reach the long-term goal of improving games and game mechanics across many domains.

ACKNOWLEDGEMENTS

This research was funded by the Simon Initiative. We thank the students and faculty of the ETC.

REFERENCES

1. Abuhamdeh, S. and Csikszentmihalyi, M. 2012. The Importance of Challenge for the Enjoyment of Intrinsically Motivated, Goal-Directed Activities. *Personality and Social Psychology Bulletin 38*, 317–330.

2. Ambinder, M. 2011. Biofeedback in Gameplay: How Valve Measures Physiology to Enhance Gaming Experience. http://www.valvesoftware.com/publications/2011/ValveBiofeedback-Ambinder.pdf.

3. Anthropy, A. and Clark, N. 2014. *A Game Design Vocabulary: Exploring the Foundational Principles Behind Good Game Design*. Pearson Education.

4. Barr, P., Noble, J., and Biddle, R. 2007. Video game values: Human–computer interaction and games. *Interacting with Computers 19*, 2, 180–195.

5. Brockmyer, J.H., Fox, C.M., Curtiss, K.A., McBroom, E., Burkhart, K.M., and Pidruzny, J.N. 2009. The development of the Game Engagement Questionnaire: A measure of engagement in video game-playing. *Journal of Experimental Social Psychology 45*, 4, 624–634.

6. Cabrera, E. 2014. League of Legends - The Potential of A/B Testing. *gamasutra.com*. http://www.gamasutra.com/blogs/EduardoCabrera/20141020/227964/League_of_Legends__The_Potential_of_AB_Testing.php.

7. Choi, J., Forlizzi, J., Christel, M., Bates, M., and Hammer, J. 2015. Compositions: Moving from Ideation to Prototyping. Games + Learning + Society 11.

8. Csikszentmihalyi, M. 1990. *Flow: The psychology of optimal performance*. Cambridge University Press.

9. Desurvire, H. and El-Nasr, M.S. 2013. Methods for game user research: Studying player behavior to enhance game design. *IEEE Computer Graphics and Applications 33*, 4, 82–87.

10. Desurvire, H. and Wiberg, C. 2009. Game usability heuristics (PLAY) for evaluating and designing better games: the next iteration. *Online communities and social computing*. Springer Berlin Heidelberg, 557-566..

11. El-Nasr, M.S., Drachen, A., and Canossa, A. 2013. *Game Analytics: Maximizing the Value of Player Data*. Springer Science & Business Media.

12. Fullerton, T. 2014. *Game Design Workshop: A Playcentric Approach to Creating Innovative Games, Third Edition*. CRC Press.

13. Hull, R. and Reid, J. 2003. Designing engaging experiences with children and artists. *Funology: From usability to enjoyment*, 179–188.

14. Hunicke, R., LeBlanc, M., and Zubek, R. 2004. MDA: A Formal Approach to Game Design and Game Research. *Workshop on Challenges in Game AI*, 1-4.

15. Isbister, K. and Schaffer, N. 2008. *Game Usability: Advancing the Player Experience*. CRC Press.

16. Jennett, C., Cox, A.L., Cairns, P., et al. 2008. Measuring and defining the experience of immersion in games. *International Journal of Human Computer Studies 66*, 9, 641–661.

17. Jr, M.W., Sathiyanarayanan, P., Nagappan, M., Zimmermann, T., and Bird, C. 2016. "What Went Right and What Went Wrong": An Analysis of 155 Postmortems from Game Development. *Proceedings of the 38th International Conference on Software Engineering Companion*, ACM Press. 280-289.

18. Lankoski, P. and Björk, S. 2015. Game Research Methods: An Overview. Lulu.com. http://press.etc.cmu.edu/files/Game-Research-Methods_Lankoski-Bjork-etal-web.pdf.

19. Lewis-Evans, B. 2013. Intro to Games User Research Methods. http://www.slideshare.net/Gortag/intro-to-games-user-research-methods-march-2013.

20. Lewis, C. and Mack, R. 1982. Learning to use a text processing system. *Proceedings of the 1982 conference on Human factors in computing systems - CHI '82*, ACM Press. 387–392.

21. Lucero, A. and Arrasvuori, J. 2010. PLEX Cards : A Source of Inspiration When Designing for Playfulness. *Fun and Games 15*, 17, 28–37.

22. McMahan, A. 2003. Immersion, Engagement, and Presence. *The video game theory reader Immersion*, 67–86.

23. Medlock, M.C., Lead, U.T., Studios, M.G., et al. 2002. Using the RITE method to improve products ; a definition and a case study. *Usability Professionals Association*.

24. Pagulayan, R.J., Keeker, K., Fuller, T., Wixon, D., Romero, R.L., and Gunn, D. V. 2002. User centered design in games, 1–46.

25. Patton, M.Q. 2005. Qualitative Research. In *Encyclopedia of Statistics in Behavioral Science*, 1633–1636.

26. Pulsipher, L. Game Playtesting: the Heart of Game Design - Udemy. *udemy.com*. https://www.udemy.com/game-playtesting/.

27. Salen, K. and Zimmerman, E. 2004. *Rules of Play: Game Design Fundamentals*.MIT Press.

28. Salen, K. and Zimmerman, E. 2005. Game Design and Meaningful Play. In *Handbook of computer game studies* The MIT Press. 59–79.

29. Schell, J. 2015. *The Art of Game Design: A Book of Lenses*. CRC Press.

30. Vorderer, P., Klimmt, C., and Ritterfeld, U. 2004. Enjoyment: At the Heart of Media Entertainment. *Communication Theory 14*, 4, 388–408.

31. Zimmerman, E. 2003. Play as Research: the iterative design process. In *Design Research: Methods and Perspectives*. 176–184.

Reward Systems in Human Computation Games

Kristin Siu and Mark O. Riedl
School of Interactive Computing
Georgia Institute of Technology
Atlanta, Georgia, USA
{kasiu, riedl}@gatech.edu

ABSTRACT

Human computation games (HCGs) are games in which player interaction is used to solve problems intractable for computers. Most HCGs use simple reward mechanisms such as points or leaderboards, but in contrast, many mainstream games use more complex, and often multiple, reward mechanisms. In this paper, we investigate whether multiple reward systems and ability to choose the type of reward affects human task performance and player experience in HCGs. We conducted a study using a cooking-themed HCG, Cafe Flour Sack, which implements four reward systems, and had two experimental versions: one which randomly assigns rewards and the other which offers players the choice of reward. Players were recruited from both Amazon Mechanical Turk and university students. We report the results across these different game versions and player audiences. Our results suggest that offering players a choice of reward can yield better *task completion* metrics and similarly-engaged *player experiences*, and may improve these metrics and experiences for audiences that are not experts in crowdsourcing. We discuss these and other results in the broader context of exploring different rewards systems and other aspects of reward mechanics in HCGs.

ACM Classification Keywords

H.5.3. Information Interfaces and Presentation (e.g. HCI): Computer-supported cooperative work; K.8.0 Personal Computing: Games

Author Keywords

human computation games; games with a purpose; rewards; game design

INTRODUCTION

Human computation games (HCGs) are games in which player interaction is used to generate data or solve problems traditionally too difficult or intractable for computers to model. These games, also called *Games with a Purpose* (GWAPs), have been effectively deployed in domains such as data classification (e.g, image labeling [24]), scientific discovery (e.g.,

protein folding [3]), and data collection (e.g., photo acquisition [23]). However, despite an increased public appetite and a growing societal benefit for games, HCGs have not seen widespread adoption. Some of this can be attributed to the fact that game design and development is still a difficult and time-consuming process.

Developing human computation games still remains challenging because like other serious games, HCGs have two often-orthogonal design goals. On the one hand, the human computation task must be solved effectively and on the other, the game should provide an entertaining player experience. Balancing the two is still a formidable task, even for experienced game designers. To complicate this, we know very little about how to design these games. Conventional game design theories often do not accommodate the additional requirements imposed by solving the task. Existing design knowledge in HCGs is limited to templates and anecdotal examples that do not easily generalize to new tasks and changing audiences. Growing this design space would enable scientists, researchers, and amateur developers to create HCGs more effectively, allowing for more games to solve many interesting problems that might otherwise be computationally intractable.

In this paper, we focus on the *reward systems* in human computation games. Without players, the underlying human computation tasks in HCGs may never be completed, and reward systems — the sets of gameplay mechanics responsible for providing positive feedback — allow us to compensate players directly for contributing their time and effort to solving these problems. This makes rewards some of the most important gameplay elements to investigate in HCGs because of their role in motivating and engaging players.

Currently, most HCGs tend to adopt simple reward systems such as point systems and leaderboards, mirroring collaborative elements of puzzle games combined with social (and sometimes competitive) mechanics. However rewards in mainstream digital games are often far more complex, and take on a wide variety of forms not seen in current HCGs. One longstanding question in HCG design is how to adopt the mechanics of modern digital games in a way that respects both the *task completion* —player performance at the task — and the *player experience* —player interaction and engagement with the game. Rewards are no exception to this, but unfortunately, we know very little about how different rewards systems behave in human computation games, let alone which ones are the most effective. Mainstream digital games often incorporate multiple, different reward systems in order to appeal to a wide variety of player motivations and allow for diverse player experiences. However, we know little about how these more-complicated systems might behave in HCGs.

This paper is a first step towards untangling the effects of using different rewards systems in human computation games. We wish to investigate the question of whether or not randomly distributing rewards to players as opposed to offering players a choice between different reward systems has any effect on the task completion and the player experience. Beyond looking at reward systems, we are interested in understanding how different reward systems affect different audiences of players.

To facilitate our investigation, we instrumented a human computation game with four kinds of reward systems. We then ran a study comparing two versions of the game: one which randomly assigns rewards to players and one which offers players the choice of different rewards. We conducted the study using two different player audiences: workers from an online crowdsourcing platform and university students. We evaluated the results as they relate to both the *task completion* and the *player experience*. Our results show significant differences between the *random* and *choice* conditions of the game, as well as differences between player audiences and interactions between these variables. For example, players in the *choice* condition completed tasks more accurately and more quickly than players in the *random* condition. We discuss these results, highlighting design recommendations around reward systems in HCGs, along with future directions for studies in this area. Ultimately, we believe this is a step to better understanding how reward systems work in HCGs, which would open possibilities for new, effective, and entertaining games.

BACKGROUND AND RELATED WORK

Rewards in HCGs
Traditionally, most human computation games have adopted simple reward systems with mechanics that focus on the collaborative nature of human computation tasks and the social features of crowdsourcing. Point and scoring systems are generally the most common form of feedback to the players. In addition to being easy to implement, they provide both a form of direct feedback to players and a way for task providers to monitor and evaluate performance at the task. Most recent survey work in HCGs [7, 16] explores rewards as different forms of incentives available to the player, although these are again in the context of scoring systems.

Design knowledge in HCGs has focused primarily on what kind of behavior players should be rewarded for, specifically as it pertains to collaboration and competition. Early design work in von Ahn and Dabbish's game templates [25] for classification tasks outlines that players should be rewarded for collaborative agreement — which maps to the divide-and-aggregate approach to solving the underlying human computation task. The respective games described [9, 24, 26] all implement collaborative scoring systems, which reward players for agreeing on task results, while leaderboards provide a social interface for players to interact, share scores, and compete. Design of scoring systems and leaderboards is further explored in *Foldit* [4], where the authors describe

the design of their scoring function and the evolution of their leaderboards to better enable collaborative sharing (of protein solutions) while still providing an interface for players to compete. Competitive play in HCGs has been explored in games such as *PhotoCity* [23], which utilized an explicit competition between students at two universities and *KissKissBan* [6], which implemented a three-person competitive variant of the original *ESP Game* [24]. Finally, a study comparing collaborative and competitive scoring systems [20] suggests that collaborative scoring systems may yield better task completion results while competitive scoring systems may provide a more engaging player experience. However, none of these design investigations and games explore different or alternative kinds of reward systems beyond point systems and leaderboards; we investigate alternative systems in this paper. This relates to a longstanding question [8, 7, 22] of how to incorporate gameplay elements of modern, commercial games into HCGs in ways that do not compromise the quality of either the *task completion* or the *player experience*.

Rewards and Motivation in Games
Outside the domain of human computation games, reward systems have been widely explored. In game design for digital games, common approaches towards understanding and designing effective rewards in games are driven by theories on motivations and incentives. Early approaches in game design sought to understand how player motivations mapped to mechanics and reward in games, often for game genres with diverse player bases such as multi-user dungeon games (MUDs) [1], tabletop roleplaying games [10], MMOs [28], and online games [2]. Models for player motivation and engagement incorporate psychological theories, such as self-determination theory [17]. A comprehensive overview of motivational theory as it applies to gamification and serious games can be found in the work of Richter et al. [18]. The authors note that point systems are the most-commonly utilized form of reward feedback, and while their discussion focuses primarily on extrinsically-motivated rewards, they note that the effect of extrinsic rewards on intrinsic motivation still remains unknown. How these existing theories might need to be modified in order to accommodate motivations unique to human computation is an open question. Unfortunately, only few attempts have been made to understand motivations in the context of HCGs. Using their game *Indagator*, Lee et al. [11] explore motivations for participating in mobile content-sharing using a model of player gratification. Similarly, in their analysis of *Foldit* [3], Cooper et al. report the results of a suvey asking a subset of users about motivations for playing the game. Their responses were categorized based on Yee's motivational components [28], amended with an additional "purpose" category to capture intrinsic motivations for participation (i.e., assisting with scientific discovery). Similar explorations appear in other serious game domains, such as educational games [12], which make adjustments to existing theories to accommodate for intrinsic motivations beyond those driven by gameplay.

Motivation in Crowdsourcing
Research in crowdsourcing, specifically in the context of paid crowdsourcing platforms, has also examined the effects of

motivation on worker performance, where extrinsic motivations are captured by financial compensation in addition to any intrinsic motivation workers may have for solving the task. Existing work shows that monetary reward may undermine the effects of intrinsic motivation in crowdsourced workers [15] and that increasing the amount of financial compensation may yield more results, though not necessarily those of higher quality [13]. Additionally, studies have examined the interchangeability between paid crowdsourcing platforms and HCGs [21, 19], suggesting that the quality of the completed work between the two is comparable. However, Sabou et al.[19] remark that maintaining player motivation in HCGs may be more difficult, suggesting that motivational findings in the context of financially-compensated crowdsourcing may not translate directly to HCGs. Thus is unclear whether how and if so, to what extent, rewards in HCGs compare with financial compensation.

EXPANDING ON REWARDS IN HCGS

Beyond point systems and leaderboards, we know very little about how other kinds of reward systems behave in human computation games. However, we know that all players are not necessarily motivated by point systems and leaderboards, but also for more immersive reasons which are not always encapsulated in the most-commonly used reward systems in HCGs. The diversity of reward and feedback systems in modern commercial games provides attractive alternatives, but how can these systems (such as customizable avatars or game narrative) be utilized in HCGs?

This raises the question of how to distribute rewards to players. If multiple reward systems are available, is it enough to randomly distribute rewards to players or allow them to pick which rewards they want? On the one hand, players who are incentivized to play for a particular type of reward may find themselves compelled to contribute for longer or faster in order to receive the rewards they prefer, at the risk of frustrating players who might not appreciate randomly-distributed rewards. On the other, giving players a choice of reward may allow players to enjoy the rewards they prefer and possibly also incentivize them to contribute better quality work, at the risk of running out of content for reward systems or distracting them from the underlying human computation task. Ideally, we desire a reward distribution system that is fair to the players (i.e., providing a quality *player experience*), but also respects any needs of the task (i.e., ensuring quality *task completion*) and the limitations of content within these systems.

To explore these questions, we built a game called *Cafe Flour Sack*. *Cafe Flour Sack* is a culinary-themed HCG that asks players to classify cooking ingredients for potential recipes. It contains four different reward systems (or reward *categories*) for players to interact with: global leaderboards, customizable avatars, unlockable narratives, and a global progress tracker. These systems were chosen to appeal to a broad audience of players and thus cover a variety of different motivations for play (e.g., such as those expressed in [28]), while remaining representative of reward systems in modern digital games. Leaderboards and customizable avatar systems have appeared in prior HCGs, while narrative was designed to address alter-

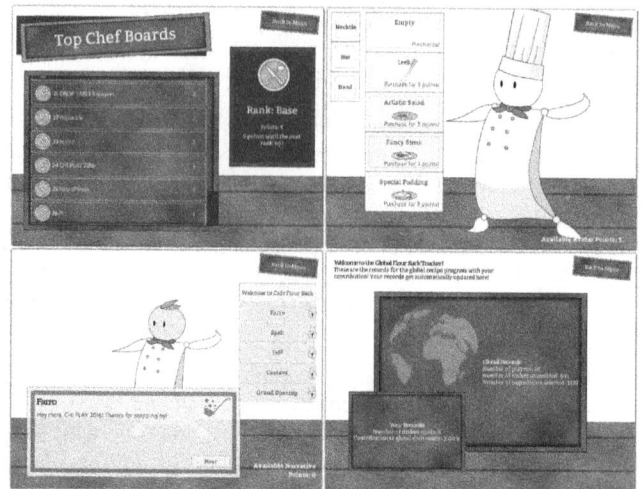

Figure 1. The four reward systems in *Cafe Flour Sack*. Starting clockwise from the upper-left: the global leaderboards, the customizable avatar, the progress tracker, and the unlockable narratives.

native motivations in a way that would not interact or interfere with the other rewards. Finally, the global tracker was added to accomodate a potential player population that derives motivation intrinsically by participating in learning or crowdsourcing, but not from extrinsic rewards.

We now describe these four reward systems:

- **Global Leaderboards** In the global leaderboards, "leaderboard" currency is automatically used to increase players' rank relative to other players. Figure 1 shows a screenshot of the leaderboards in the upper-left corner. After each round of tasks, players can check their leaderboard rank, which is represented as a medal (or badge) in the leaderboard menu. All players are added to the leaderboards by default, but players who do not receive leaderboard currency (or choose not to) remain at the default rank.

- **Customizable Avatars** In the customizable avatar system, players spend their "avatar" currency to purchase digital items that are used to customize a 2D avatar of a chef. These items include chef-themed clothing and culinary objects. While these kinds of virtual avatar systems are common in commercial games and content distribution platforms, they are rarely seen in HCGs (with one exception [5]). Figure 1 shows a screenshot of the customizable avatar in the upper-right corner.

- **Unlockable Narratives** In the unlockable narrative system, players use their "narrative" currency to unlock short stories set in the universe of the game. These stories are presented as conversational dialogue between the player and in-game characters, and are unlocked in sequential order. Figure 1 shows a screenshot of the leaderboards in the bottom-left corner.

- **Global Progress Tracker** In the global progress tracker, players may view statistics showing their overall contribution to the tasks being completed by all players in the game.

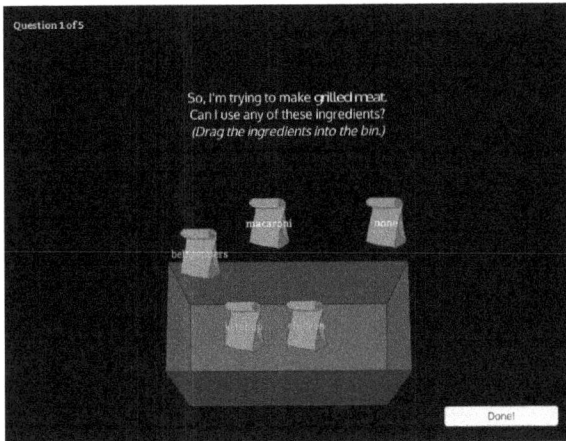

Figure 2. An example minigame from *Cafe Flour Sack*. Here, the player drags all ingredients that can be used in a corresponding recipe ("grilled meat") into a bin.

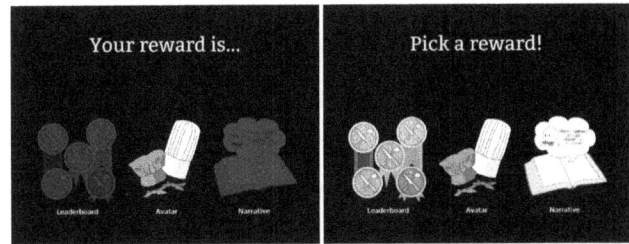

Figure 3. Screenshots of the reward selection screen between the two versions of the game. On the left, the *random* version selects a reward category (in this case, the avatar category) automatically. On the right, the *choice* version allows the player to click on their preferred category.

Figure 1 shows a screenshot of the progress tracker in the bottom-right corner. These statistics (number of players, recipes completed, etc.) are automatically updated each time a player completes a round. This system is meant to appeal to the intrinsic motivation of wanting to participate; consequently, it automatically increases when players complete tasks - and does not require any additional interaction. Instead, it exists merely to inform players of their progress relative the overall progress of the cooking task.

Cafe Flour Sack's cooking task is an artificial task with a known answer, which allows us to evaluate the efficacy of its reward mechanics without the complications of needing to simultaneously solve a human computation problem. This experimental approach of using an artificial task has been used successfully in prior HCG research in order to evaluate HCG design [14, 20]. We chose ingredient-recipe classification due to its similarity to other classification and commonsense-knowledge problems, as well as its simplicity (as players did not need actual culinary training, but merely knowledge of what ingredients could be used in classes of recipes). For this experiment, we used a gold-standard answer set containing 157 common cooking ingredients and 24 recipes. Each ingredient either belonged to a given recipe or not, and could belong to multiple recipes.

To ensure that the effects of each reward system could be measured independently of each other, each reward system has its own "currency" or point system. Currencies are not interchangeable between systems. Progression in one system does not impact progress in another - nor do any of the reward systems feed back into the gameplay of solving the task (e.g., players cannot purchase "powerups" to assist with the minigames).

METHODOLOGY

Cafe Flour Sack was released as an online game. Upon starting the game, players are placed into one of two versions of the game, *random* and *choice*, which serve as the two conditions in a between-subjects experiment. The game version

changes how players will be assigned rewards. In the *random* version, the player is automatically assigned one of the three reward categories at the beginning of each round. In the *choice* version, the player is allowed to manually select one of the three categories at the beginning of each round. Visibly and interactively, the only difference between the two game versions is the reward selection screen, as shown in Figure 3.

Players solve tasks by completing small minigames in rounds of five. Each minigame presents the player with a recipe and four possible ingredients to select from (as either belonging to the recipe or not). Figure 2 shows an example of one of these minigames. After completing a round, players are awarded currency in one of the reward systems. The amount of currency a player receives ranges from zero to five, equivalent to the number of tasks successfully completed.

The game begins with a short tutorial round of five minigames, after which players are given currency in all three possible reward categories. They are then instructed to view each of the reward menus in order to use their points, thus introducing them to all of the reward systems, before progressing further in the game. Players are then allowed to complete as many tasks as they desire throughout the duration of the experiment. At the end of the experiment, players are asked to fill out a post-game survey. Throughout gameplay, the game continually logs data for both tasks and player actions.

We recruited players (participants) from two populations. The first was through Amazon Mechanical Turk. Previous work has successfully explored the use of paid crowdsourcing platforms, such as Amazon Mechanical Turk, for distributing HCGs [14, 21]. Cafe Flour Sack was made available as a task (HIT) on Amazon Mechanical Turk's online portal where workers were compensated for playing the game, then answering the post-game survey. The second group was recruited through an undergraduate computer science class and were compensated for course credit for writing a report on the game (again, after playing the game and taking the same post-game survey).

The Amazon Mechanical Turk workers represent a group of players who are highly-skilled at crowdsourcing work, but are performing it through a monetarily-compensated interface (and thus not necessarily through HCGs). The student population represents an audience likely to be familiar with games, but not necessarily crowdsourcing work. Thus, when compared with university students, Amazon Mechanical Turk workers may be considered crowdsourcing experts and are likely to encompass a wider range of demographics (such as age range). Part of our long term goal is to broaden the accessibility of HCGs, so we deliberately chose to not only evaluate our work across two different experimental conditions, but two different audiences as well — something that has not been done in prior HCG research.

Because we are interested in understanding engagement in the context of rewards, we took some additional steps to account for the fact that players might have extrinsic motivations for completing the task quickly. First, we required all participants to play for at least 20 minutes, during which they were allowed to freely allocate their time between interacting with the reward systems and completing tasks (and thus yielding additional currency for the reward systems). This was meant to ensure that players would not be incentivized to rush through the experiment as quickly as possible, in which case it would be optimal to avoid interaction with the reward systems at all. Similarly, we also did not require that players complete a certain number of tasks.

Second, we introduced a button in the game's main menu, which we refer to as the "boredom" button. Players were explicitly asked to press the button when they would have considered quitting the game under non-experimental conditions (i.e., had they been playing the game without time enforcement or financial compensation). Pressing the button was optional and did not have any impact on whether or not players on Amazon Mechanical Turk were compensated.

Finally, we wished to ensure that players who completed the study later would not be biased by the presence and progression of earlier players in reward systems with visible social elements — namely the leaderboard and the progress tracker. In order to preserve the social elements of the study while maintaining consistency across all players, we simulated both the leaderboards and progress tracker using a set of fake players and results. After each round of the game, these players were updated (including the addition of new fake players to the game) with artificial progress in both in the leaderboards and the progress tracker.

RESULTS

The study was conducted over the course of several weeks, during which the game was made available online both to workers on Amazon Mechanical Turk and a university student population. We report on results from 78 players who took part in the study. 40 players were placed in the *random* condition and 38 were placed in the *choice* condition. 39 players were workers from Amazon Mechanical Turk (randomly selected from a larger population of 59 workers) and 39 players were students.

In total, 24 players self-reported as female and 54 players self-reported as male. Most players reported themselves as 18-40 years old. Additionally, most players reported prior gaming experience (around 80%); however only 15 players (around 20%) reported any prior experience with HCGs.

	Random	Choice
AMT Workers	0.725	0.722
Students	0.670	0.725
Total	0.696	0.724

Table 1. Mean task scores split by experimental condition, first broken down into separate player audiences and then shown in total.

Our evaluation focuses on both the results of the task (*task completion*) and the *player experience*. We investigate differences between the experimental conditions of *random* and *choice*. Additionally, we investigate differences between the two populations of our player audience — Amazon Mechanical Turk workers and students — while accounting for interaction effects with experimental condition. The majority of our dependent variables had nonparametric distributions. To measure differences and interactions between the conditions, unless otherwise stated, we used two-way ANOVAs with aligned rank transforms [27] to account for the nonparametric nature of the data. Below, we report our results; we then discuss them in the subsequent section.

Task Completion

To evaluate the *task completion*, we considered three metrics: the answer correctness, the number of tasks completed, and the timing of task completion. These metrics reflect the design considerations of task providers. For an actual human computation task, different metrics might be prioritized over others depending on the task requirements; here, we observe all metrics equally.

Correctness of Completed Tasks

To verify answer correctness, each task — the pairing of four cooking ingredients with a recipe — was assigned a score. This score was computed using our gold-standard answer set and is the ratio of correctly-assigned ingredients to the total number of ingredients in the task. A task was considered correct if 75% (a corresponding score of 0.75) or more of its ingredients belonged to the given recipe.

The results show that both experimental condition and player audience had significant effects on answer correctness. Players in the *choice* condition had higher mean scores than players in the *random* condition, 0.723 vs. 0.696 ($F = 9.474, p < 0.01$). Amazon Mechanical Turk players had higher mean scores than student players, 0.724 vs. 0.692 ($F = 9.072, p < 0.01$).

The player audience × experiment condition interaction was significant ($F = 28.648, p < 0.001$). Table 1 shows the mean task scores split across experimental condition and player audience. Amazon Mechanical Turk players in the *random* condition demonstrate the highest mean scores (0.7254) with student players in the *choice* performing closely behind (0.7245). Meanwhile, student players in the *random* condition demonstrated the lowest mean scores (0.670).

Number of Completed Tasks

We also looked at the number of tasks completed per player across both experimental condition and player audience. We broke down our observations into three categories: the *total* number of tasks completed, the number of *correct* tasks

	Random	Choice
AMT Workers	8.382	9.129
Students	14.229	12.753
Total	11.492	10.507

Table 2. Mean task completion times (in seconds) for total tasks split by experimental condition, first broken down into separate player audiences and then shown in total.

		Leaderboards	Avatar	Narrative	Tracker
Random	AMT Workers	4	8	5	0
	Students	13	6	2	2
Choice	AMT Workers	14	2	6	0
	Students	8	3	5	0
Total		39	19	18	2

Table 3. Counts of players' favorite rewards across both experimental condition and player audience.

completed, and the number of *incorrect* tasks completed. On average, Amazon Mechanical Turk players provided significantly more total answers (82.308 answers) compared with student players (70.128 answers) ($F = 5.083, p < 0.05$). Additionally, when looking only at correct answers, Amazon Mechanical Turk players also provided significantly more correct answers (57.410 answers) compared with student players (44.590 answers) ($F = 5.083, p < 0.05$). No other significant effects were observed across experimental conditions and player audience.

Timing of Completed Tasks

For our final task completion metric, we looked at the time (in seconds) it took players to complete tasks. Similarly to our observations of number of tasks completed, we evaluated these results across *total* tasks, *correct* tasks, and *incorrect* tasks.

When it came to the number of seconds it took players to complete all (total) tasks, both experimental condition and player audience had significant main effects. Players in the *choice* condition showed faster mean times for total task completion than players in the *random* condition, 10.507 seconds vs. 11.492 seconds ($F = 8.228, p < 0.01$). Meanwhile, Amazon Mechanical Turk players showed faster mean times for total task completion than student players, 8.788 seconds vs. 13.652 seconds ($F = 281.682, p < 0.001$).

There were also interaction effects. When accounting for experiment condition × player audience interaction across all tasks, we also found a significant effect ($F = 40.875, p < 0.001$). Table 2 shows the mean task completion times for all tasks split across experimental condition and player audience. Overall, Amazon Mechanical Turk players in the *random* condition demonstrated fastest mean times (8.382 seconds), and are slightly slower in the *choice* condition (9.128 seconds). This result is flipped across conditions for student players, who demonstrated faster mean times in the *choice* condition (12.753 seconds) compared with the slowest mean times in the *random* condition (14.229 seconds).

Next, when looking only at the times it took players to complete tasks correctly, we found that once again, both experimental condition and player audience had significant effects (however no interaction effects were observed). Players in the *choice* condition were faster at completing tasks correctly than players in the *random* condition, 9.773 seconds vs. 10.820 seconds ($F = 5.809, p < 0.05$). Meanwhile, Amazon Mechanical Turk players were faster at completing tasks correctly than student players, 8.348 seconds vs. 12.780 seconds ($F = 190.930, p < 0.001$).

Similarly, when looking only at the times it took players to complete tasks incorrectly, both experimental condition and player audience had significant effects. Players in the *choice* condition were slightly faster at completing tasks incorrectly than players in the *random* condition, 12.262 seconds vs. 12.726 seconds ($F = 10.222, p < 0.01$). Again, Amazon Mechanical Turk players were faster at completing tasks incorrectly compared to student players, 9.802 mean seconds vs. 15.174 mean seconds ($F = 21.868, p < 0.001$). Significant effects for experimental condition x player audience interaction were also observed ($F = 43.596, p < 0.001$). Amazon Mechanical Turk players were faster overall (at 9.371 mean seconds in the *random* condition and 10.167 mean seconds in the *choice*). Student players were slower (at 14.991 and 15.531 mean seconds in the *random* and *choice* conditions respectively).

In summary, players in the *choice* condition had faster mean times for task completion than players in the *random* condition. Additionally, Amazon Mechanical Turk players were significantly faster than completing tasks than student players at completing tasks. These findings were observed not just for all tasks, but also for tasks answered correctly and tasks answered incorrectly. For total tasks, Amazon Mechanical Turk players in the *random* condition were the fastest at completing tasks, while students in the *random* condition were the slowest. For incorrectly-answered tasks, Amazon Mechanical Turk players in the *random* condition were the fastest, while students in the *choice* condition were the slowest.

Player Experience

Our evaluation of the player experience consists of observations of player interaction, combined with player responses to questions on the post-game survey. In particular, we are interested in understanding how players engaged with the reward systems, as well as why they may have become disengaged with these systems. We first on report player survey responses regarding their favorite and least favorite reward systems in *Cafe Flour Sack*, and a question of whether or not players perceived they had a choice of reward systems. Next, we report on their their interaction time within each of the reward systems. Finally, we report their interaction with the boredom button in order to understand why they would have disengaged with the game — and if our reward systems were responsible.

Reward Preference

First, we were interested to know how players responded to each of the different reward systems available. In the post-game survey, players were asked to provide their favorite

		Leaderboards	Avatar	Narrative	Tracker
Random	AMT Workers	3	4	7	3
	Students	3	4	13	3
Choice	AMT Workers	3	4	8	7
	Students	2	6	7	1
Total		11	18	35	14

Table 4. Counts of players' least favorite rewards across both experimental condition and player audience.

reward system and their least favorite system in *Cafe Flour Sack*. For players' favorite reward system, 39 players selected the leaderboards, 19 players selected the narrative rewards, 18 players selected the customizable avatar, and 2 players selected the progress tracker. Table 3 shows the exact breakdown of players' favorite rewards across the experimental condition and player audiences.

Meanwhile, regarding players' least favorite reward system, 35 players selected the narrative, 18 players selected the customizable avatar system, 14 players selected the progress tracker, and 11 players selected the leaderboards.

We found no differences or effects on task performance based on players' favorite and least favorite reward systems.

Perception of Choice

We looked at whether or not players perceived they had a choice of rewards available, which we will refer to as "perception of reward choice". In the post-game survey, players were asked to rate the statement "I was able to choose which rewards I wanted." on a Likert-like scale from 1 to 5 (1 corresponding to "Strongly Disagree", 5 corresponding to "Strongly Agree").

Both experimental condition and player audience had significant main effects on players' "perception of reward choice." In the *choice* condition, players reported significantly higher "perception of reward choice" than in the *random* condition ($F = 73.631, p < 0.001$). Amazon Mechanical Turk players reported higher perception of reward choice than student players ($F = 5.548, p < 0.05$). No significant interaction effects were detected.

Duration of Play

As previously mentioned, interaction within the game was limited to 20 minutes. For players who were participating in this study through Amazon Mechanical Turk, it is likely that were already incentivized to participate for financial reasons. (Amazon Mechanical Turk also imposes a time limit for submitting task results, so players would have been unlikely to continue playing under this additional time pressure.) Under these limitations, we cannot look at total duration of play as an indication of engagement or retention.

Instead, we look where *how* players spent their time during those 20 minutes of play. In particular, we are interested to see how long players spent in each of the different reward systems. Each system had its own dedicated interface and we recorded how long players spent in these interfaces. Some of these systems, in particular, the leaderboards and the progress

Leaderboards	Random	Choice
AMT Workers	10.174	7.828
Students	12.829	10.174
Customizable Avatar	Random	Choice
AMT Workers	11.157	10.939
Students	12.039	12.694
Narratives	Random	Choice
AMT Workers	45.093	60.980
Students	47.070	58.036
Global Tracker	Random	Choice
AMT Workers	6.068	6.808
Students	10.278	7.654

Table 5. Mean duration (in seconds) for spent in all four reward systems across both player audience type and experimental condition.

tracker, show very short durations, as interaction is limited to viewing information such as leaderboard rank or task progress. In comparison, the narrative system required players to read and actively click through character dialogue. Table 5 shows the mean time spent in each reward menu, broken down by experimental condition and player audience.

In the leaderboards, both experimental condition and player audience had a significant main effect on the duration of interaction. Players in the *random* condition spent longer in the leaderboards than players in the *choice* condition ($F = 7.319, p < 0.01$), with a mean time of 11.904 seconds vs. 8.868 seconds. Student players spent much longer in the leaderboards than Amazon Mechanical Turk players ($F = 7.265, p < 0.01$), with a mean time of 11.795 seconds vs. 8.650 seconds. No interaction effects were observed.

No significant differences in duration of interaction were observed between experimental conditions and player audience for the remaining reward systems: the customizable avatar, the unlockable narrative, and the global progress tracker.

Boredom

62 of the 78 players pressed the boredom button. Of these players, 32 were in the *random* condition (80% press rate) and 30 were in the *choice* condition (79% press rate). 34 of these players were Amazon Mechanical Turk players and 28 were student players. When looking at the times (since the start of the game) at which the boredom button was pressed, no significant differences were detected between the experimental conditions and the player audience.

Additionally, players were asked to clarify why they had pressed the boredom button (if they had chosen to do so). Overall, 26 players (around 42% of players) described their primary reason for pressing the boredom button as due to the repetitive nature of tasks (i.e., lack of variety in the tasks or tasks that were too similar). 10 players described their main reason as due to finishing or running out of reward content. Other reasons included a lack of interest in the task and game overall (10 players), general confusion or unfamiliarity with certain ingredients (4 players), a lack of challenge (3 players), and a lack of purpose and/or learning (3 players).

Given that the task was repetitive in nature (and addressing these issues for boredom would involve looking at gameplay mechanics beyond the scope of this study), we looked more closely at the 10 players who described boredom due to finishing and running out of reward content, as this is directly related to reward systems. Of these players, 4 were in the *random* condition and 6 were in the *choice* condition, while 8 players were Amazon Mechanical Turk players and 2 were student players. A majority of these players (6 of 10) listed their favorite reward as the unlockable narrative, with 2 more preferring the customizable avatar, and the last 2 preferring the leaderboards.

DISCUSSION

What considerations for the design of reward systems in human computation games can we draw from our results?

With multiple rewards systems, offering players the choice of reward is both effective and engaging.

Overall, players in the *choice* condition demonstrated higher task correctness and were faster at completing tasks. Additionally, players in the *choice* condition perceived they had had more choice of rewards. This however, did not appear to significantly affect interactions with the reward systems themselves as we found no differences in the duration of interaction, suggesting that the lengths of player experiences were similar. The only exception to this was that players in the *random* condition spent longer in the leaderboards, but these differences, while significant, were only on the order of several seconds. We conclude that offering players the choice of reward benefits both *task completion* and the *player experience*. While other explorations of mechanics in HCGs have shown potential trade-offs in *task completion* and *player experience* [20] (and thus may require balancing design decisions for maximizing one aspect of HCGs over the other), the *choice* condition showed benefits for both.

Adjusting reward mechanics can make certain player audiences perform more effectively.

Overall, Amazon Mechanical Turk players performed significantly better than student players at all task completion metrics (task correctness, number of tasks completed, and rate of task completion), which is unsurprising given that Amazon Mechanical Turk players are considered crowdsourcing experts. As previously mentioned, Amazon Mechanical Turk players in the *random* condition were the most effective players overall, significantly so when it came to both task correctness and rate of task completion. However, these differences in *task completion* metrics, compared to the next most effective population, are significant but small. When separating students by experimental condition, students in the *choice* condition have *task completion* metrics more comparable to those of Amazon Mechanical Turk players. This is not the case with the *random* condition, where the difference in *task completion* metrics is much larger. So while our two player audiences performed very differently on *task completion* in one experimental condition (students significantly lower than Amazon Mechanical Turk players in *random*), they were comparable in the other

(*choice*). Our findings are limited because our task was selected for its simplicity, relying on primarily on commonsense knowledge without additional training. However, for more complicated tasks, such improvements could be very valuable. Combined with the previous consideration, this suggests that design decisions such as offering players choice of multiple rewards have the potential to greatly improve *task completion* metrics without negatively affecting the *player experience*.

Small changes in the design of reward mechanics can have large impacts on task completion and the player experience.

A design concern unique to HCG design is determining which gameplay elements have the most significant effects on both the *task completion* and the *player experience*. The difference between the *random* and the *choice* versions of the game was a single screen that assigned or allowed players to choose their reward before completing a round of gameplay. In this study, we showed this fairly simple design change for in the presentation and acquisition of rewards could had significant affects on both *task completion* and the *player experience*, in particular managing to improve results for a non-expert player audience. At the same time, the interaction effects between how we reward players and player audience highlight the importance of paying attention to the target player audience. This appears to be especially true in the context of reward systems and their mechanics. To the best of our knowledge, existing HCG research has not deeply examined how different player audiences might affect HCGs, not to mention tailoring subsets of HCG game mechanics within a single game to different audiences. This study helps to confirm the importance of reward mechanics to both *task completion* and the *player experience*.

LIMITATIONS AND FUTURE DIRECTIONS

Our study is limited by the number of users. This is due in part to the fact that conducting studies on Amazon Mechanical Turk is also prohibitively more expensive (both financially and logistically compared to the majority of tasks on the platform with extremely short durations). Additionally, many steps were taken to address factors in the study confounded by financial or academic compensation, which possibly affected aspects of gameplay interaction players would have had in a non-experimental setting. For example, we simulated the presence of social elements (artificial players) to avoid bias, but it is not clear how this compares to the presence of real social elements. Finally, reward systems in many digital games often contain interacting elements (e.g., exchangeable reward currencies) or are entangled with other game mechanics. Our setup necessitated keeping the systems separate to observe experimental effects, thus possibly limiting the kinds and implementations of reward systems.

Going forward, we believe there are many possible investigations enabling a better understanding of reward systems in human computation games. We utilized multiple reward systems in *Cafe Flour Sack*, some of which are present in existing HCGs and others which have never been examined before. While leaderboards were the preferred reward in *Cafe Flour Sack*, many players also expressed preferences for other underutilized systems. We also found no correlations between players who selected leaderboards with higher *task completion* or *player experience* metrics, suggesting that other reward systems might be viable for inclusion in HCGs. This raises questions such as whether leaderboards are the most effective reward system for all tasks and all audiences? Was a dislike of the unlockable narrative due to its particular implementation or because these particular audiences were unengaged by the content in this context?

Answering such questions would require undertaking a direct comparison of the different reward systems (including others not explored in this study) and seeing their effects on *task completion* and the *player experience*. Based on our explorations in this study, investigating leaderboard alternatives might focus on more neutrally-favored systems (e.g., the customizable avatar) over more polarizing systems (e.g., the unlockable narrative). This, however, comes with some considerations. Implementing many or multiple kinds of reward systems puts an additional burden on HCG developers, not just for their implementation, but generation of content as well. While the most frequently-cited reason for player boredom with the game was due to the repetitive nature of the tasks, we note that the next-most identified reason for boredom (affecting 12% of players) was due to running out of or finishing reward content. These players showed a clear preference for reward systems with finite content (the unlockable narrative and the customizable avatar), suggesting that a population of players was in fact deeply-engaged with these systems and performed enough work to exhaust all of the content in them. In order for these systems to be effective for potential player populations such as this, the amount of available reward content must match the amount of desired (or estimated) human computation work required per player, something that is of concern to HCG developers.

Other aspects of rewards, such as reward contingencies (what players were rewarded for) and schedules (when rewards were received), were kept constant for this study to reduce the number of variables, but also merit separate investigation for their effects on task performance and player engagement. Additionally, while our setup prohibited us from conducting fully qualitative interviews (i.e., not violating Amazon Mechanical Turk's Terms of Service), a deeper, detailed understanding of what motivates players to engage with HCGs — and how these findings fit within existing motivational and crowdsourcing frameworks for compensation — is imperative to making more effective and engaging HCGs based on player feedback.

CONCLUSIONS

In this paper, we explored the use of multiple reward systems in human computation games and the effect of changing how these rewards are distributed to players. Studying the impact of design decisions in HCGs is crucial to helping scientists, researchers, and game developers create more effective and engaging games. We ran a study comparing two versions of a cooking-themed HCG, *Cafe Flour Sack*, containing multiple reward systems. One version of the game (*random*) randomly distributed rewards to players and the other version of the game (*choice*) that allowed players to choose between possible reward systems. We released this game to two different player

audiences and studied the effects of the conditions as they relate to the two main design considerations of HCGs: *task completion* and the *player experience*.

We observed several main and interaction effects, such as that players in the *choice* condition solved tasks more correctly and perform tasks quicker. Unsurprisingly, we also found that Amazon Mechanical Turk players proved to be significantly better at solving tasks than student players. Overall, Amazon Mechanical Turk players in the *random* condition had the highest *task completion* metrics, but all other players in the *choice* condition were not far behind (with student players in the *random* condition demonstrating significantly lower *task completion* metrics). When it came to aspects of the *player experience*, we found that players in the *choice* condition perceived they had more choice of rewards, but there were few differences in their interaction with the reward systems (with leaderboards being the only exception). Additionally, student players were more engaged along these metrics than Amazon Mechanical Turk players.

Based on our results, we suggest that offering players *choice* of rewards leads to better *task completion* and a more engaged *player experience*. Interaction effects suggest that reward mechanics are sensitive to both our experimental conditions and player audiences, but we can leverage reward mechanics to improve *task completion* without negatively affecting the *player experience* of one audience (students) compared to another (Amazon Mechanical Turk workers). Finally, we discuss our limitations and future work in reward mechanics for HCGs. Ultimately, our goal is to help HCGs become more effective and engaging for both task providers and players, and that our investigations from this study help to clarify the design space of reward systems in these games.

ACKNOWLEDGMENTS
We thank members of the Entertainment Intelligence Lab for providing feedback on the study and the game. We also thank Eric Butler and Eleanor O'Rourke for valuable feedback and assistance.

This material is based upon work supported by the National Science Foundation under Grant No. 1525967. Any opinions, findings, and conclusions or recommendations expressed in this material are those of the author(s) and do not necessarily reflect the views of the National Science Foundation.

REFERENCES
1. Richard Bartle. 1996. Hearts, clubs, diamonds, spades: Players who suit MUDs. *Journal of MUD research* 1, 1 (1996), 19.

2. Dongseong Choi and Jinwoo Kim. 2004. Why people continue to play online games: In search of critical design factors to increase customer loyalty to online contents. *CyberPsychology & behavior* 7, 1 (2004), 11–24.

3. Seth Cooper, Firas Khatib, Adrien Treuille, Janos Barbero, Jeehyung Lee, Michael Beenen, Andrew Leaver-Fay, David Baker, Zoran Popović, and others. 2010a. Predicting protein structures with a multiplayer online game. *Nature* 466, 7307 (2010), 756–760.

4. Seth Cooper, Adrien Treuille, Janos Barbero, Andrew Leaver-Fay, Kathleen Tuite, Firas Khatib, Alex Cho Snyder, Michael Beenen, David Salesin, David Baker, Zoran Popović, and Foldit Players. 2010b. The Challenge of Designing Scientific Discovery Games. In *5th International Conference on the Foundations of Digital Games*.

5. Dion Hoe-Lian Goh, Chei Sian Lee, Alton YK Chua, Khasfariyati Razikin, and Keng-Tiong Tan. 2011. SPLASH: Blending Gaming and Content Sharing in a Location-Based Mobile Application. *Social Informatics* (2011), 328.

6. Chien-Ju Ho, Tao-Hsuan Chang, Jong-Chuan Lee, Jane Yung-jen Hsu, and Kuan-Ta Chen. 2009. KissKissBan: A Competitive Human Computation Game for Image Annotation. In *ACM SIGKDD Workshop on Human Computation (HCOMP '09)*.

7. Markus Krause and Jan Smeddinck. 2011. Human computation games: A survey. In *Signal Processing Conference, 2011 19th European*. IEEE, 754–758.

8. Markus Krause, Aneta Takhtamysheva, Marion Wittstock, and Rainer Malaka. 2010. Frontiers of a paradigm: exploring human computation with digital games. In *ACM SIGKDD Workshop on Human Computation*.

9. Edith Law and Luis von Ahn. 2009. Input-agreement: A New Mechanism for Collecting Data Using Human Computation Games. In *Proceedings of the SIGCHI Conference on Human Factors in Computing Systems*. 1197–1206.

10. Robin D Laws. 2002. *Robin's laws of good game mastering*. Steve Jackson Games.

11. Chei Sian Lee, Dion Hoe-Lian Goh, Alton YK Chua, and Rebecca P Ang. 2010. Indagator: Investigating perceived gratifications of an application that blends mobile content sharing with gameplay. *Journal of the American Society for Information Science and Technology* 61, 6 (2010), 1244–1257.

12. Brian Magerko, Carrie Heeter, and Ben Medler. 2010. Different Strokes for Different Folks: Tapping Into the Hidden. *Gaming and Cognition: Theories and Practice from the Learning Sciences: Theories and Practice from the Learning Sciences* (2010), 255.

13. Winter Mason and Duncan J Watts. 2010. Financial incentives and the performance of crowds. *ACM SigKDD Explorations Newsletter* 11, 2 (2010), 100–108.

14. Winter Mason and Duncan J Watts. 2011. Collective problem solving in networks. *Available at http://dx.doi.org/10.2139/ssrn.1795224* (2011).

15. Kou Murayama, Madoka Matsumoto, Keise Izuma, and Kenji Matsumoto. 2010. Neural basis of the undermining effect of monetary reward on intrinsic motivation. *Proceedings of the National Academy of Sciences* 107, 49 (2010), 20911–20916.

16. Ei Pa Pa Pe-Than, Dion Hoe-Lian Goh, and Chei Sian Lee. 2013. A typology of human computation games: an analysis and a review of current games. *Behaviour & Information Technology* (2013).

17. Andrew K Przybylski, C Scott Rigby, and Richard M Ryan. 2010. A motivational model of video game engagement. *Review of general psychology* 14, 2 (2010), 154.

18. Ganit Richter, Daphne R. Raban, and Sheizaf Rafaeli. 2015. *Gamification in Education and Business*. Springer International Publishing, Chapter Studying Gamification: The Effect of Rewards and Incentives on Motivation, 21–46.

19. Marta Sabou, Kalina Bontcheva, Arno Scharl, and Michael Föls. 2013. Games with a Purpose or Mechanised Labour?: A Comparative Study. In *Proceedings of the 13th International Conference on Knowledge Management and Knowledge Technologies (i-Know '13)*. ACM, New York, NY, USA, Article 19, 8 pages.

20. Kristin Siu, Alexander Zook, and Mark O. Riedl. 2014. Collaboration versus Competition: Design and Evaluation of Mechanics for Games with a Purpose. In *9th International Conference on the Foundations of Digital Games*.

21. Stefan Thaler, Elena Simperl, and Stephan Wolger. 2012. An experiment in comparing human-computation techniques. *Internet Computing, IEEE* 16, 5 (2012), 52–58.

22. Kathleen Tuite. 2014. GWAPs: Games with a Problem. In *9th International Conference on the Foundations of Digital Games*.

23. Kathleen Tuite, Noah Snavely, Dun-Yu Hsiao, Nadine Tabing, and Zoran Popović. 2011. PhotoCity: training experts at large-scale image acquisition through a competitive game. In *ACM SIGCHI Conference on Human Factors in Computing Systems*.

24. L. von Ahn and L. Dabbish. 2004. Labeling images with a computer game. In *ACM SIGCHI Conference on Human Factors in Computing Systems*. ACM, 319–326.

25. Luis von Ahn and Laura Dabbish. 2008. Designing Games with a Purpose. *Commun. ACM* 51, 8 (2008), 58–67.

26. Luis von Ahn, Ruoran Liu, and Manuel Blum. 2006. Peekaboom: A Game for Locating Objects in Images. In *Proceedings of the SIGCHI Conference on Human Factors in Computing Systems (CHI '06)*. ACM, 55–64.

27. Jacob O. Wobbrock, Leah Findlater, Darren Gergle, and James J. Higgins. 2011. The Aligned Rank Transform for Nonparametric Factorial Analyses Using Only Anova Procedures. In *Proceedings of the SIGCHI Conference on Human Factors in Computing Systems (CHI '11)*. ACM, New York, NY, USA, 143–146. DOI: http://dx.doi.org/10.1145/1978942.1978963

28. Nick Yee. 2006. Motivations for play in online games. *CyberPsychology & behavior* 9, 6 (2006), 772–775.

"The Collecting Itself Feels Good": Towards Collection Interfaces for Digital Game Objects

Zachary O. Toups,[1] **Nicole K. Crenshaw**,[2] **Rina R. Wehbe**,[3] **Gustavo F. Tondello**,[3] **Lennart E. Nacke**[3]

[1]Play & Interactive Experiences for Learning Lab, Dept. Computer Science, New Mexico State University
[2]Donald Bren School of Information and Computer Sciences, University of California, Irvine
[3]HCI Games Group, Games Institute, University of Waterloo
z@cs.nmsu.edu, crenshan@uci.edu, rina.wehbe@uwaterloo.ca, gustavo@tondello.com,
lennart.nacke@acm.org

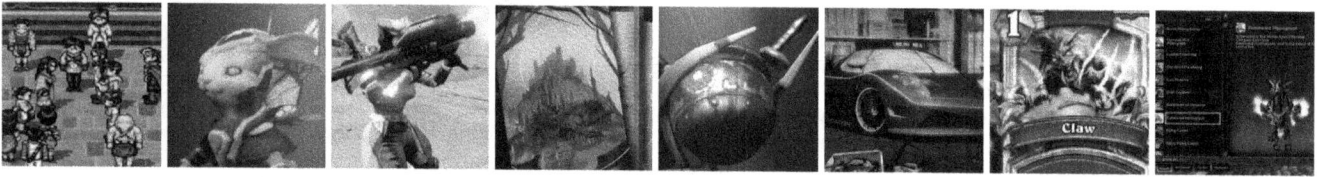

Figure 1. Sample favorite digital game objects collected by respondents, one for each code from the developed coding manual (except MISCELLANEOUS). While we did not collect media from participants, we identified representative images[0] for some responses. From left to right: CHARACTER: characters from *Suikoden II* [G14], collected by P153; CRITTER: P32 reports collecting Arnabus the Fairy Rabbit from *Dota 2* [G19]; GEAR: P55 favorited the Gjallerhorn rocket launcher from *Destiny* [G10]; INFORMATION: P44 reports *Dragon Age: Inquisition* [G5] codex cards; SKIN: P66's favorite object is the Cauldron of Xahryx skin for *Dota 2* [G19]; VEHICLE: a Jansen Carbon X12 car from *Burnout Paradise* [G11] from P53; RARE: a *Hearthstone* [G8] gold card from the Druid deck [P23]; COLLECTIBLE: *World of Warcraft* [G6] mount collection interface [P7, P65, P80, P105, P164, P185, P206].

ABSTRACT

Digital games offer a variety of collectible objects. We investigate players' collecting behaviors in digital games to determine what digital game objects players enjoyed collecting and why they valued these objects. Using this information, we seek to inform the design of future digital game object collection interfaces. We discuss the types of objects that players prefer, the reasons that players value digital game objects, and how collection behaviors may guide play. Through our findings, we identify design implications for digital game object collection interfaces: enable object curation, preserve rules and mechanics, preserve context of play, and allow players to share their collections with others. Digital game object collection interfaces are applicable to the design of digital games, gamified applications, and educational software.

ACM Classification Keywords

H.5.2. Information Interfaces and Presentation (e.g. HCI): User Interfaces; User-centered design.

Author Keywords

Digital game objects; collecting behaviors.

CHI PLAY '16, October 16 - 19, 2016, Austin, TX, USA

© 2016 Copyright held by the owner/author(s). Publication rights licensed to ACM.
ISBN 978-1-4503-4456-2/16/10. . . $15.00

DOI: http://dx.doi.org/10.1145/2967934.2968088

INTRODUCTION

People collect objects for many reasons, such as filling a personal void, striving for a sense of completion, or creating a sense of order [8, 22, 29, 34]. We find meaning in our collected objects [2, 26], and internet culture has allowed us to take our collecting practices into digital realms [16, 17, 28, 36, 37]. In digital games, we can collect explicit and improvised items including meta-game rewards (e.g., Xbox Achievements), modifications to game rules and mechanics (e.g., Pokémon), and personalization options (e.g., clothing).

We lack a clear understanding of players' collecting behaviors and how players perceive the value of their digital game objects. Prior research has explored how players value digital game characters (e.g., [20]) and general digital collections (e.g., [16, 17, 36]), yet questions remain about how players value *digital game objects*. We surveyed over 180 gamers about their digital game object collecting practices. Our research offers a broader investigation of value attribution in games, because it includes non-tangible objects (e.g., armor dyes) and games without characters (e.g., *Ingress* [G17]).

---
[0]Figure 1 source information (left to right): ⓒ⊙ YetiFreeze on YouTube (https://www.youtube.com/watch?v=cTUPNo8vBd4) (game [G14] © Konami); screenshot taken ⓒ⊙ by author Toups (game [G19] © Valve); screenshot taken ⓒ⊙ by author Nacke (with Daniel Johnson's digital game object) (game [G10] © Bungie); ⓒ⊙ Ben Pope Games on YouTube (https://www.youtube.com/watch?v=oHpywDFM464) (game [G5] © EA); screenshot provided ⓒ⊙ author Toups (game [G19] © Valve); screenshot provided ⓒ⊙ William A. Hamilton (game [G11] © EA); screenshot provided ⓒ⊙ Igor Dolgov (game [G8] © Blizzard); screenshot provided ⓒ⊙ Mark Toups (game [G6] © Blizzard).

From our data about the objects players collect, we developed a coding manual, following methods outlined by Saldaña [30]. With this manual, we are able to understand the composition of players' collections. We connect our digital object types with prior work on digital character value (e.g., [20]) to understand *why* players value digital game objects and what drives them to collect. Through our data, we develop an understanding of why players collect digital game objects, why digital game objects are valued, how sociality plays a role in digital game object collections, and how players compose their digital game object collections.

We connect our findings to data on personality and player types, conducting an exploratory analysis of multiple pairs of independent variables with players' behaviors towards digital game objects. Our data show some possible associations between player typologies and digital game object preferences that are worth investigating in future work. Players' ages were associated with their reasons for collecting objects, their reported practices towards purchasing personalization options, and their digital game object sharing behaviors. The player's BrainHex class [23] was associated with their preference for collecting rare objects and their reported practices towards sharing their digital game objects.

From our findings, we develop design implications for *digital game object collection interfaces*. Such interfaces should enable curation, preserve rules and game mechanics, preserve context of play, and enable sharing of digital game objects. The design implications support designers of digital games, gamified applications, and educational systems by offering guidance on how collection interfaces can enhance these systems, supporting users / players and driving motivation.

For those readers interested in the specifics of the survey instrument, we have supplied the instrument verbatim in the Appendix.

Reporting Conventions
In addition to references, we also supply a ludography, which provides data on the games discussed in the present research. Referenced games are prefixed with a "G" (e.g., [G6]). When we discuss game series, we only cite a single exemplar (either the specific one from our data or the first entry).

When we discuss data from participants, we use the participant's serial identifier prefixed with a "P" (e.g., [P124]); the serial identifiers match the data rows and were not modified after cleaning the data (and so there are identifiers beyond the total number of participants).

Finally, following Saldaña's convention [30], we specify codes from the coding manual in SMALL CAPITALS.

Paper Outline
We continue the present paper by discussing previous literature on game design, collections research, and prior game interfaces. We provide details of our methods, including the specific questions we are interested in in the present research, the composition of our participant population, details of our coding manual, and details of our quantitative analysis methods. Our results section describes our quantitative findings and

Code	Description
UTILITY	Enables accomplishing game tasks.
INVESTMENT	Represents player time, effort, achievements.
COMMUNICATION	An expression to a social group.
MEMORY	A record of activities in game.
ENJOYMENT	Fun to play.
RELATIONSHIPS	Represents player / group relationships.
NEW EXPERIENCES	Enables new in-game experiences.
CREATIVITY	Enables creating aesthetically pleasing forms.
SOCIABILITY	Enables engagement with friends.
SELF-EXPRESSION	Express player attitudes or beliefs.

Table 1. Livingston et al.'s [20] types of value for game characters. The value types were applied in the present study to digital game objects.

qualitative themes that provide insight into digital game object collection behaviors. We use the themes from our participants' qualitative responses to develop design implications for collection interfaces in games, address cautions about building digital game object collection interfaces, and outline plans for future work. We conclude with a call to action for developers.

BACKGROUND
The present research builds on game design and collection scholarship. We begin by discussing game mechanics, then discuss research on how players value digital game objects and how personality types are used in the game design space. We discuss collecting research in the physical and digital realms. We close the section by discussing games that provide inventory and catalog interfaces, which offer a simple means for players to collect digital game objects.

Game Mechanics
Games are made up of rules, within which players make decisions (to play) [31]. *Game mechanics* thus represent moments of player choice within those rules, modifying the game state [15,31]. One interesting element of digital game objects is that they can influence the operation of game mechanics. They may represent a combination of modifications to game rules (e.g., a sword with a specific statistics) or may enable new forms of play (i.e., mechanics) in and of themselves (e.g., a character with a range of new actions to perform).

Valuing Digital Game Objects
Prior studies have explored how players value their characters in online games. Manninen and Kujanpää [21] used Yee's [38] categories of motivational play to analyze how players valued their characters, and found that value could be categorized according to achievement- (e.g., statistics, wealth), social- (e.g., friendships, player interactions), and immersion-oriented (e.g., physical appearance, role) components. Kujanpää et al. [18] discuss financial implications of value in games by exploring how players spend real-world currencies for character customization. Guo and Barnes [10] examined *Second Life* [G15] and *EverQuest* [G12] to model why players buy digital objects in digital games for real-world currencies.

Livingston et al. [20] identified ten ways that players value characters, summarized on Table 1. We build on this work by examining the ways that players value digital game objects using Livingston et al.'s value types.

Player Personality

Previous research has examined the classification of personality types for determining human behavior. For example, the Five Factor Model (FFM) of personality developed by Costa and McCrae [6] classifies personality according to five traits: openness to new experiences, conscientiousness, extraversion, agreeableness, and neuroticism. Many variations of this personality inventory exist, varying in size; the largest of which contains 240 items [7].

Bartle defined four specific player personality types in multi-user dungeons (MUDs): Achievers, Explorers, Socializers, and Killers [1]. Players were categorized according to in-game interests and behaviors. For example, a player who finds enjoyment in player-versus-player combat might be considered a Killer, while a player who enjoys completing a map of the gameworld might be considered an Explorer. The resulting personality types have since been applied to virtual worlds and have inspired several extensions and new models [12].

BrainHex [23] is a more recent model constructed from the analysis of previous gamer typologies as well as player data. It is more general because it was built independently of game genre. Therefore, we use the BrainHex typology to measure the participants' motivations towards games. The BrainHex model classifies player motivation in seven archetypes: Achiever (goal completion), Conqueror (challenge), Daredevil (excitement), Mastermind (strategy), Seeker (exploration), Socialiser (social relations), and Survivor (fear).

However, none of BrainHex's player archetypes specifically address the activity of *collecting* in digital games. In some situations, collecting may be motivated by achievement, in others, exploration. For some players, the digital game objects that they collect may be for socializing and displaying their objects to friends. To better understand potential motivations for collecting behaviors, we use the more general Ten Item Personality Inventory (TIPI) as a measure of player personality [9], which is based on the FFM. The brevity of the TIPI allows for an economically efficient and direct assessment of player personality without assuming motivation, and allows us to analyze collecting as an activity that is not necessarily restricted to the game world.

Collecting

People collect items in the physical world for a variety of reasons [33]. Digital items, and thus digital game objects, are no different. Based on an analysis of prior collection scholars investigating collecting behaviors of physical objects, Pearce offers the following to scope the term "collection":

> From this discussion we glean that ideas like non-utilitarian gathering, an internal or intrinsic relationship between the things gathered – whether objectively 'classified' or not – and the subjective view of the owner are all significant attributes of a collection, together with the

notion that a collection is more than the sum of its parts. At some point in the process the objects have to be deliberately viewed by their owner or potential owner as a collection, and this implies intentional selection, acquisition and disposal. It also means that some kind of specific value is set upon the group by its possessor, and with the recognition of value comes the giving of a part of self-identity. But collecting is too complex and too human an activity to be dealt with summarily by way of definitions. [27, p159]

Digital Collecting Behaviors

Beyond physical object collections, researchers have begun to explore the role of digital collections as well. Previous research has explored digital collections in the cloud [24], the differences between digital and physical collecting practices [25], and design implications for technologies that might support these collections. College students collect digital data for research, which creates large, problematic collections that are infrequently used [17]. Recently, Watkins et al. [36] investigated digital collection practices in a variety of contexts (including one gamer). An interesting finding is that digital collections are more *used* that physical ones; people rarely engage with physical collections. The data suggest that game players who collect digital game objects will use them when they involve game mechanics (a finding on which the present research builds).

State of Digital Game Object Collection Interfaces

Many games offer rudimentary forms of digital game object collections, which players use (or, rather, improvise with) to develop their collections. Game catalogs, through which players unlock content, are widely available, especially in games with a complex backstory. Many games allow players to store items in inventory interfaces, generally as a means of play. Further, some meta-game systems enable players to build up collections of rewards. The present state of such interfaces does not support players' needs, as our data indicate.

Many existing collection interfaces function as *catalogs*, where players monotonically unlock data over the course of play. The *Pokémon* [G13] series provides the player with a "Pokédex", which automatically captures data about all critters encountered in the game. In the *Katamari Damacy* [G16] series, the player can review various items that were picked up during play. The *Mass Effect* [G4] series (as well as many other role-playing games) provide a means of unlocking lore about the gameworld and story as the player progresses. These interfaces address *classes* of objects (e.g., general information on Pokémon encountered), but do not enable the player to curate a collection of object *instances* (e.g., specific Pokémon with names, levels, etc.).

A primary means through which players presently develop collections are inventory interfaces. Inventory interfaces enable players to store digital game objects for the purpose of gameplay (e.g., a character may carry multiple pieces of gear to equip at different times in the *Diablo* [G9] series or *World of Warcraft* [G6]). While these interfaces address the desire to maintain collections of specific instances of digital game objects, their primary purpose is gameplay; as such, many lack features that players may desire (e.g., the ability to display collections) or offer only basic support for organization. Recently, Blizzard announced a new interface in *World of Warcraft* that allows players to collect different armor styles to "transmogrify", or change the appearance of, their current armor [3]. Previously, players needed to carry items in their inventory, creating a high demand for storage space. Blizzard paired the announcement of this new interface with the comment: "It feels good to look good" insinuating that the company is aware of players' desires to collect and display their personal armor collections.

Many game communities support meta-game reward collection interfaces. Xbox Achievements, Steam Achievements, and Playstation Trophies are unlocked by accomplishing specific tasks in-game; these meta-game rewards are visible to other players and are unlocked monotonically. Steam goes further, with the Steam Inventory and Trading Cards, which provide a set of collectible meta-game items and functions to craft new items that can be displayed in the social components of the gaming community.

Through the present research, we argue for personalized collection interfaces, in which players can curate libraries of objects, providing their own microcosm of order and knowledge [8,29].

METHODS

The present paper reports on an online survey of digital game object collecting behaviors, with a focus on specific parts of the dataset. The research protocol was approved by the New Mexico State University IRB (#12994). We build on our prior work-in-progress paper [35], using an extended dataset with 189 responses (including the 155 used previously). While our prior paper focused on game genre, we now focus on the specific objects that players value.

Survey Instrument

To understand why players collect digital game objects and what they do with them, we developed an online survey (see Appendix for the complete instrument). The survey covered the following points:

1. demographic information;

2. players' collection behaviors;

3. the BrainHex Player Typology [23]; and

4. the Ten Item Personality Inventory [9].

The present analysis specifically looks at a subset of all responses, focusing on the following questions (which are labeled as below in the Appendix):

Q1. "What is your favorite object (or collection of objects)?" [Free-response.]

Q2. "What is the main reason that you value your favorite virtual object(s)?"
[Respondents were directed to select one of the Livingston et al. [20] reasons for character value as on Table 1.]

Q3. "In what games did you collect objects that you value?" [Free-response.]

Q4. "Out of the games above, which contains your favorite object or collection of objects?"
[Refers back to Q3; free-response.]

Q5. "Have you shared the object(s) with others?"
[Responses one of: "No.";
"Yes, by showing the object(s) to other people in my game on my device." (showing in-game);
"Yes, by using the object(s) in a game online with others." (using in-game);
"Yes, by publicly displaying the object(s) online." (publicly displaying)]

Q6. "Have you purchased digital objects in one or more games with real-world currencies?"
[Responses one of: "No."; "Yes."]

Q7. "Have you ever purchased a personalization feature with real-world currencies?"
[Responses one of: "No."; "Yes."]

Participation

We recruited participants via snowball sampling through social media and posting flyers on the New Mexico State University (Las Cruces, NM, USA); University of California, Irvine (Irvine, CA, USA); and University of Ontario Institute of Technology (Oshawa, ON, Canada) campuses. The call to action was specifically aimed at recruiting participants who had an interest in collecting digital game objects. We expected our sample to be biased towards players who are actively engaging in collection practice; unsurprisingly, all responses to the opening question of "Have you collected digital objects in one or more games?" were answered in the affirmative.

Our data set contained 189 responses after cleaning. We removed responses with an age over 99, all neutrally answered questions, and entries with identical qualitative responses, which eliminated 18 entries. When referencing specific qualitative data, we refer to participants by serial number, which was determined prior to cleaning (so some values exceed 189). The sample included 126 male, 53 female, and 6 non-binary/other respondents (4 preferred not to say). Respondents were 18–58 years old ($M = 29.6$; $SD = 7.5$; respondents were required to be 18 or older to participate). Highest education attained was 21.2%: high school, 41.8%: bachelor's degree, 21.2%: master's degree, and 14.3%: Ph.D. (1.6% declined to state). Responses were collected from March–September 2015. All responses were anonymous.

Qualitative Analysis and Coding Manual

Three of the researchers developed a coding manual to analyze players' favorite digital game objects (responses to Q1). Code creation followed traditional simultaneous and attribute coding methods [30] to categorize object types and provide descriptions. Constant comparison to the data by the three researchers resulted in several iterations of the coding manual.

Following the creation of a coding manual, two independent coders read and coded all responses to Q1 using answers from Q4 to provide context for inconclusive answers. All data was coded in a fully-crossed design [11]. Following completed coding, coders addressed any discrepancies. We calculated inter-rater reliability using Cohen's Kappa [5, 11, 30]. The kappa value was 0.995, which indicates nearly perfect agreement by commonly agreed definitions [5, 11].

Each object was assigned a main code that addressed the object's type and one or more modifier codes that addressed the object's features. Modifier codes, one or both of which could be applied with any main code, were emergent during coding. Table 2 describes each of the codes in detail.

Quantitative Analysis

To investigate what factors could influence players behavior towards collecting digital game objects, we conducted an exploratory data analysis aimed at identifying possible associations between the independent variables and different indicators of player behavior. The independent variables that we considered were: age, gender, education level, BrainHex primary class (derived using the BrainHex methodology from the appropriate questions), and the five factors of personality (derived from the TIPI). The different indicators of player behavior towards digital game objects collections that were considered include: main reason for object value (Q2), type of object (Q1, coded using the coding manual), rarity of object (Q1, coded using the coding manual), purchase of digital game objects (Q6), purchase of digital personalization options (Q7), and digital game objects sharing (Q5).

The association between age with the dependent variables was calculated using one-way analysis of variance (ANOVA) tests and by calculating Eta-squared (η^2) as the effect size. However, the Kolmogorov-Smirnov test showed that the age variable is significantly not normal in our data: $D(189) = 0.86$, $p < .01$. For this reason, we also executed Kruskal-Wallis and Mann-Whitney tests as appropriate, but these non-parametric tests confirmed the significance calculated from the ANOVA tests. Thus, we conclude that the lack of normality was not enough to invalidate the ANOVA tests and in the results section we only report the ANOVA tests. The associations between each trait of the FFM with each of the dependent variables were also calculated using one-way ANOVA tests and by calculating Eta-squared. For all significant results, we also use the method suggested by Smithson [32] to calculate and report the 90% confidence interval for Eta-squared.

The association between gender, education level, and Brain-Hex class with the dependent variables was calculated using methods for categorical data. We could not use Person's Chi-square because our sample violated the test assumptions: the expected values tables frequently contained values less than one. For this reason, we employed Fisher's exact test instead. We calculated Cramer's V as the effect size. All tests were run in SPSS 23 [13] using a Monte Carlo method with a confidence level of 99% and 10,000 samples. We also report the 99% confidence intervals for p.

RESULTS

We present the analyzed results of our survey, covering the types of favored digital game objects, the reasons players valued objects, and insight into the factors of influence on player behavior. The results synthesize the quantitative data

Code	Description
CHARACTER	Party members, playable characters, or townsfolk.
CRITTER	Animal-based mounts and pets (combative or not).
GEAR	Items that can be equipped on a character.
INFORMATION	Text- or image-based items that represent in-game information.
SKIN	Items that modify the appearance of a character, but not its statistics.
VEHICLE	Technology-based modes of transportation.
MISCELLANEOUS	All other items, including achievements and other meta-game rewards. No more meaningful sub-codes were discovered through the data.
RARE*	An item that is hard to acquire or of which there are few in a game.
COLLECTIBLE*	Items of which there are a set number (either player- or game-defined).

Table 2. Coding manual developed for analyzing players' favorite digital game object and classifying by type. Un-starred codes are main codes. Modifier codes, those that are always applied in combination with a main code, are starred.

and qualitative data from the free-response questions, which we develop into themes.

Types of Favored Digital Game Objects

We analyzed which types of digital game objects appeared most frequently in players' responses to Q1, according to our coding manual. The data indicate that GEAR was the most frequently collected object type, accounting for 34.4% of the responses. The next two types in order of prevalence were CRITTERS (21.2%) and MISCELLANEOUS objects (20.6%). While the number of MISCELLANEOUS objects may seem high, these objects could not be broken down into other meaningful categories. They included object types unique to a specific game, meta-game objects, or sets of finite collectible objects. The other object types appeared less frequently: CHARACTERS (7.4%), SKINS (7.4%), VEHICLES (4.2%), and INFORMATION (2.1%) (2.6% of participants did not answer this question).

Of all participants' favorite objects, 75.6% had no modifier code, 15.9% were COLLECTIBLE, and 8.5% were RARE. COLLECTIBLE objects were valued because they completed a set of in-game objects according to a schema defined by the game developer. One participant said that they enjoyed collecting *"Pets, all of them :)"* [P106; referencing *World of Warcraft* [G6]]. Though generally not functionally useful, pets and other non-combative CRITTERS add flair to characters that differentiates them from others in the gameworld.

The COLLECTIBLE distinction was especially relevant to sets of GEAR. P174 reported that his most valued objects were *"A matching set of 'gray' rarity armor."* "Gray rarity" means that the item is neither good, nor uncommon, and is generally considered useless. However, this player reveled in the hunting and collecting of this armor set:

The armor pieces themselves are worthless[...] I enjoyed completing the set piece by piece[...] it added extra fun to get excited about [gear] I had previously considered worthless. [...] The reason I had selected this armor set[...] is because I thought it aesthetically matched another activity I enjoyed doing in *World of Warcraft* [G6]- exploring, and breaking the game's world boundaries[...] I wore [the set] while exploring, adding further value due to the memories I accrued.

RARE objects were valued because they were difficult to obtain. One participant valued *"Ultimate weapons acquired from defeating optional bosses and completing side-quests"* [P8, regarding the *Final Fantasy* series [G18]]. Collecting these objects required optional play beyond what is expected of the average player.

Other players valued RARE objects for their uniqueness. One participant described her *"druid deck, gold collected"* [P23, regarding *Hearthstone* [G8]]. "Gold" cards function similar to holographic cards in traditional trading card games. Though they offer *no difference* in game mechanics or game play, they are harder to obtain, and signal to others that the player was willing to dedicate time (or money) to acquiring rarer cards.

Reasons for Object Value

We looked at players' responses to Q2 to understand why players value their digital game objects. UTILITY (26.5%) and ENJOYMENT (23.8%) appeared most frequently in responses. INVESTMENT (12.7%), MEMORY (10.1%), and SELF-EXPRESSION (7.9%) accounted for smaller portions of the sample. All other reasons appeared in less than 5% of responses.

Beyond explicitly stating how they valued objects, participants also noted the importance of UTILITY and ENJOYMENT in their qualitative responses:

> I really enjoy collectibles that have an interesting and desirable design. I do not enjoy collectibles that have no inherent use or purpose. [P170; UTILITY]

> I like collecting objects that give the user an in-game advantage. [P190; ENJOYMENT]

Not only does the data point to digital game objects being valued for their influence on game mechanics, players also value the social elements of collecting. Based on responses to Q5, sharing digital game objects was an important practice for a majority of our participants. When asked if they had shared a digital game object with other players at least once, 65.1% responded in the affirmative. Of those that shared an object, the way it was shared was: showing in-game (23.8%), using in-game (27.0%), or publicly displayed (14.3%). This is evident through the behaviors exhibited by players who share their digital game objects through a variety of mechanisms. This suggests that some objects' primary value is a combination of SELF-EXPRESSION, SOCIALITY, RELATION-SHIPS, and/or CREATIVITY. We suggest further research on these "vanity items" that serve no practical game function, but provide aesthetic value.

DV	Age (η^2)
object value (Q2)	**.107**[**]
object type (Q1, coded)	.023
object rarity (Q1, coded)	.003
object sharing (Q5)	**.049**[*]
purchased object (Q6)	.005
purchased personalization (Q7)	**.026**[*]

* $p < .05.$ ** $p < .01.$

Table 3. Effect values and significance of age in association with different player behaviors towards digital game objects.

Object Value (Q2)	N	Mean Age	SD
UTILITY	50	31.60	7.117
ENJOYMENT	45	28.27	6.340
INVESTMENT	24	26.71	5.645
MEMORY	19	26.16	6.635
SELF-EXPRESSION	15	29.40	8.210
CREATIVITY	8	30.13	5.489
NEW EXPERIENCE	6	29.00	2.530
RELATIONSHIPS	6	35.67	11.325
total	173	29.25	7.036

Object Sharing (Q5)	N	Mean Age	SD
"No."	66	31.55	7.521
showing in-game	45	27.91	7.876
using in-game	51	28.06	5.944
publicly displaying	27	30.30	8.241
total	189	29.56	7.456

Purch. Personalization (Q7)	N	Mean Age	SD
"No."	118	30.48	7.420
"Yes."	71	28.03	7.311
total	189	29.56	7.456

Table 4. Mean values and standard deviation of age for each group of object value, object sharing, and purchased personalization.

Factors of Influence on Player Behavior

Table 3 shows the calculated effects and significance of age in association with different player behaviors towards digital game objects. Age was found to have the following significant effects:

1. a moderate effect on the main reason for collecting digital game objects: $\eta^2 = .107$, $F(7, 165) = 2.822$, $p < .01$ (90% CI $= .016 < \eta^2 < .150$);

2. a small effect on how the participants shared their objects with others: $\eta^2 = .049$, $F(3, 185) = 3.177$, $p < .05$ (90% CI $= .003 < \eta^2 < .096$); and

3. a small effect on the participants having ever purchased personalization options for their objects: $\eta^2 = .026$, $F(1, 187) = 4.906$, $p < .05$ (90% CI $= .001 < \eta^2 < .073$).

Table 4 shows the mean values and standard deviation of age for each group of the dependent variables that were significantly affected by it: object value (Q2), object sharing (Q5), and purchased personalization (Q7). The reasons for object

DV	Gender (V)	Education Level (V)	BrainHex Class (V)
object value (Q2)	.270	.210	.258
object type (Q1, coded)	.267	.183	.228
object rarity (Q1, coded)	.153	.136	**.247** *
object sharing (Q5)	.109	.166	**.230** *
purchased object (Q6)	.099	.115	.111
purchased personalization (Q7)	.039	.093	.188

* $p < .05$.

Table 5. Effect values and significance of gender, education level, and BrainHex class in association with different player behaviors towards digital game objects.

BrainHex Class	(no modifier)	COLLECTIBLE	RARE
Achiever	1.08	0.88	0.55
Conqueror	0.91	0.85	**2.00** *
Daredevil	1.32	0.00	0.00
Mastermind	**0.92** ***	**1.31** **	1.13
Seeker	**1.18** ***	**0.34** ***	0.65
Socialiser	**0.67** *	**3.12** ***	0.00
Survivor	0.67	2.00	2.00

Note. Each cell's value represents how many times that particular combination is more probable (if value > 1.0) or less probable (if value < 1.0) to occur in our sample than it would occur on an independent distribution.

* $p < .05$.   ** $p < .01$.   *** $p < .001$.

Table 6. Standardized probabilities of occurrence of each pair of BrainHex type and object rarity (Q1, coded) in comparison with an independent distribution.

BrainHex Class	"No"	using in-game	showing in-game	publicly displaying
Achiever	**0.55** ***	**1.58** ***	1.02	1.00
Conqueror	1.09	0.89	0.88	1.19
Daredevil	0.59	0.71	1.67	1.43
Mastermind	**0.88** **	1.01	**1.51** ***	**0.44** ***
Seeker	**1.44** ***	**0.61** ***	**0.55** ***	**1.41** **
Socialiser	**0.28** **	**1.85** *	0.42	3.14
Survivor	0.95	1.87	0.71	0.00

Note. Each cell's value represents how many times that particular combination is more probable (if value > 1.0) or less probable (if value < 1.0) to occur in our sample than it would occur on an independent distribution.

* $p < .05$.   ** $p < .01$.   *** $p < .001$.

Table 7. Standardized probabilities of occurrence of each pair of BrainHex type and object sharing (Q5) in comparison with an independent distribution.

value that appealed to the youngest players were MEMORY and INVESTMENT, whereas those which appealed to the oldest players were UTILITY and RELATIONSHIPS. Regarding object sharing, the oldest players reported never having shared their game object(s) or having displayed them publicly, while younger players have reported showing their object(s) to others in their game or device and using the object(s) in-game with others. Although the effect is small, this could be a result of younger players being more familiar with online game playing and mobile devices. Regarding purchase of personalization features for their digital game object(s) with real currency, younger players have more frequently reported having done so than older players. This was also a small effect, but it could suggest that younger players are more open to spend real currency on their games than the older players.

Table 5 shows the calculated effects and significance of gender, education level, and BrainHex class in association with different player behaviors towards digital game objects. The Fisher's exact tests showed no significant effect of gender and education level on the dependent variables. For BrainHex class, the tests showed the following significant effects:

1. a moderate effect for players valuing RARE collected digital game objects, Cramer's $V = .247$, $p < .05$ (99% CI $= .024 < p < .032$) (Fisher's exact test). Further analysis (see Table 6) revealed that Seekers are more inclined to collect no-modifier objects, whereas Masterminds and Socialisers are more inclined to collect COLLECTIBLE objects and Conquerors are more inclined to collect RARE objects.

2. a moderate effect on how the participants shared their objects with others, Cramer's $V = .230$, $p < .05$ (99% CI $= .015 < p < .022$) (Fisher's exact test). Further analysis (see Table 7) revealed that the classes more inclined to share their objects are Achievers (by using the objects in-game), Masterminds (by showing the objects in-game), and Socialisers (by using the objects in-game and possibly by also publicly displaying the objects, although the latter was not found to be significant in our data due to the sample size). Seekers appear to be less inclined to share their objects, unless it is by publicly displaying them on-line.

We also tested for the effects of each of the five traits of personality from the TIPI scale, namely extraversion, agreeableness, conscientiousness, emotional stability, and openness to experience, in each of the dependent variables. All the ANOVA tests showed non-significant results. Therefore, we conclude that personality traits had no effect on the participants' behaviors towards collecting digital game objects.

Themes

We connect our data points to a set of themes in the data: mechanics drive value, digital game objects represent investment, social presentation is important, and collections are esoteric and guide play.

Mechanics Drive Value

Many participants attributed collection value to how objects enabled interesting decision-making or affected game mechanics. Favorite objects were categorized as either GEAR, CHARACTER, or VEHICLES in 46.0% of responses; all such objects change how the game is played, supplying rules in the form of statistics or enabling new game mechanics. While not included in this total, many elements identified as MISCELLANEOUS *may* impact gameplay (e.g., specific buildings in simulations or location-based objects in *Ingress* [G17], both observed in our data). Further, some CRITTERS, excluded from this set, may modify game state.

When players reported their primary reason for valuing objects, UTILITY and ENJOYMENT were most frequently cited. This data, again, points to the importance of game mechanics for collected objects, suggesting that players want to make use of their objects in game, not just look at them or otherwise have the objects in their possession.

We argue that there are two main groups of players:

1. those that value their objects for their functionality and purpose, and

2. those that value their objects primarily because they bring them pleasure.

This suggestion aligns with Watkins et al.'s [36] finding that game players made more use of digital collections than other respondents.

Digital Game Objects Represent Investment
The INVESTMENT and MEMORY values accounted for 22.8% of our participants' reasons for valuing digital game objects. We expect that players' time in-game is important to them, and digital game objects serve to encapsulate these experiences.

Social Presentation is Important
Digital game objects are easily shared, and many are "shown" automatically when players go online. We observed that many participants reported having shared their digital game objects with others (65.1% did so at least once). At the same time, mechanic-oriented values were the most important; the more socially-oriented values, COMMUNICATION, RELATIONSHIPS, SOCIABILITY, and SELF-EXPRESSION, were less prevalent in the data. Our quantitative analysis also showed that participants employed different means for sharing their game objects and that this fact may have been influenced by different factors such as the player's age and style of play.

Collections are Esoteric and Guide Play
Many games offer a schema for collectible objects, such as a theme or a set of items that go together. These schemas relate to the rules of the game. However, based on our data, what players chose to collect were varied, often breaking from the originally specified schemas. A total of 10 participants reported collecting parts of specific equipment sets (GEAR). An additional three reported collecting a specific class of CRITTERS. Some collections were more esoteric; for example, P126 reported:

> I collect Teddy Bears in the *Fallout* [G2] games. The developers have put a good amount of work creating a world that feels like it was actually devastated by atomic war. I collect the bears as a kind of tribute to the massacred innocents.

P182 reported on his collection activities in *Skyrim* [G3], which functioned as a personal quest to collect unique objects:

> [...]I tracked down every item in [*Skyrim*] that could be considered unique [...]Among these was a particular[...] skull. [...]There's nothing really special about this [...]skull; it doesn't have any story significance and [...] doesn't have any utility. [...] it does have a different texture [...] more importantly there's only one of them.

Based on the data collected, we hypothesize that developing personalized schemas for collecting digital game objects provides players with the emergent ability to set their own goals.

While a game may specify a set of collection-oriented ancillary goals, such as *"Legendary Cards (Ragnaros, Leroy Jenkins, etc.)"* [P82, regarding *Hearthstone* [G8]], players may specify their own, achievable goals, for which the game provides no mechanical support (e.g., *"...all the Elemental Dragons"* [P87, regarding *DragonVale* [G1]]). Such digital game objects may or may not be COLLECTIBLE (because they are outside the game's provided schemas) and may or may not be RARE (because players may set achievable goals). Digital game objects may offer additional meaning by acting as markers of player-specified goals.

DISCUSSION
In the present paper, we investigated the collection behaviors of players. We captured information on the particular digital game objects collected and social interactions around collected objects, and developed a coding manual to categorize specific, favored objects. We also explored the value players' assigned to those objects. We found that digital game objects that influence game mechanics or provide social interest were the most commonly collected digital game objects. We provide design implications for digital game object collection interfaces, to enable them to support important player values. We recommend designing interfaces that enable curation, preserve game rules and mechanics, preserve context of play, and enable sharing. We also provide evidence that collecting is influenced by both age and BrainHex class.

Designing Digital Game Object Collection Interfaces
> [...] a game should provide a cohesive method "In Game" for identifying / locating / and organizing whatever collectibles [...] the game contains. [P106]

Digital game object collection interfaces that synthesize, sort, filter, and otherwise support interaction with collected objects would be valuable to players. Further, these interfaces should retain the informational aspects of collected objects even after a specific instance of the item has been sold, expended, or lost. Prior interfaces support players in unlocking information and gathering digital game objects for use in play, yet we observe that players develop attachment to specific instances of objects, with their own in-game statistics and even names (e.g., players' Pokémon teams: *"My current level 100 battling team"* [P74], *"My main team of Pokémon"* [P160], *"My original level 100 team from middle school"* [P178]).

Our data insinuate a set of design implications that collection interfaces could use to support games, rather than other types of archives. We expect that in a basic form, like prior collection interfaces, game collection interfaces could support INVEST-MENT, MEMORY, and CREATIVITY values. By following the proposed design implications, they could also support COMMUNICATION, SOCIABILITY, UTILITY, ENJOYMENT, and SELF-EXPRESSION, which align with how mechanics drive value and supporting the importance of social presentation.

Enable Curation

Curation is a form of authoring and creation [17] through which the author makes meaningful decisions about what elements should be acquired, displayed, and combined. It deriving from the artistic tradition of found objects, in which the act of selection is the key artistic contribution [19]. Curation serves to support the SELF-EXPRESSION and CREATIVITY values. Our data suggest collecting, in many cases, is driven by personal interest and experiences with certain objects. The first step to building a successful collection interface is the ability to curate and customize the contents within, an activity that we observe players are already undertaking informally.

The esoteric and personal nature of players' collections supports our assertion that game interfaces should be robust enough to allow players to select what objects they curate and display to others, rather than limiting what objects players are able to display. The fact that social presentation is important suggests that players desire the ability to show others what they have acquired and curated. Doing so would enable such interfaces to support the COMMUNICATION and SOCIABILITY values.

Enabling curation is likely a challenge for game designers. Curation interfaces to select items serve a meta-game purpose. This places them at odds with a gameworld's functioning as an interface to the game [14] (and not meta-game functions). Developing curation interfaces requires a means by which players can tag or otherwise access their digital game objects. The scope of such interfaces is also open: our data suggest that, since players potentially collect *anything*, such systems must be robust. Application program interfaces, like those available in *World of Warcraft* [G6] or *Destiny* [G10] enable external programmers to access those games' digital game objects and serve as exemplars of design approaches that enable the development of curation tools.

Preserve Game Rules and Mechanics

Because mechanics drive the UTILITY and ENJOYMENT values, they need to be meaningfully preserved. Players keep items because they like to use them, which we expect in digital collections [36]. We argue in favor of preserving the game rules and mechanics that players find so important, enabling players to relive and/or recreate in-game experiences and decisions.

We identify three potential implementation approaches to preserve game rules and mechanics: captured video, produced video, and simulation. The proposed methods are primarily in service to UTILITY and ENJOYMENT, but, to a lesser degree, they also support MEMORY and INVESTMENT.

Captured Video: Mechanics could be preserved by capturing video of object use. The digital game could automate this: capturing instances of use that, according to metrics defined

by the designers, are exceptional and, thus, likely to be worthy of preservation (e.g., using a favored sword to defeat 100 foes). Contemporary consoles do this for the purpose of sharing (social presentation)[1] when a player performs an exceptional act or reaches certain milestones. Captured video recordings could also be triggered manually, which is the nascent state of the ability to record and share video from modern game consoles. Voice interfaces, like on Xbox One with Kinect, are ideal for this, which enable the player to capture video clips without interrupting play.

Captured video serves to preserve exact instances of play that a player has actually experienced. It provides the player with little flexibility for experimentation, however, and, depending on camera-control algorithms, the resulting video may not highlight the digital game object well (e.g., the player's avatar might obscure a favored sword by being in front of the gameworld camera).

Produced Video: Video can also be produced in-engine, rather than captured, showing a digital game object in some predetermined context that highlights its important aspects. This offers the opportunity to record what makes the digital game object important, in terms of game mechanics, but may lack the personal experience a player desires.

An illustrative example of this is the tech-tree interface of the single-player campaign in *Starcraft 2* [G7]. While not a collection interface, a player is shown a video of each potential upgrade in a particular context that highlights its value, showing the difference it will make in gameplay.

Simulation: An alternative to video records is simulation, where a player can, through the collection interface, see multiple scenarios using a collected object. A deeper interface might even enable interactive simulation, where the player can play out (or even replay) various scenarios with one or more digital game objects, observing differences in gameplay. While simulation enables deeper interaction with objects, it has the downside of failing to capture specific contexts of use (see next section).

Preserve Context of Play

Since digital game objects represent investment by players, retaining contextual information about how or when the player collected or played with the object would be beneficial. Capturing context could be challenging, since curation likely happens after an item has been acquired or used. The need to curate the item may come much later in the game, after long-term play.

While there are many elements of context that could be automatically generated, players may also wish to attach custom, personal meaning to curated objects. This suggests the need for interfaces to customize metadata about digital game objects.

Some existing games provide the opportunity for players to add meaning to their in-game objects. For example, *Dota*

---

[1] Microsoft's Xbox One automatically records clips of exceptional gameplay, but there is no documentation of this feature. Both the Xbox One and Sony's Playstation 4 enable players to easily record and share gameplay clips.

2 [G19] provides Name Tags, tools that allow players to give their objects a customized names, and Description Tags, tools that let players write a brief description of an item. In the case of the Pokémon [G13] series, each individual CRITTER includes context details: the name of the original trainer (in case the CRITTER was traded), location in the gameworld the CRITTER was caught, ribbons acquired as rewards for gameworld contests, etc. [4].

Enable Sharing

Due to the importance of social presentation, our data imply an interest in sharing digital game object collections with others, which is an activity commonly performed by curators of other collections, digital or otherwise [8, 17, 20, 21, 28]. Enabling sharing of curated collections supports the values of COMMUNICATION and SOCIALITY.

Being digital and networked, games offer easy means to do this. Indeed, much of the infrastructure to share game moments already exists in current platforms. However, our data suggest that players might have different preferences regarding collection sharing, which can be affected by their age and personality. Future work aimed at understanding these differences could contribute to suggest more personalized options for digital game objects sharing, which could potentially appeal to a broader range of different players.

Points of Caution and Limitations

While we generally argue in favor of preserving digital game objects, doing so could have negative consequences for current collecting practices. If mechanics are preserved beyond when players have an object in their possession, this may undermine the game's mechanics overall, which could reduce the perceived INVESTMENT and UTILITY of collected digital game objects. In games where players have a limited inventory and expressly balance inventory management to preserve objects, enabling players to capture and preserve the mechanics in an archive could reduce ENJOYMENT. At the same time, the opposite may be true: players may find relief in no longer needing to manage inventory.

Another key point of caution: we expect that part of the reason that collections are meaningful are because they represent achievement in a game. This notion is backed by the observation that digital game objects represent investment; while there were not a great number of RARE items, their presence also suggests that there is importance in the challenge of acquiring certain digital game objects. A concern, then, is that poorly designed collection interfaces may enable players to collect items that they have not *earned* (undermining INVESTMENT).

Quantitative data analysis suggested that players' behaviors towards collecting digital game objects may be influenced by their age and preferred style of interacting with games, as denoted by their BrainHex class. However, there a few limitations that need to be considered. First, our analysis was mainly exploratory. In addition, all answers were self-reported and without any specific experience in mind, so they may be imprecise. Finally, some of the observed significant effects were small. For these reasons, these results must only be considered as indicators of possible effects worth investigating

in the future. However, our work provides interesting clues to direct future research.

Finally, the present research reports on data from a survey of gamers who collect digital game objects. All advertisement specifically targeted gamers who have a predisposition toward collecting. Thus, while we provide insights into collection behavior, our survey tells us little about how prevalent collecting behaviors are in digital games.

Future Work

Further research is needed to identify and reduce any deleterious effects of collection interfaces, as well as confirm their potential worth to players. Future work will continue to explore the digital game objects that players collect and identify their worth. In particular, we intend to conduct focused user studies to investigate in more detail the possible effects of player age and play style in collecting behaviors that were suggested by our quantitative analysis. We also aim to understand the prevalence of collecting behaviors.

CONCLUSION

In this paper, we provide a strong argument for the advantages of digital game object collection interfaces, and how these interfaces can foster meaning-making within games. These benefits could enhance players' value attributions for collections of game objects, and contribute to the overall play experience.

Our study shows that players are interested in collecting digital game objects with mechanics, not just meta-game rewards (which function much like catalogs of a player's successes). Ideally we would see collection interfaces rise to a meta-game level, similar to the way that meta-game rewards (e.g., Xbox Achievements, Playstation Trophies) are organized intra-platform. We would, overall, argue for a unified system to accumulate player-curated collections across games. As a starting point, we recommend that individual games support collections in way that are meaningful to players in accordance with the design implications of enabling curation, preserving rules and mechanics, preserving context of play, and enabling sharing.

We expect digital game object collection interfaces to be of benefit to individuals designing games, gamified applications, and educational software. We expect such interfaces to deepen player investment and engagement, providing a means for players to make explicit behaviors they presently undertake without support.

ACKNOWLEDGMENTS

Special thanks to Daniel Johnson, Igor Dolgov, William A. Hamilton, and Mark Toups for sharing their digital game objects for illustration purposes. Author Toups wishes to thank NMSU for its financial support of his work. Author Wehbe would like to thank the Cheriton School of Computer Science, University of Waterloo, and NSERC for funding her research. Author Tondello would like to thank the University of Waterloo and the CNPq, Brazil, for funding his research. We would like to thank NSERC (RGPIN-418622-2012) and SSHRC (895-2011-1014, IMMERSe) for funding author Nacke's research team.

REFERENCES

1. Richard Bartle. 1996. Hearts, Clubs, Diamonds, Spades: Players who suit MUDs. *Journal of MUD Research* 1, 1 (1996), 19.

2. Russell W. Belk, Melanie Wallendorf, John F. Sherry, Jr., and Morris B. Holbrook. 1991. Collecting in a Consumer Culture. *Highways and Buyways: Naturalistic Research from the Consumer Behavior Odyssey* SV-06 (1991), 178–215.

3. Blizzard Entertainment. 2016. Preview: Wardrobe Updates. (15 July 2016). `https://worldofwarcraft.com/en-us/news/20183993/preview-wardrobe-updates`.

4. Bulbapedia community. 2014. Pokémon data structure in Generation IV. (January 2014). `http://bulbapedia.bulbagarden.net/w/index.php?title=Pok%C3%A9mon_data_structure_in_Generation_IV&oldid=2049032`.

5. Jacob Cohen. 1960. A Coefficient of Agreement for Nominal Scales. *Educational and Psychological Measurement* 20, 1 (1960), 37–46. DOI: `http://dx.doi.org/10.1177/001316446002000104`

6. Paul T. Costa and Robert R. McCrae. 1992. Four ways five factors are basic. *Personality and Individual Differences* 13, 6 (1992), 653–665. DOI: `http://dx.doi.org/10.1016/0191-8869(92)90236-I`

7. Paul T. Costa and Robert R. McCrae. 2008. The revised NEO personality inventory (NEO-PI-R). In *The SAGE Handbook of Personality Theory and Assessment*, G J Boyle, G Matthews, and D Saklofske (Eds.). Vol. 2. SAGE London, 179–198.

8. Brenda Danet and Tamar Katriel. 1994. No two alike: Play and aesthetics in collecting. In *Interpreting Objects and Collections* (1st ed.), Susan M. Pearce (Ed.). Routledge, Chapter 28, 220–239.

9. Samuel D. Gosling, Peter J. Rentfrow, and William B. Swann. 2003. A very brief measure of the Big-Five personality domains. *Journal of Research in Personality* 37 (2003), 504–528.

10. Yue Guo and Stuart Barnes. 2007. Why People Buy Virtual Items in Virtual Worlds with Real Money. *SIGMIS Database* 38, 4 (Oct. 2007), 69–76. DOI: `http://dx.doi.org/10.1145/1314234.1314247`

11. Kevin A. Hallgren. 2012. Computing Inter-Rater Reliability for Observational Data: An Overview and Tutorial. *Tutor Quant Methods Psychol* 8, 1 (2012), 23–34.

12. Juho Hamari and Janne Tuunanen. 2014. Player types: A meta-synthesis. *Transactions of the Digital Games Research Association* 1, 2 (2014), 29–53.

13. IBM Corp. 2015. IBM SPSS Statistics for Windows, Version 23.0. Software [Windows]. (2015). IBM Corp., Armonk, New York, USA.

14. Kristine Jørgensen. 2013. *Gameworld Interfaces*. MIT Press, Cambridge, MA, USA.

15. Jesper Juul. 2005. *Half Real: Video Games between Real Rules and Fictional Worlds*. MIT Press, Cambridge, MA, USA.

16. Suzanne Keene. 1998. *Digital Collections, Museums and the Information Age*. Routledge.

17. Eunyee Koh and Andruid Kerne. 2006. "I Keep Collecting": College Students Build and Utilize Collections in Spite of Breakdowns. In *Proceedings of the 10th European Conference on Research and Advanced Technology for Digital Libraries (ECDL'06)*. Springer-Verlag, Berlin, Heidelberg, 303–314. DOI: `http://dx.doi.org/10.1007/11863878_26`

18. Tomi Kujanpää, Tony Manninen, and Laura Vallius. 2007. What's My Game Character Worth - The Value Components of MMOG Characters. In *DiGRA '07 - Proceedings of the 2007 DiGRA International Conference: Situated Play*. The University of Tokyo, Tokyo, Japan.

19. Lucy R. Lippard. 1971. Marcel Duchamp. In *Dadas on Art: Tzara, Arp, Duchamp, and Others*, Lucy R. Lippard (Ed.). Dover Publications, Inc., 139–154.

20. Ian J. Livingston, Carl Gutwin, Regan L. Mandryk, and Max Birk. 2014. How Players Value Their Characters in World of Warcraft. In *Proceedings of the 17th ACM Conference on Computer Supported Cooperative Work & Social Computing (CSCW '14)*. ACM, New York, NY, USA, 1333–1343. DOI: `http://dx.doi.org/10.1145/2531602.2531661`

21. Tony Manninen and Tomi Kujanpää. 2007. The Value of Virtual Assets - The Role of Game Characters in MMOGs. *International Journal of Business Science and Applied Management* 2 (2007), 21–33. Issue 1.

22. Mark B. McKinley. 2007. The Psychology of Collecting. *The National Psychologist* (2007).

23. Lennart E. Nacke, Chris Bateman, and Regan L. Mandryk. 2014. BrainHex: A neurobiological gamer typology survey. *Entertainment Computing* 5, 1 (2014), 55 – 62. DOI: `http://dx.doi.org/10.1016/j.entcom.2013.06.002`

24. William Odom, Abigail Sellen, Richard Harper, and Eno Thereska. 2012. Lost in Translation: Understanding the Possession of Digital Things in the Cloud. In *Proceedings of the SIGCHI Conference on Human Factors in Computing Systems (CHI '12)*. ACM, New York, NY, USA, 781–790. DOI: `http://dx.doi.org/10.1145/2207676.2207789`

25. William Odom, John Zimmerman, and Jodi Forlizzi. 2011. Teenagers and Their Virtual Possessions: Design Opportunities and Issues. In *Proceedings of the SIGCHI Conference on Human Factors in Computing Systems (CHI '11)*. ACM, New York, NY, USA, 1491–1500. DOI: `http://dx.doi.org/10.1145/1978942.1979161`

26. Susan M. Pearce. 1994a. Collecting Reconsidered. In *Interpreting Objects and Collections* (1st ed.), Susan M. Pearce (Ed.). Routledge, Chapter 26, 193–204.

27. Susan M. Pearce. 1994b. The Urge to Collect. In *Interpreting Objects and Collections* (1st ed.), Susan M. Pearce (Ed.). Routledge, Chapter 22, 157–159.

28. Kerry Rodden and Kenneth R. Wood. 2003. How Do People Manage Their Digital Photographs?. In *Proceedings of the SIGCHI Conference on Human Factors in Computing Systems (CHI '03)*. ACM, New York, NY, USA, 409–416. DOI: http://dx.doi.org/10.1145/642611.642682

29. Joseph Rykwert. 2001. Why Collect? *History Today* 51, 12 (December 2001).

30. Johnny Saldaña. 2012. *The Coding Manual for Qualitative Researchers* (2nd ed.). SAGE Publications Ltd.

31. Katie Salen and Eric Zimmerman. 2004. *Rules of Play: Game Design Fundamentals*. MIT Press, Cambridge, MA, USA.

32. Michael Smithson. 2002. *Confidence Intervals*. Quantitative Applications in the Social Sciences, Vol. 140. SAGE Publications, Inc.

33. Stephen Snow, Bronte McMahon, Sally McKenzie, Kenneth Radke, Ivy Verlaat, and Laurie Buys. 2015. Designing for Collections: Building Histories, Sharing the Spectacle. In *Proceedings of the Annual Meeting of the Australian Special Interest Group for Computer Human Interaction (OzCHI '15)*. ACM, New York, NY, USA, 299–303. DOI: http://dx.doi.org/10.1145/2838739.2838798

34. G. Thomas Tanselle. 1998. A Rationale of Collecting. *Studies in Bibliography* 51 (1998), 1–25.

35. Gustavo F. Tondello, Rina R. Wehbe, Zachary O. Toups, Lennart E. Nacke, and Nicole K. Crenshaw. 2015. Understanding Player Attitudes Towards Digital Game Objects. In *Proceedings of the 2015 Annual Symposium on Computer-Human Interaction in Play (CHI PLAY '15)*. ACM, New York, NY, USA, 709–714. DOI: http://dx.doi.org/10.1145/2793107.2810292

36. Rebecca D. Watkins, Abigail Sellen, and Siân E. Lindley. 2015. Digital Collections and Digital Collecting Practices. In *Proceedings of the 33rd Annual ACM Conference on Human Factors in Computing Systems (CHI '15)*. ACM, New York, NY, USA, 3423–3432. DOI: http://dx.doi.org/10.1145/2702123.2702380

37. Diane Watson, Deltcho Valtchanov, Mark Hancock, and Regan Mandryk. 2014. Designing a Gameful System to Support the Collection, Curation, Exploration, and Sharing of Sports Memorabilia. In *Proceedings of the First ACM SIGCHI Annual Symposium on Computer-human Interaction in Play (CHI PLAY '14)*. ACM, New York, NY, USA, 451–452. DOI: http://dx.doi.org/10.1145/2658537.2661322

38. Nick Yee. 2006. Motivations for play in online games. *Cyberpsychol Behav* 9, 6 (Dec 2006), 772–775.

LUDOGRAPHY

1. Backflip Studios. 2011. *DragonVale*. Game [iOS]. (14 September 2011). Backflip Studios, Boulder, Colorado, USA.

2. Bethesda Game Studios. 2008. *Fallout 3*. Game [Xbox 360]. (28 October 2008). Bethesda Softworks, Rockville, Maryland, USA.

3. Bethesda Game Studios. 2011. *The Elder Scrolls V: Skyrim*. Game [Xbox 360]. (11 November 2011). Bethesda Softworks, Rockville, Maryland, USA.

4. BioWare. 2007. *Mass Effect*. Game [Xbox 360]. (20 November 2007). Microsoft Game Studios, Redmond, Washington, USA.

5. BioWare. 2014. *Dragon Age: Inquisition*. Game [Windows]. (18 November 2014). Electronic Arts, Redwood City, California, USA.

6. Blizzard Entertainment. 2004. *World of Warcraft*. Game [OSX]. (23 November 2004). Blizzard Entertainment, Irvine, California, USA.

7. Blizzard Entertainment. 2010. *StarCraft II: Wings of Liberty*. Game [Windows]. (27 July 2010). Blizzard Entertainment, Irvine, California, USA.

8. Blizzard Entertainment. 2014. *Hearthstone: Heroes of Warcraft*. Game [Windows]. (11 March 2014). Blizzard Entertainment, Irvine, California, USA.

9. Blizzard North. 1996. *Diablo*. Game [PC]. (31 December 1996). Blizzard Entertainment, Irvine, California, USA. Last played April 2003.

10. Bungie and High Moon Studios. 2014. *Destiny*. Game [PS4]. (9 September 2014). Activision, Santa Monica, California, USA.

11. Criterion Games. 2008. *Burnout Paradise*. Game [Xbox 360]. (22 January 2008). Electronic Arts, Redwood City, California, USA. Last played July 2009.

12. Daybreak Game Company. 1999. *EverQuest*. Game [Windows]. (16 March 1999). Daybreak Game Company, San Diego, California, USA.

13. Game Freak. 2013. *Pokémon Y*. Game [3DS]. (12 October 2013). The Pokémon Company, Bellevue, Washington, USA.

14. Konami. 1999. *Suikoden II*. Game [PS1]. (29 September 1999). Konami, Tokyo, Japan.

15. Linden Lab. 2003. *Second Life*. Game [Windows]. (23 June 2003). Linden Lab, San Francisco, California, USA.

16. Namco. 2004. *Katamari Damacy*. Game [PS2]. (21 September 2004). Namco, Tokyo, Japan.

17. Niantic Labs. 2012. *Ingress*. Game [Android]. (15 November 2012). Niantic Labs, San Francisco, California, USA.

18. Square. 1987. *Final Fantasy*. Game [NES]. (18 December 1987). Square, Tokyo, Japan.

19. Valve Corporation. 2013. *Dota 2*. Game [Windows]. (9 July 2013). Valve Corporation, Bellevue, Washington, USA.

APPENDIX

The appendix includes the digital game objects survey used to collect data for the paper. The survey page includes markers (Q#) to indicate specific questions referenced in the paper. Note that in the survey we used the term "virtual objects", which was changed to "digital game objects" in the paper.

Please indicate whether or not you are 18 or older and assent to continue the survey. [select one]
Only participants age 18 and older can participate in this research project. If you are younger than 18, thank you for your interest.

○ I am 18 or older and assent to participating in this survey.
○ I am less than 18 years old or do not assent to participating in this survey.

Demographics
What is your age? [free numerical response]

What is your gender? [select one]
○ Prefer not to say.
○ Female.
○ Male.
○ Non-binary / other.

What is your highest level of education? [select one]
○ No response.
○ High school or equivalent.
○ Bachelor's degree or equivalent.
○ Master's degree or equivalent.
○ Graduate degree or equivalent.

Initial Experience
Have you collected digital objects in one or more games that you value? [select one]
For this and all future questions, an "object" might be an actual object, such as items in your inventory or worn by your character, but could also be characters/teammates, upgrades, other virtual objects, etc.

○ Yes.
○ No.

Q6. Have you purchased digital objects in one or more games with real-world currencies? [select one]
○ Yes.
○ No.

Do you enjoy unlocking achievements / trophies / etc.? [select one]
○ Yes.
○ No.
○ I am not familiar with achievements / trophies / etc.

Virtual Object Collection
In this section, we are interested in how you value virtual objects. Some reasons people value virtual objects are listed below, although they may not be exhaustive.

- Utility: the virtual object is valuable because of what it can do.
- Investment: the virtual object represented your time, effort, and achievements.
- Communication: the virtual object's appearance communicates something useful to your social group.
- Memory: the virtual object is a collection of your memories.
- Enjoyment: the virtual object is simply fun to use in game.
- Relationships: the virtual object represents relationships with other players or groups.
- New experience: the virtual object enabled new experiences.
- Creativity: the virtual object was a platform on which you could create aesthetically pleasing forms.
- Sociability: the virtual object allowed you to engage in activities with friends.
- Self-expression: the virtual object allowed you to express a wide variety of personal attributes or beliefs.

Q3. In what games did you collect objects that you value? [free response]

Q4. Out of the games above, which contains your favorite object or collection of objects? [free response]
You will use this answer as the basis for your answers to later questions.

Q1. What is your favorite object (or collection of objects)? [free response]

Why is your favorite virtual object(s) valuable to you? [check all that apply]
☐ Utility
☐ Investment
☐ Communication
☐ Memory
☐ Enjoyment
☐ Relationships
☐ New experience
☐ Creativity
☐ Sociability
☐ Self-expression
☐ Other:

Q2. What is the main reason that you value your favorite virtual object(s)? [select one]
○ Utility
○ Investment
○ Communication
○ Memory
○ Enjoyment
○ Relationships
○ New experience
○ Creativity

○ Sociability
○ Self-expression
○ Other:

For how long did you use the object(s)? [select one]
○ For a part of the game.
○ For the remainder of the game after acquiring it.
○ Beyond the game in which it was acquired and into one other game (via trading, save game transfer, etc.).
○ Beyond the game in which it was acquired and into multiple games (via trading, save game transfer, etc.).

Q5. Have you shared the object(s) with others? [select one]
○ No.
○ Yes, by showing the object(s) to other people in my game on my device.
○ Yes, by using the object(s) in a game online with others.
○ Yes, by publicly displaying the object(s) online.

What else would you like to tell us about your experiences with collecting virtual objects? [free response]

Personalization of Virtual Objects
The following questions are in regards to your personalization or customization of virtual objects.

Which of the following personalization features do you consider most important for the digital objects you have collected? [check one]
○ None
○ Dyes or color-changing features
○ Naming or name-changing features
○ Physical placement adjustments
○ Other:

Which of the following personalization features have you used for digital objects you have collected? [check all that apply]
□ None
□ Dyes or color-changing features
□ Naming or name-changing features
□ Physical placement adjustments
□ Other:

Q7. Have you ever purchased a personalization feature with real-world currencies? [check one]
○ Yes.
○ No.

What else would you like to tell us about personalization features for virtual objects? [free response]

Personality

Here are a number of personality traits that may or may not apply to you. Please select a value next to each statement to indicate the extent to which you agree or disagree with that statement. You should rate the extent to which the pair of traits applies to you, even if one characteristic applies more strongly than the other.

I see myself as: [mark one entry per row]

	disagree strongly	disagree moderately	disagree a little	neither agree nor disagree	agree a little	agree moderately	agree strongly
Extraverted, enthusiastic.	○	○	○	○	○	○	○
Critical, quarrelsome.	○	○	○	○	○	○	○
Dependable, self-disciplined.	○	○	○	○	○	○	○
Anxious, easily upset.	○	○	○	○	○	○	○
Open to new experiences, complex.	○	○	○	○	○	○	○
Reserved, quiet.	○	○	○	○	○	○	○
Sympathetic, warm.	○	○	○	○	○	○	○
Disorganized, careless.	○	○	○	○	○	○	○
Calm, emotionally stable.	○	○	○	○	○	○	○
Conventional, uncreative.	○	○	○	○	○	○	○

Brainhex Questionnaire

For each experience, choose "I love it!", "I hate it!", or "It's okay". [mark one entry per row]

	I love it.	It's okay.	I hate it.
Exploring to see what you can find.	○	○	○
Looking around just to enjoy the scenery.	○	○	○
Wondering what's behind a locked door.	○	○	○
Running away from a dangerous foe.	○	○	○
Feeling terrified.	○	○	○
Feeling relief when you escape to a safe area.	○	○	○
Feeling excited.	○	○	○
Being in control at high speed.	○	○	○
Hanging from a high ledge.	○	○	○
Cracking a challenging puzzle.	○	○	○
Devising a promising strategy.	○	○	○
Working out what to do on your own.	○	○	○
Eventually defeating a difficult boss.	○	○	○
Taking on a strong opponent in a versus match.	○	○	○
Completing a punishing challenge after failing many times.	○	○	○
Talking to non-player characters.	○	○	○
Talking to other players.	○	○	○
Co-operating with strangers.	○	○	○
Picking up every single collectible in an area.	○	○	○
Finding an item you need to complete a collection.	○	○	○
Getting 100%.	○	○	○

The Motivational Push of Games: The Interplay of Intrinsic Motivation and External Rewards in Games for Training

Max V. Birk, Regan L. Mandryk, and Cheralyn Atkins

Department of Computer Science, University of Saskatchewan

Saskatoon, SK, Canada

{firstname.lastname}@usask.ca

ABSTRACT

Games for training aim to keep interest in training activities high by making them more enjoyable, yet interest and motivation often wane over time. Games frequently employ rewards to halt waning motivation; however, research suggests that although this approach may work for less motivated players, it may backfire for players who are already enjoying a game. To explore changing motivation patterns over time, we conducted an 11-day study of a game for training executive functioning with players who were split into two groups that reflected their intrinsic motivation induced through a manipulation of identification with an in-game avatar. Although motivation waned over time, both effort and enjoyment waned more rapidly for players who identified less. After one week, when we delivered a reward (payment), the less-identified group respond positively – increasing their effort and improving performance; however, the more identified group responded negatively – decreasing their effort and declining in task performance.

Author Keywords

Motivation; training game; gamification; self-determination

ACM Classification Keywords

K.8.0 [Personal Computing]: General - Games.

INTRODUCTION

There are many domains in which people need to invest time and effort in a training activity to see future benefit. For example, consider a person who wants to learn a second language – if she puts in the work of memorizing vocabulary, over time she will be able to communicate in another language. Or consider a person who wishes to lose weight – if he makes good eating choices every day, over time he will lose excess weight. Motivation to engage in these types of training activities often starts off quite high, with the person looking forward to the future payoff that will eventually result from their invested efforts. However, over

CHI PLAY '16, October 16-19, 2016, Austin, TX, USA
© 2016 ACM. ISBN 978-1-4503-4456-2/16/10...$15.00
DOI: http://dx.doi.org/10.1145/2967934.2968091

time, motivation often wanes, resulting in people investing less effort in training, or quitting before reaching their goal.

This lost interest in training is partly because the beneficial outcome of training behaviours (e.g., being bilingual, reaching a healthy weight) takes time to achieve and is distinct from the behaviours themselves (e.g., practicing a second language, making healthy eating choices). This form of motivation – engaging in an activity because it leads to a desirable but separable outcome [48] – is called extrinsic motivation. Although extrinsic motivation can encourage participation in a training activity (e.g., [43,41,15]), it often wanes when the realization of the outcome is delayed – it takes time to become proficient at another language or lose weight. A remedy for waning extrinsic motivation over time is to make the training activity engaging enough so that people participate because they enjoy the training activity itself, and not just for the beneficial outcome that will result from sustained training. This form of motivation – engaging in an activity because it is inherently interesting – is referred to as intrinsic motivation [48]. However, the question is how to make repetitive training activities – such as verb conjugation practice – inherently enjoyable.

It has been proposed that digital games are intrinsically motivating to play [47] because they are inherently enjoyable. As such, the use of game design elements in non-game contexts – called gamification [14] – has been proposed to increase the intrinsic motivation of engaging in a training activity and avoid the waning motivation that plagues extrinsically-motivated training. However, even in games that are played solely for entertainment and are inherently enjoyable, player motivation can wane over time for a variety of reasons (e.g., loss of novelty or changes in a network of friends who play), resulting in declining participation. To retain players, many games inject rewards, tokens, or valuable in-game content. These incentives sometimes aim to increase intrinsic motivation (e.g., new game missions that are inherently enjoyable); however, a more common approach is to target extrinsic motivation (e.g., by providing a free power-up or in-game currency). Although designers intend that these doses of extrinsic rewards act as motivators to encourage players, it is unclear if they are effective at halting waning player motivation and if this approach will work in the context of gamified training activities.

Research in the psychology of motivation suggests that the effectiveness of introducing external rewards into a training activity could depend on the pre-existing motivation of the participants [55] – those motivated by a separable outcome (extrinsic) should respond well, whereas those motivated by the inherent enjoyment of the activity itself (intrinsic) may respond poorly [12]. This loss of motivation that occurs when external incentives are provided to intrinsically-motivated people has been demonstrated in other domains [11,23,1]; however, it is unclear whether the use of external rewards will improve motivation, halt waning motivation, or undermine the pre-existing intrinsic motivation of players of a training game. Loss of motivation in training games has major implications as they are used in many serious domains, such as for health [43] and safety training [49].

As such, we conducted an 11-day study to understand the effects of time and incentives on motivation and behaviour in a game-based training activity with 200 participants. We asked all participants to engage daily in a game-based version of an established task that has been used in various digital interventions [15,54] – a go/no-go task to train executive function [38]. Although we promised payment, we withheld it for the first week – replicating the context in which the beneficial outcome for an activity is separable from task engagement and is delayed. After seven days, we paid participants, delivering their expected reward. In addition, we facilitated intrinsic motivation in half of our participants using an existing induction approach of avatar identification [4] to create two groups who differed in their level of intrinsic motivation. Each day, we measured subjective motivation, affective state, and task behaviour – both before and after delivering the extrinsic motivator of payment.

The results of our study make three important contributions to understanding motivation and behaviour on repeated days of participation in a game-based training. First, we demonstrated that we can use a digital induction method (avatar identification) to foster intrinsic motivation, which lasted over repeated days of participation in the training activity. Second, we showed that motivation waned over time; however, both effort and enjoyment waned more rapidly for players who identified less with their in-game avatar. Third, when we delivered a reward (payment) after one week, the less-motivated group responded positively, increasing their effort and showing improvements in task performance. However, the more motivated group responded negatively to the reward – they showed a decrease in their invested effort and declines in performance on the training task. Explained by theories of human motivation, our findings have implications for games for training, games user researcher, and games for entertainment.

RELATED WORK
We first describe human motivation, followed by motivation in games for training and gamification.

Motivation
Human motivation describes a person's inspiration to act – as Ryan and Deci [48] note: "to be motivated means *to be moved* to do something". Nearly everyone who interacts with the world around them experiences motivation, thus it is a topic of interest in a diverse range of fields.

Spectrum of Motivation
Motivation varies by level, i.e., how much motivation is experienced, but also by orientation, i.e. what form of motivation is experienced [48]. The spectrum of different orientations of motivation is defined by how controlling or volitional an activity is (the regulatory style). Self-Determination Theory (SDT) suggests three regulatory styles of motivation: *internal motivation, external motivation, and amotivation* [48].

Amotivation suggests the complete lack of an intention to act [48], and results from not seeing an activity as valuable [19], feeling inept to do it [13], or not feeling that it will result in a desired outcome [51].

On the other end of the spectrum, *intrinsic motivation* is defined as engaging in a task for its inherent satisfaction [48] - an activity that is its own means to an end, e.g., playing endless hours of Tetris, not to beat the high score, but because implementing a clever strategy to clear the falling rows is enjoyable in and of itself.

Extrinsic motivation is defined by an activity in which behaviour and outcome are separable, e.g., studying (behaviour) to pass an exam (outcome) [48]. Extrinsic motivation varies depending on the congruency of an activity with our goals; the separable outcome may be desired because it leads to a reward (*external regulation*), leads to approval from the self or others (*introjection*), is something that is consciously valued by the individual (*identification*), or is congruent with an individual's self-view (*integration*) [48].

It is important not to confuse extrinsic motivation with external rewards. External rewards, e.g., points, or in-game currency, are representative of external regulation. Rewards are a fundamental concept in games and when combined with appropriate reward schedules, can enforce long-term retention [14]. However, once the reward or the expectation to be rewarded is removed, players would likely lose interest and retention would drop [17].

Undermining Intrinsic Motivation
There is literature from the psychology of motivation that suggests existing intrinsic motivation can be undermined by the application of an extrinsic reward [48]. As such, the efficacy of applying rewards in a training activity could depend on the existing motivation of the participants. Specifically, individuals who are extrinsically motivated to do the task should respond well to a reward, whereas intrinsically-motivated people may respond poorly.

This negative effect of an extrinsic reward on existing intrinsic motivation has been shown in multiple domains (e.g., education [11], philanthropic activities [23], workplaces [1], games [22], health [52]), and with a variety of demographics (e.g., kids [30], college students [32]). However, there has been controversy surrounding the existence of this so-called "overjustification effect". In a meta-analysis of 128 studies, including four meta-analytical studies, Deci et al. [12] confirmed that extrinsic rewards – independent of whether they are received or expected – undermine intrinsic motivation. The results showed that receiving expected tangible rewards (e.g., money or marshmallows) consistently undermined intrinsic motivation, as measured by a free choice paradigm (i.e., measuring how long participants spend on a task without any expected reward). Self-reported measures parallel results from the free-choice tasks (with weaker effect sizes), except when the rewards were based on performance (e.g., receiving a reward when a threshold score is reached).

Motivating Training Activities using Games

Motivation is a central concept in the discussion of games for both entertaining and serious purposes. With the exception of professional gamers who get financial rewards (external regulation) for playing, games are generally a leisure activity that is engaged in by choice under a player's own volition [50]. Thus players need to be motivated to participate. That motivation may be intrinsic – that is, they participate because they truly enjoy the game play – or extrinsic; they play because they get social value from gaming (introjection), value from gaming as an activity (identification), or self-identify as a gamer (integration) [48].

It is important to distinguish the motivation that people have to play games from the motivational elements that designers employ within games to encourage certain in-game behaviours. Although based in the same theories of what motivates people, design decisions grounded in motivation within games (e.g., rewarding players for in-game purchases) are conceptually distinct from design decisions used to motivate participation with the game itself (e.g., giving an in-game reward every day that the player logs in). In this paper, we focus on the latter – using game elements to motivate participation in the game in general.

Motivation in Games for Training

Motivation to participate in games for training is similar to the motivation to participate in games for leisure; however, the training game can be viewed as a means to an end. Consider the example of a person who wishes to learn German and plays a game to help her learn the genders of nouns. She may actually enjoy playing the game (intrinsic motivation), may do so because her company is paying her to learn German (external regulation), because her friends all speak German and she doesn't want to be excluded (introjection), because she sees value in speaking another language (identification), or because bilingualism is congruent with her self view (integration). Although a training activity can be inherently interesting (especially at first), they generally have instrumental value in terms of leading to a separable outcome, as opposed to intrinsic value. The application of games as training activities tries to address this intrinsic value by making them more enjoyable (e.g., [43,27]). When playing games for training, players might be motivated for multiple reasons – the motivation to play might be in service of a separable outcome, e.g., learning a language as the main purpose of engaging in the game, or because the game is inherently enjoyable, e.g., because the premise is interesting or the mechanics are enjoyable [11]. In our example, playing a learning game will likely be a more enjoyable means to learning the genders of German nouns than rehearsing them without the incorporation of game elements. As such, games for training tend not just to affect the spectrum of extrinsic motivation for learning, but address the underlying enjoyment of the activity itself.

The Motivational Pull of Games

Games are fun, because they allow us to actively participate in a compelling narrative, provide us with challenging encounters, and give us the opportunity to choose our fate [45]. A variety of models [47, 57] have tried to capture the essence of player motivation. Self-determination theory [10] is a well-grounded theoretical framework that allows us to explain how satisfying basic psychological needs leads to enjoyment in games. The traditional model proposes [10] three factors. *Competence* is the need to experience mastery and control over the outcome of a challenge, e.g., mastering the skills of a champion in *League of Legends* (2009, Riot Games), or facing the increasing challenge of *Tetris* (Pajitnov, 1984). *Autonomy* is the need to engage in a challenge under one's own volition, e.g., the diamond shaped pathways in *The Legend of Zelda* (1986, Nintendo), or through race, class, and faction choices in MMORPGs, such as *World of Warcraft* (2004, Blizzard). *Relatedness* is the universal need to feel connected to others, e.g., by playing team-matches in *Counter Strike* (2000, Valve), or by feeling connected to in-game objects or characters, e.g., bonding with the companion cube in *Portal* (2007, Valve). SDT has also been extended to capture the unique characteristics of digital games with Presence/Immersion, the experience of being transported into a virtual environment; and Intuitive Control, which describes the naturalness of the game input. Satisfying these needs has been shown to increase enjoyment [45] and play-time [4] in games.

Gamification

Because of this motivational pull of games, the use of game design elements in non-game contexts – called gamification [14] – has been proposed as a method to increase the intrinsic motivation of serious games. For example, games have been used to encourage serious behaviours, such as healthy eating [2], smoking cessation [27], lowered energy consumption [27], and understanding the challenges faced by people with disabilities [16]. In terms of promoting training activities, gamification is used to motivate people in the short term in domains from human resources system training [44] to surgical skills training [32]. In addition, serious games have also been proposed for use over the long term to motivate sustained and repeated participation, increase the effort invested by the participants, and improve the retention of participants over time, with the goal of ultimately leading to more effectives training [28].

There is some controversy surrounding the use of gamification in serious contexts and even on the use of the term *gamification* itself. Intentionally called *pointsification* [5] or *exploitationware* [6], thought leaders suggest that gamification is often a superficial application of trivial game elements – such as points, achievements, badges, and levels [40] – rather than the principled application of the mechanics, dynamics, or aesthetics [24] that create meaningful, emotional, and engaging play. As Bogost notes, "points and levels and the like are mere gestures that provide structure and measure progress within" the game system [5, 6]. For the purposes of this paper, we leverage the term gamification (and *gamify*) when we talk about the application of game-based elements in non-game contexts [14]. However, we clarify that our goal of including game elements is to increase motivation (either intrinsic or extrinsic) to engage in sustained and repeated training activities over time.

Waning Motivation in Games for Training
In games designed for long-term training, combating waning motivation is of particular importance. One way that researchers have attempted to maintain motivation in longer-term deployments is to keep enjoyment (intrinsic motivation) high because it is a good predictor for staying engaged in a task over time [17]. One approach is to inject novelty in the game over time. Hernandez et al. [20] deployed a 10-week trial of a networked multiplayer exergame for children with Cerebral Palsy to exercise and socialize together. To keep the novelty of the game high over the 10-week trial, they included six mini-games, which they introduced progressively every two weeks to maintain interest in the training activity. Logs of game choice and time played suggest that the strategy was effective [21]. Similarly, Mandryk et al. [35] deployed a 12-week trial of a neurofeedback training system for children with fetal alcohol spectrum disorder to learn to self-regulate. Rather than creating a neurofeedback game, their system turned any off-the-shelf game into a biofeedback game – this decision was largely motivated by the idea that allowing participants to select a commercial game of their choice to use for training would increase the enjoyment, i.e., intrinsic motivation, of training. In addition, the authors note that they originally deployed five game choices, but participants complained that they were bored of the games and thus two new games were added half-way through to keep interest high.

Gamification of training activities has been proposed as a means of keeping motivation high, and these few studies show how researchers attempt to employ novelty to sustain motivation over the long term. However, to our knowledge, there has been no systematic study of how motivation in game-based training wanes over time, and how methods of fostering intrinsic or extrinsic motivation within the context of gamified training activities affect waning motivation.

EXPERIMENT DESIGN
We conducted an online study to understand the effects of time and incentives on motivation and behaviour in a game-based training activity. We withheld payment for the first seven days, but paid participants each day thereafter. In addition, we facilitated intrinsic motivation in half of our participants using an existing induction approach of avatar identification [4]. Each day, we measured subjective motivation, affective state, and task behaviour.

Manipulating Identification: The Avatar Creator
To manipulate avatar identification, we used a character creator that has been shown to facilitate intrinsic motivation [4]. Participants were asked to create an avatar and adjust its appearance, personality, and attributes (characteristics). A minimum of four minutes in the character creator were required, but participants could take longer if they wished. After customizing their avatar, participants were shown a summary of their character and asked to enter a nickname.

Options for the appearance, personality and attributes are described in [4]. We additionally added customization of the size of nose, eyes, and ears (small, medium, big), the distance of the eyes (narrow, medium, far), and the shape of the head (oval, round, heart, strong jaw) to better facilitate similarity identification [4]. At the end of the creation process, the avatar was visually presented along with a summary of its personality and attributes, to give the player the sense that their avatar had a profile.

We manipulated identification by presenting half of our participants with the avatar creator. The other half were randomly assigned an avatar of the same sex, from a set of four. Following the approach used in [4], participants in the randomly-assigned avatar group watched a 4-minute video of the creation and customization of their avatar. We created four videos for each sex with four different personality and attribute configurations, similar to [4], with the additional face options set at the medium level. Participants who watched the video were not allowed to name their avatar; instead the avatar was represented as "Player 1".

Figure 1. Go/no-go task Zombie Apocalypse showing a player hiting a Zombie.

Go/No-Go Task: Zombie Apocalypse
Zombie Apocalypse is a zombie themed go/no-go task in which participants stab Zombies with a sword, and avoid stabbing moles. The game was implemented in C# using Unity 4.6 (Unity Technologies, 2014).

We chose the go/no-go task for a variety of reasons. It is used to train cognitive functions [15], so it is a representative task for a training activity that must be repeated over multiple days. It is simple to explain and does not require a steep learning curve, making it appropriate for an experiment. Go/no-go is also a common game-mechanic (e.g., whack-a-mole), making it familiar to participants in the context of a game, and also straightforward for us to gamify by adding premise, graphical assets, and a score.

Task: The participants' created or assigned avatar stood in a fixed position holding a sword (see Figure 1). Players were instructed to respond to appearing zombies (*targets*), but not to moles (*lures*). Targets and lures were intentionally visually similar to increase task difficulty. A target or a lure appeared every second (popping up from under the ground), giving participants a 500ms window to respond by pressing the spacebar. Correct or false responses to targets or lures results in four response types with different scoring: 1) correctly responding to a target: *hit*, 2) not responding to a target: *miss*, 3) responding to a lure: *false alarm*, 4) not responding to a lure: *correct rejection*. Hits increased the participant's score by 1; *misses* and *false alarms* decreased score to a minimum of zero points; *correct rejections* left the score unchanged. Stabbed zombies (hit) exhibited a death animation, whereas missed zombies (miss) walked away. Stabbed moles (false alarm) turned red before disappearing to give the participant feedback, whereas missed moles (correct rejection) popped back underground safely. Each participant was presented with 80 targets, and 20 lures, presented in a pseudorandom order. Score was displayed and incremented after each target or lure. To ensure that participants understood the task and controls, we presented a training condition with 10 stimuli total (8 targets, 2 lures) before beginning the task each day.

Applications: The go/no-go task requires participants to decide between a target and lure and initiate a response in a very short amount of time, which requires focus and quick decision-making. As a result of the 4:1 relation between targets and lures, participants get accustomed to responding to targets and are thus required to inhibit the most common response, press the spacebar, to correctly reject a lure. Assessment and training of executive functioning is used in both clinical [9] and non-clinical [15] contexts.

Measures
We collected both subjective and behavioural measures.

Identification was measured using the avatar-related subscales of similarity identification, embodied identification, and wishful identification from the Player Identification Scale (PIS, [56]). Participants rated their agreement to identification-related statements measuring similarity – "My character is like me in many ways" – on a 7-pt Likert scale.

Motivation was measured using the Intrinsic Motivation Inventory (IMI, [37]). The IMI measures the constructs *interest-enjoyment* - "I enjoyed this game very much.", *effort-importance* - "I put a lot of effort into this game.", *perceived competence* – "I think I am pretty good at this game.", and *tension-pressure* - "I felt tense while playing

the game.". Each construct was measured with multiple items using agreement with a 7-pt Likert-scale. The results were then aggregated into the four constructs of the IMI.

Task Performance
Performance in a go/no-go task is defined by *hits* and *correct rejections*. Negative performance is described as the number of *misses* and *false alarms*. Following [25, 53], *hits* and *false alarms* are used to compute *sensitivity* (d_L) and *bias* (C_L). d_L separates targets and lures and represents an index of difficulty for discriminating the two types of stimuli – a higher d_L indicates that targets and lures are more discriminable. Negative C_L scores indicate a liberal bias to respond to target or lure, while positive scores indicate a conservative bias to respond.

Participants and Deployment Platform
We conducted our experiment online. 200 participants (43.9% female) with an average age of 31.68 (SD=8.94) were recruited through Amazon's Mechanical Turk (MTurk), which connects workers willing to do Human Intelligence Tasks (HITs) with requesters of the work, and has been shown to be a valid environment for conducting user studies [26]. Participants were re-invited daily to participate in our series of HITs for 11 consecutive days. Participants received $4 for the first day (40 min), and $1 for each consecutive day (10 min). Ethical approval was obtained, and participants provided informed consent. The HIT was only made available to workers in the USA older than 18 with an approval rate above 90%.

Participants were excluded from further analysis if: they showed zero variability in more than 2 questionnaires, suggesting that they indicated the same response on all items independent of scale or reversed items; the number of *hits* in the go/no-go task exceeded 80, indicating that they reloaded the task; or they did not participate on day 4, 5, or 6, which were the days on which we measured identification (30 participants excluded).

Procedure
We recruited the initial pool of participants on the first day. Daily HITs were independent, so that people who skipped a daily HIT were not excluded from further participation.

Day 1
Participants were first informed about the amount of compensation they would receive ($4 for approximately 40 minutes); additionally, we informed them that the first payment would be delayed for 7 days, and that they were expected to answer attentively and quickly. It is important to note that by promising a reward at day 7, we introduce an anticipated extrinsic reward from day one. Therefore, participants might experience two different sources of motivation, i.e., the financial reward as an extrinsic source, and identification as a source of intrinsic motivation.

After being informed of the reward, participants were randomly assigned to either the customized or random avatar group. After creating an avatar (or watching an avatar being created), participants performed the go/no-go task, and then completed the IMI. Finally, participants provided basic demographic information, e.g., frequency of play, age, and stated the purpose of the study in their own words.

Day 2 – 11

Each day, participants were informed about the compensation they would later receive ($1 for about 10 minutes), and were asked to provide informed consent. Participants entered their MTurk identification code to load their saved avatar, and then performed the go/no-go-task, before completing the IMI. On day 4, 5, and 6, we additionally asked them to complete the avatar identification scale.

Delivery of Extrinsic Motivator

On Day 8, we paid participants for their initial HIT and continued to pay them each day thereafter. This represents us delivering on a promised (but delayed) outcome (i.e., an expected tangible reward) that is separable from the training activity. Paying a delayed reward at day 8 fulfils three purposes: 1) the separable outcome becomes salient; 2) experienced extrinsic motivation is temporarily increased; 3) paying participants reinforces trust that their efforts would be compensated. We were not interested in the specific reward, but in a proxy for receiving an expected, but delayed beneficial outcome separated from the training task.

Data Analyses

All data were logged to a database on a server at the University of Saskatchewan and were analyzed using SPSS 23. IMI data were computed after each completion of the go/no-go task. Identification was computed as average identification of Day 4 to Day 6. To create two groups that varied in their initial intrinsic motivation based on our avatar customization manipulation, we performed a median split on the average similarity identification.

To analyze changes in motivation and performance over time, we performed Hierarchical Linear Models (HLM) with *day* on level-1, and the dependent measures on level-2; *identification* was entered as the covariate. Estimates were computed using Restricted Maximum Likelihood with a maximum of 100 iterations, and a maximum step size of 10. To avoid biasing the analysis, covariance was kept unstructured for random intercepts. The α-niveau was set to .05.

To compare improvement or change over time (days) for the two identification groups separately, we computed the slopes for the daily averages within an identification group. Because we used a between-participants design, the absolute performance differences on the go/no-go task between the more- and less-identified groups is not meaningful (due to the individual differences in executive function between players in these two groups). As such, our analyses of the task performance measures calculate the difference between the day of interest and performance on Day 1. Comparisons are made using this difference, which reflects absolute improvement from Day 1 values.

RESULTS

We first present the general participation rates, followed by the results on the initial phase, and then following the re-

ward. In general, participation dropped over time (Figure 2). Day1 was a Tuesday (following a holiday Monday). The average drop-out was 30.6%. Chi-squared tests for each day showed no significant differences in participation between the two identification groups (all p>.05).

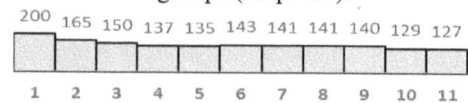

Figure 2. Participation by Day (1-11).

Initial Phase of Waning Motivation

Does motivation wane over time?

The HLM (described in the data analyses section) showed a main effect of day on invested effort ($F_{6,820.32}=6.96$, $p<.001$). Figure 4 shows that effort decreases in general over days. There was no main effect of day on enjoyment (p=.31). A general waning of effort confirms our assumptions, reflects prior research [30], and is a prerequisite for investigating the effect of a delivered reward on motivation.

Does training improve task performance?

All performance data were corrected for baseline (Day1) performance. HLMs showed that hits $(F_{6,831.33}=5.50$, $p<.001)$ increase over time, whereas false alarms decrease $(F_{6,823.14}=4.11$, $p<.001)$, indicating that players improved over time (Figure 5). Participants also showed an increase in d_L over time $(F_{6,828.76}=11.86$, $p<.001)$, suggesting that discriminating targets and lures becomes easier over time. In addition, participants were aware of their improving performance. Perceived competence increases over time $(F_{6,825.35}=4.84$, $p<.001)$. There was no difference in bias $(F_{6,829.50}=1.33$, $p=.243)$, indicating that tendency to respond to target or lures didn't change over time.

Can intrinsic motivation be fostered in a gamified training task using avatar identification?

Identification can be facilitated through a variety of methods; we chose to use customization to create variability in similarity identification. While the group differences between conditions were significant $(t_{167}=4.534$, $p<.001$, $d=.70)$, Figure 3 shows how the differences are derived from overlapping distributions of identification. We used a median split of identification in the remaining research questions to capture more-identified and less-identified participants regardless of their group assignment.

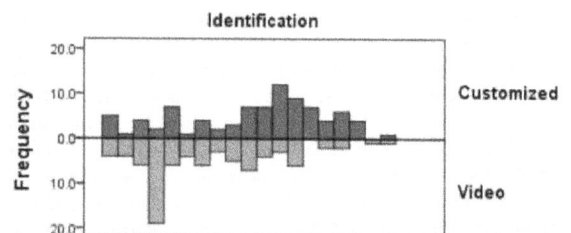

Figure 3. Split-Histogram of Identification by Condition

The HLM showed that identification is linked to motivation: players with high identification experienced more enjoyment $(F_{1,169.15}=23.19$, $p<.001)$ and invested more effort

$(F_{1,168.65}=10.96, p<.01)$ compared to those who experienced low identification (Figure 4). The results confirmed that intrinsic motivation can be fostered through identification.

Is waning motivation affected by identification?

To determine whether motivation waned at different rates for the two identification groups, we regressed a line on the daily mean of participant data from Day 1 to Day 7, separately for each group. Comparison of the slopes (explained in the data analyses section) showed significant differences for experienced enjoyment ($\beta=.074$, $p<.016$) and marginally different slopes for effort ($\beta=.058$, $p=.065$). The slope values (Figure 4) show a decline of effort and enjoyment for participants who experienced lower identification, whereas motivation was more stable for participants with higher identification. See Figure 4.

Do group differences in effort translate into performance?

We applied slope-analysis [7] to investigate differences in the improvement over days for the two identification groups. Although identified participants reported higher effort, they did not improve at a faster rate than less-identified participants (Figure 4). As Figure 5 shows, performance was initially very high on all measures, showing that there was not a lot of gains to be made from practice alone. Differences in performance would be due to training executive function. We address this further in the discussion of the results.

Response to the Delivery of an Anticipated Reward

The previous results were focused on Day 1 to Day 7 of our study to establish a differential pattern of waning motivation and determine its effects on performance. In this section, we focus on Day 7 to 11, to show the differential response of participants to receiving the external reward.

Figure 4. Means (marks), Regressions (lines), and Equations for Enjoyment and Effort from Day 1 to Day 7 (left) and Day 7 to Day 11 (right) for less and more identified participants.

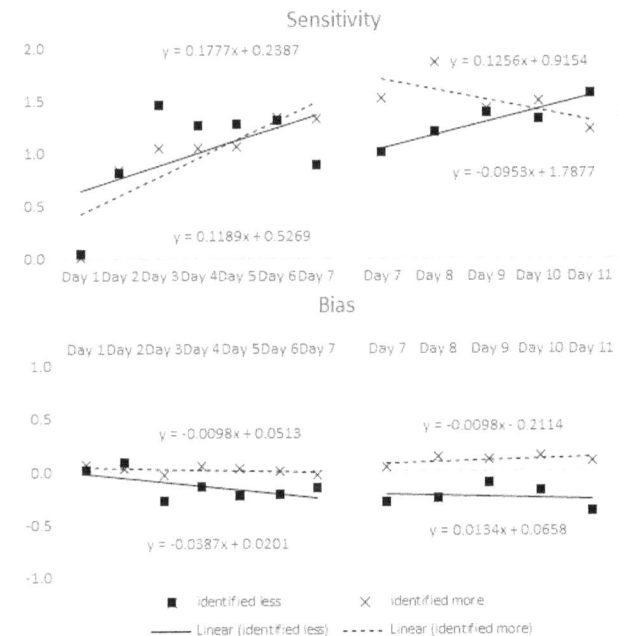

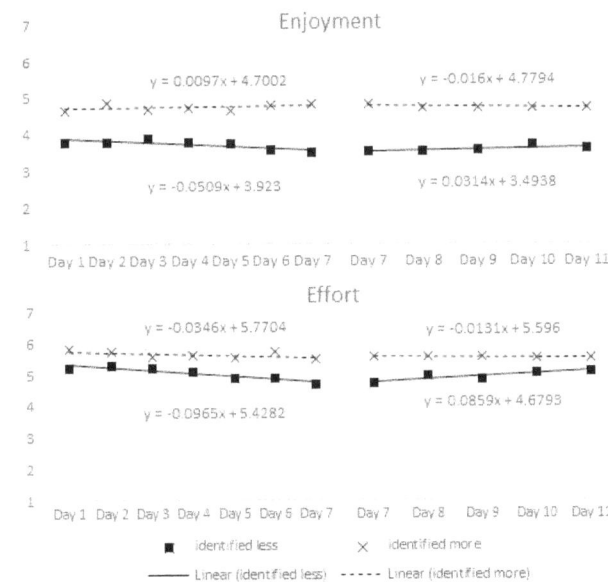

How does the delivery of an anticipated reward affect motivation for differentially motivated participants?

To investigate the impact of a reward on motivation, we compared the slopes of effort and enjoyment data on days 7-11. Figure 4 shows that the lower-identified participants report an increase in their invested effort, whereas effort reported by higher-identified participants was more stable

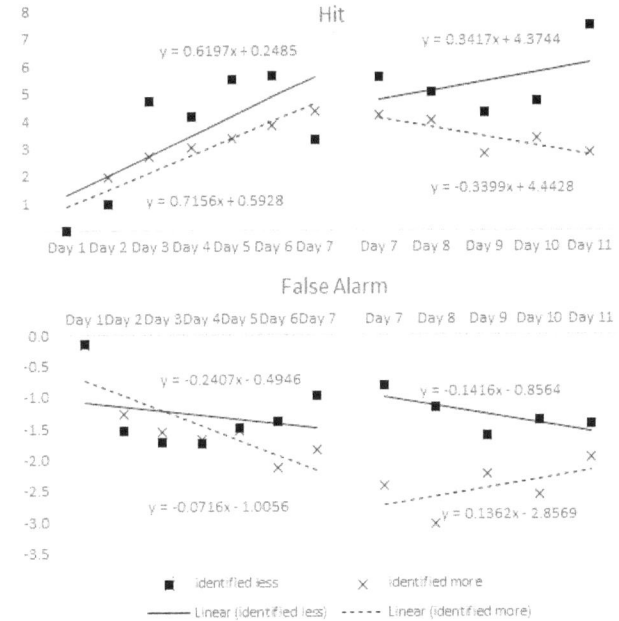

Figure 5. Means (marks), Regressions (lines), and Equations for baseline corrected Hits and False Alarms from Day 1 to Day 7 (left) and Day 7 to Day 11 (right) for less and more identified participants.

Figure 6. Means (marks), Regressions (lines), and Equations for baseline corrected Sensitivity and Bias and False Alarms from Day 1 to Day 7 (left) and Day 7 to Day 11 (right) for less and more identified participants.

(β=-.086, p=.028). There was no significant difference in the slopes for enjoyment (p=.75).

Do group differences in invested effort following the delivery of an anticipated reward translate into task performance?
We compared the slopes of task performance following the reward for the two groups. As Figure 5 shows, less-identified participants (who reported increased effort after the payment), showed improvements in performance, reflected in an increasing number of hits. However, more-identified participants showed a reversal in the improvements seen over days 1 to 7: there was a decrease in the number of hits. This difference in slopes was significant (β=-1.227, p=.012). There was a marginally-significant difference in the slopes for sensitivity (β=-.240, p=.052), showing the same trend. There was no difference in the slopes of false alarms (p=.270) or bias (p=.247).

Together, these results show that although motivation wanes for each group, identified (i.e., more motivated) participants show less of a decline in the initial 7 days in motivation and greater improvement in some measures of task performance. Following the delivery of the extrinsic motivator, the less-identified group saw improvements in motivation and performance, whereas the more-identified group actually showed declines in motivation and performance, potentially exhibiting the "overjustification effect".

DISCUSSION
We first summarize our results, and then give design recommendations for approaches to foster intrinsic and extrinsic motivation in games for training. Our discussion focuses on the application of our findings to games for training, games user research, and games for entertainment.

Summary of Results
Prior to the delivery of the external reward (i.e., on days 1-7), we found the following results.

- We first establish that motivation to invest in our game-based-training activity does wane over time. Although enjoyment of the task does not change with repeated exposure, effort – the primary measure of subjective willingness to invest in the training – decreases over time.
- Second, we show that there is improvement in the training task over time on three of the four baseline-corrected measures of behaviour (i.e., increases in hit, decreases in false alarms, increases in sensitivity). Additionally, participants were aware of their improved performance – their experienced competence also increased over time.
- Third, we demonstrate that we can foster intrinsic motivation in a gamified training task using a manipulation of avatar identification. Although prior work demonstrated this manipulation in the context of a casual game for entertainment [22], we show that the results extend to games for training. Specifically, we show benefits of identification on experienced invested effort and task enjoyment.
- Fourth, we show that the benefits of avatar identification on subjective motivation remain over repeated exposure. Although we expected differences in motivation and ef-

fort on Day 1 based on [48], we show in this study that the motivational benefits of this type of manipulation persist over time. In particular, participants with lower avatar identification experienced declining task enjoyment and invested effort over time, whereas participants with higher avatar identification show stability in both enjoyment and effort over the initial week of training.

- Fifth, we show that the group differences in invested effort do not translate into task behaviour – although the measures trend in this direction, the identified group did not improve their performance on the training task at a significantly greater rate than the non-identified group.

Following the delivery of the extrinsic reward – the delayed payment – we find the following additional results:

- Sixth, the delivery of the extrinsic reward resulted in an increase in invested effort for the non-identified participants, but not for the identified participants (i.e., those who were more intrinsically motivated).
- Seventh, the training data show that this increased effort reported by non-identified participants translated into task performance in terms of improvements in the number of target hits and marginally in greater sensitivity (i.e., a greater ability to discriminate between targets and lures).
- Finally, in a behavioural exhibition of the effect of an extrinsic reward on intrinsically-motivated people, we found that the participants who identified with their avatar showed a decrease in performance after we delivered the extrinsic reward, as reflected in a decrease in the number of target hits and marginally decreasing sensitivity.

Halting Loss of Interest through Motivational Strategies
We motivated our work with the notion that people are initially relatively enthused to begin training programs in various domains, such as to learn a new language or begin an exercise program. However, the initial enthusiasm often begins to wane after the novelty wears off, skill improvement slows down, or the person gets tired of waiting for the beneficial outcome of their efforts. Our work demonstrates that people with differing motivational engagement in a training task will respond in contrasting ways to an intervention intended to halt waning interest. Players who are less intrinsically motivated should respond well to an extrinsic reward, whereas more-intrinsically-motivated players likely will not. A good strategy of piquing the interest of less-motivated players is to provide them with a reward, whereas players who are still demonstrating interest in the task might respond better to keeping their interest high. In this section, we present different in-game strategies that could be used to engender interest in a training game.

Extrinsic Motivators
Designers wishing to use extrinsic motivators to engage players in a task can reward them explicitly, but can also choose from other approaches. Here, we provide guidance based on the spectrum of extrinsic motivation [48].

External Regulation: Rewards are the classic form of external regulation as they are disconnected from the player's goal but are salient to their interests. In-game examples of external regulation are currencies, tokens, or power-ups.

Introjection: Designing for introjection means focusing on the player receiving approval from themselves or others. Providing a player with a status item (e.g., pets in World of Warcraft), a rank that has social value (e.g., Platinum status in League of Legends), or an unlocked achievement that has personal value (e.g., Win 5000 rounds in Counter Strike:GO) target introjection.

Identification: Providing motivation for players who consciously value the activity they are undertaking should reinforce their self-endorsement of their goals. Asking a player to invest effort in service of a greater goal (e.g., grinding for a quest in World of Warcraft), or learning low-level details to achieve a desirable advantage (e.g., Champion statistics in League of Legends) are examples of identification with the personal importance of a behavior and the acceptance of the regulatory aspect.

Integration: Targeting the congruence that integrated players experience should emphasize the synthesis of the player's goals with the self-view. Challenging oneself because of internal beliefs (e.g., No-Kill run in Fall-Out 3), by accepting the demanding role to lead a team (e.g., Raid leader in World of Warcraft), or by training hard to compete in tournaments (e.g., the League of Legends World Championship) are examples of integrated motivation in games.

Intrinsic Motivation
Design choices that target intrinsic motivation should be about maintaining the interest of the players.

Enjoyment: To maintain increase of enjoyment, designers should consider adding novelty to the game [29]. This could be achieved through new game levels to play, characters to inhabit, places to explore, weapons to use, or missions to complete. Although novelty is a central concept in maintaining the interest of players, there are other ways to engender enjoyment. Self-determination theory suggests that motivation is formed through the satisfaction of the psychological needs of competence, autonomy, and relatedness. We address design options for each of these in turn.

Competence: Players should feel that they are satisfying their need for competence –that they experience mastery over challenges. Game systems use feedback in the form of scores, stars, or achievements to reinforce the experience of competence. However, a game for training (and skill acquisition in general) suffers from a fundamental problem in that improvements in skill follow a power law – that is, we see smaller improvements with more practice [39]. If we consider learning any new skill (e.g., instrument, language, game), the massive improvements seen for each unit of effort invested at the beginning begin to level off. Players often quit when the satisfaction of competence wanes (i.e., when it takes a lot of effort to see minor gains in improvement). Designers should consider how to introduce new

skills or accelerate skill acquisition to avoid the leveling off of competence satisfaction that occurs over time.

Autonomy: Players should feel like they are making choices in the game and that they are acting under their own volition to feel that their experience of autonomy is being satisfied. We manipulated feelings of autonomy using avatar customization, which previous work has shown to translate into increased effort and motivated behaviour [4]. Other examples of autonomy manipulations are the branching narratives seen in The Legend of Zelda, the character behaviour choices seen in Mass Effect 3 (Bioware, 2012), and the intensive customization of Avatars seen in Second Life (Linden Labs, 2003). Focused mainly on the choice aspect of autonomy, designers could also highlight the feeling that players are acting under their own volition in choosing to play – a potentially difficult task in a training game.

Relatedness: The feeling of making and maintaining social connections is key to the satisfaction of relatedness. Multiplayer games already have several ways in which the experience of relatedness is satisfied within gameplay. Support for clan play (e.g., League of Legends), games based on a player's social network (e.g., Farmville, PotFarm, or Clash of Clans), and matchmaking algorithms that balance the skills of players in forming a team (e.g, League of Legends, Dota 2, Fifa) all enhance the experience of relatedness in multiplayer games. In addition, relatedness can be fostered in single-player games [47] by helping the player to feel close to the characters within the game (e.g., the companion cube in Portal, or Ellie in the Last of Us).

We have presented several ways in which both extrinsic and intrinsic motivation can be fostered within games. In the next section, we discuss how to apply these motivational designs in several design contexts.

Implications for Design
Our results have several implications for the design of game-based training systems, for games user research, and for games for entertainment and leisure.

Personalizing Training
Our results demonstrate how motivational patterns change over time and how responses to a reward differ for players who are more or less motivated to begin with. Characterizing the *motivational level* of players can inform design decisions on when interactive training systems should intervene to halt waning motivation. However, our work also suggests that characterizing the *motivational orientation* of users of these training systems is just as important to inform the appropriateness and timing of interventions. Understanding that people engage in training games for differing reasons, with differing expectations, and with differing levels of interest is essential.

Previous work has suggested that the efficacy of persuasive games can be improved if they are personalized to the individual player type, because different types of players are motivated by different persuasive strategies [42]. Our work extends on this idea of tailoring games for training by suggesting that knowing the motivational level and orientation of players at any given time can – and furthermore should – inform the choice of the motivational strategy employed, for example by introducing novel content [20,35] or by providing game-based rewards [36]. As opposed to (or perhaps in addition to) the trait-based tailoring proposed in [42], our work suggests a state-based personalization that takes into account player patterns in motivation over time.

Application to Games User Research

Our findings have implications beyond games for training, including in games user research, (GUR), which is interested in understanding player experience and applying this knowledge to improve design. The methods deployed have many parallels to our context of games for training. It is common in GUR to pay people to participate in studies – sometimes over multiple days. Similar to players of games for training, gameplay testers may both enjoy the experience and be externally regulated through the payment. As such, a reward is likely to affect players' invested effort, enjoyment, and performance, depending on their level of intrinsic motivation. As such, games user researchers should be careful about how and when rewards are given to participants. In addition, researchers have to be cautious about the conclusions they draw from their tests – actual players of their games are likely to be higher in intrinsic motivation than their testers and thus will likely respond differently to the application of extrinsic in-game rewards.

Applications to Games for Entertainment

Although our research was designed to inform the area of games for training, our findings have implications in games that are designed solely for entertainment. Although the intentions of players choosing to play for leisure may differ from those engaged in games for training, there are parallels. In both cases, the goal is to retain players – the purpose in retaining players in games for training is so that they achieve a separate beneficial outcome; in games for entertainment, the purpose of retaining players is driven by the financial outcomes for the company. Next to units sold, the average revenue per paying user (ARPU) is a key metric of success for commercial games and is directly related to the number of daily active users [8]. Acquiring new players is also vital for success. A common approach to acquire new players is to leverage the existing user base through recruitment reward programs in which players receive premium currency, or vanity items (such as mounts or skins) as rewards in exchange for successfully recruiting players from their social network. Our findings suggest that the intertwined reward structure of social outreach has complex implications: the reward might be desirable for a player, but also may be perceived as externally-controlled and may negatively affect their underlying motivation and play experience if they were already enjoying the game.

Limitations and Future Work

Although our results provide several important implications for waning motivation in games for training, there are limi-

tations in our study that can be addressed in future work. First, the results that we present are not causal: we facilitate intrinsic motivation using an established induction paradigm [4]. The paradigm creates variability in avatar identification, which in turn fosters differing motivation in players; however, we cannot interpret our results as causal. Future work can address this limitation by working with existing players who are differentially motivated to participate in a game for training a specific activity; however, randomly assigning intrinsic motivation to a subset of participants in an experiment is not possible by definition. Second, our experience with the avatar identification manipulation raised ideas on how to improve the facilitation of motivation through identification. Third, while MTurk has advantages for research in general, and longitudinal research in particular, the platform is also limited in terms of conducting research on motivation. Workers have the explicit goal to work in exchange for a financial reward. When researching motivation, it would be ideal to have full control over what drives participants to engage in a task. We plan to investigate the differences in reward types such as token rewards (e.g., money), access (e.g., premium features), or social rewards (e.g., attention from others), to create a taxonomy of rewards and their effects on players. Finally, the go/no-go task has the advantage of being simple, well described, and constrained, while also training executive functioning. Most gamified training tasks are more complex and involve layers of gamification, e.g., points, leaderboards, or social reinforcement. Therefore, our results need to be shown in the context of a more complex task, ideally "in the wild'.

CONCLUSION

There are many domains in which people need to invest effort in a training activity over time to see benefit at some future point. Motivation to engage in these types of training activities often starts off quite high, but there is a loss of interest over time, and people often quit before reaching their goal. Games for training use enjoyment to keep interest in the training activity high, even when motivation to achieve the outcome starts to wane. To explore changing motivation patterns over time and to determine how rewards affect players with differing interest levels, we conducted an 11-day study of a game for training executive functioning with players who were split into two groups that reflected their intrinsic motivation induced through a manipulation of identification with an in-game avatar. We show that motivation wanes over time; however, both effort and enjoyment wane more for players who identify less. After one week, when we delivered a reward (payment), the less-motivated group respond positively – increasing their effort and showing improvements in task performance; however, the more motivated group responded negatively in terms of their invested effort and declines in performance on the training task. Explained by theories of human motivation, our findings have implications for games for training, games user researcher, and games for entertainment.

ACKNOWLEDGMENTS
We thank NSERC for funding, our participants, and members of the Interaction Lab – in particular, Jason Bowey.

REFERENCES

1. Teresa M. Amabile. 1993. Motivational synergy: Toward new conceptualizations of intrinsic and extrinsic motivation in the workplace. *Human Resource Management Review*, 3, 3, 185--201. http://dx.doi.org/10.1016/1053-4822(93)90012-s

2. Tom Baranowski, Janice Baranowski, Karen W Cullen, Tara Marsh, Noemi Islam, Issa Zakeri, Lauren Honess-Morreale, and Carl deMoor. 2003. Squire's Quest! *American Journal of Preventive Medicine*, 24, 1, 52--61. http://dx.doi.org/10.1016/s0749-3797(02)00570-6

3. Magnus Bang, Carin Torstensson, and Cecilia Katzeff. 2006. The PowerHhouse: A Persuasive Computer Game Designed to Raise Awareness of Domestic Energy Consumption. In *Persuasive Technology. Springer Science Business Media*, 123--132. http://dx.doi.org/10.1007/11755494_18

4. Max V. Birk, Cheralyn Atkins, Jason T. Bowey, and Regan L. Mandryk. 2016. Fostering Intrinsic Motivation through Avatar Identification in Digital Games. In *Proceedings of the SIGCHI Conference on Human Factors in Computing Systems*. ACM. http://dx.doi.org/10.1145/2858036.2858062

5. Ian Bogost. 2011. Gamification is Bullshit, (Blog entry). Retrieved from: http://bogost.com/writing/blog/gamification_is_bullshit/

6. Ian Bogost. 2011. Persuasive Games: Exploitationware, (Blog entry). Retrieved from: http://www.gamasutra.com/view/feature/134735/persuasive_games_exploitationware.php

7. Institute for digital research and education, UCLA. 2016. (Blog entry). Retrieved from: http://www.ats.ucla.edu/stat/spss/faq/compreg2.htm

8. Casual Games Association. 2012. Social Network Games 2012, Casual Games Sector Report.

9. B. J. Casey, Rolf J. Trainor, Jennifer L. Orendi, Anne B. Schubert, Leigh E. Nystrom, Jay N. Giedd, F. Xavier Castellanos et al. "A developmental functional MRI study of prefrontal activation during performance of a go-no-go task." Journal of cognitive neuroscience 9, no. 6 (1997): 835-847.

10. Edward L. Deci and Richard M. Ryan. 2000. The "What" and "Why" of Goal Pursuits: Human Needs and the Self-Determination of Behavior. *Psychological Inquiry*, 11, 4, 227--268. http://dx.doi.org/10.1207/s15327965pli1104_01

11. Edward L. Deci, Richard Koestner, and Richard M. Ryan. 2001. Extrinsic rewards and intrinsic motivation in education: Reconsidered once again. *Review of educational research*, 71, no. 1: 1-27. http://dx.doi.org/10.3102/00346543071001001

12. Edward L. Deci, Richard Koestner, and Richard M. Ryan. 1999. A meta-analytic review of experiments examining the effects of extrinsic rewards on intrinsic motivation. Psychological Bulletin 125, 6, 627--668. http://dx.doi.org/10.1037/0033-2909.125.6.627

13. Edward L. Deci, and Richard M. Ryan. Intrinsic motivation. John Wiley & Sons, Inc., 1975. http://dx.doi.org/10.1007/978-1-4613-4446-9

14. Sebastian Deterding, Dan Dixon, Rilla Khaled, and Lennart Nacke. 2011. From game design elements to gamefulness. In *Proceedings of the 15th International Academic MindTrek Conference on Envisioning Future Media Environments - MindTrek 11*. ACM. http://dx.doi.org/10.1145/2181037.2181040

15. Sharon M. Dowsett and David J. Livesey. 2000. The development of inhibitory control in preschool children: Effects of executive skills training. *Developmental Psychobiology*, 36, 2, 161--174. http://dx.doi.org/10.1002/(sici)1098-2302(200003)36:2<161::aid-dev7>3.0.co;2-0

16. Kathrin Maria Gerling, Regan L. Mandryk, Max Valentin Birk, Matthew Miller, and Rita Orji. 2014. The effects of embodied persuasive games on player attitudes toward people using wheelchairs. In *Proceedings of the 32nd annual ACM conference on Human factors in computing systems - CHI 14*. ACM. http://dx.doi.org/10.1145/2556288.2556962

17. John Haw. 2008. Random-ratio schedules of reinforcement: The role of early wins and unreinforced trials. *Journal of Gambling Issues*, 21, 56--67. http://dx.doi.org/10.4309/jgi.2008.21.6

18. Andy Field. 2009. *Discovering statistics using SPSS*. Sage publications.

19. Christina M. Frederick, and Richard M. Ryan. 1995. Self-determination in sport: A review using cognitive evaluation theory." *International Journal of Sport Psychology*.

20. Hamilton A. Hernandez, T.C. Nicholas Graham, Mallory Ketcheson, Adrian Schneider, Zi Ye, Darcy Fehlings, Lauren Switzer, Virginia Wright, Shelly K. Bursick, and Chad Richards. 2014. Design and evaluation of a networked game to support social connection of youth with cerebral palsy. In *Proceedings of the 16th international ACM SIGACCESS conference on Computers & accessibility - ASSETS 14*. ACM. http://dx.doi.org/10.1145/2661334.2661370

21. Hamilton A. Hernandez. 2014. Exergames for youth with cerebral palsy: Designing for Gameplay and Social Accessibility. *Queen's University*. (Thesis)

22. Hitt, Dawn D., Richard G. Marriott, and James K. Esser. 1992. Effects of delayed rewards and task interest on intrinsic motivation. *Basic and Applied Social Psychology,* 13, no. 4 : 405-414.

23. Elise Huillery, and Juliette Seban. 2014. Pay-for-Performance, motivation and final output in the health sector: Experimental evidence from the Democratic Republic of Congo. *Working Paper*, Department of Economics, Sciences Po, Paris.

24. Robin Hunicke, Marc LeBlanc, and Robert Zubek. 2004. MDA: A formal approach to game design and game research. In *Proceedings of the AAAI Workshop on Challenges in Game AI*, vol. 4, p. 1.

25. Michael J. Kane, Andrew R. A. Conway, Timothy K. Miura, and Gregory J. H. Colflesh. 2007. Working memory, attention control, and the n-back task: A question of construct validity. *Journal of Experimental Psychology: Learning, Memory, and Cognition,* 33, 3, 615--622. http://dx.doi.org/10.1037/0278-7393.33.3.615

26. Aniket Kittur, Ed H. Chi, and Bongwon Suh. 2008. Crowdsourcing user studies with Mechanical Turk. *In Proceeding of the twenty-sixth annual CHI conference on Human factors in computing systems - CHI 08*. ACM. http://dx.doi.org/10.1145/1357054.1357127

27. Rilla Khaled, Pippin Barr, James Noble, Ronald Fischer, and Robert Biddle. 2007. Fine Tuning the Persuasion in Persuasive Games. In *Persuasive Technology*. Springer Science Business Media, 36--47. http://dx.doi.org/10.1007/978-3-540-77006-0_5

28. Markus Krause, Marc Mogalle, Henning Pohl, and Joseph Jay Williams. 2015. A playful game changer: Fostering student retention in online education with social gamification." In *Proceedings of the Second (2015) ACM Conference on Learning@ Scale*, pp. 95-102. ACM.

29. Raph Koster. 2013. *Theory of fun for game design.* O'Reilly Media, Inc.

30. Lin, Dana T., Julia Park, Cara A. Liebert, and James N. Lau. 2015. Validity evidence for Surgical Improvement of Clinical Knowledge Ops: a novel gaming platform to assess surgical decision making. *The American Journal of Surgery* 209, no. 1: 79-85.

31. Mark R. Lepper, David Greene, and Richard E. Nisbett. 1973. Undermining children's intrinsic interest with extrinsic reward: A test of the" overjustification" hypothesis. Journal of Personality and social Psychology 28, no. 1: 129.

32. Yi-Guang Lin, Wilbert J. McKeachie, and Yung Che Kim. 2001. College student intrinsic and/or extrinsic motivation and learning. Learning and individual differences 13, no. 3: 251-258.

33. Conor Linehan, Ben Kirman, and Bryan Roche. 2015. Gamification as Behavioral Psychology 3. The Gameful World: Approaches, Issues, Applications: 81.

34. Andrew Macvean and Judy Robertson. 2013. Understanding exergame users physical activity, motivation and behavior over time. In *Proceedings of the SIGCHI Conference on Human Factors in Computing Systems - CHI 13*. ACM. http://dx.doi.org/10.1145/2470654.2466163

35. Regan L. Mandryk, Shane Dielschneider, Michael R. Kalyn, Christopher P. Bertram, Michael Gaetz, Andre Doucette, Brett A. Taylor, Alison Pritchard Orr, and Kathy Keiver. 2013. Games as neurofeedback training for children with FASD. In *Proceedings of the 12th International Conference on Interaction Design and Children - IDC 13*. ACM. http://dx.doi.org/10.1145/2485760.2485762

36. Regan L Mandryk, and Kevin G. Stanley. "Gemini: Accumulating context for play applications." In *Proceedings of the Ubicomp 2004 Workshop on Playing With Sensors*. 2004.

37. Edward McAuley, Terry Duncan, and Vance V. Tammen. 1989. Psychometric Properties of the Intrinsic Motivation Inventory in a Competitive Sport Setting: A Confirmatory Factor Analysis. Research *Quarterly for Exercise and Sport*, 60, 1, 48--58. http://dx.doi.org/10.1080/02701367.1989.10607413

38. John A. Nevin. 1969. Signal detection theory and operant behavior: A review of David M. Green and John A. Swets Signal detection theory and psychophysics1. *Journal of Experimental Analysis of Behavior* 12, 2, 475--480. http://dx.doi.org/10.1901/jeab.1969.12-475

39. Allen Newell, and Paul S. Rosenbloom. 1981. Mechanisms of skill acquisition and the law of practice. In *Cognitive skills and their acquisition*, 1: 1-55.

40. Scott Nicholson. 2014. A RECIPE for Meaningful Gamification. In *Gamification in Education and Business*. Springer Science Business Media, 1--20. http://dx.doi.org/10.1007/978-3-319-10208-5_1

41. Rui Nouchi, Yasuyuki Taki, Hikaru Takeuchi, Hiroshi Hashizume, Yuko Akitsuki, Yayoi Shigemune, Atsushi Sekiguchi, Yuka Kotozaki, Takashi Tsukiura, Yukihito Yomogida, and Ryuta Kawashima. 2012. Brain Training Game Improves Executive Functions and Processing Speed in the Elderly: A Randomized Controlled Trial. *PLoS ONE,* 7, 1, e29676. http://dx.doi.org/10.1371/journal.pone.0029676

42. Rita Orji, Julita Vassileva, and Regan L. Mandryk. 2014. Modeling the efficacy of persuasive strategies for different gamer types in serious games for health. *User Model User-Adapted Interaction*, 24, 5, 453--498. http://dx.doi.org/10.1007/s11257-014-9149-8

43. Dennis, Tracy A., and Laura J. O'Toole. 2014. Mental health on the go effects of a gamified attention-bias modification mobile application in trait-anxious adults. *Clinical Psychological Science.*

44. Byron Reeves, and J. Leighton Read. 2013. Total engagement: How games and virtual worlds are changing the way people work and businesses compete. Harvard Business Press.

45. Scott Rigby, and Richard M. Ryan. 2011. *Glued to Games: How Video Games Draw Us In and Hold Us Spellbound.* ABC-CLIO. http://dx.doi.org/10.5860/choice.49-0099

46. Margaret Robertson. 2010. "Can't play, won't play", (blog entry). Retrieved from: http://www.hideandseek.net/2010/10/06/cant-play-wont-play/

47. Richard M. Ryan, C. Scott Rigby, and Andrew Przybylski. 2006. The Motivational Pull of Video Games: A Self-Determination Theory Approach. *Motivation and Emotion,* 30, 4, 344--360. http://dx.doi.org/10.1007/s11031-006-9051-8

48. Richard M. Ryan and Edward L. Deci. 2000. Intrinsic and Extrinsic Motivations: Classic Definitions and New Directions. Contemporary Educational Psychology 25, 1, 54--67. http://dx.doi.org/10.1006/ceps.1999.1020

49. Lynne S. Padgett, Dorothy Strickland, and Claire D. Coles. 2006. Case study: using a virtual reality computer game to teach fire safety skills to children diagnosed with fetal alcohol syndrome. *Journal of pediatric psychology,* 31, no. 1: 65-70.

50. Katie Salen, and Eric Zimmerman. 2004. *Rules of play: Game design fundamentals.* MIT press.

51. Martin EP Seligman. 1975. *Helplessness: On depression, development, and death.* WH Freeman/Times Books/Henry Holt & Co.

52. Erin LD Seaverson, Jessica Grossmeier, Toni M. Miller, and David R. Anderson. "The role of incentive design, incentive value, communications strategy, and worksite culture on health risk assessment participation."American Journal of Health Promotion 23, no. 5 (2009): 343-352.

53. Joan G. Snodgrass and June Corwin. 1988. Pragmatics of measuring recognition memory: Applications to dementia and amnesia. Journal of Experimental *Psychology: General,* 117, 1, 34--50. http://dx.doi.org/10.1037/0096-3445.117.1.34

54. Lisa B. Thorell, Sofia Lindqvist, Sissela Bergman Nutley, Gunilla Bohlin, and Torkel Klingberg. 2009. Training and transfer effects of executive functions in preschool children. *Developmental Science,* 12, 1, 106--113. http://dx.doi.org/10.1111/j.1467-7687.2008.00745.x

55. Robert J. Vallerand and Gaétan F. Losier. 1999. An integrative analysis of intrinsic and extrinsic motivation in sport. *Journal of Applied Sport Psychology,* 11, 1, 142--169. http://dx.doi.org/10.1080/10413209908402956

56. Jan Van Looy, Cédric Courtois, Melanie De Vocht, and Lieven De Marez. 2012. Player Identification in Online Games: Validation of a Scale for Measuring Identification in MMOGs. *Media Psychology,* 15, 2, 197--221. http://dx.doi.org/10.1080/15213269.2012.674917

57. Nick Yee. 2006. Motivations for Play in Online Games. *CyberPsychology & Behavior,* 9, 6, 772--775. http://dx.doi.org/10.1089/cpb.2006.9.772

Mining for Gold (and Platinum): PlayStation Network Data Mining

Lindsay Wells; Aran Cauchi-Saunders; Ian Lewis, Lorenzo Monsif, Benjamin Geelan, Kristy de Salas
School of Engineering and ICT
University of Tasmania, Hobart, Australia
Aran.Cauchi-Saunders@utas.edu.au, Lindsay.Wells@utas.edu.au, Ian.Lewis@utas.edu.au,
Lmonsif@utas.edu.au, Benjamin.Geelan@utas.edu.au, Kristy.deSalas@utas.edu.au

ABSTRACT

Achievements are a common feature of modern video games. Early research efforts have attempted to classify achievements into taxonomies in order to identify achievement types and to learn about their potential affect on players, however, these studies have been constrained by small, manually collected samples of player data. This study describes a novel method of overcoming the lack of publicly-available achievement data, by scraping the PlayStation Network (PSN) for player profiles, including player achievement lists and progress in order to allow for a more informed analysis of players and their activities. Results of the application of this method have allowed us to source 30,227 player profiles, and subsequently learn that a number of factors can influence the earning of achievements, including PlayStation Plus subscriptions, player regions, and individual game achievement counts. We also present a wide range of future research applications which make use of this system to augment other existing datasets such as achievement taxonomies, sales figures, and review aggregators.

Author Keywords

Video Game, Game Achievements, Achievement Systems, Web Scraping

INTRODUCTION

Achievements (also known as trophies [1], badges [2], or accomplishments [3]) are a form of in-game reward and recognition for the completion of specific challenges in video games. Achievements are reliant on a centralized Achievement System that collects information across individual game titles or an entire platform (e.g. the PlayStation Network).

Despite the ubiquity of achievements in game systems, there exists a lack of publicly accessible repositories of achievements on any platform, which limits our ability to learn achievements within games. We feel that access to this data would facilitate a wide range of possible research objectives in this area, especially when linking this data to other sources. To this end, this study describes an approach to data-scraping video game achievements through the PlayStation Network, we report on what has been collected so far, and we explore the potential uses of such a dataset for future work.

Achievements integration into video games has increased steadily since the introduction of a platform-wide Achievement System on the Xbox360 in 2005 [4]. Achievement systems can now be found in many major game platforms [5, 6] including Battle.net [7], PlayStation Network (PSN) [8], Steam [7], and Facebook [6].

Unlocking or earning an achievement provides the player with a mechanism for translating gaming capital [9] into a digitally tangible [10], quantifiable, and communicable form of recognition on their profile [6, 11, 12]. We know that achievement systems record many play factors that are recorded consistently between systems such as a player's game completion statistic [6], achievement points per game [5, 6], Gamerscore for the Xbox [7], and trophy total for the PSN [1]. These metrics have been suggested to bear a form of social capital for the gaming community [9, 13]. Communities that focus on the achievement meta-game [4, 9] solely to increase personal account score and build a reputation in their gaming community have now developed [7, 9], with the aim of obtaining as many achievements as possible in the shortest amount of play time [4]. Furthermore, achievements have also been identified as an influencing factor in purchasing decisions for video games [3,15], along with being a factor in review performance by journalists [14], whilst also increasing the game's longevity [15].

Unfortunately, there are few studies which detail the motives of a player to complete achievements, possibly due to the lack of available large datasets on real-world achievements and player profiles, through which these motivations can be derived. This lack of research limits what we know about achievements and their impact, and subsequently their effective implementation into game design. Since 2005, three independent categorization studies have been conducted [3,16,12]. One study [3] conducted on Xbox achievements resulted in sixteen unique categorizations of achievements. A further study [16] focused on MMORPG achievements, resulting in fourteen unique categorizations of achievements. The most recent study [12] identified thirty-three distinct achievement types. This study focused on a much broader range of games and genres, analyzing over twelve-hundred achievements, producing a more comprehensive classification schema than the previous studies. However, there exists a lack of replication and application of these taxonomies. Low sampling rates, through manual profiling of player data, has led to categorizations without real-world validation.

In summary, achievements are an integral component of modern video games, yet we know very little of how they influence players. The body of knowledge suggests that a variety of factors influence how achievements are earned. A vital first step in exploring these issues is to empirically collect data on when and which achievements are earned, and by whom. An opportunity exists therefore to generate, and quantitatively analyze, large sets of achievement data and to preliminarily identify correlational aspects of achievements to players, and games. To this end, our paper is guided by three research questions:

- RQ1. How can a system be designed which collects en-masse achievement data about gamers?

- RQ2. What insights can be drawn solely from the data collected by the system described in RQ1?

- RQ3. What are the limitations of using only one source of usernames for the system described in RQ1, and what possible applications exist for the system when the data is supplemented with other data sources?

With this objective of collecting achievement data on a large scale in mind, data mining is the technique of analyzing large amounts of data to discover patterns and knowledge. To date, there have been no large-scale efforts to collect, analyze and report on achievement data in the public domain as there is an inherent difficulty in accessing the semi-closed Achievement Systems of the largest distribution platforms. Achievements Systems for three of the largest distribution platforms in the world, Xbox Live, PSN, and Steam boast subscription numbers in excess of 31 million [17], 72 million [18], and between seven to ten million users per day respectively [19].

Large-scale infrastructure is necessary to co-ordinate, store and confer these achievements to players on a real-time basis. While a full copy of these Achievement Systems could provide valuable insight into the nature of achievements and the players who earn them, the requirements to track these systems would fall into the realm of Big Data [20], and is an infeasible activity for smaller scale research teams. An alternative approach to this constraint is to perform semi-random sampling of the Achievement System, recognizing that while the data is not a full reflection of the Achievement System, generalizations can be inferred from the samples, and pattern evaluation can be performed to determine any relationships between achievements, games, and players.

An untapped resource for player profiling on a large scale remains unexplored: direct scraping from the Achievement System requiring automated collection and processing. The presence of a large, web-accessible, and accurate dataset which represents millions of player profiles would allow the rapid processing and analysis of trends and patterns between players, games, and achievements, without the constraints of the currently available data access format.

In summary, achievements are near-ubiquitous gaming symbols which create communities on gaming platforms that focus on the achievement-meta in an attempt to increase their social status. There has been little research into the systematic collection, processing, and analysis of achievement data. The following sections of this paper describe a novel approach to scraping and processing a large set of achievements (RQ1), the data collected so far (RQ2), followed by a discussion of the ways in which researchers might make use of such a dataset (RQ3).

METHODOLOGY

The following sections describe the mechanisms through which our systematic data collection on player profiles was performed, in pursuit of RQ1: *How can a system be designed which collects en-masse achievement data about gamers?*

Specifically, the PlayStation Network was chosen as the primary data source for this study as it has a diverse game library and provides access to an API for collecting player data. Our PSN Profile Scraper was developed based upon this API to collect data for a given set of usernames. The usernames to input into to the PSN Profile Scraper needed to be sourced and so the PSN Username Scraper was first developed to collect usernames, given that Sony does not have a published list of profiles. Given the input from the PSN Username Scraper, the PSN Profile Scraper outputs scraped data into a database. For analysis purposes, additional derived information was then added to the database by examining the relationships between players, games, and instances of earned achievements over time. The interaction between these three components is shown in Figure 1.

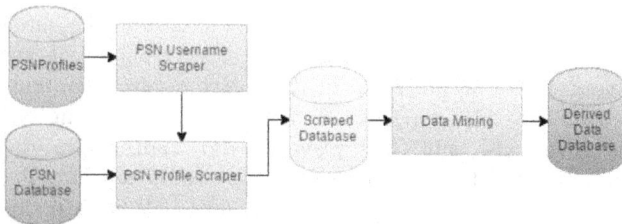

Figure 1: Program Flow: Databases, Scrapers, and Data Mining

The following sections describe each of these software components in detail.

PSN Username Scraper

To gain an accurate representation of the PSN, sampling players randomly directly from the PSN would provide an accurate cross-section of the user base. However, due to the nature of polling the PSN for profile data, a username must be provided to the PSN API. Therefore, the need for external sources of PSN usernames became apparent. A number of methods of sampling usernames were considered, all examining the rate at which names could be collected, the variety of profiles (in terms of player location, game collection, and play style), and other biases. The selected method was to collect usernames from a public source found online; the website PSNProfiles.com which lists over 2.6 million usernames of accounts on the PlayStation Network (as of April 2016) [21]. In order for an account to be listed on PSNProfiles, it must: a) be configured on the PSN to be viewable publically (this is the case by default); and b) have the username entered via the homepage of PSNProfiles. There is an inherent bias in this sampling method as accounts which are not set to be publically visible cannot be sampled this way, however this bias would be present regardless of the method as the PSN Profile Scraper would be unable to collect any data for these accounts. Another bias present in this approaches self-selection of users who have entered their name into a website, the sole purpose of which is comparison of achievements, and a better interface for listing achievement progress. Arguably this type of website attracts users who are aware of achievements, and are likely actively interested in earning them. It should be noted however that usernames can be entered by anyone (i.e. a friend, or stranger), not just the account owner.

Web scraping was utilized to acquire PSN usernames from PSNProfiles, which lists the names in a paginated leaderboard. The username scraper programmatically requested each page of the leaderboard (by simply changing an integer value for page number in the URL request) and examined the returned HTML response for entries in the leaderboard table which included the username. This name was then stored for future use as input into the PSN Profile Scraper described in the next section.

PSN Profile Scraper

The PSN Profile Scraper parses the PSN usernames retrieved from the username scraper to then acquire the respective public profile data from the PSN using a public API [22]. The API has functions for listing the games owned by a user, and the achievements the user has earned for a given game. For each username given as input, the PSN Profile Scraper requests the player's basic profile data which is stored in a table in the database, and a list of the games the player owns. For each of these games, the API is used to request the achievements for that game, and for each achievement, whether or not the player has earned the achievement, and if so, the timestamp of when the achievement was earned. This earned achievement information is stored in the database. During this process, whenever a game or achievement is encountered that isn't already present in the database, a new record is created in the game and achievements tables of the database. The structure of the resultant database is described in the following section.

Database

The data collected by the PSN Profile Scraper was stored in a relational database that facilitated the storage of: player profile data (region, PSN level, PSN progress through current level, PlayStation Plus status, and total count of bronze, silver, gold, and platinum achievements), games (title, and platform), achievements (name, icon, type (bronze, silver, gold, platinum, hidden), and PSN reported earned rate), earned achievements (including earned data). The data scraping was finalized on 14 April 2016.

A final step in the process was calculating additional information derived from the scraped data. For each game, a total count of the number of players (within the dataset) who own that game was calculated (owners), as well as the genre and release year of the game (both obtained programmatically by searching Metacritic.com). Additionally, the total and proportion of each achievement type within a game was calculated as well as the total number of achievements the game contains.

For each achievement, a percentage of the number of players (within the dataset) who had earned that achievement was calculated (earned rate). For each player, the total number of earned achievements was calculated (the sum of bronze, silver, gold, platinum, and hidden).

For every player and game relationship, we calculated the total number of achievements the player earned within that game. An additional approximate measure of game interaction was calculated as the time difference between the first and last achievement earned. We recognize that this is not an exact measure (i.e. just because a player is not earning an achievement, that doesn't mean they aren't playing the game - in particular play can continue even after earning a platinum achievement), this value still represents a definite period of time in which the player engaged with a game. A similar measure was estimated for the age of a profile, calculated as the number of days since the 19th April 2016, and the player's first achievement in any game. This would only be completely accurate if players earned an achievement on the first day their account was created. Given the weighting of achievements to the start of games, this measure is considered to be reasonably accurate if they played any game with a "normal" achievement progression on the first day of owning their account.

A more exploratory measure was calculated for players' total earned achievements within a game over time. A system was developed whereby a cumulative graph of a player's progress within a game was mapped in relative time before and after a given achievement, an approach inspired by previous work on achievements in the area of Gamification on the website StackOverflow.com [23]. The system can map this for a specific achievement across all players, or from the first or last achievement each player earned. The resultant series from this can then be averaged out for different groups of players to identify differences in how and when achievements are earned for these groups.

Legality

Web scraping exists in a grey area of data collection legality [24,25]. The uncertain nature of the legality of web scraping may be a limiting factor for deriving large datasets automatically from Achievement Systems. The methods used to scrape all data in this study do not break the terms of service of PSNProfiles.com or the PSN.

Summary

In summary, a system for obtaining usernames was developed to produce input for another system which scraped PlayStation Network profiles for the given usernames and stored the information in a relational database where further analysis and calculation was performed. The following section presents a statistical analysis of the data collected using this infrastructure, followed by a discussion of these results.

RESULTS

The PSN Username Scraper scraped all of the usernames listed on PSNProfiles.com as of February 2016 (n = 2,195,780). Due to constraints of processing time a random sample (n = 30,227) of profiles was used as the dataset for this paper. Despite this representing only 1.4% of the usernames listed on PSNProfiles.com and a small fraction of the 65 million active accounts [26], a dataset of this size has not yet been publicly examined. The following sections aim to address RQ2: *What insights cab be drawn solely from the data collected by the system described in RQ1?* by first presenting a summary of the amount of data that has been collected so far, before exploring the more interesting relationships between some of the variables collected. This section concludes with an exploratory analysis of the most

owned game in the dataset, Grand Theft Auto V. The reader is reminded to consider the bias in the sample by using profiles only from PSNProfiles.com when looking at these results—a bias which has been acknowledged in the previous section, and is considered later in the paper.

Amount of Data Collected

A total of 16,798,581 instances of players earning achievements were recorded, resulting in a total of 104,169 unique achievements from 3,212 unique games—the meta-data of which has also been stored. Of these achievements, 52.0% were bronze, 18.7% silver, 6.7% gold, 1.8% platinum, and 20.8% were hidden. The most earned type of achievement was bronze (65.1%) followed by silver (14.5%), hidden (16.9%), gold (3% gold), and platinum (0.5%).

Comparing this number of unique trophies (104,169) to the total 134,620 trophies listed on PSNProfiles.com, a 77.4% coverage was achieved from a sampling rate of 1.4% users (with a similar coverage of games at 72.1%).

The 30,227 players sampled represented a total of 60 different geographical regions. The most common regions were the United States (32%), Japan (11%), and Great Britain (10%). Players in the dataset earned an average of 555.7 trophies per player (SD = 617.36).

Games were scraped on an ownership basis, that is, at least one person owned that game for it to be reported. Players do not necessarily have to earn achievements for the game to exist in their PSN profile. There were a total of 1,059,747 player-to game relationships scraped, resulting in a mean ownership count of 330 (SD = 828.4) players per game, in the sample dataset. This corresponds to a heavily weighted ownership count of several popular games. Games owned by players in the dataset were across 3 platforms: PS4 (16.0%), PS3 (60.9%), and PSVita (23.1%).

This section has shown that even when using the data of around thirty thousand users, a considerable amount of achievement and game interaction can be gathered, highlighting further the value of collecting this data for more users in the future. The next sections examines some relationships identified between the variables collected.

Relationships between Factors

Achievement Earned Rate

The earned rate for each achievement within the users (calculated as a percentage of players within the dataset who have that achievement; M = 38.2%, SD = 0.1%) was found to be significantly higher (p < 0.001) than the percentage of players in total who have earned that achievement reported by PSN (M = 26.5%, SD = 7.8%) and a strong positive correlation (r = 0.886, p < 0.001) was found between these two factors.

In terms of distribution, 20.5% of achievements had an earned rate between 0 and 10% by players within the dataset, significantly lower (p < 0.001) than the 36.8% of achievements with the same earned rate reported by PSN. At the other end of the spectrum, 7.3% of achievements had an earned rate between 90 and 100%, which was significantly higher (p < 0.001) than the 1.6% reported by PSN.

Hidden achievements were on average earned by 44.9% (SD = 29.8%) of players in the dataset, which was significantly higher (p < 0.001) than non-hidden achievements (M = 36.5%, SD = 29.1%). This is comparable to the numbers reported by PSN for these types of achievements where the hidden achievements earned rate (M = 33.4%, SD = 25.7%) was significantly higher (p < 0.001) than that of non-hidden achievements (M = 24.7, SD = 24.7%).

Of the top 10 regions sampled, the regions with the highest average number of achievements earned per player were Italy (M = 722.1, SD = 681.8) and Germany (M = 663.2, SD = 700.5) which were both higher than the United States (M = 565.6, SD = 579.1).

PSN Level
PSN level is a public indicator of player progress in the Achievement System. Players earn levels through earning achievements, which give points (where bronze achievements afford the least points, and platinum achievements give the most). The exact value of points earned for each trophy diminishes as players progress higher through PSN level rankings. Level therefore is a rough public indicator of a player's achievement earnings for the lifetime of their account.

The average level of players recorded was 8.3 (SD = 5.4), out of a possible 100 level ranks. A small minority (0.95%) of players achieved a level of 25 or greater (M = 31.8, SD = 8.31). Figure 3 shows how the number of achievements contribute to the calculation of PSN level, and indicates a change in the calculation of level Sony uses after levels 12 and 25.

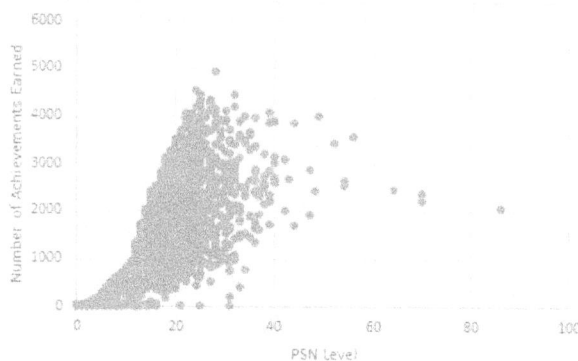

Figure 2. Plot of number of achievements earned against PSN level, showing noticeable changes in the calculation of PSN level at levels 12 and 25.

Through analyzing the relationship between players who own PlayStation Plus (PS-Plus), a paid-for subscription service, and those who do not, it was determined that PS-Plus owners had a significantly higher level than those of none PS-Plus subscribers (p = 0.00015) as shown in Figure 3. This was despite a lack of significant difference in average number of achievements earned per game, and average estimated game interaction per game.

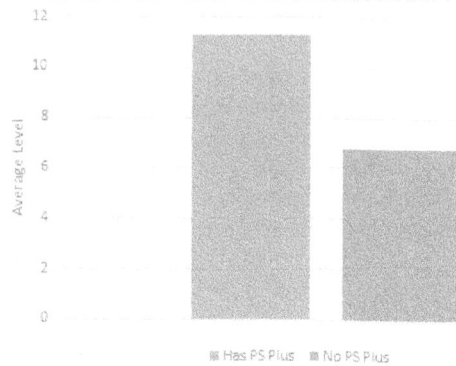

Figure 3. Graph representing the significant difference in average level between PS Plus Subscribers and Non-Subscribers

Game Interaction
The average derived game interaction of players per game was 120.3 days (SD = 97.4). The average derived age of profiles within the dataset was 1,700 days (SD = 754.3). This statistic was found to be weakly positively correlated to PSN level (r = 0.27, p < 0.05).

The average game interaction for games on the PS3 was 99.9 days (SD = 75.6) which was significantly higher than that of games on the PS4 (M = 30.9, SD = 36.1).

Game Release Year and Game Achievement Count
The number of achievements in a game was found to have a weak positive correlation to the number of players who own that game (r = 0.36, p < 0.05).

The average release year of games was 2011 (SD = 2.0), and there was a strong positive correlation between number of games released for a given year and year (r = 0.76, p < 0.05). A moderate positive correlation between year and the average number of achievements earned per game (r = 0.56, p < 0.05). There was a very weak negative correlation between the number of achievements in a game and year (r = -0.08).

Grand Theft Auto V
The most owned game in the dataset was Grand Theft Auto V (n = 13,524) making it a candidate for a further exploratory preliminary analysis in terms of player achievement progression.

For each player, a timestamp for the first achievement within the game was calculated. Then, for the 100 days after this achievement, the number of achievements the player had earned in that game were charted, resulting in a cumulative graph estimating the player's engagement with the game. These graphs were averaged out using a relative time series across different groupings of players within the dataset. Figure 4 shows a clear difference in the velocity of achievements earned can be seen for players who have a larger number of earned platinum achievements, as well as a noticeable point where achievement count does not increase, indicating a possible halt to play. Preliminary analysis on similar factors (including number of gold achievements earned, and strike rate) and on different games found similar results.

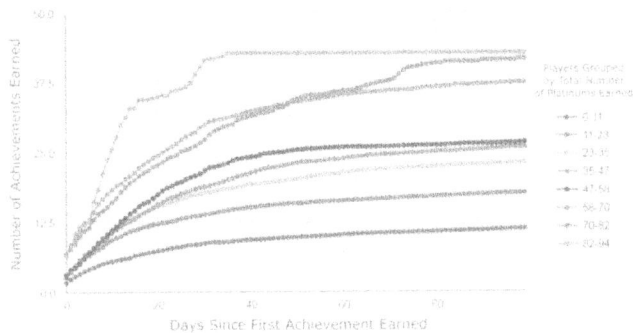

Figure 4. Cumulative graph showing the number of achievements earned in the days since a player earns their first achievement. Series are an average of all uses within a given range of platinum achievements earned on their profile for any game. A clear difference in velocity is apparent for players with 82-94 platinum achievements.

An ANOVA found there was a significant effect of number of platinum achievements on number of achievements earned at the p < .001 level for the eight groupings after 2 days [F(7,497) = 6.46, p < 0.001] and 99 days [F(7,497) = 19.63, p < 0.001].

DISCUSSION
The previous sections showed that a considerable amount of data was collected for 30,227 players, and revealed some interesting relationships between the variables collected. In the pursuit of RQ2, this section discusses the findings described in the previous section, by exploring individually the components data was collected for, achievements, players, and games.

Achievements
104,169 unique achievements were scraped for the database, and indicated that a large proportion of achievements were either bronze or silver. The PSN internally assigns a points value to the different levels of achievements with these points reflecting the difficulty of earning an achievement, which are then summed to calculated PSN score. Our findings correspond with the values Sony have determined, both in terms of the total

proportions of each type of achievement, and the rarity of these achievements within the dataset and outside the dataset.

It was also determined that players in the dataset earned trophies at a rate which strongly correlated with the PSN earned rate. Interestingly, players in the dataset were significantly more likely to have earned a given achievement, compared to a random player in the PSN. Part of this higher earned rate we believe is skewed by the existence of a number of games owned by only one person (n = 101), with achievements which were therefore only earned by one person (n = 1,001; 1%), resulting in a 100% earned rate. Further sampling should solve this, with more instances of players owning these less popular games.

Hidden achievements were earned significantly more than was the case of non-hidden achievements. This may be accounted for by the fact that hidden achievements are sometimes used for hiding story elements from players [36]. 16.9% of all achievements are classed as hidden. Due to constraints of the PSN API, earned hidden achievements are not reported by their trophy type, so an assessment of the difficulty to earn a given hidden achievement is limited.

Players
Several relationships were identified between the player cohorts in the dataset. It was observed that player level (M = 8.3, SD = 5.4) is heavily weighted to the lower quartile of the level ranking spectrum. From this it can be inferred that for the majority of players, they do not achieve close to the maximum number of levels that is possible. This fact may be due to the nature of most players in the dataset earning mostly bronze and silver trophies, compared to the higher scoring gold or platinum trophies. This speaks to the possibility that the inherent bias in selecting players from PSNProfiles.com is not as strong as it might seem on face value in that not all users on the site can be classified as achievement hunters. Indeed, as of February 2016 there exists approximately 250,000 profiles with less than 36 trophies on the site, according to their leaderboard page.

The factor of PlayStation Plus subscriptions affecting achievement earning was also explored. It was found that PS-Plus subscribers were significantly more likely to have a higher PSN level than non-subscribers. This leads to the assumption that gamers who choose to pay for PS-Plus are more likely to achieve greater levels in their profile, perhaps through the obligation to meet the cost of subscription with the greater worth of levelling up. Along with this, players who pay for a PS-Plus subscription may have access to more games, due to the fact PS-Plus provides free game access to players every month, and discounted prices on games, potentially increasing a PS-Plus player's exposure to game content.

Observing the regions for players, over 60 regions were sampled. It was determined that the United States, Japan and Great Britain were the three most common regions in the dataset. This is unsurprising due to large sales numbers of the PlayStation platform in the aforementioned countries. However, these three regions were not the highest earning regions by weighted average; Italy and Germany produced the highest average achievements earned by region. Without further demographic data, it becomes difficult to infer meaning from this relationship, however it can be stated that region ownership bears only a weak influence on the number of achievements earned.

The age of a PSN account was found to be weakly positively correlated with PSN level. This correlation can be inferred to imply that players need time to build their PSN level, and the age for the average PSN account in the dataset is 1,700 days, or 4.66 years old. From this, it can be assumed that for the majority of PSN players began collecting achievements before the release of the PS4 in late 2013.

Games
Of the total 1,059,747 game to player relationships, only 3,212 games were played by the 30,227 players in the dataset. It can therefore be stated that there is a significant overlap between players and the games they share in common. This factor may be linked to social networks of players on PSNProfiles playing similar games, along with simple game popularity. Due to the nature of popular games such as Grand Theft Auto V (the game with the highest ownership in our dataset) being owned by 13,524 players, or 44.8% of all players scraped, this explanation may be plausible. A weak positive correlation was also identified between game ownership and the total number of achievements in a game. This relationship may be weak initial evidence that achievement hunters may be more likely to purchase games that provide greater opportunities for earning achievements (i.e. games with more achievements), and this is worth exploring in future work.

Games when split into gaming platform (PS3, PS4, and PSVita) were significantly more likely to be played for longer periods on the PS3 than the PS4 or PSVita. This difference may be influenced by the relative newness of titles on the PS4 affecting how people interact with the platform and earn achievements.

FUTURE WORK
The analysis presented in this paper is preliminary in nature, and stands to benefit from additional source data, data from different sources, integration with previously published achievement taxonomies and game genres, and an interface for other researchers to interact with data. This section explores these future opportunities and limitations in turn, in order to address RQ3:

What are the limitations of using only one source of usernames for the system described in RQ1, and what possible applications exist for the system when the data is supplemented with other data sources?

A selection of 1.4% of the 2,195,780 usernames listed on PSNProfiles.com resulted in a number of outliers in the collected data, with 101 games being represented by only 1 player within the dataset. This had an impact on distribution of some variables, which we believe can be mitigated by collecting data about more players.

As identified previously, the sampling method used for source usernames has bias due to the purpose of the website the names were obtained from (i.e. achievement comparison and listing). Therefore, future work in this area of research is to obtain names from alternative sources. This presents an opportunity to examine any differences that are apparent between these groups and help describe the bias from those sources (i.e. do usernames scraped from PSNProfiles.com earn more achievements than those selected in another way?). One alternative source of names was to scrape usernames from the official PlayStation community forums, although the bias in users who have viewed the forums remains to be seen.

Another alternative method considered for obtaining names was to simply record usernames of players whose names appear in lobbies and scoreboards of a number of online games, however this would be prone to bias of what games were selected, and the locality of the servers the research team connected to within those games. Another method was to systematically traverse the friend lists of chosen profiles, however this would like attract a geological bias based upon the location of the owners of the chosen profiles. Both of these methods were also considered cumbersome in terms of efficiency, or were not likely to produce a large number of names.

Given the wide range of possibilities a dataset of this scale (not only in pure size, but geographically) presents, it is important to provide researchers with access to the data as they may take different approaches or ask different questions than our team. Therefore a user interface which allows researchers to query the data and extract results is planned for development. This interface will be presented online, as part of a service which continually scrapes PSN for up-to-date data, and data from previously unscraped users. Readers are encouraged to contact the authors for further information on obtaining access to this data. The remainder of this section explores the opportunities we have identified for further research, but given the wide reach of achievements into areas such as serious games and Gamification which are beyond the scope of this paper, our discussion here is not exhaustive.

Previous studies conducted on game Achievements have primarily focused on taxonomy [3, 12, 16]. Within a large dataset, grouping the data to explore differences is extremely valuable, and taxonomies present an opportunity to categorize achievements based upon previously developed taxonomies, and gather statistics on these categorizations. This augments the dataset, and can provide validation for the taxonomy itself if expected differences are found. Meta-data for over 100,000 achievements has been collected so far. Taxonomy designers may be able to randomly sample from this dataset, or programmatically examine all of them to produce different categorizations.

Another immediately obvious but non-trivial form of categorization is game genre. Preliminary analysis not reported within this paper has revealed that games of different genres attract differing engagement time and achievement counts.

Given the social nature of achievements [4,7,9,12], exploration of factors such as the relationship between the likelihood of an achievement being earned by a player compared to the percentage of friends who also have that achievement is an interesting avenue. Currently, the scraping program does not store friend links, however this is possible to obtain for profiles which make this available through the PSN API, a feature which will be added in future iterations of the software. Recording this information would allow researchers to visualize the PSN's social network structure, and explore how achievements are situated within that (e.g. do players with more achievements also have more friends?).

Previous studies have suggested that the number of achievements in a game may impact both player purchasing decisions [3] and reviewer scores [14]. Cross referencing the reported sales figures with the achievement data collected in the present study (not only achievement count, but also the relative rarity of the achievements available in the game) may provide some evidence toward the claim that players purchase games for their achievements. Whilst reliable sales figures may be difficult to come by, similar analysis for reviewer scores is made simpler by the existence of websites such as Metacritic.

Another possible impact of achievements according to the literature is that game longevity may be increased [15]. The current dataset provides timestamped achievement earning information, from which an estimate of the length of time a player engaged with the game may be able to infer by way of the first and last achievement dates earned. This estimate can be misleading for games which do not provide achievements early on in the progression, and does not account for play after the final trophy is earned (which may be a platinum, ensuring it is impossible to earn any more). However, if researchers wish to perform experiments on players in more controlled conditions or where actual playtime can be recorded in some way, a username can be collected from the player, which can be inputted into the scraping system to provide accurate achievement data (as well as their other profile data).

Similarly, researchers may want to use PSN usernames to link the present dataset with qualitative data, in order to overcome the non-specific nature of the data obtained (e.g. it is not discernable if players intentionally or inadvertently earned the achievements, or what feelings players had when they earned these achievements). The detail of the qualitative data collected in the present study presents an unprecedented point of comparison to self-reported feelings on achievements.

This paper presented a preliminary analysis of the timestamped data in an overview of achievement progress over time within Grand Theft Auto V using a system which is able to map the relative progress after earning the first achievement, before earning the last achievement, and before and after a specific achievement (a graphing inspired by the previous work of [23]). Future analysis using this tool will look at multiple games and different groupings to provide a visual representation of how progress can be effected, and the tool for mapping the data in this way will be provided online for researchers to explore this relative information for any achievement in any game in the dataset.

Finally, an interesting derived statistic not included in this paper due to processing time limits was a player's strike rate, calculated as the number of achievements the player has earned, divided by the maximum possible number of achievements they could earn calculated based upon the total number of achievements in the games they owned.

CONCLUSION

This paper has presented a method whereby information on players, games, and achievements from the PSN can be scraped using publicly accessible usernames. Preliminary analysis between these players, games, and their achievements was performed, and a discussion on the wide range of possible ways this dataset can be used to further the body of knowledge in this area has been presented.

It was determined through player profiling that players were significantly more likely to earn achievements if they possessed a PS-Plus subscription. Along with this, it was determined that the majority of players earn few achievements and do not rank highly on the PSN level rankings.

Through analyzing the relationship between achievements types, it was determined that hidden achievements were significantly more likely to be earned than non-hidden achievements, revealing the importance of spoiler content to game developers. It was also determined that achievements were in general homogenous between players in the dataset, whereby most players shared achievements in common with other players.

An exploratory analysis of Grand Theft Auto was also performed, where it was discovered that players with a higher number of platinums, earned achievements at a faster rate and earlier than players with fewer platinums. The preliminary analysis presents an opportunity to compare games on an individual player basis in the future.

With the mechanism for obtaining and analyzing Achievements presented in this paper, academics and industry can now undertake comprehensive studies on

Achievement data and explore the correlation between game Achievements and a wide variety of factors.

REFERENCES

1. Sony Computer Entertainment America LLC. 2014. Get Trophies. Get Recognition. Retrieved 6 January 2016 from http://us.playstation.com/community/mytrophies/.

2. Kongregate. 2013. Kongregate. Retrieved 7 January 2016 from http://www.kongregate.com/badges

3. EEDAR. 2007. Accomplishments Unlocked 2007. Retrived 7 January 2016.

4. Galli, L., and Fraternali, P. 2014 Achievement Systems Explained. In Trends and Applications of Serious Gaming and Social Media. Youngkun Baek, Ryan Ko, Tim Marsh (eds.). Springer Singapore 25–50.

5. Hamari J., and Eranti V., 2011. Framework for Designing and Evaluating Game Achievements. In Proc Digra 2011: Think Design Play

6. Lewis, I., de Salas, K., and Wells, L. 2013 Features of Achievement Systems. In Computer Games: AI, Animation, Mobile, Interactive Multimedia, Educational & Serious Games (CGAMES '13), 66–73.

7. Jakobsson, M., 2011. The Achievement Machine: Understanding Xbox 360 Achievements in Gaming Practices. In Game Studies 1, 1: 1-22

8. Lempel, E., 30 June 2008. PlayStation Blog. Retrieved 28 April 2013. from http://blog.us.playstation.coml2008/06/30/fimnware-v240-walkthroughpalt-2-trophies/.

9. Sotamaa,. O. 2009. Achievement Unlocked: Rethink Gaming Capital. In Proceedings of 3rd Vienna Games Conference: The Future and Reality of Gaming, Digital Games Research Association. 73–81.

10. Lucas Blair. 2011. The Use of Video Game Achievements to Enhance Player Performance, Self-Efficacy, and Motivation. Ph.D. Thesis, University of Central Florida, Orlanda, Florida.

11. Jakobsson, M. and Sotamaa, O. 2011. Special Issue - Game Reward Systems. In Games Studies 11, :1.

12. de Salas, K. and Lewis, I. 2013. Identifying types of Achievements. In Computer Games: AI, Animation, Mobile, Interactive Multimedia, Educational & Serious Games (CGAMES '13), 23–30.

13. Alhazmi, H., and Gokhale, S., 2015. Analysis of Structural Social Capital in Online Social Networks in The 3rd International Conference on Future Internet of Things and Cloud.

14. Griesemer, J. 2011. Undermining Achievements. Game Developer Magazine. 42–43.

15. Irwin, M. 1 April 2009. Unlocking Achievements: Rewarding Skill with Player Incentives. Retrieved 8 January 2016 from http://www.gamasutra.com/view/feature/132368/unlocking_achievements_rewarding_.php

16. Montola, M., Nulmnenmaa, T. Lucero, A., Boberg, M., & Korhonen, H. 2009. Applying Game Achievement Systems to Enhance User Experience in a Photo Sharing Service in 13th International MindTrek Conference: Everyday Life in the Ubiquitous Era.

17. Statistics Brain. 19 June 2013. Statistics Brain. Retrieved 17 January 2016 from http://www.statisticbrain.com/xbox-statistics/

18. Statistics Brain. 19 June 2013. Statistics Brain. Retrieved 17 January 2016 from http://www.statisticbrain.com/playstation-statistics/

19. Valve Corporation. 2016. Steam & Game Stats. Retrieved 7 January 2016 from http://store.steampowered.com/stats/

20. Fayyad, U., Piatetsky-Shapiro, G., Smyth, P. 1996, From Data Mining to Knowledge Discovery in Databases. AI Magazine 17, 3: 37 – 54.

21. PSNProfiles. 2016. Leaderboard. Retrieved 7 January 2016 from http://psnprofiles.com/leaderboard

22. Jhewt. 5 September 2015. Gumer-Psn. Retrieved 1 January 2016 from https://github.com/jhewt/gumer-psn/

23. Anderson, A. Huttenlocher, D., Kleinberg, J., and Leskovec, J. 2013. Steering User Behaviour with Badges. In Proceedings of the 22nd International Conference on World Wide Web, 95 – 106.

24. Mitchell, R. 2015. Web Scraping with Python: Collecting Data from the Modern Web. O'Reilly Media.

25. Xu, L., Jiang, C., Wang, J., Yuan, J., and Ren, Y. 2014. Information Security in Big Data: Privacy and Data Mining. In IEEE Access 2, 1149 – 1176.

26. Softpedia, 30 April 2015. Sony Plans to Invest Heavily in Its PlayStation Division This Year, Surprises Incoming. Retrieved 25 March 2016 from http://news.softpedia.com/news/Sony-Plans-to-Invest-Heavily-in-Its-PlayStation-Division-This-Year-Surprises-Incoming-479825.shtml

The Appeal of MOBA Games: What Makes People Start, Stay, and Stop

April Tyack
Queensland University of
Technology (QUT)
Brisbane, Australia
april.tyack@hdr.qut.edu.au

Peta Wyeth
Queensland University of
Technology (QUT)
Brisbane, Australia
peta.wyeth@qut.edu.au

Daniel Johnson
Queensland University of
Technology (QUT)
Brisbane, Australia
dm.johnson@qut.edu.au

ABSTRACT

Online multiplayer games are often rich sources of complex social interactions. In this paper, we focus on the unique player experiences (PX) created by Multiplayer Online Battle Arena (MOBA) games. We examine key phases of players' engagement with the genre and investigate why players start, stay, and stop playing MOBAs. Our study identifies how team interactions during play with friends or strangers affect PX during these phases. Results indicate the ability to play with friends is salient when beginning play and during periods of engagement. Teams that include friends support a wider range of play possibilities — socially and competitively — than teams of strangers. However, social factors appear less relevant to those choosing to stop playing, who do so for a variety of reasons. This study contributes to the field by identifying a strategy to improve the wellbeing of players.

Author Keywords

Multiplayer video games; player experience; MOBAs.

ACM Classification Keywords

K.8.0. Personal Computing: Games.

INTRODUCTION

Social experiences are essential to the structure of online video game play: in teamwork, direct communication, online scoreboards, and social media. These games create complex social worlds through which players engage in a shared experience. One of the largest emerging social game genres is the Multiplayer Online Battle Arena (MOBA), in which two teams compete to destroy each other's base. In MOBA games (henceforth referred to as MOBAs) individual players act collectively; teams coordinate to meet shared goals. MOBAs provide both collaborative (within teams) and competitive (between teams) play experiences.

While MOBAs are immensely popular [31, 38], the negative experiences associated with MOBA play are well-documented [21, 36]. The MOBA player experience (PX) is particularly influenced by the interplay between individuals and the social world created within the game; PX emerges partly as a function of the team-based interactions. Yet research into the social experiences of MOBA players, and player churn (a measure of the number of players leaving a game) is limited to a handful of exploratory studies [14, 16, 21, 36]. It is not clear the extent to which the PX issues associated with MOBAs are a function of the social dynamics that emerge through game play. A more complete understanding of the MOBA play experience is required.

Our research investigates what makes people start, stay, and stop playing MOBAs, with a focus on how team interactions impact on the player during these key phases of the MOBA experience life-cycle. The aim of this research is to understand the extent to which *who you play with* in a MOBA affects *how you play*, *your expectations*, and *how you feel* about the play experience. We investigate how PX – player mood and expectations in particular – is influenced by whether MOBA play involves friends or strangers.

By better understanding how team composition influences PX in MOBAs, we hope to gain insight into how MOBA play affects player mood, which in turn impacts wellbeing [13]. Research indicates the *quality* of social interactions, more so than the quantity, is related to subjective wellbeing among youth [27]. MOBAs are known for inducing extremes in both positive and negative social interactions, suggesting the potential to affect player wellbeing. However, further research into MOBA PX is necessary to identify the antecedents of such effects and how positive interactions may be encouraged.

Building on our previous research exploring this issue [16] we undertook this second study, with a new sample consisting exclusively of MOBA players, to consider emerging PX issues in depth. Our results indicate that players' reasons for churning are most often due to structural aspects of the genre (e.g., long game times, high commitment requirement), a considerable proportion of players appear to churn due to deviant behaviour. Motivations for beginning (and returning to) play are largely social, as expected; however, players did not often churn due to an absence of friends with whom to play.

Indeed, almost half of matches are reportedly played with a majority of strangers. This contrasts with the positive mood profile identified when playing with friends, as well as expectations of less teamwork and social interaction, and more conservative play (in order to avoid harassment or criticism) when playing with strangers. Interview responses support the idea that playing with friends is often difficult due to long, variable match times and obvious differences in skill levels. However, players appear reluctant to make friends via play, as such relationships lack a "real life" component. Our research contributes to games user research by identifying the influence that MOBA player interactions have on wellbeing [27] and the important contribution that positive social interactions play [11]. Understanding how *who we play with* affects our mood and interactions allows us to begin exploring ways to reduce the negative behaviours that pervade MOBA play. Such research may be used to start conversations with player groups and MOBA developers about ways to establish, build and maintain friendships within and communities around MOBAs.

BACKGROUND AND RELATED WORK

MOBAs are a relatively new videogame genre with influences from Role-playing games (RPGs), First-Person Shooter (FPS) games, and Real Time Strategy (RTS) games. MOBA play is typified by two teams of five players, each represented by an avatar with unique abilities, with the aim of controlling map objectives and eventually destroying their opponents' base, ending the game. They offer a wide range of strategic options in character selection, team composition, and play choices throughout each game; this variety of options in turn makes it difficult to imagine opponents' future play, increasing the level of challenge and skill required.

Player Experience

Player experience research is informed by theories from psychology or sociology to understand player behaviour and video game experiences [5, 12, 29, 33, 35]. The many different ways to measure PX [5, 7, 12, 24, 29, 33, 35, 48, 51] are designed to model game enjoyment, immersion, or motivations for play.

MOBA player experience has been identified as being highly frustrating and challenging, and cultivating less autonomy than other genres [16]. Interviews with MOBA players identified further themes of Competition, Mastery, and Teamwork as essential aspects of the genre, which exist in concert to motivate further play. Taken together, these factors contribute to intense ludic and social experiences. In League of Legends, team performance is associated both with players' familiarity with their chosen characters, and the way these characters complement each other [19], highlighting the importance of both in-game skill and knowledge of the game's triple-digit character roster. A quantitative analysis on social network formation in MOBAs, finding possible links between winning games with others and continued play together has also been

conducted; however, these findings were inconsistent across datasets [14]. Further research in this area is required to determine how players construct social networks within MOBAs, and how these relationships affect play.

PX and Player Churn

An analysis of player churn — a measure of the number of players leaving a game over a period of time — will assist in determining factors most relevant to players' enjoyment of the genre. Churn is not often studied in video game research; however, Riot Games, the developers of League of Legends, have determined that players exposed to poor player behaviour are up to 320% more likely to churn, making it a significant issue for the game's longevity [25]. This is supported by further research in the area [36], with the additional findings that long game times and deviant behaviour from teammates cause newer League of Legends players to churn. Playing with more friends was the only factor found to positively affect experienced players' long term retention. Due to the relative lack of information on the topic, our research provides a preliminary investigation of MOBA players' stated reasons for churning.

PX and mood

While many researchers have focused on the motivations for play and enjoyment in games, others have looked more specifically at effects of PX on player emotion and mood, which influence subjective wellbeing [6]. Mood can be defined as a set of feelings that vary in intensity and duration and usually involve more than one emotion [23], with potential to influence individuals in both positive and negative ways, particularly in personally important situations [41]. For example, a study of team sports [39] found positive relationships between measures of team cohesion and improved mood before competition. Existing research regarding videogames' effects on mood demonstrate their potential to reduce depression and stress [32]. Play with friends in a competitive setting has been associated with decreased vigour [30] and no significant difference in frustration [10] when compared to play with strangers. Social presence experienced in multiplayer games can also affect player mood through interaction and shared experience [5]. Such play is typically positive, but detrimental effects on mood may occur when social interaction itself is negative. The perception that social interactions in MOBAs can be negative invites exploration into relationships between PX and mood.

Social Videogame Play

Social interaction is a compelling motivation for playing games [15, 35]. Evidence suggests that videogames create a common ground that assist young people in creating and maintaining friendships [3]. New relationships formed via online play appear to have potential in offering similar support to those maintained offline [43], and these relationships are associated with increased wellbeing [45]. FPS games are often cited as contributing to social isolation; however, research consistently demonstrates that FPS game play is often socially motivated [15]. Social play may facilitate group flow, a state in which group members experience common feelings of task-associated focus, associated with communication, teamwork, and context-relevant awareness of others' abilities [18].

Voice chat, or Voice over Internet Protocol (VoIP), in online multiplayer games facilitates the communication of strategy and assists in forming social bonds [46, 47]. In-game communication features allow players to construct their own social experiences, either with strangers or friends. Players construct their own meanings around in-game events and the actions of other players, based on the perceived intent of those players [17].

PX in Online Games

Although the MOBA social experience is relatively unstudied, much has been published on social experiences in other online game genres. Massively Multiplayer Online Role-Playing Games (MMORPGs), especially World of Warcraft (WoW), have been thoroughly mined for insights on motivation, identity, and social practice in online spaces. MMORPGs structurally promote the cultivation of strong relationships with other players through shared play experiences [2, 34, 51], and many people are motivated to play in part because of the rich social experiences afforded by the genre's focus on collaboration. Of those players who attempt the most difficult challenges, some burn out and quit entirely, with the possibility of returning to play in a way demanding less of their time and energy [54].

Players may similarly form close bonds with each other through online First Person Shooter (FPS) game play, commonly through organised groups or "clans" [43]. As in MMORPGs, social interaction is a key motivator for continued play [15]. Although players may not know each other in real life, friendships made through such play can provide support for offline problems. Players may discuss real-life problems during play, which may serve to distract from the emotional weight of such issues [9].

Social interaction in online games is not always positive, and this was true even in their infancy. Poor behaviour in MMORPGs is typically called "griefing", defined by player use of in-game advantages to dominate or harass less experienced or new players, who cannot retaliate [8]. In online FPS game play, antisocial behaviour commonly takes the form of verbal harassment over voice chat, killing one's own team members, and hacking to gain an unfair advantage [44]. The most frequently reported deviant behaviour in League of Legends involves abuse of text chat or — as team killing is impossible — demonstrating their limited power by assisting the enemy team (e.g., by dying on purpose repeatedly) [1]. Analysis of text chat in MOBAs indicates that deviant players are initially less sociable than regular players [21], potentially indicating a higher focus on game outcomes for the former group. Although deviant behaviour occurs relatively often, it appears to affect player retention for newer players only [36]. While our research doesn't explicitly focus on antisocial or deviant behaviour,

we do examine how in-game social interactions, both positive and negative, are perceived by players, how these interactions differ depending on team composition, and how these differences affect the quality of the player experience.

INVESTIGATING MOBA PX

Three research questions were identified:

RQ1: What draws people to MOBAs?

RQ2: What motivates people to keep playing MOBAs?
    2a: How does PX change when playing in teams of friends, strangers, or a combination of the two groups?
    2b: How do players develop in-game friendships?

RQ3: What causes people to stop playing MOBAs?
    3a: What factors affect MOBA players' churn rates?
    3b: What factors can affect players' reasons for returning to MOBAs after long periods of absence?

A survey and interviews were used to gather quantitative and qualitative data to address these research questions. The survey was designed to provide information on all three research questions. Interview questions were chosen to help explain the data gathered from the surveys, and to clarify how different team dynamics influence the play experience.

Survey

An online survey was designed to gather information on initial reasons for play, PX differences arising from team composition, and player churn. Survey participants were sourced from a variety of online spaces, including MOBA-related forums, genre-agnostic video game forums, Facebook groups, and Twitter. It was important to draw participants from a variety of locales to reach a wide demographic range of players.

Survey Content

The survey measured typical demographic information, including gender, age, preferred MOBA, and perceived MOBA skill. We also asked participants for the number of years of experience they had with MOBAs, average MOBA play time in the previous month, and their peak MOBA play hours in a single week.

Three survey questions addressed RQ1, asking participants about their early MOBA experiences: the reason that they started playing a MOBA, how many MOBA players they knew when they started playing, and how many of these people were part of their learning experience in the game.

In addressing RQ2, we focused on how the team-based social world created in a MOBA influences PX. We asked participants their preferences with respect to team composition (i.e., friends or strangers), and subsequently the extent to which they valued particular characteristics of individual activity (i.e., skilled play and playing complementary roles) and team-based processes (i.e., positive attitude, enjoyable conversation, and communication and coordination) when playing with friends and strangers. Value was assessed on a 5-point scale ranging from "Not at all important" to "Extremely important". These characteristics of the MOBA play experience were chosen through preliminary discussion with MOBA players and previous research. The survey also examined the use of voice communication in MOBAs, as voice chat use among friends has previously been shown to strengthen these relationships [47]. Participants were asked how often they had used voice chat with friends and strangers in their most recent month of MOBA play, on a 5-point scale between "Never" and "Every time". Two further survey questions asked about the potential for friendship formation through MOBA play.

The current interest in the effects of player behaviour in MOBAs led us to examine player experience in terms of how play affects player mood. The Brunel Mood Scale (BRUMS), a validated abbreviation of the Profile of Mood States previously used in sport [40] and videogame [32] research, was employed for this purpose. Its six subscales — Tension, Vigour, Confusion, Fatigue, Depression, and Anger — were measured using a 24-item instrument, employing a 5-point Likert scale response form. Subscale reliability values (Cronbach's α) were 0.84, 0.78, 0.81, 0.81, 0.86, and 0.89, respectively. Respondents were asked to recall their mood in their most recent experience of play in a team with at least one friend, and in a team composed entirely of strangers. Players who had not experienced either occurrence in their last month of play did not answer the corresponding question.

Finally, for players who had ceased playing for more than 3 months, the survey asked why they had stopped playing (RQ3), as this measure completes the picture of long-term MOBA engagement. Multiple-choice questions assessed player reasons to stop and (then later) return to play.

Data and Analysis

A total of 966 participants began the survey. Of these, 42 respondents who did not meet the age requirement for the study (over 18) were excluded. A further 125 (of the remaining 924) were excluded for incomplete responses (they did not provide answers to any of the substantive research measures), and 37 were excluded for providing 'response set' answers (e.g., answering 1 for all items). This resulted in a final sample of 760 participants. Survey data was initially analysed using descriptive statistics to identify the main features of the information collected. These descriptives communicate properties of the survey responses, and were used to identify interesting patterns of results for further analysis. Inferential statistical analysis was undertaken on survey data relating to PX (e.g., mood) when playing with friends and strangers.

Survey Participant Demographics

Our final sample of 760 participants were aged between 18 and 40 years of age (mean age = 21.66, SD = 3.76) and 89% were male. Of those surveyed, 25% primarily play Dota 2, 23.42% play League of Legends, 40.39% play Smite, and 10.79% play Heroes of the Storm. The discrepancy between Smite players and players of other MOBAs is likely due to the increased success of the survey on the Reddit /r/Smite board over posts on /r/LeagueofLegends, /r/Dota2, and /r/HeroesoftheStorm.

Most commonly, participants have played MOBAs for two years (21.84%), while 20.79% have three years' experience and 16.84% have played MOBAs for a single year. Interestingly, 83.55% of respondents consider themselves at least "Moderately Skilled" at MOBAs — it may be that participants involved in MOBA communities are more skilful, or that players simply overestimate their own ability. The sample may be subject to bias from participant self-selection due to the nature of the places in which we advertised (i.e., Facebook groups and MOBA forums are likely to house more engaged players).

Interviews

Follow-up interviews were conducted to help explain the data generated from the surveys, and to provide insight into other aspects of the study not easily identifiable through survey measures. Interview participants were sourced from volunteer survey respondents, and willing QUT students. Snowball sampling was also employed. Interview participants were subject to the same restrictions as survey participants — that is, they were required to be aged 18 or over, and to have played a MOBA in the previous year.

Procedure

Participants were interviewed at a time and place of their choosing. Respondents sourced from the survey were interviewed using Skype, while participants found through other means were interviewed on campus. Each interview took between 45 to 90 minutes, with questions designed to probe further into the MOBA player experience, the reasons for player churn, and how social relationships emerge and are maintained within MOBAs. A semi-structured interview format was chosen, allowing for follow-up questions and discussion of topics not considered by the interview plan.

Interview Content

The interview began with questions regarding participants' basic demographic information, including their history with MOBAs and when they first played a game in the genre. We asked for opinions on factors contributing to a positive MOBA experience. Questions followed regarding players' typical PX with friends and strangers, expected and valued behaviour, and factors affecting mood when playing with friends or strangers. Given our interest in differences between play with friends and strangers, a series of questions about the transition from stranger to friend were included. Churn was explored through questions related to reasons for stopping play.

Data and Analysis

Audio of each interview was recorded and later transcribed, and notes were taken during the interview. A content analysis approach focused on identifying frequent and significant themes emerging from the raw data in relation to the research questions.

Interview Participant Demographics

Interviews were conducted with eight MOBA players, seven of whom were male. At the time of the interview, five participants were primarily playing League of Legends, one was playing Dota 2, and two were Smite players. Experience with MOBAs varied; participants had between 18 months and 7 years of experience playing MOBAs.

RESULTS AND DISCUSSION

Reasons for Starting MOBA Play

Initial survey and interview questions were designed to investigate factors drawing people to MOBAs (RQ1). A majority of survey respondents (65.22%) noted that their main reason for beginning MOBA play was that their friends were already playing the game. A substantial proportion (84.38%) indicated they knew at least one friend who played their chosen MOBA when they started to play. Another reason cited for starting to play a MOBA game was having watched someone play the game online (streaming), at 12.64%. A large (14.67%) proportion selected the "Other" option for this question and provided further detail. However, analysis of the associated reasons stated failed to produce significant themes (no category represented over 3% of responses).

Five of the eight interview participants (P1, P3, P5, P7, and P8) mentioned friends or acquaintances as a reason that they started playing a MOBA. In three cases this answer was accompanied by an associated reason (the game was free (P1), had nothing else to do at the time (P5), as a part of a LAN party (P8)). Interview participants identified trying new games as fundamental to gamer culture (P2, P7), or interest in professional tournaments (P5, P7) as motivation.

Both the survey and interview data highlight the importance of friends as a reason to begin playing MOBAs. In light of existing research into online play motivations [37, 53], this result may appear obvious; however, it is worth noting here for its contrast with other findings from the current study.

PX during MOBA Play

Nearly 70% of those surveyed reported playing with at least one friend "often" or "every time" (69.28%). The difference between who players prefer to play MOBAs with and who they typically play with is shown in Table 1.

No. of friends	Typical (%)	Preferred (%)	Difference (%)
0	17.97	4.78	13.19
1	28.99	9.13	19.86
2	30.58	20	10.58
3	10.72	6.96	3.76
4	11.74	59.13	-47.39

Table 1. Typical and preferred number of friends (same team)

A majority of respondents prefer to play with a full team of friends (59.13%); however, only 11.74% of people play games in this way. While most players have a preference to play with one friend or more, in many instances (17.97%) play games with a group of strangers. Our interview results suggest that this pattern, as might be expected, largely reflects that friends are not always available when an individual has the opportunity to play. *"The times I'll play solo queue are when I haven't been able to find anyone online"* (P2).

Importance of Player Characteristics

Survey participants indicated the level of importance they placed on five key characteristics of the team-based MOBA experience — positive attitude, skilled play, playing complementary roles or characters, enjoyable conversation, and good communication and coordination. We asked this in relation to "teammates who are friends" and "teammates who are strangers".

Wilcoxon signed-rank tests were employed to determine differences between the rated importance of player attributes when playing with strangers and friends. Asymmetric distributions of differences were found for Enjoyable Conversation violating the assumption required for the Wilcoxon signed-rank test, so for this measure a Sign test was used instead [22]. A Bonferroni correction was applied to control the experiment-wise error rate across the 11 tests conducted (for Importance of Player Characteristics and Mood), which changed the required significance level to 0.0045.

Significant differences between groups in the importance of all factors were found, with the exception of Good Communication and Coordination (Table 2). Skilled Play is more highly valued among strangers than friends, as is playing Complementary Roles or Characters. However, participants reported a preference for Positive Attitude and Enjoyable Conversation with friends, in comparison to strangers.

Variable	Strangers		Friends		z	r
	Mean	SD	Mean	SD		
Positive Attitude	4.07	1.09	4.21	0.99	-3.46*	0.10
Skilled Play	3.61	0.98	3.08	1.18	11.55**	0.32
Enjoyable Conversation	2.35	1.30	3.97	1.11	-20.66**	0.56
Complementary Roles/Characters	3.39	1.14	2.96	1.30	8.34**	0.23
Communication and Coordination	3.89	1.03	3.96	1.06	-1.63	0.04

*p < 0.01, ** < 0.001

Table 2. Importance of Player Characteristics comparisons

Thus, survey responses indicated that MOBA players value positive attitude and enjoyable conversation more in friends, while valuing skilled play and playing complementary roles or characters more in strangers. It is interesting to note that when playing with strangers, PX measures relating to how individual players' actions (e.g., execution of tasks, division of labour) affect team performance take on greater importance. In contrast, when people play with friends, the social dynamics of play are

317

more highly valued. At first glance, it may appear that a dichotomy exists for play in these modes determined by such social or competitive factors.

This is supported, to some extent, by the interview responses. Some participants (P2, P5, P8) note that strangers' individual skills directly affect their feelings about each game. *"It comes down more about how well they're playing"* (P2). However, the consequences of appearing inept appear to be more salient. Harassment and harsh criticism commonly occur. *"If someone* [makes a mistake]*, a stranger will insult them immediately"* (P1), *"Usually it starts out friendly... it can very easily escalate"* (P4), *"There's always going to be one flamer"* (P6).

The increased value placed on strangers playing complementary characters or roles also suggests a more competitive experience with this group. Some interview participants (P5, P7) enjoy collaborating in the game lobby to pick characters that work well together. With friends, a number of those interviewed (P2, P7, P8) enjoy trying new characters or strategies that would draw ire with strangers. *"It's good learning a champion* [with a team of friends]*...we don't expect you to do well"* (P2), *"*[With strangers] *there's no wiggle room* [to experiment] *without getting some flame or not having any backup"* (P7). Friends' character choices are thus less relevant when the game outcome is de-emphasised in favour of supporting experimentation, learning, and individual fun.

Enjoyable conversation is likely more highly valued with friends due to their pre-existing relationships, implying shared interests. *"*[Play with friends is] *typically a more pleasant experience, because...they're people I already like"* (P8). In contrast, the only reliable common interest among strangers is MOBA enjoyment. In-game discussions with friends are facilitated by voice chat, supporting more social experiences (P3, P4). *"If it's a skype call...that's always a great time"* (P4).

However, the idea that play with friends is *always* more casual, or play with strangers is *always* more competitive is not supported by the interview data. Participants (P1, P3, P4, P7, P8) described times where strangers made games entertaining through atypical means, such as by role-playing their character. Interviewed players (P1, P3, P5, P6, P7, P8) value strangers' social attributes and positivity, but this behaviour is believed to be rare. *"*[I value others] *responding to comments I make"* (P1), *"It's great if they're just nice"* (P3), *"I appreciate a team that can take a bit of a joke"* (P7), *"Not every game is going to go well... I like the people who can accept that"* (P8). Two participants (P4, P7) suggested they could determine the tone (e.g., casual, negative) of each game by strangers' behaviour in the game lobby, which is in line with existing research [4].

This dichotomy is further challenged by interview responses acknowledging interest in playing seriously with friends. While players noted their preference for enjoyable

conversation with friends, discussions range from topics outside of the game (P1, P2, P4, P7) to strategic considerations (P2, P3, P4, P5, P7) for which only their friends can be trusted. *"I'll ask* [friends'] *opinions more than a stranger... I know their credibility"* (P4). Similarly, some participants (P4, P8) avoid playing with friends of noticeably lower skill, or those who take the game less seriously. *"They suck at Dota... any excuse will do"* (P8). Less skilled players (P1, P7) avoid friends who are too skilled or too competitive. *"I just hate the people who take* [the game] *too seriously"* (P1).

A lack of difference in the value of communication and coordination with friends or strangers is consistent with previous findings that teamwork is essential in MOBA play and multiplayer games in general [16, 28, 42]. Interviewed players (P1, P2, P5) recognised the value of teamwork from strangers, although they do not, on the whole, *expect* such collaborative behaviours. *"People are out for themselves"* (P1). Strangers are expected to play with less regard for teamwork, and one participant discussed changing his own strategy in the same way. *"*[With strangers] *I try to play characters that don't require backup. *[A character who] *if you need to, you can take someone out"* (P1). Interview participants (P1, P2, P3, P6, P8) similarly valued team play with friends, noting that team cohesion can make otherwise negative experiences fun. *"A positive game* [occurs when] *even if the game is bad, everyone works as a team"* (P3). Strategies can be more easily communicated using voice chat rather than through text, giving teams of friends more opportunities to make exciting plays, while lowering the possibility of miscommunication. *"You can easily explain, you're not limited by how fast you can type"* (P2), *"*[Voice chat] *means that we work a lot better together and we can play a lot more aggressively"* (P8).

Mood

The survey directed participants to consider their mood during MOBA play in which they were part of a team composed "entirely of strangers". Similarly, participants were asked to describe their feelings when playing in a team including "at least one friend". Wilcoxon signed-rank tests were employed to determine differences between the two groups in their experienced mood when playing with strangers and friends. Asymmetric distributions of differences were found for four mood measures of BRUMS (Confusion, Fatigue, Depression, and Anger), violating an assumption of the Wilcoxon signed-rank test, so for these four measures Sign tests were used instead [22]. As seen in Table 3, participants reported significantly lower levels of Tension, Confusion, Fatigue, Depression, and Anger when playing with at least one friend, rather than with strangers. Significantly higher levels of Vigour were reported when playing with friends compared to strangers.

Differences in reported mood between play in teams with at least one friend and teams of strangers are striking in their consistent favour of the former group. Increased tension with strangers is likely due to their expected reprisal following mistakes, which can influence behaviours such as over-preparation (P4). In contrast, friends are more likely to be supportive after mistakes, or criticise in constructive ways (P1, P2, P4, P6, P7, P8). *"I don't mind friends telling me on occasion that I've done something terribly stupid... as long as they're somewhat civil about it"* (P2). However, one participant felt otherwise, citing a self-inflicted pressure to perform with friends. *"I feel more relaxed when I play with strangers. There's just a higher expectation when I play with friends, even if we are just goofing around"* (P5).

Variable	Strangers		Friends			
	Mean	SD	Mean	SD	z	r
Tension	1.89	0.90	1.57	0.76	-9.74*	0.33
Vigour	3.00	0.89	3.34	0.89	7.12*	0.24
Confusion	1.95	0.84	1.51	0.64	-13.69*	0.47
Fatigue	1.89	0.83	1.59	0.72	-11.22*	0.38
Depression	1.79	0.86	1.39	0.65	-12.71*	0.43
Anger	2.35	1.07	1.74	0.81	-13.63*	0.47

*$p < 0.001$

Table 3. Mood comparisons on BRUMS subscales

Increased vigour with friends is consistent with the view that MOBA play is more meaningful with friends, potentially due to the increased social element [16], or the endowed importance of experiences shared with friends (P2, P4, P5, P6). As discussed, communicating with friends, particularly when using voice chat, provides more interesting experiences than interacting with strangers limited by text. This result may also reflect a greater adherence to commonly accepted strategies with strangers, which some participants described as less engaging than having the freedom to derive their own (P2, P7, P8). More frequent risky or aggressive plays with friends (P3, P4, P5, P8) may contribute to increased vigour in a similar fashion. However, in contrast, P1 and P7 described play with strangers as more invigorating than play with friends. *"My adrenaline will be pumping* [with strangers]*, because I don't want to be the worst"* (P1).

Play with strangers may be more fatiguing due to greater concentration in this mode, related to increased pressure associated with avoiding negative feedback while retaining focus on the game outcome. Further, mental effort is required to predict strangers' strategies, whereas friends can predict each other's behaviour from previous experiences. *"I know when I'm almost dead I can still go in"* (P3), *"You usually know what they would do...you* [have] *the same understanding of what they would do in a situation"* (P6).

Increased confusion when playing with strangers reflects the difficulty of effectively communicating with the tools typically available. As players are more likely to use voice chat with friends than with strangers, up-to-date strategic information is typically better conveyed with this group.

Text chat, more commonly used with strangers, requires a combination of shorthand (e.g., "MIA" when a lane opponent is missing) and positioning such that opponents are unable to take advantage of players' inability to take action while typing. This limits communication and engenders trust less effectively than voice chat [47].

The difference in depression (here appropriately conceptualised as depressed mood rather than clinical depression) when playing with strangers may be influenced by this group's tendency towards deviant behaviour. Three interview participants (P1, P2, P4) reported that friends support them when being harassed, which could mitigate negative feelings. *"If I make a mistake, they're not going to harass me...*[if someone else does] *they'll defend me"* (P4). The reduced potential for depressed mood caused by losses or mistakes when playing with friends may also be affected by the typically more casual nature of those experiences (P1). Although player mood with friends is affected by wins and losses (P2, P4, P5, P6), the effect of losing may be mitigated by the shared experience. *"Even if they're not good, if we lose the game,* [we] *still have fun"* (P4).

Lower tolerance for mistakes may explain surveyed players' increased anger with strangers. Because strangers are less socially interested in each other than friends, their worth is determined more by their skill. *"With strangers I'm more interested in how they're playing than how they feel about playing"* (P8). In interviews, player mood with strangers was consistently related to the level of harassment or deviant behaviour displayed by others in the game (P1-P7). Anger may therefore be induced with strangers as a reaction to this behaviour. Conversely, friends are understanding of mistakes, and support each other when faced with harassment. *"When I'm playing with friends, I don't have to worry about that negative side as much"* (P4).

Team Communication
Over half (53.57%) of those surveyed always use VoIP when playing with friends. In contrast, 38.72% of survey respondents never use VoIP with strangers at all, and only 8.26% use it every time. Half of the interview participants (P2, P4, P6, P8) discussed their reluctance to use voice chat with strangers, due to the potential for negative experiences, or the associated logistic difficulties. P4 and P8 alluded to waiting to find out more about a stranger's disposition before using voice chat. *"I try to suss out whether the AD carry is going to be a dick"* (P4), *"I typically try not to* [use voice chat with strangers] *unless they come out first as friendly, talkative folk"* (P8). In contrast, most participants (P2, P3, P4, P6, P7, P8) consider voice chat a significant asset during play with friends. *"The most important fact is being able to talk to* [friends] *in TeamSpeak"* (P3).

Making Friends through Play
While a significant proportion (82.14%) of survey respondents have added a stranger to their friends list, 53.8% of participants indicated they had added a stranger with whom they never played again. Interview responses

319

support this trend, as for most respondents, new in-game friendships are only formed via pre-existing friends. A majority of interview participants (P1, P2, P5, P6, P8) have never made friends with complete strangers during MOBA play, despite their own admissions that playing with friends is more enjoyable. However, several respondents (P1, P2, P5, P7) play MOBAs at least partly to stay in contact with friends made outside the game. *"I definitely keep in contact with friends* [through the game]... *our method of communication is through League* [of Legends]*"* (P5).

The most commonly stated reason for not making in-game friends is that for many, friends are people they can meet in real life (P1, P2, P6, P8). The implausibility of playing with strangers who live in their area deters these players from making friends during play. *"I haven't met anyone who I would invite over to my place"* (P1), *"Only if I meet them in person would I consider them more than just someone on a friends list"* (P6). Others avoid forming relationships to avoid feeling obliged to play. *"I play on my own schedule... it's just less fiddly to not bother in the first place."* (P8).

Of those open to making friends through MOBA play (P3, P4, P7), relationships most often form when effectively playing together, especially when strategies are naturally well-coordinated [49]. This is in contrast to participants' recollections of typical experiences with strangers, whose behaviour they struggle to predict. Making friends through a desire to develop skill was reported by one participant (P7), who, as a new player, asked strangers for advice — people who responded positively or offered further coaching often became his friends.

Standards for in-game friends also differ from those held for friends met offline. While many such relationships revolve around MOBA play, some participants expressed desires to discuss unrelated topics. *"Someone I enjoy the idle conversation with — the non-League* [of Legends] *conversation"* (P2), *"You have to be able to talk about other things"* (P4). Relatedly, participants (P2, P7) have less tolerance for differing attitudes — if in-game friends disagree on topics close to their heart, they are unlikely to play further. A more telling outcome of the game-focused nature of these relationships is that they often end when either party disengages from MOBA play. *"I definitely feel that our relationship is tied to the game"* (P7).

However, some friendships made within the game have value similar to those developed offline, mirroring results in other genres [2, 43]. These participants (P3, P7) offer and receive emotional support when experiencing offline problems, and one (P3) recalled meeting one of her friends in real life after playing MOBAs together online. *"Just because we don't see each other doesn't mean we can't* [have] *a relationship"* (P3).

Reasons People Stop Playing MOBAs

A large proportion (48.74%) of survey respondents had previously quit MOBAs for at least three months. Of these

players, 26.94% quit because they lacked the time to play, 23.99% quit in order to play other games, 23.62% because they no longer considered the game fun, and 12.18% due to unsportsmanlike players.

The finding that just under half of survey respondents have, at some point, quit MOBAs for a significant amount of time raises a number of questions around churn in the genre. The variation in reasons for quitting suggests that players' reasons for quitting are more likely based on their individual context than their reasons for beginning MOBA play. This aligns with the experiences of the interview participants, a number of whom (P1, P2, P6) took breaks due to reasons unrelated to their game of choice. *"[It was] happenstance — we moved, my computer ended up in the lounge room for several months until I finally got around to setting it all up properly"* (P2), *"I get out of it when I don't have the time"* (P6). Relatedly, players may not consciously decide to quit at all, or have strong feelings about the game upon churning. *"I don't think I had any largely positive or negative thoughts"* (P2). It is perhaps unsurprising that a significant proportion of those surveyed stopped playing simply because their game of choice was no longer fun. Interview respondents (P1, P8) discussed feeling burnout after playing for significant amounts of time, and previous findings that MOBAs are more frustrating than other genres [16] demonstrate the potential for negative experiences to overwhelm existing reasons for play. *"I was getting quite sick of it"* (P1), *"I was just sort of bored of it overall"* (P8).

Potentially more enlightening are players' proposed reasons for returning to play. The most popular reason for returning ("Having more time to play", with 29.89% of responses) corresponds with the most popular reason for quitting ("Lack of time to play"), supporting the narrative that MOBAs can be a time-consuming pursuit. *"The amount of time I've spent in this game is absurd"* (P8). However, other results are less clear — while social factors ("I knew people who were playing") caused a significant proportion (22.99%) of players to return to MOBA play, they were seldom (4.83%) the reason for quitting ("My friends had stopped playing"). Therefore, the presence of friends is salient when choosing to play, but whether a player churns may depend on general dissatisfaction with the game, a desire to play other games, or other players' behaviour.

Previous research on MMORPG engagement supports the view that game updates assist in retaining MOBA player interest [12]. Indeed, 18.39% of returning players surveyed cited this as the main reason for their return. The novelty of new or altered game content, even cosmetic updates, can potentially draw players' attention. *"The thing that got me back into it was a cosmetic item"* (P8). For the survey question addressing reasons for returning to MOBAs, exploration of the "Other" category yielded a similar result in that 7.28% of players return due to interest in a different MOBA, especially upon its release. However, game updates can also discourage people from playing. *"They weren't bad changes, it just didn't gel"* (P8).

Returning players treat the game more casually, or have a different attitude towards play, and this is consistent with narratives of MMORPG engagement [54]. *"I look at it more as a learning experience now"* (P5), *"I sit back and enjoy the game more"* (P8). Participants who have not churned most enjoy the genre's social (P3) and competitive (P4, P5) aspects. *"I just really enjoy the competitive scene, I enjoy visiting the subreddit, I find the community interesting... I guess that's why I kept with it"* (P5).

GENERAL DISCUSSION

Starting, Stopping, and Returning to MOBA Play

As in other genres [9, 53], people most frequently begin to play MOBAs as a shared activity with friends (RQ1). Some others are mobilised to play through interest in the professional scene or by spectating games online. Although this result is not altogether new, it confirms that while MOBAs differ in a number of ways from more established genres, the reasons people begin play appear consistent.

While confirmatory, the strong social motivation for beginning play stands in sharp relief to its absence among the most popular reasons for churning. Instead, the time MOBAs appear to take up in players' lives appears highly salient (RQ3a). Whether preventing them from offline activities or simply from playing other games, MOBAs represent a significant time investment. Feelings of burnout or indifference towards future play described by interview participants may reflect the largely repetitive structure of MOBA play. While individual games differ in terms of characters chosen, player performance, and so on, the end goal and how to achieve it remain the same. Attempting to ascend through player rankings in a system in which teams are matched with an even chance to win may induce similar feelings. The effects of repetitive play on players' attitudes are documented in MMORPG research [52], although MOBA players engage in repetitive play to improve their own skills rather than to upgrade the gear of a persistent avatar. Also notable is the presence of deviant behaviour ("unsportsmanlike players") in players' stated reasons for churning, which did not clearly emerge in previous research [36]. This discrepancy likely reflects the use of different methods in each study.

In this sample, however, these problems often appear to be temporary (RQ3b). Players are more than willing to return to MOBA play when the reason for their absence is no longer salient. This may be why players are relatively unaffected when their friends churn, knowing the absence is impermanent. Further, the removal of one friend from a player's network may not affect how often they play with friends in general. Game updates may serve as a call to action for those who remain engaged with the community during their absence, or those who cited a general boredom with the game as their reason for churning.

Team Experiences

Player Characteristics

While a number of studies suggest that social interaction is an important aspect of online play [15, 50], the result that conversation in MOBA play is more valued with friends than with strangers tells of a social experience closer to unstructured online FPS play [49] than MMORPG play [50]. While survey results indicated a preference for strangers to demonstrate skilled play and to choose complementary roles or characters, interview responses suggested that play with strangers *can* elicit social outcomes if attempted. As both individual proficiency and team congruency influence win rates [19], and relate solely to game outcomes, it appears that strangers are assumed task-focused unless social interaction is attempted.

Friendship Development

This conceptualisation of strangers as primarily task-focused entities may contribute to the apparent lack of strong relationships made with strangers through play (RQ2b). MOBA players either don't expect or don't want strangers to display social characteristics, instead expecting or preferring them to embody purely play-focused attributes. Many relationships formed through play remain entirely within the context of their chosen game.

Why do MOBA players, unlike MMORPG or online FPS players, eschew making friends through play? MMORPGs encourage this behaviour by requiring cooperation to attempt their highest challenges [26]. Forming long-term groups (i.e., guilds), in which new relationships may also be developed, is the most reliable way to complete such content. While similar systems exist in most popular MOBAs, the nature of playing against people rather than AI, as in MMORPGs, means that such premade groups are matched against more skilled players to ensure teams are balanced. Therefore, the development of long-term groups which may include strangers cannot be encouraged in the same way. For online FPS games, which share the same round-based play patterns as MOBAs, the ubiquity of built-in voice chat in the former genre may provide an avenue for relationships with strangers to develop [49]. The results of this study and others [46, 47] demonstrating the importance of VoIP for social engagement support this argument. Individual MOBA games are also notably longer than online FPS rounds, which could cause difficulties when attempting to play with acquaintances on subsequent occasions. That is, it becomes less feasible to join others already playing when waiting for their game to finish could take anywhere from twenty minutes to more than an hour.

Mood

Participants experience significantly improved mood when playing with friends, as opposed to strangers (RQ2a). Our finding that players experience more vigour (and less fatigue) when playing with friends, rather than strangers, differs from research by Ravaja et al. [30]. Similarly, significant increases in self-reported anger when playing with strangers rather than friends are notable in light of previous research by Gajadhar et al. [10], which found no significant differences in frustration when playing a competitive game against a friend or stranger. Both differences appear to relate to mode of play: the mix of competition and cooperation central to MOBA play differs from the solely competitive settings of both [10] and [30]. Devising and executing strategies *with other players* may induce greater vigour beyond what competition alone can offer, and *allies* (rather than opponents) appear to be the main cause of anger in MOBA play. Taken as a whole, these results suggest that players of any genre with these structural characteristics will exhibit similar patterns of lower wellbeing when playing with strangers. Further, such high-order characteristics (e.g., those identified in [20]) are likely more specific indicators of PX differences than genre, due to the difficulty in clearly defining the latter.

Lower reported confusion with friends may relate to experiences of group flow — a state associated with communication, teamwork, and an understanding of others' abilities [18] — in this condition. Interview responses highlighting strangers' unreliability, and the potential for cohesive team play with friends (regardless of their level of seriousness), support this reading. Higher depressed mood with strangers may result from more frequent deviant behaviour with this group, in turn due to their increased focus on the importance of game outcomes. Increased anger with strangers can be seen as the inverse position, where players are more likely to become frustrated with strangers' play, potentially even becoming deviant themselves. In fact, a contradiction exists between players' expectations of strangers' in-game ability and how they prefer to be treated themselves. Players are quick to criticise strangers' mistakes, while dreading the experience of being denigrated for the same reason. The community discourages behaviour perceived as more likely to cause a loss, including experimental and more casual play, both of which appear to be desirable. Finally, our overall mood findings are in line with Terry et al. [39], who found higher values of social- and task-related cohesion within sports teams are associated with lower tension, fatigue, depression, and anger, as well as higher vigour. While this study did not directly measure team cohesion, interview responses reinforce the idea that MOBA players group with friends with similar objectives, whether this play is casual or serious in nature.

Improving the Wellbeing of MOBA Players
The relative youth of research into MOBA PX suggests that presenting multiple, concrete recommendations is premature. However, the current results, considered in tandem with related research, suggest one clear avenue for improving the PX and related wellbeing outcomes associated with MOBAs. Overall, the current results highlight that many of the positive aspects of MOBA play (mood outcomes, enjoyable conversation, absence of deviant behaviour) result from playing with friends. Clear preferences exist for playing with friends alongside

acknowledgements that this occurs less often than players would like. More broadly, previous research has established the value of social connectedness through videogame play [37, 45]. Thus, the primary recommendation offered for improving PX and wellbeing outcomes is to find ways to facilitate new friendships among MOBA players and ultimately, the formation of communities.

One possibility is public, developer-supported events focused on community building, which could help players make friends with other local players and introduce new players to the genre in a more supportive environment. Because events sponsored by MOBA developers are currently limited to amateur tournaments, less confident or more social players may feel uncomfortable attending. Non-competitive events would provide a space for players who value offline friendships to develop relationships supported by shared play experiences. Further, more casual events are likely to support discussion of topics unrelated to MOBA play, which interview participants also considered important for friendship development. Another possibility is providing matchmaking to players based less on skill or previous performance and more on, for example, preferred style of play, shared interests outside the game, or other factors that could facilitate social connection during play.

Retaining support for the competitive teamwork often at the core of MOBA PX should be prioritised in improvements such as those noted above. In future research, we are interested in exploring the extent to which social aspects of play and relationship building can be integrated into competitive matches.

Limitations and Future Work
The most promising avenues to better understand MOBAs involve targeting differences between player groups (e.g., across gender, region, level of experience), individual game aspects (e.g., Dota 2's native VoIP support), and modes of play (e.g., ranked vs. unranked). In order to avoid participant fatigue, some single item measures were used in this study. Future work, using more detailed measures, will provide a means of confirming and further exploring these initial results. Because participants were only asked about their mood during play, conclusions drawn on the effects of playing with friends or strangers on mood are relative.

CONCLUSION
This research further explores MOBA PX — specifically, in terms of social experiences during and outside of play — as a way of understanding patterns of player engagement. Through the use of a large-scale survey and corresponding interviews, this study indicates that the genre's structural characteristics (e.g., long match times, team-based competition, less expressive forms of communication) inform many of the play patterns associated with lower wellbeing and common reasons for churning. Our results also differ from established studies [10, 30] in key ways, providing avenues to further understand affective responses to multiplayer game experiences.

REFERENCES

1. Jeremy Blackburn and Haewoon Kwak. 2014. STFU NOOB! Predicting Crowdsourced Decisions on Toxic Behaviour in Online Games. In *Proceedings of the 23rd International Conference on World Wide Web* (WWW '14), 877-888.

2. Helena Cole and Mark D. Griffiths. 2007. Social Interactions in Massively Multiplayer Online Role-Playing Gamers. *CyberPsychology & Behavior* 10, 4: 575-583.

3. John Colwell, Clare Grady, and Sarah Rhaiti. 1995. Computer games, self-esteem and gratification of needs in adolescents. *Journal of Community Applied Social Psychology* 5, 3: 195-206.

4. Laura Dabbish, Robert Kraut, and Jordan Patton. 2012. Communication and Commitment in an Online Game Team. In *Proceedings of SIGCHI Conference on Human Factors in Computing Systems* (CHI '12), 879-888. http://dx.doi.org/10.1145/2207676.2208529

5. Yvonne A. W. De Kort and Wijnand A. IJsselsteijn. 2008. People, Places, and Play: Player Experience in a Socio-Spatial Context. *Computers in Entertainment* 6, 2.

6. Ed Diener, Eunkook M. Suh, Richard E. Lucas, and Heidi L. Smith. 1999. Subjective Well-Being: Three Decades of Progress. *Psychological Bulletin* 125, 2: 276-302.

7. Xiaowen Fang and Fan Zhao. 2010. Personality and enjoyment of computer game play. *Computers in Industry* 61, 4: 342-349.

8. Chek Yang Foo and Elina M. I. Koivisto. 2004. Defining grief play in MMORPGs: player and developer perceptions. In *Proceedings of 2004 ACM SIGCHI International Conference on Advances in Computer Entertainment Technology* 245-250. http://dx.doi.org/10.1145/1067343.1067375

9. Maria Frostling-Henningsson. 2009. First-person shooter games as a way of connecting to people: "Brothers in blood". *CyberPsychology & Behavior* 12, 5: 557-562.

10. Brian J. Gajadhar, Yvonne A. W. de Kort, and Wijnand A IJsselsteijn. 2008. Shared Fun Is Doubled Fun: Player Enjoyment as a Function of Social Setting. In *Fun and Games* 106-117. http://dx.doi.org/10.1007/978-3-540-88322-7_11

11. Rich Gilman. 2001. The Relationship between Life Satisfaction, Social Interest, and Frequency of Extracurricular Activities among Adolescent Students. *Journal of Youth and Adolescence* 30, 6: 749-767.

12. Christothea Herodotou, Niall Winters, and Maria Kambouri. 2014. An Iterative, Multidisciplinary Approach to Studying Digital Play Motivation The Model of Game Motivation. *Games and Culture* 10, 3: 249-268.

13. Felicia A. Huppert. 2009. Psychological Well-being: Evidence Regarding its Causes and Consequences. *Applied Psychology: Health and Well-Being* 1, 2: 137-164.

14. Alexandru Iosup, Ruud van de Bovenkamp, Siqi Shen, Adele Lu Jia, and Fernando Kuipers. 2014. Analyzing Implicit Social Networks in Multiplayer Online Games. *Internet Computing, IEEE* 18, 3: 36-44.

15. Jeroen Jansz and Martin Tanis. 2007. Appeal of Playing Online First Person Shooter Games. *CyberPsychology & Behavior* 10, 1: 133-136.

16. Daniel Johnson, Lennart Nacke, and Peta Wyeth. 2015. All about that Base: Differing Player Experiences in Video Game Genres and the Unique Case of MOBA Games. In *Proceedings of 33rd Annual ACM Conference on Human Factors in Computing Systems* (CHI '15), 2265-2274. http://dx.doi.org/10.1145/2702123.2702447

17. Daniel Johnson, Peta Wyeth, Madison Clark, and Christopher Watling. 2015. Cooperative Game Play with Avatars and Agents: Differences in Brain Activity and the Experience of Play. In *Proceedings of 33rd Annual ACM Conference on Human Factors in Computing Systems* (CHI '15), 3721-3730. http://dx.doi.org/10.1145/2702123.2702468

18. Linda K. Kaye. 2016. Exploring flow experiences in cooperative digital gaming contexts. *Computers in Human Behavior* 55: 286-291.

19. Jooyeon Kim, Brian C. Keegan, Sungjoon Park, and Alice Oh. 2016. The Proficiency-Congruency Dilemma: Virtual Team Design and Performance in Multiplayer Online Games. In *Proceedings of the 34th Annual ACM Conference on Human Factors in Computing Systems* (CHI 2016),

20. Daniel King, Paul Delfabbro, and Mark Griffiths. 2010. Video Game Structural Characteristics: A New Psychological Taxonomy. *International Journal of Mental Health and Addiction* 8, 1: 90-106.

21. Haewoon Kwak and Jeremy Blackburn. 2014. Linguistic Analysis of Toxic Behavior in an Online Video Game. In *Social Informatics*, Luca M. Aiello and Daniel McFarland (eds.). Springer International Publishing, Cham, Switzerland, 209-217.

22. Laerd. 2015. Wilcoxon Signed Rank test in SPSS. Retrieved September 4, 2015 from https://statistics.laerd.com/premium/wsrt/wilcoxon-signed-rank-test-in-spss-11.php

23. Andrew M. Lane and Peter C. Terry. 2000. The Nature of Mood: Development of a Conceptual Model with a Focus on Depression. *Journal of Applied Sport Psychology* 12, 1: 16-33.

24. Ming-Chi Lee and Tzung-Ru Tsai. 2010. What Drives People to Continue to Play Online Games? An Extension of Technology Model and Theory of Planned Behavior. *International Journal of Human-Computer Interaction* 26, 6: 601-620.

25. Jeffrey Lin. 2015. More Science Behind Shaping Player Behavior in Online Games. Video. (March 6 2015). Retrieved September 21, 2015 from http://www.gdcvault.com/play/1022160/More-Science-Behind-Shaping-Player

26. Bonnie Nardi and Justin Harris. 2006. Strangers and Friends: Collaborative Play in World of Warcraft. In *Proceedings of the 2006 20th Anniversary Conference on Computer Supported Cooperative Work* 149-158. http://dx.doi.org/10.1145/1180875.1180898

27. Nansook Park. 2004. The Role of Subjective Well-Being in Positive Youth Development. *The Annals of the American Academy of Political and Social Science* 591, 1: 25-39.

28. Nataliia Pobiedina, Julia Neidhardt, Maria del Carmen Calatrava Moreno, and Hannes Werthner. 2013. Ranking factors of team success. In *Proceedings of 22nd International Conference on World Wide Web Companion* (WWW '13), 1185-1194.

29. Karolien Poels, Yvonne A. W. De Kort, and Wijnand A IJsselsteijn. 2012. Identification and categorization of digital game experiences: a qualitative study integrating theoretical insights and player perspectives. *Westminster Papers in Communication and Culture* 9, 1: 107-129.

30. Niklas Ravaja. 2009. The Psychophysiology of Digital Gaming: The Effect of a Non Co-Located Opponent. *Media Psychology* 12, 3: 268-294.

31. Riot Games. 2015. Our Games. Retrieved September 21, 2015 from http://www.riotgames.com/our-games

32. Carmen V. Russoniello, Kevin O'Brien, and Jennifer M. Parks. 2009. The effectiveness of casual video games in improving mood and decreasing stress. *Journal of CyberTherapy and Rehabilitation* 2, 1: 53-66.

33. Richard M. Ryan, C. Scott Rigby, and Andrew Przybylski. 2006. The Motivational Pull of Video Games: A Self-Determination Theory Approach. *Motivation and Emotion* 30, 4: 344-360.

34. Diane J. Schiano, Bonnie Nardi, Thomas Debeauvais, Nicolas Ducheneaut, and Nicholas Yee. 2011. A new look at World of Warcraft's social landscape. In *Proceedings of 6th International Conference on Foundations of Digital Games* 174-179. http://dx.doi.org/10.1145/2159365.2159389

35. John L. Sherry and Kristen Lucas. 2003. Video game uses and gratifications as predictors of use and game preference. In *Proceedings of Annual Conference of the International Communication Association*

36. Kenneth B. Shores, Yilin He, Kristina L. Swanenburg, Robert Kraut, and John Riedl. 2014. The Identification of Deviance and its Impact on Retention in a Multiplayer Game. In *Proceedings of 17th ACM conference on Computer Supported Cooperative Work & Social Computing* (CSCW '14), 1356-1365. http://dx.doi.org/10.1145/2531602.2531724

37. Jeffrey G. Snodgrass, Michael G. Lacy, H. J. Francois Dengah, and Jesse Fagan. 2011. Enhancing one life rather than living two: Playing MMOs with offline friends. *Computers in Human Behavior* 27, 3: 1211-1222.

38. SteamCharts. 2015. Dota 2. Retrieved September 21, 2015 from http://steamcharts.com/app/570

39. Peter C. Terry, Albert V. Carron, Mark J. Pink, Andrew M. Lane, Glyn J. W. Jones, and Mark P. Hall. 2000. Perceptions of Group Cohesion and Mood in Sport Teams. *Group Dynamics: Theory, Research, and Practice* 4, 3: 244-253.

40. Peter C. Terry, Andrew M. Lane, and Gerard J. Fogarty. 2003. Construct validity of the Profile of Mood States — Adolescents for use with adults. *Psychology of Sport and Exercise* 4, 2: 125-139.

41. Richard C. Thelwell, Andrew M. Lane, and Neil J. V. Weston. 2007. Mood states, self-set goals, self-efficacy and performance in academic examinations. *Personality and Individual Differences* 42, 3: 573-583.

42. Jan-Noël Thon. 2006. Communication and Interaction in Multiplayer First-Person-Shooter Games. In *From Communication to Presence*, Giuseppe Riva, M. Teresa Anguera, Brenda K. Wiederhold, and Fabrizia Mantovani (eds.). IOS Press, Amsterdam, The Netherlands, 239-261.

43. Sabine Trepte, Leonard Reinecke, and Keno Juechems. 2012. The social side of gaming: How playing online computer games creates online and offline social support. *Computers in Human Behavior* 28, 3: 832-839.

44. Staci Tucker, *Griefing: Policing Masculinity in Online Games.* 2011, University of Oregon, Eugene, OR.

45. Kellie Vella, Daniel Johnson, and Leanne Hides. 2015. Playing Alone, Playing With Others: Differences in Player Experience and Indicators of Wellbeing. In *Proceedings of the 2015 Annual Symposium on Computer-Human Interaction in Play* (CHI PLAY '15), 3-12. http://dx.doi.org/10.1145/2793107.2793118

46. Greg Wadley, Martin Gibbs, and Peter Benda. 2007. Speaking in character: using voice-over-IP to communicate within MMORPGs. In *Proceedings of 4th Australasian Conference on Interactive Entertainment*

47. Dmitri Williams, Scott Caplan, and Li Xiong. 2007. Can you hear me now? The impact of voice in an online gaming community. *Human communication research* 33, 4: 427-449.

48. Richard T. A. Wood, Mark D. Griffiths, Darren Chappell, and Mark N. O. Davies. 2004. The Structural Characteristics of Video Games: A Psycho-Structural Analysis. *CyberPsychology & Behavior* 7, 1: 1-10.

49. Yan Xu, Xiang Cao, Abigail Sellen, Ralf Herbrich, and Thore Graepel. 2011. Sociable Killers: Understanding Social Relationships in an Online First-Person Shooter Game. In *Proceedings of ACM 2011 Conference on Computer Supported Cooperative Work* (CSCW '11), 197-206. http://dx.doi.org/10.1145/1958824.1958854

50. Nick Yee. 2006. The Demographics, Motivations, and Derived Experiences of Users of Massively Multi-User Online Graphical Environments. *Presence* 15, 3: 309-329.

51. Nick Yee. 2006. Motivations for Play in Online Games. *CyberPsychology & Behavior* 9, 6: 772-775.

52. Nick Yee. 2007. Player Life-Cycle: The Burnout Stage. Retrieved March 7, 2016 from http://nickyee.com/daedalus/archives/001588.php?page=6

53. Nick Yee. 2007. Player Life-Cycle: The Entry Stage. Retrieved March 7, 2016 from http://nickyee.com/daedalus/archives/001588.php?page=2

54. Nick Yee. 2007. Player Life-Cycle: The Recovery Stage. Retrieved September 22, 2015 from http://www.nickyee.com/daedalus/archives/001588.php?page=8

Crowd-Pleaser: Player Perspectives of Multiplayer Dynamic Difficulty Adjustment in Video Games

Alexander Baldwin
Queensland University
of Technology
Brisbane, Australia
alexander.baldwin@qut.edu.au

Daniel Johnson
Queensland University
of Technology
Brisbane, Australia
dm.johnson@qut.edu.au

Peta Wyeth
Queensland University
of Technology
Brisbane, Australia
peta.wyeth@qut.edu.au

ABSTRACT

Multiplayer Dynamic Difficulty Adjustment (MDDA) features are becoming increasingly common in competitive multiplayer video games as a means to balance challenge between differently-skilled players. However, without a thorough understanding of how MDDA design is perceived by players, it is difficult to predict how players may feel about its use. A mixed-methods approach combining an online survey and interviews was conducted with multiplayer game players to investigate player expectations regarding the effect of different components and attributes from the MDDA Framework on the play experience. As well as highlighting similarities and conflicts between the perspectives of low and high-performing players, patterns emerged demonstrating that players value control, personal benefit and awareness of MDDA use. Along with additional design considerations suggested, this led to the refinement of the MDDA Framework through the introduction of an 'Awareness' component.

Author Keywords

Challenge, Balancing; Video Games; Design; Multiplayer Dynamic Difficulty Adjustment;

ACM Classification Keywords

K.8.0 [Personal Computing]: General - Games

INTRODUCTION

Optimal design of video games requires a thorough understanding of the player experience and variables that affect enjoyment [22]. This holds particularly true for multiplayer games and other 'games as a service', in which long-term player retention is required for growth and profitability [6]. In competitive games, the sense of competence is a driver of motivation to play and replay intention [17]. Theories of optimal player experience such as GameFlow [22] and Player Experience of Needs Satisfaction [20], as well as more general psychological theories such as Self-Determination Theory [9] and Flow

CHI PLAY '16, October 16-19, 2016, Austin, TX, USA
© 2016 ACM. ISBN 978-1-4503-4456-2/16/10…$15.00
DOI: http://dx.doi.org/10.1145/2967934.2968100

[8], agree that the matching of player skill level to the challenge presented by the task are necessary for optimal intrinsic motivation and feelings of competence, satisfaction and engagement. Confirming this need, Clarke and Duimering [7] found that the most frequently mentioned negative aspect of play online multiplayer first-person shooter games was unmatched challenge or skill. Multiplayer 'matchmaking' systems such as TrueSkill [14] attempt to address this through matching players of similar skill together in a match. However, these systems are restricted to online play with large player populations and unable to react in real-time to differing player performance.

In single player games, reactive systems such as Dynamic Difficulty Adjustment (DDA) can dynamically balance challenge through the manipulation elements such as AI agent behaviour [1], timers [10] and the game environment [15] in real-time during play. As the game obstacles and possible variables have been planned and the bounds of their manipulation set by the designer, it is possible to predict player responses to these systems [24]. However, DDA techniques cannot be directly applied to multiplayer gameplay in which challenge is provided by competition between human players. This presents difficulties for multiplayer designers by restricting the factors available to manipulate in order to balance challenge. For a DDA system to be effective, it must be able to measure the level of difficulty the player faces at any given moment [1], a feat more easily achievable in single player games in which game-controlled obstacles are measured against player skill [18]. Multiplayer gameplay can confound this through the need to compare player skill against others. Consequently, the effect of any one change can affect the challenge and experience of other players present too.

While there is increasingly widespread usage of DDA-like features in multiplayer gameplay modes for commercial game releases, research has only recently begun to explore their use, associated impacts on the player experience and how players may perceive their inclusion. Baldwin and colleagues [3] refer to these multiplayer-specific systems as Multiplayer Dynamic Difficulty Adjustment (MDDA). An MDDA 'instance' is a gameplay feature in competitive multiplayer video games designed to reduce the difference in challenge experienced by all players through adjusting the potential performance of certain players [3]. An existing example of MDDA in a commercial game is present in the combat racer *Mario Kart 7*. During a race, lower-ranked players have an increased chance of receiving more effective weapons from 'random' weapon pickup boxes. This allows lower-performing players an increased chance of improving their ranking against high-ranked players with less powerful weapons.

Research exploring the impact of MDDA techniques has confirmed the effectiveness of some techniques (in terms of allowing differently skilled players to compete with more balanced performance) as well as positive effects on enjoyment in a variety of contexts. These include manipulating steering, speed and acceleration in racing games [5] and input assistance in a first-person shooter [23]. Beyond balancing inherent skill, dynamic performance balancing has also been tested between players with and without mobility disabilities using physical inputs for a dance game. Gerling and colleagues' [13] found MDDA features to be an effective method of balancing between players with differing physical ability and means of control. However, they note the risk of over-balancing (normalising performance too much) as a large difference between expected performance and actual in-game performance may threaten self-esteem and wellbeing. Conversely, Vicencio-Moreira and colleagues' [23] testing of different strengths of balancing suggest stronger balancing (greater performance adjustment) may be most enjoyable, although also the most noticeable.

Bateman, Mandryk, Stach and Gutwin [4] investigated differing methods of control assistance in a target shooting game and found them to be an effective method of balancing performance between differently skilled players, with combinations of methods able to provide stronger balancing. However, they caution that participants were divided on the issue of MDDA awareness with no clear consensus on whether players should be informed of the use of performance adjustment [4]. This highlights player preferences as an area of MDDA research worthy of further attention, as much dynamic balancing research has focused on specific implementations without a broad perspective on player perception of MDDA types and use. How players perceive differing types of MDDA is of particular importance compared to single player DDA, as MDDA directly adjusts the performance of the players themselves rather than simply modifying the surrounding game elements.

In our previous published work, a framework of MDDA was created to allow for the classification of MDDA instances by breaking them down into their components and attributes [2]. In this paper we seek to provide insight into the effect of individual framework components on the player experience of both low and high-performing players. This is achieved through addressing three primary aims:

- Investigate player perceptions of MDDA component attributes using the MDDA Framework.
- Determine the similarities and differences of the likely impacts of MDDA on the player experience from the perspective of low and high-performing players.
- Use player preferences and feedback to identify necessary refinements to the MDDA framework.

This study forms part of a larger program of research, in which we aim to create a more thorough understanding of player preferences for differing types of MDDA. While future studies are planned to test the effects of MDDA during gameplay, the current study focuses on player expectations regarding the impact of MDDA on the player experience. We consider expectations to be of interest as a player's expectations will inform their decision to buy/play a game in the first instance (regardless of whether player expectations align with actual in-game player experience). The findings from our larger program of research are intended to help designers make more informed decisions regarding how to balance player performance in a way that minimises interference with other aspects of the player experience. In the current study our findings are limited to players' expectations regarding balancing techniques. Additionally, by exploring preferences from differing perspectives (i.e., when a relatively low performing player vs as a high performing player) we seek to identify the aspects in which players believe an improvement in experience for one group may come at the cost of the other.

MDDA FRAMEWORK OVERVIEW

The previously-created MDDA Framework [3] consists of seven components common to all MDDA instances, irrespective of genre or game (see Table 1). Each component has several possible attributes or states, of which any particular MDDA instance will utilise one or more for every component. This allows any MDDA instance to be described using the framework by specifying its component attributes. The seven components and associated attributes are listed and defined below.

Component	Attributes
Determination	- Pre-gameplay - Gameplay
Automation	- Applied by system (automated) - Applied by player(s) (manual)
Recipient	- Individual - Team
Skill Dependency	- Skill dependent - Skill independent
User Action	- Action required - Action not required
Duration	- Single-use - Multi-use - Time-based
Visibility	- Visible to recipient - Visible to non-recipients - Not visible

Table 1. MDDA Framework overview

Determination

The Determination component refers to the game state or time in which the decision to use the MDDA instance is made. The attributes of this component are:

Pre-gameplay: the decision to use the instance is made before the multiplayer game match commences, based on past performance.

During gameplay: the decision to use the instance is made in real-time during the multiplayer match based on current performance.

Automation

This component indicates whether the decision to use the MDDA instance is automated by the game system or chosen by the player(s) themselves. The attributes of this component are:

Applied by system (automated): the game system automatically determines the need for an MDDA instance and applies it. This relies on the game possessing a means of determining relative player performance, such as TrueSkill's player rankings [21].

Applied by player(s) (manual): players choose to use an MDDA instance based on their own judgment. This is currently widely applied in the fighting game genre, with players able to choose to distribute health handicaps before a match begins by providing increased player health for low-performing players.

Recipient

The recipient of an MDDA instance refers to the player(s) intended to be affected by the instance. The attributes of this component are:

Individual: the instance is intended to affect a single player.

Team: the instance is intended to affect a group of players (only possible in team-based gameplay modes).

Skill Dependency

This component indicates whether the low-performing players are required to act with some degree of skill in order to improve performance. The attributes of this component are:

Skill dependent: the player(s) must respond, react or make-use-of the effects of the MDDA instance with a degree of skill in order for it to impact their performance. This refers to the instance providing the *opportunity* for an improvement or reduction in performance; not a guarantee. For example, providing increased movement speed in a first-person shooter game does not guarantee a higher number of player 'kills' but may allow the player a better chance to do so if they act with skill.

Skill independent: the player(s) do not need to act with any degree of skill in order for their performance to be affected by the effects of the MDDA instance. In this case the effect applied is linked to the objective and winning conditions of the game by adjusting the player's performance irrespective of their behaviour. For example, reducing damage taken

User Action

This component dictates whether the intended recipient of the MDDA instance is required to interact with the interface in order to initiate the instance's effects. The attributes of this component are:

Action required: the recipient must interact with the interface in order for the effects of the instance to begin (e.g., pressing a button to activate the effects).

Action not required: the effects of the instance will commence without player interaction with the interface.

Duration

This component indicates the time-based property of the MDDA instance. The attributes of this component are:

Single-use: the effects of the instance occur at a single moment. For example, a single boost to the player's health.

Multi-use: the effects of the instance may occur multiple times. For example, the player is given three health boosts they may activate over the course of the match.

Time-based: the effects of the instance occur continuously over a certain timeframe. For example, the player's health may recharge gradually over 30 seconds of play.

Visibility

This refers to whether players of the game are provided with feedback regarding the presence of the MDDA instance. The attributes of this component are:

Visible to recipient: feedback is provided to the recipient of the instance, with the intention to inform him/her of the potential performance adjustments enacted by the instance. This may occur via visual, audio, or tactile means within the game such as a text notification in the game's Heads-Up Display (HUD).

Visible to non-recipients: feedback is provided to the non-recipients about the effects and/or recipient of the instance. This can occur through the same methods listed above, but can additionally include the identity of the recipient.

Not visible: no feedback is provided to any players in the match that the instance is in effect. While experienced players may deduce the presence of an MDDA instance through observed variations to the game rules, no explicit feedback is provided to any players.

METHOD

To investigate player perception of the influence of MDDA features on their player experience, an online survey was crafted to reach a broad range of participants across multiple game genres and formats. Additionally, supplemental interviews with players of multiplayer games were conducted to provide better interpretation of and insights into player preferences expressed in the survey. For both methods, participants (as players of multiplayer games) were likely to have been exposed to balancing techniques in various games including examples discussed. However, no participants were familiar with the formalised MDDA Framework prior to this study.

Survey

Participants were required to be aged 17 or over with any level of multiplayer game experience. The survey was advertised via email to faculty and students of an Australian university, as well as via social media including Facebook and the official Xbox, PlayStation, Nintendo and Steam forums with a link provided for participants to share with friends. The survey consisted of two major parts.

Part 1: Participant Background

To establish background context to each participant's answers, demographic information regarding age, gender and competitive multiplayer game preferences was collected. Participants were also asked to rate their experience level playing competitive multiplayer video games on a numbered scale from 1 (not at all experienced) to 7 (extremely experienced). The use of "experience level" in opposition to asking for self-rated performance was chosen due to the potential variance in performance between different game genres. For example, while a participant may be a high-performing player in certain first-person shooter games, they may be low-performing in racing games and as such lower their self-reported performance rating.

Part 2: Effect of MDDA Framework Component Attributes on Player Experience

The earlier definition and explanation of multiplayer dynamic difficulty adjustment was provided to participants, as well as a description of the goal of these features in balancing challenge. One at a time, an explanation of a particular MDDA instance component was provided along with an example of its use in popular competitive multiplayer games *Mario Kart* and *Call of Duty: Modern Warfare 2*. Participants were asked to rate how the inclusion of differing MDDA instances would affect their player experience on a 7-point numbered scale ranging from "1 - very negatively" to "7 - very positively". All participants were asked to evaluate each MDDA attribute twice – first from the perspective of both a low-performing player (receiving assistance from the MDDA instance) and secondly from the perspective of a high-performing player (competing against the recipients of assistance from the MDDA instance). As a player's performance is relative to that of the other players in a match, they are likely to occupy the positions of both a low and high-performing player in different matches or games as their opponents vary. This makes it important to record the opinions of players from the perspective of both positions for within-groups comparison. Additionally, participants were asked for feedback on the framework, including any problems or suggestions for missing components or attributes.

Interview

Individual face-to-face interviews were conducted at Queensland University of Technology to probe player opinions on the MDDA Framework components and prior experience with MDDA in games they have personally played. Recruitment was conducted through local video game-related groups and societies in Brisbane, Australia. Participants were required to have played one or more competitive multiplayer games within the past 12 months, and each interview lasted between 20 and 50 minutes.

Interview questions were based around the same MDDA Framework components and attributes as the online survey, along with the same game examples. One at a time, each attribute was presented to the participant and they were asked how they 'feel' about MDDA instances with this attribute, as well as if they had encountered the attribute in any games they had played before. Interviews were semi-structured with participants prompted to provide reasoning behind their opinion and anecdotes where an MDDA instance of this type had been previously encountered. Suggestions for improvement or additions to the framework were also sought for further refinement.

Audio recordings and notes taken during each interview. For each framework component and attribute investigated, the reasoning behind a participant's positive or negative reaction was noted. Reasoning and concerns commonly expressed by multiple participants were then used to assist in the interpretation of the survey data by providing insights not able to be obtained through the examination of survey data alone.

RESULTS

Of the 154 valid participant responses to the survey collected, an average age of 23.70 (SD = 7.30) was recorded with 129 male and 32 female respondents. The interviews were conducted with 15 participants (10 male), 11 of whom were undergraduate students at Queensland University of Technology. Some survey participants did not complete all of the survey, in which case responses up to the last full page completed were included and any further incomplete responses removed, with 125 participants completing all pages of the survey.

Participants had first played a competitive multiplayer video games an average of 9.44 years ago and 91.56% had played within the last year. An average of 9.96 hours per week (SD = 9.20) was spent playing competitive multiplayer games by participants. First-person shooter games were the most popular genre for competitive multiplayer gameplay, played by 83.77% of those surveyed. Participants rated their experience level playing competitive multiplayer games an average of 5.28 (SD = 1.58) from '1 – not at all experienced' to '7 – extremely experienced'.

The following results explore survey participants' ratings of the effect of each component attribute on their player experience from 1 (very negatively) to 7 (very positively) from the perspectives of low and high performing players. For the purpose of clarity, results from the low-performing perspective will be abbreviated as LPP, and results from the high-performing perspective as HPP. Statistical analysis was conducted using a two-way repeated measures ANOVA, with the within-subjects factors of *component attribute* and *performance* and a dependent variable of *player experience* (operationalised as the participant's ratings of how the attribute would positively or negatively influence their experience playing the game). Significance was tested using Wilks' Lambda with an alpha of $p < 0.05$, with Bonferroni adjustment used for comparisons of *attribute* and *performance*. Mauchly's test of sphericity was used to confirm no violations of the assumption of sphericity were present, while skewness, kurtosis and residuals examination indicated normally-distributed data without outliers. Survey results are also displayed in graphs for each component with a y-axis scale of 3-5.5 to aid readability. Additional interpretation from interview participants is also noted for each framework component and individually indicated by participant codes N#. Finally, given debate regarding the suitability of parametric tests for surveys with number scales [16] all analyses were repeated with non-parametric tests and the pattern of results confirmed.

Component: Determination

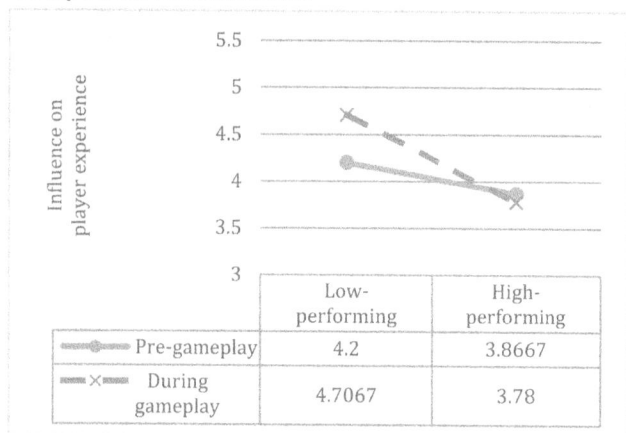

Figure 1. Influence of DETERMINATION on player experience

For the Determination component, there was a main effect for performance level as the attributes were rated higher from LPP (low-performing perspective) than HPP (high-performing perspective) ($F_{1,149} = 32.889$, $p < .001$, $\eta_p^2 = .181$). A main effect on attribute was also found ($F_{1,149} = 3.933$, $p = .049$, $\eta_p^2 = .026$), and these effects were qualified by a significant interaction between attribute and performance level on player experience ($F_{1,149} = 20.062$, $p < .001$, $\eta_p^2 = .119$) (see Figure 1). The Pre-Gameplay attribute was seen as having a more positive influence from LPP than HPP ($F_{1,149} = 6.512$, $p = .012$, $\eta_p^2 = .042$), with the same true for the During Gameplay attribute ($F_{1,149} = 54.186$, $p < .001$, $\eta_p^2 = .267$). The During Gameplay attribute was seen as having a more positive influence than the Pre-Gameplay attribute from LPP ($F_{1,149} = 15.613$, $p <$

$.001$, $\eta_p^2 = .095$), while HPP did not distinguish between pre-gameplay and during-gameplay.

One participant commented that the Determination of an MDDA instance doesn't really matter to non-recipient (high-performing players) because *"the low-scoring guys are being helped anyway, so it doesn't matter when that's chosen if it's going to happen anyway"* (N8). Interview participants raised the point that performance is not always consistent between matches, with N12 indicated that low-performing players may prefer the MDDA to be enacted during gameplay *"because if you are having a really good day or you've gotten better, you still want the chance to win on your own skill"*. Participants also highlighted the potential for reduced self-esteem from pre-gameplay MDDA, with N4 noting *"if you're already marked to be helped before the match starts it's like it's already telling you you're not good enough"*.

Component: Automation

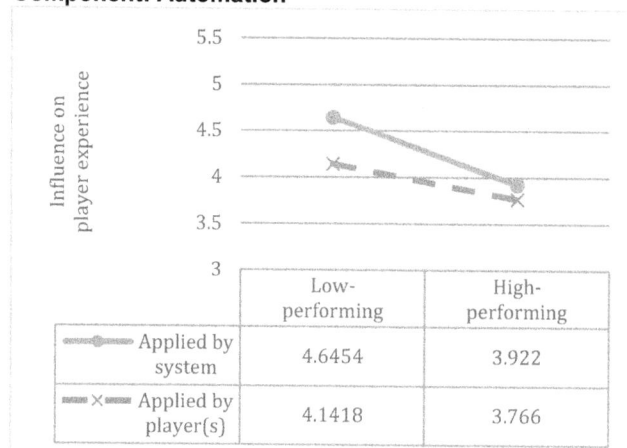

Figure 2. Influence of AUTOMATION on player experience

For the Automation component, there was a main effect for performance level as the attributes were rated higher from LPP than HPP ($F_{1,140} = 36.441$, $p < .001$, $\eta_p^2 = .207$). A main effect on attribute was also found ($F_{1,140} = 4.709$, $p = .032$, $\eta_p^2 = .033$), and these were qualified by a significant interaction between attribute and performance level on player experience ($F_{1,140} = 5.009$, $p = .027$, $\eta_p^2 = .035$) (see Figure 2). The Applied By System attribute was seen as having a more positive influence from LPP than HPP ($F_{1,140} = 43.733$, $p < .001$, $\eta_p^2 = .238$), with the same true for the Applied By Player(s) attribute ($F_{1,140} = 8.475$, $p = .004$, $\eta_p^2 = .057$). The Applied By System attribute was seen as having a more positive influence than the Applied By Player(s) attribute from LPP ($F_{1,140} = 9.014$, $p = .003$, $\eta_p^2 = .060$), while HPP did not distinguish between system or player applied.

Interview data suggests that MDDA applied by the system may be fairer than that applied by a player: the system may be *"more fair because it's not biased"* (N1); player assessment of the need for MDDA might *"not be accurate"* (N15); and some players may *"try to exploit it by giving themselves a boost so they can win*" (N1). N8 noted that these concerns are more applicable to online play against strangers, with the suggestion that "*if you're playing with your friends then it doesn't matter as much since you know the other guys*".

Component: Recipient

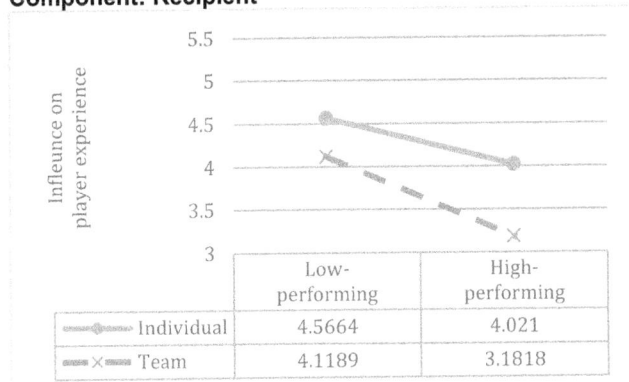

	Low-performing	High-performing
Individual	4.5664	4.021
Team	4.1189	3.1818

Figure 3. Influence of RECIPIENT on player experience

For the Recipient component, there was a main effect for performance level as the attributes were rated higher from LPP than HPP ($F_{1,142} = 44.03$, $p < .001$, $\eta_p^2 = .237$). A main effect on attribute was also found ($F_{1,142} = 28.90$, $p < .001$, $\eta_p^2 = .169$), and these effects were qualified by a significant interaction between attribute and performance level on player experience ($F_{1,142} = 7.75$, $p = .006$, $\eta_p^2 = .052$) (see Figure 3). The Individual attribute was seen as having a more positive influence from LPP than HPP ($F_{1,142} = 24.816$, $p < .001$, $\eta_p^2 = .149$), with the same true for the Team attribute ($F_{1,142} = 38.392$, $p < .001$, $\eta_p^2 = .213$). The Individual attribute was seen as having a more positive influence than the Team attribute from LPP ($F_{1,142} = 12.425$, $p = .001$, $\eta_p^2 = .080$), as well as HPP ($F_{1,142} = 31.406$, $p < .001$, $\eta_p^2 = .181$), however the difference was more pronounced for high performing players.

Interview participants indicated a preference for MDDA applied to individual recipients. N2 framed the reasoning behind this as the desire to "limit any assistance to just the person who needs it" and avoid "boosting [the performance of] a whole team just because some players aren't as good". N4 stated: "if I was on a team and not doing very well, it would be embarrassing if my whole team got helped *because my score was bad*".

Component: Skill Dependency

For the Skill Dependency component, there was a main effect for performance level as the attributes were rated higher from LPP than HPP ($F_{1,133} = 21.230$, $p < .001$, $\eta_p^2 = .138$). A main effect on attribute was also found ($F_{1,133} = 12.940$, $p < .001$, $\eta_p^2 = .089$), and these were qualified by a significant interaction between attribute and performance level ($F_{1,133} = 29.567$, $p < .001$, $\eta_p^2 = .182$) (see Figure 4).

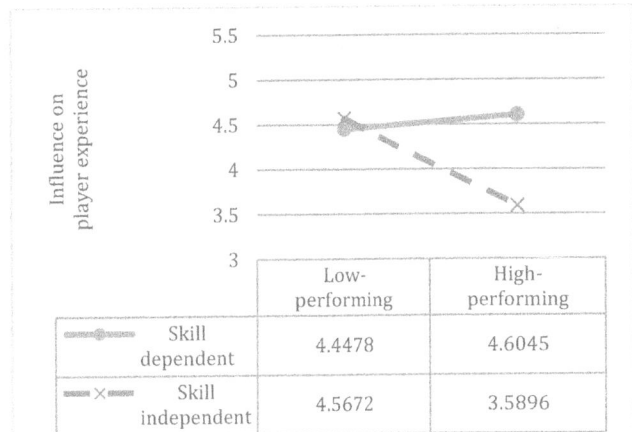

	Low-performing	High-performing
Skill dependent	4.4478	4.6045
Skill independent	4.5672	3.5896

Figure 4. Influence of SKILL DEPENDENCY on player experience

The Skill Independent attribute was seen as having a more positive influence from LPP than HPP ($F_{1,133} = 55.858$, $p <.001$, $\eta_p^2 = .296$) while LPP and HPP did not differ on the Skill Dependent attribute. The Skill Dependent attribute was seen as having a more positive influence than the Skill Independent attribute from HPP ($F_{1,133} = 45.670$, $p < .001$, $\eta_p^2 = .256$), while in contrast LPP did not distinguish between the attributes.

Interview participants indicated that high-performing players may dislike skill independent MDDA. N2 commented that it "*might look a bit like cheating* [when] *someone's score gets better without them having to actually play any better*" with N15 adding that this might be more of an issue for "*eSports [professional players] and competitions or really serious players*".

Component: User Action

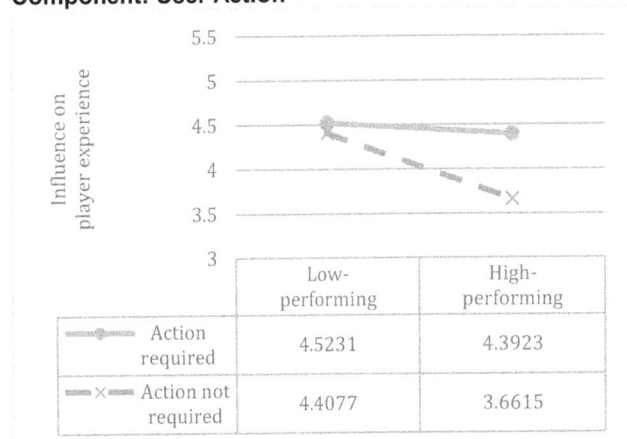

	Low-performing	High-performing
Action required	4.5231	4.3923
Action not required	4.4077	3.6615

Figure 5. Influence of USER ACTION on player experience

For the User Action component, there was a main effect for performance level as the attributes were rated higher from LPP than HPP ($F_{1,129} = 23.969$, $p < .001$, $\eta_p^2 = .157$). A main effect on attribute was also found ($F_{1,129} = 11.191$, $p =.001$, $\eta_p^2 = .080$), and these were qualified by a significant interaction between attribute and performance level ($F_{1,129} = 17.222$, $p < .001$, $\eta_p^2 = .118$) (see Figure 5). The Action Not

Required attribute was seen as having a more positive influence from LPP than HPP ($F_{1,129} = 43.912$, p < .001, η_p^2 = .254), while LPP and HPP did not differ on the Action Required attribute. The Action Required attribute was seen as having a more positive influence than the Action Not Required attribute from HPP ($F_{1,129} = 27.849$, p < .001, η_p^2 = .178) while LPP did not distinguish between these attributes.

Interview participant N1 commented that low-performing players might "*need to be helped anyway, so it should probably be automatic*". Other participants indicated that high-performing players may prefer user action be required, so that, for example "*the losing players can choose to not use it if they want to try and play just with skill instead*" (N12).

Component: Duration

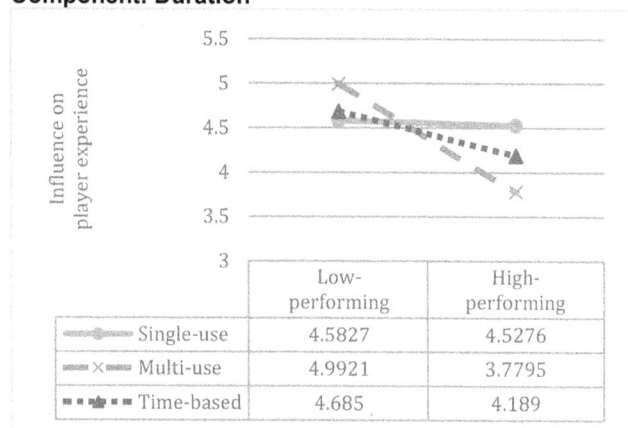

	Low-performing	High-performing
Single-use	4.5827	4.5276
Multi-use	4.9921	3.7795
Time-based	4.685	4.189

Figure 6. Influence of DURATION on player experience
Mauchly's test of sphericity indicated that the assumption of sphericity was met for attribute ($X^2(2) = 2.012$, p = .366) and the two-way interaction ($X^2(2) = 2.524$, p = .283). For the Duration component, there was a main effect for performance level as the attributes were rated higher from LPP than HPP ($F_{1,126} = 29.198$, p < .001, η_p^2 = .188), which was qualified by a significant interaction between attribute and performance level ($F_{2,252} = 36.008$, p < .001, η_p^2 = .222) (see Figure 6). The Multi-Use attribute was seen as having a more positive influence from LPP than HPP ($F_{1,126}$ = 70.603, p < .001, η_p^2 = .359), with the same true for the Time-Based attribute ($F_{1,126} = 11.659$, p = .001, η_p^2 = .085). LPP and HPP did not differ on the Single-Use attribute. An effect was present for LPP ($F_{2,252} = 6.455$, p = .002, η_p^2 = .049) who saw the Multi-Use attribute as having a more positive influence than both the Single-Use (p = .002) and Time-Based (p = .033) attributes. An effect was also present for HPP ($F_{2,252} = 22.044$, p < .001, η_p^2 = .149) who saw the Single-Use attribute as having a more positive influence than the Multi-Use (p < .001) and Time-Based (p = .011) attributes, while Multi-Use was also seen as having a more positive influence than Time-Based (P = .001).

Interview participants indicated that low-performing players may prefer multi-use MDDA instances for the additional support provided in this context, e.g., "*they have a few chances to use it properly*" (N1). However, N1 also expressed that "*obviously low-performing would want that because there would be more performance gain, but the high-performing players might not like that since it gives more boosts*" and "*could provide too much assistance so winning doesn't take skill*". Participants also expressed concerns about players "gaming' multi-use MDDA, with N11 flagging that it may be "*more open to abuse and exploitation, like if someone purposely played badly to then get something they could use multiple times over the rest of the match to win*".

Component: Visibility

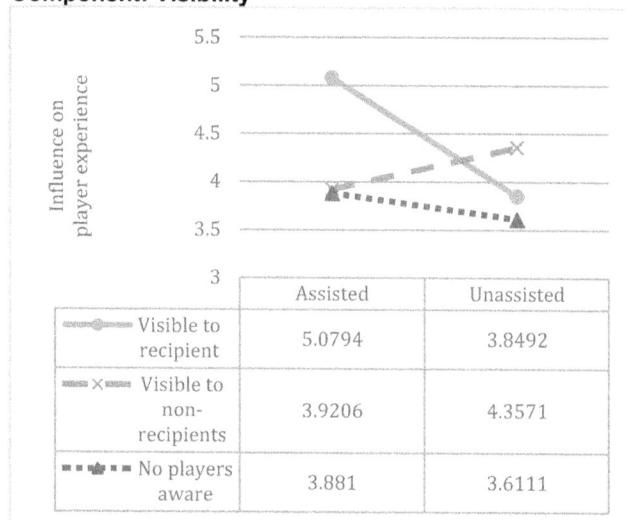

	Assisted	Unassisted
Visible to recipient	5.0794	3.8492
Visible to non-recipients	3.9206	4.3571
No players aware	3.881	3.6111

Figure 7. Influence of VISIBILITY on player experience
Mauchly's test of sphericity indicated that the assumption of sphericity was met for the two-way interaction ($X2(2) = 4.239$, p = .120), but not attribute ($X2(2) = 49.790$, p < .001) so Greenhouse-Geisser adjustment has been used with an epsilon of .751. For the Visibility component, there was a main effect for performance level ($F_{1,125} = 17.104$, p < .001, η_p^2 = .120) as the attributes were rated higher from LPP than HPP. A main effect on attribute was also found ($F_{1.503,187.870} = 10.236$, p < .001, η_p^2 = .076), and these were qualified by a significant interaction between attribute and performance level ($F_{2,250} = 47.005$, p < .001, η_p^2 = .273) (see Figure 7). The Visible to Recipient attribute was seen as having a more positive influence from LPP than HPP ($F_{1,125} = 79.362$, p < .001, η_p^2 = .388), with the same true for the Not Visible attribute ($F_{1,125} = 5.056$, p = .026, η_p^2 = .039). However, the Visible to Non-Recipients was seen as having a more positive influence from HPP than LPP ($F_{1,125}$ = 10.384, p = .002, η_p^2 = .077). An effect was present for LPP ($F_{1.631,203.887} = 28.078$, p < .001, η_p^2 = .183) who saw the Visible to Recipient (themselves) attribute as having a more positive influence than both the Visible to Non-Recipients (p < .001) and Not Visible (p < .001) attributes. An effect was also present for HPP ($F_{1.720,215.010} = 8.956$, p < .001, η_p^2 = .067) who saw the Visible to Non-Recipient (themselves) attribute as having a more positive influence

than both the Visible to Recipients (p = .005) and Not Visible (p = .002) attributes.

One participant commented that as a low-performing player, "*I would want to be told if I was being helped so I know that it's not just my skill*" (N6) while another stated "*I would probably be able to use it better if I knew what the assistance was*" (N9). However, they also noted that these players may not wish it to be visible to high-performing players for a range of reasons: "*that would make me a target and they'd probably try to hunt me down*" (N9); "*it would be really satisfying to take them down*" (N11); "*if I saw someone being helped I'd probably avoid them*" (N5).

Framework Suggestions and Refinements
A small number of survey and interview participants raised that players may become aware of the presence, effects or recipients of an MDDA instance even if not visible, with some citing games such as *Mario Kart* (where the algorithm for item selection is never shown to players). Conversely, others mentioned the possibility that a player may not become aware of an MDDA instance even though it is visible in the game (using examples include *Call of Duty* death streaks). This brought into question the validity of the Visibility component, which is discussed below.

DISCUSSION
When players of competitive multiplayer games were questioned on the effect different MDDA component attributes would have on their play experience, a general trend emerged. Participants reported an expectation that almost all forms of MDDA would have a more positive effect on the experience of low-performing players than high-performing players. As the presence of MDDA instances most often provides a performance benefit to low-performing players, this result was not surprising.

The effects on player experience reported by the participants reveal three major themes or patterns in responses across multiple attributes:
    A. Player control over the instance.
    B. Personal benefit from the effects of the instance.
    C. Awareness of the instances' presence and effects.

These themes provide insight into the values of players for the purpose of enabling a player-centric approach to designing and implementing MDDA instances, as well as highlighting the conflicts between the likely impacts on the player experience of low and high performing players.

A. Player Control
A trend across the four components of Duration, Skill Dependency, and User Action provides an indication that when high-performing, players would prefer increased control over the presence, action and properties of the MDDA instance.

From the perspective of a high-performing player, participants reported a more positive experience for instances that are *skill dependent* with *user-action required*

and only *single-use*. Each of these component attributes increase the control of the player over the assistance provided through increasing reliance on the player to make effective use of the opportunity for assistance. Through the combination of these preferences, the player would have one opportunity (single-use and skill dependent) to receive assistance at a time of their choosing (user action). A result of implementing these preferences would be increased transparency of the presence and mechanics of the MDDA instance to the players in order for the increased control to be possible. However, when taking the perspective of a low-performing player receiving performance assistance from the MDDA instance, participants did not demonstrate as much inclination for increased player control as evidenced by the lack of difference in preference for the attributes of Skill Dependency or User Action. When paired with the responses of interview participants, these results indicate players desire to still play the primary role in performance when in the position of a high-performing player. In contrast, when taking the perspective of a low-performing player, they are not as concerned by their degree of player control or the role of skill in their performance using MDDA.

Participants agreed on one particular component affecting control for both low and high-performing players: players preferred the need for activation of an MDDA instance to be automated by the game system rather than chosen by players. Interview participants noted the potential for MDDA features to be exploited or abused by players motivated by the potential performance assistance. The use of an automated game system was viewed as more impartial than relying on players to accurately judge the need for MDDA and less open to exploitation. Consequently, Automation is the only component in which participants preferred lesser control over the MDDA instance.

Additionally, the higher rating of system-automated instances from the perspective of low-performing players than high-performing is reflective of comments by interview participants concerning the effect of MDDA on pride. Participants indicated that low-performing players may experience social embarrassment when MDDA assistance is applied to them by other players. Similarly, applying MDDA assistance to oneself may be seen as an acknowledgement of lower skill or 'ranking' amongst the players or draw unwanted attention compared to the game system automating the process.

B. Personal Benefit
Trends were found between attributes that may affect the degree of personal benefit received for the Duration, Recipient, Skill Dependency and Visibility components. From the low-performing perspective, players were more likely to report a positive effect on enjoyment from component attributes that may provide more personal benefit to the recipient (e.g., the multi-use option for the Duration attribute, as opposed to only single-use or time-

based). However, a more positive effect was reported from a high-performing player's perspective for attributes which could allow high-performing players to minimize or nullify its effects. For example, an MDDA instance made visible to non-recipients would allow high-performing players to adapt to, target or take advantage of a low-performing player marked as being assisted.

Together, this paints a picture of players valuing MDDA instances that allow them the most potential performance benefit or least performance loss. However, the more positive response to attributes that may minimize the benefits to low-performing players from the perspective of a high-performing players runs contradictory to the intent of MDDA in balancing player performance. As a balance between task difficulty and player ability have been thoroughly demonstrated as key factors in achieving flow [8] and a sense of competence as key for intrinsic motivation [19], this may indicate an area in which player preferences do not match the player experience in practise. Consequently, when placing complete faith in players' abilities to align preferences with optimal experience there is a risk of players unintentionally harming their own experience in the pursuit of improved performance and increased chances of 'winning'. Testing of balancing in a multiplayer first-person shooter game by Vicensio-Moreira, Mandryk and Gutwin [23] confirmed this possibility, with the most positive experience noted by both low and high-performing players when performance was most balanced in spite of the negative effect on the stronger player's score.

C. Player Awareness

The Visibility component provided mixed results between the perspectives of low and high-performing players with differing attributes reported as having a positive effect on enjoyment. From both perspectives, the preferred attribute was that which would give them personal awareness of the presence or effects of the MDDA instance in that role. As low-performing players (the recipients), MDDA visible to recipient was seen more positively; an expected result to allow the recipient of assistance to potentially make better use of the performance enhancement. Similarly, viewed as high-performing players (non-recipients), MDDA visible to non-recipients was rated higher which echoes the values for personal benefit. This may be due to a sense of fairness through better knowledge of MDDA, but also provide the opportunity to adjust strategy to compensate for its effects.

Combined with interview responses, it is very clear that players do not wish for MDDA to be 'hidden' from view when they are playing. However, survey participants expressed a lower preference for MDDA to be visible to *other* players in the match. That is, from the low-performing perspective players did not indicate a positive effect on their experience when non-recipients were aware, while from the high-performing perspective players did indicate a positive effect if recipients were aware. Again, this suggests a bias towards the attributes with the greatest

potential to maintain or improve one's own performance; supported by the need for feelings of competence [20].

Gerling and colleagues [13] suggest these preferences may not reflect an optimal experience, as visibility of balancing may weaken an assisted player's internal attribution of success through the perception that their ability alone was not responsible. In contrast, Depping and colleagues [11] found disclosure of skill assistance to not have negative effects as players may still internally attribute success when assisted, and attribute reduced performance to the balancing system when competing against assisted players. These conflicting views highlight the potential for player preferences to differ from actual gameplay experience, and the need for further research to examine these effects.

REFINEMENT TO MDDA FRAMEWORK

As described above, our findings highlight that the component of visibility does not account for whether or not a player is aware of a particular MDDA instance (regardless of its visibility). As a result, the framework would not be able to account for cases in which players can be aware of a technique that is not intentionally communicated to them, and similarly situations in which a player does not notice or correctly interpret a technique that is made visible.

In response to the feedback and recognition of the issue, Visibility was removed from the framework in favour of a new 'Awareness' component. This component indicates a player's awareness of the MDDA instance's effects on gameplay and recipients. Unlike the other attributes, Awareness is subjective and measured during or post-play rather than defined prior to activation of the technique. A player's degree of awareness may be affected by their experience with the game, understanding of its mechanics and the MDDA instance's implementation.

A player's initial awareness of the presence of an MDDA instance is binary, as they either know of the existence of the MDDA in the match or not. Their degree of awareness of the effects and recipients of the MDDA is then represented by a two-axis matrix (see Figure 8). The horizontal 'x' axis displays the continuum of a player's awareness of the effects of the MDDA (i.e., how

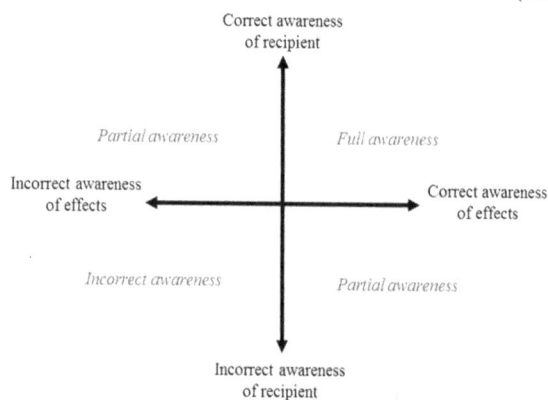

Figure 8. Awareness component matrix

performance is manipulated such as providing control assistance or a score modifier). This extends from an incorrect awareness (player is wrong about the effects), to correct awareness of the effects. The vertical 'y' axis represents awareness of the recipient of the MDDA's effects, ranging from incorrect (believes player(s) are being assisted when they are not or vice versa) to a correct identification of the recipient(s). Together, these allow player awareness to be mapped and represented independently of designer intentions of MDDA.

ADDITIONAL DESIGN CONSIDERATIONS

Along with the identified player values of *player control*, *personal benefit* and *player awareness*, survey and interview responses suggest several further considerations and for designers to contemplate when implementing MDDA features. As these are based on examination of player expectations, it is important to note actual effects in gameplay may differ.

Transparency

A concern of participants was the potential for MDDA to be seen as "cheating", particularly by the high-performing players. Combined with the preferences of participants for component attributes that increase transparency, designers should consider ensuring the presence of MDDA in their game is clearly communicated; even if when and to whom it is applied in gameplay is not visible. This may help players to view the MDDA instance like any other game mechanic rather than as 'under-the-table' interference by the designer in competitive play. Similarly, this can also help avoid a potential situation in which highly-experienced players become aware of MDDA through their own deeper understanding of the game mechanics, placing inexperienced players at a greater disadvantage.

The role of skill in match outcomes

While absolute matched challenge or performance between players may appear to be the ultimate goal in theory, the benefits to player experience may be undone by the competitive and social aspect of multiplayer games. With concerns expressed by players about the potential exploitation for performance gain and 'strength' of the MDDA effects, designers may wish to avoid assisting low-performing players to the point of completely matched performance. This can have the effect of decreasing or nullifying the contribution of skill to match outcomes, reducing gratification and intrinsic motivation to continue playing for both low and high-performing players [17].

One size does not fit all

As the results have demonstrated there can be conflicts between the perspectives of low and high-performing players. By the nature of competitive multiplayer, fulfilling these preferences for low-performing players (the recipient of assistance from MDDA instances) can conflict with the preferred play experience for the high-performing players competing against them due to the value of *personal benefit*. While the intent of balancing challenge remains, the

responses collected indicate potentially conflicting player experience effects. When designing MDDA features, it may therefore be prudent to assess and target the performance demographic most in need of the benefits of improved player experience from MDDA. For example, if an identified issue is high-performing players leaving a particular game, MDDA implementation may be weighted with the component attributes most valued by these players. In this case, a designer may seek to improve *player awareness* and *personal benefit* for high-performing player through using the 'visible to non-recipients' attribute of the Visibility component. Similarly, if designing to appeal to new players, MDDA features may be weighted towards improving *personal benefit* for low-performing players such as the 'multi-use' Duration attribute.

LIMITATIONS AND FUTURE WORK

While examination of player expectations regarding MDDA is valuable for understanding how players may perceive their use in games, it is important to consider the potential inaccuracy of participants' judgement of their play experiences as a limitation of this study. For example, from the perspective of low-performing players, survey respondents indicated MDDA visible to the recipient (themselves) to have a positive influence on their experience. However, other game balancing research found a negative effect on self-esteem and feelings of relatedness when low-performing players are aware [12]. It is suspected that the conflicts between the perspectives of low and high-performing players may be the result of players incorrectly predicting their own play experience. Future research is needed to determine if and where player expectations conflict with the actual resulting experience. Additionally, a gender imbalance was present in this study's sample which may influence the results.

CONCLUSION

The survey and interviews were conducted to evaluate player preferences and the expected player experience associated with differing implementations of MDDA. Using the MDDA Framework [2], the effects of different components were individually investigated and interpreted to allow for an understanding of player preferences for MDDA implementation and design. By determining the values consistent across players such as player control, personal benefit and player awareness, designers can better tailor their implementation of MDDA to improve the appeal of their games. Additionally, using the perspectives of both a low-performing player receiving MDDA assistance and a high-performing player competing against assisted players allowed for the identification of conflicting effects where opinions vary as a function of performance level. In response to player feedback regarding the MDDA Framework and the identification of the subjectivity of awareness, the Visibility component was removed from the framework and replaced with a new Awareness component. This has further strengthened the ability of the framework to accurately classify and differentiate MDDA instances.

REFERENCES

1. Gustavo Andrade, Hugo Santana, and Bôite Place Jussieu. 2005. Challenge-Sensitive Action Selection : an Application to Game Balancing Vincent Corruble. *Proceedings of the 2005 IEEE/WIC/ACM International Conference on Intelligent Agent Technology (IAT'05)*.

2. A. Baldwin, D. Johnson, P. Wyeth, and P. Sweetser. 2013. A framework of dynamic difficulty adjustment in competitive multiplayer video games. *Proceedings of the IEEE International Games Innovation Conference*.

3. Alexander Baldwin, Daniel Johnson, Peta Wyeth, and Penny Sweetser. 2013. A framework of dynamic difficulty adjustment in competitive multiplayer video games. *IEEE Consumer Electronics Society's International Games Innovations Conference, IGIC*: 16–19. http://doi.org/10.1109/IGIC.2013.6659150

4. Scott Bateman, R.L. Mandryk, Tadeusz Stach, and Carl Gutwin. 2011. Target assistance for subtly balancing competitive play. *Proceedings of the 2011 annual conference on Human factors in computing systems*, ACM, 2355–2364.

5. Jared E. Cechanowicz, Carl Gutwin, Scott Bateman, Regan Mandryk, and Ian Stavness. 2014. Improving player balancing in racing games. *Proceedings of the first ACM SIGCHI annual symposium on Computer-human interaction in play - CHI PLAY '14*: 47–56. http://doi.org/10.1145/2658537.2658701

6. Oscar Clark. 2014. *Games As A Service*. Focal Press, Burlington. http://doi.org/10.4324/9781315849102

7. Delwin Clarke and P Robert Duimering. 2006. How computer gamers experience the game situation: a behavioral study. *Computers in Entertainment* 4, 3: 6. http://doi.org/http://doi.acm.org/10.1145/1146816.1146827

8. Mihaly Csikszentmihalyi. 1990. *Flow: The Psychology of Optimal Experience*. Harper & Row. http://doi.org/10.1145/1077246.1077253

9. Edward L Deci and Richard M Ryan. 1985. *Intrinsic motivation and self-determination in human behavior*. Plenum Press, New York.

10. Alena Denisova and Paul Cairns. 2015. Adaptation in Digital Games: The Effect of Challenge Adjustment on Player Performance and Experience. *Proceedings of the 2015 Annual Symposium on Computer-Human Interaction in Play - CHI PLAY '15*, January: 97–101. http://doi.org/10.1145/2793107.2793141

11. Ansgar E Depping, Regan L Mandryk, Chengzhao Li, Carl Gutwin, and Rodrigo Vicencio-moreira. 2016. How Disclosing Skill Assistance Affects Play Experience in a Multiplayer First - Person Shooter Game. *Proceedings of the 2016 CHI Conference on Human Factors in Computing Systems*, ACM.

12. Kathrin M. Gerling, Matthew Miller, Regan L. Mandryk, Max Valentin Birk, and Jan D. Smeddinck. 2014. Effects of balancing for physical abilities on player performance, experience and self-esteem in exergames. *the 32nd annual ACM conference*, 2201–2210. http://doi.org/10.1145/2556288.2556963

13. Kathrin M. Gerling, Matthew Miller, Regan L. Mandryk, Max Valentin Birk, and Jan David Smeddinck. 2014. Effects of balancing for physical abilities on player performance, experience and self-esteem in exergames. *Proceedings of the 32nd annual ACM conference on Human factors in computing systems - CHI '14*: 2201–2210. http://doi.org/10.1145/2556288.2556963

14. Ralf Herbrich and Thore Graepel. 2006. TrueSkillTM: A bayesian skill rating system. *Microsoft Research*.

15. Robin Hunicke and Vernell Chapman. 2004. AI for dynamic difficulty adjustment in games. *Challenges in Game Artificial Intelligence AAAI*: 91–96. http://doi.org/10.1145/1178477.1178573

16. Susan Jamieson. 2004. Likert scales: How to (ab)use them. *Medical Education* 38, 12: 1217–1218. http://doi.org/10.1111/j.1365-2929.2004.02012.x

17. Snezhanka Kazakova, Veroline Cauberghe, Mario Pandelaere, and Patrick De Pelsmacker. 2014. Players' expertise and competition with others shape the satisfaction of competence needs, gaming gratifications, and contingent self-esteem in a gaming context. *Cyberpsychology, behavior and social networking* 17, 1: 26–32. http://doi.org/10.1089/cyber.2012.0413

18. C Pedersen, J Togelius, and G N Yannakakis. 2009. Modeling Player Experience in Super Mario Bros. *IEEE Symposium on Computational Intelligence and Games, 2009.*, 132–139.

19. Richard M Ryan, C Scott Rigby, and Andrew Przybylski. 2006. The motivational pull of video games: a self-determination theory approach. *Motivation and Emotion* 30, 4: 347–363. http://doi.org/10.1007/s11031-006-9051-8

20. Richard M. Ryan, C Rigby, and Andrew Przybylski. 2006. The Motivational Pull of Video Games: A Self-Determination Theory Approach. *Motivation and Emotion* 30, 4: 344–360. http://doi.org/10.1007/s11031-006-9051-8

21. B Schölkopf, J Platt, and T Hofmann. 2007. TrueSkill[TM]: A Bayesian Skill Rating System. *Advances in Neural Information Processing Systems*: 569–576. Retrieved January 23, 2013 from http://ieeexplore.ieee.org/xpls/abs_all.jsp?arnumber=6287323

22. Penelope Sweetser and Peta Wyeth. 2005. GameFlow: a model for evaluating player enjoyment in games. *Computer Entertainment* 3, 3: 3–24. http://doi.org/10.1145/1077246.1077253

23. Rodrigo Vicencio-Moreira, Regan L. Mandryk, and Carl Gutwin. 2015. Now You Can Compete With Anyone: Balancing Players of Different Skill Levels in a First-Person Shooter Game. *Proceedings of the 33rd Annual ACM Conference on Human Factors in Computing Systems - CHI '15*: 2255–2264. http://doi.org/10.1145/2702123.2702242

24. Haiyan Yin, Linbo Luo, Wentong Cai, Yew-soon Ong, and Jinghui Zhong. 2015. A Data-driven Approach for Online Adaptation of Game Difficulty. 146–153.

Does Helping Hurt? Aiming Assistance and Skill Development in a First-Person Shooter Game

Carl Gutwin, Rodrigo Vicencio-Moreira, and Regan L. Mandryk
Department of Computer Science, University of Saskatchewan
Saskatoon, Canada
{carl.gutwin, rodrigo.vicencio, regan.mandryk} @usask.ca

ABSTRACT

In multiplayer First-Person Shooter (FPS) games, experience can suffer if players have different skill levels – novices can become frustrated, and experts can become bored. An effective solution to this problem is aiming-assistance-based player balancing, which gives weaker players assistance to bring them up to the level of stronger players. However, it is unknown how assistance affects skill development. The *guidance hypothesis* suggests that players will become overly reliant on the assistance and will not learn aiming skills as well as they would without it. In order to determine whether aiming assistance hinders FPS skill development, we carried out a study that compared performance gains and experiential measures for an assisted group and an unassisted group, over 14 game sessions over five days. Our results show that although aim assistance did significantly improve performance and perceived competence when it was present, there were no significant differences in performance gains or experiential changes between the assisted and unassisted groups (and on one measure, assisted players improved significantly more). These results go against the prediction of the guidance hypothesis, and suggest instead that the value of aiming assistance outweighs concerns about skill development – removing one of the remaining barriers that designers may see in using player balancing techniques.

Author Keywords

Player balancing; aiming assistance; skill development

ACM Classification Keywords

H.5.m. Information interfaces and presentation (e.g., HCI).

INTRODUCTION

When people have unequal skill levels in social play situations, the gameplay experience suffers for both the weaker and the stronger player. The skill imbalance means that weaker players can become frustrated, and stronger players can become bored. *Player balancing* attempts to address this problem, by altering game mechanics and parameters to help weaker players compete with stronger players. One main type of player balancing involves artificial assistance for the weaker player – for example, faster acceleration in a driving game, different healing or damage rates, or aim adjustment to improve targeting. Several studies have shown that artificial assistance works successfully to balance games when players have unequal skill (e.g., [9, 12, 34]). In particular, aim assistance techniques can help to equalize gameplay in shooting games [9, 34, 35]; in addition, studies showed that both weaker and stronger players preferred the balanced games with the assistance techniques in place (as long as the context is social play) [14, 34].

Despite these successes, questions remain about whether assistance techniques should be used in games. In particular, the effects of assistance on skill development have not been carefully studied – that is, whether assisted players will become overly dependent on an assist, and fail to improve their skills as they play the game. The risk is that when the assist is removed, a novice player will be worse off than an unassisted novice whose performance was also initially poor, but who eventually gains the skills needed to compete.

This phenomenon has been studied in psychology and HCI as a version of the "guidance hypothesis." Bischof and colleagues summarize this hypothesis as "the more guidance given during training, the worse the learning" [6]. In the context of aim assistance in a shooting game, this translates to "the more effective that aim assistance is during training, the less a player will improve in aiming without the assist." However, this hypothesis is untested in games, and there is little known about how aim assistance affects the development of aiming skill or changes to player experience.

To explore this question, we carried out a study where we asked novices to play a first-person shooter game each day for five days, either with or without aim assistance, and then compared learning rates and experience measures across the entire week for the two groups. Our main research goals were to confirm that aiming assistance improved performance, and to explore whether either skill development or play experience was hindered for assisted players.

We compared performance in both a shooting-gallery scenario played at the start and end of the week (where players had to shoot a set of fixed targets), and in more realistic walkthroughs played each day (where players had to kill computer-controlled opponents while navigating through the map and avoiding enemy fire). We also gathered subjective measures of perceived competence, suspense, enjoyment, and attribution. In order to fairly compare any changes to skill or player experience, the first and last walkthroughs were always played without any assistance.

Our study provides several new findings:

- First, aim assistance improved performance when it was present in the walkthroughss. The Assisted group's performance significantly improved when the assist was added, and got significantly worse when it was removed.
- Second, the Unassisted group's skills did not improve more than the Assisted group during the walkthrough. There were no significant differences between the two groups in the performance gains from the first to the last walkthrough (which were always played with no assist).
- Third, adding and removing aim assistance led to instantaneous differences in some player experience measures (perceived competence and enjoyment), but there were no significant differences between the groups from the first to the last walkthrough.
- Fourth, the Unassisted group's performance also did not improve more than the Assisted group in the before-and-after shooting gallery test. There were no significant differences between the groups for improvement in Hit Ratio or Headshots – and in fact, the Assisted group showed a significantly larger improvement in Score.

Our study found no significant differences in performance or player experience to suggest that aim assistance causes a detrimental "guidance effect" in FPS games. In addition, the aim assistance also substantially improved performance while it was present, meaning that the assisted group was able to compete at a higher level during the initial sessions of the game. Because early competitiveness could increase new players' willingness to continue, our study suggests that balancing schemes based on aim assistance can play an important role in helping new players learn a game while still being able to play with more experienced friends.

RELATED WORK

Player Balancing

There are several types of balancing that can be considered in game design. Traditionally, designers attempt to balance games in terms of difficulty level – that is, a game is balanced when the difficulty level of the game matches the skill level of the player [16]. This keeps players in the "flow zone" where challenge and accomplishment are balanced [33]; games that manage to keep players at an optimal level of challenge are more enjoyable [11, 16, 21].

In multiplayer games, however, players can be at very different skill levels. If a game is balanced in the traditional sense, it means that expert players will always win over novices, and usually by a large margin – which can lead to a poor play experience for both players. *Player balancing* attempts to address this problem – it attempts to provide assistance to weaker players (or detriments to stronger players) in order to provide a more competitive game [2]. Player balancing is valuable because when players are more evenly matched, enjoyment is increased for both players [9].

One type of balancing uses *aim assistance* techniques (algorithmic changes that alter the accuracy of targeting movements) to help weaker players hit their targets. A recent study showed that this method increased enjoyment for both the stronger and weaker players [34].

Aim Assistance

There are several ways to assist targeting actions in pointer-based computer systems, and several of these can be adapted for use in FPS games. In general, all targeting actions are governed by Fitts' Law [18] (including actions in 3D virtual spaces [8, 22]). Fitts' Law states a relationship between the difficulty of targeting and the target's distance and width. Assistance techniques work either by changing the effective width of a target or by adjusting its distance.

Solutions that increase target width include Sticky Targets, which reduces the Control-to-Display ratio of the cursor when it is over the target [39], and Target Gravity, which attracts the cursor to targets using simulated gravity [9]. Both techniques have been tested in FPS games, but neither performed well due to overshooting [35]. Techniques that reduce distance can warp the cursor towards the target based on the initial movement [7], or create temporary proxies that are closer to the user's staring point [10]. In FPS games, Target Lock (i.e., snapping to a target) has been shown to be effective, but is seen as too obvious for player balancing [35].

The best balancing technique seen in previous studies [34] uses an aiming assistance technique called Bullet Magnetism (which improves accuracy by bending the path of a bullet towards nearby opponents), in addition to location awareness assistance about opponents' locations and variable damage modifiers that adjust incoming and outgoing damage. This study showed that aiming assistance alone was not enough to fully balance gameplay [34], because expertise in an FPS is made up of several skills, including the ways that players move to evade enemy fire, use cover in the environment, learn the map, and make use of resources such as ammunition and health packs, in addition to aiming accuracy.

Skill Development

Development of motor skills

A leading model of psychomotor skill acquisition is Fitts and Posner's three-stage model [17], which states that skills are developed through three phases: cognitive, associative, and autonomous. In the cognitive phase, the learner begins to form concepts about what the activity is and what needs to be done through explicit instruction and demonstrations. In the associative phase, the learner begins to improve and refine their skills, and begins to pay attention to *how* an action is done instead of just *what* is done. The autonomous phase occurs after extensive practice – in this phase, the task has a reduced mental and physical effort compared to the other phases, and results in very few errors. This frees up the learner to concentrate on other aspects of the task: for example, in FPS games players can concentrate on strategy and map navigation instead of aiming.

In order to improve at a motor skill, practice is required. The Power Law of Practice [25] indicates that large gains occur in early practice trials, and that gains gradually diminish with each subsequent trial. In order for practice to be effective, it is important for the practice to be deliberate, and focus on tasks just beyond a person's competence and comfort [15].

Skill development in games

Several researchers have investigated how learning and skill development occur in video game contexts. Kiili uses an experiential learning model to explain learning and skill development [20]; the model stresses the importance of players being in a *flow state* in order to learn most effectively [33]. When players are in the flow state, learning and skill development occur more rapidly [20] – the optimal environment for skill development is one where the game is challenging, but not so much that it disrupts game flow. This is similar to "scaffolded learning" theories from fundamental research on learning – for example, Vygotsky's idea of the "zone of proximal development" suggests that learning is most effective when a learner performs tasks that they can only complete with assistance [36]. When players compete with opponents who have much more skill, however, experiential learning is less effective [20].

Gee identified principles that lead to effective learning and skill development in video games [19]. For example, the interactivity of a video games allows for active participation, and the problems presented by games are often well ordered – problems in later levels build on what has been learned earlier in the game. Similar to Kiili's claim that learning is more effective in the flow state [20], Gee states that learning works best when challenges are "pleasantly frustrating" [19], i.e., when the challenges are hard, but not impossible.

Norman [26] identifies six different kinds of skills that are required to play most video games: perceptual-motor abilities, cognitive processing abilities, problem-solving abilities, information-utilization abilities, persistence, and human-human interaction abilities. According to Norman, the skills required to play a game vary depending on the genre. For example, FPS games mostly involve perceptual-motor, cognitive processing, and information-utilization abilities. Several tools have been developed to help people practice accuracy and targeting speed [3, 4]: for example, *Play2Improve* [28] created an FPS trainer to teach players about resource management, timing, and positioning [32].

Tutorials are another common way for skills and mechanics to be taught to new players and then subsequently trained. Research into tutorial effectiveness has indicated that their usefulness depends on the game complexity [5]; tutorials increased users' play time and engagement for complex games, but not in simple games where mechanics can be discovered through experimentation.

The Guidance Hypothesis

Practice is necessary for skill development, but the type of feedback received during practice is also important [38]. Extrinsic feedback (augmented information from an external source) is split into *knowledge of results* (KR) and *knowledge of performance* (KP) [37]. KR indicates the level of success in the action [38] (e.g., whether the player's shot hit the target), whereas KP refers to external feedback about the quality or pattern of the movement [37] (e.g., advice such as "you are pressing the trigger too early"). Studies of motor skill development have noted that the amount of KR feedback affects learning effectiveness. When KR is less frequent, motor learning improves [30,31]. When KR is frequent, the learner begins to rely on the guidance. This phenomenon has been called the *guidance hypothesis*.

This hypothesis [31] states that feedback which improves performance in early phases of learning will likely impair retention of skills once the guidance is removed [13] – due to the learner becoming dependent on the guidance. That is, the feedback can encourage "maladaptive short term correction" instead of corrections that will be effective in the long term [31]. Additionally, feedback during a motor action can result in more reliance and poorer learning than when it is displayed after the action [27]. In a study of guides for a gesture-based system [6], Bischof and colleagues suggest that the best approach is to practice with infrequent augmented feedback [31]. The study showed that retention was increased when users used an adaptive guide system that gradually disappeared during practice sessions.

STUDY METHODS

We carried out a study to test the effects of aiming assistance on skill development in first-person shooters, over a five-day period. The study extends previous work showing that aiming assistance increases performance [35] and balances play [34]. Our main goals were to confirm that aim assistance improved performance when it was present, and to explore whether changes in skill (as shown by game performance variables like hit ratio and head shots) or play experience were different when compared to players with no assistance.

Participants and Apparatus

Eighteen paid participants (8 men, 10 women) were recruited from a local university. Participants ranged in age from 18 to 47 (mean 26.8). To ensure that participants were novices, each person completed a questionnaire about gaming habits and FPS experience; we only selected participants who reported playing less than one hour per week of PC games. We verified their experience level by watching their performance during the training round, looking for markers of novice behavior such as poor aiming, difficulty navigating or remembering the map, poor evasive movement, or not using the rifle scope.

We developed a custom FPS game for the study, using the Unreal Development Kit (UDK), the UnrealScript language, and Visual Studio 2010 with the NFringe add-on. All game sessions were played on 64-bit Windows 7 machines with comparable Intel processors and NVidia graphics cards, Razor Imperator mice, and 22-inch 1080p LCD monitors with 60 Hz refresh rates. Each participant was allowed to set custom mouse sensitivity. Logging of all study data was done to a Microsoft SQL Server 2008 R2 database.

Procedure, Tasks, and Aiming Assistance

Over a five-day period, each novice participant played several rounds of the custom FPS game. Participants were first introduced to the study procedure, the game environment, and the weapons available in each of the two levels used in the study. At the beginning and end of the week, participants played a simple "shooting gallery" level (Figure 2) in order to measure their baseline and final performance. Between these two rounds, participants played through a "walkthrough" level 12 times (Figure 3). On the first day, all participants first completed the walkthrough with no aim assistance (again to get baseline performance). Participants were then divided into groups (Assisted or Unassisted), and completed two additional walkthroughs. For the Assisted group, the aiming assist was turned on for the second and third walkthroughs.

On the second, third, and fourth days, participants completed two walkthroughs each day, with aim assistance either on or off depending on their group. On the last day, participants completed two regular walkthroughs, and then played a final walkthrough that was unassisted for both groups (to assess people's final unassisted performance). All participants then played through the second shooting gallery level (also unassisted). The two shooting-gallery levels were placed at the beginning and end in order to capture the largest potential difference in pure aiming. Figure 1 shows the sequence of shooting-gallery and walkthrough levels for the study.

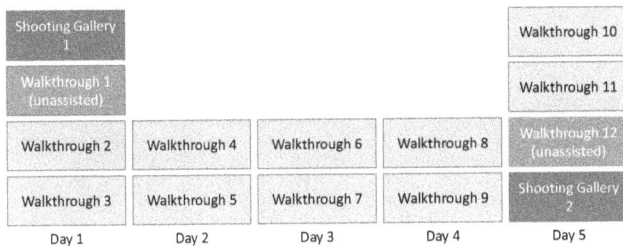

Figure 1. Sessions for each participant. Walkthroughs 2-11 were all either assisted or unassisted depending on the group. Pre-test: SG1 + W1; Training: W2-11; Post-test: W12 + SG2

Participants were told only that they would be participating in a study to investigate the learning patterns of players in FPS games. People were not informed that there would be aiming assistance, and players in the Assisted group were not warned when the assist was turned on (in the second walkthrough) or turned off (in the twelfth walkthrough).

Shooting Gallery Level

The shooting gallery constrained several game elements such as user movement and enemy actions, in order to better measure pure aiming. In the level, there were seven waves of enemies, each with six targets. Each wave stayed on the screen for 10 seconds, and the player's goal was to shoot as many enemies as possible in this period. Enemies did not shoot back at the player, and did not move after appearing. Waves 1 and 4 were close to the player; waves 2 and 5 were at a middle distance; and waves 3 and 6 were farthest (Figure 2). In wave 7, enemies were placed in varying locations at the three distances (shown in blue in Figure 2). Participants

used the sniper rifle (with the scope disabled), which took two body shots or one head shot to "kill" a target.

Figure 2. The player view of the shooting gallery; player and enemy locations are inset at top left;

Walkthrough Level

The walkthrough task was a full game-like walkthrough level set in an abandoned warehouse (Figure 3). The level contained 12 enemy bots that would move and fire at the player. To complete a walkthrough level, the player needed to move through the level and kill all 12 enemies. Participants were equipped with an assault rifle and a pistol. The assault rifle had a higher rate of fire than the sniper rifle used in the shooting gallery, but did less damage with each hit (approximately 10 body shots or 5 head shots to kill a target with the assault rifle). The pistol had a lower rate of fire than the assault rifle, but did more damage per bullet (approximately 5 body shots or 3 head shots to kill a target). Common features in FPS games (e.g., the rifle scope) were implemented, but participants were given unlimited ammunition (so no reloading was required). The level also included visual details such as lighting effects and glass shattering to look and feel like a realistic FPS game. At the end of each walkthrough, participants filled out a questionnaire about their game experience.

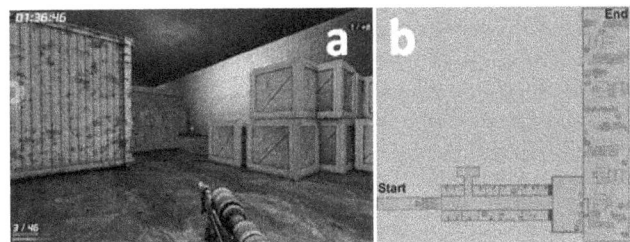

Figure 3. a) The player view of the walkthrough level b) Walkthrough Maps. Red dots represent enemies.

Aiming Assistance

The assistance provided to the Assisted group for walkthroughs 2-11 used the Bullet Magnetism technique developed and tested in earlier work [34, 35]. Bullet magnetism alters the path of a bullet toward any opponents that are within a certain angle of the initial. In the custom game, the effect was implemented by adjusting the shot vector towards the first target that is within a fixed range of the normal bullet path. The algorithm corrects shots towards the target's body; if the aim is already on the body, the path is adjusted toward the target's head. Unlike previous work, however, we did not use an adaptive assist – the strength of the technique was the same for all participants and did not change during the week. Figure 4 shows an example of the bullet magnetism effect.

The Unassisted group had no algorithmic manipulation of their shots, and all hit detection used the default methods provided by the UDK engine.

Figure 4. Bullet Magnetism adjusting the path of the bullet. Instead of going straight, the bullet bends towards the target.

Dependent Measures

For the shooting gallery levels, we looked at three measures of aiming performance:

- *Score* is the total number of enemies that the player killed during the seven waves.
- *Hit Ratio* is the number of player shots that hit a target, divided by the total number of shots.
- *Headshots* is the number of times the player hit a target's head (a shot that required higher accuracy).

For the walkthrough levels, we looked at four performance measures and six experiential measures. Performance variables were:

- *Hit Ratio*: the number of shots that hit a target, divided by the total number of shots;
- *Headshots*: the number of shots that hit a target's head;
- *Deaths*: the number of times the player died before completing the level;
- *ElapsedTime* (the amount of time in seconds that it took the player to complete the level).

The six experiential measures for the walkthrough were taken from standard instruments used in previous work, and we used only questions that were relevant to our study (e.g., removing questions about multiplayer issues):

- *Competence* and *Autonomy* using subscales from the Player Experience of Needs Satisfaction (PENS) scale of player experience [29];
- *Interest-Enjoyment* and *Pressure* from the Intrinsic Motivation Inventory (IMI) of player motivation [23];
- *Suspense* using Moulard's Suspense scale [24];
- *Attribution* using the Player Attribution scale [14] (this measure was used to determine if players attributed their performance to themselves or to external factors).

RESULTS

Results from the study are organized below in terms of three main questions: first, did the aim assist improve performance when it was present in the walkthrough levels; second, did the aim assist reduce skill development for the Assisted group compared to the Unassisted group; and third, did the aim assist change the overall play experience.

Note on analysis

Because we used a between-participants design, the absolute performance differences between the Assisted and Unassisted groups are not meaningful (due to the baseline differences between players in these groups). Therefore, our analyses below first calculate a difference between two points in time (e.g., the performance difference between the first and second shooting gallery levels), and then compare the Assisted and Unassisted groups using this difference. However, the charts in Figure 5 to Figure 12 present the original data, rather than the differences (to show actual performance for both groups).

To analyze performance differences, we used one-way ANOVA tests. To analyze differences on experiential measures, we used Wilcoxon signed-rank tests.

Did assistance improve performance when present?

To determine whether adding aim assistance led to improvements that were greater than the simple effects of practice, we compared the Assisted and Unassisted groups using the performance difference from the first walkthrough to the second. The first walkthrough was always unassisted, and the second added aim assistance for the Assisted group.

These results are summarized in Figure 5 to Figure 8. The figures clearly show that for several measures, adding aim assistance led to greater increases in performance than seen by the Unassisted group. Table 1 shows results of ANOVA for four measures of performance (all coded as the difference in the measure between Walkthough 1 and 2).

Measure (W1↔W2)	Assist (s.d.)	Unassist (s.d.)	$F_{(1,16)}$	p	η^2
Δ Completion Time	-247.8 (133.1)	-195.7 (292.4)	0.23	0.63	0.014
Δ Hit Ratio	+0.21 (.14)	+0.02 (0.08)	12.82	**0.0024**	0.44
Δ Headshots	+28.8 (7.1)	+3.9 (5.6)	68.78	**≈0.0**	0.81
Δ Deaths	-5.6 (2.1)	-1.4 (2.8)	11.87	**0.0033**	0.43

Table 1. ANOVA results when adding assist: Assisted vs. Unassisted for performance differences between first and second walkthrough (Δ = difference W1-W2).

We also looked at the effect of removing the assistance in the final walkthrough, by comparing the two groups based on the performance differential between the second-last and last walkthrough (which was unassisted for both groups). As shown in the charts below, and in the ANOVA results of Table 2, removing the assist in the final walkthrough had a substantial effect – significantly reducing performance on all four performance measures. Note that as stated above, participants in the Assisted group were not warned that the aim assist would be turned off in the final walkthrough.

Overall, our results clearly show that the aim assistance worked to improve performance when it was present.

Measure (W11↔W12)	Assist (s.d.)	Unassist (s.d.)	F(1,16)	p	η²
Δ Completion Time	+101.1 (55.3)	-1.32 (55.3)	15.4	**0.001**	0.49
Δ Hit Ratio	-0.25 (0.08)	+0.02 (0.09)	48.6	**≈0.0**	0.75
Δ Headshots	-31.5 (8.1)	+0.3 (3.8)	112.9	**≈0.0**	0.87
Δ Deaths	+3.4 (1.9)	-0.6 (1.9)	19.7	**.0004**	0.55

Table 2. ANOVA results when removing assist: comparisons between Assisted and Unassisted for performance differences between second-last and last walkthroughs.

Did aim assistance affect skill development?

Walkthrough levels

To determine whether aim assistance hindered the development of overall FPS skills (measured by performance variables in the walkthrough levels), we compared the gains for the Assisted and Unassisted group from the first to the last walkthrough (unassisted for both groups). Note that although the charts in Figure 5 to Figure 8 show results from all walkthrough sessions, our analysis used only the amount of improvement from the first to the last walkthrough.

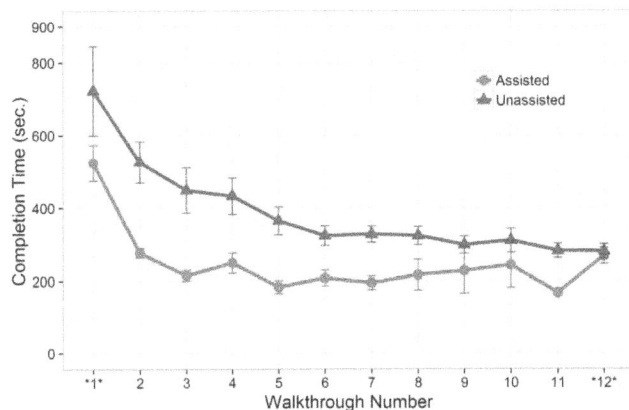

Figure 5. Walkthrough completion time (sec., ± s.e.), by group.

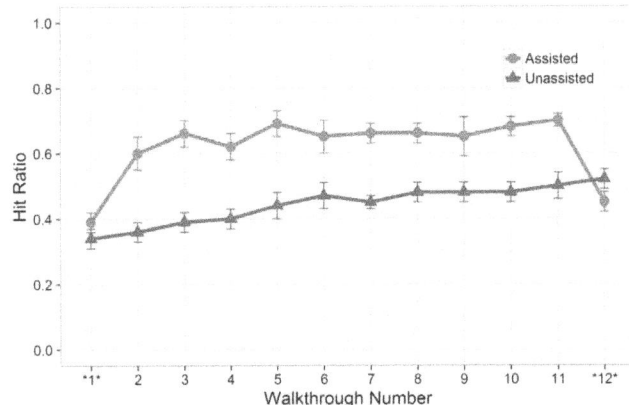

Figure 6. Walkthrough hit ratio (± s.e.), by group.

As shown by the ANOVA results in Table 3, there were no significant differences for any performance measure. These results are also visible in the charts below: even though aim assistance had a strong effect when applied, the overall improvement between the first and final walkthroughs are not substantially different for the two groups. Both groups saw large improvements in Completion Time (Figure 5) and Deaths (Figure 7), but only small changes in Hit Ratio (Figure 6) or Headshots (Figure 8).

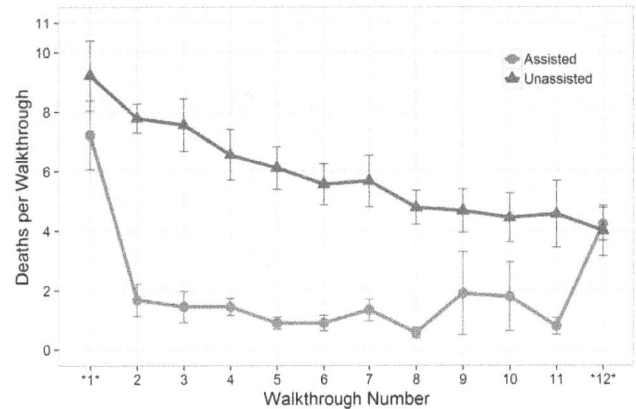

Figure 7. Walkthrough player deaths (± s.e.), by group.

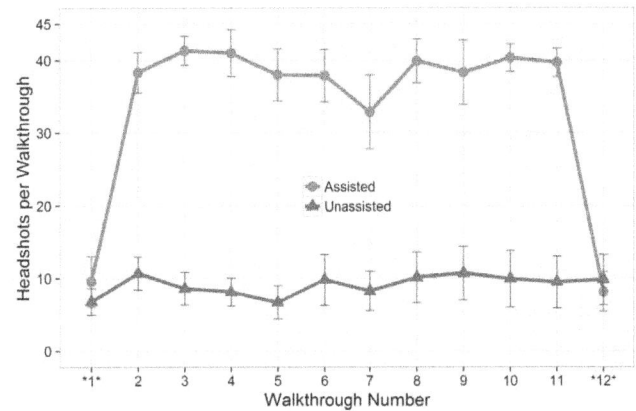

Figure 8. Walkthrough number of headshots (± s.e.), by group.

Measure (W1↔W12)	Assist (s.d.)	Unassist (s.d.)	F(1,16)	p	η²
Δ Completion Time	-256.7 (120.8)	-441.9 (361.2)	2.13	0.16	0.12
Δ Hit Ratio	+0.06 (0.12)	+0.18 (0.13)	4.08	0.061	0.20
Δ Headshots	-1.4 (8.8)	+3.0 (6.1)	1.54	0.23	0.088
Δ Deaths	-3.0 (4.2)	-5.2 (4.2)	1.27	0.28	0.074

Table 3. ANOVA results: comparisons between Assisted and Unassisted groups, considering performance differences between first and last walkthrough session (both unassisted).

Shooting gallery levels

The shooting-gallery tests focused more closely on aiming performance, and investigated whether having aiming assistance in the walkthroughs hindered the development of aiming skills in particular. We tested this hypothesis by comparing Assisted and Unassisted groups in terms of the performance gains from the first shooting gallery (the Pre-Test) to the second (the Post-Test). The results are shown in Figure 9, and the results of ANOVA tests on the three performance variables are shown in Table 4.

As shown in the ANOVA results, there were no differences found for either Hit Ratio or Headshots. However, there was a significant difference for overall Score change – but surprisingly, the larger improvement was seen in the Assisted group rather than the Unassisted group. This result goes against the expectations of the guidance hypothesis (i.e., that the development of aiming skill would be hindered by the presence of an aiming assist) – in contrast, our shooting gallery trials show that the Assisted group was not hindered, and in fact improved more in terms of overall score than the Unassisted group.

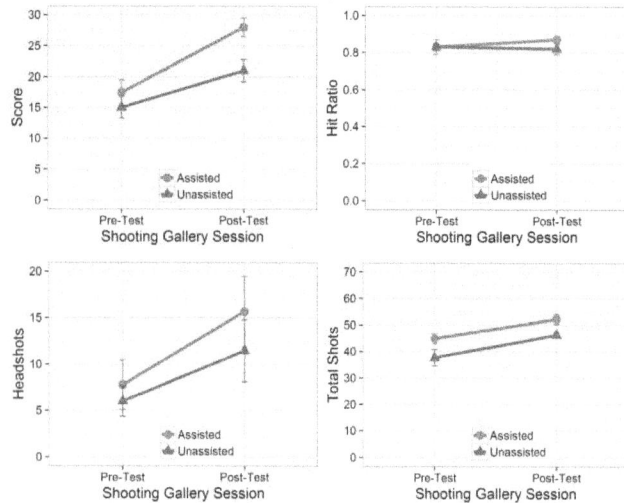

Figure 9. Pre- and Post-Test shooting gallery results

Measure (SG1↔SG2)	Assist (s.d.)	Unassist (s.d.)	F(1,16)	p	η²
Δ Score	+10.5 (4.0)	+6.0 (3.9)	5.97	**.026**	0.27
Δ Hit Ratio	+0.04 (0.08)	-0.01 (0.09)	1.45	.25	0.083
Δ Headshots	+7.9 (6.3)	+5.4 (7.5)	.56	.46	0.034

Table 4. ANOVA results: comparisons between Assisted and Unassisted for performance differences between pre-test and post-test in the shooting gallery (both unassisted).

Did aiming assistance affect play experience?

Here we consider whether the aim assist changed play experience when it was present, and whether having had the aim assist changed the Assisted group's experience compared to the Unassisted group. Note that experiential measures were only taken for the walkthrough levels.

Did aim assistance change play experience when present?

We carried out Wilcoxon signed-rank tests on several experiential variables (again, coded as the mean differences in participant responses between two walkthroughs). First, we considered whether adding aiming assistance changed experience. Tests on mean questionnaire differences between the first and second walkthroughs showed only one significant difference (to subjective Competence) between the Assisted and Unassisted groups (Table 5). As shown in Figure 10, the Assisted group's perceived Competence improved more (from 2.3 to 3.7) than the Unassisted group's (2.8 for both sessions) when the assist was added.

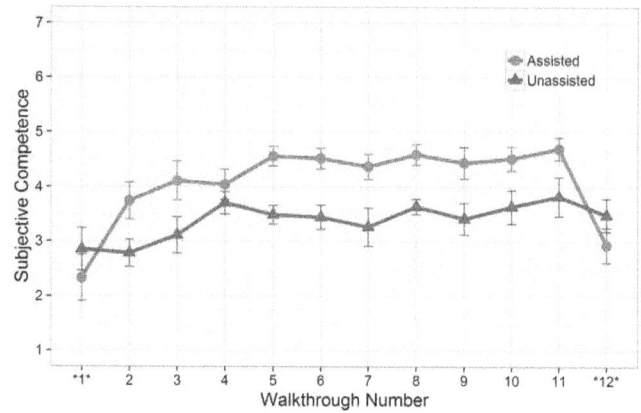

Figure 10. Perceived Competence in Walkthrough.
(1 = least competent; 7 = most competent)

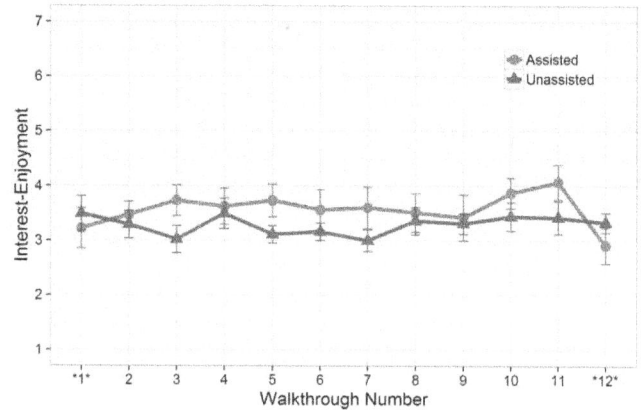

Figure 11. Perceived Interest-Enjoyment in Walkthrough.
(1 = least enjoyment; 7 = most enjoyment)

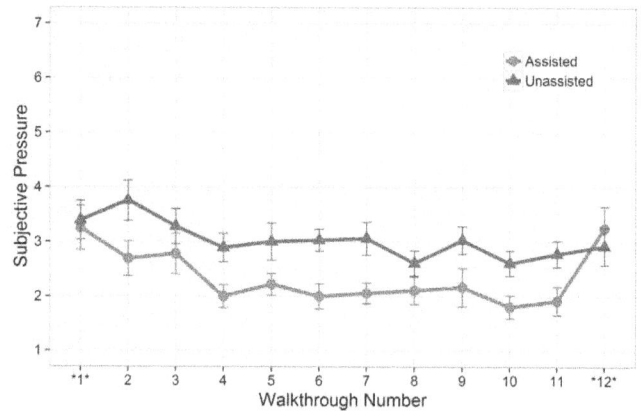

Figure 12. Perceived Pressure in Walkthrough.
(1 = least pressure; 7 = most pressure)

Measure (W1↔W2)	Assist	Unassist	W	p
Δ Competence	+1.41	-0.07	13	**.016**
Δ Interest-Enjoyment	+0.24	-0.20	28.0	.29
Δ Autonomy	-0.11	-0.22	38	.86
Δ Pressure	-0.56	+0.36	59	.11
Δ Suspense	-0.36	+0.06	54	.24
Δ Attribution	+0.25	-0.22	19	.06

Table 5. Wilcoxon test results: comparisons between Assisted and Unassisted groups, considering subjective differences between first and second walkthrough (addition of assist).

To consider whether removing the assist had similar effects, we carried out Wilcoxon tests on mean questionnaire differences between the eleventh and twelfth walkthroughs. This analysis showed significant differences in three measures: perceived Competence (Figure 10), Interest-Enjoyment (Figure 11), and Pressure (Figure 12).

Measure (W11↔W12)	Assist	Unassist	W	p
Δ Competence	-1.78	-0.33	70	**.0089**
Δ Interest-Enjoyment	-1.16	-0.09	65	**.033**
Δ Autonomy	-1.00	-0.11	51	.35
Δ Pressure	+1.33	+0.14	17	**.030**
Δ Suspense	+0.42	-0.11	20.5	.078
Δ Attribution	-0.70	-0.22	48	.52

Table 6. Wilcoxon test results: comparisons between Assisted and Unassisted groups, considering subjective differences between eleventh and twelfth walkthrough (removal of assist).

Overall, these results show that the presence of aim assistance had at least a limited effect on player experience – adding the assist led to increased feelings of competence, and removing the assist affected perceptions of competence, enjoyment, and pressure in the game.

Did aim assistance affect changes in play experience from the start to the end of the study?
We carried out Wilcoxon signed-rank tests on the experiential variables, considering differences between the first and final walkthroughs (where aim assistance was off for both groups). Our tests showed no significant differences between the Assisted and Unassisted groups for the change in any experiential measure (see Table 7).

Overall, although there are instantaneous effects of adding and removing aiming assistance on experience, having aim assistance for ten sessions of the walkthrough does not have a substantial effect on the overall change in play experience across the one-week study (from W1 to W12).

Measure (W1↔W12)	Assist	Unassist	W	p
Δ Competence	+0.59	+0.63	41.0	1.0
Δ Interest-Enjoyment	-0.31	-0.16	43.5	.82
Δ Autonomy	-0.22	+0.04	49.0	.48
Δ Pressure	0.00	-0.47	29.5	.35
Δ Suspense	-0.11	-0.17	40.0	1.0
Δ Attribution	-0.29	-0.49	40.5	1.0

Table 7. Wilcoxon test results: comparisons between Assisted and Unassisted groups, considering subjective differences between first and last walkthrough session (both unassisted).

SUMMARY OF RESULTS
There are four main results from the study:
- *The assist helped people perform better.* Performance significantly improved when the assist was added (W2), and got significantly worse when it was removed (W12).
- *Overall FPS skill development was not hindered for the Assisted group in the walkthrough.* There were no significant differences between the groups for any

performance measure (looking at performance gains from the first to the last walkthrough, W1-W12).
- *Aiming skill development was not hindered for the Assisted group in the shooting gallery.* There were no significant differences between the groups for the change in either Hit Ratio or Headshots, and the Assisted group even showed a significantly larger improvement in Score.
- *Assistance changed experience when it was added and removed, but did not affect the change in experience over the study.* Adding and removing aim assistance led to significant differences in experiential variables, but no changes in experience measures were seen between groups from the start to the end of the study.

DISCUSSION
Here we consider reasons for our results, generalization of our findings, limitations of the study, and topics for future research.

Explanations for results

Why did performance drop when the assist was removed?
The final walkthrough showed a large drop in performance for the Assisted group (e.g., see Figure 5 to Figure 8). This could point to evidence for the guidance hypothesis – that is, when the assist was removed, performance suffered. However, our data suggest that the performance drop was not due to the guidance hypothesis, and was instead due to the change in game difficulty that arises from the removal of the assist. For example, our data showed that the performance decreases seen on removal are similar to the increases seen after adding the assist. As discussed below, comparisons between the groups on the first and last walkthrough (which is a more accurate measure of the effects of aim assistance) showed no negative effects on skill development.

It is also important to note that the assist was removed abruptly and without any warning (players were not told to prepare for any change before walkthrough 12, and had no idea that aim assistance was used at all). Although a few players may have noticed the assist when it was present, most would simply have perceived this change as the game becoming suddenly more difficult (e.g., the effective hit boxes on the targets suddenly became much smaller).

The abruptness of the change may explain the drop in performance as much as the actual removal of the assist. In future studies, we will include additional walkthrough levels (also unassisted) to assess players' true performance once they are familiar with the game's actual difficulty, and not simply surprised by the changes caused by removing the assist. This would more closely approximate a real game, in which any removal of an assist would be done gradually, based on the increasing skill of the player (a strategy that is advocated by Bischof and colleagues [6] in their discussion of how to minimize the negative effects of guidance). Real game scenarios may therefore be less likely to see the large performance drop shown in our final walkthrough level. (See also the discussion of possible ordering effects below).

*Why was the assisted group's development **not** hindered?*
The main result from our study is that providing aiming assistance did not hinder skill development compared with an unassisted group. This result goes against the prediction of the guidance hypothesis, which suggests that guidance during training can limit the learning that takes place. There are several possible explanations for these results.

First, even when the assist was present, the Assisted group still had to exercise their aiming skills. The Bullet Magnetism technique does not "auto-aim" for the player, but rather provides an enhancement to the player's existing accuracy. This means that players still had to carry out all of the mechanics of aiming (e.g., seeing and tracking the target, moving the reticule to the target, and pressing the trigger), meaning that there were still opportunities for Assisted players to improve. Therefore, it is possible that the gains seen in the Assisted group result from their improvement in the other aspects of aiming that were not assisted. This idea can in fact be seen in training schemes for real-world targeting skills – for example, novice archers might start by standing closer to the target in order to maintain a basic level of success while working on the many different aspects of the skill that contribute to aiming accuracy (holding the bow, releasing the string, etc.). Previous work on the guidance hypothesis (e.g., [30]) suggests that the degree to which an assist takes over for the learner affects the amount of hindrance. The Bullet Magnetism assistance technique used in our study may therefore be a good choice, since it did not take over aiming, but rather only improved the player's existing abilities. We suspect that if our aiming assistance was more controlling (e.g., such as a "target lock" that automatically moves to and tracks the closest target), there could have been a larger hindrance than what we observed.

In the walkthrough levels, different skills were affected by aim assistance in different ways. For example, the measure of Completion Time appeared to be relatively unaffected by aim assistance – as shown in Figure 5, the improvements for the two groups follow a similar pattern, and the changes in W2 and W12 (corresponding to the addition and removal of the assist) are minor compared to those seen for other measures. This is not overly surprising, given that many of the skills involved in completing a level quickly (such as movement, navigation, and memory of the map) are not strongly affected by aiming. As indicated by previous research [34], there are several aspects to expertise in first-person shooters, and thus there are many ways for novice players to improve in addition to aiming performance.

In the shooting-gallery levels, which focused more specifically on pure aiming, the improvement in performance for the Assisted group is likely connected to these issues as well, but the fact that the assisted group had significantly higher improvement in score is surprising, and requires further consideration. We have two potential explanations. One is the possibility that the final walkthrough – which removed assistance without warning, and which resulted in a large drop in performance for the Assisted group – acted as a "wake-up call" to this group, telling them that they were going to have to put in more effort than they were used to during the assisted walkthroughs. Players in this group may therefore have tried harder in the final shooting gallery level, leading to their larger improvement in performance. We did not ask people about their effort levels, however, so this possibility is something that should be explored in future work (i.e., whether effort and performance increase immediately after a jump in difficulty).

Another potential reason for the Assisted group's strong performance in the shooting gallery is the possibility that assisted aiming may have actually provided a better learning environment than unassisted aiming. As mentioned above, different forms of guidance are part of many learning programs for aiming sports (e.g., standing closer to the target to begin), and it may be that aim assistance allowed people to learn the overall process of targeting better. For example, if players in the Unassisted group were never close with their shots in the early walkthrough sessions, they may not have had the opportunity to work on other aspects of aiming (such as tracking the target or pressing the trigger at the right time). This possibility follows the idea that learning occurs best in a "zone of proximal development" [36], as suggested by Kilii [20], Gee [19], and Ericsson [15]. That is, an optimal learning environment balances skill and challenge, and giving learners tasks that they can only complete with scaffolding leads to greater improvement. These issues have not been widely tested with aiming-based games, however, and need to be explored in additional studies.

Limitations and generalizability
Although our work involves a controlled laboratory study, there are several factors that suggest our results will generalize to real-world shooter games, and possibly to other game types as well. First, we used a realistic FPS game that used a popular commercial game engine, that used the same control scheme seen in almost all FPS games, and that included weapons and visual effects common to the genre. Our game looked and felt like a real FPS game, suggesting that our results will translate to other games of this type.

Two ways in which our study differed from the real world, however, are in the use of bots for enemies rather than real people, and in the simplification of the game (i.e., using a small map, and allowing infinite ammunition). First, the use of bots as enemies changed the gameplay somewhat from a real social-play setting (where people would be playing with more-experienced friends); our bot enemies had a fixed level of skill, rather than the range of expertise that would be seen in a real game. Although testing with full sets of real players is a clear direction for future work, our study contains all of the basic elements that would be present in a game with real players instead of bots (e.g., movement, evasion, navigation, memory of the map, and targeting), making it likely that our results will generalize to real game situations. Similarly, the smaller maps and simplified ammunition mechanics we used in our study are less likely to be affected by aiming assistance (as discussed above) than the targeting aspects of the game, which were similar to what would be seen in a real game.

In addition, elements of the study design may restrict our findings. In particular, the study used a relatively small sample (nine participants in each assistance condition), and ran for a relatively short time (five days). Therefore, it is possible that there *was* a difference in skill development between the two groups, but our study was not sensitive enough to see it. Some of our measures for the walkthrough levels (both performance and experiential) did show greater mean gains for the Unassisted group, even though none of these differences were statistically significant.

First, if we had larger participant groups, it is possible that some of the performance variables would show significant differences. Even if this situation were true, however, the differences in the means are relatively small – for example, hit ratio for Assisted players improved 0.06 over the five days, and 0.18 for Unassisted players. This implies an accuracy difference of about one shot in ten – which, although potentially valuable in an FPS game, is not the major difference that might be predicted by the guidance hypothesis. Furthermore, additional participants would not reverse the surprising result that Assisted players had significantly better improvement in score for the shooting-gallery test (and could strengthen this finding).

Second, if we had continued the study for a longer time period, it is possible that larger differences would have appeared between the two groups. However, there are several reasons to argue that our results from early-stage play are valid and valuable. We explicitly chose to study the early period of learning, since this is the period in an FPS game where skill differential is most apparent and where new players will have the most difficulty competing with more-experienced friends. We looked at the learning that occurred over twelve game sessions, and this period is likely to be critical to a new player's decision about whether or not to continue (e.g., based on principles of learning such as the Power Law of Practice, which suggests that motor skills improve more rapidly in early sessions).

It is important to note that most of our results only show no evidence of a difference between Assisted and Unassisted, rather than conclusively showing that these groups are in fact the same. Even so, these results indicate that if any effects do exist, they are not large. A small potential guidance effect must therefore be compared to the large performance benefit that we saw from the addition of the assist – this comparison suggests that the addition of aiming assistance provides a substantial net benefit. In addition, some of our results from the shooting gallery levels actually show a difference in favor of the Assisted group, further suggesting that guidance effects of aiming assistance, if they exist at all, are weak enough to be easily overshadowed by individual differences.

Lessons for designers and topics for future study
Overall, our results provide an important result that can be applied by designers of first-person shooter games who want to support social play situations. Our results indicate that one of the main concerns about assistance-based balancing techniques – that is, that these assists could prevent people from learning the game – is less of a problem than previously thought. Previous work has already shown assistance-based techniques to be highly effective at balancing game outcomes [34] and highly effective at improving the gameplay experience for both stronger and weaker players, without causing feelings of unfairness [34]. With the addition of our results about skill development, designers should clearly consider including player-balancing techniques for social play situations.

The case for assist-based player balancing is now strong. Even if skill development is hindered by a small amount, this hindrance must be weighed against the clear and significant improvement provided by the assist. That is, a novice player with assistance will be much more competitive during the critical initial sessions where they are just starting to play the game. If players are unable to compete against more-experienced friends during this early period, there is a higher chance that they will not continue playing. Assist-based balancing can therefore help to increase the audience for first-person shooter games in social-play settings.

Directions for future work in the first-person shooter genre include tests with groups of real players and full game levels, as described above, and also longer-term evaluations and tests with adaptive assistance that fades away as the player's skills increase. Our results may also generalize to other accuracy-based games, but here it is clear that further work is required. We are interested in testing the guidance hypothesis in simpler 2D shooting games (which focus more on aiming performance, and therefore may show a stronger effect), and in other genres such as driving games where similar assistance techniques have been developed [12].

CONCLUSIONS
Player balancing is an effective solution to the problem of players with widely different skill levels. However, it is unknown how assistance-based balancing techniques affect skill development or changes in player experience. To investigate this question in an FPS game, we carried out a study that compared performance gains and experiential changes for an assisted group and an unassisted group. Our results showed that although aim assistance did significantly improve performance and subjective experience when it was present, assisted players were not hindered in terms of skill development or play experience compared to unassisted players – and on one measure, the assisted group showed a greater improvement. These results go against the prediction of the guidance hypothesis, and suggest instead that the value of aiming assistance outweighs concerns about skill development. Our findings help to remove one of the remaining barriers that designers may see in using aim-assistance-based player balancing techniques.

ACKNOWLEDGMENTS
This study was supported by the Natural Sciences and Engineering Research Council of Canada.

REFERENCES

1. Sami Abuhamdeh, and Mihaly Csikszentmihalyi. 2012. The importance of challenge for the enjoyment of intrinsically motivated, goal-directed activities. In *Pers. & Soc. Psych. Bull.*, 38, 3: 317-330.

2. Ernest Adams, E. 2010. In *Fundamentals of Game Design*.

3. Aim400kg. 2015. *Reflex Training for Gamers*. Retrieved September 20, 2015, from: http://aim400kg.com/.

4. AimBooster. 2015. Retrieved September 20, 2015, from: http://www.aimbooster.com/.

5. Erik Andersen, Eleanor O'Rourke, Yun-En Liu, Rich Snider, Jeff Lowdermilk, David Truong, Seth Cooper, and Zoran Popovic. 2012. The impact of tutorials on games of varying complexity. In *CHI 2012*, 59-68.

6. Fraser Anderson, and Walter F. Bischof. 2013. Learning and performance with gesture guides. In *CHI 2013*, 1109-1118.

7. Takeshi Asano, Ehud Sharlin, Yoshifumi Kitamura, Kazuki Takashima, and Fumio Kishino. 2005. Predictive interaction using the Delphian desktop. In *UIST 2005*, 133-141.

8. Ravin Balakrishnan. 2004. "Beating" Fitt's law: virtual enhancements for pointing facilitation. In *IJHCS* 61, 857-874.

9. Scott Bateman, Regan L. Mandryk, Tadeusz Stach, and Carl Gutwin. 2011. Target assistance for subtly balancing competitive play. In *CHI 2011*, 2355-2364.

10. Patrick Baudisch, Edward Cutrell, Dan Robbins, Mary Czerwinski, Peter Tandler, Benjamin Bederson, and Alex Zierlinger. 2003. Drag-and-Pop and Drag-and-Pick: Techniques for Accessing Remote Screen Content. In *Interact*, 3: 57-64.

11. Barbaros Bostan, and Sertaç Öğüt. 2009. Game challenges and difficulty levels: lessons learned From RPGs. In *International Simulation and Gaming Association Conference*.

12. Jared E Cechanowicz, Carl Gutwin, Scott Bateman, Regan Mandryk, and Ian Stavness. 2014. Improving player balancing in racing games. In *CHI Play 2014*, 47-56.

13. Andy Cockburn, Carl Gutwin, Joey Scarr, and Sylvain Malacria. 2015. Supporting novice to expert transitions in user interfaces. In *ACM Computing Surveys (CSUR)*, 47, 2: 31.

14. Ansgar E. Depping., Regan L. Mandryk, Chengzhao Li, Carl Gutwin, and Rodrigo Vicencio-Moreira. 2016. How Disclosing Skill Assistance Affects Play Experience in a Multiplayer First-Person Shooter Game. In *CHI 2016*, 11.

15. Anders K. Ericsson, Michael J. Prietula, and Edward T. Cokely. 2007. The making of an expert. *Harvard business review*, 85, 7/8: 114.

16. Noah Falstein. 2005. Understanding fun – the Theory of Natural Funativity. In *Introduction to Game Development*, 71-98.

17. Paul Morris Fitts, and Michael I. Posner. 1967. Human performance.

18. Paul Morris Fitts. 1954. The information capacity of the human motor system in controlling the amplitude of movement. In *J.Exp. Psych.*, 47: 381-391.

19. James Paul Gee. 2005. Learning by design: Good video games as learning machines. In *E-Learning and Digital Media* 2, 1: 5-16.

20. Kristian Kiili. 2005. Digital game-based learning: Towards an experiential gaming model. *The Internet and higher education* 8, 1: 13-24.

21. Christoph Klimmt, Christopher Blake, Dorothée Hefner, Peter Vorderer, and Christian Roth. Player Performance, Satisfaction, and Video Game Enjoyment. In *ICEC 2009*, 1-12.

22. Julian Looser, Andy Cockburn, and Joshua Savage. 2005. On the Validity of Using First-Person Shooters for Fitts' Law Studies. In *People and Computers XIX*, 2: 33-36.

23. Edward McAuley, Terry Duncan, and Vance V. Tammen. 1989. Psychometric properties of the Intrinsic Motivation Inventory in a competitive sport setting: A confirmatory factor analysis. In *Res. Q. Exercise and Sport*, 60: 48-58.

24. Julie Guidry Moulard, Michael W. Kroff, and Judith Anne Garretson Folse. 2012. Unraveling consumer suspense: The role of hope, fear, and probability fluctuations. In *Journal of Business Research* 65, 3: 340-346.

25. Allen Newell, and Paul S. Rosenbloom. 1981. Mechanisms of skill acquisition and the law of practice. In *Cognitive skills and their acquisition*, 1: 1-55.

26. Kent L. Norman. 2011. Assessing the Components of Skill Necessary for Playing Video Games. *Human-Computer Interaction Technical Report 11-11-11*.

27. Jin-Hoon Park, Charles H. Shea, and David L. Wright. 2000. Reduced-frequency concurrent and terminal feedback: a test of the guidance hypothesis. In *Journal of motor behavior*, 32, 3: 287-296.

28. Play2Improve. 2010. Retrieved April 10, 2016, from: http://play2improve.com/

29. Richard M. Ryan, C. Scott Rigby, and Andrew Przybylski. 2006. Motivational pull of video games: A self-determination theory approach. In *Motivation and Emotion* 30: 347-365.

30. Alan W. Salmoni, Richard A. Schmidt, and Charles B. Walter. 1984. Knowledge of results and motor learning: a review and critical reappraisal. In *Psychological bulletin*, 95, 3: 355.

31. Richard A. Schmidt. 1991. Frequent augmented feedback can degrade learning: Evidence and interpretations. *Tutorials in motor neuroscience*, 59-75.

32. Keith Stuart. 2010. Can first-person shooter skills really be taught? *The Guardian.* December 23, 2010. Retrieved September 15, 2015, from: http://www.theguardian.com/technology/gamesblog/20 10/dec/23/first-person-shooter-skills-training

33. Penelope Sweetser, and Peta Wyeth. 2005. GameFlow: a model for evaluating player enjoyment in games. In *Computers in Entertainment* 3, 3: 3-3.

34. Rodrigo Vicencio-Moreira, Regan L. Mandryk, and Carl Gutwin. 2015. Now You Can Compete With Anyone: Balancing Players of Different Skill Levels in a First-Person Shooter Game. In *CHI 2015*, 2255-2264.

35. Rodrigo Vicencio-Moreira, Regan L. Mandryk, Carl Gutwin, and Scott Bateman. 2014. The effectiveness (or lack thereof) of aim-assist techniques in First Person Shooter games. In *CHI 2014*, 937-946.

36. Lev S. Vygotskiĭ, Eugenia Hanfmann, and Gertruda Vakar. 2012. Thought and language.

37. Carolee J. Winstein. 1991. Knowledge of results and motor learning—implications for physical therapy. In *Physical therapy 71*,2: 140-149.

38. Carolee J. Winstein, Patricia S. Pohl, and Rebecca Lewthwaite. 1994. Effects of physical guidance and knowledge of results on motor learning: support for the guidance hypothesis. In *Research quarterly for exercise and sport*, 65, 4: 316-323.

39. Aileen Worden, Nef Walker, Krishna Bharat, and Scott Hudson. Making Computers Easier for Older Adults to Use: Area Cursors and Sticky Icons. In *CHI 1997*, 266-271.

Leveraging Asymmetries in Multiplayer Games: Investigating Design Elements of Interdependent Play

John Harris
Cheriton School of Computer Science

Mark Hancock
Management Sciences

Stacey D. Scott
Systems Design Engineering

University of Waterloo, Canada
{john.harris,mark.hancock,stacey.scott}@uwaterloo.ca

ABSTRACT

Many people develop lasting social bonds by playing games together, and there are a variety of games available so that individuals are likely to find games that appeal to their specific play preferences, abilities, and available time. However, there are many instances where people might want to play together, but would normally choose vastly different games for themselves, due to these various asymmetries in play experiences, such as grandparents and grandchildren, highly skilled players and novices, or even simply two players that enjoy different games. In this work, we aim to improve the design of *asymmetric games*—games that are designed to embrace and leverage differences between players to improve multiplayer engagement. This paper builds upon prior work to describe the elements of asymmetry that can be used to design such games, and uses these elements in the design of an asymmetric game, Beam Me 'Round Scotty! We present the results of a thematic analysis of a player experience study, discuss these findings, and propose an initial conceptual framework for discussion of design elements relevant to asymmetric games.

AUTHOR KEYWORDS

Asymmetric games; game design; player experience testing

INTRODUCTION

Games and play is an important means by which we learn to socialize, communicate, and negotiate with each other. Within the realm of play, modern digital games are a uniquely flexible and multifaceted medium combining complex audio/visual presentation, narrative, interactivity, persistence, connectivity, and computation into a powerful gestalt experience unlike any other. Despite the millions of potential online play partners however, studies have shown that individualistic and ego-centric play is more common in modern online games that might otherwise be expected [8].

Further, the psychosocial benefits of anonymous online interactions are often less than that of face-to-face social interactions within player's existing social networks. [24]

For existing groups of friends and family, the diversity of individual players' game preferences and capabilities makes it even more difficult to find a mutually engaging game with which everyone can (and wants to) participate. For example, grandparents playing with grandchildren, action gamers with strategy gamer siblings, therapists with their patients, or the able-bodied with their disabled peers.

As an attempt to tackle this problem, we focus our investigation on the design of *asymmetric games*—games that adopt a design strategy that embraces differences between players, caters to them, and leverages them to create games with multi-faceted appeal while maintaining tightly-coupled social interaction.

Many commercial games include a mild form of asymmetry [20], where players can choose from a variety of characters (e.g., Magician, Thief, Warrior, etc.) or roles (e.g., attack, defense, support, etc.). However, the base mechanics of the game typically do not vary significantly between players, and it remains difficult and unsatisfying for players with more drastic preference or ability differences to play together. There are numerous ongoing discussions in both industry and academia about how best to classify players according to different typologies [1, 2, 22] as well as the importance of balancing games for different player skill levels [11, 26] but there has been little direct discussion about asymmetric games as a deliberate design paradigm.

Potentially, asymmetric games can act as the bridge between players' individual game preferences and players' desire to play with members of their pre-existing social circles. However, there is as yet no established framework for the discussion, analysis, or design of such games nor an understanding of what specific elements can be used to generate different degrees of asymmetry, and how these deliberate imbalances affect the dynamics of play.

In the absence of an existing theoretical framework for the design and discussion of asymmetric games, we adopted an exploratory approach. This work focused on what we call "strong" forms of asymmetry—experiences that afford diverse players entirely different interfaces (e.g., gamepad vs mouse, tablet vs PC), and challenges (e.g., reflexive action vs strategic planning) within the same game.

In order to begin to test and refine our emerging theories, we designed and developed our own prototype asymmetric games for use in formal player studies. In this paper, we describe one of our prototype game platforms and the player study that was conducted using it. As we have come to understand through our design, development, and testing activities, strong asymmetries introduce unique design challenges including the powerful influence of existing controller and genre familiarities, the difficulty of tuning tightly-coupled game mechanics, and the interplay between leadership, "primacy", and necessity.

Our contributions include:
1. Identifying several mechanical means of employing asymmetry to generate alternately mild or strong interdependence between players
2. Demonstration of their application in a prototype asymmetric game we have developed, called *Beam Me 'Round, Scotty!* (BMRS)
3. Discussion of the results of a player study we conducted to further explore this design space
4. A preliminary design framework that facilitates the design of future asymmetric games and understanding the complex play dynamics affecting asymmetric collaboration between players.

RELATED WORK
This paper builds on several areas of related work, namely social play in multiplayer games, player types and motivation, balancing and rubber banding, and cooperative, collaborative, and asymmetric games.

Social Play in Multiplayer Games
Research has shown that the social need to belong can be a means of kickstarting social interaction [3], that the social nature of multiplayer games can be beneficial [28], and in particular that feelings of relatedness are essential motivators for engagement and continued play [21]. However, not all multiplayer games exhibit these same benefits. Ducheneaut et al. [8] highlight the unexpectedly individualistic and ego-centric play that is often the norm in online multiplayer games. Even in so-called "massively multiplayer" games like *World of Warcraft*, they found that the multitude of other players in the shared game world are often just an audience in front of which players display their latest loot, or act as a source of idle chatter and an ambient sense of sociality via server chat.

In contrast, our research is interested in leveraging the benefits of social play by designing games that specifically encourage (and often require) players to play together, even if they may not typically enjoy the same styles of games.

Player Types and Motivation
By studying player's in-game actions and play patterns, various player typologies [1] and trait-based motivational models [21, 30] have worked to identify a wide variety of underlying player motivations such as the desire for competition, exploration, mastery, or socialization. As of yet, however, there is no widely accepted standard that fully encompasses the complexity of interactions that make up a player's experience. [2] Patterns developed from one genre of game may not necessarily carry over to other genres and player motivations have been shown to change based on time [29], environmental context [10], play partners, and even marketing awareness [25].

In our work, we build upon research into player types by identifying this as one dimension or element of asymmetry that a designer can consider when attempting to bring players together. However, we also consider other relevant elements, such as time investment, interface, and ability, as potential differences or asymmetries between players.

Balancing and Rubber Banding
The idea of encouraging players with different abilities to play together has also been studied extensively; particularly in competitive contexts. [6, 11, 26] More specifically, overt in-game balancing for skill (e.g., easy, medium, hard difficulty modes, handicaps, rubber banding) has been shown to have detrimental effects on feelings of self-esteem in player dyads [11], as the low-skilled player does not feel that they can compete on equal footing, and the high-skilled players do not feel a sense of accomplishment from winning a competition known to be unfair. Hidden balancing mechanisms (e.g., point multipliers, aiming assist) have been shown to be more effective at fostering a competitive atmosphere [26].

However, balancing for skill does not address potential mismatches in different players' underlying motivations. That is, being more competitive in a racing game through hidden speed boosts does not enhance one's experience if they dislike racing games to begin with. In our work we build on this prior research by considering differences in both ability and preference as important elements of asymmetric play.

We also distinguish these forms of in-game skill balancing from the design-time exercise of balancing or "tuning" a game's mechanics for interest/longevity. When balancing mechanics, developers tune the effectiveness of the games' available abilities and strategies to avoid the formation of a single "dominant strategy". [27] For example, when one choice of vehicle in a racing game is clearly superior in all performance metrics, every other player must also choose that same vehicle in order to compete; this makes the overall game repetitive, less interesting, and wastes the development effort that went into the many unused alternatives.

Cooperative, Collaborative, and Asymmetric Games
Researchers have also studied the effect of varying degrees of cooperation and competition in group play. Both Zagal et al. [31] and Rocha et al. [23] describe a variety of "Design Challenges for Cooperative Games" that highlight concepts such as "complementarity" between player characters, synergies between player abilities, intertwining goals, and deliberate minimization of players' competitive tendencies.

However, there is little discussion as to how designers might generate compatible game mechanics outside of the specific examples cited from existing games.

Beznosyk et al. [5] draw a distinction between "loosely-coupled" and "closely-coupled" interactions between players in casual cooperatives games. In their conceptualization, loosely-coupled cooperative games are those that "do not require tight collaboration between players and allow more independent performance" and tightly-coupled games "require a lot of waiting if the actions of one player directly affect the other player", respectively. Based on player experience surveys for six prototype games they developed around these classifications, they found that closely-coupled games tended to be rated significantly higher in terms of excitement, engagement, and replayability despite also being rated highly in terms of challenge. This highlights an exciting interplay between cooperation, challenge, and excitement, but the provided definitions of loose and tight coupling are somewhat difficult to incorporate into a design process. For example, "a lot of waiting" (a supposed virtue by the existing definition) is likely indicative of the underlying appeal of planning and coordination among teammates.

Game designer James Portnow [20] advances Beznosyk et al.'s concepts of tightly-coupled play by framing them as "signaling mechanics". Using an example of what he calls "weak asymmetry" from popular online shooter "Team Fortress 2", Portnow describes the medic character's healing beam (which can only be used on other players) as a mechanic that intuitively signals to players that medics are meant to support teammates. Portnow used *Fable: Legends* as a counter-point that exhibited much rarer "strong asymmetry", as it allowed a team of four adventurers to play against a fifth as "master of the labyrinth" who opposed the other players by spawning enemies and obstacles.

In our work, we integrate the vocabulary of *strong asymmetry*, but opt for the term *mild asymmetry* rather than "weak asymmetry" to avoid any characterization of such games as "lesser" in any way (which "weak" implies). Our game designs incorporate their ideas of collaborative and strongly asymmetric games, and we present findings from a study that investigates these asymmetries with observations from an exploratory player study.

Asymmetric Games in Research
Recent research has either explored asymmetric games directly or incorporated asymmetric design elements to achieve other goals. [4, 14, 19] Most relevant to our current work, in their game "Tabula Rasa" [13], Graham et al. presented one player with a gamepad-controlled platforming game and a second player with an interactive tabletop level editor that could alter the platforming game terrain in real time. When the players were allowed to play freely, the experimenters observed a wide variety of emergent play styles as the tabletop players alternately collaborated with, shepherded, constructed challenges for, or deliberately an-

tagonized the platforming player. Our work draws inspiration from this project while also seeking to bring a more active and deliberately cooperative role to the non-gamepad player through the use of asymmetry and pro-interdependence mechanics.

In Gerling's and Buttrick's "Last Tank Rolling" [12], a player in a wheelchair controls a powerful virtual tank that a freestanding player can hide behind for protection. Although an exciting example of allowing players with different physical abilities to leverage their unique strengths without relying on artificial skill balancing, they did not evaluate their design in a player experience study.

Asymmetric Games in Industry
Although there are numerous examples of asymmetric commercial games (e.g. *Team Fortress 2, Starcraft*), mild asymmetry (e.g. class-based character choices or weapon variants) is significantly more common than strong asymmetry, and both types are vastly outnumbered by symmetric competitive, cooperative, and single-player games.

ELEMENTS OF ASYMMETRIC PLAY
Combining this history of asymmetric game design, discourse, and research, with our own analyses, prototypes, and player studies, we have begun to build up a vocabulary of asymmetric design elements which we present now. We build upon the Mechanics, Dynamics, and Aesthetics (MDA) framework [17] framework and hope that these "elements of asymmetric play" can serve as a starting point for the further refinement and expansion of asymmetric game design practice and discussion.

Mechanics, Dynamics, and Aesthetics (MDA)
The MDA framework follows a trend in industry, where game designers have formed their own amalgam of theories from psychology, marketing, and games user research. Design frameworks such as Vandenberg's "5 Engines of Play" [25] are used as design guidelines tailored for an individual studio's culture/capabilities and refined over time based on real-world performance and sales data. In these frameworks, the efficiency of approximate but practicable guidelines often outweighs the difficulty and high cost of developing scientifically precise player motivational models. Our work builds upon the MDA framework by providing design insights specifically centered on ideas of asymmetry. As we adopt the vocabulary of the MDA framework and use it to frame our discussion of asymmetric game design elements, we briefly detail its three conceptual layers here.

Mechanics - At the Mechanics layer, the game's designers plan and implement the game's individual rules, interfaces, and algorithms. For example, how high does a player character jump? How many times can they restart if they fail a level? How many obstacles are there in a level and how difficult are they to overcome? At this layer, before the game has even begun, the game can be viewed as a series of small design decisions under the direct control of the game's designers.

Dynamics - At the Dynamics layer, the game is running and the myriad of individual Mechanics combine with the player's inputs, to form a lively and interactive whole.

Aesthetics - Finally, a game's Aesthetics are the emotional responses the game evokes in the player as a result of their individual preferences and previous experiences engaging with the game. This resultant player experience can be subtly steered and influenced by the designers' efforts but, at this layer, is furthest from their direct control.

For a player unused to third-person action games and gamepad controls, a grueling melee combat game like *Dark Souls*, with tight mechanical timing and punishing enemies, might be viewed as a frustrating and unfair slog. Alternatively, a player seeking a challenge and already familiar with complex gamepad controls might instead view such games as an invigorating odyssey through an exciting but dark fantasy landscape. Viewed within the MDA framework, it can be said that the Mechanics of the game have not changed, but each player's unique personal experiences alter the Dynamics at play and give rise to vastly different Aesthetics.

In the following sections, we employ the MDA framework to frame the insights we have gained both in analyzing existing asymmetric games and through our ongoing work designing, developing, and testing our own asymmetric games.

Mechanics of Asymmetry
In this section, we describe some of the possible mechanical manipulations that designers can employ in order to give rise to asymmetric player experiences.

Asymmetry of Ability - Where one player can do things another player cannot. E.g. one player can lift extra heavy objects while another player can leap over tall buildings.

Asymmetry of Challenge - Where the kind of challenge one player faces differs from that of other players. This is distinct from differences in the *scale* of challenges, where one player simply faces *more* obstacles than other players. E.g. one player must time a frog's jumps across a busy highway, while another player must solve a logic puzzle in order to open a treasure chest

Asymmetry of Interface - The means by which players engage with the game differs; both in terms of input and output. E.g. one player uses a dual-joystick gamepad and a VR headset while another player uses a touchscreen tablet.

Asymmetry of Information - Where one player knows something other players do not. E.g. one player has a map of a maze but is otherwise blind, while the other player can see the configuration of the local walls.

Asymmetry of Investment - The amount of time players dedicate to their roles differs. E.g. one player executes daily hour-long tactical maneuvers with their military platoon while another player take five minutes to update the overall strategic plan for the war once a week.

Asymmetry of Goal/Responsibility - Players seek to achieve different outcomes. E.g. one player is the striker on a football team while another player serves on defense.

While this list is not exhaustive, it can be used as a design tool to generate ideas for new gameplay mechanics depending on project requirements and constraints. It has been our experience that changing what type of mechanical asymmetry a game employs results in a major transformation of the overall player experience. As will be discussed next, altering more specific aspects of how individual mechanics are implemented can be used to create more subtle changes in a game's dynamics.

Interdependence and the Dynamics of Asymmetry
Particularly within cooperative play contexts, one of the most salient dynamics of asymmetric play is an emergent interdependence between players. At runtime, the asymmetries between players' mechanical abilities, interface, information, etc. force players to rely on each other for different reasons and at different times. Each must coordinate with the other and contribute where they are best able in order for the group to meet their shared goals.

In this section, we extend Beznosyk's [5] concepts of "tight" and "loose" coupling based on the player interactions we observed during our player study (presented below). Our framework introduces additional specificity regarding the directionality and timing of interdependent player relationships.

Directional Dependence
Depending on the designer's goals and specific mechanics involved, the directions of players' interdependence can be varied. Particularly when dependencies are not reciprocal, these dynamics can lead to interesting imbalances of power dynamics between players.

Mirrored Dependence - This is the simplest form of interdependence and is most commonly seen in traditional cooperative games. Often referred to simply as "teamwork", the nature of each player's reliance on each other is identical. E.g. two soldiers covering each other's back in a firefight.

Unidirectional Dependence - In this form of interdependence, Player A's progress is reliant on Player B's intervention but this dependence is not reciprocal. E.g. one player relays map information to another player.

Bidirectional Dependence (AKA Symbiosis) - In this form of interdependence, Player A and Player B rely on each other's intervention but in different ways. E.g. one player carrying a flashlight down a pitch-black, zombie infested tunnel, while a second player defends the pair with a pistol.

Synchronicity and Timing
Instances of interdependence between players in asymmetric games also have inherent time constraints. When discussing synchronicity, we are concerned with the *duration* of and *relative timing* between each player's interdependent actions at a mechanical level. Each player's actions can be

viewed as either discrete events (e.g. pulling a trigger) or continuous (e.g. remaining inside a designated zone). This is considered in combination with when each player takes their action relative to their partner (e.g. before, during, or simultaneously). Together, a number of unique combinations (Figure 1) emerge that can be applied for specific purposes in an asymmetric game's design:

Asynchronous Timing - Player A performs an action (either discrete or continuous) and Player B is unconcerned with the specifics of when. E.g. one player picks up a coin and places it in the other player's inventory.

Sequential (Disjoint) Timing - Player A completes their action some time (Δt) *before* Player B begins their action. E.g. one player removes the protective casing from an armoured enemy with a grenade, allowing the second player to finish the enemy off at their leisure.

Expectant Timing - Player A can trigger an action *if* Player B is prepared (and waiting). E.g. one player must stand atop a spring-loaded gate, weighing it down into place, while the second player locks it into place.

Concurrent Timing - Both Player A and Player B continuously perform their respective actions. E.g. one player controls the left tread of a tank while the second player controls the right tread.

Coincident Timing - Player A and Player B must perform discrete actions at the same moment (or within some small ε). E.g. Both players must throw a matching pair of switches within 1 second of each other.

Considering both the direction and timing of interdependence can be a useful design exercise for generating new play mechanics or modifying existing ones. It has been our experience that there is a general increase in "interestingness" (or at least the difficulty of execution) as one progresses down these lists. For example, actions with coincident timing are distinctly harder to execute than those with disjoint sequential timing. Considering these heuristics when designing for the generation of flow states [7] (i.e. tuning for appropriate challenge level), this would suggest for example, that pairs of more skilled players would likely prefer coincident and bidirectional interdependence over lesser demanding forms.

Aesthetics of Asymmetry

In the MDA framework, a game's aesthetics emerge during play in combination with each player's unique perspectives and expectations. As such, we incorporated several of the above mechanics and dynamics of asymmetry into our own prototype game design called *Beam Me 'Round, Scotty!* (BMRS) [15, 16]; providing us with a configurable platform with which to conduct formal player studies and explore the emergent aesthetics of asymmetric play. Primarily an exploration of asymmetries of ability, challenge, and interface, the design of BMRS focused on crafting two distinct but interdependent player experiences.

In the following sections we describe the relevant elements of *Beam Me 'Round, Scotty!*, we detail the study protocol we employed, and we discuss our observations and the feedback we gained which informed our design framework.

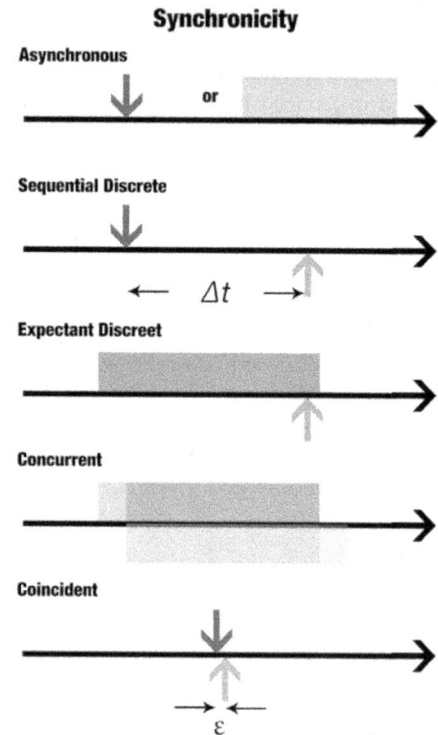

Figure 1 - Graphical timelines demonstrating different degrees of synchronized action. Player A's actions are blue. Player B's actions are green. Arrowheads and boxes represent discreet and continuous actions in time respectively.

Beam Me 'Round, Scotty!

In order to provide players with a quickly understandable narrative context, we modelled the in-game characters and scenarios of BMRS around the popular television series *Star Trek*. Previous knowledge of *Star Trek* was not required to play or understand the game however and the character names "Kirk" and "Scotty" are used in this paper as short-hand labels to encompass the respective asymmetries of interface (gamepad vs. mouse), abilities (shooting vs. teleporting), and challenges (reflex vs. planning) participants experienced in each role.

In this version of BMRS, one player controlled the courageous captain Joanna T. Kirk using a dual-joystick gamepad in an action-oriented experience that challenged the players' manual dexterity, coordination, and reaction speed. Kirk's mechanics focused on walking, aiming, and shooting a simple blaster while avoiding taking damage from hostile aliens and environmental hazards.

The second player used a mouse to assume the role of plucky engineer Scotty who deployed the orbiting starship's various abilities to assist Kirk in her adventures. The Scotty experience was designed to be low-anxiety, low-speed, and favour forethought over reflex. Scotty's mechanics employed a radial menu to select from 5 available abilities: a Shock Beam that stuns enemies in place, a Heal Beam that can restore Kirk's vitality, a Shield Wall that can erect force fields around Kirk, a Torpedo that can blast apart enemies and obstacles after a short delay, and a Teleporter which can move Kirk short distances. Each of Scotty's abilities was also tied to a slowly regenerating pool of energy which had to be carefully managed lest Kirk be left in a dangerous situation without support.

Level Configurations

BMRS consisted of five distinct levels. The Kirk Challenge and Scotty Challenge levels were tutorial levels that taught players the basics of playing as Kirk and Scotty, respectively. Both Level A and Level B were composed of a series of distinct sections that were each meant to invoke different styles of interaction between the Kirk and Scotty players. Below, we detail the aesthetic goals of each section and describe how our elements of asymmetric games were used to guide their design:

Mild Combat (Unidirectional, Asynchronous): Consisting of only a few enemies at a time, these sections were designed to be easily handled by Kirk with minimal intervention from Scotty.

Physical Obstacles (Unidirectional, Expectant): Large geographic obstacles such as chasms, steam jets, and windy walkways were designed to prompt Scotty to jump into action once Kirk reached a roadblock.

Maze (Bidirectional, Asynchronous + Concurrent): With teleportation disabled, precarious walkways, threatening laser sentries, and destructible boulders blocking the path, this section required constant attention from Scotty and required Kirk to pick up extra energy pods to fuel his partner's abilities. Scotty had to clear away the boulders with torpedoes and stun sentries while Kirk quickly and carefully walked their way through the maze.

Heavy Combat (Bidirectional, Asynchronous + Concurrent + Coincident): With many different kinds of enemies (some jumped, some shot, some were invulnerable or required special tactics) simultaneously assaulting Kirk, both Kirk and Scotty players had to work together quickly and efficiently to deploy shield walls, dodged enemy attacks, and gradually progress forward.

Teleportation Challenge (Unidirectional, Asynchronous): In Level A, pairs of enormous flaming boulders rolled down narrow side-by-side walkways with alternating timings. In Level B, an archipelago of lava fountains bridging two sections of terrain exploded intermittently. In both cases, these sections pushed the typical directional dependence of Kirk on Scotty to the limit as Scotty was forced to rapidly teleport Kirk around the shifting obstacles. Scotty had to be quick and deliberate with teleportation while Kirk essentially stood still.

Having developed a game that exhibited strong asymmetries of ability, interface, and challenge and multiple levels

that manipulated the dynamics (direction and timing) of interdependence between Kirk and Scotty players, we then mounted a player study to explore whether and how our deliberately designed play mechanics/dynamics interacted with the diverse preferences of real players and their resultant aesthetic experiences.

STUDY METHODOLOGY

In this section, we detail the experiment methodology we employed in order to investigate the player experience of our prototype asymmetric game.

Participants

Thirty-four participants (8 female) were recruited in pairs (2 female-female, 6 female-male, 9 male-male) from the local university area (21 aged 18-20, 9 aged 21-23, 4 aged 24-29). Pairs were recruited with some pre-existing relationship (e.g. friends, housemates).

Design

Our study was centered on the asymmetries introduced in the levels described in the previous section, which varied in both dependence (unidirectional or bidirectional) and timing (various combinations of: asynchronous, expectant, concurrent, coincident). However, the primary controlled factor in our study was the character that was played (either Kirk or Scotty) which varied primarily in its asymmetry of interface (Kirk was played with a game controller, and Scotty with a mouse and keyboard).

Study Procedure

Each study session lasted approximately one hour broken up into several phases (Table 1). The study was conducted in an isolated room with two large-screen displays on opposite walls, each with its own computer, speakers, mouse, keyboard, and gamepad input devices. When playing on their own computers, players could talk to each other and hear each other's in-game actions but could not see each other unless they turned around. This arrangement was chosen in an attempt to preserve the atmosphere of co-located play regardless of whether pairs were playing on the same screen or separately.

PLAYER ONE	PLAYER TWO
Intro. Survey	Intro. Survey
Kirk (gamepad) training	Kirk (gamepad) training
PENS	PENS
Scotty (mouse+kb) training	Scotty (mouse+kb) training
PENS	PENS
Level A (counterbalanced w/ Level B):	
w/ gamepad (Kirk)	w/ mouse+kb (Scotty)
PENS	PENS
Level B (counterbalanced w/ Level A):	
w/ mouse+kb (Scotty)	w/ gamepad (Kirk)
PENS	PENS
Semi-Structured Interview	

Table 1. Stages of the play study

An initial survey collected demographic information, details about each participant's game playing habits (e.g. favourite games, frequency and duration of typical play sessions), as well as a series of self-rated skill scores in various game genres (e.g. "How skilled would you consider yourself when playing first-person shooter games?")

The next four phases had participants play a particular level from the game with each play session followed by a post-gameplay experience survey. Based on the PENS questionnaire [21], the survey asked participants to rate their experience based on their feelings of autonomy, competence, relatedness, immersion, and intuitive controls during play using a 7-point Likert scale.

Each of the introductory surveys, the post-gameplay surveys, and the first two levels were completed by both participants separately on their own computer. "Level A", "Level B", and the concluding semi-structured interview were completed by both players together as a pair on the same computer.

The training levels were always completed by both players first and individually so that both players could learn to control the two different in-game characters. These levels presented a series of simple challenges that would instruct the players how to employ each character's primary abilities. For Kirk (gamepad), this included walking, aiming, and shooting with no Scotty present. For Scotty (mouse), this included the use of the five ship abilities (Teleport, Heal Beam, Shock Beam, Torpedo, and Shield Wall) as players escorted an A.I. controlled "RoboKirk" towards the level exit. RoboKirk would navigate towards the exit while shooting at any enemies within range and pause at impassable obstacles or chasms.

Levels A and B were played by both participants together with one as Kirk (gamepad, ground fighter, shooting) and the other as Scotty (mouse, teleporter, planning). When the pair played the second level in the sequence, they would switch roles (i.e. the participant who played Kirk in the first level would play Scotty in the second level and vice versa). The order of Level A and B was counterbalanced between pairs.

RESULTS

We incorporated quantitative statistical analysis into the structure of our exploratory study in order to highlight unexpected trends or future avenues of investigation. In this section, we present the statistical analysis of our player experience surveys, followed by a thematic analysis of participants' gameplay and interview recordings.

Survey Results

We designed our study with the intention that the first two single-player sessions (first as Kirk, then as Scotty) were for the purposes of training, and so the primary design involved only one factor: which character (and thereby, which distinction combination of interface, abilities and challenge) was experienced during the second two play sessions (two-player). However, because each player also played single-player versions of the game to start, we also

had data available for single-player vs. two-player experiences, and so conducted a 2 (character) $\times$ 2 (number of players) RM-ANOVA on the same subscales.

There was a significant main effect of character on autonomy ($F_{1,33} = 52.8$, $p < .001$, $\eta_p^2 = .62$) where playing as Kirk was rated as affording less autonomy than playing as Scotty. Similarly, there were significant main effects of character on ratings of intuitive controls ($F_{1,33} = 4.83$, $p < .05$, $\eta_p^2 = .13$), with the gamepad (Kirk) rated as more intuitive than the mouse (Scotty).

There were also significant main effects for number of players on autonomy ($F_{1,33} = 28.76$, $p < .001$, $\eta_p^2 = .47$), relatedness ($F_{1,33} = 135.26$, $p < .001$, $\eta_p^2 = .80$), intuitive controls ($F_{1,33} = 5.60$, $p < .05$, $\eta_p^2 = .15$), and immersion ($F_{1,33} = 36.09$, $p < .001$, $\eta_p^2 = .52$). In all cases, playing together was rated higher than playing separately.

However, it is important to note that the single-player experiences were not counterbalanced, and so this could be an order effect, and not conclusively an effect of character (i.e. interface, abilities, or challenges). Thus, survey results were inconclusive, though the thematic analysis described next provided much richer data and was the primary intent of our study design.

Thematic Analysis

A thematic analysis was performed on the gameplay footage (19.96 hours of audio + video) from all of the participant pairs. In this section, we describe the salient themes most relevant to the design of asymmetric games. When relevant, participants are labelled according to their group number and distinguished as either partner A or B (e.g. P.13A and P.13B).

Leadership and Primacy

From a narrative perspective, the character of Kirk was introduced as a marooned spaceship *captain* trying to escape from a hostile planet with remote assistance from their ship's engineer. When designing BMRS, Kirk had been envisioned as the main focus of play, but our observations of players' experiences highlighted how the dynamics of play can yield different results.

In our player study, we observed both fluid leadership dynamics, where players would trade proposed strategies back and forth, as well as heavily biased pairings where one of the players would dominate decision making and dictate the majority of actions to their partner.

In imbalanced pairings, we observed the dominant player dictating what tactics and timings to employ (e.g. "go here, do this"), regardless of which in-game character they were playing. During interview, many such pairs highlighted that the subordinate player often didn't *want* the responsibility of leadership. These players often claimed to feel less competent with the game and were happy to allow their partner to take on the additional cognitive load of coordinating their cooperation.

More common however, was a balanced and fluid leadership dynamic wherein whichever player had the most promising strategic proposal at any given moment would temporarily lead the pair. Noticing a new obstacle or recognizing a new opportunity, each player would call out suggestions as they arose and command/subordination would flow back and forth rhythmically. This cycle of observation, negotiation, decision, and action repeated on rapid time scales (e.g. "I'll deal with this enemy while you stun that one!"), large time scales ("Let's take our time and explore. We might find hidden treasure!"), and with different flavours of synchronicity. (E.g. coincident teleportation maneuvers, expectant shield wall shootouts, and sequential activation of switches.)

We also identified a distinct element of what we call "primacy" motivating many player-player negotiations. For example, if Kirk is suddenly ambushed by a group of enemies, this sudden danger would rapidly override existing team goals and a new leadership proposal would spring forth. ("Oh wow! Look out! Let's deal with those enemies first!") Alternatively, in the midst of a rapid teleportation obstacle course, Scotty's dwindling energy reserves (and the swift death Kirk would suffer should Scotty run out of energy at that time) prompted "collecting energy pods" to become the prime motivator for new action proposals.

We observed that the play partner who proposed these reactive strategies (leader) did not necessarily correlated with the player whose needs assumed primacy at that moment.

Effect of Player's Skill on Experienced Aesthetic
After playing both roles, participants generally either viewed Scotty as a helpful assistant and Kirk as a lead actor/hero/captain OR they viewed Scotty as a powerful, commanding overseer and Kirk as a fragile liability meant to be protected and shepherded to the level's exit. These sentiments are exemplified by player comments such as:

*"(As Kirk) you feel like you have more control than you give Kirk respect as Scotty. When you're playing as Scotty, you're like 'He's my pawn.' And when you're Kirk, you're like 'I need Scotty to do things. (Feebly) But I have **some** control. I have **some** self-respect! Ha! ... But I think Scotty, in this case, would be the main character, since he has so much control. Kirk was really just walking through."* [P.11B]

Which perspective was taken depended on the relative confidence and skill of the two players. Highly skilled Kirk players (accurate shots, minimal damage) could easily progress forward through enemies and hazards with minimal assistance from Scotty; typically only pausing at obstacles that *required* Scotty's abilities. (E.g. clearing a boulder away with torpedoes). Alternately, weaker Kirks tended to progress more slowly, always waiting for Scotty's tactical intervention (e.g. shield walls, stun beams).

When asked to describe the relative potency of Kirk versus Scotty, almost universally participants described Scotty as the more capable and more interesting character. With her simple "run and gun" mechanics, Kirk was described as a much more straight forward character to play as but with her own straight-forward appeal.

"(Kirk) is technically the leader but she doesn't have as much control as Scotty, really. Although...it is fun, the shooting parts." (P.11A)

In addition, participants near universally complained about Kirk's slow movement speed and suggested future improvements such as running faster, a dedicated sprint button (with limiting stamina), jumping, or a dodge-roll. These results highlight shortcomings in BMRS' current tuning of abilities, options, and excitement.

Overall, we saw that even though the underlying mechanics had not changed, the previous experience, skill, and perspectives that players brought to the game created striking differences in their ultimate aesthetic experience.

Mechanical Interactions
We also noted that interdependence between players was both an advantage and disadvantage from a design perspective. Implementing the previously mentioned player suggestions would be complicated due to the myriad of interconnected mechanical systems involved. For example, giving Kirk a jump or a dodge-roll would potentially invalidate a number of existing platforming challenges (e.g. the maze, lava boulder sections) and takes away from Scotty's responsibilities as the teleporter and primary provider of long-distance movement.

More subtly, synchronization between players' actions during heavy combat situations was consistently described as one of the most troublesome aspects of Scotty players' experiences. Scotty players said they often felt overwhelmed trying to rapidly switch between Scotty's various abilities and deploy them accurately and quickly. In essence, the reflex challenges designed for Kirk players were negatively affecting Scotty due to tight synchronicity demands.

This problem was exacerbated by an unanticipated design decision within BMRS's camera system mechanics. Because the shared camera view shifts based on *Kirk's* movements, Scotty had to attempt to counteract these movements on-the-fly in order to keep his target beneath his cursor. This is counter to the slower and more thoughtful Scotty experience original envisioned.

Familiarity with Interface
Despite our efforts to design unique player experiences that catered to distinct player preferences, our analysis highlighted the strong role our participant's gaming history played in selecting new game experiences.

Many players expressed a distinct preference for one in-game character over the other. This was primarily due to their existing familiarity with the two different control schemes and was largely unaffected by their positive or negative experiences playing as either Kirk or Scotty. Players who predominately played console games preferred the gamepad whereas players who predominately played games on PC preferred the mouse.

Familiarity with Player Partner Limits Interdependence

Similar to finding by game analytics firm Quantic Foundry [9], many of our participants described how in game frustrations could be ameliorated by having some degree of familiarity with one's play partner. In contrast, when playing with strangers online, loose coupling or outright competition was preferable to cooperative play.

"LAN games are fun if they're hard in the sense that you're relying on your friends. With online games, co-op is fun if you can do it yourself, because then you're not relying on them. But if you're trying to find a happy medium, I don't think there is one... [where] you could play online with a stranger and you're reliant on them... [but] you're not mad when they screw up. Moral of the story is I don't play co-op online." [P.11B]

Similarly, our participants claimed to play different types of games with different types of players. (i.e. Alanna would play BMRS with Bob but not with Cathy.)

When asked about playing games with their family or parents, participants typically said that they rarely played their favourite games with family members. Instead, family play typically consisted of more "casual" style games such as Just Dance or Wii Sports.

Participants reported that they essentially never played video games with their parents. However, many participants did play board/party games with their parents (such as *Yahtzee* or *Charades*).

When asked why, participants cited general disinterest from their family members or a lack of available time to invest in learning complex new game rules.

Interdependence and Necessity

Almost universally, players enjoyed needing to rely on each other. When discussing the drop-in-and-play secondary roles in games such as *Super Mario Galaxy* and *Rayman Legends* and how these roles neither require as much skill to play as the primary characters nor are strictly necessary to progress in the game, players typically stated they preferred to be dependent on each other rather than always being self-sufficient:

"[Playing an optional role] It's good in that sense but if you actually play video games, it's not great. You feel useless." [P.11B]

"Yeah, because you're not really doing anything. And you're not needed in any actual way. You can't contribute very much." [P.11A]

Many participants described how cooperative play was fun despite (and often even because of) the inherent frustration of coordination.

Participants described how the necessity of both the Kirk and Scotty roles ebbed and flowed depending on the different sections of the levels being encountered. During combat, the game progresses largely based on Kirk's skill. Scotty's contributions during these sections were appreciated but were not often viewed as strictly necessary. Alternatively, during "puzzle" sections such as the maze or teleportation challenges, Scotty's potency and necessity were pushed to the forefront by the game's mechanics and Kirk was often viewed as simply "along for the ride".

More generally, many players drew parallels with existing games such as modern *Super Mario* games which allow multiple players on screen simultaneously. In these games, players who fall off platforms or are defeated by enemies are relegated to a "bubble" which follows the surviving players around. Once the surviving player reaches a safe location, bubbled players can pop out and resume their normal play. However, participants complained that this often led to problems where imbalances between players' skills caused the less-skilled players to spend a majority of their time in-bubble and frustrated; essentially not participating in the game.

Hypothetical Mechanics

As part of the interview segment of the study, participants were asked to reflect on hypothetical iteration of BMRS where, instead of having distinct Kirk and Scotty characters, players both played as "Super Kirks" (a name we coin here to describe a new, super powerful Kirk character). In this configuration, both players would use gamepads to control identical on-screen characters similar to traditional Kirk play but would also having individual access to all of the abilities normally reserved for Scotty. (E.g. Super Kirk could teleport themselves and deploy their own shield wall.) While most participants stated that this configuration would be more individually potent, the majority of participants claimed to prefer the existing interdependent Kirk/Scotty relationship. Only those players who described themselves as particularly focused on achievement and high-skill gameplay expressed interest in the hypothetical Super Kirk configuration.

A second hypothetical configuration was also proposed. In this "Kirk + Spock" configuration, although players again used gamepads to control two on-screen characters, Scotty's abilities would be split evenly between them such that, for example, only Kirk could deploy Shield Walls but only the new Spock character could deploy torpedoes. This Kirk + Spock configuration was more warmly received than hypothetical Super Kirks in some cases but those players who had strong preferences for mouse interfaces still preferred the original Kirk + Scotty configuration.

DISCUSSION

In the previous section, we discussed several of the recurring themes we observed based on gameplay recordings and player interviews from our in-lab study of BMRS. Much of that insight directly informed the MDA-centric "Elements of Asymmetric Play" section presented earlier. Next, we discuss potential design implications and recommendations for asymmetric games based on our observations.

Leadership and Primacy

Future asymmetric game designs could leverage our observations by deliberately altering the balance of leadership and primacy between different players. Consider mechanics which introduce an asymmetry of information between players. If the imbalance were strong enough, it would become prohibitive for the less informed player (even if they were the stronger personality and the de facto leader in a particular player pairing) to constantly ask to be kept informed enough to make leadership decisions.

In theory, leadership would default to the player with the most information. If the normal social dynamic of the pair were deliberately reversed (e.g. a child in the leadership role with their parents as subordinates), such an asymmetric game could be employed as a role-taking exercise.

Familiarity

We interpret the consistency between participants' controller preference *prior* to the study and their character preference *after* the study as a mixed result. It both underscores the importance of designing games for diverse preferences as well as highlights the dominant influence of participants' previous familiarities and the limited nature of single laboratory studies.

In terms of asymmetric design and family members' hesitation to play new games together, our results speak to a need for new players to be able to intuitively osmose the game's rules, mechanics, and controls to overcome some of the likely psychological barriers at play in these scenarios. While the average age of video game players continues to rise as the first generation of "gamers" age, there are still a large number of people for whom video games remain a foreign and intimidating concept. No matter how suitable and intuitive a role a well design asymmetric game affords them, some people may still not be sufficiently enticed to participate with their friends/family.

The Difficulty of Tuning Asymmetric Mechanics

The same diversity of inputs, obstacles, information, and aesthetics that can make asymmetric games appealing can cause the playtesting, debugging, and tuning of individual play mechanics to be a significantly more complex task in asymmetric games.

Consider participants' requests to use their left hand (on the keyboard) to select abilities and their right hand (on the mouse) to deploy them. While Scotty players' ability to respond to overwhelming amounts of enemies would be greatly increased, this would also bring Scotty's aesthetic experience closer to Kirk's already action-oriented play style. Employing our conceptual framework for designing asymmetric experiences, consider instead a mechanic where Kirk throws handheld beacons throughout the environment that request specific forms of assistance which Scotty would need to manage and prepare in advance. Scotty then "authorizes" the deployment of each ability request with a single button. In this way, we can generate a cleaner and stronger asymmetry of challenge: with planning falling to Scotty and reflex/targeting falling solely to Kirk instead.

LIMITATIONS AND FUTURE WORK

The exploration and study of asymmetric games as a design paradigm is still in its infancy. This paper presents an early framework for more specific design and discussion of asymmetric games but there is still much more work to be done. For example, while related work [5] and our own exploratory observations suggest that tighter coupling or more exacting synchronization between players' action will be more engaging for highly skilled players, we have not specifically tested or quantified such experiences.

Similarly, our current work focuses primarily on mechanical asymmetries of ability, challenge, and interface but our framework has identified several other potential forms of asymmetry. We suspect each will reveal its own unique dynamic and aesthetic interactions when studied in depth.

Further, many player experience metrics have focused on individual measures such as feelings of competence and flow. Asymmetric cooperative experiences involve unique interpersonal phenomena (e.g. leadership, synchronicity, negotiation) that allude to what Kaye et. al. [18] refer to as "group flow" and a "shared aesthetic". Future work will benefit from incorporating and expanding upon these emerging, group-centric experience metrics.

CONCLUSION

Games are powerful, but many are not particularly cooperative or socially beneficial. Asymmetric games may be suitable for bridging the gaps between the psychosocial benefits of playing with pre-existing friends and finding mutually enjoyable games well-suited to everyone's preferences and capabilities.

In this paper we have presented several elements of asymmetric games that can serve as useful design tools when creating interdependent player experiences and described our application of these elements in our prototype asymmetric game *Beam Me 'Round, Scotty!* We conducted a player study to explore our theories and the thematic analysis of our participant's experiences has contributed to an initial conceptual framework for the future design, discussion, and study of asymmetric games.

ACKNOWLEDGMENTS

We thank the Natural Sciences and Engineering Council of Canada (NSERC) and the Ontario Ministry of Research and Innovation for funding. We also thank the SSHRC IM-MERSe network and the members of the Games Institute at Waterloo for their support.

REFERENCES

1. Bartle, R. (1996). Hearts, clubs, diamonds, spades: Players who suit MUDs. *Journal of MUD research*, *1*(1), 19.

2. Bateman, C., Lowenhaupt, R., & Nacke, L. E. (2011, September). Player typology in theory and practice. In *Proceedings of DiGRA*.

3. Baumeister, R. F., & Leary, M. R. (1995). The need to belong: desire for interpersonal attachments as a fundamental human motivation. *Psychological bulletin, 117*(3), 497.

4. Benford, S., Crabtree, A., Flintham, M., Drozd, A., Anastasi, R., Paxton, M., ... & Row-Farr, J. (2006). Can you see me now?. *ACM Transactions on Computer-Human Interaction (TOCHI), 13*(1), 100-133.

5. Beznosyk, A., Quax, P., Lamotte, W., & Coninx, K. (2012). The effect of closely-coupled interaction on player experience in casual games. In *Entertainment Computing-ICEC 2012* (pp. 243-255). Springer Berlin Heidelberg.

6. Cechanowicz, J., et al. "Improving Player Balancing in Racing Games" (2014), Proc. Of ACM CHI PLAY 2014, Toronto, Canada. 47-56

7. Csikszentmihalyi, M. (1990). Flow. The Psychology of Optimal Experience. New York: Harper & Row.

8. Ducheneaut, N., Yee, N., Nickell, E., & Moore, R. J. (2006, April). Alone together?: exploring the social dynamics of massively multiplayer online games. *In Proceedings of the SIGCHI conference on Human Factors in computing systems* (pp. 407-416). ACM.

9. Embaugh, K., Quantic Foundry, (2016, July 21) Local Co-Op is The Most Consistently Appealing Mode of Social Gaming Across Gender and Age, *Retrieved from http://quanticfoundry.com/2016/07/21/social-gaming/*

10. Gajadhar, B. J., De Kort, Y. A., & Ijsselsteijn, W. A. (2008). Shared fun is doubled fun: player enjoyment as a function of social setting. In *Fun and games* (pp. 106-117). Springer Berlin Heidelberg.

11. Gerling, K., et al. "Effects of balancing for physical abilities on player performance, experience and self-esteem in exergames." *Proc. of SIGCHI Conference on Human Factors in Computing Systems*. CHI '14

12. Gerling, K., Buttrick L., "Last tank rolling: exploring shared motion-based play to empower persons using wheelchairs." *Proc.of ACM SIGCHI annual symposium on Computer-human interaction in play* (CHI PLAY '14) 415-416 DOI: 10.1145/2658537.2661303

13. Graham N., et al., "Villains, architects and micro-managers: what tabula rasa teaches us about game orchestration" *Proc. of SIGCHI Conference on Human Factors in Computing Systems* (CHI '13). 705-714. http://doi.acm.org/10.1145/2470654.2470754

14. Haas, J. M. (2013). SANCTUARY: asymmetric interfaces for game-based tablet learning (Doctoral dissertation, Massachusetts Institute of Technology)

15. Harris, J., Hancock, M., & Scott, S. (2014, October). Beam Me'Round, Scotty!: Exploring the effect of in-

terdependence in asymmetric cooperative games. In *Proceedings of the first ACM SIGCHI annual symposium on Computer-human interaction in play* (pp. 417-418). ACM.

16. Harris, J., Hancock, M., & Scott, S. D. (2015, October). Beam Me'Round, Scotty!: Studying Asymmetry and Interdependence in a Prototype Cooperative Game. In *Proceedings of the 2015 Annual Symposium on Computer-Human Interaction in Play* (pp. 775-778). ACM.

17. Hunicke, R., LeBlanc, M., & Zubek, R. (2004, July). MDA: A formal approach to game design and game research. In *Proceedings of the AAAI Workshop on Challenges in Game AI* (Vol. 4, p. 1).

18. Kaye, L. K. (2016). Exploring flow experiences in cooperative digital gaming contexts. *Computers in Human Behavior*, 55, 286-291.

19. Maurer, B., Aslan, I., Wuchse, M., Neureiter, K., & Tscheligi, M. (2015, October). Gaze-Based Onlooker Integration: Exploring the In-Between of Active Player and Passive Spectator in Co-Located Gaming. *In Proceedings of the 2015 Annual Symposium on Computer-Human Interaction in Play* (pp. 163-173). ACM.

20. Portnow, J. [Extra Credits] (2015, March 18) Asymmetric Play – Can One Game Cater to Many Playstyles?, *Retrieved from* https://youtu.be/SQhxtfKH1f8

21. Przybylski, A. K., Rigby, C. S., & Ryan, R. M. (2010). A motivational model of video game engagement. *Review of general psychology*, 14(2), 154.

22. Nacke, L. E., Bateman, C., & Mandryk, R. L. (2014). BrainHex: A neurobiological gamer typology survey. *Entertainment computing*, 5(1), 55-62.

23. Rocha, J. B., Mascarenhas, S., & Prada, R. (2008). Game mechanics for cooperative games. *ZON Digital Games 2008*, 72-80.

24. Shen, C., & Williams, D. (2011). Unpacking time online: Connecting internet and massively multiplayer online game use with psychosocial well-being. *Communication Research*, 38(1), 123-149.

25. VandenBerghe, J., (201, March 14) Engines of Play, *Retrieved from* http://www.gdcvault.com/play/1023329/Engines-of-Play-How-Player

26. Vicencio-Moreira, R., et al., "Now You Can Compete With Anyone: Balancing Players of Different Skill Levels in a First-Person Shooter Game." *Proc. ACM Conference on Human Factors in Computing Systems*. CHI '15.

27. Wikipedia, "Strategic Dominance" https://en.wikipedia.org/wiki/Strategic_dominance

28. Wohn, D. Y., Lampe, C., Wash, R., Ellison, N., & Vitak, J. (2011, January). The" S" in social network

games: Initiating, maintaining, and enhancing relationships. In *System Sciences (HICSS), 2011 44th Hawaii International Conference on* (pp. 1-10). IEEE.

29. Yee, N. "As Gamers Age, The Appeal of Competition Drops the Most", http://quanticfoundry.com/2016/02/10/gamer-generation/

30. Yee, N. (2006). Motivations for play in online games. *CyberPsychology & behavior*, 9(6), 772-775.

Jofish Kaye and Paul Dourish. 2014. Special issue on science fiction and ubiquitous computing. *Personal Ubiquitous Computing*. 18, 4 (April 2014), 765-766. http://dx.doi.org/10.1007/s00779-014-0773-4

31. Zagal, J. P., Rick, J., & Hsi, I. (2006). Collaborative games: Lessons learned from board games. *Simulation & Gaming*, 37(1), 24-40.

Playing at Planning: Game Design Patterns from Disaster Response Practice

Zachary O. Toups[1], William A. Hamilton[2], Sultan A. Alharthi[1]

[1]Play & Interactive Experiences for Learning Lab, Dept. Computer Science, New Mexico State University
[2]Interface Ecology Lab, Dept. Computer Science & Engineering, Texas A&M University
z@cs.nmsu.edu, bill@ecologylab.net, salharth@nmsu.edu

ABSTRACT

We draw on years of ethnographic investigation into the disaster response practices of fire emergency response, urban search and rescue, and incident command to inform the design of games. Our objective is to support training disaster responders, yet our findings apply to general game design. We identify critical components of disaster response practice, from which we develop game design patterns: EMERGENT OBJECTIVES, DEVELOPING INTELLIGENCE, and COLLABORATIVE PLANNING. We expect that, in implementing these patterns, designers can engage players in disaster-response-style planning activities. To support the design patterns, we survey exemplar games, through case studies. The paper contributes a set of game design patterns that support designers in building games that engage players in planning activities.

ACM Classification Keywords

H.5.3. Group and Organization Interfaces: CSCW

Author Keywords

Game design; disaster response; ethnography; planning.

INTRODUCTION

A primary component of disaster response is *planning*, which is carried out by multiple individuals who each bring varied expertise and skills [14, 15, 30, 37, 38, 65, 69]. Plans, especially in large-scale disasters, must account for unseen changes and unknown variables, optimizing deployed resources. While existing games use planning as an activity, none feature disaster-response-style planning or use it as a core mechanic. Instead, fast-paced action, distributed emergent planning, and perfect information proliferate. We see an opportunity to develop games to help responders practice effective planning activities through games; thus the present research begins a new research agenda in this space.

The present research develops support for disaster response training games, building on our earlier work-in-progress [63]. Drawing on years of ethnographic observation of training

practice of fire emergency responders (FERs), urban search and rescue (USAR) operatives, and incident command (IC) teams, we identify planning activities. We draw these fields together, collectively as disaster response, observing that they are characterized by emergent objectives, the development of intelligence, and collaborative planning, which we develop into game design patterns. We then connect the patterns to existing games, through brief case studies, identifying new areas to develop gameplay. The paper contributes new game design patterns, enabling designers to build games that engage players in planning activities, either to support disaster response training, or, simply, for fun.

Scope

The present research is situated in the United States, and the findings are thus focused on practice in this region. Disaster response practice is different, but not wildly so, in other countries. Further reading on practice in other countries may be found in [8, 9, 14, 36–38].

Reporting Conventions

In the present research, we include a Ludography that, like the References section, reports on the games that we use as part of our case studies. Games from the Ludography are cited prefixed with a "G". Design patterns are identified by Alexander et al.'s [4] convention of SMALL CAPS.

Paper Outline

We next develop background that addresses collaboration, disasters, and games. We then describe our research activities and observation sites. As our main emphasis, we present and synthesize evidence from our observations to develop game design patterns. To illustrate the patterns and point to future opportunities, we present case studies of exemplar games that make use of planning, and close with discussion around the value of the developed patterns.

BACKGROUND

In this section we provide background on distributed cognition, collaborative sensemaking, disaster response, and games. Distributed cognition is our lens for understanding disaster response work practice. Our ultimate goal is to support training games to engage collaborative sensemaking. We briefly discuss game mechanics, gameworlds, and game design patterns.

Distributed Cognition

Distributed cognition theory describes cognitive processes as spread among individuals and artifacts as they mutually interact [25,27,28]. Information relevant to a task is represented in multiple forms, such as (shared) mental models, the physical environment, and information artifacts. Workers transform information to transition it between forms, enabling information seeking activities and sensemaking. Workable forms are communicated through physical and computational media, facilitating information transfer. Distributed cognition serves as a basis for understanding disaster response work practice.

Collaborative Sensemaking

A basic necessity in any incident is for responders to work in teams as part of a distributed cognition system to make sense of a situation and make decisions. Team coordination through shared mental models and situation awareness, sensemaking, and information seeking are key to success.

Team Coordination

Teams are a collection of actors, who have different assigned roles, and who collaborate and share information [49]. Teams organize their activities in order to avoid mutual interference and synchronize effort [1]. *Shared mental models* support teams in working together efficiently, enabling implicit and non-verbal communication through the use of artifacts, reference signs, and deep understanding of team activities [20,26,31,40,65].

Mental models enable individuals to predict future states of dynamic systems by mentally simulating processes and outcomes [17,33]. *Shared* mental models occur when team members have compatible mental models that predict similar future states. This supports team coordination, reducing the costs of communication (i.e. *communication overhead* [40]) and aiding the team in achieving its objectives [41,49,59]. Shared mental models are fostered through careful communication among team members and contribute to effective team *situation awareness*.

Situation awareness is the ability to comprehend a complex situation and predict its future states [10–12]. A high level of situation awareness supports decision making, enabling an actor to identify one or more correct courses of action. Awareness is critical in distributed teams where team members must inform one another of personal status. In order to move from individual situation awareness to shared situation awareness, individuals need to take into consideration each teammate's understanding and perspective of the situation, and work collaboratively together to reach a shared mental model.

Sensemaking

Weick defines *sensemaking* as a social process performed in order to understand a situation and make decisions [74]; it is an ongoing collaborative process of understanding a situation through creating meaning, situation awareness, shared mental models, and mutual understanding of different individual perspectives [1,73,74]. The need for sensemaking arises in shifting environments, when new challenges, opportunities, and tasks are emergent [2,48].

Sensemaking is often a social process [74]. Teams of different backgrounds, established or temporary, need to work together in order to make sense of critical situations. The outcome of sensemaking in teams can be affected by their team skills [29]. Each team member needs to have the knowledge and skills to work with other teammates in order to contribute productively [7]. This argues for a great need to investigate new ways and methods to contribute to the training of disaster response teams in order for them to be able to effectively work together.

A substantial body of research has studied the importance and methods of sensemaking in a number of contexts, including command and control [1–3,29], collaborative information seeking [44,45], education [47], organizational science [74], and team training [22]. Those studies together identify sensemaking as a process through which people collect, frame, and interpret information in order to understand a situation and make effective decisions.

Information Seeking

Information seeking is an essential part of the process of sensemaking [62,74]. It involves collecting, filtering, processing, authenticating, and interpreting information in order to extract what is needed in order to understand a situation [1,3]. The need to understand and make sense of the abundance of emergent information is central to making reliable decisions, therefore, the quality of information is measured by its completeness, correctness, currency, accuracy, and consistency [1]. The use of information visualization techniques (e.g., interactive maps) supports sensemaking [14,52,61], allowing teammates to easily share information.

Disaster Response

Disaster response comprises a large and complex set of activities to mitigate the effect of an incident. The term *incident* refers to "An occurrence, natural or manmade, that requires a response to protect life or property...." [69, p140]. Incident command (IC) is a set of activities that involve developing and executing plans in response to disasters and is the primary way that response is organized.

The National Incident Management System [69], accounts for how incident command structures form and disband for incidents of varying scale. For small-scale incidents (e.g., a single house fire), a lone Incident Commander makes all high-level decisions and provides direction. The same system specifies more complex hierarchies to manage large-scale incidents (e.g., multi-state wildfires), which may have a Unified Command at top and federated branches to handle aspects of response. As the need for incident response declines, the system specifies how the structure reduces its complexity.

According to the National Incident Management System, a complete IC team (e.g., one for the most complex incident) consists of the following branches: Operations, Planning, Logistics, and Finance / Administration. The branches (along with additional command staff that are not a part of any branch), report to either a singular Incident Commander or a Unified Command group. Commanders make high-level decisions with input from the branches and the command staff.

Operations converts the high-level decisions into specific objectives that can be accomplished by deploying, directing, and communicating with teams of responders. Planning gathers information and develops plan recommendations. Logistics manages supplies and equipment. Finance / Administration accounts for the costs of the response.

Crisis Informatics

Crisis informatics is an interdisciplinary area of study that focuses on how information and communication technology is used in emergency response [5,57]. It is centered around the social, technical, and information aspects of a disaster [21]. In an incident, responders, volunteers, and non-government organizations closely collaborate together on-site and online in order to effectively coordinate humanitarian assistance to those affected [18,56,58].

Applying technology to crisis mapping through the use of mobile communication and social media empowers disaster responders [43,54]. Digital volunteers are able to communicate helpful information to those who are on the ground [56]. The dissemination of geospatial information about affected areas through social media and disaster management systems helps responders, volunteers, and the general public gather data, yet sensemaking to get support to the right places at the right times remains a challenge [42,52].

Disaster management systems enable information technology support. Such systems have been used to effect crowdsourced response to incidents. Disaster management systems are of interest in the present research primarily for their map-oriented designs. Ushahidi[1] [16] and Sahana[2] [53] are web-based applications that enable collecting and visualizing information. Social media reports can be used directly on map-based interfaces to enhance situation awareness [71] and disseminate information and direct citizen response [52].

Game Design Patterns: Game Mechanics & Gameworlds

Salen and Zimmerman characterize games as systems of *rules* and *play* [50]. Rules are the structures that constrain player action, rendering it meaningful. Play is the freedom to make decisions within the scope of the rules. A *game mechanic* is a moment at which a player makes a choice and observes the outcome [35,50]. *Core mechanics* are the essence of a game, and are engaged with repeatedly. Game mechanics of digital games are fundamentally and deeply connected to user interfaces. The term *gameworlds* refers to game environments, constructed through rules, that players experience as a UI [34].

Game design patterns connect game mechanics and gameworlds in support of analyzing and designing games [6]. Design patterns support the creation of games and develop a vocabulary with which to analyze them. Each pattern consists of a name, a description, an explanation of using the pattern, consequences of using the pattern, and a set of relations to other patterns (e.g., "can implement", "may conflict with").

In the present research, we combine existing design patterns with our observations and our prior work [63] to develop new

[1] https://www.ushahidi.com/
[2] http://sahanafoundation.org/

patterns. A deep discussion of the individual game design patterns (of which there are over 500, each with a multi-page description) is beyond the scope of this paper. For details on particular game design patterns we discuss, we direct the reader to Björk's wiki: http://protagonist.sics.chalmers.se: 1337/mediawiki-1.22.0/index.php.

As in physical-world team coordination, communication is a key element of collaborative gameplay. Teammates communicate using voice, supporting fast-paced team action [60,72]. At the same time, games offer direct support for coordination through *cooperative communication mechanics* that do not rely on voice or text chat [39,64,70]. By using cooperative communication mechanics, players can more easily identify elements of the gameworld and synchronize their actions.

Games / Simulations for Training

Prior simulations and/or games for training primarily address decision making, team coordination, and sensemaking. The Distributed Dynamic Decisionmaking simulation [55] is an open-source command-and-control training simulation where participants solve problems in ambiguous situations by collaboratively managing resources. The C3Fire simulation [19] is a training environment focuses on team decision-making and team situation awareness with a focus on managing resources on a map. The generated task environment allow participants to co-operate in order to complete a specific mission, such as extinguishing forest fire. The authors' *Team Coordination Game* [68] supports players in learning how to communicate and coordinate in a gameworld. While developed from our work on fire emergency response, characteristics of the real world are not captured, focusing learning on team skills. *Levee Patroller* [22,23] is a single-player training game in which a player must find levee failures in a region and report them in a timely manner. This game is designed to target the Dutch water authorities in order to help them make sense of risks and develop decision-making skills.

Prior research primarily addresses non-disaster planning through urban and tactical planning. In urban planning simulation games (e.g., *SimCity* and *SCAPE*), players learn decision-making processes through engaging in city planning, risk assessment, and transport challenges [46]. Tactical planning assists players in dealing with uncertainty, intelligence, and decision-making [24].

DISASTER RESPONSE WORK PRACTICE

The present research is developed from years of observation by author Toups at the world-renowned disaster response training facilities operated by the Texas A&M Engineering Extension Service. Our focus is on IC, an activity that occurs in all disasters and at all scales. The complexity of IC activities vary, scaling with the scope of a disaster.

The present work synthesizes data from multiple observations of various disaster response practices. We use distributed cognition as an analytic lens to understand the information-centric activities and coordination that take place. We build on our prior work with FERs [63,65–68], while adding new insights from a previously unreported extended observation of USAR and IC practice. While we focus on IC, we bring in other "boots-on-the-ground" perspectives from operatives practicing in the field. Observed activities include firefighter live-fire training and classes, elite USAR teams practicing full-scale exercises, and a multi-day simulation of IC.

Here, we describe the observation sites, research activities, and observed practice for each disaster response domain. Collected evidence is presented in a synthesized form in the next section.

Fire Emergency Response Burn Training

Our initial (and previously reported [65–68]) observation concerned fire emergency response (2007–2010), including participant observation of classroom time with FER recruits, inside and outside live-fire burn training simulations, and discussions with expert emergency responders. Student responders undertook high-fidelity simulations of fire response, including use of apparatus[3] and radio. The objective of this project was to understand the communication practices of FERs, to drive game-based training.

Observation Site

The observation site includes the world's largest (as of 2010) collection of live-fueled training props: Brayton Fire Training Field[4] [51] in College Station, Texas. The burn training sessions were undertaken in and around props that simulated residential, commercial, and industrial buildings, as well as vehicle fires. These environments are developed to mimic physical-world locations and are constructed of fire-proof materials. Facility personnel use specially formulated fuel, as well as dry hay, to create conditions that simulate building fires. Victims are simulated using weighted dummies (for unconscious victims) or instructors in turnout gear (for conscious victims). Students effect response against real fires with real firefighting equipment, including apparatus, turnout gear and air packs, hoses, and hydrants.

Research Activities

Data presented here are derived from five burn training sessions[5] that were observed from outside the building, and three from inside, over the course of the observation period. For the outside sessions, the researcher primarily observed the Incident Commander, but was free to move and observe from multiple angles. Outside sessions were video recorded.

For the inside sessions, the investigator was equipped with turnout gear and guided by an experienced firefighter. No recordings were taken in the inside environment, which, according to the guide, would reach 1,200°F, and so was inhospitable to recording equipment. The investigator recorded observations after the experience.

Observed Practice

In the observations, students took on all FER roles: firefighter (i.e., an FER that searches a burning building, puts out fires, etc.), driver/engineer (i.e., an FER that maintains the apparatus, manages equipment, and otherwise provides outside

---

[3]"Apparatus" refers to the vehicles used in fire emergency response, such as fire engines and ladder trucks.

[4]https://teex.org/Pages/about-us/ teex-brayton-fire-training-field.aspx

[5]Our previous work reports only on the first three observed burn training sessions.

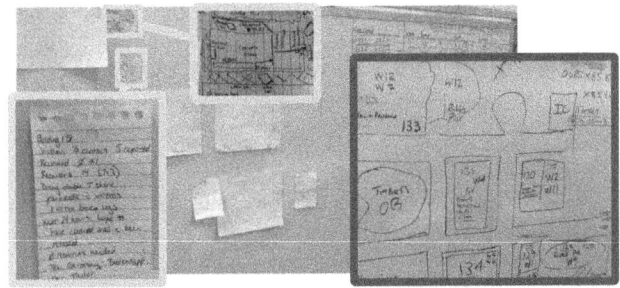

Figure 1. Planning artifacts at Multi-National USAR Exercise (October 2011). Background shows whiteboard with planning sheets and a resource-tracking chart. Left insets are taped to board: a diagram of a building (top) and plan notes (bottom). Rightmost inset is from another whiteboard, showing a drawing of the entire operation area; each rectangle is a large building and notes describe details of the area.

support), and Incident Commander. Students in the Incident Commander roles directed fellow classmates on how to fight the fire and how to search for and rescue victims. The Incident Commander was responsible for allocating resources at the scene. Upon completion of the response effort, the commander and expert instructors would run a *hotwash*, reviewing what went wrong and what went right, supporting learning. Such practice is common even outside of training.

Urban Search and Rescue Full-Scale Exercises

A second set of observations concerned USAR and took place during 2010–2012 at Disaster City[6] in College Station, Texas. In these observations, author Toups was embedded at a USAR training facility and undertook day-to-day interactions with the staff, many of whom were part of Texas Task Force 1, a combination state / US federal-level elite USAR team [15]. In addition, author Hamilton observed one of the described exercises. The purpose of this work was to understand the future role of information technology in disaster response and develop interventions for its use.

Observation Site

Disaster City is a USAR training facility that features highly realistic props; it consists of three main areas for simulations. This excludes a range of classrooms, as well as facilities used for actual operations that may be temporarily used for simulations.

One space is the Technical Skills Training Area, which provides individual props designed to hone specific skills, such as shoring and breaching walls. This area is not normally used as part of a full simulation, but for practice.

A large-scale specialized simulation environment mimics a combination of offices, homes, and commercial properties and the buildings are designed to appear as physical-world collapsed structures of an appropriate scale (including a three-story office complex with parking garage). Each building features slots for *breach plates*, interchangeable steel and concrete blocks, on which operatives practice using concrete saws and jackhammers to access inner spaces. The operational area is approximately four city blocks.

---

[6]https://teex.org/Pages/about-us/disaster-city.aspx

Finally, an Emergency Operations Training Center offers a location that serves as the base of operations in a simulated response. It provides a meeting space with information technology to support incident command.

Research Activities

During the observed practices, the researchers split time evenly between the simulation area and the simulated base of operations. They moved throughout the simulation area, taking notes and photographs and discussing activities with idle responders. As many activities take extended periods of time to complete, the observers circulated among the parallel activities, checking on progress.

Observed Practice

The investigators observed two multi-day USAR training exercises in the simulation environment. The first exercise involved an international assortment of teams from the USA, England, Germany, Belgium, and others, collaborating in the Multi-National USAR Exercise (October 2011). In the other, Texas Task Force 1 met for its annual training exercise (April 2012). Both simulations represented a large-scale disaster over four city blocks of indeterminate cause undertaken in a high-fidelity environment.

USAR operatives were tasked with gathering intelligence, shoring walls, and breaching buildings to rescue victims played by local volunteers (Figure 2).

Incident Command Simulation

Author Toups participated in an Enhanced Incident Management System simulation (June 2011). He took on the role of a student, and worked in different IC branches during the simulation.

Observation Site

The observation site for this component consisted of a large room set up to run the simulation in the Disaster City Emergency Operations Training Center. Groups of desks, each with a computer and phone, were set up for each of the IC branches. The Plans and Operations sections had access to large whiteboards. Three projected displays showed information on the status of a computer-simulated incident, unfolding in real time, showing the locations of deployed resources and problem areas. Finally, a side room was used for meetings with the heads of each branch.

The simulation was composed of special software and human operators and actors. The software managed the map and disaster simulation (e.g., realistically moving resources to specified locations, tracking the spread of damage). Human operators control the simulation, specifying how it changes over time in response to the players. Actors, expert responders with decades of experience, played remote boots-on-the-ground responders (and other humans with which the Incident Command Post would have contact, such as local officials), providing simulated reports from the field and accepting directions from the command post staff.

Research Activities

The investigator was a participant observer in the IC simulation. During the scenarios, he took on assigned roles in

Figure 2. USAR operatives breaching a rubble pile during the full-scale exercise (April 2012). After analyzing the structure for the safest entry point, the team has begun jackhammering concrete to access the interior.

different sections, including Plans, Operations, and Logistics. The researcher took notes on experiences and observations, primarily in the downtime between simulations. In addition, he took notes on the instructors' lectures. No photographs were collected.

Observed Practice

The IC simulation educated responders and officials from across the USA and across disciplines and work roles. The IC team, the students, were 40-strong and assigned roles in the Incident Command Post.

Each simulation scenario represented an extreme incident that had happened some hours prior. The scenarios are designed to be challenging for a coordination center with about 40 members. The first three scenarios were half-day events, while the last scenario was played over a full day. The scenarios were as follows:

1. **Train Wreck**: A train carrying hazardous materials has derailed and collided with an oncoming passenger train; the resulting toxic cloud is blowing toward the local state fair.

2. **Stadium Attack**: During a major sporting event, a terrorist crashed an aircraft into the stands; the aircraft contained radioactive material.

3. **Tornado Strike**: A heavily populated town has been struck by a tornado.

4. **Airport Bombing**: At a major international airport, two bombs have been detonated on passenger planes waiting to take off; the state of the airport is presently unknown.

GAME DESIGN PATTERNS FOR PLAYING AT PLANNING

In this section, we present our data and synthesize it, developing design patterns. Based on our data from disaster response training practice, we observe that planning is characterized by DEVELOPING INTELLIGENCE, EMERGENT OBJECTIVES, and COLLABORATIVE PLANNING.

Each subsection includes a design pattern description that follows Björk et al's [6] conventions of a description, using the pattern, consequences, and relations. The relations components are not exhaustive.

Sensemaking by Developing Intelligence

IC develops the concepts of information and intelligence (I&I), a concept that also materialized in the USAR component of this work. *Information* can be collected from any number of sources, but may be false. *Intelligence* is information that has been vetted and confirmed. Thus, intelligence is more reliable and actionable.

The role of I&I is to drive sensemaking and provide intelligence to Command, Plans, and Operations. Activities include information seeking to gather details and ensure accuracy, triangulating unknowns, and/or finding prior ground truths. I&I work is a distributed cognition environment, in which information is translated into usable forms, synthesized from multiple sources in multiple forms. Sensemaking in I&I work forms the basis of the DEVELOPING INTELLIGENCE design pattern.

Evidence

In USAR, I&I work was heavily connected to search, where teams of operatives need to report back findings to the base of operations. Returned data is transferred to paper maps and resource-tracking cards, in a distributed cognition process. Much information in the USAR simulations began as locations with speculation as to what might be found (e.g. chemical weapons, expected victim locations), which drove searches.

In conversations with USAR experts, we learned that there are challenges with redundancy in collecting information. As reports come in, they may be from multiple sources, but describe the same problem. The result was the unnecessary expenditure of resources to check the same victims multiple times.

A key component of I&I is the *red slice* of the pie chart of information. Information in disaster response consists of three categories: known, known unknown, and unknown unknown. This last category, the red slice, is the most dangerous. Discovering the contents of the red slice requires that IC staff constantly gather data by talking to one another, collecting remote data, investigating reference material, and otherwise undertaking research during the incident.

Information management in IC uses the intelligence cycle (which is further documented in the US military's *Joint Intelligence* [32]) involves the following five steps:

1. **Identify** essential elements of information (EEI), focusing attention;

2. **Collect** and centralize information as guided by EEI;

3. **Process** information to systematically document it;

4. **Analyze** information collected, convert it into usable intelligence to drive development of objectives and operations;

5. **Disseminate** actionable intelligence.

In all of the IC simulations, there were at least two people assigned to I&I. As questions about information from the field came in, these students would find relevant members of the IC team and hunt down documents that pertained to the question. At one point, during the Airport Bombing exercise, I&I was needed to assess the locations of various populations on a map of the airport and verify locations of suspected bombs. In multiple instances in all the simulations, I&I was called upon to determine clear routes for resources into the incident site.

Design Pattern Description

In order to engage players in DEVELOPING INTELLIGENCE, players should make informed decisions about how to collect information in a gameworld, and need to make judgements of its authenticity and value. They should engage in filtering processes to identify EEI. This pattern makes sensemaking, information seeking, and authentication key elements of play.

Using the Pattern: To design for DEVELOPING INTELLIGENCE, a game needs to supply information the player collects. This information need not be accurate, yet sources of accurate information must be discoverable. Players should be able to act without first engaging with DEVELOPING INTELLIGENCE (i.e., it should not be an OBSTACLE that impedes progress), but, without intelligence, it will be challenging for a player to succeed.

Consequences: A concern for DEVELOPING INTELLIGENCE game mechanics is the need for intelligence that **cannot** be reused across play sessions. If intelligence can be reused, it poses a risk to REPLAYABILITY, even in the short term (e.g., when one might sacrifice a unit to gain intelligence, then restart and use that intelligence without making the same sacrifice).

Imperfect information should be discovered ecologically through the gameworld; players need to make active decisions about what is valid and what is not. This argues against corrective game rules that mark information as verified and/or discard false information automatically.

Relations: DEVELOPING INTELLIGENCE can be instantiated by RANDOMNESS or other forms of unpredictability (e.g., SOLUTION UNCERTAINTY, UNCERTAINTY OF INFORMATION, PERFORMANCE UNCERTAINTY, PLAYER UNCERTAINTY, UNPREDICTABLE BEHAVIOR). Involving other players (e.g., MULTIPLAYER GAMES) is a straightforward instantiation. Further, RECONFIGURABLE GAME WORLDS, which can be changed between plays, offer a meaningful way to create the uncertainty that drives the need to DEVELOP INTELLIGENCE.

DEVELOPING INTELLIGENCE modulates UNCERTAINTY OF OUTCOME by reducing that uncertainty.

It can partially instantiate GAME WORLD EXPLORATION.

It potentially conflicts with MEMORIZING.

Emergent Objectives

Our data in all three domains indicates that objectives are emergent and their priority depends on level of danger. While some objectives materialize as the incident progresses, most already exist, but are undiscovered until the environment is investigated by operatives and/or with sensors. These observations lead to the EMERGENT OBJECTIVES design pattern.

Evidence

FERs work in environments that change rapidly, which shifts objectives. For example, objectives may involve rescuing victims and putting out the fire, but, the latter may shift to containment, preventing damage beyond the burning structure. A key part of decision making between putting out a fire and containing it, we learned from informants, depended upon the structure in question: many structures are not designed to withstand even short fires, which means it is safer for FERs to stay outside. Another informant explained that losing a single structure is often acceptable if all victims have been rescued, but only if the loss is limited to that structure.

USAR environments feature clear general objectives (e.g., rescue all civilians in the region). However, our USAR contacts explained that intelligence must drive the development of more detailed objectives and activities. Reports for the activity may come from multiple people, but those reports may be inaccurate or the problem may have already been solved. Thus, a solution must be considered in light of the problem being unclear, unsolvable, or already solved. Additionally, plans may need to change in real-time to respond to new intelligence.

Much of USAR practice is devoted to search, where operatives move through the environment, looking for damaged areas where people might be in need of rescue. Sensing tools and search dogs support this activity [15]. USAR work involves shoring walls [13], a process of in-the-field on-the-fly situated engineering, to prevent further collapse and opening up spaces using lifting equipment and cutting tools to further search for victims. Through the laborious process of searching, USAR operatives discover where to direct effort.

IC works with emergent objectives at various levels: Plans identifies long-term objectives, while Operations works with a smaller scope. In the observed Stadium Attack simulation, Operations learned that the crashed airplane was loaded with radioactive material. Mitigating exposure to the material, supporting exposed responders and victims, and bringing specialized teams to remove the material became new objectives. This caused Plans to respond by requesting details on the material to drive intelligence on the appropriate response.

An emphasis in the IC simulation involved training command staff in how to develop objectives for an incident. We learned that Command does not dictate what Operations is doing, but provides guiding objectives. A key part of ensuring that objectives are attainable and realistic involves developing objectives that can be completed using the currently available resources.

Design Pattern Description
As players progress through a game, EMERGENT OBJECTIVES may be discovered, developed, and/or lost as a scenario plays out. EMERGENT OBJECTIVES arise through engaging with DEVELOPING INTELLIGENCE. Such play could appear at either end of the process: players may identify new objectives through developed intelligence or computer-controlled agents could gather information to trigger new objectives for players.

Using the Pattern: EMERGENT OBJECTIVES likely require that a game feature multiple paths to victory [50], where the player can accomplish some, but not all, objectives and still succeed. Players may find that some EMERGENT OBJECTIVES become cut off, or new ones open, as implemented through the EPHEMERAL GOALS pattern. Alternative objectives might be substituted for one another.

Consequences: EMERGENT OBJECTIVES suggests that **not** all objectives should be achievable, which may frustrate players. Such designs mean that not all players experience all events in a game.

Relations: EMERGENT OBJECTIVES can be implemented through DEVELOPING INTELLIGENCE, EPHEMERAL GOALS, SECRET GOALS, and FOG OF WAR.

Spatio-Temporal Collaborative Planning
Iterative, careful planning activities characterize USAR and IC, domains, where events typically emerge more slowly than FER practice. Planning activities are undertaken by multiple people, enacting distributed cognition, to make sense of an incident and effect change. We expect such activities to be interesting sources of play for the COLLABORATIVE PLANNING implication, creating situations in which players collaboratively coordinate activity in advance.

Evidence
We observed collaborative planning in the USAR and IC domains, with similar activities occurring in both. FER practice is fast-paced; while we expect that larger incidents require collaborative planning, the size of the ones we observed resulted in single Incident Commanders doing most of the work.

In observed USAR activities, a remote coordination center and local base of operations collaboratively developed plans to execute a response, following the National Incident Management System [69]. These command structures developed plans, a sample of which appear in Figure 1, that spanned 12-hour periods; tracked and requested resources; and followed progress using a collection of printed and hand-drawn paper maps and other information artifacts.

In the IC simulation, we observed groups gathered around whiteboards, drawing maps, and positioning resources. Plans were developed in the long-term by the Plans section, while the Operations section tended to gather together, develop a small plan of attack, then execute it.

In long-term incidents, objectives are connected to physical spaces where activity takes place. Objectives must be laid out such that they account for expected progress of deployed operatives, with contingencies to account for changes in the incident and/or the success or failure of deployed teams.

Design Pattern Description
A key component of COLLABORATIVE PLANNING involves the development of mechanics and interfaces that support time and space synchronization, as well as limited programming that can respond to successes and failures of events. This enables players to consider converging and diverging lines of activity that happen in the field. Players should learn how to plan for contingencies when activities enter exceptional states, such as failure modes, faster-than-expected completion, or slower-than-expected completion. Various failure modes are further buoyed by the design of EMERGENT OBJECTIVES that enable the player to recover and succeed, even after failures.

Using the Pattern: Players should interact with space, typically on maps, to specify future activities that will be undertaken by players or agents. COLLABORATIVE PLANNING should involve accounting for emergent changes in state.

Figure 3. Planning interfaces in *Due Process* (left), *Rainbow Six* (middle), and *Transistor* (right), all of which feature a map on which the player draws paths and specifies activities spatiotemporally. The planning phase in *Due Process* (left) gives each team the ability to plan breach/defensive positions, here they have identified locations for activities and paths to follow in the action phase (screenshot from the developer's press kit). In *Rainbow Six* (middle) and *Breach & Clear* (not pictured), the player specifies what actions game units will take when play begins (screenshot taken ⓒⓣ author Toups). In *Transistor* (right), the player may stop time to specify a set of actions the avatar can take (screenshot taken ⓒⓣ author Toups).

Consequences: Players need to communicate to succeed at COLLABORATIVE PLANNING. Voice and chat communication enable players to coordinate with language [72], but cooperative communication mechanics [64, 70] offer a means of coordinating with the game interface directly. Implementing the COLLABORATIVE PLANNING pattern likely requires some level of artificial intelligence or other reasoning, to enable computer agents to be involved in the collaborative component or to execute developed plans.

Relations: COLLABORATIVE PLANNING can be implemented by STIMULATED PLANNING, STRATEGIC PLANNING, and TACTICAL PLANNING (though these relate heavily to the structure of the game rules and do not address collaboration). Further patterns for implementation are those relating to location (e.g., STRATEGIC LOCATIONS, SNIPER LOCATIONS, RESOURCE LOCATIONS) and time (e.g., REAL-TIME GAMES, TIME PRESSURE, TIME LIMITS, DEVELOPMENT TIME). COOPERATION is also an essential pattern, and SYMBIOTIC PLAYER RELATIONS, MUTUAL GOALS, and opposing teams (e.g., having one or more GAME SYSTEM PLAYERS and/or working on TEAMS in MULTIPLAYER GAMES) motivate players to cooperate.

GAME PLANNING INTERFACE CASE STUDIES

A number of existing games feature planning interfaces and mechanics; the authors identified these based on experiences playing and on game reviews. To connect to our deep investigation of planning practices in disaster response and accompanying design patterns, we develop case studies of games that offer implementations of the patterns, using them as analytic lens. We highlight a breadth of exemplars in this section, as brief case studies of their planning interfaces.

Transistor

Transistor [G9] is an isometric-perspective action game in which combat is played through a combination of a real-time mode and a planning-oriented strategy mode, Turn() (Figure 3, right). In Turn() mode, the player may move the avatar and select a set of actions, each of which consume time. During Turn() mode, enemies are frozen, and the game supplies a simulated expected outcome for each action. Movement paths and actions can be undone during the Turn(), usually without

consequence. Later enemies can interfere with Turn() mode, altering the game mechanic and engaging players in careful meta-planning when engaging such enemies. While executing, Turn()s cannot be interrupted.

Transistor enables the player to try out strategies, think critically, and plan ahead, but sometimes penalizes the player while using Turn() mode. Simulated outcomes inform players' plans, but may provide unreliable results; players have little means to DEVELOP INTELLIGENCE except through trial and error. While players can engage in planning tasks, there is no TIME PRESSURE or need for COLLABORATIVE PLANNING.

Due Process

Due Process [G5] is a multiplayer first-person shooter (FPS) focused on COOPERATION, STRATEGIC PLANNING, and TACTICAL PLANNING; it does a good job of implementing spatiotemporal COLLABORATIVE PLANNING. At the beginning of a game, two opposing teams are given a planning phase to collaboratively establish strategy. During this phase, each team is given a top-down view of the map detailing walls and doors (Figure 3, left). The offensive team identifies means of ingress and progression through the environment, while the defensive team can specify defensive positions and responsive strategies.

During the planning phase, team members may draw plans on the map. The drawing system serves as a novel cooperative communication mechanic, allowing players to point out which walls/doors will be breached, or which walls/doors the defenders suspect the attacking team might use. Teams are also able to show where they will be defending from and draw out the best defensive positions to take, to cover points of entry.

The planning phase map drawing is made visible on the ground during the execution phase, enabling use during action gameplay. This gives the players the ability to know exactly where to place themselves to breach/take cover. Players may communicate via voice during the planning and action phases to discuss strategy (at first) and tactics (during the action phase).

Due Process's innovative map-drawing mechanic makes COLLABORATIVE PLANNING usable in action play. The superimposed map drawings enable the players to establish a shared mental model of gameworld and execute the developed plan.

Figure 4. The smart ping menu in *League of Legends* provides players with four types of map pings, which they can use to warn teammates about threats or to communicate map-based information. Neutral monsters, like Baron Nashor (seen here), serve as EMERGENT OBJECTIVES for opposing teams to contest. Screenshot taken ⓒ① author Alharthi.

As the game progresses, players are subject to EMERGENT OB-JECTIVES as information about the opposing team is revealed through play (defense / attack points and maneuvers). DEVEL-OPING INTELLIGENCE and sharing of emergent information is supported through a voice communication channel.

Breach & Clear

Breach & Clear [G6] is a tactical strategy SWAT-team sim-ulation game developed in consultation with special forces members, an exemplar of the genre. The game is a single-player isometric-view turn-based strategy game. Each turn includes a planning phase where the player issues directions to individual units; once planning is finished, the player waits for all units to complete their actions. This next phase is only reached when every member of a squad has either reached a designated position or died. While not COLLABORATIVE PLANNING, players engage in contingency planning, respond-ing to EMERGENT OBJECTIVES as play progresses.

Like many strategy games, *Breach & Clear* uses the FOG OF WAR pattern to hide information. While the position of ene-mies is hidden until a unit obtains line of sight, players know the layout of the gameworld. A design to address DEVEL-OPING INTELLIGENCE might incorporate false information, requiring that the player engage in information seeking.

League of Legends

League of Legends (*LoL*) is a popular multiplayer online battle arena [G8]; a highly successful exemplar of the genre. Dur-ing a match, five-player teams battle to control territory. To succeed, players coordinate and engage in COLLABORATIVE PLANNING; *LoL* also provides some support for EMERGENT OBJECTIVES and DEVELOPING INTELLIGENCE.

LoL is designed so that not all objectives can be achieved im-mediately, even though they are known in advance. Teams must prioritize objectives. While the main objective in the game is to destroy the opposing team's base, the game features EMERGENT OBJECTIVES discovered as the match progresses. For example, Baron Nashor, a neutral monster (Figure 4), is

an EMERGENT OBJECTIVE; by killing it, the team gains an increase in strength, helping them achieve the main objec-tive. The Baron only appears 15 minutes into the game, and respawns seven minutes after being killed by a team. The team must complete this objective while fending off the enemy, who will mostly likely try to contest the objective.

The *LoL* mini-map (Figure 4, lower right) provides a UI for DEVELOPING INTELLIGENCE through concise information access. It provides a summary of the gameworld, detailing the position and condition of defenses, allies, and enemies. *LoL* uses FOG OF WAR to only show activity near a team's avatars or defenses. Additionally, players can engage mechan-ics that provide vision on the gameworld, temporarily granting extra intelligence. Gaining vision at strategic locations (e.g., Baron Nashor's lair), helps the team engage in DEVELOPING INTELLIGENCE about the enemy team's behavior.

To support COLLABORATIVE PLANNING, *LoL* provides coop-erative communication mechanics in the form of pings. Pings allow players to focus one another's attention, warning about a threat or to pass on a message during the game [39, 64]. *LoL* provides two regular pings and four smart pings, each of which represents a different message (Figure 4). Pings en-able lightweight spatio-temporally referenced communication, supporting COLLABORATIVE PLANNING.

Tom Clancy's Rainbow Six

The original *Rainbow Six* [G7] is an FPS that focuses on the development and execution of tactical plans. Play occurs over missions, each consisting of planning and execution stages. During the planning stage, the player is presented with vari-ous information sources including a biography on opposition forces and a map of the mission (Figure 3, middle). The map shows obstacles, objectives, and probable enemy locations. This information is presented as intelligence, and the player must create a detailed plan for four assault teams. The player makes plans by defining a spatio-temporal path for each team and specifying actions (e.g., breach a door, use a flash-bang grenade). We note that the provided planning information is not comprehensive or perfect, which leads to EMERGENT OBJECTIVES during play, but that, since all intelligence is true, the game does not implement DEVELOPING INTELLIGENCE.

During the mission, the player may directly control one team at a time, switching between teams, while the other teams are computer-controlled. Missions typically progress slowly and methodically, while encounters with enemy forces are usually won or lost in short, rapid exchanges. During play, the only way for the player to deviate from the plan to handle EMER-GENT OBJECTIVES is to directly control a team. During plan-ning, teams can be ordered to wait for specific commands at waypoints enabling a limited degree of contingency response and management of spatio-temporal synchronization.

The fast-paced nature of exchanges, difficulty in deviating from plans, and limited control over each team during the mis-sion makes it difficult to respond to EMERGENT OBJECTIVES. While there are mechanics in *Rainbow Six* for assembling and executing plans, there is no need to engage in COLLABORA-TIVE PLANNING through communication with others. There

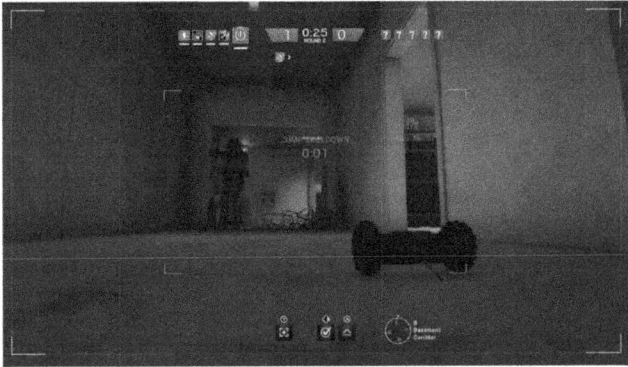

Figure 5. *Siege* players engage in DEVELOPING INTELLIGENCE by piloting drones to gather and share information (e.g., objective locations). Screenshot taken ⓒⓟ author Hamilton.

are also limited means for players to engage in DEVELOPING INTELLIGENCE beyond what is provided.

Tom Clancy's Rainbow Six Siege

Tom Clancy's Rainbow Six Siege (*Siege*) is another tactical FPS [G10]. In contrast with the original *Rainbow Six*, *Siege* emphasizes competitive, team-based play. In *Siege*, teams of five players play against each other over a series of rounds in alternating offensive and defensive conditions. The offensive team tries to secure or eliminate an objective the defensive team is protecting (e.g., a hostage or bomb). Players communicate through built-in text or voice chat.

Siege incorporates several novel mechanics that support exercising planning activities. For example, at the beginning of each round, a short fortification/scouting period allows the offensive team to use remote-controlled drones to scout the gameworld and gather information (e.g., enemy and objective locations; see Figure 5). This encourages team members to engage in DEVELOPING INTELLIGENCE by sharing their individually discovered information with one another.

Objective locations change from round to round and provide constrained but guided objectives for players to defend or attack. During the fortification period, and throughout the round, defensive players can modify the gameworld to block approaches. Conversely, throughout each round, both teams can destroy parts of the gameworld to open up new approaches. The dynamic nature of the gameworld forces both teams must identify and address EMERGENT OBJECTIVES.

Additionally, the defensive and offensive team maintain access to security cameras and drone feeds. After a player is killed by the opposing team, they can still participate in COLLABORATIVE PLANNING and DEVELOPING INTELLIGENCE with the remaining teammates through information seeking.

Together, these mechanics and information sources create an environment in which players must engage in COLLABORATIVE PLANNING, DEVELOPING INTELLIGENCE, and addressing EMERGENT OBJECTIVES in order to succeed.

DISCUSSION

Existing games minimally support our design patterns. To educate responders, we argue for games incorporating DE-

VELOPING INTELLIGENCE, EMERGENT OBJECTIVES, and COLLABORATIVE PLANNING. While we anticipate that systems to support disaster response training will benefit most from incorporating these design implications, we expect them to be a fun source of play. Future research will investigate the effectiveness of designs based on these patterns.

Games typically supply true information to players, limiting opportunities to DEVELOP INTELLIGENCE. Further, gathered intelligence rarely changes in games, which limits replayability. While players expect games to be truthful about game state, we expect that, as long as games are truthful about the presence of false information, DEVELOPING INTELLIGENCE can make compelling play. *Papers, Please* [G1], for example, makes information seeking and the detection of consistency in information a core mechanic.

We rarely observe EMERGENT OBJECTIVES in play. Many games use the FOG OF WAR pattern (e.g., *XCOM: Enemy Unknown* [G4], the *StarCraft* series [G2, G3]) to obscure objectives on a map. While compelling, we argue for a deeper engagement with EMERGENT OBJECTIVES, dealing with objective timing and even being able to fail at some objectives. Mutually exclusive objectives, where only one of a set of objectives *can* be completed, are an interesting implementation.

COLLABORATIVE PLANNING relies on multiple players working together, but not all players need to be human. While we have observed many examples of COLLABORATIVE PLANNING, few are the kind of iterative, careful activity found in USAR or have the focus on planning that characterizes IC. Some games do offer the ability to direct other players or identify a single waypoint, but none offer longer-term planning.

CONCLUSION

We developed an understanding of distributed cognition in multiple disaster response domains, using it to drive game design patterns to support disaster response learning through game play: DEVELOPING INTELLIGENCE, EMERGENT OBJECTIVES, and COLLABORATIVE PLANNING. Our primary guiding principle is a need for better long-term planning game mechanics, with the objective of developing new games for disaster response education. Interfaces that make clear a series of planned events and contingencies for the success or failure of those activities are a useful space for future design. We believe these essential disaster response activities and characteristics need to be made available for play, and future games will serve to validate the value of these design patterns.

ACKNOWLEDGMENTS

Thanks to the Texas A&M Engineering Extension Service for access to its training facilities and to Texas Task Force 1 for access to its members. This material is based upon work supported by the National Science Foundation under Grant Nos. IIS-0803854, IIS-0742947. Author Toups wishes to thank NMSU for its financial support of his work.

REFERENCES

1. David S. Alberts, John J. Garstka, Richard E. Hayes, and David A. Signori. 2001. *Understanding information age warfare*. Technical Report. DTIC Document.

2. David S. Alberts and Richard E. Hayes. 2006. *Understanding command and control*. Technical Report. DTIC Document.

3. David S. Alberts and Richard E. Hayes. 2007. *Planning: complex endeavors*. Technical Report. DTIC Document.

4. Christopher Alexander, Sara Ishikawa, Murray Silverstein, Max Jacobson, Ingrid Fiksdahl-King, and Shlomo Angel. 1977. *A Pattern Language: Towns, Buildings, Construction*. Center for Environmental Structure, Vol. 2. Oxford University Press, New York, NY, USA.

5. Kenneth M. Anderson and Aaron Schram. 2011. Design and Implementation of a Data Analytics Infrastructure in Support of Crisis Informatics Research (NIER Track). In *Proceedings of the 33rd International Conference on Software Engineering (ICSE '11)*. ACM, New York, NY, USA, 844–847. DOI:
http://dx.doi.org/10.1145/1985793.1985920

6. Staffan Björk, Sus Lundgren, and Jussi Holopainen. 2003. Game Design Patterns. In *Level Up - Proceedings of Digital Games Research Conference 2003*.

7. Bryan L. Bonner, Michael R. Baumann, and Reeshad S. Dalal. 2002. The effects of member expertise on group decision-making and performance. *Organizational Behavior and Human Decision Processes* 88, 2 (2002), 719 – 736. DOI:
http://dx.doi.org/10.1016/S0749-5978(02)00010-9

8. Sebastian Denef and David Keyson. 2012. Talking About Implications for Design in Pattern Language. In *Proceedings of the SIGCHI Conference on Human Factors in Computing Systems (CHI '12)*. ACM, New York, NY, USA, 2509–2518. DOI:
http://dx.doi.org/10.1145/2207676.2208418

9. Sebastian Denef, Leonardo Ramirez, Tobias Dyrks, and Gunnar Stevens. 2008. Handy Navigation in Ever-changing Spaces: An Ethnographic Study of Firefighting Practices. In *Proceedings of the 7th ACM Conference on Designing Interactive Systems (DIS '08)*. ACM, New York, NY, USA, 184–192. DOI:
http://dx.doi.org/10.1145/1394445.1394465

10. Mica R. Endsley. 1988. Design and evaluation for situation awareness enhancement. In *Proceedings of the Human Factors and Ergonomics Society Annual Meeting*, Vol. 32. SAGE Publications, 97–101.

11. Mica R. Endsley. 1995. Toward a theory of situation awareness in dynamic systems. *Human Factors* 37, 1 (1995), 32–64.

12. Mica R. Endsley. 2000. Theoretical Underpinnings of Situation Awareness: A Critical Review. In *Situation Awareness Analysis and Measurement*, Mica R. Endsley and D J Garland (Eds.). Lawrence Erlbaum Associates, Mahwah, NJ, USA, 3–6.

13. FEMA US&R Structures Sub-Group and U.S. Army Corps of Engineers US&R Program Office. 2013. *Urban Search & Rescue Shoring Operations Guide* (3rd ed.). U.S. Army Corps of Engineers.

14. Joel E. Fischer, Stuart Reeves, Tom Rodden, Steve Reece, Sarvapali D. Ramchurn, and David Jones. 2015. Building a Birds Eye View: Collaborative Work in Disaster Response. In *Proceedings of the 33rd Annual ACM Conference on Human Factors in Computing Systems (CHI '15)*. ACM, New York, NY, USA, 4103–4112. DOI:
http://dx.doi.org/10.1145/2702123.2702313

15. Bud Force. 2011. *Texas Task Force 1: Urban Search and Rescue*. Texas A&M University Press, College Station, TX, USA.

16. Huiji Gao, Geoffrey Barbier, and Rebecca Goolsby. 2011. Harnessing the Crowdsourcing Power of Social Media for Disaster Relief. *IEEE Intelligent Systems* 26, 3 (2011), 10–14. DOI:http://dx.doi.org/10.1109/MIS.2011.52

17. Dedre Gentner and Albert L. Stevens. 1983. *Mental Models*. Lawrence Earlbaum Associates, Hillsdale, NJ, USA.

18. Sean Goggins, Christopher Mascaro, and Stephanie Mascaro. 2012. Relief Work After the 2010 Haiti Earthquake: Leadership in an Online Resource Coordination Network. In *Proceedings of the ACM 2012 Conference on Computer Supported Cooperative Work (CSCW '12)*. ACM, New York, NY, USA, 57–66. DOI:
http://dx.doi.org/10.1145/2145204.2145218

19. Rego Granlund, Björn Johansson, and Mats Persson. 2001. C3Fire: A microworld for collaboration training in the ROLF environment. In *42nd Conference on Simulation and Modelling, Simulation in Theory and Practice, 8-9 October 2001, Porsgrunn, Norway*.

20. Carl Gutwin and Saul Greenberg. 2004. The Importance of Awareness for Team Cognition in Distributed Collaboration. In *Team Cognition: Understanding the Factors that Drive Process and Performance* (1st ed.), Eduardo Salas and Stephen M. Fiore (Eds.). American Psychological Association, Washington, DC, USA, Chapter 9, 177–201.

21. Christine Hagar. 2013. Crisis informatics: Perspectives of trust–is social media a mixed blessing? *iSchool Student Research Journal* 2, 2 (2013), 2.

22. Casper Harteveld. 2012. *Making Sense of Virtual Risks*. Deltares Select Series, Vol. 11. IOS Press.

23. Casper Harteveld, Rui Guimarães, Igor S Mayer, and Rafael Bidarra. 2010. Balancing play, meaning and reality: The design philosophy of LEVEE PATROLLER. *Simulation & Gaming* 41, 3 (June 2010), 316–340.

24. Marko A. Hofmann and Bodo Junge. 2008. Dealing with Structural Uncertainty in Tactical Wargaming. In *Proceedings of the 2008 Summer Computer Simulation Conference (SCSC '08)*. Society for Modeling and Simulation International, Vista, CA, Article 10, 13 pages.

25. James Hollan, Edwin Hutchins, and David Kirsh. 2000. Distributed cognition: Toward a new foundation for human-computer interaction research. *ACM Transactions on Computer-Human Interaction* 7, 2 (2000), 174–196. DOI:http://dx.doi.org/10.1145/353485.353487

26. Edwin Hutchins. 1990. The Technology of Team Navigation. In *Intellectual Teamwork*, Jolene Galegher, Robert E. Kraut, and Carmen Egido (Eds.). L. Erlbaum Associates Inc., Hillsdale, NJ, USA, 191–220.

27. Edwin Hutchins. 1995a. *Cognition in the Wild*. MIT Press, Cambridge, MA, USA.

28. E. Hutchins. 1995b. How a Cockpit Remembers Its Speeds. *Cognitive Science* 19, 3 (1995), 265–288. DOI: http://dx.doi.org/10.1207/s15516709cog1903_1

29. Eva Jensen. 2007. Sensemaking in military planning: a methodological study of command teams. *Cognition, Technology & Work* 11, 2 (2007), 103–118. DOI: http://dx.doi.org/10.1007/s10111-007-0084-x

30. Xiaodong Jiang, Jason I. Hong, Leila A. Takayama, and James A. Landay. 2004. Ubiquitous computing for firefighters: Field studies and prototypes of large displays for incident command. In *CHI '04: Proceedings of the SIGCHI Conference on Human Factors in Computing Systems*. ACM Press, 679–686. DOI: http://dx.doi.org/10.1145/985692.985778

31. Matthew W. Johnson. 2010. Supporting Collaborative Real-time Strategic Planning in Multi-player Games. In *Proceedings of the Fifth International Conference on the Foundations of Digital Games (FDG '10)*. ACM, New York, NY, USA, 265–267. DOI: http://dx.doi.org/10.1145/1822348.1822388

32. Joint Chiefs of Staff. 2013. *Joint Publication 2-0, Joint Intelligence*. U.S. Department of Defense, Washington, DC, USA.

33. David H. Jonassen and Philip Henning. 1996. Mental models: Knowledge in the head and knowledge in the world. In *ICLS '96: Proceedings of the 1996 International Conference on Learning Sciences*. International Society of the Learning Sciences, 433–438.

34. Kristine Jørgensen. 2013. *Gameworld Interfaces*. MIT Press, Cambridge, MA, USA.

35. Jesper Juul. 2005. *Half Real: Video Games between Real Rules and Fictional Worlds*. MIT Press, Cambridge, MA, USA.

36. Markus Klann. 2007. Playing with Fire: Participatory Design of Wearable Computing for Fire Fighters. In *CHI '07 Extended Abstracts on Human Factors in Computing Systems (CHI EA '07)*. ACM, New York, NY, USA, 1665–1668. DOI: http://dx.doi.org/10.1145/1240866.1240878

37. Jonas Landgren. 2006. Making Action Visible in Time-critical Work. In *Proceedings of the SIGCHI Conference on Human Factors in Computing Systems (CHI '06)*. ACM, New York, NY, USA, 201–210. DOI: http://dx.doi.org/10.1145/1124772.1124804

38. Jonas Landgren and Urban Nulden. 2007. A Study of Emergency Response Work: Patterns of Mobile Phone Interaction. In *Proceedings of the SIGCHI Conference on Human Factors in Computing Systems (CHI '07)*. ACM, New York, NY, USA, 1323–1332. DOI: http://dx.doi.org/10.1145/1240624.1240824

39. Alex Leavitt, Brian C. Keegan, and Joshua Clark. 2016. Ping to Win?: Non-Verbal Communication and Team Performance in Competitive Online Multiplayer Games. In *Proceedings of the 2016 CHI Conference on Human Factors in Computing Systems (CHI '16)*. ACM, New York, NY, USA, 4337–4350. DOI: http://dx.doi.org/10.1145/2858036.2858132

40. Jean MacMillan, Elliot E. Entin, and Daniel Serfaty. 2004. Communication Overhead: The Hidden Cost of Team Cognition. In *Team Cognition: Understanding the Factors that Drive Process and Performance* (1st ed.), Eduardo Salas and Stephen M. Fiore (Eds.). American Psychological Association, Washington, DC, USA, 61–82.

41. John E Mathieu, Gerald F Goodwin, Tonia S Heffner, Eduardo Salas, and Janis A Cannon-Bowers. 2000. The Influence of Shared Mental Models on Team Process and Performance. *Journal of Applied Psychology* 85, 2 (2000), 273–283.

42. Patrick Meier. 2011. New information technologies and their impact on the humanitarian sector. *International Review of the Red Cross* 93 (12 2011), 1239–1263. Issue 884. DOI: http://dx.doi.org/10.1017/S1816383112000318

43. Patrick Meier. 2012. Crisis Mapping in Action: How Open Source Software and Global Volunteer Networks Are Changing the World, One Map at a Time. *Journal of Map & Geography Libraries* 8, 2 (2012), 89–100. DOI: http://dx.doi.org/10.1080/15420353.2012.663739

44. Sharoda A. Paul and Meredith Ringel Morris. 2009. CoSense: Enhancing Sensemaking for Collaborative Web Search. In *Proceedings of the SIGCHI Conference on Human Factors in Computing Systems (CHI '09)*. ACM, New York, NY, USA, 1771–1780. DOI: http://dx.doi.org/10.1145/1518701.1518974

45. Sharoda A. Paul and Madhu C. Reddy. 2010. Understanding Together: Sensemaking in Collaborative Information Seeking. In *Proceedings of the 2010 ACM Conference on Computer Supported Cooperative Work (CSCW '10)*. ACM, New York, NY, USA, 321–330. DOI: http://dx.doi.org/10.1145/1718918.1718976

46. Nicole Podleschny. 2008. Playing Urban Sustainability: The Ecology of a Simulation Game. In *Proceedings of the 20th Australasian Conference on Computer-Human Interaction: Designing for Habitus and Habitat (OZCHI '08)*. ACM, New York, NY, USA, 231–234. DOI: http://dx.doi.org/10.1145/1517744.1517749

47. Yvonne Rogers, Kay Connelly, William Hazlewood, and Lenore Tedesco. 2009. Enhancing learning: a study of how mobile devices can facilitate sensemaking. *Personal and Ubiquitous Computing* 14, 2 (2009), 111–124. DOI: http://dx.doi.org/10.1007/s00779-009-0250-7

48. Daniel M. Russell, Mark J. Stefik, Peter Pirolli, and Stuart K. Card. 1993. The Cost Structure of Sensemaking.

In *Proceedings of the INTERACT '93 and CHI '93 Conference on Human Factors in Computing Systems (CHI '93)*. ACM, New York, NY, USA, 269–276. DOI: http://dx.doi.org/10.1145/169059.169209

49. Eduardo Salas, Terry L. Dickinson, Sharolyn A. Converse, and Scott I. Tannenbaum. 1992. Toward an understanding of team performance and training. In *Teams: Their Training and Performance*, Robert W Swezey and Eduardo Salas (Eds.). Ablex Publishing Corporation, Norwood, NJ, USA, 3–29.

50. Katie Salen and Eric Zimmerman. 2004. *Rules of Play: Game Design Fundamentals*. MIT Press, Cambridge, MA, USA.

51. Texas Engineering Extension Service. 2000. *A Legacy of Service: The Texas Fire School 1930-2000*. Emergency Services Training Institute.

52. Irina Shklovski, Leysia Palen, and Jeannette Sutton. 2008. Finding Community Through Information and Communication Technology in Disaster Response. In *Proceedings of the 2008 ACM Conference on Computer Supported Cooperative Work (CSCW '08)*. ACM, New York, NY, USA, 127–136. DOI: http://dx.doi.org/10.1145/1460563.1460584

53. Thushari Silva, Vilas Wuwongse, and Hitesh Nidhi Sharma. 2012. Disaster mitigation and preparedness using linked open data. *Journal of Ambient Intelligence and Humanized Computing* 4, 5 (2012), 591–602. DOI: http://dx.doi.org/10.1007/s12652-012-0128-9

54. Robert Soden and Leysia Palen. 2016. Infrastructure in the Wild: What Mapping in Post-Earthquake Nepal Reveals About Infrastructural Emergence. In *Proceedings of the 2016 CHI Conference on Human Factors in Computing Systems (CHI '16)*. ACM, New York, NY, USA, 2796–2807. DOI: http://dx.doi.org/10.1145/2858036.2858545

55. Alan A. Song and David L. Kleinman. 1994. A distributed simulation system for team decisionmaking. In *AI, Simulation, and Planning in High Autonomy Systems, 1994. Distributed Interactive Simulation Environments., Proceedings of the Fifth Annual Conference on*. IEEE, 129–135.

56. Kate Starbird and Leysia Palen. 2011. "Voluntweeters": Self-organizing by Digital Volunteers in Times of Crisis. In *Proceedings of the SIGCHI Conference on Human Factors in Computing Systems (CHI '11)*. ACM, New York, NY, USA, 1071–1080. DOI: http://dx.doi.org/10.1145/1978942.1979102

57. Kate Starbird and Leysia Palen. 2012. (How) Will the Revolution Be Retweeted?: Information Diffusion and the 2011 Egyptian Uprising. In *Proceedings of the ACM 2012 Conference on Computer Supported Cooperative Work (CSCW '12)*. ACM, New York, NY, USA, 7–16. DOI: http://dx.doi.org/10.1145/2145204.2145212

58. Kate Starbird and Leysia Palen. 2013. Working and Sustaining the Virtual "Disaster Desk". In *Proceedings of the 2013 Conference on Computer Supported Cooperative Work (CSCW '13)*. ACM, New York, NY, USA, 491–502. DOI: http://dx.doi.org/10.1145/2441776.2441832

59. Renee J. Stout, Janis A. Cannon-Bowers, Eduardo Salas, and Dana M. Milanovich. 1999. Planning, shared mental models, and coordinated performance: An empirical link is established. *Human Factors* 41, 1 (March 1999), 61–71.

60. Anthony Tang, Jonathan Massey, Nelson Wong, Derek Reilly, and W. Keith Edwards. 2012. Verbal Coordination in First Person Shooter Games. In *Proceedings of the ACM 2012 Conference on Computer Supported Cooperative Work (CSCW '12)*. ACM, New York, NY, USA, 579–582. DOI: http://dx.doi.org/10.1145/2145204.2145292

61. Anthony Tang, Michel Pahud, Kori Inkpen, Hrvoje Benko, John C. Tang, and Bill Buxton. 2010. Three's Company: Understanding Communication Channels in Three-way Distributed Collaboration. In *Proceedings of the 2010 ACM Conference on Computer Supported Cooperative Work (CSCW '10)*. ACM, New York, NY, USA, 271–280. DOI: http://dx.doi.org/10.1145/1718918.1718969

62. James B. Thomas, Shawn M. Clark, and Dennis A. Gioia. 1993. Strategic sensemaking and organizational performance: Linkages among scanning, interpretation, action, and outcomes. *Academy of Management Journal* 36, 2 (1993), 239–270.

63. Zachary O. Toups, William A. Hamilton, Christian Keyes-Garcia, Stepheny Perez, and Richard Stanton. 2015. Collaborative Planning Gameplay from Disaster Response Practice. In *Proceedings of the 2015 Annual Symposium on Computer-Human Interaction in Play (CHI PLAY '15)*. ACM, New York, NY, USA, 715–720. DOI: http://dx.doi.org/10.1145/2793107.2810287

64. Zachary O. Toups, Jessica Hammer, William A. Hamilton, Ahmad Jarrah, William Graves, and Oliver Garretson. 2014. A Framework for Cooperative Communication Game Mechanics from Grounded Theory. In *Proceedings of the First ACM SIGCHI Annual Symposium on Computer-human Interaction in Play (CHI PLAY '14)*. ACM, New York, NY, USA, 257–266. DOI: http://dx.doi.org/10.1145/2658537.2658681

65. Zachary O. Toups and Andruid Kerne. 2007. Implicit Coordination in Firefighting Practice: Design Implications for Teaching Fire Emergency Responders. In *Proceedings of the SIGCHI Conference on Human Factors in Computing Systems (CHI '07)*. ACM, New York, NY, USA, 707–716. DOI: http://dx.doi.org/10.1145/1240624.1240734

66. Zachary O. Toups, Andruid Kerne, and William Hamilton. 2009. Game Design Principles for Engaging Cooperative Play: Core Mechanics and Interfaces for Non-mimetic Simulation of Fire Emergency Response. In *Proceedings of the 2009 ACM SIGGRAPH Symposium on Video Games (Sandbox '09)*. ACM, New York, NY, USA, 71–78. DOI: http://dx.doi.org/10.1145/1581073.1581085

67. Zachary O. Toups, Andruid Kerne, William Hamilton, and Alan Blevins. 2009. Emergent Team Coordination: From Fire Emergency Response Practice to a Non-mimetic Simulation Game. In *Proceedings of the ACM 2009 International Conference on Supporting Group Work (GROUP '09)*. ACM, New York, NY, USA, 341–350. DOI: `http://dx.doi.org/10.1145/1531674.1531725`

68. Zachary O. Toups, Andruid Kerne, and William A. Hamilton. 2011. The Team Coordination Game: Zero-fidelity Simulation Abstracted from Fire Emergency Response Practice. *ACM Trans. Comput.-Hum. Interact.* 18, 4, Article 23 (Dec. 2011), 37 pages. DOI: `http://dx.doi.org/10.1145/2063231.2063237`

69. U.S. Department of Homeland Security. 2008. *National Incident Management System*. U.S. Department of Homeland Security, Washington, DC, USA.

70. Deepika Vaddi, Zachary O. Toups, Igor Dolgov, Rina Wehbe, and Lennart E. Nacke. 2016. Investigating the Impact of Cooperative Communication Mechanics on Player Performance in *Portal 2*. In *Proceedings of Graphics Interface*. In press.

71. Sarah Vieweg, Amanda L. Hughes, Kate Starbird, and Leysia Palen. 2010. Microblogging During Two Natural Hazards Events: What Twitter May Contribute to Situational Awareness. In *Proceedings of the SIGCHI Conference on Human Factors in Computing Systems (CHI '10)*. ACM, New York, NY, USA, 1079–1088. DOI: `http://dx.doi.org/10.1145/1753326.1753486`

72. Greg Wadley, Marcus Carter, and Martin Gibbs. 2015. Voice in Virtual Worlds: The Design, Use, and Influence of Voice Chat in Online Play. *Human–Computer Interaction* 30, 3-4 (2015), 336–365. DOI: `http://dx.doi.org/10.1080/07370024.2014.987346`

73. Karl E. Weick. 1993. The Collapse of Sensemaking in Organizations: The Mann Gulch Disaster. *Administrative Science Quarterly* 38, 4 (1993), 628–652. `http://www.jstor.org/stable/2393339`

74. Karl E. Weick. 1995. *Sensemaking in Organizations*. Foundations for Organizational Science, Vol. 3. SAGE Publications.

LUDOGRAPHY

1. 3909. 2013. *Papers, Please*. Game [Windows]. (2013). 3909.

2. Blizzard Entertainment. 1998. *StarCraft*. Game [Windows]. (31 March 1998). Blizzard Entertainment, Irvine, CA, USA.

3. Blizzard Entertainment. 2010. *StarCraft II: Wings of Liberty*. Game [Windows]. (27 July 2010). Blizzard Entertainment, Irvine, California, USA.

4. Firaxis Games. 2012. *XCOM: Enemy Unknown*. Game [PS3]. (9 October 2012). 2K Games, Novato, CA, USA.

5. Giant Enemy Crab. 2016. *Due Process* [pre-Alpha]. Game [Windows]. (2016). Giant Enemy Crab, Seattle, WA, USA.

6. Mighty Rabbit Studios. 2014. *Breach & Clear*. Game [Windows]. (21 March 2014). Gun Media, Lexington, KY, USA.

7. Red Storm Entertainment. 1998. *Tom Clancy's Rainbow Six*. Game [Windows]. (21 August 1998). Red Storm Entertainment, Cary, NC, USA.

8. Riot Games. 2009. *League of Legends*. Game [Windows]. (27 October 2009). Riot Games, Los Angeles, CA, USA.

9. Supergiant Games. 2014. *Transistor*. Game [PS4]. (20 May 2014). Supergiant Games, San Jose, CA, USA.

10. Ubisoft Montreal. 2015. *Tom Clancy's Rainbow Six Siege*. Game [Windows]. (1 December 2015). Ubisoft, Paris, France.

Playification: The PhySeEar case

Elena Márquez Segura
Annika Waern
Uppsala University
Uppsala, Sweden
elena.marquez@im.uu.se
annika.waern@im.uu.se

Luis Márquez Segura
Fonserrana S.C.A de interés
social
Tocina (Sevilla), Spain
luismarquezsegura@
gmail.com

David López Recio
Mobile Life Centre,
Royal Institute of Technology
Stockholm, Sweden
dalore1es@gmail.com

ABSTRACT

The concept of playification has recently been proposed as an extension of, or alternative to, gamification. We present a playification design project targeting the re-design of physiotherapy rehabilitative sessions for elderly inpatients. The menial and repetitive nature of the physical exercises targeted for design might seem ideal for shallow widespread gamification approaches that add external rewards to entice usage. In the PhySeEar project, we introduced a "third agent" instead, in the form of technology that would take over some of the work typically carried out by the physiotherapist. This technological intervention triggered the emergence of playfulness, when inpatients and the therapist re-signified the ongoing activity by engaging in playful role-taking, such as blaming the technology for mistakes, or for sensitivity to the inpatient's inaccurate movements. Based on the experiences from this project, we discuss some of the major differences between playification and gamification.

Author Keywords

Gamification; Playification; Physiotherapy; Physical training; Rehabilitative therapy; NAO; Robot; Technology-supported design.

ACM Classification Keywords

H.5.m. Information interfaces and presentation (e.g., HCI): Miscellaneous.

INTRODUCTION

The concept of gamification has received much attention but also critique [19], for taking into account only a narrow perspective of what makes games fun and engaging. Today, research on gamification has oriented towards tapping into the players' intrinsic motivations and playful engagement, opening for a wider scope of play activities than challenge-based play. Nicholson [45] argued that designing for

CHI PLAY '16, October 16 - 19, 2016, Austin, TX, USA
Copyright is held by the owner/author(s). Publication rights licensed to ACM.
ACM 978-1-4503-4456-2/16/10...$15.00
DOI: http://dx.doi.org/10.1145/2967934.2968099

playful engagement without adding game challenges could be an important enough strategy to motivate a different name – *playification*.

However, so far there are only a few examples of projects that have attempted to encourage playful engagement in serious activities, without adding game challenges.

This article contributes to the investigation of playification by addressing a domain that may seem ideal for classic, shallow gamification. In the PhySeEar project, we investigated physiotherapy training for elderly patients; a form of menial, repetitive training for which the patients show low interest and receive little reward. Instead of adding any game challenge or external reward schema, we designed an intervention that allowed the physiotherapist and inpatients to engage playfully together, through the addition of an external artificial 'referee' that took over the task of presenting feedback on training exercises. We report on how the therapist and the inpatients would engage in playful but also more challenge-oriented forms of play. However, in contrast with traditional gamification these were under constant negotiation and re-negotiation between the inpatients and their trainer. The PhySeEar case study illustrates how playification can offer a way to open up for playful and yet challenging engagement in training in a more flexible way than what is typical of gamification.

BACKGROUND

Design for play

Play design research has a long history in HCI. While early work presented useful approaches to design for fun or pleasurable experiences [1,4,26], more recent work has chartered play experiences in particular [32]. However, these approaches focus on the individual experience and present little support for designing for the unfolding play activity. The work presented here is more closely related to the strand of design research that focuses on play as a creative and typically social activity, such as the work on design for open-ended play [3,60], and that of Gaver and his group on 'ludic design' [20,21]. What these approaches have in common is that the technology is seen as a tool for fostering creative play in a social context, rather than directly creating a particular experience. The work on exertion games by Mueller et al. [43,44] is also relevant due to its focus on movement and engagement.

Playification

The concept of playification has emerged recently as an alternative to, or generalization of, the more widespread concept of gamification. In an overview of work branded as gamification, Deterding et al. [15] suggests a definition of gamification as "the use of game design elements in non-game contexts". To this, Lieberoth et al. [34] adds the observation that the word has increasingly become used as an overarching term for using games and game-like phenomena in non-leisure settings. The goal behind gamification is to draw people into a pre-existing activity that the designer wants people to like more, do for longer, repeat more, or engage more deeply with. In this last aspect, it has become similar to the concept of "serious gaming" [42], with the difference that the latter is typically focused on the development of full games for serious purposes.

The most widespread approaches to gamification have met with extensive critique. The most vocal criticism concerns how gamification typically takes the form of adding a superficial "game layer" to existing systems, in the form of external rewards such as points, badges or competitions [13–15,41,45,46]. Arguments for this type of gamification are based in behavioral psychology [50]. Apart from being ethically questionable [5], adding a thin game layer to motivate an otherwise uninteresting activity might not work. Based in a meta-analysis of motivational factors in the educational setting [11], Nicholson [45,46] pointed out how extrinsic rewards may work against intrinsic motivations especially in a longer term perspective; a very similar concern was voiced by McGonigal [41]. A more fruitful approach is thus looking at the core activity itself, and designing it to be intrinsically motivating through appealing to intrinsic motivation [52] or simply our inherent drive to be playful. Deterding [13] framed the core design challenge for gamification as "not how to include game mechanics, but how to induce a playful stance in the user towards the activity they are engaging in."

The suggestion to instead discuss *playification* originates in such concerns. While some authors consider playification to be a wider concept than gamification (in a way analogous to how playing is often seen as a wider concept than playing games) [55], we here follow Nicholson [45,46] to consider playification a form of design that fosters *playful*, rather than *gameful*, behavior. This distinction originates in how Deterding et al. [15] proposed to focus on "gameful design", i.e. on designs that foster a goal-oriented and competitive attitude (also called "ludus" [7]). They argued that such an approach would be beneficial for learning and training applications by tapping into the common response to game challenges (when they are at the right level to the skills of the player): to try again, to try harder. In gameful design, mastering a challenge is intrinsically rewarding in the way it fosters a sense of competence. What Nicholson proposes stands in stark contrast: he suggests that playification could remove all goals and rewards, to focus entirely on play engagement. He discusses how play emerges not only when mastering a challenge but when "having boundaries, bumping up against them, and occasionally crossing them" [46]. Boundaries (usually in the form of goals and rules) are not static, but players should be free to change their rules when they become boring or don't work. This is an approach that foregrounds a form of player empowerment, which is also recognized within the New Games Movement [18]. At the center of this is the maxim of *playing well together* [12], being open to adapting the rules of the game to the players, which contrasts with playing a game well by having the players adhering to fixed, pre-set rules and challenges.

SETTING: PHYSIOTHERAPY TRAINING

This paper adopts Nicholson's overarching perspective on playification as fostering open-ended playfulness rather than goal-oriented gamefulness. But the type of playification addressed here is very different from the open-ended explorative play for learning that Nicholson is proposing: we are looking into what playification can achieve when applied to a repetitive, menial task that needs to be done. This is the kind of domain that is typically targeted by shallow gamification, as adding rewards is simple to implement (with or without technological aids). Hence, this case is useful in illustrating the difference between playification and gamification. In this section, we go through the setting in some detail to present the reader with an understanding of the kind of challenges that the domain posed.

The setting and the challenges

The PhySeEar project was carried out in collaboration with the physiotherapist of an assisting living facility, Nuestra Señora de la Soledad (NSS), in Tocina (Seville, Spain). The project has previously been reported in [36,38,39], but here we analyze the design process and their solutions from the perspective of playification.

The motivation for initiating the project originated in the physiotherapist's frustration with challenges arising from both technical and social aspects of the rehabilitation setting. To start with, most of the inpatients presented multiple medical conditions, with some non-specific symptoms, as well as secondary complications to their main diseases. This corresponds to normal medical conditions in geriatric healthcare [29,47,58] but adds an extra challenge to the creation of physiotherapy treatment plans [6]. At NSS, the therapist focused on working with functional limitations related to age through physical rehabilitative sessions focused on helping them maintain their physical abilities and independency as long as possible. They typically involved repetitions of mobility exercises meant to restore or maintain the inpatients' range of motion, flexibility, and balance, and also to improve their strength and endurance. These activities are not intrinsically motivating: they are repetitive [49], and often painful for the inpatients [51]. In addition, extrinsic rewards in the form of physical improvement are not apparent, given the elderly's deteriorated health and physical impairments [6,28]. Essentially, the patients only get marginally better; they must train to *not get worse*.

In physical rehabilitative therapy in general, motivation and engagement are very important for creating impact in the improvement of the physical condition of the inpatients [57].

In an interview session with the physiotherapist, we found that such motivation was often lacking, which decreased the attendance of inpatients to the non-compulsory rehabilitative sessions offered. In addition, the therapist told us that one of the major reasons why the inpatients showed up to the sessions was to socialize with him: to tell him about their day, to gossip, and to complain about their (lack of) health.

Social support and interpersonal relationships are key for the elderly's satisfaction and their positive self-esteem [17,25] and hence receiving humane and personal treatment can be beneficial for their therapy. However, the therapist considered this aspect was taking too much attention away from the actual physical rehabilitative exercises. Some of the inpatients that would attend to the sessions showed little interest in the actual movement performance, and would sometimes use their emotional bonds with the physiotherapist to get away with less exercises or repetitions. The therapist articulated other social challenges around communication and joint action. The typical sessions required the physiotherapist to instruct, motivate, and provide feedback about performance. On the inpatients' side, they had to understand and follow these instructions and feedback. Hence, the sessions required the joint effort and coordination of the physiotherapist and the inpatient to be successful.

An additional issue was that many of the patients had never participated in instructed fitness activities before, and that many of them exhibited deteriorated physical abilities as well as physical and cognitive impairments. In most cases, this resulted in low proprioceptive skills, i.e. low awareness and ability to track and control the position, orientation, an motion of one's body parts [33]. This made it challenging for the physiotherapist to provide feedback, corrections, and movement goals in ways they could understand.

Taken together, these challenges shaped the design goals in the PhySeEar project: to increase the inpatients' focus, motivation, and understanding of their performance, and to help the physiotherapist to facilitate this.

METHOD
The approach taken in this project is a Research through Design (RtD) one [10,66,67], wherein the iterative design process and the designs themselves drive research and knowledge production.

The particular RtD approach in this work takes from user-centered design [48] that both the therapists and the

inpatients were considered as users. By taking this design approach rather than a participatory one [53], the design team put itself in a privileged position, making central design decisions informed by observations and user feedback. To counter this effect, we sought to develop open-ended designs [16]. The openness of such designs empowers users by opening up for appropriation.

Furthermore, we used a technology-supported approach to design [62], meaning that the added technology would partially support but not fully sustain the activity in focus. In the context of co-located physical and social activities, this means considering as design resources the technology as well other elements present in the setting. This includes physical artifacts, the roles of users involved, and their spatial distribution and use of the space [38,40]. What is targeted in design is therefore a closely knit ecosystem of technological, physical, and socio-spatial elements that together facilitate and support a particular activity [38,40], in this case the rehabilitative sessions. Furthermore, a technology-supported approach to design helps to empower users in their capacity of shaping the activity [38,40].

Data collection and analysis
The two design iterations were evaluated in actual rehabilitative training sessions. All rehabilitative sessions were recorded with a camera setup using two cameras that captured two different angles of the room. A researcher onsite would also take field notes. Finally, the physiotherapist was continuously consulted during the design process, mostly after user studies, once the design team had conducted an initial analysis over the video material.

The analysis was inspired in ethnomethodology, and in particular in Conversation Analysis (CA) [2,27,54] and Interaction Analysis (IA) [23,24]. From CA it borrows the type of phenomenon studied and the theoretical underpinnings and approach, taking users as sociologists in practice who understand, leverage, and make use of the fact that social action is ordered in interaction. The analysis borrows from IA an attention to, and coding of, other aspects than conversation to coordinate joint action (e.g., proxemic aspects such as gaze and bodily orientation [37]).

Inspired by Goodwin [24] we used clear central questions or aspects to drive the analysis: these were performance, motivation, and playfulness (the last one emerging after the first design iteration). Similar to Goodwin's embodied participation framework [24], we looked into the semiotic resources the users employed for joint action. Goodwin's proposed focus on the how users use and configure the semiotic resources is highly useful in a technology-supported design approach, as many of these can become design resources in subsequent design iterations. In particular, we focused on what Goodwin calls "contextual organizations", the way the resources are "oriented to at a particular moment as relevant to the organization of a particular action" [24]. We also looked at how users

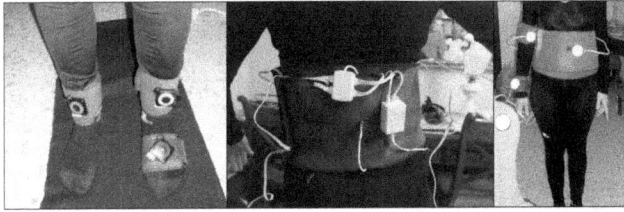

Figure 1. The wearable prototypes used in the first design iteration. Left: prototype for lower limb exercises. Center and right: prototype for upper limb exercises. The waist band (center) was used to attach a wireless receiver that communicated with a remote control triggering the output.

rearranged contextual onsite elements to appropriate and make sense (and the most) of the ongoing activity. Key moments analyzed were those that worked particularly well or badly from the perspective of performance, engagement and playfulness. After identifying such moments, they were also discussed with the physiotherapist, to gain further knowledge from an inside perspective.

FIRST DESIGN ITERATION

The first design prototypes were conceived as wearables that the inpatients would use during the rehabilitative exercise sessions [39] attached to the body part that was being trained. They presented audio-visual signals indicating if the movement was correctly or incorrectly performed.

Implementation

Two prototypes were developed at this stage with initial feedback from the physiotherapist. The first was meant to assist in upper limb rehabilitative exercises, whereas the second prototype was attached to lower limbs to assist during walking exercises (see Fig. 1).

For the upper body wearable, a commercial light set from IKEA was used. It consisted of four LED lamps, three of which were attached to the inpatients using armbands (see Fig. 1), while one was fixed on a lampshade in front of the inpatients (see Fig. 2). The light set connected all four lamps together to an infrared receiver attached to a waistband, which was controlled by a remote control that handled all lights together, with different colors and intensities. The therapist would control the lamps, using the color green as an output to indicate a correctly performed

exercise, orange to indicate a performance that could be improved, and red to indicate an incorrect performance that required the inpatient's immediate attention.

The legs wearable used sound for feedback instead. This was motivated by the fact that inpatients were usually told to look forward when performing walking exercises for stabilization, and wouldn't be able to see visual indicators attached to their legs. Again, off-the-shelf commercial technology was used, in this case radio tags. Each of them would produce a different sound when activated with a remote control. Just like with the lights system, these small devices were attached to the inpatients' bodies (see Fig. 1, left). Their feedback was more complex than the arms wearables: each tag would assess one of the five walking parameters that the therapist would usually evaluate: the size, length, height, and symmetry of the step, as well as any deviation from walking in a straight line. The physiotherapist would trigger the sound of the corresponding device whenever one of these measurements deviated from the stipulated measure for each inpatient.

Study

From the perspective of the inpatients, these designs were trialed in a Wizard of Oz manner [9]: While it was the therapist who controlled the system's feedback using the remotes, to the eye of the inpatients it appeared to be working autonomously (see Fig. 2, left).

Even though this was a qualitative explorative study, below we present the demographics of the participants to give a sense of their physical condition and abilities. Twenty-six inpatients at NSS participated this first study. Of those 26, there were 11 men, and 15 women. One patient was 57 years old, the rest were between 72 to 96 years old. Five inpatients suffered from Parkinson's disease, three from Alzheimer's, and two suffered from stroke. Sixteen required mobility aids, of which six were dependent on wheelchairs. Apart from physical impairments, six suffered severe or very severe cognitive impairment and 12 were likely to be depressed or very depressed (in the geriatric depression scale, GDS, used in [64]). Twelve of them were highly dependent, six moderately dependent, and seven scarcely dependent or independent (in the Barthel test of independency [8]). Regarding demographics related to

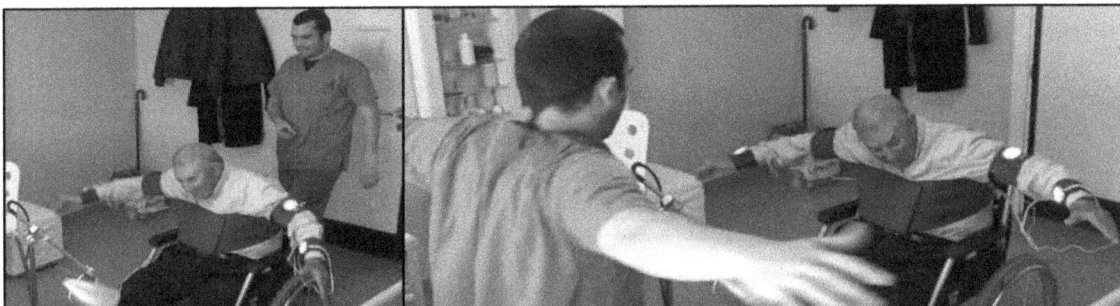

Figure 2. Training with the arms wearable. Left: the physiotherapist is triggering the output of the lights with a remote control. Right: the physiotherapist is helping the inpatient to perform the movement right by modeling it for him.

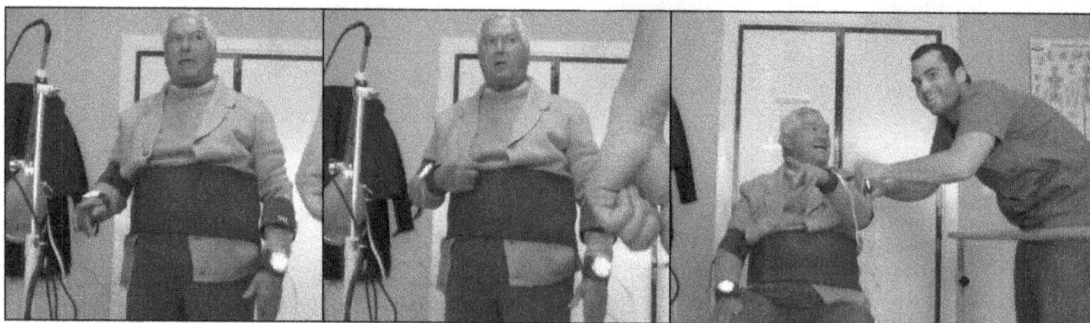

Figure 3. Inpatient teasing the system.

technology usage, they all considered themselves computer illiterates, but some of them were just starting a basic computer course.

In the study, 9 participants interacted with the lights system and 8 with the sound system. The rest would go through a standard therapy session with the therapist without technology support.

Insights

The arms wearable succeeded to create an understanding of the rehabilitative exercises, although, as we shall see below, this was to a large extent dependent on the usage patterns that the therapist and inpatient developed around the technology.

The legs wearable did not work as intended. Many of the inpatients had difficulties distinguishing between the different feedback sounds. Moreover, the sound attracted their attention down towards their lower limbs in a similar way we envisioned visual feedback would, which the therapist saw as problematic.

Play, playfulness, and motivation

The most interesting observation in this trial related to how the therapist, without any previous instruction or explicit reflection, started to use the technology to take the role of "the bad cop". Whenever negative feedback was required, the therapist would attribute it to the technology. The therapist would say things like (see Fig. 2):

"Be careful..." –the lights would turn orange, and he continued saying: "See? I was about to tell you"

This allowed the therapist to be "on the patients' side" as "the good cop", which allowed him to stay very understanding with their mistakes, helping and explaining them what they were doing wrong. The inpatients seemed to enjoy the physiotherapist's siding with them "against the system":

"This one, this one is a tattletale!" – inpatient laughing and pointing to the light on the lampshade.

"It knows too much" – physiotherapist, also laughing (see Fig. 3, right)

This division of roles between the therapist and the system changed the social dynamics of the situation. Not only did it

eliminate the inpatients' attempts to get away with easier or less exercises, but many of them actually displayed the opposite behavior. None of them complained about the number of repetitions. While five of the inpatients complained about their inability to perform well, this was not done in the beginning of the session (in an attempt to get away with less effort), but as a justification towards the end. It seemed like they felt they had to justify that they weren't as good as "expected", although there had not been any such expectation set. Some showed a determined will to continue with the exercises longer than required. For example, after finishing a session, an inpatient continued performing the exercises, to which the physiotherapist commented (see Fig. 3, left and center):

"You won't stop, will you?"

"This one, this one does not punish me, I punish him!" – patient, laughing and pointing to the light.

Finally, at the end of the session, many inpatients showed signs of assessing their own performance, with comments such as "It got red the two first times". To this, the therapist would continue in the "good cop" role, with a positive appraisal, decreasing the importance of "those reds", acknowledging their effort, and setting goals for following sessions.

It should be noted that the role distribution between technology and therapist was here created on the fly by the therapist, in a manner that must be considered playful. From the inpatients' reactions we can see that this was appreciated in an equally playful manner, in how the technology was spoken of as an active agent - and in one case "punished".

The physiotherapist's tasks

The improvised role distribution motivated our looking closer at the different tasks that the physiotherapist did during the sessions, as these could potentially be taken over by the technology in subsequent design iterations. This analysis revealed the different techniques the physiotherapist used to correct and provide feedback, which would appear alone and in combination. The later post-debrief session with the physiotherapist clarified when and why he used these.

The therapist would use *verbal* communication to explain what the inpatients needed to correct, or to call their attention to a particular body part, or to the trajectory they were following. He would also use verbal utterances of affection and motivation, acknowledging and praising their effort. *Deitic* (pointing) gestures were used to point out problematic body parts, to draw a particular movement trajectory, or to indicate speed. He used *his own body* to *model* movements for the inpatients to encourage them to continue moving, and to explain and correct movements, e.g. by showing both the correct movement performance and the incorrect performance of the inpatient, emphasizing what was wrong.

Finally, the therapist would provide *tactile feedback* to the inpatients. Sometimes, this was done tapping a particular body part so that they would focus their attention to it; and sometimes he would mobilize their body limbs. According to the therapist, tactile feedback was useful when the other strategies didn't work, and allowed the inpatients to understand how to move a particular body part by passively feeling its movement. Last, but not least, there were some physical contact of affection and support. For example, the therapist would put a hand over the inpatient's shoulders or back. He mentioned that he did this frequently with inpatients that had stability issues, since this gave them a feeling of safety, but also in general as a way of expressing support and encouragement.

SECOND DESIGN ITERATION

The core insight from the first trials concerned the many instances of playful behavior from both sides, which both the designers and the therapist suspected to be a major reason behind the success of the trial in terms of motivation and engagement. Hence, the project picked up on the incidental emergence of playfulness, moving towards a deliberate playification design. The second design iteration was decided to support playful behavior, while maintaining the focus on movement performance and assessment. The wearable devices were then substituted by a NAO robot. We anticipated that the robot could be seen as a plaything as well as a social agent [30]. The latter was inspired by how research has shown that both children and adults engage with robotic toys and connect emotionally to them [30,59,61]. In particular, we tried to capitalize on the observed behavior of the therapist and the inpatients siding together to fight "the system". By substituting the neutral and inanimate LED technology with an anthropomorphic robot, we hoped to further enhance this relation.

The NAO robot was chosen over other robot alternatives due to the similarity in movement functionality to the human body, in that it shared its major joints and their movement with the human body. We saw in the NAO the potential of extending the discrete and binary type of

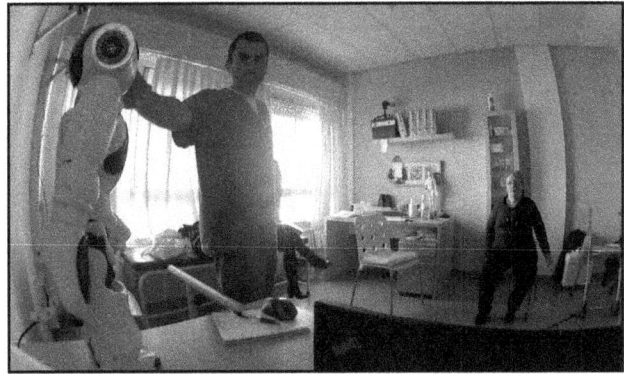

Figure 4. The physiotherapist controls the movements of the robot by pressing buttons on its head.

feedback inherent in our first design iteration, and of helping the physiotherapist in some of his tasks reported above. In particular, we saw a clear opportunity for the technology to take over the modeling task we had observed the therapist do. The robot could supply the inpatients with continuous visual stimuli encouraging them to keep moving, reminding them of the correct performance of these movements, and showing if and how their movements deviated from the ideal.

So as to maintain the binary feedback that worked well in the first trial, the design team programmed the color of the eyes of the NAO to turn green when demoing the "correct" movement, and red when the inpatients performed a movement wrong or inaccurately. The robot would also mimic the faulty movement in an exaggerated way. With the help of the therapist, the design team was able to trial this functionality by preprogramming a set of nine movements that the physiotherapist often used during his exercise sessions. Furthermore, the most typical movement errors were implemented [35].

The Wizard of OZ setup was maintained in this trial in the sense that the physiotherapist triggered the different movements of the robot, either via a computer keyboard, or by touching the control buttons on the top of the NAO's head (see Fig. 4). In the case that other errors than those preprogrammed appeared, the therapist would use any of his ordinary methods to correct the inpatients.

For comparison, the trial also included a virtual screen-based version of the robot, implemented using the NAOSim provided by Aldebaran (see Fig. 5). Here, this design will be called ViNAO. It was programmed to behave exactly like its physical counterpart [35]. The reason for including ViNAO in the study was to investigate how important it was that the robot had a physical presence in the space of the therapy session. The ViNAO was controlled through the computer keyboard.

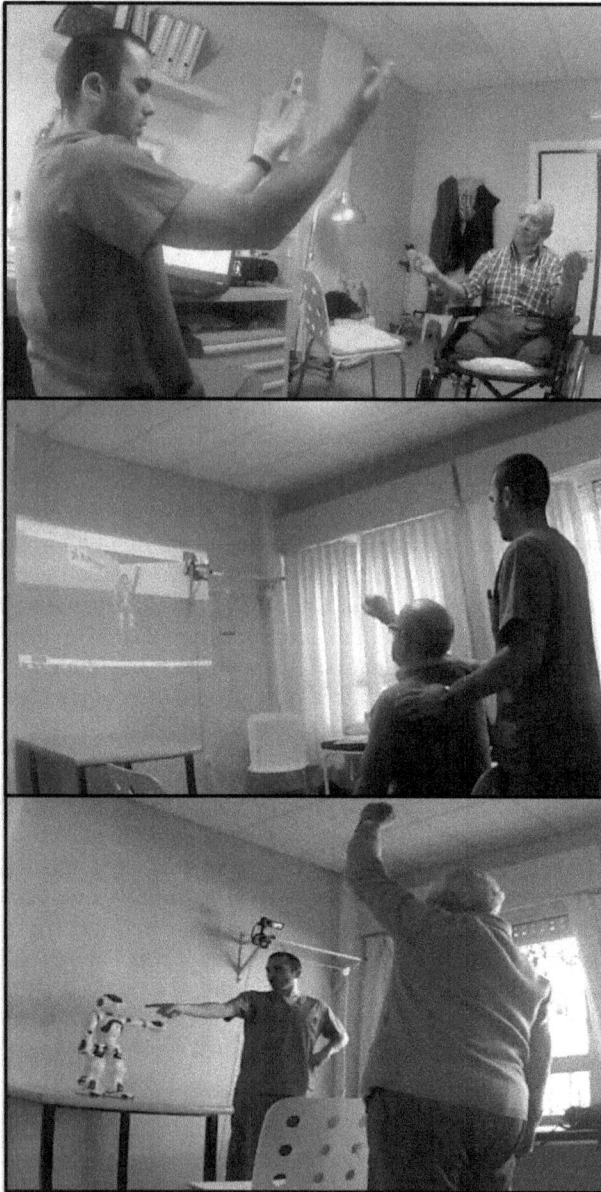

Figure 5. The three conditions. Top: without technology. Center: with ViNAO. Bottom: with the NAO robot.

Study

The study in the second design iteration was organized in the same way as the first. The inpatients were of roughly the same age and had similar medical conditions as in the previous study and many of them had participated in the previous trial. Thirteen inpatients participated in total, divided into three groups, where the first group would do an ordinary training session, the second group would interact with the therapist assisted by the NAO robot, and the third group would meet the therapist assisted by the ViNAO system. The exercises were randomly picked from the repertoire that had been implemented in the NAO.

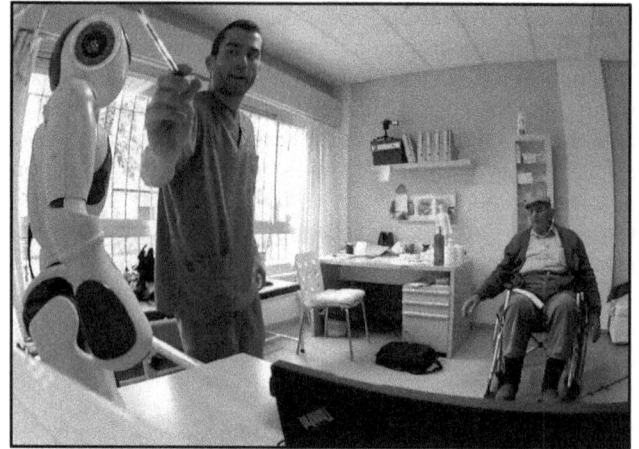

Figure 6. Physiotherapist explains body planes with relation to the robot.

Insights

The NAO as a modeling tool

The study showed that the introduction of the NAO robot changed the therapist's tasks. In the condition without technology intervention, he would model the movements almost continuously, complementing it with verbal feedback. Modeling was interrupted only once, when the physiotherapist prioritized tactile feedback by mobilizing an inpatient's body limb.

In the ViNAO group, the physiotherapist used mobilization as the main feedback technique. It was used twice as much in this condition, 15 times, as in the robot condition, 7 times. The faulty mode of the ViNAO was only triggered once, compared to the robot condition, where it was triggered 13 times.

In the robot condition, the therapist used all of the preprogrammed NAO movements. In a debrief session, the therapist commented that he felt relieved by the robot and able to focus on other tasks. We saw less movement modeling on his side, and an increased usage of other techniques for feedback. Expressive gestures of encouragement and appraisal were also more common in these sessions (13 instances, compared to 2 when not assisted by any technology, and 7 in the ViNAO condition). A particularly interesting use of the NAO robot was that of a pedagogical tool: the therapist would use it to explain some characteristics of the movements, such as the relative position of a body part with respect to others, or the plane of movement wherein a limb should be moving (see Fig. 6).

It was also interesting to see how the physical robot affected the behavior of the inpatients. For example, unless told otherwise, the inpatients would follow the robot's movement pace, which was not observed in the ViNAO group. An illuminating anecdote in this regard happened before one session with the robot. Usually the NAO started the sessions sitting down on the table in front of the inpatient. Once the physiotherapist initiated the program

Figure 7. Mimicking the robot standing up.

that controlled the NAO's movements, the robot would stand up to assume its initial default position. One inpatient who was sitting down waiting for the session to start, stood up following the robot without being told so (see Fig. 7).

For some movements, the physical limitations of the NAO robot became apparent and in those, mobilizations became important. For example, halfway through the robot's abduction of the shoulder[1], while the arms where parallel to the floor, the robot would stop the movement to rotate its elbows' internal joints to be able to continue the movement. Some inpatients noticed this, and talked about these singularities. One inpatient asked puzzled whether he had to "do the same" when he reached his open arms position, to which the physiotherapist chuckled. The therapist commented later about how this realization had surprised him given this inpatient had a severe cognitive impairment.

The robot as a playmate
During the session, playfulness emerged in the robot group in the form of a playful competition with, and joyful mocking of, the NAO. The therapist used the NAO's limitations to challenge some inpatients. He would set goals, such as performing some movements with a greater movement range, or faster. This mode of in-the-moment competition seemed to both amuse and motivate the inpatients, sparking off a playful competitive atmosphere. Some inpatients teased the robot when performing the jerky clumsy movements mentioned above. This did not happen in the ViNAO condition.

In line with previous findings, there were instances of the therapist siding with the inpatients. When the therapist talked about incorrect or wrong movements, he would often blame the NAO, saying for example: "The NAO is doing the movement wrong", despite the fact that the robot was correctly mimicking the inpatients' performance.

Figure 8. Inpatient teasing and "complaining" to the robot.

The NAO clearly became a joint plaything. The inpatients first, and later also the therapist, would refer to it as "the doll" (the ViNAO version was instead called "the movie"). Some inpatients would playfully complain to the robot (see Fig. 8), some gave it names such as "smart-arse", or "tattletale", like happened in the first design iteration. Some of them praised the robot's capabilities instead.

One inpatient, curious about the robot, asked at the end of his session about what else the NAO could do. A researcher triggered its automatic pre-set Tai Chi mode, to which the inpatient reacted by mimicking the complex movements, which amazed the therapist (See Figure 9).

In a post-session interview, the therapist said that he particularly enjoyed the activity in the NAO group, and that he thought that the inpatients did so too. Based on the observations detailed above, we can see how a combination of factors allowed the therapist to use more physical forms of encouragement and support, and how the therapy became more a social act, while still one focused on movement performance. This was, to a large extent, due to the appearance of playful behavior in the robot condition.

Differences between the virtual and the physical NAO
As discussed above, we observed some differences in how the physical and the virtual NAO were used. Firstly, the physical properties of the robot seemed to help the physiotherapist to explain nuances of movements and the inpatients to understand the targeted movement and theirs better. In the debrief session, the therapist commented about how he thought the inpatients did not understand the movement cues from the ViNAO, and he suspected this was due to the two-dimensional character of the virtual NAO. We relate this to his more frequent mobilization of inpatients. The physiotherapist also commented about how he disliked the way that the faulty mode in ViNAO was triggered (from his computer, which was placed on his desk. This made him turn his back to the inpatient, which is something he usually avoids). Both aspects together made him reluctant to use this faulty mode. In total, the physical NAO was more effective both as a training tool and to foster play.

---

[1] Having the arms close to the body, this movement involves opening them to the sides and up over the head.

DISCUSSION

Technology-supported play and the socio-spatial configuration

Designing for playfulness rather than for gamefulness rely on radically more open designs; designs that make space for players to create their own play activity through exploration, transgression, and creative negotiation of the rules of play. In this respect, the work here is inspired by DeValk and colleagues [3,60], who developed a framework for the design of interactive play tools that emphasizes open-ended design strategies. In open-ended play, the rules and goals of the activity are not predefined, but they emerge during play. Their designs still offer a framing play structure, designed mainly through the interactivity of the technology. In PhySeEar, due to the serious use of playification, the core activity itself could not be changed – it had to be movement-based training. Instead, the solution was to choose a technology-supported approach. By developing technology to only support *part* of the training session (modeling and presenting feedback), the design left room for the participants to design their own activity with and around the technological intervention.

But the technology-supported approach has another effect as well: the technology becomes one tool among many, integrated in a socio-spatial configuration where it matters where people are and what they do, apart from interacting with the technology [38]. In the description of the PhySeEar studies, we have placed a certain emphasis on the social and physical behaviors of therapist and inpatients. These behaviors had a large influence over which functions the technology could, and was allowed to, take over; they were often also key elements in the playful interactions that evolved, such as when a patient interacted with the technology to "punish" it.

Re-keying an activity as play

The core goal of playification is the re-keying of an activity as play [22]. Such re-keying is difficult to achieve in a task that is necessary to perform, as we will not perceive something as play unless it has an element of voluntary engagement. In this sense, it is difficult to understand how play could emerge in PhySeEar, with its menial but necessary task of physical training. The authors would suggest that this re-keying emerged from *voluntary role-taking*, allowing the therapist and the inpatients to be "on the same team" against the technology. This role-taking was further enhanced by the introduction of the NAO robot in the second design cycle, as it could play a role much similar to that of a doll (and was indeed referred to as such). This role-taking allowed the training movements to be re-keyed as playful interaction with the NAO.

Although we used a Wizard of Oz setting in both trials, it should be noted that it was much more obvious that the physiotherapist was in control in the latter setup, as he would manipulate the robot or the computer to control feedback in plain view. A few inpatients picked this up, but

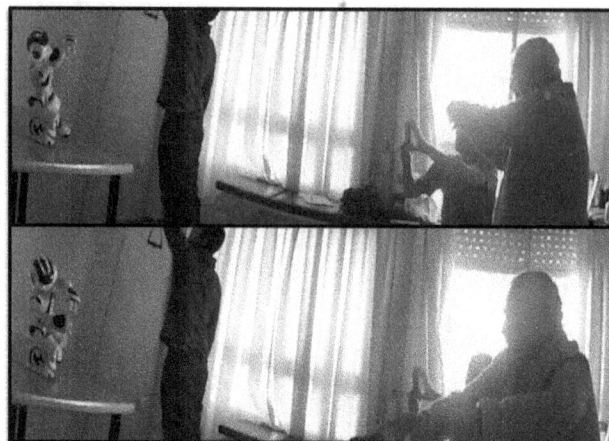

Figure 9. Inpatient mimicking a Tai Chi move.

some of them still pretended to take no notice of the physiotherapist's actions, playing along with the setup. For these patients, the whole session thus acquired an element of pretense play that was enjoyed by therapist and inpatients alike.

Within this setting, some elements of competitive and almost gameful play emerged, like when the physiotherapist would challenge the inpatients to e.g. perform their movements faster than the robot, or when the inpatients assessed their own performance at the end of the session. But in contrast to gameful approaches, such challenges were not the main goal of the intervention but were voluntarily adopted in the moment. They were not implemented in the technology, and could be changed at any time if they ceased to be relevant for the ongoing activity. Again, the technology-supported approach was key in creating room for playful creativity.

A playful approach to the design process

Above, we have described how the open-ended design strategy presented ample room for participants to negotiate and re-negotiate what form of play they engaged in. This, we consider to lie at the core of playification, and it also has implications for the design process.

The PhySeEar project was originally not intended as a playification project, but as a technological augmentation to support the therapist in presenting more understandable feedback to the in-patients. We were able to identify an opportunity for playification only through the way *the design process* itself allowed playful explorations to emerge. The trials in the first design iteration were deliberately very open, allowing the therapist and the inpatients to appropriate the technology in any way they saw fit. It was this openness that left room for playful engagement. Furthermore, we were careful to document and analyze instances of enjoyment and playful engagement.

We think that this openness for emerging phenomena is a critical element in all designs for play. Play is always creative and can be transgressive [56,65]. A good play design should always continue to surprise the designer, as players invent new ways to play. However, once play is observed, the designer can start to deconstruct what made it happen and find ways to further support that form of play. A successful redesign will encourage this mode of engagement further, while still leaving sufficient room for new and unforeseen forms of play. This happened in PhySeEar when the introduction of the NAO robot started to inspire mimicking, or when inpatients noticed clumsy movements of the robot or its limitations. Movements could be programmed to show limitations that can be exploited both from a pedagogical point of view (inpatients noticing details of the performance), and from a playful one. Following design iterations in this project could capitalize on these observations.

Rather than striving for precise design goals and predictable play behavior, we think that design for playification should place this phenomenon at its core: play emerging from the exploration, appropriation, and occasional transgression of the designed structures and setting.

The challenge of sustained play
The PhySeEar project did not explore the long-term effect of introducing the NAO robot in physiotherapy training. The living facility had the robot on loan for only a few training sessions. In line with most studies of gamified systems and play installations, it is likely that the interest in the robot would subside over time. Playification may even face larger problems with the novelty effect [31] than gamification if there is no element of gameful engagement, which can encourage players to try again and again, and to finally succeed and by that reach a sense of achievement. However, such a gameful experience was not easily accessible in PhySeEar as there was very little room for a tangible achievement; the patients were training to maintain physical status rather than to improve it.

Yet, tapping into the in-the-moment experience makes sense also in such settings. Playification brings forth another aspect that may potentially compensate for the lack of gameful engagement: the space for collective reinvention of the activity. Were the NAO robot used repeatedly in training, its role would most likely change over time. It may be attributed new levels of competence (or stupidity), the therapist could play it as "tired" one day and "happy" another, it could have been dressed up differently one day, etcetera. New challenges could be created. Quoting DeKoven [12]: "if an activity ceases to be fun, change it!"

CONCLUSION
Playification has been proposed both as an alternative to, and as a wider concept than, gamification. In this article, we have used a case example from the domain of physiotherapy training to argue that playification, in some crucial aspects, is *different* from gamification. We have shown how tapping into playful re-keying of an activity can

work to increase motivation in and by itself, without adding either any game challenge or external rewards.

A central aspect of such playful re-keying relates to the role distribution between the parties involved, including the technology. While it would be presumptuous to draw conclusions from this study alone, a pattern emerges when we compare it to previous work: it seems to be useful to offload *socially awkward* roles to technology. In this study, this is seen in how the role of the "bad cop" was assigned to the technology by the physiotherapist. In previous work on designing social dance games [40], we reported on how pre-teen children preferred to offload the socially awkward role of judging the correctness of a game move to the technology, even if the technology would not be particularly good at it. In the design of B.U.T.T.O.N. [63], Wilson deliberately designed a computer game that was easy to cheat at. By that, he was able to eradicate the social cost for cheating and to foster a playful mode of engagement. The potential for using technology as a "scapegoat" in social play is worthy of further exploration.

The aspects brought forward in this article all center on the way playification needs to leave room for players to create their own form of play engagement. In this, the approach is similar to previous work on open-ended design for play. However, when play is used in a domain such as training, there is a stricter structure framing play, as much of the activity is prescribed. This contrasts with free play (no structure) and with open-ended play (light structure mainly in the form of technology interactivity). Playification must in this case achieve a re-keying of the activity as something else, which can be appropriated in a playful manner. In PhySeEar, this re-keying was achieved through a playful redistribution of the roles between the therapist, the inpatients, and the technology.

Finally, the article has stressed how playful engagement is always creative and sometimes transgressive. Placing this phenomenon at the core of playification requires that designers acknowledge and cherish that they will not be able to predict all modes of play engagement that their designs will foster. This places requirements on the design process that are rather, and possibly radically, different than those adopted in game design.

ACKNOWLEDGMENTS
Thanks to the elderly who participated in this project. Some of you are not with us today, but your laughter will remain in our hearts. Thanks to the staff at Nuestra Señora de la Soledad, especially Inés Gallego. Thanks to Lola Segura and Francisca Peña for modeling.

REFERENCES
1. Juha Arrasvuori, Marion Boberg, Jussi Holopainen, Hannu Korhonen, Andrés Lucero, and Markus Montola. 2011. Applying the PLEX Framework in Designing for Playfulness. *Proceedings of the 2011 Conference on Designing Pleasurable Products and*

Interfaces, ACM, 24:1–24:8.
http://doi.org/10.1145/2347504.2347531

2. J. Maxwell Atkinson and John Heritage (eds.). 1984. *Structures of social action: studies in conversation analysis*. Cambridge University Press, New York, NY, USA.

3. Tilde Bekker and Janienke Sturm. 2009. Stimulating physical and social activity through open-ended play. *Proceedings of the 8th international conference on interaction design and children*, ACM, 309–312.

4. M. A. Blythe, K. Overbeeke, A. F. Monk, and P. C. Wright (eds.). 2003. *Funology: From Usability to Enjoyment*. Springer, New York.

5. Ian Bogost. 2013. Exploitationware. In *Rhetoric/Composition/Play through Video Games*. Springer, 139–147.

6. Cynthia J. Brown and Claire Peel. 2009. Rehabilitation. In *Hazzard's Geriatric Medicine and Gerontology* (6th ed.), Jeffrey B. Halter, Joseph G. Ouslander, Mary E. Tinetti, Stephanie Studenski, Kevin P. High and Sanjay Asthana (eds.). The McGraw-Hill Companies, New York, NY. Retrieved December 11, 2015 from http://mhmedical.com/content.aspx?aid=5113374

7. Roger Caillois. 1961. *Man, play, and games*. University of Illinois Press.

8. Javier Cid-Ruzafa and Javier Damián-Moreno. 1997. Valoración de la discapacidad física: el índice de Barthel. *Revista española de salud pública* 71, 2: 127–137.

9. Nils Dahlbäck, Arne Jönsson, and Lars Ahrenberg. 1993. Wizard of Oz Studies: Why and How. *Proceedings of the 1st International Conference on Intelligent User Interfaces*, ACM, 193–200. http://doi.org/10.1145/169891.169968

10. Peter Dalsgaard. 2010. Research In and Through Design: An Interaction Design Research Approach. *Proceedings of the 22nd Conference of the Computer-Human Interaction Special Interest Group of Australia on Computer-Human Interaction*, ACM, 200–203. http://doi.org/10.1145/1952222.1952265

11. Edward L. Deci, Richard Koestner, and Richard M. Ryan. 2001. Extrinsic rewards and intrinsic motivation in education: Reconsidered once again. *Review of educational research* 71, 1: 1–27.

12. Bernie DeKoven. 2002. *The well-played game: a playful path to wholeness*. iUniverse.

13. Sebastian Deterding. 2010. Just add points? What UX can (and cannot) learn from games. conftitle> *Slide show presented at UX Camp Europe</conftitle>, Berlin, May* 30.

14. Sebastian Deterding. 2011. Getting Gamification right. Retrieved October 5, 2015 from http://www.slideshare.net/dings/meaningful-play-getting-gamification-right

15. Sebastian Deterding, Dan Dixon, Rilla Khaled, and Lennart Nacke. 2011. From game design elements to gamefulness: defining gamification. *Proceedings of the 15th International Academic MindTrek Conference: Envisioning Future Media Environments*, ACM, 9–15.

16. Linda De Valk, Tilde Bekker, and Berry Eggen. 2013. Leaving room for improvisation: towards a design approach for open-ended play. *Proceedings of the 12th International Conference on Interaction Design and Children*, ACM, 92–101.

17. Rocío Fernández-Ballesteros, María Dolores Zamarrón, and Miguel Ángel Ruiz. 2001. The contribution of socio-demographic and psychosocial factors to life satisfaction. *Ageing and Society* 21, 01: 25–43.

18. A Fluegelman. 1976. *The New Games Book*. The Headlands Press, Dolphin Books/Doubleday, Garden, City, New York.

19. Mathias Fuchs, Sonia Fizek, Paolo Ruffino, and Niklas Schrape (eds.). 2014. *Rethinking Gamification*.

20. William Gaver. 2002. *Designing for homo ludens, still*.

21. William Gaver, John Bowers, Andrew Boucher, et al. 2004. The drift table: designing for ludic engagement. *CHI'04 extended abstracts on Human factors in computing systems*, ACM, 885–900.

22. Erving Goffman. 1961. Fun in Games. In *Encounters: Two studies in the sociology of interaction*. Bobbs-Merrill, Oxford, UK, 15 – 81.

23. Charles Goodwin. 1979. The Interactive Construction of a Sentence in Natural Conversation. In *Everyday Language: Studies in Ethnomethodology*, G. Psathas (ed.). Irvington Publishers, New York, NY, USA, 97–121.

24. Charles Goodwin. 2000. Action and embodiment within situated human interaction. *Journal of Pragmatics* 32, 10: 1489–1522. http://doi.org/10.1016/S0378-2166(99)00096-X

25. Amanda Lundvik Gyllensten, Gunvor Gard, Eva Salford, and Charlotte Ekdahl. 1999. Interaction between patient and physiotherapist: a qualitative study reflecting the physiotherapist's perspective. *Physiotherapy Research International* 4, 2: 89–109.

26. Marc Hassenzahl. 2003. The thing and I: understanding the relationship between user and product. In *Funology*. Springer, 31–42.

27. John Heritage. 2008. Conversation Analysis as Social Theory. In *The New Blackwell Companion to Social Theory*, Bryan S. Turner (ed.). Wiley-Blackwell, Oxford, UK, 300–320. Retrieved January 10, 2016 from http://onlinelibrary.wiley.com/doi/10.1002/9781444304992.ch15/summary

28. Michael A. Horan and John E. Clague. 1999. Injury in the aging: recovery and rehabilitation. *British Medical Bulletin* 55, 4: 895–909.

29. Arti Hurria. 2011. Embracing the complexity of comorbidity. *Journal of Clinical Oncology* 29, 32: 4217–4218.

30. Mattias Jacobsson. 2009. Play, belief and stories about robots: A case study of a pleo blogging community. *RO-MAN 2009, 18th International Symposium on Robot and Human Interactive Communication*, IEEE Computer Society.

31. Jonna Koivisto and Juho Hamari. 2014. Demographic differences in perceived benefits from gamification. *Computers in Human Behavior* 35: 179–188.

32. Hannu Korhonen, Markus Montola, and Juha Arrasvuori. 2009. Understanding playful user experience through digital games. *International Conference on Designing Pleasurable Products and Interfaces*, 274–285.

33. James R. Lackner and Paul DiZio. 2005. Vestibular, proprioceptive, and haptic contributions to spatial orientation. *Annu. Rev. Psychol.* 56: 115–147.

34. Andreas Lieberoth, Max Møller, and Andreea Catalina Marin. 2015. Deep and Shallow Gamification in Marketing: Thin Evidence and the Forgotten. *Engaging Consumers through Branded Entertainment and Convergent Media*: 110.

35. David López Recio. 2013. Designing a new model for the elderly in an assisted living facility: Iterative programming of the NAO robot within a multidisciplinary design environment. Retrieved from http://www.diva-portal.org/smash/get/diva2:826536/FULLTEXT02

36. David López Recio, Elena Márquez Segura, Luis Márquez Segura, and Annika Waern. 2013. The NAO models for the elderly. *Proceedings of the 8th ACM/IEEE international conference on Human-robot interaction*, IEEE Press, 187–188.

37. N. Marquardt and S. Greenberg. 2015. *Proxemic Interactions: From Theory to Practice*. Morgan & Claypool Publishers, San Rafael, CA, USA. Retrieved March 24, 2016 from http://ieeexplore.ieee.org/xpl/articleDetails.jsp?arnumber=7056253

38. Elena Márquez Segura. 2016. *Embodied core mechanics. Designing for movement-based co-located play*. Ph.D. Dissertation. Uppsala University, Uppsala, Sweden.

39. Elena Márquez Segura, Luis Márquez Segura, and Clara Lopez Torres. 2012. PhySeEar Moving yourself to shine and sound in geriatric physiotherapy interventions. *Pervasive Computing Technologies for Healthcare (PervasiveHealth), 2012 6th International Conference on*, IEEE, 179–182.

40. Elena Márquez Segura, Annika Waern, Jin Moen, and Carolina Johansson. 2013. The design space of body games: technological, physical, and social design. *Proceedings of the SIGCHI conference on Human Factors in computing systems*, ACM, 3365–3374.

41. Jane McGonigal. 2011. *Reality is broken: Why games make us better and how they can change the world*. Penguin.

42. David R. Michael and Sandra L. Chen. 2005. *Serious games: Games that educate, train, and inform*. Muska & Lipman/Premier-Trade.

43. Florian'Floyd' Mueller, Martin R. Gibbs, and Frank Vetere. 2009. Design influence on social play in distributed exertion games. *Proceedings of the SIGCHI Conference on Human Factors in Computing Systems*, ACM, 1539–1548.

44. Florian Mueller, Martin R. Gibbs, and Frank Vetere. 2010. Towards understanding how to design for social play in exertion games. *Personal and Ubiquitous Computing* 14, 5: 417–424.

45. Scott Nicholson. 2012. A user-centered theoretical framework for meaningful gamification. Retrieved from scottnicholson.com/pubs/meaningfulframework.pdf

46. Scott Nicholson. 2015. A recipe for meaningful gamification. In *Gamification in education and business*. Springer, 1–20.

47. Jay F. Piccirillo, Anna Vlahiotis, Laurel B. Barrett, Kellie L. Flood, Edward L. Spitznagel, and Ewout W. Steyerberg. 2008. The changing prevalence of comorbidity across the age spectrum. *Critical reviews in oncology/hematology* 67, 2: 124–132.

48. Jenny Preece, Helen Sharp, and Yvonne Rogers. 2015. *Interaction Design-beyond human-computer interaction*. John Wiley & Sons.

49. Niels Quinten. 2015. The Design of Physical Rehabilitation Games: The Physical Ambient Abstract Minimalist Game Style.

50. Felix Raczkowski. 214AD. Making points the point: Towards a history of ideas of gamification. In *Rethinking gamification*. 141–160.

51. Barbara Resnick. 1999. Motivation to perform activities of daily living in the institutionalized older adult: can a leopard change its spots? *Journal of Advanced Nursing* 29, 4: 792–799. http://doi.org/10.1046/j.1365-2648.1999.00954.x

52. Richard M. Ryan and Edward L. Deci. 2000. Self-determination theory and the facilitation of intrinsic motivation, social development, and well-being. *American psychologist* 55, 1: 68.

53. Elizabeth B.-N. Sanders. 2002. From user-centered to participatory design approaches. *Design and the social sciences: Making connections*: 1–8.

54. Emanuel A. Schegloff. 1987. Analyzing Single Episodes of Interaction: An Exercise in Conversation Analysis. *Social Psychology Quarterly* 50, 2: 101–114. http://doi.org/10.2307/2786745

55. Katie Seaborn and Deborah I. Fels. 2015. Gamification in theory and action: A survey. *International Journal of Human-Computer Studies* 74: 14–31.

56. Miguel Sicart. 2014. *Play Matters*. MIT Press.

57. Stephanie A. Studenski. 1999. Principles of Rehabilitation in Older Patients. In *Principles of Geriatric Medicine and Gerontology* (4th edition),

William R. Hazzard, John P. Blass and Walter H. Ettinger (eds.). McGraw-Hill, New York, NY, USA.

58. Stephanie A. Studenski, Pamela Duncan, and J. H. Maino. 1999. Principles of rehabilitation in older patients. *Principles of geriatric medicine and gerontology. 4th ed. New York: Mc-Graw-Hill*: 435–55.

59. Sherry Turkle, Will Taggart, Cory D. Kidd, and Olivia Dasté. 2006. Relational artifacts with children and elders: the complexities of cybercompanionship. *Connection Science* 18, 4: 347–361. http://doi.org/10.1080/09540090600868912

60. Linda de Valk, Tilde Bekker, and Berry Eggen. 2013. Leaving Room for Improvisation: Towards a Design Approach for Open-ended Play. *Proceedings of the 12th International Conference on Interaction Design and Children*, ACM, 92–101. http://doi.org/10.1145/2485760.2485771

61. K. Wada and T. Shibata. 2006. Living with Seal Robots in a Care House - Evaluations of Social and Physiological Influences. *2006 IEEE/RSJ International Conference on Intelligent Robots and Systems*, 4940–4945. http://doi.org/10.1109/IROS.2006.282455

62. Annika Waern. 2009. Information technology in pervasive games. In *Pervasive games: Theory and design*. Morgan Kaufmann, 163–174.

63. Douglas Wilson. 2011. Brutally unfair tactics totally ok now: On self-effacing games and unachievements. *Game Studies* 11, 1.

64. Jerome A. Yesavage, T. L. Brink, Terence L. Rose, et al. 1983. Development and validation of a geriatric depression screening scale: a preliminary report. *Journal of psychiatric research* 17, 1: 37–49.

65. Eric Zimmerman. 2004. *Narrative, interactivity, play, and games: Four naughty concepts in need of discipline*. MIT Press, Cambridge, MA.

66. John Zimmerman, Jodi Forlizzi, and Shelley Evenson. 2007. Research Through Design As a Method for Interaction Design Research in HCI. *Proceedings of the SIGCHI Conference on Human Factors in Computing Systems*, ACM, 493–502. http://doi.org/10.1145/1240624.1240704

67. John Zimmerman, Erik Stolterman, and Jodi Forlizzi. 2010. An Analysis and Critique of Research Through Design: Towards a Formalization of a Research Approach. *Proceedings of the 8th ACM Conference on Designing Interactive Systems*, ACM, 310–319. http://doi.org/10.1145/1858171.1858228

Squeezy Green Balls: Promoting Environmental Awareness through Playful Interactions

Charlene Jennett[1], Ioanna Iacovides[2], Anna L. Cox[1], Anastasia Vikhanova[3], Emily Weigold[3], Layla Mostaghimi[3], Geraint Jones[1], James Jenkins[4], Sarah Gallacher[5], Yvonne Rogers[1]

[1]UCL Interaction Centre
University College London,
London, UK
charlene.jennett, anna.cox,
geraint.jones, y.rogers
@ucl.ac.uk

[2]Institute of Educational
Technology, The Open
University, Milton Keynes, UK
jo.iacovides@open.ac.uk

[3]UCL Psychology Department,
University College London,
London, UK
emily.weigold.14,
anastasia.vikhanova.14,
layla.mostaghimi.14 @ucl.ac.uk

[4]Department of Biological & Environmental
Sciences, University of Hertfordshire,
Hertfordshire, UK
j.o.jenkins@herts.ac.uk

[5]Intel Labs Europe,
ICRI-Cities, 1 Sekforde Street,
London, UK
sarah.m.gallacher@intel.com

ABSTRACT
We need collective action to tackle global warming. However, research shows that people switch off from being concerned about the environment because they are often too busy, or fail to appreciate their ability to make a difference. An alternative approach is to run campaigns that are able to engage large numbers of people and engender feelings of concern and empowerment. This could then kick-start a range of pro-environmental habits. We present the development and evaluation of a playful installation that aimed to attract attention, and stimulate discussion about environmental issues amongst university staff and students. The first prototype was shown to successfully attract people to engage and interact with the installation. The second prototype was deployed in-the-wild, over the course of a week. We evaluated the extent to which the installation was successful at attracting attention, and in encouraging people to interact with it, to reflect on their habits and to discuss environmental issues with others. We found the Green Ball Kiosk was a fun way to raise discussions about green issues, to encourage the adoption of new environmentally friendly behaviours and to prompt people to maintain existing ones. We suggest that interactive installations such as this can be effective at promoting awareness and generating a 'social buzz' about environmental topics when exhibited as a temporary installation.

Author Keywords
Physical computing; environmental awareness; public spaces; engagement; play.

ACM Classification Keywords
H.5.m. Information interfaces and presentation (e.g., HCI): Miscellaneous.

INTRODUCTION
Climate change is becoming an increasingly urgent issue with the Intergovernmental Panel on Climate Change calling for global actions to mitigate the problem [21]. Within the European Union, a target has been set to reduce greenhouse gases by at least 20% by 2020 [10] and it is clear that meeting this will require major changes across all levels of society. In the UK, it is estimated that lifestyle changes contribute up to a 30% reduction in greenhouse gases [41] but questions remain about how to effectively persuade people to change their environmentally related behaviours on a collective level.

Though individuals are increasingly aware of climate change, they do not necessarily view it as a priority [26; 30]. It has even been suggested that concern about the issue has actually been diminishing within the UK [31]. A study in the UK [27] suggests that degree-level educated people may be more willing to take environmentally-motivated principled actions (e.g. buy recycled paper products, avoid the purchase of over-packaged products), but are less willing than others to take relatively small actions that may be of a personal inconvenience (e.g. turn the TV off overnight, switch off lights in unused rooms).

What are effective methods that can be used at scale? Information campaigns have been criticized for being ineffective at leading to large scale change due to levels of apathy [33] and for making people feel helpless through relying on fear inducing content [32]. There is also a problem of information overload, as people are constantly bombarded with a variety of messages and advertisements. Similarly, in universities and other organisations, it is easy for an environmental poster to get lost among the many other posters on display.

Previous approaches by the HCI community to raise awareness of environmental issues have attempted to encourage individual behaviour change via interactive systems that track personal information [e.g. tracking household energy usage; 12; 24; 35; 38] and through mechanisms such as gamification [e.g. using competition as a way to reduce energy usage between households; 19; 13]. While these approaches may provide useful tools for those who already want to track and reduce their energy usage, they do not attempt to create initial engagement in, and reduce levels of apathy towards, environmental issues.

Brynjarsdóttir et al. [3] argue that another approach would be to design persuasive technologies that act as a catalyst for reflection on environmental issues. We suggest that the deployment of playful physical computing technologies [e.g. 15] might be a good candidate for this. By locating interactions in a public space, such interventions would be available to large numbers of people, and could be designed in a way as to prompt discussion on the wide range of sustainable actions that individuals can make within their day-to-day lives. In this paper we describe the development of a playful physical computing installation, the Green Ball Kiosk that was deployed in a university setting. We explore whether a playful technology could engage university students and staff to reflect on and re-engage with environmental issues that could lead them to taking small actions. We present the results of our evaluations of the intervention, discussing the extent to which it was successful at getting people to engage with the serious topic of climate change and environmentally friendly living.

RELATED WORK

Information campaigns
Froehlich [14] notes that one of the most widely used approaches to promote changes in environmental behaviours is to communicate information to the public through mediums such as leaflets, websites or social media. However, campaigns based on the "information deficit model" have been criticised as being ineffective for bringing about wide spread change due to the different ways in which problems can be framed, and for not considering the wider social contexts in which attitudes and behaviours are formed [33]. Framing is not just important in terms of whether actions are presented as avoiding loss or leading to a gain but also in terms of how relevant communication is on a personal level and the emotive quality of a message [39]. Fear appeals are particularly

prevalent in climate change campaigns as a way of attracting attention to the issue [32]. However, fear can run the risk of desensitising individuals [32] or potentially lead to helplessness [25].

In the context of behaviour change, one strategy which may be particularly effective is to use "binding communication" which consists of pairing a persuasive message with a low-cost preparatory act [34]. Parant et al. [34] asked groups of participants to watch a climate change film about the effects of melting glaciers (the persuasive message) and found that those in the binding communication condition, who were asked to write down at least three actions they could take to reduce their carbon footprint, were much more likely to engage in behaviour follow-through than those in the control condition. They also suggest that binding communication with action helped to reduce the fear appeal of the film, resulting in a positive effect on attitude.

When it comes to raising awareness about climate change and promoting the adoption of sustainable behaviours, it is clear that how information is presented and interpreted is likely to impact on the success of the approach.

Tracking energy usage
In addition to attempting to change behaviours through providing information, technology can provide a more interactive way to engage people. Environmental sustainability has become an increasingly popular topic in HCI, where behaviour change interventions have ranged from embedding twinkly lights in the floor to lead people towards taking the stairs (as opposed to the lift) [36], to using ambient light displays to illustrate electricity usage in the work place [23]. The use of sensing and tracking technologies has been particularly prevalent [3], with a focus on developing systems that collect and visualise information e.g. about energy consumption [12; 24; 35; 38]. The aim of these systems is to deliver data in such a way that users become more aware of their activities and try to reduce their environmental impact [14].

For example, Costanza et al. [5] present FigureEnergy, an interactive visualization tool that allows users to annotate graphical representations in order to make sense of their own electricity consumption. However, research involving tracking systems often involves people who are already eco-friendly [14] and has been criticised for supporting a narrow set of prescribed behaviours, normally around reducing energy consumption [3].

Game based approaches
In an effort to motivate users, other tracking approaches have included game based elements. Froehlich [13] notes that commercial applications such as the Nest smart thermostat are implementing gamification techniques, e.g. awarding users with virtual leaves for setting energy efficient temperature levels. Video games have also been developed where sensor data is used as input to gameplay. For instance, Gustafsson et al. [19] present an energy conservation game for mobile phones that collects data

from an electric power meter in the home. The game involves missions and competition between households to encourage users to behave in particular ways (e.g. switching off lights, unplugging appliances when not in use). However, while the game was found to be engaging, the evaluation also indicated that players may have been more concerned about how to win than they were about energy conservation in the long term.

In addition, digital games have also been used to prompt reflection and discussion through delivering forms of "serious experience" that resonate with players [e.g. 20; 28]. With respect to the topic of climate change, games have focused on raising general awareness and educating players [e.g. 4, 6, 9, 11, 16]. For instance, Fate of the World [11] is a serious game, based on real climatic models, where the player has to set policy initiatives over a 200-year period and watch the social and environmental impact of their decisions play out. Another example is EnerCities [9], where players are challenged to develop an eco-friendly city while maintaining a budget and dealing with issues such as pollution and energy shortages.

However, with respect to serious games, debriefing (i.e. discussing gameplay content and the player experience) has been shown to be integral to a game's effectiveness [7; 8] but this is not usually supported outside formal educational contexts such as classrooms. Furthermore, many freely available online games focus on higher level issues (such as making policy and planning decisions) and have not been subject to a rigorous evaluation [22]. Thus it is unclear how far they engage people in reflecting on the issue of climate change or supporting individuals in considering direct ways to reduce their environmental impact.

Playful physical computing

Whilst each of the approaches described above aims to engage people in behaviour change, it is less clear how any of them might reach those who are apathetic about environmentally friendly behaviours. In order to increase the level of engagement with such issues we need to consider how to design interventions that can reach these people and that can encourage reflection and discussion around a wider range of environmentally friendly actions.

A promising method for engaging a diversity of people is through locating physical computing installations within public spaces. Through the 'honeypot effect', participants can be attracted by others who are interacting with a technology [2]. These approaches can be designed to be deliberately playful in order to stimulate curiosity and intrigue. For instance, the VoxBox [18] was designed as a playful physical questionnaire that comprises a range of physical input controls, such as sliders, dials, buttons, and spinners; real-time visualisations of collected data; and a tube which delivers a ball to the users when they have completed the survey. The installation has been used to gather opinions from members of the public at a number of events such as the Tour de France in London, and has been shown to incentivise participation through the range of playful and tangible interactions it offers [18]. A similar system, Sens-Us [17] has also been used in a quite different context, to gather data for the UK census (which can include questions about more sensitive topics).

Physical computing technologies have also been used to deliver playful interactions within the workplace. Gallacher et al. [15] developed the Mood Squeezer, consisting of a squeeze kiosk of differently coloured balls, which invites users to squeeze according to their mood. Through creating opportunities for people to socialise, the intervention was able to create a more positive and open work environment, providing employees with opportunities for self-reflection and to engage in conversation with others.

These examples indicate the potential of using tangible systems for attracting attention and encouraging discussion through locating playful interventions in public work spaces. In the following sections, we describe how we adapted an existing intervention and deployed it in order to attract the attention of students and staff, to get people talking about environmental issues and encourage them to reflect on their own behaviours.

OUR STUDY

In this paper we describe the development of a physical computing installation. We include a description of the interactive element – prototype #1, the Green SqueezeBox; the evaluation of this intervention at two events in order to determine whether it is effective at attracting the attention of attendees; the further development of the installation to create prototype #2, the Green Ball Kiosk; and the in-the-wild evaluation of this installation when it was deployed in a university setting for a week.

PROTOTYPE #1: DESIGN OF THE GREEN SQUEEZE BOX

Given the success of the Mood Squeezer study [15], we decided to adapt the original design by changing the colours of the six balls to different shades of green, varying from light to dark (see Figure 1).

Figure 1. Images of the input and output devices; Green SqueezeBox and a laptop showing the webpage

The Green SqueezeBox used Force Sensitive Resistors (FSRs) in each ball to detect squeezes, which were monitored and transmitted to a backend server by an Ardunio Uno (an electronics prototyping platform). Squeeze data was processed and logged by the backend server and relayed in real time to a web-page. See Figure 2 for an example of the webpage output.

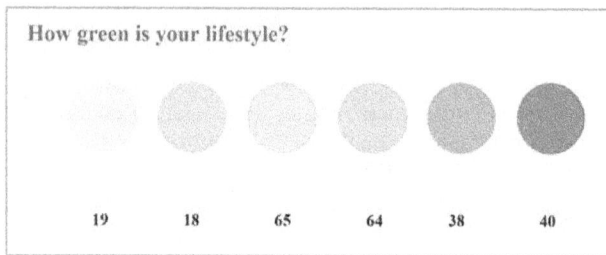

Figure 2. Green SqueezeBox webpage, showing the number of squeezes for each ball

EVALUATING THE GREEN SQUEEZE BOX AT EVENTS

We evaluated the Green SqueezeBox at two events: 1) a Welcome Fair targeted at new university students, and 2) a Professional Services Conference targeted at university staff.

The UCL Welcome Fair is a two-day event that took place on Saturday 3rd October and Sunday 4th October 2015. Over 250 clubs and societies booked stalls so that they could get an opportunity to interact with university students and distribute promotional materials. It is one of the UK's biggest welcome fairs. The Green SqueezeBox was utilized as part of the UCL Green Stand.

The UCL Professional Services Conference is a one-day event that took place on Tuesday 2nd February 2016. The conference celebrates the achievements of university staff across departments. It provides an opportunity for hundreds of colleagues to come together to hear about exciting collaborative and cross-faculty projects. During the one-hour lunch break, conference attendees were invited to visit various stands in the "Market Place" and to network with others. The Green Squeezebox was utilized as part of the UCL Psychology and Language Sciences (PALS) stand.

At both events, the goal was to attract interest to the stand, by providing something physical that visitors would want to interact with. The staff running the stand asked visitors to squeeze the balls in response to the question "How green is your lifestyle?" The question was deliberately opened-ended to encourage conversations between the staff running the stand and those attending the events. The six green balls represented a Likert scale response, varying from "not green" (left balls) to "fairly green" (middle balls) to "very green" (right balls).

Results: On Day 1 of the Welcome Fair, 168 squeezes were recorded and on Day 2, 77 squeezes were recorded (see Table 1). The middle balls (representing "fairly green") were squeezed the most often; in particular, the 4th green ball was squeezed by 33.3% of visitors on Day 1 and 33.8% visitors on Day 2. For the Professional Services Conference, 25 squeezes were recorded. The middle balls (representing "fairly green") were squeezed the most often; in particular, the 3rd green ball was squeezed by 40% of visitors.

In a follow-up interview, the staff member running the Welcome Fair stand said that he found the Green Squeezebox to be a good way of attracting students and it was different to the typical approach of just handing out leaflets. He described how some students approached to ask "what is that?" and how others were intrigued by seeing them squeeze one of the balls. He was then able to lever this initial interest to engage them in a casual conversation about green issues. For example, some students talked about how they used to be greener before they came to London. For many it was their first time living away from home, buying things for themselves. They talked about food choices, e.g. buying cheaper products rather than buying free-range. They also talked about travel choices and pollution. Many viewed themselves as in the middle – they were a bit "green", but they could do better.

	Not green		Fairly green		Very green	
WF 1	10	7	51	56	28	16
N=168	*6%*	*4.2%*	*30.4%*	*33.3%*	*16.7%*	*9.5%*
WF 2	6	10	16	26	14	5
N=77	*7.8%*	*13%*	*20.8%*	*33.8%*	*18.2%*	*6.5%*
PSC	0	1	10	7	5	2
N=25	*0%*	*4%*	*40%*	*28%*	*20%*	*8%*

Table 1. Squeeze data for the Welcome Fair (WF) and the Professional Services Conference (PSC). Red font indicates modal response.

The person running the PALS stand at the Professional Services Conference agreed that the Green SqueezeBox was a good way of attracting visitors to the stand. He described how he was able to make jokes with visitors, asking them "Do you want to squeeze my balls?" This helped to lighten the mood and get visitors to open up about what being green means to them, and the things they do (and don't do) that were green. For example, staff talked about green issues such as recycling, switching off lights, wearing a jumper instead of turning up the heating, shopping for organic food, cycling/walking to work. Some staff felt that they still used too much paper in their office and more effort was needed before they were truly "paperless". Packaging waste was another concern.

Overall, our study of the Green Squeezebox in the different university settings indicates it was effective as a novel way of attracting students and staff, and prompting conversations about green issues. The use of the different shades of green to represent a Likert scale response was understood by visitors and did not require further explanation. Next we decided to explore how the Green Squeezebox could be utilized as a stand-alone installation, as part of a study exploring the effectiveness of different environmental messages.

PROTOTYPE #2: DESIGN OF THE GREEN BALL KIOSK

In the Green Ball Kiosk we combined the Green Squeezebox with different environmental messages. Our goal was to create an engaging installation that would attract passers-by and encourage discussion about green issues without being co-located with a manned stall [similar to 15].

As this was to act as a stand-alone intervention, we decided to combine the Kiosk with a TV screen and handout which suggested different actions for mitigating climate change. These actions were combined in a persuasive message [33] which framed information in a negative, neutral or positive way. In line with previous literature [37, 39, 40], we chose images and messages that would be relevant to our participants (staff and students living in London, UK). See Table 2 for the five messages and related questions. The six green balls represented a Likert scale response, varying from "never" (left balls) to "sometimes" (middle balls) to "always" (right balls).

Day	Message	Question
1	Producing, harvesting, transporting, and packaging food produces tons of carbon dioxide... One thing you can do to save energy and mitigate climate change is to avoid wasting food.	How often do you plan ahead to avoid throwing away leftovers or expired food?
2	Big Ben could be underwater by 2100... One thing you can do to save energy and mitigate climate change is to put a layer on, not the heating.	How often do you put another layer on when it gets colder, instead of putting on the heating?
3	Spend more time watching Netflix and less time cooking in the kitchen... One thing you can do to save energy and mitigate climate change is to put a lid on your pots.	How often do you put a lid on your pots when you are cooking?
4	As early as 2030, mosquitoes could bring deadly tropical diseases to the UK... One thing you can do to save energy and mitigate climate change is to take the stairs, not the lift.	How often do you choose to take the stairs, not the lift?
5	Increase your chances for romance... One thing you can do to save energy and mitigate climate change is to switch off lights and appliances.	How often do you switch off lights and appliances that you don't need?

Table 2. Green Ball Kiosk messages and questions

Message 1 (with a picture of trucks transporting food) was designed to be neutral. Messages 2 (with an image of Big Ben going underwater) and 4 (with an image of a mosquito) were designed to be negative and uncomfortable. Messages 3 (with a picture a living room with Netflix on TV) and 5 (with a photo of a candle lit dinner) were designed to be more positive and playful. In line with research on "serious experience" [20; 29] and climate change communication [32] we predicted that negative messages would be more memorable than positive ones. The messages were piloted with 19 participants to ensure the emotive tone was in line with the way they had been framed.

In contrast to our previous use of the Green Squeezebox at events, we did not share the live webpage alongside the Green Ball Kiosk. The main reason for this was practical: in our study we planned to use a large LCD screen to show the message and question for the day as part of a PowerPoint slideshow, and we were unable to include a webpage as part of this slideshow.

RESEARCH QUESTIONS

We aimed to answer five research questions:

1. How does interaction with the Green Ball Kiosk vary over the course of five days?
2. Does the positive/negative phrasing of a message affect how memorable it is?
3. What factors motivate people to interact with the Green Ball Kiosk?
4. Is the Green Ball Kiosk successful in encouraging environmental discussions?
5. Does interacting with the Green Ball Kiosk lead to attitude/behaviour change?

METHODOLOGY

The Green Ball Kiosk was set up outside of the UCL Psychology common room (see Figure 2) for five consecutive days in early 2016. It was a typical week of the year, where staff are in offices and students attend lectures. We chose to set up the Kiosk outside of the common room because it is a social hub used by Psychology students and staff alike, and we wanted a location where people would naturally chat to others and be sociable.

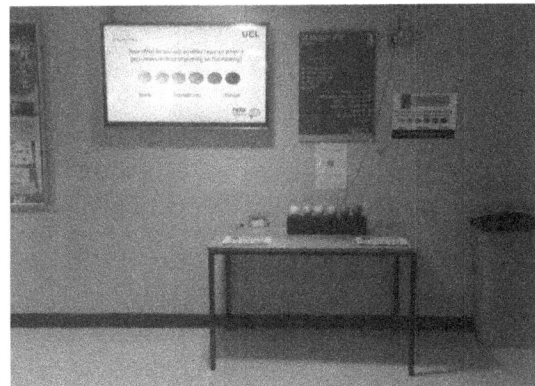

Figure 2. Green Ball Kiosk setup

On each day, a new environmental message was displayed, followed by a question was presented on the LCD screen which invited passers-by to squeeze a ball in response. Several nearby posters repeated the information displayed on the LCD screen. The posters also displayed a QR code and a web link, allowing visitors to find out more information presented in the messages if they wished.

An email was sent to all staff and students on the first day of the installation, informing them about the arrival of the Green Ball Kiosk, that it would be present for one week only, and that messages and questions would change each day. No further emails were sent that week.

The following week, an online survey was sent to all staff and students. The survey consisted of 13 questions asking respondents about their interactions with the Kiosk, whether they could recall any of the messages and/or questions, and whether they would be willing to take part in follow-up interviews. To incentivize participation, we announced that 2 survey participants and 2 interview participants would be selected at random to receive £10 gift vouchers.

We collected 41 survey responses. Regarding occupation, 35 (85%) were students (24 undergraduates, 4 postgraduates, 7 doctoral) and 6 (15%) were staff (5 support staff, 1 'other'). Regarding gender, 28 were female (68%) and 13 were male (32%). Their ages ranged from 18 to 53 years, mean age = 24.5 years (SD = 8.5).

Out of the 41 survey respondents, 15 (37%) agreed to take part in follow-up interviews. Regarding occupation, 12 were students and 3 were staff. Regarding gender, 11 were female and 4 were male. Their ages ranged from 19 to 53 years, mean age = 24.5 years (SD = 10.3).

The interviews were exploratory and semi-structured, though a script was used to ensure consistency between the three researchers who carried out the interviews. Each interview was audio recorded and lasted approximately 15 minutes. The resulting transcripts were coded and analysed using thematic analysis [1].

RESULTS

Below we present our results structured around our 5 research questions.

1. How does interaction with the Green Ball Kiosk vary over the course of five days?

Table 3 shows squeeze data for each day. The most active day was Monday (241 squeezes). The number of squeezes declines for subsequent days, Wednesday and Friday recording half as many squeezes (125 and 120 respectively). The data is generally skewed towards positive answers (i.e. "sometimes" or "always").

Analysis of the time of day for squeezes reveals that the frequency of squeezes is normally distributed, centering around lunchtime (13:00 to 14:00). There is a second peak around 16:00, possibly indicating a popular time that staff and students take a coffee break.

	Never		Sometimes		Always	
Day 1	29	18	27	52	64	51
N=241	*12%*	*7.5*	*11.2*	*21.6*	*26.6*	*21.2*
Day 2	23	9	17	29	39	40
N=157	*14.6%*	*5.7*	*10.8*	*18.5*	*24.8*	*25.5*
Day 3	12	22	28	33	11	19
N=125	*9.6%*	*17.6*	*22.4*	*26.4*	*8.8*	*15.2*
Day 4	18	19	43	45	35	20
N=180	*10%*	*10.6*	*23.9*	*25*	*19.4*	*11.1*
Day 5	12	9	16	17	46	20
N=120	*10%*	*7.5*	*13.3*	*14.2*	*38.3*	*16.7*

Table 3. Squeeze Data for the Green Ball Kiosk. Red font indicates modal response.

Survey Data

Survey respondents were asked to recall which days they saw the Green Ball Kiosk and which days they squeezed one (or more) of the balls. Generally, when they saw the Green Ball Kiosk they also squeezed one or more of the balls; see Figure 3. On average, they interacted with the Kiosk for 2 days out of the 5. Only 9 survey respondents (22%) saw the Kiosk on all 5 days, and only 3 respondents (7.3%) squeezed one (or more) of the balls on all 5 days.

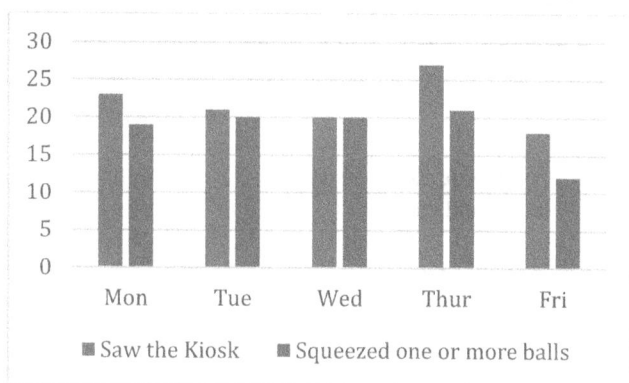

Figure 3. Number of survey respondents that saw the Green Ball Kiosk each day and squeezed one or more balls

Survey respondents were also asked about the QR code and web link provided on the poster. Only 18 respondents (44%) answered 'yes' that they noticed these links, and only 1 person answered 'yes' that they used it to find more information about the topic. The majority of participants (39 out of 41; 95%) answered 'no' that they did not check the link; 1 participant answered 'not sure'.

2. Does the positive/negative phrasing of a message affect how memorable it is?

Survey respondents were asked to recall as much as possible about the Green Kiosk messages. We tallied the number of respondents who recalled the message for each day, then considering the number of respondents that had seen the message that day we calculated percentages. On average, 49% of respondents who saw the Kiosk on any given day were able to recall the message. As can be seen in Figure 4, uncomfortable messages (Tuesday 48%, Thursday 44%) and comfortable messages (Wednesday 55%, Friday 50%) were recalled at roughly the same rate.

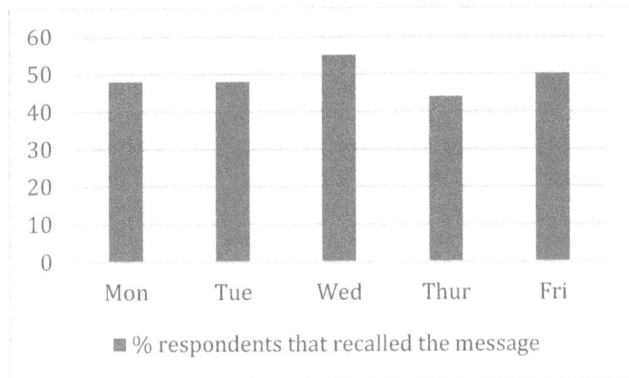

Figure 4. Percentage of survey respondents that recalled the Green Ball Kiosk message each day

In our follow-up interviews, participants suggested possible reasons for why they remembered some messages but not others. One theme was **personal relevance** (n=6). P1 said *"The lift one made me a bit uncomfortable as I'd literally just got out of the lift"*. Similarly, P8 said *"I think some of the questions were more personal to me like the one about taking the stairs rather than the lift"*. P2 remembered turning off electrical appliances and lights, using the stairs instead of the lift: *"probably because these are things I do"*.

Another theme was **learning new information** (n=3). P6 remembered putting lids on pans: *"I thought it was interesting because although I don't regularly cook I would never think to put a cover over the pan to conserve heat"*. P5 remembered wearing a jumper instead of turning the heating up: *"...realizing that I put the heating on for the whole day, and it's not really good for the environment"*. Conversely, P4 suggested that the messages weren't memorable because *"it wasn't new information, I wasn't learning anything, just reinforcing what I knew."*

Emotional reactions were mentioned only in relation to uncomfortable messages (n=2). P8 said *"There was one with the Big Ben underwater [...] I remember thinking oh that's a bit depressing"*. Similarly, P15 said *"some of the messages were quite shocking like the flooding one. I thought it was quite strange because on the outlook it looks like a really fun experiment that's going to make me feel happy but then it's actually just a bit scary and depressing."*

There was also a tendency to recall the **questions** rather than the full message. One possible explanation is that interactions with the Green Ball Kiosk were short, so people focused more on the information they needed to respond to. P4 explains *"I read questions quite quickly, I wouldn't actually stay there to think about it at all"*. **Font size** could be another factor. P5 said *"I know I saw the question because it was in a big font, and it was quite eye-catchy. I'm not sure how big the messages were..."* Similarly, P2 said *"I think the message could have been bigger and more obvious, maybe like in big writing on the wall behind the Kiosk, because clearly it didn't grab enough of my attention!"*

Additionally, five participants recalled a question that wasn't present in the Green Ball Kiosk: *"I'm assuming that there was something about cycling... probably recycling too"* (P15); *"Bottled water... if you use the reusable plastic container for water. Oh, it wasn't there?"* (P3).

3. What factors motivate people to interact with the Green Ball Kiosk?

In our follow-up interviews, participants discussed how they felt motivated to interact with the Green Ball Kiosk for multiple reasons. They also explained why they did not interact with the installation on some days.

Novelty and fun

Nine participants mentioned that they were first drawn to interact with the installation because it was novel, fun and made them curious: *"I was curious, it seemed like a fun thing to do"* (P13); *"I thought it looked different and I was like ooh intrigued"* (P7); *"I thought it looked very appealing, they're like squidgy"* (P15). Interactivity was an important aspect: *"it wasn't something that people saw every day, so they noticed something that was interactive"* (P3); *"it seems a lot more interactive and engaging than other things like that I've seen"* (P15). Two participants also mentioned that they liked the playful innuendo around being invited to 'squeeze balls': *"I thought the name was quite funny and it did make me and my friends laugh!"* (P12).

However, some participants (n=3) questioned how long this novelty effect would last: *"I think five days was enough, if it was longer, people might get bored and irritated by it, like they might see it as something negative or even just feel lazy"* (P2); *"I expect you would see use of it to drop off as time goes on, I don't think it would work as a permanent installation"* (P1). Similarly, P12 said that she became less interested over time: *"Because it was not new, I knew what it was about, no curiosity anymore"*.

Helping research

Seven participants said that they took part because they wanted to help with research. Some felt that they were helping environmental research, while others were more concerned with helping colleagues in their department: *"it's good to help with any research that might improve environment stuff"* (P1); *"I knew it was an experiment and I could help people with the data collection"* (P5).

Convenience

Participants liked that it was quick and convenient to take part (n=8): *"short and sweet"* (P9); *"it was cool, just a novelty thing that didn't take too much time and effort"* (P1); *"I liked that it was easy, convenient and very well placed, so people could casually wander off and it's a good way of getting people to think about their behaviour"* (P11). Two participants described getting into the habit of squeezing as they walked past: *"Became slightly habitual - like come out of the lift, squeeze the ball, get a coffee in the common room"* (P1); *"Each day I had in the back of my mind that I should do it. And well also it's in between my office and the toilet, so I sort of had to pass by it every day"* (P4).

Despite it being quick to engage with, a common reason that participants gave for not interacting with the Green Ball Kiosk was lack of time (n=5): *"I think I was in a rush one day"* (P5); *"Probably because that time I was rushing for a class"* (P10); *"I'd be running into the cafe for lunch break before I had a double lecture"* (P14). Also two participants said they did not pass by the Green Ball Kiosk on some days: *"because I did not go to the cafe, and I had other things to do on different floors"* (P11); *"Well I was not in the building the other times"* (P13).

Honey-pot effect

One participant described how she became intrigued when she saw another person interacting with the Green Ball Kiosk: *"I saw [name] squeeze one of the green balls and I thought oh that looks really interesting so I squeezed one and encouraged my friend to do the same so we could compare our results"* (P6). Another participant described how there was a 'buzz' of activity round the installation: *"I definitely saw a lot of people buzzing around it especially in the first couple of days. People generally looked quite curious and giggly about squeezing the balls"* (P1).

Two participants described visiting the Kiosk as part of a group: *"my group of friends was expecting the balls to be there so once they were there it was definitely a feeling of excitement"* (P9); *"there were several of us and we stood in front of it trying to figure out what it is"* (P12). On the other hand, sometimes group dynamics discouraged interaction: *"it was quite crowded at certain points of the day and it made it quite difficult to approach it"* (P15).

4. Is the Green Ball Kiosk successful in encouraging environmental discussions?

20 out of 41 survey respondents (48.8%) answered 'yes' that they spoke to others about their experience with the Green Ball Kiosk. In our follow-up interviews, we were able to find out more about the conversations that people had. P10 told her friends about it in case they were interested in taking part: *"I just said something like the Kiosk is very interesting, it will be there for a week so maybe if you're free you can pop by and have a go"*.

Other conversations focused more on the environment. P2 said that she talked about the message she had read about

that day: *"we were talking about how we cooked over the weekend so we wouldn't be cooking for these days now"*. P13 said that she talked about that day's Kiosk message and also other pro-environmental actions that she knew of: *"I did have a conversation later about taking the stairs if it's only going up or down one floor. Also using ceramic mugs instead of Styrofoam plastic cups, things like printer control measures for people that use too much paper"*.

P9 describes how her experience with the Kiosk prompted her to engage her flat mate in a conversation they had had previously, but this time she was more opening to listening to her flat mate's advice: *"I did discuss one which was about food wastage with my flat mate who always tried to make me reduce the amount of food I waste, and the fact that it came from my university and not one of the people I live with sort of made the message even stronger"*.

Four of our interview participants said that they did not talk about the installation with others. P2 explains that she did not think about it much afterwards: *"I didn't discuss it and [the messages] haven't really been on my mind, no."* P14 thought that her friends would not find environmental discussions interesting: *"that would have been a really boring conversation"*.

5. Does interacting with the Green Ball Kiosk lead to attitude/behaviour change?

Out of the 41 survey respondents, 18 (43.9%) answered 'yes' that their attitudes had been influenced because of the Kiosk, and 28 (68.3%) answered 'yes' that they had changed their behaviours due to the Kiosk. In our follow-up interviews, we were able to find out more about the changes that participants experienced, and factors that motivated these changes.

Reflection

The Green Ball Kiosk encouraged participants to reflect on their habits and whether they align with their values. Two participants described squeezing a light green ball (i.e. "never") and feeling like they could be doing more: *"I squeezed the ball and I was thinking it shouldn't be the one that I'm squeezing so it did make me think I should be doing better for the environment"* (P7); *"I didn't like it because I couldn't press one of the darker balls, so I try to use the stairs more. But only going down the stairs. Still too lazy to use them going up!"* (P2)

Similarly, three participants describe changing their behaviour after reading one of the messages: *"I've recently adjusted the heating based on the temperature. I was like oh I am cold now, I could do the jacket, instead of increasing the heating"* (P5); *"some of the questions were more personal to me, like the one about taking the stairs rather than the lift, I do actually take the stairs more now, it's had a bit of an impact"* (P8); *"it's actually stayed in my mind, I actually took the stairs"* (P10).

New knowledge

One participant describes how he learned something new from the Kiosk: *"I'm sure now if I see my flat mates cooking I'll bring up that point to them because I didn't realise you know how much impact just a little cover on your pan can have so I guess it has impacted my knowledge about pro-environmental behaviour somewhat"* (P6).

Good reminder
For other participants, the Green Ball Kiosk served as a useful reminder of pro-environmental behaviours they already wanted to engage in. P1 describes how it reminded him to take the stairs: *"They did remind me to take the stairs down rather than the lift! You kind of just go on autopilot and before you know it you're in a lift going down [...] that statement kind of reminded me to turn off that autopilot."*

Four participants said that were already engaged in these pro-environmental behaviours, but they still felt that it was good to get a reminder: *"I didn't change my behaviour probably because I'm already doing those things. But it reminded me of the things, so I think that was good"* (P3); *"I haven't really changed my behaviour really, no. But maybe made me aware and made me think more about it."* (P4); *"I already took reasonable actions for those such as turning the lights off [...] I sort of do that thing generally but yeah it's nice as a little reminder"* (P8); *"I guess it just reminded me of the need to be environmentally friendly"* (P13).

The Kiosk also served as a reminder of environmental issues in general. P15 recalls a message that wasn't present (recycling) and that she's thinking about volunteering for charity work: *"There was one message I think about recycling [...] I was thinking of volunteering for a good cause and I guess it got me thinking that I could volunteer for an environmental charity"* (P15).

No change
Several participants (n=5) stated that the Green Ball Kiosk made no difference to their behaviour because they were already 'green'. P15 said *"I was already aware of the environmental issues, so it just reinforced my beliefs rather than changed them."* In addition, there appeared to be a risk of 'green information overload'. P14 said *"I've always been an environmentally friendly person anyway so squeezing a ball to say that I know about recycling didn't necessarily change anything [...] the media and everything bombards you of images of like, polar bears falling off icebergs and people telling you to turn your lights off and, you know, the Kiosk didn't really offer anything that I haven't really heard or seen before. I mean every time I leave a room I think, 'oh I better turn that light off' but that's just me being habitual rather than me being reminded of squeezing the ball".*

Another issue was that participants did not remember all of the messages: *"Though in the moment I did pay attention to them, they didn't stick with me"* (P1); *"it was like a whole week ago, it's not really fresh in my mind anymore"* (P2). P11 viewed the Kiosk as just a 'mild distraction': *"I think all of them made me think about things I wouldn't normally*

think about at that particular time of day, but not in a way that would make me want to change my behaviour, just more that I hadn't evaluated those things before [...] if anything I think it was an extremely mild and possibly pleasant distraction, it was something to think about whilst I came out of the lift".

Suggested Improvements
Participants made several suggestions for improvements and further developments to the installation. Seven participants mentioned that they would like to receive feedback when they squeezed the ball. P3 suggests *"when people answer question it would give you some results and statistics, you responded like 83% of your peers and stuff like that. And that's also a very important thing, because I think there are studies showing that if you are convinced that other people do something you are more likely to do it, because of social pressure."* A few participants said that competition between people, or even buildings, would support their willingness to be 'greener' and engage in environmentally friendly behaviour.

Three participants suggested the need for various events and talks to make people discuss environmentally friendly issues. They did not feel that the Kiosk encouraged them to discuss the messages and felt that the experience could be improved by having the Kiosk be manned: *"someone could stay next to the station [...] and encourage people to squeeze or read the messages"* (P5). Four participants also mentioned that the Kiosk should be monitored in order for people *"not to get crazy squeezing the balls"* (P12) and to analyse peoples' reactions more efficiently.

Two participants suggested the use of the same technology as a Kiosk, but making it more portable and usable for a longer period of time: *"like a website or something that asks you a few questions to determine how green you were this day or week"* (P5). Five participants also mentioned that a poster would not be as effective, as it is not interactive enough and people just ignore the information.

DISCUSSION
A challenge facing society is that many people have trouble linking their current behaviour to long term consequences [26] or that they rapidly become desensitized to the issue [32]. A further challenge is that some people may be less willing than others to take relatively small actions that may be of a personal inconvenience (e.g. turn the TV off overnight, switch off lights in unused rooms) [27]. How can we try to overcome these barriers to behavioural change? Our study has shown that using a playful physical installation that is striking can help to prompt discussion about and reinvigorate engagement with environmental issues.

In particular, as a stand-alone installation, the Green Ball Kiosk was successful at attracting attention, where participation rates remained high throughout the week. Participants felt motivated to interact with the Green Ball Kiosk because it appeared that the novelty of the device drew them in, followed by discovering that it only required them squeezing one. However, this low level of commitment was enough to provoke reflection on the issues that were represented.

As our survey results revealed, the Green Ball Kiosk was successful at encouraging nearly 50% of participants to have conversations about the environment. As a result of their experience, nearly half also said that they changed their attitudes, while many said that they changed their behaviour, by becoming more environmentally friendly. This finding suggests that this kind of simple playful device, that requires minimal effort, may be able to trigger a big increase in environmental awareness. Part of the effect can also be down to how it encourages the 'honeypot effect', where people take part in groups and a 'social buzz' is created around the installation (cf Gallacher et al. [15]).

Another factor that appeared to make an impact was the way the messages were worded. While our hypothesis, that uncomfortable messages would be more memorable than comfortable messages was not supported, this did not seem to matter. It may have been that the overall positivity of the approach reduced any discomfort the uncomfortable messages elicited [similar to 34]. Either way, our findings not only showed evidence that the installation prompted conversations about environmental behaviours, but that it was also able to positively influence attitudes and behaviour change. In addition, these findings illustrate how playful physical computing approaches [e.g. 17] have the potential to engage people in serious topics through creating opportunities for people to reflect on their habits and how they align with their values [25].

In general, the squeeze data tended to skew towards positive answers (i.e. "sometimes" or "always"). This suggests that many participants were already engaged in pro-environmental behaviours where rather than teaching new knowledge, the Kiosk served as a useful reminder of good behaviour. For those that had become complacent, it reminded them to re-engage with environmentally friendly behaviours, e.g. taking the stairs instead of the lift.

An alternative explanation is that the social context may have influenced responses, where people wanted to appear more environmentally friendly than they might be in practice. However, the fact that some participants 'recalled' messages that were not there suggests that the installation was able to activate existing schemas of related environmental concepts. Therefore, for ideas that are already ingrained into the minds of the general public, then this kind of public kiosk can help to reinforce particular behaviours and to prompt discussions with others.

In sum, we propose that our installation was successful because it looked fun, it was quick to engage with, and it provided physical interaction. Novelty is important, so we recommend that similar installations should be of a short-term nature (e.g. one week only) so that they stand out.

Limitations
One of the main limitations of the study is that our findings our dependent on self-report data. In the case of behaviour change, it would be useful to consider more objective measurements and carrying out pre and post-intervention assessments. It is also possible that participants were more likely to take part if they had a strong interest in the environment. However, using raffle prizes to motivate completion of the questionnaire and interviews, we were able to recruit 3 interviewees who only interacted with the Kiosk once, suggesting that our sample did not only consist of people who were highly engaged.

Another limitation is that none of the participants were motivated enough to scan the QR codes and read further information. It appears that the 'short and sweet' nature of the installation was a double edged sword: participants took part because it was quick and easy, but they soon forgot about the messages and did not think about them very deeply. Added to the fact that a small number of participants considered the humorous tone of the intervention to be at odds with the serious nature of the subject matter, there are questions yet to be answered around the extent to which this approach is likely to resonate with individuals [29] and lead to long term changes.

Further Research
It is vital to develop engaging ways of presenting 'old' information so that it does not feel repetitive to people. Future work needs to include different ways of leveraging social effects to encourage more behaviour change. We are planning to organise a Green Squeezy Environmental Awareness Week where we host a competition between different buildings, and participants can see how those from other departments squeezed. Future work could also explore deploying the installation with a larger, potentially more diverse audience, outside of the university setting.

CONCLUSION
Overall the Green Ball Kiosk was a fun way to remind university staff and students about green issues, to encourage them to take small actions to help the environment and to prompt them to maintain existing habits. We suggest that interactive installations displayed as a temporary exhibit can be effective at drawing people in again to environmental messages in a playful way, and in doing so can generate a 'social buzz' about environmental topics. In sum, as well as serving as a reminder of good practices, it helps people to tap into their existing knowledge, to think about environmental issues in general and encourages the adoption of new behaviours.

ACKNOWLEDGMENTS
Special thanks to all the participants and to the following people for their help and support: Alex Green, John Draper, Harriet Lilley, Louise Gaynor, George Joseph, Dave Hetherington, Morgan Douglas, Neil Daeche.

REFERENCES

1. Virginia Braun and Victoria Clarke. 2006. Using thematic analysis in psychology. *Qualitative Research in Psychology, 3 (2)*, 77-101.

2. Harry Brignull and Yvonne Rogers. 2003. Enticing people to interact with large public displays in public spaces. Proceedings of INTERACT 2003, 17-24.

3. Hronn Brynjarsdottir, Maria Håkansson, James Pierce, Eric Baumer, Carl DiSalvo and Phoebe Sengers. 2012. Sustainably Unpersuaded: How Persuasion Narrows our Vision of Sustainability. *Proceedings of the SIGCHI Conference on Human Factors in Computing Systems,* 947-956. http://dx.doi.org/10.1145/2207676.2208539

4. Clim'Way. Accessed July 29, 2016: http://climway.cap-sciences.net/us/index.php

5. Enrico Costanza, Sarvapali D. Ramchurn and Nicholas R. Jennings. 2012. Understanding domestic energy consumption through interactive visualisation: a field study. *Proceedings of the 2012 ACM Conference on Ubiquitous Computing,* UbiComp '12, 216-225. http://dx.doi.org/10.1145/2370216.2370251

6. Paul Coulton, Rachel Jacobs, Dan Burnett, Adrian Gradinar, Matt Watkins and Candice Howarth. 2014. Designing data driven persuasive games to address wicked problems such as climate change. In *Proceedings of the 18th International Academic MindTrek Conference: Media Business, Management, Content & Services*, 185-191. doi>10.1145/2676467.2676487

7. David Crookall. 2010. Serious games, debriefing, and simulation/gaming as a discipline. *Simulation & Gaming*, 41, 898-920. http://dx.doi.org/10.1177/1046878110390784

8. Sara de Freitas and Martin Oliver. 2006. How can exploratory learning with games and simulations within the curriculum be most effectively evaluated? *Computers and Education, Special Issue on Gaming*, 46, 249-264. http://dx.doi.org/10.1016/j.compedu.2005.11.007

9. Enercities. Accessed July 29, 2016: http://www.enercities.eu/

10. European Commission. 2011. A *roadmap for moving to a competitive low carbon economy in 2050*. Article No. 52011DC112. Retrieved April 16, 2016 from http://eur-lex.europa.eu/legal-content/EN/ALL/?uri=CELEX:52011DC0112

11. Fate of the World. 2011. Soothsayer Games.

12. Geraldine Fitzpatrick and Greg Smith. 2009. Technology-enabled feedback on domestic energy consumption: articulating a set of design concerns. *Pervasive Computing* 8, 1(2009), 37-44.

    http://dx.doi.org/10.1109/MPRV.2009.17

13. Jon Froehlich. 2015. Gamifying green: gamification and environmental sustainability. In *The Gameful World*, Steffen P. Walz and Sebastian Deterding (eds.). MIT Press Cambridge, CA, USA, 563–596.

14. Jon Froehlich, Leah Findlater and James Landay. 2010. The design of eco-feedback technology. Proceedings of the SIGCHI Conference on Human Factors in Computing Systems, CHI '10, 1999-2008. http://dx.doi.org/10.1145/1753326.1753629

15. Sarah Gallacher, Jenny O'Connor, Jon Bird, Yvonne Rogers, Licia Capra, Daniel Harrison and Paul Marshall. 2015. Mood squeezer: lightening up the workplace through playful and lightweight interactions. *Proceedings of the 18th ACM Conference on Computer Supported Cooperative Work & Social Computing,* CSCW '15 , 891-902. http://dx.doi.org/10.1145/2675133.2675170

16. Luciano Gamberini, Nicola Corradi, Luca Zamboni, Michela Perotti, Camilla Cadenazzi, Stefano Mandressi, Giulio Jacucci, Giovanni Tusa, Ann Spagnolli, Christoffer Bjokskog, Marja Salo and Pirkka Aman. Saving is fun: designing a persuasive game for power conservation. *Proceedings of the 8th International Conference on Advances in Computer Entertainment Technology,* ACE'11, Article no. 16. http://dx.doi.org/10.1145/2071423.2071443

17. Connie Golsteijn, Sarah Gallacher, Licia Capra and Yvonne Rogers. 2016. Sens-Us: Designing innovative civic technology for the public good. To appear in *Proceedings of the Conference on Designing Interactive Systems*, DIS 2016. http://dx.doi.org/10.1145/2901790.2901877

18. Connie Golsteijn, Sarah Gallacher, Lisa Koeman, Lorna Wall, Sami Andberg, Yvonne Rogers and Licia Capra. 2015. VoxBox: A tangible machine that gathers opinions from the public at events. *Proceedings of the Ninth International Conference on Tangible, Embedded, and Embodied Interaction*, TEI '15, 201-208. http://dx.doi.org/10.1145/2677199.2680588

19. Anton Gustafsson, Cecilia Katzeff and Magnus Bang. 2009. Evaluation of a pervasive game for domestic energy engagement among teenagers. *Computers in Entertainment*, 7(4), Article No. 54. http://dx.doi.org/10.1145/1658866.1658873

20. Ioanna Iacovides and Anna L. Cox. 2015. Moving beyond fun: Evaluating serious experience in digital games. *Proceedings of the 33rd Annual ACM Conference on Human Factors in Computing Systems,* CHI'15, 2245-2254. http://dx.doi.org/10.1145/2702123.2702204

21. Intergovernmental Panel on Climate Change. 2014. *Climate Change 2014 Synthesis Report: Summary for Policymakers*. Retrieved July 29, 2016 from http://www.ipcc.ch/pdf/assessment-report/ar5/wg1/WGIAR5_SPM_brochure_en.pdf

22. Korina Katsaliaki and Navonil Mustafee. 2010. A survey of serious games on sustainable development, *Proceedings of the Winter Simulation Conference*, 1528-1540. http://dx.doi.org/10.1109/WSC.2012.6465182

23. Cecilia Katzeff, Loove Broms, Li Jönsson, Ulrika Westholm and Minna Räsänen. 2013. Exploring sustainable practices in workplace settings through visualizing electricity consumption. ACM Transactions on Computer-Human Interaction (TOCHI), 20(5):1–22. http://dx.doi.org/10.1145/2501526

24. Tanyoung Kim, Hwajung Hong and Brian Magerko. 2009. Coralog: use-aware visualization connecting human micro-activities to environmental change. *CHI '14 Extended Abstracts on Human Factors in Computing Systems*, 4303-4308. http://dx.doi.org/10.1145/1520340.1520657

25. Bran Knowles, Lynne Blair, Stuart Walker, Paul Coulton, Lisa Thomas and Louise Mullagh. 2014. Patterns of persuasion for sustainability. *Proceedings of the 2014 conference on Designing interactive systems*, DIS '14, 1035-1044. http://dx.doi.org/10.1145/2598510.2598536

26. Irene Lorenzoni, Sophie Nicholson-Cole, Lorraine Whitmarsh. 2007. Barriers perceived to engaging with climate change among the UK public and their policy implications. *Global Environmental Change*, 17, 445–459. http://dx.doi.org/10.1016/j.gloenvcha.2007.01.004

27. Peter Lynn and Simonetta Longhi. 2011. Environmental attitudes and behaviour: who cares about climate change? In: McFall, Stephanie L and Garrington, Chris, (eds.) *Understanding Society: early findings from the first wave of the UK's household longitudinal study*. ISER, Colchester, p. 7.

28. Tim Marsh. 2015. Slow serious games, interactions and play: Designing for positive and serious experience and reflection. *Entertainment Computing*, 14, 45–53 http://dx.doi.org/10.1016/j.entcom.2015.10.001

29. Tim Marsh and Brigid Costello. 2013. Lingering serious experience as trigger to raise awareness, encourage reflection and change behavior. *Proceedings of the 8th international conference on Persuasive Technology*, PERSUASIVE'13, 116-124. http://dx.doi.org/10.1007/978-3-642-37157-8_15

30. Pew Research Center. 2014. *Thirteen years of the public's top priorities*. Retrieved July 29, 2016 from http://www.people-press.org/interactive/top-priorities/

31. Nick Pidgeon. 2012. Climate change risk perception and communication: addressing a critical moment? *Risk Analysis*, 32(6), 951-956. http://dx.doi.org/10.1111/j.1539-6924.2012.01856.x

32. Saffron O'Neill and Sophie Nicholson-Cole. 2009. 'Fear won't do it': Promoting positive engagement with climate change through visual and iconic representations. *Science Communication,* 30(3), 355-379. http://dx.doi.org/10.1177/1075547008329201

33. Susan Owens and Louise Driffill. 2008. How to change attitudes and behaviours in the context of energy. *Energy Policy*, 36, 4412 - 4418.

34. Aymeric Parant, Alexandre Pascual, Milena Jugel, Myriam Kerroume, Marie-Line Felonneau and Nicolas Gueguen. 2016. Raising students awareness to climate change: An illustration with binding communication. *Environment and Behavior*. Online before Print. http://dx.doi.org/10.1177/0013916516629191

35. Petromil Petkov, Felix Köbler, Marcus Foth, and Helmut Krcmar. 2011. Motivating domestic energy conservation through comparative, community-based feedback in mobile and social media. *Proceedings of the 5th International Conference on Communities and Technologies*, C&T '11, 21-30. http://dx.doi.org/10.1145/2103354.2103358

36. Yvonne Rogers, William Hazlewood, Paul Marshall, Nick Dalton and Susana Hertrich. 2010. Ambient influence: can twinkly lights lure and abstract representations trigger behavioral change? *Proceedings of the 12th ACM international conference on Ubiquitous computing,* UbiComp '10, 261-270 . http://dx.doi.org/10.1145/1864349.1864372

37. Leila Scannell and Robert Gifford. 2013. Personally relevant climate change: the role of place attachment and local versus global message framing. *Engagement. Environment and Behavior, 45(1),* 60-85.

38. Tobias Schwartz, Sebastian Denef, Gunnar Stevens, Leonardo Ramirez and Volker Wulf. 2013. Cultivating energy literacy: results from a longitudinal living lab study of a home energy management system. *Proceedings of the SIGCHI Conference on Human Factors in Computing Systems,* CHI'13, 1193-1202 http://dx.doi.org/10.1145/2470654.2466154

39. Alexa Spence and Nick Pidgeon. 2010. Framing and communicating climate change: The effects of distance and outcome frame manipulations. *Global Environmental Change,* 20, 656–667. http://dx.doi.org/10.1016/j.gloenvcha.2010.07.002

40. Alexa Spence, Wouter Poortinga, Catherine Butler and Nick Pidgeon. 2011. Perceptions of climate change and willingness to save energy related to flood experience. *Nature Climate Change, 1(1),* 46- 49.

41. UK Energy Research Centre, 2009. *Making the transition to a secure and low-carbon energy system: synthesis report*, UKERC Energy 2050 Project. UKERC, UK. Retrieved July 29, 2016 from http://www.ukerc.ac.uk/publications/energy-2050-synthesis-report.html

Designing Play to Support Hospitalized Children

Ruth Sancho Huerga, Jennifer Lade, Florian 'Floyd' Mueller
Exertion Games Lab
RMIT University
Melbourne, Australia
{ruth, jennifer, floyd}@@exertiongameslab.org

ABSTRACT

Play as a form of complementary care is increasingly considered to support sick children with their hospital experience. Prior work around digital play is mostly focusing on distracting the child from the hospital experience. In contrast, we propose an alternative approach. We seek to engage the children with the hospital experience through play that utilizes the hospital environment and materials. We present findings from two hospital play workshops with 23 children with severe diseases. Based on these findings, we derive four lenses (reframing, ownership, privilege, body) through which researchers can examine these types of play experiences. We then use these lenses to articulate six practical strategies to aid designers in developing play that supports hospitalized children. Ultimately, our work extends our understanding of how play can be designed as a form of complementary care.

Author Keywords

Children; hospital; play; games; complementary care

ACM Classification Keywords

H.5.2. [Information Interfaces and Presentation]: User Interfaces - Miscellaneous.

INTRODUCTION

In this paper, we explore how play can be used to support the hospital experience for children with severe diseases such as cancer. While hospitals have the ability to offer specialized medical treatment to support children's recovery, the hospital experience itself can be very stressful: hospitalized children often experience anxiety and fear which can intensify their illness and negatively interfere with medical treatment [15]. In response, complementary care programs have emerged that aim to support patients from both a medical and experiential perspective. Complementary care is aimed at enhancing the

wellbeing of patients and often used in conjunction with specialized medical treatments such as chemotherapy. Examples of complementary care are meditation, acupuncture, and music therapy. Research has shown that these approaches can support a patient's wellbeing and speed up the recovery process [36].

A range of complementary care approaches exist specifically for children: for example the humor therapy program, made famous by the Clown Doctors [9], and play therapy, renowned due to the work by Axline [3]. We believe emerging interactive technology can offer further benefits to complement these programs. For example, practitioners are introducing commercial game consoles into the children's ward while researchers are designing games specifically for children in hospital [38]. We find that these approaches predominantly work with the assumption that they can help the children by distracting them from the hospital environment [16, 38, 47, 49]; an extreme example of this approach is the work using head-mounted displays to detach patients from the hospital environment through alternative virtual realities [11]. We propose a complementary approach through which we aim to engage the children directly with the hospital environment to support them in experiencing the hospital not as a space of diseases and illness that contrasts their prior playful life outside, but rather as another place for play that is part of life. Our work aims to carve out a niche between purely entertaining games and toys that distract children from the hospital experience and serious games that educate children about their hospital experience. The games we present are related to both but are not explicitly either of the two. Instead, we aim to focus on the hospital experience itself and propose games that are integrated into the hospital experience. As such, our approach takes a holistic play perspective that engages the children's families, the hospital staff and environment and is conducted in a play workshop format. The play workshop includes craft activities (as suggested by prior work [32]) in which children and their families create play elements out of hospital materials in order to interact with two novel play systems we developed specifically for the play workshops. We present the results of two play workshops from two different hospitals with 23 inpatient children.

We note that although parents and hospital staff reported these play workshops impacted positively on the children's wellbeing and their recovery process, it is difficult to assess to what extent (as with all complementary care approaches [7]). Nevertheless, we provide results from the workshops that suggest the children embraced the opportunity to play; were able to reframe their relationship with the hospital; showed signs of claiming ownership of their hospital experience; were able to experience a sense of privilege; and also experienced their body as a resource for play rather than just a source of illness.

We use these results to derive four lenses through which researchers can examine play for hospitalized children. We then draw on the lenses to articulate six practical strategies based on our craft knowledge to aid designers developing play for hospitalized children. Our work makes the following contributions: it presents a novel holistic play approach of aiming to engage children with their hospital experience. It exemplifies this approach through the design of two novel play systems. We also present four lenses for analysis for researchers and six practical strategies for designers interested in our approach. Our work is useful for game designers and complementary care staff interested in utilizing digital play for young patients. Furthermore, game design practitioners interested in applying their existing play and game systems to support children in hospital could also benefit from the work. Ultimately, our work extends our understanding of how play can be designed as a form of complementary care.

RELATED WORK: CHILDREN, HEALTH AND PLAY
Prior work has contributed significantly to our understanding of how to design interactive systems for children [8, 19, 28]. However, existing works do not offer much guidance on how to design for sick children suffering from severe diseases such as cancer. A notable exception is the work by Hoiseth et al. [17] who find that health games should elevate the "child as expert"; a strategy we applied in our play workshops. Contrasting our approach, this prior work highlights the importance of distracting the child; however, their focus is on utilizing games to support specific treatments, rather than considering the specific intricacies of the hospital experience.

We also learned from emerging complementary care programs in children's hospitals [15, 16], especially those who aim to assist children in realizing the potential of play. We are inspired by Stagnitti and Copper who say: "If a child is admitted into hospital it is important that their play is not left behind [...] Play facilitates comprehension, enhances coping and provides emotional support for children undergoing medical procedures" [44]. Past research has demonstrated that play can be effective when it comes to managing a child's anxiety resulting from the hospital environment [25]. An example is the "ChildLife Program" [27] that aims to help children cope with the emotional and bodily changes caused by medical procedures. Other complementary care programs such as

"Payasospital" [37] and "Therapeutic Clowns" [25] aim to support children through the use of magic, props, and physical play. Research around these programs suggest that clowns performing with children who require surgery can be effective for managing their anxiety [44]. The most well-known of these programs is the "Clown Doctors" [9] who bring laughter to hospital wards [25]. The Clown Doctors inspired our work, including the use of crafting activities to inform play, building on work in art therapy [7]. According to Rubin [40], hospitalized children can find crafting an opportunity to organize their thinking and to express and cope with the powerful feelings experienced during illness. Furthermore, our play workshop facilitator (first author and artist, dancer and actor with a certification in laughter therapy), with prior experience developing therapeutic projects with children, performed as a clown character during the play workshops.

Interactive technology, children and health
We know from previous research that children respond well to digital technology [38] and engagement with new media provides them with an enjoyable platform to engage their imagination and creativity [6]. In particular, hospitalized children can find emotional and physical relief through virtual play [13]. Consequently, organizations such as "Juegaterapia" [20] supply digital game consoles to sick children to alleviate their anxiety. Supplying children with commercial digital games can successfully distract them from painful treatment procedures [41]. While these and related approaches [47, 49] focus on using play to distract the child from the hospital experience, we in contrast are aiming to engage the child with the hospital experience.

A few researchers have designed games specifically for sick children, such as "Operation IBD" [46], "Bronkie the Bronchiasaurus" [24] and "Glucoboy" [42]. These games aim to help children understand their treatments [46]. Such games can be useful as part of complementary care [43, 46]. While these games focus on supporting specific treatments, our work aims to support children's overall hospital experience, regardless of an individual treatment. Prior research has also begun to support patients by going beyond screen-based interactions. Watters et al. combined digital media with physical objects for emotional recovery treatment [46]. "Elements" [48] is an interactive tabletop that can be placed in hospitals to support rehabilitation. The biofeedback "BrightHearts Project" [23] uses heart rate and aesthetic visuals to help children manage the anxiety experienced during medical procedures. Similarly, Bucolo et al. designed a tangible device to alleviate anxiety in paediatric burns patients [5]. "Magic Land" [38] combines toys with a smart table to help children overcome feelings of anxiety. These works suggest that combining digital and physical elements can be beneficial to therapeutic play [38], and in response, we also drew on both physical and digital play activities.

In sum, prior works highlight the potential of play to support sick children's experiences in hospital. However, most projects did not consider digital play or only utilized play as a distraction method. There appears to be a lack of knowledge on how digital play can support children with their hospital experience. In response, we ask: how do we design digital play to support sick children's hospital experience?

THE PLAY WORKSHOPS

Fig. 1. The workshops' crafting activities (faces obscured)

We conducted our play workshop (which ran for two days, lasting three hours each) twice in two different hospitals. With the support of the hospital administration, we used flyers to invite all 7-13 year-old inpatients and their families. Before the play workshops, the children and parents were given a short questionnaire (i.e. when they are available, how many family members will join, etc.) and asked for consent as per our ethic guidelines. Supporting the social environment is key for children in hospital [30], we therefore were eager to include the children's families. This contrasts prior work that has focused on stand-alone applications (such as [47, 49]), however, we see our work not replacing, but complementing existing work around children's solo play in hospital. We recruited 23 children and 17 family members (40 participants in total). The children were between 7 and 12 years (average: 8 years). The children's health conditions were considered severe, with the most common disease being cancer (13), but the children also had different traumatic injuries (6) as well as neurological diseases (4). There were a total of 6 families, with 10 parents, 1 grandmother, 1 aunt and 5 siblings present. All participants were encouraged to engage equally in all activities.

The games were designed through an iterative process, where early mock-ups where shown to children, game designers and researchers to elicit informal feedback. We did not have access to the sick children at this stage, so this is a limitation of our work, however, one of the authors has worked with sick children before so we drew on this

expertise. We presented the games at the beginning and asked participants to explore them before starting the crafting activities. This initial step included a short tutorial that explained the key elements of the games. We then showed the crafting materials that allowed participants to create their own play elements. Once these play elements were created we incorporated them into the games. We did not explicitly encourage the children to interact with each other; however, we observed the children and family members starting to create and play together without being prompted. Also, the children and parents helped each other during the activities. Conducting play workshops in hospital means considering that treatment always takes priority, hence attendance was rather fluid: two children had to cancel at the last minute as they were too unwell, and three children had to leave early to undergo medical treatment.

Doctor Giggles

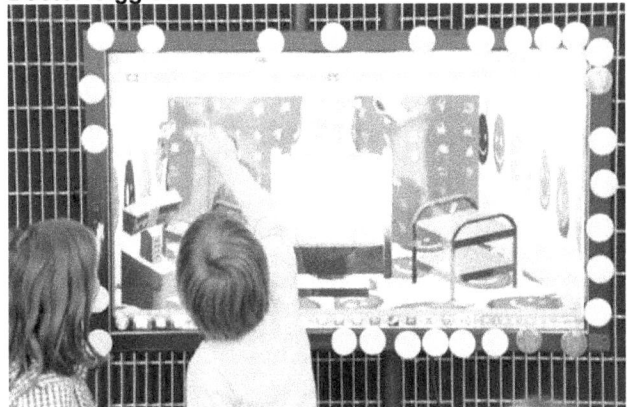

Fig. 2. Doctor Giggles

On the first day, the focus was on "Doctor Giggles", which we designed inspired by laughter therapy (Fig. 2). Playing with Doctor Giggles means to first create the play characters (drawing on the benefits of crafting for wellbeing [32]): we invited our participants to create play characters out of X-ray sheets to be used in the digital play system (Fig. 1, 3 & 4). Instead of simply providing the players with a ready-to-go game, we aimed to support their autonomy in play [39] by allowing them to create their own personal play characters. Thus enabling the children to engage with hospital material frequently encountered as part of their hospital stay through the act of crafting (instead of seeing such material only being handled by doctors).

Fig. 3. X-ray play characters

We brought along some examples we had created to inspire our participants and guide them in how they could use the X-ray shading as a way to create texture for their play characters. The children were invited to use their own X-ray sheets of their bodies, which the staff helped provide. Then the X-ray play characters were quickly scanned in order to use them in the digital play system. We used a large touch screen accommodating multiple children to support social play (Fig. 4&5).

In the game, the children see a virtual operating room, with a doctor character (whose face is one of the doctors from the hospital), dressed in children pajamas who jumps up and down and around the room. In the virtual operating room there are various items the children know from their hospital experience, such as a hospital bed, an operating light, a table with medical tools and an X-ray machine.

Fig. 4. Setup in the hospital

The aim is to make the doctor laugh as much as possible (indicated through visuals and sound). To achieve this, the children are invited to freely explore the elements in the operating room: for example, if the child operates the X-ray machine, the X-ray play characters appear on the screen, bouncing around. If the child touches those characters, they make silly sounds. The children can then use the characters to perform a medical procedure with the tools from the table, however, the tools have different functions in the game than they normally would: the scissors are made from feathers that tickle rather than cut; the syringe is a magic wand that changes the color of the room's lighting; and the gas mask releases perfume to relax the doctor. The typical functions of the hospital tools are swapped such that the real patient (the sick child) is in control, while the virtual doctor is the patient that needs to be treated with laughter.

X-Safari

The second day was similar to the first, but the focus was on creating play characters in the form of hand puppets to play "X-Safari". The play characters were made out of familiar medical equipment, for example medical gloves, cotton, bandages, band-aids, and medical tape. Again, we brought along examples to inspire the children. "X-Safari" uses an augmented glove system we developed (Fig. 6). The children put it on and then slide their gloved hand into their characters to play. Although glove control input devices already exist, our system is novel as it is low-cost and allows for a "dressing up" with the play characters; the benefits of being able to "dress up" technology with personalized material has previously been highlighted [21].

Fig. 5. The virtual world of X-Safari

Our intention was to enable the children to perceive that they are crafting (at least a part of) their play interface controller out of hospital material (Fig. 7). Using the glove, the children are able to control a horse avatar in a 3D virtual fantasy world.

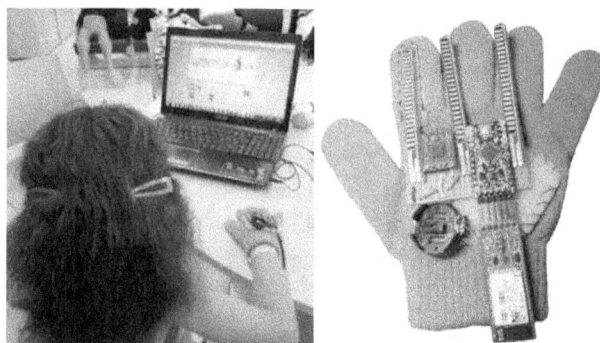

Fig. 6. The play characters are put on top of this augmented glove to control the game

The virtual world is connected to an Arduino that controls the avatar's movement, direction and speed based on sensors attached to the inner glove's fingers and palm. When the children move their fingers in a walking fashion the avatar moves. By tilting their hand, the child controls the direction the horse moves. The children use their virtual horse to explore a fantasy island through their play characters; on this fantasy island the children can explore and encounter additional characters that are the play characters created the day before.

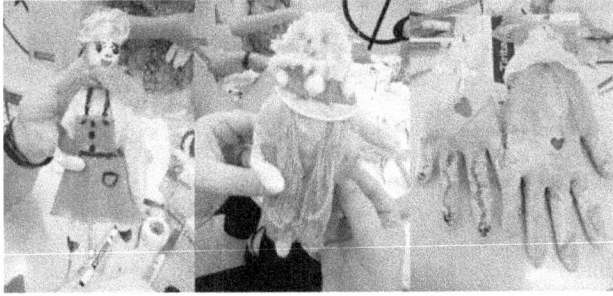

Fig. 7. Glove play characters

Data collection & analysis
We invited all participants for an interview right after the play workshops and were able to speak to 17 children and five parents (the other children and parents had to leave for treatments and prior commitments). We also captured pictures of the play characters the children made (Fig. 7), documented the play workshops by camera and video and took notes. The first author analyzed the data using an open coding process [35] to derive analytic categories. We were interested in how our designed play engaged children with their hospital environment and if, and how, it supported their hospital experience. The resulting categories were discussed with two senior researchers and then further refined using affinity diagrams to identify key groupings. We then described these groupings in an elaborative language to facilitate "thinking through writing" [35], which allowed us to derive four lenses we describe below. This approach is similar to other qualitative work in hospitals [45], providing intermediate-level knowledge [18] that is aimed to be readily applicable to designers.

RESULTS
Overall, the participants appeared to enjoy the play workshops with the hospital materials. The children answered they felt creative, happy, "normal" again and had fun (referring to their "normal" life outside the hospital). An indicator the play workshops were a success could be that many asked unprompted if they could take part in more. We now articulate key groupings of our results to describe how the play workshops engaged the children with their hospital environment and in consequence supported their hospital experience.

Engagement in and with the hospital environment
Laughter in the hospital
An important element of each play workshop and a key factor to their success was the laughter that emerged out of them. There were many jokes told and much laughter present throughout the play workshops. The children told jokes to each other about their play characters and their digital play experiences accompanied by the laughing sounds from Doctor Giggles. Similarly, X-Safari elicited much laughter through the horse-movement control. The parents commented positively that they enjoyed seeing their

children laugh, which contrasted their usual hospital experience: firstly, laughing is inexplicitly inhibited due to the "mute" hospital environment and secondly due to the seriousness of the health context. Parents described it as a relief that they were able to laugh with their children *in* the hospital environment, and also laugh with them *at* the hospital environment and the associated medical tools that were now encountered from their "*silly*" side in the virtual world.

Children decorated their hospital environment with the play characters
After the conclusion of the workshops, the children continued to engage with the play characters they had created to decorate their hospital environment. They set them up in their rooms and attached them to their hospital equipment such as their wheelchairs and IV-drips (Fig. 8). Others gave their play characters as gifts to their families, other patients and hospital staff. Maribel (12) described how the play characters facilitated an interaction with her brother, and furthermore, how the play character, coming out of the hospital, became part of her home environment: *"I've shown my giraffe puppet to my brother and he really liked it. He studies visual arts. We have put it in my bedroom."*

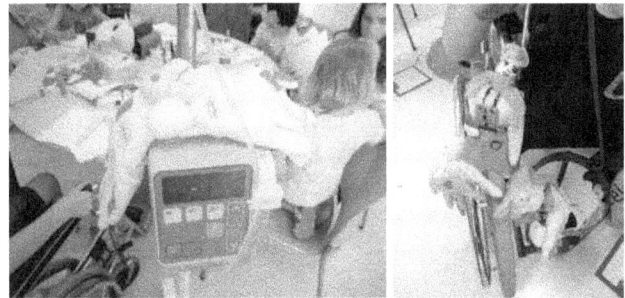

Fig. 8. IV-drip and wheelchair decorated with play characters

Children enjoyed being able to use hospital material
The children enjoyed using items for play such as the virtual medical scissors and physical X-ray sheets. The hospital environment usually does not allow children to interact with such material, as they "belong" to hospital staff and are generally seen as a symbol of illness. The children described the use of hospital material as *"nice"* and considered it *"different" (Pau, 10)*. Pilar (12) noted that: *"I like [the play characters] because they are funny and because we have used things from the hospital"*. Similarly, Maribel (12) said that *"it was very interesting to use the bones from people to make shadow puppets"*.

Children seeing hospital material and treatment as a resource for play
The sick children appeared to really enjoy the fact that they had knowledge and expertise of hospital materials and equipment that their family members, especially their non-sick siblings, had not, and as such were able to be in a more guiding position during the play workshops.

Children explained hospital material
One particular way this guiding position unfolded was through the children explaining the hospital material to the other participants. For example, with Doctor Giggles, we noticed children explained to family members the names and uses of the virtual hospital materials, just to burst into laughter when the tools in the virtual world performed very different functions. It appeared to empower children placing them in a position where they could explain to family members aspects of the hospital experience that often their siblings did not know about, which filled them with pride. We noticed this especially when explained to an older sibling, as it appeared to elevate the sick child to a superior position.

Children were proud of being able to contribute to the virtual play system
The children found the virtual operation room of Doctor Giggles fun and engaging: they liked being able to interactively change the color of the lights in the operation room and triggering the different sounds the IV-drip in the game made: *"It is like a room for medical procedures but it is a little bit crazy... Haha... It is fun" (Maribel, 12)*. Such enjoyment of interactive opportunities was expected, however, the children also reported enjoying seeing their own play characters coming out of the *"crazy"* and *"silly"* digital X-ray machine. When asked about the use of the play characters within the play system, all children confirmed that they found Doctor Giggles more engaging when they saw their own characters appear. It seemed the children were proud that they were able to contribute to the play system's content and manipulate their physical characters in the virtual world. The connection between the physical and virtual environment was not always immediately apparent (as others have previously observed [4]), probably due to the delay caused by the scanning process. As such, we note that reframing a physical hospital environment is a complex design process that goes beyond simply reproducing it in the virtual world. However, children enjoyed much more their contribution in designing and playing a game set in a hospital, which contrasts their usual video game experience, where all visual game content is usually pre-created and set in environments different to the child's.

Children seeing treatment as a resource for play
The children began seeing treatments as opportunities to collect hospital material for play
Being in hospital means treatment occurs frequently. As a result of the play workshops, the children began to see their treatments as an opportunity to gain access to hospital material that later could be used for play. For example, when Pilar was taken for an X-ray examination during the play workshop, one of the other children exclaimed: *"Ask for the X-rays for the puppets!"* Similarly, Abdul received his usually stressful and painful dialysis treatment during the play workshop. However, this time, he started clapping

his hands and shouted: *"Party, party! Yes, yes, let's do puppets!" (Abdul, 7)*. During the treatment, he asked for more bandages for later play: *"I want more bandages for my dolphin!" (Abdul, 7)*.

The children's excitement interfered sometimes with treatments
However, the heightened engagement and excitement the children experienced made administering treatments like demo-dialysis more difficult. A nurse complained about the play workshop because when the children shouted and clapped, the machines for treatment had to be readjusted several times. Usually, administering treatments benefit from the patients being calm and still, so the nurse explained to us that she felt uncomfortable with the amount of extra work involved to set up treatments for excited children.

Children engaged bodily with the hospital environment
Although the children had illnesses that affect their bodily abilities, we found they still engaged very much using their bodies, as you would expect from children that age. Besides moving around the hospital environment, the children embodied their play characters' behavior. The parents were excited to photograph their children embodying such behavior, contrasting it with the non-active behavior the children usually exhibit when back in their hospital beds.

Moving around
The opportunity to leave their hospital beds and move to another part of the hospital to attend the play workshop was welcomed. The children also enthusiastically moved around the workshop room to go back and forth between the craft table and the screen setup. In particular, the parents appreciated this opportunity to help their children leave their room and move around the hospital motivated by play.

Embodying behavior
We observed how eight children embodied the behavior of the characters they created out of hospital materials. For example, Javier, while playing with his hospital vampire character, was trying to bite the workshop facilitator, which resulted in a lot of shouting and laughing. Similarly, the children reported to like playing X-Safari because they were able to move their avatar with their hand. However, we also observed some challenges: four children found the glove difficult to operate. The others, though, said they liked the glove input because, even though it was difficult, they enjoyed the challenge.

Picture-taking
The parents enthusiastically took pictures of their children during and after the play workshops and shared them with relatives through social media. Medical staff also helped to send photos of the play workshops to the children's friends, relatives, and teachers. It appeared the parents enjoyed photographing their children "doing something nice" related to the hospital experience, which highlights the

child being active and engaged, compared to the pictures they usually take with the child being "inactive" or lying in bed, which highlights the illness, rather than the child.

Children can be exhausted
Due to their illness and treatments the children were often exhausted. We observed one child falling asleep during the play workshop as a result of her cancer treatment. In another case, a girl became so tired that two nurses had to pick her up to return her to her room. The bodily engagement during the play workshops probably only amplified such exhaustion. From our experiences with children, we know that children can get exhausted during play workshops, however, this exhaustion can occur much quicker in hospital. Luckily, our format was structured in such a way that it could accommodate such situations easily, for example it did not require two players to play in the virtual world simultaneously, so that if one player would drop out, the play would not end.

Children might not want to go back to their rooms
The bodily engagement resulting from the play workshop also led to challenges: Some children enjoyed the play workshops so much that they did not want to leave the play space and go back to their rooms. They enjoyed moving around (and of course being in a social environment with their families etc.) that they would have rather stayed there than return to their rooms (which is associated with boredom, pain, stress etc.). Although the children knew that the room would be vacated after the play workshops, they wanted to stay, even after knowing they were allowed to play digital games on their consoles in their rooms.

Reversing roles in the hospital environment
The children enjoyed being able to "treat" their doctor in Doctor Giggles and to help family members with their knowledge of hospital material, highlighting how reversed roles contributed to the success of the workshops.

Experiencing hospital authority in an alternative way
The children reported that they enjoyed Doctor Giggles especially because the patient was an adult, in particular their doctor, rather than a child (which is the usual role they are accustomed to) and that they were able to manipulate, i.e. tickle, the adult: *"Look, he is an adult!" Javier (7)* said, while the other children laughed. Although the doctor in the game was not familiar to all children, those who knew him recognized him and referred to him and his practice as a doctor, often imitating some of the ways they encountered when he treated them.

Helping others
We observed that the children eagerly helped their siblings and parents with making the play characters. It appeared that both the children and especially their parents enjoyed this opportunity of a reversal of the usual roles where the parents and the doctors are in control; in contrast, here the child felt more in control as they had prior knowledge about

the hospital material and therefore knew more about what can and cannot be done with it during crafting and play activities. The child's ability to help others due to this knowledge appeared to result in feelings of empowerment.

Diverting attention from the everyday hospital reality
The participants appreciated the play workshops facilitating a diversion of attention away from the everyday hospital reality, allowing them to talk about something other than sickness and form as well as strengthen social bonds beyond the common denominator of illness.

Talking about something other than sickness
The parents appreciated meeting other families and talking about being creative and playful, which was a welcomed relief compared to the usual discussions about the health of their children. Instead, the parents talked about the materials and the play systems while laughing and helping each other with the play workshop activities. Having their parents enjoy talking with other parents about the hospital environment appeared to have contributed also to the children's positive experience of the play workshops.

The play workshops facilitating social bonds
The parents thanked us after the play workshops, congratulated us on its execution and asked if there would be more. Furthermore, the parents from the first play workshop invited other families to come to the second. One father highlighted how the play workshop was not only a success for his child, but also for him. He was enjoying it more than he expected and described the experience as *"very relaxing"*. He found that playing with hospital materials with his daughter could relieve some of the family stress that comes with having a hospitalized child. Similarly, Pablo's mother expressed delight how the play workshop supported her son's relationship with his sibling: *"Many times siblings don't know how to feel [...] they don't understand. This is a way to make things much more personal and easygoing [...] I like it very much [...] all the activities we did."*

LENSES
Based on our findings, we derive four lenses through which researchers can examine the design of play that aims to engage children with the hospital environment to support their hospital experience. We then use these lenses to articulate six practical strategies to aid game designers developing such play systems.

Reframing
Our first lens provides a perspective of examining play for hospitalized children through the notion of reframing. Our play workshops successfully supported a reframing of the hospital experience by allowing the children to engage with medical materials, the hospital environment and tasks in a different way, here it was a playful way that contrasted with their usual hospital experience that focuses on disease and

illness. This reframing helped the children reimagine what the hospital experience can be for them. This was achieved through three key ways:

- by reframing various hospital materials commonly associated with illness, e.g. turning X-rays, bandages, and other hospital items into crafting resources for play;
- by reframing the hospital environment through reversing the role of the patient and doctor in the virtual world; and
- by reframing hospital tasks into a resource for play, for example the children perceived that through participating in treatments, they could control the operating theatre light switch illuminating the theatre with night club lighting.

As such, game designers should think about reframing the hospital materials and swapping medical staff roles, both in the physical and virtual world. We now describe such thinking as strategies in more detail.

Strategy: Opportunities for reframing can be found by exploring the hospital environment
The participants enjoyed using the hospital materials as a craft resource, partially because the children were very familiar with the materials. Using materials from the hospital was not an act of convenience or of minimizing cost, but rather an opportunity to reframe the hospital material through turning it into craft resource for play. Opportunities can be found by exploring the hospital environment. For example we examined if medical material could be turned into craft material, but other approaches could include exploring the hospital bed as a theatre stage or the corridor as playground. The children also enjoyed how the hospital material became a resource for digital content, allowing them to feel like junior game designers when their creations appeared in the virtual world. Virtual worlds are usually designed by adults, so being able to contribute to Doctor Giggles was a welcomed change for the children.

The reframing of hospital material reminds us of the desensitization methods that are often employed in hospitals. Desensitization refers to the presentation and use of a frightening object so that it becomes less stressful [40]. Prior work has shown that a hospitalized child who familiarizes themselves with a medical object can in response have a less emotionally disturbing relationship with it [31]. It appears that by reframing the hospital material through play our participants experienced a desensitization effect, resulting in a less stressful relationship with the material that in consequence positively affected the hospital experience as a whole. Furthermore, the reframing of the hospital material led to a reframing of the treatment task: the children saw their treatments as a resource to generate and gain access to play material. For example, by undergoing an X-ray scan, they would gain material for one of the X-ray shadow characters.

However, although the play workshops facilitated a reframing of the hospital tasks that the children experienced as positive, it made administering the treatments more challenging for the staff: sitting still is a requirement for many medical procedures, which is not easy to achieve with an excited child. As such, it is important for designers to consider not only the positive effects reframing can have on children, but also any consequences for medical staff.

We highlight to designers that our approach was to reframe the hospital tasks as a resource for generating play material, however, we can also envision other approaches where the task itself becomes a resource for play; for example reframing a dialysis treatment into an activity that is experienced as a form of play could be an exciting area of future work.

Strategy: Reframing the hospital environment by reversing roles through play
Doctor Giggles supported a reframing of the hospital environment as the play system allowed the children to take control of the virtual hospital environment reversing the role of the patient and doctor. This reframing supported the children's fantasy to imagine opportunities for play throughout the hospital experience: what role could nurses and parents take on in their play, for example?

The digital aspect of our play workshops played to its strength here: it was relatively easy for us to change the face of the virtual doctor in Doctor Giggles to elicit a fantasy of the doctor being the patient, in contrast, changing the "face" of the play workshop facilitator, i.e. dressing up as a clown, took much longer (and we doubt the senior medical staff would dress up for the children, for example). As such, reframing the hospital environment by reversing roles through play lends itself to the virtual world, as we know from game design research that one of the strengths of digital games is their ability to support the fantasy element [26].

Ownership of hospital experience
The play workshops facilitated the children gaining a sense of control over their hospital experience, as evident by them showing their siblings what some of the hospital material is for. This sense of control can lead to feelings of ownership of the hospital experience, which we believe is a positive development. Therefore we propose examining play for children in a hospital context as an opportunity to promote this feeling of ownership. As a result of the play workshops, the children were able to gain confidence in moving from a more passive role (in which the doctors have all the say) to one in which they can see themselves as having (at least partial) ownership. Two key strategies facilitated this: supporting autotopography and supporting autonomy.

Strategy: Supporting autotopography
Miller [33] explains that people like to express themselves with material artifacts that embody their lives, personalities,

emotions and achievements. The children were no different: they expressed themselves by decorating their rooms, wheelchairs and IV drips with the play characters they had created. Such an arrangement of material artifacts as physical signs to spatially represent the identity of an individual is known as "autotopography" [14]. An autotopographical collection of material artifacts put on display not only becomes the public representation of the self and craftsmanship [12], but also serves as a memory landscape to the owner allowing for the triggering of reminiscence.

Opportunities for hospitalized children to express themselves are often very limited, as such, the opportunity to decorate their rooms with artifacts they had created was very welcomed. We note that this opportunity to support autotopography existed for the physical play characters but not the virtual ones: they disappeared with us dismantling the screen setup, and were also not able to travel to the children's room and could not be put on display there. As such, we highlight that the physical play artifacts were supporting autotopography, however, the digital elements were not. We believe there is an opportunity for physical-digital material such as tangibles to support hospitalized children's desires to engage with autotopography (similar opportunities have been expressed in related work with dementia patients [45] and children with limited physical activity [1]). For example, we can envision utilizing 3D printers to print 3D objects based on children's play as personalized decorations to be placed in their rooms to support this experience of autotopography (inspired by prior work around 3D printing and autotopography [22]).

Strategy: Supporting autonomy
The play workshops appeared to facilitate the children gaining a sense of ownership of the hospital experience, especially as it provided the children with control over their play, for example they could use the play characters any way they wanted, and both digital components supported open-ended play. The sense of control during play has been previously described by Rigby et al. as "autonomy" [39], it refers to people's innate desire to take action based on personal volition, and not because one is "controlled" by circumstances [39]. Hospitalized children in particular might feel "controlled" by their sickness, and as such, we feel offering experiences of autonomy might be a welcoming and beneficial contrast. Studies have shown that if young people feel their autonomy is supported, rather than feeling they are being controlled, there is greater sustained engagement and an improved sense of wellbeing [39]. Similarly, the play workshops supported autonomy by creating activities that were non-prescriptive and allowed the children to control the direction of their play. This included a) having no predefined desirable game states, b) having no winning or losing condition, c) supporting open-ended play, d) us being responsive to the participants during play (as suggested by [32]) and e) allowing children to

pause play anytime, for example when they felt exhausted or when a treatment was due. When play was stopped for whatever reason, children were able to re-enter the play environment easily. However, it is important to note that supporting autonomy can interfere with the constraints of the hospital: the example of the children who did not want to go back to their rooms suggests supporting autonomy could be a source for conflict that designers need to keep in mind.

Feeling privileged
The play workshops facilitated the children feeling privileged, as shown through the enjoyment the children felt in knowing something about the hospital environment and tools (both physical and virtual) they could then teach other family members as part of play. It appeared to make them proud and put them in a privileged role; in other words, they became the experts who controlled the proceedings. This parallels the recommendation by Hoiseth et al. [17] who find that health games for children should elevate the "child as expert" in digital play. The feeling of being privileged contrasts with the sick child's usual situation. The play workshops facilitated this feeling of being privileged through a strategy of asymmetrical play.

Strategy: Asymmetrical play
The play workshops featured asymmetrical play [29] in which the children had prior intimate knowledge about the hospital material, environment and tasks that their siblings and parents often had not. As such, the play participants were not treated equally, which contrast the current trend of game balancing, where game designers aim to balance players with different abilities. For example, Gerling et al. balanced a game in order to give children with and without wheelchairs an equal chance to win [10]. Here, we work against this trend by highlighting that identifying (and stressing) advantages of the hospitalized child could be a valuable resource to enable asymmetrical play, so that the sick child has an opportunity to inhabit a privileged position.

The body as resource for play
It appeared the play workshops were an affirmation that the children were able to bodily engage in play despite their illnesses: they were moving around, clapping and generally being very active, seemingly forgetting that this is not how a sick child "is meant to" behave. We suggest the children realized that even though their bodies are affected by disease, they could still draw on their bodies as a resource for play. The fact the parents photographed their children engaging in physical play seemed to underline the notion of the body as a resource for play despite being ill. The play workshops aimed to facilitate this notion of the body as a resource for play through a strategy of supporting embodied play.

Strategy: Embodied play

The play workshops facilitated seeing the body as a resource for play – rather than primarily as a source of disease – via embodied play. This was facilitated by a) throughout all the activities the children engaged with physical materials that were concerned with bodily aspects of the hospital experience, b) the artifacts they crafted had embodied characteristics (i.e. all play characters were either animals or people), reminding them of bodily aspects, c) the location of craft tools and the large display required the children to get up and move about, d) the horse character in X-Safari was controlled using the children's hand movements, e) the characters in Doctor Giggles were controlled via big arm movements along a large touchscreen, aiming to bodily engage with (i.e. tickle) a virtual doctor, and f) the virtual worlds featured 3-dimensional embodied characters. This embodied play focus contrasts prior work highlighting cognitive-focused play (e.g. [47, 49]) to accommodate the limited bodily abilities of children in hospital. We note that our play workshops were designed with the knowledge that the children would not be able to engage in intense exertion activities as part of gameplay (as, for example, afforded by games like Remote Impact [34]), however, we promoted engagement with embodied activities as much as possible. The benefits of embodied play to support children has been previously highlighted [2], however, we point out that embodied play for hospitalized children means making a shift from seeing the body as a source of disease to a resource for play, not only significant for the children, but also their families and medical staff.

LIMITATIONS

Supporting children in hospital is multifaceted and therefore riddled with challenges; as such we acknowledge that our work has several limitations. So far, we have only conducted two play workshops, and we also do not have conducted comparisons with workshops that facilitate "generic" or non-hospital specific play. Extending the target age and the number of play workshops could reveal further insights. Furthermore, we have yet to test our lenses with other designers to examine their utility.

We believe that supporting the development of emotional wellbeing can positively affect a child's physical recovery. Our work focused on highlighting knowledge for the design of play to support such wellbeing, however, this needs to be complemented with evidence-based research into the efficacy of play as part of complementary care. This is required to ensure the continuation and increased support of such complementary care programs in hospital and is therefore an important avenue for future work.

CONCLUSION

We have presented the results of two play workshops designed to support hospitalized children. Our approach was to engage children with the hospital environment through play in order to support them to experience the hospital not just as a place of distress and diseases, but as another space for play that is part of life. The work therefore contrasts prior work that has sought to use play as a method of distraction from the hospital experience. Although measuring the success of complementary care is always challenging, we believe our results provided indicators that our play workshops were successful in supporting the children's experience in hospital. Through our results, we derived four lenses through which to see the design of play for hospitalized children, which we complemented with a set of strategies that designers can hopefully readily apply to future work.

Although we do not have data from outpatient children, we believe our contribution might also be useful to them and other user groups such as disabled children, children who need to undergo rehabilitation treatments and children who need to regularly see a GP as they might also benefit from reframing the experience of being sick. We also believe our work furthers our understanding of the design of play that aims to support hospitalized children from a perspective of complementary care. In particular, our work complements existing approaches by providing an interaction design perspective on the potential of interactive technology to support existing non-technical approaches such as play therapy. Our work is aimed at designers interested in creating interactive technologies and play for children in hospital, and hospital staff and medical practitioners interested in the power of digital play to support complementary care. Furthermore, we believe our work through its four lenses is useful for researchers to analyze approaches that aim to support complementary care for children and compare different approaches. Lastly, our work through its six strategies might be useful for game designers and researchers who want to utilize their design knowledge to support hospitalized children and contribute to their wellbeing.

Overall, our work aims to inspire other designers and researchers to consider supporting play as complementary care so that ultimately more children and their families can profit from its benefits.

ACKNOWLEDGEMENTS

Florian 'Floyd' Mueller appreciates the support from the Australian Research Council (DP110101304 & LP130100743).

REFERENCES

1. Swamy Ananthanarayan, Katie Siek and Michael Eisenberg. 2016. A Craft Approach to Health Awareness in Children. In *Proceedings of the 2016 ACM Conference on Designing Interactive Systems*. ACM, 724-735. http://dx.doi.org/10.1145/2901790.2901888

2. Alissa Antle. Embodied Child Computer Interaction: Why Embodiment Matters. ACM Interactions March+April (2009), 27-30.

3. Virginia Axline. Play Therapy. Churchill Livingstone, 1989.

4. Steve Benford, John Bowers, Lennart E Fahlén, Chris Greenhalgh and Dave Snowdon. 1995. User Embodiment in Collaborative Virtual Environments. In *Proceedings of the SIGCHI conference on Human factors in computing systems*. ACM, 242-249.

5. Sam Bucolo, Jonathan Mott and Roy Kimble. 2006. The Design of a Tangible Interaction Device to Alleviate Anxiety and Pain in Paediatric Burns Patients. In *Proceedings of CHI '06 Extended Abstracts on Human Factors in Computing Systems*. ACM, 129-134. http://dx.doi.org/10.1145/1125451.1125482

6. Eduardo H Calvillo-Gámez and Paul Cairns. 2008. Pulling the Strings: A Theory of Puppetry for the Gaming Experience. In *Proceedings of the Philosophy of Computer Games*. 308-323.

7. Alain De Botton and John Armstrong. Art as Therapy. Phaidon Press, 2013.

8. Allison Druin. The Role of Children in the Design of New Technology. Behaviour and information technology 21, 1 (2002), 1-25.

9. The Humour Foundation. 2011. Clown Doctors. http://www.humourfoundation.com.au.

10. Kathrin Maria Gerling, Matthew Miller, Regan L Mandryk, Max Valentin Birk and Jan David Smeddinck. 2014. Effects of Balancing for Physical Abilities on Player Performance, Experience and Self-Esteem in Exergames. In *Proceedings of the SIGCHI Conference on Human Factors in Computing Systems*. ACM, 2201-2210.

11. Jonathan Gershon, Elana Zimand, Melissa Pickering, Barbara Olasov Rothbaum and Larry Hodges. A Pilot and Feasibility Study of Virtual Reality as a Distraction for Children with Cancer. Journal of the American Academy of Child & Adolescent Psychiatry 43, 10 (2004), 1243-1249.

12. Erving Goffman. The Presentation of Self in Everyday Life. Garden City, 1959.

13. Jeffrey I Gold, Seok Hyeon Kim, Alexis J Kant, Michael H Joseph and Albert" Skip" Rizzo. Effectiveness of Virtual Reality for Pediatric Pain Distraction During Iv Placement. CyberPsychology & Behavior 9, 2 (2006), 207-212.

14. Jennifer A González. Autotopographies. Prosthetic territories: Politics and hypertechnologies (1995), 133-150.

15. Robyn Hart and Judy Rollins. Therapeutic Activities for Children and Teens Coping with Health Issues. John Wiley & Sons, 2011.

16. Catherine Hendon and Lisa Bohon. Hospitalized Children's Mood Differences During Play and Music Therapy. Child: care, health and development 34, 2 (2008), 141-144.

17. Marikken Høiseth, Michail N Giannakos, Ole A Alsos, Letizia Jaccheri and Jonas Asheim. 2013. Designing Healthcare Games and Applications for Toddlers. In *Proceedings of the 12th International Conference on Interaction Design and Children*. ACM, 137-146.

18. Kristina Höök and Jonas Löwgren. Strong Concepts: Intermediate-Level Knowledge in Interaction Design Research. ACM Trans. Comput.-Hum. Interact. 19, 3 (2012), 1-18. http://dx.doi.org/10.1145/2362364.2362371

19. Juan Pablo Hourcade. Interaction Design and Children. Foundations and Trends in Human-Computer Interaction 1, 4 (2008), 277-392.

20. Juegaterapia. 2015. http://www.juegaterapia.org/

21. Oskar Juhlin and Yanqing Zhang. 2011. Unpacking Social Interaction That Make Us Adore: On the Aesthetics of Mobile Phones as Fashion Items. In *Proceedings of the 13th International Conference on Human Computer Interaction with Mobile Devices and Services*. ACM, 241-250. http://dx.doi.org/10.1145/2037373.2037410

22. Rohit Ashok Khot, Larissa Hjorth and Florian Mueller. 2014. Understanding Physical Activity through 3d Printed Material Artifacts. In Proceedings of the SIGCHI Conference on Human Factors in Computing Systems. ACM, 3835-3844. http://dx.doi.org/10.1145/2556288.2557144

23. George Poonkhin Khut, Angie Morrow and Melissa Yogui Watanabe. 2011. The Brighthearts Project: A New Approach to the Management of Procedure-Related Paediatric Anxiety. In Proceedings of OZCHI Workshops Program, Canberra.

24. Jared Knauf. Bronkie the Bronchiasaurus for the Super Nintendo Entertainment System. Respiratory Care 41, 8 (1996), 748-749.

25. Donna Koller and Camilla Gryski. The Life Threatened Child and the Life Enhancing Clown: Towards a Model of Therapeutic Clowning. Evidence-Based Complementary and Alternative Medicine 5, 1 (2008), 17-25.

26. Nicole Lazzaro. 4 Fun Keys: Testing Emotions and Player Experiences. In Game Usability: Advice from the Experts for Advancing the Player Experience, Morgan Kaufmann (San Francisco, CA), 2008.

27. Child Life. 2012. Child Life. http://www.childlife.org.

28. Henrik Hautop Lund and Patrizia Marti. Designing Manipulative Technologies for Children with Different Abilities. Artificial Life and Robotics 9, 4 (2005), 175-187.

29. Sus Lundgren, Joel E Fischer, Stuart Reeves and Olof Torgersson. 2015. Designing Mobile Experiences for Collocated Interaction. In *Proceedings of the 18th ACM Conference on Computer Supported Cooperative Work & Social Computing*. ACM, 496-507.

30. Cathy A Malchiodi. Medical Art Therapy with Children. Jessica Kingsley Publishers, 1999.

31. Cathy A Malchiodi. Art Therapy and Health Care. Guilford Press, 2012.

32. Kevin Marshall, Anja Thieme, Jayne Wallace, John Vines, Gavin Wood and Madeline Balaam. 2014. Making Wellbeing: A Process of User-Centered Design. In *Proceedings of the 2014 conference on Designing interactive systems*. ACM, 755-764.

33. Daniel Miller. The Comfort of Things. Polity, 2008.

34. Florian Mueller, Martin Gibbs, Frank Vetere, Stefan Agamanolis and Darren Edge. 2014. Designing Mediated Combat Play. In *Proceedings of the 8th International Conference on Tangible, Embedded and Embodied Interaction*. ACM, 149-156.

35. W. L. Neuman. Social Research Methods. Pearson Education, USA, 2006.

36. Eva Nwokah. Clowns and Jokers Can Heal Us. Comedy and Medicine. International Journal of Play 2, 3 (2013), 301-304.

37. Payasospital. 2012. Payasospital: Payasos De Hospital. http://payasospital.com.

38. Olga Pykhtina, Madeline Balaam, Gavin Wood, Sue Pattison, Ahmed Kharrufa and Patrick Olivier. 2012. Magic Land: The Design and Evaluation of an Interactive Tabletop Supporting Therapeutic Play with Children. In *Proceedings of Designing Interactive Systems*. ACM, 136-145.

39. Scott Rigby and Richard Ryan. Glued to Games: How Video Games Draw Us in and Hold Us Spellbound. Praeger, 2011.

40. Judith A Rubin. 2005. Child Art Therapy. Hoboken.

41. Soumitri Sil, Lynnda M Dahlquist and Andrew J Burns. Case Study: Videogame Distraction Reduces Behavioral Distress in a Preschool-Aged Child Undergoing Repeated Burn Dressing Changes: A Single-Subject Design. Journal of pediatric psychology 38, 3 (2013), 330-341.

42. Susan G Slater. New Technology Device: Glucoboy®, for Disease Management of Diabetic Children and Adolescents. Home Health Care Management & Practice 17, 3 (2005), 246-247.

43. Tobias Sonne and Mads Møller Jensen. 2016. Chillfish: A Respiration Game for Children with ADHD. In *Proceedings of the TEI'16: Tenth International Conference on Tangible, Embedded, and Embodied Interaction*. ACM, 271-278.

44. Karen Stagnitti and Rodney Cooper. Play as Therapy: Assessment and Therapeutic Interventions. Jessica Kingsley Publishers, 2009.

45. Jayne Wallace, Anja Thieme, Gavin Wood, Guy Schofield and Patrick Olivier. 2012. Enabling Self, Intimacy and a Sense of Home in Dementia: An Enquiry into Design in a Hospital Setting. In *Proceedings of the SIGCHI Conference on Human Factors in Computing Systems*. ACM, 2629-2638.

46. Carolyn Watters, Sageev Oore, Michael Shepherd, Azza Abouzied, Anthony Cox, Melanie Kellar, Hadi Kharrazi, Fengan Liu and Anthony Otley. 2006. Extending the Use of Games in Health Care. *In Proceedings of System Sciences* (HICSS'06). IEEE, 88b-88b.

47. Karen E Weiss, Lynnda M Dahlquist and Karen Wohlheiter. The Effects of Interactive and Passive Distraction on Cold Pressor Pain in Preschool-Aged Children. Journal of pediatric psychology 36, 7 (2011), 816-826.

48. Peter H Wilson, Jonathan Duckworth, Nick Mumford, Ross Eldridge, Mark Guglielmetti, Patrick Thomas, David Shum and Heiko Rudolph. 2007. A Virtual Tabletop Workspace for the Assessment of Upper Limb Function in Traumatic Brain Injury (Tbi). In Proceedings of Virtual Rehabilitation, 2007. IEEE, 14-19.

49. Karen A Wohlheiter and Lynnda M Dahlquist. Interactive Versus Passive Distraction for Acute Pain Management in Young Children: The Role of Selective Attention and Development. Journal of pediatric psychology (2012). http://dx.doi.org/doi: 10.1093/jpepsy/jss108

1.

Author Index

414